Jacqueline Griot

Fodor's

France

" "When it comes to information on regional history, what to see and do, and shopping, these guides are exhaustive."

—*USAir Magazine*

"Usable, sophisticated restaurant coverage, with an emphasis on good value."
—Andy Birsh, *Gourmet Magazine* columnist

"Valuable because of their comprehensiveness."
—*Minneapolis Star-Tribune*

"Fodor's always delivers high quality...thoughtfully presented...thorough."

—*Houston Post*

"An excellent choice for those who want everything under one cover."

—*Washington Post* "

Fodor's Travel Publications, Inc.
New York • Toronto • London • Sydney • Auckland

Fodor's France '96

Editor: Conrad Little Paulus

Editorial Contributors: Steven K. Amsterdam, Rob Andrews, Robert Blake, Nancy Coons, William Echikson, Nigel Fisher, Janet Foley, Echo Garrett, Elva Harding, Simon Hewitt, Laura M. Kidder, Corinne LaBalme, Dawn Lawson, Lisa Leventer, Alexander Lobrano, Kristen D. Perrault, Mary Ellen Schultz, M. T. Schwartzman, George Semler, Dinah Spritzer

Creative Director: Fabrizio La Rocca

Cartographers: David Lindroth; Mapping Specialists Ltd.

Cover Photograph: Jean-Paul Nacivet/Leo de Wys, Inc.

Design: Between the Covers

Copyright

Copyright © 1995 by Fodor's Travel Publications, Inc.

Fodor's is a registered trademark of Fodor's Travel Publications, Inc.

All rights reserved under International and Pan-American Copyright Conventions. Published in the United States by Random House, Inc., New York, and simultaneously in Canada by Random House of Canada Limited, Toronto. Distributed by Random House, Inc., of New York. *No maps, illustrations, or other portions of this book may be reproduced in any form without written permission from the publisher.*

ISBN 0–679–03022–0

Special Sales

Fodor's Travel Publications are available at special discounts for bulk purchases for sales promotions or premiums. Special editions, including personalized covers, excerpts of existing guides, and corporate imprints, can be created in large quantities for special needs. For more information, contact your local bookseller or write to Special Markets, Fodor's Travel Publications, 201 East 50th Street, New York, NY 10022. Inquiries from Canada should be directed to your local Canadian bookseller or sent to Random House of Canada, Ltd., Marketing Department, 1265 Aerowood Drive, Mississauga, Ontario L4W 1B9. Inquiries from the United Kingdom should be sent to: Fodor's Travel Publications, 20 Vauxhall Bridge Road, London, England SW1V 2SA.

MANUFACTURED IN THE UNITED STATES OF AMERICA

10 9 8 7 6 5 4 3 2 1

CONTENTS

IV   **Contents**

ON THE ROAD WITH FODOR'S

A GOOD TRAVEL GUIDE IS LIKE A wonderful traveling companion. It's charming, it's brimming with sound recommendations and solid ideas, it pulls no punches in describing lodging and dining establishments, and it's consistently full of fascinating facts that make you view what you've traveled to see in a rich new light. In the creation of *France '96,* we at Fodor's have gone to great lengths to provide you with the very best of all possible traveling companions— and to make your trip the best of all possible vacations.

About Our Writers

The information on these pages is a collaboration of a roster of extraordinary writers.

Simon Hewitt, who first wrote much of this book and whose words come to you straight from Paris, where he has lived since 1984, is a youthful curmudgeon; an expert in architecture, wine, and history; and impatient with sloppiness and fuzzy thinking. Such is his devotion to duty that in the wettest winter in memory he slogged through the drenched streets of Charleville-Mézières as the water rose. Days later the town was 6 feet under. From the heights of his Paris apartment (you climb no fewer than 150 narrow steps), you can see the Eiffel Tower. Perhaps it's that breadth of vision that informs his work.

Lots of this book is updated by **Nigel Fisher,** the peripatetic writer and knowledgeable publisher of "Voyager International," a newsletter on world travel. His particular interests are in telling his readers about art, about divine places to stay, and about the most delicious food. Everywhere he goes, he talks to people and makes friends; so he always knows which chefs are striving for the second Michelin star and which are resting on their laurels.

In Paris, while Simon Hewitt updates Exploring, **Corinne LaBalme** pounds the sidewalks, seeking charming hotels and the best shopping. Corinne has lived in Paris since 1984 and is half French. Though she sometimes splurges on clothes she can't really afford in places like the rue de Rivoli, her savvy French frugality leads her to spend most of her annual budget at the August sales and the *marché aux puces.*

George Semler actually lives over the border in Spain, but he's acquainted with each trout in the Pyrénées, of Spanish *and* French persuasion. He loves every bump in those mountainy roads and has contributed a grand tour of the region, cannily feeding and lodging us along the way.

Conrad Paulus, remembering Mme. Duvallier's teaching from the third grade, still compulsively pronounces French signs and headlines under her breath and is a pushover for all things Gallic. Her latest trip was to the enchanting streets and neighborhoods of Lyon—not to mention its ravishing restaurants. Never mind the calories, and hang the cholesterol!

We'd especially like to thank the French Government Tourist Office in New York; Air France; and Amaury de Varax, Véronique Charpenet, and Laurence Soleymieux of the Office du Tourisme, Lyon.

What's New

Nigel Fisher has added a new chapter to this edition, covering central France from the lower Loire Valley to Provence; Simon Hewitt has given us new material on the north, including the city of Lille; and George Semler has supplied a fresh tour of the Atlantic Pyrénées.

A New Design

If this is not the first Fodor's guide you've purchased, you'll immediately notice our new look. More readable and easier to use than ever? We think so—and we hope you do, too.

Travel Updates

Just before your trip, you may want to order a Fodor's Worldview Travel Update. From local publications all over France, the lively, cosmopolitan editors at Worldview gather information on concerts, plays, opera, dance performances, gallery and museum shows, sports competitions, and other special events that coincide with your visit. See the order blank at the back of this book, call 800/799–9609, or fax 800/799–9619.

And in France

As Louis XIV marked his absolute power at Versailles and Napoléon celebrated victories with the Invalides and Arc de Triomphe, so former Président François Mitterand built his way into the history books, with a giant arch at La Défense, the huge science museum at La Villette, the shining new opera at the Bastille, and I. M. Pei's dazzling, decade-long remodelling of the Louvre. The $800-million reconstruction, begun with the sleek glass pyramid, will continue into this year.

The major project completed in 1995 was the **Très Grande Bibliothèque,** or Very Large Library, sprawling over 17 acres along the Left Bank and designed to anchor previously underdeveloped Eastern Paris. Critics deride the $1.5-billion project as a Very Large Mistake, asking how France can afford it at a time of economic austerity and unemployment. The powers that be maintain that if Paris is to be a business center to challenge London, a diplomatic crossroads to rival Brussels, and a cultural magnet to match New York, it must add a sparkling modern layer to its 2,000 years of history.

Disneyland Paris, having lost more than $900 million in its first year of operation, despite being Europe's No. 1 tourist attraction, is still struggling to correct its problems, principally by reducing prices.

You may now make reservations at Relais & Châteaux properties by calling the New York office: 212/856–0015 or by fax: 212/856–0193. They'll send you a free catalogue, or you can browse through it on the Internet: http://www.calvacom.fr/relais/acqueil.html.

A new motorway now links L'Isle-Adam (45 km/28 mi north of Paris) to Amiens, in the north; and in 1995 the world's largest cable-stayed bridge, the **Pont de Normandie,** opened across the Seine between Honfleur and Le Havre, uniting north and south Normandy.

Since the arrival of the TGV in 1994, the northern city of **Lille** can be reached from Paris (140 mi/225 km) in just one hour. A high-tech commercial center, Euralille, has sprung up around the new train station, but the city is not neglecting its heritage: The **Vieille Bourse** and the giant **Musée des Beaux-Arts,** two of Lille's venerable attractions, reopened late in 1995 after massive renovation.

Catastrophic flooding hit eastern France in January 1995. **Charleville-Mézières** went 6 feet under, but luckily the sumptuous **Musée de l'Ardennes,** which opened in 1994 after a $6-million transformation, emerged unscathed. The other big news from the unjustly neglected Ardennes region is the May 1995 launch of a new multilingual tour of Europe's largest castle at **Sedan,** using infrared headsets.

In December 1994, in the **Combe d'Arc grotto** at Vallon-Pont-d'Arc in the Ardèche, **20,000-year-old cave paintings** were discovered, including unusual depictions of a hyena and a jaguar. They have been heralded as the most important prehistoric finds since Lascaux, but worries about their conservation suggest that the cave won't be open to the general public any time soon.

Bear in mind that the wonky and skewed economy has caused crime to flow out of Paris. Though the French are not broadcasting the news, professional thieves have been migrating to the once peaceful and secure countryside. Take care of your possessions!

U.S. visitors alarmed by the weak dollar will be pleased to learn that inflation in France remains negligible. Dining can be particularly affordable, as the trend toward budget bistros shows no sign of abating. The French are flocking to these eateries for traditional dishes such as pot-au-feu, mashed potatoes, and crème brûlée—comfort foods for an uncertain fin de siècle.

How to Use This Guide

Organization

Up front is the **Gold Guide,** comprising two sections on gold paper that are chockfull of information about traveling within your destination and traveling in general. Both are in alphabetical order by topic. **Important Contacts A to Z** gives addresses and telephone numbers of organizations and companies that offer destination-related services and detailed information or publications. Here's where you'll find information about how to get to France from wherever you are. **Smart Travel Tips A to Z,** the Gold Guide's second section, gives specific tips on how to get the most out of your travels, as well as information on how to accomplish what you need to in France.

Chapters in *France '96* are arranged geographically, starting in Paris and the surrounding Ile de France, moving west down the Loire Valley and on to Brittany; thence, roughly clockwise around the hexagon. Each chapter covers exploring, shopping, sports, dining, lodging, and arts and nightlife, and ends with a section called Essentials, which tells you how to get there and get around and gives you important local addresses and telephone numbers.

At the end of the book you'll find Portraits: wonderful essays about French cooking, wine, and architecture and "France at a Glance: A Chronology," followed by suggestions for pretrip reading, both fiction and nonfiction.

Stars

Stars in the margin are used to denote highly recommended sights, attractions, hotels, and restaurants.

Restaurants and Hotels

Restaurants and lodging places are chosen with a view to giving you the cream of the crop in each location and in each price range. In all restaurant price charts, costs are per person, excluding drinks, but including service and tax. In hotel price charts, rates are for standard double rooms, including service and the 18.6% tax.

Hotel Facilities

Note that in general you incur charges when you use many hotel facilities. We indicate what facilities a hotel has to offer, but we don't always specify whether or not there's a charge, so when planning a vacation that entails a stay of several days, it's wise to ask what's included in the rate.

Hotel Meal Plans

Assume that hotels operate on the **European Plan** (EP, with no meals) unless we note that they use the **American Plan** (AP, with all meals), the **Modified American Plan** (MAP, with breakfast and dinner daily), the **Continental Plan** (CP, with a Continental breakfast daily), or are **all-inclusive** (all meals and most activities).

Dress Codes in Restaurants

Look for an overview in the Dining section of Smart Travel Tips A to Z in the Gold Guide pages at the front of this book. The **What to Wear** section at the beginning of the Paris dining section tells you what's most common there. Elsewhere, we note a dress code only when men are required to wear a jacket or a jacket and tie.

Credit Cards

The following abbreviations are used: **AE,** American Express; **DC,** Diners Club; **MC,** MasterCard; and **V,** Visa. Discover is not accepted outside the United States.

Please Write to Us

Everyone who has contributed to *France '96* has worked hard to make the text accurate. All prices and opening times are based on information supplied to us at press time, and the publisher cannot accept responsibility for any errors that may have occurred. The passage of time will bring changes, so it's always a good idea to call ahead and confirm information when it matters—particularly if you're making a detour to visit specific sights or attractions. When making reservations at a hotel or inn, be sure to speak up if you have a disability or are traveling with children, if you prefer a private bath or a certain type of bed, or if you have specific dietary needs or any other concerns.

Were the restaurants we recommended as described? Did our hotel picks exceed your expectations? Did you find a way to make your trip more enjoyable? We would love your feedback, positive and negative. If you have complaints, we'll look into them and revise our entries when the facts warrant it. If you've happened upon a special place that we haven't included, we'll pass the information along to the writers, so they can check it out. So please send us a letter or postcard (we're at 201 East 50th Street, New York, New York 10022). We'll look forward to hearing from you. And in the meantime, have a wonderful trip!

Karen Cure
Editorial Director

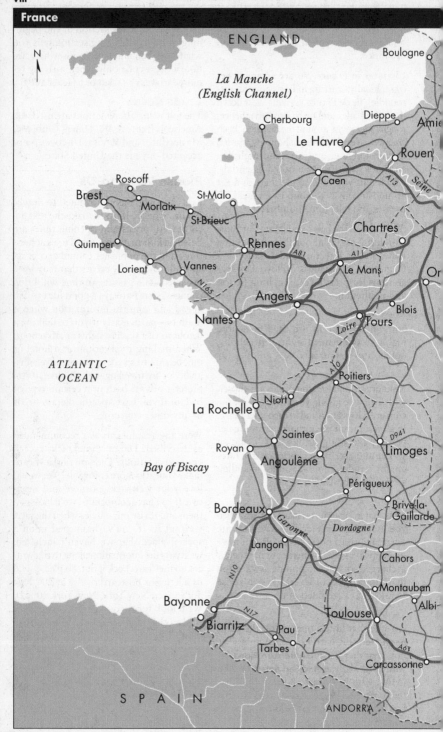

France

ENGLAND

La Manche
(English Channel)

N

Boulogne

Dieppe

Amie

Cherbourg

Le Havre

Rouen

Seine

Caen

A13

Roscoff

Brest

Morlaix

St-Malo

St-Brieuc

Chartres

Quimper

Rennes

A81

A11

Le Mans

Or

Lorient

Vannes

N165

Angers

Blois

Loire

Tours

Nantes

A10

ATLANTIC
OCEAN

Poitiers

Niort

La Rochelle

Saintes

D941

Royan

Angoulême

Limoges

Bay of Biscay

Périgueux

Brive-la-
Gaillarde

Bordeaux

Garonne

Dordogne

Cahors

N10

Langon

A62

Montauban

Albi

Bayonne

N17

Toulouse

Biarritz

Pau

Tarbes

A61

Carcassonne

SPAIN

ANDORRA

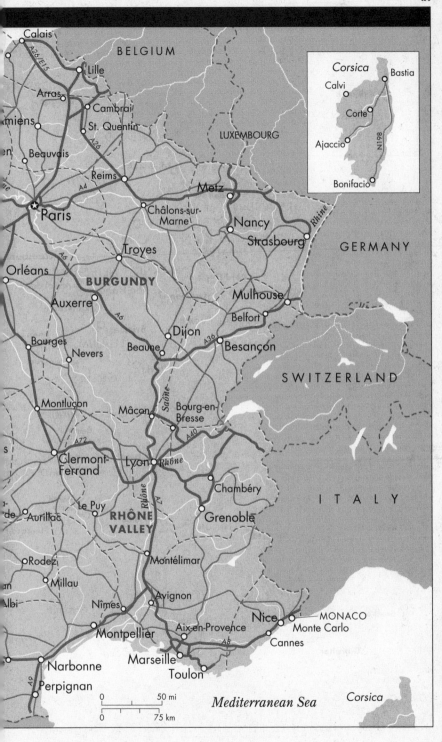

Europe

ICELAND

Reykjavík

NORWAY

Bergen

NORTHERN
IRELAND

SCOTLAND

Edinburgh

*North
Sea*

Skagerra

Belfast

IRELAND

*Irish
Sea*

DENMARK

Dublin

UNITED
KINGDOM

WALES

Hamburg

ENGLAND

NETHERLANDS

Cardiff

The Hague

Amsterdam

London

Rotterdam

GER

*ATLANTIC
OCEAN*

English Channel

Brussels

Bonn

BELGIUM

Frankfurt

Paris

LUXEMBOURG

F R A N C E

Zürich

Muni

Bern

SWITZERLAND

Lyon

LIECHTENSTE

Milan

Ven

Monte
Carlo

PORTUGAL

ANDORRA

Marseille

Nice

MONACO

Florence

Lisbon

Madrid

Corsica

Barcelona

S P A I N

Sardinia

Seville

Granada

*Balearic
Islands*

Tyrrheni

Gibraltar

Mediterranean Sea

MOROCCO

ALGERIA

0   400 miles

TUNISIA

0   600 km

World Time Zones

Numbers below vertical bands relate each zone to Greenwich Mean Time (0 hrs.).
Local times frequently differ from these general indications,
as indicated by light-face numbers on map.

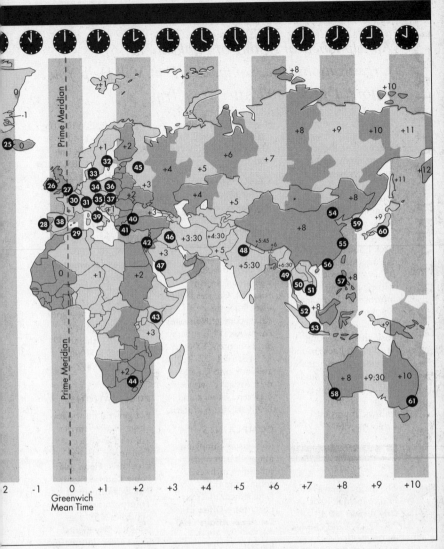

Prime Meridian

Prime Meridian

Greenwich
Mean Time

IMPORTANT CONTACTS A TO Z

An Alphabetical Listing of Publications, Organizations, and Companies That Will Help You Before, During, and After Your Trip

No single travel resource can give you every detail about every topic that might interest or concern you at the various stages of your journey—when you're planning your trip, while you're on the road, and after you get back home. The following organizations, books, and brochures will supplement the information in *France '96*. For related information, including both basic tips on visiting France and background information on many of the topics below, study Smart Travel Tips A to Z, the section that follows Important Contacts A to Z.

A

AIR TRAVEL

The major gateways to France include Paris's **Orly Airport** (☎ 49–75–52–52) and **Charles de Gaulle** (Roissy) **Airport** (☎ 48–62–22–80). Flying time is 7½ hours from New York, 9 hours from Chicago, and 11 hours from Los Angeles.

CARRIERS

Carriers serving France include **Air France** (☎ 800/237–2747), **American Airlines** (☎ 800/433–7300), **British Airways** (☎ 800/247–9297), **Continental** (☎ 800/231–0856), **Delta** (☎ 800/241–4141), **TWA** (☎ 800/892–

4141), **United Airlines** (☎ 800/241–6522), and **USAir** (☎ 800/428–4322).

Carriers from the United Kingdom include **Air France** (☎ 0181/759–2311), **British Airways** (☎ 0181/759–2313), and **Caledonian Airways** (☎ 0293/567100), the charter division of British Airways. Charter flights often offer the best value; contact **Nouvelles Frontières** (11 Blenheim St., London W1Y 0QP, ☎ 0171/629–7772), and look into Caledonian Airways' service between Gatwick and Beauvais, north of Paris.

COMPLAINTS

To register complaints about charter and scheduled airlines, contact the U.S. Department of Transportation's **Office of Consumer Affairs** (400 7th St. NW, Washington, DC 20590, ☎ 202/366–2220 or 800/322–7873).

CONSOLIDATORS

Established consolidators selling to the public include **BET World Travel** (841 Blossom Hill Rd., Suite 212-C, San Jose, CA 95123, ☎ 408/229–7880 or 800/747–1476); **Euram Tours** (1522 K St. NW, Suite 430, Washington DC, 20005, ☎ 800/848–6789); **TFI Tours International** (34 W. 32nd St.,

New York, NY 10001, ☎ 212/736–1140 or 800/745–8000); **Uni-Travel** (Box 12485, St. Louis, MO 63132, ☎ 314/569–0900 or 800/325–2222); **Council Charter** (205 E. 42nd St., New York, NY 10017, ☎ 212/661–0311 or 800/800–8222); and **Travac Tours and Charter** (989 6th Ave., 16th Floor, New York, NY 10018, ☎ 212/563–3303 or 800/872–8800; 2601 E. Jefferson, Orlando, FL 32803, ☎ 407/896–0014 or 800/872–8800).

PUBLICATIONS

For general information about charter carriers, ask for the Office of Consumer Affairs' brochure **"Plane Talk: Public Charter Flights."** The Department of Transportation also publishes a 58-page booklet, **"Fly Rights"** (Consumer Information Center, Dept. 133-B, Pueblo, CO 81009; $1.75).

For other tips and hints, consult the Consumers Union's monthly **"Consumer Reports Travel Letter"** (Box 53629, Boulder CO 80322, ☎ 800/234–1970; $39 annually); the newsletter **"Travel Smart"** (40 Beechdale Rd., Dobbs Ferry, NY 10522, ☎ 800/327–3633; $37 annually); *The Official Frequent Flyer Guide-*

book, by Randy Petersen (4715-C Town Center Dr., Colorado Springs, CO 80916, ☎ 719/597–8899 or 800/487–8893; $14.99 plus $3 shipping); *Airfare Secrets Exposed,* by Sharon Tyler and Matthew Wonder (Universal Information Publishing; $16.95 plus $3.75 shipping from Sandcastle Publishing, Box 3070-A, South Pasadena, CA 91031, ☎ 213/255–3616 or 800/655–0053); and *202 Tips Even the Best Business Travelers May Not Know,* by Christopher McGinnis (Irwin Professional Publishing, Box 1333, Burr Ridge Pkwy., Burr Ridge, IL 60521, ☎ 708/789–4000 or 800/634–3966; $10 plus $3 shipping).

WITHIN FRANCE

France's domestic airline service, **Air Inter** (☎ 45–46–90–00), has flights from Paris to all major cities. For long journeys—from Paris to the Riviera, for instance—air travel is a time saver, though train travel is always much cheaper. Most domestic flights from Paris leave from **Orly Airport.**

B

BARGE TRAVEL

For information on cruising France's inland waterways, contact **Bourgogne Voies Navigables** (1 quai de la République, 89000 Auxerre, ☎ 86–52–18–99). For tours of France that travel by barge, *see* Theme Trips *in* Tour Operators, below.

BETTER BUSINESS BUREAU

For local contacts in the home town of a tour operator you may be considering, consult the **Council of Better Business Bureaus** (4200 Wilson Blvd., Arlington, VA 22203, ☎ 703/276–0100).

BICYCLING

For information on cycling in France, contact the **Fédération Française de Cyclotourisme** (8 rue Jean-Marie-Jégo, 75013 Paris, ☎ 44–16–88–88). The yellow Michelin maps (1:200,000 scale) are fine for roads, but the best large-scale maps are prepared by the **Institut Géographique National** (IGN, 107 rue La Boétie, 75008 Paris, ☎ 42–56–06–68). Try their blue series (1:25,000) or orange series (1:50,000). Both indicate elevations and steep grades. Several good bike routes are described in detail in the chapters that follow. Also *see* Theme Trips *in* Tour Operators, *below.*

BIKE RENTALS

Among firms that rent bikes are **Bicyclub** (8 pl. Porte-de-Champerret, 75017 Paris, ☎ 47–66–55–92), at 60 francs per day or 350 francs per week, and **Paris Vélo** (4 rue du Fer-à-Moulin, 75005 Paris, ☎ 43–37–59–22), at 80 francs per day or 360 francs per week. Both stores require a 1,000-franc deposit, though they may accept a credit card.

BUS TRAVEL

For service from the United Kingdom, contact **Eurolines** (☎ 0171/730–3499), the international affiliate of **National Express.**

WITHIN FRANCE

Excursions and bus holidays are organized by the **SNCF** (88 rue St-Lazare, 75009 Paris, ☎ 45–82–50–50) and other tourist organizations, such as **Horizons Européens.** Ask for the brochure at any major travel agent, or contact **France-Tourisme** (3 rue d'Alger, 75001 Paris, ☎ 42–61–85–50).

C

CAR RENTAL

Major car-rental companies represented in France include **Alamo** (☎ 800/327–9633, 0800/272–2000 in the United Kingdom); **Avis** (☎ 800/331–1084, 800/879–2847 in Canada); **Budget** (☎ 800/527–0700, 0800/181181 in the United Kingdom); **Hertz** (☎ 800/654–3001, 800/263–0600 in Canada, 0181/679–1799 in the United Kingdom); and **National** (sometimes known as Europcar InterRent outside North America; ☎ 800/227–3876, 0181/950–5050 in the United Kingdom). Rates for an economy car in Paris begin at $27 a day and $180 a week, with unlimited mileage. This does not include VAT, which in France is 18.6%.

Local car-rental firms in Paris include **Rent-A-Car** (79 rue de Bercy, 75012, ☎ 43–45–15–15), which offers small Fiat

Pandas or larger Rover 214s. Other outfits include **Dergi** (60 blvd. St-Marcel, 75005, ☎ 45–87–27–04); **Locabest** (104 blvd. Magenta, 75010, ☎ 44–72–08–05); and **ACAR** (99 blvd. Auguste-Blanqui, 75013, ☎ 45–88–28–38), with economy cars and Renault Espace minivans.

RENTAL WHOLESALERS

Contact **Auto Europe** (Box 7006, Portland, ME 04112, ☎ 207/828–2525 or 800/223–5555); **Europe by Car** in New York City (write 1 Rockefeller Plaza, 10020; visit 14 W. 49th St.; or call 212/581–3040, 212/245–1713, or 800/223–1516) or Los Angeles (9000 Sunset Blvd., 90069, ☎ 800/252–9401 or 213/272–0424 in CA); **Foremost Euro-Car** (5658 Sepulveda Blvd., Suite 201, Van Nuys, CA 91411, ☎ 818/786–1960 or 800/272–3299); or the **Kemwel Group** (106 Calvert St., Harrison, NY 10528, ☎ 914/835–5555 or 800/678–0678).

THE CHANNEL TUNNEL

For information, contact **Le Shuttle** (☎ 01345/353535 in the United Kingdom, 800/388–3876 in the United States), which transports cars, or **Eurostar** (☎ 0171/922–4486 in the United Kingdom, 800/942–4866 in the United States), the high-speed train service between London (Waterloo) and Paris (Gare du Nord). Euro-

star tickets are available in the United Kingdom through **InterCity Europe**, the international wing of BritRail (London's Victoria Station, ☎ 0171/834–2345 or 0171/828–8092 for credit-card bookings), and in the United States through **Rail Europe** (☎ 800/942–4866) and **BritRail Travel** (1500 Broadway, New York, NY 10036, ☎ 800/677–8585).

CHILDREN AND TRAVEL

BABY-SITTING

Paris agencies include the **American University of Paris** (31 av. Bosquet, 75007 Paris, ☎ 40–62–06–00, FAX 47–05–33–49, only during school year); **Bébé Cool Services** (4 rue Faustin-Hélie, 75016 Paris, ☎ 45–04–27–14); **Home Service** (2 rue Pierre-Semard, 75009 Paris, ☎ 42–82–05–04); **Institut Catholique** (21 rue d'Assas, 75006 Paris, ☎ 44–39–52–00, only during school year).

DISCOUNT RAIL PASSES

The **SNCF** allows children under 4 to travel free (provided they don't occupy a seat) and children 4 to 11 to travel at half fare. The Carte Kiwi (280 francs) allows children under 16 and as many as four accompanying adults to make four journeys at half fare.

FLYING

Look into **"Flying with Baby"** (Third Street Press, Box 261250, Littleton, CO 80126, ☎ 303/595–5959;

$5.95 plus $1 shipping), cowritten by a flight attendant. **"Kids and Teens in Flight,"** free from the U.S. Department of Transportation's Office of Consumer Affairs, offers tips for children flying alone. Every two years the February issue of *Family Travel Times* (*see* Know-How, *below*) details children's services on three dozen airlines.

KNOW-HOW

Family Travel Times, published 4 times a year by Travel with Your Children (TWYCH, 45 W. 18th St., New York, NY 10011, ☎ 212/206–0688; $40 annually), covers destinations, types of vacations, and modes of travel.

The *Family Travel Guides* catalogue (☎ 510/527–5849; 1$ postage) lists about 200 books and articles on family travel. Also check *Take Your Baby and Go! A Guide for Traveling with Babies, Toddlers and Young Children,* by Sheri Andrews, Judy Bordeaux, and Vivian Vasquez (Bear Creek Publications, 2507 Minor Ave., Seattle, WA 98102, ☎ 206/322–7604 or 800/326–6566; $5.95 plus $1.50 shipping). *Innocents Abroad: Traveling with Kids in Europe,* by Valerie Wolf Deutsch and Laura Sutherland (Penguin USA, 120 Woodbine St., Bergenfield, NJ 07621, ☎ 201/387–0600 or 800/253–6476; $15.95 or $4.95 paperback), covers child- and teen-friendly activities, food, and transportation.

LODGING

Novotel (☎ 800/221–4542) and **Sofitel** hotels (☎ 800/221–4542) offer discounts for families; some properties have special programs for children. **Club Med** (40 W. 57th St., New York, NY 10019, ☎ 800/258–2633) has a "Baby Club" (from age four months) at its resort in Chamonix, "Mini Clubs" (for ages four to six or eight, depending on the resort), and "Kids Clubs" (for ages eight and up during school holidays) at all its resort villages in France except in Val d'Isère. Some clubs are only French-speaking, so check first.

TOUR OPERATORS

Contact **Grandtravel** (6900 Wisconsin Ave., Suite 706, Chevy Chase, MD 20815, ☎ 301/986–0790 or 800/247–7651), which has tours for people traveling with grandchildren ages 7 to 17; **Families Welcome!** (21 W. Colony Pl., Suite 140, Durham, NC 27705, ☎ 919/489–2555 or 800/326–0724); or **Rascals in Paradise** (650 5th St., Suite 505, San Francisco, CA 94107, ☎ 415/978–9800 or 800/872–7225).

CUSTOMS

U.S. CITIZENS

The **U.S. Customs Service** (Box 7407, Washington, DC 20044, ☎ 202/927–6724) can answer questions on duty-free limits and publishes a helpful brochure, **"Know Before You Go."** For information on registering foreign-made articles, call 202/927–0540.

CANADIANS

Contact **Revenue Canada** (2265 St. Laurent Blvd. S, Ottawa, Ontario, K1G 4K3, ☎ 613/993–0534) for a copy of the free brochure **"I Declare/Je Déclare"** and for details on duties that exceed the standard duty-free limit.

U.K. CITIZENS

HM Customs and Excise (Dorset House, Stamford St., London SE1 9NG, ☎ 0171/202–4227) can answer questions about U.K. customs regulations and publishes **"A Guide for Travellers,"** detailing standard procedures and import rules.

D
FOR TRAVELERS
WITH DISABILITIES

COMPLAINTS

To register complaints under the provisions of the Americans with Disabilities Act, contact the U.S. Department of Justice's **Public Access Section** (Box 66738, Washington, DC 20035, ☎ 202/514–0301, FAX 202/307–1198, TTY 202/514–0383).

LOCAL INFORMATION

Contact the **Comité Nationale Français de Liaison pour la Réadaptation des Handicapés** (38 blvd. Raspail, 75007 Paris, ☎ 53–80–66–66) or the **Association des Paralysés de France** (17 blvd. Auguste-Blanqui, 75013 Paris, ☎ 40–78–69–00), which publishes a useful Paris hotel list.

ORGANIZATIONS

FOR TRAVELERS WITH HEARING IMPAIRMENTS➤ Contact the **American Academy of Otolaryngology** (1 Prince St., Alexandria, VA 22314, ☎ 703/836–4444, FAX 703/683–5100, TTY 703/519–1585).

FOR TRAVELERS WITH MOBILITY IMPAIRMENTS➤ Contact the **Information Center for Individuals with Disabilities** (Fort Point Pl., 27–43 Wormwood St., Boston, MA 02210, ☎ 617/727–5540, 800/462–5015 in MA, TTY 617/345–9743); **Mobility International USA** (Box 10767, Eugene, OR 97440, ☎ and TTY 503/343–1284; FAX 503/343–6812), the U.S. branch of an international organization based in Belgium (*see below*) that has affiliates in 30 countries; **MossRehab Hospital Travel Information Service** (1200 W. Tabor Rd., Philadelphia, PA 19141, ☎ 215/456–9603, TTY 215/456–9602); the **Society for the Advancement of Travel for the Handicapped** (SATH, 347 5th Ave., Suite 610, New York, NY 10016, ☎ 212/447–7284, FAX 212/725–8253); the **Travel Industry and Disabled Exchange** (TIDE, 5435 Donna Ave., Tarzana, CA 91356, ☎ 818/344–3640, FAX 818/344–0078); and **Travelin' Talk** (Box 3534, Clarksville, TN 37043,

☎ 615/552–6670, FAX 615/552–1182).

FOR TRAVELERS WITH VISION IMPAIRMENTS➤ Contact the **American Council of the Blind** (1155 15th St. NW, Suite 720, Washington, DC 20005, ☎ 202/467–5081, FAX 202/467–5085) or the **American Foundation for the Blind** (15 W. 16th St., New York, NY 10011, ☎ 212/620–2000, TTY 212/620–2158).

IN EUROPE

Contact the **Royal Association for Disability and Rehabilitation** (RADAR, 12 City Forum, 250 City Rd., London EC1V 8AF, ☎ 0171/250–3222) or **Mobility International** (Rue de Manchester 25, B1070 Brussels, Belgium, ☎ 00–322–410–6297), an international clearinghouse of travel information for people with disabilities.

PUBLICATIONS

Several free publications are available from the U.S. Information Center (Box 100, Pueblo, CO 81009, ☎ 719/948–3334): **"New Horizons for the Air Traveler with a Disability"** (address to Dept. 355A), describing legally mandated changes; the pocket-size **"Fly Smart"** (Dept. 575B), good on flight safety; and the Airport Operators Council's worldwide **"Access Travel: Airports"** (Dept. 575A).

The 500-page **Travelin' Talk Directory** (Box 3534, Clarksville, TN 37043, ☎ 615/552–6670; $35) lists people

and organizations who help travelers with disabilities. For specialist travel agents worldwide, consult the **Directory of Travel Agencies for the Disabled** (Twin Peaks Press, Box 129, Vancouver, WA 98666, ☎ 206/694–2462 or 800/637–2256; $19.95 plus $2 shipping).

TRAVEL AGENCIES AND TOUR OPERATORS

The Americans with Disabilities Act requires that travel firms serve the needs of all travelers. However, some agencies and operators specialize in making group and individual arrangements for travelers with disabilities, among them **Access Adventures** (206 Chestnut Ridge Rd., Rochester, NY 14624, ☎ 716/889–9096), run by a former physical-rehab counselor. In addition, many general-interest operators and agencies (*see* Tour Operators, *below*) can also arrange vacations for travelers with disabilities.

FOR TRAVELERS WITH HEARING IMPAIRMENTS➤ One agency is **International Express** (7319-B Baltimore Ave., College Park, MD 20740, ☎ and TTY 301/699–8836, FAX 301/699–8836), which arranges group and independent trips.

FOR TRAVELERS WITH MOBILITY IMPAIRMENTS➤ A number of operators specialize in working with travelers with mobility impairments: **Flying Wheels Travel** (143 W. Bridge St., Box 382, Owa-

tonna, MN 55060, ☎ 507/451–5005 or 800/535–6790), a travel agency that specializes in European cruises and tours; **Hinsdale Travel Service** (201 E. Ogden Ave., Suite 100, Hinsdale, IL 60521, ☎ 708/325–1335 or 800/303–5521), a travel agency that will give you access to the services of wheelchair traveler Janice Perkins; **Nautilus Tours** (5435 Donna Ave., Tarzana, CA 91356, ☎ 818/344–3640 or 800/345–4654); and **Wheelchair Journeys** (16979 Redmond Way, Redmond, WA 98052, ☎ 206/885–2210), which can handle arrangements worldwide.

FOR TRAVELERS WITH DEVELOPMENTAL DISABILITIES➤ Contact the nonprofit **New Directions** (5276 Hollister Ave., Suite 207, Santa Barbara, CA 93111, ☎ 805/967–2841).

DISCOUNTS

Options include **Entertainment Travel Editions** (Box 1068, Trumbull, CT 06611, ☎ 800/445–4137; $28–$53, depending on destination); **Great American Traveler** (Box 27965, Salt Lake City, UT 84127, ☎ 800/548–2812; $49.95 annually); **Moment's Notice Discount Travel Club** (163 Amsterdam Ave., Suite 137, New York, NY 10023, ☎ 212/486–0500; $25 annually, single or family); **Privilege Card** (3391 Peachtree Rd. NE, Suite 110, Atlanta GA 30326, ☎ 404/262–0222 or 800/236–9732; $74.95 annually); **Travelers**

Advantage (CUC Travel Service, 49 Music Sq. W, Nashville, TN 37203, ☎ 800/548–1116 or 800/648–4037; $49 annually, single or family); and **Worldwide Discount Travel Club** (1674 Meridian Ave., Miami Beach, FL 33139, ☎ 305/534–2082; $50 annually for family, $40 single).

E
ELECTRICITY

Send a SASE to the **Franzus Company** (Customer Service, Dept. B50, Murtha Industrial Park, Box 142, Beacon Falls, CT 06403, ☎ 203/723–6664) for a copy of the free brochure "Foreign Electricity Is No Deep Dark Secret."

F
FERRY TRAVEL

DOVER–CALAIS

Contact **P&O European Ferries** (Channel House, Channel View Rd., Dover, Kent CT17 9TJ, ☎ 0181/575–8555); **Sealink** (Charter House, Park St., Ashford, Kent TN24 8EX, ☎ 01233/646801); or **Hoverspeed** (International Hoverport, Marine Parade, Dover CT17 9TG, ☎ 01304/240241).

OTHER CROSSINGS

Folkestone–Boulogne crossings are available from Hoverspeed. Newhaven–Dieppe crossings are available from Sealink. The Portsmouth–Le Havre crossing is offered by P&O. For Ramsgate–Dunkerque crossings, contact **Sally Line** (Ar-

gyle Centre, York St., Ramsgate, Kent CT11 9DS, ☎ 01843/595522).

Driving distances from the French ports to Paris are as follows: from Calais, 290 kilometers (180 miles); from Boulogne, 243 kilometers (151 miles); from Dieppe, 193 kilometers (120 miles); from Dunkerque, 257 kilometers (160 miles). The fastest routes to Paris from each port are via the N43, A26, and A1 from Calais and the Channel Tunnel; via the N1 from Boulogne; via the N15 from Le Havre; via the D915 and N1 from Dieppe; and via the A25 and A1 from Dunkerque.

G
GAY AND
LESBIAN TRAVEL

ORGANIZATIONS

The **International Gay Travel Association** (Box 4974, Key West, FL 33041, ☎ 800/448–8550), a consortium of 800 businesses, can supply names of travel agents and tour operators.

PUBLICATIONS

The premiere international travel magazine for gays and lesbians is **Our World** (1104 N. Nova Rd., Suite 251, Daytona Beach, FL 32117, ☎ 904/441–5367; $35 for 10 issues). The 16-page monthly **"Out & About"** (☎ 212/645–6922 or 800/929–2268; $49 for 10 issues) covers gay-friendly resorts, hotels, cruise lines, and airlines.

TOUR OPERATORS

Toto Tours (1326 W. Albion, Suite 3W, Chicago, IL 60626, ☎ 312/274–8686 or 800/565–1241) has group tours worldwide.

TRAVEL AGENCIES

The largest agencies serving gay travelers are **Advance Travel** (10700 Northwest Freeway, Suite 160, Houston, TX 77092, ☎ 713/682–2002 or 800/695–0880); **Islanders/Kennedy Travel** (183 W. 10th St., New York, NY 10014, ☎ 212/242–3222 or 800/988–1181); **Now Voyager** (4406 18th St., San Francisco, CA 94114, ☎ 415/626–1169 or 800/255–6951); and **Yellowbrick Road** (1500 W. Balmoral Ave., Chicago, IL 60640, ☎ 312/561–1800 or 800/642–2488). **Skylink Women's Travel** (746 Ashland Ave., Santa Monica, CA 90405, ☎ 310/452–0506 or 800/225–5759) works with lesbians.

H
HEALTH ISSUES

FINDING A DOCTOR

The best bet is to ask the **American Hospital** (63 blvd. Victor-Hugo, Neuilly-sur-Seine, just outside Paris, ☎ 46–41–25–25, FAX 46–24–49–38) to recommend an English-speaking doctor. A midnight visit to a local public hospital could be frightening and confusing, as the interns on duty often speak little English.

For members, the **International Association for Medical Assistance to Travellers** (IAMAT, 417 Center St., Lewiston, NY 14092, ☎ 716/754–4883; 40 Regal Rd., Guelph, Ontario, Canada N1K 1B5, ☎ 519/836–0102; 1287 St. Clair Ave., Toronto, Ontario, Canada M6E 1B8, ☎ 416/652–0137; 57 Voirets, 1212 Grand-Lancy, Geneva, Switzerland; membership free) publishes a worldwide directory of English-speaking physicians meeting IAMAT standards.

MEDICAL-ASSISTANCE COMPANIES

Contact **International SOS Assistance** (Box 11568, Philadelphia, PA 19116, ☎ 215/244–1500 or 800/523–8930; Box 466, Pl. Bonaventure, Montréal, Québec, Canada H5A 1C1, ☎ 514/874–7674 or 800/363–0263); **Medex Assistance Corporation** (Box 10623, Baltimore, MD 21285, ☎ 410/296–2530 or 800/573–2029); **Near Services** (Box 1339, Calumet City, IL 60409, ☎ 708/868–6700 or 800/654–6700); and **Travel Assistance International** (1133 15th St. NW, Suite 400, Washington, DC 20005, ☎ 202/331–1609 or 800/821–2828). Because these companies also sell death-and-dismemberment, trip-cancellation, and other insurance coverage, there is some overlap with the travel-insurance policies sold by the companies listed under Insurance, *below*.

HIKING

For details on hiking in France, contact the **Club Alpin Français** (24 av. Laumière, 75019 Paris, ☎ 42–02–68–64) or the **Fédération Française de la Randonnée Pédestre** (64 rue de Gergovie, 75014 Paris, ☎ 45–45–31–02), which publishes good topographical maps and guides. The IGN maps sold in many bookshops are also invaluable (*see* Bicycling, *above*).

I

INSURANCE

Travel insurance covering baggage, health, and trip cancellation or interruptions is available from **Access America** (Box 90315, Richmond, VA 23286, ☎ 804/285–3300 or 800/284–8300); **Carefree Travel Insurance** (Box 9366, 100 Garden City Plaza, Garden City, NY 11530, ☎ 516/294–0220 or 800/323–3149); **Near Services** (Box 1339, Calumet City, IL 60409, ☎ 708/868–6700 or 800/654–6700); **Tele-Trip** (Mutual of Omaha Plaza, Box 31716, Omaha, NE 68131, ☎ 800/228–9792); **Travel Insured International** (Box 280568, East Hartford, CT 06128, ☎ 203/528–7663 or 800/243–3174); **Travel Guard International** (1145 Clark St., Stevens Point, WI 54481, ☎ 715/345–0505 or 800/826–1300); and **Wallach & Company** (107 W. Federal St., Box 480, Middleburg, VA 22117, ☎ 703/687–3166 or 800/237–6615).

IN THE U.K.

The **Association of British Insurers** (51 Gresham St., London EC2V 7HQ, ☎ 0171/600–3333; 30 Gordon St., Glasgow G1 3PU, ☎ 0141/226–3905; Scottish Provident Bldg., Donegall Sq. W., Belfast BT1 6JE, ☎ 01232/249176; call for other locations) gives advice by phone and publishes the free **"Holiday Insurance,"** which sets out typical policy provisions and costs.

L

LODGING

APARTMENT AND VILLA RENTAL

Among the companies to contact are **At Home Abroad** (405 E. 56th St., Suite 6H, New York, NY 10022, ☎ 212/421–9165); **Europa-Let** (92 N. Main St., Ashland, OR 97520, ☎ 503/482–5806 or 800/462–4486); **Hometours International** (Box 11503, Knoxville, TN 37939, ☎ 615/588–8722 or 800/367–4668); **Interhome** (124 Little Falls Rd., Fairfield, NJ 07004, ☎ 201/882–6864); **Property Rentals International** (1008 Mansfield Crossing Rd., Richmond, VA 23236, ☎ 804/378–6054 or 800/220–3332); **Rental Directories International** (2044 Rittenhouse Sq., Philadelphia, PA 19103, ☎ 215/985–4001); **Rent-a-Home International** (7200 34th Ave. NW, Seattle, WA 98117, ☎ 206/789–9377 or 800/488–7368); **Vacation Home Rentals Worldwide** (235

Kensington Ave., Norwood, NJ 07648, ☎ 201/767–9393 or 800/633–3284); **Villas and Apartments Abroad** (420 Madison Ave., Suite 1105, New York, NY 10017, ☎ 212/759–1025 or 800/433–3020); and **Villas International** (605 Market St., Suite 510, San Francisco, CA 94105, ☎ 415/281–0910 or 800/221–2260). Members of the travel club **Hideaways International** (767 Islington St., Portsmouth, NH 03801, ☎ 603/430–4433 or 800/843–4433; $99 annually) receive two annual guides plus quarterly newsletters, and arrange rentals among themselves.

HOME EXCHANGE

Principal clearinghouses include **HomeLink International/Vacation Exchange Club** (Box 650, Key West, FL 33041, ☎ 305/294–1448 or 800/638–3841; $60 annually), which gives members four annual directories, with a listing in one, plus updates; **Intervac International** (Box 590504, San Francisco, CA 94159, ☎ 415/435–3497; $65 annually), which has three annual directories; and **Loan-a-Home** (2 Park La., Apt. 6E, Mount Vernon, NY 10552-3443, ☎ 914/664–7640; $35–$45 annually), which specializes in long-term exchanges.

HOTELS

Directories to small, inexpensive hotels can be obtained from **Logis de France** (83 av. d'Italie, 75013 Paris, ☎ 45–84–83–84, FAX 44–24–08–74; 75 francs) and **France-Accueil** (163 av. d'Italie, 75013 Paris, ☎ 45–83–04–22, FAX 45–86–49–82). Write to **Relais & Châteaux** (15 rue Galvani, 75017 Paris, ☎ 45–72–90–00, FAX 45–72–90–30 or, in the United States, call 212/856–0015 or fax 212/856–0193) for a guide to the group's network of prestigious inns and hotels.

For reservations and information on the **Gîtes Ruraux,** contact either the **Federation National des Gîtes de France** (35 rue Godot-de-Mauroy, 75009 Paris, ☎ 49–70–75–75, FAX 49–70–75–76), naming which region interests you, or the **French Government Tourist Office** in London (178 Piccadilly, W1V OAL, ☎ 0891/244–123 [39p per minute cheap rate and 49p per minute at other times]), which runs a special reservation service.

M

MONEY MATTERS

ATMS

For specific foreign **Cirrus** locations, call 800/424–7787; for foreign Plus locations, consult the **Plus** directory at your local bank.

CURRENCY EXCHANGE

If your bank doesn't exchange currency, contact **Thomas Cook Currency Services** (41 E. 42nd St., New York, NY 10017 or 511 Madison Ave., New York, NY 10022, ☎ 212/757–6915 or 800/223–7373 for locations) or **Ruesch International** (☎ 800/424–2923 for locations).

WIRING FUNDS

Funds can be wired via **American Express MoneyGram℠** (☎ 800/926–9400 from the United States and Canada for locations and information) or **Western Union** (☎ 800/325–6000 for agent locations or to send using MasterCard or Visa, 800/321–2923 in Canada).

P

PASSPORTS AND VISAS

U.S. CITIZENS

For fees, documentation requirements, and other information, call the **Office of Passport Services** information line (☎ 202/647–0518).

CANADIANS

For fees, documentation requirements, and other information, call the Ministry of Foreign Affairs and International Trade's **Passport Office** (☎ 819/994–3500 or 800/567–6868).

U.K. CITIZENS

For fees, documentation requirements, and to get an emergency passport, call the **London Passport Office** (☎ 0171/271–3000).

PHOTO HELP

The **Kodak Information Center** (☎ 800/242–2424) answers consumer questions about film and photography. An informative book on taking expert-quality travel photographs is

Kodak Guide to Shooting Great Travel Pictures (Fodor's Travel Publications, 800/533–6478 or from bookstores; $16.50).

R

RAIL TRAVEL

Train-ferry travel from the United Kingdom is provided by **Sealink** (☎ 0233/647047) and **British Rail International** (☎ 0171/834–2345).

For information on rail travel within France, contact the **SNCF** (88 rue St-Lazare, 75009 Paris, ☎ 45–82–50–50).

DISCOUNT PASSES

Buying a rail pass can save you money if you plan to do a lot of traveling by train. The French Flexipass allows you unlimited train travel on any four days within a one-month period; cost is $180 in first class, $125 in second. The France Rail 'n' Drive Pass buys you three days of unlimited train travel and three days use of an Avis car within a one-month period; cost is $195 in first class, $159 in second class, with up to six additional days' use of the car available at $39 per day. With both passes, you can buy up to six additional days of train travel for $40 a day in first class, $29 a day in second class. The BritFrance Rail Pass covers both France and Britain (and Hovercraft Channel crossings); cost for unlimited travel on any five days of a month is $359 in first class, $259 in second class; $539 and $399 for any 10 days in a 30-day period. All these passes must be purchased stateside and are sold by travel agents as well as **Rail Europe** (226–230 Westchester Ave., White Plains, NY 10604, ☎ 914/682–5172 or 800/438–7245; 2087 Dundas East, Suite 105, Mississauga, Ontario L4X 1M2, ☎ 416/602–4195).

France is also one of 17 countries in which you can use EurailPasses, which provide unlimited first-class rail travel during their period of validity. If you plan to rack up the miles, they can be an excellent value. Standard passes are available for 15 days ($498), 21 days ($648), one month ($728), two months ($1,098), and three months ($1,398). Eurail Saverpasses valid for 15 days cost $430 per person; for 21 days, $550; for one month, $678 per person; you must do all your traveling with at least one companion (two companions from April through September). Eurail Youthpasses, which cover second-class travel, cost $578 for one month, $768 for two; you must be under 26 on the first day you travel. Eurail Flexipasses allow you to travel first class for five ($348), 10 ($560), or 15 ($740) days within any two-month period. Eurail Youth Flexipasses, available to those under 26 on their first travel day, allow you to travel second class for five ($255), 10 ($398), or 15 ($540) days within any two-month period. Another option is the Europass, featuring a minimum of five and a maximum of 15 days (within a two-month period) of unlimited rail travel in your choice of three, four, or all five of the participating countries (France, Germany, Italy, Spain, and Switzerland); cost for five days is $280 first class, $198 second class (three countries); for eight days, $394 first class, $284 second class (four countries); and for 11 days, $508 first class, $366 second class (all five countries). Each extra rail day costs $38 for first class and $28 for second class. Apply through your travel agent or **Rail Europe** (*see above*); **DER Tours** (Box 1606, Des Plaines, IL 60017, ☎ 800/782–2424); or **CIT Tours Corp.** (342 Madison Ave., Suite 207, New York, NY 10173, ☎ 212/697–2100 or 800/248–8687; 310/670–4269 or 800/248–7245 in western United States).

Senior citizens (over 60) and young people (under 26) are eligible for reduced fares with the Carte Vermeil and Carrissimo, respectively, which carry up to 50% discounts on travel within France. They can be purchased at SNCF stations (135 francs for four trips or 255 francs for unlimited discount travel for Carte Vermeil; 190 francs or 350 francs, for 4 or 8 trips respectively, for Carrissimo) with proof of identity and two passport photos. The reductions are 50% during "blue" periods (most of the time) and 20%

during "white" periods (noon Friday through noon Saturday; 3 PM Sunday through noon Monday). Every station can give you a calendar of white/blue periods and sell you the appropriate tickets. Note that there is no reduction for buying an *aller-retour* (round-trip) ticket rather than an *aller simple* (one-way) ticket, with one exception: Rail travelers get a 25% discount for a return ticket (ask for a *billet de séjour*) between stations at least 500 kilometers apart, providing journeys do not take place at peak times and include at least part of a Sunday. For further information contact the **SNCF** (88 rue St-Lazare, 75009 Paris, ☎ 45–82–50–50).

S
SENIOR CITIZENS

DISCOUNT PASSES
See Rail Travel, *above.*

EDUCATIONAL TRAVEL
The nonprofit **Elderhostel** (75 Federal St., 3rd Floor, Boston, MA 02110, ☎ 617/426–7788), for people 60 and older, has offered inexpensive study programs since 1975. The nearly 2,000 courses cover everything from marine science to Greek myths and cowboy poetry. Fees for two- to three-week international trips—including room, board, and transportation from the United States—range from $1,800 to $4,500.

For people 50 and over and their children and grandchildren, **Interhostel** (University of New Hampshire, 6 Garrison Ave., Durham, NH 03824, ☎ 603/862–1147 or 800/733–9753) runs 10-day summer programs involving lectures, field trips, and sightseeing. Most last two weeks and cost $2,125–$3,100, including airfare.

ORGANIZATIONS
Contact the **American Association of Retired Persons** (AARP, 601 E St. NW, Washington, DC 20049, ☎ 202/434–2277; $8 per person or couple annually). Its Purchase Privilege Program gets members discounts on lodging, car rentals, and sightseeing.

For other discounts on lodgings, car rentals, and other travel products, along with magazines and newsletters, contact the **National Council of Senior Citizens** (1331 F St. NW, Washington, DC 20004, ☎ 202/347–8800; membership $12 annually) and *Mature Outlook* (6001 N. Clark St., Chicago, IL 60660, ☎ 312/465–6466 or 800/336–6330; subscription $9.95 annually).

PUBLICATIONS
The 50+ Traveler's Guidebook: Where to Go, Where to Stay, What to Do, by Anita Williams and Merrimac Dillon (St. Martin's Press, 175 5th Ave., New York, NY 10010, ☎ 212/674–5151 or 800/288–2131; $12.95), offers many useful tips. **"The Mature Traveler"** (Box 50400,

Reno, NV 89513, ☎ 702/786–7419; $29.95), a monthly newsletter, covers travel deals.

STUDENTS

DISCOUNT PASSES
See Rail Travel, *above.*

GROUPS
Major tour operators include **Contiki Holidays** (300 Plaza Alicante, Suite 900, Garden Grove, CA 92640, ☎ 714/740–0808 or 800/466–0610) and **AESU Travel** (2 Hamill Rd., Suite 248, Baltimore, MD 21210-1807, ☎ 410/323–4416 or 800/638–7640).

HOSTELING
Contact **Hostelling International–American Youth Hostels** (733 15th St. NW, Suite 840, Washington, DC 20005, ☎ 202/783–6161) in the United States, **Hostelling International–Canada** (205 Catherine St., Suite 400, Ottawa, Ontario K2P 1C3, ☎ 613/237–7884) in Canada, and the **Youth Hostel Association of England and Wales** (Trevelyan House, 8 St. Stephen's Hill, St. Albans, Hertfordshire AL1 2DY, ☎ 01727/855215 and 01727/845047) in the United Kingdom. Membership ($25 in the United States, C$26.75 in Canada, and £9 in the United Kingdom) gets you access to 5,000 hostels worldwide that charge $7–$20 nightly per person.

Information is also available from the French headquarters, **Fédération Unie des Auberges de Jeunesse**

(27 rue Pajol, 75018 Paris, ☎ 44–89–87–28, FAX 44–89–87–10).

ID CARDS

To get discounts on transportation and admissions, get the **International Student Identity Card** (ISIC) if you're a bona fide student or the **International Youth Card** (IYC) if you're under 26. In the United States, the ISIC and IYC cards cost $16 each and include basic travel accident and illness coverage, plus a toll-free travel hot line. Apply through the Council on International Educational Exchange (*see* Organizations, *below*). Cards are available for $15 each in Canada from **Travel Cuts** (187 College St., Toronto, Ontario M5T 1P7, ☎ 416/979–2406 or 800/667–2887) and in the United Kingdom for £5 each at student unions and student travel companies.

ORGANIZATIONS

A major contact is the **Council on International Educational Exchange** (CIEE, 205 E. 42nd St., 16th Floor, New York, NY 10017, ☎ 212/661–1450) with locations in Boston (729 Boylston St., 02116, ☎ 617/266–1926); Miami (9100 S. Dadeland Blvd., 33156, ☎ 305/670–9261); Los Angeles (1093 Broxton Ave., 90024, ☎ 310/208–3551); 43 other college towns nationwide; and the United Kingdom (28A Poland St., London W1V 3DB, ☎ 0171/437–7767). Twice a year, it publishes *Student Travels*

magazine. The CIEE's Council Travel Service is the exclusive U.S. agent for several student-discount cards.

Campus Connections (325 Chestnut St., Suite 1101, Philadelphia, PA 19106, ☎ 215/625–8585 or 800/428–3235) specializes in discounted accommodations and airfares for students. The **Educational Travel Centre** (438 N. Frances St., Madison, WI 53703, ☎ 608/256–5551) offers rail passes and low-cost airline tickets, mostly for flights departing from Chicago. For air travel only, contact **TMI Student Travel** (100 W. 33rd St., Suite 813, New York, NY 10001, ☎ 800/245–3672).

In Canada, also contact **Travel Cuts** (*see above*).

PUBLICATIONS

See the *Berkeley Guide to France* (Fodor's Travel Publications, 800/533–6478 or from bookstores; $17.50).

T

TOUR OPERATORS

Among the companies selling tours and packages to France, the following have a proven reputation, are nationally known, and have plenty of options to choose from.

GROUP TOURS

Super-deluxe escorted tours to France are available from **Abercrombie & Kent** (1520 Kensington Rd., Oak Brook, IL 60521, ☎ 708/954–2944 or 800/323–7308) and **Travcoa** (Box 2630, Newport Beach, CA, 92658, ☎

714/476–2800 or 800/992–2003). For deluxe programs, try **Tauck Tours** (11 Wilton Rd., Westport, CT 06881, ☎ 203/226–6911 or 800/468–2825) or **Maupintour** (Box 807, Lawrence, KS 66044, ☎ 913/843–1211 or 800/255–4266). Another operator falling between deluxe and first-class is **Globus** (5301 S. Federal Circle, Littleton, CO 80123, ☎ 303/797–2800 or 800/221–0090). For first-class and first-class superior tours, try **Trafalgar Tours** (21 E. 26th St., New York, NY 10010, ☎ 212/689–8977 or 800/854–0103); **Brendan Tours** (15137 Califa St., Van Nuys, CA 91411, ☎ 818/785–9696 or 800/421–8446); and **Insight International** (745 Atlantic Ave., Boston, MA 02111, ☎ 617/482–2000 or 800/582–8380).

PACKAGES

The French Experience (370 Lexington Ave., Suite 812, New York, NY 10017, ☎ 212/986–1115) has the greatest variety of packages, from canal barging to stays in countryside cottages. Just about every airline that flies to France sells packages that include round-trip airfare and hotel accommodations. Among U.S. carriers, contact **American Airlines Fly AAway Vacations** (☎ 800/321–2121), **Continental Airlines Grand Destinations** (☎ 800/634–5555), **Delta Dream Vacations** (☎ 800/872–7786), and **United Airlines Vacation Plan-**

ning Center (☎ 800/ 328–6877). Other packagers include: **Abercrombie & Kent** (*see* Group Tours, *above*); **Brendan Tours** (*see* Group Tours, *above*); **Alek's Travel** (103 N.W. Second Ave., Fort Lauderdale, FL 33311, ☎ 305/462– 6757 or 800/ 929– 7768); **Five Star Touring** (60 E. 42nd St., Suite 612, New York, NY 10165, ☎ 212/818– 9140 or 800/792– 7827); **DER Tours** (11933 Wilshire Blvd., Los Angeles, CA 90025, ☎ 310/479–4140 or 800/782–2424); and **Jet Vacations** (1775 Broadway, New York, NY 10019, ☎ 212/474– 8740 or 800/538– 2762).

THEME TRIPS

Travel Contacts (45 Idmiston Rd., London SE27 9HL, England, ☎ 011/44–81766–7868, FAX 011/44–81766– 6123), with 135 member operators, can satisfy virtually any special interest in France.

ADVENTURE➤ **All Adventure Travel** (5589 Arapahoe, No. 208, Boulder, CO 80303, ☎ 800/537–4025) can book biking, hiking, kayaking, diving, rafting, and many other adventures in France. **Uniquely Europe** (2819 1st Ave., No. 280, Seattle, WA 98121, ☎ 206/441–8682 or 800/ 426–3610) has hiking, walking, biking, and skiing tours.

ARCHAEOLOGY➤ **4th Dimension Tours** (1150 N.W. 72nd Ave., Suite 250, Miami, FL 33126, ☎ 305/477–1525 or

800/343–0020) will lead you to France's Roman ruins.

ART AND ARCHITECTURE➤ **Esplanade Tours** (581 Boylston St., Boston, MA 02116, ☎ 617/ 266–7465 or 800/426– 5492) has art treasure and nature tours of Romanesque France, Champagne, Burgundy and the upper Loire, the Côte d'Azur, and the Dordogne.

BALLOONING➤ **Bombard European Balloon Adventures** (855 Donald Ross Rd., Juno Beach, FL 33408, ☎ 800/862–8537 or 407/ 775–0039) is the leader in hot-air balloon tours of France.

BARGE TRAVEL➤ **Barge & Voyage Associates** (140 E. 56th St., Suite 4C, New York, NY 10022, ☎ 800/546– 4777) represents 13 barges that carry 6 to 12 passengers; hot-air ballooning and bicycling are available from most barges. For barges with room for up to 50 passengers in Burgundy, Alasace-Lorraine, Bordeaux, and the south of France, try the **Kemwel Group** (106 Calvert St., Harrison, NY 10528, ☎ 800/ 234–4000). **Le Boat** (215 Union St., Hackensack, NJ 07601, ☎ 201/342–1838 or 800/992–0291) has one of France's most diverse barge fleets and runs theme tours around food and wine, gardens, golf, horseback riding, and sketching and art. **French Country Waterways** (Box 2195, Duxbury, MA 02331, ☎ 617/934–2454 or

800/222–1236) books four luxury barges in Burgundy and France. **Fenwick & Lang** (900 4th Ave., Suite 1201, Seattle, WA 98164, 206/382–1384 or 800/243–6244) has more than 35 years experience in booking barge tours of France.

BICYCLING➤ Bike tours of the French countryside are available for five days to two weeks. Contact **Backroads** (1516 5th St., Suite L101, Berkeley, CA 94710, ☎ 510/527– 1555 or 800/462– 2848); **Châteaux Bike Tours** (Box 5706, Denver, CO 80217, ☎ 303/393–6910 or 800/678–2453); **Bridges Tours** (2855 Capital Dr., Eugene, OR 97403, ☎ 503/ 484–1196); **Butterfield & Robinson** (70 Bond St., Suite 300, Toronto, Ontario, M5B 1X3, Canada, ☎ 416/864– 1354 or 800/268– 8415); **Euro-Bike Tours** (Box 990, De Kalb, IL 60115, ☎ 800/321– 6060); and **Progressive Tours** (224 W. Galer, Suite C, Seattle, WA 98119, 206/285–1987 or 800/245–2229).

FOOD AND WINE➤ Culinary theme tours are available from **Annemarie Victory Organization** (136 E. 64th St., New York, NY 10021, ☎ 212/ 486–0353); **Avalon Wine Tours** (Box 473, Jamestown, RI 02835, ☎ 401/423–3730 or 800/662–2628); and **European Culinary Adventures** (5 Ledgewood Way, Apt. 6, Peabody, MA 01960, ☎ 508/535–5738 or 800/

852–2625). If you want to learn French cooking, **Le Cordon Bleu** (404 Irvington St., Pleasantville, NY 10570, ☎ 800/457–2433 in U.S.), one of the world's best-known cooking schools, has courses for beginners and connoisseurs. The prestigious **Ritz-Escoffier** cooking school in Paris's Ritz hotel (☎ 800/966–5758) schedules 1- to 12-week courses in cooking and bread and pastry making.

GOLF➤ **ITC Golf Tours** (4134 Atlantic Ave., Long Beach, CA 90807, ☎ 310/595–6905 or 800/257–4981) custom designs golf itineraries in France.

HORSEBACK RIDING➤ For weeklong tours through Beaujolais, the Dordogne, Brittany, and the Loire Valley, contact **FITS Equestrian** (685 Lateen Rd., Solvang, CA 93463, ☎ 805/688–9494 or 800/666–3487).

LEARNING VACATIONS➤ **Earthwatch** (680 Mt. Auburn St., Watertown, MA 02272, ☎ 617/926–8200) recruits volunteers to serve in its EarthCorps as short-term assistants to scientists on research expeditions.

MUSIC➤ **Dailey-Thorp Travel** (330 W. 58th St., New York, NY 10019, ☎ 212/307–1555; book through travel agents) specializes in classical music and opera programs throughout France; its packages include tickets that are otherwise very hard to get. Also try **Keith Prowse Tours** (234 W. 34th St., Suite 1000, New York, NY 10036, ☎ 212/398–1430 or 800/669–8687).

TENNIS➤ **Steve Furgal's International Tennis Tours** (11828 Rancho Bernardo Rd., San Diego, CA 92128, ☎ 619/487–7777 or 800/258–3664) can take you to the French Open and arrange for a variety of accommodations and activities in Paris.

VILLA RENTALS➤ Contact **Eurovillas** (☎ 707/648–2066); **Barge & Voyage Associates** (*see* Barge Travel, *above*); **Chez Vous** (220 Redwood Hwy., Suite 129, Mill Valley, CA 94941 ☎ 415/331–2535); and **Villas International** (605 Market St., No. 510, San Francisco, CA 94105, ☎ 415/281–0910 or 800/221–2260).

ORGANIZATIONS

The **National Tour Association** (546 E. Main St., Lexington, KY 40508, ☎ 606/226–4444 or 800/682–8886) and **United States Tour Operators Association** (USTOA, 211 E. 51st St., Suite 12B, New York, NY 10022, ☎ 212/750–7371) can provide lists of member operators and information on booking tours.

PUBLICATIONS

Consult the brochure **On Tour** and ask for a current list of member operators from the National Tour Association (*see* Organizations, *above*). Also get a copy of the **"Worldwide Tour & Vacation Package Finder"** from USTOA (*see above*) and the Better Business Bureau's **"Tips on Travel Packages"** (Publication No. 24-195; 4200 Wilson Blvd., Arlington, VA 22203; $2).

TRAVEL AGENCIES

For names of reputable agencies in your area, contact the **American Society of Travel Agents** (1101 King St., Suite 200, Alexandria, VA 22314, ☎ 703/739–2782).

U
U.S.
GOVERNMENT
TRAVEL BRIEFINGS

The U.S. Department of State's Overseas Citizens Emergency Center (Room 4811, Washington, DC 20520; enclose SASE) issues **Consular Information Sheets,** which cover crime, security, political climate, and health risks as well as embassy locations, entry requirements, currency regulations, and other routine matters. For the latest information, stop in at any U.S. passport office, consulate, or embassy; call the interactive hot line (☎ 202/647–5225 or FAX 202/647-3000); or, with your PC's modem, tap into the Bureau of Consular Affairs' computer bulletin board (☎ 202/647–9225).

V
VISITOR
INFORMATION

Contact the **French Government Tourist Office** in the United States at 610 5th Ave., New York, NY 10020 (☎ 212/315–0888 for travel professionals or 900/990–0040 [50¢ per minute] to reach an operator who can send you information and itineraries for your specific destination); 676 N. Michigan Ave., Chicago, IL 60611 (☎ 312/751–7800); 2305 Cedar Springs Rd., Dallas, TX 75201 (☎ 214/720–4010); 9454 Wilshire Blvd., Suite 303, Beverly Hills, CA 90212 (☎ 310/271–

2358); in Canada at 1981 McGill College, Suite 490, Montréal, Québec H3A 2W9 (☎ 514/288–4264); 30 St. Patrick St., Suite 700, Toronto, Ontario M5T 3A3 (☎ 416/593–4723); or in the United Kingdom at 178 Piccadilly, London WIV OAL, England (☎ 0891/244–123 [39p per minute cheap rate and

49p per minute at other times]).

W
WEATHER

For current weather and forecasts, plus the local time and helpful travel tips, call the **Weather Channel Connection** (☎ 900/932–8437; 95¢ per minute) from a Touch-Tone phone.

SMART TRAVEL TIPS A TO Z

Basic Information on Traveling in France and Savvy Tips to Make Your Trip a Breeze

The more you travel, the more you know about how to make trips run like clockwork. To help make your travels hassle-free, Fodor's editors have rounded up dozens of tips from our contributors and travel experts all over the world, as well as basic information on visiting France. For names of organizations to contact and publications that can give you more information, *see* Important Contacts A to Z, *above.*

A
AIR TRAVEL

If time is an issue, **always look for nonstop flights,** which require no change of plane. If possible, **avoid connecting flights,** which stop at least once and can involve a change of plane, although the flight number remains the same; if the first leg is late, the second waits.

CUTTING COSTS

The Sunday travel section of most newspapers is a good source of deals.

MAJOR AIRLINES➤ The least-expensive airfares from the major airlines are priced for round-trip travel and are subject to restrictions. You must usually **book in advance and buy the ticket within 24 hours** to get cheaper fares, and you may have to **stay over a Saturday night.** The

lowest fare is subject to availability, and only a small percentage of the plane's total seats are sold at that price. It's good to **call a number of airlines**—and **when you are quoted a good price, book it on the spot**—the same fare on the same flight may not be available the next day. Airlines generally allow you to change your return date for a $25 to $50 fee, but most low-fare tickets are nonrefundable. However, if you don't use it, you can apply the cost toward the purchase price of a new ticket, again for a small charge.

CONSOLIDATORS➤ Consolidators, who buy tickets at reduced rates from scheduled airlines, sell them at prices below the lowest available from the airlines directly—usually without advance restrictions. Sometimes you can even get your money back if you need to return the ticket. Carefully read the fine print detailing penalties for changes and cancellations. If you doubt the reliability of a consolidator, **confirm your reservation with the airline.**

FROM THE U.K.➤ The route from London to Paris is the busiest in Europe, with up to 17 flights making the hour-long trip daily from Heathrow and four or five from Gatwick, all to Charles de Gaulle.

There are also regular flights from the new London City Airport in the Dockland and several regional airports, including Manchester, Birmingham, Glasgow, Edinburgh, and Southampton; and flights from London to Nice, Lyon, Bordeaux, Marseille, Clermont-Ferrand, Caen, Quimper, Nantes, Montpellier, and Toulouse, as well as from Manchester to Nice. Flying to France is much cheaper than it used to be, and lower prices on scheduled flights have elbowed out most of the charters, but **look for charter flights to the south of France in the summer.**

TRAVEL PASSES➤ You can **save on air travel** within Europe if you plan on traveling to and from Paris aboard Air France. As part of its Euro Flyer program, you can then buy between three and nine flight coupons, which are valid on Air France flights to more than 100 European cities. At $120 each, these coupons are a good deal, and the fine print still allows you plenty of freedom.

ALOFT

AIRLINE FOOD➤ If you hate airline food, **ask for special meals when booking.** These can be vegetarian, low-cholesterol, or kosher, for example; commonly prepared to order in smaller quantities than standard catered fare, they can be tastier.

JET LAG➤ To avoid this syndrome, which occurs when travel disrupts your body's natural cycles, try to maintain a normal routine. At night, **get some sleep.** By day, move about the cabin to **stretch your legs, eat light meals, and drink water—not alcohol.**

SMOKING➤ Smoking is banned on all flights within the United States of less than six hours' duration and on all Canadian flights; the ban also applies to domestic segments of international flights aboard U.S. and foreign carriers. Delta has banned smoking system-wide. On U.S. carriers flying to France and other destinations abroad, a seat in a no-smoking section must be provided for every passenger who requests one, and the section must be enlarged to accommodate such passengers if necessary as long as they have complied with the airline's deadline for check-in and seat assignment. If smoking bothers you, request a seat far from the smoking section.

Foreign airlines are exempt from these rules but do provide no-smoking sections. British Airways has banned smoking; some nations have banned smoking on all domestic flights, and others may ban smoking on some flights. Talks continue on the feasibility of broadening no-smoking policies.

B

BARGE TRAVEL

France has Europe's densest inland waterway system, and canal and river vacation trips are popular. You can take an all-inclusive organized cruise or simply rent a boat and plan your own leisurely route. Some of the most picturesque waterways are in Brittany, Burgundy, and the Midi. The Canal du Midi between Toulouse and Sète, constructed in the 17th century, is a historic marvel. For further information, contact a travel agent; ask for a "Tourisme Fluvial" brochure in any French tourist office; or contact Bourgogne Voies Navigables. Also *see* Tour Operators *in* Theme Trips *in* Important Contacts A to Z.

BUS TRAVEL

France's excellent train service means that long-distance buses are rare; regional buses are found mainly where the train service is spotty. Excursions and bus holidays are organized by the SNCF and other tourist organizations.

FROM THE U.K.

A London-to-Paris bus journey can be a rewarding experience (and typically costs only a little more than £60 round-trip). Eurolines, the international affiliate of National Express, runs four daily *Citysprint* buses in summer from Victoria Coach Station to the rue Lafayette in Paris near the Gare du Nord; these buses use the Hovercraft crossing, and the journey time is around 7½ hours. Three daily buses from Victoria to Bagnolet (métro Gallieni) on the outskirts of Paris use traditional ferries for the Channel crossing and take a bit longer (9 to 10 hours).

Eurolines has buses to the Riviera, leaving Victoria three times a week for such resorts as Nice and Cannes. The round-trip fare to Cannes starts at £109 in low season. The Atlantic coast is also served by Eurolines, with two buses a week to Bordeaux and Biarritz in mid-summer (journey time 24 hours; price approximately £99 round-trip); the Bordeaux service can be extended to Lourdes via Tarbes. There is also regular service from London to Chamonix and the Alps (22½ hours; from around £97 round-trip).

In addition, Eurolines operates an express bus that runs overnight to Grenoble, where there are connecting buses to Nice and Marseille (round-trip to Nice costs about £109); as well as a fast bus to Lyon six days a week in summer, leaving London mid-evening and reaching Lyon the following afternoon (about £85 round-trip).

BUSINESS HOURS

BANKS

Banks are open weekdays but have no strict pattern regarding times. In general, though,

THE GOLD GUIDE / SMART TRAVEL TIPS

hours are from 9:30 to 4:30. Most banks, but not all, take a one-hour, or even a 90-minute, lunch break. Note that many 24-hour exchange offices have sprung up around Paris (particularly along the rue de Rivoli) and the larger French cities.

MUSEUMS

Most are closed one day a week (usually Tuesday) and on national holidays. Usual opening times are from 9:30 to 5 or 6. Many museums close for lunch (noon–2); many are open only afternoons on Sunday.

SHOPS

Large stores in big towns are open from 9 or 9:30 until 7 or 8 (without a lunch break). Smaller shops often open earlier (8 AM) and close later (8 PM) but take a lengthy lunch break (1–4). This siesta-type schedule is routine in the south of France. Corner groceries, often run by immigrants (*"l'Arabe du coin"*), frequently stay open until around 10 PM. Many Paris stores (small and large alike) are beginning to open on Sundays.

C

CAMERAS, CAMCORDERS, AND COMPUTERS

LAPTOPS

Before you depart, **check your portable computer's battery,** because you may be asked at security to turn on the computer to prove that it is what it appears to be. At the

airport, you may prefer to **request a manual inspection,** although security X-rays do not harm hard-disk or floppy-disk storage. Also, **register your foreign-made laptop with U.S. Customs.** If your laptop is U.S.-made, call the consulate of the country you'll be visiting to find out whether or not it should be registered with local customs upon arrival. You may want to **find out about repair facilities at your destination** in case you need them.

PHOTOGRAPHY

If your camera is new or if you haven't used it for a while, **shoot and develop a few rolls of film** before you leave. Always **store film in a cool, dry place**—never in the car's glove compartment or on the shelf under the rear window.

Every pass through an X-ray machine increases film's chance of clouding. To protect it, carry it in a clear plastic bag and **ask for hand inspection at security.** Such requests are virtually always honored at U.S. airports, and usually are accommodated abroad. Don't depend on a lead-lined bag to protect film in checked luggage—the airline may increase the radiation to see what's inside.

VIDEO

Before your trip, **test your camcorder, invest in a skylight filter to protect the lens, and charge the batteries.** (Airport security personnel may ask you to

turn on the camcorder to prove that it's what it appears to be). The batteries of most newer camcorders can be recharged with a universal or worldwide AC adapter charger (or multivoltage converter), usable whether the voltage is 110 or 220. All that's needed is the appropriate plug.

Videotape is not damaged by X-rays, but it may be harmed by the magnetic field of a walk-through metal detector, so **ask that videotapes be hand-checked.** Videotape sold in France is based on the SECAM standard, which is different than the one used in the United States. You will not be able to view your tapes through the local TV set or view movies bought there in your home VCR. Blank tapes bought in France can be used for camcorder taping, but they are pricey. Some U.S. audiovisual shops convert foreign tapes to U.S. standards; contact an electronics dealer to find the nearest.

CAR RENTAL

Renting cars in France is expensive—usually at least twice the cost of renting in the United States. In addition, the price doesn't usually take into account the whopping 18.6% VAT tax. If you are flying into Paris first and are planning to spend time there, pick up your car the day you're leaving. You won't need a car in the capital, and it may be more of a hassle than a convenience.

CUTTING COSTS

To get the best deal, **book through a travel agent and shop around.** When pricing cars, **ask where the rental lot is located.** Some off-airport locations offer lower rates—even though their lots are only minutes away from the terminal via complimentary shuttle. You may also want to **price local car-rental companies,** whose rates may be lower still, although service and maintenance standards may not be up to those of a national firm. Also **ask your travel agent about a company's customer-service record.** How has it responded to late plane arrivals and vehicle mishaps? Are there often lines at the rental counter, and, if you're traveling during a holiday period, does a confirmed reservation guarantee you a car?

Always **find out what equipment is standard** at your destination before specifying what you want; **do without automatic transmission or air-conditioning** if they're optional. In Europe, manual transmissions are standard and air-conditioning is rare and often unnecessary.

Also in Europe, **look into wholesalers**—companies that do not own their own fleets but rent in bulk from those that do and often offer better rates than traditional car-rental operations. Prices are best during low travel periods, and rentals booked through wholesalers must be paid for before you leave the United States. If you use a wholesaler, **know whether the prices are guaranteed** in U.S. dollars or foreign currency, and if unlimited mileage is available; find out about required deposits, cancellation penalties, and drop-off charges; and confirm the cost of any required insurance coverage.

INSURANCE

When you drive a rented car, you are generally responsible for any damage or personal injury that you cause as well as damage to the vehicle. Before you rent, **see what coverage you already have** through your personal auto-insurance policy and credit cards. For about $14 a day, rental companies sell insurance, known as a collision damage waiver (CDW), that eliminates your liability for damage to the car; it's always optional and should never be automatically added to your bill.

REQUIREMENTS

In France your own driver's license is acceptable; an International Driver's Permit, available from the American or Canadian Automobile Association, is a good idea.

SURCHARGES

Before picking up the car in one city and leaving it in another, **ask about drop-off charges or one-way service fees,** which can be substantial. Note, too, that some rental agencies charge extra if you return the car before the time specified on your contract. To avoid a hefty refueling fee, **fill the tank just before you turn in the car.**

THE CHANNEL TUNNEL

The Channel Tunnel provides the fastest route across the Channel—25 minutes from Folkestone to Calais, 60 minutes from motorway to motorway. It consists of two large, 50-kilometer-long (31-mile-long) tunnels for trains, one in each direction, linked by a smaller service tunnel running between them.

Le Shuttle, a special car, bus, and truck train, operates continuously, with trains departing every 15 minutes at peak times and at least once an hour through the night. No reservations are necessary, although tickets may be purchased in advance from travel agents. Most passengers travel in their own car, staying with the vehicle throughout the "crossing," with progress updates via radio and display screens. Motorcyclists park their bikes in a separate section with its own passenger compartment, while those on foot must book passage by coach.

Eurostar high-speed train service whisks passenger-only trains between stations in Paris (Gare du Nord) and London (Waterloo) in 3 hours and between London and Brussels (Midi) in 3¼ hours. At press time, fares were $154 for a one-way, first-class ticket and

$123 for an economy fare.

The Tunnel is reached from exit 11a of the M20/A20. Tickets for either Tunnel service can be purchased in advance (see Important Contacts A to Z, above.)

CHILDREN AND TRAVEL

The easiest way to break down any Gallic arrogance is to show up with a child. Normally stiff salesmen go ga-ga and become immediately helpful. Bakers are often known to give young children free sweets, and children are accepted in both fancy and informal restaurants with little fuss. Changing compartments for infants are available on all TGVs. In short, don't worry about bringing a child to France.

BABY-SITTING

For recommended local sitters, **check with your hotel desk.** See also Children and Travel in Important Contacts A to Z, above.

DRIVING

If you are renting a car, **arrange for a car seat when you reserve.** Sometimes they're free.

FLYING

Always **ask about discounted children's fares.** On international flights, the fare for infants under age 2 not occupying a seat is generally either free or 10% of the accompanying adult's fare; children ages 2 through 11 usually pay half to two-thirds of the adult fare.

On domestic flights, children under 2 not occupying a seat travel free, and older children currently travel on the "lowest applicable" adult fare.

BAGGAGE

In general, the adult baggage allowance applies for children paying half or more of the adult fare. Before departure, **ask about carry-on allowances** if you are traveling with an infant. In general, those paying 10% of the adult fare are allowed one carry-on bag, not to exceed 70 pounds or 45 inches (length + width + height), and a collapsible stroller; you may be allowed less if the flight is full.

SAFETY SEATS

According to the Federal Aviation Administration (FAA), it's a good idea to **use safety seats aloft.** Airline policy varies. U.S. carriers allow FAA-approved models, but airlines usually require that you buy a ticket, even if your child would otherwise ride free, because the seats must be strapped into regular passenger seats. Foreign carriers may not allow infant seats, may charge the child's rather than the infant's fare for their use, or may require you to hold your baby during takeoff and landing, thus defeating the seat's purpose.

FACILITIES

When making your reservation, **ask for children's meals and a freestanding bassinet** if you need them; the latter are available only to those with seats at the bulkhead, where there's enough legroom. If you don't need the bassinet, **think twice before requesting bulkhead seats**—the only storage for in-flight necessities is in inconveniently distant overhead bins.

LODGING

Most hotels allow children under a certain age to stay in their parents' room at no extra charge, while others charge them as extra adults; be sure to **ask about the cut-off age.**

CUSTOMS AND DUTIES

IN FRANCE

There are two levels of duty-free allowance for travelers entering France: one for goods obtained (tax paid) within another European Union (EU) country and the other for goods obtained anywhere outside the EU or for goods purchased in a duty-free shop within the EU.

In the first category, you may import duty-free: 300 cigarettes or 150 cigarillos or 75 cigars or 400 grams of tobacco; 5 liters of table wine and (1) 1½ liters of alcohol over 22% volume (most spirits), (2) 3 liters of alcohol under 22% by volume (fortified or sparkling wine), or (3) 3 more liters of table wine; 90 milliliters of perfume; 375 milliliters of toilet water; and other goods to the value of 2,400 francs (620 francs for those under 15).

In the second category, you may import duty-free: 200 cigarettes or 100 cigarillos or 50 cigars or 250 grams of tobacco (these allowances are doubled if you live outside Europe); 2 liters of wine and (1) 1 liter of alcohol over 22% volume (most spirits), (2) two liters of alcohol under 22% volume (fortified or sparkling wine), or (3) 2 more liters of table wine; 60 milliliters of perfume; 250 milliliters of toilet water; and other goods to the value of 300 francs (150 francs for those under 15).

BACK HOME

IN THE U.S.➤ You may bring home $400 worth of foreign goods duty-free if you've been out of the country for at least 48 hours and haven't already used the $400 exemption, or any part of it, in the past 30 days.

Travelers 21 or older may bring back 1 liter of alcohol duty-free, provided the beverage laws of the state through which they reenter the United States allow it. In addition, 100 non-Cuban cigars and 200 cigarettes are allowed, regardless of your age. Antiques and works of art more than 100 years old are duty-free.

Duty-free, travelers may mail packages valued at up to $200 to themselves and up to $100 to others, with a limit of one parcel per addressee per day (and no alcohol or tobacco

products or perfume valued at more than $5); outside, identify the package as being for personal use or an unsolicited gift, specifying the contents and their retail value. Mailed items do not count as part of your exemption.

IN CANADA➤ Once per calendar year, when you've been out of Canada for at least seven days, you may bring in C$300 worth of goods duty-free. If you've been away less than seven days but more than 48 hours, the duty-free exemption drops to C$100 but can be claimed any number of times (as can a C$20 duty-free exemption for absences of 24 hours or more). You cannot combine the yearly and 48-hour exemptions, use the C$300 exemption only partially (to save the balance for a later trip), or pool exemptions with family members. Goods claimed under the C$300 exemption may follow you by mail; those claimed under the lesser exemptions must accompany you.

Alcohol and tobacco products may be included in the yearly and 48-hour exemptions but not in the 24-hour exemption. If you meet the age requirements of the province through which you reenter Canada, you may bring in, duty-free, 1.14 liters (40 imperial ounces) of wine or liquor *or* 24 12-ounce cans or bottles of beer or ale. If you are 16 or older, you may bring in, duty-

free, 200 cigarettes, 50 cigars or cigarillos, and 400 tobacco sticks or 400 grams of manufactured tobacco. Alcohol and tobacco must accompany you on your return.

An unlimited number of gifts valued up to C$60 each may be mailed to Canada duty-free. These do not count as part of your exemption. Label the package "Unsolicited Gift—Value Under $60." Alcohol and tobacco are excluded.

IN THE U.K.➤ If your journey was wholly within EU countries, you no longer need to pass through customs when you return to the United Kingdom. If you plan to bring large quantities of alcohol or tobacco, check in advance on EU limits.

DINING

France is two-big-meals-a-day country, with good restaurants around every corner. If you prefer to eat lighter, you can **try a brasserie for rapid, straightforward fare** (steak and french fries remains the classic) or a picnic (the long, skinny loaf of bread known as a baguette, with ham, cheese, or pâté makes a perfect combination). There is no shortage of possibilities for snacks—from pâtisseries (pastry shops) to street vendors hawking roast chestnuts or thin pancakes known as crêpes.

French breakfasts are relatively skimpy: good coffee, fruit juice if you request it, bread, butter, and croissants. You can "breakfast" in cafés as well as hotels. If you're in the mood for bacon and eggs, you're in trouble.

Dinner, the main meal, usually begins at 8 PM. Lunch, which can be as copious as you care to make it, starts at 12:30 or 1.

Tap water is safe, though not always appetizing (least of all in Paris). The more palatable alternative is mineral water—there is a vast choice of both *eau plate* (still) and *eau gazeuse* (fizzy).

FOR TRAVELERS
WITH DISABILITIES

The French government is doing much to ensure that public facilities provide for visitors with disabilities. A number of monuments, hotels, and museums—especially those constructed within the past decade—are equipped with ramps, elevators, and special toilet facilities. Lists of regional hotels include a symbol to indicate which hotels have rooms that are accessible to people using wheelchairs. Similarly, the SNCF has special cars on some trains that have been reserved exclusively for people using wheelchairs and can arrange for those passengers to be escorted on and off trains and assisted in making connections (the latter service must be requested in advance).

When discussing accessibility with an operator or reservationist, **ask hard questions.** Are there any stairs, inside *or* out? Are there grab bars next to the toilet *and* in the shower/tub? How wide is the doorway to the room? To the bathroom? For the most extensive facilities, meeting the latest legal specifications, **opt for newer properties,** which more often have been designed with access in mind. Older properties or ships must usually be retrofitted and may offer more limited facilities as a result. Be sure to **discuss your needs before booking.**

DISCOUNT CLUBS

Travel clubs offer members unsold space on airplanes, cruise ships, and package tours at as much as 50% below regular prices. Membership may include a regular bulletin or access to a toll-free hot line giving details of available trips departing from three or four days to several months in the future. Most also offer 50% discounts off hotel rack rates. Before booking with a club, **make sure the hotel or other supplier isn't offering a better deal.**

DRIVING

Roads marked *A,* for *autoroutes,* are expressways. There are excellent links between Paris and most other French cities, but poor ones between the provinces (principal exceptions: the A62 between Bordeaux and Toulouse, and the A9/A8 that runs the length of the Mediterranean). It is often difficult to avoid Paris when crossing France; this need not cause too many problems if you steer clear of rush hours (7–9:30 AM and 4:30–7:30 PM). Most expressways require you to pay a *péage* (toll); the rates vary and can be steep. The *N,* or *Route Nationale,* roads and the *D, Route Départementale,* roads are usually wide, unencumbered, and fast (you can average 80 kph/50 mph with luck). The cheap, informative, and well-presented regional yellow Michelin maps are an invaluable navigational aid. You can find them in most bookshops and newsagents.

BREAKDOWNS

If you break down on an expressway, go to the nearest roadside emergency telephone and call the breakdown service. If you break down anywhere else, find the nearest garage or, failing all else, contact the police (dial 17).

FUEL AVAILABILITY AND COSTS

Gas is more expensive on expressways, cheaper in rural areas. Don't let your tank get too low, as you can go for many miles in the country without hitting a gas station. Keep an eye on pump prices, which vary enormously: anything between 5.50 and 6.30 francs per liter. At the pumps, opt for "super" (high-grade/four-star) rather than "essence" (low-grade/two-star).

PARKING

Parking is a nightmare in Paris and is often

difficult in large towns. Meters and ticket machines (pay and display) are commonplace (be sure to have a supply of 1-franc coins). As a summer gift, parking is free during August in most of Paris, but be sure to check the signs. In smaller towns, parking may be permitted on one side of the street only, alternating every two weeks: Pay attention to signs. The French park as anarchically as they drive, but don't follow their example: If you're caught out of bounds, you could be subject to a hefty fine and your vehicle may be unceremoniously towed away to the dread compound (at least 500 francs to retrieve it).

RULES OF THE ROAD

In France, you **drive on the right.** Be aware of the erratically followed French tradition of giving way to drivers coming from the right, unless there is an international stop sign. Seat belts are obligatory, and children under 12 may not travel in the front seat. Speed limits: 130 kph (81 mph) on expressways; 110 kph (68 mph) on major highways; 90 kph (56 mph) on minor rural roads; 50 kph (31 mph) in towns. French drivers break these limits and police dish out hefty on-the-spot fines with equal abandon. You may use your home driver's license in France.

G
GAY AND
LESBIAN TRAVEL

The French are relatively open-minded about sex, and their liberal attitudes are reflected in their outlook toward homosexuals. The largest gay and lesbian communities, which are in cosmopolitan Paris, are low-key and reserved in public, although active and easily accessible to visitors. Discos and nightclubs are numerous and popular; it takes a serious *couchetard* (night owl) to keep up with the hip scene (*see also* Arts and Nightlife *in* Chapter 2).

I
INSURANCE

Travel insurance can protect your investment, replace your luggage and its contents, or provide for medical coverage should you fall ill during your trip. Most tour operators, travel agents, and insurance agents sell specialized health-and-accident, flight, trip-cancellation, and luggage insurance as well as comprehensive policies with some or all of these features. Before you make any purchase, **review your existing health and homeowners policies** to find out whether they cover expenses incurred while traveling.

BAGGAGE

Airline liability for your baggage is limited to $1,250 per person on domestic flights. On international flights, the airlines' liability is $9.07 per pound or $20 per kilogram for checked baggage (roughly $640 per 70-pound bag) and $400 per passenger for unchecked baggage. However, this excludes valuable items such as jewelry and cameras that are listed in your ticket's fine print. You can buy additional insurance from the airline at check-in, but first **see if your homeowner's policy covers lost luggage.**

FLIGHT

You should **think twice before buying flight insurance.** Often purchased as a last-minute impulse at the airport, it pays a lump sum when a plane crashes, either to a beneficiary if the insured dies or sometimes to a surviving passenger who loses eyesight or a limb. Supplementing the airlines' coverage described in the limits-of-liability paragraphs on your ticket, it's expensive and basically unnecessary. Charging an airline ticket to a major credit card often automatically entitles you to coverage and may also embrace travel by bus, train, and ship.

HEALTH

If your own health insurance policy does not cover you outside the United States, **consider buying supplemental medical coverage.** It can reimburse from $1,000 to $150,000 worth of medical and/or dental expenses incurred as a result of an accident or illness during a trip.

These policies also may include a personal-accident, or death-and-dismemberment, provision, which pays a lump sum ranging from $15,000 to $500,000 to your beneficiaries if you die or to you if you lose one or more limbs or your eyesight, and a medical-assistance provision, which may either reimburse you for the cost of referrals, evacuation, or repatriation and other services, or may automatically enroll you as a member of a particular medical-assistance company. (*See* Health Issues *in* Important Contacts A to Z, *above.*)

FOR U.K. TRAVELERS➤ You can buy an annual travel-insurance policy valid for most vacations during the year in which it's purchased. If you go this route, make sure it covers you if you have a preexisting medical condition or are pregnant.

TRIP

Without insurance, you will lose all or most of your money if you must cancel your trip due to illness or any other reason. Especially if your airline ticket, cruise, or package tour is nonrefundable and cannot be changed, it's essential that you **buy trip-cancellation-and-interruption insurance.** When considering how much coverage you need, look for a policy that will cover the cost of your trip plus the nondiscounted price of a one-way airline ticket should you need to return home early. Read the fine print carefully, especially sections defining "family member" and "preexisting medical conditions." Also **consider default or bankruptcy insurance,** which protects you against a supplier's failure to deliver. However, such policies often do not cover default by a travel agency, tour operator, airline, or cruise line if you bought your tour and the coverage directly from the firm in question.

L
LANGUAGE

The French study English at school for a minimum of four years (often longer) but to little general effect. However, English is widely understood in major tourist areas, and no matter what the area, at least one person in most hotels can explain things to you. Young people usually speak more than their parents' generation. Be patient, and speak slowly.

The French may appear prickly at first to English-speaking visitors, but they usually will try to help out, especially when you at least make an effort to speak their language. So even if your own French is terrible, try to master a few words. *See* the French Vocabulary and Menu Guide at the back of the book.

LODGING

France has a wide range of accommodations, ranging from rambling old village inns that cost next to nothing to stylish converted châteaus that cost the earth. Prices must, by law, be posted at the hotel entrance and should include taxes and service. Prices are always by room, not per person, and you should always check what bathroom facilities that includes, if any. Because replumbing drains is often prohibitive, if not impossible, old hotels may have added bathrooms—often with showers, not tubs—to the guest rooms, but not toilets. Breakfast is not always included in the price, but you are usually expected to have it and are often charged for it regardless. In smaller rural hotels you may be expected to have your evening meal at the hotel, too. Ask for a *grand lit* if you want a double bed. Negotiating rates has become acceptable in Paris and the provinces. Although you may not be able to reduce the price, you might get an upgrade to a newly redecorated, larger, or deluxe room.

APARTMENT AND VILLA RENTALS

If you want a home base that's roomy enough for a family and comes with cooking facilities, **consider a furnished rental.** It's generally cost-wise, too, although not always—some rentals are luxury properties (economical only when your party is large). Home-exchange directories do list rentals—often second homes owned by prospective house swappers—and some services search for a house or apartment for you (even a castle if that's your fancy) and handle the paperwork. Some send an illustrated catalogue and others send photographs of specific properties, sometimes at a charge; up-front registration fees may apply.

BED-AND-BREAKFAST

B&Bs, known in France as *chambres d'hôte*, are increasingly popular, especially in rural areas. Check local tourist offices for details.

HOME EXCHANGE

If you would like to find a house, an apartment, or other vacation property to exchange for your own while on vacation, **become a member of a home-exchange organization,** which will send you its annual directories listing available exchanges and will include your own listing in at least one of them. Arrangements for the actual exchange are made by the two parties to it, not by the organization.

M

MAIL

Airmail letters to the United States and Canada cost 4.30 francs for 20 grams, 7.90 francs for up to 40 grams, and 12.50 francs for up to 60 grams. Letters to the United Kingdom cost 2.80 francs for up to 20 grams. Letters cost 2.80 francs within France; postcards cost 2.80 francs within France and if sent to Canada, the United States, the United Kingdom, and EU countries; 4.30 francs if sent airmail to

North America. Stamps can be bought in post offices and cafés sporting a red TABAC sign outside.

RECEIVING MAIL

If you're uncertain where you'll be staying, **have mail sent to the local post office,** addressed as "poste restante," or to American Express, but remember that during peak seasons, American Express may refuse to accept mail.

MEDICAL ASSISTANCE

No one plans to get sick while traveling, but it happens, so **consider signing up with a medical assistance company.** These outfits provide referrals, emergency evacuation or repatriation, 24-hour telephone hot lines for medical consultation, dispatch of medical personnel, relay of medical records, cash for emergencies, and other personal and legal assistance.

MONEY AND EXPENSES

The units of currency in France are the franc (fr) and the centime. Bills are in denominations of 500, 200, 100, 50, and 20 francs. Coins are 20, 10, 5, 2, and 1 francs and 50, 20, 10, and 5 centimes. Note that the old 10-franc coin has been changed and replaced by a smaller, two-tone version. At press time (spring 1995), the exchange rate was about 5.35 francs to the U.S. dollar, 3.75 to the Canadian

dollar, and 8.35 to the pound sterling.

ATMS

Cirrus, Plus, and many other networks connecting automated-teller machines operate internationally. Chances are that you can **use your bank card at ATMs** to withdraw money from an account and get cash advances on a credit-card account if your card has been programmed with a personal identification number, or PIN. Before leaving home, **check in on frequency limits** for withdrawals and cash advances. Also **ask whether your card's PIN must be reprogrammed** for use in France. Four digits are commonly used overseas. Note that Discover is accepted only in the United States.

On cash advances you are charged interest from the day you receive the money, whether from a teller or an ATM. Although transaction fees for ATM withdrawals abroad may be higher than fees for withdrawals at home, Cirrus and Plus exchange rates are excellent because they are based on wholesale rates only offered by major banks.

COSTS

The following prices are for Paris; other cities and areas are often cheaper. Coffee in a bar: 5 francs (standing), 10 francs (seated); beer in a bar: 10 francs (standing), 13 francs (seated); Coca-Cola: 6–10 francs a can; ham sandwich: 14–29 francs; one-mile taxi ride: 35 francs; movie-theater seat: 45 francs (20%–30% cheaper on Monday and Wednesday); foreign newspaper: 9–12 francs.

EXCHANGING CURRENCY

For the most favorable rates, **change money at banks.** You won't do as well at exchange booths in airports, rail, and bus stations, or in hotels, restaurants, and stores, although you may find their hours more convenient. To avoid lines at airport exchange booths, **get a small amount of currency before you leave home.**

TAXES

All taxes must be included in posted prices in France. The initials TTC (*toutes taxes comprises*—taxes included) sometimes appear on price lists but, strictly speaking, are superfluous. By law, restaurant and hotel prices must include 18.6% taxes and a service charge. If you discover that these have rematerialized as additional items on your bill, kick up a fuss.

VAT➤ A number of shops, particularly large stores and shops in holiday resorts, offer VAT refunds to foreign shoppers. You are entitled to an Export Discount of 18.6%, depending on the item purchased, but it is often applicable only if your purchases in the same store reach a minimum of 2,800 francs (for U.K. and EU residents) or 1,200 francs (other residents,

including U.S. and Canadian residents). Remember to ask for the refund, as some stores—especially larger ones—offer the service only upon request.

TRAVELER'S CHECKS

Whether or not to buy traveler's checks depends on where you are headed; **take cash to rural areas and small towns, traveler's checks to cities.** The most widely recognized are American Express, Citicorp, Thomas Cook, and Visa, which are sold by major commercial banks for 1% to 3% of the checks' face value— it pays to **shop around.** Both American Express and Thomas Cook issue checks that can be counter-signed and used by you or your traveling companion, and they both provide checks, at no extra charge, denominated in francs. You can cash them in banks without paying a fee (which can be as much as 20%) and use them as readily as cash in many hotels, restaurants, and shops. So you won't be left with excess foreign currency, **buy a few checks in small denominations** to cash toward the end of your trip. Record the numbers of the checks, cross them off as you spend them, and keep this information separate from your checks.

WIRING MONEY

You don't have to be a cardholder to send or receive funds through MoneyGram^{SM} from American Express. Just go to a MoneyGram^{SM} agent, located in retail

and convenience stores and in American Express Travel Offices. Pay up to $1,000 with cash or a credit card, anything over that in cash. The money can be picked up within 10 minutes in the form of U.S. dollar traveler's checks or local currency at the nearest Money-Gram agent, or, abroad, the nearest American Express Travel Office. There's no limit, and the recipient need only present photo identification. The cost runs from 3% to 10%, depending on the amount sent, the destination, and how you pay.

You can also send money using Western Union. Money sent from the United States or Canada will be available for pickup at agent locations in 100 countries within 15 minutes. Once the money is in the system, it can be picked up at any one of 25,000 locations. Fees range from 4% to 10%, depending on the amount you send.

P PACKAGES AND TOURS

A package or tour to France can make your vacation less expensive and more convenient. Firms that sell tours and packages purchase airline seats, hotel rooms, and rental cars in bulk and pass some of the savings on to you. In addition, the best operators have local representatives to help you out at your destination.

A GOOD DEAL?

The more your package or tour includes, the better you can predict the ultimate cost of your vacation. Make sure you know exactly what is included, and **beware of hidden costs.** Are taxes, tips, and service charges included? Transfers and baggage handling? Entertainment and excursions? These can add up.

Most packages and tours are rated deluxe, first-class superior, first class, tourist, or budget. The key difference is usually accommodations. If the package or tour you are considering is priced lower than in your wildest dreams, **be skeptical.** Also, **make sure your travel agent knows the hotels** and other services. Ask about location, room size, beds, and whether the facility has a pool, room service, or programs for children, if you care about these. Has your agent been there or sent others you can contact?

BUYER BEWARE

Each year consumers are stranded or lose their money when operators go out of business—even very large ones with excellent reputations. If you can't afford a loss, take the time to **check out the operator**—find out how long the company has been in business, and ask several agents about its reputation. Next, **don't book unless the firm has a consumer-protection program.** Members of the United States Tour Operators Association and the National Tour Association are required to set aside funds exclusively to cover your payments and travel arrangements in case of default. Nonmember operators may instead carry insurance; look for the details in the operator's brochure—and the name of an underwriter with a solid reputation. Note: When it comes to tour operators, **don't trust escrow accounts.** Although there are laws governing those of charter-flight operators, no governmental body prevents tour operators from raiding the till.

Next, **contact your local Better Business Bureau and the attorney general's office** in both your own state and the operator's; have any complaints been filed? Last, **pay with a major credit card.** Then you can cancel payment, provided that you can document your complaint. Always **consider trip-cancellation insurance** (*see* Insurance, *above*).

BIG VS. SMALL➤ An operator that handles several hundred thousand travelers annually can use its purchasing power to give you a good price. Its high volume may also indicate financial stability. But some small companies provide more personalized service; because they tend to specialize, they may also be experts on an area.

USING AN AGENT

Travel agents are an excellent resource. In fact, large operators accept bookings only through travel agents. But it's good to **collect brochures from several agencies,** because some agents' suggestions may be skewed by promotional relationships with tour and package firms that reward them for volume sales. If you have a special interest, **find an agent with expertise in that area;** the American Society of Travel Agents can give you leads in the United States. (Don't rely solely on your agent, though; agents may be unaware of small-niche operators, and some special-interest travel companies only sell direct).

SINGLE TRAVELERS

Prices are usually quoted per person, based on two sharing a room. If traveling solo, you may be required to pay the full double occupancy rate. Some operators eliminate this surcharge if you agree to be matched up with a roommate of the same sex, even if one is not found by departure time.

PACKING
FOR FRANCE

Pack light: Baggage carts are scarce in airports and railroad stations, and luggage restrictions on international flights are tight.

Over the past few years, the French have become less formal in their dress. Paris is still the world's fashion capital and both men and women spend a lot on clothes. But there is no need to wear a tie and jacket at most of even the fanciest restaurants, and jeans are de rigueur at the new Bastille Opéra. However, sneakers are seldom worn in cities, even with casual clothing; the same goes for shorts, which are seen as vulgar. Men who wear them will probably be denied admission to churches and cathedrals, as will women (though they no longer need to cover their heads and arms to enter).

For beach resorts, take a cover-up, as wearing bathing suits on the street is frowned upon. Most casinos and nightclubs along the Riviera require jackets and ties. If you like to dress formally, take a cocktail dress or tuxedo.

Most of France is hot in the summer, cool in the winter—and rainy all year round. Do not forget a raincoat and umbrella. You'll need a sweater or warm jacket for the Mediterranean in winter.

If you are staying in budget hotels, take along small bars of soap; many either do not provide it or limit guests to one tiny bar per room. Zip-closure bags, a pocket calculator, and a small flashlight are also indispensable.

Bring an extra pair of eyeglasses or contact lenses in your carry-on luggage, and if you have a health problem, **pack enough medication** to last the trip or have your doctor write a prescription using the drug's generic name, because brand names vary from country to country (you'll then need a prescription from a doctor in the country you're visiting). **Don't put prescription drugs or valuables in luggage to be checked,** for it could go astray. To avoid problems with customs officials, carry medications in original packaging. Also, don't forget the addresses of offices that handle refunds of lost traveler's checks.

ELECTRICITY

To use your U.S.-purchased electric-powered equipment, **bring a converter and an adapter.** The electrical current in France is 220 volts, 50 cycles alternating current (AC); wall outlets take Continental-type plugs, with two round prongs.

If your appliances are dual voltage, you'll need only an adapter. Hotels sometimes have 110-volt outlets for low-wattage appliances marked "For Shavers Only" near the sink; don't use them for high-wattage appliances like blow-dryers. If your laptop computer is older, carry a converter; new laptops operate equally well on 110 and 220 volts, so you need only an adapter.

LUGGAGE

Free airline baggage allowances depend on the airline, the route, and the class of your ticket; ask in advance. In general, on domestic flights and on international flights between the United States and foreign destinations, you are entitled to check two bags— neither exceeding 62 inches, or 158 centimeters (length + width + height), or weighing more than 70 pounds (32 kilograms). A third piece may be brought aboard; its total dimensions are generally limited to less than 45 inches (114 centimeters), so it will fit easily under the seat in front of you or in the overhead compartment. In the United States, the Federal Aviation Administration gives airlines broad latitude to limit carry-on allowances and tailor them to different aircraft and operational conditions. Charges for excess, oversize, or overweight pieces vary.

If you are flying between two foreign destinations, note that baggage allowances may be determined not by piece but by weight— generally 88 pounds (40 kilograms) in first class, 66 pounds (30 kilograms) in business class, and 44 pounds (20 kilograms) in economy. If your flight between two cities abroad *connects* with your transatlantic or transpacific flight, the piece method still applies.

SAFEGUARDING YOUR LUGGAGE➤ Before leaving home, **itemize your bags' contents** and their worth, and label them with your name, address, and phone number. (If you use your home address, cover it so that potential burglars can't see it.) Inside your bag, **pack a copy of your itinerary.** At check-in, **make sure that your**

bag is correctly tagged with the airport's three-letter destination code. If your bags arrive damaged or not at all, file a written report with the airline before leaving the airport.

PASSPORTS
AND VISAS

If you don't already have one, **get a passport.** While traveling, **keep one photocopy of the data page** separate from your wallet and leave another copy with someone at home. If you lose your passport, promptly call the nearest embassy or consulate, and the local police; having the data page can speed replacement.

U.S. CITIZENS

All U.S. citizens, even infants, need a valid passport to enter France for stays of up to 90 days. New and renewal application forms are available at any of the 13 U.S. Passport Agency offices and at some post offices and courthouses. Passports, which are valid for ten years, are usually mailed within four weeks; allow five weeks or more in spring and summer.

CANADIANS

You need a valid passport to enter France for stays of up to 90 days. Application forms are available at 28 regional passport offices as well as post offices and travel agencies. Whether for a first or a renewal passport, you must apply in person. Children under 16 may be included on a parent's passport but must have their own to travel

alone. Passports are valid for five years and are usually mailed within two to three weeks of application.

U.K. CITIZENS

Citizens of the United Kingdom need a valid passport to enter France for stays of up to 90 days. Applications for new and renewal passports are available from main post offices as well as at the passport offices located in Belfast, Glasgow, Liverpool, London, Newport, and Peterborough. You may apply in person at all passport offices, or by mail to all except the London office. Children under 16 may travel on an accompanying parent's passport. All passports are valid for 10 years. Allow a month for processing.

R
RAIL TRAVEL

To save money, **look into rail passes** (*see* Important Contacts A to Z, *above*). But be aware that if you don't plan to cover many miles, you may come out ahead by buying individual tickets.

Many travelers assume that rail passes guarantee them seats on the trains they wish to ride. Not so. You need to **book seats ahead even if you are using a rail pass;** seat reservations are required on some European trains, particularly high-speed trains, and are a good idea on trains that may be crowded—particularly in summer on popular routes. You

will also need a reservation if you purchase overnight sleeping accommodations.

The SNCF is generally recognized as Europe's best national rail service: It's fast, punctual, comfortable, and comprehensive. The high-speed TGVs, or *Trains à Grande Vitesse* (average 255 kph/160 mph on the Lyon/southeast line, 300 kph/190 mph on the Lille and Bordeaux/southwest lines), are the best domestic trains. They operate between Paris and Lille, Paris and Brussels, Paris and Lyon/Switzerland/the Riviera, and Angers/Nantes, and Tours/Poitiers/Bordeaux. As with other main-line trains, a small supplement may be assessed at peak hours. You must **always make a seat reservation for the TGV**—easily obtained at the ticket window or from an automatic machine. Seat reservations are reassuring but seldom necessary on other main-line French trains, except at certain busy holiday times.

If you know what station you'll depart from, you can get a free schedule there (while supplies last), or you can access the new multilingual computerized schedule information network at any Paris station and many provincial ones. You can also make reservations and buy your ticket while at the computer.

If you are traveling from Paris (or any other terminus), **get to the station half an hour** before departure to ensure that you'll have a good seat. The majority of intercity trains in France consist of open-plan cars and are known as *Corail* trains. They are clean and extremely comfortable, even in second class. Trains on regional branch lines are currently being spruced up but lag behind in style and quality. The food in French trains can be good, but it's poor value for the money.

Before boarding, you must punch your ticket (but not EurailPass) in one of the orange machines at the entrance to the platforms, or else the ticket collector will fine you 100 francs on the spot.

It is possible to get from one end of France to the other without traveling overnight. Otherwise you have the choice between high-priced *wagons-lits* (sleeping cars) and affordable *couchettes* (bunks, six to a compartment in second class, four to a compartment in first, with sheet and pillow provided, priced at around 89 francs). Special summer night trains from Paris to Spain and the Riviera, geared to young people, are equipped with disco and bar.

S

SENIOR-CITIZEN DISCOUNTS

Older travelers to France can take advantage of many discounts, such as reduced admissions of 20%–50% to museums and movie

theaters. Seniors 60 and older should **buy a Carte Vermeil,** which entitles the bearer to discounts on the French domestic airline (Air Inter), rail travel outside Paris, the bus and Métro, and reduced admission prices for films and many cultural events. Cards are available at any rail station in France (cost: 140 francs).

To qualify for age-related discounts, **mention your senior-citizen status up front** when booking hotel reservations, not when checking out, and before you're seated in restaurants, not when paying your bill. Note that discounts may be limited to certain menus, days, or hours. When renting a car, **ask about promotional car-rental discounts**—they can net lower costs than your senior-citizen discount.

SHOPPING

Shop prices are clearly marked and bargaining isn't a way of life. Still, at outdoor and flea markets and in antiques stores, you can try your luck. If you're thinking of buying several items, you've nothing to lose by cheerfully suggesting to the proprietor, *"Vous me faites un prix?"* ("How about a discount?").

SPORTS

France has no shortage of sports facilities. Many seaside resorts are well equipped for water sports, such as windsurfing and water-skiing, and there are swimming pools in

every French town. In winter, the Alps and the somewhat less pricey Pyrénées and Vosges boast excellent skiing facilities—both for *ski alpin* (downhill) and *ski de fond* (cross-country).

Bicycling (*see* Bicycling *in* Important Contacts A to Z) is popular and, like *équitation* (horseback riding), possible in many rural areas. The many rivers of France offer excellent fishing (check locally for authorization rights) and canoeing. Tennis is phenomenally popular in France, and courts are everywhere: Try for a typical *terre battue* (clay court) if you can. Golf and squash have caught on; you may be able to find a course or a court not too far away. The French are not so keen on jogging, but you'll have no difficulty locating a suitable local park or avenue.

STUDENTS ON THE ROAD

For students, France holds special allure, particularly Paris. During the summer, young people from all over Europe congregate in the French capital. During the school year, students dominate the Left Bank. Cheap food and lodging is easy to find throughout the country, so there's little need to scrounge. In addition, there are student bargains almost everywhere, on train and plane fares, and for movie and museum tickets. All you need is an International Student Identity Card (*see*

Students *in* Important Contacts A to Z).

To save money, **look into deals available through student-oriented travel agencies** to those with a bona fide student ID card, and to members of international student groups. *See* Students *in* Important Contacts A to Z.

T

TELEPHONES

For the moment, all French phone numbers have eight digits; a code is required only when calling the Paris region from the provinces (add 16–1 for Paris) and for calling the provinces from Paris (16, then the number). The number system was changed only in 1985; therefore, you may still come across some seven-digit numbers in Paris and some six-digit ones elsewhere. Add 4 to the beginning of such Paris numbers, and the former two-figure area code to provincial ones.

Because more phone lines are now needed, **in October 1996 all numbers will get a prefix of two new digits.** In Paris and Ile de France, 01 will precede the number (replacing the 16–1); in the northwest, 02; in the northeast, 03; in the southeast, 04; and in the southwest, 05.

LONG-DISTANCE

The country code for dialing France is 33.

To make a direct international call from France, dial 19 and wait for the tone, then dial the country code (1 for the United States

and Canada; 44 for the United Kingdom), area code (minus any initial 0), and number.

OPERATORS AND INFORMATION

When calling home from France, local access numbers to the English-speaking operators of U.S. long-distance carriers are: **AT&T:** 19–0011; **MCI:** 19–0019, and **Sprint:** 19–0087.

To find a number in France or to request other information, dial 12. For international inquiries, dial 19–33 plus the country code.

PAY PHONES

The French telephone system is modern and efficient. Telephone booths are plentiful; they can almost always be found at post offices and often in cafés. A local call costs 80 centimes for every three minutes; half-price rates apply weekdays between 9:30 PM and 8 AM, from 1:30 PM Saturday, and all day Sunday.

Most French pay phones are operated by *télécartes* (phone cards), which you can buy from post offices, métro stations, and some tobacco shops (cost: 40 francs for 50 units; 96 francs for 120). Some pay phones accept 1-, 2- and 5-franc coins (1-franc minimum). Lift the receiver, insert the télécarte or coins in the appropriate slots, and dial.

TIPPING

The French have a clear idea of when they should be tipped. Bills

in bars and restaurants include service, but it is customary to leave some small change unless you're dissatisfied. The amount of this varies: 30 centimes if you've merely bought a beer, or a few francs after a meal. Tip taxi drivers and hairdressers about 10%. Give ushers in theaters and movie theaters 1 or 2 francs. In some theaters and hotels, coat check attendants may expect nothing (if there is a sign saying POURBOIRE INTERDIT—tips forbidden); otherwise give them 5 francs. Washroom attendants usually get 5 francs, though the sum is often posted.

If you stay in a hotel for more than two or three days, it is customary to leave something for the chambermaid—about 10 francs per day. In expensive hotels you may well call on the services of a baggage porter (bell boy) and hotel porter and possibly the telephone receptionist. All expect a tip: Plan on about 10 francs per item for the baggage boy, but the other tips will depend on how much you've used their services—common sense must guide you here. In hotels that provide room service, give 5 francs to the waiter (this does not apply to breakfast served in your room). If the chambermaid does some pressing or laundering for you, give her 5 francs on top of the charge made.

Gas-station attendants get nothing for gas or oil, and 5 or 10 francs

THE GOLD GUIDE / SMART TRAVEL TIPS

for checking tires. Train and airport porters get a fixed 6–10 francs per bag, but you're better off getting your own baggage cart if you can (a 10-franc coin—refundable—is sometimes necessary). Museum guides should get 5–10 francs after a guided tour, and it is standard practice to tip tour guides (and bus drivers) 10 francs or more after an excursion, depending on its length.

W
WHEN TO GO

June and September are the best months to be in France, as both are free of the midsummer crowds. June offers the advantage of long daylight hours, while cheaper prices and frequent Indian summers, often lasting well into October, make September attractive. Try to avoid the second half of July and all of August, when almost all of France goes on vacation. Huge crowds jam the roads and beaches, and prices are jacked up in resorts. Don't travel on or around July 14 and August 1, 14, and 31.

July and August in southern France can be stifling. Paris can be stuffy in August, too, but it is pleasantly deserted. Many restaurants, theaters, and small shops close, but enough stay open these days to make a low-key, unhurried visit a pleasure. If you want to go to the countryside at this time, stay away from the coast. Hotels and restaurants are less crowded inland.

The ski season in the Alps and Pyrénées lasts from Christmas to Easter; if you can, avoid February, when school holidays mean crowds. Anytime between March and November will offer you a good chance to soak up the sun on the Riviera. If Paris and the Loire are among your priorities, remember that the weather is unappealing before Easter. If you're dreaming of Paris in the springtime, May is your best bet, not rainy April. But the capital remains a joy during mid-winter, with plenty of things to see and do.

CLIMATE

What follows are average daily maximum and minimum temperatures for Paris and Nice.

Climate in France

PARIS

Jan.	43F	6C	May	68F	20C	Sept.	70F	21C
	34	1		49	10		53	12
Feb.	45F	7C	June	73F	23C	Oct.	60F	16C
	34	1		55	13		46	8
Mar.	54F	12C	July	76F	25C	Nov.	50F	10C
	39	4		58	15		40	5
Apr.	60F	16C	Aug.	75F	24C	Dec.	44F	7C
	43	6		58	15		36	2

NICE

Jan.	55F	13C	May	68F	20C	Sept.	77F	25C
	39	4		55	13		61	16
Feb.	55F	13C	June	75F	24C	Oct.	70F	21C
	41	5		61	16		54	12
Mar.	59F	15C	July	81F	27C	Nov.	63F	17C
	45	7		64	18		46	8
Apr.	64F	18C	Aug.	81F	27C	Dec.	55F	13C
	46	8		64	18		41	5

1 Destination: France

THE BEST OF ALL POSSIBLE WORLDS

FRANCE IS NEITHER TOO HOT nor too cold, neither too wet nor too dry, neither too flat nor too crammed with inconvenient mountains. At any rate, that is what the French say. They think that countries should be hexagonal in shape and about 600 miles across. Spain is too square, Norway is frayed at the edges, l'Angleterre (which is what they usually call Great Britain) is awkwardly surrounded by cold water, Switzerland landlocked and too small, and the United States too large (you cross three time zones and then get the same depressing dinner). After God created France, He belatedly realized that He had gone too far: It was too near perfection. "How can I restore the balance?" He asked Himself. Then He saw what to do—He created the French. That is a French story. The French enjoy grumbling about themselves or, rather, about other French people, but in the same breath they admit that there is only one civilized way for people to live, and that is the French way, *la civilisation française*.

My wife and I have lived in France for more than 15 years, and we have come to the conclusion that there is something to be said for this view. Our fellow villagers are kind, patient, and friendly, behaving with natural dignity and good manners, like most of the other French people we meet (except Parisians in the rush hour). Visitors to France, particularly Anglo-Saxon visitors, whether they stay a week or a year, will have a better time if they "go native" as far as they find it practicable—and when and where they don't, they should be philosophically aware of the drawbacks of trying to behave as in dear old Birmingham, AL or U.K. (I am using the word "Anglo-Saxon" as the French use it. To them, Louis Armstrong, Robert Burns, James Joyce, and Frank Sinatra are representative Anglo-Saxons; Beowulf and King Alfred have nothing to do with it.).

Let's look at the French timetable. Most of the French are up early, gulping a *café au lait* and getting to work by 8. By 10, Parisian executives are fuming because their London contacts haven't yet answered the phone (it's only 9 in England). There is no coffee break.

At noon, they are hungry. Work stops for two hours or longer. Museums and small shops close. *Le déjeuner* (called *le dîner* in the country) is a sacred rite. Fast-food outlets have multiplied, but the norm is a proper meal, taking an hour and a half; a surprising number, even of those who work in central Paris, manage to get home for it. However, the increasing number of women at work means that six lunches out of ten are eaten at restaurants or canteens—substantial, freshly cooked affairs, eaten with serious critical attention. The French grew rich in the '60s: Back in 1920, they each ate nearly three pounds of bread a day—now it is just under a pound, with a corresponding increase in the consumption of meat, fish, and cheese. Less wine is drunk, but more of it is of higher quality.

There is a typical restaurant in our nearest market town (pop. 6,000). It has only one menu: copious hors d'oeuvres, a fish dish or a light meat dish, a more serious meat dish, vegetables in season, a good cheese board, fruit or ice cream. It's always full by 12:30. A couple from San Francisco who stayed in a rented cottage in our village were hardly ever able to use it. They used to get up at 9 and have an Anglo-Saxon sort of breakfast, and so they were hopelessly out of phase with the commercial travelers (up at 6) who form the restaurant's main clientele. You can't start your lunch there at 1:30 or 2, and there are no doggy bags in France. We are in the Midi, where an early start and a siesta are convenient (many of the shops don't reopen until 3:30). However, the couple happily developed the picnic habit: France is God's own country for picnicking, if only you get to the *charcuterie* and the *boulangerie* and the *pâtisserie* well before they close at noon.

Back to work for another four-hour stretch. No tea or coffee break. Are the French mighty toilers? Yes and no. I have conducted oral language examinations in France and in England. The French expect me to keep on examining nonstop from 8 to 12:30 and again from 2 to 6:30. The merciful (lazy?) English think six hours of attentive interviewing per day, with breaks midmorning and mid-afternoon, are all the human mind can stand. French schoolchildren have a much longer day than do Anglo-Saxon ones and have more to learn.

On the other hand, wage earners and schoolchildren have many leisure days. In the '80s, the average industrial worker put in 1,872 hours of work in the United States, 1,750 in Great Britain, but only 1,650 in France. Five weeks' paid vacation is the official minimum, and there are many public holidays. The French have become addicts of leisure in the past two decades. One family in ten has a second house in the country, where they go on weekends and vacations, causing astounding traffic jams as they flee the cities.

If he finishes his day's work at 6 or 6:30, will our average Frenchman call in at his favorite café for a chat and an aperitif on his way home? Probably not, nowadays. In the past, the café was used as a sort of extra living room for meeting friends or professional contacts, or even for writing novels if you were Jean-Paul Sartre or Simone de Beauvoir. But today an average of two hours and 50 minutes is spent watching television at home, which reduces the time available for social life.

This is sad. The number of cafés has diminished. Fortunately, there are still a lot left, and how convenient they are for the visitor! On the terrace of a French café, you can bask in the sun or enjoy the shade of a multicolored parasol, sipping a cool beer and keeping an eye on life's passing show, while your near and dear toy with Popsicles or write letters. A small black coffee entitles you to spend an hour or two—no hurry.

While we are on the subject: It seems odd to the Anglo-Saxon that in France beer is generally considered a nonalcoholic drink. When you tell the French that some people at home succeed in getting nastily drunk on it, they say, "But they must drink several glasses!" Indeed. A Frenchman will spend half an hour sipping a quarter of a liter. One sees few drunks in France, except in the north, and then very rarely.

I mentioned the aperitif hour to talk not only about cafés but about friendliness. Some people—notably Americans—complain that the French are inhospitable and standoffish. The fact is that they are great respecters of privacy. If the Englishman's home is his castle, the Frenchman's apartment or house is his lair. People simply do not pop into one another's lairs, drinking casual cups of coffee and borrowing half a pound of sugar. They need a neutral place in which to socialize. Britons come somewhere between typical French people and the American middle class. According to Paul Fussell (*Caste Marks*, 1983): "Among the [American] middles there's a convention that erecting a fence or even a tall hedge is an affront."

It's different in France. People in the Midi, where we live, just love to talk, and even to listen. But our village neighbors are timid about entering our house. If they want to ask us something, they will wait until we meet, or stay on the doorstep, or phone (from 50 yards away). They penetrate our house, and we penetrate theirs, when specifically invited. That is how they behave among themselves, too. It's not because we are foreigners.

So when do we talk? There are benches everywhere, in the sun and in the shade. The villagers—and we—sit there for hours, chatting. The locals really are interested in you, your habits and tastes, the number and ages of your children, your work, where you come from, and so forth, and are longing to impart a discreet selection of their own personal details. Of course you *may* be invited home. There are no rules about this sort of thing. And if there were, the French would take pleasure in breaking them.

When talking with the French, there are conventions that should be observed if you don't want to be thought a barbarian by people who are unaware of Anglo-Saxon attitudes. You must say *"Bonjour"* followed by *Monsieur, Madame, Mademoiselle, Messieurs, Mesdames,* or *Messieurs-dames* much more often than you would think necessary (on entering a small shop, for instance) and *"au revoir, Monsieur"* (etc.). Hands are shaken frequently (by colleagues at work, morning and evening, and by the most casual acquaintances). *Bon appétit* can replace *au revoir* shortly before mealtimes. On going through a door, a certain amount of *après-vous*-ing is normal, with *pardon* if you go through first, turning your back. Getting on first-name terms is a sign of much greater intimacy than in England or the United States. Rush-hour Parisian life is more brutal, of course, and, as elsewhere in the world, the driving seat of a car exerts a malign influence. In England, a headlight flash sometimes means "After you"; in France, it means either "After me" or "I am a criminal and I expect you are, too, so watch it, chum, the cops are round the corner."

Back home from the café, *le dîner* (called *le souper* in the country) is served around 8, for rich and poor. It's a lighter meal than at midday, with soup replacing hors d'oeuvres. The schoolchildren will have finished their homework by then. Bed follows not long after. But the movies, after a sharp fall as television established itself in every home, have resisted well. Except in Paris, films are dubbed into French, a practice deplored by intellectuals.

Almost all employed people now have a two-day weekend, usually Saturday and Sunday, but Sunday and Monday for many shop workers. Schoolchildren have Wednesday free, but may attend Saturday morning, instead. In recent years, the French have revolutionized their leisure habits: Jogging, swimming, soccer, gymnastics, tennis, and vigorous bicycling (for fun, not transport) are practiced, mainly on weekends, by large numbers of all social classes.

Sunday is a day for enjoying oneself. Though 85% of the population declare themselves Catholics, only 15% of those go to church every week. There is a fairly strong anti-church sentiment among many, even among those who say they are Catholics, but the traditional warfare between priest and primary-school teacher—the one reactionary and the other attached to Republican ideals—is a thing of the past. Divorce, the pill, and legal abortion are widely accepted, even by practicing Catholics.

The great Sunday ritual takes place at noon or soon after. Four out of 10 will visit friends or relations. Sixty percent of families do more cooking on Sundays than on other days. This is also a big day for restaurants that feature a special Sunday menu. Half the French end their Sunday lunch with a fresh fruit tart or some sort of *gâteau*, which is why the pastry shops are open in the morning and why you see Frenchmen carefully carrying flat cardboard boxes. Then a quarter of the population takes a little siesta.

An essay such as this has to contain rash generalizations. Is there an average French person? Obviously not. There are the rich and the poor, for example. The poor, in France, like champagne, oysters, and foie gras, but they get them less often than do the rich. The same is true of other aspects of life. The gulf between one class and another is not one of tastes and aspirations; rich and poor are in broad agreement on what constitutes a pleasant life. The poor are simply further away from it than are the rich.

Changing France . . . I was there in 1947, and I said to myself: "How wonderful! But it can't last." On the whole it has. The surge of prosperity in the '60s brought improvements to French life, with some drawbacks (traffic in Paris, for example), but basic traditions die hard. The young ape foreign fashions, with a fast-food/motorcycle/mid-Atlantic pop noise/comic-strip culture, but they grow out of it. Official morality has changed. Contraception used to be forbidden; Paris was famed for its elegant brothels, but women had to go to London for diaphragms and to Switzerland for abortions. All that has gone. In 1988, the rise of AIDS caused a quickly smothered quarrel among bishops about the sinfulness of condoms, which are readily available. *Le topless* is seen on most beaches, and total nakedness on some. But the family remains a powerful, cohesive unit.

What do they think of us? Corresponding to the Anglo-Saxon stereotype that depicts all Frenchmen wearing berets and pointed beards, waving their arms wildly and being saucy with the girls, the French picture Americans as rich, generous, overweight, and likely in world politics or personal relationships to behave like well-meaning bulls in china shops and the English as either tall, silent, inhibited, masochistic, and scrupulously honest or as drunken, sadistic, soccer-watching vandals. Of course nobody really believes any of this, but if you are going to attach a national label to yourself, you might as well be aware of the cliché lurking at the back of the mind.

"Happy as God in France" say the Germans, exaggerating a bit. Anglo-Saxons come in two sorts: those who love France and those who don't. It's a matter of taste and character. The former find it easy to slip into the French way of life for a week or a month or permanently. The latter are better off in Paris or on the Riviera. But really, the French are canny operators when it comes to enjoying *la douceur de vivre,* the sweetness of life. If you follow their example while in France, you can't go far wrong. (One way to go wrong would be to quote almost any paragraph from this essay to them; at any rate, it will start a vigorously French argument.)

—*John P. Harris*

Born in England, John P. Harris has lived in a small village in the south of France since 1975. He has written numerous articles for both French and British newspapers and magazines, including the London Times, *and is the author of* France—a Guide for the Independent Traveler *(Macmillan, London 1987).*

WHAT'S WHERE

Alsace and Lorraine

In Alsace, France's Germanic northeast corner, the beautiful Route de Vin winds through vineyards and villages among the Vosges foothills, and medieval half-timber houses lend a storybook air. Strasbourg rivals Paris in culture (it's the EU capital), history and architecture, not to mention foie gras. Nancy, in Lorraine, is home to Baccarat and St-Louis crystal and adds Art Nouveau to its decorative mix, while remembering Joan of Arc. In the Jura, you can ski and visit pretty little towns to buy wooden toys, clocks, and pipes.

Atlantic Coast

Whatever you want is what you get in Aquitaine. Castles and châteaus recall medieval battles; Romanesque abbeys and cathedrals echo with history. The glossy resort of Biarritz may draw you, or the vast beaches, marshy "Green Venice" in the north, and Basque villages high in the Pyrénées.

Come to elegant Bordeaux in May for the music festival, or any time to sip the splendid wines with your oysters, Périgord truffles, foie gras, and Dordogne caviar.

Brittany

Nationalistic Brittany, the northwest arm of France, is full of the sound of the sea. It also has massive castles, vast beaches, and prehistoric standing stones. You'll be charmed, as well, by Rennes (medieval, Renaissance, *and* classical buildings), walled St-Malo, Quimper with its pottery, Dinan's Old Town, and tranquil Nantes. Come to Finisterre (land's end) in August for the classic sailboat rally in the Bay of Douarnenez, then visit Ste-Anne-la-Palud during the *pardon,* where you'll see traditional Breton lace *coiffes.*

Burgundy

Drive southeast from Paris to the land of medieval dukes more powerful than kings, noble vineyards, Gothic cathedrals, and fabulous food. Stop first in Troyes (Champagne) to wander the pedestrian streets, see the old churches, timber houses, and museums. Circle the Morvan Forest, stopping in Autun, once a Roman town, and picturesque Vézelay with its basilica, and push on to Dijon, where the Palais des Ducs now houses the wonderful Musée des Beaux-Arts. Be sure to taste the wines at the Marché aux Vins in Beaune, and maybe buy some as you head south, visiting the Abbey of Cluny on your way to Mâcon's wine fair in May.

Corsica

This island in the Mediterranean, about 100 miles southeast of Monaco, is wonderful in spring and fall, crowded in July and August. You'll need a week to circle it; visit Bastia's Old Town, explore the mountains along the Scala di Santa Regina, see Corte's citadelle, laze on a beach, hear folk songs in Pigna, tour Napoléon's birthplace, Ajaccio, visit fortified Bonifacio, and splurge at the Grand Hôtel de Cala Rossa in the walled town of Porto-Vecchio.

Ile de France

The green surround of Paris, lushly forested and islanded by meandering rivers, is studded with royal and noble châteaus. Versailles and Fontainebleau, Thoiry, Chantilly, and Maintenon are only a few. From sublime Chartres to Monet's Giverny, then to Disneyland Paris, you can traverse the centuries, all within an hour or so of Paris.

The Loire Valley

Sometimes owned by England, and fought over for centuries, this stretch of the Loire southwest of Paris resounds today with the noise of contented tourists, music festivals, and *son et lumière* spectacles at the extraordinary châteaux. Amboise, Blois, Chenonceau, Chambord—there are hundreds. Joan of Arc captured Orléans, and here you can learn her history, while at Angers, 130 miles downriver, you can ride, fish, canoe, take a boat or a balloon, visit the fortress and the cathedral, and get to know the wines of Anjou at the Maison du Vin.

Lyon and the Alps

You can zip down from Paris on the TGV in a couple of hours, and plant yourself in wonderful Lyon while you take in the rest of the region, from the wine villages of Beaujolais to the lakes and marshes of the Dombes and the medieval hilltop village of Pérouges. Then, venture down the Rhone to Vienne for Roman ruins and Renaissance facades and to the river town of Serrières. Pass through Grenoble with its fine museum en route to the Alps. Aix les Bains has ruined Roman baths and modern ones, and Annecy has lively Tuesday and Friday markets. Picturesque Talloires and chic Chamonix, with its cable car up the Aiguille du Midi, are two more enticing spots.

The Massif Central

This unspoiled region, newly accessible on good roads, has volcanoes and ravines, thermal springs, and the dramatic and beautiful Gorges du Tarn. Visit the exquisite cathedral in the market town of Bourges, elegant Vichy, and the museums and cathedral of Clermont-Ferrand; the Parc des Volcans (but not in summer), and wonderful medieval towns and villages like Salers, high-perched Rocamadour, St-Cirq-Lapopie, Figeac, and Ste-Foy.

Normandy

With miles of sandy beaches along the English Channel, Normandy also has seaside towns like Dieppe, Fécamp, Honfleur, and the Trouville and Deauville resorts. Continue west to reach fabulous Mont-St-Michel, the medieval abbey and village on a rock offshore that's an island at high tide. Inland, you must see Rouen's cathedral and its museums, visit charming Pont-Audemer on a market day, the lace museum in Alençon, and stay a while in Bayeux for the legendary tapestry and the harmonious cathedral. And don't forget the Calvados, the Camembert, and other marvelous cheeses.

Paris

The Eiffel Tower gives you an overview; the Louvre, a good look at the art of the past (with a peek, too, at architecture's present and future). Say a prayer at Notre-Dame, buy a dress you'll love forever, and eat an unforgettable meal anywhere at all. Open your eyes; there's something beautiful or amusing at every step; dawdle around the Latin Quarter, climb up to Montmartre for a peek at Sacré Coeur, spend a morning at the marché aux puces, and sail down the Seine on a bâteau mouche.

Provence

Hot, fragrant Provence, full of well-preserved Roman ruins, feels like summer, with dozens of produce and flower and fish markets, and outdoor sports (even bullfighting). Come to Nîmes (in Languedoc) to see the Pont du Gard aqueduct, the amphitheater, the museums, and the beautiful Maison Carré temple. You might spot wild horses in the marshy Camargue en route to Arles, with its Roman arena and theater. Visit Daudet's Moulin in charming Fontvieille, inspect the tiny medieval streets and ancient houses in Les Baux, and stop in Avignon to see the Papal Palace and the famous bridge. Orange has a Roman theater and triumphal arch, and elegant Aix-en-Provence has museums, fountains, and the beautiful Cours Mirabeau boulevard.

The Riviera

Invisible celebrities, pebbly beaches, backed-up traffic, hordes of sunburned bathers—why do people come? Medieval hilltop villages (St-Paul-de-Vence, Mougins, Gassin, Vence, Peillon, even touristy Eze), fields of fragrant flowers that supply the Grasse perfume factories, wonderful museums, and the lovely, limpid light are still as magnetic as ever. Stylish boutiques, great art, splendid food, exciting nightlife, and spectacular views of crystal bays and cliff-side villas don't hurt either. Wander the cobble streets of Nice's old town, visit its Shell Museum, and have a flutter at Monte Carlo's casino.

Toulouse, the Midi-Pyrénées, and Roussillon

Sports and nature lovers flock to southwest France, by the Spanish border, where lively Toulouse, a university town of rosy pink brick, is the cultural star. Visit fortified Cordes, with its medieval houses, and Albi's huge cathedral, the fine cloister at Moissac, and the old Roman town of Lectoure. Appealing spa towns and wonderful views enliven the Pyrénées' twisting roads, and Carcassonne, within its medieval walls, draws all the world, but should not be missed. When you see picturesque Collioure's stunning Mediterranean setting you'll know why artists love it, and in the Grotte de Niaux you can see marvelous prehistoric paintings in the underground gallery.

PLEASURES & PASTIMES

Beaches

It is ironic that France's most famous coastline should possess the country's worst beaches. But there it is: Sand is in shorter supply along the Riviera than pebbles. There are sandy beaches, of course, but they are seldom large or particularly clean, as the Mediterranean behaves like a large lake, with minimal tide to wash away the litter.

By far the best French beaches are those facing north (toward the Channel) and west (toward the Atlantic). Many are so vast that you can spread out even at the most popular resorts (like Biarritz, Royan, Dinard, or Le Touquet). The most picturesque beaches are those of Brittany.

Best bets for family vacations include the coast west of Bordeaux around Arcachon (with a good selection of accommodations and amusements) and the northern coast between Calais and Le Touquet (for a more invigorating climate and tranquil beachcombing). The larger resorts invariably have golf, tennis, and horseback riding; Le Touquet is unbeatable.

Bicycling

There is no shortage of wide, empty roads and flat or rolling countryside in France suitable for biking. The French themselves are great bicycling enthusiasts. Bikes can be hired from many train stations for around 40 francs a day (ask for a list at any station); you need to show your passport and leave a deposit of 500 francs (unless you have Visa or MasterCard). In general, you must return the bike to a station within the same *département* (county or region). Bikes may be sent as accompanied luggage from any station in France; some trains in rural areas transport them without any extra charge. *See also* Bicycling *in* Important Contacts A to Z.

Boules

The sport that is closest to French hearts is *boules* or *pétanque*—an easy-to-grasp version of bowling, traditionally played beneath plane trees with a glass of *pastis* (similar to anisette) at hand. The local *boulodrome* is a social focal point in southern France.

Camping

French campsites have a high reputation for organization and amenities, but they tend to be jam-packed in July and August. More and more campsites now welcome advance reservations; if you're traveling in summer, it makes good sense to book ahead. A guide to the country's campsites is published by the **Fédération Française de Camping et de Caravaning** (78 rue de Rivoli, 75004 Paris, ☎ 42–72–84–08). They'll send it to you directly for 70 francs plus shipping.

Hiking

France has a huge network of footpaths—some 40,000 kilometers (25,000 miles). The most popular are in such hilly regions as the Vosges, Massif Central, Pyrénées, Alps, Ardennes, Jura, Beaujolais, and Champagne. Other good bets include windswept Brittany, the picturesque Dordogne Valley, and forested areas of the Ile de France (Fontainebleau, St-Germain, Rambouillet). *See also* Hiking, *in* Important Contacts A to Z.

Shopping

If you ask any Frenchman to identify a region by product, he'd probably think first in terms of alcohol—of such local wines and brandies as cognac, Armagnac, Calvados, and marc (brandy made from grape skins). Food would be next on the list: foie gras in the southwest, mussels and oysters on the Channel and Atlantic coasts, olives and herbs in Provence, sausages and sauerkraut in Alsace, and nougat in Montélimar. Most regions have their own cheeses.

As for clothes, Paris is the firm fashion capital. Traditional regional strongholds (Lille for textiles, Calais for lace) have little clout these days, though good clothes can be bought everywhere and are invariably cheaper outside Paris (*see* Shopping *in* individual chapters for details).

FODOR'S CHOICE

Châteaus and Castles

★ **Chenonceau, Loire Valley.** The most romantic of them all, with arched galleries spanning the Cher, this palace owes its gardens to Catherine de' Medici.

★ **Citadelle, Corte, Corsica.** From its spectacular site high over the junction of three rivers, the fortress protects the earlier "Eagle's Nest" château and contains the **Musée de la Corse.**

★ **Fontainebleau, Ile de France.** François I, Henri II, and Napoléon, and the best artists of their day all contributed to make this the quintessential royal château, a work of art inside and out.

★ **Hautefort, Périgord.** Part medieval, part Renaissance, vast Hautefort raises an eclectic skyline above its gardens and is full of 17th-century furnishings.

★ **Josselin Castle, Brittany.** The castle presents an almost blank face to the River Oust, but from the medieval town it welcomes you into gardens presided over by pinnacles, turrets, and gables.

★ **Pierrefonds, Oise.** This huge château, begun in the 12th century, was restored in the 1860s by the fairy-tale imagination of Viollet-le-Duc and the money of Napoléon III.

★ **Vitré, Brittany.** This triangular fortress, with fat, round towers, has stood guard at the gateway to Brittany since the 11th century.

Churches and Abbeys

★ **Basilica of Ste-Madeleine, Vézelay.** Look up and marvel at the miniature figures on the carved capitals in the nave—the Romanesque cathedral was restored by Viollet-le-Duc.

★ **Cathedral, Amiens.** Spacious Cathédrale Notre-Dame was built in 44 years during the 13th century; note the rose window and humorous carved misericords.

★ **Cathedral, Bourges.** Look for the towers of Cathédrale St-Etienne as you approach on N151; inside, note its stained glass and the slender columns rising to extraordinary height.

★ **Chapelle Nôtre-Dame-du-Haut, Ronchamp.** Some say it's Le Corbusier's masterpiece—utterly individual, yet imbued with peace and calm.

★ **Mont-St-Michel, Normandy.** From its silhouette against the horizon to the abbey and gardens at the peak of the rock, you'll never forget this awe-inspiring sight.

★ **Notre-Dame, Guebwiller.** A wonderfully exuberant and well-preserved example of 18th-century Baroque.

Lodging

★ **La Cité, Carcassonne.** Tucked into the old city, this ivy-covered hotel will wrap you in luxury, in its library, the garden, its quiet, spacious rooms, and its deep tubs. $$$$

★ **La Cour des Loges, Lyon.** The wonderful atrium lobby is a surprise here, in Old Lyon, but the design of this stylish hotel, carved out of four Renaissance buildings, is an all-round delight. Relax in the *tapas* bar, and swim in the heated pool. $$$$

★ **Le Crillon, Paris.** Once the windows of this most historic palace hotel overlooked the guillotine, set up in the great square below, but today all is marble and crystal in the sumptuous salons. $$$$

★ **Le Palais, Biarritz.** The enormous rooms, vast lawns, and the elegant mirrored dining room overlooking the sea recall the grandeur of the days of the Empress Eugénie. $$$$

★ **Saint James, Paris.** What could be nicer than a weekend in Paris, hidden away in this elegant mansion in its own enclosed garden? A stylish restaurant reserved for guests and drinks in the leather-bound library complete the scene. $$$$

★ **Manoir de Lan Kerellec, Trébeurden.** Warm hospitality and excellent food await you at this Relais & Châteaux hotel on the Breton coast. $$$–$$$$

Le Vieux Logis, Trémolat. The romantic, charmingly furnished rooms in the old stone house, the pool in the garden, and the wonderful meals (it's a Relais & Châteaux house) make this a lodging worth waiting for. $$$–$$$$

★ **Château de Camon, Mirepoix.** This medieval castle in the Pyrénées foothills is full of ornate antiques, tapestries, and red velvet—which contrasts nicely with the modern tiled baths and comfortable family-style meals with the charming owner. $$$

★ **La Colombe d'Or, St-Paul de Vence.** Once a hangout for the likes of Klee, Picasso, and Utrillo, whose works are still on the walls, this country inn in the hills now draws the rich and famous, for a meal or a stay. $$$

★ **Fleurie, Paris.** This cool, quiet family-run hotel on the Left Bank supplies comforts like private safes, heated towel racks, marble baths, and CNN. $$$

★ **Mas du Langoustier, Ile de Porquerolles.** Come by boat or by ferry, and you'll be met and taken to your hideaway on the island's westernmost point, where the rooms and the views and the meals are superb. $$$

★ **Grand Hôtel de Cala Rossa, Porto-Vecchio.** Good taste shows all over this luxurious modern hotel, from the paintings to the furnishings to the nouvelle Corsican cuisine. $$–$$$$

★ **L'Hostellerie du Vieux Cordes, Cordes.** You'll love this old house around a wisteria-draped courtyard, and not least because of the splendid meals in the opulent crimson dining rooms. $$

★ **Gutenberg, Strasbourg.** This centrally located hotel, in an 18th-century mansion, is full of charm. $–$$

★ **Hôtels St-Albert et Montaigne, Sarlat.** These comfortable lodgings on the delightful town square share a good regional restaurant and the services of the pleasant Garrigou family. $–$$

★ **Esméralda, Paris.** It's right across from Notre-Dame and noisy, but it's really cheap and charming. $

Dining

★ **Boyer, Reims.** The innovative cuisine of Gérard Boyer and his extensive wine list draw sophisticated diners (and lodgers) to this opulent dining room in a 19th-century château. $$$$

★ **Georges Blanc.** At this simple country inn, appealing as it is, you'd not expect to find a great culinary talent. But Georges Blanc does everything right. (He can also put you up for the night if you plan well ahead). $$$$

★ **Le Centenaire.** Roland Mazère's accomplishments with the regional specialties, like foie gras, scampi, truffles, and snails, keep them coming back again and again—and sometimes to spend the night. $$$

★ **La Chenevière, Bayeux.** Peach linen and shining glass will enhance your mood of festive anticipation of chef Claude Esprabens' wonderful food. He has a sure hand and a lightness of style. $$$

★ **L'Assiette, Honfleur.** The harbor-front setting here gives a hint that seafood is a strong point, but all Gérard Bonnefoy's food is to die for—including the delectable desserts. $$–$$$

★ **A l'Ami Fritz, Ottrott.** The owner-chef here serves succulent local specialties and his own wine. The rustic charm is both chic and warm—well worth a trip to this unspoiled village. $$

★ **Les Muses, Lyon.** You sit behind enormous statues of the muses on the roof of the opera house, while lunching or dining on Philippe Chavent's inspired dishes. $$

★ **Pigeons Blancs.** Chef Jacques Tachet's cooking would be worth a detour even if the handful of rooms weren't charming and reasonable. His three-course *carte du jour* is a find. $$

★ **Le Brouage, Brouage.** This restaurant (with a few rooms), which serves as the village bar, is just the place to settle the affairs of the world and have a wonderful regional meal. $

★ **La Régalade, Paris.** You must reserve a month ahead, but you'll be glad you found this bargain-priced outpost of haute cuisine—that of Yves Camdeborde, formerly of the Crillon. $

★ **Au Tire Bouchon, Strasbourg.** This cozy "winstub" serves classic local fare, some lighter options, and local carafe wines. $

Museums

★ **Fondation Maeght, St-Paul-de-Vence.** A small gem of a museum of modern art, blending its stunning holdings with stylish presentation.

★ **Musée des Arts Décoratifs, Lyon.** You can see the well-displayed furniture, silverware, ceramics, and objects of early Lyonnaise life in a satisfying couple of hours.

★ **Musée Condé, Chantilly.** The château houses a remarkable collection of illuminated manuscripts, tapestries, furniture, paintings, Fouquet miniatures, and stained glass.

★ **Musée Fesch, Ajaccio, Corsica.** Wonderful Italian Old Masters.

★ **Musée Ingres, Montauban.** Drawings and paintings by the great French classicist and works from his own collection, housed in the Bishop's Palace.

★ **Musée Matisse, Le Cateau-Cambrésis.** The Palais Fénelon is now home to paintings, sculpture, and drawings by the native son.

★ **Musée de l'Oeuvre Notre-Dame, Strasbourg.** Much more than just weathered statues rescued from the cathedral; different presentations evoke cloisters, workshops, and chapels; objects are carefully displayed.

★ **Louvre, Paris.** No matter how many times you've visited, be sure to come again; the new construction is stunning.

GREAT ITINERARIES

France for First-Timers

So, you want to taste France, gaze at its beauty, and inhale its special joie de vivre—all in a one-week to 10-day trip. Let's assume at least that you've seen Paris, and you're ready to venture out into the country-side. A first-time visitor should try to get a feel for France's tremendous variety—its Continental heart in the north and its Mediterranean soul in the south. This is the route Parisians used to follow, slowly, surely, heading south to the Mediterranean, feasting and sightseeing along the way.

Take Highway A6 (Autoroute du Soleil) southeast out of Paris and follow signs to Lyon. You might have lunch in Fontainebleau or Vézelay, depending on what time you set off, or stop for a snack in the picture-postcard village of **Barbizon,** center of a 19th-century naturalist school of artists. Napoléon loved the castle at **Fontainebleau,** especially its ornamental staircase, and you'll find the beautiful gardens in back perfect for picnicking. Leave Highway A6 at the exit marked **Vézelay;** the hilltop village's Romanesque basilica is one of Europe's most important early medieval buildings.

Next, take small roads southeast through the Morvan Forest to **Beaune,** a stylish town in the Burgundy wine country. Don't miss the medieval hospital—the Hôtel-Dieu—with its perfect gothic proportions and colorful tapestry of a roof. You might visit **Saulieu** en route, for a good meal. Also take in the famous wine-producing villages of **Pommard, Meursault,** and **Volnay.** Continue south through Beaujolais to Lyon—the hills along this route are lovely.

Lyon, which competes with Marseilles to be France's second city, is uncontested as a gastronomic capital. Have at least one meal, either at an inexpensive neighborhood *bouchon* or an expensive culinary landmark like Restaurant Paul Bocuse. Take a walk in Old Lyon between the Saône and Rhône rivers, where the old silk merchants' mansions are painted rose and ocher. Around here the land begins to change; the forests and farmlands of northern France cede place to the olive and cypress trees of the south, as butter and cream give way to olive oil, amid the sweet smells of the Mediterranean.

Continue south on the national roads or the autoroute (now A7) through the Rhône Valley to **Avignon,** site of the Papal Palace. Visit the nearby Roman ruins, the theater at **Orange,** the aqueduct at **Pont du Gard,** the coliseum in **Nîmes,** and the old marketplace in **Vaison-la-Romaine.** Whatever you do, don't miss the amazing medieval village of **Les Baux,** perched on high cliffs, with views for miles over the Camargue to the sea. If you're short on time, your trip can end in Provence with a taste of modern-day France—a return to Paris on the TGV.

If time permits, continue east through the charming university town of **Aix-en-Provence** to **St-Tropez,** the ultimate Riviera resort. Not far away are **Nice; Cannes,** chic home of the famous film festival; and the tiny principality of **Monaco.** Be sure to explore the hilltop villages, like **Eze** and **St-Paul-de-Vence,** where the slower, more traditional way of life provides a nice contrast to the flashy high living down at sea level.

DURATION➤ 7–10 days

GETTING AROUND➤ It's best to rent a car in Paris for this itinerary. The TGV speeds through Burgundy and Lyon to the coast, stopping in major cities along the way. You'll have to arrange transport into the countryside or rent a bicycle at the train station.

THE MAIN ROUTE➤ **Two nights: Véze-lay, Saulieu,** or **Beaune.** Visit the medieval basilica and Beaune's Hôtel-Dieu. En route note the virgin forests and the hills and small family-tended vineyards of Burgundy, easing your passage with the memorable *dégustation* (tasting) available free at many of them. Dine in Lyon.

Two to three nights: Avignon and **Provence.** Visit the Roman ruins and medieval towns, the fields of aromatic lavender and of the towering sunflowers that Van Gogh painted.

Two to three nights: Cannes and the **Côte d'Azur.** Take a swim in the Mediterranean at one of the trendy (even topless) French beaches. Walk through Eze or another medieval hilltop village. Depending on your inclination, say a prayer at the Matisse Chapel near Vence, or lose your remaining francs at Monte Carlo's Belle Epoque casino.

INFORMATION➤ *See* chapters on Burgundy, Lyon, Provence, and the Riviera.

Palatial France

The French Revolution ended the old regime, but many of the buildings remain—palaces of local seigneurs and châteaus reserved for the king. **Versailles,** the most

famous of all, was built just outside Paris for Louis XIV, and it originally housed an army of 20,000 servants and courtiers. These days, the château in its ritzy suburb is reachable by car on the A13 highway or by rail from St-Lazare and Montparnasse stations or the Left Bank's RER stations. You can walk to the château from the station. The fabulous gardens designed by Le Nôtre are perfect for a picnic.

From Versailles, head southwest on N10 into the lush Chevreuse Valley. You'll come to the handsome 17th-century stone-and-brick château of **Dampierre,** where the duc de Luynes' descendants live. You're invited to inspect the attractive interior (for a small charge), and also at the **Château de Breteuil,** a little farther on, where the owners have set up life-size wax figures depicting the building's history. Head next to **Rambouillet,** now a leafy suburb, but formerly a royal hideout. The château is attractive, but the real draw is its gardens and woods. Take time out to visit the magnificent cathedral at **Chartres,** one of the country's greatest treasures.

Of the hundreds of châteaus in the wooded Loire Valley, the following four represent the range of architectural development from early Renaissance to late Classical. Make your base at **Tours,** the region's largest city. If you have time for only a short visit, go first to the attractive town of **Blois,** whose palace, one of the most interesting, was built over several architectural periods and saw much royal intrigue. The next day, go east to **Chambord,** the largest of all Loire châteaus, which stands in an extensive forest. The structure's vast interiors were emptied during the Revolution.

Then visit nearby **Cheverny.** Though its formal neoclassicism may be a bit forbidding, its proportions are perfect and the rooms sparkle with splendid 18th-century furniture. Don't miss the spectacle of the hunting dogs kept at the residence. A fitting finale is the unforgettable **Chenonceau,** built across the River Cher. The setting is spectacular and the building graceful and romantic. If possible, stay for the evening sound-and-light show. If you have time on the way back to Paris, make a short detour to visit **Fontainebleau** and **Vaux le Vicomte.**

DURATION➤ 5–7 days

GETTING AROUND➤ Versailles is a 20-minute drive from downtown Paris (avoid rush hours). The Loire Valley is three hours from the city via A10, or you can take N10 via Chartres to Tours.

The TGV gets to Blois and Tours in little more than an hour, and buses run from the train stations to most of the châteaus. You can also rent bicycles at the train stations; the valley is flat and easy to navigate.

THE MAIN ROUTE➤ **One to two nights: Versailles** and the **Valley of the Chevreuse.** Visit the châteaus and **Chartres Cathedral.**

Three nights: Tours. Visit Blois, Chambord, Cheverny, and Chenonceau in the Loire Valley.

One night: Fontainebleau and **Vaux le Vicomte.**

INFORMATION➤ *See* chapters on Ile de France and the Loire Valley.

Sporting France

France is a country blessed with many natural wonders, ideal for outdoor sports. The skier can enjoy the Alps and the Pyrénées; the swimmer has some of the continent's most pristine lakes and Europe's longest coastline; cyclists are challenged by the varied terrain that is the site of the Tour de France; golf is burgeoning; and almost every village has public tennis courts.

Though the Alps and the Riviera are better known recreational areas, the southwest is less commercialized and crowded (except in August, when all France is on vacation). Start in **Arcachon,** near Bordeaux, a low-key resort famous for the local oysters and for Europe's biggest dunes, at nearby Pyla-sur-Mer. On the Atlantic coast you can relax on miles of sand, unlike the pebble beaches of the Côte d'Azur. The **Aquacity** complex off N250 south of Arcachon offers water slides, a wave machine, a warm-water swimming pool, and a heated pool. And as a foil to your active life you can take a pleasant detour to the nearby Bordeaux vineyards.

Head south through the magnificent **Landes** forest, where pines stretch to the horizon. The area has a pleasant climate and a tremendous variety of outdoor activities: hiking, fishing, canoeing, sand-skiing, golf, tennis, surfing, sailing, and swimming. As the forest ends, you enter the Basque country, coming first to **Bayonne,** its capital, and then the celebrated resort of **Biarritz.** A chic resort in the 19th century—Victoria's son Edward summered here—it has been at the center of the recent French golfing boom. Many of France's dozens of new courses are open to the public, though most have steep green fees ($40 and up).

Explore the Basque coastline, especially the resort and fishing town of **St-Jean-de-Luz,** where the local sport is *pelote* (related to jai alai). Finish the trip with a hike in the beautiful **Pyrénées,** with their rustic appeal. You can still see shepherds leading their flocks to graze, and stay in wooden chalets with bright red shutters. Visit the charming Basque village of **St-Jean-Pied-de-Port** in the foothills; it's a picturesque starting point for the higher altitudes ahead.

DURATION➤ 6–8 days

GETTING AROUND➤ Arcachon is a six-hour drive from Paris. The road south to Biarritz along the coast is only two lanes, and the trip takes a couple of hours. From there to St-Jean-Pied-de-Port takes less than an hour.

The TGV gets you from Paris to Bordeaux in three hours, and in summer continues to Arcachon, through some of France's most beautiful scenery. It also goes from Bordeaux to Biarritz and St-Jean-de-Luz, though not at *très grande vitesse.*

THE MAIN ROUTE➤ **Two to three nights: Arcachon.** Spend one day at the beach, perhaps another visiting the vineyards. Consider taking a boat out on the bay with an oyster fisherman.

Three nights: Biarritz. Enjoy the beach, visit the rugged Basque coastline, play a round of golf, and take in a pelote match.

Two nights: St-Jean-Pied-de-Port. Hike into the Pyrénées along the Spanish border, or if you are courageous, bike: the Tour de France is often won by those who survived the Pyrénées!

France for the Family

Sophisticated and suave may be what comes to mind when thinking of France, but there's another side to this varied country: It has a love for children that extends to even the youngest. Unlike many big cities, Paris is a great place for kids. Even the swankiest eating places usually offer a *menu des enfants*. Children love riding to the top of the **Eiffel Tower** and sailing toy boats in the **Luxembourg Gardens.** You can squeeze in a museum or two, and **Disneyland Paris** is only a half-hour away by RER railroad.

To get a well-rounded view of the country, begin with a summer trip through Normandy and Brittany, the prime family resort areas. Take one of the roads that follow the Seine northwest out of Paris, and stop at Vernon to visit **Giverny,** where painter Claude Monet lived. One of the joys of Impressionism is its accessibility to children, and Monet's water lilies and other natural subjects are captivating even to those with no artistic bent. A stunning new museum in the village is dedicated to the American artists who came to study with the French master. Serious art students will be enthralled.

On the Normandy coast, kids will love climbing the chalk cliffs of **Etretat** and **Fécamp,** though the beaches here are rather rocky. You'll find sandy beaches farther south at **Deauville, Trouville,** and **Cabourg,** resorts captured in Marcel Proust's elaborate prose. Lessons in history abound here, from the famous tapestry of medieval **Bayeux** to the D-Day beaches. **Mont-St-Michel** in Brittany, farther west along the coast, is an unforgettable sight for everyone, although the climb to the abbey may be tough for small children.

Brittany, with its rugged coastline and simple cuisine (particularly the crêpes) is bound to please families. Kids love scampering along the stone ramparts of **St-Malo,** and low-key, informal resorts like **Dinard** and **Perros Guirec** are also ideal destinations.

DURATION➤ 6–8 days

GETTING AROUND➤ Normandy is only a few hours from Paris, although it takes up to six hours to reach its far end. Traveling around Normandy and Brittany is almost impossible without a car.

Trains leave from Gare St-Lazare for Deauville and other Normandy destinations; trains to Brittany leave from Gare Montparnasse.

THE MAIN ROUTE➤ **One or two nights: Etretat and Fécamp.** Take a walk on Etretat's cliffs and explore Fécamp's fishing port.

Two nights: Deauville. Visit the casino and the beach. Make an excursion to the charming fishing town of Honfleur.

One night: Bayeux. Visit the medieval tapestries and the D-Day beaches.

Three nights: Brittany. Start at Mont-St-Michel and make your way west. Sample the crêpes and enjoy the views.

INFORMATION➤ *See* chapters on Normandy and Brittany.

FESTIVALS AND SEASONAL EVENTS

France is a festival all year round, with special events taking place throughout the country. For full museum, theater, and concert information, be sure to check the listings in *Pariscope* (which includes reviews in English of the week's main events and new restaurants) or *Spectacles* on arrival in Paris. *The International Herald Tribune* also lists special events in its weekend edition, but not in great detail. The most complete listing of festivals comes in a small pamphlet published by **Maison de la France** (8 avenue de l'Opéra, Paris 75001, ☎ 42–96–10–23).

Annual highlights include the Monte Carlo Motor Rally in January, Nice's Carnival in February, the Cannes Film Festival and French Open Tennis Championships in May, the Festival du Marais and Bastille Day in July, and the September Autumn Festival in Paris.

WINTER

Dec.➤ On the 24th, a Christmas celebration known as the **Shepherd's Festival**, featuring midnight Mass and picturesque "living crèches," is held in Les Baux, Provence. From late in the month to early January, **Christmas in Paris** spells celebrations, especially for children, during the school holiday. A giant crèche is set up on the square in front of the Hôtel de Ville (City Hall), and there are automated window displays in the *grands magasins* (department stores) on boulevard Haussmann.

Jan.➤ The **International Circus Festival**, featuring top acts from around the world, and the **Monte Carlo Motor Rally,** one of the motoring world's most venerable races, are held in Monaco. The **St. Vincent Tournament,** a colorful Burgundy wine festival, takes place on the third weekend in a different wine village each year. Visitors buy a cup for about $7 and then drink as much as they like–or just frolic in the decorated streets. Angoulême hosts the world's biggest and most popular **comic book festival.**

Feb.➤ The **Carnival of Nice** provides an exotic blend of parades and revelry during the weeks leading up to Lent. Other cities and villages also have their own smaller versions. Rugby matches pitting France against teams from Scotland, Wales, England, and Ireland in the **Five Nation Tournament,** Europe's most prestigious **rugby championship,** take place at Parc des Princes in Paris.

SPRING

March➤ In Paris, the **Salon de Mars,** a modern art festival, is held at the Champs de Mars, and the **Salon du Livre,** France's biggest book festival, takes place at the Grand Palais.

April➤ The **Monte Carlo Open Tennis Championships** get under way at the ultraswank Monte Carlo Country Club. From then until September, there are **Sound and Light Shows** (*son et lumière*), historical pageants featuring special lighting effects, at many châteaus in the Loire Valley. The show at Beaune's Hôtel-Dieu is also very well done.

May➤ The **Cannes Film Festival** sees two weeks of star-studded events. Classical concert festivals get underway throughout the country. At the end of the month, the **French Open Tennis Championships** are held at Roland Garros Stadium in Paris.

SUMMER

June➤ The **Festival du Marais,** including everything from music to dance to theater, is held in Paris. **Strasbourg's International Music Festival** features concerts in the cathedral and various halls. This is a popular time for horse races: The **Prix du Président de la République** is run at the Hippodrome de Vincennes, the **Grand Steeplechase de Paris** is at the Auteuil Racecourse, and the **Grand Prix de Paris,** for equine three-year-olds, is at Longchamp Racecourse. Most important, the **Tour de France,** the world's most famous bicycle race, gets underway.

JULY➤ **Summer arts festival season** gets into full swing, particularly in Provence. Avignon offers a month of top-notch theater, Aix-en-Provence specializes in opera, Carpentras in religious music, Châteauvallon in dance, and Nice holds a big Jazz Festival, starting with a Grand Parade. Arles mounts a big photography festival. On the last Sunday in the month, the Tour de France crosses the finish line on the Champs-Elysées.

On **July 14,** all of France celebrates Bastille Day,

commemorating the Storming of the Bastille in 1789—the start of the French Revolution. Look out for fireworks, free concerts, and street festivities beginning the evening of the 13th.

AUTUMN

SEPT.➤ The **Music Festival of Besançon and Franche-Comté** hosts a series of chamber music concerts in and around Besançon. The **Festival of Autumn,** a major arts and film festival, opens in Paris and continues until December. The **Vendanges,** grape

harvests, begin and festivals are held in the country's wine regions.

OCT.➤ The **Prix de l'Arc de Triomphe,** a venerable annual horse race, is held at Longchamp Racecourse in Paris. A giant contemporary art exhibition called FIAC takes place at the Grand Palais.

NOV.➤ **Les Trois Glorieuses,** Burgundy's biggest wine festival, features the year's most important wine auction and related merriment in several Burgundy locations. On the third Thursday in November, France—especially Paris—celebrates the arrival of the Beaujolais Nouveau.

2 Paris

IF THERE'S a problem with a trip to Paris, it is the embarrassment of riches that faces the visitor. A city of vast, noble perspectives and winding, hidden streets, Paris remains a combination of the pompous and the intimate. Whether you've come looking for sheer physical beauty, cultural and artistic diversions, world-famous dining and shopping, history, or simply local color, you will find it here in abundance.

The city's 20 districts, or *arrondissements,* have their own distinctive character, as do the two banks of the Seine, the river that weaves its way through the city's heart. The tone of the Rive Droite (Right Bank) is set by spacious boulevards and formal buildings, while the Rive Gauche (Left Bank) is more carefree and bohemian.

The French capital is also, for the tourist, a practical city: It's relatively small as capitals go, and its major sites and museums are within walking distance of one another. The city's principal tourist axis is less than 6 kilometers (4 miles) long, running parallel to the north bank of the Seine from the Arc de Triomphe to the Bastille.

There are several "musts" that any first-time visitor to Paris should try not to miss: the Eiffel Tower, the Champs-Elysées, the Louvre, and Notre-Dame. It is only fair to say, however, that a visit to Paris will never be quite as simple as a quick look at a few landmarks. Every *quartier* has its own treasures, and travelers should adopt the process of discovery—a very pleasant prospect in this most elegant of French cities.

EXPLORING

Orientation

Because the best method of getting to know Paris is on foot, we've divided our coverage into six walking tours. Use our routes as a base; concentrate on the areas that are of particular interest to you; and, above all, enjoy to the fullest the sights, sounds, and smells of this exciting city.

To make your days run more smoothly (not to mention cheaply) you might want to buy the *Carte Musées et Monuments,* a one-, three-, or five-day pass (60, 120, or 170 francs) that allows you unlimited access to the permanent collections of 65 museums and monuments in Paris and the surrounding area. Not only that, you can say good-bye to the long ticket lines. The pass is sold at any of the participating museums and monuments (many of which are described below), the main métro and RER stations, the tourist office (127 av. des Champs-Elysées, 8e), and Musée & Compagnie (49 rue Etienne-Marcel, 75001), and it comes with an information-packed leaflet and a métro plan.

Tour 1: The Historic Heart

Numbers in the margin correspond to points of interest on the Paris map.

Of the two islands in the Seine—the Ile St-Louis and Ile de la Cité—it is the latter that forms the historic heart of Paris. It was here that the earliest inhabitants, the Gaulish tribe of the Parisii, settled around 250 BC. Whereas the Ile St-Louis is largely residential, the Ile de la Cité is the site of the great, brooding cathedral of Notre-Dame. Few of the island's other medieval buildings have survived, most having fallen victim to Baron Haussmann's ambitious rebuilding of the city in the mid-

19th century. Among the rare survivors are the jewel-like Sainte Chapelle, a vision of shimmering stained glass, and the Conciergerie, the grim former city prison.

The tour begins at the western tip of the Ile de la Cité, at the sedate ❶ **square du Vert Galant.** The statue of the *Vert Galant* himself, literally the "vigorous [by which was really meant the amorous] adventurer," shows Henri IV sitting sturdily on his horse. Henri, king of France from 1589 until his assassination in 1610, was something of a dashing figure as well as a canny statesman.

Crossing the Ile de la Cité, just east of the Vert Galant, is the oldest bridge in Paris, confusingly called the **Pont Neuf,** or New Bridge. Completed in the early 17th century, it was the first bridge in the city to be built without houses lining either side. Turn left onto it. Once across the river, turn left again and walk down to rue Amiral-de-Coligny, opposite the massive eastern facade of the Louvre. Before heading for the museum, however, stay on the right-hand sidewalk and duck into the ❷ church of **St-Germain-l'Auxerrois.** This was the French royal family's Paris church in the days before the Revolution, when the Louvre was a palace rather than a museum. The fluid stonework of the facade reveals the influence of 15th-century Flamboyant Gothic, the final, exuberant fling of the Gothic before the Classical takeover of the Renaissance. Note the unusual double aisles and the exceptionally wide windows—typical of the style. The triumph of Classicism is evident, however, in the 18th-century fluted columns around the choir, the area surrounding the altar.

The Louvre colonnade across the road screens one of Europe's most ❸ dazzling courtyards, the **Cour Carré,** a breathtakingly monumental, harmonious, and superbly rhythmic ensemble. In the crypt below, excavated in 1984, sections of the defensive towers of the original, 13th-century fortress can be seen.

Stroll through the courtyard and pass under the **Pavillon de l'Horloge,** the Clock Tower, and you'll come face-to-face with I. M. Pei's **Great Pyramid,** surrounded by three smaller pyramids, in the Cour Napoléon. The pyramid marks the new entrance to the Louvre and houses a large museum shop, café, and restaurant. It is also the terminal point for the most celebrated city view in Europe—a majestic vista stretching through the Arc du Carrousel, the Tuileries Gardens, across place de la Concorde, up the Champs-Elysées to the towering Arc de Triomphe, and ending at the giant modern arch at La Tête Défense, 4 kilometers (2½ miles) away. Needless to say, the architectural collision between classical stone blocks and pseudo-Egyptian glass panels has caused a furor.

The pyramid, unveiled in 1989, marks the first completed objective of former president François Mitterrand's **Grand Louvre Project,** a plan for the restoration of the museum launched in 1981 and expected to cost $1.3 billion by its completion in 1996. In November 1993, exactly 200 years since the Louvre first opened its doors to the public, Mitterrand cut the ribbon on the completed second phase. This includes the renovation of the **Richelieu Wing,** former home of the Ministry of Finance, which was gutted by Pei and his associates and reopened to house more than 12,000 artworks (a third of them brought out from storage), notably the Islamic and Mesopotamian collections, French painting and sculpture, and the sumptuous Napoléon III apartments. The new wing is characterized by its sunlit exhibition spaces surrounding airy courtyards, a marked contrast to the formal Denon and Sully wings. Also open now is the **Carrousel du Louvre,** a subterranean shopping complex with a wide range of stores, a food court, an auditorium, and a large parking garage. The third and final phase of the project includes improvement of the air-conditioning and lighting, the restoration of the Tuileries Gardens, and a pedestrian bridge that will connect the Tuileries with the Musée d'Orsay.

★ ❹ Today's **Louvre** is the end product of many generations and purposes. Philippe-Auguste built it in the early 13th century as a fortress to protect the city's western flank. The earliest parts of the current building date from the reign of François I at the beginning of the 16th century, while subsequent monarchs—Henri IV (1589–1610), Louis XIII (1610–43), Louis XIV (1643–1715), Napoléon (1802–14), and Napoléon III (1851–70)—all contributed to its construction. The open section facing the Tuileries Gardens was once the site of the Palais des Tuileries, the main residence of the royal family in Paris.

Over the centuries, the Louvre has been a royal residence and a home for minor courtiers; at one point, it was taken over by a rabble of artists, whose chimneys projected higgledy-piggledy from the otherwise severe lines of the facades. After a stint as headquarters of the French Revolution, it was finally established, in Napoléon's time, as a museum, though the country's last three monarchs continued to make it their home.

The number-one attraction for most visitors is Leonardo da Vinci's enigmatic **Mona Lisa,** "*La Joconde*" to the French; be forewarned that you will find it encased in glass and surrounded by a mob of tourists. The collections are divided into seven sections: Oriental antiquities; Egyptian antiquities; Greek and Roman antiquities; sculpture; paintings, prints, and drawings; furniture; and objets d'art. Don't try to see it all at once; try, instead, to make repeat visits—the admission is reduced on Sunday. Some other highlights of the paintings are *Shepherds in Arcadia,* by Nicolas Poussin (1594–1665); *The Oath of the Horatii,* by Jacques-Louis David (1748–1825); *The Raft of the Medusa,* by Théodore Géricault (1791–1824); and *La Grande Odalisque,* by Jean-Auguste Dominique Ingres (1780–1867). The *Winged Victory of Samothrace* seems poised for flight at the top of the stairs, and another much-loved piece of sculpture is Michelangelo's pair of *Slaves,* intended for the tomb of Pope Julius II. These can be admired in the Denon Wing, where a new Medieval and Renaissance sculpture section, housed partly in the former imperial stables, opened in October 1994. The French crown jewels (in the objets d'art section of the Richelieu Wing) include the mind-boggling 186-carat Regent diamond. *Palais du Louvre,* ☎ 40–20–53–17. ☛ *40 frs adults, 20 frs ages 18–25, after 3 PM, and on Sun.* ☺ *Wed.–Mon. 9–6, Mon. and Wed. until 9:45. Métro: Palais Royal.*

Stretching westward from the main entrance to the Louvre and the glass pyramid is an expanse of stately, formal gardens, the **Jardins des Tuileries** (*see* Tour 3, *below*).

TIME OUT Your best bet for refreshment in the Louvre is the trendy new **Café Marly** (93 rue de Rivoli, 75001, ☎ 49–26–06–60) in two ornate salons of the Richelieu Wing. Here you'll find cheeseburgers, sushi, and oysters on the half shell. It's owned by the proprietor of Café Beaubourg. Or you can try the mall-style food court at the recently opened **Carrousel du Louvre,** the underground shopping center on the Tuileries side. The offerings of its 13 counters range from brasserie-style to Italian and Chinese.

Running the length of the Louvre's northern side is Napoléon's arcaded rue de Rivoli. Cross it and you're in **place des Pyramides,** face-to-face with its gilded statue of Joan of Arc on horseback. Walk up rue des

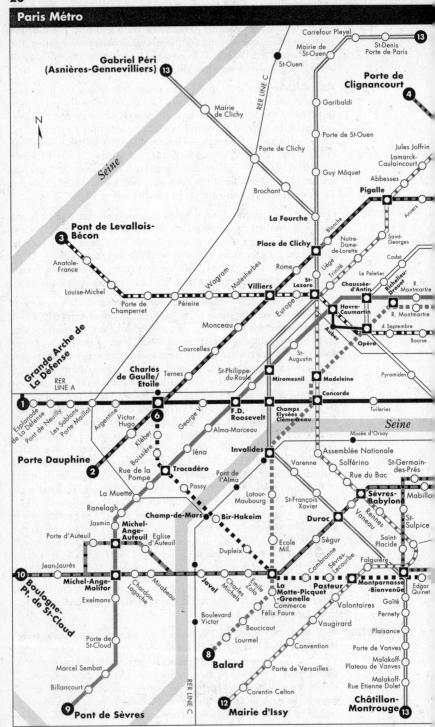

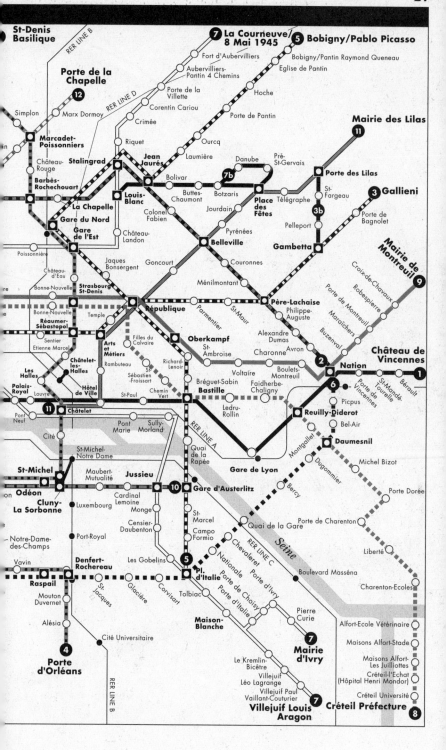

Paris Arrondissements

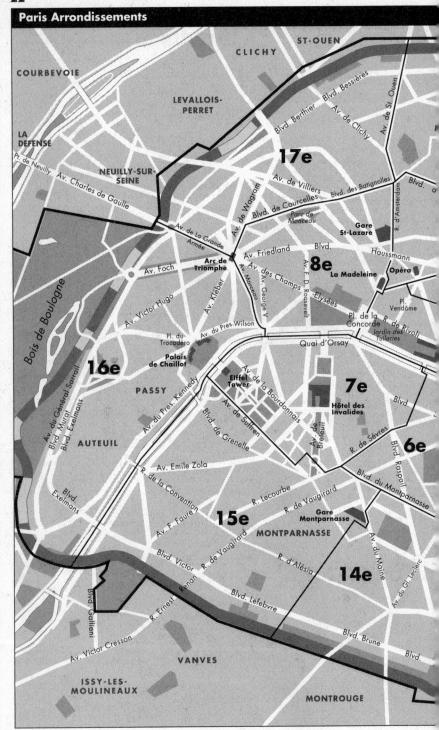

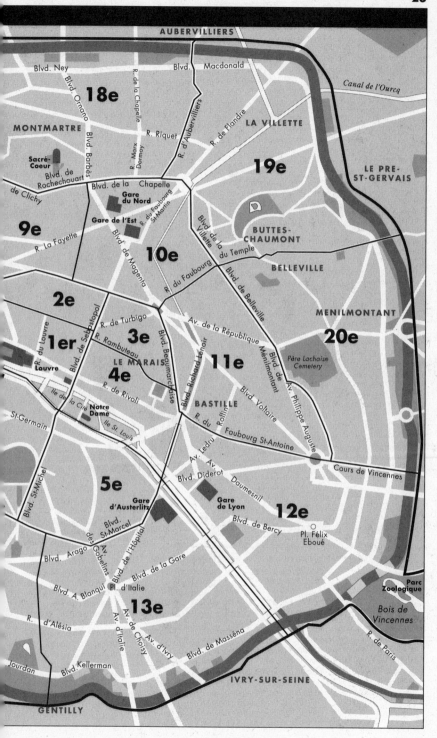

AUBERVILLIERS

Blvd. Ney

Blvd. Macdonald

18e

Canal de l'Ourcq

R. de la Chapelle

MONTMARTRE

R. Riquet

R. d'Aubervilliers

R. de Flandre

LA VILLETTE

Blvd. Ornano

Blvd. Barbès

R. Marx Dormoy

19e

LE PRE-
ST-GERVAIS

Sacré-
Coeur

Blvd. de
Rochechouart

de Clichy

Blvd. de la Chapelle

Gare
du Nord

Gare de l'Est

R. du Faubourg
St-Martin

Blvd. de la
Villette

BUTTES-
CHAUMONT

9e

R. La Fayette

10e

R. du Faubourg

du Temple

BELLEVILLE

Blvd. de Magenta

Blvd. de Belleville

MENILMONTANT

2e

R. de Turbigo

Av. de la République

20e

1er

Blvd. de Sébastopol

R. Rambuteau

3e

Blvd. Beaumarchaise

Blvd. Richard Lenoir

11e

Blvd. de
Ménilmontant

Av. Philippe Auguste

Père Lachaise
Cemetery

R. du Louvre

Louvre

LE MARAIS

4e

R. de Rivoli

Blvd. Voltaire

Ile de la Cité

Notre
Dame

BASTILLE

St-Germain

Ile St. Louis

R. du
Rollin

R. du Faubourg St-Antoine

Cours de Vincennes

Blvd. St-Michel

5e

Av. Ledru

Av.
Daumesnil

Blvd. Diderot

Gare
d'Austerlitz

Gare
de Lyon

12e

Blvd.
St-Marcel

Blvd. de Bercy

Pl. Félix
Eboué

Blvd. Arago

Av. des Gobelins

Blvd. de l'Hôpital

Blvd. de la Gare

Parc
Zoologique

Blvd. A. Blanqui

Pl. d'Italie

Bois de
Vincennes

R. d'Alésia

13e

Av. d'Italie

Av. de Choisy

Av. d'Ivry

Blvd. de Masséna

R. de Paris

Jourdan

Blvd. Kellerman

IVRY-SUR-SEINE

GENTILLY

Paris

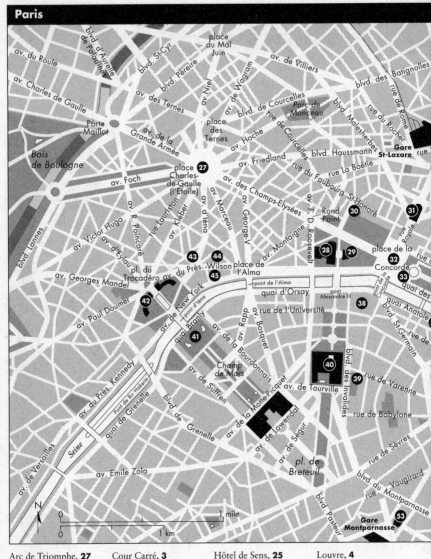

Montmartre see detail map

blvd. de Clichy · place Pigalle · blvd. de Rochechouart · blvd. Barbès · blvd. de la Chapelle · Canal de l'Ourcq · av. Jean Jaurès

rue d'Amsterdam · rue de Clichy · rue St-Lazare · rue de Châteaudun · **Gare du Nord** · rue La Fayette · **Gare de l'Est** · Canal St-Martin · blvd. de la Villette

blvd. Haussmann · blvd. de la Madeleine · blvd. des Italiens · blvd. Montmartre · blvd. Poissonnière · r. du Fg. Poissonnière · blvd. St-Denis · blvd. St-Martin · blvd. de Strasbourg · blvd. de Magenta · blvd. de la Villette · blvd. du Faubourg-du-Temple

av. de l'Opéra · rue de Richelieu · rue Réaumur · r. St-Denis · r. St-Martin · rue de Turbigo · place de la République · av. de la République

rue de Rivoli · rue Etienne Marcel · rue du Louvre · r. St-Honoré · r. Berger · r. Rambuteau · rue des Archives · rue du Temple · blvd. Beaumarchais · blvd. Voltaire

des Tuileries · Seine · place de France · quai du Louvre · rue de Rivoli · pl. du Châtelet · rue des Francs-Bourgeois · **LE MARAIS** · blvd. Richard Lenoir · r. de la Roquette · r. Ledru Rollin

pont du Carrousel · pont de l'Université · r. Jacob · pont des Arts · pont Neuf · quai de l'Hôtel de Ville · Île de la Cité · rue St-Antoine · rue du Faubourg St-Antoine

rue de Rennes · rue Bonaparte · blvd. St-Germain · pl. St-Michel · Île St-Louis · blvd. Henri IV · av. Ledru Rollin · av. Daumesnil · blvd. Diderot · **Gare de Lyon**

Palais du Luxembourg · Jardin du Luxembourg · blvd. St-Michel · rue St-Jacques · place Maubert · quai de la Tournelle · pont de Sully · Seine

blvd. Raspail · av. de l'Observatoire · rue Monge · rue Descartes · rue Mouffetard · rue Lacépède · **Gare d'Austerlitz**

⑤ Pyramides and take the first left, rue St-Honoré, to the Baroque church of **St-Roch.** The church was completed in the 1730s, the date of the cool, Classical facade. It's worth having a look inside to see the bombastically Baroque altarpiece in the circular Lady Chapel.

⑥ Return to rue des Pyramides and follow rue St-Honoré to **place André-Malraux,** with its exuberant fountains. The Opéra building is visible down the avenue of the same name, while, on one corner of the square, at rue Richelieu, is the **Comédie-Française,** the time-honored setting for performances of classical French drama. The building dates from 1790, but the Comédie-Française company was created by Louis XIV in 1680. If you understand French and have a taste for the mannered, declamatory style of French acting, you will appreciate an evening here (*see* The Arts and Nightlife, *below*).

⑦ To the right of the theater (as you face it from the Louvre) is the unobtrusive entrance to the gardens of the **Palais Royal.** The buildings of this former palace date from the 1630s and are royal only in that the builder, Cardinal Richelieu (1585–1642), magnanimously bequeathed them to Louis XIII. Today the Palais Royal is home of the French Ministry of Culture and is not open to the public. But don't miss the **gardens,** divided by rows of perfectly trimmed small trees, a surprisingly little-known oasis in the heart of the city. There's not much chance that you'll miss the black-and-white striped columns in the courtyard or the revolving silver spheres that slither around in the two fountains at either end, the controversial early 1980s work of architect Daniel Buren. Walk to the end, away from the main palace, and peek into the opulent, Belle Epoque, glass-lined interior of **Le Grand Véfour** (*see* Dining, *below*). One of the poshest restaurants in the city, it's probably the most sumptuously appointed, too.

⑧ Around the corner, on rue de Richelieu, stands France's national library, the **Bibliothèque Nationale,** containing more than 7 million printed volumes. Visitors can admire Robert de Cotte's 18th-century courtyard and peep into the 19th-century reading room. *58 rue de Richelieu.* ☺ *Daily 10–8. Métro: Bourse.*

TIME OUT Wine bars, which sprang to prominence in London a decade ago, have caught on less quickly in Paris. A splendid trendsetter is English-run **Willi's,** behind the Palais-Royal. Sample a glass of wine on a stool at the bar or eat a sit-down meal in the restaurant (the inexpensive menu changes daily). *13 rue des Petits-Champs.*

⑨ From the library, walk along rue des Petits-Champs to the circular **place des Victoires.** It was laid out in 1685 by Jules Hardouin-Mansart (1646–1708), a leading proponent of French 17th-century Classicism, in honor of the military victories of Louis XIV. You'll find some of the city's most upscale fashion shops here and on the surrounding streets.

⑩ Head south down rue Croix-des-Petits-Champs. The second street on the left leads to the circular 18th-century **Bourse du Commerce,** or Commercial Exchange. Alongside it is a 100-foot-high fluted column, all that remains of a mansion built here in 1572 for Catherine de' Medici. The column is said to have been used as a platform for stargazing by her astrologer, Ruggieri.

⑪ You can easily spot the bulky outline of the church of **St-Eustache,** away to the left. It is a huge church, the "cathedral" of Les Halles, built, as it were, as the market people's Right Bank reply to Notre-Dame. Under construction from 1532 to 1637 and modified over the centuries, the church is a curious architectural hybrid. Its flying buttresses, for example, are solidly Gothic, yet its column orders, rounded arches, and comparatively simple window tracery are unmistakably Classical. Few buildings bear such eloquent witness to stylistic transition. St-Eustache is the site of occasional organ concerts. *2 rue du Jour,* ☎ *46–27–89–21. Métro: Les Halles.*

If Notre-Dame and the Louvre represent Church and State, respectively, Les Halles (pronounced "lay al") stands for the common man. For centuries, this was Paris's central market. Closed in 1969, it was replaced ⑫ by a striking shopping mall, the **Forum des Halles.** The surrounding streets have since undergone a radical transformation, much like the neighboring Marais, and the shops, cafés, restaurants, and chic apartment buildings make it an example of successful urban redevelopment.

TIME OUT A few blocks south of Les Halles and just north of place du Châtelet is **Le Trappiste,** where 20 different international beers are available on draft, along with well over 180 bottled varieties. Mussels and french fries are the traditional accompaniment, although various other snacks (hot dogs and sandwiches) are also available. There are tables upstairs and on the pavement. *4 rue St-Denis.*

From place du Châtelet, cross back over the Seine on the Pont-au-Change ⑬ to the Ile de la Cité. To your right looms the imposing **Palais de Justice,** the Courts of Law, built by Baron Haussmann in his characteristically weighty Classical style around 1860. The main buildings of interest on the Ile de la Cité, however, are the medieval parts of the complex, spared by Haussmann in his otherwise wholesale destruction.

The **Conciergerie,** the northernmost part of the complex, was originally part of the royal palace on the island. Most people know it, however, as a prison, the grim place of confinement for Danton, Robespierre, and Marie Antoinette during the French Revolution. Inside you'll see the guardroom (the Salle des Gens d'Armes), a striking example of Gothic monumentality; the cells, including the one in which Marie Antoinette was held; and the chapel, where objects connected with the ill-fated queen are displayed. ☛ *26 frs adults, 17 frs children, students, and senior citizens. Joint ticket (with Ste-Chapelle): 40 frs (20 frs).* ☾ *Daily 9:30–6:30 (10–4:30 in winter). Métro: Cité.*

★ The other perennial crowd-puller in the Palais de Justice is the **Sainte-Chapelle,** the Holy Chapel, one of the supreme achievements of the Middle Ages. It was built by the genial and pious Saint Louis (Louis IX, 1226–70) to house what he took to be the Crown of Thorns and fragments of the True Cross from Christ's crucifixion. For all its delicate and ornate exterior decoration, the design of the building is simplicity itself: in essence, no more than a thin, rectangular box much taller than it is wide. Some clumsy 19th-century work has added a deadening touch, but the glory of the chapel—the stained glass—is spectacularly intact: The walls consist of at least twice as much glass as masonry. Try to attend one of the regular, candle-lit concerts given here. ☎ *43–54–30–09.* ☛ *26 frs adults, 17 frs children under 17.* ☾ *Daily 9:30–6:30 (10–5 in winter). Métro: Cité.*

Take rue de Lutèce opposite the Palais de Justice down to place Louis-Lépine and the bustling **Marché aux Fleurs,** the flower market. Around ★ ⑭ the corner is the most enduring symbol of Paris, the cathedral of **Notre-Dame.** The building was started in 1163, with an army of stonemasons, carpenters, and sculptors working on a site that had previously seen a Roman temple, an early Christian basilica, and a Romanesque church. The chancel and altar were consecrated in 1182, but the magnificent sculptures surrounding the main doors were not put into position until 1240. The north tower was finished 10 years later. Despite various changes in the 17th century, principally the (temporary) removal of the rose windows, the cathedral remained substantially unaltered until the French Revolution, when much destruction was wrought, mainly to statuary.

Stand in place du Parvis, in front of the cathedral, to gaze first at the building's famous facade, divided neatly into three levels. At the first level are the three main entrances: the Portal of the Virgin on the left, the Portal of the Last Judgment in the center, and the Portal of St. Anne on the right. Above the portals the restored statues of the kings of Israel, the Galerie des Rois (which took a beating during the French Revolution), complete the first level. A large rose window centers the second level, and at the third level, the Grande Galerie is a series of pointed double arches at the base of the twin towers. The south tower houses the great bell of Notre-Dame, the one tolled by Quasimodo, Victor Hugo's fictional hunchback.

The interior of the cathedral, with its vast proportions, soaring nave, and gentle, multicolored light filtering through the stained-glass windows, inspires awe, despite the inevitable throngs of tourists. (There is no charge to visit the interior of the cathedral.) On the south side of the chancel is the **Treasury,** with a collection of vestments, reliquaries, and silver and gold plate. ☞ *15 frs adults, 10 frs students and senior citizens, 5 frs children.* ☉ *Weekdays 9:30–6. Métro: Cité.*

The 387-step climb to the top of the **towers** is worth the effort for the close-up view of the famous gargoyles and the expansive view over the city. *Entrance via the north tower.* ☞ *31 frs adults, 20 frs students and senior citizens, 7 frs children.* ☉ *Daily 9:30–12:15 and 2–6 (5 in winter).*

The **Crypte Archéologique,** the archaeological museum under the square, contains structural remains unearthed during excavations in the 1960s. The foundations of the 3rd-century Gallo-Roman rampart and the 6th-century Merovingian church can also be seen. ☞ *26 frs adults (40 frs including Notre-Dame towers), 17 frs students and senior citizens, 6 frs children 7–17.* ☉ *Daily 10–6:30, 10–5 in winter.*

If your interest in the cathedral is not yet sated, duck into the **Musée Notre-Dame,** which displays artwork and documents tracing the cathedral's history. *10 rue du Cloître Notre-Dame.* ☞ *12 frs, 6 frs students and senior citizens, 4 frs children under 14.* ☉ *Wed. and weekends only, 2:30–6.*

Tour 2: The Marais and Ile St-Louis

The history of the Marais ("marsh") began when Charles V, king of France in the 14th century, moved the French court from the Ile de la Cité. However, it wasn't until Henri IV laid out the place Royale, today the place des Vosges, in the early 17th century that the Marais became *the* place to live. Following the French Revolution, however, the Marais rapidly became one of the most deprived, dissolute areas in Paris. It was spared the attentions of Baron Haussmann in the mid-19th century, so that, though crumbling, its ancient golden-hued buildings and squares remained intact. The influx of central and eastern European immigrants at the beginning of the century, and then a wave of Sephardic Jews from Algeria, after its independence in the 1960s, gave the neighborhood around the Rue des Rosiers its distinctly Jewish flavor, which endures—despite the displacement of kosher butchers and family storefronts by chic boutiques and restaurants—in the occasional smells of pastrami and borscht. Most of the marais's spectacular *hotels particuliers* (meaning, simply, "private houses"), one-time mansions of aristocratic families, have been restored and transformed into museums. Today's Marais once again has staked a convincing claim as the city's most desirable district. Try to visit during the Festival du Marais, held every June and July, when concerts, theater, and ballet are performed.

⓯ Begin your tour at the **Hôtel de Ville** (City Hall), overlooking the Seine. It was in the square on the Hôtel de Ville's west side that Robespierre, fanatical leader during the period of the French Revolution known as the Reign of Terror, came to suffer the fate of his many victims when a furious mob sent him to the guillotine in 1794. Following the accession of Louis-Philippe in 1830, the building became the seat of the French government, a role that came to a sudden end with the uprisings in 1848. In the Commune of 1871, the Hôtel de Ville was burned to the ground. Today's exuberant building, based closely on the Renaissance original, went up between 1874 and 1884.

From the Hôtel de Ville, head north across rue de Rivoli and up rue du Temple. On your right, you'll pass one of the city's most popular department stores, the **Bazar de l'Hôtel de Ville,** or BHV as it's commonly known. The first street on your left, rue de la Verrerie, will take you to the stores, restaurants, and galleries of the rue St-Martin.

⓰ The **Beaubourg**—also known as the **Pompidou Center** (short for Centre National d'Art et de Culture Georges Pompidou)—is next. The center hosts an innovative and challenging series of exhibits, in addition to housing the world's largest collection of modern art. Its brash architectural style—it has been likened to a gaudily painted oil refinery—has caused much controversy, however. Many critics think it is beginning to show its age (it only opened in 1977) in a particularly cheap manner: Witness the cracked and grimy plastic tubing that encases the exterior elevators and the peeling, skeletal interior supports. Probably the most popular thing to do at Beaubourg is to ride the escalator up to the roof to see the Paris skyline unfolding as you are carried through its clear plastic piping. There's a sizable restaurant and café there. Aside from the art collection (from which American painters and sculptors are conspicuously absent), the building houses a movie theater; a language laboratory; an extensive collection of tapes, videos, and slides; an industrial design center; and an acoustics and musical research center. *Plateau Beaubourg,* ☎ *42–77–12–33.* ☛ *Free; Modern Art museum: 35 frs, slightly more for special exhibitions.* ☯ *Wed.–Mon. noon–10 PM, weekends 10–10. Guided tours in English during summer and Christmas seasons only: weekdays 3:30, weekends 11. Métro: Rambuteau.*

TIME OUT   Don't leave the plateau without stopping for coffee at the **Café Beaubourg** on the corner of rue St-Merri, designed by the trendy Philippe Starck. A staircase takes you from the first floor to a *passerelle*, or footbridge, linking the two sides of a mezzanine. The severe, high-tech design is lightened by the little glass-top tables, which are covered with etchings, drawings, and paintings.

Stroll over to the right side of the Pompidou Center as you're facing it and look at the large digital clock, dubbed the **Genitron,** which counts down the seconds to the year 2000 at what seems like an apocalyptic pace. From here turn right into the café-lined **square Stravinsky**; kids will delight at the lively, eponymous fountain animated by the colorful and imaginative sculptures of French artist Niki de Saint-Phalle and the aquatic mechanisms of Jean Tinguely.

Leave plateau Beaubourg by its southwestern corner and head east on little rue Ste-Croix de la Bretonnerie to visit the Marais's Jewish quarter. You'll see the more obvious of the area's historical highlights if you take rue Rambuteau, which runs along the north side of the center (to your left as you face the building). The **Quartier de L'Horloge,** the Clock Quarter, opens off the plateau here. An entire city block has been rebuilt, and despite the shops and cafés, it retains a resolutely artificial quality. The mechanical clock around the corner on rue Clairvaux will amuse children, however: St. George defends Time against a dragon, an eagle-beaked bird, or a monstrous crab (symbolizing earth, air, and water, respectively) every hour, on the hour. At noon, 6 PM, and 10 PM, he takes on all three at once.

You are now poised to plunge into the elegant heart of the Marais. The historic homes here are now private residences and apartment buildings; don't be afraid to push through the heavy doors, or *portes-cochère,* to glimpse the discreet courtyards that lurk behind.

From the little market on rue Rambuteau, take the first left, up rue du Temple, to the 17th-century **Hôtel de Montmor,** at No. 79. It was once the scene of an influential salon—a part-social, part-literary group—that included the philosopher Descartes (1596–1650) and the playwright Molière (1622–73).

Take rue de Braque (opposite) down to the Hôtel de Soubise, now the ⑰ **Archives Nationales** (its collections form part of the **Musée de l'Histoire de France,** whose entrance is at the far end of the courtyard). The museum's highlights are the Edict of Nantes (1598), Louis XIV and Napoléon's wills, and the Declaration of Human Rights (1789). Louis XVI's diary is also in the collection, containing his sadly ignorant entry for July 14, 1789, the day the Bastille was stormed at the start of the French Revolution: *Rien* (nothing), he wrote. You can also visit the apartments of the Prince and Princess de Soubise: Don't miss them if you have any interest in the lifestyles of 18th-century French aristocrats. The Archives buildings also include the elegant **Hôtel de Rohan,** built for the archbishops of Strasbourg in 1705 (open only during temporary exhibits). *60 rue des Francs-Bourgeois,* ☎ *40–27–62–18.* ☛ *15 frs adults, 10 frs students.* ☉ *Wed.–Mon. 1:45–5:45. Métro: Rambuteau.*

Turn right into rue des Archives, then take the first right into rue des ⑱ Quatre-Fils, which becomes rue de la Perle. At No. 1 is the **Musée Bricard de la Serrure,** the Lock Museum. The museum's sumptuous building is perhaps more interesting than the assembled locks and keys within; it was built in 1685 by Bruand, the architect of Les Invalides. If you have a taste for fine craftsmanship, you will appreciate the intricacy and ingenuity of many of the older locks. One represents an early security system—it would shoot anyone who tried to open it with the wrong key. *Hôtel Bruand, 1 rue de la Perle.* ☛ *20 frs adults.* ☉ *Weekdays 2–5. Métro: St-Sébastien.*

From here it is but a step to the Hôtel Salé, built between 1656 and ⑲ 1660, and today the popular **Musée Picasso;** be prepared for long lines. The collection encompasses pictures, sculptures, drawings, prints, ceramics, and other assorted works of art given to the French government after the painter's death, in 1973, in lieu of death duties. What's notable about it—other than its being the world's largest collection of works by Picasso—is that these were works that the artist himself owned and especially valued. There are works from every period of his life, as well as paintings by Paul Cézanne, Joan Miró, Pierre Auguste Renoir, Georges Braque, Edgar Degas, Henri Matisse, and others. The palatial surroundings add greatly to the visit. *5 rue de Thorigny,* ☎ *42–71–25–21.* ☛ *26 frs adults.* ⊘ *Wed.–Mon. 9:30–6. Métro: St-Sébastien.*

⓴ Cut across place Thorigny and take rue Elzévir. Halfway down on the left is the **Musée Cognacq-Jay,** transferred here in 1990 from its original home near the Opéra. The museum is devoted to the arts of the 18th century: furniture, porcelain, and paintings (Watteau and Boucher notably). The Hôtel Donon, a 15th-century mansion, was virtually in ruins before its tasteful transformation by the City of Paris. *8 rue Elzévir,* ☎ *40–27–07–21.* ☛ *17 frs adults, 9 frs students and children.* ⊘ *Tues.–Sun. 10–5:30. Métro: St-Paul.*

㉑ Continue down rue Elzévir to rue des Francs-Bourgeois, where the substantial **Hôtel Carnavalet** became the scene, in the late 17th century, of the most brilliant salon in Paris, presided over by Madame de Sévigné. She is best known for the hundreds of letters she wrote to her daughter during her life; they've become one of the most enduring chronicles of French high society in the 17th century. In 1880, the house was transformed into the **Musée de l'Histoire de Paris,** and to celebrate the bicentennial of the French Revolution in 1989, the museum annexed the neighboring Hôtel Peletier St-Fargeau. Together the two museums chronicle the entire history of Paris, with material dating from the city's origins until 1789 housed in the Hôtel Carnavalet, and objects from that time to the present in the Hôtel Peletier St-Fargeau. The latter contains some fascinating macabre models of guillotines. *23 rue de Sévigné,* ☎ *42–72–21–13.* ☛ *27 frs adults, 19 frs children and senior citizens.* ⊘ *Tues.–Sun. 10–5:30. Métro: St-Paul.*

★ ㉒ Now walk a minute or two farther along rue des Francs-Bourgeois to **place des Vosges,** or place Royale, as it was originally known, the oldest square in Paris. Laid out by Henri IV at the beginning of the 17th century, it is the model for all the later city squares of most French urban developments. The harmonious balance of the square, with its lush greenery and symmetrical town houses of pale pink stone, makes it a pleasant place in which to spend a hot summer's afternoon. At No. 6 is the **Maison de Victor Hugo,** which commemorates the workaholic French writer. ☛ *18 frs. Métro: St-Paul.*

㉓ From place des Vosges, follow rue du Pas-de-la-Mule and turn right down rue des Tournelles until you reach **place de la Bastille,** site of the infamous prison destroyed in 1789 during the French Revolution. Until 1988, there was little more to see here than a huge traffic circle and the **Colonne de Juillet,** the July Column, but as part of the bicentennial celebrations, a 3,000-seat **opera house** boasting five moving stages and a gleaming curved-glass facade was erected on the south side of the square. Redevelopment projects have changed what used to be a humdrum neighborhood into one of the city's most chic and attractive areas.

The **Bastille** was built by Charles V in the late 14th century as a fortress to guard the eastern entrance to the city. By the reign of Louis XIII (1610–43), however, it was used almost exclusively to house political prisoners, including, in the 18th century, Voltaire and the marquis de Sade. This obviously political role led the "furious mob" (in all probability no more than a largely unarmed rabble) to break into the prison on July 14, 1789, kill the governor, steal what firearms they could find, and set the seven remaining prisoners free. The ground plan of the prison is marked by paving stones set into the modern square.

Return toward the Hôtel de Ville down rue St-Antoine, forking left down
(24) rue François-Miron to the church of **St-Gervais–St-Protais,** named after
two Roman soldiers martyred by the Emperor Nero in the 1st century
AD. The original church—one of the earliest in Paris; no trace remains
of it now—was built in the 7th century. The present building, a riot of
Flamboyant decoration, went up between 1494 and 1598, making it
one of the last Gothic constructions in the country. Pause before you
go in to look at the facade, added between 1616 and 1621. Although
the interior is late Gothic, the exterior is one of the earliest examples
of the Classical, or Renaissance, style in France. ☉ *Tues.–Sun. 6:30–
8. The church holds occasional choral and organ concerts; call 47–
26–78–38 for information. Métro: Hôtel de Ville.*

Don't cross the Seine to Ile St-Louis yet. Take rue de l'Hôtel de Ville
(25) east to rue de Figuier. The painstakingly restored **Hôtel de Sens** (1474)
on the corner is one of a handful of Parisian homes to have survived
since the Middle Ages. With its pointed corner towers, Gothic porch,
and richly carved decorative details, it is a strange mixture: half defensive stronghold, half fairy-tale château. Built at the end of the 15th
century for the archbishop of Sens, it was once the home of Henri IV
and his queen, Marguerite, philanderers both. While Henri dallied with
his mistresses—he is said to have had 56—at a series of royal palaces,
Marguerite entertained her almost equally large number of lovers here.
Today the building houses a fine arts library, the **Bibliothèque Forney.**
☛ *Free.* ☉ *Tues.–Fri. 1:30–8:30, Sat. 10–8:30. Métro: Pont Marie.*

(26) Cross pont Marie to the residential **Ile St-Louis,** linked to the Ile de la
Cité by pont St-Louis. There are no standouts here and no great sights,
but for idle strolling, window shopping, or simply sitting on one of
the little quays and drinking in the views, the Ile St-Louis exudes a
quintessentially Parisian air.

TIME OUT   **Berthillon** has become a byword for delicious ice cream. Cafés all over
Ile St-Louis sell its glamorous products, but the place to try them is still the
little shop on rue St-Louis-en-l'Ile. Expect to wait in line. *31 rue St-Louis-
en-l'Ile. Closed Mon. and Tues. Métro: Pont Marie.*

Tour 3: From the Arc de Triomphe to the Opéra

This tour takes in grand, opulent Paris—the Paris of imposing vistas;
long, arrow-straight streets; and plush hotels and jewelers. It begins at
the Arc de Triomphe, standing sturdily at the top of the most famous
street in the city, the Champs-Elysées.

Place Charles-de-Gaulle is known by Parisians as **l'Etoile,** the star—a
reference to the streets that fan out from it. It is one of Europe's most
chaotic traffic circles, and short of a death-defying dash, your only way
of getting to the Arc de Triomphe in the middle is to take an underground passage from the Champs-Elysées or avenue de la Grande-Armée.

★ (27) The colossal, 164-foot **Arc de Triomphe** was planned by Napoléon to
celebrate his military successes. Unfortunately, the great man's strategic and architectural visions were not entirely on the same plane:
When it was required for the triumphal entry of his new empress, Marie
Louise, into Paris in 1810, it was still only a few feet high. To save face,
he ordered a dummy arch of painted canvas to be put up. (The real
thing wasn't finished until 1836.) After recent, extensive cleaning, its
magnificent elaborate relief sculptures now gleam. The highlight is the
scene by François Rude, illustrated to the right of the arch when viewed
from the Champs-Elysées. Called *Departure of the Volunteers in 1792,*

it's commonly known as *La Marseillaise* and depicts *La Patrie,* or the Fatherland, with outspread wings exhorting the volunteers to fight for France.

If you like elevated views, go up to the platform at the top of the monument, from which you can look down the Champs-Elysées toward place de la Concorde and the distant Louvre. A small museum halfway up the arch is devoted to its history. France's *Unknown Soldier* is buried beneath the archway; the flame is rekindled every evening at 6:30. *Pl. Charles-de-Gaulle.* ☛ *31 frs adults, 20 frs students and senior citizens, 7 frs children.* ⊙ *Daily 10–5:30, 10–5 in winter; closed public holidays. Métro: Etoile.*

Laid out by landscape gardener Le Nôtre in the 1660s as a garden sweeping away from the Tuileries, the cosmopolitan **Champs-Elysées** reached its pinnacle at the turn of the century when the tree- and café-lined avenue was the main drag for Paris's beau monde. The city of Paris has now completed an ambitious reconstruction program reestablishing this once glorious thoroughfare as one of the world's most beautiful avenues. Improvements include underground parking to alleviate congestion, tree-lined walkways along each side, designer street furniture (coordinated benches, signs, trash cans), Belle Epoque newsstands, and stricter regulations to control the garishness of business storefronts. The avenue also occupies a central role in French national celebrations. It witnesses the finish of the Tour de France cycle race on the last Sunday of July and is the site of vast ceremonies on Bastille Day, July 14 (France's national holiday), and November 11, Armistice Day. Start by walking east from l'Etoile on the left-hand side, where 300 yards along, at No. 116-B, is the famous **Lido** nightclub: Foot-stomping melodies in French and English, and champagne-soaked, topless razzamatazz pack in the crowds every night. Opposite is the red-awning **Fouquet's** café, an 1899 landmark, which still caters to a highbrow clientele. Inside, look for the bronze plaques that line the booths, honoring faithful patrons past and present, including François Truffaut, Marcel Pagnol, and Orson Welles. Avenue George-V leads south to the **Prince de Galles** (Prince of Wales) at No. 33 (with the red awning) and the **George V** (with the blue awning), two of the city's top hotels. Continue down avenue George-V and turn right on Pierre-Ier-de-Serbie to the church of **St-Pierre de Chaillot** on avenue Marceau. The monumental frieze above the entrance, depicting scenes from the life of St. Peter, is the work of Henri Bouchard and dates from 1937. Returning to avenue George-V, continue south toward the slender spire of the **American Cathedral of the Holy Trinity,** built by G. S. Street between 1885 and 1888. ⊙ *Weekdays 9–12:30 and 2–5, Sat. 9–noon. Services: weekdays 9 AM, Sun. 9 AM and 11 AM; Sun. school and nursery. Guided tours Sun. and Wed. at 12:30. Métro: George V.*

At the bottom of avenue George-V is the place de l'Alma and the Seine. Just across the Alma bridge, on the left, is the entrance to **Les Egouts,** the Paris sewers. Aside from the unpleasant smell, the Egouts are surprisingly interesting. Several underground passages and footbridges carry you along the banks of Paris sewers, marked with signs to mirror the streets above. ☛ *24 frs.* ⊙ *Sat.–Wed. 11–5. Métro: Pont de l'Alma.*

Or stay on the Right Bank and head east down the sloping side road to the left of the bridge, for the embarkation point of the *Bâteaux Mouches* motorboat tours of the Seine.

Stylish avenue Montaigne leads from the Seine back toward the Champs-Elysées at the Rond Point circle.

TIME OUT   Although power brokers and fashion models make up half the clientele at the **Bar des Théâtres,** its blasé waiters refuse to bat an eyelid. This is a fine place for an aperitif or a swift, more affordable lunch than you'll find around the corner at the luxury restaurants on place de l'Alma. *Opposite the Théâtre des Champs-Elysées at 6 av. Montaigne.*

Two blocks east, along the Champs-Elysées and on the side of avenue Winston-Churchill, sit the **Grand Palais** and the Petit Palais, erected before the Paris World Fair of 1900. Like the Eiffel Tower, there was never any intention that these two buildings would be anything other than temporary additions to the city. Together they recapture the opulence and frivolity of the Belle Epoque. Today the atmospheric iron-and-glass interior of the Grand Palais plays regular host to major exhibitions. *Av. Winston-Churchill.* ☛ *Varies according to exhibition. Usually open 10:30–6:30, often until 10 PM on Wed. Métro: Champs-Elysées–Clemenceau.*

The **Petit Palais** has a beautifully presented permanent collection of lavish 17th-century furniture and French 19th-century painting, with splendid canvases by Courbet and Bouguereau. Temporary exhibits are often held here, too. The sprawling entrance gallery contains several enormous turn-of-the-century paintings on its walls and ceiling. *Av. Winston-Churchill.* ☛ *26 frs adults, children under 18 free (temporary exhibits: 40 frs adults, 30 frs children under 18).* ⊗ *Tues.–Sun. 10–5:30. Métro: Champs-Elysées–Clemenceau.*

Cross the Champs-Elysées and head north on avenue de Marigny to **rue du Faubourg St-Honoré,** a prestigious address in the world of luxury fashion and art galleries. High security surrounds the French president in the **Palais de l'Elysée.** This "palace," where the head of state lives, works, and receives official visitors, was originally constructed as a private mansion in 1718. It has known presidential occupants only since 1873; before then, Madame de Pompadour (Louis XV's influential mistress), Napoléon, Josephine, and Queen Victoria all stayed here. Today the French government, the *Conseil des Ministres,* meets here each Wednesday. *Not open to the public.*

Continue east to rue Royale. This classy street, lined with jewelry stores, links place de la Concorde to the **Eglise de la Madeleine.** With its rows of uncompromising columns, the Madeleine's sturdy neoclassical edifice looks more like a Greek temple than a Christian church. The only natural indoor light comes from three shallow domes. The inside walls are richly and harmoniously decorated, and gold glints through the murk. The church was designed in 1814 but not consecrated until 1842. The portico's majestic Corinthian colonnade—cleaned and renovated in 1991 and 1992—supports a gigantic pediment with a sculptured frieze of the *Last Judgment.* From the top of the steps, stop to admire the view down rue Royale across the Seine.

Alongside the Madeleine, a **kiosk** sells tickets for same-day theater performances at greatly reduced prices. ⊗ *Tues.–Fri. 12:30–8; Sat. 12:30 for matinees and 2–8 for evenings. Métro: Madeleine.*

At the far end of rue Royale, on the right (as you look from La Madeleine), is the legendary **Maxim's** restaurant. Unless you choose to eat here—an expensive and not always rewarding experience—you won't be able to see the interior decor, a riot of crimson velvet and florid Art Nouveau furniture.

TIME OUT   **L'Ecluse,** on the west side of the square around the church, is a select, wood-paneled wine bar where you can order a whole range of Bordeaux by the glass. Stylish snacks, such as foie gras or carpaccio, make this a great place for a light lunch. *15 pl. de la Madeleine.* ⊙ *Noon–2 am.*

32 There is a striking contrast between the gloomy locked-in feel of the high-walled rue Royale and the broad, airy **place de la Concorde.** This huge square is best approached from the Champs-Elysées: The flower beds, chestnut trees, and sandy sidewalks of the avenue's lower section are reminders of its original leafy elegance. Place de la Concorde was built in the 1770s, but there was nothing in the way of peace or concord about its early years. From 1793 to 1795, it was the scene of more than 1,000 deaths by guillotine; victims included Louis XVI, Marie Antoinette, and Danton. The obelisk, a present from the viceroy of Egypt, was erected in 1833. The handsome, symmetrical 18th-century buildings facing the square include the deluxe **Hôtel Crillon** (far left), though there's nothing so vulgar as a sign to identify it—just an inscribed marble plaque. East from place de la Concorde stretch the Tuileries Gardens. Two smallish buildings stand sentinel here. The one nearer rue de Rivoli is the **Jeu de Paume,** fondly known to many as the former home of the Impressionists now in the Musée d'Orsay. It underwent extensive renovation in 1990–91 and is now home to temporary exhibits of contemporary art. The identical building nearer the Seine is
33 the recently restored **Orangerie,** containing some early 20th-century paintings by Monet (*Water Lilies*) and Renoir, among others. *Pl. de la Concorde.* ☛ *Orangerie: 27 frs (18 frs students, senior citizens, and Sun.).* ⊙ *Wed.–Mon. 9:45–5:45.* ☛ *Jeu de Paume: 35 frs adults, 25 frs children.* ⊙ *Wed.–Fri. noon–7, Tues. noon–9:30, weekends 10–7. Métro: Concorde.*

34 As gardens go, the formal and greatly patterned **Jardin des Tuileries** is typically French, a charming place for strolling and surveying the surrounding cityscape. As part of the Grand Louvre Project, the garden renovation is scheduled to restore the fountains, statues, and shady groves by the end of 1996. Leave the Tuileries by the rue de Rivoli gateway across from rue de Castiglione, leading to place Vendôme.

TIME OUT For something to sweeten your day, stop at **Angelina** (226 rue de Rivoli). Founded in 1903, this elegant *salon de thé* and *pâtisserie* (tea and pastry shop) is famous for its *Chocolat L'Africain*—a cup of hot chocolate so thick you'll need a fork to eat it (a delight, even in the summer months).

35 The opulent **place Vendôme,** a perfectly proportioned example of 17th-century urban architecture (by Mansart), now holds numerous upscale jewelers and the **Ritz.** The square recently benefitted from a facelift, which included a new granite pavement, Second Empire-style streetlamps, and an underground garage. Napoléon had the square's central column made from the melted bronze of 1,200 cannons captured at the battle of Austerlitz in 1805. That's him standing vigilantly at the top.

36 The **Opéra,** begun at the behest of Napoléon III and completed in 1875 by Charles Garnier, typifies the pompous Second Empire style of architecture. The monumental foyer and staircase are a stage in their own right, where, on first nights, celebrities preen and prance. If the lavishly upholstered auditorium (ceiling painted by Marc Chagall in 1964) seems small, it is only because the stage is the largest in the world—more than 11,000 square yards. Constructed over a subterranean lake for fire safety, the Opéra Garnier inspired Gaston Leroux's penny dreadful **The Phantom of the Opera** (it was rumored that a diabolical genius who lived in the cellar lured the singers down to his damp, murky chambers). The **opera museum,** containing a few paintings and theatrical mementos, is unremarkable. ☎ 47–42–57–50. ☛ 30 frs adults, 18 frs students and senior citizens. ☉ Daily 10–4:30; closed occasionally. Métro: Opéra.

Tour 4: From Orsay to Trocadéro

The Left Bank has two faces: the cozy, ramshackle Latin Quarter (see Tour 5, below) and the spacious, stately Seventh Arrondissement, covered in this tour. The latest addition to this area is already the most ★ ㉗ popular: the **Musée d'Orsay,** the stylishly converted train station on the Seine across from the Tuileries. It shows the Impressionist paintings formerly housed in the Jeu de Paume and important examples of other 19th- and 20th-century schools. The chief artistic attraction here is the collection of Impressionist works on the top floor. Highlights include Whistler' portrait of his mother, Arrangement in Gray and Black, and Renoir's Le Moulin de la Galette. The Post-Impressionists—Paul Cézanne, Vincent Van Gogh, Paul Gauguin, and Henri de Toulouse-Lautrec—are also represented on this floor.

On the first floor, you'll find the work of Edouard Manet and the delicate nuances of Edgar Degas. Pride of place, at least in art-history terms, goes to Manet's Déjeuner sur l'Herbe, the painting that scandalized Paris in 1863. If you prefer modern developments, head for the exhibit of paintings by the early 20th-century group known as the Fauves (meaning wild beasts, as they were dubbed by an outraged critic in 1905)—particularly Henri Matisse, André Derain, and Maurice de Vlaminck. Sculpture at the Orsay means, first and foremost, Auguste Rodin. Two further highlights are the faithfully restored Belle Epoque restaurant and the model of the entire Opéra quarter, displayed beneath a glass floor. Prepare for huge crowds: The best times for relatively painless viewing are at lunchtime or on Thursday evening. 1 rue de Bellechasse, ☎ 40–49–48–14. ☛ 35 frs, 24 frs students, senior citizens, and on Sun., children under 18 free. ☉ Tues.–Wed. and Fri.–Sat. 10–5:45, Thurs. 10–9:30, Sun. 9–5:45. Métro: Solférino.

㊳ Continue west along the Seine to the 18th-century **Palais Bourbon** (directly across from place de la Concorde), home of the Assemblée Nationale (French Parliament). The colonnaded facade was commissioned by Napoleon. Though it's not open to the public, there is a fine view from the steps across to place de la Concorde and the church of the Madeleine.

Head south on rue de Bourgogne to rue de Varenne and the Hôtel Biron, ㊴ better known as the **Musée Rodin.** The splendid house, with its spacious vestibule and light, airy rooms, retains much of its 18th-century atmosphere and makes a handsome setting for the sculpture of Rodin (1840–1917), including the famous Thinker (Le Penseur) and Kiss (Le Baiser). Don't leave without visiting the garden, to see both its rosebushes (more than 2,000) and its sculptures. 77 rue de Varenne, ☎ 47–05–01–34. ☛ 27 frs, 18 frs Sun. ☉ Tues.–Sun. 10–6, 10–5 winter. Métro: Varenne.

★ ㊵ From the Rodin Museum, you can see the **Hôtel des Invalides** along rue de Varenne, founded by Louis XIV in 1674 to house wounded veterans. Only a handful of old soldiers live there today, but the building contains one of the world's foremost military museums, **Musée de l'Armée,** which has a vast, musty collection of arms, armor, uniforms, banners, and military pictures. The **Musée des Plans-Reliefs,** on the fifth floor of the right-hand wing, contains a fascinating collection of scale models of French towns made to illustrate the fortifications planned by the 17th-century military engineer Sébastien de Vauban. The largest and most impressive is Strasbourg, which takes up an entire room.

The museums are not the only reason for visiting the Invalides, however. The building itself is an outstanding monumental ensemble in late-17th-century Baroque, designed by Libéral Bruant (1635–97) and Jules Hardouin-Mansart (1646–1708). The main, cobbled courtyard is a fitting scene for the parades and ceremonies still occasionally held here. The most impressive dome in Paris towers over the **Eglise du Dôme,** designed by Mansart and built between 1677 and 1735. Napoléon is buried here, in a series of six coffins, one inside the next, within a bombastic tomb of red porphyry. Among others commemorated in the church are French World War I hero Marshal Foch and fortification builder Vauban, whose heart was brought to the Invalides at Napoléon's behest. *Hôtel des Invalides.* ☛ *Tomb and museum: 34 frs adults, 24 frs children and senior citizens.* ⊙ *Daily 10–6, 10–4:45 in winter. Métro: St-François Xavier.*

★ ④ Turn right out of the Dôme church and follow avenue de Tourville to the Champ de Mars. At the far end looms Paris's best-known landmark, the **Eiffel Tower.** Built by Gustave Eiffel for the World Exhibition of 1889, the centennial of the French Revolution, it was still in good shape to celebrate its own 100th birthday. Such was Eiffel's engineering wizardry that, even in the strongest winds, his tower never sways more than 4½ inches. Today it exudes a feeling of mighty permanence. As you stand beneath its huge legs, you may have trouble believing that it nearly became 7,000 tons of scrap iron when its concession expired in 1909. Only its potential use as a radio antenna saved the day; it now bristles with a forest of radio and television transmitters. The energetic can stride up the stairs as far as the third deck. If you want to go to the top, 1,000 feet up, you'll have to take the elevator. *Pont d'Iéna.* ☛ *By elevator: 2nd floor, 20 frs; 3rd floor, 36 frs; 4th floor, 53 frs.* ☛ *By foot: 12 frs (2nd and 3rd floors only).* ⊙ *Daily 9:30 AM–11 PM (until midnight in July and Aug.). Métro: Bir-Hakeim.*

④ Just across the Seine by Pont d'Iéna from the Eiffel Tower, on the heights of Trocadéro, is the massive, sandy-colored **Palais de Chaillot,** a cultural center built in the 1930s. The gardens between the Palais de Chaillot and the Seine contain an aquarium and some dramatic fountains, and the terrace between the two wings of the palace offers a wonderful view of the Eiffel Tower.

The Palais de Chaillot contains four large museums, two in each wing. In the southwest wing are the **Musée de l'Homme,** an anthropological museum, with artifacts, costumes, and domestic tools from around the world dating from prehistoric times to the recent past (admission: 25 frs adults, 15 frs children; open Wed.–Mon. 10–5), and the **Musée de la Marine,** a maritime museum with exhibits on French naval history right up to the age of the nuclear submarine (admission 31 frs adults, 16 frs senior citizens and children; open Wed.–Mon. 10–6).

The other wing is dominated by the **Musée des Monuments Français,** without question the best introduction to French medieval architecture. Its long first-floor gallery pays tribute to French buildings, mainly of the Romanesque and Gothic periods (roughly AD 1000–1500), in the form of painstaking copies of statues, columns, archways, and frescoes. Substantial sections of a number of French churches and cathedrals are represented here, notably Chartres and Vézelay. Murals and ceiling paintings—copies of works in churches around the country—dominate the other three floors. ☛ *21 frs, 14 frs on Sun.* ☉ *Wed.–Mon. 9:45–5:15. Métro: Trocadéro.*

The **Musée du Cinema Henri Langlois,** tracing the history of motion pictures from the 1880s, is located in the basement. ☛ *25 frs adults, 15 frs children and senior citizens.* ☉ *Wed.–Mon., guided tours only, on the hr at 10, 11, 2, 3, 4, and 5.*

43 The area around the Palais de Chaillot offers a feast for museum lovers. The **Musée Guimet** has three floors of Indo-Chinese and Far Eastern art, including stone Buddhas, Chinese bronzes, ceramics, and painted screens. *6 pl. d'Iéna.* ☛ *26 frs adults, 17 frs students, senior citizens, and on Sun.* ☉ *Wed.–Mon. 9:45–5:10. Métro: Iéna.*

44 Nearby is the **Palais Galliera,** home of the **Musée de la Mode et Costume** (Museum of Fashion and Costume), a late-19th-century town house that hosts revolving exhibits. *10 av. Pierre-Ier-de-Serbie.* ☛ *26 frs.* ☉ *Tues.–Sun. 10–5:40. Métro: Iéna.*

45 The **Musée de l'Art Moderne de la Ville de Paris** has both temporary exhibits and a permanent collection of modern art. Among the earliest works in the vast galleries are Fauvist paintings by Vlaminck and Derain, followed by Picasso's early experiments in Cubism. Other highlights include works by Robert Delaunay, Georges Braque, and Amedeo Modigliani. There is also a large room devoted to Art Deco furniture and screens; a pleasant, if expensive, museum café; and an excellent bookshop with many books in English. *11 av. du Président-Wilson.* ☛ *15 frs, free Sun. for permanent exhibitions only, varies for special exhibitions.* ☉ *Tues.–Sun. 10–5:40, Wed. 10–8:30. Métro: Iéna.*

Tour 5: The Left Bank

The most piquant images of Paris, those evoked by the Left Bank, have never lost their power to stir us. Although the *vie de Bohème* that once flourished here has lost much of its vigor, people who choose to live and work here today are, in effect, turning their backs on the formality and staidness of the Right Bank.

The Left Bank's geographic and cerebral hub is the Latin Quarter, which takes its name from the university tradition of studying and speaking in Latin, a practice that disappeared at the time of the French Revolution. The area is populated mainly by students and academics from the Sorbonne, the headquarters of the University of Paris.

46 **Place St-Michel** (named for architect Davioud's grandiose fountain, which depicts St-Michel striking down the dragon) is a good starting point for exploring the rich slice of Parisian life that the Left Bank offers. Leave your itineraries at home and wander along the neighboring streets lined with restaurants, cafés, galleries, old bookshops, and all sorts of clothing stores, from tiny boutiques to haute-couture showrooms.

Pick up the pedestrian rue St-André des Arts at the southwest corner of place St-Michel. Just before you reach the carrefour de Buci crossroads at the end of the street, turn onto the cour du Commerce St-André. Jean-Paul Marat printed his revolutionary newspaper, *L'Ami du Peuple,* at No. 8, and it was here that Dr. Guillotin conceived the idea for a new "humane" method of execution that, to his horror, was used during the French Revolution.

47 Continue to the **carrefour de Buci,** once a notorious Left Bank landmark. By the 18th century, it contained a gallows, an execution stake, and an iron collar for punishing troublemakers. Many Royalists and priests lost their heads here during the bloody course of the French Revolution. Nearby rue de Buci has one of the best food markets in Paris. The stands close by 1 PM and do not open at all on Monday.

Several interesting, smaller streets of some historic significance radiate from the carrefour de Buci. Rue de l'Ancienne-Comédie is so named because No. 14 was the first home of the now legendary French theater company, the *Comédie-Française*. Across the street sits the oldest café in Paris, the **Procope** (now a classy restaurant). Opened in 1686, it has been a watering hole for many of Paris's literati, including Voltaire, Victor Hugo, and Oscar Wilde. Ben Franklin was a patron, as were the fomenters of the French Revolution—Marat, Danton, Desmoulins, and Robespierre. Napoléon's hat, forgotten here, was encased in a glass dome.

Stretching north toward the Seine is the rue Dauphine, the street that singer Juliet Greco put on the map when she opened the **Tabou jazz club** here in the '50s. The club attracted a group of young intellectuals who were to become known as the Zazous, a St-Germain movement prompting the jazz culture, complete with all-night parties and "free love."

The next street that shoots out of the carrefour (moving counter-clockwise) is rue Mazarine, leading north to the **Hôtel des Monnaies,** formerly the national mint. Louis XVI transferred the Royal Mint to this imposing mansion in the late 18th century, and although the mint was moved in 1973, weights and measures, and limited-edition coins are still made here. You can see the vast collection of coins, documents, engravings, and paintings at the **Musée de la Monnaie**. *11 quai Conti.* ☛ *20 frs adults, 15 frs students, senior citizens, and children and Sun.* ⊙ *Tues., Thurs.–Sun. 1–6, Wed. 1–9. Métro: Pont Neuf.*

Next door is the **Institut de France,** a revered cultural institution and one of the Left Bank's most impressive waterside sights, with its distinctive dome and commanding position overlooking the quai. It was built as a college in 1661; in the early 19th century, Napoléon stipulated that the Institut de France be transferred here from the Louvre. The **Académie Française,** the oldest of the five academies that comprise the Institut de France, was created by Cardinal Richelieu in 1635. Its first major task was to edit the French dictionary; today, among other functions, it is still charged with safeguarding the purity of the French language. Membership is the highest literary honor in France. Not until 1986 was a woman, author Marguerite Yourcenar, elected to its ranks. *Guided visits are reserved for cultural associations only.*

Just west along the waterfront, on quai Malaquais, stands the **Ecole Nationale des Beaux-Arts,** whose students can usually be seen painting and sketching on the nearby quais and bridges. The school, once the site of a convent, was established in 1816 and is still the breeding-ground for many of France's foremost painters, sculptors, and architects. Allow yourself time to wander into its courtyard and galleries to see the casts and copies of the statues that were once stored here, or stop in at one of the temporary exhibitions of professors' and students' works. *14 rue Bonaparte.* ⊙ *Daily 1–7. Métro: St-Germain des Prés.*

Tiny **rue Visconti,** running east–west off rue Bonaparte (slightly south of the Beaux-Arts), has a lot of history packed into its short length. In the 16th century, it was known as Little Geneva—after Europe's foremost Protestant city—because of the Protestant ghetto that formed here. Jean Racine, one of France's greatest playwrights and tragic poets, lived at No. 24 until his death in 1699. Honoré Balzac set up a printing shop at No. 17 in 1826, and the fiery Romantic artist Eugène Delacroix (1798–1863) worked here from 1836 to 1844.

TIME OUT   The terrace at **La Palette** beckons as you reach the rue de Seine, at the end of rue Visconti. This popular café has long been a favorite haunt of Beaux-Arts students. One of them was allowed to paint an ungainly portrait of the patron, François, which rules over the shaggy gathering of clients with mock authority. *43 rue de Seine.*

Farther south on gallery-lined rue de Seine, swing right onto the pretty rue Jacob, where both Wagner and Stendhal once lived. Then turn left onto rue de Fürstemberg, which leads to one of Paris's most delightful and secluded little squares, the place Fürstemberg. Delacroix's studio here has been turned into the charmingly tiny **Musée Eugène Delacroix**; it contains a small collection of sketches and drawings, while the garden at the rear is almost as interesting. *6 rue Fürstemberg.* ☛ *12 frs adults over 25, 7 frs adults 18–25 and senior citizens over 60.* ⊙ *Wed.–Mon. 9:15–5:15. Métro: St-Germain des Prés.*

❷ Continue south and take rue de l'Abbaye to **St-Germain-des-Prés,** Paris's oldest church, which began as a shelter for a relic brought back from Spain in 542. Only the church and the adjoining building, the former **Abbey Palace,** remain from the powerful Benedictine monastery that stood here for centuries. Parts of the church date from 990. Interesting interior details include colorful 19th-century frescoes in the nave by Hippolyte Flandrin, a pupil of the Classical painter Ingres. The church stages superb organ concerts and recitals; programs are displayed outside.

Across the cobbled place St-Germain-des-Prés stands the celebrated **Les Deux Magots** café, still thriving on its '50s reputation as one of the Left Bank's prime meeting places for the intelligentsia. These days, you're more likely to rub shoulders with tourists than with philosophers, but a sidewalk table still affords a perfect view of Left Bank life.

In the years after World War II, Jean-Paul Sartre and Simone de Beauvoir would meet "The Family"—their intellectual clique—two doors down at the **Café de Flore,** on the boulevard St-Germain. Today the Flore has become more of a gay hangout, but it is a scenic spot that never lacks for action, often in the form of the street entertainers performing in front of the church.

If you now pick up the long rue de Rennes and follow it south, or travel three stops on the métro to Montparnasse-Bienvenüe, you'll soon arrive in the heart of Montparnasse. The opening of the **Tour Maine-Montparnasse** in 1973 forever changed the face of this former painters' and poets' haunt. The tower, containing offices and a branch of the Galeries Lafayette department store, was part of a vast redevelopment plan that aimed to make the area one of Paris's premier business and shopping districts. As Europe's tallest high-rise, it claims to have the fastest elevator in Europe and affords stupendous views of Paris. ☛ *40 frs adults, 32 frs students and senior citizens, 22 frs children 5–14.* ⊙ *Daily 9:30 AM–10:30 PM weekdays, 10 AM–9:30 PM in winter. Métro: Montparnasse-Bienvenüe.*

Southeast on boulevard du Montparnasse and across from the Vavin métro station are two of the better-known gathering places of Montparnasse's bohemian heyday, the **Dôme** and **La Coupole** brasseries. La Coupole opened in 1927 and soon became a home away from home for luminaries such as Guillaume Apollinaire, Max Jacob, Jean Cocteau, Erik Satie, Igor Stravinsky, and Ernest Hemingway.

Continue along boulevard du Montparnasse, to the intersection with boulevard St-Michel, where the verdant avenue de l'Observatoire sweeps north to the Luxembourg Gardens. Here you'll find perhaps **54** the most famous bastion of the Left Bank café culture, the **Closerie des Lilas.** Now a pricey but pretty bar-restaurant, the Closerie remains a staple on all literary tours of Paris, not least because of the commemorative plaques on the bar, marking the places where renowned writers used to sit. Charles Baudelaire, Paul Verlaine, Ernest Hemingway, and Guillaume Apollinaire are just a few.

Turn left on avenue de l'Observatoire and then take the first right down **55** rue du **Val-de-Grâce** to the mighty domed Baroque church of the same name, extensively restored in the early 1990s and famous for its cupola frescoes and rhythmic two-story facade. Retrace your steps and head **56** down to the **Jardin du Luxembourg,** one of the city's few large parks. Its fountains, ponds, trim hedges, precisely planted rows of trees, and gravel walks are typical of French formal gardens. At the far end is the **Palais du Luxembourg,** gray and formal, built, like the park, for Marie de Médicis, widow of Henri IV, at the beginning of the 17th century. The palace remained royal property until the French Revolution, when the state took it over and used it as a prison. Danton, the painter Jacques Louis David, and American political philosopher and writer Thomas Paine (1737–1809) were all detained here. Today it is the site of the French Senate and is not open to the public.

If you follow rue Vaugirard two blocks east to boulevard St-Michel, you will soon be at the place de la Sorbonne, nerve center of the Left Bank's student population. The square is dominated by the **Eglise de la Sorbonne,** whose outstanding exterior features are its 10 Corinthian columns and cupola. Inside is the white marble tomb of Cardinal Richelieu. (The church is open to the public only during exhibitions and cultural events.) The university buildings of La Sorbonne spread out around the church from rue Cujas down to the visitor's entrance on rue des Ecoles.

57 The **Sorbonne** is the oldest university in Paris—indeed, one of the oldest and most important in Europe. It is named after Robert de Sorbon, a medieval canon who founded a theological college here in 1253 for 16 students. By the 17th century, the church and university buildings were becoming dilapidated, so Cardinal Richelieu undertook to have them restored; the present-day Sorbonne campus is largely a result of that restoration. For a glimpse of a more recent relic of Sorbonne history, look for Puvis de Chavannes's painting of the *Sacred Wood* in the main lecture hall, a major meeting point during the tumultuous student upheavals of 1968.

Behind the Sorbonne, bordering its eastern reach, is the rue St-Jacques. The street leads south toward rue Soufflot, named in honor of the man **58** who built the vast, domed **Panthéon,** set atop place du Panthéon. One of Paris's most physically overwhelming sites—it was commissioned by Louis XV as a mark of gratitude for his recovery from a grave illness in 1744—the Panthéon is now a seldom-used church with monumental frescoes by Puvis de Chavannes and a crypt that holds the remains of such national heroes as Voltaire, Emile Zola, and Jean-Jacques Rousseau. *Entrance on rue Clothilde.* ☞ *26 frs adults over 24, 17 frs adults 18–24, 6 frs children under 18.* ☼ *Daily 10–5:30. Métro: Cardinal Lemoine.*

East of the Panthéon is **St-Etienne-du-Mont,** a church with two claims to fame: its ornate facade and its curly Renaissance rood screen (1521–

35) separating nave and chancel—the only one of its kind in Paris. Take time to check out the fine 17th-century glass in the cloister at the back of the church.

★ ❺❾ Walk north on rue St-Jacques and turn left on the rue des Ecoles to reach the square Paul-Painlevé and the distinguished **Musée National du Moyen-Age** (formerly the Musée du Cluny). Built on the site of the city's enormous Roman baths, it is housed in a 15th-century mansion that originally belonged to the monks of Cluny Abbey in Burgundy. But the real reason anyone comes to the museum is to see its superb tapestry collection. The most famous series is the graceful *Dame à la Licorne* (*Lady and the Unicorn*), woven in the 15th or 16th century, probably in the southern Netherlands. There is also an exhibition of decorative arts from the Middle Ages; a vaulted chapel; and a deep, cloistered court-yard with mullioned windows, set off by the *Boatmen's Pillar,* Paris's oldest sculpture, at its center. ☛ *27 frs, 18 frs students and senior citizens and on Sun., under 18 free.* ☉ *Wed.–Mon. 9:45–5:15. Métro: Cluny–La Sorbonne.*

❻⓿ Across boulevard St-Germain, rue St-Jacques runs north toward the Seine, past the elegantly proportioned church of **St-Séverin,** the parish church of the entire Left Bank during the 11th century. Rebuilt in the 16th century and noted for its width and its Flamboyant Gothic architecture, the church dominates a close-knit neighborhood filled with quiet squares and pedestrian streets. Note the splendidly deviant spiraling column in the forest of pillars behind the altar. ☉ *Weekdays 11–5:30, Sat. 11–10. Métro: St-Michel.*

Running riot around the relative quiet of St-Séverin are streets filled with restaurants of every description, serving everything from take-out souvlaki to five-course haute cuisine. Rue de la Huchette is the most heavily trafficked of the restaurant streets and is especially good for its selection of cheaper Greek food houses and Tunisian patisseries.

TIME OUT If you are in the mood for entertainment with your supper, duck into **Le Cloître** (19 rue St-Jacques). This old, heavily wood-beamed bar stages a one- and sometimes two-woman revue in the cellar, performing songs of old Paris from the '20s, '30s, and '40s. For a quieter diversion, stop at **Pub St-Jacques** (11 rue St-Jacques), where you can drink whiskey until the wee hours.

Cross to the east side of rue St-Jacques. In square René-Viviani, which surrounds the 12th-century church of **St-Julien-le-Pauvre,** stands an acacia that is supposedly the oldest tree in Paris (although it has a rival claim from another acacia at the Jardin des Plantes). This tree-filled square also gives you one of the more spectacular views of Notre-Dame.

Behind the church, to the east, are the tiny, elegant streets of the recently renovated Maubert district, bordered by quai de Montebello and boulevard St-Germain. Walk south on rue Lagrange, which becomes rue Monge across boulevard St-Germain.

❻❶ Public meetings and demonstrations have been held in place Maubert ever since the Middle Ages. Nowadays, most gatherings are held inside or in front of the **Palais de la Mutualité** on the corner of the square, also a venue for jazz, pop, and rock concerts. On Tuesday, Thursday, and Saturday, the square is transformed into a colorful outdoor food market.

❻❷ The **Jardin des Plantes,** several blocks southeast via rue des Ecoles and rue de Jussieu, is an enormous swath of greenery containing spacious botanical gardens and a number of natural-history museums (admission prices vary; all are open Wed.–Sun.). It is stocked with plants dating from the first collections of the 17th century and has since been enhanced by subsequent generations of devoted French botanists. The garden claims to shelter Paris's oldest tree, an *Acacia robinia*, planted in 1636. It also contains a small, old-fashioned zoo, an alpine garden, an aquarium, a maze, and a number of hothouses. ☛ *Zoo: 25 frs.* ☉ *Daily 9–5 (until 6 in summer). Métro: Monge.*

63 In 1994 the **Grande Galerie de l'Evolution** reopened to popular acclaim. The vast, handsome iron-and-glass structure, built, as was the Eiffel Tower, in 1889, contains a mind-blowing collection of stuffed animals, including some that are now extinct. Stunning lighting effects change automatically to mimic climatic shifts. ☛ *40 frs.* ☉ *Wed. and Fri.–Mon. 10–6, Thurs. 10–10. Métro: Monge.*

TIME OUT At the back of the gardens, in place du Puits-de-l'Hermite, you can drink a restorative cup of sweet mint tea in **La Mosquée,** a beautifully kept white mosque complete with minaret. The Muslim restaurant here serves copious quantities of couscous. The sunken garden and tiled patios are open to the public—the prayer rooms are not—and so are the luxurious *hammams,* or Turkish baths (open Fri. and Sun. 11–8 men only; Mon., Wed., Thurs., and Sat. 11–8 women only; 65 frs for bath). ☛ *Mosque: 15 frs adults, 10 frs students and senior citizens.* ☉ *Sat.–Thurs., guided tours 10–noon and 2–6:30 (5:30 in winter). Métro: Monge.*

Tour 6: Montmartre

Numbers in the margin correspond to points of interest on the Montmartre map.

The hill of **Montmartre** rises dramatically above the city, crowned by the basilica of Sacré-Coeur—Paris's best-known landmark after the Eiffel Tower—and home to a once-thriving artistic community, now reduced to gangs of third-rate painters clustered in the place du Tertre. Despite their presence and the fact that the fabled nightlife of old Montmartre has fizzled to some glitzy nightclubs and porn shows, the area still exudes a sense of history.

64 Begin your tour at **place Blanche** (White Square), which takes its name from the clouds of chalky dust churned up by the windmills that once dotted Montmartre. The windmills were set up here not just because the hill was a good place to catch the wind—at over 300 feet, it's the highest point in the city—but because Montmartre was covered with cornfields and quarries right up to the end of the 19th century. Today only two of the original 20 windmills are intact. The most famous, immortalized by painter Toulouse-Lautrec, is the **Moulin Rouge,** or Red Windmill, on place Blanche, built in 1885 and turned into a dance hall in 1900; the place is still trading shamelessly on the notion of Paris as a city of sin (*see* Arts and Nightlife, *below*).

For a taste of something more authentically French than the Moulin Rouge's computerized light shows, walk up rue Lepic, a colorful and tempting **food market** (closed Mon.).

Turn left onto rue Joseph-de-Maistre and walk along to the small **Montmartre cemetery.** It contains the graves of many prominent French men and women, including Edgar Degas and Adolphe Sax, inventor of the saxophone. The Russian ballet dancer Vaslav Nijinsky is buried here as well.

Montmartre

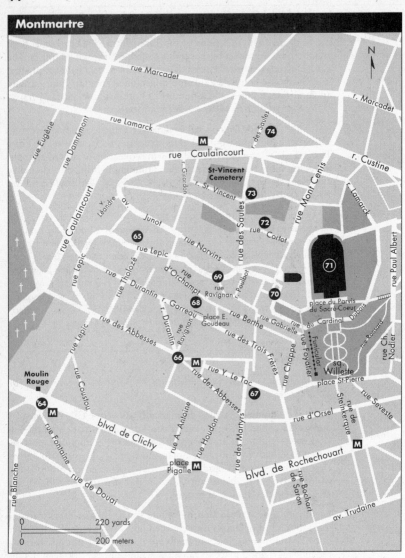

Basilique du Sacré-Coeur, **71**

Bateau-Lavoir, **68**

Chapelle du Martyre, **67**

Lapin Agile, **73**

Moulin de la Galette, **65**

Musée d'Art Juif, **74**

Musée du Vieux Montmartre, **72**

Place des Abbesses, **66**

Place Blanche, **64**

Place Jean-Baptiste Clément, **69**

Place du Tertre, **70**

⑥⑤ Walk back along rue des Abbesses, then turn onto rue Tholozé, which leads to the **Moulin de la Galette,** one of the two remaining windmills, now unromantically rebuilt. To reach it you pass **Studio 28**: This seems no more than a generic little movie theater, but when it opened in 1928, it was the first *art et essai,* or experimental theater, in the world, and it has shown the works of such directors as Jean Cocteau, François Truffaut, and Orson Welles before the films' official premieres.

⑥⑥ Return to rue des Abbesses, turn left, and walk to **place des Abbesses.** Though commercial, the little square has the kind of picturesque and slightly countrified architecture that has made Montmartre famous.

There are two competing attractions just off the square. Theater buffs should head down the tiny rue André-Antoine. At No. 37, you'll see what was originally the **Théâtre Libre,** the Free Theater, which was influential in popularizing the ground-breaking works of naturalist playwrights Henrik Ibsen and August Strindberg. The other attraction is **rue Yvonne Le Tac,** scene of a vital event in Montmartre's early history and linked to the disputed story of how this quarter got its name. Some say the name Montmartre comes from the Roman temple to Mercury that was once here, called the Mound of Mercury, or *Mons Mercurii.* Others contend that it was an adaptation of *Mons Martyrum,* a name inspired by the burial here of Paris's first bishop, St-Denis. (The popular version of his martyrdom is that after he was beheaded by the Romans in AD 250, he arose to carry his severed head from rue Yvonne Le Tac 4 miles north, to an area now known as St-Denis.) He is commemorated by the 19th-
⑥⑦ century **Chapelle du Martyre** at No. 9. It was in the crypt of the original chapel that the Italian priest Francis Xavier founded the Jesuit order in 1534, a decisive step in the efforts of the Catholic Church to reassert its authority in the face of the Protestant Reformation.

From rue Yvonne Le Tac retrace your steps through place des Abbesses. Take rue Ravignon on the right, climbing to the summit via place Emile-
⑥⑧ Goudeau, an enchanting little cobbled square. Your goal is the **Bateau-Lavoir,** or Boat Wash House, at its northern edge. Montmartre poet Max Jacob coined the name for the old building on this site, which burned down in 1970: Not only did it look like a boat, he said, but the warren of artists' studios within were always paint spattered and in need of a good hosing down. The drab, present-day concrete building also contains art studios, though none so illustrious as those of Cubist painters Picasso and Braque, who worked here in years gone by.

⑥⑨ Continue up the hill to **place Jean-Baptiste Clément.** The Italian painter and sculptor Modigliani (1884–1920) had a studio here at No. 7. Some people have claimed that he is the greatest Italian artist of the 20th century, the man who fused the genius of the Italian Renaissance with the modernity of Cézanne and Picasso. Modigliani claimed he would drink himself to death—he eventually did—and chose the wildest part of town in which to do it.

Rue Norvins, formerly rue des Moulins, runs behind and parallel to the north end of the square. Turn right, walk past the bars and tourist shops,
⑦⓪ and you'll reach **place du Tertre.** At most times of the year, you'll have to fight your way through the crowds to the southern end of the square and the breathtaking view over the city. The real drawback here, though, is the swarm of artists clamoring to dash off your portrait. Most are licensed, but there is a fair share of con men. If one produces a picture of you without having asked first, you're under no obligation to buy it!

La Mère Catherine, the restaurant at the north end of the square, was a favorite with the Russian cossacks who occupied Paris after Napoléon's

1814 exile to the island of Elba. Little did the cossacks know that when they banged on the tables and shouted "bistro," the Russian word for "quick," they were inventing a new breed of French restaurant. Now fairly touristic, La Mère Catherine is surprisingly good, though prices are high.

TIME OUT **Patachou** sounds the one classy note in place du Tertre. It offers exquisite, if expensive, cakes and teas.

It was in place du Tertre that one of the most violent episodes in French history began, one that colored French political life for generations. Despite popular images of late 19th-century France—and Paris especially—as a time of freedom and prosperity, the country was desperately divided into two camps for much of this period: a militant underclass, motivated by resentment of what they considered an elitist government, and a reactionary and fearful bourgeoisie and ruling class. In March 1871, the antimonarchist Communards clashed with soldiers of the French government leader, Adolphe Thiers. The Communards formed the Commune, which ruled Paris for three months. Then Thiers ordered his troops to take the city, and upwards of 10,000 Communards were executed after the Commune's collapse.

★ ⑦ Looming behind the church of St-Pierre on the east side of the square, the **Basilique du Sacré-Coeur** was erected in 1873 (after Thiers's death) as a kind of guilt offering for the ruthless killing of the Communards. Even so, the building was to some extent a reflection of political divisions within the country, financed by French Catholics fearful of an anticlerical backlash and determined to make a grand statement on behalf of the Church. Stylistically, the Sacré-Coeur borrows elements from Romanesque and Byzantine models, fusing them under its distinctive Oriental dome. The gloomy, cavernous interior is worth visiting for its golden mosaics; climb to the top of the dome for the view over Paris.

⑦ More of Montmartre beckons north and west of the Sacré-Coeur. Take rue du Mont-Cenis down to rue Cortot, site of the **Musée du Vieux Montmartre.** Like the Bateau-Lavoir, the building that is now the museum sheltered an illustrious group of painters, writers, and assorted cabaret artists in its heyday toward the end of the 19th century. Foremost among them were Pierre-Auguste Renoir and Maurice Utrillo, who was the Montmartre painter par excellence. Taking the gray, crumbling streets of the quarter as his subject matter, Utrillo discovered that he worked much more effectively from cheap postcards than from the streets themselves. Look carefully at the pictures in the museum here and you will see the plaster and sand he mixed with his paints to help convey the decaying buildings of the area. The next best thing about the museum is the view over the tiny vineyard on neighboring rue des Saules. *12 rue Cortot.* ☞ *25 frs adults, 20 frs children and senior citizens.* ☾ *Tues.–Sun. 11–6. Métro: Lamarck Caulaincourt.*

⑦ There's an equally famous Montmartre landmark on the corner of rue St-Vincent, just down the road: the **Lapin Agile,** or the Nimble Rabbit. It's a bar-cabaret, originally one of the raunchiest haunts in Montmartre. Today it manages against all odds to preserve at least something of its earlier flavor, unlike the Moulin Rouge.

⑦ Behind the Lapin Agile is the **St-Vincent Cemetery,** whose entrance is off little rue Lucien Gaulard. It's a tiny graveyard, but serious students of Montmartre may want to visit to see Utrillo's burial place. Continue north on rue des Saules, across busy rue Caulaincourt, and you'll come to the **Musée d'Art Juif,** the Museum of Jewish Art, containing devotional items, models of synagogues, and works by Camille Pissarro and Marc Chagall. *42 rue des Saules.* ☛ *30 frs adults, 20 frs students, 15 frs children under 12.* ⊙ *Sun.–Thurs. 3–6; closed Aug.*

Excursion: Rueil-Malmaison

Rueil-Malmaison is today a faceless, if pleasant, western suburb of Paris, but the memory of star-crossed lovers Napoléon and Joséphine still haunts its Malmaison château on avenue Napoléon-Bonaparte. To get there by car, take N13 from Porte Maillot; or, alternatively, catch the RER-A to La Défense, then Bus 258 to Bois-Préau.

Built in 1622, **La Malmaison** was bought by the future Empress Joséphine in 1799 as a love nest for Napoléon and herself (they had married three years earlier). After the childless Joséphine was divorced by the heir-hungry emperor in 1809, she retired to La Malmaison and died here on May 29, 1814.

The château has 24 rooms furnished with exquisite tables, chairs, and sofas of the Napoleonic period; of special note are the library, game room, and dining room. The walls are adorned with works by contemporary artists of the day, such as Jacques-Louis David, Pierre-Paul Prud'hon, and Baron Gérard. Take time to admire the clothes and hats that belonged to Napoléon and Joséphine, particularly the display of the empress's gowns. Their carriage can be seen in one of the garden pavilions, and another pavilion contains a unique collection of snuffboxes donated by Prince George of Greece. The gardens themselves are delightful, especially the regimented rows of spring tulips. *15 av. du Château.*

The **Bois Préau,** which stands close to La Malmaison (and is included in the same admission ticket), is a smaller mansion that dates from the 17th century. It was acquired by Joséphine in 1810, after her divorce, but subsequently reconstructed in the 1850s. Today its 10 rooms, complete with furniture and objects from the Empire period, are devoted mainly to souvenirs of Napoléon's exile on the island of St. Helena. *Entrance from av. de l'Impératrice.* ☛ *27 frs adults, 18 frs students and senior citizens.* ⊙ *Wed.–Mon. 10:30–1 and 2–5:30.*

For other excursions from Paris, *see* Chapter 3, Ile de France.

What to See and Do with Children

Amusement Parks

Jardin d'Acclimatation. This charming children's play park in the Bois de Boulogne boasts a miniature train, boat rides, and a zoo. ☛ *10 frs adults, 5 frs children.* ⊙ *Daily 10–6, 10–4 in winter. Métro: Les Sablons.*

Parc Floral de Paris. The east Paris equivalent of the Jardin d'Acclimatation, the Parc Floral is situated in the Bois de Vincennes, near the château. It features a miniature train, a games area, and miniature golf. *Rte. de la Pyramide, Vincennes.* ☛ *10 frs, children under 6 free.* ⊙ *Daily, summer 9:30–8; winter 9:30–5. Métro: Château de Vincennes.*

Aquariums

Fish gazing is a soothing, mesmerizing experience for young and old alike. There are two principal aquariums in Paris: **Centre la Mer et des Eaux** (195 rue St-Jacques, 5e; admission 25 frs adults, 15 frs children; open Tues.–Fri. 10–12:30 and 1:15–5:30, weekends 10–5:30; RER: Luxembourg) and **Aquarium Tropical** (293 av. Daumesnil, 12e; admission

27 frs, 18 frs Sun.; open Wed.–Mon. 10–noon and 1:30–5:30; Métro: Porte Dorée).

Boat Trips

An hour on the Seine on a *Bateau Mouche* or *Vedette* is a fun way to get to know the capital. The cost is 40–45 francs for adults, 20 francs for children under 10. Departures are every half hour from **Square du Vert Galant** (1er; Métro: Pont-Neuf), **Eiffel Tower** (7e; Métro: Bir-Hakeim), and **Pont de l'Alma** (8e; Métro: Alma-Marceau).

Boating

Rowboats can be rented at the **Lac Inférieur** in the Bois de Boulogne and at **Lac des Minimes** and **Lac Daumesnil** in the Bois de Vincennes.

Circus

There's no need to know French to enjoy a circus. Tickets range from 60 francs to 180 francs. There are evening and weekend matinee performances. Check for details with **Cirque Grüss** (21 av. de la Porte de Chatillon, 14e, ☎ 45–42–37–77; Métro: Porte d'Orléans) or **Cirque d'Hiver** (110 rue Amelot, 11e, ☎ 48–78–75–00; Métro: Chemin Vert).

Eiffel Tower

See Tour 4, *above.*

Fairs

Twice a year—usually in August and at Christmas—the rue de Rivoli side of the Tuileries Gardens is transformed into a *foire,* or fairgrounds, complete with rides, shooting galleries, and a huge Ferris wheel. The **Foire du Trône,** every spring in the Bois de Vincennes (Métro: Porte Dorée), is a big fair that goes until the wee hours. The **Fête à Neu Neu** is the September equivalent in the Bois de Boulogne (Métro: Porte d'Auteuil). Consult the weekly *Pariscope* for details.

Ice-Skating

Every winter a small skating rink is erected on the Rivoli side of the Tuileries Gardens (admission 35 frs including rental; open 10–10, with special hrs for children only). Otherwise try the Buttes-Chamont rink (30 rue Edouard-Pailleron, 19e, ☎ 42–08–72–26; admission 25 frs adults, 20 frs children under 16, 15 frs skate rental).

Museums

Cité des Sciences et de l'Industrie de la Villette. Children love this extensive and imaginatively laid out museum devoted to industry, with dozens of "try-it-yourself" contraptions. Don't miss the **Geode** cinema, the huge silver golf ball that houses a 180-degree curved movie screen. *Parc de la Villette.* ☛ *45 frs adults, 35 frs children, 25 frs after 4 PM, planetarium 15 frs extra.* ☾ *Tues.–Sun. 10–6 (Geode open Tues.–Sun. 10–9). Métro: Porte de la Villette.*

Musée de la Curiosité. This new museum contains antique magic paraphernalia, including some objects from Houdini's bag of tricks, and features an hourly magic show. *11 rue St-Paul.* ☛ *45 frs adults, 30 frs children.* ☾ *Wed., Sat., and Sun. 2–7. Métro: St-Paul.*

Musée de la Femme et Collection d'Automates. The collection of automata and clockwork dolls bursts into life each afternoon. It's well worth making the short trip to Neuilly, especially since the Jardin d'Acclimatation (*see above*) and the Bois de Boulogne are close at hand. *12 rue du Centre, Neuilly.* ☛ *20 frs adults, 10 frs children and senior citizens.* ☾ *Wed.–Mon. 2:30–5; guided tours Wed.–Mon. 3 PM. Métro: Pont de Neuilly.*

Musée Grévin. The long-established boulevard Montmartre museum concentrates on waxwork imitations of the famous, while the newer one in les Halles recaptures the Belle Epoque. *10 blvd. Montmartre, 9e.* ☛ *50 frs adults, 34 frs children under 14. Métro: Rue Montmartre. Forum des Halles, 1er.* ☛ *42 frs adults, 36 frs children under 14. Métro: Les Halles.* ☼ *Both Mon.–Sat. 10:30–7, Sun. 1–7 (blvd. Montmartre museum closed mornings in winter).*

Puppet Shows

On most Wednesday, Saturday, and Sunday afternoons, **Guignol,** the French equivalent of Punch and Judy, performs at various parks, including the Champ de Mars and the Luxembourg.

Zoos

Monkeys, deer, birds, and farm animals star at the **Jardin d'Acclimatation** (*see above*), while the **Ménagerie** in the Jardin des Plantes boasts elephants, lions, and tigers. *57 rue Cuvier, 5e.* ☛ *25 frs adults, 13 frs children.* ☼ *Daily 9–6 (9–5 in winter). Métro: Jussieu.*

Paris's biggest zoo is the **Parc Zoologique de Paris** in the **Bois de Vincennes;** in addition to wild beasts, it includes a museum, films, and exhibitions. *53 av. de St-Maurice, 12e.* ☛ *40 frs adults, 20 frs children.* ☼ *Daily 9–7. Métro: Porte Dorée.*

SHOPPING

By Corinne
LaBalme

Window-shopping is one of Paris's great spectator sports. Tastefully displayed wares—luscious cream-filled éclairs, lacy lingerie, rare artwork, gleaming copper pots—entice the eye and awaken the imagination. And shopping is one of the city's greatest pastimes, a chance to mix with Parisians and feel the heartbeat of the country. Who can understand the magic of French cuisine until they've explored a French open-air produce market on a weekend morning? Or resist the thrill of seeing a Chanel evening dress displayed in it own glossy Paris boutique—where the doorknobs are shaped like Chanel crystal perfume bottle stoppers?

Happily, the shopping opportunities in Paris are endless and geared to every taste. You can price emerald earrings at Cartier, spend an afternoon browsing through bookstalls along the Seine, buy silk-lined gloves at Dior, tour the high-gloss department stores, or haggle over prices in the sprawling flea markets on the outskirts of town. For many, perfume and designer clothing are perhaps the most coveted Parisian souvenirs. However, even on haute couture's home turf, bargains are surprisingly elusive. Foreign visitors, subject to the slings and arrows of international exchange rates, are advised to know prices in their own country before arrival. A Pierre Cardin tie or a Lalique bottle of *L'Air du Temps* may possibly be cheaper at the mall back home . . . although it won't be as much fun to buy.

Credit Cards

Even stores that accept currency other than francs will generally give you a lower rate of exchange than banks or exchange offices. You're better off using credit cards, which are widely used. Even the corner newsstand or flea market salesperson is likely to honor plastic. Visa is the most common and preferred card, followed closely by MasterCard/Euro Card. American Express, Diners Club, and Access are accepted in the larger international stores.

Duty-Free Shopping

Visitors from outside the European Union, aged 15 and over, whose stay in France and/or the EU is less than six months, can benefit from VAT (Value Added Tax) reimbursements, known in France as TVA or *détaxe*. To qualify, non-EU residents must spend at least 2,000 francs in a single store. Refunds vary from 13% to 18.6% and are mailed to you by check or credited to your charge card.

Shopping Areas

Avenue Montaigne

The names atop the showcase windows lining this elegant boulevard are the honor roll of haute couture: Chanel, Dior, Nina Ricci, Christian Lacroix, Emanuel Ungaro, Céline, Valentino, Per Spook, Escada, Thierry Mugler, Hanae Mori. Here you'll also find accessorists S. T. Dupont and Louis Vuitton, and the lively boutique run by former Chanel super-model Inès de la Fressange. Yves St-Laurent's salon is nearby at 5 avenue Marceau.

Left Bank

Browsing through the antique shops, bookstores, and art galleries of St-Germain-des-Prés, Paris's intellectual core, is window-shopping at its most varied. High fashion arrived here in the '70s, when YSL opened Rive Gauche boutiques for men and women on the place Saint-Sulpice. The area around rue de Grenelle and rue Saint-Pères is known for intimate designer boutiques (Sonia Rykiel, Claude Montana) and shoe shops (Maud Frizon, Charles Jourdan, Stéphane Kélian, and Carel).

Le Marais

The elegant mansions and tiny kosher food stores that characterized the low-lying area between the Beaubourg and place des Vosges were overtaken by New Wave fashion and trendy gift shops in the 1980s. Avant-garde designers Azzedine Alaïa, Lolita Lempicka, Issey Miyake, and Romeo Gigli have boutiques within a few blocks of the stately Picasso and Carnavalet museums. Shopping for off-beat decorative household items is also excellent here. A bonus: Many Marais shops are open Sunday afternoon.

Les Halles

Most of the narrow pedestrian streets on the former site of Paris's wholesale food market are lined with fast-food joints, sex shops, jeans outlets, and garish souvenir stands, but the rue du Jour (home of the Agnès b. boutiques) is an attractive exception. Street artists claim the plaza in front of the Pompidou Center, and prostitutes rule the nearby rue St-Denis. In the middle of the action, the **Forum des Halles**—a multi-level underground shopping mall—caters to a noisy teenage clientele.

Opéra to Madeleine

Three major department stores—Au Printemps, Galeries Lafayette, and the British Marks & Spencer are clustered behind Paris's ornate 19th-century opera house. The place de la Madeleine is home to two luxurious food stores, Fauchon and Hédiard, plus a 75-shop mall, Les Trois Quartiers. Lalique and Baccarat Crystal also have opulent showrooms near the Madeleine Church.

Montparnasse

The bohemian mecca for artists and writers in the '20s and '30s, Montparnasse is better known for bars and restaurants than shops. A commercial center near the train station boasts a Galeries Lafayette outlet but is too charmless to attract many tourists. The rue d'Alésia on the southern fringe of Montparnasse is known for discount clothing shops.

Place des Victoires

Françoise Chassagnac, the canny retailer who "discovered" Azzedine Alaia and Angelo Tarlazzi, put this graceful, circular plaza near the Palais-Royal on the fashion map when she opened her Victoires boutique in 1967. Kenzo, Thierry Mugler, and Cacharel soon followed. Avant-garde boutiques like Chantal Thomass, Jean-Charles de Castelbajac, and En Attendant les Barbares have since fanned into the sidestreets, while Jean-Paul Gaultier (Madonna's favorite dresser) has his shop in the nearby Galerie Vivienne arcade.

Place Vendôme and the Rue de la Paix

Here's where Holly Golightly would eat breakfast. The magnificent 17th-century place Vendôme, and the rue de la Paix leading north from Vendôme, have attracted the world's most elegant jewelers: Cartier, Boucheron, Buccellati, Van Cleef and Arpels, Répossi, Mellerio, Mauboussin, and Mikimoto. This superposh pedestrian square was repaved with silver-gray granite in 1992, and shines brighter than ever.

Rue du Faubourg St-Honoré

The presence of the Elysée Palace and the official residences of the American and British ambassadors mean this chic shopping and residential street is well patrolled by the police. The Paris branch of Sotheby's and renowned antique galleries such as Didier Aaron and Odermatt-Cazeau add artistic flavor. Boutiques included Hermés, Lanvin, Karl Lagerfeld, Revillon Furs, Louis Féraud, and Christian Lacroix.

Champs-Elysées

Cafés and movie theaters keep the once-chic Champs-Elysées active 24 hours a day, but the invasion of exchange banks, car showrooms, and fast-food chains has lowered the tone. Four glitzy 20th-century arcade malls (Galerie du Lido, Le Rond-Point, Le Claridge, and Elysées 26) capture most of the retail action.

Bastille

The faddiest (and most ephemeral) teenager boutiques are clustered between art galleries, bars, and furniture outlets in this rapidly gentrifying neighborhood. Jean-Paul Gaultier established his "Junior" boutique on the rue Faubourg St-Antoine in 1995.

Louvre-Palais Royal

The elegant and eclectic shops clustered in the 18th-century arcades of the Palais Royal sell antiques, toy soldiers, Shiseido cosmetics, art jewelry . . . even vintage designer dresses. The Carrousel du Louvre—beneath the Louvre gardens—is a sleek, upscale mall housing outlets for Virgin Megastore, the Body Shop, Esprit, and several museum gift shops. It's open every day except Tuesday, including Sunday afternoon.

Department Stores

Paris's top department stores offer both convenience and chic. Some are open until 10 PM one weekday evening, and all five major stores listed below have multilingual guides, international welcome desks, détaxe offices, and restaurants.

Opéra Area

Au Printemps (64 blvd. Haussmann, 9e, ☎ 42–82–50–00; Métro: Havre-Caumartin, Opéra, Auber) is a glittery three-store complex that includes "La Maison," for housewares and furniture; "La Mode," for women and children; and "Brummel," a six-floor emporium devoted to menswear. Flo Prestige, the celebrated Parisian brasserie chain, caters the in-house restaurants. ☉ *Mon.–Sat. 9:30–7.*

Galeries Lafayette (40 blvd. Haussmann, 9e, ☎ 42–82–34–56; Métro: Chaussée d'Antin, Opéra, Havre-Caumartin) is equally elegant, and it spices up its Parisian aura with periodic exhibits featuring crafts from exotic countries. Be sure to look up while in the main store: The glorious Belle Epoque stained-glass dome is a Paris landmark. Stylish private-label fashions (Briefing and Jodphur) offer good value, and the elegant floor-wide gourmet shop includes several sophisticated snack/wine bars. ⊙ *Mon.–Sat. 9:30–6:45. Another branch is at Centre Commercial Montparnasse, 15e,* ☎ *45–38–52–87.*

Louvre-Pont Neuf
La Samaritaine (19 rue de la Monnaie, 1er, ☎ 40–41–20–20, Métro: Pont-Neuf), a sprawling four-store complex, is rapidly shedding its fusty, grandmotherly image. Especially good for kitchen supplies, housewares, and furniture, it's famous for its rooftop snackbar, which offers a marvelous view of Notre-Dame. ⊙ *Mon.–Wed. and Fri.–Sat. 9:30–7, Thurs. 9:30–10.*

Hotel de Ville/Marais area
Bazar de l'Hotel de Ville (52–64 rue de Rivoli, 4e, ☎ 42–74–90–00; Métro: Hôtel de Ville), affectionately called BHV, houses an enormous basement hardware store that sells everything from doorknobs to cement mixers! The fashion offerings are minimal, but BHV is noteworthy for quality household goods, home decor materials, and office supplies. ⊙ *Mon., Tues., and Thurs.–Sat. 9:30–7, Wed. 9:30–10.*

Marks and Spencer (88 rue de Rivoli, 4e ☎ 44–61–08–00; Métro: Hotel de Ville) started this five-floor outlet in 1994. ⊙ *Mon.–Tues. 9:30–8, Wed.–Fri. 9:30–8:30, Sat. 9:30–7:30.*

Left Bank
Au Bon Marché (22 rue de Sèvres, 7e, Métro: Sèvres-Babylone, ☎ 44–39–80–00), founded in 1852, is chiefly known for linens, table settings, and high-quality furniture. La Grande Epicerie, a grocery store and deli here, is a gourmet's delight, and the sleek restaurant was designed by jet-set decorator Andrée Putman. The basement is a treasure trove for books, records, and arty gifts. ⊙ *Weekdays 9:30–6:30, Sat. 9:30–7.*

Shopping Arcades and Markets

Paris's 19th-century commercial arcades, called *passages,* are the forerunners of the modern mall. Glass roofs, decorative pillars, and mosaic floors give the passages great charm. Shops range from the trendy (**Jean-Paul Gaultier** and **Yukii Tori** fashions in the freshly restored Galerie Vivienne) to the genteel (embroidery supplies and satin ribbons at **Au Bonheur des Dames** in the Passage Jouffroy).

The major arcades are on the Right Bank in central Paris and include **Galerie Vivienne** (4 rue des Petits-Champs, 2e), **Galerie Véro-Dodat** (19 rue J-J Rousseau, 1er), and **Passage des Pavillons** (6 rue de Beaujolais, 1er). Near the Montmartre métro you'll find the very old **Passage des Panoramas**—built in 1800 (11 blvd. Montmartre, 2e)—and the **Jouffroy** (12 blvd. Montmartre, 2e).

Flea Markets
The **Marché aux Puces** on Paris's northern boundary (Métro: Porte de Clignancourt) still attracts the crowds, but its once unbeatable prices are now a feature of the past. This century-old labyrinth of alleyways packed with antiques dealers' booths and junk stalls now spreads for over a square mile. Early birds pick up the most worthwhile loot; the

pros get out to Clignancourt before breakfast. But be warned—if
there's one place in Paris where you need to know how to bargain, this
is it! For lunch, stop for mussels and fries in one of the rough-and-ready
cafés. ☯ *Sat.–Mon.*

There are other, less-impressive flea markets on the southern and eastern slopes of the city—at **porte de Montreuil** and **porte de Vanves**—
but they have a depressing amount of real junk and are best avoided,
except by obsessive bargain hunters.

Food Markets

Paris's open-air food markets are among the city's most colorful attractions.
Every *quartier* (district) has one, although many are open only a few days
each week. Sunday morning, till 1 PM, is usually a good time to go; Monday is the day these markets are likely to be closed. The local markets
usually concentrate on food, but they always have a few brightly colored flower stalls. Fruits and vegetables are piled high in vibrant pyramids. The variety of cheeses is always astounding. The lively—sometimes
chaotic—atmosphere that reigns in most markets makes them a sight worth
seeing even if you don't want or need to buy anything.

Many of the better-known markets are in areas you'd visit for sightseeing; our favorites are on **rue de Buci,** 6e (open daily); **rue Mouffetard,** 5e; and **rue Lepic** in Montmartre (the latter two best on weekends).
The **Marché d'Aligre** (open Sat., Sun., and Mon. mornings) is a bit farther out, beyond the Bastille on rue d'Aligre in the 12th arrondissement, but you won't see many tourists in this less-affluent area of town,
and Parisians from all over the city know it and love it. The prices come
tumbling down as the morning draws to a close.

SPORTS AND THE OUTDOORS

Bicycling

The Bois de Boulogne and the Bois de Vincennes, with their wide, leafy
avenues, are good places for biking. Bikes can be rented from **Paris Vélo**
(2 rue du Fer-à-Moulin, 5e, ☎ 43–37–59–22) for around 90 francs
a day or 160 francs a weekend.

Fitness Centers

The best hotel-fitness facilities are in the newer properties on the edges
of the city center. The Vitatop Club on the top floors of the **Sofitel Paris**
(8 rue Louis-Armand, 15e, ☎ 45–54–79–00), free for its guests, offers a 15-meter pool, sauna, steamroom, and Jacuzzi, plus a stunning
view of the Paris skyline. Next door is the **Parc Suzanne Lenglen,** with
plenty of room for running, plus indoor and outdoor tennis courts. The
Bristol (112 rue du Faubourg St-Honoré, 8e, ☎ 42–66–91–45) has a
large pool, plus a sauna, free for its guests.

The **Aquaboulevard** complex (46 rue Louis-Armand, 15e, ☎ 40–60–
10–00), opened in 1989, has gyms, Turkish baths, a solarium, and
the city's finest swimming pool, complete with a giant slide and a wave
machine.

Several gyms and clubs in Paris offer one-day or short-term member-
ships. **Espace Vit-Halles** (Place Beaubourg, 48 rue Rambuteau, 1er, ☎
42–77–21–71; open weekdays 9 AM–10 PM, Sat. 11–7, and Sun. 11–
3) has a broad range of aerobics classes at 90 francs a class (800 francs
for 10 classes), an exercise machine area, sauna, and steambath (60
francs per day). **Club Quartier Latin** (19 rue de Pontoise, 5e, ☎ 43–
54–82–45; open Mon.–Thurs. 10–midnight, Fri. 10–10, weekends
9:30–7:30) boasts a 30-meter skylighted pool, a climbing wall, squash

courts, and exercise equipment (70 francs per day and 70 francs an hour for squash).

Jogging

The best inner-city running is in the **Champ-de-Mars,** next to the Eiffel Tower, measuring 1½ miles around the perimeter. Shorter and more crowded routes are found in the **Luxembourg Gardens,** with a 1-mile loop just inside the park's fence; in the **Tuileries,** also measuring about 1 mile; and in the **Parc Monceau,** which has a loop of two-thirds of a mile. The **Bois de Boulogne,** on the western edge of Paris, offers miles of trails through woods, around lakes, and across grassy meadows. The equally bucolic **Bois de Vincennes,** on the eastern side of the city, offers a 9-mile circuit or a 1-mile loop around the château de Vincennes itself.

Tennis

There are few tennis courts in Paris. Your best bet is to try the public courts in the **Luxembourg Gardens.** There is also a large complex of courts at the Polygone sportsground in the **Bois de Vincennes.** It's a 20-minute walk down route de la Pyramide from the château de Vin-cennes métro stop. There are also 11 covered courts (and six squash courts) at **Aquaboulevard** (*see above*).

The **French Open** is held during the last two weeks in May at the **Roland Garros** stadium on the eastern edge of the Bois de Boulogne (take the métro to Porte d'Auteuil). Center-court tickets are difficult to obtain, especially for the second week; try your hotel or turn up early in the morning (play starts at 11) and buy a general ground ticket. Expect to pay between 100 and 300 francs, depending on the day and seat.

DINING

By Robert Noah

Updated by Alexander Lobrano

Whether your dream meal is savoring truffle-studded foie gras on Limoges china, or breaking the crust of a steaming cassoulet in a thick crockery bowl, you can find it in Paris. Despite rumblings about low-ered standards and increasingly bland fare, Paris remains one of the world's great food capitals. For most visitors, the prospect of eating here is exciting; for many, it's the main reason for a trip.

It's not unusual to hear of mediocre food, haughty service, and out-rageous prices in Paris restaurants. It's certainly possible to have a bad meal here. Yet the city's restaurants exist principally for the de-manding Parisians themselves, for whom every meal is an event wor-thy of their undivided attention. Most restaurants that cannot attain the high standard of their French patrons will not last long. If you want to dine well, therefore, look for restaurants where the French go, and avoid places that cater to tourists. Keep in mind, however, that world-famous restaurants are bound to be frequented by foreigners as well as Parisians and that a midwestern accent at the next table is not always a bad sign.

In making the selections for this guide, we have tried to include restau-rants with a variety of styles and price levels, from formal dining rooms serving haute cuisine to cheery wine bars offering open-face sand-wiches and not much more. More than half are in the 1st–8th ar-rondissements, within easy reach of hotels and sights; many others are in the 14th and 16th, also popular visitor areas. In addition, we have included a number of restaurants with excellent food, atmosphere, and service that are off the beaten tourist path. In this we follow the lead of the French, for whom a good meal is worth a trip. As restaurant prices increasingly follow higher rents in the heart of the city, young chefs striking out on their own are seeking affordable locations in out-lying, often residential neighborhoods; here you'll find good food at reasonable prices, and you'll have the opportunity to discover little-known parts of the city that the great majority of Parisians call home. Because space is at a premium, our selection is limited to places with primarily French rather than ethnic dishes, but if you crave something exotic, you can easily find terrific Vietnamese spring rolls, North African couscous, or even a simple pizza.

Generally, Paris restaurants are open from noon to about 2 and from 7:30 or 8 to 10 or 10:30. We urge you to make reservations. If you want no-smoking, make this clear; the mandatory no-smoking area is sometimes limited to a very few tables. Brasseries have longer hours and often serve all day and late into the evening; some are open 24 hours. The iconoclastic wine bars do as they want, frequently serving hot food only through lunch and cold assortments of *charcuterie* and cheese until a late afternoon or early evening close.

Assume a restaurant is open every day unless otherwise indicated. Sur-prisingly, many prestigious restaurants close on Saturday as well as Sun-day. July and August are the most common months for annual closings, but Paris in August is no longer the wasteland it used to be.

What to Wear

We note those places where men will feel more comfortable with a jacket and tie and those where it is de rigueur. Otherwise, use common sense—jeans and T-shirts are not suitable in Paris restaurants, nor are shorts or running clothes, except in the most casual bistros.

Most restaurants offer two basic types of menu: à la carte and fixed price (*prix fixe,* or *un menu*). The prix fixe menu will usually be the best value, though choices are limited. Most menus begin with a first-course section, followed by fish and poultry, then meat; it's rare today that anyone orders something from all three. However, outside of brasseries, wine bars, and other simple places, it's inappropriate to order just one dish, as you'll understand when you see the waiter's expres-sion. The popular *menu dégustation,* with many small courses, allows for a wide sampling of the chef's offerings. In general, consider the sea-son and the daily specials when ordering. *See* our Menu Guide at the end of the book. Although prices include tax and tip, pocket change left on the table in simple places, or an additional 5% in better restau-rants, is appreciated.

CATEGORY	COST*
$$$$	over 550 frs
$$$	300 frs–550 frs
$$	175 frs–300 frs
$	under 175 frs

*per person for a three-course meal, including 18.6% tax and service but not drinks

1st Arrondissement

$$$$ **Le Grand Véfour.** Luminaries from Napoléon to Colette to Jean Cocteau have frequented this intimate address under the arcades of the Palais-Royal; you can request to be seated at their preferred table. This sump-tuously decorated restaurant, with its mirrored ceiling and painted-glass panels, is perhaps the prettiest in Paris, and its 18th-century origins make it one of the oldest. Chef Guy Martin impresses with his unique blend of sophisticated yet rustic dishes, including roast lamb in a juice of herbs. ✗ *17 rue Beaujolais,* ☎ *42–96–56–27. Reservations advised*

Paris Dining

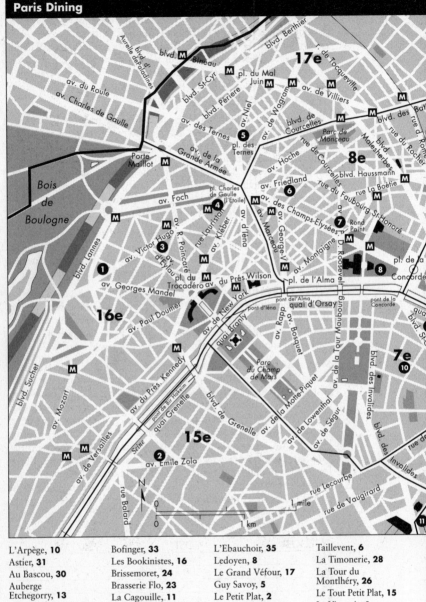

L'Arpège, **10**

Astier, **31**

Au Bascou, **30**

Auberge
Etchegorry, **13**

Au Trou Gascon, **29**

Aux Crus de
Bourgogne, **25**

Aux Fins Gourmets, **9**

Baracane, **32**

La Bastide Odéon, **14**

Bofinger, **33**

Les Bookinistes, **16**

Brissemoret, **24**

Brasserie Flo, **23**

La Cagouille, **11**

Campagne et
Provence, **27**

Chardenoux, **34**

Chartier, **20**

Chez Bruno, **21**

Chez Pauline, **18**

L'Ebauchoir, **35**

Ledoyen, **8**

Le Grand Véfour, **17**

Guy Savoy, **5**

Le Petit Plat, **2**

Le Petit Rétro, **3**

Le Petit Yvan, **7**

Pile ou Face, **22**

Prunier, **4**

La Régalade, **12**

Le Restaurant, **19**

Taillevent, **6**

La Timonerie, **28**

La Tour du
Montlhéry, **26**

Le Tout Petit Plat, **15**

Le Vivarois, **1**

Les Zygomates, **36**

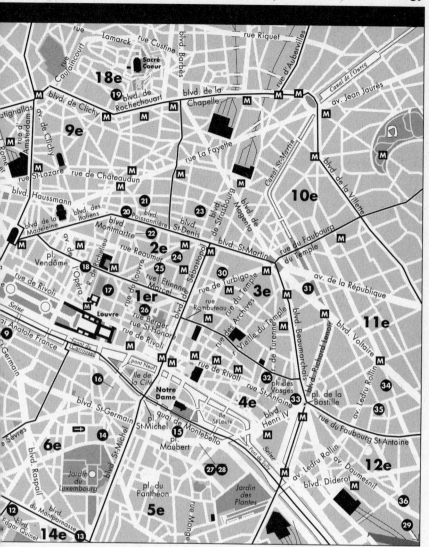

1 wk in advance. Jacket and tie. AE, DC, MC, V. Closed weekends and Aug. Métro: Palais-Royal.

$$–$$$ **Chez Pauline.** This classic restaurant near the Palais Royale has become
★ a neighborhood institution. The setting, with wood-paneled walls, is warm and welcoming. The cooking is bourgeois, old-fashioned, and delicious. Chef André Gelin has been here for decades and his touch is sure and swift. Try the oysters in cream sauce. The wine list is filled with classic Burgundies, and the lunch menu provides good value. ✕ 5 rue Villedo, ☎ 42–96–20–70. Reservations advised. AE, MC, V. Closed Sun., and 2 wks in Aug. No dinner Sat. Métro: Pyramides or Palais Royal.

$$ **Aux Crus de Bourgogne.** The din of a happy crowd fills this delightful, old-fashioned bistro with bright lights and red-check tablecloths. It opened in 1932 and quickly became popular by serving two luxury items—foie gras and cold lobster with homemade mayonnaise—at surprisingly low prices, a tradition that happily continues. Among the bistro classics on the menu, the boeuf au gros sel (beef boiled in bouillon with vegetables and garnished with rock salt) and confit de canard (duck confit) are very satisfying. Tempting desserts include fruit tarts, flan, and chocolate mousse. ✕ 3 rue Bachaumont, ☎ 42–33–48–24. Reservations advised. V. Closed weekends and Aug. Métro: Sentier.

$–$$ **La Tour du Montlhéry.** When the centuries-old Les Halles marketplace became an aseptic shopping mall, many neighborhood bistros closed or went upscale. With sagging wood-beam ceilings, red-check tablecloths, and exposed-brick walls lined with imaginative portraits, the Montlhéry has managed to hang on to the old-market feel. If you don't mind passing under hanging samples of your future meal (sausages, etc.) on your way into the dining room, jovial waiters will serve you simple grilled food. Try the côte de boeuf (T-bone steak) and wash it down with a good Beaujolais. ✕ 5 rue des Prouvaires, ☎ 42–36–21–82. Reservations advised. MC, V. Closed weekends and July 14–Aug. 15. Métro: Les Halles.

2nd Arrondissement

$$–$$$ **Pile ou Face.** This restaurants serves the most interesting and creative food around the stock exchange. Housed on two floors in a narrow building, it offers an intimate setting for discussing big business. The cooking is inventive, the service attentive. Try to the rabbit pâté or the scrambled eggs with mushrooms, then move on to the sweetbreads or the exquisite roast chicken. ✕ 52 bis rue de Notre Dame des Victoires, ☎ 42–33–64–33. Reservations advised. MC, V. Closed weekends and Aug. Métro: Bourse.

$$ **Brissemoret.** There's a lot of timeless Parisian ambience in this pocket-size bistro with only nine tables. It's crowded to capacity at lunch and dinner—25 diners in a real pinch—but the dinner crowd is more relaxed and cosmopolitan than the stockbrokers and journalists who come at noon. Feast on fresh artichoke hearts, veal in lemon, sautéed duck breast garnished with clementines, and crème caramel. ✕ 5 rue St-Marc, ☎ 42–36–91–72. Reservations required. V. Closed weekends. Métro: Bourse.

3rd Arrondissement

$ **Au Bascou.** Gregarious proprietor Jean-Guy Lousteau enthusiastically shares his knowledge of the wines of southwestern France at this fashionable little bistro with a simple but imaginative decor, including mosaics of broken mirror. The sturdy, savory cuisine of the Basque country stars on the menu, and the country ham, cod with broccoli puree, and sautéed baby squid are particularly flavorful. ✕ 38 rue Reaumur, ☎ 42–72–69–25. Reservations advised. MC, V. Closed weekends. Métro: Arts et Metiers.

4th Arrondissement

$$ Bofinger. Founded in 1864, this may be Paris's oldest brasserie. It's also one of the prettiest, with its authentic Belle Epoque decor, white linen tablecloths, black leather banquettes, and beautiful stained-glass dome (ask to be seated on the main floor). The menu offers excellent shell-fish and *choucroute garnie* (including a lighter version with fish), and there's a large selection of Alsatian beers. Only steps from the place de la Bastille and open until 1 AM, Bofinger makes a good postopera rendezvous. ✕ *5 rue de la Bastille,* ☎ *42–27–87–82. Reservations advised. AE, DC, MC, V. Métro: Bastille.*

$ ★ Baracane. This small, simple place is one of the best values in the Marais district. The owner oversees the menu, full of the robust specialties of his native southwestern France, including rabbit confit, veal tongue, and pear poached in wine and cassis. A reasonable dinner menu and cheaper menu at lunch keep the Baracane solidly affordable, and the service is friendly. ✕ *38 rue des Tournelles,* ☎ *42–71–43–33. Reservations advised. MC, V. Closed Sun. No lunch Sat. Métro: Bastille.*

5th Arrondissement

$–$$ ★ La Timonerie. Only a few steps along the quay from La Tour d'Argent, this small, elegant restaurant avoids all theatrics and sticks to fine cooking. Philippe de Givenchy works with a small staff, but his creations are consistently interesting and well executed. In his hands, a simple dish such as rosemary and lemon mackerel is turned into a high-class eating experience. ✕ *35 Quai de la Tournelle,* ☎ *43–25–44–42. Reservations advised. Jacket and tie. MC, V. Closed Sun., Mon. Métro: Maubert Mutualité.*

$$ ★ Campagne et Provence. The talented young owners of the Miravile (4th Arr.) also run this small establishment on the quai across from Notre-Dame. The fresh, colorful, Provençal-inspired cuisine includes ratatouille and vegetables stuffed with cod *brandade* (ragout). The list of reasonably priced regional wines helps keep prices down. ✕ *25 quai de la Tournelle,* ☎ *43–54–05–17. Reservations advised. MC, V. Closed Sun. No lunch Sat. and Mon. Métro: Maubert-Mutualité.*

$ Le Tout Petit Plat. This charming and conveniently located wine bar, where the food's as good as the wine, occupies the tiny former quarters of the very popular Le Petit Plat (*see below*). All the dishes are paired with a suggested glass of wine, allowing you to discover such mellifluous combinations as a plate of country ham, nutty *tête de moine* (monk's head) cheese, and a glass of crisp, white Vouvray. Other savory, light offerings include tomatoes and fennel Provençal and a delicious stewed chicken with five spices. ✕ *3 rue des Grands Degrés,* ☎ *40–46–85–34. Reservations advised. MC, V. Closed Thurs. Métro: Maubert-Mutualité.*

6th Arrondissement

$$ ★ La Bastide Odéon. This little corner of Provence in Paris is just a few steps from the Luxembourg Gardens. The cooking of southern France continues to increase its popularity in the capital, and this sunny yellow room with old oak tables and chairs is one of the best places to sample the soothing Mediterranean food. Chef Gilles Ajuelos, formerly of Michel Rostang's kitchen at Le Bistrot d'à Côté, is a fine fish cook who also prepares wonderful pastas, such as tagliatelle in *pistou* (basil and pine nuts) with wild mushrooms, and main courses such as peppered tuna steak with ratatouille or roast cod with capers. The best bet on the slightly pricey wine list is the red Côteaux du Tricastin. ✕ *7 rue Corneille,* ☎ *43–26–03–65. Reservations advised. MC, V. Closed weekends. Métro: Odéon or Luxembourg RER.*

$$ **Les Bookinistes.** Talented chef Guy Savoy's fifth bistro annex—his
★ first on the Left Bank—is a big success with the locals. The cheery post-
modern room is painted peach, with red, blue, and yellow wall sconces,
and it looks out on the Seine. The menu of French country cooking
changes seasonally and might include mussel and pumpkin soup, ravi-
oli stuffed with chicken and celery, or baby chicken roasted in a casse-
role with root vegetables. The reasonable prices are challenged by a
somewhat pricey wine list. The service is friendly and efficient. ✕ *53
quai des Grands-Augustins,* ☎ *43–25–45–94. Reservations advised.
AE, DC, MC, V. Closed Sun. No lunch Sat. Métro: St-Michel.*

7th Arrondissement

$$$$ **L'Arpège.** This small, striking restaurant one block from the Rodin Mu-
★ seum is currently one of the most talked-about in Paris. Young chef-
owner Alain Passard's cuisine is both original (lobster-turnip starter
in a sweet-sour vinaigrette, stuffed sweet tomato) and classic (beef Bur-
gundy, pressed duck). The problem here is inconsistency: One sublime
meal can be followed by a mediocre one. With its curving, handcrafted
wood panels and wrought-iron window frames, the decor is unusu-
ally minimalist. The staff, although young and energetic, sometimes
falls behind. The fixed-priced lunch is a steal. ✕ *84 rue de Varenne,*
☎ *45–51–47–33,* fax *47–05–09–06. Reservations advised. AE, DC,
MC, V. Closed Aug. No lunch Sat. Métro: Varenne.*

$ **Aux Fins Gourmets.** What would the western end of boulevard St-Ger-
main be without this comforting bistro? Solid country dishes prevail:
pipérade (a mixture of eggs, peppers, onions, tomatoes, and garlic),
duck confit, and cassoulet. Pastries come from the excellent Peltier shop.
In warm weather, dinner or lunch on the terrace, under the shady plane
trees, is a delight. ✕ *213 blvd. St-Germain,* ☎ *42–22–06–57. Reser-
vations advised. No credit cards. Closed Sun. and Aug. No lunch
Mon. Métro: Bac.*

8th Arrondissement

$$$$ **Ledoyen.** Chef Ghislaine Arabian is the most talked-about up-and-com-
★ ing chef in Paris. She sets gastronomic fashion by concentrating on north-
ern French cuisine and creates specialties featuring beer sauces, including
coquilles St-Jacques à la bière (scallops in a beer sauce). The elegant
restaurant, with its gilded ceilings and walls, plush armchairs, and ta-
bles with candelabra, is set in a posh location off the Champs-Elysées
near place de la Concorde. ✕ *1 av. du Tuit, on the Carré des Champs-
Elysées,* ☎ *47–42–23–23. Reservations essential. AE, DC, MC, V.
Closed weekends. Métro: Place de la Concorde or Champs-
Elysées–Clemenceau.*

$$$$ **Taillevent.** Many say it's the best restaurant in Paris. Within the pan-
★ eled main dining rooms of this mid-19th-century mansion you will find
exceptional service that is never overbearing, a stellar wine list, and
the tempered classic cuisine of young chef Philippe Legendre. Among
his signature dishes are lobster boudin and lamb with cabbage. Pastry
chef Gilles Bajolle is one of the finest in Paris. Try his *nougatine glacée
aux poires* (thin layers of nougat, pastry, and pear sherbet) or tarte Tatin
with quince. ✕ *15 rue Lamennais,* ☎ *45–63–39–94. Reservations es-
sential, 3–4 wks ahead. Jacket and tie. AE, MC, V. Closed weekends,
Aug. Métro: Charles de Gaulle/Etoile.*

$ **Le Petit Yvan.** Personable Yvan, much loved by fashionable Paris, has
opened a new annex to his other eponymous restaurant nearby. The
decor (unremarkable, but comfortable and casual) and menu are both
simpler than at his star-studded main outpost, but this place is excep-
tional and has become very stylish for lunch. The prix fixe menu of-
fers very good value and might include dishes such as lemon-marinated

salmon and steak tartare. ✕ *1 bis rue Jean-Mermoz,* ☎ *42–89–49–65. Reservations advised. MC, V. Closed Sun. No lunch Sat. Métro: St-Philippe-du-Roule.*

9th Arrondissement

$ Chartier. People come here more for the bonhomie than the food, which is often rather ordinary. This cavernous turn-of-the-century restaurant enjoys a huge following among the budget-minded, including students, solitary bachelors, and tourists. You may find yourself sharing a table with strangers as you study the long, old-fashioned menu of such favorites as hard-boiled eggs with mayonnaise, pâté, and roast veal with spinach. ✕ *7 rue du Faubourg-Montmartre,* ☎ *47–70–86–29. No reservations. No credit cards. Métro: rue Montmartre.*

$ Chez Bruno. In a theater neighborhood with few good, inexpensive restaurants, this jazzy bistro stands out. The dim interior, the photos and posters, and the soft music all bow to jazz. A solid 79-franc menu gets you three courses that change daily; 130 francs will buy you homemade foie gras with the house special of fondu Bourguignonne. There's also an interesting, inexpensive afternoon tea, with a good selection of pastries. ✕ *5 rue Bergère,* ☎ *45–23–24–42. Reservations advised. AE, MC, V. Closed Sun. No lunch Sat. Métro: rue Montmartre.*

10th Arrondissement

$$ Brasserie Flo. This, the first of brasserie king Jean-Paul Bucher's seven Paris addresses, is hard to find down its passageway near the Gare de l'Est but worth the effort. The rich wood-and-stained-glass interior is typically Alsatian, the service enthusiastic, and the brasserie standards, such as shellfish, steak tartare, and choucroute savory. Order one of the carafes of Alsatian wine. It's open until 1:30 AM, with a special night-owl menu from 11 PM. ✕ *7 cour des Petites Ecuries,* ☎ *47–70–13–59. Reservations advised. AE, DC, MC, V. Métro: Château d'Eau.*

11th Arrondissement

$$ ★ Chardenoux. A bit off the beaten track but well worth the effort, this cozy neighborhood bistro with amber walls, etched-glass windows, dark bentwood furniture, tile floors, and a long zinc bar attracts a cross section of savvy Parisians with its first-rate traditional cooking. Start with one of the delicious salads, such as the green beans and foie gras, and then try the veal chop with morels, or a game dish. Savory desserts and a nicely chosen wine list with several excellent Côtes-du-Rhônes complete the experience. ✕ *1 rue Jules-Valles,* ☎ *43–71–49–52. Reservations advised. AE, V. Closed weekends and Aug. Métro: Charonne.*

$ Astier. You'll find remarkable value at this pleasant restaurant, where the prix fixe menu (there's no à la carte) includes first and main courses, cheese (excellent), and dessert. Among high-quality seasonal dishes, try mussel soup with saffron, fricassée of beef cheeks, and plum *clafoutis* (tart). Service can be rushed, but the enthusiastic crowd does not seem to mind. Study the excellent wine list, which has some surprising buys. ✕ *44 rue Jean-Pierre Timbaud,* ☎ *43–57–16–35. Reservations advised. AE, MC, V. Closed weekends and Aug. Métro: Parmentier.*

$ L'Ebauchoir. A trendy, laid-back local crowd is complemented by a sprinkling of fashionable types who know a bargain when they see one, at this old-fashioned bistro with classic prewar decor. Don't expect dainty service, but come instead for a hearty feed and good inexpensive wines. The salad with poached eggs and bacon bits and the *confit de canard* (duck confit) are delicious, as are the steaks and the homemade tarts for dessert. ✕ *43–45 rue des Citeaux,* ☎ *43–42–49–31. Reservations advised. MC, V. Closed Sun. Métro: Faidherbe-Chaligny.*

12th Arrondissement

$$$ **Au Trou Gascon.** The success of this pretty Belle Epoque establishment off the place Daumesnil enabled owner Alain Dutournier to open the now-renowned Carré des Feuillants (1st Arr.). He's still the owner here, too, and continues to serve his personal version of the cuisine of Gascony, a region of outstanding ham, foie gras, lamb, and poultry. His white chocolate mousse is now a classic. ✕ *40 rue Taine,* ☎ *43–44– 34–26. Reservations advised. AE, DC, MC, V. Closed weekends, Christmas wk, Aug. Métro: Daumesnil.*

$ **Les Zygomates.** When this handsome old butcher's shop with marble counters was converted into a bistro a few years ago, it became instantly popular with a local, young, more-dash-than-cash crowd. Since it's deep in a part of the city few tourists venture to, you'll find yourself surrounded by Parisians, and if you don't speak French, the menu pages in the back of this guide will be a help. You'll experience delicious modern bistro food, such as terrine of rabbit with tarragon, chicken in cream with chives, and a very fairly priced catch-of-the-day selection. ✕ *7 rue Capri,* ☎ *40–19–93–04. Reservations advised. V. Closed Sun., Sat. June–Sept., 1st 3 wks in Aug. No lunch Sat. Oct.–May. Métro: Michel-Bizot or Daumesnil.*

13th Arrondissement

$$ **Auberge Etchegorry.** Pull up a chair under the rafters festooned with braids of dried peppers and garlic, cured ham and sausages, and experience the lively flavors of traditional Basque country cooking in Paris. This friendly spot serves up generous portions of Basque classics, like pipérade, along with other southern favorites, like paella and succulent pan-sautéed duck breast with wild mushrooms. ✕ *41 rue Croulebarbe,* ☎ *43–31–63–05. Reservations advised. AE, DC, V. Closed Sun. Métro: Corvisart or Gobelins.*

14th Arrondissement

$$$ **La Cagouille.** This is one of the best fish restaurants in Paris. Though bearlike Gérard Allemandou's intimate and very successful *bistro à poissons* overlooks the somewhat sterile place Brancusi, Parisians continue to flock here for his intriguingly Zen-like cooking. Few sauces or adornments mask the fresh, clean flavors of fish—from elegant sole and turbot to more-pedestrian sardines and mackerel. An aquarium and a long wooden bar are almost the only decoration in the large, simple, modern dining room. Besides its excellent wine list, La Cagouille has the finest collection of Cognacs in the city. There's a large terrace for warm-weather dining. ✕ *10–12 pl. Brancusi,* ☎ *43–22–09–01. Reservations advised. AE, MC, V. Métro: Gaîté.*

$ **La Régalade.** This is one of the most talked about new restaurants in
★ Paris. The location, in a remote, colorless residential neighborhood, is a nuisance, but Yves Camdeborde's cooking is stunning. Although a veteran of the Crillon, he has kept his prices remarkably low—$35 for a three-course feast. Tables are booked far in advance, but service does continue until midnight, and you can often sneak in late in the evening. ✕ *49 av. Jean-Moulin,* ☎ *45–45–68–58. Reserve 1 month in advance. MC, V. Closed Sun., Mon., Aug. No lunch Sat. Métro: Alesia.*

15th Arrondissement

$ **Le Petit Plat.** Originally squeezed in a tiny space in the Latin Quarter (*see Le Tout Petit Plat, 5th Arrondisement, above*), this bistro was so popular that the owners found a bit more space in a quiet residential area; it's still small, but now the feel is intimate rather than crowded. The kitchen turns out generous portions of the slightly urbanized French country cooking that Parisians are currently mad about: Try the terrine of rabbit in tarragon aspic, sausage with potato salad in shallot vinaigrette, or roast chicken with sautéed mushrooms. The excellent wine list was selected by Henri Gault of Gault-Millau, the famous French food guide (his daughter is one of the three owners). ✗ *45 av. Emile-Zola,* ☎ *45–78–24–20. Reservations advised. V. Closed Mon. No lunch Tues. Métro: Charles-Michel.*

16th Arrondissement

$$$$ ★ **Le Vivarois.** Chef-owner Claude Peyrot is one of the most inspired and creative of contemporary French chefs, though his cooking can be uneven. He is a master with fish and puff pastry, his *bavarois* of red bell pepper (a creamy, molded concoction) is oft-imitated, and his original dishes shine: scallops with sesame and ginger, *rissolette* (small meat patty) of lamb's feet with artichokes and basil, and chocolate soufflé with chicory ice cream. Service is not always up to par. ✗ *192 av. Victor Hugo,* ☎ *45–04–04–31. Reservations advised. AE, DC, MC, V. Closed weekends, Aug. Métro: rue de la Pompe.*

$$–$$$ **Prunier.** When Prunier reopened in late 1994, Parisians were thrilled to find that one of their favorite and most glamorous restaurants had not only been sensitively renovated—the famous Art Deco mosaics have never looked better—but that the kitchen, too, had been resurrected with skill and creativity. Founded in 1925, this was one of the best—and surely the prettiest—seafood restaurants in Paris for more than 50 years. Now the white marble counters again display impeccably fresh shellfish like precious jewelry, and the kitchen not only excels at classic French fish cooking but has added some variety, with dishes like a *Saintongeaise* plate—raw oysters with grilled sausages—as eaten in Bordeaux. The pan-fried langoustines and turbot in hollandaise sauce are superb. The well-balanced wine list echoes director Jean-Claude Vrinat's acclaimed cellar at his other restaurant, Taillevent. No reservations are needed for the raw bar on the main level, but book for lunch or dinner in the upstairs dining room. ✗ *16 av. Victor-Hugo,* ☎ *44–17–35–85. Reservations advised for main dining room. Jacket and tie. AE, DC, MC, V. Closed Sun., Mon. Métro: Etoile.*

$ **Le Petit Rétro.** Two different clienteles—mostly men in expensive suits at noon and well-dressed local couples in the evening—frequent this immaculate little bistro with Art Nouveau tiles and bentwood furniture. You can't go wrong with the daily special, which is written on a chalkboard presented by one of the friendly waitresses. Come in some night when you want a good solid meal, such as the perfect *pavé de boeuf* (thick steak) in a ruddy red-wine and stock sauce, accompanied by a baked disk of au gratin potatoes and some deliciously caramelized braised endive. ✗ *5 rue Mesnil,* ☎ *44–05–06–05. Reservations advised. MC, V. Closed Sun. No lunch Mon. Métro: Victor Hugo.*

17th Arrondissement

$$$$ **Guy Savoy.** Guy Savoy is one of a handful of top chefs in Paris today, and his four bistros have not managed to distract him too much from his handsome luxury restaurant near the Arc de Triomphe. Savoy's oysters in aspic, sea bass with spices, and poached and grilled pigeon reveal the magnitude of his talent. His mille-feuille is a contemporary classic. ✗ *18 rue Troyon,* ☎ *43–80–40–61. Reservations advised. AE, MC, V. Closed Sun. No lunch Sat. Métro: Charles de Gaulle/Etoile.*

18th Arrondissement

$$ **Le Restaurant.** Here's a real oasis just steps from the place Pigalle, an area where it's not easy to find a good meal. The simply decorated storefront dining room is popular with the artists and media types who've been quietly moving into this otherwise touristy and slightly tawdry

neighborhood. The food's interesting and generally good; try the omelet of oysters or the lamb with fennel and black olives. For dessert, the shortbread tart filled with melted chocolate is delicious. The service is often slow, though, especially on weekends. ✗ *32 rue Veron,* ☎ *42–23–06–22. Reservations advised. AE, MC, V. Closed Mon. Métro: Abbesses.*

LODGING

Updated by
Corinne
LaBalme

At last count, the Paris Tourist Office's official (albeit incomplete) hotel guide listed 1,478 hotels in 20 arrondissements alone. Despite this huge choice, you should always be sure to make reservations well in advance, except, paradoxically, during July and August, when the trade fairs, conventions, and conferences that crowd the city the rest of the year come to a halt.

Our listings have been compiled with the aim of identifying hotels that offer maximum atmosphere, convenience, and comfort. We do not include many chain hotels for the simple reason that the ones in Paris aren't very different from those in other major cities. We prefer to list special, one-of-a-kind hotels that will, in themselves, contribute greatly to the charm of your stay. For the most part, hotels on the Right Bank offer greater luxury, or at any rate formality, than those on the Left Bank, where small size and a certain old-fashioned parisian charm are the drawing cards.

With the exception of the largest and most expensive hotels, almost all Paris hotels have certain idiosyncrasies. Plumbing can be erratic, though rarely to the point where it becomes a problem. Air-conditioning is the exception rather than the rule. This can cause difficulties chiefly because of noise in summer, when on stuffy, sultry nights you may have no choice but to open the windows. Ask for a room *sur cour*—overlooking the courtyard (almost all hotels have one)—or, even better, if there is one, *sur le jardin*—overlooking the garden.

There is almost always an extra charge for breakfast, anything from about 20 francs per person in the least expensive hotels to 90 francs per person in the most expensive. If you want more than the standard French breakfast of *café au lait* (coffee with milk) and a croissant, the price will almost certainly be increased. A nominal **séjour** tax (per person, per night) was introduced in 1994 to pay for increased promotion of tourism in Paris.

CATEGORY	COST*
$$$$	over 1,200 frs
$$$	750 frs–1,200 frs
$$	450 frs–750 frs
$	under 450 frs

All prices are for a standard double room, including tax and service.

1st Arrondissement

$$$$
★

Ritz. Surrounded by the city's finest jewelers, the Ritz is the crowning gem on the newly sparkling place Vendôme. Festooned with gilt and ormolu, dripping with crystal chandeliers and tapestries, and swathed in heavy silk, this dazzling hotel, which opened in 1896, is the epitome of fin-de-siècle Paris. It's surprisingly intimate, too. The hotel has no lobby, for the express purpose of discouraging paparazzi and sightseers who could annoy the privileged clientele. Legendary suites are named after ritzy former residents, like Marcel Proust and Coco Chanel. The famous Hemingway Bar (which the writer claimed to have "liberated" in 1945) reopened in 1994. The handsome Vendôme Bar and the Espadon restaurant remain elite meeting spots, and the lower-level health club has a magnificent indoor swimming pool surrounded by bucolic frescoes and towering columns. There's warm-weather seating in the charming adjacent garden. ☎ *15 pl. Vendôme, 75001,* ☎ *42–60–38–30,* FAX *42–86–00–91. 142 rooms and 45 suites, all with bath. English spoken. 2 restaurants, 2 bars, indoor pool, health club, shopping gallery, cooking school, beauty salon. AE, DC, MC, V. Métro: Madeleine.*

$$ **Britannique.** A friendly, family-owned hotel in a restored 19th-century building, the Britannique has a handsome winding staircase and nicely decorated, soundproofed rooms. During World War I the hotel was the headquarters of a Quaker mission. Ask for a room on one of the top three floors. ☎ *20 av. Victoria, 75001,* ☎ *42–33–74–59,* FAX *42–33–82–65. 31 rooms with bath, 9 with shower. English spoken. AE, DC, MC, V. Métro: Châtelet.*

2nd Arrondissement

$$ **Gaillon-Opéra.** The oak beams, stone walls, and marble tiles of the Gail-
★ lon-Opéra single it out as one of the most charming hotels in the Opéra neighborhood. The plants throughout and a flower-filled patio also delight. ☎ *9 rue Gaillon, 75002,* ☎ *47–42–47–74,* FAX *47–42–01–23. 26 rooms and 1 suite, all with bath. English spoken. AE, DC, MC, V. Métro: Opéra.*

3rd Arrondissement

$$$$ **Pavillon de la Reine.** The best hotel in the Marais, it's set around two
★ flower-filled courtyards behind the historic Queen's Pavilion on the 17th-century place des Vosges. Although this cozy mansion looks old, it was actually reconstructed from scratch in 1986 following original plans and using period timbers, rough-hewn paving stones, Louis XIII fireplaces, and antiques. Ask for a duplex with French windows overlooking the first courtyard (there are no rooms overlooking the place des Vosges). Breakfast is served in a vaulted cellar. ☎ *28 pl. des Vosges, 75003,* ☎ *42–77–96–40,* FAX *42–77–63–06. 31 rooms and 24 suites, all with bath. English spoken. Parking. AE, DC, MC, V. Métro: Chemin Vert.*

4th Arrondissement

$$$ **Deux-Iles.** This converted 17th-century mansion on the Ile St-Louis has
★ long won plaudits for charm and comfort. Flowers and plants are scattered around the stunning hall. The fabric-hung rooms, though small, have exposed beams and are fresh and airy. Ask for a room overlooking the little garden courtyard. The lounge is dominated by a fine chimneypiece and doubles as a bar. If the hotel is full, go to the Lutèce down the road; it belongs to the same owners. ☎ *59 rue St-Louis-en-l'Ile, 75004,* ☎ *43–26–13–35,* FAX *43–29–60–25. 8 rooms with bath, 9 with shower. English spoken. No credit cards. Métro: Pont-Marie.*

$$ **Bretonnerie.** This small three-star hotel is located on a tiny street in the Marais, a few minutes' walk from the Beaubourg. The snug rooms are decorated in Louis XIII style but vary considerably in size from spacious to cramped. Some boast antiques, beamed ceilings, and marble-clad bathrooms. There's a breakfast room in the vaulted cellar. ☎ *22 rue St-Croix-de-la-Bretonnerie, 75004,* ☎ *48–87–77–63,* FAX *42–77–26–78. 30 rooms with bath and 2 suites. English spoken. MC, V. Closed Aug. Métro: Hôtel de Ville.*

$ **Castex.** This family-run, two-star hotel in a 19th-century building is a real find. It was remodeled from top to bottom in 1989, and rooms are squeaky clean. The decor is strictly functional, but the extremely friendly owners and rock-bottom prices mean the Castex is often fully

Paris Lodging

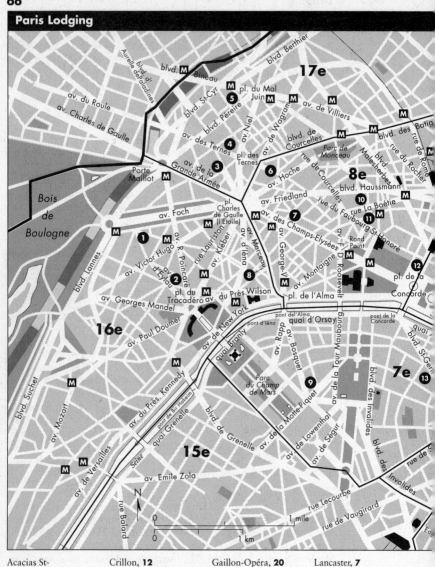

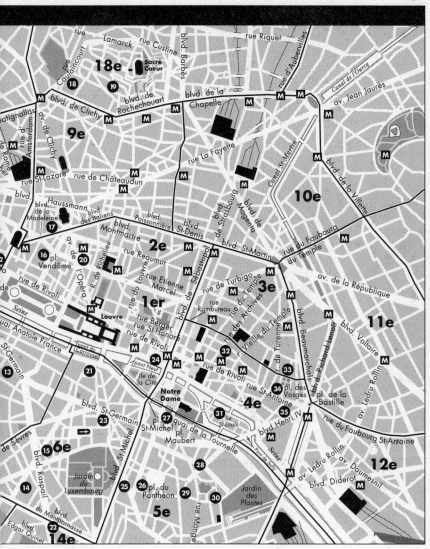

booked months ahead. There's a large American clientele. The eight least expensive rooms, two per floor, share toilets on the immaculate, well-lit landings. There's no elevator, and TV is in the lobby only. ☎ *5 rue Castex, 75004,* ☎ *42–72–31–52,* FAX *42–72–57–91. 4 rooms with bath, 23 with shower. English spoken. MC, V. Métro: Bastille.*

$ **Place des Vosges.** A loyal American clientele swears by this small hotel
★ on a charming street just off the exquisite square of the same name. Oak-beam ceilings and rough-hewn stone in public areas and some of the guest rooms add to the atmosphere. Ask for the top-floor room, the hotel's largest, with a view of Marais rooftops. There's a welcoming little breakfast room. ☎ *12 rue de Birague, 75004,* ☎ *42–72–60–46,* FAX *42–72–02–64. 11 rooms with bath, 5 with shower. English spoken. AE, DC, MC, V. Métro: Bastille.*

5th Arrondissement

$$ **Elysa Luxembourg.** The Elysa is what the French call an *hôtel de charme*. Though the building is not large, most rooms are surprisingly spacious, and all are exquisitely maintained and refurbished yearly. Cream-color furniture is set against pale blue or pink fabrics. There's no restaurant or bar, but you'll find a minibar in every room and a breakfast lounge serving Continental or buffet breakfasts. Moreover, the Elysa is one of the rare hotels in the city with a sauna. ☎ *6 rue Gay-Lussac, 75005,* ☎ *43–25–31–74,* FAX *46–34–56–27. 25 rooms with bath, 5 with shower. English spoken. Sauna. AE, MC, V. Métro: Luxembourg.*

$$ **Grandes Ecoles.** This delightful hotel in three small old buildings is set far off the street in a beautiful garden. There are parquet floors, antiques, and a (non-working) piano in the breakfast area. Most rooms have beige carpets and flowery wallpaper. It's hard to find a quieter, more charming hotel for the price. There's a faithful American clientele, including some backpackers. The rooms with bathroom facilities on the well-lit landings are inexpensive. ☎ *75 rue du Cardinal Lemoine, 75005,* ☎ *43–26–79–23,* FAX *43–25–28–15. 29 rooms with bath, 10 with shower, 9 with shared bath. English spoken. AE, MC, V. Métro: Cardinal Lemoine.*

$$ **Jardin des Plantes.** Across the street from the lovely Jardin des Plantes
★ botanical gardens on the edge of the Latin Quarter, this pleasant two-star hotel offers botanical-theme decor and very reasonable prices. There's a fifth-floor terrace, where you can breakfast or sunbathe in summer, and a sauna and ironing room in the cellar. ☎ *5 rue Linné, 75005,* ☎ *47–07–06–20,* FAX *47–07–62–74. 29 rooms with bath, 4 with shower. English spoken. Bar-tearoom, sauna. AE, DC, MC, V. Métro: Jussieu.*

$$ **Panthéon.** In a handsome 18th-century building facing the Panthéon, this excellent three-star hotel has prices that range from moderate to expensive. Some of the charming rooms have exposed beams, balconies, and stunning views all the way to Sacré-Coeur; a vaulted breakfast room, an impressive lobby, and air-conditioning are additional attractions. The desk staff is very helpful. ☎ *19 pl. du Panthéon, 75005,* ☎ *43–54–32–95,* FAX *43–26–64–65. 34 rooms with bath. English spoken. AE, DC, V. Métro: RER Luxembourg.*

$ **Esméralda.** One either loves it or hates it. The Esméralda, which boasts a fine (but noisy) location in a fusty 17th-century building across from Notre-Dame, is famed for its cozy, eccentric charm. Some closet-size rooms are nearly overpowered by gaudy imitation antiques. Request a room with a view of the cathedral. Animal lovers will enjoy the friendly dogs and cats that snooze in the lobby. The price of the best rooms creeps upward; singles with shower on the landings are very cheap. ☎ *4 rue St-Julien-le-Pauvre, 75005,* ☎ *43–54–19–20,* FAX *40–51–00–*

68. *15 rooms with bath, 4 with shower on the landing. Some English spoken. No credit cards. Métro: St-Michel.*

$ **Familia.** The Gaucheron family runs this pretty, hospitable hotel with great panache. A mural painted by a local art student adorns the lobby, and its 30 clean, neat rooms are equipped with minibars, cable TV (CNN), and hair dryers in the bathrooms. Rooms looking out on the pretty Left Bank street have double-glazed windows. Seven have balconies; highly prized, these must be booked well in advance. ☎ *11 rue des Ecoles, 75005,* ☎ *43–54–55–27,* FAX *43–29–61–77. 14 rooms with bath, 16 with shower. English spoken. MC, V. Métro: Jussieu, Maubert-Mutualité, Cardinal–Lemoine.*

6th Arrondissement

$$$$ **L'Hôtel** Rock idols and movie stars adore this expensive and eccentric
★ Left Bank hotel filled with flowers and antiques. Oscar Wilde died here in room 16 ("I am dying beyond my means," he wrote). One small double is decorated entirely in leopardskin; another handsome suite features the mirrored, Art Deco boudoir furniture that belonged to vaudeville star Mistinguett. Many rooms are extremely small. The hotel has a fine restaurant, Le Belier, whose decor includes a fountain and a live tree. The bar, open until 1 AM, is popular with a well-heeled international crowd. ☎ *13 rue des Beaux-Arts, 75006,* ☎ *43–25–27–22,* FAX *43–25–64–81. 16 rooms with bath, 8 with shower, 3 suites with bath. English spoken. Restaurant, bar. AE, DC, MC, V. Métro: St-Germain-des-Prés.*

$$$ **L'Abbaye St-Germain.** This delightful hotel, entirely renovated in 1993, is a former 18th-century convent near St-Sulpice, in the heart of the Left Bank. The first-floor rooms open onto flower-filled gardens. Some rooms on the top floor have oak beams and alcoves. The entrance hall is sturdily authentic, with stone vaults. All bathrooms are decorated with colored marble. The bar is for guests only. ☎ *10 rue Cassette, 75006,* ☎ *45–44–38–11,* FAX *45–48–07–86. 42 rooms and 4 suites, all with bath. English spoken. Bar. AE, MC, V. Métro: St-Sulpice.*

$$$ **Fleurie.** Entirely air-conditioned, this spiffy family-run hotel, established
★ in 1988, offers good location (a quiet side street near the place de l'Odéon), prettily furnished pastel rooms, and many luxury amenities: built-in hair dryers, minibars, private safe deposit boxes, marble-clad bathrooms, heated towel racks, and color TV with CNN. ☎ *32–34 rue Grégoire-de-Tours, 75006,* ☎ *43–29–59–81,* FAX *43–29–68–44. 29 rooms with bath. English spoken. Bar-salon. AE, DC, MC, V. Métro: Odéon.*

$$ **Acacias St-Germain.** This three-star hotel in a 19th-century building near Montparnasse is steadily remodeling its English-style rooms. It offers spotlessly clean rooms decorated in summery fabrics and colors and a small, flower-filled patio. Look into the remarkable low-season and weekend discounts. All rooms have CNN and hair dryers. ☎ *151 bis rue de Rennes, 75006,* ☎ *45–48–97–38,* FAX *45–44–63–57. 24 rooms with bath, 17 with shower. English spoken. Room service, baby-sitting, meeting room, laundry service and dry cleaning, airport shuttle. AE, DC, MC, V. Métro: St-Placide.*

7th Arrondissement

$$$$ **Duc de Saint-Simon.** Set back from a peaceful little street leading to boule-
★ vard St-Germain, the Saint-Simon is both quaint and classy. Parts of the building date back to the 17th century, others to the 18th. Try for one of the rooms with a terrace; they look over the courtyard and neighboring gardens. There's a pleasant bar and a cellar lounge for breakfast. The regular doubles are significantly less expensive than the suites. ☎ *14 rue St-Simon, 75007,* ☎ *45–48–35–66,* FAX *45–48–68–25. 29*

rooms and 5 suites, all with bath. English spoken. Bar. No credit cards. Métro: Bac.

$ **Champ de Mars.** This simple, clean two-star hotel has one-star prices. Don't expect luxury or atmosphere, just a very good deal, in a nice neighborhood near the Eiffel Tower and Invalides. ☎ *7 rue du Champ-de-Mars, 75007,* ☎ *45–51–52–30. 19 rooms with bath, 6 with shower. Some English spoken. MC, V. Closed 2 wks in mid-Aug. Métro: Ecole Militaire.*

8th Arrondissement

$$$$ **Crillon.** Among Parisian "palace" hotels, only the Crillon can provide a front-row seat to history, set as it is in two 18th-century town houses on the place de la Concorde, site of the French Revolution's infamous guillotine. Marie-Antoinette, who met her end there, took singing lessons at the Hôtel de Crillon, where one of the original *grands appartements,* now sumptuous salons protected by the French National Historic Landmark Commission, has been named for the queen. Guests must pay dearly for a balcony overlooking the great square, with seemingly all of Paris at their feet; only the suites have them. Lesser mortals still get magnificent digs, individually decorated with Rococo and Directoire antiques, crystal and gilt wall sconces, and gold fittings. Most double rooms have separate sitting rooms, and the bathrooms, stocked with wonderful Annick Goutal toiletries, are clad in marble. The sheer quantity of the marble downstairs—in the lobby, the adjacent lounge, and especially the grand, top-rated Les Ambassadeurs restaurant—is staggering. The staff anticipates your every need. ☎ *10 pl. de la Concorde, 75008,* ☎ *44–71–15–00,* FAX *44–71–15–02. 120 rooms and 43 suites, all with bath. English spoken. 2 restaurants, 2 bars. AE, DC, MC, V. Métro: Concorde.*

$$$$ **Lancaster.** The phrase "Small is beautiful" sums up the appeal of the
★   Lancaster, just off the Champs-Elysées. This charming, old-fashioned hotel—behind a now-gleaming facade—offers all the same services as its bigger and better-known sisters but with the atmosphere of a luxurious private house. All rooms are individually decorated with Louis XV and Louis XVI furniture. Bathrooms vary, but most are clad with marble. A fountain, statues, and flowers fill the pretty garden. ☎ *7 rue de Berri, 75008,* ☎ *40–76–40–76,* FAX *40–76–40–00. 58 rooms and 8 suites, all with bath. English spoken. Restaurant, 2 private dining rooms. AE, DC, MC, V. Métro: George V.*

$$$$ **Le Bristol.** Luxury and discretion are the Bristol's trump cards. The un-
★   derstated facade on rue du Faubourg St-Honoré might mislead the unknowing, but the Bristol ranks among Paris's top four hotels. Some of the air-conditioned and spaciously elegant rooms have authentic Louis XV and Louis XVI furniture. Moreover, the management has filled public areas with Old Master paintings, sculptures, sumptuous carpets, and tapestries. The marble bathrooms are simply magnificent. Nonguests can take tea in the vast garden or dine in the tented summer restaurant or paneled winter restaurant; later, you can listen to the pianist in the bar, open till 1 AM. There's an enclosed pool on the roof, complete with solarium and sauna, for guests only. The service throughout is impeccable. ☎ *112 rue du Fbg. St-Honoré, 75008,* ☎ *42–66–91–45,* FAX *42–66–68–68. 155 rooms and 45 suites, all with bath. English spoken. Restaurant, bar, pool, sauna, fitness machines, solarium. AE, DC, MC, V. Métro: St-Philippe du Roule.*

$$$ **Ceramic.** Formerly a shabby student hangout near the Arc de Triomphe, this hotel was totally renovated in 1994, with double rooms priced near the low end of this category. The new room decor reflects the Art Nouveau period, matching the hotel's glorious landmark 1904

facade. ☎ *34 av. de Wagram, 75008,* ☎ *42–27–20–30,* ⒻⒶⓍ *46–22–95–83. 51 rooms with bath, 6 with shower. English spoken. AE, DC, MC, V. Métro: Etoile.*

$ **Argenson.** This friendly family-run hotel provides what may well be the best value in the swanky 8th Arrondissement. Some of the city's greatest sights are just a 10-minute walk away. Old furniture, molded ceilings, and skillfull flower arrangements add to the charm. Ongoing room-by-room renovation means new bathrooms in many. The best rooms have full baths, but they are pricier; reserve well in advance for one of these. The smallest rooms have shared baths. ☎ *15 rue d'Argenson, 75008,* ☎ *42–65–16–87,* ⒻⒶⓍ *47–42–02–06. 5 rooms with bath. 19 with shower, 3 with shared bath. Some English spoken. MC, V. Métro: Miromesnil.*

9th Arrondissement

$$$$ **Grand Hotel Inter-Continental.** Paris's biggest luxury hotel has endless hallways and a facade that seems as long as the Louvre. And after a thorough restoration completed mid-1991, this 1862 gem sparkles like new. The grand salon's Art Deco dome and the painted ceilings of the Opéra and Café de la Paix restaurants are registered landmarks. Rooms are spacious and light, decorated in Art Nouveau style with pastel colors. The famed Café de la Paix is one of the city's great people-watching spots. ☎ *2 rue Scribe, 75009,* ☎ *40–07–32–32,* ⒻⒶⓍ *42–66–12–51. 470 rooms, 23 suites, all with bath. English spoken. 3 restaurants, 2 bars, health club. AE, DC, MC, V. Métro: Opéra.*

14th Arrondissement

$$$ **Raspail.** All the rooms in this glossy, recently remodeled Art Deco hotel
★ are named for the artists who made Montparnasse the art capital of the world in the '20s and '30s. All the pastel-tinted rooms have AC, TV with CNN, safes, minibars, and hair dryers. The five "panoramic" rooms have three windows and offer spectacular views of Montparnasse and the Eiffel Tower. Prices for most rooms are at the low end of this category. ☎ *203 blvd. Raspail, 75014,* ☎ *43–20–62–86,* ⒻⒶⓍ *43–20–50–79. 28 rooms with bath, 10 with shower. English spoken. AE, DC, MC, V. Métro: Raspail.*

16th Arrondissement

$$$$ **Parc Victor Hugo.** The newest (1992) luxury hotel on the Right Bank
★ was decorated by Nina Campbell with cozy chintz. Perfumed by floral potpourri, with sleek lighting and up-to-date amenities (CNN, air-conditioning, VCRs), the Victor Hugo is a gracious tribute to English country-house charm. A gourmet plus: Joël Robuchon's celebrated restaurant is right next door. ☎ *55–57 av. Raymond-Poincaré, 75116,* ☎ *44–05–66–66,* ⒻⒶⓍ *44–05–66–00. 104 rooms with bath, 11 suites. English spoken. Restaurant, bar, no-smoking floor, room service. AE, DC, MC, V. Métro: Victor Hugo.*

$$$$ **Saint James Paris.** Billed as the only château hotel in Paris, the Saint James lives up to expectations. The gracious late-19th-century neoclassical mansion is surrounded by greenery in a lush private park. Although the lavish interior decor, created by jet-set designer Andrée Putman, is mostly Art Deco style, some rooms are being done newly traditional. The restaurant is reserved for guests. In summer, meals are served in the garden. Ten rooms on the third floor open onto a winter garden. The plushest option? Renting a small freestanding gatehouse on the property. ☎ *5 place du Chancelier-Adenauer, 75116,* ☎ *44–05–81–81,* ⒻⒶⓍ *44–05–81–82. 48 rooms, suites and duplexes, all with bath. English spoken. Restaurant, bar, piano bar, room service, health club, billiards. AE, DC, MC, V. Métro: Porte Dauphine.*

$$ **Keppler.** Ideally located on the edge of the 8th and 16th arrondissements near the Champs-Elysées, this small two-star hotel in a 19th-century building boasts many three-star features (room service, small bar) at extremely reasonable prices. The spacious and airy rooms are simply decorated with modern furnishings. Some rooms with shower are less expensive. ⌧ *12 rue Keppler, 75116,* ☎ *47–20–65–05,* ꜰᴀˣ *47–23–02–29. 31 rooms with bath, 18 with shower. English spoken. Bar. AE, MC, V. Métro: Kléber, Georges V.*

17th Arrondissement

$$$ **Regent's Garden.** The large number of repeat visitors is a safe indication that this is a special place. Near the Arc de Triomphe, the hotel was built in the mid-19th century by Napoléon III for his doctor. Inside, it is every bit as you would imagine, with marble fireplaces, mirrors, gilt furniture, and stucco work. But the real attraction is the garden—a room overlooking it is something to be treasured. The levels of service match the spectacular architecture and decor. ⌧ *6 rue Pierre-Demours, 75017,* ☎ *45–74–07–30,* ꜰᴀˣ *40–55–01–42. 39 rooms with bath, 1 with shower. English spoken. AE, DC, MC, V. Métro: Etoile.*

$$ **Etoile-Péreire.** Pianist Ferrucio Pardi, owner and manager here, has cre-
★   ated a unique small hotel, set behind a quiet, leafy courtyard in a chic residential district. Renovated in 1986, rooms and duplexes are decorated in soothing pastels—pinks, grays, and apricots—with Laura Ashley curtains and chair covers, and prints on the walls. There's no house restaurant, but room service can be arranged, and a copious breakfast is available—with 40 different jams and jellies. The bar is always busy in the evening. For a lively, personally run hotel, few places beat this likable spot. ⌧ *146 blvd. Péreire, 75017,* ☎ *42–67–60–00,* ꜰᴀˣ *42–67–02–90. 18 rooms with bath, 3 with shower; 4 duplexes and 1 suite. English spoken. Bar. AE, DC, MC, V. Métro: Péreire.*

$ **Palma.** This prim and proper two-star hotel, between the Arc de Triomphe and Porte Maillot, is run by the friendly and efficient Couderc family. Small and charming, it is one of the best modest hotel deals in the city. Ask for a top-floor room with a view. All rooms have cable TV with CNN. Breakfast is included in the price. ⌧ *46 rue Brunel, 75017,* ☎ *45–74–74–51,* ꜰᴀˣ *45–74–40–90. 15 rooms with bath, 22 with shower. English spoken. MC, V. Métro: Argentine.*

18th Arrondissement

$ **Regyn's Montmartre.** Despite small rooms (all recently renovated), this owner-run hotel on Montmartre's place des Abbesses is rapidly gaining an enviable reputation for simple, comfortable accommodations. A predominantly young clientele and a correspondingly relaxed atmosphere have made this an attractive choice for some. Try for one of the rooms on the upper floors, with great views of either the Eiffel Tower or Sacré-Coeur. All rooms have safes and hair dryers. ⌧ *18 pl. des Abbesses, 75018,* ☎ *42–54–45–21,* ꜰᴀˣ *42–23–76–69. 14 rooms with bath, 8 with shower. English spoken. AE, MC, V. Métro: Abbesses.*

$ **Utrillo.** Newly renovated, the Utrillo is on a quiet side street at the foot of Montmartre, near the colorful rue Lepic markets. The decor is appealing, with prints in every room and a marble-topped breakfast table. Because the color white is emphasized throughout, the hotel seems light, clean, and more spacious than it actually is. Two rooms have views of the Eiffel Tower. ⌧ *7 rue Aristide-Bruant, 75018,* ☎ *42–58–13–44,* ꜰᴀˣ *42–23–93–88. 5 rooms with bath, 25 with shower. English spoken. Sauna. AE, DC, MC, V. Métro: Blanche.*

THE ARTS AND NIGHTLIFE

The Arts

Parisians consider their city a bastion of art and culture, and indeed it is. But surprisingly, much of the theater, opera, music, and ballet here is not on a par with what you'll find in London, New York, or Milan. Mime and contemporary dance performances are often better bets, and they pose no language problems.

The music season usually runs from September to June. Theaters stay open during the summer, but many productions are at summer festivals elsewhere in France. The weekly magazines *Pariscope, L'Officiel des Spectacles,* and *Figaroscope* are published every Wednesday and give detailed entertainment listings. The Paris Tourist Office has set up a **24-hour hot line** (☎ 49–52–53–56) in English with information about weekly events. The best place to buy tickets is at the box offices. Otherwise, try your hotel or a travel agency, such as **Paris-Vision** (214 rue de Rivoli). Tickets for some events can be bought at the **FNAC** stores—especially Alpha-FNAC (1–5 rue Pierre-Lescot, 1er, Forum des Halles, 3rd level down). **Virgin Megastore** (52 av. des Champs-Elysées) sells theater and concert tickets. Half-price tickets for many same-day theater performances are available at the **Kiosque Théâtre** across from 15 place de la Madeleine (open Tues.–Sat. 12:30–8, Sun. 12:30–6); expect a line. There's another branch at Châtelet RER station (closed Sun.).

Concerts

Before the new Opéra de la Bastille opened, the **Salle Pleyel** (252 rue du Faubg. St-Honoré, 8e, ☎ 45–63–07–96), near the Arc de Triomphe, was Paris's principal home of classical music. The Paris Symphony Orchestra and other leading international orchestras still play here regularly. Paris isn't as richly endowed as New York or London, when it comes to orchestral music, but the city compensates with a never-ending stream of inexpensive lunchtime and evening concerts in churches. The candlelit concerts held in the **Sainte-Chapelle** are outstanding—make reservations well in advance. **Notre-Dame** is another church where you can combine sightseeing with good listening. Others that offer concerts are **St-Eustache,** near Les Halles; **St-Germain-des-Prés,** on the Left Bank; **St-Louis-en-l'Ile; St-Roch,** north of the Louvre; and the lovely **St-Louis des Invalides.**

Dance

The highlights of the Paris dance year usually take place at the **Opéra Garnier,** which, in addition to being the sumptuous home of the well-reputed Paris Ballet, also bills dozens of major foreign troupes, ranging from classical to modern. Other major venues include the **Théâtre de la Ville** at Châtelet (☎ 42–74–22–77), the **Palais des Congrès** at Porte Maillot (☎ 40–68–00–05) and the **Palais des Sports** at the Porte de Versailles (☎ 48–28–40–48).

Films

Parisians are far more addicted to the cinema as an art form than are Londoners or New Yorkers. There are hundreds of movie theaters in the city, and a number of them run English films. Check the *Officiel du Spectacle* or *Pariscope,* and look for the initials "v.o.," which mean *version originale;* i.e., not subtitled or dubbed. Cinema admission runs from 40 francs to 55 francs; there are reduced rates on Monday and, in some cinemas, for morning shows. Most theaters will post two show times: The first is the *séance,* or period of commercials and previews. The film usually starts 10–25 minutes later. Real movie buffs should visit the **Pompidou Center,** which screens lots of classics and obscure films.

Opera

The **Opéra** itself, or **Palais Garnier** (pl. de l'Opéra, 9e, ☎ 47–42–53–71) has conceded its role as Paris's main opera house to the **Opéra Bastille** (pl. de la Bastille, ☎ 44–73–13–00). The old Opéra now devotes itself to classical dance; French ballet superstar Patrick Dupont is the reigning artistic director. The Opéra Bastille, meanwhile, has had its share of start-up and management problems, and many feel it is not living up to its promise of grand opera at affordable prices. In the lofty old hall of the **Opéra Comique** (5 rue Favart, 2e, ☎ 42–60–04–99), you'll hear often excellent comic operas and lightweight musical entertainments. The **Théâtre Musical de Paris,** better known as the Théâtre du Châtelet (2 pl. du Châtelet, 1er, ☎ 40–28–28–28), offers opera and ballet for a wider audience, at more reasonable prices.

Theater

A number of theaters line the Grands Boulevards between Opéra and République, but there is no Paris equivalent to Broadway or the West End. Shows are mostly in French. Classical drama is performed at the distinguished **Comédie Francaise** (Palais-Royal, 1er, ☎ 40–15–00–15). You can reserve seats in person about two weeks in advance, or turn up an hour beforehand and wait in line for returned tickets.

Ionesco admirers should visit the tiny Left Bank **Théâtre de la Huchette** (23 rue de la Huchette, 5e, ☎ 43–26–38–99), where the playwright's short modern plays make a deliberate mess of the French language.

A particularly Parisian form of theater is **Café-Théâtre**—a mixture of satirical sketches and variety riddled with slapstick humor, in a café setting. It's fun if you have a good grasp of French. We suggest either the **Café de la Gare** (41 rue du Temple, 4e, ☎ 42–78–52–51) or Montmartre's pricier **Chez Michou** (80 rue des Martyrs, 18e, ☎ 46–06–16–04).

Nightlife

The French are definitely nightbirds, though these days that means smart, elegant *bars de nuit* rather than frenetic discos. The **Champs-Elysées,** that ubiquitous cabaret land, is making a comeback, though the clientele remains predominantly foreign. The tawdry **Pigalle** and down-at-the-heels **Bastille** areas are trendy these days, and the **Left Bank** boasts a bit of everything. During the week, people usually go home after the closing hour of 2 AM, but weekends mean late-night partying.

Bars and Nightclubs

The more upscale Paris nightclubs tend to be both expensive (1,000 francs for a bottle of gin or whiskey) and private—in other words, you'll usually need to know someone who's a member. It helps to be famous—or look like a model—to get into **Les Bains** (7 rue du Bourg-l'Abbé, 3e) or **Niel's** (27 av. des Ternes, 17e). **Keur Samba** (73 rue La Boétie, 8e) has a jungle setting. The Pigalle area in Montmartre is becoming the place to be nowadays, despite its reputation as a seedy red-light district. Among hot places here are **Moloko** (26 rue Fontaine, 9e), a smoky late-night bar with a small dance floor; **Le Dépanneur** (next door at 27 rue Fontaine), which caters to more of a gin-drinking yuppie crowd; **Lili la Tigresse** (98 rue Blanche, 9e), a sexy bar with a trendy crowd; and—not to be missed—the brasserie **Pigalle** (22 blvd. de Clichy, 18e), whose '50s frescoes and ceramics have been classified as a national treasure.

The nightlife is still hopping in and around the Bastille: The **China Club** (50 rue de Charenton, 12e) is a trendy bar with an Orient Express theme; **La Casbah** (18 rue de la Forge Royale, 11e) a bar and dance club with a touch of Casablanca; **Café de la Plage** (59 rue de Charonne, 11e) an arty-jazzy bar; **Le Wah-Wah** (11 rue Daval, 11e) a jewel of a bar with strange, religious imagery on the walls; and **Le Pistou Pelican** (15 rue de Bagnolet, 20e) a favorite among Beaux-Arts students with a laid-back ambience and occasional live music.

Literary types will head for **Harry's Bar** (5 rue Daunou, 2e), a cozy, wood-paneled hangout for Americans that's haunted by the ghosts of Ernest Hemingway and Scott Fitzgerald. Also highly popular among the nostalgic set are the many hotel bars in the city, including those at the **Ritz** (15 pl. Vendôme, 1er), the **Lutétia** (45 blvd. Raspail, 6e), the **Bristol** (112 rue du Fbg. St-Honoré, 8e), the **Normandy** (7 rue de l'Echelle, 1er), and the **Bélier** at **L'Hotel** (13 rue des Beaux Arts, 6e).

Other popular spots are **Le Rosebud** (11 bis rue Delambre, 14e), a cult spot for the Jeunesse Dorée (young and fashionable) of the Left Bank; **Le Comptoir** (4 rue Vauvilliers, 1er), a popular locale that draws a hip Les Halles crowd and features a drink aptly called a Sexy; and **Le Forum** (4 blvd. Malesherbes, 8e), an archetypical French cocktail bar with one of the best selections of drinks in Paris.

Cabaret

Paris's nightclubs are household names, shunned by wordly Parisians and beloved of foreign tourists, who flock to the shows. Prices can range from 200 francs (simple admission plus one drink) to more than 800 francs (dinner plus show). The **Crazy Horse** (12 av. George V, 8e, ☎ 47–23–32–32) is one of the best-known clubs for pretty girls and dance routines, lots of humor, and few clothes. The **Moulin Rouge** (pl. Blanche, 18e, ☎ 46–06–00–19), that old favorite in Montmartre, mingles the can-can and crocodiles in an extravagant spectacle. The **Lido** (116 bis av. des Champs-Elysées, 8e, ☎ 40–76–56–10) stars the famous Blue-bell Girls and underwent a $10 million face-lift in 1994. The legendary **Folies Bergères** (32 rue Richer, 9e, ☎ 44–79–98–98) reopened at the end of 1993 after closing briefly because of financial trouble. The new and improved cabaret includes ornate costumes, masterful lighting, and a show that returns to its music hall origins.

Gay and Lesbian

Gay and lesbian bars and clubs, mostly concentrated in the Marais, are some of the most happening addresses in the city. You'll find many clubs, discos, and restaurants on or near rue Vieille-du-Temple. The trendy clubs fall in and out of favor at lightning speed, however, and one-night discos and tea dances are always popping up, so check the local papers to see what's hot. Prepare for a late (and expensive) night; most discos don't open until 11:30 and don't get rolling until the bars close, around 2. The very trendy **Banana Café** (13 rue de la Fer-ronnerie, 1er) attracts an energetic and scantily clad mixed crowd; dancing on the tables is the norm. **Queen** (102 av. des Champs-Elysées, 8e) is currently one of the most talked about nightclubs in all of Paris. Everybody is lining up to get in. Dress to the hilt and bring lots of francs. **Les Planches** (36 rue Doudeauville, 18e) offers two roomy lounges and a summer terrace for evening get-togethers; or you might try the friendly, arty atmosphere (and reasonable prices) of **Le Central** (33 rue Vieille-du-Temple, 4e). **Amnesia Café**'s (42 rue Vieille-du-Temple, 4e) under-lit bar and Art Deco ceiling paintings attract a young, yuppie gay and lesbian crowd, and it's a great place for a light lunch salad.

For men: **Le Quetzal** (10 rue de la Verrerie, 4e), which features a chrome-and-blue-light atmosphere, gets very crowded and smoky on weekends. For 26 years now, men have been meeting at **Club 18** (18 rue du Beaujolais, 1er), the oldest gay disco in Paris. It took on a new, modern look in 1993 but is as popular and casual as ever, particularly on theme nights. **The Trap** (10 rue Jacob, 6e) contains a ground-floor video bar with a staircase that leads to a darker, more social area. For a relaxed atmosphere, try **Subway** (35 rue St-Croix-de-la-Bretonnerie, 4e), a popular hangout with pinball and pool.

For women: **La Champmeslé** (4 rue Chabanais, 2e), the hub of lesbian nightlife, has a back room reserved for women only; **Le Memorie**'s (2 pl. de la Porte-Maillot, 17e), though in a staid neighborhood, is Paris's most renowned lesbian dance club. **Katmandou** (21 rue du Vieux Colombier, 7e), which has been around for years, is still a favorite nightspot for women; and **El Scandalo** (21 rue Keller, 11e) gets started late but is always lively.

Jazz Clubs

The French take jazz seriously, and Paris is one of the great jazz cities of the world, with plenty of variety, including some fine, distinctive local coloring. (You're in Europe now, so why insist on American performers?) For nightly schedules, consult the specialty magazines *Jazz Hot* or *Jazz Magazine*. Remember that nothing gets going till 10 or 11 PM and that entry prices can vary from about 40 francs to more than 100 francs.

Start on the Left Bank at the **Caveau de la Huchette** (5 rue de la Huchette, 5e), a smoke-filled shrine to the Dixieland beat. **Le Petit Journal** (71 blvd. St-Michel, 5e), opposite the Luxembourg gardens, serves up good food and traditional jazz. **Le Bilboquet** (13 rue Saint-Benoît, 6e) plays mainstream jazz in a faded Belle Epoque decor. Nearby, the **Montana** (28 rue Saint-Benoît, 6e) is a well-known spot for jazz lovers. **La Villa** (29 rue Jacob, 6e), a newcomer on the jazz scene, has been attracting serious musicians.

Elsewhere in the city, **Au Duc des Lombards** (42 rue des Lombards, 1er) is an ill-lit, romantic venue. **Le Petit Opportun** (15 rue des Lavandières-Ste-Opportune, 1er) is a converted bistro that sometimes features top-flight American soloists with French backup. **The Slow Club** (130 rue de Rivoli, 1er) plays swing, bebop, and Dixieland jazz. **New Morning** (7 rue des Petites-Ecuries, 10e) is a premier spot for visiting musicians and French bands.

Pubs

The number of Paris bars that woo English-speaking clients with a pub atmosphere and dark beer are becoming increasingly popular with Parisians, too. The **Académie de la Bière** (88 bis blvd. de Port-Royal, 5e) serves more than 100 foreign brews to accompany good french fries and *moules marinières* (mussels cooked in white wine). The **Bar Belge** (75 av. de Saint-Ouen, 17e) is an authentically noisy Flemish drinking spot, while the **Mayflower** (49 rue Descartes, 5e) is a classy Left Bank spot, British-style. **Connolly's Corner** (8 rue Mirbel, 5e) and **Finnegans Wake** (9 rue des Boulangers, 5e) are two of the city's numerous Irish pubs.

PARIS ESSENTIALS

Arriving and Departing by Plane

Airports and Airlines

Paris is served by two international airports: **Charles de Gaulle,** also known as Roissy, 26 kilometers (16 miles) northeast of the downtown area, and **Orly,** 16 kilometers (10 miles) south. Major carriers, among them **TWA, American Airlines,** and **Air France,** fly daily from the United States, while **Air France** and **British Airways** between them offer hourly service from London. For more information on getting to Paris by air, *see* Arriving and Departing in Chapter 1.

Between the Airports and Downtown

The easiest way to get into Paris from **Charles de Gaulle** (Roissy) airport is on the **RER-B** line, the suburban express train. A new station opened right beneath Terminal 2 in 1994. Trains to central Paris (Les Halles, St-Michel, Luxembourg) leave every 15 minutes; the fare is 44 francs, and the journey time is 30 minutes. **Buses** operated by Air France (you don't have to have flown with the airline) run every 15 minutes between Charles de Gaulle and western Paris (Porte Maillot and the Arc de Triomphe). The fare is 48 francs, and the journey time is about 40 minutes, though rush-hour traffic often makes this a slow and frustrating trip. Additionally, the **Roissybus,** operated by RATP, runs directly between Roissy and rue Scribe at Paris Opera every 15 minutes and costs 35 francs. **Taxis** are readily available; the fare will be around 180–230 francs, depending on traffic.

From **Orly** airport, the simplest way to get into Paris is on the **RER-C** line; there's a free shuttle bus from the terminal building to the train station, and trains leave every 15 minutes. The fare is 40 francs, and the journey time is about 30 minutes. The **Orlyval** service, introduced in 1991, involves a new shuttle train that runs between Orly and the Antony **RER-B** station every seven minutes. A ticket from Paris is 50 francs. **Buses** operated by Air France (you need not have flown with the airline) run every 12 minutes between Orly airport and the Air France air terminal at Les Invalides on the Left Bank; the fare is 32 francs, and the trip can take from 30 minutes to an hour. RATP also runs the **Orlybus** between Denfert-Rochereau métro station and Orly every 15 minutes for 30 francs. A 25-minute **taxi** ride costs 130–180 francs.

Arriving and Departing by Car, Train, and Bus

By Car

In a country as highly centralized as France, it is no surprise that expressways converge on the capital from every direction: A1 from the north (England/Belgium); A13 from Normandy/the northwest; A4 from the east; A10 from Spain/the southwest; and A7 from the Alps/Riviera/Italy. Each connects with the *périphérique,* the beltway, whose exits into the city are named, not numbered.

By Train

Paris has six international train stations: **Gare du Nord** (northern France, northern Europe, and England via Calais or the Channel Tunnel); **Gare St-Lazare** (Normandy and England via Dieppe); **Gare de l'Est** (Strasbourg, Luxembourg, Basel, and central Europe); **Gare de Lyon** (Lyon, Marseille, the Riviera, Geneva, Italy); and **Gare d'Austerlitz** (Loire Valley, southwest France, Spain). **Gare Montparnasse** has taken over as the main terminus for Bordeaux- and southwest-bound domestic trains since the introduction of the new TGV-Atlantique service.

By Bus

Paris has no central bus depot. Long-distance bus journeys are rare compared with train travel. The leading Paris-based bus company is **Eurolines** (28 av. du Général-de-Gaulle, Bagnolet, ☎ 49–72–51–51).

Getting Around

To help you find your way around, we suggest that you buy a *Plan de Paris par arrondissement,* a city guide available at most kiosks with separate maps of each district, including the whereabouts of métro stations and an index of street names. Maps of the métro/RER network are available free from any métro station and many hotels. They are also posted on every platform, as are maps of the bus network. Bus routes are also marked at bus stops and on buses.

By Métro

The métro, by far the quickest and most efficient way of getting around the city, runs from 5:30 AM until 1:15 AM (be careful—this means that the famous "last métro" can pass your station anytime after 12:30). Stations are recognizable either by a large yellow "M" within a circle or by their distinctive curly, green Art Nouveau railings and archway entrances bearing the full title (Métropolitain).

With 13 lines crisscrossing Paris and its environs, the métro is fairly easy to navigate. It is essential to know the name of the last station on the line you take, however, since this name appears on all signs. A connection (you can make as many as you like on one ticket) is called a *correspondance.* At junction stations, illuminated orange signs bearing the name of the line terminus appear over the correct corridors for *correspondance.* Illuminated blue signs marked *sortie* indicate the station exit. Some lines and stations in the less salubrious parts of Paris are a bit risky at night: lines 2 and 13 in particular. In general, however, the métro is safe throughout.

The métro network connects with the RER network at several points in Paris. RER trains, which race across Paris from suburb to suburb, are a sort of supersonic métro and can be great time-savers. All métro tickets and passes are valid for RER and bus travel within Paris. Tickets cost 7 francs each, and a *carnet* containing 10 tickets costs 41 francs). They can be bought in the métro and at most TABAC stands.

If you're staying for a week or more, the best deal is the weekly (*coupon jaune*) or monthly (*carte orange*) ticket, sold according to zone. Zones 1 and 2 cover the entire métro network; tickets cost 63 francs a week or 219 francs a month. If you plan to take suburban trains to visit places in the Ile-de-France, consider a four-zone (Versailles, St-Germain-en-Laye; 113 francs a week) or six-zone (Rambouillet, Fontainebleau; 150 francs a week) ticket. Weekly and monthly passes are available from rail and major métro stations. The monthly pass requires a passport-size photograph.

Alternatively, there are one-, three-, and five-day unlimited-travel tickets for the métro, bus, and RER (*Formule 1* and *Paris Visite*). The advantage is that unlike the *coupon jaune,* good from Monday morning to Sunday evening, the unlimited ticket is valid starting any day of the week and gives you discounts on a limited number of museums and tourist attractions. The prices are, respectively, 38, 95, and 150 francs for Paris only; 95, 210, and 285 francs for suburbs.

Access to métro and RER platforms is through an automatic ticket barrier. Slide your ticket in and pick it up as it pops up. Keep your ticket during your journey; you'll need it to leave the RER system.

By Bus

Paris buses are green and are marked with the route number and destination in front and major stopping places along the sides. Most routes operate from 6 AM to 8:30 PM; some continue until midnight. Ten *Noctambus,* or night buses, operate hourly (1 to 6 AM) between Châtelet and various nearby suburbs. The brown bus shelters, topped by red-and-yellow circular signs, contain timetables and route maps.

You can use your métro ticket on the buses, or you can buy a one-ride ticket on board. If you have individual tickets (as opposed to weekly or monthly tickets), state your destination and be prepared to punch one or more tickets in the red-and-gray machines on board the bus.

By Taxi

Paris taxis may not have the charm of their London counterparts—there is no standard vehicle or color—but they're cheaper. Daytime rates (7 AM to 7:30 PM) are around 2.80 francs per kilometer, and night-time rates are around 4.50 francs. There is a basic charge of 12 francs for all rides and a 6-franc charge per piece of luggage. Rates are about 40 percent higher in the suburbs than in the city. You are best off asking your hotel or restaurant to call for a taxi; cruising cabs can be hailed but are annoyingly difficult to spot. Note that taxis seldom take more than three people at a time.

By Bicycle

You can rent bikes in the Bois de Boulogne (Jardin d'Acclimatation), Bois de Vincennes, some RER stations, and from the Bateaux-Mouches embarkation point by place de l'Alma. Or try Paris-Vélo (2 rue du Fer-à-Moulin, 5e, ☎ 43–37–59–22). Rental rates vary from about 90 to 140 francs per day, 160 to 220 francs per weekend, and 420 to 500 francs per week. The 1,000 francs deposit per bike can be left on a credit card.

Guided Tours

Orientation

The two largest bus-tour operators are **Cityrama** (4 pl. des Pyramides, 1er, ☎ 44–55–61–00) and **Paris Vision** (214 rue de Rivoli, 1er, ☎ 42–60–31–25). Tours are generally in double-decker buses with either a live or a tape-recorded commentary (English is available) and last two hours. Expect to pay about 150 francs.

For a more intimate—albeit expensive—tour of the city, **Cityrama** also runs several minibus excursions per day. The bus can take eight people and can pick up or drop off at hotels. Cost is 210 francs for a two-hour tour, 350 francs for three hours. Make reservations through **Cityrama** or the tourist office.

The **RATP** (Paris Transport Authority) has many guide-accompanied excursions in and around Paris. Inquire at its Tourist Service Board (pl. de la Madeleine, 8e, ☎ 40–06–71–45) or at its office (53 quai des Grands-Augustins, 6e, ☎ 40–46–41–41). *See* Guided Tours *in* Chapter 3.

For sightseeing at your own pace, take **Paris Bus,** a red double-decker with nine pick-up and drop-off points around Paris. Tours start from Trocadero at 10:20 AM and every 50 minutes until 5. Tickets are good for two days and cost 120 francs for adults, 60 francs for children under 12.

Special-Interest

Cityrama and **Paris Vision** offer a variety of theme tours ("Historic Paris," "Modern Paris," "Paris by Night") lasting from 2½ hours to all day and costing 150 to 450 francs (more if admission to a cabaret show is included).

Hour-long **boat trips** on the Seine are a must for the first-time visitor. Some boats serve lunch and dinner; make reservations in advance. The following services operate regularly: **Bateaux-Mouches** leaves from Pont de l'Alma (Right Bank, 8e, ☎ 42–25–96–10); **Vedettes du Pont-Neuf** leaves from Square du Vert Galant (Ile de la Cité, 1er, ☎ 46–33–98–38); **Bateaux Parisiens-Tour Eiffel** departs from Pont d'Iéna (Left Bank, 7e, ☎ 47–05–50–00), and **Canauxrama** (☎ 42–39–15–00) organizes half- and full-day barge tours along picturesque canals in east Paris (departures from 5 bis quai de la Loire, 19e, or from Bassin de l'Arsenal, 12e, opposite 50 blvd. de la Bastille).

Walking

There are plenty of guided tours of specific areas of Paris, often concentrating on a historical or architectural topic—"Restored Mansions of the Marais," for instance, or "Private Walled Gardens in St-Germain." The guides are enthusiastic and dedicated, though not always English-speaking. Charges range from 40 francs to 60 francs, and tours last about two hours. Details are published in the weekly magazines *Pariscope* and *L'Officiel des Spectacles* under "Conférences." You can sometimes make reservations for walking tours organized by the **Caisse Nationale des Monuments Historiques,** Bureau des Visites/Conférences (Hôtel de Sully, 62 rue St-Antoine, 4e, ☎ 44–61–20–00).

Bike

Paris by Cycle (78 rue de l'Ouest 14e, ☎ 40–47–08–04) organizes daily bike tours around Paris and the environs (Versailles, Chantilly, and Fontainebleau) for about 220 francs, 120 francs for bike rental.

Personal Guides

Espace Limousines (18 rue Vignon, 9e, ☎ 42–65–63–16) has guides with luxury cars or minibuses (holding up to seven passengers) who will take you around Paris and the environs for a minimum of three hours. Reservations are required, and the cost is about 250 francs per hour.

Important Addresses and Numbers

Embassies

U.S. (2 av. Gabriel, 8e, ☎ 42–96–12–02), **Canada** (35 av. Montaigne, 8e, ☎ 44–43–29–00), and **U.K.** (35 rue du Fbg. St-Honoré, 8e, ☎ 42–66–91–42).

Emergencies

Police (☎ 17), **ambulance** (☎ 15 or 45–67–50–50), **doctor** (☎ 43–37–77–77), and **dentist** (☎ 43–37–51–00).

English-Language Bookstores

If you need some English reading matter try **W.H. Smith** (248 rue de Rivoli, 1er, ☎ 42–60–37–97), **Galignani** (224 rue de Rivoli, 1er, ☎ 42–60–76–07), **Brentano's** (37 av. de l'Opéra, 2e, ☎ 42–61–52–50), and **Shakespeare and Co.** (37 rue de la Bûcherie, 5e).

Hospitals

The **American Hospital** (63 blvd. Victor-Hugo, Neuilly, ☎ 47–45–71–00) has a 24-hour emergency service.

The **Hertford British Hospital** (3 rue Barbès, Levallois-Perret, ☎ 47–58–13–12) also offers a 24-hour service.

Pharmacies

Pharmacie des Champs-Elysées (Galerie des Champs, 84 av. des Champs-Elysées, 8e, ☎ 45–62–02–41), open 24 hours; **Drugstore** (corner of blvd. St-Germain and rue de Rennes, 6e), open daily until 2 AM; **Pharmacie des Arts** (106 blvd. Montparnasse, 14e), open daily until midnight.

Travel Agencies

American Express (11 rue Scribe, 9e, ☎ 47–77–70–00), **Air France** (119 av. des Champs-Elysées, 8e, ☎ 44–08–24–24), and **Wagon-Lits** (32 rue du Quatre-Septembre, 2e, ☎ 42–66–15–80).

Visitor Information

There is the main Paris tourist office (127 av. des Champs-Elysées, 8e, ☎ 49–52–53–54; open daily 9 AM–8 PM; closed Christmas Day and New Year's Day) and branches at all mainline train stations, except Gare St-Lazare. Dial 49–52–53–56 for recorded information in English.

3 Ile de France

*Versailles, Chartres,
Fontainebleau*

PARIS IS small as capital cities go, with just over 2 million inhabitants. The Paris region, however, contains more than 10 million people—almost one-fifth of France's entire population. That type of statistic conjures up visions of a gray, never-ending suburban sprawl. Nothing could be farther from the truth.

The official name for the region sets the tone. "Ile de France" has a poetic ring to it; there is no island here, but the region is figuratively isolated from the rest of France by the three rivers—the Seine, Oise, and Marne—that weave majestic, meandering circles around its limits.

The broad, ambling waters of those rivers, along with a network of brooks and streams, serves to defend the area and make it lush. This precious combination has always enticed settlers; an entire country was to spring from the Ile de France fountainhead. Indeed, the kings and clerics who ruled the medieval roost refused to be sequestered in Paris: Castles and palaces went up in the towns of Vincennes, St-Germain-en-Laye, and Provins; abbeys and cathedrals sprang skyward in Chartres, Senlis, and Royaumont.

The Ile de France never lost favor with the powerful, partly because its many forests—large chunks of which still stand—harbored sufficient game for even bloated, cosseted monarchs to achieve a regular kill. First Fontainebleau, in humane Renaissance proportions, then Versailles, on a minion-crushing, Baroque scale, reflected the royal desire to transform hunting lodges into palatial residences.

The 17th century was a time of prodigious building in the Ile de France—a period that bequeathed a vast array of important sights to admire and explore. The château, gardens, and well-preserved town of Versailles should not be overlooked. But do not neglect Versailles's slightly lesser neighbors; Vaux-le-Vicomte, Dampierre, Rambouillet, and Chantilly would bask in superstar status anywhere else. And, after the crowds of Versailles in midsummer, you will welcome the relative tranquillity of these smaller châteaus.

Euro Disney opened in 1992 to an explosion of fanfare and anticipation which, unfortunately, has faded away. The powers at Disney situated their theme park poorly, 32 kilometers (20 miles) east of Paris, a convenient but rather cold location, and, as the resort's dismal financial returns show, they overestimated the Disney draw. In 1995, after renaming the site Disneyland Paris, they reduced admission prices to halt the slide.

On the whole, however, the architectural impact of the 20th century is discreet in the Ile de France, and you may find it disorienting that so many rural backwaters exist within 30 minutes' drive of the capital. There is no miracle involved with this, however, just some commonsensical forethought: With the Gallic mania for centralized planning, new developments are assigned to restricted areas. Students of modern architecture may find food for thought in such so-called new towns as Cergy-Pontoise or St-Quentin-en-Yvelines (near Versailles), and sociologists won't lack material in the concrete ghettos of the "red belt" north of Paris (so called because its working-class population traditionally votes communist), but the average visitor can comfortably avoid them.

EXPLORING

Numbers in the margin correspond to points of interest on the Ile de France and Versailles maps.

Orientation

Our four tours take you east to Marne-la-Vallée and Disneyland, southeast to Fontainebleau, north to Chantilly, and west—the most favored point on the regional touring compass—to Versailles, Chartres, and Giverny. We have occasionally transgressed the administrative limits of Ile de France along the way.

Tour 1: West to Versailles, Chartres, Giverny, and Thoiry

No visit to Paris is complete without an excursion to Versailles—easy to reach either by train (*see* Getting Around in Essential Information, *above*) or car (A13 expressway from Porte d'Auteuil) in about 25 minutes. On this tour, however, Versailles is only the starting point for a trip through the west of the Ile de France, a region of forests, wheat fields, lush valleys, and imposing châteaus.

If, after days of museum lines and crowded métros, you feel a sense of escape as you leave Paris, you won't be the first. Back in the 17th century, Louis XIV, the Sun King, no sooner had a firm grip on the throne than he cast his cantankerous royal eye over the Ile de France in search

❶ of a new power base. Marshy, inhospitable **Versailles,** 24 kilometers (15 miles) to the west of Paris, was the place of his dreams. Down came his father's modest royal hunting lodge and up, up, and along went the new château.

★ ❷ Today the **château** of Versailles seems outrageously big—but it wasn't nearly big enough for the army of 20,000 noblemen, servants, and hangers-on who moved in with Louis. A new capital had to be constructed from scratch. Tough-thinking town planners dreamed up vast avenues broader than the Champs-Élysées—all in bicep-flexing Baroque.

It is hardly surprising that Louis XIV's successors soon felt out of sync with their architectural inheritance. Louis XV, who inherited the throne from the Sun King in 1715, transformed the royal apartments into places to live rather than pose in. The unfortunate Louis XVI—reigning monarch at the time of the French Revolution—cowered in the Petit Trianon in the leafy depths of Versailles's gardens, out of the mighty château's shadow. His queen, Marie-Antoinette, had lost her head well before her trip to the guillotine in 1793, pretending to be a peasant shepherdess amid the ersatz rusticity of her oh-so-cute Potemkin hamlet.

The château was built by architects Louis Le Vau and Jules Hardouin-Mansart between 1662 and 1690. Enter through the gilt iron gates from the huge place d'Armes. On the first floor of the château, right in the middle as you approach across the sprawling cobbled forecourt, is Louis XIV's bedchamber. The two wings were occupied by the royal children and princes of the blood, with courtiers making do in the attics.

The highlight for many on a visit to the palace is the **Galerie des Glaces** (Hall of Mirrors), fully restored to sparkling glory. It was here, after France's capitulation, that Prince Otto von Bismarck proclaimed the unified German Empire in 1871 and here, too, that the controversial Treaty of Versailles, asserting Germany's responsibility for World War I, was signed in 1919.

The **Grands Appartements** (State Rooms) that flank the Hall of Mirrors retain much of their original Baroque decoration: gilt stucco, painted ceilings, and marble sculpture. Perhaps the most extravagant of these rooms is the **Salon d'Apollon,** the former throne room, dedicated to the sun god Apollo, Louis XIV's mythical hero. Equally interesting are the **Petits Appartements,** where the royal family and friends lived in (relative) privacy.

In the north wing of the château can be found the solemn white-and-gold **chapel,** designed by J. H.-Mansart and completed in 1710; the intimate **opera house,** the first oval hall in France, built by J.A. Gabriel for Louis XV in 1770; and, connecting the two, the 17th-century **Galleries,** with exhibits retracing the château's history. The south wing contains the majestically proportioned **Galerie des Batailles** (Gallery of Battles), lined with gigantic canvases extolling French military glory. ☛ *40 frs adults, 26 frs students and senior citizens. ☉ Tues.–Sun. 9–6:30, 9–5:30 in winter. Galerie des Glaces: 9:45–5; Opéra Royal 9:45–3:30 (tours every 15 min.).*

★ After the awesome feast of interior decor, the **park** outside is an ideal place to catch your breath. The gardens were designed by the French landscape architect Lenôtre, whose work here represents classical French landscaping at its most formal and sophisticated. The 250-acre grounds include woods, lawns, flower beds, statues, artificial lakes, and fountains galore. They are at their golden-leafed best in the fall but are also enticing in summer—especially on Sundays when the fountains are in full flow. They become a spectacle of rare grandeur during the **Fêtes de Nuit** floodlighting and fireworks shows held in July and September. ☉ *Grounds daily,* ☎ *39–50–36–22 for details of the Fêtes de Nuit.* ☛ *20 frs Sun., May–Sept., free other times.*

If you wander too far into the park woods, you can easily get lost. Follow signs to skirt the numerous basins (or ponds) until you reach the **Grand Canal.** Move down the right bank, along gravelly paths beneath high-plinthed statues, until you discover that the canal is in the form of a cross—with two smaller arms known as the **Petit Canal.** At the crossing, bear right toward the Grand Trianon (in all, about a mile from the château).

❸ The **Grand Trianon,** built by Mansart in 1687, is a scaled-down, pink-marble pleasure palace now used to entertain visiting heads of state. When it is not in use, the palace is open so that visitors can admire its lavish interior and early 19th-century furniture. ☛ *21 frs adults, 14 frs students and senior citizens. ☉ Oct.–Apr., Tues.–Sun. 10–5:30; May–Sept., Tues.–Sun. 10–6:30.*

❹ The **Petit Trianon,** close by, was built in the neoclassical style by architect Gabriel in 1768. It is a mansion, not a palace, and is modest by Versailles standards—though still sumptuously furnished. It contains mementos of its most illustrious inhabitant, Marie-Antoinette. Look for her initials wrought into the iron railings of the main staircase. ☛ *12 frs adults, 8 frs students and senior citizens. ☉ Hours same as for Grand Trianon.*

Beyond the Petit Trianon and across the Petit Lac, which looks more like a stream as it describes a wriggly semicircle, is the queen's so-called ❺ hamlet (**Hameau**). With its watermill, genuine lake (Grand Lac), and pigeon loft, this make-believe village is outrageously pretty; it was here that Marie-Antoinette lived out her romanticized dreams of peasant life.

Ile de France

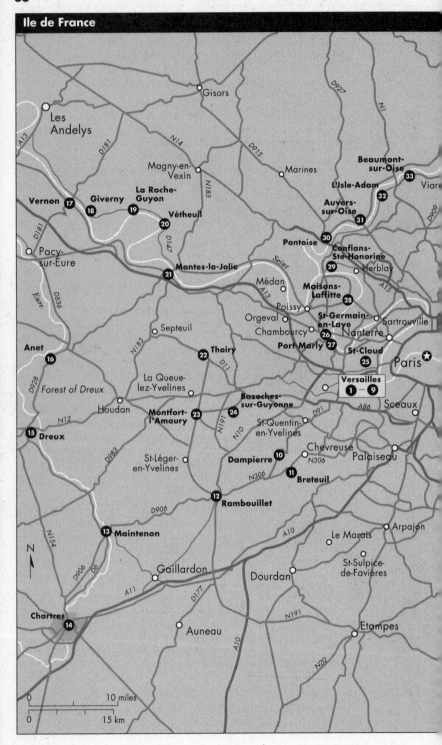

Gisors

Les Andelys

Magny-en-Vexin

Marines

Beaumont-sur-Oise 33

L'Isle-Adam 32

Viar

Vernon 17

Giverny 18

La Roche-Guyon 19

Vétheuil 20

Auvers-sur-Oise 31

Pacy-sur-Eure

Mantes-la-Jolie 21

Pontoise 30

Conflans-Ste-Honorine 29

Herblay

Médan

Maisons-Laffitte 28

Poissy

St-Germain-en-Laye

Sartrouville

Septeuil

Orgeval

Chambourcy 26

Nanterre

Anet 16

Thoiry 22

Port-Marly 27

St-Cloud 25

Paris

La Queue-lez-Yvelines

Bazoches-sur-Guyonne 24

Versailles 1 — 9

Sceaux

Houdan

Montfort-l'Amaury 23

St-Quentin-en-Yvelines

Chevreuse

Palaiseau

Dreux 15

St-Léger-en-Yvelines

Dampierre 10

Breteuil 11

Rambouillet 12

Maintenon 13

Gaillardon

Dourdan

Le Marais

Arpajon

St-Sulpice-de-Favières

Chartres 14

Auneau

Etampes

Forest of Dreux

Seine

0   10 miles

0   15 km

N

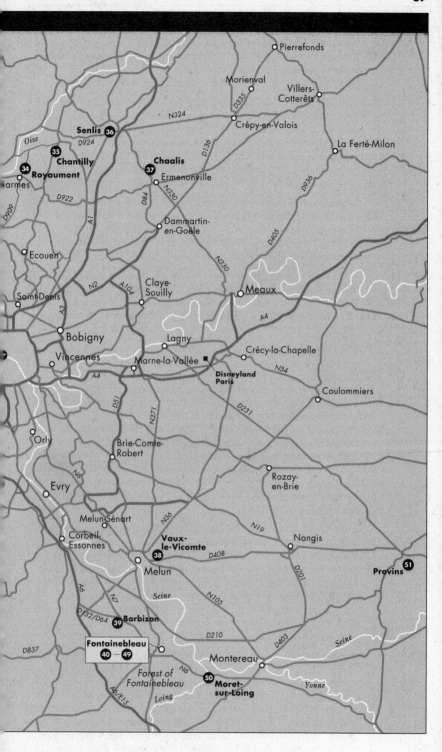

The town of Versailles is attractive, and its broad, leafy boulevards make **(6)** agreeable places for strolling. Facing the château are the **royal stables,** buildings of regal dimensions and aspect. Take avenue de Sceaux, to **(7)** the right, and turn left onto rue de Satory, which leads to the **Cathédrale St-Louis,** an austere edifice built between 1743 and 1754 by Mansart's grandson, with notable paintings and an organ loft.

Turn right out of the cathedral, then left down avenue Thiers, which cuts through the town's three major boulevards—avenues de Sceaux, de Paris, and de St-Cloud—to the ancient market square, where rue **(8)** de la Paroisse heads left to the **Eglise Notre-Dame.** This sturdy Baroque monument was built from 1684 to 1686 (and is therefore older than the cathedral) by Mansart, who is buried here, as parish church for the Sun King's new town. Louis XIV himself laid the foundation stone.

Behind the church, in an imposing 18th-century mansion on boulevard **(9)** de la Reine, is the **Musée Lambinet,** a museum with a wide-ranging collection—a maze of cozy, finely furnished rooms replete with paintings, weapons, fans, and porcelain. *54 blvd. de la Reine,* ☎ *39–50–30–32.* ☛ *19 frs adults, 13 frs students and senior citizens.* ⊙ *Tues.–Sun. 2–6.*

The fast N10 heads down from Versailles to another famous château town—Rambouillet (*see below*). But if you're in no rush, take the attractive D91 south from Versailles through the glades and folds of the **(10)** Chevreuse Valley to the unspoiled village of **Dampierre,** 18 kilometers (11 miles) away.

The **château** of Dampierre is a handsome stone-and-brick structure, surrounded by a moat and set 100 yards back from the road behind 18th-century iron railings. Rebuilt in the 1670s by J. H.-Mansart for the duc de Luynes, it is still the family seat. Much of the interior has kept its 17th-century decoration—portraits, wood paneling, furniture, and works of art. But the main staircase, with its trompe l'oeil murals, and the richly gilded Salle des Fêtes date from the last century. The Salle des Fêtes, on the second floor, contains a huge wall painting by the celebrated artist Jean-Auguste Ingres (1780–1867): a mythical evocation of the Age d'Or (Golden Age). The large park was designed by Le Nôtre. ☎ *30–52–53–24.* ☛ *46 frs adults, 28 frs children over 7 and senior citizens. Grounds only: 28 frs, 20 frs.* ⊙ *Apr.–Oct., Mon.–Sat. 2–6, Sun. 11–noon and 2–6.*

From Dampierre take D58 (signposted to Chevreuse) for 2½ kilometers (1½ miles) before forking off toward N306. A couple of miles farther south (follow signs), close to the village of Choisel, is the steep-roofed **(11)** château of **Breteuil.** Like the Luynes of Dampierre, the Breteuil family have owned and lived in their château since the early 17th century. And, like the Panouses of Thoiry (*see below*), they have been innovative in their attempts to woo visitors: Life-size wax figures—including the English King Edward VII and one-time guest Marcel Proust, the French novelist (1871–1922)—lurk in many of the rooms.

Interior highlights range from Swedish porcelain to Gobelin tapestries and a richly inlaid Teschen table, encrusted with pearls and precious stones—an 18th-century present to the Breteuils from Austrian empress Maria Theresa. The basement kitchens contain a gleaming array of copper pots and pewterware, while the vast wooded park offers picnic areas and playgrounds. ☎ *30–52–05–02.* ☛ *(château and grounds): 48 frs adults, 36 frs children and senior citizens.* ☛ *(grounds): 28 frs, 20 frs.* ⊙ *Château Mon.–Sat. 2:30–6, Sun. 11–6); grounds daily 10–6.*

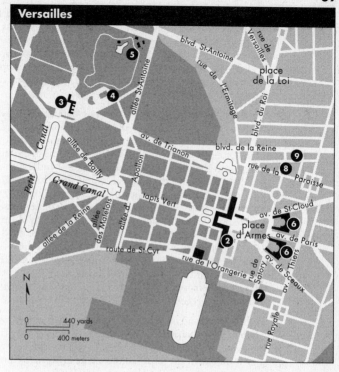

Versailles

⑫ Get back onto N306 and head southwest to **Rambouillet,** 14 kilometers (9 miles) away and surrounded by a magnificent 30,000-acre forest (reason enough for hikers and bikers to plan an excursion out this way). Rambouillet is a haughty town, once favored by kings and dukes. Today it is home to affluent gentry and, occasionally, the French president. When he's not entertaining visiting bigwigs, the château and its grounds are open to all.

Leave your car in the spacious parking lot next to the **Hôtel de Ville** (town hall), an imposing Classical building in red brick, and wander around the corner to the **château.** Most of the buildings you see date from the early 18th century, but the muscular **Tour François I** (Tower of François I), named after the king who breathed his last therein in 1547, once belonged to a 14th-century castle. ☞ *Grounds free; château (guided tours only): 28 frs.* ✆ *Wed.–Mon. 10–11:30 and 2–4:30 (until 5:30 Apr.–Sept.).*

If your appetite for château interiors has already been satisfied, you'll be able to forgo Rambouillet's without feeling too guilty. The château's exterior charms are hidden as you arrive, but if you head to the left of the buildings—and if nature is in bloom—you are in for two pleasant surprises. A splendid lake, with several enticing islands, spreads out for you, beckoning you to explore the extensive grounds beyond. Before you do, however, turn around: There, behind you, across trim flower beds awash with color, is the facade of the château—a sight of unsuspected serenity, asymmetry, and, as more flowers spill from its balconies, cheerful informality.

If time allows, veer left around the lake and carry on until you reach two interesting groups of outbuildings: the **Laiterie de la Reine** (built as a dairy for Marie-Antoinette), with its small temple, grotto, and shell-lined **Chaumière des Coquillages** (Shell Pavilion); and the **Bergerie Nationale** (National Sheepfold), site of a more serious agricultural venture. The merino sheep reared here, prized for the quality and yield of their wool, are descendants of beasts imported from Spain by Louis XVI in 1786. ☛ *14 frs (Laiterie), 21 frs (Bergerie).* ☉ *Laiterie Wed.–Mon. 10–11:30 and 2–4:30 (until 4 in winter). The Bergerie can be visited Fri.–Sun. 2–5 (Oct.–June Sun. only, 2–5).*

⑬ D906 links Rambouillet to the town of **Maintenon,** 24 kilometers (15 miles) west. The Renaissance **château** of Maintenon once belonged to Louis XIV's mistress (and future morganatic spouse), Madame de Maintenon, whose private apartments form the hub of the short interior visit. A round brick tower (16th century) and a 12th-century keep are all that remain of the buildings on the site. The formal gardens ease their way back from the château to the unlikely ivy-covered arches of a ruined aqueduct, one of the Sun King's most outrageous projects. His aim: to provide the ornamental lakes in the gardens of Versailles (some 50 kilometers, or 30 miles, away) with water from the River Eure. In 1684, 30,000 men were signed up to construct a three-tiered, 5-kilometer (3-mile) aqueduct as part of the project. Many died of fever in the process, and construction was called off in 1689. ☛ *28 frs adults, 22 frs students and senior citizens.* ☉ *Apr.–Oct., Wed.–Mon. 2–6, Nov.–Mar., weekends only 2–5. Closed Jan.*

⑭ The River Eure, accompanied by picturesque D6, snakes southwest from Maintenon to **Chartres,** 19 kilometers (12 miles) away. Try to spot the **★** noble, soaring spires of **Chartres Cathedral** before you reach the town; they form one of the most famous sights in Western Europe.

Worship on the site of the cathedral goes back to before the Gallo-Roman period; the crypt contains a well that was the focus of Druid ceremonies. In the late 9th century, Charles II (known as the Bald) presented Chartres with what was believed to be the tunic of the Virgin, a precious relic that attracted hordes of pilgrims. Chartres swiftly became a prime destination for the Christian faithful; pilgrims trek here from Paris to this day.

Today's cathedral dates primarily from the 12th and 13th centuries, having been built after the previous, 11th-century edifice burned down in 1194. A well-chronicled outburst of religious fervor followed the discovery that the Virgin's relic had miraculously survived unsinged, and reconstruction moved ahead at a breathtaking pace: Just 25 years were needed for the cathedral to rise from the rubble.

The lower half of the facade is a survivor of the earlier Romanesque church: This can be seen most clearly in the use of round arches rather than the pointed Gothic type. The main door (**Portail Royal**) is richly sculpted with scenes from the Life of Christ, and the flanking towers are also Romanesque. The taller of the two spires (380 feet versus 350 feet) dates from the start of the 16th century; its fanciful Flamboyant intricacy contrasts sharply with the stumpy solemnity of its Romanesque counterpart across the way. The **rose window** above the main portal dates from the 13th century, while the three windows below it contain some of the finest examples of 12th-century stained glass in France.

The interior is somber, and your eyes will need time to adjust to the dimness. The reward: the gemlike richness of the stained glass, with the famous deep "Chartres blue" predominating. The oldest window is arguably the most beautiful: **Notre-Dame de la Belle Verrière,** in the south choir. The cathedral's windows are being gradually cleaned—a lengthy, painstaking program—and the contrast with those still covered in the grime of centuries is staggering. *Pl. Notre-Dame.*

Just behind the cathedral stands the **Musée des Beaux-Arts** (Museum of Fine Arts), a handsome 18th-century building that used to be the Bishop's Palace. Its varied collection includes Renaissance enamels; a portrait of the Dutch scholar Erasmus by German painter Hans Holbein; tapestries; armor; and some fine paintings, mainly French, dating from the 17th to the 19th century. There is also an entire room devoted to the forceful 20th-century land- and snowscapes of Maurice de Vlaminck, who lived in the region. *29 cloître Notre-Dame.* ☎ *10 frs adults (20 frs for special exhibitions in summer only), 7 frs students and senior citizens.* ☉ *Nov.–Mar., Wed.–Mon. 10–noon and 2–5; Apr.–Oct., Wed.–Mon. 10–6.*

The **museum gardens** overlook the old streets that tumble down to the River Eure. Take rue Chantault down to the river, cross over, and head right along rue de la Tannerie (which, in turn, becomes rue de la Foulerie) as far as rue du Pont St-Hilaire. From here, there is a picturesque view of the roofs of old Chartres nestling beneath the cathedral. Cross over the bridge and head up to the Gothic **Eglise St-Pierre,** whose magnificent windows date to the early 14th century. There is more stained glass (17th century) to admire at the **Eglise St-Aignan** nearby, just off rue St-Pierre. Wander at will among the steep, narrow surrounding streets, using the spires of the cathedral as your guiding landmark.

⑮ Thirty-two kilometers (20 miles) north of Chartres (via N154) is the charming and ancient town of **Dreux.** The downtown area has several old houses and monuments, notably the **Eglise St-Pierre** on place Métézeau, and the **Beffroi** (Belfry) just across the road. St-Pierre, an interesting jumble of styles with good stained glass and a 17th-century organ loft, presents a curious silhouette, with its unfinished classical towers cut off in midcolumn. The Beffroi, standing at one end of a lively shopping square, is a hefty tower built between 1512 and 1531; though there is a fine view from the top, the tower is closed for extensive restorations.

Dreux was a prosperous place in the 16th century—it was awarded the title of Royal Borough in 1556—but the early 19th century conferred lasting glory on the town. In 1816, the Orléans family, France's ruling house from 1830 to 1848, began the construction of a chapel-mausoleum on the hill behind the center of town. The circular chapel, known as the **Chapelle Royale de St-Louis,** is built in sugary but not unappealing neo-Gothic: Superficial ornament rather than structure recalls the medieval style. Unfortunately, the sumptuously decorated interior can be visited only with a French-speaking guide, but no linguistic explanations are needed to prompt wonder at either the Sèvres-manufactured "stained glass"—thin layers of glass coated with painted enamel (an extremely rare, fragile, and vivid technique)—or the funereal statuary. Some of the tombs—an imploring hand reaching through a window to a loved one or an infant wrapped in a cloak of transparent gauze—may evoke morbid sentimentality, but their technical skill and compositional drama belie sculpture's reputation as one of the fustier visual arts. *Rue de Billy.* ☎ *30 frs.* ☉ *Feb.–Dec., daily 9–11:30 and 2:30–5 (4 in winter).*

⑯ D928 runs straight through the **Forest of Dreux** to the tiny village of **Anet,** 16 kilometers (10 miles) to the north. Only picturesque ruins now remain of what was reputedly the finest **château** of the French Renaissance, begun in 1548 for Henri II's mistress Diane de Poitiers. Her bedchamber can be visited in the Left Wing, the finest surviving building with its 17th-century **Escalier d'Honneur** (Grand Staircase) and tapestries in the **Salle des Gardes** (Guard Room), depicting the adventures of the huntress Diana. The chapel is of note, thanks to its 16th-century dome, one of the earliest in France. As you enter the grounds, look up at the tympanum over the gate to admire the cast of Benvenuto Cellini's *Nymph with a Stag* (the original is now in the Louvre). ☎ *16/37–41– 90–07.* ☛ *35 frs.* ☉ *Apr.–Oct., Mon.–Sat. 2:30–6:30, Sun. 10–11:30 and 2:30–6:30; Nov.–Mar., Mon.–Sat. 2–5, Sun. 10–11:30 and 2–5.*

From Anet, keep to the road that winds along the River Eure (D836) and follow signs north to Pacy-sur-Eure, 24 kilometers (15 miles) away. Here D181 heads off to the old town of **Vernon,** 13 kilometers (8 miles) distant. Together with its pleasant riverside location on the Seine, Vernon boasts several medieval timber-frame houses; the best of these has been chosen by local authorities to house the Tourist Office, in rue Carnot. Alongside is the arresting rose-windowed facade of **Notre-Dame** church. The facade, like the high nave, dates from the 15th century, but the rounded Romanesque arches in the choir attest to the building's 12th-century origins. The church is a fine sight when viewed from behind—Impressionist painter Claude Monet painted it several times from across the Seine.

A few minor Monet canvases, along with other late-19th-century paintings, can be admired in the **Musée Poulain** (Town Museum) at the other end of rue Carnot. This rambling old mansion is seldom crowded, and the helpful curators are happy to explain local history to visitors who are intrigued by the town's English-sounding name. *Rue du Pont,* ☎ *16/32–21–28–09.* ☛ *15 frs.* ☉ *Tues.–Sun. 2–6.*

Most people stop off at Vernon simply because of its proximity to the village of **Giverny** across the Seine (turn right along D5 after the bridge). A place of pilgrimage for art lovers, this was the village in which Claude Monet lived during the second half of his life and died in 1926 at age 86. After decades of neglect, his pretty pink-washed house, with its green shutters; studios; and, above all, the wonderful garden with its famous lily pond, have been lovingly restored.

Monet was brought up in Normandy, in northwestern France, and, like many of the Impressionists, was stimulated by the soft light of the Seine Valley. After several years at Argenteuil, just north of Paris, he moved downriver to Giverny in 1883, along with his two sons, mistress Alice Hoschedé (whom he later married), and her own six children. By 1890, a prospering Monet was able to buy the house outright; three years later, he purchased another plot of land across the road to continue his gardening experiments, diverting the little River Epte to make a pond.

Soon the much-loved and oft-painted waterlilies and Japanese bridges were special features of Monet's garden. They readily conjure up the image of the grizzle-bearded painter dabbing cheerfully at his canvas— pioneering a breakup of form that would have a major impact on 20th-century art.

Provided you steer clear of the tourist battalions that tramp through Giverny on weekends and hot summer days, Monet's house—which you enter from the modest country lane that masquerades as Giverny's major thoroughfare—feels refreshingly like a family home, after the formal French châteaus. The rooms have been restored to Monet's original designs: the kitchen with its blue tiles, the buttercup-yellow dining room, Monet's bedroom containing his bed and desk. Walls are lined with the Japanese prints he avidly collected, as well as with reproductions of his works.

The exuberant **garden** breaks totally with French tradition, with flowers spilling over the paths. You can reach the enchanting **water garden,** with its lilies, bridges, mighty willow, and rhododendrons, via an attractively decorated tunnel. *84 rue Claude-Monet,* ☎ *16/32–51–28–21.* ☛ *35 frs (garden only, 24 frs).* ☉ *Apr.–Oct., Tues.–Sun. 10–noon and 2–6 (garden open 10–6).*

Close by is the **Musée Américain,** opened in 1993 and endowed by Chicago art patrons Daniel and Judith Terra. On view are works by American Impressionists influenced by Claude Monet. *99 rue Claude-Monet,* ☎ *16/32–51–94–65.* ☛ *32 frs adults; 21 frs children, students, and senior citizens.* ☉ *Apr.–Oct., Tues.–Sun. 10–6.*

South of Giverny, the French road network has difficulty matching the extravagant bends of the meandering Seine. If you follow the signs to Mantes, you will next encounter the river at the charming village of
⑲ **La Roche-Guyon,** dominated by chalky cliffs and its Classical **château.**

⑳ A few miles farther, just after the tumbling village of **Vétheuil,** with its
12th-century church, the road (now D147) again abandons the river-
㉑ bank until it reaches prettily named **Mantes-la-Jolie,** these days a sullen suburban town but once favored by 19th-century landscape artist Camille Corot. Corot would set up his easel within sight of the town's principal attraction, the vast 12th-century church of **Notre-Dame,** with a twin-towered facade strikingly similar to that of Notre-Dame in Paris. The small, circular windows that ring the east end are a rare local characteristic; you may have noticed them at the church of nearby Vétheuil. (There are other attractive medieval churches upriver at Poissy and Orgeval.)

N183 runs 13 kilometers (8 miles) south of Mantes to Septeuil, where we suggest that you head east along D11 (follow signs to Versailles)
★ ㉒ to **Thoiry,** 9 kilometers (5½ miles) away.

The **château** of Thoiry, just 40 kilometers (25 miles) west of Paris, makes an excellent day outing in its own right, especially if you are traveling with children. Owners Vicomte de La Panouse and his American wife, Annabelle, have restored the château and park, opening both to the public. The result is a splendid combination of history, culture, and adventure. The superbly furnished 16th-century château has archive and gastronomy museums and overlooks a safari park, where you can picnic with the bears and lions.

The château was built in 1564. Its handsome Renaissance facade is set off by gardens landscaped in typically disciplined French fashion by Lenôtre. The discipline has unexpected justification: The château is positioned to be directly in line with the sun as it sets in the west at the winter solstice (December 21) and as it rises in the east at the summer solstice (June 21). Heightening the effect, the central part of the château appears to be a transparent arch of light, owing to its huge glass doors and windows.

The viscountess is a keen gardener and enjoys experimenting in the less formal **Jardin à l'Anglaise** (English Garden), where cricket is played on weekend afternoons during the summer, and in her late-flowering **Autumn Garden.** Visitors are allowed to wander at leisure, although few dare stray from the official footpath through the **animal reserve!** Note that the parts of the reserve that contain the wilder beasts—deer, zebra, camels, hippos, bears, elephants, and lions—can be visited only by car.

The reserve hit the headlines when the first-ever ligrons—a cross between a lion and a tiger—were born here a few years ago. These new-look beasts (bigger than either a lion or a tiger) are now in their second generation and can be seen from the safety of a raised footbridge in the **Tiger Park.** Nearby, as emus and flamingos stalk in search of tidbits, a **children's play area** features an Enchanted Burrow to wriggle through and a huge netted Cobweb to bounce around in.

Highlights of the château's interior include the **Grand Staircase,** with its 18th-century Gobelins tapestries, and the **Green** and **White salons,** with their antique painted harpsichord and portraits, and the **Salon de la Tapisserie,** with its monumental Don Quixote tapestry bearing the blood-curdling arms (three severed raven's heads) of former owner Machault d'Arnouville. An authentic, homey, faintly faded charm pervades these rooms, especially when log fires crackle in their enormous hearths on damp afternoons.

The distinguished history of the Panouse family—a Comte César even fought in the American Revolution—is retraced in the **Archive Museum,** where papal bulls and Napoleonic letters mingle with missives from Thomas Jefferson and Benjamin Franklin.

The château pantries house a **Museum of Gastronomy,** whose tempting display of *pièces montées*—virtuoso banquet showpieces—recreate the designs of famed 19th-century chef Antoine Carême. Early recipe books, engravings, and old copper pots are also displayed. ☎ *34–87–52–25.* ☞ *Château 30 frs adults, 25 frs children; animal reserve plus gardens 95 frs adults, 75 frs children. ⊙ Easter–Oct., weekdays 10–6, weekends 10–6:30; Nov.–Easter, weekdays 10–5, weekends 10–5:30.*

㉓ From Thoiry, continue briefly along D11 south, then turn right on D76 to **Montfort-l'Amaury,** 11 kilometers (7 miles) away. With its twisting, narrow streets clustered around an old church, whose bulky Renaissance tower dominates the town square, Montfort is, in property jargon, one of the most desirable places to live in the Ile de France. The composer Maurice Ravel must have thought so; he lived here from 1921 until his death in 1937. His tiny house has been reconstituted with many of his souvenirs and furnishings (including his piano), and you can explore the "Japanese" garden where he composed his famous *Bolero* in 1928. *Le Belvédère, rue Maurice-Ravel,* ☎ *34–86–00–89.* ☞ *21 frs adults, 11 frs children. ⊙ Mon.–Thur. 2–5, weekends 10–noon and 2–5.*

㉔ Take D13 east from Montfort to **Bazoches-sur-Guyonne,** 5 kilometers (3 miles) away, to visit the home of another famous man: politician Jean Monnet, often known as the Father of Europe, who is said to have conceived the idea of a European Community in 1950, shortly after moving into this attractive, thatched house, where he lived until his death in 1979 (he was accorded the supreme state accolade of burial in the Paris Panthéon). His Bazoches retreat (now owned by the European Parliament), where Monnet hobnobbed with world leaders, displays information on the present European Union, Monnet mementos, and a film on his life and ideas—all in more than 10 different languages, in time-honored Eurocrat tradition. *Houjarray,* ☎ *34–86–12–43.* ☞ *Free. ⊙ Wed.–Sun. 2–6.*

TIME OUT The area west of Paris is littered with châteaus, and there are two more close to Bazoches: at Pontchartrain (visible from afar but not open to the public) and in the neighboring village of **Le Tremblay-sur-Mauldre,** where you can lunch or dine in style at a 17th-century château converted into a top-ranking hotel-restaurant (*see* Dining, *below*).

Return to D11 and follow the signs back to Paris.

Tour 2: North to St-Germain-en-Laye and Chantilly

Although this second Ile de France tour explores the north of the region, we suggest that you again leave Paris by the A13 from Porte d'Auteuil. A spectacular curving bridge soon whisks you across the Seine, **25** past the chic suburb of **St-Cloud.** To the right are the steep streets of the old town, pierced by a church spire; to the left, the rolling, wooded St-Cloud Park, once the site of the favorite palace of the emperor Napoléon III; it was burned down by invading Prussians in 1870. Only its ground plan and the imposing, tiered waterfall known as the **Grande Cascade** (the lower portion designed by architect Jules Hardouin-Mansart in the 17th century) now remain. The park commands fine views of Paris, and its grassy expanses and broad, wooded paths are delightful for walks. The château's history and architecture are retraced in the **Musée Historique,** near the main entrance. ☞ *Free. Grounds open daily 7 AM–9 PM (7:30–8 in winter). Museum open Easter–mid-Nov., Wed. and weekends, 2–6; mid-Nov.–Easter, Wed. and weekends 2–5.*

Just after St-Cloud, A13 veers right through a depressingly long, dirty tiled tunnel, emerging into a corridor of tall trees that lasts several miles. Instead of continuing to Versailles, take the N186 exit just beforehand, signposted to St-Germain-en-Laye, 5 kilometers (3 miles) away.

26 The elegant town of **St-Germain-en-Laye,** perched on a hill above the Seine and encircled by forest, has lost little of its original cachet, despite the invasion of wealthy Parisians who commute to work on the RER. Next to the train station is the town's chief attraction—its stone-and-brick **château.**

Most of the defensive-looking château, with its dry moat and intimidating circular towers, dates from the 16th and 17th centuries. Yet a royal palace has existed here since the early 12th century, when Louis VI—known as *Le Gros* (The Fat)—exploited St-Germain's defensive potential in his bid to pacify the Ile de France. A hundred years later, Louis IX (Saint Louis) added the elegant **Sainte-Chapelle,** the château's oldest remaining section. The figures on the tympanum (the inset triangular area over the main door) are believed to be the first known representations of French royalty, portraying Louis with his mother, Blanche de Castille, and other members of his family.

Charles V (1364–80) built a powerful defensive keep in the mid-14th century, but from the 1540s, François I and his successors transformed St-Germain into a palace of more domestic, and less warlike, vocation. Louis XIV was born here, and it was here that his father, Louis XIII, died. Until 1682—when the court moved to Versailles—it remained the country's foremost royal residence outside Paris. Since 1867, the château has housed a major **Musée des Antiquités Nationales** (Museum of Ancient History), holding a trove of artifacts, figurines, brooches, and weapons from the Stone Age to the 8th century. ☞ *20 frs, 13 frs on Sun.* ☉ *Wed.–Mon. 9–5:15.*

Another place to visit in St-Germain is the quaint **Musée du Prieuré** (Priory Museum), some 600 yards from the château (follow rue au Pain from the church). This museum is devoted to the work of the artist Maurice Denis (1870–1943) and his fellow symbolists and Nabis—painters opposed to the naturalism of their 19th-century Impressionist contemporaries. Denis found the calm of the former Jesuit priory suited to his spiritual themes, which he expressed in stained glass, ceramics, and frescoes, as well as oils. *2 bis rue Maurice-Denis.*

☛ *25 frs adults, 15 frs children and senior citizens.* ☉ *Wed.–Fri. 10–5:30, weekends 10–6:30.*

Those with a bent for the swashbuckling novels of Alexandre Dumas should make a 2-kilometer (1-mile) detour south to **Port-Marly,** to visit the **Château de Monte-Cristo,** reopened in 1994 after a four-year renovation program. Purists may find its fanciful exterior, where pilasters, cupolas, and stone carvings compete for attention, a classic example of parvenu tastelessness, but—as in *The Count of Monte-Cristo* and *The Three Musketeers*—swagger, not subtlety, is what counts. Dumas built the château after his books' surging popularity made him rich in the 1840s. Construction costs and lavish partying meant he got unrich just as quickly, and he had skedaddled to a Belgian exile by 1849. The château contains pictures, Dumas mementos, and the luxurious Moorish Chamber, with spellbinding, interlacing plasterwork executed by Arab craftsmen (lent by the Bey of Tunis) and recently restored by a donation from Moroccan king Hassan II. The château park has a miniature version in a small lake of the Château d'If, off Marseille, scene of the Count of Monte-Cristo's most heroic exploits. *Ave. du Président-Kennedy,* ☎ *30–61–61–35.* ☛ *30 frs adults, 23 frs students and senior citizens.* ☉ *Apr.–Oct., Tues.–Sun. 10–6.*

Six and a half kilometers (4 miles) north of St-Germain along the River Seine, via D157, is the town of **Maisons-Laffitte.** The early Baroque **château** of Maisons, constructed by architect François Mansart from 1642 to 1651, is one of the least-known châteaus in the Ile de France. This was not always the case: Sun King Louis XIV came to the housewarming party, and Louis XV, Louis XVI, the 18th-century writer Voltaire, and Napoléon all stayed here. The interior clearly met their exacting standards, thanks to the well-proportioned entrance vestibule with its rich sculpture; the winding **Escalier d'Honneur,** a majestic staircase adorned with paintings and statues; and the royal apartments, above, with their parquet floors and elegant wall paneling. ☛ *26 frs adults, 17 frs students and senior citizens.* ☉ *Daily 10–6.*

Cross the bridge that links Maisons-Laffitte to Sartrouville and take the first left along the banks of the Seine. Parts of this river road, particularly at the neighboring town of La Frette, retain surprising pastoral charm, given the proximity of industrial suburbs. At Herblay, the road leaves the river; head up through the housing development to the main road and turn left for Conflans, a couple of miles away.

The town of **Conflans-Ste-Honorine,** 32 kilometers (20 miles) northwest of Paris, reflects the importance of waterways to the Ile de France region. Boats and barges arrive from as far afield as the ports of Le Havre and Dunkerque, on France's northern coast, and are often moored up to six-abreast along the mile-long quayside, near the *conflans* (confluence, and hence the town's name) of the Rivers Seine and Oise. The **Musée de la Batellerie** (Boat Museum), next to an old church high above the river, explains the historic role of the barges and waterways with the help of its collection of pictures and scale models. ☛ *Free.* ☉ *Easter–Oct., Wed.–Mon. 9–noon and 1:30–6, weekends 3–6; Nov.–Easter, Wed.–Mon. 9–noon and 1:30–5, weekends 2–5.*

The road that crosses the Seine at Conflans continues 8 kilometers (5 miles) north toward **Pontoise,** a pleasant old town on the banks of the Oise. One of the town's most illustrious past residents was Impressionist painter Camille Pissarro (1830–1903). The small **Musée Pissarro,** high up in the old town (17 rue du Château, admission free, open Wed.–Sun. 2–6) has an unexciting collection of prints and drawings. The town's other museum, the **Musée Tavet-Delacour,** housed in a turreted mansion, stages good exhibitions and has a permanent collection that includes landscapes by other local painters and intriguing abstract geometric compositions by Otto Freundlich. *4 rue Lemercier.* ☛ *20 frs.* ⊙ *Wed.–Mon. 10–noon and 2–6.*

The tranquil Oise Valley, which runs northeast from Pontoise, retains much of the charm that attracted Pissarro and other Impressionists to this area a century ago. In the second half of the 19th century, Pissarro, Paul Cézanne, Camille Corot, Charles-François Daubigny, and Berthe ❸ Morisot all painted in **Auvers-sur-Oise,** 6 kilometers (4 miles) from Pontoise along D4, but it is Vincent van Gogh whose memory haunts every nook and cranny of this pretty riverside village. After years of indifference and neglect, the inn where van Gogh eked out the last 10, penniless weeks of his life has been turned into a shrine, and the whole village is peppered with plaques, enabling you to compare his final works with the scenes as they are today. Little has changed since he was buried in 1890 in a simple grave in the village cemetery, now covered with ivy. You can also visit the medieval village church, subject of one of van Gogh's most famous paintings, and admire Osip Zadkine's powerful modern statue of him in the village park.

The Auberge Ravoux, the inn where van Gogh lodged, was opened to the public in 1993, after painstaking restoration, as the **Maison de Van Gogh.** A dingy staircase leads up to the tiny, spartan, wood-floored attic where van Gogh stored some of modern art's most famous pictures under the bed in which he died after shooting himself. A short film retraces van Gogh's short time at Auvers, where he painted no fewer than 70 pictures. There is a well-stocked souvenir shop. *8 rue de la Sansonne.* ☛ *25 frs adults, 15 frs students and senior citizens.* ⊙ *Daily 10–6.*

TIME OUT Stop for a drink or for lunch on the ground floor of the Auberge Ravoux, where the window glass, lace curtains, and wall decor have been carefully modeled on designs that Van Gogh would have known. The 140-franc three-course menu has a small choice of fish and meat dishes and changes regularly; there is also a good-value wine list. *52 rue Gal-de-Gaulle,* ☎ *34-48-05-47. Reservations advised.*

The elegant 17th-century village **château,** set above split-level gardens, opened in 1994 as home to a *Voyage au Temps des Impressionistes.* Each visitor receives a set of infrared headphones (available in English), with commentary that reacts to your progress through various tableaus of Belle Epoque life. Although there are no Impressionist originals—500 reproductions pop up on screen—this is an imaginative, enjoyable, and innovative museum. Some of the special effects—talking mirrors, computerized cabaret dancers, a train ride past Impressionist landscapes—are worthy of Disney. *Rue de Léry,* ☎ *34-48-48-48.* ☛ *50 frs adults, 40 frs senior citizens, 35 frs students, 100 frs family.* ⊙ *May–Oct., daily 10–8; Nov.–Apr. Tues.–Sun. 10–5.*

Serious art lovers should also consider a visit to the modest **Musée Daubigny** (upstairs from the Tourist Office and opposite the Maison de Van Gogh) to admire the drawings, lithographs, and occasional oils by local 19th-century artists. *Manoir des Colombières, rue de la Sansonne.* ☛ *15 frs adults, 10 frs students and senior citizens.* ⊙ *Tues.–Wed. and Fri.–Sun. 2:30–6:30 (5:30 in winter).*

Daubigny, a precursor of Impressionism, lived in Auvers from 1861 until his death in 1878. Visit his studio, the **Atelier Daubigny,** to admire the remarkable array of mural and roof paintings by Daubigny

Corot, and Honoré Daumier. *61 rue Daubigny.* ☛ *20 frs.* ⊘ *Easter–Oct., Tues.–Sun. 2–6:30.*

Another small museum, the **Musée de l'Absinthe,** near the château, uses publicity posters and Belle Epoque artifacts to trace the story of what was once France's most popular drink—a forerunner of today's anise-based aperitifs like Ricard and Pernod—until it was banned during World War I as a source of alcoholism. Van Gogh no doubt downed the odd glass at the Auberge Ravoux. *44 rue Callé,* ☎ *30–36–83–26.* ☛ *25 frs adults, 20 frs students and senior citizens.* ⊘ *Apr.–May and Oct., weekends 11–6; June–Sept., Wed.–Sun. 11–6.*

㉜ Six and a half kilometers (4 miles) upstream from Auvers, across the bridge at Parmain, is residentially exclusive **L'Isle-Adam,** one of the most picturesque towns in the entire Ile de France. Paris lies just 40 kilometers (25 miles) south, but it could be 100 miles and as many years away. There is a sandy **beach** along one stretch of the River Oise and (via rue de Beaumont) a curious pagoda-like folly, the **Pavillon Chinois de Cassan.** An unassuming local museum, the **Musée Louis-Senlecq,** on the main street, often stages painting exhibitions and contains numerous attractive works by local landscapists. *46 Grande-Rue,* ☎ *34–69–45–44.* ☛ *15 frs.* ⊘ *May–Oct., Sat.–Mon. 3–6; Nov.–Apr., tours by appointment.*

㉝ From L'Isle-Adam, take N322/D922 to the small hilltop town of **Beaumont-sur-Oise**—worth a quick peek if only for its attractive 12th- to 13th-century **church of St-Laurent,** transformed into a cathedral by 19th-century French writer Emile Zola as the setting for his romantic novel *Le Rêve* (*The Dream*). From Beaumont, take D922 to Viarmes, then ㉞ turn left along D909 to the Cistercian Abbey of **Royaumont,** 2½ kilometers (1½ miles) away. The abbey was founded by the only canonized French King, Louis IX, known as Saint Louis, in 1228; 5 of his 11 children are buried here. You can visit the only part of the abbey church still standing (the south transept), along with the ivy-clad cloisters, the refectory where Saint Louis occasionally served the monks their meals, and the vaulted kitchens. The monks' dormitories, chapterhouse, and library are now part of an international cultural center and are rarely open to the public (☎ 30–35–30–16 for details of the concerts held here in summer). ☛ *20 frs.* ⊘ *Easter–Oct., Wed.–Mon. 10–12:30 and 2–6; Nov.–Easter, weekends 10–12:30 and 2–5.*

★ ㉟ Ten kilometers (6 miles) northeast via D909 lies the town of **Chantilly,** with its romantic, golden-stone **château,** sitting snugly behind an artificial, carp-stocked lake. Despite appearances, much of the current building is not old but is 19th-century Renaissance pastiche, rebuilt in the 1870s. The lavish interior contains the outstanding **Condé Collection** of illuminated medieval manuscripts, tapestries, furniture, and paintings. The most famous room, the **Santuario,** boasts two celebrated works by Italian painter Raphael (1483–1520)—the *Three Ages of Woman* and *The Orleans Virgin*—plus an exquisite ensemble of 15th-century miniatures by the most illustrious French painter of his time, Jean Fouquet (1420–81). Farther on, in the Cabinet des Livres, is the **Book of Hours** of the duc de Berry, one of the finest medieval manuscripts.

Other highlights of this unusual museum are the **Galerie de Psyché,** with 16th-century stained glass and portrait drawings by Flemish artist Jean Clouet II; the **chapel,** with sculptures by Jean Goujon and Jacques Sarrazin; and the extensive **collection of paintings** by 19th-century French artists, headed by Jean-Auguste Ingres. ☛ *35 frs adults, 27 frs students, 10 frs children under 12. Park only: 15 frs.* ⊘ *Mar.–Oct.,*

Wed.–Mon. 10–6; Nov.–Feb., Wed.–Mon. 10:30–12:45 and 2–5. Orchestra performance every afternoon during the summer and Christmas holidays. ☛ *80 frs.*

Behind the château is a large **park,** based on that familiar combination of formal bombast (neatly planned parterres and a mighty straight-banked canal) and romantic eccentricity (the jardin anglais, with its waterfall, or the make-believe village that inspired Marie-Antoinette's version at Versailles).

Across the lake from the château is the Chantilly racecourse, inaugurated in 1834 by the prestigious French Jockey Club. In one corner (to the right as you leave the château) are the majestic 18th-century stables (**Grandes Ecuries**), where up to 240 horses and 400 hounds for stag and boar hunts could be accommodated in straw-lined comfort. Today the stables host the **Musée Vivant du Cheval** (Live Horse Museum), with 40 horses and ponies and dressage presentations thrice daily, and a glittering array of carriages. ☛ *45 frs adults, 35 frs students and senior citizens, 32 frs children. ⊙ Apr.–Oct., Wed.–Mon. 10:30–6:30; Nov.–Mar., Wed.–Mon. 2–4:30, weekends 2–5:30.*

TIME OUT   Since the château of Chantilly is a fair walk from the town's main street, it makes sense to have a quick lunch on the spot—at the self-service **Capitainerie restaurant** in the château's medieval basement (adorned with old kitchen utensils). The buffet is available nonstop from 10:30 through 6:30: mostly salads, cheeses, and desserts, complemented by a few hot dishes. *Closed Tues.*

36   Ten kilometers (6 miles) east of Chantilly, along the picturesque, gently turning D924, is **Senlis,** an exceptionally well preserved medieval town whose crooked, mazelike streets are dominated by the svelte, soaring spire of the Gothic cathedral of **Notre-Dame,** recently cleaned and looking glorious.

As we noticed at Chantilly, this is prime hunting country. On the grounds of the ruined royal castle opposite the west front of the cathedral is the **Musée de la Vénerie,** a full-fledged hunting museum. Suitable artifacts, prints, and paintings rekindle the atmosphere of the kingly pursuit. *Château Royal.* ☛ *14 frs adults, 7 frs children. ⊙ For guided visits on the hr, Feb.–mid-Dec. Wed. 2–6, Thurs.–Mon. 10:30–noon and 2–6.*

No one with even a glimmer of interest in antiquities should miss the town's **Musée d'Art et Archéologie,** built atop an ancient Gallo-Roman residence. The excavated foundations are on display in the museum's basement. Fascinating, too, are Gallo-Roman votive objects, unearthed in the neighboring Halatte Forest. Upstairs, the museum presents paintings by—among others—Thomas Couture, Manet's teacher, who lived in Senlis. *Place du Parvis-Notre-Dame.* ☛ *15 frs. ⊙ Mar.–Oct., weekdays except Tues. 9–noon and 1:30–5:30, weekends 10–noon and 2–7; Nov.–Apr., Wed.–Mon. 1:30–6:30; closed 3 wks in winter.*

Down the lane behind the cathedral is the former church of **St-Pierre,** with its Flamboyant facade, while across place Notre-Dame, the large square beside the cathedral, is the **Fondation Cziffra:** the former church of St-Frambourg, converted into an exhibition center by Hungarian-born pianist Gyorgy Cziffra in 1977, with a concert auditorium and a small adjoining museum devoted to regional archaeological finds. *1 pl. St-Frambourg.* ☛ *20 frs adults, 10 frs students. ⊙ Mid-Apr.–Oct., Sun. 3–5.*

TIME OUT   Senlis is not the liveliest place for taking a quick drink or lunch, but if you head down rue du Châtel from the cathedral you'll find cafés and bars in **rue l'Apport-du-Pain** (No. 16), **rue Vieille de Paris** (No. 19), and **place de la Halle** (No. 37).

Just off N330, some 11 kilometers (7 miles) southeast of Senlis, stand
⚫️ the ruins of the 18th-century abbey of **Chaalis,** built on the site of a
13th-century Cistercian abbey. The landscaped park has been restored
to its 18th-century appearance, and the château, which dates from the
same period, has an eclectic collection of Egyptian antiquities and medieval paintings, together with three rooms devoted to the 18th-cen-
tury French philosopher and writer Jean-Jacques Rousseau, who died
at nearby Ermenonville. ☛ *30 frs.* ☯ *Mar.–Oct., weekdays except
Tues. 2–6:30, weekends 10:30–12:30 and 2–6:30; Nov.–Mar., Sun.
2–6:30. Park admission: 12 frs. Park open year-round 9–7.*

To return to Paris, take D84 about 8 kilometers (5 miles) due south to
Dammartin, then follow the signs for Paris on the fast N2.

Tour 3: South to Fontainebleau

Fontainebleau, which forms the hub of our final tour, can be reached
from Paris (65 kilometers, or 40 miles, away) in as little as half an
hour via A6 and N37. But we urge you not to bypass nearby Vaux-
le-Vicomte, a masterpiece of 17th-century architecture and design. It
is best reached from Paris (Porte de Bercy) via N6, leaving this road
at Melun and continuing to Vaux, 5 kilometers (3 miles) northeast,
along N36 and D215.

★ ⚫️ The château of **Vaux-le-Vicomte** was built between 1656 and 1661 for
finance minister Nicolas Fouquet. The construction process was monstrous even for those days: Entire villages were razed, 18,000 workmen called in, and architect Louis Le Vau, painter Charles Le Brun,
and esteemed landscape architect André Le Nôtre hired to prove that
Fouquet's supremely refined tastes matched his business acumen. Unfortunately, his housewarming party was too lavish for the liking of
star guest Louis XIV. King Louis threw a fit of jealousy, hurled the tact-
less Fouquet in jail (where he died penniless 19 years later), and
promptly set Le Vau, Le Brun, and Lenôtre to work on Versailles.

The high-roofed château, partially surrounded by a moat, is set well
back from the roadside behind iron railings topped with sculpted
heads. A cobbled avenue stretches up to the entrance. Stone steps lead
to the entrance hall, which, given the noble scale of the exterior, seems
small. There is no grand staircase, either—the stairs are tucked away
in the left wing and lead to the private apartments—rooms designed
on an intimate scale for daily living.

Painter Charles Le Brun's lush interior decoration captivates the eye.
One major achievement is the ceiling of the **Chambre du Roi** (Royal
Bedchamber), depicting *Time Bearing Truth Heavenward,* framed by
stucco work by sculptors François Girardon and Legendre. Along the
frieze you can make out small squirrels—known as *fouquets* in local
dialect. But surely his masterwork is the ceiling in the **Salon des Muses,**
a brilliant allegorical composition painted in glowing, sensuous colors that surpasses anything Le Brun did at Versailles.

The **Grand Salon** on the ground floor impresses as well. With its unusual oval form and 16 caryatid pillars symbolizing the months and seasons, it possesses harmony and style despite its unfinished state. In fact,
the lack of decoration only points up Le Vau's architectural genius.

A clever exhibition, complete with life-size wax figures, explains the rise and fall of Nicolas Fouquet. The version is, not surprisingly, favorable to the château's founder—accused by Louis XIV and subsequent historians of megalomania and shady financial dealings, but apparently condemned on little evidence by a court anxious to please the jealous, irascible monarch. The exhibition continues in the basement, whose cool, dim rooms were used to store food and wine and house the château's staff. The **kitchens,** a more cheerful sight, with their gleaming copperware and old menus, are also down here.

Although the château's interior is in some respects incomplete, there is no mistaking the grandeur of Lenôtre's **gardens,** which have been carefully restored. Visit the **Musée des Equipages** in the stables and inspect a host of carriages and coaches in wonderful condition. ☎ 60–66–97–09. ☛ *50 frs adults, 40 frs students and senior citizens. Gardens only: 28 frs.* ☉ *Apr.–Oct., daily 10–6; Nov.–Mar., daily 11–5; closed Dec.–mid-Feb. except Dec. 25 and Jan. 1. Candlelight visits: 68 frs adults, 54 frs students.* ☉ *May–Oct., Sat. 8:30–11* PM.

TIME OUT To the right of the château entrance is an imposing barn that has been transformed into a self-service **cafeteria.** Here, beneath the ancient rafters of a stout wood-beam roof, you can enjoy coffee, cheap pitchers of wine, and good steaks. Insist on *bien cuit* if you don't want your meat extremely rare.

㊴ From Vaux, return to Melun (take the beltway around the north of the town) and head along D132 (which becomes D64) to **Barbizon,** 10 kilometers (6 miles) south. Barbizon stands on the western edge of the 62,000-acre Forest of Fontainebleau and retains the atmosphere of a small village, despite the intrusion of expensive art galleries, tacky souvenir shops, and weekending Parisians.

Barbizon owes its renown to the colony of landscape painters—Camille Corot, Jean-François Millet, and Théodore Rousseau, among others—who lived here from the 1830s on. Their innovative commitment to working outdoors paved the way for the Impressionists, as did their willingness to accept nature on its own terms, rather than use it as an idealized base for carefully structured compositions.

After working hours, the Barbizon painters repaired to the **Auberge du Père Ganne.** The inn is still standing—now closed indefinitely for restoration—but you can soak up the arty mood at the houses of Millet and Rousseau farther along the single main street (rue Grande) and admire some of their works at the **Ecole de Barbizon** museum. *55 rue Grande.* ☛ *15 frs.* ☉ *Wed.–Mon. 10–12:30 and 2–5.*

㊵ Eight kilometers (5 miles) southeast of Barbizon (via the fast N7) lies the town of **Fontainebleau.** Like Chambord in the Loire Valley or Compiègne to the north, Fontainebleau earned royal esteem as a hunting base. Today's château was begun under the flamboyant Renaissance prince François I, the French contemporary of England's Henry VIII. The king hired Italian artists Il Rosso (a pupil of Michelangelo; 1494–1540) and Francesco Primaticcio (1504–70), to embellish his château. In fact, they did much more: by introducing the pagan allegories and elegant lines of Mannerism to France, they revolutionized French decorative art. Their extraordinary frescoes and stuccowork can be admired in the Galerie François I and the glorious Salle de Bal, completed under Henri II, François's successor. Napoléon spent lavishly to make a Versailles, as it were, out of Fontainebleau. The château's collection of Empire furniture is the finest anywhere.

Numbers in the margin correspond to points of interest on the Fontainebleau map.

Walk past the Parterre, east of the Etang des Carpes (Carp Pond), and turn into an alley that leads to the **Cour Ovale**—a courtyard shaped like a flattened oval with, at its east end, the domed **Porte du Baptistère.** The gateway's name commemorates the fact that the Dauphin—the heir to the throne, later to become Louis XIII—was baptized under its arch in 1606. Opposite is the **Cour Henri IV,** a large, severe square built at the same time as the place des Vosges in Paris (1609).

The hedge-lined alley continues to the Jardin de Diane (Garden of Diana), with its peacocks and statue of the hunting goddess surrounded by mournful hounds. Cross this informal garden and enter the palace's most majestic courtyard, the **Cour du Cheval-Blanc,** or Cour des Adieux, dominated by the famous **horseshoe staircase** built by Jean Androuet du Cerceau in the early 17th century, where Napoléon bade his troops farewell. Climb the steps to the château's entrance.

In **Napoléon's apartments** on the second floor is a lock of his hair, his Légion d'Honneur medal, his imperial uniform, the hat he wore on his return from Elba in 1815, and a bed in which he once slept.

There is also a **throne room**—Napoléon spurned the one at Versailles, a palace he disliked, and established his imperial seat here in the former King's Bedchamber, a room with a suitably majestic decor—and the **Queen's Boudoir,** known as the Room of the Six Maries. The sweeping **Galerie de Diane,** built during the reign of Henri IV (1589–1610), was converted to a library in the 1860s. Other salons boast 17th-century tapestries, marble reliefs by Jacquet de Grenoble, and paintings and frescoes by Primaticcio, Niccolò dell'Abbate, and other members of the Fontainebleau School.

The jewel of the interior, though, is the ceremonial ballroom—the **Salle de Bal**—nearly 100 feet long, with wood paneling, 16th-century frescoes and gilding, and, reputedly, the first coffered ceiling in France, its intricate pattern echoed by the splendid 19th-century parquet floor. *Pl. du Général de Gaulle,* ☎ *60–71–50–70.* ☛ *31 frs adults, 20 frs students and senior citizens.* ☺ *Wed.–Mon. 9:30–12:30 and 2–5; closed holidays.*

If time permits, complete your visit with a stroll around the leafy **Jardin Anglais** (English Garden) to the west of the Etang des Carpes. *Gardens open 9–dusk; admission free.*

Numbers in the margin correspond to points of interest on the Ile de France map.

Ten kilometers (6 miles) southeast of Fontainebleau on N6, close to the confluence of the Rivers Seine and Yonne, is the charming village of **Moret-sur-Loing,** immortalized by Impressionist painter Alfred Sisley, who lived here for 20 years at 19 rue Montmartre (not open to the public), around the corner from the church of Notre-Dame. Close by, across the river, is the thatched **house-museum** of another illustrious former inhabitant: truculent World War I leader Georges Clemenceau (1841–1929), known as the Tiger. His taste for Oriental art and his friendship with Impressionist Claude Monet are evoked. *Follow signs to La Grange-Batelière.* ☎ *60–70–51–21. Guided tours only: 35 frs.* ☺ *Easter–mid-Nov., weekends 3–6.*

The best view of Moret is from the far banks of the Loing. Cross the narrow bridge (one of the oldest in France and invariably clogged with

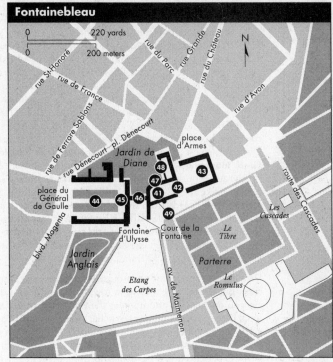

Fontainebleau

traffic) to gaze back at the walls, rooftops, and church tower. A good time to visit Moret is on a Saturday evening in summer when locals stage *son-et-lumière* (sound-and-light) pageants illustrating the town's history.

After crossing the Loing, take N6 east for 6½ kilometers (4 miles), then turn left along D403 (via Montereau) to the picturesque medieval town of **Provins,** another 37 kilometers (23 miles) away. Provins developed on the hilltop site of a Roman camp before acquiring international renown as a rose-growing center. Under the influence of the counts of Champagne during the Middle Ages, it became an important commercial town, the third most important in France (after Paris and Rouen). Upper Provins sleeps in the past, tucked in behind its defensive walls at the foot of the solid 12th-century **Tour de César,** a circular keep on a sturdy mound. Climb to the top for a view of the town. ☛ *15 frs adults, 7 frs children.* ⊙ *Daily 10–5.*

Beneath the tower is the 12th-century Gothic church of **St-Quiriace,** with its incongruous 17th-century Classical dome. Close by is a pleasant garden, the **Jardin des Brébans.** From here, rue du Palais leads up to place du Châtel, a sloping square with restaurants at the far end. Veer left down rue de Jouy; on the first corner is the 13th-century tithe-barn, or **Grange aux Dîmes,** whose vaulted ground floor contains a collection of stone sculptures. ☛ *Free.* ⊙ *Weekends 2–6.*

Rue St-Jean leads to the Porte St-Jean gateway. Here you can survey some of the best-preserved **medieval ramparts** in France. In a bid to liven up its image, Provins now stages "medieval evenings" in summer; call the Tourist Office (☎ 64–60–26–26) for details.

N19 links Provins to Paris, 72 kilometers (45 miles) away.

What to See and Do with Children

A bit of American pop culture now anchors the eastern suburbs of the City of Light: **Disneyland Paris** (known originally as **Euro Disney**). This 4,800-acre development comprises six themed hotels, all with restaurants, shops, and sports facilities from tennis to ice-skating, Festival Disney (an entertainment complex with American-style restaurants, a dinner theater, bar, disco, and shops), and the main draw, the 136-acre theme park that combines features of Tokyo Disneyland, California Disneyland, and Florida's Walt Disney World. It offers rides and attractions, live entertainment, Disney souvenirs galore, restaurants, and Disney's newest attractions, **Indiana Jones et le Temple de Peril** and **Space Mountain** (opened 1995). The entrance to Euro Disneyland is off the A4 expressway and is clearly marked; it takes about 30 minutes to make the 32-kilometer (20-mile) drive from Paris. Parking is available 600 yards from the theme park entrance. A new suburban train station (Marne-la-Vallée-Chessy) stops just 100 yards from the entrance and Festival Disney. Board the train at Charles-de-Gaulle-Etoile, Auber, Châtelet, or the Gare de Lyon in Paris; the journey takes about 40 minutes and costs 72 francs, round-trip.

Disneyland Paris is not what most people travel to France to experience. But if you have a child in tow, the promise of a day there may get you through an afternoon at the Louvre. If you're a dyed-in-the-wool Disney fan, you'll want to make a beeline for the park to see how it has been molded to appeal to the tastes of European visitors. (Disney's "imagineers" call it their most lovingly detailed park.) And if you've never experienced this particular form of Disney showmanship, you may want to put in an appearance, if only to see what the fuss is all about. *32 km (20 mi) east of Paris, off A4,* ☎ *64–74–30–00 (information). Admission (prices vary according to season): 175–250 frs adults (335—475 frs for 2-day Passport, 440–630 frs for 3-day Passport), 125–175 frs children under 12 (240–335 frs for 2-day Passport, 315–440 frs for 3-day Passport), including admission to all individual attractions within the park but not meals; AE, DC, MC, and V accepted in payment of admission, sit-down restaurant meals, and purchases in shops.* ⊙ *Mid-June–mid-Sept., daily 9–10, mid-Sept.–mid-June, daily 10–6, Dec. and spring school holidays, daily 10–9 (hours may lengthen if demand warrants).*

A special treat for youngsters are meals at which Disney characters put in appearances, held in the Disneyland Hotel or Hotel New York. For details, call 49–41–49–41. The cost is normally under 200 francs, but beware of premium prices for special themes or holiday meals.

Opposite the abbey of Chaalis, 11 kilometers (7 miles) southeast of Senlis, is the **Mer de Sable playground**—a cheerful place for children, with its miniature train, giant slide, small zoo, and curious natural "desert" of white sand. *Parc d'Attractions Jean-Richard, Forêt d'Ermenonville, off N330.* ☎ *44–54–00–96.* ☛ *69 frs adults, 48 frs children 6–16, 38 frs children 3–5, 22 frs children under 3.* ⊙ *Apr., May, and Sept., weekdays 11–6:30, weekends 11–7; June, weekdays 10–6, weekends 11–7; July–Aug., daily 10:30–6:30, Sun. 10:30–7; closed Oct.–Mar.*

The theme park known as **Parc Astérix** (recently spruced up to compete with Disneyland Paris) takes its cue from a French comic-book figure whose adventures are set during the Roman invasion of France 2,000 years ago. Highlights include a mock Gallo-Roman village, a dolphin lake, and a giant roller coaster. *Just off A1 at Plailly, 32 km (20* *mi) north of Paris.* ☎ *44–62–31–31.* ☛ *150 frs adults, 100 frs children under 12.* ○ *Apr.–Oct., daily 10–6.*

Some 4,000 models and more than 1,300 feet of track make the **Musée Rambolitrain,** in Rambouillet, France's leading model-train museum. There are historic steam engines, old-time stations, and a realistic points and signaling system. *4 pl. Jeanne-d'Arc,* ☎ *34–83–15–93.* ☛ *20 frs adults, 10 frs children.* ○ *Wed.–Sun. 10–noon and 2–5:30.*

Five hundred species of exotic butterflies flutter freely, in a lush jungle setting of rare orchids and carnivorous plants, at **La Serre aux Papillons** in La Queue-lez-Yvelines, near Montfort-l'Amaury. *Jardinerie Poullain,* ☎ *34–86–42–99.* ☛ *25 frs.* ○ *Daily Apr.–Nov. 9:15–noon and 2:15–5:45.*

The animal reserve, Tiger Park, and play area of the **Château de Thoiry** (*see* Tour 1, *above*) are also popular with children.

Off the Beaten Track

Take a short literary pilgrimage down the Seine Valley one Sunday to the little town of **Médan,** where Emile Zola moved in 1877 after the runaway success of his novel *L'Assommoir.* Until recently, his house was used as an orphanage, but it is now open to the public. *26 rue Pasteur.* ☛ *25 frs.* ○ *Sat. 3–5, Sun. 2–6.*

In **Chambourcy,** 5 kilometers (3 miles) northwest of St-Germain-en-Laye, is the stately 17th-century Maison André-Derain, where the versatile Derain (1880–1954), best known for his pioneering, hotly colored Fauve paintings, lived from 1935 until his death. You can admire his well-preserved studio and a smattering of his works, and watch a 12-minute film about his career. *64 Grande Rue,* ☎ *30–74–70–04.* ☛ *20 frs.* ○ *Weekends 2–4:30.*

Fans of church architecture should not miss the venerable basilica in **Saint-Denis,** even if it means taking the Paris métro into a dowdy northern suburb. It was at Saint-Denis that dynamic builder-prelate Abbé Suger pioneered the Gothic rib vaults and pointed arches around 1140. Many French kings are buried in the basilica, and their richly sculpted tombs—along with what remains of Suger's part of the church—can be seen in the choir at the east end. The vast 13th-century nave is a brilliant example of scholastic logic, with its harmonious integration of columns, capitals, shafts, and vaults. *Métro: St-Denis Basilique.* ☛ *Choir: 26 frs adults, 17 frs students and senior citizens.* ○ *Daily 9–7 (10–5 in winter). Choir closed during services.*

Ecouen, a wooded suburb 19 kilometers (12 miles) north of Paris, is known for its château, containing a museum devoted to the Renaissance that's particularly strong on 16th- and 17th-century tapestry and furniture from France, Italy, and Holland. *Musée de la Renaissance, Château d'Ecouen.* ☛ *21 frs (14 frs Sun.).* ○ *Wed.–Mon. 9:45–12:30 and 2–5:15.*

The Orge Valley southwest of Paris presents an attractive mixture of hills, fields, and forest, with two outstanding man-made attractions: an enormous, airy 13th-century church in the tiny village of **St-Sulpice-de-Favières** and the enticing château of **Le Marais,** with a lake, extensive grounds, and a small museum devoted to onetime inhabitant Talleyrand (a romantic but unscrupulous 19th-century diplomat). A car is the only means of access to these two sites, though the RER-C trains from Paris stop at nearby St-Chéron, where taxis can be hired. *Le Marais:* ☎ *25 frs (park only: 20 frs).* ☉ *Mar. 15–Nov. 15, Sun. and holidays 2–6:30.*

Students of urban planning and modern architecture will have a field day in the Ile de France. **La Défense,** just west of Paris, is renowned for its steel-and-glass, Manhattan-style skyline, but five bigger developments—in fact, whole **new towns** (*villes nouvelles*)—have been undertaken in the past 20 years: at St-Quentin-en-Yvelines, Cergy-Pontoise (with its ambitious vista, or Axe Majeur), Evry, Melun-Sénart, and Marne-la-Vallée. All can be reached by train or RER from Paris within 45 minutes.

SHOPPING

Most of the Ile de France's working population either commutes to Paris or cultivates farmland. There is little in the way of regional specialties, and, with Paris never more than an hour away, serious shopping—particularly for clothes—means heading back to the capital. Beware: With the exception of the Disneyland shops, most stores are closed Sunday (except in December and peak seasons) and often close for lunch.

Food Items
Versailles is perhaps the region's most commercial town. After visiting the château, you may want to stop in at **Aux Colonnes,** a highly rated *confiserie* with an astounding array of chocolates and candies (14 rue Hoche; closed Mon.). A huge choice of cheeses—including one of France's widest selection of goat cheeses—can be smelled, admired, and eventually purchased from **Eugène Le Gall** (15 rue Ducis; closed Sun. afternoon and Mon.). For the makings of an impromptu picnic (cold cuts, cheese, salads, and such), try **Les Délices du Palais** (4 rue Maréchal-Foch, closed Sun. PM and Mon.).

Antiques
Anyone in the mood for antiques hunting should visit Versailles's passage de la Geôle, site of a good thrice-weekly flea market (10 rue Rameau; open Fri.–Sun. 9–7). Antiques shops in other major towns include **A La Cour Des Adieux** (3 rue Dénecourt, Fontainebleau); **Formanoir** (6 pl. Notre-Dame, Senlis); **Susen Antiquités** (18 rue des Coches, St-Germain-en-Laye); and **Ambiance & Style** (17 rue des Changes, Chartres).

Souvenirs
There are notably fine souvenir shops at Vaux-le-Vicomte, Giverny, and Thoiry (where you can sample cookies and jams made by the American viscountess herself).

Disney souvenirs are available throughout Disneyland, but pirate hats can be bought only in Adventureland and cowboy items only in Frontierland. For the best generic Disney souvenirs, do your shopping on **Main Street;** the **Emporium** has the broadest selection of everything from T-shirts to Mickey Mouse ears.

Gift Items
Stained glass being the key to Chartres's fame, enthusiasts may want to visit the **Galerie du Vitrail** (17 rue Cloître Notre-Dame), which specializes in the noble art. Pieces range from small plaques to entire windows, and there are books on the subject in English and French.

SPORTS AND THE OUTDOORS

Bicycling

Biking is an enjoyable and healthy way to explore the area. The generally flat terrain has occasional slightly rolling hills, but the real pleasure is that here (unlike the plains of northern France) the wind is negligible. Recommended itineraries include the 90 kilometers (55 miles) of cycling paths in the Rambouillet Forest, the route from Barbizon to the Gorges d'Apremont in the Fontainebleau Forest, or, for an easy ride, the path around the canal on the grounds of Versailles. Apply at local Tourist Offices for information on bicycle rental and itineraries, and *see also* the Gold Guide.

Golf

Golf is a new, expensive cult sport in France, but there are several clubs open to the general public and accessible via public transportation: **Golf de l'Ile Fleurie** (☎ 39–52–61–61) in Chatou, **Golf National de St-Quentin-en-Yvelines** (☎ 30–57–65–65) **Fontainebleau** (☎ 64–22–22—95), and **St-Germain-en-Laye** (☎ 34–51–75–90). An 18-hole par-72 course is open to the public at Disneyland; rental clubs are available, and some special golf packages are available through travel agents.

Hiking

Confirmed trekkers and Sunday strollers alike will appreciate the region's 4,200 kilometers (2,600 miles) of marked hiking trails, notably the GR 1 (*Grande Randonnée* means a long hike) that loops through Paris's surrounding forests. There are paths for short jaunts (*Petite Randonnée*) too, as well as nature trails in the Regional Park of the Haute Vallée de Chevreuse (for information, ☎ 30–52–09–09). Entrance to the trails is often conveniently near a train station. For maps and detailed itineraries, purchase a copy of the *Ile de France Topo Guides,* available at many bookshops. If you'd like to hike with a convivial group, contact the Hiking Association (64 rue de Gergovie, Paris 14e, ☎ 45–45–31–02).

Horseback Riding

Veteran riders who wish to explore the region on horseback should get in touch with the **Equestrian Touring Association** (ARTEIF, 170 quai de Stalingrad, ☎ 40–93–01–77), just south of Paris in Issy-les-Moulineaux. It offers exciting excursions that combine cultural sightseeing with gallops through the woods. Both beginners and experienced riders are welcome at the **Club Hippique de Versailles** (59 rue Rémont, ☎ 39–51–17–02) or the **Club Hippique des Etangs** (☎ 46–30–35–02) in Meudon-la-Forêt.

Rock Climbing

The Forest of Fontainebleau is famed for its fascinating rock formations, where many a novice alpinist first caught the climbing bug. For more information about Sunday bus excursions to Fontainebleau, contact the **Club Alpin Français** (24 av. Laumière, 75019 Paris, ☎ 42–02–75–94).

Swimming

You'll never be too far away from a public swimming pool. The following are just a few of the options: route de l'Ermitage, Fontainebleau, ☎ 64–22–16–85; blvd. Courtille, Chartres, ☎ 37–28–05–87; 3 rue Léon-Gatin, Versailles, ☎ 39–50–65–71.

Tennis

A tennis fanatic's best bet is to visit one of the many **Bases de Plein Air** (Outdoor Recreation Centers) sprinkled throughout the Ile de France. Most include tennis courts as well as a wide array of sports and leisure activities. Three centers easily accessible from Paris are Bois-Le-Roi (Seine-et-Marne, via train from the Gare de Lyon, ☎ 64–87–83–00); Moisson (Yvelines, via train from the Gare St-Lazare to Bonnières, ☎ 34–79–33–34); and Etampes (Essonne, via RER C to St-Martin-d'Etampes, ☎ 64–94–76–18).

DINING AND LODGING

Dining

The smart restaurants of Ile de France can be just as pricey as their Parisian counterparts. But in smaller towns, and for those prepared to venture only marginally off the beaten tourist track, nourishing, good-value meals are not hard to find. The style of cuisine mirrors that of Paris. The "local delicacies" cited by earnest textbooks—navarin lamb stew, pâté Pantin (pastry filled with meat, chicken, game, or fish), pig's trotters, or vegetable soup—tend to be either banal or obsolete. In season, sumptuous game and asparagus are found in the south of the region; the soft, creamy cheese of Brie hails from Meaux and Coulommiers to the east. More generally, the Ile de France is a prolific producer of vegetables, and at table or the market, you should refuse all but the freshest produce.

CATEGORY	COST*
$$$$	over 400 frs
$$$	200–400 frs
$$	100–200 frs
$	under 100 frs

*per person for a three-course meal, including tax (18.6%) and tip but not wine

Lodging

Remember two things: In summer, hotel rooms are at a premium and reservations are essential; the relative lack of choice means that almost all accommodations in the swankier towns—Versailles, Rambouillet, and Fontainebleau—are on the costly side. Take nothing for granted. Picturesque Senlis, for instance, does not have a single hotel in its historic downtown area. Some of the smaller hotels in the region may not accept credit cards, although the Carte Bleue and its international equivalents (MasterCard and Visa) are widely recognized—unlike American Express, which is often refused in all but the plushest establishments.

Several packages that include Disneyland lodging, entertainment, and admission are available through travel agents in Europe. Disneyland hotels take all major credit cards and are open daily throughout the year. To book your room, contact the Central Reservations Office, BP 104, 77777 Marne-la-Vallée, Cedex 4, ☎ 49–41–49–41, FAX 49–30–71–00.

CATEGORY	COST*
$$$$	over 800 frs
$$$	400–800 frs
$$	200–400 frs
$	under 200 frs

*All prices are for a standard double room for two, including tax (18.6%) and service charge.

Barbizon

DINING

Le Relais de Barbizon. Delicious country-French specialties are served here in large portions, and there is a good choice of fixed-price menus. The restaurant is spacious, with a big open fire and paintings and hunting trophies adorning the walls. The owner is rightly proud of the large terrace, where diners can eat in the shade of lime and chestnut trees. ✕ *2 av. Charles-de-Gaulle,* ☎ *60–66–40–28. Reservations required weekends. MC, V. Closed Tues. evening, Wed. $–$$*

DINING AND LODGING

★ **Auberge des Alouettes.** This delightful family-run 19th-century inn is set in 2 acres of grounds (which the better rooms overlook). The interior has been redecorated in '30s style, but many rooms still have their original oak beams. The popular restaurant (reservations are essential), with its large open terrace, features light cuisine (succinct sauces) and barbecued beef in summer. 🏨 *4 rue Antoine-Barye, 77630,* ☎ *60–66–41–98,* FAX *60–66–20–69. 22 rooms with bath. Restaurant (jacket and tie; closed Sun. evenings in winter), tennis. AE, DC, MC, V. $$*

Chantilly

DINING

Relais Condé. What is probably the classiest restaurant in Chantilly is pleasantly situated opposite the racecourse, in a building that originally served as an Anglican chapel. An adroit chef has introduced a roster of elegant dishes, including duck with honey and spices and lobster terrine. A reasonably priced menu makes it a suitable lunch spot. There is an attractive wine list. ✕ *42 av. du Maréchal-Joffre,* ☎ *16/44–57–05–75. Reservations required. AE, V. Closed Tues. $$*

Relais du Coq Chantant. The discreet, upmarket style of this well-established restaurant attracts a classy clientele of golfers and horse fanciers. They may be willing to splash out à la carte, but we suggest that you opt for the set menu (which changes weekly) to sample a traditional meal based on fowl or rabbit. ✕ *21 rte. de Creil,* ☎ *16/44–57–01–28. Reservations advised. Jacket required. AE, DC, MC, V. $$*

LODGING

La Calèche. This small, underwhelming hotel and restaurant is conveniently placed on the avenue leading from the train station to the château. It's cheap and acceptable for a night's stopover, though your reception may be somewhat lacking in warmth. 🏨 *3 av. du Maréchal-Joffre, 60500,* ☎ *16/44–57–02–55. 10 rooms, some with shower. MC, V. $$*

Campanile. This functional, modern motel is set in a quiet, relaxing location just outside Chantilly, on the edge of the forest. (The forest setting goes far to compensate for the lack of interior atmosphere.) There's a grillroom for straightforward, if unexciting, meals. 🏨 *Les Huits Curés, on the N16 to Creil, 60500,* ☎ *16/44–57–39–24,* FAX *44–58–10–05. 50 rooms, most with bath. Terrace for outdoor dining. MC, V. $$*

Chartres

DINING

La Vieille Maison. Occupying a pretty 14th-century building just 100 yards from the cathedral, this restaurant is a fine choice for either lunch or dinner. The decor is intimate, and the setting, centered on a flower-decked patio, is lovely. The menu changes regularly but invariably includes regional specialties—such as asparagus or rich duck-flavored pâté de Chartres. The homemade foie gras is superb. Prices, though justified, can be steep, but the 160-franc lunch menu is a good bet. ✕

5 rue au Lait, ☎ *16/37–34–10–67. Reservations advised. Jacket and tie. AE, MC, V. Closed Mon., Sun. evening. $$$*

★ **Le Buisson Ardent.** A wood-beamed, second-floor restaurant, Le Buisson Ardent offers robust, low-priced menus, imaginative food, and a view of Chartres cathedral (it's just opposite the south portal). The service is gratifyingly attentive. Try the fruity Gamay de Touraine, an ideal wine for lunchtime. ✗ *10 rue au Lait,* ☎ *16/37–34–04–66. Reservations advised. AE, DC, MC, V. Closed Sun. evening. $–$$*

DINING AND LODGING

★ **Grand Monarque.** The venerable 18th-century Monarque provides guest with the level of consistent comfort you expect from a member of two hotel chains (Best Western and Mapotel). The most atmospheric rooms overlook a small garden or are tucked away in the attic of this former coaching inn. There's also a stiffly formal restaurant, known for its classic seasonal fare. ☎ *22 pl. des Epars, 28000,* ☎ *16/37–21–00–72,* FAX *16/37–36–34–18. 54 rooms, 52 with bath. AE, DC, MC, V. $$$*

Dreux
DINING AND LODGING

Le Beffroi. This is a modest country hotel, excellently situated on the historic square that links the church to the belfry; ask for a room with a view. A cozy restaurant, Auberge Normande, is a couple of doors farther along the square. ☎ *12 pl. Métézeau, 28100,* ☎ *16/37–50–02–03,* FAX *37–42–07–69. 16 rooms with shower. AE, DC, MC, V. Closed Dec. 25. $$*

Ermenonville
DINING AND LODGING

★ **Auberge de la Croix d'Or.** For lunch or an overnight stop in tiny Ermenonville (just a few miles outside Senlis), why not try the Croix d'Or? Its small rooms and homey restaurant have the welcoming feel of a village inn, and the attractive park where Jean-Jacques Rousseau was buried is nearby. ☎ *2 rue du Prince-Radziwill, 60950,* ☎ *44–54–00–04. 11 rooms, some with bath or shower. MC, V. Restaurant closed Mon. and (winter only) Sun. evening; hotel closed mid-Dec.–first wk Feb. $–$$*

Fontainebleau
DINING

La Route du Beaujolais. The food is cheap and the atmosphere cheerful at this jolly eatery near the château, where Lyonnais-style cold cuts and pots of Beaujolais are the mainstays. For something a little more upscale, try the beef fillet with Brie or the braised veal kidney. Set meals are priced at 88 and 130 francs. ✗ *3 rue Montebello,* ☎ *64–22–27–98. Reservations advised. AE, DC, MC, V. $–$$*

DINING AND LODGING

★ **Aigle-Noir.** This may be Fontainebleau's costliest hotel, but you can't go far wrong: Most rooms overlook either the garden or the château and have late-18th- or early-19th-century reproduction furniture to evoke a Napoleonic mood. The grand hotel restaurant, **Le Beauharnais,** serves subtle, imaginative cuisine, generously apportioned. The set menus are recommended. ☎ *27 pl. Napoléon-Bonaparte, 77300,* ☎ *64–22–32–65,* FAX *64–22–17–33. Restaurant reservations required; jacket and tie. 56 rooms with bath. Pool, sauna, exercise room, convention center. AE, DC, MC, V. $$$*

Napoléon. Strategically situated opposite the château, this is not the cheapest hotel in town, but it is surely one of the most charming. Pastel-color guest rooms, with minibars and televisions, have modern furniture and marble baths and look out onto terraces or an indoor garden. The restaurant, **La Table des Maréchaux,** serves satisfying, deftly prepared classics, and the 130-franc menu is an excellent deal. Choose a wine from its fine cellar. ☎ *9 rue Grande, 77300,* ☎ *64–22–20–39,* FAX *64–22–20–87. 57 rooms with bath. Restaurant. Restaurant reservations advised. AE, DC, MC, V. Closed end of Dec. $$$*

LODGING

Hôtel de Londres. The balconies of this tranquil, family-style hotel overlook the château and the Cour des Adieux, where Napoléon bade his troops an emotional farewell; the austere 19th-century facade is a registered landmark. In 1994 the hotel interior was being renovated but has maintained its Louis XV decor. ☎ *1 pl. Général-de-Gaulle, 77300,* ☎ *64–22–20–21. 22 rooms with bath. Restaurant, bar. AE, DC, MC, V. Closed Dec. 20–Jan. 5. $$*

Giverny

DINING

Les Jardins de Giverny. This commendable restaurant, with an old-fashioned dining room that overlooks a rose garden, is close to Monet's house. Enjoy the 120-franc lunch menu, or choose from a repertoire of inventive dishes such as foie gras spiked with applejack or scallops with wild mushrooms. ✕ *1 rue Milieu,* ☎ *16/32–21–60–80. Reservations advised. AE, V. Closed Sun. evening and Mon. $$*

L'Isle-Adam

DINING AND LODGING

Le Cabouillet. The riverside Cabouillet aptly reflects the quiet charm of L'Isle-Adam, thanks to its pretty views over the Oise. You can savor these from each of its eight rooms or from the chic restaurant, where the cooking can be inspired (if it's on the menu, go for the crawfish in Sauternes sauce). ☎ *5 quai de l'Oise, 95290,* ☎ *34–69–00–90,* FAX *34–69–33–88. 8 rooms with bath. Restaurant reservations advised. AE, DC, MC, V. Hotel closed Dec. 25–early Feb. Restaurant closed Wed. $$–$$$*

Maintenon

DINING AND LODGING

Château d'Esclimont. Nineteen kilometers (12 miles) southeast of Maintenon (take D116 to the village of Gaillardon, keep an eye out for its magnificent old church, and then turn left) is the restored Renaissance Château d'Esclimont. The château is well worth seeking out if you wish to eat (or slumber) like royalty. Set in luxurious grounds, with lawns, a lake, and a heliport, this member of the Relais & Châteaux chain is a regular target for Parisian power brokers. The cuisine is sophisticated and varied: Quail, lamb, game in season, and lobster top the menu. Guest rooms are luxuriously furnished (several were recently renovated), and there are two private tennis courts and a heated swimming pool. The 16th-century château makes an admirable base for visiting Rambouillet and Chartres. ☎ *28700 St-Symphorien-le-Château,* ☎ *16/37–31–15–15,* FAX *16/37–31–57–91. 48 rooms with bath. Hotel and dinner reservations essential. Jacket and tie. Restaurant, pool, tennis, fishing. MC, V. $$$*

Montfort l'Amaury

DINING AND LODGING

Les Voyageurs. This small, homely hotel at the bottom of Montfort's cobbled main street, with wood-beam bedrooms, a good-value restaurant, and a cheerful bar with incongruous but appealing '50s decor, is a handy base for exploring Thoiry, Dreux, or Rambouillet. ☎ *49 rue de Paris, 78490,* ☎ *34–86–00–14,* FAX *34–86–14–56. 7 rooms with shower. MC, V. Closed Aug. 15–31. $$*

Provins

DINING AND LODGING

Vieux Remparts. Old wood beams inside and a cheerful, leafy courtyard for outdoor eating in the summer help to create a charming atmosphere at the Vieux Remparts, housed in an attractive old building in the Ville Haute. The creative menus offer good value for the money, and meals are sustaining. ☎ *3 rue Couverte, 77160,* ☎ *64–08–94–00,* FAX *60–67–77–22. 25 rooms with bath. Reservations accepted. 2 rooms accessible to people in wheelchairs. AE, DC, MC, V. $$–$$$*

Rambouillet

DINING

La Poste. You can bank on traditional, unpretentious cooking at this former coaching inn right in the center of town. Service is good, as is the selection of fixed-price menus, weekends included. Game is a specialty in season. ✕ *101 rue du Général-de-Gaulle,* ☎ *34–83–03–01. Reservations advised. Jacket and tie. AE, MC, V. $*

St-Germain-en-Laye

DINING

★ **La Feuillantine.** Friendly service and an imaginative, good-value fixed-price menu have made this restaurant a success with locals as well as tourists. Gizzard salad, salmon with endive, and herbed chicken fricassee with morels are among the specialties. ✕ *10 rue des Louviers,* ☎ *34–51–04–24. Reservations advised. MC, V. Closed Dec. 25. $$*

La Petite Auberge. The specialty here is farmhouse-style cooking from the Aveyron region of southwest France. Aged beef is cooked over an open fire throughout the year, and cheerful red wine (Chinon, from the Loire Valley) is drawn straight from the barrel. Game is served in season. ✕ *119-bis rue Léon-Desnoyer,* ☎ *34–51–03–99. Reservations accepted. Jacket required. MC, V. Closed Tues., Sat. lunch, mid-July–mid-Aug. $$*

LODGING

★ **La Forestière.** St-Germain is no stopover point for those watching their wallets. The town is obsessed with style, and this is its most stylish hotel, a member of the deluxe Relais & Châteaux chain. Its forest setting, 18th-century-style furniture, and a fine, if pricey, restaurant, the **Caza-udehore,** contribute to a sense of well-being. ☎ *1 av. Président-Kennedy, 78100,* ☎ *39–73–36–60,* FAX *39–73–73–88. 25 rooms and 5 suites, all with bath. MC, V. Restaurant closed to nonguests Mon. (except holidays). $$$*

Senlis

DINING

★ **Les Gourmandins.** This cozy, two-floor restaurant in old Senlis serves some interesting dishes—try the marjoram-scented rabbit with tiny vegetable ravioli—and offers a fine wine list. The fixed-price menus served at lunch and dinner offer great value for your money. ✕ *3 pl. de la Halle,* ☎ *16/44–60–94–01. Weekend reservations advised. V. Closed Tues. $$*

LODGING

Hostellerie Porte-Bellon. This is the closest you'll get to spending a night in the historic center of Senlis. A modest yet efficient hotel, the Porte-Bellon is just a five-minute walk from the cathedral and is close to the bus station. ☎ *51 rue Bellon, 60300, ☎ 16/44–53–03–05, ℻ 16/44–53–29–94. 20 rooms, most with bath. Restaurant. MC, V. Closed mid-Dec.–mid-Jan., Fri. (except in summer). $*

Vernon
DINING AND LODGING

★ **Château de Brécourt.** This 17th-century stone-and-brick château, with its high-pitched roofs and imposing forecourt, is set in extensive grounds 10 kilometers (6 miles) south of Vernon along D181 near Douains. Inventive food in the august atmosphere of the tasteful dining room makes it a popular spot with visitors to Giverny, just across the Seine from Vernon. And, as such hotel-cum-châteaus go, guest rooms can represent a relatively good value. ☎ *27120 Douains, ☎ 16/32–52–40–50, ℻ 16/32–52–69–65. 24 rooms and 5 suites, all with bath. Pool, tennis, parking. AE, DC, MC, V. $$$*

Versailles
DINING

★ **Les Trois Marches.** The most famous restaurant in Versailles is also recognized as one of the best in the Ile de France, thanks to its subtle and creative cuisine. Even the most sophisticated foodophiles salivate at the thought of Gérard Vié's bisque of lobster, salmon with fennel, or turbot *galette*, impeccably served in the sumptuous surroundings of the Trianon Palace hotel (*see* Lodging, below). ✗ *1 blvd. de la Reine, ☎ 39–50–13–21. Reservations required. Jacket and tie. AE, DC, MC, V. Closed Sun., Mon., and Aug. $$$$*

La Grande Sirène. The addition of an appealing 150-franc lunch menu (wine included), served every day but Sunday, makes this pretty spot near the château a popular noontime choice. Try the zesty simmered snails or deftly prepared fish accompanied by fine wines and fine service. ✗ *25 rue du Maréchal-Foch, ☎ 39–53–08–08. Reservations advised. AE, MC, V. Closed Mon. $$*

Quai N° 1. Fish and seafood rule supreme amid the sails, barometers, and model ships of this quaintly decked-out restaurant. Home-smoked salmon, and sauerkraut with fish are specialties. Eating à la carte isn't too expensive, and there are value-priced set menus. ✗ *1 av. de St-Cloud, ☎ 39–50–42–26. Reservations advised. MC, V. Closed Sun. dinner, Mon. $$*

LODGING

Trianon Palace. This deluxe hotel is set in its own huge garden close to the château park. It is a turn-of-the-century creation of imposing size whose once-faded charm was given a thorough overhaul in 1991 by its new Japanese owners, who were determined to turn it into one of Europe's most prestigious hotels. The results are spectacular: The health club alone is worth the price of admission. The restaurant (*see* Les Trois Marches, *above*) offers an inventive cuisine, served in fine weather on the huge outdoor terrace. ☎ *1 blvd. de la Reine, 78000, ☎ 30–84–38–39, ℻ 39–51–57–79. 97 rooms and 32 suites, all with bath. Restaurant, pool, health club, business services. AE, DC, MC, V. $$$$*

Sofitel. Opened in 1992 (as the Pullman), this luxury hotel, nestled behind a giant triumphal arch dating from the Sun King's era, is handier (and slightly cheaper) than the Trianon Palace for exploring the old town, and the château is just 5 minutes' walk away. Rooms are spacious and decor subdued to the point of blandness. Set menus in the Manèges restaurant start at around 160 francs. ☎ *2 bis av. de Paris, 78000, ☎ 39–53–30–31, ℻ 39–53–87–20. 146 rooms and 6 suites, all with bath. Restaurant, bar, business services. AE, DC, MC, V. $$$$*

Le Versailles. This unpretentious modern hotel, ideally situated close to the château, is warmly recommended if you plan to explore the town on foot (or balk at the palatial prices of the Trianon Palace, *above*). Guest rooms have comfort but lack character. There's no restaurant. 🖭 *7 rue Ste-Anne, 78000,* ☎ *39–50–64–65,* 🆑 *39–02–37–85. 50 rooms with bath. AE, DC, MC, V. $$–$$$*

Home St-Louis. The small, recently modernized Home St-Louis is a good, cheap, quiet bet—close to the cathedral and not too far from the château. There's no restaurant. 🖭 *28 rue St-Louis, 78000,* ☎ *39–50–23–55,* 🆑 *39–21–62–45. 27 rooms with bath. MC, V. $$*

THE ARTS AND NIGHTLIFE

The Arts

With Paris so close, it seems pointless to detail the comparatively minor offerings of the towns of the Ile de France in the domains of theater, music, or cinema (*see* The Arts in Chapter 3). There are, however, a number of arts festivals staged in the Ile de France that have earned esteem in their own right. Of these, the largest is the **Festival de l'Ile de France** (Sept.–Oct.), famed for concerts held at châteaus (for details, ☎ 42–96–02–32). There are also music festivals in **Provins** (June), **St-Denis** (June–mid-July, with concerts in the basilica, ☎ 42–43–30–97), **Versailles** (May–June, concerts and operas, details available at the Tourist Office, ☎ 30–97–81–03), and at the abbey of **Royaumont** (mid-Aug.–mid-Oct., ☎ 34–68–05–50).

An invaluable list of monthly regional events is the *Tourisme Loisirs* brochure, produced by the **Comité Régional du Tourisme Ile-de-France** (26 av. de l'Opéra, 75001 Paris, ☎ 42–60–28–62).

Nightlife

We recommend that anyone interested in painting the town red do so in Paris; there's precious little to choose from in the small towns of the Ile de France, although a few bars and clubs in Versailles and St-Germain-en-Laye stay open late (especially on Friday and Saturday). (*See* Nightlife in Chapter 2.)

However, if you're visiting Disneyland, plan to take in **Buffalo Bill's Wild West Show,** a two-hour dinner extravaganza with a menu of sausages, spareribs, and chili and performances by a talented troupe of stunt riders, bronco busters, tribal dancers, and musicians, plus some 50 horses, a dozen buffalo, a bull, and Annie Oakley, Princess of the Winchester Rifle, with a golden-maned Buffalo Bill as emcee. A re-creation of a show that dazzled Parisians a hundred years ago, it's corny but great fun for those who can manage the appropriate suspension of disbelief. *Reservations:* ☎ *60–45–71–00. Show and dinner 305 frs adults, 205 frs children. Two shows nightly.*

ILE DE FRANCE ESSENTIALS

Arriving and Departing

By Plane

Visitors to the Ile de France can arrive at **Charles de Gaulle** (Roissy), 25 kilometers (16 miles) northwest of the city (☎ 48–62–22–80), or **Orly,** 16 kilometers (10 miles) south (☎ 49–75–15–15). Shuttle buses link Disneyland to the airports at Roissy, 56 kilometers (35 miles) away, and Orly, 50 kilometers (31 miles) distant; buses taking 45 minutes run every 45 minutes from Roissy, every 60 minutes from Orly (less frequently in low season), and cost 75 francs.

By Train

Many of the sights mentioned in our exploring text can be reached by train from Paris. Both regional and mainline (Le Mans–bound) trains leave the **Gare Montparnasse** for Chartres; the former also stop at Versailles, Rambouillet, and Maintenon. Gare Montparnasse is also the terminus for trains to Dreux (Granville line) and for the suburban trains that stop at Montfort-l'Amaury, the nearest station to Thoiry.

Some mainline trains from **Gare St-Lazare** stop at Mantes-la-Jolie and Vernon on their way to Rouen and Le Havre. Mantes and Pontoise are termini for the frequent suburban trains from St-Lazare, most of which stop at Conflans-Ste-Honorine. Suburban trains leave St-Lazare for Maisons-Laffitte and Versailles, and the **Gare du Nord** for L'Isle-Adam and Beaumont-sur-Oise. Chantilly is on the main north-bound line from Gare du Nord (Senlis can be reached by bus from Chantilly) and Provins on a suburban line from **Gare de l'Est.** Fontainebleau—or, rather, neighboring Avon, 2 kilometers (1½ miles) away (there is frequent bus service)—is 45 minutes from **Gare de Lyon.**

St-Germain-en-Laye is a terminus of the **RER-A express metro** that tunnels through Paris (main stations at Etoile, Auber, and Les Halles). The RER-A also accesses Conflans, Maisons-Laffitte, and at the other end, the new suburban station for Disneyland Paris (Marne-la-Vallée-Chessy), which is within 100 yards of the entrance to both Disneyland, the theme park, and Festival Disney. Journey time to the theme park is around 40 minutes and trains operate every 10–30 minutes, depending on the time of day. A mainline TGV station opened next to the RER station in 1994, providing direct access from Lille, Lyon, and ultimately London and Brussels. The handiest of Versailles's three train stations is the one reached by the **RER-C** line (main stations at Austerlitz, St-Michel, Invalides, and Champ de Mars).

Getting Around

By Car

Although a comprehensive rail network ensures that most towns in the Ile de France can make comfortable day excursions from Paris, the only way to crisscross the region without returning to the capital is by car. There is no shortage of expressways or fast highways, but be prepared for delays close to Paris and during the morning and evening rush hours.

Guided Tours

Orientation

Paris Vision (214 rue de Rivoli, 1er, ☎ 42–60–31–25) and **Cityrama** (4 pl. des Pyramides, 1er, ☎ 44–55–61–00) run half-day guided trips to Chartres on Tuesday, Thursday, and Saturday afternoons (250 francs), combined excursions to Chartres plus Versailles (440 francs), and half-day trips to Fontainebleau and Barbizon (departures 1:30 Wednesday, Friday, and Sunday; price 300 francs; additional departures are scheduled in summer).

Guided excursions to Giverny are organized by **American Express** (11 rue Scribe, 9e, ☎ 47–77–77–37) from April through October and the **RATP**, either half-day or full-day when combined with Rouen. *See* Guided Tours *in* Chapter 2.

Personal Guides

For touring in style, get in touch with **Alliance Autos** (5 bis av. Foch, St-Mandé, near the Bois de Vincennes, ☎ 43–28–20–20, FAX 43–28–27–27). Bilingual guides with luxury cars or a minibus will take you around Paris or the surrounding area for a minimum of four hours at around 500 francs an hour (though call to check details and prices).

Important Addresses and Numbers

Car Rental

Avis (☎ 46–07–82–45); **Hertz** (☎ 45–74–97–39); **Europcar** (☎ 45–51–21–11). All in Paris.

Visitor Information

For written inquiries only, contact the **Comité Régional de Tourisme d'Ile de France** (26 av. de l'Opéra, 75001 Paris, ☎ 42–60–28–62). Local offices are in **Barbizon** (55 rue Grande, ☎ 60–66–41–87), **Chartres** (pl. de la Cathédrale, ☎ 16/37–21–50–00), **Fontainebleau** (31 pl. Napoléon-Bonaparte, ☎ 64–22–25–68), **Rambouillet** (8 pl. de la Libération, ☎ 34–83–21–21), and **Versailles** (7 rue des Réservoirs, ☎ 39–50–36–22). Information on Disneyland Paris is available from the **Euro Disneyland Central Reservations Office** (BP 104, 77777 Marne-la Vallée, Cedex 4, ☎ 49–41–49–10, FAX 49–30–71–00).

4 The Loire Valley

THE LOIRE is the longest river in France, rising deep in the heart of the southern Massif Central and winding its way north and then west for over 960 kilometers (600 miles) before reaching the Atlantic at Nantes. Halfway along, just outside the town of Orléans, the river makes a wide, westward bend, gliding languidly through low, rich country known as the Val de Loire—the Loire Valley. In this temperate "garden" region—a 224-kilometer (140-mile) stretch between Orléans and Angers—hundreds of châteaus rise from the rocky banks of the Loire and its tributaries: the Rivers Cher, Indre, Vienne, and Loir (with no *e*).

For centuries the Loire River was the area's principal means of transportation and an important barrier to invading armies. Cities rose at strategic bridgeheads, and fortresses—the earliest châteaus—appeared on the slopes of towering hills. The Loire Valley was hotly disputed by France and England during the Middle Ages, belonging to England (under the Anjou Plantagenet family) between 1154 and 1216 and again during the Hundred Years' War (1337–1453). It was the example of Joan of Arc, the Maid of Orléans, (where she had her most rousing military successes), that finally prompted the French to expel the English.

The Loire Valley's golden age came under François I (1515–47), flamboyant contemporary of Henry VIII. His salamander emblem is to be seen in many châteaus, including Chambord, the mightiest of them all. He hired Renaissance craftsmen from Italy and hobnobbed with the aging Leonardo da Vinci, his guest at Amboise. Although the nation's power base shifted to Paris around 1600, aristocrats continued to erect luxurious palaces along the Loire until the end of the 18th century. Since that time, many châteaus—too expensive now for even the wealthiest to maintain—have fallen to the care of the state and are now preserved as cultural and historic monuments.

Besides the châteaus, the Loire Valley offers visitors all kinds of sports and outdoor activities. Horseback riding, fishing, canoeing, and swimming facilities abound. In summer, tourists and natives alike flock to concerts, music festivals, fairs, and the celebrated *son-et-lumière* (sound-and-light) extravaganzas held on the grounds of many châteaus.

EXPLORING

Orientation

For touring purposes, we've divided the Loire Valley into two regions: the western Loire, from Angers to Tours, and the eastern Loire, from Amboise to Orléans. The Loire is for gentle exploring, picnicking, sampling wines, retelling history, and visiting France's most grand, if not grandiose, aristocratic country homes. If you have only two or three days in the Loire, concentrate on the region between Amboise and Orléans. If you will be relying on public transportation, it's a good idea to use one of the region's four major cities—Tours, Blois, Angers, or Orléans—or the town of Saumur as your base.

Tour 1: The Western Loire Valley—Angers to Tours

Numbers in the margin correspond to points of interest on the Loire Valley and Tours maps.

❶ Angers, former capital of the Anjou region, lies on the banks of the River Maine, just north of the Loire, about 106 kilometers (66 miles) west of Tours and 210 kilometers (130 miles) from Orléans. In addition to a towering medieval fortress filled with extraordinary tapestries, the town has a fine Gothic cathedral; a choice of art galleries; and a network of pleasant, traffic-free shopping streets. Well served by public transportation, Angers is the starting point for numerous bus, riverboat, hiking, biking, horseback, and ballooning excursions.

The town's principal sights lie within a compact square formed by the three main boulevards and the River Maine. When you arrive, head for the castle, just off the river between boulevard De Gaulle and quai Ligny. Before you go in, stop at the **Maison du Vin** (5 bis pl. Kennedy; open 9–noon and 2–5, closed Sun.), the organization that represents Anjou's wine producers. It can provide lots of leaflets about wines, suggestions on which vineyards to visit, and even a free sample or two. The tourist office is next door, so you may want to drop in there for maps and information.

The massive **château,** dating from the 13th century, glowers over the town from behind turreted moats, which are now laid out as gardens, overrun with deer and blooming flowers. As you explore the grounds, note the startling contrast between the thick, defensive walls and the formal garden, with its delicate, white tufa-stone chapel, erected in the 16th century. For a sweeping view of the city and surrounding countryside, climb one of the castle towers.

A new gallery within the castle grounds houses the great **Tapestry of the Apocalypse,** completed in 1390. Measuring 16 feet high and 120 yards long, it shows a series of 70 horrifying and humorous scenes from the Book of Revelation. In one, mountains of fire fall from heaven while boats capsize and men struggle in the water; another shows an intriguing, seven-headed beast. *Pl. Kennedy,* ☎ *41–87–43–47.* ☛ *31 frs adults, 15 frs students and senior citizens, 5 frs children.* ☉ *July–Aug., daily 10–7; Sept.–June, daily 9:30–12:30 and 2–5:30.*

Just east of the château is the **Cathédrale St-Maurice** (pl. Freppel), a 12th- and 13th-century Gothic cathedral noted for its curious Romanesque facade and original stained-glass windows; you'll need binoculars to appreciate both fully. A few steps north, practically in the cathedral's shadow, lies Angers's large covered food market, **Les Halles** (pl. Mondain; open Tues.–Sun. 9–7). Treat it as a gourmet museum, or stop in for an exotic lunch. A modern shopping mall sits right above it.

Just south of the cathedral, in a house that once sheltered Cesare Borgia and Mary, Queen of Scots, is the **Musée des Beaux-Arts** picture gallery. Among the museum's attractions is an impressive collection of Old Masters from the 17th and 18th centuries, including paintings by Raphael, Watteau, Fragonard, and Boucher. *10 rue du Musée,* ☎ *41–88–64–65.* ☛ *12 frs.* ☉ *Tues.–Sun. 10–noon and 2–6.*

Around the corner, in the refurbished Eglise Toussaint, is the **Musée David d'Angers,** housing a collection of dramatic sculptures by Jean-Pierre David (1788–1859), the city's favorite son. *33 rue Toussaint,* ☎ *41–87–21–03.* ☛ *10 frs adults.* ☉ *Tues.–Sun. 10–noon and 2–6.*

❷ The château of **Plessis-Bourré** lies 20 kilometers (12 miles) north of Angers by N162 and D768. Built between 1468 and 1473 by Jean Bourré, one of Louis XI's top-ranking civil servants, the château looks like a traditional grim fortress: The bridge across its moat is nearly 50 yards long. Once you step into the central courtyard, however, the gentler mood of the Renaissance takes over.

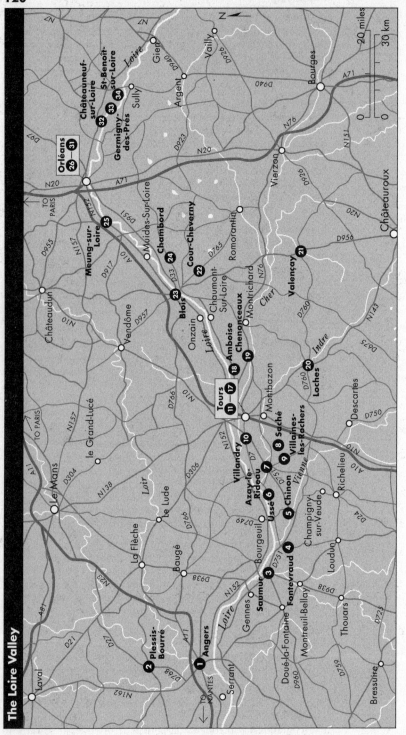

What makes this place special is the painted wooden ceiling in the Salle des Gardes (Guard Room). Jean Bourré's hobby was alchemy—an ancient branch of chemistry with more than a touch of the occult—and the ceiling's 24 hexagonal panels are covered with scenes illustrating the craft. Some have overtones of the grotesque dreamworld of late-medieval Dutch painter Hieronymus Bosch (1450–1516), while others illustrate folktales or proverbs. A few must have been painted just for the fun of it: A topless lady steers a land-yacht with wooden wheels (thought to be an allegory of spirit and matter); people urinate ceremoniously (ammonia was extracted from urine); an emaciated wolf takes a bite out of a startled lady (according to folk legend, the wolf's diet was faithful wives, apparently in short supply); and Thurberesque dogs gambol in between. You may want to ignore the guide's lecture on furniture and spend your time gazing upward. ☎ *41–32–06–01.* ☛ *35 frs adults, 28 frs students, 18 frs children.* ◎ *Sept.–Nov. and Apr.–June, Thurs.–Tues. 10–noon and 2–6; Dec.–Mar., Thurs.–Tues. 2–5.*

★ ❸ About 83 kilometers (52 miles) east of Angers by road, and accessible by train, **Saumur** is an excellent base for exploring the western Loire Valley. The town is known for its flourishing mushroom industry, which produces 100,000 tons per year. La Musée du Champignon (*see* Guided Tours, *above*) tells all. The same cool tunnels in which the mushrooms grow also provide an ideal storage place for the local *mousseux* (sparkling wines).

You will find an efficient tourist office on place Bilange. Perched high above town and river is Saumur's elegant, white 14th-century **château,** and if you arrive in the evening, the sight of the floodlit castle will take your breath away. Though you can reach it by car, it's only a 10-minute walk from the tourist office. The route takes you through the pretty old town and place St-Pierre, with its lively Saturday market.

TIME OUT When you get to the top of the hill, why not stop for a picnic on the grass outside the château? If you've forgotten your picnic provisions, there's a café just beside the parking lot.

If the château looks familiar, it's probably because you've seen it in countless reproductions from the famous *Très Riches Heures (Book of Hours)* painted for the duc de Berri in 1416, now in the Musée Condé at Château de Chantilly (*see* Tour 2 in Chapter 3, Ile de France). Inside it's bright and cheerful, with its fairy-tale gateway and plentiful potted flowers. Two museums, the **Musée des Arts Décoratifs** and the **Musée du Cheval** (Horse Museum), are housed here, the former with a fine collection of medieval objets d'art and 18th- and 19th-century porcelain. Both are included in the guided tour. Afterward, climb the **Tour de Guet** (Watchtower) for an impressive view. ☎ *41–51–30–46.* ☛ *33 frs adults, 24 frs children and senior citizens.* ◎ *July–Sept., daily 9–6:30; Oct. and Apr.–June, daily 9–11:30 and 2–6; Nov.–Mar., Wed.–Mon. 10–12 and 2–5.*

The old powder house at the château holds the **Musée de la Figurine-Jouet,** which has more than 2,000 figures on display. ☎ *41–67–39–23.* ☛ *12 frs adults, 7 frs children.* ◎ *Wed.–Mon., June and Sept. 2–6, July–Aug. 10–6.*

At **Montreuil-Bellay,** about 17 kilometers (11 miles) south of Saumur on D938, you can visit a 15th-century **château** with majestic towers and pointed roofs. The interior is equally fascinating, offering a fine collection of rich furniture and tapestries, a fully equipped medieval kitchen, and a chapel adorned with frescoes of angelic musicians. For a memorable view, take a stroll in the private gardens; graceful white turrets tower high above the trees and rosebushes, and down below, the little River Thouet winds its lazy way to the Loire. *Pl. des Ormeaux,* ☎ *41–52–33–06.* ☛ *38 frs.* ☉ *Apr.–Nov., Wed.–Mon. 10–noon and 2–5:30.*

Even if the château is closed, be sure to visit the **public gardens** beside the river. Cafés and little restaurants abound in the village.

About 16 kilometers (10 miles) southeast of Saumur is the town of ❹ **Fontevraud,** famous for its large, medieval **abbey,** which was of central importance in the history of both England and France. Founded in 1099, the abbey offered separate churches and living quarters for nuns, monks, lepers, "repentant" female sinners, and the sick. Between 1115 and the French Revolution in 1789, 39 different abbesses—among them a granddaughter of William the Conqueror—directed its operations. The abbey church contains the tombs of Henry II of England; his wife, Eleanor of Aquitaine; and their son, Richard Coeur de Lion—Richard the Lionhearted. Though their bones were scattered during the Revolution, their effigies remain. Napoléon turned the abbey church into a prison, and so it remained until 1963, when historical restoration work—still under way—was begun.

The great 12th-century abbey church is one of the most eclectic architectural structures in France. The medieval section is built of simple stone and topped with a series of domes; the chapter house, with its collection of 16th-century religious wall paintings (prominent abbesses served as models), is unmistakably Renaissance; and the paving stones bear the salamander emblems of François I. Next to the long refectory, you will find the unusual octagonal kitchen, its tall spire, the **Tour d'Evrault,** serving as one of the abbey's 20 faceted stone chimneys. ☎ *41–51–71–41.* ☛ *26 frs adults, 17 frs senior citizens, 7 frs children.* ☉ *May–mid-Sept., daily 9–noon and 2–6:30; mid-Sept.–Apr., daily 9:30–12:30 and 2–5:30.*

★ ❺ **Chinon** lies in the fertile countryside between the Loire and the Vienne rivers, 29 kilometers (18 miles) southeast of Saumur, via Fontevraud. Several trains a day run from Tours, stopping at Azay-le-Rideau on the way. Bicycles can be rented at Chinon station.

The town—birthplace of the author François Rabelais (1494–1553)—is dominated by the towering ruins of its medieval **fortress-castle,** perched high above the River Vienne. Though the main tourist office is in the town below, during the summer months a special annex operates from the castle grounds. Both the village and the château stand among steep, cobbled slopes, so wear comfortable walking shoes.

The vast fortress dates from the time of Henry II of England, who died here in 1189 and was buried at Fontevraud. Two centuries later, the castle witnessed an important historic moment: Joan of Arc's recognition of the disguised dauphin, later Charles VII. In the early 17th century, the castle was partially dismantled by its then-owner, Cardinal Richelieu (1585–1642), who used many of its stones to build a new palace 21 kilometers (13 miles) away (*see* Off the Beaten Track, *below*).

At Chinon, everything except the royal chambers—which house a small museum—is open to the elements. For a fine view of the region, climb the **Coudray Tower,** where, in 1307, leading members of the crusading Knights Templar were imprisoned before being taken to Paris, tried, and burned at the stake. The **Tour de l'Horloge,** whose bell has been sounding the hours since 1399, houses a small **Joan of Arc museum.** ☎ *47–93–13–45.* ☛ *23 frs adults, 18 frs senior citizens and* *children under 19 years.* ☉ *Daily Nov.–mid-Mar. 9–noon and 2–5; mid-Mar.–June and Sept. 9–6; July and Aug. 9–7; Oct. 9–5. Closed Wed. Jan.–Feb.*

Follow the signposted steps down into the old town, or drive your car to the River Vienne pathway. **Place de l'Hôtel**—the main square—is the best place to begin exploring. Stop by the tourist office and pick up a town plan to help you explore the town's fine medieval streets and alleys. While you are there, visit **Le Musée du Vin** (Wine Museum) in the vaulted cellars. This is a fascinating exhibit, full of information on vine growing and wine and barrel making. An English commentary is available, and the admission charge entitles you to a sample of the local product. *12 rue Voltaire,* ☎ *47–93–25–63.* ☛ *22 frs.* ☉ *Apr.–Oct., Fri.–Wed. 10–noon and 2–6.*

★ ❻ About 10 kilometers (6 miles) northeast of Chinon, set between the Forest of Chinon and the Loire, is the archetypal fairy-tale château of **Ussé,** with its astonishing array of delicate towers and turrets. Tourist literature describes it as the original Sleeping Beauty castle—the inspiration for Charles Perrault's beloved 17th-century story. Though parts of the castle date from the 1400s, most of it was completed two centuries later. It is a flamboyant mix of Gothic and Renaissance styles—stylish and romantic, built for fun, not fighting. Its history supports this playful image: It suffered no bloodbaths—no political conquests or conflicts. And a tablet in the chapel indicates that even the French Revolution passed it by.

After admiring the château's luxurious furnishings and 19th-century French fashion exhibit, climb the spiral stairway to the tower to view the River Indre through the battlements. Here you will also find a waxwork effigy of Sleeping Beauty herself. Before you leave, visit the 16th-century chapel in the garden; its door is decorated with pleasingly sinister skull-and-crossbone carvings. ☎ *47–95–54–05.* ☛ *54 frs.* ☉ *Mid-Mar.–Nov. 11., daily 9–noon and 2–6.*

❼ Continuing east about 11 kilometers (7 miles) from Ussé, you'll soon arrive at **Azay-le-Rideau.** Nestled in a sylvan setting on the banks of the River Indre, this 16th-century white château was—like Ussé—a Renaissance pleasure palace rather than a serious fortress.

A financial scandal forced its builder, royal financier Gilles Berthelot, to flee France shortly after its construction in 1520. For centuries, it passed from one private owner to another and was finally bought by the state in 1905. Though the interior offers an interesting blend of furniture and artwork, you may wish to spend most of your time exploring the enchanting private park. During the summer, visitors can enjoy delightful son-et-lumière shows on the castle grounds. *Rue Balzac,* ☎ *47–45–42–04.* ☛ *26 frs adults, 17 frs senior citizens and students, 6 frs children.* ☉ *Apr.–Sept., daily 9:30–6; Oct.–Mar., 10–12:30 and 2–4:45.*

❽ About 6 kilometers (4 miles) east of Azay-le-Rideau is the village of **Saché,** best known for its associations with the novelist Honoré de Balzac. Though the town had a real castle during the Middle Ages, the present **château,** built between the 16th and 18th centuries, is more of a comfortable country house than a fortress. Balzac came here—to the home of his friends, the Marjonnes—during the 1830s, both to write and to escape his creditors. The château houses a substantial **Balzac museum,** with exhibits ranging from photographs to original manuscripts to the coffeepot he used to help keep him writing up to 16 hours a day. Those who have never read Balzac and don't understand spoken French may find little of interest in Saché; those who have, and do, will return to the novels with fresh enthusiasm and understanding. ☎ 47–26–86–50. ☞ *21 frs adults, 17 frs senior citizens, 14 frs children under 19 years.* ☉ *Feb.–mid-Mar., Thurs.–Tues. 9:30–11:45 and 2:15–4:30; mid-Mar.–Sept., daily 9–noon and 2–6; Oct.–Nov., Thurs.–Tues. 9:30–11:45 and 2:15–4:30.*

❾ From Saché, it's worth making a brief detour to **Villaines-les-Rochers,** about 6 kilometers (4 miles) southwest, to see the village's interesting **wickerwork cooperative.** Local people have been producing *osier* (willow) products for centuries. In 1849, when the craft was threatened with extinction, the parish priest persuaded 65 small groups of basketweavers to form France's first agricultural workers' cooperative. A small museum, **Musée de l'Osier et de la Vannerie** (☎ 47–50–02–09; admission 7 frs), tells the cooperative's story, but it is only open weekend afternoons from mid-June to mid-September. However, all year the surrounding shops have lots of handmade objects—from sofas to cat baskets to babies' rattles. *Société Coopérative de Vannerie.* ☞ *Free.* ☉ *Most of the year, Mon.–Sat. 10–noon and 2–6, Sun. 10–noon and 2–7.*

❿ After leaving Villaines-les-Rochers, head for **Villandry,** following D57 back through Azay-le-Rideau to the junction with D7 and take a right. The **Château de Villandry** stands on the south side of the Loire, about 19 kilometers (12 miles) southwest of Tours. Its extravagant, terraced ★ **gardens** are renowned and well worth a visit.

Both the gardens and the château date from the 16th century, but, over the years, they fell into disrepair. In 1906, Spanish doctor Joachim Carvalla and his wife, American heiress Ann Coleman, bought the property and began a long process of restoration. The gardens were replanted according to a rigorous, geometric design, with zig-zagging hedges enclosing flower beds, vegetable plots, and gravel walks. The result is an aristocratic 16th-century *jardin à la française.* Below an avenue of 1,500 precisely pruned lime trees lies an ornamental lake filled with swans: Not a ripple is out of place. The aromatic and medicinal garden, with plots neatly labeled in three languages, is especially appealing.

The château itself has a remarkable gilded ceiling—imported from Toledo, in Spain—and a collection of fine Spanish paintings. However, the garden is unquestionably the main attraction, and since it is usually open during the two-hour French lunch break, you can have it to yourself for a good part of the afternoon. ☎ 47–50–02–09. ☞ *Château and gardens, 37 frs adults, 28 frs students and senior citizens; gardens only, 24 frs adults, 18 frs students and senior citizens.* ☉ *Château mid-Mar.–mid-Nov., daily 9–6; garden all year, daily 9–sunset (or 8, whichever is earlier).*

⓫ About 20 kilometers (12 miles) east of Villandry lies the city of **Tours,** an ideal center from which to tour the Loire Valley's attractions by public transportation. Trains from Tours run along the river in both directions, and regular bus services radiate from here; in addition, the city is the starting point for a variety of organized bus excursions (many with English-speaking guides). The former town has mushroomed into a city of a quarter of a million inhabitants, with an ugly modern sprawl of factories, high-rise blocks, and overhead expressway junctions cluttering up the outskirts. Thanks to current mayor M. Jean Royer's enthusiasm for restoring the old buildings, the city center remains pleasant and manageable. Tours is easy to get around by public buses. Travelers with cars may prefer to base themselves in any of a dozen smaller towns within a half hour's drive of Tours (Montbazon and Amboise in particular, are recommended for their hotels and restaurants—*see* Dining and Lodging, *below*) but should certainly explore the city during their stay.

⑫ Start your tour at place du Maréchal Leclerc, usually called the **place de la Gare.** Here you'll find the fine Belle Epoque train station, with its cast-iron curlicues; the bus station; and the tourist office. Many of the most convenient hotels are situated here or just around the corner.

The layout of the city is fairly simple. Turn left from place du Maréchal Leclerc; go down boulevard Heurteloup, to reach place Jean-Jaurès and the imposing Hôtel de Ville; then turn right into rue Nationale. This street holds many of the city's major shops, and if you continue along it for just over a half mile, you'll reach the River Loire. Turning right near the river end, you'll soon reach the cathedral, the château, and the Musée des Beaux-Arts. If you turn left off rue Nationale, you'll come to place Plumereau and a quaint pedestrian precinct in the area known as Vieux Tours.

⑬ The **Cathédrale St-Gatien,** built between 1239 and 1484, reveals a mixture of architectural styles. Its majestic two-tower facade was cleaned and restored in 1990. The stained glass, in particular, deserves binoculars, and you will want to visit the little children's tomb, with its kneeling angels, built in memory of the two children of Charles VIII and Anne of Brittany. *Rue Lavoisier. Closed noon–2.*

What is left of the château is of minor interest, but, within it, you will
⑭ find the **Historial de la Touraine**—a group of more than 150 waxwork models representing historic figures like St. Martin and Joan of Arc, whose deeds helped shape this region over 15 centuries. There's also a small aquarium. *Quai d'Orléans,* ☎ *47–61–02–95.* ☛ *Wax museum, 29 frs adults, 25 frs students, 22 frs children; aquarium, 25 frs adults, 20 frs students, 15 frs children.* ☉ *Daily, mid-Sept.–mid-Nov. 9–11:30 and 2–6:30; mid-Nov.–mid-Mar. 2–5:30; mid-Mar.–mid-June 9–11:30 and 2–6:30; mid-June–mid-Sept. 9–6:30.*

⑮ Next door, in what was once the archbishop's palace, is the **Musée des Beaux-Arts** (Fine Arts Museum). It houses an eclectic selection of treasures: works by Rubens, Rembrandt, Boucher, Degas, sculptor Alexander Calder—even Fritz the Elephant, stuffed in 1902. *18 pl. François-Sicard,* ☎ *47–05–68–73.* ☛ *30 frs adults, 15 frs students and senior citizens, 12 frs children.* ☉ *Wed.–Mon. 9–12:45 and 2–6.*

⑯ Two small museums stand at the river end of rue Nationale: the **Musée des Vins** (Wine Museum) and the **Musée du Compagnonnage** (Guild Museum). You may wish to see the latter, at least. *Compagnonnage* is a sort of apprenticeship-trade-union system, and here you see the masterpieces of the candidates for guild membership: virtuoso craftwork, some of it eccentric (an Eiffel Tower made of slate, for instance, or a varnished noodle château). These stand as evidence of the devotion to craftsmanship that is still an important feature of French life. Both the guild and the wine museum are set in and around the cloisters of an old church—a pleasant setting, and you are free to visit them at your own pace. *8 rue Nationale,* ☎ *47–61–07–93.* ☛ *20 frs adults, 10 frs students.* ☉ *Wed.–Mon. 9–noon and 2–5.*

From rue Nationale, narrow rue du Commerce leads you to the oldest and most attractive part of Tours, the area around **place Plumereau.** It's a great area for strolling, largely traffic-free, and full of little squares, small, inexpensive hotels, intimate restaurants, open-air cafés,

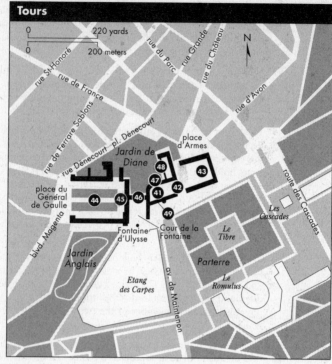

and pricey antiques shops. It is here that the young at heart congregate in the evening, and a good place to do that is at the Café du Vieux
Marier (11 place Plumereau, ☎ 47–61–04–77), where earnest con-
versationalists cram in among the cluttered decor night after night. From
place Plumereau, head one block along rue Briconnet and take the first
left into rue du Mûrier. The **Musée du Gemmail,** halfway down on the
right in the imposing 19th-century Hôtel Raimbault, houses an unusual
collection of three-dimensional colored-glass window panels. Depicting patterns, figures, and even portraits, the panels are both beautiful
and intriguing, since most of the gemlike fragments of glass come
from broken bottles. Incidentally, Jean Cocteau coined the word Gemmail by combining *gemme* (gem) with *émail* (enamel). *7 rue du Mûrier,*
☎ *47–61–01–19.* ☛ *28 frs adults, 18 frs students.* ⊙ *Mar.–mid-Oct.,*
Tues.–Sun. 10–noon and 2:30–6.

Tour 2: The Eastern Loire Valley—Amboise to Orléans

Numbers in the margin correspond to points of interest on the Loire
Valley and Orléans maps.

★ **18** On the south side of the Loire, about 26 kilometers (16 miles) due east
of Tours, is **Amboise,** a picturesque little town with bustling markets,
narrow medieval streets, plenty of hotels and restaurants, and a historic **château,** looking over the Loire. A lively little town, Amboise can
make a superb base from which to explore.

The history of Amboise is really the history of its château. A Stone Age
fortress stood here, and an early bridge gave the stronghold strategic
importance. In AD 503, Clovis, king of the Franks, met with Alaric,
king of the Visigoths, on an island (now the site of an excellent campground). In the years that followed, the Normans attacked the fortress

repeatedly. The 15th and 16th centuries were Amboise's golden age, and during this time, the château, enlarged and embellished, became a royal palace. Charles VII stayed here, as did the unfortunate Charles VIII, best remembered for banging his head on a low doorway (you will be shown it) and dying as a result. François I, whose long nose appears in so many château paintings, based his court here. In 1560, his son, young François II, settled here with his wife, Mary Stuart (otherwise known as Mary, Queen of Scots), and his mother, Catherine de' Medici. The castle was also the setting for the Amboise Conspiracy, an ill-fated Protestant plot organized against François II; visitors are shown where the corpses of 1,200 conspirators dangled from the castle walls. In later years, a decline set in, and demolition occurred both before and after the Revolution. Today only about a third of the original building remains standing.

The château's interior is partly furnished, though not with the original objects; these vanished when the building was converted into a barracks and then a button factory. The great round tower contains a spiral ramp rather than a staircase; designed for horsemen, it is wide enough to accommodate a small car. You are free to explore the grounds at your own pace, including the little chapel of St-Hubert, with its carvings of the Virgin and Child, Charles VIII, and Anne of Brittany. There are frequent son-et-lumière pageants on summer evenings. ☎ 47–57–00–98. ☛ 30 frs adults, 20 frs students, 10 frs children. ☉ Oct.–Mar., 9–noon and 12–5; Apr.–June and Sept., 9–noon and 2–6:30; July and Aug., 9–6:30; closed Tues.

Up rue Victor-Hugo, five minutes uphill from the château, is the **Clos Lucé,** a handsome Renaissance manor house. François I lent the house to Leonardo da Vinci, who spent the last four years of his life here, dying in 1519. You can wander from room to room at will. The basement houses an extraordinary exhibition: working models of some of Leonardo's inventions. Though impractical in his own time, when technology was limited, they were built recently by engineers from IBM, using the detailed sketches contained in the artist's notebooks. Mechanisms on display include three-speed gearboxes, a military tank, a clockwork car, and even a flying machine complete with designs for parachutes. *At the eastern end of rue Victor-Hugo,* ☎ 47–57–62–88. ☛ 34 frs adults, 25 frs students and senior citizens, 16 frs children. ☉ Sept.–June, daily 9–6; July and Aug., daily 9–7.

TIME OUT After you've marveled at Leonardo's genius, you can explore the garden and grab a quick bite at the convenient creperie.

★ ⑲ About 10 kilometers (6 miles) southeast of Amboise lies the village of **Chenonceaux.** (For some reason, the village is spelled Chenonceaux and the château, Chenonceau.) You could happily spend half a day wandering through the château and grounds, but the village is small. It nevertheless has ample eateries and several hotels (*see* Dining and Lodging, *below*). From long-ago historical figures, such as Diane de Poitiers, Catherine de' Medici, and Mary, Queen of Scots, to a host of modern travel writers, many have called Chenonceau the "most exciting" and the "most romantic" of all the Loire châteaux. You are free to wander about (there are attendants to answer questions). During the peak summer season the château is open—unlike many others—all day. The only drawback is its popularity: If you want to avoid a roomful of English schoolchildren, take a stroll in the grounds and come back when they stop for lunch.

More pleasure palace than fortress, Chenonceau was built in 1520 by Thomas Bohier, a wealthy tax collector. When he went bankrupt, it passed to François I. Later, Henri II gave it to his mistress, Diane de Poitiers. After his death, Henri's not-so-understanding widow, Catherine de' Medici, expelled Diane to nearby Chaumont and took back the château. It is to Catherine that we owe the lovely gardens and the handsome three-story extension whose arches span the river Cher.

Before you go inside, pick up an English leaflet at the gate. Then walk around to the right of the main building and admire the peaceful, delicate architecture; the formal garden; and the river gliding under the arches. The romantically inclined may want to rent a rowboat and spend an hour drifting. Inside the château are splendid ceilings, colossal fireplaces, and authentic furnishings. Paintings include works by Rubens, Andrea del Sarto, and Correggio. And as you tour the rooms, be sure to pay your respects to former-owner Madame Dupin, whose face is captured in Nattier's charming portrait. Thanks to the great affection Madame Dupin inspired among her proletarian neighbors, the château and its treasures survived the Revolution intact.

A waxwork exhibition (**Musée des Cires**), housed in one of the outbuildings, illustrates four centuries of French history. There are also excellent son-et-lumière shows (admission 50 frs) throughout the summer. ☎ 47–23–90–07. ☛ *Château, 45 frs adults, 25 frs students and children; wax museum 10 frs.* ⊘ *Mid-Feb.–mid-Nov., daily 9–5, 6, or 7, depending on the season; mid-Nov.–mid-Feb., daily 9–noon and 2–4:30.*

TIME OUT   If you feel like spending the day at Chenonceau, refuel in the inexpensive self-service restaurant in the former stables.

About 18 kilometers (11 miles) due south of Chenonceaux lies the town **㉑** of **Loches,** set on a rocky spur just beside the River Indre. Like Chinon, Loches is a walled citadel dominating a small medieval village. But although Chinon's citadel is a ruined shell, much of Loches's is well preserved and stands as a functioning part of the town.

As you approach the citadel, the first building you will come across is the church of **St-Ours:** Note its striking roof formed of octagonal pyramids, dating from the 12th century; the doorway sculpted with owls, monkeys, and mythical beasts; and the baptismal font converted from a Roman altar.

The **Logis Royaux**—the château—has a terrace that provides a fine view of the roofs and river below and the towers and swallows' nests above. Inside, keep an eye out for the vicious, two-man crossbow that could pierce an oak door at 200 yards. There are some interesting pictures, too, including a copy of the well-known portrait that shows an extremely disgruntled Charles VII and one of his mistresses, Agnes Sorel, poised as a virtuous Virgin Mary (though semitopless). Her alabaster image decorates her tomb, guarded by angels and lambs. Agnes died in 1450, at age 28, probably the result of poisoning by Charles's son, the future Louis XI. The little chapel was built by Charles VIII for his queen, Anne of Brittany, and is lavishly decorated with sculpted ermine tails, the lady's emblem.

After the tour, amble over to the *donjon,* or tower keep. One 11th-century tower, half-ruined and roofless, is open for individual exploration, though the others require guided supervision. These towers contain dungeons and will delight anyone who revels in prison cells and torture chambers. *Pl. Charles-VII,* ☎ *47–59–01–32.* ☛ *26 frs adults, 19 frs children, students, and senior citizens.* ⊘ *Jan.–mid-Mar., Thurs.–Tues. 9–noon and 2–5, mid-Mar.–June, daily 9–noon and 2–6; July and Aug., daily 9–6; Sept.–Nov., Thurs.–Tues. 9–noon and 2–5.*

As a side trip, 30 kilometers (18 miles) to the southwest on D750 is the small town of **Descartes,** the birthplace of René. His home is now a small museum. *29 rue Descartes,* ☎ *47–59–79–19.* ☛ *10 frs.* ☉ *Nov.–Sept., Wed.–Mon. 2–6.*

㉑ The town of **Valençay,** with its pleasant château, lies just over 40 kilometers (25 miles) southeast of Chenonceaux and 48 kilometers (30 miles) east of Loches. Although it is some distance south of the Loire, it is well worth a visit.

A palace rather than a castle, Valençay was started in the 16th century, though most of the surviving structure was added later. Talleyrand (1754–1838), the opportunistic statesman and diplomat, who managed to survive whatever the regime, left his mark here. A young but not very pious bishop under Louis XVI, Talleyrand played a leading role in the French Revolution and was foreign minister under Napoléon. After Napoléon's fall he helped reshape Europe at the Congress of Vienna, supporting the return of the Bourbon monarchy. While serving as Napoléon's foreign minister, he was instructed to buy a suitable palace to impress visiting royalty and ambassadors: The result was Valençay. In these grandiose and seductive surroundings, he wove his political spells and enjoyed himself for a quarter of a century. The many rooms that are open to the public have luscious furnishings and decorations.

The grounds at Valençay include a formal French garden with statues, peacocks, and precisely cut hedges; a park where kangaroos and llamas roam; and the **Musée de l'Automobile Ancienne,** exhibiting more than 80 polished cars and motorcycles dating from 1898. ☎ *54–00–10–66.* ☛ *30 frs adults, 25 frs senior citizens, 16 frs children. Admission to park only: 7 frs.* ☉ *Mid.-Mar.–mid-Nov., daily 9–noon and 2–dusk or 8; château and museum closed mid-Nov.–mid-Mar.*

㉒ On your journey north, stop off for an afternoon at the village of **Cour-Cheverny,** just over 20 kilometers (12 miles) outside Blois. The main attraction is the classical **château of Cheverny,** finished in 1634. The interior, with its painted and gilded rooms, splendid furniture, and rich tapestries depicting the labors of Hercules, is one of the grandest in the Loire region. American visitors will spot a bronze of George Washington in the gallery, alongside a document bearing his signature.

One of the chief delights of Cheverny is that you can wander freely at your own pace. Unfortunately, the gardens are off-limits, as is the Orangery, where the *Mona Lisa* and other masterpieces were hidden during World War II. But you are free to contemplate the antlers of 2,000 stags in a nearby Trophy Room. Hunting, called "venery" in the leaflets, continues vigorously here, red coats, bugles, and all. In the kennels next door, hordes of hungry hounds lounge about dreaming of their next kill. Feeding times—*la soupe aux chiens*—are posted on a noticeboard, and visitors are welcome to watch the dogs gulp down their dinner. ☎ *54–79–96–29.* ☛ *29 frs adults, 20 frs children and senior citizens.* ☉ *June–mid-Sept., daily 9–6:30; mid-Sept.–mid-June, daily 9:30–noon and 2:15–5.*

★ ㉓ As you leave Cheverny, follow D765 north to **Blois,** a quaint yet convenient touring center off A10, about midway between Tours and Orléans. Perched on a steep hillside overlooking the Loire, its white facades, redbrick chimneys, and blue-slate roofs create a cheerful, tricolor effect. The town is also quite accessible, posing few traffic problems and offering direct train links to Paris and all the major towns along the Loire.

The **château** at Blois is among the valley's finest. Your ticket entitles you to a guided tour—in English when there are enough visitors who can't understand French—but you are more than welcome to roam around without a guide if you visit between mid-March and August. Before you enter the building, stand in the courtyard and admire four centuries of architecture. On one side stands the 13th-century hall and tower, the latter offering a stunning view of town and countryside. The Renaissance begins to flower in the Louis XII wing (built between 1498 and 1503), through which you enter, and comes to full bloom in the François I wing (1515–24). The masterpiece here is the openwork spiral staircase, painstakingly restored. The fourth side is the Classical Gaston d'Orléans wing (1635–38).

At the bottom of the staircase there's a *diaporama*, an audiovisual display tracing the château's history. Upstairs you'll find a series of enormous rooms with tremendous fireplaces, decorated with the gilded porcupine, emblem of Louis XII; the ermine of Anne of Brittany; and, of course, François I's salamander, breathing fire and surrounded by flickering flames. There are intricate ceilings; carved and gilded paneling; and a sad little picture of Mary, Queen of Scots. In the great council room, the duc de Guise was murdered on the orders of Henri III in 1588. Don't miss the **Musée des Beaux-Arts,** the art gallery, in the Louis XII wing. The miscellaneous collection of paintings from the 16th to the 19th century is interesting and often amusing. The château also offers a son-et-lumière display most summer evenings. ☎ *54–78–06–62.* ☛ *30 frs adults, 15 frs children and senior citizens.* ⊙ *Apr.–Aug., daily 9–6; Sept.–Mar., daily 9–noon and 2–5.*

If you have time, take a walking tour of the city, along the signposted route. (Maps are available from the tourist office.) Be sure to make a point of going up to the galleries of the Hôtel de Ville (Town Hall) for the best view of the old town, the château, and the river.

★ ㉔ The château of **Chambord** lies 18 kilometers (11 miles) east of Blois on D33, in the middle of a royal game forest. The largest of the Loire châteaus, Chambord is also one of the valley's two most popular touring destinations (Chenonceau being the other). But although everyone thinks Chenonceau is extravagantly beautiful, reactions are mixed as to the qualities of Chambord. Chambord is the kind of place William Randolph Hearst would have built if he had had more money: It's been described as "megalomaniac," "an enormous filmset extravaganza," and, in its favor, "the most outstanding experience of the Loire Valley."

A few facts set the tone: The facade is 420 feet long, there are 440 rooms and 365 chimneys, and a wall 32 kilometers (20 miles) long encloses the 13,000-acre forest (you can wander in 3,000 of these, the rest being reserved for wild boar and other game). François I started building in 1519, a job that took 12 years and required 1,800 workmen. His original grandiose idea was to divert the Loire to form a moat, but someone (probably his adviser, Leonardo da Vinci) persuaded him to make do with the River Cosson. François used the château only for short stays; yet when he first arrived, 12,000 horses were required to transport his luggage, servants, and hangers-on! Later kings also used Chambord as an occasional retreat, and Sun King Louis XIV had Molière perform here. In the 18th century, Louis XV gave the château to Maréchal de Saxe as a reward for his victory over the English and

Dutch at Fontenoy in 1745. When not besporting himself with wine, women, and song, the marshal stood on the roof overseeing the exercises of his own regiment of 1,000 cavalry.

Now, after long neglect—all the original furnishings vanished during the French Revolution—Chambord belongs to the state. Vast rooms are open to visitors (you can wander freely) and have been filled with a variety of exhibits—not all concerned with Chambord, but interesting nonetheless. Children will enjoy repeated trips up and down the enormous **double-helix staircase:** It looks like a single staircase, but an entire regiment could march up one spiral while a second came down the other, and they would never meet. Also be sure to visit the roof terrace, whose forest of towers, turrets, cupolas, gables, and chimneys was described by 19th-century novelist Henry James as "more like the spires of a city than the salient points of a single building."

Chambord also offers a short son-et-lumière show, for 50 frs, in French, English, and German, successively, on many evenings from mid-May to mid-October. ☎ 54–20–31–32. ☛ *31 frs adults, 17 frs students and senior citizens, 7 frs children.* ☉ *July and Aug., daily 9:30–6:30; Sept.–June, daily 9:30–4:30, 5:30, or 6:30 depending on the season.*

The remainder of this last leg of our Loire Valley tour follows the
㉕ river itself. **Meung-sur-Loire** lies about 30 kilometers (20 miles) northeast, though you may want to backtrack to Blois and continue along the river road from there. It is a small, intimate town without the commercialism of places like Amboise. The town's most famous citizen was Jehan de Meung, born in 1260 and author of the best-selling *Roman de la Rose.* (Later, Geoffrey Chaucer produced a well-known English translation.)

The **château** at Meung is part 12th-century fortress, part 18th-century residence. From the 12th century to the French Revolution, it served mainly as the official residence of the bishops of Orléans, although in 1429, Lord Salisbury used it as his headquarters during the seige of Orléans. (When he was killed in the fray, Lord Talbot took over but could not prevent Joan of Arc from capturing the château.) It was sold after the French Revolution, and when its present owner, M. Tachon, bought it in 1970, it had stood empty and derelict for years. Tachon began a long process of restoring, furnishing it with a diverse collection of items ranging from 12th-century antiquities to souvenirs from his own life. The weapons room contains cross-bows, World War II submachine guns, and military helmets from the Middle Ages to 1945.

The most unusual part of the château is underground, where the owner is in the process of exploring and reopening a network of tunnels, dungeons, and storehouses, with a chapel and torture chamber. *16 pl. du Martroi,* ☎ *38–44–36–47.* ☛ *29 frs adults, 12 frs children.* ☉ *Apr.–Oct., daily 9:30–5; Nov.–Mar., Sun. and national holidays only, 2:30–5.*

Give yourself time in Meung to wander down rue Jehan de Meung, the street leading off the main square in the opposite direction from the château, to see the marvelous half-timbered houses. At one of them, Herbaudière Claude (☎ 38–44–43–41), you can select delicious pastries.

Leaving Meung, follow N152 northeast about 18 kilometers (11 miles)
㉖ to **Orléans,** a thriving commercial city. Its strategic position as a natural bridgehead over the Loire has long made it the target of hostile confrontations and invasions. Julius Caesar slaughtered its inhabitants and burned it to the ground. Five centuries later, Atilla and his Huns did much the same. Next came the Normans; then the Valois kings

turned it into a secondary capital. The story of the Hundred Years' War, Joan of Arc, and the siege of Orleáns is widely known. During the Wars of Religion (1562–98), much of the cathedral was destroyed, and a century ago, ham-fisted town planners razed many of the city's fine old buildings. During World War II, both German and Allied bombs helped finish the job. In recent years, dedicated and sensitive planners have done much to bring the city back to life, though perhaps you may not want to give it top priority in your Loire explorations.

The tourist office is on boulevard de Verdun, right in front of the train station. From here, rue de la République takes you 400 yards south to the main square—the **place du Martroi,** with its statue of Joan of Arc. A block farther south, turn left for the cathedral, down rue Jeanne-d'Arc, or continue south down **rue Royale;** the latter is lined with an excellent variety of shops. Rue Royale brings you to the quai du Châtelet and the banks of the Loire. Make a left turn here to arrive at

27 the **Nouvelle Halle,** the covered market, with its tempting food displays. (Drivers would do best to park in the underground parking lot at the Campo Santo, beside the cathedral.)

28 **Cathédrale Ste-Croix** is a riot of pinnacles and gargoyles, both Gothic and pseudo-Gothic, the whole embellished with 18th-century wedding-cake towers. In the 16th century most of the cathedral was destroyed during the religious wars and then rebuilt by Henry IV and his successors. Novelist Marcel Proust (1871–1922) called it France's ugliest church, but most people find it impressive. Inside you'll see vast quantities of stained glass and 18th-century wood carving, plus the modern **Chapel of Joan of Arc,** with plaques in memory of the British and American war dead. *Rue Jeanne-d'Arc.* ⊙ *Daily 9–noon and 2–6.*

29 The modern **Musée des Beaux-Arts** (the art gallery) is just across the street from the cathedral. Take the elevator to the top of the five-story building, and work your way down, seeing works by such artists as Tintoretto, Velázquez, Watteau, Boucher, Rodin, and Gauguin. The museum's richest collection is in 17th-century French paintings. *1 rue Ferdinand-Rabier,* ☎ *38–53–39–22.* ☛ *20 frs adults, 12 frs students and senior citizens.* ⊙ *Wed.–Mon. 10–noon and 2–6.*

30 Retrace your steps along the rue Jeanne-d'Arc and turn left into place Abbé Desnoyers for a visit to Orléans's **Musée Historique.** This Renaissance town house, Hôtel Cabu, restored after World War II, contains both "fine" and "popular" works of art connected with the town's history and a remarkable collection of pagan bronzes of animals and dancers. These last were hidden from zealous Christian missionaries in the 4th century and discovered in a sand pit near St-Benoît in 1861. *Hôtel Cabu, pl. de l'Abbé-Desnoyers,* ☎ *38–53–39–22.* ☛ *12 frs adults, 6 frs students.* ⊙ *Wed.–Mon. 10–noon and 2–6 (until 5 Oct.–Mar.).*

31 Another block west on rue Jeanne-d'Arc, in place du Général-de-Gaulle, is **La Maison de Jeanne-d'Arc.** Seventeen-year-old Joan stayed on the site during the 10-day siege of Orléans in 1429, in a house that underwent many changes before it was bombed flat in 1940. This reconstruction contains exhibits about her life, costumes of her time, and models of siege engines. Several dioramas modeled by Lucien Harmey recount the main stages on her life, from the audience at Chinon to the coronation at Reims; her seizure at Compiegne; and the stake at Rouen. *Pl. du Général-de-Gaulle,* ☎ *38–79–65–45.* ☛ *12 frs adults, 6 frs students.* ⊙ *Tues.–Sun. 10–noon and 2–6 (2–6 only Nov.–Apr.).*

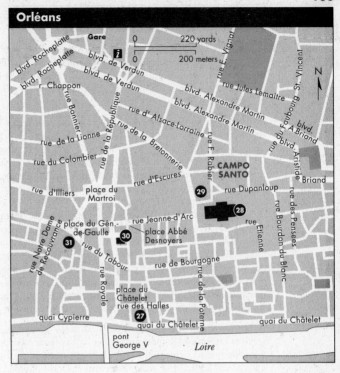

About 25 kilometers (15 miles) east of Orléans, the leafy village of
Châteauneuf-sur-Loire is a convenient base from which to explore the
towns and countryside of the eastern Loire.

Although the **château** was destroyed during the French Revolution, its
outbuildings and garden survive. Beyond them stretches a delightful
public park, laid out *à l'anglaise*—in a "natural" way—with giant tulip
trees, magnolias, weeping willows, and rhododendrons, especially
beautiful in late May and early June. Little streams snake their way
across the parkland, passing benches, shady copses, and scenic picnic
spots on their way to the Loire.

You may also want to visit the **Musée de la Marine,** whose exhibits
chronicle the history of navigation on the Loire. Paintings, photographs,
documents, and model boats illustrate the boatman's life. *In the basement of the Mairie (town hall), 1 pl. Aristide-Briand,* ☎ *38–58–41–
18.* ☛ *14 frs adults, 8 frs students.* ☉ *July and Aug., Wed.–Mon.
10–noon and 2–5:30; June and Sept., Mon. and Wed.–Fri. 2–5:30;
Apr.–May, weekends 10–noon and 2–5:30; Oct.–Mar., Sun. 2–6.*

On the north bank of the Loire, just 5 kilometers (3 miles) southeast
of Châteauneuf, is the little village of **Germigny-des-Prés**. Around AD
800, Theodulf, an abbot of St-Benoît, built a tiny **church** here that is
often cited as the oldest in France. A square Byzantine arrangement of
rounded arches on square pillars, with indirect lighting filtering from
smaller arches above the central square, it was carefully restored to its
original condition during the last century. Though Theodulf himself
brought most of the original mosaics from Italy, only one—covered in
plaster and discovered in 1848—survives. Made of 130,000 cubes of
colored glass, it shows the Ark of the Covenant transported by angels

with golden halos. The Latin inscription asks us not to forget Theo-dulf in our prayers. ☉ *Daily 9–noon and 2–5.*

34 The little town of **St-Benoît-sur-Loire** lies about 10 kilometers (6 miles) southeast of Châteauneuf and 5½ kilometers (3½ miles) from Ger-migny-des-Prés. Its highlight is the ancient **Abbey of St-Benoît,** often hailed as the greatest Romanesque church in France; village signposts refer to it as *la Basilique.*

St-Benoît, or St. Benedict, was the founder of the Benedictine monas-tic order. In AD 650, a group of monks chose this safe and fertile spot for their new monastery, returning to Monte Cassino, Italy, to retrieve the bones of St. Benedict with which to bless the site. Despite demands for their return from priests at the church at Monte Cassino, some of the relics remain here, in the 11th-century abbey church bearing his name. Following the Hundred Years' War of the 14th and 15th cen-turies, the monastery fell into a decline, and the Wars of Religion (1562–98) wrought further damage. During the French Revolution, the monks dispersed and the buildings were destroyed, all except the abbey church itself, which became the parish church. Monastic life here began anew in 1944, when the monks rebuilt their monastery and re-gained the abbey church for their own use. The pillars of the tower porch are noted for their intricately carved capitals, and the choir floor is an amazing patchwork of many-colored marble.

Gregorian chant can be heard daily, at mass or vespers, and Sunday services attract worshipers and music lovers from all around. Visitors are welcome to explore the church crypt. *Mass and vespers Sun. 11 AM and 6:15 PM, Mon.–Sat. noon and 6:15 PM.* Guided English-lan-guage tours of the monastic buildings can be arranged; inquire at the monastery shop.

What to See and Do with Children

Older children should enjoy visiting a handful of châteaus—especially **Chambord** (Tour 2), with its extravagant staircase and wild parkland, and the eerie tunnels and dungeons at **Meung** (Tour 2). Make-it-your-self cardboard models of the famous palaces—available in most gift shops—are also popular and help enrich children's visits.

For a fun family outing, try the **Zoo de Doué,** a privately run zoo in a garden setting surrounded by golden limestone quarries. The deer, emu, monkeys—even the vultures—all look happy and well cared for; the hefty admission charge goes to safeguard endangered species. *Rte. de Cholet, 49700 Doué-la-Fontaine, about 16 km (10 mi) west of Saumur,* ☎ *41–59–18–58.* ☛ *45 frs adults, 20 frs children.* ☉ *May–Sept., daily 9–7:30; Oct.–Apr., daily 10–noon and 2–6.*

Off the Beaten Track

The 16th-century château of **Gué-Péan** is hidden amid wooded grounds near the village of Monthou-sur-Cher, about 10 kilometers (6 miles) from Montrichard. It's neither museum nor showcase, but the ancestral home of the marquis de Keguelin, whose family still lives here. Inside you'll find a miscellany of furniture, paintings, and interesting *objets.* To off-set the cost of maintaining the château, the marquis also runs an ex-cellent bed-and-breakfast service; dinner, if wanted, is often taken in his company. *41400 Monthou-sur-Cher,* ☎ *54–71–43–01.* ☛ *26 frs.* ☉ *Mid-Mar.–Sept., daily 9–5; Oct.–mid-Mar., daily 9–noon and 2–5.*

Thirty-two kilometers (20 miles) northwest of Blois via D957 is the town of **Vendôme.** It's not on most tourists' itineraries, but its picturesque appeal amply merits the detour. Vendôme's château is in ruins, but the **gardens** surrounding it offer knockout views of the town center. From place du Château, head down to admire the Flamboyant Gothic abbey church of **La Trinité,** with its unusual 12th-century clock tower and fine stained glass. Take time to stroll through the narrow streets of this enchanting little town.

The fortress-castle of **Châteaudun** lies 45 kilometers (28 miles) northeast of Vendôme via the fast N10. Its austere facade is decidedly grim, but the internal courtyard is overlooked by buildings of a more welcoming aspect, thanks to 16th-century restoration work. The interior contains period furniture and tapestries, but the highlight is the **Sainte-Chapelle** (holy chapel), with its collection of 15th-century statues. Except for this attraction, Châteaudun is not worth driving out of your way for. ☎ 37–45–22–70. ☛ 32 frs. ⊘ Easter–Sept., daily 8–11:45 and 2–6; Oct.–Easter, Sun. 10–11:45 and 2–6.

Le Mans, 200 kilometers (125 miles) west of Paris, is close to—but not part of—four separate regions: Brittany, Normandy, the Ile de France, and the Loire Valley. Le Mans is best known for its 24-hour automobile race. The hilltop city center and the cathedral are well worth a visit.

The sumptuous moated **Château de Serrant** is only 16 kilometers (10 miles) southwest of Angers, near St-Georges-sur-Loire. Begun in 1546, and gaining additions during the 17th and 18th centuries, it contains lush interiors, paneled and hung with tapestries. The library, which contains more than 10,000 volumes, is magnificent. Like the château de Gué-Péan, Château de Serrant is a private residence. ☎ 41–39–13–01. ☛ 32 frs. ⊘ Easter–Oct., Wed.–Mon. 9–11:30 and 2–6.

Champigny-sur-Veude is just 13 kilometers (8 miles) south of Chinon along D749, but visitors to its **Sainte-Chapelle** are few. What many miss is some of the best Renaissance stained glass in the world. The chapel was originally part of a château built between 1508 and 1543 but razed a century later by order of jealous neighbor Cardinal Richelieu. Its 16th-century windows relate scenes from the Passion, Crucifixion, and life of the 13th-century French king St-Louis; note the vividness and harmony of the colors, especially the purplish blues. ☛ 30 frs (includes château and chapel). ⊘ Apr.–Sept., daily 9–noon and 2–6.

Five miles farther down D749 is the town of **Richelieu,** founded by Cardinal Richelieu in 1631, along with a huge château intended to be one of the most lavish in Christendom. All that's left of the latter are a few buildings and some parklands, though the town remains a rare example of rigid, symmetrical, and unspoiled Classical town planning—with 28 identical mansions lining the main street—well worth seeing: Its bombastic scale and state of preservation are unique. The severe, straight streets have not changed for 350 years, give or take the occasional traffic sign.

Anyone interested in mushrooms, a specialty of the region, will be intrigued by an unusual subterranean tour through fossil-filled caverns where edible fungi are grown; it's offered by **La Musée du Champignon** (Mushroom Museum, Flines, rte. de Gennes, St-Hilaire, ☎ 41–50–31–55), just outside Saumur. Tours are available daily from mid-February through mid-September, daily 10–7. The cost is 30 francs, 18 francs for children under 14.

SHOPPING

Wine

The region's extraspecial produce is Loire wine. It's not a practical buy for tourists—except for instant consumption—but if wine-tasting tours of vineyards inspire you, enterprising wine makers will arrange shipment to the United States; think in terms of hundreds rather than dozens. Try the **Maison du Vin** in Angers (5 pl. Président-Kennedy, next to the tourist office), and **Maison des Vins de Touraine** in Tours (4 bis blvd. Heurteloup), or, near Saumur, the wine-making firms of **Ackerman** (19 rue Léopold-Palustre, 49400 St-Hilaire, ☎ 41–50–25–33) and **Veuve Amiot** (21 rue Jean-Ackerman, 49400 St-Hilaire, ☎ 41–50–25–24), which also offer organized tours.

Gift Ideas

Loire food specialties include barley sugar (*sucre d'orge*) and prunes stuffed with marzipan (*pruneaux fourrés*); both are widely available at food shops throughout the valley. A sweet-toothed specialty of the Orléans district is *cotignac*—an orangey-red molded jelly made from quinces. It, too, can be bought from most local patisseries and is produced almost exclusively by **Gilbert Jumeau** (1 rue Voisinas, St-Ay), 8 kilometers (5 miles) west of Orléans. For fine chocolates, try the **Chocolaterie Royale** in Orléans (53 rue Royale), and for a bottle of **Cointreau,** that heartwarming liqueur which comes from Angers, go right to the factory (rue Croix-Blanche, 49124 St-Barthélémy d'Anjou, ☎ 41–43–25–21).

Antiques

All major towns have high-quality antiques for sale. There are numerous antiques shops in **rue de la Scellerie** in Tours, and you can also pick up some fine pieces at **Au Vieux Tours** (91 rue Colbert). In Saumur, try **Au Vieux Saumur** (21 rue Dacier); in Fontevraud, **Christian Saulnier** (2 pl. des Plantagenêts). Angers has an interesting **flea market** on Saturdays (pl. Imbach).

Arts and Crafts

Gien, on the north bank of the Loire a few miles past Sully and St-Benoît, is a major earthenware center; the factory, **Faïenceries de Gien** (78 pl. de la Victoire, ☎ 38–67–00–05), can be contacted for private visits. In addition to its wines, **La Maison de Touraine** in Tours (4 bis blvd. Heurteloup; closed Sun. and Mon. mornings) offers a wide selection of local products and crafts, including ceramics. For fine wickerwork, visit the shop at the **Société Coopérative de Vannerie** in Villaines-les-Rochers, near Saché.

SPORTS AND THE OUTDOORS

Bicycling

The Loire region is excellent country for biking. The roads meander through wooded countryside and along river banks. The short distances between châteaus and other attractions will appeal to the cyclist who does not want to spend all day pedaling. For the more ambitious, the Tourist Office in Tours has a booklet listing 68 country rides ranging from 20 km to 90 km. Also delightful in the Loire are ample places for picnics—and the local wine is refreshing. Bikes can be rented at most train stations and at dozens of other outlets for about 40 francs (try **Au Col de Cygne,** 46 bis rue du Dr-Fournier, Tours, ☎ 47–46–00–37; and **Leprovost,** 13 rue Carnot, Azay-le-Rideau, ☎ 47–45–40–94). **Loisirs Accueil** offices in Blois and Orléans offer organized trips;

these often include luggage transportation and camp or youth-hostel accommodations. Ask at the nearest tourist office or contact Loisirs Accueil (3 rue de la Bretonnerie, Orléans, ☎ 38–62–04–88; or 11 pl. du Château, Blois, ☎ 54–78–55–50).

Fishing and Shooting
The **Loisirs Accueil** office in Orléans (*see above*) organizes week-long and weekend fishing and shooting outings in the Forest of Orléans. Some include accommodations in two-star hotels.

Hiking
Scenic footpaths abound. Long-distance walking paths (*sentiers de grande randonnée*) pass through the Loire Valley and are marked on Michelin maps with broken lines and route numbers. Tourist offices will supply sketch maps of interesting paths in their area.

Horseback Riding
The region offers abundant facilities and activities, including pony-trekking trips and week-long equestrian tours. Try the **Centre de Tourisme Equestre** at Gennes near Saumur (☎ 41–67–93–28). You can also rent a horse at **Chambord,** from the former stables of the marshal of Saxe, and ride in the vast national park surrounding the château (☎ 54–20–31–01).

Water Sports
Good facilities for canoeing, sailing, fishing, and windsurfing can be found at the **Centre Nautique du Lac de Maine** (☎ 41–48–12–47) in Angers and the **Lac de Loire** (☎ 54–78–82–05) near Blois. The Loire itself has swift and dangerous currents, so swim only at official beaches (signposted *plages*), which are safe and supervised. Package canoeing and kayaking trips can be arranged through local Loisirs Accueil offices (*see* Bicycling, *above*).

DINING AND LODGING

Dining

The Loire region, known as the "garden of France," produces a cornucopia—from beef, poultry, game, and fish to butter, cream, wine, fruit, and vegetables. It sends its early crops to the best Parisian tables, yet keeps more than enough for local use. Loire wines can be extremely good—and varied. Among the best: Savennières, Cheverny (dry white); Coteaux du Layon (sweet white); Cabernet d'Anjou (rosé); Bourgueil, Chinon (red); and Saumur, Vouvray (white, still or sparkling).

CATEGORY	COST*
$$$$	over 400 frs
$$$	250–400 frs
$$	125–250 frs
$	under 125 frs

per person for a three-course meal, including tax (18.6%) and tip but not wine

Lodging

Even before the age of the train, the Loire Valley drew visitors from far and wide, anxious to see the great châteaus and sample the sweetness of rural life. Hundreds of hotels of all kinds have sprung up to accommodate today's travelers. At the higher end of the price scale is the **Relais & Châteaux** group; some of their best hotels are converted châteaus.

Chateaux-Hotels Independents are usually somewhat less expensive, supervised by their live-in owners; though some are less efficient than ordinary hotels, they offer much individuality and charm. Two smaller groups, the **Château-Accueil** and **La Castellerie,** offer pleasant accommodations for a limited number of guests. Illustrated lists of these groups are available from French Government Tourist Offices abroad, as well as in France. At the lower end of the price scale are the **Logis de France** hotels. These small, traditional hotels are located in towns and villages throughout the region and usually offer terrific value for the money. The Logis de France handbook is available free from French Tourist Offices abroad and for about 65 francs in French bookshops.

The Loire Valley is one of the country's most popular vacation destinations, so always make reservations well in advance.

CATEGORY	COST*
$$$$	over 800 frs
$$$	550–800 frs
$$	300–550 frs
$	under 300 frs

*All prices are for a standard double room for two, including tax
(18.6%) and service charge.*

Amboise

DINING

Manoir St-Thomas. Between the château and the Clos Lucé, this restaurant occupies a fine Renaissance building with an adjacent garden. Chef François Le Coz serves elegantly traditional food. Try his *ravioli avec huitres* (ravioli stuffed with oysters and peppered with caviar) or his *suprême de pintade farci* (stuffed guinea-fowl breast). The list of Touraine wines is enticing. ✕ *Pl. Richelieu,* ☎ *47–57–22–52. Reservations advised. Jacket and tie. AE, DC, MC, V. Closed Sun. dinner, Mon., and mid-Jan.–mid-Feb. $$$*

DINING AND LODGING

Château de Pray. This former 13th-century fortress was transformed during the Renaissance into a pleasing manor. Two kilometers (about ½ mile) east of Amboise on the south bank of the Loire, it is surrounded by a 25-acre park and a lovely garden. Inside you'll appreciate the cozy, hunting-lodge ambience. The elegantly appointed guest rooms are equipped with carved wooden furniture and modern conveniences. One drawback is the hotel's lack of comfortable lounges, but if your room faces the Loire, you will be content. The restaurant is only adequate, but diners can enjoy a roaring fire and fine views of the river. 🖭 *On D751, route de Chargé, 37530 Chargé,* ☎ *47–57–23–67,* 🖷 *47–57–32–50. 17 rooms, 2 suites, all with bath. Restaurant. AE, DC, MC, V. Closed Jan.–mid-Feb. $$$*

Choiseul. Amboise's Relais & Châteaux hotel offers classical elegance and also a superb restaurant. Choiseul sits on the banks of the Loire, just below the château. Though the guest rooms have recently been modernized, they retain an old and distinctive charm. Built against the cliff side, the grounds are neat but small. Be sure to visit the caverns, whose enormous galleries often contain an art exhibition. 🖭 *36 quai Charles-Guinot, 37400,* ☎ *47–30–45–45,* 🖷 *47–30–46–10. 32 rooms with bath. Restaurant, pool. MC, V. Closed Jan.–mid-Mar. $$$*

★ **Le Blazon.** This delightful, small hotel, enlivened by the enthusiasm of the owners, is behind the château, a four-minute walk from the center of town. The old building has been well converted into guest rooms of different shapes and sizes, whose compact, prefabricated bathroom units have showers and toilets. Most rooms have twin beds, though a few have queens. Room 229, with exposed beams and a cathedral ceiling, has special charm; Room 109 is comfortably spacious and has a good view of the square. There's superior fare in the pretty little restaurant, with menus beginning at 95 francs. The menu changes with the seasons and may include roast lamb with garlic or medallions of pork, and appetizers of carpaccio of salmon with mustard dressing or air-dried duck breast scented with herbs and spices. ⌕ *14 rue Joyeuse, 37400,* ☎ *47–23–22–41,* 𝖥𝖠𝖷 *47–57–56–18. 29 rooms. Restaurant. MC, V. $–$$*

Angers

DINING

★ **Toussaint.** Chef Michel Bignon dishes up nouvelle versions of traditional local dishes, plus fine wines and tasty desserts. Loire River fish with *beurre blanc* (white butter sauce) is a particular specialty. There are two dining rooms: The ground floor is less formal, but upstairs the neo-classical room has a better view of the castle. Reserve your table accordingly. ✕ *7 pl. Kennedy,* ☎ *41–87–46–20. Reservations required. Jacket required. AE, MC, V. Closed Sun. evening, Mon., part of Feb. $$–$$$*

California Street Line. If you hanker after Texas fare—chili, buffalo wings, spicy burgers—in a party atmosphere with American posters and the young of Angers, make tracks to this small new restaurant run by a French couple. It's not a place you'd come to France to visit, but it is a humorous way to satisfy nostalgia! ✕ *13 rue des Poëliers,* ☎ *41–87–18–42. Closed Sun. lunch, Mon. No credit cards. $*

Le Boucherie. This is the place for those of you with an appetite for steak and good value. There are various menus with different cuts of beef, but for 49 francs you can get a sirloin, a small salad, crusty bread, and a ¼-liter carafe of wine. Service is friendly, cheerful, and swift. If there is a wait for a table, don't despair: The action is fast; dishes are swept away quickly, and a new paper tablecloth laid in a matter of moments. Tables are close together, and lively conversation adds to the robust atmosphere. ✕ *27 blvd. Foch,* ☎ *41–87–27–85. No reservations. MC, V. $*

Maître Kanter. This chain restaurant, located at the covered market, provides simple food and swift service. It's a convenient refueling spot, and the firm's own beer is available on tap. Try the steak and french fries or the sauerkraut with sausages and ham. ✕ *Les Halles,* ☎ *41–87–93–30. No reservations. V. $*

La Treille. For traditional, simple fare at very affordable prices, try this small two-story mom-and-pop restaurant just off the place Ste-Croix and across from Maison d'Adam, Angers's most charming timbered house. The prix-fixe menu may start with a *salade au chèvre chaud* (warm goat cheese salad), followed by confit of duck and an apple tart. Madame runs the small bar while Monsieur, with a welcoming smile, serves the food. The upstairs dining room draws a lively crowd; downstairs is better for quiet conversation. ✕ *12 rue Montault,* ☎ *41–88–45–51. Closed Sun. MC, V. $*

DINING AND LODGING

Pavillon Paul Le Quéré. The city's only four-star hotel, in a renovated mansion set back from the main avenue, opened in 1992 just next door to the traditional Hotel d'Anjou. Paul Le Quéré, a former student of Joël Robuchon, has created a luxurious and expensive boutique hotel to complement his restaurant. His wife, Martine, who is also the sommelier, has done the rooms in classic modern style, with flashy marble bathrooms. Dining is a pleasure, with recipes happily juggling tradition with modern innovations: you might have roast lobster tails, fillet of sole sautéed in the juice of oysters, or diced beef with mussels. One dining room is in a glass rotunda, splendid for lunch, while the formal dining room with trompe-l'oeil marble and Charles X fireplace sets a classic tone for dinner. ⊡ *3 blvd. Foch, 49100,* ☎ *41–20–06–20,* FAX *41–20–00–20. 6 rooms, 4 suites (1 accessible to people using wheelchairs). Restaurant. AE, DC, MC, V. $$$–$$$$*

Bleu Marine. You won't find individuality in this standardized chain hotel, but, then again, you won't find problems either. The soundproof rooms are bright and modern, furnished with a copious amount of Formica. There's a spacious lobby and a good classical restaurant on the ground floor that looks out on to Angers's main boulevard. For breakfast, there is a large and splendid buffet. ⊡ *18 blvd. Foch, 49000,* ☎ *41–87–37–20, 800/888–4747 in the U.S.,* FAX *41–87–49–54. 75 rooms with bath. Restaurant, health club. AE, DC, MC, V. $$$*

Anjou. In business since 1850, the Anjou has recently been redecorated in a vaguely 18th-century style, including stained-glass windows in the lobby. Each room is individually styled, and all are quite spacious with high ceilings, double doors, double-glazed windows, and modern bathrooms with terrycloth bathrobes. The restaurant, Salamandre, with Renaissance-style decor, serves carefully prepared classical cuisine. ⊡ *1 blvd. Foch, 49000,* ☎ *41–88–24–82, 800/528–1324 in the U.S.,* FAX *41–87–22–21. 53 rooms with bath. Restaurant. AE, DC, MC, V. $$*

Azay-le-Rideau

DINING AND LODGING

Grand Monarque. Just yards from the château, this mildly eccentric, popular hotel draws hundreds of visitors, playing host to celebrities, royals, and tourists alike. The owners, M. and Mme. Forest, have, over the last eight years, renovated the old buildings on either side of a courtyard—which is a pleasant place for breakfast in the summer. Rooms vary in size and style; most are simply decorated with an antique or two, and many have exposed beams. Mattresses vary between firm and flexible: There are hard, smooth ones for the American taste and, for Europeans, less-dense ones. The restaurant serves good, traditional food, and the selection of Loire wines is extensive. The special 115-franc, four-course luncheon menu is particularly good value, and there are more elaborate menus, up to the *gastromonique* at 395 francs. Weekend stays must include dinner. Restaurant service can be erratic at times. ⊡ *3 pl. de la République, 37190,* ☎ *47–45–40–08,* FAX *47–45–46–25. 30 rooms, 27 with bath. AE, DC, MC, V. Restaurant closed mid-Nov.–mid-Mar. Hotel closed mid-Dec.–Jan. 15. $$*

Blois

DINING

★ **Au Rendez-vous des Pêcheurs.** This extremely modest restaurant on the right bank of the Loire, below the castle, has simple decor but offers excellent value for its creative cooking. Chef Eric Reithler studied under Guy Savoy in Paris and has brought inventiveness to his fish-based specialties. ✗ *27 rue du Foix,* ☎ *54–74–67–48. Reservations advised. MC, V. Closed Mon. dinner, Sun. $$*

La Péniche. This innovative restaurant is actually a luxurious barge moored along the banks of the Loire. Charming chef Germain Bosque serves up beautifully presented fresh seafood specialties (notably lobsters and oysters). ✗ *Promenade du Mail,* ☎ *54–74–37–23. Reservations advised. AE, DC, MC, V. $$–$$$*

DINING AND LODGING

Le Médicis. The rooms at this smart and friendly hotel, 1,000 yards from the château, are comfortable, air-conditioned, and soundproof from the main avenue. If you wish to splurge, the suite has a whirlpool; the regular rooms simply have modern bathrooms with such amenities as hair dryers. The rooms, newly decorated, are furnished individually, but all share a common joyous color scheme. The restaurant, in itself, makes staying here worthwhile. Chef-owner Christian Garanger makes each dish a presentation, and his cooking is innovative classical—coquilles St-Jacques with a pear fondue, and thin slices of roast hare with black-currant sauce, for example. The maître d' happily guides you through the menu, and, in fact, the whole staff is keen and helpful. ☎ *2 allée François-1er, 41000,* ☎ *54–43–94–04,* FAX *54–42–04–05. 12 rooms with bath, 1 suite. Restaurant (closed Sun. dinner in low season), Hotel closed Jan. 3–24. AE, DC, MC, V. $$*

LODGING

Anne de Bretagne. Although this simple, two-star pension is nothing to rave about, the rooms, up rather steep stairs, are clean and neat, with bright bedspreads and curtains. It's on a small square across the road from the cathedral and up the hill from the town center, a quiet place to spend the night. The price is a little on the high side for what you get, so you might try Le Medicis (*see above*) first. There's space to keep your car on the street, which is a plus, and a small bar next door, which is a congenial spot to have refreshment and a nightcap. ☎ *31 av. du Dr-Jean-Laigret, 41000,* ☎ *54–78–05–38. 29 rooms, most with bath. AE, DC, MC, V. Closed mid-Feb.–mid-Mar. $$*

Bourgeuil

DINING

★ **L'Atlantique.** This exceedingly good restaurant lies between Bourgeuil and Chinon and is worth a trip from either town. The small dining room, with only eight tables, dressed in white tablecloths, potted plants, and a Grecian statue, has a classic simplicity that allows the focus to stay on the food. Chef Jean-Claude creates excellent dishes at very reasonable prices. His 99-franc fixed menu of three courses includes chicken *à la chinoise* with a thick mushroom wine sauce, a delicate goat cheese salad, and a *tarte Normandie.* One fears his consequent discovery and success, which will surely double the prices. ✕ *17 rue Nationale, Avoine,* ☎ *47–58–81–85. Reservations advised. MC, V. $$*

LODGING

Château des Reaux. At Mme. Goupil de Bouille's 15th-century château, a moat still separates the splendid house from the rolling green lawns. Its turreted facade shows off step-pattern bricks exposed on white stucco. Guest rooms in the château and renovated stables vary greatly in size and character. The feminine "Olympe" is a modest-size room whose window overlooks the moat, while the spacious "Bon Maman" accommodates two queen-size beds and a view over the back lawns. In the grand salon, de Bouille ancestral paintings peer down as guests flip through *Paris Match* and other glossy magazines. They dine on a fixed menu at tables with other guests, and conversation flows with the wine. Though this is a member of the Château d'Accueil group, whose members usually act as personal hosts, the owners tend to run this as a hotel and business enterprise. But don't let that detract from your enjoyment here, and don't be annoyed by the day visitors, who pay 15 francs to see the château. ☎ *Le Port-Boulet, 37140,* ☎ *47–95–14–40,* FAX *47–95–18–34. 13 rooms and 4 suites, all with bath. Bar, table d'hôte dinner with reservations. MC, V. $$–$$$*

Chambord

DINING

Bernard Robin. Residents of Bracieux, 8 kilometers (5 miles) from Chambord, rate this as one of the country's best restaurants. From his gleaming kitchens, chef Bernard Robin produces fine nouvelle cuisine, but connoisseurs savor his simpler dishes: carp, game in season, and salmon with beef marrow. The attentive staff brings delicious tidbits to keep you busy between courses. ✕ *1 av. de Chambord, Bracieux,* ☎ *54–46–41–22. Reservations required. Jacket and tie. AE, MC, V. Closed Tues. dinner, Wed., and late Dec.–Jan. $$$$*

LODGING

St-Michel. Guests enjoy simple and comfortable living in this revamped country house at the edge of the woods across from Chambord château. A few rooms boast spectacular views, and there's a pleasant café-terrace for contemplative drinks. ⌂ *103 pl. St-Michel, 41250,* ☎ *54–20–31–31. 39 rooms, 31 with bath. Restaurant, tennis. MC, V. Closed mid-Nov.–Dec. 20 $–$$*

Chaumont-sur-Loire
DINING AND LODGING

★ **Domaine des Hauts de Loire.** Nearly midway between Amboise and Blois, just over the bridge from Chaumont, this exquisite hotel occupies an 18th-century turreted, vine-covered manor house set amid 180 acres of parkland. Guest rooms in the main house are furnished with antique period pieces, creating an aristocratic air. Rooms in the adjacent carriage houses have a mix of old and classically modern furnishings that harmonize with exposed brick walls and gabled ceilings. Under M. Bonneval's attention, the service is relaxed and unpretentious; the restaurant is first-class, and in 1993 the chef justifiably was awarded his second Michelin star. ⌂ *Rte. Mesland, 41150 Onzain,* ☎ *54–20–72–57,* 𝗙𝗔𝗫 *54–20–77–32. 28 rooms and 7 suites with bath. AE, DC, MC, V. Closed Dec.–Feb. $$$$*

Pont d'Ouchet. English-speaking owners have recently taken over this wonderfully inexpensive restaurant-hotel in the small village of Onzain on the banks of the Loire between Tours and Blois. The simple, clean rooms are comfortable, though not all have private baths, and the restaurant serves good, basic fare. There is also a patio off the garden for lighter fare. ⌂ *50 Grande-Rue, 41150 Onzain,* ☎ *54–20–70–33,* 𝗙𝗔𝗫 *54–20–71–79. 20 rooms, some with bath. MC, V. Closed Dec.–Feb.; restaurant closed Sun. dinner and Mon. $*

Chenonceaux
DINING AND LODGING

★ **Bon Laboureur et du Château.** In 1882, it won Henry James's praise as a simple, rustic inn. Since then, through four generations of the Jeudi family, the Bon Laboureur, just steps from Chenonceau, has come up in the world: It's elegantly modern, with a few old oak beams surviving, and a pretty garden where you can eat in summer. Recent renovations in the main house, in the former stables, and in a manor house across the street have produced a variety of individually decorated rooms: comfortably traditional in the old house; larger, with contemporary appeal in the former stables and very large and more formally elegant in the manor. For honeymooners there are rooms in a small separate house across the road, whose garden contains a swimming pool. Another, much larger garden at the back of the manor house supplies vegetables and herbs for the kitchen, and fountains, streams, and shrubs for admiring. The food is commendable—you can dine on excellent turbot with hollandaise or braised rabbit with dried fruits. The *poêle de St-Jacques* (sautéed scallops) with fresh cèpes from the forest is a must in the autumn. Make your dinner reservations early, for a table in the original dining room rather than in the annex. ⌂ *6 rue du Dr-Bretonneau, 37150,*

☎ 47–23–90–02, FAX 47–23–82–01. *36 rooms with bath. 2 restaurants, pool, bicycles. AE, DC, MC, V. Closed Dec.–mid-Mar.* $$

Chinon

DINING

★ **Au Plaisir Gourmand.** Gourmets from all around come here to celebrate, and lucky tourists will get a table only if they make reservations (the dining room in this charming old house seats only 30). Chef Jean-Claude Rigollet makes inventive use of fresh, local produce. For a real treat, try the Vienne River trout. Au Plaisir Gourmand gives top quality without frills and features exceptional local wines. Surprisingly, Chinon has few outstanding restaurants, so if you do not splurge here, consider driving over to Avoine (on the way to Bourgueil) for dinner at L'Atlantique (*see* Bourgueil Dining, *above*). ✕ *2 rue Parmentier,* ☎ *47–93–20–48. Reservations required. Jacket and tie. MC, V. Closed Sun. dinner, Mon., last 3 wks in Feb., and 2nd half of Nov.* $$–$$$

Jeanne de France. Local families and swarms of young people patronize this lively little pizzeria in the town's main square. But it's a far cry from an American pizza joint: Here you can also buy jugfuls of local wine, steaks, and french fries. ✕ *12 pl. Général-de-Gaulle,* ☎ *47–93–20–12. Reservations accepted. Closed Wed., Jan.* $

DINING AND LODGING

★ **Château de Marcay.** An efficient staff serves the fashion-conscious guests at this smartly renovated château, the most sophisticated hotel in the western Loire. Rooms in the newly constructed "pavilion," 50 yards from the hotel, though pleasantly furnished, have little charm; those in the château, though more expensive, have a lot more to offer. Beams and gables add a cozy warmth to the spacious rooms, which are decorated with valuable antiques. The marble bathrooms are also large. Dinner turns into an occasion, with chef Pascal Bodin preparing an excellent *carpaccio de canard* (thin slices of marinated cold duck) for a starter, which may be followed by tournedos of salmon bathed in a Chinon wine sauce and served with a confit of aubergine. An extensive cheese board (try the Ste-Marie chèvre) and wine list round out a truly wonderful meal. 🏨 *6 km (4 mi) south of Chinon by D49 and D116. Marcay, 37500,* ☎ *47–93–03–47,* FAX *47–93–45–33. 35 rooms (27 in château). Restaurant, pool, tennis. AE, DC, MC, V. Closed 2nd wk Jan.–mid-Mar.* $$$$

Hostellerie Gargantua. In the 15th century, the building housing the Gargantua was a bailiff's palace. Today this small, quiet hotel, in the center of the medieval city and close to the church of St-Maurice, offers an array of rooms in various sizes and styles. Half of them are spacious and have baths; the other half are without bath but cost under 250 francs. Rooms 7 and 9, with views of the château, are particularly good choices. Simple good taste prevails throughout. The charming old dining room serves delicious local specialties in a setting more appropriate for dinner than lunch. On Friday and Saturday evenings, waitresses dress up to give a medieval flavor to dinner. The omelets are famous and the fillet of *barbue* (a white fish) with a marmalade, thyme, and citron sauce is excellent. In summer, you may dine outside and admire the view of Chinon's castle. 🏨 *73 rue Voltaire,* ☎ *47–93–04–71. 10 rooms, 5 with bath. AE, DC, MC, V. Closed mid-Nov.–mid-Mar.* $–$$

Hotel de France. Just off the main square of Chinon stands one of the oldest buildings in town. Built in the 16th century, it was home to many notables until the revolution, when it became known as the Hotel de France. The current owners have been working continuously to restore it, most recently by refurbishing 8 of the 30 rooms. Ask for one of these, though all the rooms are comfortable and have private baths. On the ground floor, the restaurant doubles as a bar, a congenial place to re-group your energies for the next adventure. ☎ *47–49 pl. du Général-de-Gaulle, 37500, ☎ 47–93–33–91, FAX 47–98–37–03. 30 rooms with bath or shower. Restaurant. No credit cards. $–$$*

Meung-sur-Loire

DINING AND LODGING

★ **Auberge St-Jacques.** Located on Meung's busy main road, this inn is just a five-minute walk from the château and river. Its restaurant is one of the glories of France, a family-run affair where excellent fresh food, prepared by chef-owner M. Le Gall, is served without fuss at deliciously low prices. A very acceptable three-course menu is available for 90 francs, but for 150 francs you can have a hearty four-course meal of half a dozen oysters, fillet of duck in a raspberry vinaigrette, lamb or fish, followed by cheese and dessert. The clean and simple rooms either have a shower or, for 20 francs more, a full bath. ☎ *60 rue Général-de-Gaulle, 45130, ☎ 38–44–30–39, FAX 38–45–17–02. 12 rooms with shower or bath. Reservations advised. AE, MC, V. Restaurant closed Mon.; hotel and restaurant closed last 2 wks in Jan. $*

Montbazon

DINING AND LODGING

Château d'Artigny. One of the first members of the Relais & Châteaux properties lies just outside town on D17. Built by the Coty perfume tycoon in 1912 as a vast pseudo-Louis XV house, it is now a suavely run, expensive hotel appealing to the nouveau riche. Ironically, the am-bience recalls a perfume ad: Gilt, marble, and plush abound, creating a perfect backdrop for the frequent celebrity guests. The nouvelle restaurant is excellent but expensive. You can jog away the calories in the 60-acre park. ☎ *Rte. d'Azay-le-Rideau, 37250 Montbazon, ☎ 47–26–24–24, FAX 47–65–92–79. 55 rooms with bath. Restaurant, pool, tennis. DC, MC, V. Closed Dec.–early Jan. $$$$*

★ **Domaine de la Tortinière.** Although this charming little 19th-century château is more intimate and less expensive than the Château d'Artigny, it's hardly a country cousin. The Domaine's brand of elegance is sim-pler and subtler, but it still has everything you could want in a country hotel. Rooms in the main building exude a quiet, rustic luxury; those in the modern annex are less desirable. Some negatives in the old house: The morning gurgle of the water pipes serves as an alarm clock, and the opening and closing of doors along the corridor tells you it is time to descend to the breakfast room. Never mind; the beds, with their Egyp-tian cotton sheets, are so comfy it's a pleasure to be awake in them. No. 15, a small but pleasant room (665 francs), is quieter than some of the others. Dinner is a delightful occasion, even if the fare does not quite live up to its reputation. Start with an aperitif of sparkling white wine with cassis and raspberry in the high-ceiling lounge before descending to the brightly lit dining room, redecorated in 1995. The lobster bisque with a pastry top is delicious, and the strong hint of vanilla gives it spe-cial distinction. The *sandre* (white fish) in a white wine sauce can be rather bland, so you may wish to choose the lamb or the excellent pi-geon in a rich wine sauce. ☎ *10 rte. Ballan, Veigné, 37250 Montbazon, ☎ 47–26–00–19, FAX 47–65–25–70. 21 rooms with bath. Restaurant, pool, tennis. MC, V. Closed mid-Dec.–mid-Mar. $$$*

★ **Moulin Fleuri.** This is really a restaurant with rooms in a converted wa-termill 5 kilometers (3 miles) from Montbazon. The Indre sweeps by the garden terrace, where aperitifs and post prandial drinks are served. The delightful dining room is overseen by Mme. Chaplin, while her husband, Alain, masterminds the kitchen. An enthusiastic chef, he creates, among other specialties, excellent coquilles St-Jacques, fillet de sandre in a shellfish butter, and maigret de canard. Guest rooms vary in price according to size, but even the small ones are bright and cheerful. For value, quality, and personality, the Moulin Fleuri is a treat. ☎ *Rte. du Ripault, Veigné, 37250 Montbazon,* ☎ *47–26–01–12. 12 rooms, 8 with shower. Restaurant (MAP offered and suggested), Continental and English breakfasts, fishing. AE, MC, V. Closed Feb.; restaurant closed Mon. $–$$*

Muides-sur-Loire

LODGING

★ **Château de Colliers.** It's the ambience that makes this 18th-century manor so special. Enter through the courtyard and you'll be greeted by M. and Mme. Gelis's golden labrador, Goldie. The current owners are a bit shyer, but if you make a reservation to dine with the English-speaking couple, you'll soon be treated like friends. The dining room is a gem, with murals on the walls and ceilings, and although the food isn't elaborate, it's a pleasant meal indeed. Rooms are simply furnished with queen-size beds and functional bathrooms—the tub has a hand-held shower—holding true to the country-house style. The newly refurbished Empire Room not only has marvelous antiques but also a private rooftop terrace with views of the Loire (it's quite a climb up here). Afternoon tea or an aperitif on the terrace overlooking the Loire is an ideal way to end the day after visiting Blois, Chambord, Cheverny, Meung-sur-Loire, and Orléans—all close by. ☎ *41500 Muides-sur-Loire,* ☎ *54–87–50–75,* FAX *54–87–03–64. 5 rooms. Table d'hôte dinner with reservation, pool, tennis. MC, V. Closed Dec.–mid-Mar. $$*

Orléans

DINING

L'Assiette. This is a brisk but comfortable place, on the corner of place du Martroi (the main square). Choose your main course (simple grilled meats, mostly), and while it's cooking, help yourself to a wide variety of hors d'oeuvres and table wine from the barrel. You're entitled to as much of both as you want—and desserts are "free," too: The price of your meal depends on the main dish. ✗ *12 pl. du Martroi,* ☎ *38–53–46–69. Reservations advised. V. $*

DINING AND LODGING

Le Rivage. This small, white-walled hotel in Olivet makes a pleasant, affordable base for exploring Orléans, 4 kilometers (3 miles) to the north. All the rooms face the gently flowing, tree-lined Loiret, and each has a small balcony, just large enough to stand on and survey the scene of rowing sculls sweeping their oars up and down river. The rooms are compact and the bathrooms even tinier, with space for a shower, toilet, sink, and not much else but a hair dryer. Walls between rooms are thin, so expect to awake in the morning when your neighbors do. There is no elevator. Though the rooms are simple, meals are quite elaborate, and the cuisine of the two chefs, François Tassain and Patrice Ponsolle, is notable. The dining room is light and airy, with windows on three sides, with one of the sides opening to a terrace facing the river—a wonderful place to sit with an aperitif. The menu adapts to the seasons, and if you're lucky enough to find the crayfish (in a delectable sauce that heightens the taste), you will remember it for a long time. The lamb, marinated in paprika, is equally memorable, and the desserts—perhaps the aspic of orange and grapefruit in a banana syrup or the glazed green apple soufflé with apple marmalade—are the final indulgence. ☎ *635 rue de la Reine-Blanche, 45160 Olivet,* ☎ *38–66–02–93,* FAX *38–56–*

31–11. 20 rooms, some with bath. Restaurant, tennis court. AE, DC, MC, V. Closed Dec. 25–mid-Jan. $$

Saumur

DINING AND LODGING

Le Prieuré. In a Renaissance manor 8 kilometers (5 miles) from Saumur on D751 toward Anger, Le Prieuré offers elegant and gracious accommodations. The original structure dates from medieval times, but renovations over the centuries make it look more modern than old. The large guest rooms feature tasteful reproductions, and the nicest are in the main building. Room 5 has a delightful little alcove with a table and a window that looks over the Loire. Though the garden chalets are luxurious inside, and are neatly appointed, they are short on character. In the spacious dining room, crystal and silver clink discreetly, and diners can gaze at the river through large windows. Behind the scenes, chef Jean-Noël Lumineau produces his well-executed classics. ⌧ *Le Prieuré, 49350 Chênehutte,* ☎ *41–67–90–14, ℻ 41–67–92–24. 33 rooms with bath. Restaurant, pool, tennis. AE, MC, V. Closed early Jan.–early Mar. $$$$*

Anne d'Anjou. For proximity to the château and the center of town, this 18th-century hotel facing the river is your best choice. When you step inside you'll be astounded as you look up at the curving staircase with its wrought-iron railing. It circles up and up to the top floor and is capped by a truly impressive mural painting. Most of the rooms are simple and reasonably priced, either with old furniture (No. 201, 410 frs) or done in contemporary style (No. 205, 415 frs). Room 101 (450 frs) is large, and its big windows looking onto the quay and the white walls and bedspreads make it seem even larger. The pride and joy of the hotel's owners, Yves and Anne-Marie Touzé, is No. 102 (640 frs); with its wood-panel paintings and Empire furnishings; it is quite special. In the restaurant, Les Menestreles, chef Christophe provides very acceptable fare, and his wife, Catherine, guides you through the menu. ⌧ *32–33 quai Mayaud, 49400 Saumur,* ☎ *41–67–30–30, ℻ 41–67–51–00. 50 rooms with bath. Restaurant. AE, DC, MC, V. $$*

Loire. This member of the Best Western chain wins no prizes for charm or friendly service, but it is clean, spacious, and functional, and there is a stunning view of the château from the restaurant, Les Marineis. A drawback is that the hotel is across the river from the main part of town, though this makes for easier parking. ⌧ *Rue de Vieux-Pont, 49400,* ☎ *41–67–22–42, ℻ 41–67–88–80. U.S. reservations,* ☎ *800/528–1234; U.K. reservations,* ☎ *0181–541–0033. 44 rooms with bath. AE, DC, MC, V. $$*

Tours

DINING

Les Tuffeaux. This restaurant facing the château retains its place as one of Tours's best, without breaking the budget. Chef Gildas Marsollier has been winning customers with his delicious fennel-perfumed salmon, his oysters with an egg sauce seasoned with Roquefort, and remarkable desserts. Gentle lighting and a warm, understated decor provide a soothing background. ✕ *19 rue Lavoisier,* ☎ *47–47–19–89. Reservations advised. Jacket required. MC, V. Closed Sun., Mon. lunch, part of Jan. $$*

DINING AND LODGING

Jean Bardet. This restaurant is the brainchild and namesake of one of France's top-20 chefs. Try the eight-course *menu dégustation,* or order à la carte, oysters poached in muscadet on a puree of watercress. Or why not a simple grilled lobster, some fine cheese, and a hot baked apple filled with cinnamon ice cream? Both the food and the service can be erratic, something not to be expected when the tab for two will be approximately 975 francs. The Bardets also offer 5 luxurious suites and 16 rooms, which, at 700 to 1,300 francs, are on the exorbitant side. For real style, you can hire Jean Bardet's Rolls Royce *Silver Shadow II* to take you on a tour of the Loire. ☎ *57 rue Groison, 37000,* ☎ *47–41–41–11,* FAX *47–51–68–72. 21 rooms. Reservations essential. Jacket and tie. AE, DC, MC, V. Closed Sun. dinner, Mon., and late Feb.–early Mar. $$$$*

★ **Hotel de L'Univers.** A renovation completed in spring of 1993 has made the most of this building's old charm and turned it into the best hotel in town. Murals in the salon depict some of the famous who have stayed here: Winston Churchill, Sarah Bernhardt, Maurice Chevalier, Rudyard Kipling, and the Duke of Windsor. A clever use of space in the guest rooms creates desk and sitting areas apart from the beds, which are usually twins. Wood panels and soft colors add a traditional warmth. Bathrooms, many with a mirrored window that opens into the bedroom, are spacious, with large baths and separate toilet cabinets. Only 10 rooms face the street; the others, away from the traffic noise, look onto a flower garden. ☎ *5 blvd. Heurteloup, 37000,* ☎ *47–05–37–12,* FAX *47–61–51–80. 89 rooms with bath, 10 suites. Restaurant, bar, meeting rooms. AE, DC, MC, V. Restaurant closed Sat. $$$*

Valençay

DINING

Chêne Vert. If you want a reliable restaurant that serves good, simple meals at rock-bottom prices, look no further. The Green Oak is a basic little tavern offering hearty regional specialties. The four-course meal will fill you up, and in fine weather, you can eat outside. ✗ *55 rue Nationale,* ☎ *54–00–06–54. Reservations accepted. MC, V. Closed Sun. dinner, Sat. (except July–mid-Sept.), and 3 wks in June. $*

DINING AND LODGING

★ **Hôtel d'Espagne.** A recent addition to the Relais & Châteaux group, this intimate hotel retains the feel of an elegant provincial residence. The Fourré family has run it since 1875. A former coaching inn, covered in Virginia creeper, it is built around a landscaped courtyard with yews and flowers. Guest rooms are individually decorated, and many have balconies. Dining is on classical cuisine with novel twists, such as escalope de foie gras on a bed of ravioli. ☎ *9 rue du Château, 36600,* ☎ *54–00–00–02,* FAX *54–00–12–63. 16 rooms with bath. Restaurant, pool, tennis. AE, DC, MC, V. Closed Mon. and Jan.–Feb. $$$*

Villandry

DINING AND LODGING

Cheval Rouge. This is a fine, old-fashioned hotel whose restaurant is popular with the locals. It boasts an excellent Loire wine list and surprisingly good classical food, considering its touristy location right next to the château. Good bets are the terrine of foie gras, the calf sweetbreads, and the wood-fired grills. The 20 modern guest rooms are tidy, and all have bath or shower. ☎ *9 rue de la Mairie, 37510 Villandry,* ☎ *47–50–02–07,* FAX *47–50–08–77. Reservations advised. MC, V. Closed Mon. out of season, and Nov.–mid-Mar. $$*

THE ARTS AND NIGHTLIFE

Son-et-Lumière

The Loire Valley's favorite form of cultural entertainment is son-et-lumière, a dramatic spectacle that takes place after dark on summer evenings on the grounds of major châteaus. Programs sometimes take the form of historical pageants, with huge casts of people in period costume and caparisoned horses, the whole floodlit and backed by music and commentary, often (as at **Amboise**) in English. They may also take the form of spectacular lighting and sound shows, with spoken commentary and dialogue but no visible figures, as at **Chenonceau.** The most magnificent son-et-lumière occurs at **Le Lude,** on the River Loir (not the Loire), 48 kilometers (29 miles) northeast of Saumur and 50 kilometers (30 miles) northwest of Tours. Here more than 100 performers present a pageant chronicling the history of the château and region from the Hundred Years' War on. The spectacle is enhanced by fountains and fireworks.

Open-Air Festivals

For four weeks beginning in mid-June, the **Festival d'Anjou** enlivens the area around Angers with music, theater, and dance. In July, the château grounds at **Loches** are the setting for a series of open-air concerts. And in the medieval **Grange du Meslay** near Tours, top-class international musicians gather in late June and July for the **Fêtes Musicales de Touraine.**

LOIRE VALLEY ESSENTIALS

Arriving and Departing

By Plane

The closest airports are Paris's Charles de Gaulle and Orly.

By Train

The Loire region is served by fast, regular trains from Paris and other major cities. Trains run every two hours from Paris's Gare d'Austerlitz to Orléans (usually you must change at Les Aubrais) and Blois; from Gare Montparnasse, TGV trains leave for Tours (change at St-Pierre-des-Corps) and Angers every two hours.

By Car

A10 runs from Paris to Orléans—a distance of 130 kilometers (78 miles)—and on to Tours, with exits at Meung, Blois, and Amboise. After Tours, the A10 veers south, toward Poitiers and Bordeaux. A11 links Paris to Angers via Le Mans.

Getting Around

By Car

Slower but more scenic routes than A10 run from the western Channel ports down through Normandy into the Loire region. You can arrange to rent a car in all the large towns in the region or at train stations in Orléans, Blois, Tours, or Angers.

By Train

The Loire region has a good local network. The main line follows the Loire itself, running from Orléans through Blois, Tours, Saumur, and Angers to Nantes.

By Bus

Local bus services are extensive and reliable and are a link between train stations and scenic areas off the river. Inquire at tourist offices for information about routes and timetables.

Guided Tours

Orientation

Accueil de France in Angers (pl. Président-Kennedy, ☎ 41–87–72–50) and Blois (pl. du Maréchal-Leclerc, ☎ 54–74–06–49) organizes numerous tours of the Loire Valley, including car and bus excursions, and even hot-air balloon and boat trips. The office in Blois also offers equestrian, bike, and horse-drawn carriage tours of the Loire-et-Cher region. **Reservations Loisirs Accueil** in Blois (11 pl. du Château, ☎ 54–78–55–50) also arranges guided visits to the region's châteaus, as well as balloon and bicycle trips.

Personal Guides

The tourist offices in **Tours** and **Angers** (*see* Visitor Information, *below*) arrange city and regional excursions with personal guides. A walking tour sets out from Tours' tourist office every morning at 10 AM from mid-April through October for 35 francs. English-speaking guides will conduct visitors around the historic city of **Blois** during a walk that starts from the château at 4; the cost is about 30 francs.

Important Addresses and Numbers

Travel Agencies

American Express (12 pl. du Martroi, Orléans, ☎ 38–53–84–54) and **Wagons-Lits** (9 rue Marceau, Tours, ☎ 47–20–40–54).

Car Rental

Avis (6 rue Jean-Moulin, Blois, ☎ 54–74–48–15; 13 rue San-sonnières, Orléans, ☎ 38–62–27–04; and Gare SNCF, Tours, ☎ 47–20–53–27), **Hertz** (5 rue du Dr-Desfray, Blois, ☎ 54–74–03–03; and 57 rue Marcel-Tribut, Tours, ☎ 47–20–40–24), and **Europcar** (81 rue André-Dessaux, Fleury-les-Aubrais, near Orléans, ☎ 33–73–00–40; and 76 rue Bernard-Palissy, Tours, ☎ 47–64–47–76).

Visitor Information

The Loire region has two area tourist offices, for written inquiries only. For Chinon and points east, the regional office is **Comité Ré-gional du Tourisme du Centre-de-Loire** (8 rue Etienne-Dolet, 45050 Orléans). For Fontevraud and points west, contact **Comité Régional du Tourisme des Pays-de-Loire** (2 rue de la Loire, 44000 Nantes). Others are as follows: **Amboise** (quai Général-de-Gaulle, ☎ 47–57–09–28), **Angers** (pl. Kennedy, ☎ 41–91–96–56), **Blois** (3 av. Jean-Laigret, ☎ 54–74–06–49), **Orléans** (pl. Albert-Ier, ☎ 38–53–05–95), **Saumur** (pl. de la Bilange, ☎ 41–51–03–06), and **Tours** (rue B. Palissey, ☎ 47–05–58–08).

5 Brittany

THANKS TO its proximity to Great Britain, its folklore, and its spectacular coastline, Brittany (Bretagne in French) is a favorite destination among English-speaking vacationers. The French love the area, too, but don't worry about hordes of tourists—Brittany's vast beaches aren't easily crowded.

Occupying the bulbous portion of western France that juts far out into the Atlantic, the stubborn, independent-minded Bretons have more in common—both historically and linguistically—with the Celts of Cornwall, Wales, and Ireland than with their French countrymen. Both Brittany and Cornwall claim Merlin, King Arthur, and the Druids as cult figures, while huge Stonehenge-like menhirs and dolmens (prehistoric standing stones) litter the Breton countryside. As in Wales, nationalistic fervor has been channeled into gaining official acceptance for the local language.

Brittany became part of France in 1532, but regional folklore is still very much alive. An annual village *pardon* (a religious festival) will give you a good idea of Breton traditions: Banners and saintly statues are borne in colorful parades, accompanied by hymns, and the whole event is rounded off by food of all kinds. The most famous pardon is held on the last Sunday of August at Ste-Anne-la-Palud, near Quimper. The surrounding Finistère (from *Finis Terrae,* or Land's End) département, Brittany's westernmost district, is renowned for the costumes worn on such occasions—notably the lace bonnets, or *coiffes,* which can tower 15 inches above the wearer's head.

Geographically, Brittany is divided in two: maritime Armor ("land of the sea") and hinterland Argoat ("land of the forest"). The north of Brittany tends to be wilder than the south, where the countryside becomes softer as it descends toward Nantes and the Loire. Wherever you go, the coast is close by; the frenzied, cliff-bashing Atlantic surf alternates with sprawling beaches and bustling harbors. Islands, many inhabited and within easy reach of the mainland, dot the coastal waters.

Although Brittany's towns took a mighty hammering from the retreating Nazis in 1944, most have been nicely restored, the large concrete-cluttered naval base at Brest being an exception. Rennes, the only Breton city with more than 200,000 inhabitants, retains its traditional charm, as do the towns of Dinan, Quimper, and Vannes. Many ancient man-made delights are found in the region's villages, often in the form of *calvaries* (ornate burial chapels). Other architectural highlights include castles and cathedrals, the most outstanding examples being those of Fougères and Dol, respectively.

EXPLORING

Orientation

Our first tour is confined to northeastern Brittany, which stretches from Rennes to the fortified harbor of St-Malo. This region played a front-line role in Brittany's efforts to repel French invaders during the Middle Ages, as can be seen in the massive castles of Vitré, Fougères, and Dinan. Our second tour begins 144 kilometers (90 miles) farther west, at the town of Morlaix, before swinging southeast down the Atlantic coast to the city of Nantes at the mouth of the River Loire. Though Nantes is officially part of the Pays de la Loire, it has historic ties with Brittany, embodied in the imposing Château des Ducs de Bretagne.

Tour 1: Northeast Brittany

Numbers in the margin correspond to points of interest on the Brittany map.

★ ❶ Built high above the Vilaine Valley, **Vitré** (pronounced vee-*tray*) is one of the age-old gateways to Brittany: There's still a feel of the Middle Ages about its dark, narrow alleys and tightly packed houses. The town's leading attraction is its formidable **castle,** shaped in an imposing triangle with fat, round towers. An 11th-century creation, it was first rebuilt in the 14th and 15th centuries to protect Brittany from invasion and proved to be one of the province's most successful fortresses: During the Hundred Years' War (1337–1453) the English repeatedly failed to take it, even though they occupied the rest of the town.

Time, not foreigners, came closest to ravaging the castle, which was heavily, though tastefully, restored during the past century. The town hall, however, is an unfortunate 1913 addition to the castle courtyard. You can visit the wing to the left of the entrance, beginning with the Tour St-Laurent and continuing along the walls via Tour de l'Argenterie, with its macabre collection of stuffed frogs and reptiles preserved in glass jars, to Tour de l'Oratoire. ☛ *18 frs.* ☉ *Apr.–June, Wed.–Mon. 10–noon and 2–5:30; July–Sept., daily 10–12:30 and 2– 6:15; Oct.–Mar., Wed.–Fri. 10–noon and 2–5:30, Mon. 2–5:30.*

Vitré's castle is a splendid sight, especially from a vantage point on rue de Fougères across the river valley below. The castle stands at the west end of town, facing the narrow, cobbled streets of the remarkably preserved old town. Rue Poterie, rue d'Embas, and rue Beaudrairie, originally the home of tanners (the name comes from *baudoyers*—leather workers), make up a web of medieval streets as picturesque as any in Brittany; take time to stroll through them, soaking up the quaint atmosphere. Fragments of the town's medieval ramparts remain, including the 15th-century **Tour de la Bridolle** on place de la République, five blocks up from the castle. Built in the 15th and 16th centuries, **Notre-Dame** church has a fine, pinnacled south front and dominates a large square of the same name.

❷ Thirty-two kilometers (20 miles) due north of Vitré via D178 and D798 is **Fougères,** a traditional cobbling and cider-making center. For many centuries, it was a frontier town, valiantly attempting to guard Brittany against attack. Perhaps one of the reasons for its conspicuous lack of success is the site of the **castle:** Instead of sitting high up on the hill, it spreads out down in the valley, though the sinuous River Nançon does make an admirable moat. The 13-tower castle, one of the largest in Europe, covers over five acres. Although largely in ruins, it is an excellent example of the military architecture of the Middle Ages, impressive both inside and out. The thick walls—20 feet across in places—were intended to resist 15th-century artillery fire, but the castle was to prove vulnerable to surprise attacks and sieges. A visit inside the castle walls reveals three lines of fortification, with the keep at their heart. There are charming views over Fougères from the Tour Mélusine and, in the Tour Raoul, a small shoe museum. The second and third stories of the Tour de Coigny were transformed into a chapel during the 16th century. *East end of town on pl. Raoul II.* ☛ *13 frs (18 frs with guide).* ☉ *Daily Feb.–June and Sept.–Dec., 9:30–noon and 2–5; July–Aug. 9–7.*

The oldest streets of Fougères are alongside the castle, clustered around the elegant slate spire of **St-Sulpice** (rue de Lusignan), a Flamboyant

Gothic church with several fine altarpieces. A number of medieval houses line rue de la Pinterie, which leads directly from the castle up to the undistinguished heart of town.

In the 1790s, Fougères was a center of Royalist resistance to the French Revolution. Much of the action in 19th-century writer Honoré de Balzac's bloodcurdling novel *Les Chouans* takes place hereabouts; the novel's heroine, Marie de Verneuil, had rooms close to the church of **St-Léonard** (follow the river left from the castle), which overlooks the Nançon Valley. Both path and church, with its ornate facade and 17th-century tower, have changed little; the garden through which the path leads is known today as the **Jardin Public.**

Another man who was inspired by the scenery of Fougères was locally-born Emmanuel de La Villéon (1858–1944), a little-known Impressionist painter. His works are displayed in the **Musée La Villéon,** in one of the oldest surviving houses (dating from the 16th century) in hilltop Fougères; to reach it from the Jardin Public, head left past St-Léonard and cross the square into the adjacent rue Nationale. The more than 100 paintings, pastels, watercolors, and drawings suggest serene, underestimated talent. The artist's work ranges from compassionate studies of toiling peasants to pretty landscapes in which soft shades of green melt into hazy blue horizons. *51 rue Nationale.* ☛ *8 frs.* ☉ *Easter–mid-June, weekends only, 11–12:30 and 2:30–5; mid-June–mid-Sept., weekdays 10:30–12:30 and 2:30–5:30, weekends and holidays 11–12:30 and 2:30–5.*

★ ③ **Rennes** (pronounced *wren*), lying 48 kilometers (30 miles) southwest, is the traditional capital of Brittany. It has a different flavor from other towns in the region, mainly because of a terrible fire in 1720, which lasted a week and destroyed half the city. The remaining cobbled streets and half-timbered, 15th-century houses form an interesting contrast to the Classical feel of Jacques Gabriel's disciplined granite buildings, broad avenues, and spacious squares.

Start at the west end of the old town, bordered by the River Rance. The **Cathédrale St-Pierre,** a 19th-century building in Classical style that took 57 years to construct, looms above rue de la Monnaie. Stop in to admire its richly decorated interior and outstanding 16th-century Flemish altarpiece. *Pl. St-Pierre.* ☉ *Mon.–Sat. 8:30–noon and 2–5, Sun. 8:30–noon.*

The surrounding streets are filled with 15th- and 16th-century houses in both medieval and Renaissance styles. Many have been converted into shops, boutiques, restaurants, and crepe houses; a lively **street market** is held in and around place des Lices on Saturday morning.

The pedestrian rue Lafayette and rue Nationale lead to the **Palais de Justice** (Law Courts), the palatial original home to the Breton Parliament, designed in 1618 by Salomon de Brosse, architect of the Luxembourg Palace in Paris. It was the most important building in Rennes to escape the 1720 fire, but in February 1994, following a massive demonstration by Breton fishermen demanding state subsidies, a disastrous fire broke out at the Parliament building that left it just a charred shell. Much of the art work—though damaged—was saved by firefighters, who arrived at the scene only when the fire was in full flow. It was a case of the fire bell that cried "fire" once too often; a faulty bell, which went off regularly for no reason, had led the man on duty to ignore the ringing. As for the cause of the fire itself, rumors abound, but an investigation is still underway. The Parliament has been indefinitely closed for a major restoration.

On the nearby place de la Mairie, next door to the imposing 19th-century Municipal Theatre, is the oddly named **Piccadilly Tavern.** Its huge, sunny terrace is a perfect place to people-watch while enjoying an aperitif or—why not?—a half dozen of the superfresh oysters.

Head down from the Palais de Justice and left across quai Émile-Zola to the **Palais des Musées,** a huge building containing two museums— the **Musée des Beaux-Arts** and **Musée de Bretagne.** The Fine Arts Museum on the second floor houses one of the country's best collections of paintings outside Paris, featuring works by Georges de La Tour, Jean-Baptiste Chardin, Camille Corot, Paul Gauguin, and Maurice Utrillo, to name only a few. The ground-floor Museum of Brittany retraces the region's history, period by period, by way of costumes, models, porcelain, furniture, coins, statues, and shiny push-button visual displays. 20 quai Émile-Zola. ☛ Joint ticket 18 frs adults, 9 frs children under 14. ⊗ Wed.–Mon. 10–noon and 2–6.

Northeast of the museum building, a five-minute walk via rue Gambetta and rue Victor-Hugo, is the **Jardin du Thabor,** a large, formal French garden with regimented rows of trees, shrubs, and flowers. Even the lawns are manicured—not often the case in France. There is a notable view of the church of **Notre-Dame-en-St-Mélaine** in one corner.

North of Rennes, the landscape is dotted with hefty castles and enticing châteaus. Twenty-four kilometers (15 miles) away via N137 and D27 is the castle of **Montmuran,** closely associated with Brittany's warrior-hero Bertrand du Guesclin, whose name is commemorated in countless squares and hostelries across the province. Bertrand was quite a fellow. Cast as the ugly son of a noble family, he became tough and cunning by playing with the peasants. Ashamed of his rough manners, his family kept him hidden from society. However, at the age of 17, he entered a jousting tournament in disguise and successfully unseated several knights. When his identity was discovered, Bertrand's father proudly brought his son back into the fold. Bertand du Guesclin went on to become one of France's greatest warriors of all time. Here, he was knighted in 1354 and married his second wife in 1372. An alley of oak and beech trees leads up to the main 18th-century building, which is surrounded by a moat and flanked by four towers, two built in the 12th century, two in the 14th. You can visit the towers and a small museum devoted to the castle's history. ☛ 16 frs. ⊗ Easter–Oct., daily 2–7; Nov.–Easter, weekends only, 2–6.

⑤ Just 8 kilometers (5 miles) west is **Caradeuc,** a classical château ambitiously dubbed the Versailles of Brittany. Visitors can't go inside to check out this claim, unfortunately, but to compensate, explore the surrounding park—Brittany's largest—and admire its statues, flower beds, and leafy alleys. ☛ 12 frs. ⊗ Apr.–Oct., daily 9–noon and 1:30–8; Nov.–Mar., weekends only, 2–6.

⑥ Take D20 to Tinténiac, then N137 north to **La Bourbansais,** a total of 19 kilometers (12 miles) from Caradeuc. This castle has remained in the same family since it was founded by local lord Jean de Breil in 1583. It, too, has extensive gardens, containing a small zoo and a pack of hunting hounds. The buildings were enlarged in the 18th century, and the majority of the interior furnishings date from that period. There are fine collections of porcelain and tapestries. ☛ 32 frs. Castle open Apr.–Oct., daily 2–6; Nov.–Mar., weekends only, 2–6. Park open daily 10–noon and 2–7.

❼ Combourg, best known as the boyhood home of Romantic writer viscount Chateaubriand (1768–1848), is 11 kilometers (7 miles) east along D75 and D794. The thick-walled, four-tower castle dates mainly from the 14th and 15th centuries and contains a roomful of Chateaubriand archives. You can visit the writer's austere bedroom in the Tour du Chat (Cat's Tower). The castle grounds—ponds, woods, and half-tended lawns—are suitably mournful and can seem positively desolate under leaden skies. ☛ *22 frs, park only 11 frs.* ☉ *Castle Mar.–Nov., Wed.–Mon. 2–5; park Mar.–Nov., Wed.–Mon. 9–noon and 2–5.*

Seventeen kilometers (10 miles) north via D795, the ancient town of **❽ Dol-de-Bretagne** looks out from its 60-foot cliffs over Le Marais, a marshy plain stretching across to Mont-St-Michel, 21 kilometers (13 miles) northeast. The **Promenade des Douves,** laid out along the northern part of the original ramparts, offers extensive views of Le Marais and Mont Dol, a 200-foot granite mound, 3 kilometers (2 miles) north, legendary scene of combat between St. Michael and the devil.

At the end of the promenade, note the **Cathédrale St-Samson** (pl. de la Cathédrale), a damp, soaring, fortresslike bulk of granite dating mainly from the 12th to the 14th century. This mighty building shows just how influential the bishopric of Dol was in days gone by. The richly sculpted Great Porch, carved wooden choir stalls, and stained glass in the chancel deserve close scrutiny.

Turn down rue des Écoles to the small **Musée Historique d'Art Populaire.** During a short, cheerful guided tour, you'll see costumes, weapons, and a series of scale models retracing life in Dol since prehistoric times. The glory of the museum, though, is its assembly of colored wooden religious statues. *Rue des Écoles.* ☛ *23 frs.* ☉ *Easter–Oct., Wed.–Mon. 9–noon and 1:30–6:30.*

Rue des Écoles leads to Dol's picturesque main street, Grand-Rue des Stuarts, lined with medieval houses. The oldest, at No. 17, boasts a chunky row of Romanesque arches.

★ **❾** From Dol, take N176 to **Dinan,** 24 kilometers (15 miles) southwest. Dinan has close links with Brittany's 14th-century anti-English warrior-hero Bertrand du Guesclin, whom we heard of in Montmuran. Du Guesclin won a famous victory here in 1359 and promptly married a local girl, Tiphaine Raguenel. When he died in the siege of Auvergne (central France) in 1380, his body was dispatched home to Dinan. Owing to the great man's popularity, however, only his heart completed the journey—the rest of him having been confiscated by devoted followers in towns along the route.

Begin your stroll around the old town at the tourist office, housed in a charming 16th-century building in rue de l'Horloge. For a superb view of the town, climb to the top of the medieval clock tower, the **Tour de l'Horloge.** ☛ *10 frs.* ☉ *July–Aug., 10:45–1:15 and 3–6.*

Turn left and head half a block along to admire the triangular-gabled wooden houses in **place des Merciers, rue de l'Apport,** and **rue de la Poissonnerie.** With their overhanging balconies and black-and-white half-timbered houses, these cobbled streets are so pretty you may think you've stumbled into a Hollywood movie set. Restore your faith with a visit to the nearby church, the **Basilique St-Sauveur** (turn right out of place des Merciers along rue Haute-Voie, then take the second left into the church square). The church is a mixture of styles, ranging from the Romanesque south front to the Flamboyant Gothic facade and Renaissance side chapels. Du Guesclin's heart lies in the north transept.

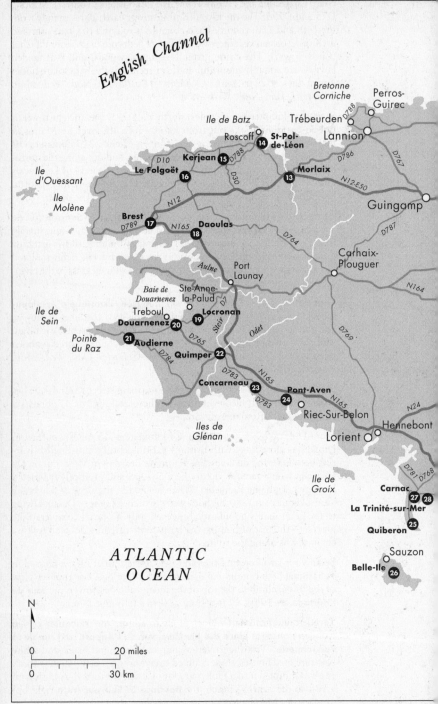

English Channel

Bretonne Corniche

Perros-Guirec

Trébeurden

Ile de Batz

Roscoff

St-Pol-de-Léon

14

Lannion

Ile d'Ouessant

Ile Molène

Kerjean **15**

D10

Le Folgoët

16

Morlaix

13

N12-E50

D786

D788

D788

D30

D767

Guingamp

N12

Brest **17**

D789

N165

Daoulas

18

D764

Carhaix-Plouguer

D787

Aulne

Port Launay

N164

Ste-Anne-la-Palud

Baie de Douarnenez

Locronan **19**

D7

Ile de Sein

Treboul

Douarnenez **20**

Steir

Odet

D769

21 **Audierne**

Pointe du Raz

D765

D784

Quimper **22**

D783

N165

Concarneau **23**

24 **Pont-Aven**

Riec-Sur-Belon

N165

N24

Iles de Glénan

D783

Hennebont

Lorient

Ile de Groix

D781

D768

Carnac

27 **28**

La Trinité-sur-Mer

Quiberon **25**

Sauzon

ATLANTIC OCEAN

Belle-Ile **26**

N

0   20 miles

0   30 km

Golfe de St-Malo

CÔTE EMERAUDE

Cap Fréhel

Coutances

Granville

Avranches

Mont-St-Michel

Cancale **12**

St-Malo **11**

Dinard **10**

Dol-de-Bretagne **8**

St-Brieuc

Dinan **9**

La Bourbansais **6**

Combourg **7**

Tinténiac

Fougères **2**

Loudéac

St-Méen-le-Grand

Caradeuc **5** **4** Montmuran

Vitré **1**

Pontivy

3 Rennes

TO PARIS →

Josselin

Ploërmel

La Chapelle

Elven

Rochefort-en-Terre

Châteaubriant

Auray

Vannes **29**

28

Golfe du Morbihan

30 Redon

Muzillac

Billiers

31

Missillac

Ile Houat

St-Lyphard

Ile Hoëdic

La Baule **32**

St-Nazaire

St-Marc-sur-Mer

Nantes
33 — 40

Pornic

Rance river

Vilaine

Vilaine

Loire

Couesnon

Nançon

Oust

TIME OUT Every evening at **Le Prélude,** Bernard Benoit sings traditional Breton songs, accompanying himself on guitars, Breton harp, and hammer dulcimer. The welcome is warm, the '60s atmosphere is intimate, and you can take home a CD or cassette as a souvenir. *20 rue Haute Voie, no cover or minimum.*

The **Jardin Anglais** (English Garden) is just behind the church; it's not really much of a garden, but its old trees nicely frame the east end of St-Sauveur. More spectacular views can be found at the bottom of the garden, which looks down the plummeting Rance Valley to the river 250 feet below.

The cobblestone rue du Jerzual leading down to the harbor, is a beautifully preserved medieval street. It's lined with boutiques and crafts shop in 15th- and 16th-century houses, and divided halfway down by the town walls and massive Porte du Jerzual gateway.

TIME OUT Woolens by the yard and English cakes and scones by the dozen: That's the unlikely combination you'll find at this strange little American-run outfit, **La Toison d'Or** (rue du Jerzual), where long wooden benches add to the atmosphere, if not the comfort, as you settle down for a cup of coffee and a snack.

Dinan's harbor seems somewhat forlorn; although there are sailings in summer up the River Rance to Dinard and St-Malo, abandoned warehouses bear witness to vanished commercial activity, with only an occasional restaurant to brighten up the place.

Amble back up the hill (it's steep) and turn right, well after the Porte du Jerzual, onto rue de l'École. This street leads down to another gateway, the Porte St-Malo, from which the leafy Promenade des Grands Fossés heads left on a tour of the best-preserved section of the town walls. Follow these walls around as far as the **castle.** Here you can visit the two-story Coëtquen Tower and 100-foot 14th-century keep, containing varied displays of medieval effigies and statues, Breton furniture, and local lace *coiffes. Porte de Guichet.* ☎ *15 frs.* ⊙ *March–Jan., daily 9–noon and 2–6.*

❿ **Dinard** is the most elegant resort on this stretch of the Brittany coast. It's only 22 kilometers (14 miles) north on D266, but a bit farther away if you follow the picturesque meanderings of the Rance. The town's picture-book setting on the Rance Estuary opposite the walled city of St-Malo is probably what lured the English aristocracy here in droves after it was discovered in the 1850s by an American named Coppinger. What started out as a small fishing port soon became a seaside mecca of lavish turn-of-the-century villas, grand hotels, and a bustling casino. A number of more modern establishments punctuate the landscape, but the town still retains something of an Edwardian tone. Walking along Dinard's sandy, crescent-shaped beaches, it's easy to see why people love the place.

To make the most of Dinard's exhilarating setting, head down to the town's southern tip, the **Pointe de la Vicomte,** where cliffs offer panoramic views across the Baie du Prieuré and Rance Estuary. The **Plage du Prieuré,** named after a priory that once stood here, is a sandy beach ringed by yachts, dinghies, and motorboats. The **Clair de Lune Promenade** hugs the seacoast on its way toward the English Channel, passing in front of the small jetty used by boats crossing to St-Malo. Shortly after, the street reaches the **Musée de la Mer** (Marine Museum and Aquarium). Virtually every known species of Breton bird and sea creature is on display here, in two rooms and 24 pools. Another room is devoted to the polar expeditions of explorer Jean Charcot, one of the first men to chart the Antarctic; there are poignant souvenirs of his last voyage, in 1936, from which he never returned. *Clair de Lune Promenade.* ☛ *10 frs.* ⊘ *Pentecost Sun.–Sept., daily 10–noon and 2–6.*

The Clair de Lune Promenade, lined with luxuriant semitropical vegetation, really hits its stride as it rounds the Pointe du Moulinet to the Prieuré Beach. River meets sea in a foaming mass of rock-pounding surf, and caution is needed as you walk along the slippery path. Your reward: the calm and shelter of the **Plage de l'Écluse,** an inviting sandy beach, bordered by a casino and numerous stylish hotels. The coastal path picks up again on the far side, ringing the Pointe de la Malouine and Pointe des Etêtés before arriving at Dinard's final beach, the **Plage de St-Enogat.**

★ ⑪   Little more than a mile from Dinard by water, but 13 kilometers (8 miles) by road, is the ancient walled town of **St-Malo.** The stone ramparts of this onetime pirate base have stood firm against the Atlantic since the 12th century, but were considerably enlarged and modified in the 18th. The town itself has proved less resistant: A week-long fire in 1944, kindled by retreating Nazis, wiped out nearly all the old buildings. Restoration work was more painstaking than brilliant, but the narrow streets and granite houses of the old town, known as *Intra Muros* ("within the walls"), have been satisfactorily re-created, enabling St-Malo to regain its role as a busy fishing port and seaside resort.

North American visitors can pay homage to Jacques Cartier, who set sail from St-Malo in 1535 to discover the St. Lawrence River and found Québec. Cartier's tomb is in the church of **St-Vincent** (off Grande-Rue), while his statue looks out over the town ramparts, four blocks away—along with that of swashbuckling corsair Robert Surcouf, hero of many daring 18th-century raids on the British navy (he's the one pointing an accusing finger over the waves at *l'Angleterre*). The ramparts extend from the castle in St-Malo's northeast corner and ring the old town, with a total length of over a mile. The views from there are stupendous, especially at high tide. Five hundred yards offshore is the **Ile du Grand Bé,** a small island housing the somber military tomb of viscount Chateaubriand, who was born in St-Malo. The islet can be reached by a causeway at low tide, as can the **Fort National,** a massive fortress with a dungeon constructed in 1689 by that military-engineering genius Sébastien de Vauban. ☛ *10 frs.* ⊘ *Easter–Sept. Call ahead:* ⊘ *Hours and times of the half-hour guided tours depend on the tides.*

At the edge of the ramparts, overlooking the Fort National, is **St-Malo Castle,** whose great keep and watchtowers command an impressive view of the harbor and coastline. It houses two museums: the **Musée de la Ville,** devoted to local history, and the **Quic-en-Grogne,** a tower where various episodes and celebrities from St-Malo's past are recalled by way of waxworks. *Porte St-Vincent. Musée de la Ville, admission: 16 frs.* ⊘ *Mar.–Nov., Wed.–Mon., 9:30–noon and 2–6:30. Tour Quic-en-Grogne, admission: 17 frs.* ⊘ *Easter–Oct., daily 9–11:30 and 2–6.*

⑫   Anyone who enjoys eating oysters should make the 13-kilometer (8-mile) trip east on D355 to **Cancale,** renowned for its oyster beds. You'll find lots of quayside restaurants in which to sample this delicacy. The town's delightful seaside setting is also an attraction.

Stretching out into La Manche (the English Channel) west of Dinard and St. Malo, the Emerald Coast is followed by D786 and D34 to Val André and down to St-Brieuc. The winding, narrow road, continuously offering grand views and lookout points, is less than 97 kilometers (60 miles), but it can take five hours to drive. If time makes you selective, choose **Cap Fréhel,** the most dramatic site along the coast, with red, gray, and black cliffs rising vertically from the sea. The colors are best in the evening, but any time of day the sight is formidable. Duck the seagulls and cormorants and walk down past the small restaurant to the platform for a look at the Fauconnière rocks below. And go up to the lighthouse, whose beam winks at ships more than 100 kilometers away.

After the Emerald Coast comes the **Bretonne Corniche,** whose particular attraction is the pink granite rocks that have been eroded into distinctive shapes by the battering sea and wind. To avoid some of the winding roads, you can take N12 west to Guingamp and then D767 northwest to Lannion, and continue on to **Trébeurden.** As you travel up the peninsula to Trégastel, Ploumanach, and Perros-Guirec, the weird profiles of the rocks and the names assigned to them will enable your imagination to see such shapes as the Tête de Mort (Death's Head), La Tortoise, Le Sentinel, and Wellington's Hat. The scene is forever changing with the play of sunlight and the vast tides, which sweep in to shore and then retreat, stranding fishing boats among islands that were, hours ago, hidden beneath the surface of the sea.

Tour 2: Brittany's Western Coast

⓭ Our second tour begins at **Morlaix** (pronounced mor-*lay*), far to the west of St-Malo—144 kilometers (90 miles) by the fast N12. Morlaix's town-spanning, 19th-century stone railroad viaduct is an unforgettable sight—300 yards long and 200 feet high. Though there are no other major sights in Morlaix, the old town is an attractive mix of half-timbered houses and low-fronted shops that rewards unhurried exploration. The pedestrian Grand' Rue is its commercial heart, lined with quaint 15th-century houses. The **Maison de la Reine Anne,** in adjacent rue du Mur, is a three-story 16th-century building adorned with statuettes of saints.

Just off rue d'Aiguillon, which runs parallel to Grand' Rue, is the town museum, known as the **Musée des Jacobins** because it is housed in the former Jacobin church; an early 15th-century rose window survives at one end as a reminder. The museum's eclectic display ranges from religious statues to archaeological finds and modern paintings. *Pl. des Jacobins.* ☛ *16 frs.* ⊙ *Apr.–Oct., daily 10–noon and 2–6; Nov.–Mar., Wed.–Mon. 2–5.*

⓮ D73 hugs the riverbank north of Morlaix; branch left at Kerdanet and follow signs for **St-Pol-de-Léon,** 10 kilometers (6 miles) farther away. St-Pol is a lively market town dominated by three spires: Two belong to the cathedral, the highest to the Chapelle du Kreisker. The **Ancienne Cathédrale,** built between the 13th and 16th centuries, is pleasingly proportioned, and its finely carved 16th-century choir stalls are worth a trip inside. Rue du Général-Leclerc, with its large wood-framed houses, links the cathedral to the **Chapelle du Kreisker,** originally used for meetings by the town council. Its magnificent 250-foot 15th-century granite spire, flanked at each corner by tiny spirelets known as *fillettes* ("young girls"), is the prototype for countless bell towers in Brittany. From the top there is a rewarding view across the Bay of Morlaix toward the English Channel. ☛ *5 frs. Access to the tower mid-June–mid-Sept., daily 10–noon and 2–5.*

Just 5 kilometers (3 miles) north of St-Pol along D58 is the burgeoning port of Roscoff. From here, head 24 kilometers (15 miles) southwest toward Brest before turning right onto D30 and making for the nearby ⓯ 15th-century château of **Kerjean.** With its vast park, ditch, and 40-foot-thick defensive walls, Kerjean at first looks like a fortress until you see the large windows, tall chimney stacks, and high-pitched roofs of its main buildings. The chapel, kitchens, and main apartments, full of regional furniture, can be visited. Temporary exhibitions are held in the stable wing. Notice the old well in the main courtyard. ☛ *22 frs.* ☉ *Sept.–June, Wed.–Mon. 10–noon and 2–7; July–Aug., daily 10–7.*

16 Sixteen kilometers (10 miles) west of Kerjean along D788 is **Le Folgoët** and its splendid **Notre-Dame basilica,** whose sturdy north tower, visible from afar, beckons pilgrims to the *pardon* (religious festival) held here in early September. On this occasion, many pilgrims drink at the Salaün fountain against the wall behind the church; its water comes from a spring beneath the altar, which can be reached through a sculpted porch. Inside the church is a rare, intricately worked, granite rood screen separating the choir and nave.

17 Continue along D788 to the maritime city of **Brest,** 24 kilometers (15 miles) southwest, but don't plan to spend much time here; you may even want to bypass the town altogether. Brest's enormous, sheltered bay is strategically positioned close to the Atlantic and the English Channel. During World War II, Brest was used by the Germans as a naval base; it was liberated in 1944 by American forces, after a 43-day siege that left the city in ruins. Postwar reconstruction, resulting in long, straight streets of reinforced concrete, has left latter-day Brest with the unenviable reputation of being one of France's ugliest cities. Its waterfront, however, is worth visiting for the few old buildings and museums, as well as for dramatic views across the bay toward the Plougastel Peninsula.

Begin your visit at one of the town's oldest monuments, the **Tour Tanguy.** This bulky, round 14th-century tower, once used as a lookout post, is a majestic sight in its own right; the interior contains a museum of local history with scale models of the Brest of yore. ☛ *Free.* ☉ *Oct.–May, Wed.–Sun. 2–6; June–Sept., daily 10–noon and 2–7.*

Next to the tower is the River Penfeld and, crossing it, the Pont de Recouvrance, at 95 yards Europe's longest lift-bridge. On the other side, Brest's medieval castle is home to the **Musée de la Marine** (Naval Museum), containing boat models, sculpture, pictures, and naval instruments. A section is devoted to the castle's 700-year history. The dungeons can also be visited. ☛ *22 frs.* ☉ *Wed.–Mon. 9:15– noon and 2–6.*

A short walk inland leads to the **Musée Municipal** on rue Traverse. French, Flemish, and Italian paintings, spanning the period from the 17th to the 20th century, make up the collection. *Rue Émile-Zola.* ☛ *Free.* ☉ *Wed.–Sat. and Mon. 10–11:45 and 2–6:45, Sun. 2–6:45.*

Farther east, overlooking the Moulin Blanc marina, is the brand-new, futuristic **Océanopolis** center. Maritime technology, fauna, and flora are the themes of its exhibits, but the biggest attraction is the aquarium—the largest in Europe. *Rue Alain-Colas.* ☛ *40 frs.* ☉ *Tues.–Sun. 9:30–6, Mon. noon–6.*

18 Southbound N165, which leaves Brest for Quimper, 104 kilometers (65 miles) away, soon passes through **Daoulas,** where you can stop off to admire the *Enclos Paroissial* (literally, "parish enclosure") and the 12th-century Romanesque abbey, with its cloisters and herbal garden. Stay on N165 until you reach Port Launay, then branch off southwest **19** along scenic D7 to **Locronan,** a typical old weaving town, where the great canvas sails were made to supply the French fleet. There's a magnificently preserved ensemble of houses and main square, all dominated by the 15th-century Church and Chapel of Le Pénity.

Before heading southwest on D7, you might take a detour toward the coast for some fresh sea air and a look at Brittany as it has been for centuries. As you approach the cliffs and inlets of **Ste-Anne-la-Palud,** the roads become blissfully free of cars and are lined with the charming stone cottages that are typical of the area.

⓴ **Douarnenez,** 10 kilometers (6 miles) west of Locronan via D7, is a quaint old fishing town of quayside paths and zigzagging narrow streets. Boats come in from the Atlantic to offload their catches of mackerel, sardines, and tuna. Sailing enthusiasts will be interested in the town's biennial classic boat rally in mid-August (scheduled for this summer), when traditionally rigged sailing boats of every description ply the waters of the picturesque Bay of Douarnenez. Across the bridge over the Port-Rhu estuary is Tréboul, a seaside resort town for French families.

In 1993, the town opened a unique **Port-Musée** (Maritime Port/Museum) in one of its three harbors. Along the wharves, you can visit the workshops of wooden-boatwrights, sail makers, and other old-time craftspeople, then go aboard the historic trawlers, lobster boats, Thames barges, and a former lightship anchored alongside. Visitors can also take a sail on an antique fishing boat. *Quai du Port-Rhu.* ☞ *60 frs (June–Sept.), 50 frs (Oct.–May) adults; 25 frs (June–Sept.), 15 frs (Oct.–May) children 7–16.* ☼ *Daily 10–7.*

Due west of Douarnenez, parts of the coast look more like the breezy bluffs of Ireland than like France, especially around **Pointe du Raz.** This is the westernmost tip of the country, marked by a dramatic 300-foot drop; the spectacular view is worth the detour. Plan on an hour to walk along the edge of deep chasms. The deepest is called L'Enfer de Plogoff (the Plogoff Inferno), where the tide rushes in and out with a deafening roar. Go out all the way to the end for broad views of the horizon and coastline and to tremble a while as you become hypnotized by the Raz de Sein, a tidal race whose rip puts fear into everyone's heart.

㉑ Just inland from Pointe du Raz is the small working port of **Audierne,** where the fishermen come daily bearing the day's catch of langoustines. In summer, it is a busy pleasure-boat center that is never overcrowded; most of the visitors are locals, which makes for a nontouristy, welcoming atmosphere.

㉒ From Douarnenez, take D765 southeast to **Quimper.** This lively commercial town is the ancient capital of the Cornouaille province, founded, it is said, by King Gradlon 1,500 years ago. Quimper (pronounced cam-*pair*) owes its strange-looking name to its site at the confluence (*kem-per* in Breton) of the Odet and Steir rivers. The banks of the Odet are a charming place for strolling. Highlights of the old town include **rue Kéréon,** a lively shopping street; the medieval rue de Guéodet (note the house with caryatids), rue St-Mathieu, and rue du Salle; and the stately **Jardin de l'Evêché** (Bishop's Gardens) behind the cathedral in the center of the old town.

The **Cathédrale St-Corentin** is a masterpiece of Gothic architecture and the second-largest cathedral in Brittany (after that of Dol). Legendary King Gradlon is represented on horseback just below the base of the spires, harmonious mid-19th-century additions to the medieval ensemble. The luminous 15th-century stained glass is particularly striking. *Pl. St-Corentin.*

Two museums flank the cathedral. Works by major masters, such as Rubens, Corot, and Picasso, mingle with pretty landscapes from the local Gauguin-inspired Pont-Aven school in the **Musée des Beaux-Arts** (Fine Arts Museum; admission 25 frs; open July–Aug., daily 9–7, Sept.–June, Wed.–Mon. 10–noon and 2–6), while local furniture, ceramics, and folklore top the bill in the **Musée Départemental** (Regional Museum) in adjacent rue du Roi-Gradlon (admission 20 frs; open June–Sept., daily 9–6, Oct.–May, Wed.–Mon. 9:30–noon and 2–6).

Quimper sprang to nationwide attention as an earthenware center in the mid-18th century, when it began producing second-rate imitations of the Rouen ceramics known as faience, featuring blue Oriental motifs. Today's more colorful designs, based on floral arrangements and marine fauna, are still often handpainted. Plan on looking at some pottery shops; a particularly good one is Maison A. Breton at 16 bis, rue de Parc, a block away from the cathedral. There are guided visits to the main pottery, the **Faïencerie Henriot,** and its museum, situated on the banks of the Odet south of the old town. *Allée de Locmaria. ☛ 25 frs. ☉ Mid-Apr.–Oct. and school vacations, Mon.–Sat. 10–6.*

★ ㉓ **Concarneau,** 21 kilometers (13 miles) from Quimper along D783, is the third-largest fishing port in France. A busy industrial town, it has a grain of charm and an abundance of tacky souvenir shops. The town's main attraction, the **Ville Close,** is a fortified islet in the middle of the harbor that you enter by a quaint drawbridge. The view of the harbor from here is splendid. From early medieval times, Concarneau was regarded as impregnable, and the fortifications were further strengthened by the English under John de Montfort during the War of Succession (1341–64). This enabled the English-controlled Concarneau to withstand two sieges by Breton hero Bertrand du Guesclin; the third siege was successful for the plucky du Guesclin, who drove out the English in 1373. Three hundred years later, Sébastien de Vauban remodeled the ramparts into what you see today: half a mile long and highly scenic, offering views across the two harbors on either side of the Ville Close. *☛ Ramparts: 4 frs. ☉ Easter–mid-June, 10–12:30 and 2–7, mid-June–Sept., 10–7:30.*

At the end of rue Vauban closest to the drawbridge is the **Musée de la Pêche** (Fishing Museum), which houses aquariums and offers historical explanations of fishing techniques around the world. *☛ 30 frs adults, 20 frs children. ☉ Mid-June–mid-Sept., 9:30–7, mid-Sept.–mid-June, 9:30–12:30 and 2–6.*

If you're in Concarneau during the second half of August, you will be able to enjoy the Fête des Filets Bleus (Blue Net Festival) in the Ville Close. This festival is a week-long folk celebration in which Bretons in costume swirl and dance to the wail of bagpipes.

㉔ **Pont-Aven,** just a few kilometers down coastal backroads or D783, is a former artists' colony that was headquarters for Paul Gauguin before he headed off to the exotica of the South Seas. The group was known as the Pont-Aven School, and the **Musée Municipal** has a permanent photography exhibition documenting it all, as well as shows of different artists who participated in the movement. *Pl. de l'Hotel de Ville, ☏ 98–06–14–43. ☛ 25 frs July–Aug., 15 frs Apr.–June and Sept.–Dec. ☉ July–Aug., daily 10–7; hours vary other times.*

Gourmets will want to push on to **Belon,** the town famous for its oysters, just 16 kilometers (10 miles) down D783, then take D24 at Riec-sur-Belon.

Boat trips down the estuary from Pont-Aven are a relaxing way to cool off in summer breezes, or you can walk up a hill among the pastures to the Tremalo chapel, where there is a crucifix that has been attributed to Gauguin.

N165 speeds down the coast, past the industrial port of Lorient, as far as Auray. Here, take D768 southwest toward Carnac at the northern end of the 16-kilometer-long (10-mile-long) Quiberon Peninsula, dangling off the Brittany coast. The Côte Sauvage (Wild Coast) on the west of the peninsula is a savage mix of crevices, coves, and rocky grottoes lashed by violent seas.

㉕ **Quiberon** itself is famed for more soothing waters: It is a spa town with fine, relaxing beaches on the protected side.

TIME OUT In a country where gourmandism is virtually a cultural pursuit, **Henri Le Roux** (18 rue du Port-Maria) has taken the art of chocolateering to dizzying heights. Check out his delicious displays—created before your very eyes—at his shop near Quiberon Harbor.

The cheerful harbor of Port-Maria is the base for boat trips to nearby Belle-Ile, at 18 kilometers (11 miles) long the largest of Brittany's islands. Because of the cost and inconvenience of reserving car-berths on the ferry, it's best to cross to Belle-Ile as a pedestrian and rent a car—or, better still, a bicycle—on the island.

㉖ Although it's just a 45-minute boat trip from Quiberon, **Belle-Ile** is much less commercialized, and exhilarating scenery is its main appeal. Near Sauzon, the island's prettiest settlement, is a view across to the Quiberon Peninsula and Gulf of Morbihan from the **Pointe des Poulains,** home of Belle Epoque actress Sarah Bernhardt. The nearby **Grotte de l'Apothicairerie** is a grotto whose name derives from the local cormorants' nests, said to resemble apothecary bottles. Farther south, near Port Goulphar, is another dramatic sight—the **Grand Phare** (lighthouse), built in 1835 and rising 275 feet above sea level. Its light is one of the most powerful in Europe, visible from 75 miles across the Atlantic. If the keeper is available, you may be able to climb to the top and admire the view.

★ ㉗ Once back on the mainland, return to **Carnac** at the north end of Quiberon Bay. Carnac is famed for its beaches and, especially, its **megalithic monuments** dating from the Neolithic/Early Bronze Ages (3500–1800 BC). The whys and wherefores of their construction remain as obscure as those of their English contemporary, Stonehenge, although religious beliefs and astrology were doubtless an influence. The 2,395 menhirs that make up the three *Alignements* (Kermario, Kerlescan, and Ménec) are positioned with astounding astronomical accuracy in semicircles and parallel lines over half a mile long. There are also smaller-scale dolmen ensembles and three tumuli (mounds or barrows), including the 130-yard-long, 38-foot-high **Tumulus de St-Michel,** topped by a small chapel affording fine views of the rock-strewn countryside. *Guided tours of the tumulus daily Apr.–Sept.* ☛ *5 frs.* ☉ *Easter–Oct.*

㉘ Just east of Carnac lies the yachtsman's paradise of **La Trinité-sur-Mer,** a resort town ringed by sandy beaches and oyster beds, and much favored by wealthy Parisians seeking a home-away-from-home vacation. From La Trinité, head up D781 and D28 to Auray, then take N165 ㉙ east to **Vannes** (pronounced *van*). Scene of the declaration of unity between France and Brittany in 1532, Vannes is one of the few towns in Brittany to have been spared damage during World War II, so its authentic regional charm remains intact. Be sure to visit the **Cohue** (medieval market hall—now a temporary exhibition center) and the picturesque **place Henri IV** and browse in the small boutiques and antiques shops in the surrounding pedestrian streets. The ramparts, Promenade de la Garenne, and medieval washhouses are all set against the backdrop of the much-restored **Cathédrale St-Pierre,** with its 1537 Renaissance chapel, Flamboyant Gothic transept portal, and treasury in the old chapterhouse. *Pl. du Cathédrale.* ☞ *3 frs.* ☉ *Treasury mid-June–mid-Sept., Mon.–Sat. 10–noon and 2–6.*

③⓪ From Vannes, N165 goes to Muzillac, 19 kilometers (12 miles) away, from which D20 veers 43 kilometers (27 miles) east to the little town of **Redon,** built at the junction of the River Vilaine and the Nantes–Brest canal. These days, Redon Harbor is used exclusively by pleasure boats, but it was once a busy commercial port. A number of stylish 17th–19th-century mansions, with large windows and wrought-iron balconies, line the adjacent quays. Wood-framed medieval houses line the main street, Grande Rue, which is dominated by the slender spire and magnificent Romanesque tower of the church of **St-Sauveur,** all that remains of a once-powerful Benedictine abbey.

③① Head due south from Redon, via D114, to **Missillac,** at the edge of the **Grande Brière Regional Park.** This low-lying marshy area, criss-crossed by narrow canals, can be explored either by boat (trips are organized from St-Nazaire) or by car along D51 as you head southwest toward La Baule. Ever since a ducal edict of 1461, La Brière has been the common property of its inhabitants, who live in distinctive and picturesque white thatched cottages. Highlights include the panoramic view from the church tower at **St-Lyphard** and the curious **Kerbourg dolmen** 5 kilometers (3 miles) south, just off D47.

③② **La Baule,** 18 kilometers (11 miles) from St-Lyphard, is one of the most fashionable resorts in France, with a 5-kilometer (3-mile) seafront promenade lined with resort hotels. Like Le Touquet and Dinard, it is a 19th-century creation, founded in 1879 to make the most of the excellent sandy beaches that extend 10 kilometers (6 miles) around the broad, sheltered bay between Pornichet and Le Pouliguen. A pine forest, planted in 1840, keeps the shifting local sand dunes firmly at bay.

★ ③③ From La Baule head 72 kilometers (45 miles) east, past St-Nazaire and its struggling shipyard, to **Nantes,** a tranquil, prosperous city that seems to pursue its existence without too much concern for what's going on elsewhere in France. Although Nantes is not really part of Brittany— officially it belongs to the Pays de la Loire—the dukes of Brittany were in no doubt that Nantes belonged to their domain, and the castle they built is the city's principal tourist attraction.

Numbers in the margin correspond to points of interest on the Nantes map.

③④ The **Château des Ducs de Bretagne** is a massive, well-preserved 15th-century fortress with a neatly grassed moat. The duke responsible for building most of it was François II, who led a hedonistic existence here, surrounded by ministers, chamberlains, and an army of servants. Numerous monarchs later stayed in the castle, where, in 1598, Henry IV signed the famous Edict of Nantes advocating religious tolerance.

Within the Harnachement—a separate building inside the castle walls— you'll find the **Musée des Salorges** (Naval Museum), devoted principally to the history of seafaring; a separate section outlines the triangular trade that involved transportation of African blacks to America to be sold as slaves. As you cross the courtyard to the Grand Gouvernement

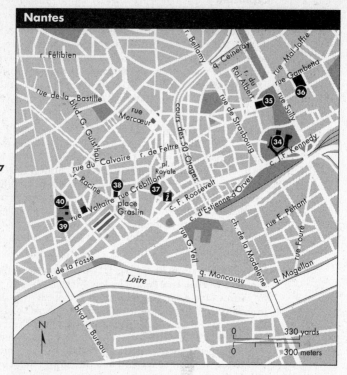

wing, home to the **Musée d'Art Populaire Régional** (Regional Folk Art Museum), look for the old well, where the ducal coat of arms is entwined in a magnificent wrought-iron decoration. The Musée d'Art Populaire features an array of armor, furniture, 19th-century Breton costumes, and reconstituted interiors illustrating the former life of the Vendée region to the south. *Just off rue du Château.* ☛ *30 frs, free Sun.* ☻ *Castle and museums Sept.–June, Wed.–Mon. 10–noon and 2–6; July–Aug., daily 10–noon and 2–6.*

35 Opposite the castle is the **Cathédrale St-Pierre,** one of France's latest Gothic cathedrals; building began only in 1434, well after most other medieval cathedrals had been completed. The facade is ponderous and austere, in contrast to the light, wide, elegant interior, whose vaults rise higher (120 feet) than those of Notre-Dame in Paris. In the transept, notice Michel Colombe's early 16th-century tomb of François II and his wife, Marguerite de Foix, which is one of France's finest examples of funerary sculpture. *Pl. St-Pierre.*

36 Behind the cathedral, past the 15th-century Porte St-Pierre, is the **Musée des Beaux-Arts,** with a fine collection of paintings from the Renaissance on, featuring works by Jacopo Tintoretto, Georges de La Tour, Jean-Auguste Ingres, and Gustave Courbet. *10 rue G-Clemenceau.* ☛ *20 frs, free Sun.* ☻ *Mon., Wed.–Sat. 10–noon and 1–5:45, Sun. 11–5.*

The cobbled streets around the castle and cathedral make up the town's medieval sector. Across cours des 50 Otages, a broad boulevard, is the 19th-century city. From place Royale stroll and windowshop down busy **37** rue Crébillon. Halfway down on the left is the **Passage Pommeraye,** an elegant shopping gallery erected in 1843, and at the far end, on place **38** Graslin, stands the **Grand Théâtre,** built in 1783.

TIME OUT   Miniature palm trees, gleaming woodwork, colorful enamel tiles, and painted ceilings have led to the official recognition of **La Cigale** (4 pl. Graslin) as a *monument historique*. You can savor its Belle Epoque ambience without spending a fortune: The 69- and 120-franc menus are just right for a quick lunch, although the banks of fresh oysters and the well-stacked dessert cart may tempt you to go for a leisurely meal à la carte.

㊴ Just along rue Voltaire from place Graslin is the 15th-century **Manoir de la Touche,** once home to the bishops of Nantes. Its medieval silhouette
㊵ is offset by the mock-Romanesque **Palais Dobrée,** next door, built by arts connoisseur Thomas Dobrée during the past century. Among the treasures within are miniatures, tapestries, medieval manuscripts, and enamels, while one room is devoted to the Revolutionary Wars in Vendée. *Pl. Jean V.* ☛ *20 frs, free Sun.* ☉ *Wed.–Mon. 10–noon and 1:30–5:30.*

What to See and Do with Children

Boat trips make entertaining excursions for old and young alike. Some of the most scenic include the tour of the Golfe du Morbihan (depart from Vannes), sea jaunts from Dinard or St-Malo to the Ile de Cézembre or along the rugged coast to Cap Fréhel, cruises up the River Rance from Dinard to Dinan, and the frequent 10-minute crossings between Dinard and St-Malo.

These other attractions are described in the Exploring section:
Château des Ducs de Bretagne, Nantes, Tour 2.
Fougères Castle, Tour 1.
Grand Phare (Lighthouse), Belle-Ile, Tour 2.
Musée de Bretagne, Rennes, Tour 1.
Musée de la Mer, Dinard, Tour 1.
Musée de la Pêche, Concarneau, Tour 2.
Port-Musée, Douarnenez, Tour 2.
Océanopolis, Brest, Tour 2.
Vitré Castle, Tour 1.

Off the Beaten Track

You may enjoy visiting the inland countryside, particularly some of the spectacular castles north of Vannes. The first of these castles, set in a wooded park 19 kilometers (12 miles) from Vannes via N166, is the **Fortress of Largoët** near Elven. Its 170-foot 14th-century octagonal keep is the highest in France; its walls are up to 30 feet thick. Alongside is a faithfully restored 15th-century tower. Henry Tudor was held prisoner here before his return to England and the triumphant 1485 military campaign that led to his becoming Henry VII. ☛ *13 frs.* ☉ *Mid-Jan.–mid-Nov., daily 8–6.*

Continue along N166 past Brignac—a round 15th-century tower is all that remains of the fortress that once stood here—to La Chapelle. The elegant, nearby château of **Le Crêvy** houses a collection of costumes dating from 1730.

Sixteen kilometers (10 miles) northwest along D4 is **Josselin,** a picturesque medieval town. **Josselin Castle** has two faces. Overlooking the River Oust is a defensive stronghold with three stout turreted towers linked by austere, near-windowless walls. The landward facade, however, is a riot of intricate pinnacles, gables, and stone ornament, surrounded by gardens. You can visit the library, wood-paneled dining room, portrait gallery, and Grand Salon, with its ornate fireplace (only the ground floor is open to the public). ☛ 22 frs. ⊗ July–Aug., daily 10–noon and 2–6, June and Sept., daily 2–6, Apr.–May, Wed. and Sun. 2–6.

Another attraction in Josselin is the 500-strong collection of old dolls displayed in the former castle stables. Many are dressed in traditional costume; most date from the 18th century, and one dates from the 17th century. ☛ 22 frs (separate from castle). ⊗ June–Sept., daily 10–noon and 2–6, Mar.–May and Oct., Wed. and weekends 2–6.

The cheerful old town of **Rochefort-en-Terre,** 45 kilometers (28 miles) southeast of Josselin, boasts a cozy, ivy-clad 14th-century castle. The interior holds tapestries, armor, chests, and furniture; earthenware statuettes; and paintings by Alfred and Trafford Klots, American artists who lived here and restored the castle. ☛ 15 frs. ⊗ Apr.–May and Oct., weekends 10–12:30 and 2–6:30; June–Sept., daily 10–12:30 and 2–6:30.

SHOPPING

Folk Costumes and Textiles

When it comes to distinctive Breton folk costumes, **Quimper** is the best place to look. The streets around the cathedral (especially **rue du Parc**) are full of shops, several selling the woolen goods (notably thick marine sweaters) in which the region also specializes. Addresses for good textiles in **Rennes** are **Tidreiz** (pl. du Palais) and **Au Roy d'Ys** (29 blvd. de Magenta).

Gift Ideas

The commercial quarter of **Nantes** stretches from place Royale to place Graslin. For antiques, try **Cibot** (7 rue Voltaire). Don't miss chocolate specialist **Georges Gautier** (9 rue de la Fosse), with his *Muscadets Nantais*—grapes dipped in brandy and covered with chocolate. Since 1803, the Devineau family has been selling wax fruit and vegetables at **Maison Devineau** (6 pl. Ste-Croix). For 75 francs, you can take home a basket of purple grapes or a cauliflower. They also sell handmade candles and wildflower honeys. **Quimper** is best known for its faïence—hand-painted earthenware—which can be bought at the **Kéraluc Faïencerie** (14 rue de la Troménie on the Bénodet road), at **Maison A Breton** (16 bis, rue de Parc), or at **Henriot** (12 pl. St-Corentin). Keep an eye out for such typical Breton products as woven or embroidered cloth, brass and wooden goods, puppets, dolls, and locally designed jewelry.

Markets

Among Brittany's most colorful markets are the ones held at Talensac in **Nantes** and in the streets of old **St-Malo** (Tuesday and Friday only). The most interesting street for arts and crafts is the cobbled, sloping **rue de Jerzual** in **Dinan,** whose medieval houses contain an assortment of wood-carvers, jewelers, leather workers, glass specialists, and silk painters.

SPORTS AND THE OUTDOORS

Beaches and Water Sports

From St-Malo to Brest, then south to Nantes, the Brittany coast has any number of clean sandy **beaches**—the best are found at Dinard, Perros-Guirec, Trégastel-Plage, Douarnenez, Carnac, and La Baule. Resorts offer numerous sports facilities ranging from **underwater diving** and **spearfishing** to **canoeing** and **sand-sailing** (at St-Pierre Quiberon). To rent **sailboats,** try St-Malo (☎ 99–82–00–78), Carnac (☎ 97–52–

02–41), Douarnenez (**Iroise Nautique,** ☎ 98–74–29–38), Dinard (**Yacht Club,** ☎ 99–46–14–32), or Morlaix (**Loisirs 3000,** ☎ 98–88–27–30).

Windsurfing (boards can be rented in Carnac from **De Petigny** at 90 rte. du Pô, ☎ 97–52–02–41), the **Wishbone Club** in Dinard (Pont d'Emeraude), and the **Centre Nautique** in Brest (☎ 98–02–11–93). **Waterskiers** can try Concarneau (☎ 98–97–41–03).

Bicycling
Bikes can be rented at the train stations in Brest (☎ 98–44–21–55), Morlaix (☎ 98–88–60–47), and Quimper (☎ 98–80–50–50); in St-Malo, from **Diazo** (☎ 99–40–31–63); in Dol, from **Cycles Nicole** (☎ 99–48–03–20); or at Carnac (☎ 97–52–02–33) and Dinard (**Duval Cycles,** ☎ 99–46–19–63).

Horseback Riding
There are riding stables in St-Malo (**Société Hippique,** ☎ 99–81–20–34), Dinan (☎ 96–27–14–62), Carnac (**Centre Equestre des Menhirs,** ☎ 97–55–73–45), and Dinard (**Centre Equestre de la Cote d'Emeraude,** ☎ 99–46–23–57).

DINING AND LODGING

Dining

Not surprisingly, Breton cuisine is dominated by fish and seafood. Shrimp, crayfish, crabs, oysters, and scallops are found throughout the region, but the linchpin of Breton menus is often lobster, prepared in sauce or cream or grilled. Popular meats include ham and lamb, frequently served with kidney beans. Fried eel is a traditional dish in the Nantes district. Brittany is particularly famous for its crepes, served with both sweet and savory fillings. Accompanied by a glass of local cider, they make an ideal basis for a light, inexpensive meal.

CATEGORY	COST*
$$$$	over 400 frs
$$$	250–400 frs
$$	125–250 frs
$	under 125 frs

*per person for a three-course meal, including tax (18.6%) and tip but not wine

Lodging

Brittany's economy is heavily dependent on tourism, and its hotel infrastructure is correspondingly dense. Recent TGV train links make the area easily accessible from Paris, bringing larger crowds in the summer, so it is always best to make reservations far in advance. The charm of many of the region's lodging places is that they are family-run and can be quite small, encouraging the friendly, personal service for which the Bretons are known. Brittany also has a growing number of luxury hotels and beautiful old châteaus converted into lodgings, many of which offer thalassatherapy (sea water) treatments, sporting facilities, swimming, and top-notch dining. Dinard, on the English Channel, and La Baule, on the Atlantic, are the two most expensive resorts.

CATEGORY	COST*
$$$$	over 800 frs
$$$	500–800 frs
$$	300–500 frs
$	under 300 frs

All prices are for a standard double room for two, including tax (18.6%) and service charge.

Audierne

DINING AND LODGING

★ **Le Goyen.** This modern hotel sits just across the street from the bustling fishing port, and in the early morning you can watch the activity below from the balcony of your very pretty room (or ultramodern suite). Take your aperitifs in the lounge, surrounded by marine decorations, and prepare yourself for the haute Breton cuisine of chef Adolphe Bosser. You can watch the port from every table as you dine on his seafood specialties: baked turbot with a sauce made from beef stock, or Breton lobster, or you might opt for one of his other superb dishes, perhaps the aromatic *ris de veau* (veal sweetbreads). ☎ *Portside, 29770,* ☎ *98–70–08–88,* FAX *98–70–18–77, 126 rooms with bath, 3 suites. Reservations advised. AE, MC, V. Closed mid-Nov.–mid-Dec. and Mon. off-season. $$$*

La Baule

DINING

La Marcanderie. This warm, yellow-walled restaurant is widely considered the best in town, helped by the cheerful welcome of Jean-Luc Girard and his wife. Potato and scampi tart, lobster salad, lotte in cider, and scallops in endive figure on the menus, which start at 190 francs. ✗ *5 av. d'Agen,* ☎ *40–24–03–12,* FAX *40–11–08–21. Reservations required. Jacket and tie. AE, MC, V. Closed Mon., Sun. evening. $$$*
Le Nossy Be. Sitting directly on the beach, at the foot of the seawall, this plant-filled pavillion offers a seafood menu that includes bouillabaisse and a selection of the oysters for which the region is famous. ✗ *Across from 14 blvd. Darlu,* ☎ *40–60–42–25. AE, MC, V. $$*

LODGING

Concorde. This establishment numbers among the least expensive good hotels in pricey La Baule. It's calm, comfortable, recently modernized, and a short block from the beach (ask for a room with a sea view). There's no restaurant. ☎ *1 bis av. de la Concorde, 44500,* ☎ *40–60–23–09,* FAX *40–42–72–14. 47 rooms with bath or shower. Closed Oct.–Easter. $$*

Belle-Ile

DINING

La Forge. A sure bet for lunch or dinner, La Forge specializes in traditional cuisine, based on seafood and fish, at affordable prices. Old wooden beams and remnants of the building's original purpose—blacksmithing—contribute to the pleasant, rustic atmosphere. ✗ *Rte. de Port-Goulphar, Bangor,* ☎ *91–31–51–76. Reservations required in summer. AE, DC, MC, V. Closed Wed. and Jan.–Feb. $$*

Billiers

DINING AND LODGING

Domaine de Rochevilaine. At the tip of the Pen-lan headland (take D5 out of Billiers for 3 kilometers, or 2 miles) you'll find this resort hotel, whose rooms are arranged on two sides of a courtyard, surrounded by terraced gardens. The rooms all have modern furnishings, but they vary in size and not all face the sea. The lounge and dining room make up the third wing. With the arrival of chef Patrice Caillaut, the cuisine has become excitingly creative but the prices are somewhat inflated—menus start at 250 francs. The view over the ocean with the sun dipping low on summer evenings is magnificent. Wealthy Parisians come here for a few days of relaxation, and in the off-season, the hotel is sometimes taken over for business seminars. ⌖ *56190 Billiers,* ☎ *97–41–61–61,* ⊠ *97–41–44–85. 25 rooms with bath, 2 suites. Restaurant, pool. Closed Feb.–mid-Mar. AE, DC, MC, V. $$$$*

Cancale

DINING AND LODGING

★ **De Bricourt** The picturesque fishing village of Cancale is the setting for one of the region's best restaurants, from whose windows there's a view of Mont-St-Michel. The highly rated young chef, Olivier Roellinger, opened the restaurant in the large stone house in which he grew up, and the murals, stone fireplaces, and antique tiles create an atmosphere that is both appetizing and cozy. Local seafood dishes are his specialty, but his are seasoned with exotic spices more indigenous to Indonesia than to the Côte d'Emeraude. Desserts are not to be missed. There are 19 very attractive guest rooms for those wishing to dine and sleep in style, 3 in the main building, 16 in an annex. ⌖ *1 rue Duguesclin,* ☎ *99–89–64–76,* ⊠ *99–89–88–47. Reservations advised. AE, DC, MC, V. Restaurant closed Tues. and Wed. in winter, Tues. in July and Aug. $$$$*

LODGING

Hotel Richeux. This, one of two hotels in Cancale owned by Jane and Olivier Roellinger of Restaurant DeBricourt, occupies an imposing turn-of-the-century waterfront mansion built on the ruins of an 11th-century château of the duGuesclin family. Try for one of the tower rooms, which have stunning views across the Bay of Mont-St-Michel. The small restaurant specializes in the renowned local oysters and other shellfish. ⌖ *St. Meloir des Ondes, 35350,* ☎ *99–89–64–76,* ⊠ *99–89–88–47. 11 rooms with bath, 2 suites. Restaurant. AE, DC, MC, V.* ☉ *All year, restaurant closed Nov. 15–Dec. 15. $$$$*

Les Rimains. The Roellingers' other hotel is tucked among towering trees at the end of a rocky point, with the surf directly below. Every room has a direct ocean view, and you breakfast at a table in the flower-filled garden. There is no restaurant, but Restaurant DeBricourt is just a 10-minute walk away, through quiet lanes. ⌖ *1 rue Duguesclin, 35260,* ☎ *99–89–64–76,* ⊠ *99–89–88–47. 6 rooms with bath. AE, DC, MC, V. Closed Oct.–Mar. $$$$*

Dinan

DINING

Relais des Corsaires. The old hilltop town of Dinan is full of restaurants and crepe houses, but we suggest that you wander down to the old port on the banks of the Rance to dine at this spot, quaintly named after the pirates who apparently raided the wharves of Dinan. The mid-range fixed-price menu provides an ample four-course meal, with alternative menus at higher and lower prices. The welcoming proprietors, Jacques and Barbel Pauwels, have also created a more informal grill, Au Petit Corsair, in the 15th-century building next door. ✕ *7 rue du Quai,* ☎ *96–39–40–17. Reservations accepted. AE, DC, MC, V. Closed Jan., Feb. $*

LODGING

D'Avaugour. This hotel, splendidly situated opposite Dinan Castle's Tour du Connétable, has its own flower garden with a southern exposure, where breakfast and afternoon teas are served on sunny days. Most of the cozy guest rooms look out onto either the garden or the castle and all are being redecorated (completion in 1997). Now, that Mme. Quinton is a widow, sadly, the restaurant is no more, but agreements with nearby restaurants ensure her guests top-quality local fare. She offers a full buffet breakfast at the former Continental breakfast rate. Mme. Quinton is fluent in English and enjoys helping guests plan their trips. ⌨ *1 pl. du Champ-Clos, 22100,* ☎ *96–39–07–49,* ℻ *96–85– 43–04. 27 rooms with bath. Garden. AE, DC, MC, V. $$*

LODGING

Arvor. An English couple, the Bundys, converted an 18th-century convent building into a comfortable, charming hotel across from the tourist office that overlooks the quiet cobbled streets of Dinan's old town. ⌨ *5 rue A. Pavie, 22100,* ☎ *96–39–21–22,* ℻ *96–39–83– 09. 23 rooms with bath or shower. AE, MC, V. $*

Dol-de-Bretagne

DINING AND LODGING

Logis de la Bresche Arthur. With its crisp outlines, white walls, and glassed-in terrace, the hotel may not look quite as historic as it sounds, but it's the coziest place in Dol to spend a night. The rooms are functional and inexpensive; local character, a certain smartness, and a sense of indulgence are reserved for the restaurant. Here chef-owner Phillipe Martel serves classically inspired dishes, like roast pigeon with black currant and ginger sauce, lightly poached scallops with herbs, and ravioli stuffed with *petits gris* (small snails) in a cream sauce. ⌨ *36 blvd. Deminiac, 35120,* ☎ *99–48–01–44,* ℻ *99–48–16–32. 24 rooms with bath. Restaurant. AE, DC, MC, V. $$*

Douarnenez

DINING AND LODGING

★ **Hotel Ty Mad.** Artists and writers like Picasso and Breton native Max Jacob have been coming to this small hotel, in a quiet residential area, since the 1920s. The rooms are small, but the views of the sea and the meals in the glass-enclosed restaurant are great. Try the seafood terrine with langoustine sauce, and don't miss the pumpkin *flan.* ⌨ *Plage St-Jean, 29100,* ☎ *98–74–00–53,* ℻ *98–74–15–16. 23 rooms with bath or shower. Restaurant. MC, V. Closed Nov.–late Mar. $$*

Hennebont

DINING AND LODGING

Château de Locquenole. The architecture here is monstrous—one can only marvel. It's squat, cold, and imposing, but all that is forgiven for the peaceful, natural setting of lawns and woods with the River Blavet flowing through. Design takes a turn for the better inside the manor house, with traditional 19th-century furnishings and great tapestries on the high walls. The spacious guest rooms are similarly done; those with a view over the lawns to the river are especially appealing. Some prefer to stay at La Chaumière, the renovated stables at the farm, 3 kilometers (2 miles) away. The rooms here are rustic, warm, and cozy, making romance where there was none. Dining at the château has always been an event, but three years ago it lost its second Michelin star. In 1995 one of France's top chefs, Marc Angelle, was hired to win it back. Thus, you may expect a keenness of creativity that may sometimes be lacking on "established" restaurants' menus. ⌨ *D781 3 km (2 mi) south of Hennebont. Rte. de Port-Louis, 56700,* ☎ *97– 76–29–04,* ℻ *97–76–39–47. 31 rooms, 4 suites. Restaurant, pool, sauna. Closed Jan.–mid-Feb. Restaurant also closed Mon. AE, DC, MC, V. $$$$*

Morlaix

DINING AND LODGING

★ **Europe.** Occupying an old building in the town center, the Europe is easily the best hotel in town, with simple, modernized guest rooms. Its restaurant (low-cost fixed-price menus, higher à la carte) provides an exuberant welcome, sumptuous many-mirrored decor, and exciting recipes featuring lobster (try the fricassee of Breton lobster with chervil and garlic confit), warm oysters, and smoked salmon. ☎ *1 rue d'Aiguillon, 29210,* ☎ *98–62–11–99,* FAX *98–88–83–38. 67 rooms, some with bath. Restaurant. AE, DC, MC, V. $–$$*

Nantes

DINING

★ **L'Embellie.** Chef Claude Scheiber has taken over this small, modern bistro, formerly Le Colvert, serving interesting dishes based on seafood or game. The cooking is serious and traditional, making the most of herbs to bring out the natural flavors. The lunchtime menu is particularly good value. ✕ *14 rue Armand-Brossard,* ☎ *40–48–20–02. Reservations advised. MC, V. Closed Sat. lunch, Sun., and first wk in Sept. $$*

Mon Rêve. Fine food and a delectable parkland setting are offered at this cozy little restaurant about 8 kilometers (5 miles) east of town. Chef Gérard Ryngel concocts elegantly inventive regional fare (the duck or rabbit in muscadet are good choices), while his wife, Cécile, presides over the dining room with aplomb. ✕ *506 blvd. de la Loire, Basse-Goulaine,* ☎ *40–03–55–50,* FAX *40–06–05–41. Reservations advised. AE, DC, MC, V. Closed Tues. evening and Wed. Oct.–Mar. $$–$$$*

LODGING

Hotel Graslin. This hotel, on a quiet street just off the central Place Graslin, is distinctly French: modest, cozy, and comfortable and run with discreet efficiency by the couple who own it. The rooms feature soundproof windows, individual safes, and satellite TV (CNN, etc.). M. and Mme. Roche also manage to keep their prices reasonable. ☎ *1 rue Piron, 44000,* ☎ *40–69–72–91,* FAX *40–69–04–44. 47 rooms with bath. AE, DC, MC, V. $$*

Pont-Aven

DINING

La Taupinière. On the road from Concarneau, in the outskirts of Pont-Aven, is a roadside inn with an attractive garden. The food doesn't come cheap, but, then, chef Guy Guilloux doesn't dabble in mediocrity. Fish, crab, crayfish, and Breton ham (perhaps grilled over the large, open fire) are the bases of his inventions, while his wine cellar is renowned. ✕ *Rte. de Concarneau,* ☎ *98–06–03–12. Reservations required. Jacket required. MC, V. Closed Mon. dinner, Tues., and mid-Sept.–mid-Oct. $$$*

DINING AND LODGING

Moulin de Rosmadec. This faithfully restored old mill sits in the middle of the rushing, rocky Aven River. There are only a handful of newly appointed rooms attached to the original establishment, but in each of these you'll fall asleep to the sound of water gently spilling over the stones beneath your window. The restaurant is one of the best in France, serving such seafood dishes as lobster- or langoustine-stuffed ravioli in a rustic dining room decorated with sturdy Breton furnishings. ☎ *Town center, 29930,* ☎ *98–06–00–22,* FAX *98–06–18–00. 4 rooms with bath. Reservations required. Jacket required. MC, V. Closed Oct. 15–31, Sun. evening and Wed. mid-Sept.–mid-June. $$$*

Rennes

DINING

★ **Palais.** The best, though not the most expensive, restaurant in Rennes must thank its highly inventive young chef, Marc Tizon, for its considerable reputation. Specialties include roast rabbit and, during winter, fried oysters in crab sauce. The menu changes according to the season and what's freshest in the market. The decor is sharp-edged contemporary, the site conveniently central. ✕ *7 pl. du Parlement de Bretagne,* ☎ *99–79–45–01. Dinner reservations required. Jacket required. AE, DC, MC, V. Closed Sun. dinner, Mon., and Aug. $$*

★ **Le Grain de Sable.** Situated on the corner of a tiny, winding street in the oldest part of town is a thoroughly unusual restaurant. Plants, candelabra, faded photographs, and a settee in the middle of the dining room create an ambience that escapes tackiness only by sheer eccentricity (a rocking horse sways in one corner). The cuisine is equally off-beat; expect garlic puree or endive with melted cheese to accompany the grilled meats that dominate the menu. Piped music, from opera to Louis Armstrong, warbles in the background as the playful waitresses receive noisy reprimands from Hervé in the kitchen. ✕ *2 rue des Dames,* ☎ *99–30–78–18. Reservations advised. MC, V. Closed Sun., Mon. dinner. $–$$*

LODGING

Central. This stately, late-19th-century hotel lives up to its name and sits in a quiet, narrow back street close to Rennes Cathedral. The individually decorated guest rooms look out over the street or courtyard. The owners have recently renovated the hotel, adding 35 rooms and off-street parking, a big plus so close to the town center. ☎ *6 rue Lanjuinais, 35000,* ☎ *99–79–12–36,* FAX *99–79–65–76. 43 rooms, most with bath. AE, DC, MC, V. $$*

Riec-sur-Belon

DINING

Chez Jacky. From the town center, follow the arrows west 8 kilometers (5 miles) to this picturesque wharf-side restaurant directly on the Belon River, the source of some of the country's best oysters. Whatever you eat here is as fresh as it can possibly be. ✕ *Rive Droite,* ☎ *98–06–90–32. Reservations advised. MC, V. Closed Mon., Oct.–Mar. $–$$*

Ste-Anne-la-Palud

DINING AND LODGING

Hotel de la Plage. At what seems like the end of the earth (it is indeed very near the end of Brittany), this former private house sits nestled in a cove on a quiet strip of smooth, sandy beach. Some of the comfortably furnished rooms face the sea and are afforded magnificent sunsets. The remote setting is great for long, restorative walks— the sort that work up an appetite for the seafood specialties served in the hotel's highly rated restaurant, where the food is consistently good, though not very innovative. Certainly this is a very comfortable hotel, though with less charm or feeling of Brittany than one might want. ☎ *29127 Plonevez-Porzay,* ☎ *98–92–50–12,* FAX *98–92–56–54. 26 rooms with bath. Tennis courts, private beach. Reservations required. Jacket required. AE, DC, MC, V. Closed Oct. 15–Apr. 1. $$$–$$$$*

St-Malo

DINING

La Métairie de Beauregard. It is worth driving south on N137 and then D4 toward Château-Malo to find this restaurant in a small, attractive manor of 1653, when it was the home of a privateer. Jacques

Gonthier and his wife, Marie-Claire, have created a warm, cozy ambience in their Louis XIII–style dining room. Jacques's cuisine is classical, but he travels the world, frequently to Arizona, and comes back with new flavors to excite his creations. His skill is in producing light fare, and many of his specialties use freshly caught fish—crab millefeuille with a puree of crab, and John Dory with a cream of prawns, for example. Service is charmingly personal, particularly when young Rozenne is helping her mother, Marie-Claire, in the dining room. Another plus is that the price is very reasonable. ✕ *St-Etienne, St-Servan via N137, D4.* ☎ *99–81–37–06.* ☉ *Daily in summer; often closed in winter. AE, DC, MC, V. $$*

Café de la Bourse. Wherever you eat in the old town of St-Malo, you will feel caught in a commercialized tourist trap. This restaurant, where prawns and oysters are downed by the shovelful, is no exception. Although its wooden seats and tacky nautical paraphernalia— ships' wheels and posters of grizzled old sea dogs—are hardly artistic, the large, L-shape dining room makes amends with genuinely friendly service and a seafood platter for two that includes at least three tanklike crabs, plus an army of cockles, whelks, and periwinkles. ✕ *1 rue de Dinan,* ☎ *99–56–47–17. Reservations accepted. AE, V. Closed Wed. low season. $–$$*

Le Chalut. For fish and only fish, this simple, casual, and friendly restaurant in the northeast corner of the walled town attracts locals and tourists alike. As you walk by, you can inspect the night's fare laid out on a stand in front, and a large tank for the shellfish dominates the dining room. There's not much else—the emphasis is on the fish, not the decor. ✕ *8 rue Corne de Cerf,* ☎ *99–56–71–58. No reservations. Closed Jan., 2 wks in Oct., and Sun. dinner out of season. MC, V. $*

LODGING

La Digue. Many of the rooms and the breakfast terrace at this hotel face the sea, offering magnificent views over St-Malo's long beach. The largest and most luxurious apartments are pricey, but many others are quite reasonable. A bar with a magnificent view of the sea, and a *salon de thé* add to the hotel's attractions. ⊞ *49 chaussée du Sillon, 35400,* ☎ *99–56–09–26,* FAX *99–56–41–65. 53 rooms, some with bath. Bar, tearoom. AE, V. Closed Jan. $$–$$$*

Hôtel Elizabeth. In this very touristy and slightly honky-tonk town, the Elizabeth, near the porte St-Louis, is a little gem of sophistication. It is small, as you would expect of a town house built into the ramparts of the city wall, but each of the small rooms is furnished in taste and the rate varies with the size of the room. The hotel is obviously Mme. Raverat's pride and joy, and perhaps for that reason she keeps the rates down. ⊞ *2 rue des Cordeliers, 35400,* ☎ *99–56–24–98,* FAX *99–56– 39–24. 17 rooms with bath. AE, DC, MC, V. $$*

Jean-Bart. This clean, quiet hotel next to the ramparts, whose decor makes liberal use of cool blue, bears the stamp of diligent renovation: The beds are comfortable, the bathrooms shiny-modern, but the rooms are somewhat small. (Some offer sea views.) ⊞ *12 rue de Chartres, 35400,* ☎ *99–40–33–88. 17 rooms with bath. MC, V. Closed mid- Nov.–mid-Feb. $$*

St-Marc-sur-Mer

LODGING

Hôtel de la Plage. This comfortable hotel has two distinctions. It is one of very few on the Atlantic coast actually built on the beach, and it was the setting of Jacques Tati's classic film, *Mr. Hulot's Holiday.* The place has been updated since then, and no, *hélas,* the swinging door to the dining room is no longer there, but the sea view and the sound of the surf are still the same. ☎ *37 rue du Commandant Charcot, 44600,* ☎ *40–91–99–01,* 𝔽𝔸𝕏 *40–91–92–00. 33 rooms, most with bath. Restaurant. V. Closed Jan. 2–20. $$*

Trébeurden

DINING AND LODGING

Manoir de Lan Kerellec. Not only is the land around Trébeurden splendid, with its dramatic rocks carved by wind and rain, but so is this Relais & Châteaux hotel. Too many of the hotels in this chain prissy themselves up and lose touch with their environment. Not so with the Manoir de Lan Kerellec. It offers a comfortable range of accommodations, warm hospitality, and excellent dining while embracing the beauty of the Breton coastline. Dinner is served in a circular dining room, overhung by a ship's model, the *Saint Yves*, suspended from the ceiling. This delightful piece lessens the tone of formality and makes you relax and enjoy your meal. The menu makes the most of the sea's products, but you should also try the incredibly good roast lamb. ☎ *22560 Trébeurden,* ☎ *96–23–50–09,* 𝔽𝔸𝕏 *96–23–66–88. 16 rooms with bath, 2 suites. Restaurant, tennis. Closed Nov. 15–Mar. 15. AE, DC, MC, V. $$$–$$$$*

Vannes

DINING AND LODGING

Image Ste-Anne. This charming hotel is in a suitably old, rustic building in the center of historic Vannes. The warm welcome and comfortable guest rooms make the price of a night here seem more than acceptable, as a varied foreign clientele has realized. Mussels, sole in cider, and duck are featured in the restaurant; set menus are very reasonable, beginning at 78 francs. This hotel offers good value, in both accommodations and food, and is also extremely attractive. ☎ *8 pl. de la Libération, 56000,* ☎ *97–63–27–36,* 𝔽𝔸𝕏 *97–40–97–02. 32 rooms with bath or shower. Restaurant. MC, V. Restaurant closed Sun. dinner, Nov.–Mar. $$*

Vitré

LODGING

Chêne Vert. Vitré is badly placed in the hotel stakes, but we suggest this establishment, which is convenient to D857, just opposite the train station and a 10-minute stroll from Vitré Castle. It is the epitome of a French provincial hotel: creaky stairs, fraying carpets, oversoft mattresses, and less-than-enthusiastic service—all, including a copious dinner, for next to nothing. Look carefully, however, and you will notice some intriguing touches—an enormous model ship on the second floor, for example, and the zinc-plated walls that submerge the dining room in art deco/ocean-liner pastiche. ☎ *2 pl. du Général-de-Gaulle, 35500,* ☎ *99–75–00–58. 22 rooms, a few with bath. Closed mid-Sept.–mid-Oct.; restaurant closed Fri. dinner and Sat., Oct.–May. $*

THE ARTS AND NIGHTLIFE

The Arts

Pardons

These traditional religious parades-cum-pilgrimages that invariably showcase age-old local costumes are the backbone of Breton culture. Two of the biggest take place at Ste-Anne d'Aurau (July 26) and Ste-Anne la Palud (last Sunday in August). Further manifestations of local tradition, often with dancers and folk singers, occur at the various Celtic summer festivals, of which the **Festival de Cornouaille** in Quimper (late July) is the biggest.

Theater
The region's principal theaters are the **Théâtre de la Ville** in Rennes (pl. de la Mairie, ☎ 99–28–55–87), the **Théâtre Châteaubriand** in St-Malo (6 rue Groult-St-Georges, ☎ 99–40–98–05), and the **Théâtre Graslin** in Nantes (rue Scribe, ☎ 40–69–77–18).

Concerts
Of particular note is the **Festival de la Musique Sacrée** (sacred music) held in St-Malo in August.

Nightlife

Bars and Nightclubs
In Saint-Malo: **Le Faubourg** (7 rue St-Thomas), **La Selle** (24 rue Ste-Barbe), or **La Belle Epoque** (11 rue de Dinan). In Rennes, try **Le Pym's** (27 pl. du Colombier); in Nantes, the piano bar **Le Tie Break** (1 rue des Petites-Ecuries); and in Brest, **Le Stendhal** (18 rue Colbert).

Jazz Clubs
Two regional jazz venues are the **Cave du Louisiane** in St-Malo (14 rue des Cordiers) and the **Pub Univers** in Nantes (16 rue J. J. Rousseau).

Discos
Les Chandelles in Carnac (av. de l'Atlantique) attracts a cosmopolitan crowd and enjoys a reputation as one of the country's leading discos. You could also try **L'Escalier** in St-Malo (rue du Tour-du-Bonheur) or **L'Espace** in Rennes (45 blvd. de la Tour d'Auvergne).

Casinos
There are casinos in **Dinard** (☎ 99–46–15–71), **Fréhel** (☎ 96–41–49–05), **Perros-Guirec** (☎ 96–23–20–51), **Quiberon** (☎ 97–50–23–57), and **La Baule** (☎ 40–60–20–23).

BRITTANY ESSENTIALS

Arriving and Departing

By Plane
There are domestic airports at Rennes, Brest, Nantes, Morlaix, Dinard, Quimper, and Lorient.

By Car
Rennes, the gateway to Brittany, lies 310 kilometers (193 miles) south-west of Paris. It can be reached in about four hours, via Le Mans and the A81/A11 expressways (A11 continues from Le Mans to Nantes).

By Train
There are numerous daily TGVs between Paris (Gare Montparnasse) and both Nantes and Rennes. They take from two hours to two hours 20 minutes to cover the 403 kilometers (250 miles). There is regular train service up the west coast to Nantes from La Rochelle and Bordeaux.

Getting Around

By Car
Rennes, a strategic base for penetrating Brittany, is linked by good roads to Morlaix and Brest (E50), Quimper (N24/N165), and Vannes (N24/N166).

By Train

Some trains from Paris stop at Vitré before forking at Rennes on their way to either Brest (via Morlaix) or Quimper (via Vannes). Change at Rennes for Dol and St-Malo; at Dol for Dinan and Dinard (bus link); at Morlaix for Roscoff; at Rosporden, 19 kilometers (12 miles) south of Quimper, for Concarneau; and at Auray for Quiberon.

Guided Tours

France Tourisme (3 rue de'Alger, 75001 Paris, ☎ 42–61–85–50) organizes three-day tours of Normandy and Brittany from April through October. Sites include the châteaus on the Loire, Mont-St-Michel, and the walled city and spa town of St-Malo. Further details of organized tours of Brittany can be had from the **Maison de la Bretagne** in Paris (Centre Commercial Maine-Montparnasse, 17 rue de l'Arrivée, B.P. 1006, 75737 Paris, Cedex 15, ☎ 45–38–73–15, FAX 43–20–45–07) or from the regional tourist offices in Brest (☎ 98–44–24–96) and Quimper (☎ 98–53–04–05).

Important Addresses and Numbers

Travel Agencies

Wagons-Lits (22 rue du Calvaire, Nantes, ☎ 40–08–29–18 and 2 rue Jules-Simon, Rennes, ☎ 99–79–45–96).

Car Rental

Avis (pl. de la Gare, La Baule, ☎ 40–60–36–28; 3 blvd. des Français-Libres, Brest, ☎ 98–43–37–73; aéroport, Dinard, ☎ 99–46–25–20; 18 blvd. de Stalingrad, Nantes, ☎ 40–74–07–65; and 8 av. de la Gare, Quimper, ☎ 98–90–31–34).

Visitor Information

The principal regional tourist offices are at **Rennes** (Pont de Nemours, ☎ 99–79–01–98, FAX 99–79–31–38), **Brest** (8 av. Georges-Clemenceau, ☎ 98–44–24–96), and **Nantes** (pl. du Commerce, ☎ 40–47–04–51, FAX 40–89–11–89). The addresses of other tourist offices are as follows: **Carnac** (74 av. des Druides, ☎ 97–52–13–52), **Concarneau** (quai d'Aiguillon, ☎ 98–97–01–44), **Dinan** (6 rue de l'Horloge, ☎ 96–39–75–40), **Dinard** (2 blvd. Féart, ☎ 99–46–94–12), **Dol-de-Bretagne** (3 Grand Rue, ☎ 99–48–15–37), **Douarnenez** (town center, ☎ 98–92–13–35, FAX 98–74–46–09), **La Baule** (9 pl. de la Victoire, ☎ 40–24–34–44, FAX 40–11–08–10), **Morlaix** (pl. des Otages, ☎ 98–62–14–94), **Quiberon** (7 rue de Verdun, ☎ 97–50–07–84), **Quimper** (pl. de la Résistance, ☎ 98–53–04–05, FAX 98–53–31–33), **St-Malo** (Esplanade St-Vincent, ☎ 99–56–64–48, FAX 99–40–93–13), **Vannes** (1 rue Thiers, ☎ 97–47–24–34), and **Vitré** (pl. St-Yves, ☎ 99–75–04–46).

6 Normandy

Rouen to Mont-St-Michel

NORMANDY (or Normandie, as the French spell it), the coastal region lying northwest of Paris, probably has more associations for English-speaking visitors than does any other part of France. William the Conqueror, Joan of Arc, the Bayeux Tapestry, and the D-Day landing beaches have become household names in English, just as they have in French.

Normandy is one of the country's finest gastronomic regions, producing excellent cheeses, such as Camembert, and Calvados, a powerful apple brandy. The area has become popular with British vacationers not only because it's right across the Channel but also because of its charming countryside, from the wild, granite cliffs in the west to the long sandy beaches along the Channel coast, from the wooded valleys of the south to the lush green meadows and apple orchards in the center.

Historic buildings—castles, churches, and monuments—crown the Norman countryside as reminders of its rich and eventful past. Following the 1066 invasion of England by the Norman duke, William (the Conqueror), Normandy switched between English and French dominion for several centuries. In Rouen in 1431, Joan of Arc was burned at the stake, marking a turning point in the Hundred Years' War, the last major medieval conflict between the French and the English. The most celebrated building in Normandy is the abbey of Mont-St-Michel, erected on a 264-foot mound of granite cut off from the mainland at high tide; it's an architectural marvel and the most visited site in provincial France.

Normandy features 375 miles of coastline bordering the English Channel, four major ports—Le Havre, Rouen, Dieppe, and Cherbourg—and coastal towns with seafaring pasts, such as Honfleur, with its picturesque old harbor, and former fishing villages like Fécamp. Sandwiched between are the beaches of such fashionable resorts as Deauville, Cabourg, and Etretat, where visitors can be found reclining in deck chairs, gin and tonic in hand.

EXPLORING

Orientation

We've divided our Norman coverage into three separate tours. The first tour leads northwest from Paris to Rouen, the capital of Upper Normandy. From here, we meander west to the port town of Le Havre before heading up along the impressive coastline of chalky cliffs and pebble beaches known as the Alabaster Coast.

Lower Normandy covers a much larger area, and we explore its sights in two itineraries. The first starts in the market town of Lisieux before heading north to the coastal resort of Honfleur, then west through the region's swankiest resort towns along the Calvados Coast. From here, we turn inland, to Caen and Bayeux. This area saw some of the fiercest fighting after the D-Day landings, as many monuments and memorials testify. The last stop is at the fabled Mont-St-Michel, which lies at the western edge of Normandy.

Finally, there's a scenic drive along the River Orne south of Caen, through the hilly region called La Suisse Normande.

Tour 1: Upper Normandy

Numbers in the margin correspond to points of interest on the Normandy and Rouen maps.

❶ Setting out from Paris, take the A13 expressway and branch off left, just after Bonnières-sur-Seine, to **Evreux,** capital of the Eure *département*. From the 5th century on, the town was ravaged and burnt by a succession of armies—first the Vandals, then the Normans, the English, and various French kings. World War II played its part as well. These days, the town has been well restored and is embellished by a number of gardens and overgrown footpaths by the banks of the River Iton.

Evreux's principal historic site is the **Cathédrale Notre-Dame,** (pl. Notre-Dame), in the heart of town just off rue Corbeau. Unfortunately, it was an easy victim of the many fires and raids that took place over the centuries; all that's left of the original 12th-century construction are the nave arcades. The lower parts of the chancel date from 1260, the chapels from the 14th century. Still, it's an outstanding example of Flamboyant Gothic inside and out. Don't miss the choir triforium and transept, the 14th-century stained-glass windows in the apse, or the entrance to the fourth chapel.

❷ If you have time, rather than go directly to Rouen, get on D316 heading for **Les Andelys,** 36 kilometers (21 miles) away on the north bank of the River Seine. The pretty little town is set against magnificent chalky cliffs in one of the most picturesque loops of the river. Overlooking the town from the clifftops and affording spectacular views in both directions are the remains of the **Château Gaillard,** a formidable fortress built by English king Richard the Lionhearted in 1196. Despite its solid defenses, the castle fell to the French in 1204. It had suffered considerable damage during the assault, and sections were later torn down at the end of the 16th century; only one of its five main towers remains intact. ☛ *15 frs.* ☉ *Thurs.–Mon. 10–noon and 2–5, Wed. 2–5.*

❸ Instead of taking the most direct road from Les Andelys to Rouen (D126/D138), continue along D313 around the Seine for about 14 kilometers (9 miles), crossing it at St-Pierre-du-Vauvray. You can then either stop at the busy town of **Louviers** on the Eure River to see its old houses and its Flamboyant Gothic Notre-Dame church, a mixture of 13th-, 15th-, and 16th-century styles, or turn straight onto N15. Eight kilometers (5 miles) from Louviers, you'll cross the Pont de l'Arche, where the Eure and Seine rivers merge; from here, it's another 18 kilometers (11 miles) to Rouen. On the way, you'll pass through **Bonsecours,** now a suburb of the town and the site of the Basilique Notre-Dame, built in the early 1840s and one of the finest neo-Gothic churches in France. It is also the home of the Auberge de la Butte (*see* Rouen dining, *below*), a fine place for an indulgent lunch.

★ ❹ The city of **Rouen** is a blend of ancient and modern, a large part having been destroyed during World War II. Even before its massive postwar reconstruction, the city had expanded outward during the 20th century with the development of industries spawned by its increasingly busy port, now the fifth largest in France. In its more distant past, Rouen gained celebrity when Joan of Arc was burned at the stake here in 1431.

Rouen is known as the City of a Hundred Spires, and many of its important edifices are churches. Lording it over them all, in place du Cathé-
❺ drale, is the magnificent **Cathédrale Notre-Dame,** one of the masterpieces of French Gothic architecture. If you are familiar with the works of Impressionist Claude Monet, you will immediately recognize the cathe-

Normandy

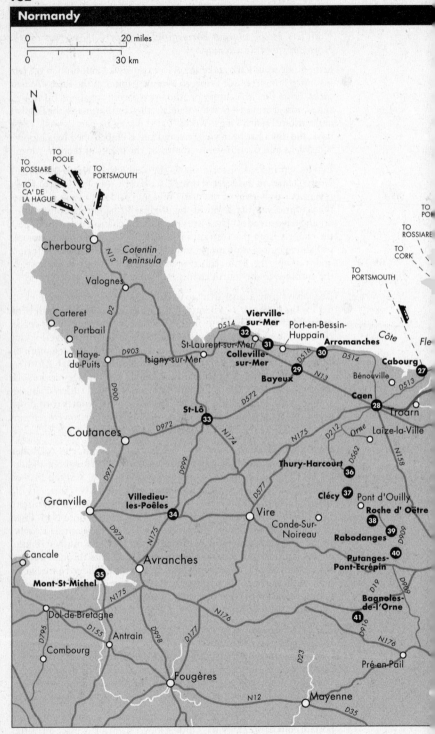

0 _____ 20 miles
0 _____ 30 km

N

TO ROSSIARE
TO POOLE
TO PORTSMOUTH
TO CA' DE LA HAGUE

TO PO
TO ROSSIARE
TO CORK
TO PORTSMOUTH

Cherbourg
Cotentin Peninsula
N13

Valognes

Carteret
Portbail
D2

La Haye-du-Puits
D903
Isigny-sur-Mer

St-Laurent-sur-Mer
Vierville-sur-Mer
D514
Port-en-Bessin-Huppain
Arromanches
Côte
Fle
Colleville-sur-Mer
D514
Cabourg **27**

30
31
32
29
D514

Bayeux
Bénouville
D513
N13

D900
D572

Caen **28**
Troarn

Coutances
D972
St-Lô **33**
D574
N174
N175
D212
Orne
Laize-la-Ville
N158

D971
D999
Thury-Harcourt **36**
D562

Granville
Villedieu-les-Poêles
34
D577
Clécy **37** Pont d'Ouilly
Roche d' Oëtre
38
39
D90

D973
N175
Vire
Condé-Sur-Noireau
Rabodanges
40

Cancale
Avranches
Putanges-Pont-Ecrépin
D19
D90

Mont-St-Michel **35**
N175
Bagnoles-de-l'Orne
41
D976

Dol-de-Bretagne
D155
Antrain
D908
D177
N176
N176
Pré-en-Pail

D795
Combourg
D23

Fougères
Mayenne
N12
D35

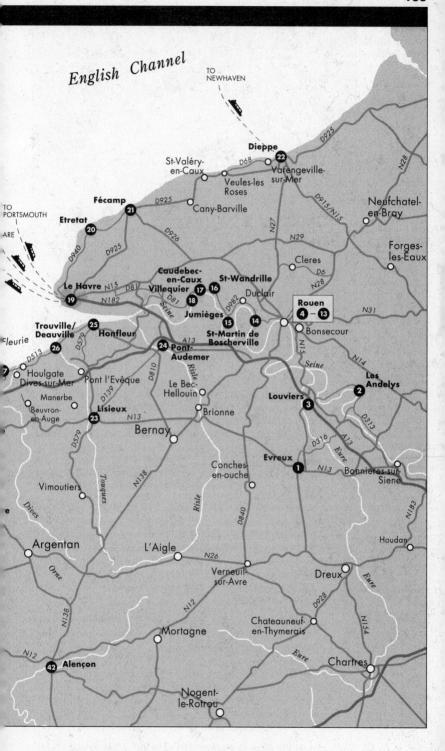

English Channel

TO NEWHAVEN

TO PORTSMOUTH

ARE

Dieppe **22**

St-Valéry-en-Caux

Varengeville-sur-Mer

Veules-les-Roses

D68

D925

Neufchatel-en-Bray

Fécamp **21**

Cany-Barville

D925

Etretat **20**

D926

Cleres

D6

Forges-les-Eaux

D940

D925

N27

N29

N28

D915/N15

Caudebec-en-Caux **17** **16** St-Wandrille

Villequier

Le Havre N15

D81

Duclair

Rouen **4** — **13**

N31

18 Jumièges

15 **14**

Seine

N182

D982

Bonsecour

Trouville/Deauville **25**

Honfleur

24 Pont-Audemer

A13

St-Martin de Boscherville

N15

N14

Seine

Les Andelys **2**

fleurie

D513

D579

Risle

Seine

Houlgate **26**

Dives-sur-Mer

Pont l'Evêque

Le Bec-Hellouin

Louviers

Brionne

3

D313

Manerbe

D139

D810

Beuvron-en-Auge

Lisieux **23**

N13

Bernay

Evreux **1**

N13

Bonnières-sur-Siene

D316

A13

Eure

Vimoutiers

N138

Touques

Conches-en-ouche

Risle

D840

N183

Dives

e

Argentan

Orne

L'Aigle

N26

Verneuil-sur-Avre

Dreux

Eure

Houdan

N138

N12

N12

Chateauneuf-en-Thymerais

D928

Eure

N154

Mortagne

Alençon **42**

Chartres

Nogent-le-Rotrou

184

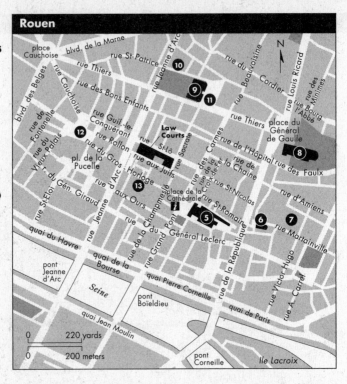

dral's immense west facade, rendered in an increasingly misty, yet always beautiful, fashion in his series "Cathédrales de Rouen." The original 12th-century construction was replaced after a terrible fire in 1200; only the left-hand spire, the Tour St-Romain, survived the flames. The imposing 250-foot iron steeple on the right, known as the Butter Tower, was added in the 15th and 16th centuries and completed in the 17th, when a group of wealthy citizens donated large sums of money—for the privilege of eating butter during Lent.

Interior highlights include the 13th-century choir, with its pointed arcades; vibrant stained glass depicting the crucified Christ (restored after heavy damage during World War II); and massive stone columns topped by some intriguing carved faces. The first flight of the famous Escalier de la Librairie (Booksellers' Staircase) rises from a tiny balcony just to the left of the transept and is attributed to Guillaume Pontifs, who is also responsible for most of the 15th-century work seen in the cathedral. *Pl. de la Cathédrale.*

Leaving the cathedral, head east, and cross rue de la République to place St-Maclou, an attractive square surrounded by picturesque half-timbered houses with steeply pointed roofs. The square's late-Gothic

❻ **Eglise St-Maclou** bears testimony to the wild excesses of Flamboyant architecture; take time to examine the central and left-hand portals under the porchway on the main facade, covered with little bronze lion heads and pagan engravings. Inside, note the 16th-century organ, with its Renaissance wood carving, and the fine marble columns. *Pl. St-Maclou.* ☉ *Daily 7:30–noon and 2:30–6.*

❼ Walk east to the **Aître St-Maclou** (184–186 rue Martainville), a former ossuary that is one of the last reminders of the plague that devastated Europe during the Middle Ages; these days, it holds Rouen's

School of Art and Architecture. The ossuary (a charnel house used for the bodies of plague victims) is said to have inspired the French composer Camille Saint-Saëns (1835–1921) when he was working on his *Danse Macabre*. The building's massive double frieze is especially riveting, carved with some graphic skulls, bones, and gravediggers' tools.

(8) Turn north up rue de la République to place du Général-de-Gaulle, site of the **Eglise St-Ouen,** a fine example of late Gothic architecture. The stained-glass windows, dating from the 14th to the 16th centuries, are the most spectacular features of the otherwise spare structure. The church's 19th-century pipe organs have few equals in France. ☉ *Daily 8–noon and 2–6. Closed Dec. 15–Jan. 15 and Mon., Tues., and Thurs. Jan. 16–Mar. 14 and Nov. 1–Dec. 14.*

(9) Walk west on rue Thiers to get to a cluster of Rouen's fine museums, the most important of which is the **Musée des Beaux-Arts** (Fine Arts Museum), on square Verdrel (☎ 35–71–28–40). It contains a fine collection of French paintings from the 17th and 19th centuries, including works by Claude Monet, Alfred Sisley, and Auguste Renoir. An entire room is devoted to Rouen-born Théodore Géricault, and there are impressive works by Delacroix and Chassériau. A superb collection of Norman ceramics **(10)** is now housed separately in the **Musée de la Céramique**, a few steps down the road (rue Faucon, ☎ 35–07–31–74; ☛ 21 frs for both museums). **(11)** The **Musée de Ferronerie Le Secq des Tournelles** (☎ 35–07–31–74), right behind the Musée des Beaux-Arts claims to possess the world's finest collection of wrought iron, with exhibits spanning the 3rd through the 19th century. Displays include a range of items used in daily life, accessories, and professional instruments used by surgeons, barbers, carpenters, clockmakers, and gardeners. ☛ *13 frs.* ☉ *All three museums Thurs.–Mon. 10–noon and 2–6, Wed. 2–6.*

(12) Continue down rue Thiers, then turn left onto rue Jeanne-d'Arc and head toward place du Vieux-Marché, dominated by the thoroughly modern **Eglise Jeanne d'Arc.** Dedicated to the saint, the church was built on the spot where she was burned to death in 1431. Not all is spanking new, however; the church is graced with some remarkable 16th-century glass windows taken from the former Eglise St-Vincent, destroyed in 1944. ☉ *Daily 10–12:15 and 2–6, except Fri. and Sun. mornings.*

(13) Leading out of place du Vieux-Marché is Rouen's most popular attraction, the rue du Gros-Horloge. The name of this little pedestrian street comes from the **Gros-Horloge** itself, a giant Renaissance clock; in 1527, the Rouennais had a splendid arch built especially for it, and today its golden face looks out over the street (the ticket to the Musée des Beaux-Arts includes admission to the ornate belfry). Though the ancient thoroughfare is crammed with boutiques and fast-food joints, a few old houses, dating from the 16th century, remain. Wander through the surrounding old town, a warren of tiny streets lined with more than 700 half-timbered houses. Instead of standing simply as monuments to the past, these cobbled streets have been successfully transformed into a lively pedestrian shopping precinct, and the old buildings now contain the most fashionable shops in the city.

The Seine Valley between Rouen and Le Havre and along the route called Val de Seine et des Abbayes is full of interesting sights, old and new, dotted amid some lovely scenery. Within 10 minutes of Rouen, **(14)** along D982, is the 11th-century abbey church of St-George in **St-Martin de Boscherville.** From here, follow D982 and D65 around the Seine **(15)** for some 19 kilometers (12 miles) to **Jumièges** to see the imposing ruins of its once-mighty Benedictine abbey, the **Abbaye de Jumièges,** founded in 654 by Saint Philbert and plundered by Vikings in 841. The abbey was rebuilt by William Longswood, Duke of Normandy, around 940, though not until it was fully consecrated in 1067 did it regain its prosperity. Seven centuries later, the French Revolution forced the evacuation of the remaining 16 monks, whereupon the abbey was auctioned off to a timber merchant, who promptly demolished a large part of the building to sell the stones. ☎ *35–37–24–02.* ☞ *24 frs.* ☉ *Daily 10– noon and 2–6 (until 4 in winter).*

About 16 kilometers (10 miles) farther along the right bank of the Seine, then 5 kilometers (3 miles) inland on D22, there's another Benedictine ⑯ abbey in **St-Wandrille.** The **Abbaye de St-Wandrille** survives as an active monastery to this day; like Jumièges, it was founded in the 7th century, sacked (by the Normans), and rebuilt in the 10th century, though what you see today is an ensemble of styles from the 11th century through the early 18th—predominantly the 18th. You can still hear the monks sing their Gregorian chants at morning Mass if you're there early in the day (9:25 weekdays and 10 Sunday and holidays). Be sure to visit the abbey shop down the hill. It sell goods—everything from floor polish to spiritual aids— made by Benedictine monks. ☎ *35–96–23–11. Guided tour at 3 and 4 weekdays;* ☞ *18 frs adults, children free.*

From St-Wandrille, it's only a couple of miles to the charming little vil- ⑰ lage of **Caudebec-en-Caux**; if the day is sunny, you should leave the car and walk along the banks of the Seine. The village's 15th-century Eglise Notre-Dame was described by French monarch Henri IV (1589– 1610) as "the most beautiful chapel in the kingdom." A huge modern bridge, the Pont de Brotonne, spans the Seine just before Caudebec. Instead of crossing it, however, drive west around the north bank of ⑱ the Seine for a couple of miles to **Villequier,** a peacefully situated riverside village dominated by its château. Villequier is famous as the place where 19th-century writer Victor Hugo lost his daughter, Léopoldine, and her husband, Charles Vacquerie, who drowned in the Seine's notorious seasonal tidal wave (these days it is held at bay by a dam). A museum, the **Musée Victor Hugo,** has been created in the couple's old house; exhibits include the manuscript of Hugo's poem *Contemplations,* a lament. *Quai Victor-Hugo,* ☎ *35–56–78–31.* ☞ *12 frs.* ☉ *Wed.–Mon. 10–12:30 and 2–5:30.*

TIME OUT   If the weather's fine when you are in Villequier, stop off for a light lunch at **Le Grand Sapin** (rue Louis-le-Graffic). The food is plain, traditional fare, but the riverside terrace is delightful.

About 16 kilometers (10 miles) before reaching Le Havre, you'll see the turnoff to the new suspension bridge (toll 40 frs), the Pont de Nor- ⑲ mande, across the Seine, to Honfleur. Then comes the port of **Le Havre,** which lies 53 kilometers (33 miles) west by D81 and N182. A bustling modern town, largely rebuilt after 1945, Le Havre is France's second-largest port (after Marseille). It was bombarded no fewer than 146 times during World War II, and reinforced concrete and bleak open spaces have not done much for the town's atmosphere. The old seafaring quarter of Ste-Adresse is worth a visit if you find yourself with some time to spare. From its fortress, you have panoramic views of the port and the Seine estuary.

At the opposite end of the seafront, at the tip of boulevard François-Ier, ★ sits the metal-and-glass **Musée des Beaux-Arts.** On the ground floor there's a remarkable collection of Raoul Dufy's work, including oils, watercolors, and sketches. Dufy (1877–1953) was born in Le Havre and devoted a lot of time to his native region: views of Norman beaches and of Le Havre itself. If you can't spend much time in Normandy, go upstairs to have a look at works by one of the forerunners of Impressionism—Eugène Boudin. Boudin's compelling beach scenes and Norman countrysides will give you a taste of what you're missing. *23 blvd. Clemenceau,* ☎ *35–42–33–97.* ☛ *Free.* ☉ *Wed.–Mon. 10–noon and 2–6.*

★ ⑳ The first stop on the coast between Le Havre and Dieppe (a stretch known as the Alabaster Coast) is **Etretat,** about 30 kilometers (18 miles) away along D940. The town's white cliffs are almost as famous in France as Dover's are in England. Although the promenade running the length of Etretat's pebble beach has been spoiled by a proliferation of seedy cafés and french-fry stands, the town retains its vivacity and charm. There is a small casino with blackjack, roulette, and slot machines, in case you'd like to try your luck (1 rue Baissaye, ☎ 35–27–00–54). Etretat's landmarks are two arched cliff formations, the **Falaise d'Amont** and the **Falaise d'Aval,** which jut out over the sea on either side of the bay, and a 300-foot needle of rock, the **Aiguille,** which thrusts up from the sea near the Falaise d'Amont. Through the huge archways carved by the sea into the cliffs, you can walk to neighboring beaches at low tide. For a breathtaking view of the whole bay, take the path up to the Falaise d'Aval on the southern side, from which you can hike for miles across the Manneporte hills.

㉑ Seventeen kilometers (11 miles) from Etretat along D940 is **Fécamp,** an ancient fishing port that was Normandy's primary place of pilgrimage before Mont-St-Michel stole all the glory. Fécamp no longer has a commercial fishing fleet, but you will still see lots of boats in the private yachting marina. The magnificent **Eglise La Trinité** (just off blvd. de la République) bears witness to the town's religious past. The Benedictine abbey was founded by the duke of Normandy in the 11th century and became the home of the monastic order of the Précieux Sang et de la Trinité (referring to Christ's blood, which supposedly arrived here in the 7th century). Fécamp is also the home of the liqueur Benedictine. The **Musée de la Bénédictine,** seven blocks across town on rue Boufart, was rebuilt in 1892 in a florid mixture of neo-Gothic and Renaissance styles and remains one of Normandy's most popular attractions. *110 rue Alexandre-le-Grand,* ☎ *35–28–00–06.* ☛ *30 frs (including a tasting).* ☉ *Easter–mid-Nov., daily 9:30–noon and 2–6.*

From Fécamp you can cut down south on D926 to the main roads for Lisieux and Honfleur or continue along the coast for about 65 kilometers (40 miles) to Dieppe; take D925 via Cany-Barville to St-Valery-en-Caux and Veules-les-Roses and then the scenic coast road, D68, the rest of the way. Just before reaching Dieppe, you'll pass through **Varengeville-sur-Mer.** Look for the tiny church perched on a hill: The 20th-century painter Georges Braque—who, with Picasso, is credited with inventing Cubism—is buried in its graveyard. If you like gardens, don't miss the **Parc Floral des Moustiers,** with its rare flowers and giant 100-year-old rhododendrons. *La Haie des Moustiers,* ☎ *35–85–10–02.* ☛ *40 frs in season, less off-season.* ☉ *Daily 10–noon and 2–6.*

㉒ **Dieppe** is a bustling blend of a fishing and commercial port and a Norman seaside town, though its fashionable era is past and its hotels have seen better days. The boulevard du Maréchal-Foch, a seafront promenade, separates an immense lawn from an unspoiled pebble beach where, in 1942, many Canadian soldiers were killed during the so-called Jubilee raid. Overlooking the Channel, at the western end of the bay, stands the 15th-century **Château de Dieppe,** which dominates the town from its clifftop position. It contains the town museum, well known for its collection of ivories. In the 17th century, Dieppe imported vast quantities of elephant tusks from Africa and Asia, and as many as 350 craftsmen settled here to work the ivory; their efforts can be seen in the form of ship models, nautical accessories, or, upstairs, in religious and day-to-day objects. The museum also has a room devoted to sketches by Georges Braque. *Sq. du Canada,* ☎ 35–84–19–76. ☛ 20 *frs.* ☾ *Mid-Sept.–mid-June, Wed.–Mon. 10–noon and 2–5 (until 6 Sun.).*

Sterna ferries run from Dieppe three times a day across the Channel to Newhaven (16 kilometers, or 10 miles, from Brighton). Consequently, much of Dieppe is geared to last-minute shopping by Brits for wine, cheeses, and souvenirs. There is even a casino (☎ 35–82–33–60) at the Grand Hotel to take away any remaining francs.

Tour 2: The Calvados Coast and Mont-St-Michel

㉓ **Lisieux** is the main market town of the prosperous Pays d'Auge, an agricultural region famous for cheeses named after such towns as Camembert, Pont l'Evêque, and Livarot. It is also a land of apple orchards, from which the finest Calvados brandy comes. Lisieux emerged relatively unscathed from World War II, though it boasts few historic monuments beyond the **Cathédrale St-Pierre,** built in the 12th and 13th centuries. It is also famous for its patron saint, Ste-Thérèse, who was born and died in the last quarter of the 19th century, having spent the last 10 of her 25 years as a Carmelite nun. Thérèse was canonized in 1925, and in 1954 a basilica—one of the world's largest 20th-century churches—was dedicated to her; to get there from the cathedral, walk up avenue Victor-Hugo and branch left onto avenue Jean-XXIII. A son-et-lumière show, giving a run through 2,000 years of history, is presented every evening except Sunday at 9:45 from June to September. ☛ *35 frs.*

㉔ From Lisieux, take D139 to **Pont-Audemer** on the banks of the River Risle. This town has escaped the destruction of warfare and bulldozers, and still retains its authentic charm. Many of its buildings are as they were in the 16th century when it made its mark as a trading town. Although the church has pleasing modern stained-glass windows, which blend with the combination of Romanesque and Perpendicular architecture, Pont Audemer's charm lies not in specific sights but in the totality of its buildings, its colorful market, held twice a week, its antiques shops, book stores, and the multitude of mouthwatering grocery shops. After taking in the market square, be sure to stroll along two classic streets, rue de la Licorne and rue de l'Epée, both medieval delights. Almost without trying, Pont Audemer attracts tourists who want a rural base from which to explore Calvados. From Pont-Audemer, take N175 west and pick up D312 for a 20-kilometer (12-mile)

★ ㉕ run into **Honfleur.** This colorful port on the Seine estuary epitomizes Normandy for many people. It was once an important departure point for maritime expeditions, and the first voyages to Canada in the 15th and 16th centuries embarked from here. Its 17th-century harbor is fronted on one side by two-story stone houses with low, sloping roofs and on the other by tall, narrow houses whose wooden facades are topped by slate roofs. The whole town is a museum piece, full of half-timbered houses and cobbled streets.

Today Honfleur is one of the most popular vacation spots in northern France, and it is likely to become even more crowded now that the new suspension bridge directly links Honfleur and Le Havre. During the summer, its hotels rarely have vacancies and its cafés and restaurants are always packed. Soak up the seafaring atmosphere by strolling around the old harbor and pay a visit to the **Eglise Ste-Catherine,** which dominates the harbor's northern corner (rue des Logettes). The wooden church was built by townspeople to show their gratitude for the departure of the English at the end of the Hundred Years' War (1453), when masons and architects were occupied with national reconstruction.

★ ㉖ Leave Honfleur by D513 west and follow the coast for 14 kilometers (9 miles) until you arrive at the twin seaside resorts of **Trouville** and **Deauville,** separated only by the estuary of the River Touques. Although Trouville is now considered an overflow town for its more prestigious neighbor, it became one of France's first seaside resorts when Parisians began flocking here in the mid-19th century.

Deauville is a chic watering hole for the French bourgeoisie and would-be fashionable personalities from farther afield, who are attracted by its racecourse, casino, marina and regattas, palaces and gardens, and, of course, its sandy beach. The **Promenade des Planches**—the boardwalk extending along the seafront and lined with deck chairs, bars, and striped cabanas—is the place for celebrity spotting. With high-priced hotels, designer boutiques, and one of the smartest, gilt-edge casinos in Europe, Deauville's fashionable image attracts the wealthy throughout the year. In contrast, Trouville is more of a family resort with few pretensions. So, if you'd like to see a typical French holiday spot rather than look for glamour, stay in Trouville. It, too, has a casino and boardwalk, a bustling fishing port, and a native population that makes it a livelier place out of season than Deauville.

TIME OUT One of the most popular places in Trouville is **Les Vapeurs,** a friendly, animated brasserie with neon-lit '50s decor. It serves good, fresh food at any time, day or night, and both the famous and not so famous like to meet here after dark. *160 blvd. Fernand-Moureaux. Closed Tues. dinner and Wed.*

㉗ Continue west along D513, which takes you through a number of family seaside resorts, such as pretty Houlgate and nearby Dives-sur-Mer, before reaching the larger and more elegant resort of **Cabourg,** just across the River Dives. Cabourg's streets fan out from a central hub near the seafront where the casino and the Grand Hôtel are situated. The early 20th-century novelist Marcel Proust, author of *Remembrance of Things Past,* was a great admirer of the town's pleasant seaside atmosphere and spent much of his time here. One of the volumes in his epic paints a perfect picture of life in the resort, to which the town responded by naming its magnificent seafront promenade after him.

㉘ Leave Cabourg by D513, which veers inland and after 24 kilometers (15 miles) brings you to **Caen,** the capital of Lower Normandy. Caen, with its abbeys and castle, presents a strong contrast to the somewhat uniform coastal resorts.

William of Normandy ruled from Caen in the 11th century before he conquered England. Nine hundred years later, the two-month Battle of Caen devastated the town in 1944. Much of the city burned in a fire that raged for 11 days, and the downtown area was almost entirely rebuilt after the war. Caen is now a busy, traffic-congested commercial city, the administrative center for the region. Depending upon the extent of your involvement with William, you may be tempted to bypass the city.

★ A good place to begin exploring is at the town's main tourist attraction, the **Abbaye aux Hommes,** a monastery built by William the Conqueror. "The Men's Abbey" was begun in Romanesque style in 1066 and was added to during the 18th century. Note the magnificent facade of the abbey church, the Eglise St-Etienne, whose spareness is enhanced by two 11th-century towers topped by Norman Gothic octagonal spires. Inside, what had been William the Conqueror's tomb was destroyed by 16th-century Huguenots during the Wars of Religion, but the choir still stands; it was the first to be built in Norman Gothic style, and many subsequent choirs were modeled after it. *Pl. Louis-Guillouard,* ☎ *31–30–41–00. Guided tours of the abbey cost 10 frs.* ☉ *Daily 9– noon and 2–5.*

Head right up Fosses St-Julien to the Esplanade du Château. The ruins of William the Conqueror's **fortress,** built in 1060 and sensitively restored after the war, glower down on all who approach. The castle gardens are a perfect spot for strolling, and the ramparts afford good views of the city. Within the rampart walls lies the **Musée des Beaux-Arts,** a Fine Arts Museum whose impressive collection includes Rembrandts and Titians. Also within the castle are the **Musée de Normandie,** displaying regional arts, and the chapel of St-George. *Entrance by the Porte sur la Ville,* ☎ *31–86–06–24.* ☛ *Each: 10 frs (free Sun.).* ☉ *Wed.–Mon. 9:30–12:30 and 2–6.*

Take rue des Chanoines right to the **Abbaye aux Dames,** the "Ladies' Abbey," built by William the Conqueror's wife, Matilda, in 1062. The abbey is now a hospital and not open to visitors, but you can visit its Eglise de la Trinité. This squat church is a good example of 11th-century Romanesque architecture, though its original spires were replaced by bulky balustrades in the early 18th century. The 11th-century crypt once held Matilda's tomb, which was destroyed during the French Revolution. Note the intricate carvings on columns and arches in the chapel. *Pl. Reine-Mathilde.* ☛ *Free. Guided tours daily at 2:30 and 4.*

Head back down the rue des Chanoines and continue on rue Montoir-Poissonnerie. Turning left onto place St-Pierre, you'll come face-to-face with the Caen Tourist Office. It merits a visit not only for its excellent information resources, but for its splendid site in the **Hôtel d'Escoville,** a 16th-century mansion built by a wealthy town merchant, Nicolas le Valois d'Escoville. The building was badly damaged during the war but has since been restored; the austere facade conceals an elaborate inner courtyard, reflecting the Italian influence on early Renaissance Norman architecture.

A good introduction to the Normandy landings of 1944 can be had at the **Mémorial,** a museum opened in the north of the city in 1988. Videos, photos, arms, paintings, and prints detail the Battle of Normandy and the French Liberation within a historical context, from the 1930s to the 1960s. Multimedia screens also depict the events of D-Day and the Battle of Normandy. *Esplanade Général-Eisenhower,* ☎ *31–06–06–44.* ☛ *58 frs adults, 32 frs students.* ☉ *Wed.,–Mon. 9–7.*

㉙ From Caen, N13 heads 28 kilometers (17 miles) northwest to **Bayeux,** an attractive town steeped in history and the first town to be liberated during the Battle of Normandy. Today, its small-town medieval charm has made Bayeux a popular base, especially among British travelers, from which to make day visits to the Normandy D-Day beaches, Mont-St-Michel, Deauville, Honfleur, La Suisse Normande, Caen, the Cotentin Peninsula, and even to Jersey. The tourist office (pont St-Jean, ☎ 31–92–16–26, open Mon.–Sat. 10–6:30) can help plan your trips.

Bayeux's long history stretches back many centuries before World War II, however, and we begin our tour at the **Musée de la Tapisserie** (Tapestry Museum), located in an 18th-century building on rue de Nesmond and showcasing the world's most celebrated piece of needle-

★ work, the **Bayeux Tapestry.** The medieval work of art—stitched in 1067—is really a 225-foot-long embroidered scroll, which depicts, in

58 separate scenes, the epic story of William of Normandy's conquest of England in 1066, a watershed in European history. The tapestry's origins remain obscure, though it was probably commissioned from Saxon embroiderers by the count of Kent—also the bishop of Bayeux—to be displayed in his newly built cathedral. Despite its age, the tapestry is in remarkably good condition; the extremely detailed, often homey scenes provide an unequaled record of the clothes, weapons, ships, and lifestyles of the day. *Centre Guillaume Le Conquérant, 13 bis, rue de Nesmond,* ☎ *31–92–05–48.* ☛ *32 frs.* ☉ *June–Sept., daily 9–7; Oct.–May, daily 9:30–12:30 and 2–6.*

Your ticket also gains you entrance to the **Musée Baron Gérard.** Head up rue de Nesmond to rue Larchet, turning left into lovely place des Tribuneaux. The museum contains fine collections of Bayeux porcelain and lace, ceramics from Rouen, a marvelous collection of apothecary jars from the 17th and 18th centuries, and 16th- to 19th-century furniture and paintings. *1 rue la Chaîne,* ☎ *31–92–14–21.* ☛ *18 frs.* ☉ *June–mid-Sept., daily 9–7; mid-Sept.–May, 10–12:30 and 2–6. Closed two wks in Jan.*

Behind the museum, with an entrance on rue de Bienvenu, sits Bayeux's most important historic building, the **Cathédrale Notre-Dame.** The cathedral is a harmonious mixture of Norman and Gothic architecture. Note the portal on the south side of the transept, which depicts the assassination of English Archbishop Thomas à Becket in Canterbury Cathedral in 1170, following his opposition to King Henry II's attempts to control the church. *Closed Sept.–June 12:30–2:30.*

Return to the 20th century by turning left, walking to the place au Blois, and continuing down rue St-Loup. Turn right on boulevard du Général-Fabian-Ware, site of the **Musée de la Bataille de Normandie,** whose detailed exhibits trace the story of the Battle of Normandy from June 7 to August 22, 1944. The ultramodern museum contains an impressive array of war paraphernalia, including uniforms, weapons, equipment, 150 waxworks, and a film depicting scenes and tactics of the invasion. However, if you plan on visiting the war museum at Arromanches, you may want to pass by this one. *Blvd. Général-Fabian-Ware,* ☎ *31–92–45–55.* ☛ *24 frs.* ☉ *June–Aug., daily 9–7; Sept.–Oct. and Mar.–May, daily 10–12:30 and 2–6:30; and Nov.–Feb., weekends 10:30–12:30 and 2–6:30.*

Operation Overlord, the code name for the Invasion of Normandy, called for five beachheads—dubbed Utah, Omaha, Gold, Juno, and Sword—to be established along the Calvados Coast, to either side of Arromanches. Preparations started in mid-1943, and British shipyards worked furiously through the following winter and spring building two artificial harbors (called Mulberries), boats, and landing equipment.

The British troops that landed on Sword, Juno, and Gold quickly pushed inland and joined with parachute regiments that had been dropped behind the German lines. U.S. forces met with far tougher opposition on Omaha and Utah beaches, however, and it took them six days to secure their positions and meet the other Allied forces. From there, they pushed south and west, cutting off the Cotentin Peninsula on June 10 and taking Cherbourg on June 26. Meanwhile, British forces were encountering fierce resistance at Caen and did not take it until July 9; St-Lô was finally liberated on July 19.

After having boned up on the full story of the Normandy invasion, you'll want to go and see the area where it all took place. There's little point in visiting all five sites, since not much remains to mark the furious fighting waged hereabouts. In the bay of Arromanches, however, some elements of the floating harbor are still visible.

30 Head north from Bayeux along D516 to **Arromanches,** 10 kilometers (6 miles) away. Linger here awhile, contemplating those seemingly insignificant hunks of concrete protruding from the water, and try to imagine the extraordinary technical feat involved in towing the two floating harbors across the Channel from England. (The other was moored at Omaha Beach but was destroyed on June 19, 1944, by an exceptionally violent storm.) If you're interested in yet more battle documentation, visit the **Musée du Débarquement** (Normandy Landings Museum), right on the seafront, whose exhibits include models, mock-ups, and photographs depicting the invasion. *Pl. du 6-Juin,* ☎ *31–22–34–31.* ☛ *30 frs adults, 18 frs students.* ⏲ *July and Aug., daily 9–7; Sept.–June, 9–11:30 and 2–6; closed Jan. 1–22.*

From Arromanches, take D514 west.

TIME OUT About 10 kilometers (6 miles) along, you'll reach Port-en-Bessin-Huppain, a little fishing port that has a striking restaurant called **La Marine** (quai Letourneur). The fish and seafood are fresh, and the upstairs dining room offers terrific views of the port.

31 Continue along D514 for another 8 kilometers (5 miles) to **Colleville-sur-Mer,** then turn right to **Omaha Beach,** scene of a bloody battle in which nearly 10,000 American soldiers lost their lives. Many of the fallen are buried at the American cemetery above the beach (open daily 9–6). A little farther along D514, at St-Laurent-sur-Mer, turn right onto D517, which takes you back to the seafront at the site of the **Monument du Débarquement** (Monument to the Normandy Landings). You may want to park the car and stroll around the beaches and the grassy tops of the dunes overlooking them, from which you'll see sad remnants of the war—ruined bunkers, rows of trenches, and the remains
32 of barbed-wire defenses. Continue along the beachfront to **Vierville-sur-Mer,** which has a monument to the members of the U.S. National Guard who fought in both world wars.

Unless you decide to drive into the Cotentin Peninsula, past Utah Beach and on to Cherbourg, where ferries cross the Channel to England, you can conclude your tour of the Calvados Coast either by returning to Bayeux via Isigny-sur-Mer, known for its small, tasty oysters,
33 about 19 kilometers (12 miles) from Vierville, or by continuing to **St-Lô,** 29 kilometers (18 miles) from Isigny. Given its sad sobriquet of the "capital of ruins," you won't be surprised that St-Lô played a strategic role in the Battle of Normandy and was almost completely destroyed in July 1944. The town was largely and unattractively rebuilt after the war, and its only relic of the past is the ruined 13th- to 17th-century Eglise Notre-Dame.

If you're interested in cathedral architecture, you'll want to make a trip to **Coutances,** 29 kilometers (18 miles) west of St-Lô along D972. Many consider the largely 13th-century Cathédrale Notre-Dame, with its famous octagonal lantern rising 135 feet above the nave, to be the most harmonious and impressive Gothic building in Normandy.

34 Otherwise, take D999 from St-Lô, which joins with N175 at **Villedieu-les-Poêles,** famous for its copperware. It is said that every kitchen worth its salt in France buys its pans from Villedieu. The temptation is great, with shops lining the main street and smaller outlets, with better buys, on the parallel rue du Dr. Harvard. The same copper frying pan bought here will cost triple in New York!

★ Continue on through Avranches and follow the road around the bay to the Abbey of **Mont-St-Michel.** Before you visit this awe-inspiring monument, be warned that the sea that separates the rock from the mainland is extremely dangerous: It's subject to tidal movements that produce a difference of up to 45 feet between low and high tides, and because of the extremely flat bay bed, the water rushes in at an incredible speed. Also, there are nasty patches of quicksand, so tread with care!

The dramatic silhouette of Mont-St-Michel against the horizon may well be your most lasting image of Normandy. The wonder of the abbey stems not only from its rocky perch a few hundred yards off the coast (it's cut off from the mainland at high tide), but from its legendary origins in the 8th century and the sheer exploit of its construction, which took more than 500 years, from 1017 to 1521. The abbey stands at the top of a 264-foot mound of rock, and the granite used to build it was transported from the Isles of Chausey (just beyond Mont-St-Michel Bay) and Brittany and laboriously hauled up to the site.

Legend has it that the Archangel Michael appeared to Aubert, bishop of Avranches, inspiring him to build an oratory on what was then called Mont Tombe. The original church was completed in 1144, but new buildings were added in the 13th century to accommodate the monks, as well as the hordes of pilgrims who flocked here even during the Hundred Years' War, when the region was in English hands. The Romanesque choir was rebuilt in an ornate Gothic style during the 15th and 16th centuries. The abbey's monastic vocation was undermined during the 17th century, when the monks began to flout the strict rules and discipline of their order, a drift into decadence that culminated in the monks' dispersal and the abbey's conversion into a prison well before the French Revolution. In 1874, the former abbey was handed over to a governmental agency responsible for the preservation of historic monuments; only within the past 20 years have monks been able to live and work here once more.

A causeway—to be replaced eventually by a bridge, thus allowing the bay waters to circulate freely—links Mont-St-Michel to the mainland. Leave your car in the parking lot (10 francs) at the foot of the mount, outside the main gateway. If you are staying the night in Mont-St-Michel, take what you need in a small valise and leave the rest of your baggage out of sight in the trunk. You cannot gain access to your hotel by car.

The climb to the abbey is hard going, but it's worth it. Head first for the Grand Degré, the steep, narrow staircase on the north side. Once past the ramparts, you'll come to the pink-and-gray granite towers of the Châtelet and then to the Salle des Gardes, the central point of the abbey. Guided tours start from the Saut Gautier terrace (named after a prisoner who jumped to his death from it): You must join one of these groups if you want to see the beautifully wrought Escalier de Dentelle (Lace Staircase) inside the church. ☛ 32 frs. ☉ Mid-May–Sept., daily 9:30–11:30 and 1:30–6; Oct.–mid-May, Wed.–Mon. 9–11 and 1:30–4.

The island village, with its steep, narrow streets, is best visited out of season, from September to May. The hordes of souvenir sellers and tourists can be stifling in summer months, but you can always take refuge in the abbey's gardens. The ramparts in general and the North Tower in particular offer dramatic views of the bay. Mont-St-Michel is truly a marvel of human undertaking made magnificent by nature. Give yourself at least a couple of hours here. However, with the mount's inflated prices you may want to stay elsewhere. The Manoir de la Roche Turin nearby at Courtils (see Lodging, below) is a charming alternative.

Tour 3: La Suisse Normande

Caen is the best starting point for a trip through La Suisse Normande, or Swiss Normandy, a rocky expanse of hills and gullies in the heart of Lower Normandy, containing lots of natural beauty and few man-made wonders. Striking as the scenery is, however, you'll need to exert all your powers of imagination to see much resemblance to the Swiss Alps. Taking D562 south for 45 kilometers (28 miles), you'll come to **36 Thury-Harcourt** on the Orne River, the gateway to La Suisse Normande. If you're not in a hurry and you enjoy twisting country roads, turn right off D562 at Laize-la-Ville, cross the Orne, and take the more scenic D212, which runs alongside the river and enters Thury-Harcourt from the opposite bank. This little country town is famous for the beautiful gardens of its ruined castle.

37 Continue down D562, following the Orne, to **Clécy,** the area's main tourist center. It's a good base for visiting the sights of the Orne Valley; take the steep roads up to the clifftops overlooking the river, where there are lovely views of the woods on the other bank.

TIME OUT   You'll find an open-air, riverbank café in Clécy, **La Potinière,** which is great for drinks or snacks. Crepes top the bill, either sweet or with savory fillings such as ham and cheese, and there's a good selection of tarts and homemade ice cream. On Friday evening, you can enjoy a rowdy musical backdrop of jazz or rock. *On the river. Closed Oct.–Apr.*

From Clécy, continue for a couple of miles along D562 and then turn left at Le Fresne onto D1, which winds its way through the valley of the Noireau to another riverside resort, Pont d'Ouilly, situated at the point where the River Noireau flows into the Orne. Heading south along the Orne on D167, veer right at le Pont-des-Vers onto D43 and head ★ **38** into the most mountainous part of La Suisse Normande to the **Roche d'Oëtre;** from here, you'll get the most spectacular views of the craggy hills that give the region its name.

Continue along D301 for a few miles and then turn left across the Orne, **39** joining D21 before turning almost immediately right along D239 to **Rabodanges.** Turn down any of the side roads leading to the riverside, where you'll be rewarded with a fine view of the river gorge (the Gorges de St-Aubert). A little farther upstream is the Rabodanges dam; from here, D121 skirts the eastern side of the lake. The road crosses the lake by **40** the Ste-Croix bridge and takes you to **Putanges-Pont-Ecrépin.**

The Orne River now swings east to Argentan, a peaceful little town that was badly damaged during the last days of the Battle of Normandy. Rather than follow the river, however, it's more rewarding to head south from **41** Putanges, along D909 and then D19, to **Bagnoles-de-l'Orne,** the most important spa town in the region. Forty-five hotels and a casino (☎ 33–37–84–00) with blackjack, roulette, baccarat, and slot machines are only part of what draws visitors here. During the season from April through October some 20,000 people come to cure their blood-related ailments by soaking in the chemical laden waters. Indeed, the nickname for Bagnoles-de-l'Orne is the Capital of Veins. The town nestles in a beautiful setting overlooking a lake formed by the River Yée and is surrounded by forests and parkland that are well worth touring.

42 From Bagnoles-de-l'Orne, it's a fairly straight road to **Alençon;** follow D916 south, then turn left onto N176 to Pré-en-Pail and take N12 from there. The road runs through the middle of the Normandie-Maine Nature Park. Alençon lies on the eastern edge of the park, south of the

Forest of Ecouves and west of the Forest of Perseigne. An attractive town with many historic buildings, Alençon has been a lace-making center since 1665; by the end of the 17th century *point d'Alencon* was de rigueur in all fashionable circles. The **Musée des Beaux-Arts et de la Dentelle** (Museum of Fine Arts and Lace) contains a sophisticated collection of lace from Italy, Flanders, and France, along with paintings from the French school that span the 17th to the 20th century. *Rue Charles-Aveline,* ☎ *33–32–40–07.* ☛ *12 frs.* ⊙ *Tues.–Sun. 10–noon and 2–6.*

What to See and Do with Children

The **Parc Zoologique de Clères,** 16 kilometers (10 miles) north of Rouen, is a wildlife park that's home to more than 750 species of birds, plus a motley assortment of free-roaming antelope, deer, kangaroos, and gibbons. Clères is a tiny village; you can't miss the park. ☎ *35–33–23–08.* ☛ *25 frs adults, 15 frs children under 15.* ⊙ *Mar.–May and Sept.–Nov., daily 9–noon and 3:30–sunset; June–Aug., daily 9–sunset.*

A **vintage-car museum** is found at Le Bec-Hellouin, southwest of Rouen (*see below*). Even those who are long past childhood will appreciate the 50 racing and touring automobiles from as early as 1920; the highlights must be the seven Bugattis. ☎ *32–44–86–06.* ☛ *25 frs.* ⊙ *9–noon and 2–7; closed Wed. and Thurs. in winter.*

Off the Beaten Track

Connoisseurs of the apple brandy Calvados will be interested in a visit to the **Vallée d'Auge,** on the west side of the Pays d'Auge. This is the heart of Calvados country, between Troarn and Lisieux, through which the River Dives and its tributaries flow. You don't need a fixed itinerary; just follow your nose and look for local farmers offering Calvados for sale. However, there is a pretty, winding route to follow from Manerbe, north of Lisieux, which meanders west along D270, D117, and D85 to Beuvron-en-Auge, where you take D117 again across the River Dives to Troarn. Local Calvados producers will be delighted to let you taste their products, especially if you then buy a few bottles. They use traditional methods to distill the brandy, so you can be sure of finding something superior to the brands available in most shops.

Northwest of Evreux is **Le Bec-Hellouin,** near Brionne. Its famous Abbaye du Bec-Hellouin dates from the 11th century, but the monks were driven out during the French Revolution and the original abbey was demolished during the 19th century. Only the 15th-century St-Nicolas tower, part of the south transept, and the bases of some pillars remain, together with a 13th-century Gothic door and some statues from the 14th and 15th centuries. Next to the abbey is a vintage-car museum. *Abbaye du Bec-Hellouin,* ☎ *32–44–86–09.* ☛ *22 frs.* ⊙ *Guided tours only, Wed.–Mon. June–Sept. at 10, 11, 3, 4, and 5; on Sun. and holidays, tours at 12:15, 3:30, 4, and 6; Oct.–May at 11, 3:15, 4:30; Sun. and holidays at noon, 3, and 4.*

SHOPPING

Lace

Handmade lace is a great rarity, and admirers will certainly think it's worth spending some time searching it out. Prices are high, but then, this kind of labor-intensive, high-quality creation never comes cheap. In Alençon, try the **Musée de la Dentelle** (31 rue du Pont-Neuf). In Bayeux, try the **Centre Normand de la Dentelle** on rue Leforestier.

Food Items

Normandy is a food-lover's region, and some of the best buying is to be done in food markets and charcuteries. Gastronomes will want to drop by **La Ferme Normande** (13 rue Breney, Deauville) for regional delicacies, while those with a weakness for sweets should go straight to **Raten** (115 Grande-Rue, Dieppe). For France's famed copper cookware, head for Villedieu-les-Poêles.

Spirits

It's true that you can buy Benedictine anywhere in the world, but if you've visited the **Musée de la Bénédictine** (110 rue Alexandre-le-Grand) in Fécamp, the bottle you buy there will have a certain sentimental value. Calvados is harder to find outside France, and although it's generally available in wine shops around the country, you'll find a wider choice of good-quality Calvados in Normandy itself. If possible, buy Calvados that comes from the Vallée d'Auge, the area of Normandy reputed to produce the best (*see* Off the Beaten Track, *above*).

Antiques Fairs and Markets

If you enjoy the hunt as much as the prize, try the following: Caen hosts a bric-a-brac and antiques fair in June, while Cabourg has one in mid-August. Caen also has two morning flea markets: on Sunday in place Courtonne and on Friday in place St-Saveur.

SPORTS AND THE OUTDOORS

Beaches

Wherever you go on the Normandy Coast, you'll look at the chilly waters of the English Channel: Those used to warmer climes may need all their resolve to take the plunge, even on hot, sunny days. The most fashionable Norman resorts lie along the Floral Coast, the eastern end of the Calvados Coast between Deauville/Trouville and Cabourg; it's virtually one long, sandy beach, with the different towns overlapping. The rest of the Calvados Coast is also a succession of seaside resorts, though the beaches that saw the Normandy landings have not been so developed as those farther east. While the resort towns of the western Calvados Coast don't lack for charm, they don't have the character of Honfleur or the unspoiled and rugged beauty of the pebbly Alabaster Coast, stretching from Le Havre to beyond Dieppe. The resorts here are more widely spaced, separated by craggy cliffs, and even in the summer months, beaches are relatively uncrowded.

Bicycling

The Cotentin Peninsula is well suited for easy cycling and its west coast has little vehicular traffic. The rolling hills of La Suisse Normande are dotted with numerous little villages connected by small country roads and picnic spots along the Orne that make the area ideal for touring by bike. You can reserve bicycles from train stations in Bayeux, Caen, Dieppe, and Le Tréport that rent for about 40 francs per day. Or try **Family Home** in Bayeux (39 rue du Gal-Dais, ☎ 31–92–15–22). At Argentan, Bueil, Granville, Pontorson, Verñon, and 30 other stations bicycles may be hired when you arrive.

Golf

The most spectacular golf course in Normandy is at **Le Vaudrueil,** in a park that nestles between two branches of the River Eure; the course takes you past the ruins of a number of castles. Other 18-hole courses are found in Cabourg, Deauville, Etretat, Dieppe, Le Havre, Port-en-Bessin, and Rouen, and there are 9-hole courses in Deauville, Houlgate, and Bagnoles-de-l'Orne.

Hiking

There are 10 long-distance, signposted itineraries and countless well-indicated footpaths for shorter walks; overnight hostels are found at many points. Contact the **Comité Départemental de la Randonnée Pedestre de Seine-Maritime** (B.P. 666, 76008 Rouen).

Horseback Riding

Normandy is a leading horseracing and training region, with numerous stud farms, Thoroughbred stables, and racecourses. The most important race of the year is the Grand Prix at Deauville, on the last Sunday in August. If you prefer riding to watching, contact Upper Normandy's center for equestrian tourism, the **Association Régionale de Tourisme Equestre** in Caen (Chambre d'Agriculture, 4 promenade Mme-de-Sévigné, 14039 Caen, ☎ 31–84–47–19).

Water Sports

With its miles of coastline, its rivers, and its lakes, Normandy offers a multitude of water activities. Many resorts have yachting marinas, where you can rent sailing dinghies and Windsurfers as well as water-ski. At the **Deauville Yacht Club** (quai de la Marine, ☎ 31–88–38–19), hiring the smallest boat (16 feet) costs just 100 francs, while a day on an 80-foot yacht will set you back about 500 francs per person. Similar prices are encountered at **Le Club Nautique de Trouville** (Digue des Roches Noires, ☎ 31–88–13–59). For swimmers, there are 60 outdoor and 20 indoor pools, in addition to the many safe bathing beaches; you can find public swimming pools in Bayeux, Cabourg, Caen, Deauville, Trouville, and Lisieux. The charming resort of Granville, 26 kilometers (16 miles) northwest of Avranches, is a center for aquatic sports; inquire about sailboat jaunts at the **Centre Regional de Nautisme de Granville** (Anse de Hérel, 50400 Granville, ☎ 33–50–18–95). **Lepesqueux Voile** (3 rue Clément-Desmaisons, 50400 Granville, ☎ 33–50–18–97) rents boats and yachts for vacation cruises.

DINING AND LODGING

Dining

Normandy is the land of butter, cream, cheese, and Calvados. The Normans are notoriously big eaters: In the old days, on festive occasions they wouldn't bat an eye at tucking into as many as 24 courses. Between the warm-up and the main course there was a *trou* (hole), often lasting several hours, during which lots of Calvados was downed, giving rise to the expression *le trou normand*.

Many dishes are cooked with rich cream sauces; the description *à la normande* usually means "with a cream sauce." The richness of the milk makes for excellent cheese: Pont-l'Évêque (known since the 13th century) is made in the Pays d'Auge with milk that is still warm and creamy, while Livarot (also produced for centuries) uses milk that has stood for a while; don't be put off by its strong smell. Then there are the excellent Pavé d'Auge and the best known of them all, Camembert, a relative newcomer, invented by a farmer's wife in the late 18th century. Now so popular that it is produced all over France, the best Camembert is still made in Normandy (known as *Camembert au lait cru*).

There are many local specialties. Rouen is famous for its *canard à la Rouennaise* (duck in blood sauce); Caen, for its *tripes à la mode de Caen* (tripe cooked with carrots in a seasoned cider stock); and Mont-St-Michel, for *omelette Mère Poulard* (a hearty omelette made by a local hotel manager in the late 19th century for travelers to Mont-St-Michel).

Then there are *sole dieppoise* (sole poached in a sauce with cream and mussels), excellent chicken from the Vallée d'Auge, and lamb from the salt marshes. Those who like *boudin noir* (blood sausage) have come to the right region, and for seafood lovers, the coast provides oysters, lobster, and shrimp.

Normandy is not a wine-growing area, but it produces excellent hard cider. The best comes from the Vallée d'Auge and is 100% apple juice; when poured into the glass, it should fizz a bit without frothing.

CATEGORY	COST*
$$$$	over 400 frs
$$$	250–400 frs
$$	125–250 frs
$	under 125 frs

per person for a three-course meal, including tax (18.6%) and tip but not wine

Lodging

There are accommodations to suit every taste in Normandy. In the beach resorts the season is very short, July and August only, but weekends are busy for much of the year. In June and September, accommodations are usually available at short notice, and good discounts are given off-season, especially for stays of more than one night.

CATEGORY	COST*
$$$$	over 800 frs
$$$	550–800 frs
$$	300–550 frs
$	under 300 frs

All prices are for a standard double room for two, including tax (18.6%) and service charge.

Bagnoles-de-l'Orne

DINING AND LODGING

★ **Le Manoir de Lys.** This warm, inviting Norman country house presides over a beautifully landscaped park on the edge of a forest. Although the rooms' size varies, all are neat with a separate toilet and compact tiled bathroom. Some have French windows that open onto the gardens; others, in the new wing, have exposed beams, cheerful fabrics, and are slightly larger. The lounge area, with a small bar, fireplace, and leather settees, beckons you to relax in the afternoons or to have an aperitif before a gourmet treat. Chef-owner Paul Quinton and his son are winning accolades for their creations, all made from the freshest of local produce. Try the tournedos of lobster or the ravioli with frogs' legs. Quinton offers week-long cooking seminars several times a year for those with culinary ambitions. ✉ *Croix Gauthier, rte. de Juvigny (2 km, or 1 mi, from the casino), 61140,* ☎ *33–37–80–69,* FAX *33–30–05–80. 20 rooms with bath. Restaurant, tennis. AE, MC, V. Closed Jan.–Feb.; restaurant closed Sun. dinner and Mon.* $$

Bayeux

DINING

L'Amaryllis. This small restaurant with fewer than 15 tables produces good Norman fare at very reasonable prices. A 98-franc, three-course dinner with six or so choices for each course will place before you such pleasures as a half dozen oysters, fillet of sole with a cider-based sauce, and pastries for dessert. Decor is simple with white tablecloths and glistening glasses ready to be filled with wine of modest cost. ✗ *32 rue*

St-Patrice, ☎ *31–22–47–94. Reservations accepted. Closed Mon., and Dec. 20–Jan. 15. AE, DC, MC, V. $*

★ **Château d'Audrieu.** Fifteen kilometers (9 miles) from Bayeux off N13, this family-owned property fulfills Hollywood's idea of a palatial château. An avenue leads to an imposing, elegant 18th-century facade, which sets the tone for what lies within. The bedrooms and salons are the last word in Old World opulence, with wall sconces, overstuffed chairs, and antiques. Most rooms have been renovated in modern style with rich, warm fabrics and large tiled baths. A few, slightly larger, are duplexes. Rooms 50 and 51 have gabled ceilings with exposed-wood beams that set a romantic mood. Everything runs with smooth, practiced efficiency, and the staff is mostly English-speaking. The restaurant has an extensive wine list, and chef Alain Cornet keeps to a classical repertoire of dishes. His sauces for fish tend to be rather bland, but otherwise he has a well-balanced menu. A Calvados in the bar or lounge after dinner, where you can meet other guests if you wish, is the culmination of a fine dinner. ⌨ *14250 Audrieu,* ☎ *31–80–21–52,* FAX *31–80–24–73. 30 rooms with bath. Restaurant, bar, pool. MC, V. Closed Dec. 20–Feb.; restaurant closed Mon. $$$$*

★ **Le Chenevière.** This grand manor of the late 19th century, set in parkland between Bayeux and the coast, was converted into an elegant hotel in 1988. Its smooth operation sets out to challenge the nearby Château d'Audrieu. The rooms have modern furnishings, with plain draperies on the floor-to-ceiling windows and flowered bedspreads to give a splash of color. The marble bathrooms are spanking fresh. Chef Claude Esprabens strives for a Michelin star, and dinner is worth a detour. His Norman recipes are prepared with a lightness of style: The roasted scampi with sesame seed and fresh chanterelles is delicious, but you will find it hard to resist the warm *escalope de foie gras de canard* (warm sliced duck liver) with raspberry sauce. The Chausey Island lobster with morels is a favorite, but you may also try the justifiably famous rack of lamb with truffle sauce. For dessert, be sure to taste the warm goat cheese in puff pastry or the warm apple stuffed with Camembert. The large wine list covers most bases and has a reasonable selection of moderately priced bottles and a large selection of half bottles. To end with total satisfaction, order the 40-year-old Calvados. The sophisticated setting is underscored with peach tablecloths and glittering glassware. Service is professional. ⌨ *Escures-Commes, 14520 Port-en-Bressin,* ☎ *31–21–41–96,* FAX *31–21–47–98. 19 rooms. Restaurant, golf. AE, DC, MC, V. $$$*

Grand Hôtel du Luxembourg. Bayeux has three hotels classified with a three-star rating that are virtually the same, but the Luxembourg, a Best Western affiliate, stays open all year and its restaurant, Les Quatre Saisons, currently has the best cuisine in town. Chef Daniel Rivière's classic Norman repertoire draws inspiration from the seasons. You may have a salmon galette, chicken roasted with cider, or veal in a sauce strongly scented with Calvados. The hotel's guest rooms are fairly small, but adequate, with a toilet separate from the freshly tiled bathroom. All but two face the courtyard garden away from any street noise. Off-season rates are only slightly higher than at the town's two-star hotels, which makes this hotel a good choice during the winter months. Adjoining the hotel and under the same ownership is the more modest, but quite pleasant, two-star Hôtel de Brunville (☎ 31–21–18–00). ⌨ *25 rue des Bouchers, 14403,* ☎ *31–92–54–26, 800/528–1234 for U.S. reservations,* FAX *31–92–54–26. 19 rooms, 3 suites. Restaurant, bar, dance club. AE, DC, MC, V. $$*

Hôtel d'Argouges. This 18th-century hotel is an oasis of calm in the city center, and many rooms offer views of the well-tended flower garden. The rooms are simply furnished with the ubiquitous candlewick bedspreads. You can lie on the bed and ponder the sagging wood beams supporting the weight of centuries. The rooms in the main house are quieter than those in the town house that abuts the street, and they have garden views. Most but not all have minibars and television. Each of the two suites has a small room with twin beds that is ideal for children. Continental breakfast is the only meal. ⌂ *21 rue St-Patrice, 14400,* ☎ *31–92–88–86,* FAX *31–92–69–16. 25 rooms (20 with bath, 5 with shower), 2 suites. AE, DC, MC, V. $$*

Le Lion d'Or. The Lion d'Or is a handsome '30s creation, conveniently situated in the center of town. Palm trees arch over the garden courtyard, while flowers cascade from balcony window boxes. The rooms are comfortable and well furnished with pretty fabrics. Fine Norman cuisine is served in the chic wood-beam restaurant, decorated in shades of apricot. Specialties include *andouille chaude Bovary,* no doubt Madame Bovary's own recipe for hot sausages, and fillet of sole in a creamy lobster sauce. If you can't make a reservation here, try the nearby Churchill Hotel (14 rue St-Jean, ☎ 31–21–31–80, FAX 31–21–41–66), which has 32 rooms. It maintains a similar standard and offers the same range of amenities at about the same cost. ⌂ *71 rue St-Jean, 14400,* ☎ *31–92–06–90,* FAX *31–22–15–64. 22 rooms with bath. Restaurant. AE, DC, MC, V. Closed Dec. 25–mid-Jan. $$*

Le Bec-Hellouin

DINING AND LODGING

Auberge de l'Abbaye. You'll enjoy traditional Norman cooking in this rustic inn with a classic *colombage* facade (exposed timber in stucco walls). Inside, beamed ceilings and stone walls are hung with ornamental copper pans. Charming Madame Sergent has been in charge for more than a quarter of a century; she also has eight delightfully old-fashioned bedrooms but says they are reserved for her diners (though you don't have to stay here to eat at the restaurant). According to one famous TV personality, this restaurant serves the best apple tart in France. ⌂ *Pl. de l'Eglise, 27800,* ☎ *32–44–86–02. Reservations advised. MC, V. Closed Mon. and Tues. out of season and mid-Jan.–Feb. $$*

Bénouville

DINING AND LODGING

Le Manoir d'Hastings. One of Normandy's most celebrated restaurants is in a little village 10 kilometers (6 miles) northeast of Caen. The 17th-century building was originally a Norman priory. In addition to the main dining room, there are 11 private rooms for more intimate (and expensive) occasions. Aperitifs and coffee are served in the garden. The considerable reputation of owner-chef José Aparicio is based mainly on his fish and seafood dishes. He also has 11 expensive (800 francs) rooms, which he offers to those who dine at his restaurant. ⌂ *18 av. de la Côte-de-Nacre, 14970,* ☎ *31–44–62–43,* FAX *31–44–76–18. Reservations required. Jacket and tie. AE, DC, MC, V. Closed Sun. dinner, Mon., and first half of Feb. $$$*

Cabourg

LODGING

Pullman Grand Hôtel. This luxurious white-stucco hotel is set right on the seafront at the heart of town, and many guest rooms have balconies overlooking the sea. There's a lively piano bar during the summer season, and the hotel is connected to the casino. Its restaurant, Le Balbec, offers traditional French cuisine of a high standard but no great sophistication, though the *navarin d'agneau* (thinly sliced lamb) is quite delicious. ☎ *Promenade Marcel-Proust, 14390,* ☎ *31–91– 01–79,* FAX *31–24–03–20. 70 rooms with bath. Restaurant, bar. AE, DC, MC, V. $$$$*

Caen

DINING

★ **La Bourride.** Normandy boasts a number of excellent restaurants; La Bourride, close to the castle down one of Caen's oldest streets, is one of the best. Chef Michel Bruneau's inventive and delicate dishes are inspired mainly by local produce, but the cooking is essentially modern. Specialties include baked St. Pierre (white fish) with green mango and baby pigeon in a salted bean crust. The small dining room is typically Norman, with stone walls, beamed ceilings, and a large fireplace. ✕ *15 rue du Vaugueux,* ☎ *31–93–50–76. Reservations required. Jacket and tie. AE, DC, MC, V. Closed Sun., Mon., first 3 wks in Jan., second half of Aug. $$$*

DINING AND LODGING

★ **Le Dauphin.** Despite its downtown location—beware one-way streets as you arrive—Le Dauphin offers peace and quiet. The building is a former priory dating from the 12th century, though the smallish guest rooms are briskly modern. Those overlooking the street are soundproof, while the rooms in back have views of the serene garden courtyard. The service is especially friendly and efficient, both in the hotel and in the excellent, though rather expensive, restaurant, which specializes in traditional Norman cooking. Fish is featured on the menu, though the veal sweetbreads in a mushroom sauce are a good choice as well. ☎ *29 rue Gémare, 14000,* ☎ *31–86–22–26,* FAX *31–86–35–14. 21 rooms with bath or shower. Restaurant. AE, DC, MC, V. Restaurant closed Sat. $$*

Le Relais des Gourmets. One of the best hotels in town also has a terrific restaurant. The luxurious modern guest rooms are spacious and airy, and an Old World atmosphere reigns in the public rooms, which are dotted with charming antiques. Rooms vary in size, and those with only showers (350 francs) cost less than the larger rooms with full baths (520 francs). The plus restaurant offers a sophisticated level of service and classic local cuisine. The gratinéed lobster with crayfish and the turbot with cêpe mushrooms are memorable. Meals are served in the garden during summer months. ☎ *15 rue de Geôle, 14000,* ☎ *31– 86–06–01,* FAX *31–98–66–23; for U.K. reservations, 0181/541–0033; for U.S. reservations, 800/528–1234. 32 rooms with bath or shower. Restaurant. AE, DC, MC, V. $$*

Deauville

DINING AND LODGING

Normandy. Built in 1912, the hotel, with a traditional Norman facade and an underground passage to the casino, has attracted the fashionable and monied from Paris since its opening. A luxurious sense of well-being pervades the hotel, from the chandeliers and columns in the reception rooms to the haute bourgeois decor of the guest rooms. Ask for a room with a sea view at the time of your reservation. Breakfast (90 francs) is served around the indoor pool. The gourmet restaurant, La Potinière, has innovative Norman cuisine, while the large hotel dining room, often used by groups, has simpler and more classic Norman fare. ☎ *38 rue Jean-Mermoz, 14800,* ☎ *31–98–66–22, 800/223–5652 for U.S. reservations,* FAX *31–98–66–22. 271 rooms with bath. 2 restaurants, pool, sauna. AE, DC, MC, V. $$$$*

Le Royal. This gigantic five-star hotel, overlooking the sea and close to the casino, is stately and more than a trifle self-important. Americans prefer this hotel over its sister property, the Normandy, because the Royal appears larger and more palatial. Many of its rooms face the sea, and half of them have been redecorated in more traditional and warmer colors, with dark wood cabinetry and improved bathrooms (some have a separate shower stall). Of the two dining rooms, L'Etrier is more intimate and emphasizes haute cuisine, while Le Royal is a vast dining hall that often caters to the groups that dominate the hotel in early spring and late autumn. ☏ *Blvd. Cornuché, 14800,* ☎ *31–98–66–33, 800/223–5652 for U.S. reservations,* ℻ *31–98–66–34. 281 rooms with bath. Restaurants, pool, sauna, tennis. AE, DC, MC, V. Closed mid-Nov.–Easter. $$$$*

LODGING

Le Continental. One of Deauville's oldest buildings is home to this provincial hotel, four blocks from the sea; it's within easy walking distance of the town center and even of downtown Trouville. The guest rooms are small, but all were refurbished in 1990 to offer simple, pristine accommodation at prices that are reasonable for Deauville. *Petit déjeuner* (breakfast) is served in your room. The Continental is placed between the port and the casino, but it doesn't have a restaurant. ☏ *1 rue Désiré-le-Hoc, 14800,* ☎ *31–88–21–06,* ℻ *31–98–93–67. 48 rooms with bath or shower. AE, DC, MC, V. Closed mid-Nov.–mid-Mar. $$*

Dieppe
DINING AND LODGING

Windsor. Because Dieppe, once a popular resort, is today a transit port for crossing the Channel, the quality of the hotels has declined. Of the hotels facing the sea, the Windsor is currently the best kept, with modern rooms, functional furniture, and bathrooms of reasonable size. Do take a room with a sea view rather than one at the back. The restaurant on the second floor is popular for its panoramic view of the Channel. ☏ *18 blvd. de Verdun, 76200,* ☎ *35–84–15–23. 50 rooms, 45 with bath or shower. Restaurant. AE, DC, MC, V. Closed Dec. 25 and Jan. $$*

Duclair
DINING

Le Parc. Pierre Le Patezour, one of the region's most acclaimed chefs, has created an excellent restaurant in Duclair, about 20 kilometers (12 miles) west of Rouen, on the road to Caudebec-en-Caux. The dining room features plush Art Nouveau decor, and the menu offers such classic regional dishes as *canard à la Rouennaise* (duck in blood sauce). Le Patezour's subtle preparation of fillet of sole is an eye-opener, and the oysters served in a creamy sauce with a hint of tartness are scintillating. ✗ *721 av. du Président-Coty,* ☎ *35–37–50–31. Reservations advised. Jacket and tie. AE, DC, MC, V. Closed Sun. dinner, Mon., and Dec. 20–Jan. 20. $$$$*

Etretat
DINING

Les Roches Blanches. The exterior of this family-owned restaurant, situated back from the beach, is most unattractive—a concrete post–World War II eyesore. But take a table by the window with a view of the sea and the cliffs and order the superbly fresh seafood—you'll be glad you came. Other dishes, like the veal escalope with mushrooms, flambéed in Calvados, are good, too, but be sure at least to try the mussels. ✗ *Rue Abbé-Cochet,* ☎ *35–27–07–34. Reservations advised, especially* *for Sun. lunch. MC, V. Closed Tues., Wed., and Thurs. (Wed. only July–early Sept.), and Jan. and Oct. $$*

LODGING

★ **Le Donjon.** This charming little château, set in a large park overlooking the resort, offers lovely bay views. The individually furnished guest rooms are huge, comfortable, and quiet. Reliable French cuisine is served with flair in the cozy restaurant. ⌖ *Chemin de St-Clair, 76790,* ☎ *35–27–08–23,* FAX *35–29–92–24. 8 rooms, 6 with bath. Restaurant, pool. AE, DC, MC, V. $$–$$$*

Fécamp

DINING

★ **L'Escalier.** This delightfully simple little restaurant overlooks the harbor and serves traditional *cuisine à la normande.* The several inexpensive fixed-price menus offer mainly fish and seafood. ✕ *101 quai Bérigny,* ☎ *35–28–26–79. Reservations essential in summer. DC, MC, V. Closed Mon. and 2 wks in Nov. $*

DINING AND LODGING

★ **Auberge de la Rouge.** The quaint Auberge de la Rouge is in a little hamlet a mile or so south of Fécamp. Its menu features a good mix of classic and modern dishes and includes many local specialties; the lobster is always a good bet, but the *coquilles St-Jacques* (scallops in a sherry cream sauce) with a scent of herbs or the wild pressed duck are the true temptations. There are eight moderately priced guest rooms, all with bath, should you wish to sleep well after your dinner. ⌖ *Commune de St-Léonard, 76400,* ☎ *35–28–07–59,* FAX *35–28–70–55. Reservations advised. AE, DC, MC, V. Closed Sun. dinner and Mon. $$*

Honfleur

DINING

L'Absinthe. The Absinthe's 17th-century dining room, with stone walls and beamed ceilings, is a magnificent setting in which to enjoy chef Antoine Ceffrey's masterly creations, though on sunny days you'll probably want to eat outside on the terrace. Ceffrey has a delicate way with fish and seafood; try the *barbet,* a freshwater cod, prepared with ginger. ✕ *10 quai de la Quarantaine,* ☎ *31–89–39–00. Reservations advised. Jacket and tie. AE, DC, MC, V. Closed Mon. evenings, Tues., and mid-Nov.–Dec. 25. $$$*

★ **L'Assiette Gourmande.** Next door to the Cheval Blanc stands Honfleur's unsung top restaurant, under the skillful and creative chef Gérard Bonnefoy. He is also a master at deciding what you would enjoy most, after a few minutes of culinary conversation. The menu changes with the season, of course, but you might be lucky enough to have the superb coquilles St-Jacques grilled with sautéed asparagus in a raspberry vinaigrette and reduced orange sauce, or the *noix de St-Jacques* (huge succulent scallops) with a hazelnut risotto. But then, everything is delectable, from the lobster salad to the smoked-salmon tartare in a caviar-based cream, from the turbot marinated in a basil mussel sauce to the roast lamb from the salt marshes. Desserts are a pleasure both to the eye and to the palate. ✕ *2 quai des Passagers,* ☎ *31–89–24–88. Reservations accepted. Closed Mon. dinner, Tues. $$–$$$*

L'Ancrage. Massive seafood platters top the bill at this delightful old restaurant, which occupies a two-story 17th-century building overlooking the harbor. The cuisine is authentically Norman—simple but good. If you want a change from fish and seafood, try the succulent calf sweetbreads. ✕ *12 rue Montpensier,* ☎ *31–89–00–70. Reservations advised, especially in summer. MC, V. Closed Tues. dinner, Wed., and Jan. $$*

La Terrasse de l'Assiette. In the square shared by the Eglise Ste-Catherine and several other restaurants, the newcomer is La Terrasse, offering excellent fare at reasonable prices. Go with the fixed menu at 120 francs, choosing perhaps the appetizer of local oysters or the salmon and haddock marinated in anis. Follow this with the grilled tuna with a tart lemon sauce or the roast maigret of duck. End with a fondue of apple ice cream blessed with Calvados or a black chocolate mousse cake with an orange cream sauce. The wine list is limited but extremely well priced. ✗ *8 pl. Ste-Catherine,* ☏ *31–89–31–33. AE, MC, V. Closed Wed. in low season. $$*

DINING AND LODGING

Ferme St-Siméon. A 19th-century manor house—commonly held to be the birthplace of Impressionism—is set in the park that inspired such 19th-century luminaries as Claude Monet and Alfred Sisley. The guest rooms are individually decorated in a style that attempts to be opulent, but the high prices reflect more the reputation of the hotel than its comfort level. Pastel colors and floral wallpaper create a garden-like aura in some rooms, while antiques and period decor are featured in others. You have the option of staying in the main house or in the converted stables. The latter is quieter, though the rooms have somewhat less character. The sophisticated restaurant specializes in fish, and in good weather you can eat out on the terrace. The cheese board does justice to this region's superior products. ☎ *Rue Adolphe-Marais, on D513 to Trouville, 14600 Honfleur,* ☏ *31–89–23–61,* FAX *31–89–48–48. 22 rooms, 16 suites, all with bath. Restaurant, pool, tennis. MC, V. Restaurant closed Wed. lunch Nov.–Mar. $$$$*

LODGING

Le Cheval Blanc. Occupying a renovated 15th-century building on the harborfront, this hotel has a new owner, Alain Petit, a humorous Frenchman who speaks excellent English. You'll find him a jack of all trades, helping out everywhere as he and his wife run this friendly, warm inn. All the guest rooms have recently been redecorated and offer fine views of the stubby fishing boats in the port across the road. Room 34 is very special (and slightly more expensive than the others). It has a table and chairs and small couch along with a queen-size bed, and its gabled ceilings are held up by triangle and cross beams. The bathroom is large and the tub has Jacuzzi-style air nozzles. ☎ *2 quai des Passagers, 14600,* ☏ *31–81–65–00,* FAX *31–89–52–80. 35 rooms, 14 with bath. Breakfast room. MC, V. Closed Jan. $$*

DINING AND LODGING

★ **Hostellerie Lechat.** One of the best-known and loved establishments in Honfleur stands in a pretty square just behind the harbor in a typical 18th-century Norman building. The well-maintained, spacious guest rooms are done in pretty French provincial decor that makes good use of cheerful prints, with warm blue and rose predominating. Foreign guests are given a warm welcome, especially in the American bar. The rustic, beamed restaurant serves top-notch Norman cuisine: lobster and locally caught fish, but also such pleasures as breast of quail with apples and Calvados, and diced duck with a ginger confit and lime. There is a menu in English. ☎ *3 pl. Ste-Catherine, 14600,* ☏ *31–89–23–85,* FAX *31–89–28–61. 23 rooms with bath, 1 suite. Restaurant, bar. AE, DC, MC, V. Restaurant closed Jan., Wed., and Thurs. lunch mid-Sept.–May. $$*

Houlgate

DINING AND LODGING

Mon Castel. If you want to stay on the Calvados coast but don't fancy pricey Deauville or Cabourg, cheerful Houlgate is your best bet. The down-to-earth Mon Castel, three blocks from the sea, offers the best value in town, especially if you secure the large-windowed Room 1 on the second floor. Seafood reigns in the old-fashioned dining room. ▥ *1 blvd. des Belges, 14510,* ☎ *31–24–83–47. 12 rooms, 9 with bath or shower. MC, V. $*

Mont-St-Michel

DINING AND LODGING

Mère Poulard. The hotel of the most celebrated restaurant on the mount consists of adjoining houses whose small rooms, up three steep flights of narrow stairs, have simple furnishings and clean bathrooms with narrow tubs. Room prices start low, but for a room of decent size, you'll pay 850 francs. The restaurant's reputation derives partly from Mère Poulard's famous omelet recipe and partly from its dramatic location, and the prices are exorbitant. Nor does the posted menu accurately reflect what you will pay. So be forewarned. The owner, M. Vannier, is trading on past reputation and his captive market. Also, you are usually requested to book MAP, rather than taking only the room. ▥ *50116 Mont-St-Michel,* ☎ *33–60–14–01,* FAX *33–48–52–31. 26 rooms with bath. Restaurant (reservations required), piano bar. AE, DC, MC, V. $$$$*

Terrasses Poulard. M. Vannier bought this popular restaurant first and later acquired its more prestigious sister establishment (*see above*). The hotel is a recent addition, a result of buying up and renovating the neighboring houses to create an ensemble of buildings that exude charm and character, clustered around a small garden in the middle of the mount. The large restaurant attracts hordes of tourists, but you'll no doubt enjoy the traditional cuisine. ▥ *On the main road opposite the parish church, 50116,* ☎ *33–60–14–09,* FAX *33–60–37–31. 29 rooms with bath. Restaurant, library, billiards. AE, DC, MC, V. $$–$$$*

★ **Le Manoir de la Roche Turin.** A delightful alternative to the high price of staying in Mont-St-Michel is this small ivy-clad manor house on 4 acres of parkland 9 kilometers (5 miles) away. Rooms are pleasantly old-fashioned, but the bathrooms are modern. The owners, M. and Mme. Barraux, run a delightful beamed dining room with an open fireplace: The *agneau pré-salé* (lamb from the salt marshes) is superb, and lobster and fresh fish are available. In the warmer months, aperitifs are served in the garden, where you can look onto the majestic sight of Mont-St-Michel. ▥ *50220 Courtils,* ☎ *33–70–96–55,* FAX *33–48–35–20. 11 rooms and 1 suite, all with bath. Restaurant (closed Mon.). Closed mid-Nov.–mid-Mar. MC, V. $$*

Pont Audemer

DINING AND LODGING

Belle Isle sur Risle. This country hotel, the child of charming Mme. Yazbeck, is a civilized retreat from frenetic Paris and not tarted up like some of the Relais & Châteaux group. Neither the furnishings nor the service is polished to the point of removing personality—even the cracked tiles in the bar and the peeling wallpaper add to the feeling that you are a guest in a private manor. Guest rooms are new and modern or old and traditional. The latter, with rugs on wood floors, have assorted furnishings purchased at auction; the former, with wall-to-wall carpeting, have furnishings ordered from department stores. The traditional rooms on the first floor have balconies. All bathrooms are spacious, with hair dryers and terrycloth bathrobes. The café veranda has outdoor tables; the semicircular dining room faces the sunset. The young chef, Laurent Matuit, is remarkably good. Using the inspirations of Mme. Yazbeck, he creates tasty finished products: foie gras blinis; coquilles St-Jacques (scallops), with a coulis of mushrooms; a sorbet of Roquefort and port; and, to end, a light pastry tart with honeyed apples and sorbet. The delightful village of Pont Audemer is a stiff 15-minute walk away. ⌑ *112 Rte. de Rouen, 27500,* ☎ *32–56–96–22,* FAX *32–42–88–96. 15 rooms, and 4 suites. Restaurant, indoor and outdoor pool, sauna, tennis court. MC, V. \$\$\$*

Le Petit Coq aux Champs. The owners recently purchased this Norman-style, thatch-roof farmhouse and made it into a small luxury hotel with a swimming pool in the attractive garden. The bedrooms are not large but their balconies make them appear larger. Room 39 has two superbly comfortable beds and a good-size bathroom with a porthole window into the bedroom. Aperitifs are served before dinner in a comfortable lounge area in front of a crackling fire. Try the house specialty, made from apple and pear. Dinner is served in a cozy, beamed dining room full of the owners' antiques, but the food is not worth a special trip. Although the produce is fresh and of top quality, the preparation and the sauces are unexciting. Your best bet is the lamb chops, whose quality is tops. The lady owner speaks excellent English, and her husband manages the kitchen. ⌑ *Campigny, 27500 Pont Audemer (use D 810 and then D 29),* ☎ *32–41–04–19,* FAX *32–56–06–25. 12 rooms with bath. Restaurant, pool. Closed Jan. AE, DC, MC, V. \$\$*

Auberge du Vieux Puits. This is a quaint little cottage of a hotel, whose trellised and beamed exterior can't have changed much in the past 300 years. Gustave Flaubert, an early admirer, gave the hotel a few lines in *Madame Bovary.* The guest rooms make use of heavy wooden furniture with pretty curtains and bedspreads to reflect the traditional feel of the architecture. The simple rooms, in two wings overlooking the courtyard, are quiet, but don't expect elegant comfort. Chef Geffroy's restaurant offers first-rate, innovative cuisine based on the bountiful Normand provender, and since the owners consider their inn primarily a restaurant, you are expected to dine here when you stay overnight. The Menu Vieux Puits (290 francs) offers trout in champagne sauce, Calvados sherbet, duckling stew with sour cherries, local cheeses, and a fresh fruit tart with cream. Look out for the richness of this Norman food. ⌑ *6 rue Notre-Dame-du-Pré, 27500 Pont-Audemer,* ☎ *32–41–01–48. 7 rooms, 5 with shower. MC, V. Closed Dec. 20–Jan. 22; restaurant closed Mon. evening and Tues., except June–Aug. \$\$–\$\$\$*

Rouen

DINING

★ **Auberge de la Butte.** Chef Pierre Hervé is renowned for his subtle way with fish and seafood; his best dishes include poached oysters wrapped in spinach leaves and fricasseed fillet of sole. The magnificent Norman dining room's half-timbered walls are adorned with paintings and shining copper pots, and the ceiling features exposed beams. It's well worth the 3-kilometer (2-mile) drive out of Rouen to find this former 18th-century post house. ✕ *69 rte. de Paris, Bonsecours,* ☎ *35–80–43–11. Reservations advised. Jacket and tie. AE, DC, MC, V. Closed Sun., Mon., Dec. 22–Jan. 5, and Aug. \$\$\$*

La Couronne. The dining room of this 15th-century Norman building features beamed ceilings, leather-upholstered chairs, wood-panel walls, and a scattering of sculpture. The traditional Norman cuisine makes few concessions to modernism; specialties include crayfish salad with foie gras and caviar, duck with orange, and turbot in puff pastry. ✕

31 pl. du Vieux-Marché, ☎ *35–71–40–90. Reservations advised. Jacket and tie. AE, DC, MC, V. $$$*

La Grande Brasserie. A friendly, bustling bistro, La Grande Brasserie is just beside the market and Joan of Arc's memorial church. It has a motherly staff and a huge menu with some worthwhile specialties. This is the place for succulent oysters and mussels and delicious tripe cooked the local way. There are tables outside in summer. ✗ *2 pl. du Vieux-Marché,* ☎ *35–15–14–24. Reservations advised. AE, DC, V. $$*

DINING AND LODGING

Mercure Rouen Centre. This modern hotel built into the jumble of narrow streets of downtown Rouen near the cathedral offers small modern rooms that are comfortable and breezily furnished in pastels. The efficient service is the standard for this national chain of hotels. There's an American bar, and the restaurant, Le Tournebroche, serves classic Norman cooking with creamy and cheesy sauces, as well as plain grilled and spit-roast dishes. ☎ *Rue Croix-de-Fer, 76000,* ☎ *35–52–69–52,* FAX *35–89–41–46. 125 rooms with bath. Restaurant, bar. AE, DC, MC, V. $$–$$$*

Hôtel de Dieppe. Dating from the late 19th century, the Dieppe remains fresh and up-to-date, thanks to frequent redecoration under the proud management of four generations of the same family. The fairly compact rooms have been furnished in a cheerful modern style. Double-glazed windows keep out the traffic noise (which stops at 10 PM, when the last train arrives from Paris), but you might want to open them to the breeze in summer. The restaurant, Les Quatre Saisons, has a well-earned reputation and offers English-style roasts, as well as such traditional French dishes as duckling *à la presse,* a Norman dish of crispy duck prepared at your table. ☎ *Pl. Bernard-Tissot, 76000,* ☎ *35–71–96–00,* FAX *35–89–65–21. U.S. reservations 800/528–1324. 42 rooms with bath. Restaurant, breakfast room. AE, DC, MC, V. $$*

LODGING

Hotel de la Cathédrale. On a narrow pedestrian street behind the cathedral stands a very appealing hotel in a medieval building. Rooms are petite but neat and comfortable, and all have a private bath or shower. Guests can sleep soundly, too; the cathedral bells do not boom out the hour during the night. Breakfast is served in a wonderfully beamed dining room. The owner, who is on hand at the desk, is extremely cordial and will give you tips on exploring Rouen and advice on dining options. ☎ *12 rue St-Romain, 76000,* ☎ *35–71–57–95,* FAX *35–70–15–54. 25 rooms. Breakfast room. MC, V. $–$$*

St-Pierre-du-Vauvray

DINING AND LODGING

Hostellerie St-Pierre. If you're looking for a hotel between Paris and Rouen in charming countryside, this can suit the need. Choose Room 27, and you'll have a view of the Seine quietly flowing by its wooded banks, and French windows opening onto a terrace. Its size (and that of most of the others) is modest, but there's enough space around the queen-size bed for a coffee table, chairs, and a desk. Bathrooms are tiled and accommodate a tub and shower; the bathroom is separate. Dinner is a pleasant occasion. A good dish to select is the *rable de lapin farci* (saddle of rabbit) stuffed with mushrooms in a cider sauce and served with roasted apples, or the *boudin de poisson* (fish mousse) in a beurre blanc sauce, scented with herbs. Desserts are generally good, though the *assiette tout chocolat* (all-chocolate plate) with crème anglaise is less luscious than you might expect. The Crozes Hermitage, at 120 francs, is a find among the limited selection of reasonably

priced wines. ☎ *1 chemin des Amoureux, 27430,* ☎ *32–59–93–29,*
FAX *32–59–41–93. 14 rooms. Restaurant. Closed mid-Nov.–mid-Mar.*
MC, V. $$$

St-Valéry-en-Caux

DINING

Les Hêtres. The most fashionable chef in Rouen has moved up the coast
to Ingouville, just south of St-Valéry. Bertrand Warin has created an
elegant dining room that contrasts half-timbered walls and Louis XIII
chairs with sleek, modern furnishings. The tables are widely spaced,
and large windows look out onto an extensive landscaped garden. ✗
Ingouville, ☎ *35–57–09–30. Reservations required. Jacket and tie.*
No credit cards. Closed Sun. evening, Mon., first half of Jan., and last
2 wks in Aug. $$$

Trouville

LODGING

Hotel Le Beach. Hotels in Trouville are a mixed bag. Those popular in
the 1930s have fallen into tattered decay while still charging premium
rates. The newer hotels lack character but have fresher paint and not-
so-stained carpets. Hotel Le Beach (1985) is one such hotel and is listed
here because of its location, behind the casino. Guest rooms face the
English Channel; Room 605, for example, overlooks the swimming pool
and, beyond, the harbor, where small sailboats beat their way past the
lighthouse. All the rooms have pristine white walls and print fabrics
for color. The public rooms are designed for the flow of guests who
often arrive on package tours or with seminar groups, so expect efficiency rather than personal service. ☎ *Quai Albert-1er, 14360 Trou-*
ville, ☎ *31–98–12–00,* FAX *31–87–30–29. 110 rooms. Restaurant,*
pool, meeting rooms. AE, DC, MC, V. $$–$$$
Carmen. This straightforward, unpretentious little hotel is just around
the corner from the casino and a block from the sea. The rooms range
from plain and inexpensive to comfortable and moderate, and the
owners, the Bude family, are always on hand to advise their guests. The
restaurant offers good home cooking at value-for-the-money prices. ☎
24 rue Carnot, ☎ *31–88–35–43,* FAX *31–88–08–03. 18 rooms with*
bath. Restaurant. AE, DC, MC, V. Closed Jan.–mid-Feb., and 10 days
in Oct. Restaurant closed Mon. dinner and Tues. $–$$

Vernon

DINING AND LODGING

Normandy. Good accommodations near Giverny have long been in short
supply, so this hotel, opened in 1990, is good news. The service is friendly,
the breakfasts substantial, and the rooms well equipped and calm (ask
for one away from the street). ☎ *1 av. Mendès-France, 27200,* ☎ *32–*
51–97–97. 50 rooms with bath. Restaurant, bar. AE, MC, V. $$–$$$

THE ARTS AND NIGHTLIFE

The Arts

Music

Normandy's cultural activities revolve around music, both classical and
modern. Many churches host evening concerts; organ recitals are especially popular. Particularly good programs are featured at the church
of **St-Ouen** in Rouen, **St-Etienne** in Caen, and **St-Pierre** in Lisieux (get
details from the tourist office). Rouen's **St-Maclou** hosts an annual series of organ recitals in August; even the venerable abbey of **Mont-St-**
Michel gets into the act during July and August. Jazz aficionados will

be interested in the **European Traditional Jazz Festival** held in mid-June at Luneray, 8 kilometers (5 miles) southwest of Dieppe. For those who like spectacle with their music, the **Théâtre des Arts** (☎ 35–71–41–36) in Rouen stages numerous operas.

Festivals

A **Joan of Arc Commemoration** takes place in Rouen at the end of May, with a variety of parades, street plays, concerts, and exhibitions that recall the life—and death—of France's patron saint.

Film

One of the biggest cultural events on the Norman calendar is the **American Film Festival,** held in Deauville during the first week of September.

Nightlife

The hot spots of Normandy nightlife are, predictably enough, such resorts as Deauville, Trouville, and Cabourg, where discos and clubs vie with casinos for space.

Casinos

The region is dotted with nearly 30 casinos, five of which—**Deauville, Forges-les-Eaux, Trouville, Dieppe,** and **Bagnoles-de-l'Orne**—rank among France's best, with floorshows and cabarets, as well as gaming rooms.

Bars and Nightclubs

Try **Le Revoir** (14 bis rue Désiré-le-Hoc) in Deauville or Dieppe's **Casino** (3 blvd. de Verdun). Night owls will enjoy the smoky ambience of **Club Melody** in Deauville (13 rue Albert-Fracasse) and the jiving crowd at the **Green Onions Café** (29 blvd. des Belges) in Rouen.

NORMANDY ESSENTIALS

Arriving and Departing

By Plane

Paris's Charles de Gaulle (Roissy) and Orly airports will be American visitors' closest link with the region. From the United Kingdom, there are regular flights to Caen and Deauville (from London) and to Cherbourg (from Southampton and the Channel Islands).

By Boat

Car ferries connect several Normandy ports with England and Ireland: Newhaven to Dieppe (Sealink; ☎ 01273/51–6699 in Newhaven, ☎ 35–06–39–00 in Dieppe); Portsmouth to Cherbourg and Le Havre (P&O European Ferries; in Portsmouth, ☎ 0130/21–0004; in Le Havre, ☎ 35–19–78–50; in Cherbourg, ☎ 33–88–65–70); Portsmouth to Ouistreham, near Caen; Poole to Cherbourg (Brittany Ferries; in Poole, ☎ 01705/827701; in Ouistrehan, ☎ 31–36–36–39; in Cherbourg, ☎ 33–22–38–98); Southhampton to Cherbourg (Stena Sealink Line; in Southhampton, ☎ 01703/23–5506; in Cherbourg, ☎ 33–20–43–38); Rosslare and Cork to Le Havre and Cherbourg (Irish Ferries; in Le Havre, ☎ 35–53–28–23; in Cherbourg, ☎ 33–22–38–98). Ferries also leave from Carteret, Portbail, and Granville for the Channel Islands.

By Car

The A13 expressway from Paris spears its way to Rouen in 1½ hours (toll 33 frs) and to Caen in 2½ hours (toll 86 frs). A13/N13 takes you to Cherbourg via Bayeux in another two hours.

By Train

From Paris's St-Lazare station, express trains stop at Rouen and Dieppe, Le Havre, or Fécamp, and at Caen and Cherbourg via Evreux and Lisieux. For Mont-St-Michel (nearest station: Pontorson), take the express from Paris's Montparnasse station to Rennes or to Caen (from St-Lazare) and switch to a local train.

Getting Around

By Plane

Normandy's domestic airports are at Rouen, Le Havre, and Evreux.

By Car

A13/N13 travels from Rouen to Cherbourg via Bayeux in two hours. Main roads also branch off from A13 to Le Havre (A15) and Dieppe (N27). To get to Mont-St-Michel, take A11 to Rennes, then N175 north.

Guided Tours

Orientation

Viking Voyages (16 rue du Général-Giraud, 14000 Caen, ☎ 31–27–12–34) specializes in two-day packages by car, with overnight stays in private châteaus. Itineraries include "Normandy: From Rouen to Cherbourg"; "William the Conqueror's Route"; "Discovering the Manche," which includes a trip to Mont-St-Michel; a "D-Day Beaches" tour; and "From Lisieux to Suisse Normande." An all-inclusive tour, with car and English-speaking driver, is 1,850 francs. The **French Association of Travel Agents** offers a two-day tour of Mont-St-Michel and St-Malo, which includes a visit to Honfleur, the resorts of Deauville and Cabourg, the D-Day beaches, and Caen. The excursion, offered from April to October, costs 1,800 francs; contact **Clamageran Voyages** (4 rue Rollon, 76000 Rouen, ☎ 35–07–39–07) for details.

Train Excursions

Both **Paris-Vision** (214 rue de Rivoli, 75001 Paris, ☎ 42–60–31–25) and **Cityrama** (4 pl. des Pyramides, 75001 Paris, ☎ 42–60–30–14) organize one-day train excursions to Mont-St-Michel, with a two-day option that takes in the châteaus of the Loire on the second day. Costing 990 francs, the one-day trips leave Paris at 7:15 PM on Saturday, arriving in Mont-St-Michel in time for lunch (included in the cost). Following a guided tour of the mount and the abbey, you return to Paris—with a stop for dinner (also included in the cost) on the way—about 10:30 PM.

Special-Interest

Viking Voyages in Caen (*see above*) organizes bike trips around the region, as well as a "Normandy Antiques" tour by car. A two-day bike tour, without guide, costs 995 francs, while a guided antiques excursion costs 1,795 francs. **Trans Canal** in Caen (13 rond-point de l'Orne, ☎ 31–34–00–00) arranges two-hour cruises on Caen's canal.

Important Addresses and Numbers

Travel Agencies

American Express (1–3 pl. Jacques-Lelieur, Rouen, ☎ 35–98–19–80; 57 quai George V, Le Havre, ☎ 35–42–59–11) and **Havas** (25 Grande-Rue, Alençon, ☎ 33–32–88–88; 80 rue St-Jean, Caen, ☎ 31–86–04–01; 14 pl. Nationale, Dieppe, ☎ 35–84–29–16).

Car Rental

Avis (44 pl. de la Gare, Caen, ☎ 31–87–31–84; 24 rue Malouet, Rouen, ☎ 35–72–77–50) and **Europcar** (25 cours de la République, Le Havre, ☎ 35–25–21–95).

Visitor Information

Each of Normandy's five *départements* has its own central tourist office: **Alençon** (Orne, 88 rue St-Blaise, ☎ 33–28–88–71), **Caen** (Calvados, pl. St-Pierre, ☎ 31–27–14–14), **Evreux** (Eure, blvd. Georges-Chauvin, ☎ 32–31–05–98), **Rouen** (Seine-Maritime, 25 pl. de la Cathédrale, ☎ 35–71–41–77), and **St-Lô** (Manche, rte. Villedieu, ☎ 33–05–98–70). Tourist offices of other major towns covered in this chapter are as follows: **Bayeux** (1 rue des Cuisiniers, ☎ 31–92–16–26), **Dieppe** (1 blvd. du Général-de-Gaulle, ☎ 35–84–11–77), **Fécamp** (pl. Bellet, ☎ 35–28–20–51), **Le Havre** (1 pl. de l'Hôtel-de-Ville, ☎ 35–21–22–88), and **Honfleur** (9 rue de la Ville, ☎ 31–89–23–30).

7 The North and Champagne

Lille, Reims, and the Ardennes

TOO FEW people visit northern France. The crowd-following French head south each year in search of a suntan. The millions of foreign tourists who flock through the Channel ports of Calais, Boulogne, and Dunkerque make a beeline to Paris. The Channel Tunnel, perhaps the most ambitious engineering project of the late 20th century, will change this; local tourist authorities are banking on an influx of British day-trippers and weekenders. The English are already busy buying homes in the region, many with an eye to commuting to London on the TGV.

Northern France was in the frontline of battle during the world wars and suffered heavily. The city of Reims was shelled incessantly during World War I, and such names as the Somme and Vimy Ridge evoke the bloody, deadlocked battles that raged from 1914 to 1918. Cemeteries and war memorials may not be the most cheerful items on a tourist's itinerary, but they do have a melancholy, thought-provoking beauty.

The Channel coast—mile upon mile of empty, sandy beaches—is featured in our first tour. Calais and Dunkerque, the first ports of call for many visitors to France, are among the country's uglier towns. The old sectors of neighboring Boulogne are far more appealing, while there is a startling clash between the narrow streets of ancient Montreuil and the posh avenues of fashionable Le Touquet.

The north of France is an industrial region, but don't look for slag heaps and smokestacks everywhere; the heavy industry is highly centralized. This is a green and pleasant land where wooded, restful landscapes predominate. Lille, the regional capital, on the TGV line, has plenty to see. To the east, the plains give way to hills. The grapes of Champagne flourish on the steep slopes of the Marne Valley and on the so-called Mountain of Reims. Reims is the only city in Champagne, and one of France's richest tourist venues. The kings of France were crowned in its cathedral until 1825, and every age since the Roman period has left an architectural mark. The thriving champagne business has conferred wealth and, sometimes, an arrogant reserve on the region's inhabitants. The down-to-earth folk of the north provide a warmer welcome.

EXPLORING

Orientation

We have divided the vast region covered in this chapter into two tours. The first covers the north of France proper, stretching from the River Somme up to the English Channel, including Lille. We chart a circular tour you can join anywhere, although we start at the exciting new Channel Tunnel. The second tour covers Reims and the Champagne area northeast of Paris, with an excursion to the Ardennes by the Belgian border.

Tour 1: The North

Numbers in the margin correspond to points of interest on The North and Lille maps.

❶ Napoléon dreamed of it and the Victorians even started digging it, but it was only in May 1994 that the **Channel Tunnel** was finally inaugurated by Queen Elizabeth II and former president François Mitterrand. Then, elaborate safety checks and production delays put off the *Eurostar* rail service between Paris and London until the fall of 1994. Begun with two trains a day in each direction, it aims for hourly service by the end of 1995. *Le Shuttle*'s special double-decker trains for cars run continually—every 15 minutes at peak times—and there is no need to book ahead. Drivers arriving from England disembark at **Coquelles,** 3 kilometers (2 miles) from the coast, where the terminal's Centre d'Information (open daily 10–7) has brochures on the tunnel and the region.

Nearby Calais is best known these days for its giant hypermarkets, where the British stock up on cheap drink. It is no tourist mecca, and we suggest that, from Coquelles, you head back to the coast at Sangatte, site of the Chunnel's giant shaft, and make your way along picturesque D940 to the cliffs of Cap Blanc-Nez and Cap Gris-Nez. It's worth making ❷ the short detour to **Cap Gris-Nez** for a bracing stroll along the cliff tops beneath the shadow of the lighthouse and the ominous outlines of a World War II concrete bunker. From here you get the best views of the White Cliffs of Dover across the Channel.

Return to D940 and continue along the coast past Ambleteuse, with its 17th-century fort, and Wimereux, a Belle Epoque resort.

❸ Just before you arrive in **Boulogne** (another stamping ground for cross-Channel visitors), spin off left toward the **Colonne de la Grande Armée.** Work began on this 160-foot marble column in 1804 to commemorate Napoléon's soon-to-be abandoned plans to invade England, but it was finished 30 years later under Louis-Philippe. The 263 steps take you to the top and a wide-reaching panoramic view. If the weather is clear and you're blessed with Napoleonic vision, you may be able to make out the distant cliffs of Dover. ☛ *Free.* ⊙ *Daily 10–noon and 2–5.*

The contrast between the lower and upper sections of Boulogne is startling. The rebuilt concrete streets around the port are gruesome and sinister, but the Ville Haute—the old town on the hill—is a different world, and you will begin to understand why Napoléon chose Boulogne as his base while preparing to cross the Channel. The Ville Haute is dominated by the formidable **Notre-Dame** basilica, its distinctive elongated dome visible from far out at sea. Surrounding the basilica are charming cobbled streets and tower-flanked ramparts, dating from the 13th century and offering excellent views. The four main streets of the old town intersect at place Bouillon, where you can see the 18th-century brick town hall, and the Hôtel Desandrouins, where Napoléon spent many long nights pondering how to invade Britain.

★ ❹ **Le Touquet,** 27 kilometers (17 miles) down the coast from Boulogne, at the mouth of the Canche estuary, is a total contrast: a superb example of an elegant Victorian seaside resort that sprang out of nowhere in the 19th century, adopting the name Paris-Plage. Mainly because gambling laws were stricter in Victorian England than in France, Englishmen, not Parisians, were the town's mainstay. A cosmopolitan atmosphere remains, although many Frenchmen, attracted by the airy, elegant avenues and invigorating climate, have moved here for good. To one side lies a fine sandy beach; to the other, an artificial forest planted in the 1850s. A casino, golf courses, and racetrack cater to fashionable pleasure, but the swimming is none too safe.

TIME OUT   The **Aqualud** waterpark has an unpretentious bar and restaurant, as well as numerous water-sports facilities, half outdoors, half in; you can shoot the rapids, thunder down a toboggan run, or just relax in the sauna. *Blvd. Thierry-Sabine,* ☎ *21–05–63–59.* ☛ *Waterpark: 46 frs for 3 hours, 54 frs for 4 hours, 62 frs for 5 hours, 70 frs all day. Persons*

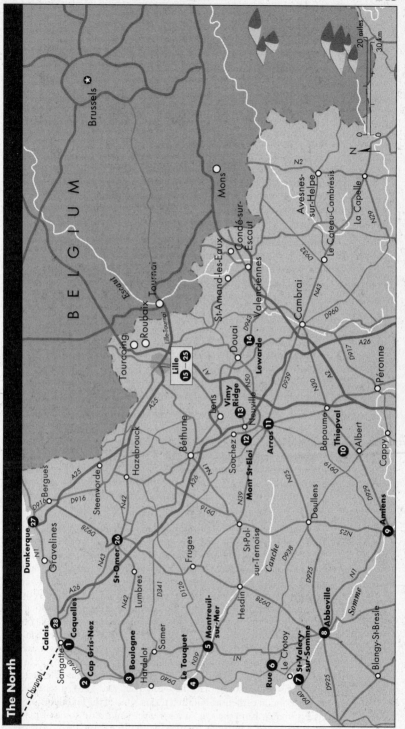

under 1 meter (39″) in height free. ⊘ *Mid-Feb.–Oct., daily 10–6; July and Aug., daily 10–7.*

❺ Despite its seaside-sounding name, **Montreuil-sur-Mer** lies 16 kilometers (10 miles) inland from Le Touquet by N39. It was once a port, but the Canche silted up and left it high and dry. The ancient town features majestic walls and ramparts, as well as a faded, nostalgic charm to which various authors, notably Victor Hugo, have succumbed; an important episode of his epic work *Les Misérables* is set here.

Wherever citadels and city walls loom on the French horizon, it's a fair bet that Vauban had a hand in their construction. Montreuil is no exception. In about 1690, Vauban supplemented the existing 16th-century towers of the **citadel** with an imposing wall, whose grassy banks and mossy flagstones can be explored at leisure. There are extensive views on all sides. ☎ *21–06–10–83.* ☛ *8 frs adults, 5 frs children under 18.* ⊘ *Wed.–Mon. 10–noon and 2–6.*

❻ Some 28 kilometers (17 miles) south along N1/D938 is the small town of **Rue,** home to the extravagantly sculpted Chapelle du St-Esprit, with lacelike stonework and stellar patterned vaulting of luxuriant complexity. The chapel is said to have been built with the money of pilgrims attracted by a miraculous crucifix from Jerusalem, washed up on the coast nearby.

❼ D940 leads south to the bustling harbor of Le Crotoy and around the Bay of the Somme, where sheep graze peacefully on the salt marshes, to **St-Valery-sur-Somme,** a pretty fishing resort (squid and shellfish are specialties) with a shady seaside promenade, medieval fortifications, and the flint-and-sandstone-checkerboard Chapelle des Marins, an 18th-century chapel housing the tomb of St. Valery himself.

❽ The historic town of **Abbeville,** 11 kilometers (7 miles) inland along the Somme, was heavily reconstructed after being reduced to rubble in 1940. It has a lively Thursday and Saturday market. The church of **St-Vulfran,** begun in 1488, was one of the last cathedral-size churches to be constructed in the Gothic style. Its much-mauled facade, still undergoing renovation, is a riot of Flamboyant Gothic tracery and ornament. It was here that, according to 19th-century art historian John Ruskin, Gothic "lay down and died."

❾ The Gothic cathedral can be admired in all its glory down the Somme Valley in **Amiens,** 46 kilometers (29 miles) away along N1. Much of the city counts as a catastrophic example of postwar reconstruction, **★** but the **Cathédrale Notre-Dame** has survived unscathed through the ages. It is by far the largest church in France; Notre-Dame of Paris could fit inside twice! Although it lacks the stained glass of Chartres or the sculpture of Reims, for architectural harmony, engineering proficiency, and sheer size, it has no peer. The soaring, asymmetrical facade boasts a notable Flamboyant Gothic rose window and dominates the surrounding nondescript brick streets. Inside, the overwhelming sensation of space is enhanced by the absence of pews in the nave, a return to medieval tradition. There is no stylistic disunity to mar the perspective: Construction took place between 1220 and 1264, a remarkably short period in cathedral-building terms. One of the highlights of your visit is hidden from the eye, at least until you lift up some of the 110 choir stalls and admire the humorous, skillful misericord (seat) carvings executed between 1508 and 1518. *Pl. Notre-Dame,* ☎ *22–92–77–29.* ⊘ *All day except noon–2.*

Turn left on rue Cormant and take the second right onto rue Victor-Hugo. Midway down, you'll discover the **Hôtel de Berny,** an elegant 1634 mansion filled with period furniture and devoted to local art and regional history. *36 rue Victor-Hugo,* ☎ *22–91–81–12.* ☛ *16 frs, free on Sun.* ⊙ *Tues.–Sun. 10–12:30 and 2–6.*

If you've any spare time in Amiens, head for the waterfront quarter called **Saint-Leu,** behind the cathedral: Its colorful, restored houses and eclectic shops make this a lively spot to explore. Also in Amiens are the **Hortillonnages,** commercial gardens where the more than 700 acres, cultivated since Roman times, can be visited on foot or by small boat (La Capitainerie, quai Bélu, ☎ 22–97–88–55). Jules Verne lived in Amiens for some 35 years, and his former home has become the **Centre de Documentation Jules Verne.** It contains some 15,000 documents about Verne's life as well as original furniture and a reconstruction of the writing studio where he created his science fiction classics. True fans might also want to visit his dramatically sculpted tomb in the **Cimetière de la Madeleine** (2 rue de la Poudrière, ☎ 22–91–90–15).

Amiens is the major city of the *département* of the Somme, a name forever etched into history as the site of one of the bloodiest battles of World War I. On July 1, 1916, whole regiments of Allied soldiers went "over the top" only to be mowed down by a hail of German machine-gun fire. The major encounters took place northeast of Amiens near **Albert.**

To reach the former Somme battlefields, take D929 from Amiens to Albert, 24 kilometers (15 miles), then D151 north to the British War Memorial at **Thiepval,** 8 kilometers (5 miles) away. This brick memorial, shaped like a triumphal arch, dominates the Ancre Valley and bears the names of the 73,000 British soldiers who were killed nearby. A little over 2 kilometers (1 mile) northwest is the **Beaumont-Hamel** memorial park, where trenches, parapets, and barbed wire recall the fighting waged here by Newfoundland regiments in July 1916.

TIME OUT The white-painted, vine-covered exterior of **L'Escale** (22 Chaussée Léon-Blum, ☎ 22–76–02–03), in the tiny village of Cappy, 12 kilometers (7½ miles) southeast of Albert, marks it as a restaurant with a difference. The dining room, decorated with antiques and needlework tablecloths, has the feel of a country cottage, and the menu is illustrated with poems and old photos. The regional dishes (smoked eel, duck, and black pudding) are chosen according to season and accompanied by subtle, refined sauces.

War cemeteries dot the countryside as you head north along D919 to **Arras,** 32 kilometers (20 miles) away. Capital of the historic Artois region between Flanders and Picardy, Arras has grown into something of a sprawling industrial town. Its historic core bears witness to the grandeur of another age, however, when the town enjoyed medieval importance as a trading and cloth-making center.

Grand' Place and **place des Héros,** separated by a short block, are the two main squares, harmonious examples of 17th- and 18th-century Flemish civil architecture. The gabled facades recall those in Belgium and Holland and are a reminder of the unifying influence of the Spanish colonizers of the "Low Lands" during the 17th century. The smaller, arcaded place des Héros is dominated by the richly worked—and much restored—**Hôtel de Ville,** capped by a 240-foot belfry.

Turn left out of the square, then right into rue Paul-Doumer. Walking a block along brings you to the imposing 18th-century premises of a former abbey, now the **Musée des Beaux-Arts.** The Fine Arts Museum houses a rich collection of porcelain and, especially, painting, with several major 19th-century French works. *22 rue Paul-Doumer,* ☎ *21–71–26–43.* ☛ *20 frs adults, 12 frs children and senior citizens.* ⊙ *Apr.–mid-Oct., Wed.–Mon. 10–noon and 2–6; mid-Oct.–Mar., Mon. and Wed.–Fri. 10–noon and 2–5, Sat. and Sun. 10–noon and 2–6.*

The 19th-century **Cathédrale St-Vaast,** a short block farther on, is a white-stone classical building, every bit as vast as its name (pronounced "va") suggests. It replaced the previous Gothic cathedral that was destroyed in 1799; though it was half-razed during World War I, restoration was so skillfully done you'd never know.

At first glance you might not guess that Arras was badly mauled during World War I. Not far off, though, are parks and memorials recalling the fierce battles. Arras is a convenient base for visiting the area's numerous superbly cared for cemeteries and memorials, which number among the most poignant sights in northern France.

⓬ Eight kilometers (5 miles) northwest of Arras via D341 lies the ruined abbey of **Mont St-Eloi.** Legend has it that this once-vast abbey is connected to Arras by an enormous underground tunnel. Ghostly towers are all that remain of the abbey, which was destroyed during the French Revolution. They peer mournfully over the tiny village and surrounding countryside and are visible for miles around. Just 3 kilometers (2 miles) away, with gentle slopes, trees, and manicured lawns, is perhaps the most beautiful and moving of all the French war cemeteries—**La Targette.**

⓭ From nearby Neuville-St-Vaast, D55 winds up to the Canadian War Memorial on top of **Vimy Ridge.** Thanks to its woods and lush grass, the Vimy memorial park has become a popular picnic spot, yet the preserved trenches and savagely undulating terrain are harsh reminders of the combat waged here in 1917. The simple, soaring, white-stone Canadian War Memorial, a cleft rectangular tower adorned with female figures in tearful lament, is highly effective. Its base is inscribed with thousands of names of the fallen.

Head back to Neuville and take D937 right shortly afterward, past the beautiful circular cemetery of the Cabaret Rouge and the village of **Souchez.** Turn left up to **Notre-Dame de Lorette,** a colossal cemetery standing on a windswept hill 500 feet above the plains of Artois. There is a mock-Byzantine church and a huge tower containing a small war museum; from the top of the tower, treat yourself to some superb views of the surrounding countryside.

⓮ Get onto southbound A26, branching off at N50 (follow signs for Douai). From Douai, it's just a 5-kilometer (3-mile) drive east on D943 to **Lewarde,** whose abandoned coal mine has been skillfully converted into the **Centre Historique Minier,** a museum documenting the mining industry. You can admire the beefy mine machinery, stroll around an interesting photographic exhibit, and take a train ride through reconstructed coal galleries. ☎ *27–98–03–89.* ☛ *46 frs adults, 16 frs children and students under 18.* ⊙ *Apr.–Sept., 10–5; Oct.–Mar., daily 10–4.*

TIME OUT   If you find yourself at the Mining Museum around lunchtime, make for the on-site brasserie, **Le Briquet.** The menu offers excellent value and regional specialties, including carbonnade, rabbit in prunes, and cock in beer.

⓯ **Lille,** 40 kilometers (24 miles) north, is quickly reached via D943 and the A1 expressway. For a big city supposedly reeling beneath the problems of its main industry, textiles, Lille is a remarkably dynamic, attractive place. It is also horrendous to drive in, and parking is nigh impossible. Sunday, when the sights are open but the offices are closed, may be your best time to visit the old town. Lille—the name comes from *l'isle* ("the island") in the Deûle River, where the city began—experienced Flemish, Austrian, and Spanish rule before passing into French hands for good in 1667. Since the arrival of the TGV in 1994, it is again a European crossroads, a quick trip by train from Paris, London, and Brussels. Traditionally, the liveliest time to be in Lille is the first weekend of September for its three-day street fair, **La Grande Braderie.** For local ambience at other times, visit the down-to-earth Wazemmes Market south of the city center (Métro: Gambetta).

16 The shiny glass towers of the new **Euralille** complex, the high-tech commercial center, that is Lille's answer to La Défense near Paris, greet travelers arriving at the new TGV station, Lille-Europe. Hotels and shops dominate the complex, and students of modern architecture will find it stimulating.

Avenue Le Corbusier links Euralille to the original rail station, still used for non-TGV services and now renamed Lille-Flandres. The station building, originally the Gare du Nord in Paris, was moved brick by brick to **17** Lille in 1866! Just off place de la Gare is the sumptuous **Eglise St-Maurice,** a large, five-aisle church built between the 15th and 19th centuries.

TIME OUT   **Les Brasseurs,** (22 pl. de la Gare) is a brasserie that brews its own beer on the spot. There are four types—blond (lager), amber, dark (stout), and white (wheat beer)—and *La Palette du Barman* lets you sample all four. The hearty menu includes andouillettes, black pudding, leg of pork, kippers, *mousse à la blanche de Lille* (dessert made from beer), and even a beer-based digestif.

Walk south along rue de Paris down to the majestic Porte de Paris, a cross between a mansion and a triumphal arch, built by Simon Vollant in 1685 and overlooked by the 340-foot brick tower of the Hôtel de Ville, alongside. Turn right (west) and take boulevard de la Liberté **18** north to the **Musée des Beaux-Arts,** the largest fine arts museum in France outside Paris, reopened in 1995 after extensive renovation. It houses a noteworthy collection of Dutch and Flemish painting (Anthony Van Dyck, Peter Paul Rubens, Flemish Primitives, and Dutch landscapists) as well as some charmingly understated still lifes by Chardin, works by the Impressionists, a few bombastic 19th-century French painters, and dramatic canvases by El Greco, Goya, Tintoretto, and Paolo Veronese. A ceramics section displays some fine examples of Lille faience, which uses opaque glazing techniques to achieve remarkable effects. *Pl. de la République,* ☎ *20–57–01–84.*

Continue along boulevard de la Liberté, then right along rue Jean-Sans-Peur to place Rihour. The tourist office is housed in the former chapel **19** of the 15th-century **Palais Rihour,** built for the dukes of Burgundy. Exhibitions are often staged here, and you should take a look at the staircase, famed for its intricate, swirling-pattern brickwork.

Next door to place Rihour is Lille's most famous square, the Grand' **20** Place, now officially called **place du Général-de-Gaulle** (Charles de Gaulle was born in Lille in 1890; his house, at 9 rue Princesse, is a museum). The Déesse (Goddess) atop her giant column, clutching a linstock (used to fire a cannon), has dominated the square since 1845; she commemorates Lille's heroic resistance to an Austrian siege in 1792. Other landmarks include the handsome, gabled 1932 facade of *La Voix du*

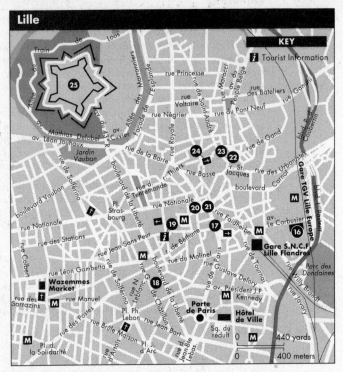

Nord (the main regional newspaper), topped by three gilded statues symbolizing the three historic regions of Flanders, Artois, and Hainaut; and the Furet du Nord, which immodestly claims to be the world's largest bookshop.

㉑ At the far side of the square is the elegant **Vieille Bourse,** the old commercial exchange built in 1653 by Julien Destrées to rival those of the Netherlands. The bronze busts, sculpted medallions, and ornate stonework of its arcaded quadrangle can now be fully appreciated after a wholesale cleaning in 1994–95.

Cross through the Bourse and take Grande Chaussée, turning right onto the quaintly named rue des Chats-Bossus (Street of the Hunchbacked Cats) to place du Lion d'Or. On the adjacent place Louise-de-Bettignies (No. 29) is the ornate **Maison de Gilles de la Boë,** built in the 1630s for a rich grocer.

㉓ Turn the corner onto rue de la Monnaie. A short way up on the right is the **Hospice Comtesse,** founded by Jeanne de Constantinople, countess of Flanders, as a hospital in 1237, and rebuilt in the 15th century after a fire destroyed most of the original building. Local artifacts from the 17th and 18th centuries form the backbone of the museum now housed here, but its star attraction is the Salle des Malades (Sick Room), featuring a majestic wooden ceiling. *32 rue de la Monnaie,* ☎ *20–51–02–62.* ✆ *12 frs adults.* ⊘ *Wed.–Mon. 10–12:30 and 2–6.*

㉔ Take the passage opposite the hospice to **Notre-Dame de la Treille.** The original medieval church here was dismantled at the revolution, and the present building was only begun—in a suitably neo-Gothic style—in 1856. Building was halted from 1869 to 1893, and by World War I only the choir was finished. In the meantime, the church was made a basilica, then the unfinished basilica became a cathedral, none of which did much to speed construction. The roof vaults were only finished in 1973, and the west front, with its dismal expanses of gray concrete, remains despairingly incomplete. Grandiose plans for a new, glass facade seem unlikely to come to fruition, and so this mighty edifice stands like a colossal wreck, admonishing the quaint, cozy streets of old Lille like some latter-day Ozymandias.

Head west (via rue Basse and rue de la Barre) from Notre-Dame to an equally ambitious but rather more convincing architectural undertaking: the gigantic **citadel,** which glowers down on the whole of the old town. Construction started in the mid-17th century; of course that genius of military engineering, Sébastien de Vauban, got the commission. Some 60 million bricks were baked in record time—Louis XIV's prime northern outpost needed urgent defending—and the result is a fortified town in its own right, with monumental towers and walls. These days, the citadel is used as a barracks. *Visits on Sun. afternoons, Apr.–Oct. Contact tourist office, Palais Rihour,* ☎ *20–30–81–00.*

From Lille, take the A25 expressway northwest toward Steenvorde, then N42 to St-Omer via Hazebrouck. **St-Omer** is a delightful small town, too often neglected by hasty motorists on their way south. It is not the archetypal northern industrial town; with its yellow-brick buildings it even looks different from its neighbors, and a distinct air of 18th-century prosperity hovers about the place. Stroll through the narrow streets surrounding the Basilique Notre-Dame and, if time allows, visit the **Hôtel Sandelin.** Now the town museum, the 1777 mansion is furnished with 18th-century furniture and paintings and contains an exceptional collection of porcelain and faience. *14 rue Carnot,* ☎ *21–38–00–94.* ☛ *15 frs.* ☽ *Wed. and weekends 10–noon and 2–6, Thurs. and Fri. 10–noon and 2–5.*

From St-Omer drive 28 kilometers (18 miles) north on D928 to **Bergues,** captured from the Spanish in 1668 and fortified by Vauban at the end of the 17th century. He used the Colme River to irrigate a complex network of ditches and moats, which were effective enough to keep the English at bay in 1793. Parts of the old town walls remain, protecting a maze of crooked streets.

The D916 leads from Bergues to **Dunkerque,** 9 kilometers (6 miles) away. It is renowned for its rumbustious Carnival, when the inhabitants take to the streets in fancy dress and the mayor flings herrings at the crowd from the town-hall balcony. For English-speaking visitors, Dunkirk conjures up the evacuation of 1940, when 338,000 men escaped the Nazi advance, ferried to safety across the Channel by an impromptu fleet consisting in large part of small private boats. Dunkerque was three-quarters destroyed in World War II but remains the third largest port in France. Its few historic buildings include the 14th-century **Leughenaer,** one of 28 towers that once ringed the town; the 16th century **Eglise St-Eloi;** and the 190-foot **Beffroi** (belfry), built in 1440, whose peal of 48 bells chimes every quarter hour.

The N1 follows the coast west from Dunkerque, skirting the fortified town of Gravelines, to **Calais,** 40 kilometers (25 miles) distant.

Few vestiges remain of the old, once-pretty port that owed its wealth to the lace industry rather than to day-trippers who come across the Channel by ferry to shop for tax-free wine and beer (nearly 8 million visitors each year). You won't want to stay here long, but there are a few sights to see before you dash off.

You don't need to be a sculpture fanatic to appreciate Auguste Rodin's powerful bronze **Monument des Bourgeois de Calais,** which dominates the east end of the Parc St-Pierre next to place du Soldat-Inconnu. The bourgeois in question were townspeople who, in 1347, when Calais fell to English king Edward III after an eight-month siege, offered their lives in exchange for his sparing the town. Edward's queen, Philippa, intervened on their behalf, and the courageous men were saved. Calais, on the other hand, remained in English hands for another 200 years, and was the last English toehold in France.

Head up traffic-clogged boulevard Jacquard, turning right onto rue Richelieu. Three blocks along, at No. 25, is the **Musée des Beaux-Arts et de la Dentelle** (Fine Arts and Lace Museum), which contains some fine 19th- and 20th-century pictures, Rodin bronzes, local historical displays, and exhibits documenting the Calais lace industry. *25 rue Richelieu,* ☎ *21–46–63–17.* ☞ *10 frs (free Wed.)* ◷ *Wed.–Mon. 10–noon and 2–5:30.*

Turn left at the next block, making for the much-restored **Eglise Notre-Dame,** where Général de Gaulle was married in 1921. Take time to admire the simple, vertical elegance of the windows and the ornate fan vaulting inside. From Calais it's just 4 kilometers (2½ miles) to the Channel Tunnel; the A26 expressway arrows inland, joining the Paris-bound A1 near Arras, and continuing on for Tour 2.

Tour 2: Champagne Country

Numbers in the Margin Correspond to points of interest on the Champagne and Reims maps.

㉙ Our second tour starts in the village of **Morienval,** 72 kilometers (45 miles) from Paris via A1, N324, and D335. It is hard to imagine, when you first see the elegant but relatively modest church of Morienval, its three towers rising amid verdant parkland 8 kilometers (5 miles) from Crépy, that you are face-to-face with one of the key buildings in architectural history. The 11th-century Romanesque church became a center of pilgrimage when, in 1122, the relics of St-Annobert were translated here. The need for a new ambulatory (so everyone could get a look at the saintly remains) was obvious, but no one knows why the masons at Morienval, when extending the church, hit on the innovative idea of using stone vaults, supported on "ribs" springing diagonally from column to column. Few dispute, however, that this architectural breakthrough, the structural basis of the Gothic style (along with pointed arches), did occur in Morienval, about 1135. It was promptly adopted at the great basilica of St-Denis near Paris and swept through northern France during the years that followed (as we shall shortly see at Noyon, Laon and Reims).

Much of the original church remains, notably the east tower and the columns in the nave, whose astonishing carved capitals feature spirals, stars, masks, and animals.

㉚ Continue along D335 for 10 kilometers (6 miles) to the attractive lakeside village of **Pierrefonds,** dominated by its huge 12th-century **château,** comprehensively restored to imagined former glory by Viollet-le-Duc at the behest of upstart emperor Napoléon III in the 1860s. What he left is a crenellated fortress with a fairy-tale silhouette. (Like the fortified town of Carcassonne, which Viollet-le-Duc also restored, Pierrefonds is considered more a construct of what le-Duc thought it should have looked like than what it really was.) A visit takes in the chapel, barracks, and the majestic keep holding the lord's bedchamber and re-

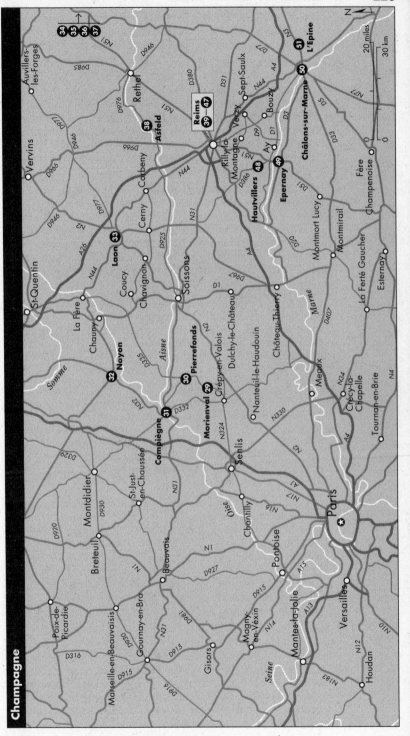

ception hall. ☎ 44–42–80–77. ☛ *30 frs adults, 10 frs children 7–17. Guided tours only.* ⊘ *May–Aug., daily 10–6; Apr. and Sept., daily 10–noon and 2–6; Oct.–Mar., Thurs.–Mon. 10–noon and 2–4:30.*

㉛ Compiègne can be reached from Pierrefonds via D975. A bustling town of some 40,000 people, it stands at the northern limit of the Ile de France forest, on the edge of the misty plains of Picardy: prime hunting country, a sure sign that there's a former royal palace in the vicinity. The one here enjoyed its heyday in the mid-19th century under Napoléon III. But the town's place in history looks both farther back—Joan of Arc was captured in battle and held prisoner here—and farther forward: The World War I armistice was signed in Compiègne Forest on November 11, 1918.

★ The 18th-century **Palais de Compiègne** was restored by Napoléon I and favored for wild weekends by his nephew Napoléon III. The first Napoléon's legacy can be more clearly felt, however. His state apartments have been refurnished, using the original designs for wall hangings and upholstery; brightly colored silk and damask adorn every room. Much of the elegant mahogany Empire furniture gleams with ormolu, and the chairs sparkle with gold leaf. (In contrast, Napoléon III's furniture looks ponderously ostentatious.)

In the gardens a gently rising, 4-kilometer (2½-mile) vista leads back from the palace, inspired by the park at Schönbrunn in Vienna, where Napoléon I's second wife, empress Marie-Louise, was brought up. You should also visit the **Musée de la Voiture** to admire its large collection of carriages, coaches and old cars, including the *Jamais Contente* ("Never Satisfied"), the first car to reach 100 kph (62 mph). *Pl. du Palais,* ☎ 44–40–04–37. ☛ *32 frs.* ⊘ *Wed.–Mon. 9:30–5.*

One of the central highlights of Compiègne is the late-15th-century town hall, or **Hôtel de Ville,** which possesses an exceptional Flamboyant Gothic facade with fine statuary. Make time to visit the **Musée de la Figurine** for its amazing collection of 85,000 lead soldiers depicting military uniforms through the ages. *28 pl. de l'Hôtel de Ville,* ☎ 44–40–72–55. ☛ *12 frs.* ⊘ *Mar.–Oct., Wed.–Sun. 9–noon and 2–6; Nov.–Feb., Wed.–Sun. 9–noon and 2–5.*

A short distance east of Compiègne, near Rethondes (take N31), is the **Clairière de l'Armistice,** where a railway car was run out on a spur line especially for the signing of the World War I armistice. In 1940, the Germans turned the tables and made the French sign their own surrender in the same place—accompanied by Hitler's famous jig for joy. The car you can visit these days is a replica—the original was destroyed during the war. *Wagon de l'Armistice, Forêt de Compiègne,* ☎ 44–40–09–27. ☛ *10 frs.* ⊘ *Apr.–Oct., Wed.–Mon. 9–noon and 2–6:30; Nov.–Mar., Wed.–Mon. 9–noon and 2–5:30.*

㉜ Noyon, 26 kilometers (16 miles) northeast of Compiègne on N32, is a frequently overlooked cathedral town that owed its medieval importance to the cult of 7th-century saint Eloi, patron of blacksmiths and a former town bishop. The **Cathédrale St-Eloi** was constructed between 1150 and 1290. Its four-story nave; the intermittent use of rounded as well as pointed arches; and the thin, pointed lancet (as opposed to rose) windows in the austere facade all mark it as one of the earliest attempts at what was to become "the Gothic Cathedral."

From Noyon, head east on N32 to **Chauny,** with its colossal town hall and handsome 1920s buildings, then head south on D1 to Coucy-le-Château, a hilltop village whose majestic walls—once punctuated by

28 towers—took a hammering during World War I. Continue on D5 to Chavignon, turn right onto N2, then left along D18. This hilltop road separating the valleys of the Aisne and the Ailette, known as the **Chemin des Dames,** was the site of a disastrous French offensive in April 1917 that led to futile slaughter and mutiny. Follow D18 past the French memorial in Cerny-en-Laonnois to the dank, dismal **Caverne du Dragon,** used as an arsenal and living quarters by the Germans and now the site of an eerie underground war museum. ☎ 23–22–44–90. ☛ 12 frs. ⊙ Daily Wed.–Mon. 10:30–noon and 2–5:30.

Stay on the road to Corbeny, stopping at the **Plateau de Californie** for a panoramic view of the scene of combat, then take N44 northwest to Laon.

❸❸ **Laon,** on a splendid hilltop site, is called the "crowned mountain"—a reference to the forest of towers sprouting from its ancient cathedral. The site, cathedral, and enchanting old town are well worth a visit. Strangely, though, very few people come here; few Parisians, for instance, have ever heard of the place.

★ In the middle of the old town, just off place Aubry, is **Cathédrale Notre-Dame,** constructed between 1160 and 1235 and a superb example of early Gothic. The recently cleaned, light interior gives the impression of order and immense length (120 yards in total). The flat east end, an English-inspired feature, is unusual in France. The upper galleries that extend around the building are typical of early Gothic; what isn't typical is that you can visit them (and the towers) with a guide from the tourist office on the cathedral square (tours last about two hours and are held on weekend afternoons). The filigreed elegance of the five remaining towers is audacious by any standard and rare: French medieval architects preferred to concentrate on soaring interiors, with just two towers at the west end. Even those not usually affected by architecture will appreciate the sense of movement imparted by Laon's majestic west front; compare it with the more placid, two-dimensional feel of Notre-Dame in Paris. Look, too, for the stone oxen protruding from the towers—a tribute to the stalwart, 12th-century beasts who carted up blocks of stone from quarries far below.

TIME OUT The **Café du Parvis** on place du Parvis is unremarkable in every respect but one: its location, just opposite the cathedral. What better place to drink in one of France's most exciting medieval facades with your morning coffee? 4 pl. du Parvis, ☎ 23–20–26–10.

★ The medieval **ramparts,** virtually undisturbed by passing traffic, provide a ready-made itinerary for a tour of old Laon. Panoramic views, sturdy gateways, and intriguing glimpses of the cathedral lurk around every bend. Another notable survivor from medieval times is the **Chapelle des Templiers,** a small, well-preserved octagonal 12th-century chapel on the grounds of the town museum, which has a fine collection of Greek terra-cotta vases. Porte d'Ardon. ☛ 10 frs. ⊙ Apr.–Oct., Wed.–Mon. 10–noon and 2–6; Nov.–Mar., Wed.–Mon. 10–noon and 2–5.

We now make an excursion into the French Ardennes, a neglected region tucked away by the Belgian frontier. Take N2 north to pretty **Vervins** (site of a fine hotel restaurant; see Dining and Lodging, below), then ❸❹ N43 east to **Charleville-Mézières** (104 kilometers, or 65 miles), officially united in 1966 but separated by a branch of the capricious Meuse River, which burst its banks in January 1995, in the worst flooding since records began in 1794. Mézières, an administrative and military center, has a more regimented feel than folksy Charleville, where a warren of narrow pedestrian streets encircles the large, shambling Ducal Square.

With its pink brick, arcades, and steep slate roofs, the **place Ducale,** designed around 1610, by Clément Métezeau, recalls the place des Vosges in Paris, designed by his elder brother Louis. Place Ducale has no trees or railings to mask the view; its original symmetry, however, has been zapped by rooftop accretions and a 19th-century church and town hall. The square is at its liveliest at market time on Tuesday, Thursday, and Saturday mornings.

Head down rue Moulin to the **Vieux Moulin,** a majestic 1626 watermill straddling a branch of the Meuse. The giant wheel turns no more, but the mighty facade, with its broken pediment and rusticated Ionic columns, has been restored. Inside, along with temporary art exhibitions, is a museum devoted to Charleville's most famous son: precocious punk poet Arthur Rimbaud. Pictures, souvenirs, and photographs chart his turbulent career, revealing that he fled Charleville at age 17, after writing his masterpiece, "Le Bateau lure" (*The Drunken Boat*). He died in 1891 in Marseille at age 37 but is buried in Charleville town cemetery. *Quai Arthur-Rimbaud,* ☎ *24–32–44–65.* ☛ *10 frs.* ☉ *Tues.–Sun. 10–noon and 2–6.*

A passageway at 31 place Ducale leads to the stylish, new **Musée de l'Ardenne,** opened in 1994. Subtle lighting and spacious, imaginative layout lend the displays of guns, coins, keys, pottery, and archaeological findings an almost abstract aesthetic appeal. There is also a clutch of local paintings and a re-created rustic regional interior. *31 pl. Ducale,* ☎ *24–32–44–60.* ☛ *22 frs adults, 11 frs students and senior citizens.* ☉ *Tues.–Sun. 10–noon and 2–6.*

Turn left out of the museum and, just as you head into place Winston-Churchill, look up to your left to see a huge turquoise frame, topped by a clock and a gold mask peeping out of the roof. In the alleyway you will notice a pair of giant gold legs. This is **Le Grand Marionnettiste** (The Giant Puppeteer), commissioned in 1991 by the International Puppet Institute. Every hour from 10 AM to 9 PM, the red stage curtains slide open to reveal gold hands pulling the strings of a plethora of puppets enacting the local legend of *Aymon & His Four Sons.* On Saturday at 9:15 PM, all 12 tableaus appear in sequence.

Return to place Ducale and head south along rue de la République to Mézières (take your car). Turn right after crossing the Meuse, then left

★ up to **Notre-Dame de l'Espérance.** This 16th-century basilica, where Charles IX married Elizabeth of Austria in 1570, has a four-square Renaissance tower topped by a fancy 19th-century spire. But the real attraction lies inside. "The church of Mézières is reputed for its stained glass," wrote Victor Hugo in 1838. Alas, the windows he admired have long since been blasted into oblivion during repeated invasions, but today you can admire the most ambitious modern stained glass anywhere in France: an entire churchful of abstract, geometric designs by René Dürrbach. The overall effect is a breathtaking collision of old and new, one of the most homogeneous displays of stained glass outside Chartres. A guidebook to its biblical symbolism is available from the presbytery.

North of Charleville-Mézières you might explore the tortuous, wooded Meuse Valley as it twines toward Belgium. The D1 hugs the river past slate quarries and metalworks, through oak and evergreen forest, home to deer and boar. Near Château-Regnault rise the four spiky quartzite summits of the **Rocher des Quatre Fils Aymon.** Stroll through the old streets of **Monthermé,** tucked in beneath Longue Roche and the Roche à Sept Heures. A few miles north, the 900-foot **Roches de Laifour** surge into view at the bridge across the Meuse, with an imposing row of rolling peaks, the **Dames de Meuse,** to your left.

35 The fame of **Sedan,** 14 kilometers (9 miles) east of Charleville, far outweighs its modest size. To English speakers its name has become associated with cars and chairs—accidentally, say sedan-tary etymologists. In France, Sedan is forever written into the national psyche because here, in 1870, Napoléon III's Second Empire came crashing down as the Prussian army smashed through, taking Napoléon and 83,000 soldiers prisoner, then steaming on toward Paris. Emile Zola captures the mayhem in his epic novel *La Débâcle.*

★ The grim, massive **castle** that dominates Sedan may not be the most impregnable in Europe, but it claims to be the largest. The colossal front, illuminated at night, dominates the town like a Wall of Jericho; the daunting courtyard is hemmed in by bleak walls seven stories high and up to 24 feet thick. (The castle was used as a prison during World War II, and you can see why). It was virtually a town in its own right and could house 4,000 soldiers. Its sturdy walls withstood sieges in 1495 and 1521, when Charles V was forced to seek a truce, though he was attacking with more than 30,000 men.

The castle was founded in 1424 by the Lords of Sedan, local rulers, and it dates mainly from the 15th and 16th centuries. Elizabeth of Austria stayed here in 1570 before her marriage to Charles IX in Mézières, as did Henri II and Catherine de Médicis, and Henri IV and Marie de Médicis. Sedan became part of France only in 1642; Louis XIV stayed here during the siege of Stenay.

Documents relating the castle's history can be examined in a museum in the south wing, along with archaeological findings. At press time, in May 1995, the castle was preparing to launch a **Historium,** with tableaus depicting its history, and a self-guided tour with infrared headsets and multilingual commentary. Try to visit at nightfall on Friday, Saturday, or Sunday in summer for a guided tour by torchlight. ☎ *24–27–73–73.* ☛ *25 frs.* ☾ *Daily mid–Mar.–mid–Sept., 10–6; mid–Sept.–mid–Mar., 1:30–5:30.*

The center of Sedan is spoiled by the five skyscrapers that glower down from the hill behind place Turenne, although from there you can glimpse remnants of the awesome walls and catch a rooftop view of higgledy-piggledy chimneys gushing smoke in a satisfyingly Dickensian manner. In the oldest part of town, from the castle down to the Meuse, several streets are pedestrian-only, especially around place d'Armes, which is dominated by the Eglise St-Charles, with its pepperpot towers. The triangular place de la Halle leads into rue du Ménil, lined with 17th- and 18th-century houses.

TIME OUT Stop off for a drink at **Au Roy de la Bière** (19 pl. de la Halle), a warm, wood-panel bar that tries to resemble an English pub (a red London phone box stands in the square opposite). The wide choice of draught beers includes Irish Guinness and Belgian *bière blanche* (wheat beer).

36 From Sedan take N43 east to **Douzy.** The small aerodrome's **Musée des Débuts de l'Aviation** is devoted to the pioneering exploits of Roger Sommer (1877–1965), who edged past Wilbur Wright's previous best to set a flight record of 2 hours, 27 minutes at Châlons-sur-Marne on August 7, 1909. ☎ *24–26–38–70.* ☛ *12 frs.* ☾ *June–Aug., Tues.–Sun. 10–noon and 2–6; May and Sept., Tues.–Sun. 2–6; Apr. and Oct., weekends 2–6.*

Continue 8 kilometers (5 miles) south, via D964, to the village of
③⑦ **Mouzon,** dwarfed beneath the twin towers of its 13th-century abbey
church of **Notre-Dame.** With fat, round monostyle columns and a sec-
ond-story gallery, this imposing edifice, 215 feet long and 70 feet high,
is a stylistic successor to the cathedrals of Laon and Notre-Dame in
Paris. Mouzon's **Musée du Feutre** (Felt Museum) outlines the 8,000-
year history of felt, from its immemorial manufacture in Turkey,
Afghanistan, and Mongolia to its latter-day use in games, decorations,
cars, and pens, with exhibits of dolls, dresses, and tapestries. *Pl. du
Colombier,* ☎ *24–26–19–91.* ☛ *12 frs.* ☉ *Daily July–Aug., 10–
noon and 2–6; June and Sept., daily 2–6; Apr., May, and Oct., weekends 2–6.*

Return to Sedan, head west along D764/D864/N51 to Rethel, turn right
③⑧ and take D926 along the Aisne Valley to **Asfeld,** home to one of
France's most surprising buildings, the **Eglise St-Didier.** This brick
church, designed by Father François Romain for the Count d'Avaux
in 1683, is a whimsical essay in Roman Baroque, with curves, cupolas, a rotunda, colonnades, oval side chapels, and hardly a straight line
in sight. The ground plan is said to be based on a viola, and the individual bricks are not rectangular but concave or convex. The church
would look swell in a swanky sector of Rome; in this tiny village it
hovers between the sublime and the ridiculous. ☎ *24–72–94–97.* ☉
Daily 8–7.

③⑨ Head 22 kilometers (14 miles) south from Asfeld to **Reims,** the capital of the champagne industry. Several major producers are headquartered here, and you won't want to miss the chance to visit the chalky
maze of cellars that tunnel under the city center.

Reims cathedral, one of the most famous in France, is the age-old setting for the coronations of the French kings. Clovis, king of the Franks
in the 6th century, was baptized in an early structure on this site; Joan
of Arc led her recalcitrant dauphin here to be crowned King Charles
VII; Charles X's coronation, in 1825, was the last. The glory of the
★ ④⓪ **Cathédrale Notre-Dame** is its facade: It's so skillfully proportioned that
initially you have little idea of its monumental size. Above the north
(left) door hovers the *Laughing Angel,* a delightful statue whose famous smile threatens to melt into an acid-rain scowl. Pollution has succeeded war as the ravager of the building's fabric. Restoration is an
ongoing process.

The high, solemn nave is at its best in summer when the light shows
up the plain lower walls adorned by 16th-century tapestries relating
the life of the Virgin. The east-end windows have stained glass by Marc
Chagall. Admire the vista toward the west end, with an interplay of
narrow pointed arches of different sizes.

With the exception of the 15th-century towers, most of the original building went up in the 100 years after 1211. A stroll around the outside
will reinforce the impression of harmony, discipline, and decorative richness. The east end presents an idyllic sight across well-tended lawns.
There are spectacular light shows both inside (45 francs) and outside
(free) in July and August. *Pl. du Cardinal-Luçon.* ☉ *Daily 7:30–7:30.*

④① Next door, the **Palais du Tau** (former archbishop's palace) houses an
impressive display of tapestries and coronation robes, as well as several statues "rescued" from the cathedral facade. The second-floor views
of Notre-Dame are terrific. *2 pl. du Cardinal-Luçon,* ☎ *26–47–74–
39.* ☛ *25 frs adults, 13 frs senior citizens, 5 frs children.* ☉ *July–Aug.,
daily 9:30–6:30; mid-Mar.–June and Sept.–mid-Nov., daily 9:30–*

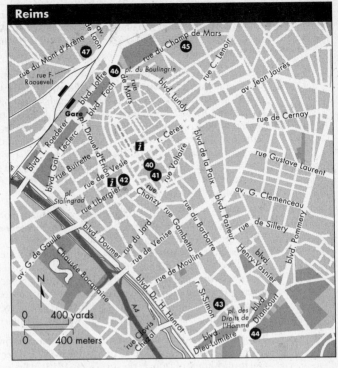

12:30 and 2–6; mid-Nov.–mid-Mar., weekdays 10–noon and 2–5, weekends 10–noon and 2–6.

TIME OUT Something out of the ordinary is always happening at the **Café du Palais** (14 pl. Myron-Herrick), just around the corner from the cathedral: a jazz quartet, a fashion-modeling session, or the screening of a silent movie. There's a piano, a veranda, and a choice of baguette sandwiches with such fillings as duck mousse or warm goat cheese. Closing at 8:30, this is no place for late dinners.

42 Two blocks southwest of the cathedral, on the right, is the **Musée des Beaux-Arts,** with an outstanding collection of paintings: no fewer than 27 Corots, and Jacques-Louis David's celebrated portrait of Marat stabbed in his bath by Charlotte Corday. 8 rue Chanzy, ☎ 26–47–28–44. ☛ 11 frs, or 16 frs for joint ticket with the Salle de Reddition (Surrender Room). ☼ Wed.–Mon. 10–noon and 2–6.

43 As you leave the museum, turn right and walk southeast on rue Chanzy and rue Gambetta to the 11th-century **Basilique St-Rémi,** honoring the 5th-century saint who gave his name to the city. St-Rémi is nearly as long as the cathedral, and its interior seems to stretch into the endless distance, an impression created by its relative murk and lowness. The airy, four-story Gothic choir contains some fine original 12th-century stained glass.

44 Several champagne producers organize visits to their cellars, combining video presentations with guided tours of their cavernous, chalk-hewn underground warehouses. **Taittinger** has the most spectacular. 9 pl. St-Nicaise, ☎ 26–85–45–35. ☼ Weekdays 9:30–1 and 2–5:30, weekends 9–noon and 2–6. Closed weekends Dec.–Feb.

Few show much generosity when it comes to pouring samples, though,
45 so we recommend that you double back across town to **Mumm,** which
does. *34 rue du Champ-de-Mars,* ☎ *26–49–59–70.* ⊙ *Mar.–Oct., daily
9–11 and 2–5.*

Head down rue du Champ-de-Mars toward the train station and you'll
46 see, looming up, the **Porte Mars,** an unlikely but impressive 3rd-cen-
tury Roman arch adorned by faded bas-reliefs depicting Jupiter, Ro-
mulus, and Remus. Turn north onto avenue de Laon, then left onto
47 rue Franklin-Roosevelt. A short way along is the **Salle de Reddition**
(Surrender Room), where General Eisenhower established Allied headquarters at the end of World War II. It was here, in a well-preserved,
map-covered room, that the German surrender was signed in May 1945.
12 rue Franklin-Roosevelt, ☎ *26–47–84–19.* ☛ *11 frs adults.* ⊙
Wed.–Mon. 10–noon and 2–6.

Your first encounter with the champagne vineyards can be had 10 kilometers (6 miles) south of Reims via N51 on the **Montagne de Reims,** a
lofty, forest-topped plateau whose slopes are a tangle of vines. D26
winds around the eastern face of the plateau, through wine villages such
as Chigny-les-Roses, Rilly-la-Montagne, Mailly-Champagne, and Verzy,
each as pretty as its name. Pride of place goes to the unforgettable **Bouzy,**
where a fashionable but overpriced still red wine is produced. South of
Bouzy, D1 runs along the banks of the River Marne to Ay, once capital
of the champagne vineyards; Henry VIII was a keen tippler of its wines.

To understand how traditional still wine became exciting, sparkling
48 champagne, detour up D386 to nearby **Hautvillers,** a gem of a village
and former home of Dom Pérignon (1638–1715), who invented champagne as we know it. This able monk, a cellar master whose blindness
enhanced his taste buds and sense of smell, is the supposed discoverer
of the use of corks for stoppers, the blending of wines from different
vineyards, and the systematic (rather than occasional) production of
champagne bubbles. Dom Pérignon's simple tomb-slab, in the damp,
forlorn Benedictine Abbey church (now owned by Moët et Chandon),
is a modest memorial to the hero of one of the world's most lucrative
drink industries.

49 Across the Marne lies **Epernay,** a town that, unlike Reims with its numerous treasures, appears to live only for champagne. Unfortunately,
no relation exists between the fabulous wealth of Epernay's illustrious
winehouses and the drab, dreary appearance of the town as a whole.
Most of the champagne houses are spaced out along the long, straight
avenue de Champagne and, although their names may provoke sighs
of wonder, their facades are either functional or overdressy.

The attractions are underground, in the cellars. Of the various houses
open to the public, **Mercier** offers the best deal; its sculpted, labyrinthine
caves contain one of the world's largest wooden barrels (with a capacity
of over 200,000 bottles); you can tour the cellars in the speed and comfort of a small train. A generous glass of champagne is your post-visit
reward. *75 av. de Champagne,* ☎ *26–54–71–11.* ☛ *Free.* ⊙ *Mar.–Oct.,
daily 10–noon and 2–5; Nov.–Feb., Mon.–Sat. 10–noon and 2–5.*

TIME OUT Champagne is not the only Epernay specialty. At **La Chocolaterie,** Monsieur Thibaut performs confectionery miracles before your eyes. If you
feel the urge to indulge, take a seat in the adjoining Salon de Thé. *9 rue
Gallice,* ☎ *26–51–54–43. Closed Sun. and Mon.*

Strangely enough, the official administrative center of the champagne
50 industry is not Reims or Epernay but **Châlons-sur-Marne.** Yet this

large town is of principal interest to fans of medieval architecture. The **Cathédrale St-Etienne** is pure, harmonious 13th-century, with large nave windows and tidy flying buttresses; the overall effect is marred only by the bulky 17th-century Baroque west front. Of equal merit is the church of **Notre-Dame des Vaux,** with its twin spires, Romanesque nave, and early Gothic choir and vaults. The small **museum** beside the excavated cloister contains outstanding medieval statuary. *Rue Nicolas-Durand,* ☎ *26-64-03-87.* ☛ *20 frs adults, 6 frs children 7-18.* ⊙ *Apr.–Sept., Wed.–Mon. 10–noon and 2–6; Oct.–Mar., Wed.–Mon. 10–noon and 2–5.*

51 Another architectural treat lies east of Châlons at **L'Epine,** where the twin-towered Flamboyant Gothic basilica of **Notre-Dame de l'Epine** dominates the tiny village. The ornament here, weaving intricate patterns over the facade and spires, seems effortless, while the interior exudes elegance and restraint. L'Epine is an ideal spot for lunch, especially if you eat outside at Aux Armes de Champagne (*see* Dining and Lodging, *below*).

D1 west of Epernay along the north bank of the Marne twists its way high above the river valley, providing the most spectacular views of the entire champagne region. It continues almost to **Château-Thierry,** birthplace of French fabulist Jean de La Fontaine (1621–95). Pay a visit to the ruined castle and old gateway, the Porte St-Pierre, through which Joan of Arc passed in 1429 after delivering the town from the English.

From here you can return to Paris on A4, or continue along the banks of the Marne to **Meaux,** site of another medieval cathedral.

What to See and Do with Children

The most obvious source of youthful amusement is found on the seaside, along the huge, sandy **beaches** that stretch from Calais to Le Touquet. The latter has a spectacular water-sports center, **Aqualud** (*see* Tour 1, *above*). Stop off at **Cap Gris-Nez,** as well, for a walk along the Channel cliffs. The **automated Métro** in Lille fascinates children with its tiny cars and no driver.

The marshy Bay of the Somme has two attractions to entice youthful visitors from nearby Abbeville. The first is the **Chemin de Fer de la Baie de Somme,** a steam railway that runs between Le Crotoy and St-Valéry-sur-Somme (☎ 22-26-96-96; tickets 54 frs adults, 42 frs children under 12; operates July–Aug., Tues., Wed., and weekends; May, June, and Sept., Sun. only). In 1994 the railway acquired the *130T* locomotive used during construction of the Panama Canal, owned by Detroit's Ford Museum until 1977. Just off D204 between St-Valéry and Cayeux is the **Maison de l'Oiseau,** with its collection of 400 stuffed birds and video presentation of their local habitat. *Carre-four du Hourdel,* ☎ *22-26-93-93.* ☛ *29 frs adults, 24 frs children 6–12.* ⊙ *Mar.–Nov., daily 10–6.*

Minitrain tour of the **Mercier** cellars, Epernay (Tour 2).

Centre Historique Minier (Mining Museum), Lewarde (Tour 1).

Musée de la Figurine (Toy Soldier Museum), Compiègne (Tour 2).

Off the Beaten Track

The cathedral town of **Beauvais,** 72 kilometers (45 miles) north of Paris on N1, still bears the painful scars of two world wars, and the ramshackle streets of the old town have been rebuilt as characterless modern blocks. One survivor is the beautiful old Bishop's Palace, now the **Musée Départemental de l'Oise,** where you'll find a varied collection of painting, ceramics, and regional furniture. Highlights include an epic canvas of the French Revolution by 19th-century master Thomas Couture, complete with preparatory sketches, and the charming attic under the sloping roofs, one of the loveliest rooms in all France. *1 rue du Musée,* ☎ *44–48–48–48.* ☛ *16 frs adults.* ☺ *Wed.–Mon. 10–noon and 2–6.*

★ The town's showpiece is unquestionably the **Cathédrale St-Pierre,** adjacent to the art museum. You may have an attack of vertigo just gazing up at its vaults, which, at 153 feet, are the highest in France. Such daring engineering was not without risk: The choir collapsed in 1284, shortly after completion. The transept, an outstanding example of Flamboyant Gothic, was not attempted until the 16th century. It was crowned by an improbable 450-foot spire that promptly came crashing down. With funds rapidly dwindling, the nave was never begun, delivering the final coup de grâce to Beauvais's ambition of becoming the largest church in Christendom. Experts now say the cathedral is starting to lean and worry about cracks that have appeared in the choir vaults. The 10th-century church, known as the **Basse Oeuvre** (closed to the public), juts out impertinently where the nave should have been. *Pl. St-Pierre,* ☎ *44–48–11–60.* ☺ *9–12:30 and 2–6.*

From 1664 to 1939, Beauvais was one of France's leading tapestry centers; it reached its zenith in the mid-18th century. The **Galerie Nationale de la Tapisserie,** a modern museum next to the cathedral, has examples from all periods. *1 rue St-Pierre,* ☎ *44–05–14–28.* ☛ *20 frs.* ☺ *Mar.–Oct., Tues.–Sun. 9:30–11:30 and 2:30–6; Nov.–Feb., Tues.–Sun. 10–11:30 and 2:30–4:30.*

Midway between the two regions covered in our Exploring section is **Cambrai,** a name the French associate with minty candies known as *bêtises.* Cambrai would be a typical northern French industrial town were it not for its white, chalky stone, a total contrast with the red brick so prevalent elsewhere. Showcasing that stone are age-old town gateways, such as the 14th-century Porte de Paris and the 17th-century Porte Notre-Dame, and three bell towers—those of St-Géry, the cathedral, and the former church of St-Martin. Above the sprawling main square looms the town hall's strange-looking cupola, flanked by an exotic pair of be-turbaned attendants who look as if they've just arrived from India.

★ Twenty-four kilometers (15 miles) east of Cambrai along N43 is **Le Cateau-Cambrésis.** Its most important building is the **Palais Fénelon,** former home to the archbishops of Cambrai and today a museum devoted to the artist Henri Matisse (1869–1954), born in Le Cateau. Along with a number of early oil paintings and sculptures, there is a superb collection of 50 drawings selected by Matisse himself and arranged in a carefully lit room on the second floor. The enthusiastic curator, Dominique Szymusiak, will show you around (her English is excellent). ☎ *27–84–13–15.* ☛ *16 frs adults, 4 frs children under 18.* ☺ *Wed.–Sat. and Mon., 10–noon and 2–6; Sun. 10–noon and 2:30–6. Free guided tour Sun. at 3.*

St-Quentin, just off the Calais–Reims expressway 24 kilometers (15 miles) south of Cambrai, has two claims to fame: its cathedral-size Gothic **Basilica** and the riotously sculpted facade of its 16th-century **Hôtel de Ville** (Town Hall). Make that three if you count one of the most famous restaurants in northern France—Le Président, in the Grand Hôtel (*see* Dining and Lodging, *below*).

Soissons lies 32 kilometers (20 miles) southwest of Laon along the Paris-bound N2. Not to be outdone, it, too, possesses a sizable Gothic cathedral, nearly 130 yards long. The interior, with its pure lines and restrained ornament, creates a more harmonious impression than does the asymmetrical, one-tower facade. The most remarkable feature, however, is the rounded, two-story transept, a feature more frequently found in the German Rhineland than in France.

SHOPPING

Northern France and shopping are intimately associated in the minds of many visitors, especially the English. The cross-channel ferry trip to Calais and Boulogne has become something of an institution, with one rather ignoble aim: to stock up on as much tax-free wine and beer as possible. You may see some travelers heading home to England astoundingly laden. You might want to consider local juniper-based *genièvre* brandy, which is a more original choice. Boulogne is famous for its kippers (smoked herring).

Arts and Crafts
Calais has long been renowned as a lace-making center. Lace shops still abound; try **La Dentellière** (30 blvd. de l'Egalité). Near Montreuil, the wickerwork tradition prevails at **Régis Quiénot** in Marlessur-Canche. For individual paintings on silk, visit **Claudine Decq** at La Calotterie, again near Montreuil. Wooden puppets are a specialty at Amiens, and glazed earthenware is part of St-Omer's historical heritage.

Antiques
Antiques dealers are legion; some of the best buys, though, can be made at the busy auction houses (*commissaires-priseurs*) at Douai, Lille, and Calais.

Champagne
You'll find the best buys at small producers in the villages along the Montagne de Reims between Reims and Epernay (not at Bouzy, though).

SPORTS AND THE OUTDOORS

Beaches and Water Sports
The northern French coast, from Calais to Le Touquet, is one long, sandy beach, known as the Côte d'Opale. The **Aqualud** complex on Le Touquet beach (blvd. Thierry-Sabine, ☎ 21–05–63–59) has slides, toboggans, a wave machine, sauna, and solarium.

Apart from ocean swimming (backed up by indoor and outdoor pools throughout the region), you may care to try speed sailing or handling a sand buggy, those windsurf-boards on wheels that race along the sands at up to 70 mph. Known as *Char à Voile*, the sport can be practiced at Le Touquet, Hardelot, Dunkerque, Bray-Dunes, and Berck-sur-Mer. For details, contact amiable Claude Wantier at the **Drakkars** club in Hardelot, south of Boulogne (☎ 21–91–81–96); the cost is 60–80 francs per hour.

Bicycling
Bicycles, well suited to the sea-level lowlands, can be rented from many train stations for around 40 francs a day. Get details of special circuits from the **Comité Départemental de Cyclotourisme** (75 rue Louis-Drouart, Les Ageux, 60700 Pont-Ste-Maxence). Mountain biking is also popular in the Noyon area; get in touch with **Patrick Drocourt** (8 bis ave. Alphonse-Chauvet, 60200 Compiègne, ☎ 44–76–40–49).

Golf

You'll find courses at Hardelot, Le Touquet (three courses), Wimereux, Lille, and Compiègne.

Horseback Riding

Horseback riding is possible in many places, including Hardelot (L'Eperon, ☎ 21–83–71–28) and St-Amand-les-Eaux (Centre Equestre du Parc Naturel, ☎ 27–48–56–62).

Parachuting

Sky-diving thrills can be had at Hardelot (☎ 21–91–81–86).

DINING AND LODGING

Dining

The cuisine of northern France is robust and hearty, like that of neighboring Belgium. Beer predominates and is often used as a base for sauces (notably for chicken). French fries and mussels are featured on most menus, and vans selling fries and hot dogs are a common sight. Great quantities of fish, notably herring, are eaten along the coast, while inland delicacies include *andouillettes* (chitterling sausages), tripe, and pâté made from duck, partridge, or woodcock. Smoked ham and, in season, boar and venison are specialties of the Ardennes. Be sure to sample the region's creamy cheeses: *Maroilles,* soft squares with a dark red rind; buttery, high-fat *Chaource*; and the one true *lait-cru* (raw-milk) *Brie de Meaux*—likely to astound Americans who think they know their Brie. Anyone with a sweet tooth will enjoy the region's ubiquitous macaroons and minty Cambrai bêtises. Ham, pigs' feet, gingerbread, and a champagne-based mustard are specialties of the Reims area, as is *ratafia,* a sweet aperitif made from grape juice and brandy. To the north, a glass of *genièvre* (a brandy made from juniper berries and sometimes added to black coffee to make a drink called a *bistoul*) is the typical way to conclude a good meal.

CATEGORY	COST*
$$$$	over 400 frs
$$$	250–400 frs
$$	125–250 frs
$	under 125 frs

*per person for a three-course meal, including tax (18.6%) and tip but not wine

Lodging

Northern France is overladen with old hotels, often rambling and simple, seldom pretentious. Good value is easier to come by than top quality, except in major cities (Amiens, Lille, and Reims) or at Le Touquet, whose Westminster Hotel numbers among the country's best.

CATEGORY	COST*
$$$$	over 800 frs
$$$	550–800 frs
$$	300–550 frs
$	under 300 frs

*All prices are for a standard double room for two, including tax (18.6%) and service charge.

Amiens

DINING

Joséphine. This unpretentious, good-value restaurant in central Amiens is a reliable choice. Solid fare, decent wines, and rustic decor (a bit on the stodgy side, like the sauces) pull in many foreign customers, notably the British. ✕ *20 rue Sire-Firmin-Leroux,* ☎ *22–91–47–38. Reservations advised in summer. AE, MC, V. Closed Sun. evening, Mon., and 3rd wk in Aug. $$*

Les Marissons. This restaurant, in the prettiest and oldest section of Amiens, near the cathedral, has been earning fine reviews thanks to chef Antoine Benoît's willingness to experiment with regional ingredients. Few of the burbot swimming in the Somme can ever have dreamed they would be cooked with apricots, for example; rabbit is accompanied by mint and goat cheese, while black currants add tang to the local pigeon. To avoid a pricey à la carte, try one of the three set menus. ✕ *68 rue des Marissons,* ☎ *22–92–96–66. Reservations advised. Jacket and tie. MC, V. Closed Mon., Sat. lunch, Sun. evening, and part of Jan. $$*

LODGING

Hôtel de la Paix. Near the Picardy Museum, the hotel is housed in a building that was reconstructed after World War II. Private parking and the view of a nearby church from some of the rooms offset a certain lack of personality, although the breakfast room tries valiantly to suggest an 18th-century Louis XV salon. Foreign visitors are frequent, and English is spoken. 🏠 *8 rue de la République, 80000,* ☎ *22–91–39–21,* FAX *22–92–02–65. 26 rooms, 11 with bath. Breakfast room. AE, MC, V. $*

Arras

DINING

La Faisanderie. This sumptuous restaurant, in a former stable, offers memorable variations on international fare: *pied de veau* (calf's foot), pike baked with frogs' legs, and lobster casserole are among the offerings. A loyal clientele supports its long-standing gastronomic reputation, so reserve in advance. ✕ *45 Grand'Place,* ☎ *21–48–20–76. Reservations required. Jacket and tie. Closed Sun. evening, Mon. AE, DC, MC, V. $$$*

La Rapière. This lively alternative to its posh neighbor, La Faisanderie, offers distinctly local dishes, such as andouillettes, poule à la bière, and tourte au Maroilles, as well as a broad range of specialties like escalope de veau au Camembert and foie gras maison, all in a casual setting. ✕ *44 Grand'Place,* ☎ *21–55–09–92. Closed Sun. evening. AE, MC, V. $*

LODGING

★ **Univers.** An 18th-century monastery has been converted into a stylish hotel with a pretty garden and a charming restaurant. Its central position and views of the courtyard and garden make it a favorite stopover. The interior has recently been modernized, but it retains its rustic provincial furniture. 🏠 *5 pl. de la Croix-Rouge, 62000,* ☎ *21–71–34–01,* FAX *21–71–41–42. 36 rooms, most with bath. Restaurant. AE, MC, V. Restaurant closed Sun. in Aug. $$*

Auvilliers-les-Forges

DINING AND LODGING

Hostellerie de Lenoir. Of the wonderful village inns that are the pleasure of France, this is a good example. Jean and Maryse Lenoir started in 1953 with a little bistro about 30 kilometers (19 miles) east of Vervins, and over the years it developed into a cozy, welcoming hotel, with a restaurant where guests linger in comfort over Jean's classic cooking. You'll see an occasional oddity on the menu, though—like fillet of sole with bean sprouts and soybean sauce—because Jean makes an annual trip to Asia. Guest rooms are smallish but comfy and warmly decorated with chintzes. ⌑ *Grand-Rue, 08260,* ☎ *24–54–30–11,* FAX *24–54–34–70. 18 rooms (15 with bath) and 3 suites. Restaurant (closed Thurs.) Closed Jan.–Feb. AE, DC, MC, V. $$*

Boulogne-sur-Mer

DINING

★ **Brasserie Liègeoise.** Good food spiced with delicious nouvelle touches helps this old, established restaurant remain at the top of the Boulogne eating scene. The decor is modern—an eccentric contrast of black and yellow—and so are the prices for both à la carte and set-menu meals. Chef Alain Delpierre justifies the cost with his delicate sauces and flair for seafood: Watch for the *menu poisson,* the list of available fish. ✕ *10 rue Monsigny,* ☎ *21–31–61–15. Reservations required on weekends. Jacket required. AE, DC, MC, V. Closed Wed., Sun. dinner, and second half of July. $$$*

DINING AND LODGING

Cléry. Eight kilometers (5 miles) inland from Boulogne, along N1, is the tiny village of Hesdin-l'Abbé, its 18th-century château now transformed into a stylish hotel. Extensive lawns, lined with tulips, rose beds, and an avenue of trees, create a favorable impression, enhanced by the entrance hall, with its old wooden staircase and wrought-iron banisters. As the vast price range indicates, each guest room is different; those in the former stables have been particularly well converted. It was here at the château that Napoléon decided to abandon his plans to invade England. As you bask in the peace and quiet of the beautiful grounds, you'll understand why. ⌑ *62360 Hesdin-l'Abbé,* ☎ *21–83–19–83,* FAX *21–87–52–59. 18 rooms with bath or shower. Breakfast room, tennis. AE, V. $$–$$$*

LODGING

Métropole. This small hotel is handy for ferry passengers, but like most of the Ville Basse (lower town), no great architectural shakes. While no exciting views are to be had from the rather faceless '50s building, there is a small garden (pleasant for breakfast in the summer) and the guest rooms are adequately furnished and individually decorated. There is no restaurant. ⌑ *51 rue Thiers, 62200,* ☎ *21–31–54–30,* FAX *21–30–45–72. 27 rooms, some with bath. AE, DC, MC, V. Closed Dec. 25 and Jan. 1. $$*

Calais

DINING

Sole Meunière. As its name ("sole fried in butter") suggests, the Sole Meunière is a temple of fish and seafood—not that anything else could be expected from a restaurant next to Calais Harbor! The good-value menus start at a very low price; the dining room's intimate decor is a medley of soft grays and pinks. ✕ *1 blvd. de la Résistance,* ☎ *21–34–43–01. Reservations advised. AE, DC, MC, V. Closed Mon. $–$$*

Châlons-sur-Marne

DINING AND LODGING

★ **Angleterre.** This stylish venue in central Châlons, close to the church of Notre-Dame-en-Vaux, has fully renovated rooms (most with marble bathrooms) and elaborate decor. Rooms in the back are quieter than those in the front. The restaurant, in particular, stands apart: The creations of chef Jacky Michel have reached new levels of inspiration and technical accomplishment. Watch for *blanc de turbot au Champagne*; veal kidneys in local Bouzy rouge; lobster salad in truffle vinaigrette; and *tout-pommes*, a dessert featuring five variations on the humble apple. Breakfast is a superb buffet. ⌸ *19 pl. Monseigneur-Tissier, 51000,* ☎ *26–68–21–51,* FAX *26–70–51–67. 19 rooms with bath or shower. AE, DC, MC, V. Closed Sun., Dec. 25., and second half of July. $$–$$$*

Charleville-Mézières

DINING

La Côte à l'Os. Although you can order lamb or steak if you wish, fish is the specialty here: Sea bass, marinated salmon, and braised pike with mushrooms often figure on the menu. Service is welcoming but low-key, and the long, cheerful dining room, decked out with fresh flowers, is popular with locals for its 79-franc lunchtime menu. ✕ *11 cours Aristide-Briand,* ☎ *24–59–20–16. Reservations recommended. Jacket required. AE, DC, MC, V. $$*

Compiègne

DINING AND LODGING

Rôtisserie du Chat qui Tourne. Three factors help this hotel stand out: It's central, it's cheap, and it has a silly name (The Cat That Turns the Spit). In fact, it's the epitome of the French provincial hotel. The rooms have creaky, uneven floors; metal plaques awarded by long-gone guidebooks adorn the wonky facade, erected in 1665; the prim *patronne,* Mme. Robert, appears from nowhere as you cross the threshold, with all the officious alacrity of a Paris concierge. The restaurant, with its brass wall lights and plush curtains, tries vainly to resemble an antechamber from the nearby palace as blasé waiters potter around, failing to be discreet. But it also has charm, not all of it faded. Valiant efforts have been made to modernize the bathrooms (new showers and retiled walls), and although you should avoid the smaller bedrooms, some rooms can sleep four and are ideal for families with young children. Modern pictures line the staircase. The cuisine is inventive (braised turbot, scallops in crab sauce, duck with figs) and the 128-franc and 210-franc menus copious (avoid the skimpy 89-franc lunchtime menu). ⌸ *17 rue Eugène-Floquet, 60200,* ☎ *44–40–02–74,* FAX *44–40–48–37. 21 rooms, some with bath or shower. Bar. MC, V. $$*

Epernay

DINING AND LODGING

La Briqueterie. Epernay has a severe lack of good lodging, but just outside town toward the village of Vinay stands a very commodious hotel, set in large, pretty grounds. The owners, Catherine and Georges Guillon, have taken a modern rustic approach, decorating with lots of wood, luxury, and comfort. The bedrooms are quite spacious and furnished in modern style with marble bathrooms. Choose one overlooking the garden. The cooking is a mix of classical and neoclassical, with such creations as *navarin de turbot et langoustines* (stew of turbot and Dublin Bay prawns) and *aiguillettes de pintade* (thin slices of guinea fowl in a wine sauce). ⌸ *4 rte. de Sézanne, 51530 Vinay,* ☎ *26–59–99–99,* FAX *26–59–92–10. 40 rooms with bath. Restaurant, pool, sauna. Closed Christmastime. AE, DC, MC, V. $$$*

L'Epine

DINING AND LODGING

★ **Aux Armes de Champagne.** Just opposite the sumptuous facade of Notre-Dame de l'Epine, 10 kilometers (6 miles) east of Châlons, this cozy coaching inn, with solid, traditional furniture (ask for Room 21 with its wooden beams), is renowned for Patrick Michelon's imaginative, and often spectacular, cuisine. Try his delicate rabbit terrine, veal with braised lettuce, or grilled sole and lobster with artichokes. ⌖ *Pl. de la Basilique, 51460,* ☎ *26–69–30–30,* FAX *26–66–92–31. 39 rooms with bath. MC, V. Closed Jan. and Sun. evening, Mon. out of season. $$–$$$*

Laon

DINING

La Petite Auberge. Young chef Willy-Marc Zorn dishes up modern, imaginative cuisine at this 18th-century-style restaurant close to the train station in Laon's Ville Basse. Try his hare stew or salmon with pigs' feet. The recherché 160-franc menu is a good bet, as à la carte prices continue to climb. Those in search of inexpensive fare can have a satisfying meal in the adjoining wine bar, **Le Saint-Amour,** where good steaks and local andouillettes accompany a staggering variety of wines. ✕ *45 blvd. Pierre-Brossolette,* ☎ *23–23–02–38. Reservations advised. AE, DC, MC, V. $$*

DINING AND LODGING

Bannière de France. In business since 1685, the old-fashioned, uneven-floored Bannière de France is just five minutes' walk from Laon's picturesque cathedral and the medieval Ville Haute (upper town). Madame Lefèvre, the *patronne,* speaks fluent German and English. The guest rooms are cozy and quaintly decorated, and the restaurant's venerable dining room features sturdy cuisine (trout, guinea fowl, lemon sole à la Normande) and good-value menus. ⌖ *11 rue Franklin-Roosevelt, 02000,* ☎ *and fax 23–23–21–44. 18 rooms, a few with bath or shower. Restaurant. AE, DC, MC, V. Closed Dec. 25 and Jan. 1; restaurant closed Dec. 20–Jan. 20. $$*

Lille

DINING

L'Huîtrière. Behind a magnificent Art Deco fish shop, you'll find an elegant seafood restaurant offering that rarity of rarities: fresh, local seafood, simply prepared in regional (Flemish) style—turbot hollandaise, *waterzooie* (a mild, creamy fish stew), and, of course, oysters from La Manche. The clientele is chic, well heeled; the decor sumptuous, with waxed oak, linens, and elaborate china; and prices are justifiably high. ✕ *3 rue des Chats-Bossus,* ☎ *22–55–43–41. Reservations advised. Jacket and tie. Closed Sun. evening. $$$*

Le Hochepot. Just two blocks from the Place de Gaulle, this is a cozy, old-fashioned source of simple, homey regional food, much of it cooked in (and served with) locally made beer. ✕ *6 pl. Mendès-France,* ☎ *20–54–17–59. Reservations suggested. Closed Sat. noon, Sun. $$*

LODGING

Bellevue. This central, elegant prewar hotel has many large, comfortable Art Deco rooms, impeccably modern baths, and the sort of deferential service you can no longer take for granted. It's favored by British travelers and has a leather-lined *bar américain.* ⌖ *5 rue Jean-Roisin, 59800,* ☎ *20–57–45–64,* FAX *20–40–07–93. 80 rooms, most with bath. Bar. AE, MC, V. $$*

Montreuil Sur Mer

DINING AND LODGING

Château de Montreuil. It's worth coming to Montreuil just to stay at this former manor house facing the citadelle, a member of the Relais & Châteaux group. Its decor has a personality of its own—a clublike atmosphere that makes you feel you belong. The owner, Lindsay Germain, spent many years in England, including a few as a head chef, and his cooking demonstrates that excellent food should not be pretentious, nor pursue the visual at the cost of the taste. Bringing out the natural flavor is his forte. For example, the scallops lightly sautéed and served with *pompadour* (a special variety of potato) and the lamb chops with a glazing of wine sauce are simple perfections. The wine list, too, is commendable, especially for its broad selection of half bottles. The guest rooms are furnished with 18th- and 19th-century antiques, and details, like lights for reading in bed, are given attention. Room 208 is a choice room, looking onto the garden, with a large sitting area. Bathrooms are luxurious. The splendid breakfasts, with freshly squeezed juices and home-baked breads, are wheeled into your room. The less expensive rooms, in the converted stables, are pleasantly furnished but smaller. ⊞ *4 Chaussée des Capucins, 62170 Montreuil,* ☎ *21–81–53–04,* FAX *21–81–36–43. 12 rooms and 1 suite, all with bath. Restaurant (closed Thurs.). Closed mid-Dec.–Feb. $$$*

Noyon
LODGING
St-Eloi. Under new ownership, this downtown institution underwent a complete transformation, reducing its capacity in order to expand its rooms and include new baths in all. Several rooms have garden views, and the restaurant still offers affordable menus. It's handily located between the station and the cathedral. ⊞ *81 blvd. Carnot, 60400,* ☎ *44–44–01–49,* FAX *44–09–20–90. 17 rooms with bath. Restaurant, bar. MC, V. Closed Dec. 25; restaurant closed Sun. dinner. $$*

Pierrefonds
DINING AND LODGING
Etrangers. An attractive lakeside terrace, château views, and a welcoming restaurant make this an ideal stopping place beneath the mighty castle of Pierrefonds. The three-story hotel was recently modernized, although it still lacks an elevator; American and English visitors are frequent. In the restaurant watch for monkfish in blueberries and slow-cooked veal-kidney casserole. Menus begin at 95 francs. ⊞ *10 rue Beaudon, 60350,* ☎ *44–42–80–18,* FAX *44–42–86–74. 18 rooms, 10 with bath. Restaurant (closed Sun. dinner and Mon. mid-Nov.–mid-Mar.), horseback riding, bicycles. AE, DC, MC, V. $–$$*

Reims
DINING AND LODGING
★ **Boyer.** Gérard Boyer, justifiably one of the country's most highly rated chefs, continues to produce gasps of appreciation for the simplicity of his highly personal preparations, from wild mushrooms in cream or scallops with endive confit to grilled St-Pierre (John Dory) or oysters with turbot. The extensive wine list, with more than 100 selections, pays homage to Reims's champagne heritage. The small bar is sometimes very crowded, but the veranda extension to the dining room is delightful. The building is magnificent, too: a 19th-century château surrounded by an extensive, well-tended park. The decor is opulent, typified by ornate chandeliers, towering ceilings, gilt mirrors, intricate cornices, and glossy paneling. There are 19 luxurious suites as well, which have wonderful views of the park from their bay windows. ⊞ *Les Crayères, 64 blvd. Henry-Vasnier,* ☎ *26–82–80–80,* FAX *26–82–65–52. 19 rooms. Restaurant (reservations required, jacket and tie, closed Mon., Tues. lunch, and Dec. 25–Jan. 1), indoor pool. AE, DC, MC, V. $$$$*

Gambetta. Attracting foreign visitors for its successful restaurant, the Vonnelly, as well as its central location by the cathedral, this modest, comfortable establishment offers simple rooms with all the creature comforts and a dinner menu with specialties like duck in fig vinegar, fillet of sea bream in a zesty sauce and vegetables perfumed with anise, the wonderful pear soufflé with strawberry sherbet, and crème brûlée with lime. The guest rooms are small and somewhat featureless but clean and acceptable for the very reasonable price. ☎ *9 rue Gambetta, 51000,* ☎ *26–47–41–64,* FAX *26–47–22–43. 14 rooms with bath. Restaurant (closed Sun. dinner and Mon.). AE, MC, V. $*

DINING

Florence. This elegant, well-run restaurant occupies a high-ceilinged mansion where pictures and tapestries festoon the walls. Chef Laurent Helleu serves wonderfully light versions of the classical French repertoire as well as some creations of his own: Try the rouget with orange and fennel or John Dory with truffles and leeks. Prices have risen, but the weekday menu remains a good value. ✗ *43 blvd. Foch,* ☎ *26–47–12–70. Reservations advised. Jacket required. AE, DC, MC, V. Closed most of Aug. $$$*

★ **Le Vigneron.** This friendly little brasserie in a 17th-century mansion is cozy and cheerful, with two tiny dining rooms that display a jumble of champagne-related paraphernalia—from old advertising posters to venerable barrels and tools of the trade. The food is delightful as well: relatively cheap, distinctly hearty, and prepared with finesse. Try the pigs' feet or *andouillettes* (chitterling sausages), and be sure to slather on lots of Reims's delicious mustard made with champagne. ✗ *Pl. Paul-Jamot,* ☎ *26–47–00–71. Reservations advised. MC, V. Closed Sat. lunch, Sun., Dec. 25–Jan. 1, and most of Aug. $$*

LODGING

Hôtel de la Paix. A modern, eight-story hotel, 10 minutes' walk from the cathedral, La Paix boasts stylish rooms, plus a pretty garden, swimming pool, and a rather incongruous chapel. Its brasserie-style restaurant, Drouet, serves good, though not inexpensive, cuisine (mainly grilled meats and seafood). The breakfasts are generous. ☎ *9 rue de Buirette, 51000,* ☎ *26–40–04–08,* FAX *26–47–75–04. 105 rooms with bath. Restaurant, bar, pool. AE, DC, MC, V. Restaurant closed Sun. $$*

St-Omer

DINING

Le Cygne. Duck breast (*magret de canard*), not swan, tops the menu at Le Cygne, in the old section of St-Omer near the cathedral. There are two menus—one three-course, the other four-course. Traditional, regional cooking holds sway—nothing fancy, but honest fare from hot duck sausage to smoked salmon with strips of trout. Be sure to try the local Olivier cheeses. ✗ *8 rue Caventou,* ☎ *21–98–20–52. Reservations accepted. MC, V. Closed Tues., Sat. lunch, and Dec. 25–Jan. 20. $$*

DINING AND LODGING

★ **Moulin de Mombreux.** Huge cogs and waterwheels, skillfully integrated into the decor, reflect the 18th-century watermill origins of the Moulin, west of St-Omer at Lumbres. Jean-Marc Gaudry has hoisted these old premises into the top league with his tasteful renovation and even tastier cuisine. Try his poached oysters in fennel, lamb in foie gras sauce, and raspberry soufflé. There are three set menus, with wine included. Silver candlesticks and original wooden beams lend the dining room atmosphere. Guest rooms occupy the second floor and an annex across the grounds, where the discreet if unoriginal charm in pastel shades is augmented by a spacious breakfast room, with large windows and wicker chairs. ☎ *62380 Lumbres,* ☎ *21–39–62–44,* FAX *21–93–61–34. 30 rooms with bath. Restaurant. AE, DC, MC, V. Closed Dec. 25–Jan. 1. $$$*

St-Quentin

DINING AND LODGING

★ **Grand.** After undergoing head-to-toe restoration, the Grand Hôtel hopes to underline its status as the best hotel in town. Its restaurant, Le Président, already has a reputation as one of the finest in northern France, with elegant decor and a highly rated new chef, Jean-Marc Le Guénnec, trained by the legendary Parisian Joël Robuchon. His gastronomic creations—roast pigeon with artichoke, for instance—don't come cheap, but there is also a less expensive menu available. ☎ *6 rue Dachery, 02100,* ☎ *23–62–69–77. 26 rooms with bath. AE, DC, MC, V. Closed Aug. and Dec. 25–Jan. 1. Restaurant closed Sat. lunch and Sun. $$$*

Sedan

DINING AND LODGING

L'Europe. Rather than brave the narrow, one-way streets of central Sedan, you will find it more convenient to stay at this modern hotel by the train station on the outskirts of the town. Rooms are clean, comfortable, soundproof, and a little characterless. The spacious bar is a fine place to unwind with an aperitif before dining on boar or venison (in season) at the hotel restaurant. ☎ *2 pl. de la Gare, 08200,* ☎ *24–27–18–71,* FAX *24–29–32–00. 24 rooms with bath or shower. Restaurant (closed Sun. dinner), bar. Closed Dec. 25–Jan. 1. AE, DC, MC, V. $*

Sept Saulx

DINING AND LODGING

Le Cheval Blanc. This hotel, in a small village just south of Reims with easy access to the autoroute, is a popular stop for the British en route to Burgundy. Each of five generations of the Robert family has added to this hospitable, cheery inn, and the accommodations are now across the road in a parklike setting on the small River Vesle—a delightful place for families to relax, with swings for kids and tennis. Some rooms are quite small, but opening the French doors onto the garden helps. Some refurbishment of the carpets and draperies is in order. The newer suites, in a renovated house near the river, are larger and are furnished with a romantic blend of modern design that goes well with the elements of the original building. Dinner is elaborate and well presented, though perhaps not worth a detour. Even so, the *escargot* and *champignon* (snail and mushroom) salad is a treat, and the *pintade* (roast pigeon) with plum sauce is flavorful. Service is smart and friendly. ☎ *Rue du Moulin, 51400 Sept–Saulx,* ☎ *26–03–90–27,* FAX *26–03–97–09. 25 rooms with bath. Restaurant, tennis, fishing. MC, V. Closed mid-Jan.–mid-Feb. $$–$$$*

Le Touquet

DINING

Flavio. Fish is the star at this elegant spot near the casino. Chef Guy Delmotte specializes in lobster and charges aficionados-only prices for his lobster menu. The other two menus will please most (wine is included in the 190-franc weekday carte). Cut glass and Oriental carpets add an appropriate note of dated glamour. ✕ *2 av. du Verger,* ☎ *21–05–10–22. Reservations required except weekday lunch. Jacket and tie. AE, DC, MC, V. Closed Mon. in low season. $$$*

DINING AND LODGING

★ **Westminster.** The Westminster's mammoth redbrick facade looks as if it were built just a few years ago; in fact, it dates from the 1930s and, like the rest of the hotel, has been extensively restored by its new owners, the personable Flament brothers. The hotel offers a modestly priced coffee bar (serving lunch and dinner), a swanky dining room (classic but well-prepared French cuisine), and an "American bar" that serves cocktails for around 50 francs. The enormous double rooms represent good value, and the bridal suite is the last word in thick-carpeted extravagance. ☎ *Av. du Verger, 62520,* ☎ *21–05–48–48,* FAX *21–05–45–45. 115 rooms with bath. Restaurants, bar, indoor pool, hot tub, sauna, solarium, squash. AE, DC, MC, V. $$$*

Vervins

DINING AND LODGING

La Tour du Roy. This converted manor house, built of stone from the ramparts of the small town, is run by garrulous Claude Desvignes, who rattles away amusingly in English. While he acts as the host, his wife, Annie, holds sway in the kitchen; an excellent cook, she is one of the few female Michelin-starred chefs. Her cooking is classical, with emphasis on the local produce of the region and such dishes as turbot with sorrel. Try the *flamiche aux poireaux* (puff pastry tart with cream and leeks). The rooms have recently been refurbished and all display the character of the owners: a blend of the traditional and the modern. One choice room has a private roof terrace. ☎ *45 rue du Général-Leclerc, 02140,* ☎ *23–98–00–11,* FAX *23–98–00–72. 12 rooms, 3 suites, all with bath. Restaurant. Restaurant closed Sun. dinner and Mon. lunch Dec.–Feb. AE, DC, MC, V. $$*

THE ARTS AND NIGHTLIFE

The Arts

Lille is the hub of cultural activity in northern France—lively and exotic happenings can take place at any time (a recital of traditional music by Tibetan monks, for example). There are various local fairs, notably the **Dunkerque Carnival** in January, the **Roses Festival** in Arras in May, and the **Grande Braderie** in Lille and the **Kermesse de la Bêtise** festival in Cambrai in early September.

Theater

Théâtre d'Animation Picard in Amiens (theatre, rue Edouard David; ticket information, 24 rue St-Leu, ☎ 22–92–42–06) presents a rare glimpse of the traditional Picardy Marionettes. Shows take place on weekends in French, with plot synopses in English.

Concerts

The **Orchestre National de Lille** is a well-respected symphony orchestra (3 pl. Mendès-France, ☎ 20–54–67–00).

Opera

Lille boasts one of France's few regional opera houses, the **Opéra du Nord** (pl. du Théâtre, ☎ 20–55–48–61).

Nightlife

Bars

We suggest **Solitaire Club** (188 rue Riolan, ☎ 22–91–61–40) in Amiens; **Cave du Vieux Lille** (55 rue Basse, ☎ 20–06–61–31) in Lille; and **La Boîte à Cocktails** (6 pl. au Forum, ☎ 26–47–56–58) in Reims. In Amiens, there's music and a waterfront terrace at **La Lune des Pirates** (17 quai Bélu, ☎ 22–97–88–47).

Nightclub

Try **Croque-Notes** (24 rue Ernest-Renan, ☎ 26–88–41–28) in Reims.

Casinos
Gamblers should head for the casinos at **Berck-Plage** (☏ 21–84–09–39), **Boulogne** (☏ 21–83–88–00), **Calais** (☏ 21–34–64–18), and **Dunkerque** (☏ 28–59–18–23).

Discos
Good bets include **Cosy Club** (25 rue de l'Hôpital) in Epernay, **La Renardière** (227 blvd. Victor-Hugo, ☏ 20–57–03–46), **Le Crypton** (32 pl. Louise de Bettignies, ☏ 20–06–58–33), and **Le Pirogue** (16 rue Jean-Jacques Rousseau, ☏ 20–31–70–82) in Lille, and **L'Echiquier** (110 av. Jean-Jaurès, ☏ 20–30–62–62) in Reims.

THE NORTH AND CHAMPAGNE ESSENTIALS

Arriving and Departing

By Plane
American visitors should count on arriving at Paris's Charles de Gaulle or Orly airport; there are direct flights from London's Heathrow to Lille and from Gatwick to Beauvais.

By Car
The A1 expressway from Paris passes close to Compiègne (N32 heads off to Noyon) and Arras (where the A26 branches off to Calais) before reaching Lille, where there are expressways to Brussels (E42) and Ghent (E3). British drivers arriving via the Chunnel disembark at Coquelles, near Calais.

By Train
TGV trains whistle from Paris to Lille (256 kilometers, or 160 miles) in just one hour. A separate TGV service links Paris to Arras (50 mins) and Dunkerque (2 hrs). The Paris–Calais train chugs unhurriedly around the coast, taking nearly three hours to cover 300 kilometers (190 miles) and stopping at Amiens, Abbeville, Etaples (bus link to Le Touquet 6½ kilometers, or 4 miles, away), Montreuil-sur-Mer, and Boulogne. There is frequent daily service from Paris to Compiègne and Noyon. The train from the Gare du Nord to Laon takes two leisurely hours to cover 140 kilometers (90 miles). Regular trains cover the 175 kilometers (110 miles) from Paris (Gare de l'Est) to Reims in 1½ hours, continuing to Charleville and Sedan. TGV trains link London to Lille in 2 hours.

Getting Around

By Plane
There are domestic airports at Le Touquet, Calais, and Reims.

By Car
A26 heads inland from Calais and St-Omer to Arras (where it intersects with A1), Laon, and Reims, which is directly linked to Paris by A4. N1 follows the railroad around the coast from Belgium and Dunkerque through Calais, Boulogne, Montreuil-sur-Mer, Amiens, and Beauvais to Paris.

By Train
The branch line between Lille and Calais stops at St-Omer. Trains run daily, though slowly, from Amiens to Reims by way of Laon.

Guided Tours

Bus Excursions

The main tourist office in Lille (pl. Rihour, ☎ 20–30–81–00) is a mine of information about companies that offer bus tours of northern France. **Loisirs-Accueil Nord** (15 rue du Nouveau-Siècle, Lille, ☎ 20–54–88–73) offers bus trips to Boulogne and Flanders.

Special-Interest

Loisirs-Accueil Nord (*see above*) specializes in outdoor pursuits and can arrange fishing and walking tours. It also provides beer-tasting tours.

Personal Guides

Renaissance du Vieux Boulogne (rue Bernet, Boulogne-sur-Mer, ☎ 21–92–11–52) arranges trips to Boulogne's old town and port for groups of up to four; the cost for two hours is 330 francs.

Important Addresses and Numbers

Travel Agencies

Wagons Lits, (1 rue Paul-Bert, Calais, ☎ 21–34–79–25; and 74 bis rue Nationale, Lille, ☎ 20–57–72–45).

Car Rental

Avis (36 pl. d'Armes, Calais, ☎ 21–34–66–50; Calais car ferry terminal, ☎ 21–96–47–65; Calais Hoverport, ☎ 21–96–66–52; Cour de la Gare, Reims, ☎ 26–47–10–08), **Europcar** (32 pl. de la Gare, Lille, ☎ 20–06–18–80), and **Hertz** (5 blvd. d'Alsace-Lorraine, Amiens, ☎ 22–91–26–24; 10 blvd. Daunou, Boulogne, ☎ 21–31–53–14).

Visitor Information

The principal regional tourist offices are in **Lille** (pl. Rihour, ☎ 20–30–81–00), **Reims** (2 rue Guillaume-de-Machault, ☎ 26–77–45–25), and **Amiens** (20 pl. Notre-Dame, ☎ 22–91–16–16). The addresses of other tourist offices in towns mentioned on this tour are as follows: **Abbeville** (1 pl. de l'Amiral-Courbet, ☎ 22–24–27–92), **Arras** (pl. des Héros, ☎ 21–51–26–95), **Beauvais** (1 rue Beauregard, ☎ 44–45–08–18), **Boulogne** (Forum Jean-Noël, quai de la Poste, ☎ 21–31–68–38), **Calais** (12 blvd. Clemenceau, ☎ 21–96–62–40), **Charleville-Mézières** (22 pl. Ducale, ☎ 24–56–06–08), **Compiègne** (pl. de l'Hôtel-de-Ville, ☎ 44–40–01–00), **Laon** (pl. du Parvis, ☎ 23–20–28–62), **Montreuil-sur-Mer** (pl. Darnétal, ☎ 21–06–04–27), **Le Touquet** (Palais de l'Europe, pl. de l'Hermitage, ☎ 21–05–21–65), **Noyon** (pl. de l'Hôtel-de-Ville, ☎ 44–44–21–88), **Pierrefonds** (rue Louis-d'Orléans, ☎ 44–42–81–44), **St-Omer** (pl. Paul-Painlevé, ☎ 21–98–08–51), and **Sedan** (pl. du Château, ☎ 24–27–73–73).

8 Alsace and Lorraine

Strasbourg, Nancy, and Franche-Comté

THOUGH THE NAMES "Alsace" and "Lorraine" to this day are often linked, the two regions, long distinct geologically and politically, have always had strong individual cultures, cuisines, and architectural styles. Only their recent past ties them together: In 1871, after France's defeat in the Franco-Prussian War, Alsace and Lorraine, sutured together by Kaiser Wilhelm I, were ceded to Germany as part of the spoils of war. The region was systematically (but unsuccessfully) teutonized, and two generations grew up culturally torn—until 1919, when, after World War I, France reclaimed the territory.

But no matter how forcefully the French tout its Frenchness, Alsace's German roots go deeper than the late 19th century, as one look at its storybook medieval architecture will prove. In fact, this strip of flatland and vine-covered hills squeezed between the Rhine and the Vosges mountains was called Prima Germania by the Romans and belonged to the fiercely German Holy Roman Empire for more than 700 years. A heavy German influence is still evident. Regional dialect is widespread; conversations between locals are incomprehensible even to most Frenchmen; town names look German; and the main daily paper, *Les Dernières Nouvelles d'Alsace,* is published in both languages.

The prettiest parts of Alsace are the vineyards that nestle amid the Vosges foothills. The Route du Vin (Wine Road) weaves its way through flower-strewn villages with medieval towers, walls, and houses built in the unmistakable red Vosges sandstone. The pointed, half-timbered houses, ornate wells and fountains, oriels, and carved-wood balustrades would serve well on a film set for William Tell. Noble storks flutter overhead; their large, distinctive nests crown the spires of church towers. Strasbourg, the capital and unofficial "capital" of Europe—and the symbol of Franco-German reconciliation—is a city of great cultural, historic, and architectural interest, perhaps France's most fascinating outside Paris. And throughout Alsace, hotels are well scrubbed, with tiled bathrooms, good mattresses, and geraniums spilling from every windowsill. Sauerkraut, foie gras, and tobacco are among the region's specialties, and though France's major breweries are here, Alsace is more famous for its white wine, named not by locality but by grape variety.

Lorraine, west of the Vosges, creased by the cheerful Moselle Valley, evolved as decidedly less German than its neighbor. It served French and Burgundian lords as well as the Holy Roman Empire, coming into its own under the powerful Dukes of Lorraine in the Middle Ages and the Renaissance. The present-day decline of the steel and coal industries and the miseries of its small farmers have left much of it tarnished and neglected—or, some might say, unspoiled. At its heart is majestic Nancy, a city of great appeal imbued with medieval, classical, and Art Nouveau elegance. And the rich, rolling countryside is dotted with orchards of the yellow, plumlike mirabelle and with crumbling stucco villages, abbeys, fortresses, and historic towns. It is the home of Baccarat and St-Louis crystal, the birthplace of Joan of Arc, Gregorian chant, and Art Nouveau. Yes, it lacks the Teutonic comforts of Alsace, subscribing to the more Latin laissez-faire school of innkeeping (concave mattresses, dusty bolsters, creaky floors), but it serves its regional delicacies with flair: *tourte Lorraine* (a pork and beef pie), madeleines, mirabelles, and the famous quiche Lorraine.

In the Jura–Franche Comté region to the south, the Jura Mountains form a natural border more than 100 miles long between France and

Switzerland and provide a winter-sports alternative to the Alps. Birthplace of Louis Pasteur and Victor Hugo and home to the celebrated aperitif, Pernod, the Jura is dotted with pretty little towns where local craftsmen still make wooden toys, clocks, and pipes. The area is renowned for its wine and cheese, and for a cuisine that draws on the plentiful local lake and river fish—especially trout.

EXPLORING

Orientation

Our tour begins in Strasbourg, a city of such historic and cultural importance that it is well worth exploring in detail. From here, our second tour takes you through the rest of Alsace, south through the charming villages along the Route du Vin (Wine Road) to Mulhouse. The third tour covers the region of Lorraine, with a thorough look at the artistic town of Nancy and the battlegrounds of Verdun. Tour 4 heads south to Belfort, Besançon, and the spectacular scenery of Franche-Comté and the Jura.

Tour 1: Strasbourg

Numbers in the margin correspond to points of interest on the Alsace and Strasbourg maps.

① **Strasbourg** is perhaps the most interesting and attractive French city after Paris—an irresistible mixture of old houses; waterways; museums; the European Parliament; and, looming above them all, the colossal single spire of the cathedral.

The Romans knew Strasbourg as Argentoratum before it came to be known as Strateburgum, or city of (cross) roads. After centuries as part of the Germanic Holy Roman Empire, the city was united with France in 1681, but retained independence regarding legislation, education, and religion under the honorific title Free Royal City. Since World War II, Strasbourg has become a symbolic city, embodying Franco-German reconciliation and the wider idea of a united Europe. It plays host to the European Parliament and Council of Europe and acts as a neutral stamping ground for controversial political figures.

If you're approaching by car, follow signs to the "centre" and "cathédrale" and park in the garage under place Gutenberg, near all the central sights. At the hub of Strasbourg, on place de la Cathédrale, is the ★ **②** **Cathédrale Notre-Dame,** with its splendid openwork spire. Pink masonry covers the ornately sculpted facade—a triumph of gothic art, completed in 1284. Not content with the outlines of the walls themselves, medieval builders stuck huge, slender, rodlike shafts of stone everywhere: You feel as if you can reach up and snap one off. The spire, finished in 1439, looks absurdly fragile as it tapers skyward like some elongated, 466-foot wedding cake.

The interior presents a stark contrast to the facade. For a start, it is older, virtually finished by 1275. Then, the nave's broad windows emphasize the horizontal rather than the vertical. Note Hans Hammer's ornately sculpted pulpit (1484–86), with its 50 statuettes, and the richly painted 14th- to 15th-century organ loft that rises from pillar to ceiling. The choir is not ablaze with stained glass, but framed by chunky masonry, the original brickwork of the cupola visible, as if no one had ever gotten around to decorating it. The fact that the choir is raised

248

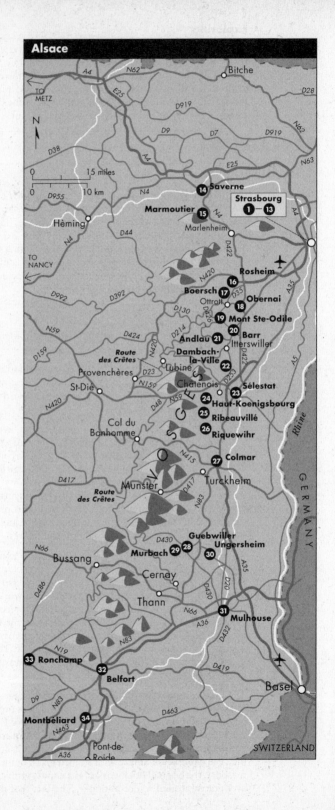

Alsace

TO METZ

TO NANCY

N

0 — 15 miles
0 — 10 km

Bitche

Saverne **14**

Strasbourg **1** — **13**

Marmoutier **15**
Marlenheim

Hèming

Rosheim

Boersch **16** **17**
Ottrott **18** Obernai
19 Mont Ste-Odile
20 Barr
Andlau **21** Itterswiller
Dambach-la-Ville
Lubine **22**
Chatenois **23** Sélestat
Provenchères **24** Haut-Koenigsbourg
St-Dié **25** Ribeauvillé
26 Riquewihr

Route des Crêtes

Col du Bonhomme

27 Colmar
Munster
Route des Crêtes
Turckheim

Guebwiller
Ungersheim
Murbach **29** **28**
Bussang **30**
Cernay
Thann
31 Mulhouse

Ronchamp **33** **32**
Belfort

Montbéliard **34**

Pont-de-Roide

GERMANY

Rhine

Basel

SWITZERLAND

Strasbourg

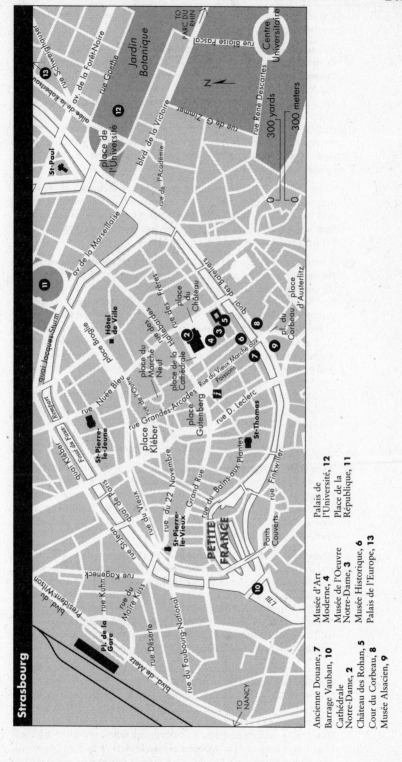

Ancienne Douane, **7**
Barrage Vauban, **10**
Cathédrale
Notre-Dame, **2**
Château des Rohan, **5**
Cour du Corbeau, **8**
Musée Alsacien, **9**

Musée d'Art
Moderne, **4**
Musée de l'Oeuvre
Notre-Dame, **3**
Musée Historique, **6**
Palais de l'Europe, **13**

Palais de
l'Université, **12**
Place de la
République, **11**

above the level of the rest of the church reinforces an aura of murky mystical sanctity.

The elaborate 16th-century **Chapelle St-Laurent,** to the left of the choir, merits a visit, but most visitors turn to the right to admire the **Angels' Column,** an intricate pillar dating from 1230, formed by clustering, tube-like colonnettes harboring three tiers of delicate statues. Nearby, the daring Renaissance machinery of the 16th-century **Astronomical Clock** whirs into action at 12:30 PM daily: Macabre clockwork figures—including a skeletal Father Time and the screeching rooster that reminds the Apostle Peter of his broken promise—enact the story of Christ's Passion. *Visit to clock at performance time: 5 frs. Entrance daily at noon by south door; line forms from 11:45 on.*

There is a *son-et-lumière* (sound-and-light) performance in the cathedral every evening from April through the end of September. The text is in French or German, but virtuoso lighting effects translate into any language. ☛ *29 frs adults, 16 frs children under 18. Performances at 8:15 PM in German and 9:15 PM in French.*

③ A worthy complement to the cathedral is the **Musée de l'Oeuvre Notre-Dame,** opposite the south front. There is more to this museum than the usual assembly of dilapidated statues rescued from the local cathedral before they fell off. A conscious effort has been made to create a church atmosphere and to provide an appropriate setting for the works of art. Part of one room evokes a narrow, low-roofed cloister. A dimly lit, high-walled chamber, reached through a creaky wooden door, is ringed by stone screens with pinnacles and pointed gables. Soon you'll find yourself in the stonemasons' workshop. A polished wooden staircase leads to a suite of small passages and large rooms, with drawings, stained glass, and gold objects. All the architectural elements of the Renaissance—pediments, spiral pillars, and cornices—can be found on the bulky wardrobes and cupboards produced by local cabinetmakers. *3 pl. du Château,* ☎ *88–32–88–17.* ☛ *15 frs adults, 8 frs students and children.* ☉ *Tues.–Sun. 10–noon and 1:30–6, Sun. 10–5.*

④ Next door the **Musée d'Art Moderne** features high-quality temporary expositions of new esoteric and unsung modern art, and its permanent collection ranges from the Impressionists to postwar abstract painters. Native son Jean Arp, the Dadaist, is prominently featured. *5 pl. du Château,* ☎ *88–52–50–00.* ☛ *15 frs adults, 8 frs children.* ☉ *Wed.–Mon. 10–noon and 1:30–6.*

⑤ Alongside the Musée de l'Oeuvre Notre-Dame, between the cathedral and the river, is the **Château des Rohan,** onetime palace of the powerful Rohans, a dynasty of prince-bishops who held both political and spiritual sway over the city and region. While the exterior of Robert de Cotte's neoclassical building (1732–42) is starkly austere, the glamour is inside, in Robert le Lorrain's magnificent ground-floor rooms, led by the great **Salon d'Assemblée** (Assembly Room) and the book- and tapestry-lined **Bibliothèque des Cardinaux** (Cardinals' Library).

The library leads to a series of less august rooms that house the **Musée des Arts Décoratifs** (Decorative Arts Museum) and its elaborate display of ceramics. Works by Hannong, a porcelain manufacturer active in Strasbourg from 1721 to 1782, are comprehensively represented; dinner services by other local kilns reveal the influence of Chinese porcelain in their delicate patterns. Furniture, tapestries, and silver-gilt complete the collection. The **Musée des Beaux-Arts** (Fine Arts Museum), also in the château, features masterworks of European paintings from Giotto and Memling to El Greco, Rubens, and Goya. Downstairs, the

Musée Archéologique displays regional findings. *2 pl. du Château,* ☏ *88–52–50–00.* ☛ *30 frs adults, 16 frs students and children for all museums; per museum, 15 frs adults, 8 frs students.* ◷ *Wed.–Sat. and Mon. 10–noon and 1:30–6; Sun. 10–5.*

About 50 yards north of the cathedral, and running parallel to it, is rue des Hallebardes, Strasbourg's most stylish pedestrian-only shopping street. It leads to **place Gutenberg,** dominated by an elegant three-story building with large windows, constructed between 1582 and 1585, now used as the Chamber of Commerce and city tourist office. Johannes Gutenberg (1400–68), for whom the square is named, invented the printing press in Strasbourg in 1434.

⑥ If you walk south from place Gutenberg to the river, the **Musée Historique** (Local History Museum) stands on your left. Closed for renovations until the end of 1997, it will then reopen its collection of maps, armor, arms, bells, uniforms, printing paraphernalia, cardboard toy soldiers, and two huge relief models of Strasbourg, one made in 1727, the other in 1836. *2 rue du Vieux-Marché-aux-Poissons,* ☏ *88–32–25–63. Postrenovation prices and hours to be announced.*

⑦ The **Ancienne Douane,** opposite, was constructed in 1358 to serve as a customs house. It is now a small gallery, mounting temporary exhibitions. A popular restaurant adjoins it. *1A rue du Vieux-Marché-aux-Poissons,* ☏ *88–75–10–77. Admission and hours vary with exhibitions.*

⑧ Across the river is the **cour du Corbeau,** a ramshackle 14th-century courtyard whose hostelry once welcomed kings and emperors. Facing the An-
⑨ cienne Douane is the **Musée Alsacien.** If you want a glimpse of how Alsatian families used to live, this is the place to visit. Local interiors—kitchens, bedrooms, and sitting rooms (the latter two often combined)—have been faithfully reconstituted. The diverse activities of blacksmiths, clog makers, saddlers, and makers of artificial flowers are explained with the help of old-time artisans' tools and equipment. *23 quai St-Nicholas,* ☏ *88–35–55–36.* ☛ *15 frs adults, 8 frs students and children.* ◷ *Wed.–Sat. and Mon. 10–noon and 1:30–6, Sun. 10–5.*

Stroll across the river two bridges farther west to admire the church of **St-Thomas** (quai Finkwiller), particularly the mausoleum of Marshal Maurice of Saxony (1696–1750), a key figure in the 1740–48 War of Austrian Succession. Follow the banks of the River Ill toward the picturesque quarter of **Petite France,** lined with carved, half-timbered Renaissance houses and cobbled streets. The Ill, which branches into several canals, is spanned by the **Ponts Couverts,** three connected 14th-century covered bridges, each with its tall, stern stone tower. Just
⑩ beyond lies the grass-roof dam, the **Barrage Vauban,** built by its namesake in 1682; climb to the top for a stunning view across the roofs of old Strasbourg. ☛ *Free.* ◷ *Mid-Oct.–mid-Mar., daily 9–7; mid-Mar.–mid-Oct., daily 9–8.*

Continue along the waterfront to the church of **St-Pierre-le-Vieux,** whose choir is decorated with scenes from the Passion (circa 1500) by local painter Henri Lutzelmann. Follow the quay around to **St-Pierre-le-Jeune,** consecrated in 1320, to admire its painted rood screen, immense choir, and 14th-century frescoes.

Alsace provided the French Revolution with 64 generals and marshals. One of the most famous was Jean-Baptiste Kléber (1753–1800), who was assassinated in Cairo after being left in charge of Egypt by Napoléon in 1799. Kléber's statue lords it over Strasbourg's busiest square, **place Kléber,** up rue des Grandes-Arcades from St-Pierre-le-Jeune.

Rue des Orfèvres, one of the lively pedestrian streets leading off from rue des Hallebardes, is connected to the noisy, commercial rue des Grandes-Arcades by a cobbled, leafy square—the **place du Marché-Neuf**—seldom discovered by visitors. This peaceful oasis is a fine place to stop for a drink; its two open-air cafés don't close till late at night.

Rue de l'Outre heads down to another large square, **place Broglie,** home of the city hall, the 18th-century Municipal Theater, and the Banque de France. The bank occupies the site of the house where "La Marseillaise" (composed by Rouget de Lisle, and originally entitled "Battlesong of the Rhine Army") was sung for the first time, in 1792.

⑪ The spacious layout and ponderous architecture of **place de la République** have nothing in common with the old town across the river, except the local red sandstone. A different hand was at work here—that of occupying Germans, who erected the former Ministry (1902); the Academy of Music (1882–92); and the Palais du Rhin (1883–88).

Much of northern Strasbourg bears the German stamp. Head east out of place de la République, past the handsome neo-Gothic church of
⑫ **St-Paul,** to the pseudo-Renaissance **Palais de l'Université**—constructed between 1875 and 1885. Heavy, turn-of-the-century houses, some betraying the whimsical curves of the Art Nouveau style, frame allée de la Robertsau, a tree-lined boulevard that would not look out of place
⑬ in Berlin; follow its length to reach the modern **Palais de l'Europe,** designed by Paris architect Henri Bernard in 1977. The Palais houses the European Court of Human Rights and the Council of Europe (founded in 1949 and independent of the European Union). *Av. de l'Europe. Guided tours by appointment only (☎ 88–41–20–29).*

Just across the street from the Palais de l'Europe is the **Orangerie,** a delightful park laden with flowers and punctuated by imperial copper beeches. It contains a lake and, close by, a small reserve of rare birds, including flamingos and noisy local storks.

Tour 2: Alsace

⑭ Leaving **Strasbourg,** take the fast A4 autoroute 40 kilometers (24 miles) northwest to **Saverne,** gateway to the northern Vosges. Its 18th-century **Château des Rohan,** built in red sandstone, is renowned for its majestic north facade, lined by fluted pilasters and a Corinthian colonnade. The right wing houses an interesting, newly renovated museum devoted to archaeology, religious statuary, and local history, with a new section devoted to 20th-century events. Don't miss the 1,000 types of rose in the **Roseraie,** 300 yards from the château on Route de Paris. ☎ *88–91–06–28.* ☛ *8 frs adults, 4 frs children; 16 frs. for special exhibitions. Guided tours and cassette tours may be available this year.* ☼ *Mid-June–mid-Sept., Wed.–Mon. 2–6.*

⑮ Head south from Saverne along N4 through **Marmoutier,** where a marvelous Romanesque **église abbatiale** (abbey church) stands in the town's charming old center. The facade, dating from the 11th and 12th centuries, is pure Lombard Romanesque, built from local Vosges sandstone. Continue on N4 to **Marlenheim** and the start of the great Alsace **Route du Vin** (Wine Road), which forms the backbone of this tour. Regular signs marked ROUTE DU VIN will help you keep your bearings on the twisty way south to Thann, a bit west of Mulhouse.

⑯ D422 connects Marlenheim with **Rosheim,** a pleasant village with medieval ramparts, gateways, and a sturdy Romanesque church with an octagonal tower. The two-story, stone **Heidehuss,** indicated by signs marked "Maison Romane," is reputedly the oldest house in Alsace (circa 1170). It's novel to see a family residence in Romanesque style, complete with carved faces trimming the windows and sculpted stone. Look for it outside the clock-tower gate.

(17) **Boersch,** 3 kilometers (2 miles) from Rosheim on D35, conserves three medieval gateways and the 16th-century Hôtel de Ville (Town Hall).

(18) **Obernai,** a thriving, colorful Renaissance market town well-developed for tourism, can be reached from Boersch via D322 (about 6 kilometers, or 4 miles). At its heart is the medieval place du Marché, dominated by the stout, square 13th-century **Kappellturm Beffroi** (Belfry), topped by a pointed steeple flanked at each corner by frilly openwork turrets added in 1597. The nearby **Puits à Six-Seaux,** constructed in the 1570s, is an elaborate Renaissance well whose name recalls the six buckets suspended from its metal chains.

North of the town hall, the twin spires of the parish church of **St-Pierre–St-Paul** compete with the belfry for skyline preeminence. They date, like the rest of the church, from the 1860s, although the 1504 Holy Sepulcher altarpiece in the north transept is a survivor from the previous church, along with some 15th-century stained glass.

D426 from Obernai heads back west to cross the Route du Vin at the medieval hill town of Ottrott, renowned for its crisp, cool, Pinot Noir–like red wine. From Ottrott, D109 winds its way 6 kilometers
★ **(19)** (4 miles) up to **Mont Ste-Odile,** a 2,500-foot mound that has been an important religious and military site for 3,000 years. An eerie 9½-kilometer-long (6-mile-long) pagan wall, up to 12 feet high and, in parts, several feet thick, rings the summit; its mysterious origins and purpose still baffle archaeologists. The Romans established a settlement here, and at the start of the 8th century, Odile, daughter of Duke Etichon of Obernai, founded a monastery on the same spot after recovering her sight while being baptized (she had been born blind). Odile—venerated as the patron saint of Alsace—died here in AD 720; her sarcophagus rests in the chapel. The **monastery** still remains, rescued by the bishop of Strasbourg in 1853, after repeated plunder, military vandalism, and the expulsion of its monks during the French Revolution.

(20) D854 tumbles down the hillside to **Barr,** another 6 kilometers (4 miles) farther, a thriving little town surrounded by vines, with some charming narrow streets (notably rue des Cigognes, rue Neuve, and the tiny rue de l'Essieu) and the cheerful Hôtel de Ville. Most buildings in Barr date from after a catastrophic fire of 1678; the only medieval survivor is the Romanesque tower of St-Martin, the Protestant church.

The **Musée de la Folie Marco,** up rue du Dr. Sultzer from the town hall, is housed in a steep-tiled mansion built by local magistrate Félix Marco in 1763. You can admire lots of original furniture here, plus local porcelain, earthenware, and pewter. One section of the museum explains the traditional process of *schlittage*: Sleds, bearing bundles of freshly sawn tree trunks, once slid down forest slopes along a "corduroy road" made of logs. *30 rue du Dr. Sultzer,* ☎ *88–08–94–72.* ☛ *10 frs.* ☺ *July–Sept., Wed.–Mon. 10–noon and 2–6; June and Oct., weekends 10–noon and 2–6.*

A small road leads from Barr through the vineyards and the tiny vil-
(21) lage of Mittelbergheim to **Andlau,** 3 kilometers (2 miles) away. The abbey church of **St-Pierre–St-Paul** was built in the mid-12th century. The spire above the octagonal bell tower was finished only in 1737. The west front boasts the richest ensemble of Romanesque sculpture in Al-

sace. Sculpted vines wind their way around the doorway as a reminder of the time-honored importance of wine to the local economy.

The 15th-century abbey choir stalls are adorned with the coats of arms of the princess abbesses. A statue of a female bear, the mascot of the abbey—bears used to roam local forests and were bred at the abbey until the 16th century—can be seen in the north transept. Legend has it that Queen Richarde founded the abbey in 887 after being enjoined by an angel to construct a church on the spot where a female bear appeared to her.

Take D253 from Andlau, past the parish church, to the junction with D603. From here, you can enjoy a splendid view down the valley toward Andlau. A mile later, turn right, then left through the overly cute village of Itterswiller (its many restaurants are outrageously expensive) before turning right toward **Dambach-la-Ville,** a fortified medieval town protected by ramparts and three powerful 13th-century gateways. Dambach is particularly rich in half-timbered, high-roofed houses from the 17th and 18th centuries, clustered mainly around place du Marché and its 16th-century Hôtel de Ville.

En route from Dambach to Sélestat, you'll see the imposing **Château Ortenburg** on the hilltop to your right. Constructed in 1000 by Wernher d'Ortenburg, it was rebuilt by his successors in the 12th century, then restored in 1258 by Rodolphe de Habsbourg. The climb to the castle up a steep forest trail is well worth taking.

D35 continues to Châtenois, from which it's just a 3-kilometer (2-mile) detour along N59 to **Sélestat,** a busy town with two impressive churches. **St-Foy** dates from between 1155 and 1190; its Romanesque facade remains largely intact (the spires were added in the 19th century), as does the 140-foot octagonal tower over the crossing. Sadly, the interior was mangled during the centuries, chiefly by the Jesuits; their most inspired legacy is the Baroque pulpit of 1733 illustrating the life of St. Francis Xavier. Note the Romanesque bas-relief next to the baptistery, originally the lid of a sarcophagus. *On the place du Marché Vert.*

Take rue de Babil one block south to the later, Gothic church of **St-Georges.** Head left down rue du Sel to the **Bibliothèque Humaniste,** a major library founded in 1452 and installed in the former Halle aux Blés. Among the precious manuscripts on display are a 7th-century lectionary and a 12th-century Book of Miracles. Altarpieces, jewelry, sculpture, and earthenware are also exhibited. *1 rue de la Bibliothèque,* ☎ *88–92–03–24.* 🎫 *10.50 frs adults, 5.50 frs students.* ⊙ *Weekdays 9–noon and 2–6, Sat. 9–noon; July–Aug. also weekends 2–5.*

★ ㉔ D159 now makes the steep, twisting climb to **Haut-Koenigsbourg.** This romantic, crag-top castle looks just as a kaiser thought it should: In 1901, German emperor Wilhelm II was presented with the 13th-century ruins by the town of Sélestat (or Schelestadt; the German name was used then) and restored them with some diligence and no lack of imagination—squaring the main tower's original circle, for instance. Today Haut-Koenigsbourg is besieged by tourists and should be avoided on sunny summer weekends. At other times, the site, panorama, drawbridge, and amply furnished imperial chambers merit a visit. ☎ *88–92–11–46.* 🎫 *35 frs adults, 10 frs children 7–17.* ⊙ *Daily June–Sept. 9–6; Apr.–May 9–noon and 1–6; Oct. and Mar. 9–noon and 1–5; Nov.–Feb. 9–noon and 1–4.*

㉕ Head south from Haut-Koenigsbourg to **Ribeauvillé,** a beautifully preserved, half-timbered wine town surrounded by vineyards and guarded by three imposing châteaus. Walk the length of the Grand'Rue, stopping in *winstubs* (wine bar/tearooms), pausing for a tasting, shopping for local pottery, and admiring the fountain, clock tower, and architectural details. This is the home of Trimbach wines, among the most respected in Alsace.

TIME OUT At **Caveau l'Ami Fritz** (1 pl. de l'Ancien-Hôpital), a casual restaurant, you can opt for light, one-course meals—tarte flambée (a crisp pizzalike cheese torte topped with crème fraîche, onions, and bacon), onion tart, and salads—or a heftier regional menu, served at odd hours in an easy-going, local atmosphere: paisley linens on the plank-tables, a barrel-vaulted stone ceiling, and a roaring fire.

★ 26 Follow D1 south to **Riquewihr,** whose steep main street, ramparts, and winding back alleys have scarcely changed since the 16th century and could easily serve as film sets. Overlook the plethora of kitschy souvenir shops, and peep into courtyards at massive wine presses, study the woodwork and ornately decorated houses, or stand in the narrow old ghetto at the cours des Juifs. When it's time to eat and drink, sample the local goods: Riquewihr's famous wineries include Dopff & Irion and the venerable Hugel et Fils.

27 From Riquewihr, continue south to the proud merchant city of **Colmar.** The heart of Colmar remains intact: A web of pedestrian streets fans out from the beefy-towered church of **St-Martin.** To the east lies Grand'Rue, with its 15th-century **Ancienne Douane** (Customs House) and twin-turreted **Maison aux Arcades** (1609). To the south is the pretty, water-crossed district known as **Petite Venise.**

Alongside St-Martin's, on rue Mercière (No. 11), is the **Maison Pfister** (1537), which, with its decorative frescoes and medallions, counts as one of the most impressive dwellings in town. On the other side of rue des Marchands is the **Musée Bartholdi,** former home of Frédéric-Auguste Bartholdi (1834–1904), the local sculptor who designed the Statue of Liberty. *30 rue des Marchands, ☎ 89–41–90–60. ☛ 20 frs adults, 10 frs students. ⏲ Apr.–Dec., Wed.–Mon. 10–noon and 2–6.*

In the nearby **Église des Dominicains** (Dominican Church), the Flemish-influenced *Madonna of the Rosebush* (1473) by Martin Schongauer (1445–91), a talented engraver as well as a painter, can be seen. This work, stolen from St-Martin's in 1972 and later recovered and hung here, has almost certainly been reduced in size from its original state. Realistic birds, buds, thorns, and flowers add life to the gold-background solemnity. *Pl. des Dominicains, ☎ 89–24–46–57. ☛ 8 frs adults, 5 frs students. ⏲ Mid-Mar.–Dec., daily 10–6.*

Take rue des Têtes past the Maison des Têtes (1608)—so called because of the carved heads proliferating on its facade—to the **Musée d'Unterlinden,** France's best-attended provincial museum. The star attraction ★ of this former medieval convent is the **Isenheim Altarpiece** (1512–16) by Matthias Grünewald, majestically displayed in the convent's Gothic chapel. The altarpiece was originally painted for the Antoine convent at Isenheim, 32 kilometers (20 miles) south of Colmar, and was believed to have miraculous healing powers over ergotism, a widespread disease in the Middle Ages. The altarpiece's emotional drama moves away from the stilted restraint of earlier paintings toward the humanistic realism of the Renaissance: The blanched despair of the Virgin, clutched by a weeping St. John, is balanced, on the other side of the cross, by the grave expression of John the Baptist. The blood of the crucified Christ gushes forth, while his face is racked with pain.

The altarpiece was closed and folded according to the religious calendar and contains several other scenes apart from the *Crucifixion.* Modern art, stone sculpture, and local crafts cluster around the 13th-century cloisters to complete Unterlinden's folksy charm. *1 rue Unterlinden,* ☎ *89–20–15–50.* ☛ *28 frs adults, 18 frs students.* ☯ *Apr.–Oct., daily 9–noon and 2–6; Nov.–Mar., Wed.–Mon. 9–noon and 2–5.*

From Colmar, you can end your Alsace tour and head west on D417 toward Gérardmer and Lorraine (*see* Tour 3, *below*), stopping to explore the charms of **Turckheim,** a Renaissance village surrounded by an ancient fortification wall. About 15 kilometers (9 miles) west, on the forested edge of the Vosges, you'll reach **Munster,** where its famous cheese is sold in savory rounds on the place du Marché. Steps from the marketplace, a sizeable population of storks has been encouraged by an *enclos* (reserve).

㉘ If you choose to continue south through Alsace toward the Jura, head 25 kilometers (15 miles) south on N83 to the **Guebwiller** exit. The town's **Eglise St-Léger** (1180–1280) is one of the most harmonious Romanesque churches in Alsace, though its original choir was replaced by the current Gothic one in 1336. The bare, solemn interior is of less interest than the three-tower exterior. The towers of the facade match—almost: The one on the left has small turrets at the base of its steeple, whereas the one on the right is ringed by triangular gables. The octagonal tower over the crossing looms above them both, topped by a seldom-visited stork's nest.

The surrounding square, home to a lively weekly market, faces rue de la République, Guebwiller's main street. Head left upon leaving the church: One hundred yards down the road stands the Renaissance **Hôtel de Ville,** with its small spire and crenellated oriel (or bay) window, built by wealthy draper Marquart Hesser. Continue down the main street before turning left into rue de l'Hôpital. The **Église Dominicain** (Dominican Church) is unmistakable, thanks to the thin, lacy lantern that sticks out of its roof like an effeminate chimney. Its large, 14th-century nave is adorned with frescoes and contains a fine rood screen.

Rue de la République continues to Guebwiller's third and largest church, **Notre-Dame** (1762–85). The church possesses a Baroque grandeur that would not be out of keeping in a chic district of Paris—a reflection of the wealth of the Benedictine abbey at nearby Murbach, whose worldly friars, fed up with country life, opted for the bright lights of Guebwiller in the mid-18th century. The monks—who needed a noble pedigree of four generations to take the cloth—outmaneuvered church authorities by pretending to take temporary exile in Guebwiller while "modernizing" Murbach Abbey, thus circumnavigating the papal permission required before abbeys could move. As a token gesture, the crafty clerics smashed the nave of Murbach Abbey but failed to replace it and refused to budge from their "temporary" home. Instead, they commissioned Louis Beuque to design a new church in Guebwiller—Notre-Dame.

The church's facade, with its double layer of cornice-bearing columns, is devoid of ornament except for the statues halfway up. The interior is majestic but not overbearing, thanks to the cheerful pale pink of the stone and the survival of much of the original decoration. The gold-and-marble high altar fits in better, perhaps, than does the trick 3-D-effect stucco *Assumption,* which puffs its way out of a half-open coffin behind the altar before erupting over the walls and balcony and mak-

ing for the roof, an example of Baroque craftsmanship at its most outlandish. *Rue de la République.*

The **Musée du Florival,** on one side of the church square, occupies one
of the 18th-century canon's houses. It has a fine collection of ceramics designed by Théodore Deck (1823–91), a native of Guebwiller and
director of the renowned porcelain factory at Sèvres near Paris. *1 rue
du 4-Février,* ☎ *89–74–22–89.* ☛ *15 frs.* ☉ *Mon. and Wed.–Fri. 2–
6, weekends 10–noon and 2–6.*

㉙ D430 now heads up the valley toward Lautenbach; at Buhl, take the
exit to **Murbach.** This road is a dead end, so it's all the more surprising to discover a vast rump of a church towering above the hillside.
Only the east end remains of the **Eglise St-Léger,** once part of the most
powerful abbey in Alsace. Roofs and towers create a geometric interplay of squares and triangles, lent rhythm and variety by those round-
arched windows and arcades so loved by Romanesque architects. Note
the tympanum above the door to the south transept: Its elongated lions,
seen in profile, resemble stone images found more commonly in the
Middle East.

㉚ Make your way back to Guebwiller and take the Ensisheim road,
passing over N83, as far as **Ungersheim,** home of the **Ecomusée de Haute-
Alsace.** This "open-air museum," a small village created from scratch
in 1980, includes 35 historic peasant houses typical of the region that
have been transferred here lock, stock, and barrel (or more precisely,
stable, barn, and pigeon loft) to escape demolition. A low-season visit
is a study in local architecture; in high season the place comes alive
with entertaining demonstrations of the old ways, from communal laundering to pottery making and blacksmithing. Storks, another example
of the local heritage, are nurtured here in a reserve. *Chemin Gross-
wald,* ☎ *89–74–44–74.* ☛ *65 frs adults, 57 frs students and children.*
☉ *Daily July–Aug. 9–7; June and Sept. 9–6; Apr., May, and Oct. 10–
6; Nov.–Mar. 11–5.*

㉛ From the old town of Ensisheim, D20 spears south to **Mulhouse,** 16
kilometers (10 miles) away. Mulhouse, a pleasant if unremarkable industrial town, rates a visit for its museums. Dutch and Flemish masters of the 17th to 18th centuries top the bill at the **Musée des
Beaux-Arts.** *4 pl. Guillaume-Tell,* ☎ *89–45–43–19.* ☛ *20 frs adults,
15 frs children 6–16.* ☉ *Oct.–mid-June, Fri.–Mon., and Wed. 10–noon
and 2–5, Thurs. 10–5; mid-June–Sept., Fri.–Mon., and Wed. 10–
noon and 2–6, Thurs. 10–5.*

But it is cars and trains that attract most visitors. Some 500 vintage and
modern cars, dating from the steam-powered Jacquot of 1878 and
spanning 100 different makes, are featured in the **Musée National de
l'Automobile.** The highlights are the two Bugatti Royales. Only a handful of these stately cars were ever made; one was auctioned in 1987 for
$8 million. *192 av. de Colmar,* ☎ *89–42–29–17.* ☛ *56 frs adults, 26
frs students.* ☉ *Oct.–May, Wed.–Mon. 10–6; June–Sept., daily 10–6.*

A reconstructed Stephenson locomotive of 1846 sets the wheels rolling
at the **Musée Français du Chemin de Fer** (National Train Museum), a
10-minute walk west down rue J.-Hofer. Rolling stock is spread over
12 tracks, including a vast array of steam trains and the BB 9004 electric train that held the rail speed record of 207 mph from 1955 to 1981.
A section of the museum also houses a display of firefighters' equipment. *2 rue Alfred-de-Glehn,* ☎ *89–42–25–67.* ☛ *43 frs adults, 20
frs students.* ☉ *Daily 9–5.*

From Mulhouse head 34 kilometers (21 miles) down the A36 expressway to the stubborn warrior-town of **Belfort.** Here, on place des Bourgeois in the heart of the town, is the celebrated 36-foot-high **Lion of Belfort,** sculpted in red sandstone by Frédéric-Auguste Bartholdi, best known as the sculptor of the Statue of Liberty in New York. The lion was commissioned to celebrate Belfort's heroic resistance during the Franco-Prussian War (1870–71) when the town of Belfort, under the leadership of General Denfert-Rochereau, withstood a 103-day siege and surrendered only after the rest of France had capitulated. The Prussian leader Otto von Bismarck was so impressed by Belfort's plucky resistance that he declined to incorporate it into the German Empire along with neighboring Alsace, granting Belfort independent status. Although Alsace was returned to France in 1918, Belfort maintained its special status—meaning that the *Territoire de Belfort* remains by far the smallest *département* in France. *To visit the Lion close up there's a charge of 3 frs.*

Belfort's Lion sits proudly at the foot of Vauban's impregnable hilltop **château,** now home to the **Musée d'Art & d'Histoire,** containing Vauban's 1687 scale model of the town, plus a detailed section on military history. From the castle you can look out over the old town, toward the Vosges Mountains to the north and the Jura to the south. ☎ *84–28–52–96.* ☛ *Château free.* ☛ *Museum: 11 frs (free Wed.).* ☉ *May–Sept., daily 10–7; Oct.–Apr., Wed.–Mon. 10–noon and 2–5.*

★ ㉝ Now make an architectural pilgrimage to the little town of **Ronchamp,** 21 kilometers (13 miles) west of Belfort via N19, and our sole excursion into the windswept *département* of Haute-Saône. Once renowned for having France's deepest coal-mine shaft (3,300 feet), whose huge chimney still towers above the valley, Ronchamp is now the site of one of Europe's most famous postwar buildings, the hilltop chapel of **Notre-Dame-du-Haut,** designed by Swiss-born French architect Le Corbusier in 1951 to replace the church destroyed here during World War II. The chapel's curved, sloping white walls; small, irregularly placed windows; and unadorned slug-shape gray concrete roof are unique. Many consider it to be Le Corbusier's masterpiece—utterly individual, yet imbued with peace and calm. ☎ *84–20–65–13.* ☛ *10 frs.* ☉ *Mid-Mar.–Oct., daily 9–7; Nov.–mid-Mar., daily 9–4.*

㉞ From Ronchamp, double back to Belfort and take the A36 expressway south to **Montbéliard,** 14 kilometers (9 miles) away. Industrial Montbéliard, base for the giant Peugeot automobile company, is redeemed by a stately, round-tower château. Its museum is devoted to insects, geology, archaeology, and traditional local crafts (clocks and musical boxes). *Rue du Château,* ☎ *81–99–22–61.* ☛ *Free except during special exhibitions.* ☉ *Wed.–Mon. 10–noon and 2–6.*

In the neighboring suburb of Sochaux, Peugeot's production methods and colorful history can be explored at the **Musée de l'Aventure Peugeot,** and you can tour the factory. *Carrefour de l'Europe, Sochaux,* ☎ *81–94–48–21.* ☛ *30 frs adults, 15 frs children.* ☉ *Daily 10–6. Free guided 2-hr tours of factory (*☎ *81–33–47–80; weekdays 8:30 AM; no children; English on request).*

Tour 3: Lorraine

Numbers in the margin correspond to points of interest on the Lorraine and Nancy maps.

Our tour of Lorraine begins at the southern tip of the Vosges range, accessible from Colmar, Mulhouse, or Belfort. From Colmar, head west on D417, then continue over the mountain pass, **Col de la Schlucht.** Chalet-like mountain homes and deep fir forest epitomize the heart of the Vosges wilderness. This is a vacation and resort area for French

㉟ hikers, casual skiers, and water-sports fans. At **Gérardmer,** dozens of resort hotels surround a clear mountain lake. Gérardmer is famous as the source of good household linens.

㊱ Follow the circuitous but well-marked route on to **Épinal,** and head for the town center. Épinal, seated on the Moselle at the feet of the Vosges, has been a printing center since 1735, publishing popular illustrations, prints, and hand-colored stencils on its Gutenberg press. You can visit **L'Imagerie Pellerin,** the artisanal workshop, and see a slide show tracing its history. *42 bis quai de Dogneville,* ☎ *29–34–21–87.* ☞ *Free. Guided tour with slide show: 25 frs adults, 15 frs children 6– 16. Tours depart 10, 11, 3, and 4:30 and last 45 min. Gallery/salesroom open between tours Mon.–Sat. 8:30–noon and 2–6:30, Sun. 2–6:30.*

On an island in the Moselle in the center of town, Epinal's spectacular new (1992) **Musée Départemental d'Art Ancien et Contemporain** is an all-contemporary metamorphosis of a 17th-century hospital, whose classical traces are still visible under a dramatic barrel-vaulted skylight that runs the length of the museum and sheds light into adjoining galleries. There are minor collections of Gallo-Roman artifacts; rural tools and local faience; and Old Masters, including some fine drawings and watercolors by Fragonard and Boucher. Most important, however, is the comprehensive survey of contemporary art, the fourth largest in France, which includes works of Andy Warhol and Donald Judd. *1 pl. Lagarde,* ☎ *29–82–20–33.* ☞ *30 frs adults, 15 frs students 13 and older.* ☼ *Apr.–Sept., Wed.–Mon. 10–noon and 2–6; Oct.–Mar., Wed.–Mon. 10–noon and 2–5. No wheelchairs or strollers.*

In the oldest section of town, visit the **Basilique St-Maurice,** whose Romanesque-Gothic styles combine the influences of the four regions that have ruled Épinal: Lorraine, Alsace, Burgundy, and Champagne. The deep, atmospheric, 13th-century entry portal is Champenois, the three-level nave is Burgundian, and the 14th-century choir is Lorraine Gothic.

㊲ From Épinal, take D166 and D28 west through **Vittel,** the famous thermal source. For centuries the popular mineral water has been used for ailments of the liver and kidneys, and nowadays it's served up in a luxurious country setting of golf greens, parklands, and spring-fed swimming pools. You will pass the bottling center, where some 4 million bottles are prepared daily for shipping worldwide. Five kilometers (3 miles) west,

㊳ **Contrexéville,** the namesake of another popular mineral water, has drawn visitors to its forests and glamorous baths since Stanislas, the 18th-century Polish duke of Lorraine, took the waters. Contrexéville is a convenient base for excursions into the pretty countryside.

Follow D164 northwest toward Neufchâteau, where you enter the gentle **Meuse Valley**—its rolling green hills peppered with Lorraine's beloved mirabelle orchards. In September, any farmer will sell you crates of the sweet yellow-pink globes (somewhere between a Queen Anne cherry and a greengage plum). Out of season, pick up some jam or some jars of the preserved fruit; or try a taste (or buy a liter) of mirabelle eau-de-vie, which concentrates the musky-sweet essence of the fruit in a fiery, crystal-clear liquid.

Continue north onto hallowed ground: the countryside where Joan of Arc (Jeanne d'Arc) tended her father's sheep. Her mother was born in Coussey, her father in Maxey-le-Meuse, but Joan herself was born in

㊴ a simple stone hut in **Domrémy-la-Pucelle.** The church where she was

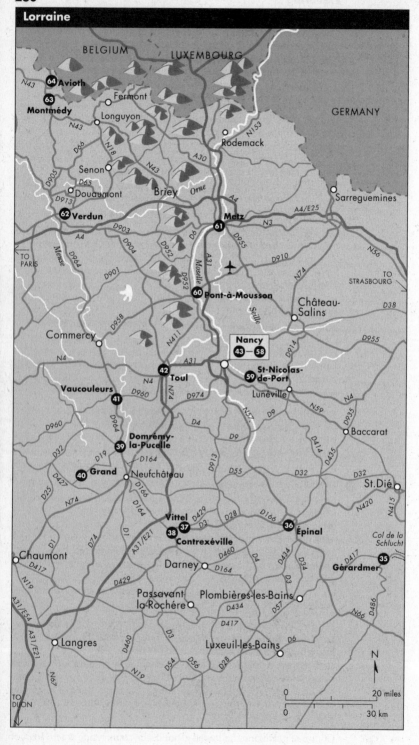

Lorraine

BELGIUM   LUXEMBOURG

GERMANY

N43

64 Avioth
63
Montmédy
Fermont
Longuyon
N43
D66
N118
Rodemack
N153
Senon
D65
D905
Douaumont
D913
Briey
Orne
A30
A4
Metz
A4/E25
Sarreguemines
62 Verdun
61
N3
A4
D903
D6
D955
N56
Meuse
D964
D904
D952
D901
Moselle
A31
D910
N74
TO
PARIS
60 Pont-à-Mousson
Seille
Château-Salins
D38
TO
STRASBOURG
D958
D952
N411
Nancy
43 — **58**
D914
D955
Commercy
A31
N4
42 Toul
St-Nicolas-de-Port
59
N4
D960
D974
Lunéville
N59
N4
Vaucouleurs
41
D964
D4
N57
D9
N59
D435
Baccarat
D960
Domrémy-la-Pucelle
39
D19
D164
D9
D414
D435
D32
D32
40 Grand
Neufchâteau
D166
D613
D55
D32
D32
St.Dié
D25
N74
D164
D166
N420
N415
Vittel
37
D429
D3
D28
D166
36 Épinal
Col de la Schlucht
38 Contrexéville
D3
D429
Chaumont
D417
Darney
D460
D164
D4
D434
D34
Gérardmer
35
D417
D1
A31/E21
D74
D429
Passavant-la-Rochère
D434
D57
Plombières-les-Bains
D3
N19
A31/E54
Langres
D460
D3
D417
D6
D486
N66
N67
D54
D56
D28
Luxeuil-les-Bains
D6
TO
DIJON

N

0   20 miles
0   30 km

baptised still holds the figure of Ste-Marguerite she prayed before, and you can visit the hillside where the devout girl first heard voices telling her to take up arms and save France from the English. The events of her story are still considered historic fact, whatever forces may have empowered her. Following her voices, Joan of Arc walked the 19 kilometers (12 miles) to Vaucouleurs and into history. Dressed and mounted like a man, she led her forces to lift the siege of Orléans, defeated the English, and escorted the unseated Charles VII to Reims, to be crowned king of France. That was, unfortunately, her own crowning moment as well. Military missions after Orléans failed—including an attempt to retake Paris—and she was captured at Compiègne. The English, dodging responsibility, turned her over to the Church, which sent her to be tried by the Inquisition for witchcraft and heresy. She was convicted in one of the best-documented trials in history, excommunicated, and burned at the stake in Rouen. Her humble stone-and-stucco **maison natale** (birthplace)—an irregular, slope-roofed former cowshed—has been preserved with some reverence, and an attached museum retells her story. *2 rue de la Basilique, ☎ 29–06–95–86. ☛ 6 frs adults, 3 frs students. ☉ Apr.–Sept., daily 9–12:30 and 2–7; Sept.–Mar. 30, Wed.–Mon. 9:30–12 and 2–5.*

From the birthplace it's a pleasant walk up a country road to the magnificent late 19th-century **Basilique du Bois-Chenu.** Its enormous painted panels tell Joan's story in glowing pre-Raphaelite tones and at the time of its construction, salved the wounds of the recent national defeat by the Prussians.

40 From Domrémy, follow signs down country roads west toward the tiny, enigmatic architectural treasure of **Grand.** Here a famous spring developed into a center for the worship of the Gallo-Roman sun god Apollo-Grannus, important enough to draw the Roman Emperors Caracalla and Constantine. A marvelously expressive floor mosaic, a partially restored amphitheater once seating 20,000, and scraps of exotic stone and relics transported from across two continents bear witness to this isolated village's opulent past. *☎ 29–06–63–43. ☛ Amphitheater (at entrance to village) free. Mosaic in upper village 6 frs adults, 3 frs students. ☉ Both open Apr.–Aug. 9–noon and 2–5; Sept.–Apr. 10–noon and 2–5.*

41 Return to Domrémy and continue up D164 toward **Vaucouleurs,** stopping 5 kilometers (3 miles) along to heave open the ancient gate and enter the magical secret-garden enclosure of the **Château de Goussain-court,** still inhabited by a genteel lady of a certain age who sells handmade blue-and-white faience to passersby. At **Vaucouleurs,** below the medieval walls and ruins of the ancient château of Robert de Baudricourt, you can see the **Porte de France,** through which—as depicted in many art works—Joan of Arc led her armed soldiers to Orléans. From **42** Vaucouleurs, head east on D960 to the old town of **Toul,** nestled behind mossy, star-shaped ramparts. A bishopric since 365 AD, Toul merited visits from the Frankish king Clovis to study the Christian faith; from Charlemagne in passing; and from a young, pre-military Joan of Arc, who was sued in the Toul court for breach of promise, when she threw over a beau for the voices of God. In 1700, under Louis XIV, the military engineer Vauban built the thrusting ramparts around the town.

The ramshackle streets of central Toul haven't changed much for centuries—not since the embroidered, twin-towered facade, a Flamboyant Gothic masterpiece, was woven onto the **cathédrale St-Etienne** in the second half of the 15th century. The cathedral's interior, begun in 1204, is long (321 feet), airy (105 feet high), and more restrained than its exuberant facade. *Place Charles-de-Gaulle.* ✆ *Daily, summer 9–6; winter until dark.*

On one side the cathedral is flanked by vast 14th-century **cloisters** (spend some time with the gargoyles, as the cloisters never close) and on the other by a pleasant garden behind the **Hôtel de Ville** (Town Hall), built in 1740 as the Bishop's Palace. Continue down rue de Rigny, turn right onto rue Michâtel, and then take a second right onto rue de Ménin, which winds its way down to the Porte de Metz. Veer left at the gateway, then left again onto rue Gouvion St-Cyr; at No. 25 is the **Musée Municipal** (Town Museum), housed in a former medieval hospital. The museum's well preserved *Salle des Malades* (Patient's Ward) dates from the 13th century and displays archaeological finds, ceramics, tapestries, and medieval sculpture. *25 rue Gouvion St-Cyr,* ☎ *83–64–13–38.* ☞ *16 frs.* ✆ *Apr.–Oct., Wed.–Mon. 10–noon and 2–6; Nov.–Mar., 2–6 only.*

Fork right onto rue de la Boucherie, which, over a 300-yard stretch lined with old houses, becomes successively rue du Collège, rue Pont-de-Vaux, and rue Gengoult. Eventually rue Sonaire leads off to the right to the attractive church of **St-Gengoult,** whose choir has a vast group of beautifully preserved 13th-century stained glass windows. Unfortunately, because of repeated vandalism, the cathedral is closed to the public, although attending Sunday Mass (10:30 AM) will reward the devout, especially on sunny mornings. The adjoining Flamboyant Gothic **cloisters,** later than those of the cathedral but equally picturesque, stay open at all hours.

43 **Nancy,** 23 kilometers (14 miles) east of Toul via A31, is one of France's richest cities architecturally. Medieval ornament, 18th-century grandeur, and Belle Epoque fluidity rub shoulders in a town center that mingles commercial bustle with stately elegance. Its majesty derives from a long history as home to the powerful dukes of Lorraine, whose double-barred crosses figure prominently on statues and building around town. It was at the Battle of Nancy (1476) that the Burgundian warlord Charles the Bold—having swept as far east as Fribourg, Switzerland—was defeated and killed by René II, Duke of Lorraine, who celebrated victory by constructing a church and restoring the ducal palace.

★ **44** The symbolic heart of Nancy is **place Stanislas,** among the finest examples of 18th-century architecture in the country. The severe, gleaming-white classical facades of this stylish square are given a touch of rococo jollity by fancifully wrought gilt-iron railings. Stanislas Leszczynski, twice dethroned as King of Poland, was offered the throne of Lorraine by Louis XV (his son-in-law) in 1736. Knowing that after his death the independent duchy of Lorraine would fall under French rule, Stanislas sweetened the transition with a legacy of spectacular buildings, undertaken between 1751 and 1760 under the artistry of architect Emmanuel Héré and ironwork-genius Jean Lamour. A sculpture of Stanislas dominates the square's center, though he didn't commission the work himself; his grand statue of Louis XV, which ornamented what was then called the place Royale, was destroyed in the Revolution. In the 1830s, the statue of the beloved Polish king was erected when the place was named after him.

45 One side of place Stanislas is occupied by the **Hôtel de Ville** (Town Hall), usually the focal point of a summer night son et lumière (call the **46** tourist office for schedule). Across the square stands the **Musée des Beaux-Arts,** where on the ground floor you'll find 19th- and 20th-century paintings by Monet, Manet, Utrillo, and Modigliani, as well as

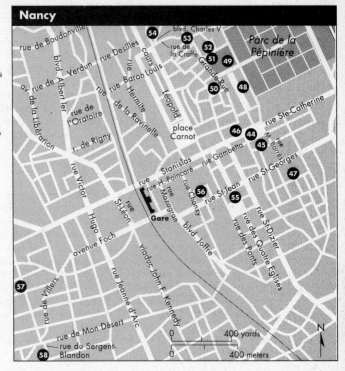

impressive Art Nouveau glass by Nancy-native Antonin Daum. A
hefty *Transfiguration* by Rubens adorns the staircase that leads to the
second floor with its wealth of Old Masters from the Italian, Dutch,
Flemish, and French schools. *Pl. Stanislas,* ☎ *83–85–30–72.* ☛ *20
frs adults (30 frs for joint admission with the Musée de l'Ecole de Nancy,
see below).* ⊙ *Wed.–Sun. 10:15–12:30 and 1:30–5:45; Mon. 1:30–
5:45; closed Tues.*

47 Before leaving place Stanislas, take a look down rue Maurice-Barrès
(to the left of the Hôtel de Ville) at the twin towers of the **cathedral.**
This vast, frigid edifice was built in the 1740s in a ponderous Baroque
style that has none of the ease and grace of the 18th-century place Stanislas. Its most notable interior feature is a murky 19th-century fresco in
the dome. The promised restoration is sorely needed.

48 From place Stanislas, the **place de la Carrière,** lined with pollards and
handsome 18th-century mansions (another successful collaboration be-
49 tween Stanislas and Héré), leads to the colonnaded facade of the **Palais
du Gouvernement,** former home of the governors of Lorraine. To the
east are some spacious formal gardens known as La Pépinière, a graceful urban playground complete with zoo and carousel. A couple of blocks
50 west is the 275-foot spire of **St-Epvre,** a splendid neo-Gothic church
rebuilt in the 1860s. Thanks to the efforts of Monsignor Trouillet, an
entrepreneurial builder-priest, St-Epvre embodies craftsmanship of a
cosmopolitan kind. Most of the 2,800 square yards of stained glass
were created by the Geyling workshop in Vienna; the chandeliers were
made in Liège, Belgium; many carvings are the work of Margraff of
Munich; the heaviest of the eight bells was cast in Budapest; and the
organ, though manufactured by Merklin of Paris, was inaugurated in
1869 by Austrian composer Anton Bruckner.

Running north–south near St-Epvre is Nancy's principal medieval thoroughfare, the **Grande-Rue,** lined with bookshops, antiques dealers, restaurants, and bakeries; and dominated by the majestic **Palais Ducal,** built in the 13th century and completely restored at the end of the 15th century by René II, the hero who defeated Charles the Bold in 1476. Duke Antoine, his heir, contributed the elaborate front entry (that's his statue, on a rearing horse, above the door) and the Galerie des Cerfs. The main entrance to the palace, and the **Musée Historique Lorrain,** which it now houses, is 80 yards farther down the street. The museum has a delightfully far-flung collection of exhibits. A low building across the palace lawn has several showcases of archaeological finds ranging from Stone Age implements and ancient pottery to Roman coins and sculpture.

Across the courtyards is the poorly indicated entrance to the main building. A spiral stone staircase leads up to the palace's most impressive room, the **Galerie des Cerfs.** Exhibits here (including pictures, armor, and books) recapture the Renaissance mood of the 16th and 17th centuries—one of elegance and merry-making, though not devoid of stern morality: An elaborate series of huge tapestries, *La Condemnation du Banquet,* expounds on the evils of drink and gluttony. In a series of attic rooms, posters, proclamations, and the inevitable tricolor banners retrace local history from Napoléon up to World War I. *64 Grande-Rue,* ☎ *83–32–18–74.* ☛ *Musée des Arts et Traditions Populaires and Eglise des Cordeliers (see below): 20 frs adults, 15 frs children.* ☼ *May–Sept., Wed.–Mon. 10–6; Jan.–Apr. and Oct.–Dec., 10–noon and 2–5, Sun. to 6.*

Continue along the Grande-Rue to the Convent des Cordeliers, which now contains the **Musée des Arts et Traditions Populaires,** a branch of the history museum that's a minutely researched combination of scholarship and theatrical realism. It shows how local people lived in a series of rural interiors equipped with craftsmen's tools, colorful crockery, and regional furniture stained a rich black brown with pigs' blood. There are butter molds, cheese presses, choucroute graters, rush-woven beehives, and massive stone fireplaces with iron firebacks that, through open cupboard doors in the adjoining room, warmed the children in their carved-box beds. The dukes of Lorraine are buried in the crypt of the adjoining **Eglise des Cordeliers,** a Flamboyant Gothic church; the *gisant* (death portrait in repose) of Philippa de Gueldra, second wife of René II, is a moving example of Renaissance portraiture, executed in limestone in flowing detail. The tomb of her husband stands against the south wall. The octagonal Ducal Chapel was begun in 1607 in the classical style, modeled on the Chapel of the Medicis in Florence. *66 Grande-Rue,* ☎ *83–32–18–74.* ☛ *See above.* ☼ *May–Sept., Wed.–Mon. 10–6; Oct.–Apr., Wed.–Mon. 10–noon and 2–5, Sun. to 6.*

Wander to the end of the Grande-Rue to the **Porte de la Craffe,** the last vestige of Nancy's medieval fortifications. Built in the 14th and 15th centuries, this striking group of towers served as a prison through the Revolution.

Nancy has yet another face: It was a principal source of the revolution in decorative arts that produced Art Nouveau and Jugendstil. Inspired and coordinated by the glass master Emile Gallé, the local movement, formalized in 1901 as l'Ecole de Nancy, nurtured the floral *pâte de verre* (literally, glass dough) and stained glass works of Daum and Gruber as well as Gallé; the fluid furniture of Louis Majorelle; and the sinuous architecture of Lucien Weissenburger, Emile André, and Eugène Vallin. With a good pair of walking shoes, you can head from the Porte de la Craffe along a route that takes in many of Nancy's best Art Nouveau buildings and end up at the Musée de l'Ecole de Nancy (*see below*). Allow a good hour and a half for the stroll; in poor weather, you may opt for Bus No. 5 from the gare, which heads directly to the museum.

54 Around the corner from rue de la Craffe, at **1 boulevard Charles-V,** is a house by Lucien Weissenburger (1904) with windows by Jacques Gruber—one in the form of the double-armed cross of Lorraine. The adjacent **cours Léopold** has another Weissenburger creation (1905) at No. 52, and you'll see more Gruber windows at No. 40.

Continue to the end of cours Léopold, past **place Carnot,** turn left onto rue Stanislas, then take a second right into the busy shopping district along **rue St-Dizier.** At No. 42 is a bank designed in 1903 by architects Georges Biet and Eugène Vallin; its interior can be inspected during working hours (weekdays 9–5). Turn west onto rue St-Jean, then a left **55** onto **rue Raugraff.** At No. 86 is a house by Vallin (1906). Return to **56** rue St-Jean and continue to **rue Bénit.** At No. 2 is the first building in Nancy with a metallic structure; not just iron girders, but intricately wrought metal pillars, the work of Schertzer to the design of Gutton. There is more stained glass by Gruber, while the exterior decoration tells us that the building began life as a seed shop. The next street along, parallel to rue Bénit, is **rue Chanzy;** at No. 9 is another bank, designed by Emile André, with interior furnishings by Majorelle and yet more Gruber windows.

No. 40 on **rue Henri-Poincaré,** a street running parallel to rue Stanislas, is a commercial building by Toussaint and Marchal (1908), with metal structure by Schertzer, glass by Gruber, and wrought iron by Majorelle. The facade is adorned with the Lorraine thistle, while hops—used to make beer—symbolize local breweries. **Rue Mazagran** greets you at the far end of the street with, at No. 5, the **Excelsior Brasserie;** its rhythmic facade, severe by Art Nouveau standards, is invitingly illuminated at night.

TIME OUT For once, a landmark offers more than food for thought: Lunch or an evening meal in the hushed bustle of the **Excelsior** can make you feel part of the Belle Epoque. *Corner of av. Foch,* ☎ *83–33–12–79.*

At the south end of rue Mazagran, **avenue Foch,** a busy boulevard, heads past the train station into a district lined with solid, serious mansions clearly built for Nancy's affluent 19th-century middle class. At No. 41, more ironwork by Majorelle can be admired; yet another architect, Paul Charbonnier, was responsible for the overall design in 1905. At No. 69, the occasional pinnacle suggests Gothic influence on a house built in 1902 by Emile André, who designed the neighboring No. 71 two years later.

57 On the right, past rue de Villers, is **rue Louis-Majorelle.** At No. 1 stands a villa built in 1902 by Paris architect Henri Sauvage for Majorelle himself. Sinuous metal supports seem to sneak up on the unsuspecting balcony like swaying cobras, leading up to the grand windows of Jacques Gruber.

58 End your Art Nouveau survey at the **Musée de l'Ecole de Nancy,** at 36 rue du Sergent-Blandon, about four blocks south. This airy, turn-of-the-century garden–town house was built by Eugène Corbin, an early patron of the School of Nancy. His personal collection forms the basis of this, the only museum in France devoted to Art Nouveau. Lamps, pianos, stained glass, paintings, silverware, and whole ensembles of worked-wood furniture are arrayed over two creaky stories. There isn't a right angle in the place—all forms ooze, bulge, and flow. *36 rue Sergent-Blandon,* ☎ *83–40–14–86.* ☛ *20 frs adults, 15 frs students; 30 frs for joint ticket with Musée des Beaux-Arts, above.* ☉ *Apr.–Oct., Wed.–Mon. 10–noon and 2–6; Nov.–Mar., Wed.–Mon. 10–noon and 2–5.*

⑤⑨ Leaving Nancy, head southeast 20 kilometers (12 miles) to **St-Nicolas-de-Port,** a small industrial town saved from mediocrity by its colossal **basilica** (1495–1555), expanded on the base of the 11th-century original, in the flush of victory by Duke René II. Legend has it that a finger of St. Nicholas was brought here during the 11th-century Crusades. (St-Nicholas, old Saint Nick himself, is the patron saint of Lorraine. Every December 6 Lorraine schoolchildren reenact the legend of his macabre miracle: A greedy butcher slaughtered and salted down three children as hams, but when St-Nicholas dropped by his place for a meal, he discovered the deed and brought them back to life. (You'll find his statue, with three children in a *saloir,* or salt-box, throughout Lorraine.) Holding such a priceless relic, the church was rapidly besieged by pilgrims, including Joan of Arc who, like a good Lorrainer, came to ask St-Nicholas' blessings on her famous journey to Orléans.

Architecture buffs will recognize in the simplified column capitals and elaborate rib vaulting a shining example of Flamboyant Gothic enjoying a final fling before the gathering impetus of the Renaissance. But you don't need specialized knowledge to sense the excitement of the 280-foot onion-domed towers, almost symmetrical but, as was the Gothic wont, not quite. There's excitement inside, too: The slender, free-standing 90-foot pillars in the transept (the "arms" of the church's cruciform shape) are the highest in France.

⑥⓪ En route between Nancy and Metz on the A31 expressway, exit at **Pont-à-Mousson** to see the charming 16th-century arcaded town center. Stroll across the bridge over the Moselle to visit the ornate Gothic **église St-Martin,** built in the 15th century with the maximum of gravity-defying sculptures and gargoyles. Just downstream, the splendid Baroque **Abbaye des Prémontrés,** begun in 1608, offers sharp contrast between its serene, classical exterior and its flamboyant interior decor. The *pont* (bridge) itself, a key Moselle crossing, was dynamited by the Germans as Patton's army, having bombed the town in preparation, routed them to the east bank in 1944.

From the town center, head back up N57, then turn right on D910. After about 2 kilometers (1 mile), veer left toward Lesménils and double back to D34 toward, simply, Mousson. A steep climb leads you to the summit of the **Butte de Mousson,** a feudal stronghold of the dukes of Bar. Ruins of a chapel and fortification walls frame spectacular views over the Moselle valley. The Germans profited from the natural power of the position, holding out against two weeks of pounding artillery before retreating yet farther east.

★ **⑥①** Return to A31 and head north for **Metz,** the capital of the Moselle region. Despite its industrial background, it is officially classed as one of France's greenest cities: Parks, gardens, and leafy squares crop up everywhere. At its heart, towering above the Hôtel de Ville (Town Hall) and the 18th-century place d'Armes, you'll find the **Cathédrale St-Etienne,** one of the finest Gothic cathedrals in France.

At 137 feet from floor to roof, Metz Cathedral is also one of the highest; and, thanks to nearly 1½ acres of window space, one of the lightest. The narrow 13th- to 14th-century nave channels the eye toward the dramatically raised 16th-century choir, whose walls have given way to huge sheets of richly colored, gemlike glass by masters old and modern, including Russian-born artist Marc Chagall (1887–1985). The oldest windows actually date from the 12th century and, in their dark, mosaiclike simplicity, offer stark contrast to the ethereal new stained glass. You'll find them on the right rear wall of the transepts, over the modern organ. Binoculars magnify moving details and reveal, flanking the full length of the clerestory above the nave, marvelously quirky gargoyles. A pair of symmetrical 290-foot towers flank the nave, marking the medieval division between two churches that were merged to form the cathedral. The tower, with a fussy 15th-century pinnacle, houses **Dame Mutte,** an enormous bell cast in 1605 and tolled on momentous occasions. The Grand Portal beneath the large rose window was reconstructed by the Germans at the turn of the century; the statues of the prophets include, on the right, *Daniel,* sculpted to resemble Kaiser Wilhelm II (his unmistakable upturned mustachios were shaved off in 1940). Be sure to walk the length of the exterior to take in the web of flying buttresses that arc airily down from the apse. *Pl. d'Armes.*

TIME OUT On your way from the cathedral to the museum, stop at the charming bistro/tearoom, **Dauphiné** (8 rue du Chanoine-Collin), where under a low barrel vault you can sample *tourte lorraine* (meat pie), an inexpensive *plat du jour,* or a slice of fruit tart.

Up the street, in a 17th-century former convent, is the **Musée d'Art et d'Histoire**: turn left out of the cathedral and take rue des Jardins. The museum's wide-ranging collections encompass French and German paintings from the 18th century on, military arms and uniforms, and archaeology; local finds evoke the city's Gallo-Roman, Carolingian, and medieval past. Religious works of art are stored in the **Grenier de Chèvremont,** a granary built in 1457, with a many-windowed façade and stone-arcade decoration. An Escher-like labyrinth of stairways automatically excludes wheelchairs, strollers, and poor navigators. *2 rue du Haut-Poirier,* ☎ *87–75–10–18.* ☛ *20 frs adults, 10 frs students.* ☉ *Daily 10–noon and 2–5.*

Now walk back past the cathedral, continuing for another two blocks. Down the Esplanade is the small, heavily restored church of **St-Pierre-aux-Nonnains** (rue Poncelet, adjoining the concert hall called l'Arsenal). The round stones and rows of red bricks are thought to date from the 4th century, predating Attila the Hun's sacking of Metz; thus, Metz claims the oldest church in France. The best of the rare Merovingian ornaments salvaged from the 6th-century version of the chapel are displayed in a full reproduction of the interior in the Museum of Art and History. The neighboring **Chapelle des Templiers** (blvd. Poincaré), from the 13th century, is the only octagonal church in Lorraine.

★ ⑫ From Metz, head west on the A4 tollway to **Verdun** and follow signs to the battlefields northeast of the town's center. A key strategic site along the Meuse Valley, Verdun is famous, above all, for the 18-month battle between the French and the Germans in World War I. It left more than 700,000 dead and nine villages wiped off the map. Both sides fought with suicidal fury, and in the end, no significant ground was gained or lost. To this day, the scenes of battle are scarred by bomb craters, stunted vegetation and thousands of unexploded mines and shells, rendering the area permanently uninhabitable.

Circuits of the major war sites extend on either side of the River Meuse, with the leading memorial—a huge **chapel and ossuary** surrounded by an endless cemetery—at Douaumont, 10 kilometers (6 miles) to the north. The bizarre, evocative structure—a little like a cross, a lot like a bomb—rears up over the graves, its ground-level windows revealing undignified heaps of human bones and skulls riveted with bullet holes, harvested from the killing fields. A climb to the top of the tower (6 frs) affords a view over the ocean of graves, and in the basement, a film dwells on the agony and futility of the pointless butchery. ☎ 29–84–54–81. ☛ Film: 13 frs adults, 8 frs children under 16. ☉ Daily Mar.–Apr. and Oct.–Nov. 9–noon and 2–5:30; Apr.–June 9–6; July–Aug. 9–6:30; Sept. 9–noon and 2–6.

The square, moderne **mémorial de Verdun** is a more complete museum, with emotionally charged texts and video commentary. Panoramas, uniforms, weapons, and the pathetic artwork of trenchbound soldiers (Art Nouveau vases hammered from artillery shells) prevail. Fleury-devant-Douaumont, ☎ 29–84–35–34. ☛ 20 frs adults, 10 frs children 11–16. ☉ Apr.–mid-Sept., daily 9–6; mid-Sept.–mid-Dec. and mid-Jan.–Apr., 9–noon and 2–5:30.

Head north from Verdun on D905. When Louis XVI was arrested at Varennes in 1791, he was fleeing by coach toward the refuge of **Montmédy,** a historic hilltop citadel redesigned and reinforced by the great military architect Vauban. His signature star-shaped fortifications still thrust out over the valley, and drivers still enter the tiny upper village over a drawbridge. Once inside, there's not much to see but a sleepy, undeveloped neighborhood, but the military architecture itself remains in nearly mint condition.

Some 8 kilometers (5 miles) north of Montmédy on N43, then D110, you'll find the sumptuous **basilica** at **Avioth.** A miraculous statue of the Virgin was discovered in this tiny village in the 11th century, and the faithful poured in for the next 300 years, which explains the church's surprising richness. Construction of the church lasted from the late 13th to the early 15th centuries, finishing amid the elaborate stone lace of the Flamboyant Gothic style. The interior contains a 14th-century altar, and recent restoration has revealed medieval frescoes on the choir vaults. The recevresse, a free-standing Flamboyant tower in front of the main entrance, once held the miraculous statue and received the offerings of pilgrims.

Tour 4: Franche-Comté

Numbers in the margin correspond to points of interest on the Franche-Comté map

Our tour starts in **Besançon,** the capital of Franche-Comté (the province roughly covering the French extent of the Jura mountains), nestled in a vast bend of the River Doubs. Besançon's defensive potential was quickly spotted by Vauban, whose imposing citadel remains the town's architectural highlight. Besançon has long been a clock-making center and is the more recent birthplace of the synthetic silk (rayon) industry. The town's famous offspring include Auguste and Louis Lumière, the inventors of a motion-picture camera, and the poet Victor Hugo, born while his father was garrisoned here in 1802. Hugo is no local hero, though, having dismissed Besançon as an "old Spanish town," a disparaging reference to the lip service the town's inhabitants paid to the Austro-Spanish Habsburgs during medieval times. A 75-minute trip along the River Doubs on a 110-seat vedette boat provides a good introduction to the town. Boats leave from Pont de la République and take in a lock and the 400-yard tunnel under the citadel. ☎ 81–68–13–25. ☛ Ticket: 43 frs adults, 33 frs children 3–10. July–early Sept.,

*weekdays 10:30, 2:30, 4:30, weekends also at 6:15; May–June, week-
ends 2:30 and 4:30.*

Wander around the quayside and continue to the nearby Pont Battant
and the start of Grande-Rue, Besançon's oldest street. This leads to the
citadel, past fountains, wrought-iron railings, and stately 16th- to
18th-century mansions, the most stunning of which is the Renaissance
Palais Granvelle (1540). Hugo was born at No. 140, the Lumière
brothers just opposite. At the foot of the citadel, notice the **Horloge
Astronomique,** a stupendous 19th-century astronomical clock with 62
dials and an array of automatons that spurt into action just before the
hours are sounded. *2 rue du Chapitre,* ☎ *81–81–12–76.* ☛ *20 frs.*
☺ *Wed.–Mon. 9:45–11:45 and 2:45–5:45; closed Wed. in winter.*

In the summer, a small independent tourist train carries you (with commentary) on a round-trip to the Citadelle, but the fare does not include
admission (☎ 81–68–13–25; 30 frs adults, 19 frs children; daily 9–
6 in summer). The **Citadelle** is perched on a rocky spur 350 feet above
the town. Its triple ring of ramparts, now laid out as promenades and
peppered with Vauban's original watchtowers, offers extensive views
of the city and the countryside. The buildings contain a series of museums devoted to natural history, regional folklore, agricultural tools,
and the French Resistance during World War II. There also are shops
and restaurants, though no hotels as yet: The gates close at night. *Rue
des Fusillés,* ☎ *81–65–07–44. Admission to citadel and museums: 30
frs adults, 20 frs students and senior citizens.* ☺ *Late Mar.–Sept.,
Wed.–Mon. 9–6:30; Oct.–Mar., Wed.–Mon. 9:45–4:45.*

From Besançon, make the 26-kilometer (16-mile) drive along N57/D67
⓺ to **Ornans.** There are two reasons to visit this pretty village: the view
of the steep-roofed old houses that line the River Loue and the **Maison Natale** of Gustave Courbet (1819–77), the pioneering French Realist painter who influenced Edouard Manet. Courbet is best known
for his *Burial at Ornans* (now in the Musée d'Orsay), with its procession of somber peasants. He also enjoyed painting local landscapes (often
featuring deer), unblushing erotic compositions for Asian clients, and
self-portraits. This assertive, full-bearded radical spent his last years
in Swiss exile after toppling the Napoléonic column on Place Vendôme
during the Paris Commune of 1871. Courbet's original home—a rambling 18th-century mansion—hardly goes with this radical image, but
it provides a pleasant setting for the collection of souvenirs, documents,
drawings, sculptures, and paintings housed there. *Pl. Robert-Fernier,*
☎ *81–62–23–30.* ☛ *20 frs adults, 10 frs children 6–14; temporary
exhibits 40 frs.* ☺ *Apr.–June and Sept.–Oct., daily 10–noon and 2–
6; July–Aug., daily 10–6; closed Tues. in winter.*

Continue down the steeply banked Loue Valley along D67, through
the picturesque villages of Vuillafans (with its 16th-century bridge and
restored watermill), Lods, and Mouthier-Haute-Pierre, as far as La Main.
Turn right onto D41, and right again in Ouhans 4 kilometers (2.5 miles)
⓺ later, following signs to the **Source de la Loue.** Leave your car at the
parking lot; it's a 15-minute walk along a stony path to the spectacular river source, where the Loue gushes forth from a cliff face, cascading
past ruined watermills. You can get good close-up photographs if you
take care not to slip on the mossy vantage points.

Return to La Main and head south on N57. If you're keen on church
architecture, turn left on D130 just before Pontarlier, left again on D437,
⓺ and continue to the tiny village of **Montbenoît,** 14 kilometers (9 miles)
northeast. Its **Ancienne Abbaye** dates from the 11th century, although

Franche-Comté

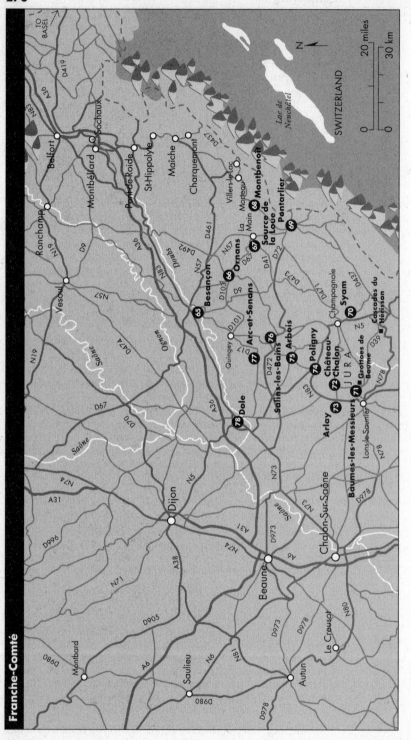

N

20 miles

30 km

TO
BASEL

SWITZERLAND

Lac de
Neuchâtel

Belfort

Ronchamp

Sochaux

Montbéliard

Pont-de-Roide

St-Hippolyte

Vesoul

Maîche

Charquemont

Villers-le-Lac

Mortequ

La Main

64 Montbenoît

Pontarlier

69

Source de
la Loue

63

Ornans

67

66

Besançon

65

Arc-et-Senans

Champagnole

Syam

70

Cascades du
Hérisson

76 Arbois

75 Poligny

Château
Chalon

74

72

J U R A

Grottoes de
Baume

71

77
Quingey

Salins-les-Bains

78 Dole

Arlay

73

Baumes-les-Messieurs

Lons-le-Saunier

Dijon

Beaune

Chalon-Sur-Saône

Montbard

Saulieu

Le Creusot

Autun

the cloisters and chapter house were built 300 years later. Note the superbly carved wooden choir stalls (1525–27), which often offer a Renaissance interpretation of biblical tales. Samson, for instance, wears natty hose and a lace ruff collar as Delilah takes to his flowing locks with a pair of oversize scissors. ☎ 81–38–10–32. ☛ *15 frs adults, 4 frs children. Church and cloisters ⊘ daily 9–noon and 2–6. Guided tours with kitchen and refectory July–Aug., on request.*

You may want to continue along the Doubs Valley to Villers-le-Lac, to spend the night at its fine hotel-restaurant (*see below*), or you can head back to **Pontarlier,** with its old streets, churches, and gateways. Absinthe—a notorious anise-based aperitif, the forerunner of Ricard and Pernod—was produced in Pontarlier until it was banned in 1915 for inducing alcoholism. Learn more about the *fee verte* (green fairy), as absinthe was called, at the **Musée Municipal** (Town Museum), which also displays porcelain, pictures, and artifacts from local excavations. *2 pl. d'Arçon,* ☎ 81–46–73–68. ☛ *10 frs adults, 5 frs children 12– 18. ⊘ Weekdays 10–noon and 2–6, Sat. 2–6, Sun. 3–7.*

Just south of town via N57 lies the **Château de Joux,** a beefy fortress perched on a steep hill, glowering across the Jura landscape toward the Swiss border. Founded in the 11th century, it retains its round medieval towers, drawbridges, and 17th-century ramparts. You can visit the dungeon and a sturdy collection of old guns and weapons (guided tours only; allow one hour). ☎ 81–69–47–95. ☛ *28 frs. ⊘ Daily, July–Aug. 9–6; Apr.–June and Sept. 10–noon and 2–5; Oct.–Mar. tours at 10, 11:15, 2, and 3:30.*

From Pontarlier, head 43 kilometers (27 miles) southwest on D72/D471 to Champagnole, then briefly take N5 south (toward Geneva) before bearing left on D127 to **Syam,** nestling in the lush Ain Valley. Here you can visit the ironworks, **Les Forges de Syam,** built in 1813 and still in operation. Nearly 50 people work here, making nails, locks, tools, and machinery; the techniques of "hot-rolling" and "hard drawing" are explained at a museum (with video presentation), and you can visit the blacksmiths' former dwellings. ☎ 84–51–61–00. ☛ *12 frs adults, 6 frs children. ⊘ July–Aug., Wed.–Mon. 10–6; May–June and Sept., weekends only 10–6.*

The adjacent **Château de Syam,** a sturdy, square, yellow-fronted neo-Palladian villa built in 1818, has outsize Ionic pilasters at each corner and, inside, a theatrical, colonnaded rotunda ringed with balconies. Guided tours take you through restored rooms, furnished in Louis-Philippe/Biedermeier style. ☎ 84–51–61–25. ☛ *20 frs adults, 10 frs children. ⊘ July–Sept., Sat.–Mon. 2–6.*

From Syam, rejoin N5 south then take D75 to Ilay, turn right (west) on D39 to Doucier and follow signs to the **Cascades du Hérisson,** via the narrow, winding D326. From the parking lot it's an uphill 10-minute walk to the first waterfall (L'Eventail), with its 210-foot drop. If you come after heavy rains, the noise is deafening, and the path is slippery with spray. It's exhilarating but drenching, so dress accordingly. In summer you can usually progress beyond L'Eventail, along a rugged path past five more cascades, all the way to Le Saut Girard, 3 kilometers (2 miles) away (allow three hours for the round-trip).

Return to Doucier and continue along D39 until it joins D471. Then, instead of turning left toward Lons-le-Saunier, turn right and look for signs to the Belvedere des Roches de Baume: a vantage point with a plummeting view of the ring of chalky cliffs that hem in the village of

Baume-les-Messieurs—our next port of call (continue east on D471 and take the first left).

㉑ Quite apart from its breathtaking setting, **Baume-les-Messieurs** is a quaint old village in its own right; the pick of its ancient buildings is a 12th-century abbey, still fully functional, with rickety courtyards and an early 16th-century Flemish altarpiece donated by the Belgian town of Ghent. The church is closed in winter; the abbey is open year-round. ☎ 84–47–26–93 or 84–44–61–41. ☛ *Abbey free.* ⊙ *Daily 9–8.*

Don't miss another local attraction: the 40-minute tour of the **Grottes de Baume,** 650 yards of skillfully lit galleries 400 feet underground, containing a river, a lake, and weird-shaped stalactites and stalagmites (the temperature is chilly, so bring a sweater). The largest cave is more than 200 feet high, and classical music blasts out to heighten the dramatic effect. ☎ 84–44–61–58. ☛ *25 frs adults, 12 frs children.* ⊙ *Apr.–Sept., 9:30–noon and 2–6.*

㉒ Follow D70 north from Baume to the medieval village of **Château-Chalon,** perched on a rocky promontory high above local vineyards, whose legendary *vin jaune* (yellow wine), said to keep for 200 years without losing its vigor, is considered the Jura's finest wine. A charming place to sample it is on the tiny square opposite the 12th-century church, where the Fruitière Vinicole runs generous tastings in an old cellar. Walk off any aftereffects with a stroll through Château-Chalon's narrow, twisting streets. The restored stonework, restrained shopfronts, and archaic street signs help to keep out the 20th century, and beguiling views await you around every corner.

㉓ Then push west along D120 to **Arlay,** 6 kilometers (4 miles) past Voiteur, with the **Château d'Arlay** on your left just before you reach the village. The 18th-century château contains sumptuously carved regional furniture dating from the same period. The outstanding wine produced here can be sampled (and purchased) in the château's cellar (open Mon.–Sat. 8–noon and 2–6). Combine your visit with a walk around the park and a visit to the **Volerie des Rapaces,** where (at 4 and 5 PM) trained eagles and other birds of prey perform wide-winged acrobatics overhead. *Rue Haute du Bourg,* ☎ 84–85–04–22. ☛ *Château and volerie: 45 frs.* ⊙ *July–Aug., Mon.–Sun. 2–6. Volerie also open Apr.–Oct., Wed. and weekends 2–6.*

㉔ Backtrack and take N83 northeast 18 kilometers (11 miles) to **Poligny,** home of the largely 15th-century **Collégiale St-Hippolyte,** filled with medieval statues, and the **Maison du Comté,** a museum devoted to the production and aging of a famous, slow-maturing Comté cheese. *Av. de la Résistance,* ☎ 84–37–23–51. ☛ *14 frs adults, 9 frs children under 12.* ⊙ *Daily 9–noon and 2–6; guided tours July–Aug. at 10, 11, 2, 3:15, and 4:30.*

㉕ Carry on up N83 to nearby **Arbois,** a pretty wine village, worth an overnight stop for its fine hotel-restaurant, Jean-Paul Jeunet (*see* Dining and Lodging, *below*). The famous bacteriologist Louis Pasteur (1822–95) grew up here and returned each year on vacation. His family home with many of his possessions—his inkstand, school prizes, science books, and laboratory—is being renovated to honor the centennial of his death. *83 rue de Courcelles,* ☎ 84–66–11–72. *New admission and opening hours to be announced.*

The Arbois vineyard is one of the finest in eastern France; to learn more about it, visit the newly remounted **Musée de la Vigne et du Vin de Franche-Comté** and peruse its collection of tools and documents.

Château Pecauld, ☎ *84–66–26–14.* ☛ *17 frs age 13 and over.* ☉
Feb.–Nov., Wed.–Mon. 10–noon and 2–6.

While in Arbois, make the short excursion south along D469 to two
beautiful spots: the **Reculée des Planches,** a rocky valley created by glacial
erosion and peppered with caves and waterfalls (admission to caves
30 frs, 15 frs children 4–12; open Apr.–Sept., daily 10–noon and 2–
6; Oct., Sat.–Thurs. 10–noon and 2–6), and the rocky **Cirque du Fer
à Cheval** (Horseshoe Circus), with its panoramic view of U-shaped cliffs.

⓵ Next, follow D54/D94 8 kilometers (5 miles) northeast to **Salins-les-
Bains,** tucked away in the steep valley of the River Furieuse. At the saltworks here, which functioned until modern times (1962), you can
learn how local salty water was pumped to the surface and then evap-
orated; it was a sticky, sweaty process that you can fully appreciate in
the humid "heating room." *Pl. des Salines,* ☎ *84–73–01–34.* ☛ *23
frs adults, 13 frs children. Guided tours only, hourly Easter–mid-Sept.,
mid-Sept.–Nov. and Feb.–Easter at 10:30, 2:30, and 4.*

★ ⓷ For a glimpse of the palatial pretensions of the erstwhile salt industry,
drive northwest 18 kilometers (11 miles) on D472/D121 (via Cramans)
to **Arc-et-Senans.** The **royal saltworks,** built 1774–79 by Claude-
Nicolas Ledoux, are an extraordinary example of neoclassical industrial architecture. With their Palladian porticoes, rustication, and
towering columns, the buildings—arranged in a gracious semicircle
around sweeping lawns—have an almost palatial grandeur. Originally
they were intended to form part of a rationally planned, circular *ville
idéale* (ideal town). Wander around the various buildings, admire their
intricate wood-beam roofs, and learn about the long-gone salt industry. *Saline Royale,* ☎ *81–54–45–45.* ☛ *29 frs adults, 22 frs students,
12 frs children 8–15.* ☉ *July–Aug., daily 9–7; Mar.–June and Sept.–Oct.,
daily 9–noon and 2–6; Nov.–Feb., daily 10–noon and 2–5.*

⓸ Head west from Arc-et-Senans 28 kilometers (17 miles) on D17/D7 to
Dole, another sturdy old hilltop town. It climbs above the River Doubs,
with the muscular 250-foot tower of its 16th-century Eglise Notre-Dame
visible above the rooftops for miles around. The warren of dank alleyways beneath the church invites exploration, and you may want to
track down the **Maison Natale de Pasteur,** where Louis Pasteur (last
encountered in Arbois) was born in 1822. The museum, recently restored to its 1744 look, with original beams and waxed plank floors,
contains documents and mementos, plus the restored tanner's workshop of Pasteur's father who, like most of his neighbors, was a leather
worker. *43 rue Pasteur,* ☎ *84–72–20–61.* ☛ *20 frs.* ☉ *Apr.–June and
Sept.–Oct., Wed.–Sat. and Mon. 10–noon and 2–6, Sun. 2–6; July–Aug.,
Wed.–Sat. and Mon. 10–6, Sun. 10–5.*

What to See and Do with Children

Children should be delighted by the **Walibi Schtroumpf** theme park,
featuring the cuddly blue dwarves known in English as Smurfs. *Voie
Romaine, 57210 Maizières-les-Metz, just off A31 north of Metz,* ☎
87–51–73–90. ☛ *105 frs adults, children under 1 meter (39 inches)
free.* ☉ *Mid-Apr.–May 1, daily 10–6; May and Sept., Wed. and weekends 10–6; June, daily 10–6; July–Aug., daily 10–7.*

Astronomical Clock, Strasbourg, Tour 1
Automobile and Train Museums, Mulhouse, Tour 2
Haut-Koenigsbourg, Tour 2
Horse and Harness Museum, near Boersch, Tour 2
Musée Alsacien, Strasbourg, Tour 1

Ecomusée de Haute-Alsace, Ungersheim, Tour 2
Volerie des Rapaces, Château d'Arlay, Tour 4

Off the Beaten Track

You can watch glassblowing in the tiny town of **Passavant-la-Rochère,** 37 kilometers (23 miles) southeast of Contrexéville via D164/D5. The **Verrerie de la Rochère** has been in operation since 1475. A wide selection of glassware is sold in an adjoining 17th-century building with a majestic wooden roof. *Rue de la Verrerie,* ☎ *84–78–61–00.* ☉ *Apr.–Sept., daily 2:30–6. No glassblowing Sun. or Aug.*

Forty or so kilometers (25 miles) due north from Metz toward Luxembourg lies the tiny medieval village of **Rodemack,** which touts itself with only slightly exaggerated pride as the Carcassonne of Lorraine. Its 600 meters (650 yards) of 13th-century ramparts, chapel, private château, and medieval garden remain picture perfect, and the Auberge de la Petite Carcassonne (12 pl. de la Porte-de-Sierck) serves excellent regional menus.

SHOPPING

Gift Ideas

Among the specialties of Alsace are the handwoven checkered napkins and tablecloths known as **kelches** and the hand-painted **earthenware molds** for *kouglof* bread. You'll also see thousands of products adorned with Hansi, a beclogged Alsatian folk character, in every village souvenir shop. In Obernai, try **Dietrich** (pl. du Marché) for useful and beautifully crafted household goods. Besançon is a traditional clockmaking center. Pipes, wood carvings, and automatons are Jura specialties. The **Faïenceries** in Salins-les-Bains have a wide choice of local pottery.

Shopping Districts

The lively city centers of Strasbourg and Colmar are crammed with specialized shops and boutiques. **Rue des Hallebardes** next to the cathedral, the adjacent **rue des Grandes Arcades** (with its shopping mall), and **place Kléber** form the commercial heart of Strasbourg; chocolate shops and delicatessens selling local foie gras are delicious places for browsing. In Nancy the streets next to the cathedral are full of life; the ancient Grand' Rue features antiques, bouquinistes, and independent bakers; and the covered market could occupy foodies for hours.

Glass

Glass and crystal are produced by skilled artisans at **Passavant-la-Rochère** (*see* Off the Beaten Track, *above*). At **Baccarat** (60 kilometers, or 37 miles, east of Nancy on N59), the town center is dominated by attractive crystal shops, including the factory's opulent showroom. ☎ *83–76–60–22. Museum* ☉ *Apr.–Oct., daily 10:30–noon and 2–6; Nov.–Mar. weekends 10:30–noon and 2–6. Salesroom open Oct.–Apr., Mon.–Sat. 9–12:30 and 1:30–7; May–Sept., Mon.–Sat. 9–7, Sun. 10–12:30 and 2:30–7.* The **Daum** glassworks in Nancy (17 rue des Cristalleries) carry on the city's Art Nouveau *pâte de verre* (colored matte glass) tradition.

Linens

Household linens made in Gérardmer enjoy some prestige in France. Watch for the mark Linvosges both in shops and at factory outlets in Xonrupt-Longemer and Gérardmer.

Food and Wine

Throughout Alsace, streetfront *dégustations* (tastings) encourage you to stop, sample, and buy the local wares. Excellent eaux-de-vie are also available. We recommend **Schwach & Fils** (28 rte de Ribeauvillé, 68150 Hunawihr) or **Jean-Paul Metté** (9 rue des Tanneurs, 68150 Ribeauvillé). For superb foie gras and pâté, hunt out **Schiffmacher** (Les Champs Colnot, 88540 Bussana, ☎ 29–61–54–68) between Mulhouse and Gérardmer, off N66); enjoy them en route, however—farm meat products may not be exported. Portable treats from Lorraine include handsomely packaged bergamot candies from Nancy, buttery madeleines from **Gros-Jean** in Commercy, and any number of mirabelle products, from jams and conserves to eaux-de-vie.

SPORTS AND THE OUTDOORS

Bicycling

The southern regions of Lorraine make for pleasant bicycle touring. A guide is available from the **Comité Départemental de Cyclotourisme** (33 rue de la République, 54950 Laronxe). For information on biking in the rolling, low mountains of the Jura, contact the **Comité Régional de Cyclotourisme VTTde Franche-Comté** (12 rue Charles-Dornuer, 25000 Besançon, ☎ 81–52–18–13). In Alsace, the north–south route between Strasbourg and Colmar is relatively flat.

Canoeing

Canoes and kayaks can be rented (130–190 francs per day) from **Sport Nautique** (2 av. Chardonnet, 25000 Besançon, ☎ 81–80–56–01).

Fishing

Franche-Comté is an angler's paradise. Write to the **Comité Départemental du Tourisme** (Hôtel du Département, 39021 Lons-le-Saunier) for their brochure—"Pêche Gratuite."

Golf

There are 18-hole courses at Epinal, Vittel, Mamirolle (near Besançon), Liverdun (near Nancy), the Château of Cherisey (near Metz), La Wantzenau (north of Strasbourg), and Ammerschwihr (near Colmar).

Hiking

For a list of signposted trails in the Vosges foothills, contact the **Sélestat** tourist office (*see* Essential Information, *above*). The **Comité Régional de Tourisme** (9 rue de Pontarlier, 25000 Besançon) provides full details on hiking in Franche-Comté; write to the **Fédération Jurassienne de Randonnée Pédestre** (Hôtel du Département, BP652, 39021 Lons-le-Saunier) for their brochure on trails in the Jura.

Horseback Riding

There are many possibilities for renting horses for a forest sortie. For further details, contact the **Association Départementale de Tourisme Equestre** (4 rue des Violettes, 67201 Eckbolsheim, ☎ 88–77–39–64). In the Jura, contact the **Poney Club des Chênes** (39110 Andelot, ☎ 84–51–45–97), north of Champagnole, or **Le Petit Cheval Blanc** (39800 Fay-en-Montagne, ☎ 84–85–32–07), near Poligny.

Skiing

Both downhill and—especially—cross-country skiing are possible in winter in the Vosges and Jura mountains at Le Bonhomme, Gérardmer, Valley of Munster, Champ du Feu, Le Hohwald, Jougne, and Les Rousses. Altitudes range from 2,800 to 4,300 feet.

DINING AND LODGING

Dining

Alsatian cooking is distinctive in its marriage of German and French tastes. It tends to be heavy: *Choucroute* (sauerkraut), served with ham and sausages, or *baeckoffe* (a hearty meat and potato casserole), washed down with a mug of local beer or a pitcher of wine. But there is some sophistication, too. The local foie gras is admirably accompanied by a glass of Gewurztraminer, preferably late-harvested (*vendanges tardives*) for extra sweetness. Riesling, the classic wine of Alsace, is often used to make a sauce that goes exceptionally well with trout or chicken. Snails and seasonal game (pheasant, partridge, hare, venison, and boar) are other favorites, as are Munster cheese (often served with pungent cumin seeds), salty *bretzel* loaves, and flaky, briochelike *kouglof* bread.

Local salmon, pike, eel, and trout are plentiful. Carp fried in breadcrumbs is a specialty of southern Alsace. Lorraine, renowned for quiches, is also famous for its dumplings, madeleines, almond candies (*dragées*), and macaroons. Lorraine shares the Alsatian love of pastry and fruit tarts, often made with mirabelles, but only in German-influenced Alsace will you find *winstubs* (cozy paneled inns serving wine and snacks or meals). Restaurant prices tend to be lower in Lorraine than in Alsace.

Beef and freshwater fish (trout, pike, carp, perch) are menu mainstays in the Jura. Hard, flavorsome Comté is the choice local cheese, along with Morbier, Vacherin, and Cancoillotte. Bread dipped in melted cheese (fondue) is a popular winter dish. Jura wines, notably Vin Jaune and Vin de Paille, can be superb.

CATEGORY	COST*
$$$$	over 500 frs
$$$	250–500 frs
$$	125–250 frs
$	under 125 frs

*per person for a three-course meal, including tax (18.6%) and tip but not wine

Lodging

Hotel accommodations are easier to find in Lorraine and the Jura than in Alsace, where advance reservations are essential during summer months (especially in Strasbourg and Colmar). Alsace is rich in *gîtes*, or rented country houses, which provide excellent value for families or small groups. Local tourist offices or the regional office in Strasbourg (17 place de la Cathédrale, ☎ 88–52–28–28) can provide full details. For the "Gîtes de France" Jura brochure, write to Service Tourisme, Chambre d'Agriculture, B.P. 417, 39016 Lons-le-Saunier.

CATEGORY	COST*
$$$$	over 800 frs
$$$	500–800 frs
$$	250–500 frs
$	under 250 frs

*All prices are for a standard double room for two, including tax (18.6%) and service charge.

Arbois

DINING AND LODGING

Jean-Paul Jeunet. This ancient stone convent, its massive beams enhanced with subtle lighting and contemporary art, has surged to the fore as the most popular and recognized eatery in the Jura. Chef Jean-Paul Jêunet's devotion to the flora and fauna of the local wilderness has evolved a bold, earthy, high-flavored cuisine: smoked carp pancakes, snails in anise sauce, prawns with heather flowers, crisp beet chips, even sheeps' milk sorbet—though, occasionally, his classic *coq au vin jaune* (made with cream and a flavorful regional wine) reappears. The chef's father, once an award-winning sommelier himself, has laid down a worthy *cave* (cellar) that focuses, naturally, on regional treasures. The hotel rooms have pleasant modern fittings and pretty pine furniture. ☎ *9 rue de l'Hôtel-de-Ville, 39600,* ☎ *84–66–05–67,* FAX *84–66–24–20. 17 rooms with bath or shower. Restaurant (closed Tues. and Wed. lunch, Dec.–Jan.). DC, MC, V. Closed Dec.–Jan. $$$*

Belfort

DINING

Pot au Feu. This rustic, red-sandstone bistro at the foot of the citadel serves tasty salads, smoked fish, pot-au-feu, and roast turbot. Two lunch menus include wine. ✕ *27 bis Grande-Rue,* ☎ *84–28–57–84. Reservations advised. MC, V. Closed Sun., Mon., and 1 wk in Aug. $$*

DINING AND LODGING

Château Servin. You'll find surprises at this quiet, traditional hotel, set on expansive grounds. The Louis XV rooms are comfortable and modern, although some are small; many overlook the garden. The dining room has plush, thick carpeting and gleaming silverware. Chef Dominique Mathy serves up such dishes as spicy duck soup, caramelized spider crab, foie gras with raspberry vinegar, smoked salmon with cabbage, and steaming cherry soufflé. ☎ *9 rue du Général Négrier, 90000,* ☎ *84–21–41–85,* FAX *84–57–05–57. 10 rooms with bath or shower. Restaurant (closed Sun. evening and Fri.). AE, DC, MC, V. $$*

Besançon

DINING

Mungo Park. This former warehouse on the banks of the River Doubs is now a welcoming two-story restaurant combining Old World beams and stonework with exotic African wall hangings and empty tortoise shells. Locals and Parisians pile in to appreciate the inspired work of partners Jocelyne Choquart and Benoît Rotchi, who brilliantly marry local and exotic ingredients—carp, tongue, and Vin Jaune meet ginger, curry, and citrus leaf. Be sure to explore the extensive local wine list. ✕ *11 rue Jean-Petit,* ☎ *81–81–28–01. Reservations required. MC, V. Closed Sat. lunch, Sun., Mon. lunch, and first half of Aug. $$$*

Poker d'As. Wood carvings and gleaming brasswork lend a folkloric feel to this popular restaurant. But judging from such adventurous cuisine as mussels in kirsch, salmon and herring tartare, and rhubarb soup, we suspect that Benoît Ferreux is something of a city slicker. Menus offer excellent value for such brave forays into *cuisine du terroir* (regional cooking). Jura wines are showcased. ✕ *14 rue du Clos St-Amour,* ☎ *81–81–42–49. Reservations advised. AE, DC, MC, V. Closed Sun. dinner, Mon., and most of July. $$*

LODGING

Paris. There are few decent hotels in the attractive heart of Besançon. This one is the best; it's well run, unpretentious, old-fashioned, and brightened by a tree-lined garden courtyard. ☎ *33 rue des Granges,*

25000, ☎ 81–81–36–56, FAX 81–61–94–90. *60 rooms, most with bath or shower. Breakfast room. AE, DC, MC, V. $$*

Colmar

DINING

Schillinger. Displaying not a trace of Alsatian influence in either his menu or decor, genial Jean Schillinger lords it over one of the smoothest-run restaurants in Alsace. Impeccable service, velvet upholstery, and gleaming silver cutlery complement an exhaustive wine list and the increasingly adventurous cooking: monkfish with garlic and bacon, squid salad with herb pasta, rouget with marrow, and salt-cooked pigeon. ✕ *16 rue Stanislas, ☎ 89–41–43–17. Reservations required. Jacket and tie. AE, DC, MC, V. Closed Sun. dinner and Mon. $$$$*

Caveau Hansi. Appropriately named for the ubiquitous little beclogged child who decorates everything around here, this hypertraditional tavern in the old town offers excellent down-home classics (choucroute, pot-au-feu) prepared and served with a sophisticated touch. ✕ *23 rue des Marchands, ☎ 89–41–37–84. MC, V. Closed Jan. $$*

Koïfhus. On a beautiful old-town summer terrace, you'll dive into a massive, classic choucroute, *baeckoffe* (meat and potato stew), or tender-crisp tarte flambée without dealing with stuffy service or heavy *additions* (bills). Have another pitcher of Riesling and spend the evening. Reserve in summer for a seat outdoors. ✕ *2 pl. de l'Ancienne-Douane, ☎ 89–23–04–90. DC, MC, V. Closed Thurs. and Jan. $*

La Cave Gourmande. Just across from Hansi and a few steps downstairs (pricewise as well), this atmospheric vaulted crypt tries a little harder to break away from local standards (snails with pasta, Muenster pastry, cod in mustard sauce). The weekday lunch is a bargain. ✕ *22 rue des Marchands, ☎ 89–24–37–94. MC, V. Closed Jan. $*

DINING AND LODGING

★ **Hostellerie Le Maréchal.** A maze of corridors connects the three Renaissance town houses that make up this charming hotel near the River Lauch. Some of the rooms are small, decorated predominantly in light, cheerful colors; some are endearingly rustic, with beams and curvy walls and floors; those in back have good river views. The restaurant, A l'Echevin, offers atmospheric, if pricey, garden meals along the canal. ⌂ *5 pl. des Six-Montagnes-Noires, 68000, ☎ 89–41–60–32, FAX 89–23–73–61. 40 rooms with bath. Restaurant. AE, MC, V. Closed Jan. and Feb. Restaurant $$–$$$, hotel $$$*

LODGING

Colbert. The convenient location is a plus here, halfway between the train station and the ancient town center. Ask for one of the quieter rooms along rue des Taillandiers. The guest rooms are well equipped and air-conditioned, though the decor is a little loud. ⌂ *2 rue des Trois-Epis, 68000, ☎ 89–41–31–05, FAX 89–23–66–75. 50 rooms with bath or shower. Bar. MC, V. $$*

Dole

DINING

Les Templiers. With its vaulted stone ceiling and pointed Gothic archways, this restaurant in a 16th-century building on the main street offers the archetypal Old World setting. The feeling is enhanced by tapestry-upholstered high-back chairs and stained-glass windows masking the kitchen. Chef Joël Césari's cuisine is a shade more nouvelle: pike-perch with onions and juniper berries, or snails cooked with chicken liver. ✕ *35 Grande-Rue, ☎ 84–82–78–78. Reservations advised. DC, MC, V. Closed Sun. dinner, Mon. lunch. $$*

Domrémy-la-Pucelle

LODGING

Jeanne d'Arc. Pilgrims to the birthplace of France's holy heroine can stay next door to her childhood church and wake to the bells that summoned her voices. Accommodations are considerably less evocative, in jazzy '60s tile and paneling, but bathrooms are spotless and state-of-the-art, and breakfasts (in-room only) generous. ⌖ *Domrémy-la-Pucelle, 88630,* ☎ *29–06–96–06. 12 rooms with bath. No credit cards. $*

Lons-le-Saunier

DINING AND LODGING

Parenthèse. It's worth the 3-kilometer (2-mile) trip from Lons-le-Saunier to the hillside village of Chillé to stay at this sturdy, rustic mansion in a large garden. The rooms are fully modernized and individually decorated; the good, cheap restaurant menu features liver salad and morel mushrooms with chicken and Vin Jaune. ⌖ *111 Grande-Rue, 39570 Chillé,* ☎ *84–47–55–44,* FAX *84–24–92–13. 21 rooms with bath or shower. Restaurant (closed Sun. evening and Mon.). MC, V. Restaurant $, hotel $$*

Metz

DINING

La Dinanderie. Chef Claude Pieriorgi serves clever cuisine—salmon cooked in mustard and chives, crayfish with olive piperade, zucchini fritters, and kiwi with lime and banana sorbet—for modest prices at this intimate restaurant, attractively refurbished in pastels, just across the River Moselle from the Metz cathedral. ✕ *2 rue de Paris,* ☎ *87–30–14–40. Reservations advised. AE, MC, V. Closed Sun., Mon., mid-Feb., and last 3 wks in Aug. $$–$$$*

A La Ville de Lyon. Just behind the cathedral in a venerable vaulted setting, this charming eatery is well worth checking out for its fabulous wine list (30,000 bottles in stock) and no-nonsense menu. Dishes range from juicy grilled veal kidneys to the ubiquitous local mirabelle soufflé glacé. ✕ *7 rue des Piques,* ☎ *87–36–07–01. Reservations advised. AE, DC, MC, V. Closed Sun. dinner, Mon., and most of Aug. $$*

Auberge de Mazagran. In an isolated farmhouse redecorated some time back with a heavy hand (glossy beams, farm tools, stuffy floral prints of all kinds, massive oil paintings), you'll find ageless farm-kitchen classics with a slightly dated bourgeois touch: *vol au vent* (puff pastry shell) with creamed lamb sweetbreads, cocks' combs and morels; tiny copper *cassoulettes* of snails in anise-garlic butter; seared game or beef garnished with cranberries and savory flan; baked Alaska in sugary sabayon sauce. There's a pricey wine list, strong on locals. Weekly menus offer by far the best value. It's east of the A-31 freeway, just north of Metz, in the heart of the Moselle countryside. ✕ *D-954, rte. de Boulay, at Mazagran, between Ste-Barbe and Les Etangs.* ☎ *87–76–62–47. Reservations advised. AE, MC, V. $$*

La Baraka. Below the cathedral, this classic French-Moroccan couscous spot with a lively, unstuffy ambience offers a fiery but digestible break from heavy *cuisine bourgeoise*. If you burned out on couscous in Paris, venture toward *méchoui* (lamb shish kebab) or *tajine,* a meat stew simmered in terra-cotta. ✕ *24 pl. de Chambre,* ☎ *87–36–33–92. MC, V. Closed Wed. $*

LODGING

★ **Royal Bleu Marine.** The fully modernized Royal Bleu Marine, taken over and buffed up by the Campanile chain, occupies a sumptuous Belle Epoque building not far from the train station and provides a choice of style (old-fashioned luxury versus simpler modernity). All rooms are soundproof. ⌨ *23 av. Foch, 57011,* ☎ *87–66–81–11,* FAX *87–56– 13–16. 76 rooms with bath. Restaurant, bar. AE, DC, MC, V. $$–$$$*

Mittelbergheim

DINING AND LODGING

Gilg. Looking over a tiny medieval village outside Barr, this historic inn specializes in a pleasant mix of classic and regional cuisine (fish *presskopf,* or head cheese, foie gras in brioche pastry), served in a timbered and vaulted "winstub." Choose wines from the neighboring vineyards. Guest rooms are more atmospheric than comfortable; young romantics will like the 17th-century stone spiral staircase that leads upstairs better than will bag-toting retirees. ⌨ *1 rte. du Vin,* ☎ *88– 08–91–37,* FAX *88–08–45–17. 10 rooms with bath. Restaurant. AE, DC, MC, V. Closed most of Jan. and first half July. $$*

Munster

DINING

La Cigogne. Despite a remarkably funereal old-hotel atmosphere—silverplate, white damask, and maroon velvet Louis XIII chairs, compounded by stuffy service—this is an excellent place for regional specialties, from trout in Riesling wine to mild choucroute. The incredibly fresh creamy Muenster (its cumin seeds served in a silver urn) must have come straight from one of the farm stands in the market across the street. ✗ *4 pl. du Marché,* ☎ *89–77–32–27. Reservations advised in season. Jacket suggested. MC, V. $–$$*

Nancy

DINING

★ **Capucin Gourmand.** A sinuous Art Nouveau decor and faultless service set the tone at Capucin Gourmand, one of Nancy's finest restaurants. Chef Gérard Veissière's menu includes such regional specialties as foie gras, game *en casserole,* and an excellent rendition of the classic quiche Lorraine. Desserts are superb, and Toul wines make an admirable accompaniment to your meal. ✗ *31 rue Gambetta,* ☎ *83– 35–26–98. Reservations required. Jacket and tie. V. Closed Sun., Mon., and Aug. $$$*

Petit Gastrolâtre. Admirers of regional cuisine shouldn't pass up a visit to Nancy's most famous purveyor of the art, under the direction of chef Patrick Tanesy. Recommended dishes include *baeckoffe* (meat and potato stew) with foie gras, salmon—try it any way it's offered— and a delectable fricassee of snails. ✗ *7 rue des Maréchaux,* ☎ *83– 35–51–94. Reservations required. Jacket and tie. V. Closed Sun., Mon. lunch. $$*

La Gourmandière. In this tiny garden-decor storefront opposite St-Epvre, a friendly young couple serves up an inexpensive daily lunch menu with a surprising variety of choices, from quiche and crudités to turkey in tarragon, pork chop in mustard sauce, and a delicate fish *feuilleté* in lemon sauce with saffron rice. With paper mats over pink linens, a mustard pot on every table, good pitcher wines and concerned service, it's a far cry from the touristy lunch scene off place Stanislas. ✗ *13 pl. du Colonel-Fabien,* ☎ *83–32–80–95. MC, V. $*

LODGING

★ **Grand Hôtel de la Reine.** This hotel is every bit as swanky as the place Stanislas on which it stands; the magnificent 18th-century building it occupies is officially classified as a historic monument. The guest rooms are decorated in a suitably grand Louis XV style, and the most luxurious look out onto the square. The classic-nouvelle restaurant,

Le Stanislas, is costly, although there is a good-value set menu at weekday lunch. Try the foie gras, the cod in bacon cream sauce, and the briochelike *kouglof*, a local delicacy made with mirabelles. ⊞ *2 pl. Stanislas, 54000,* ☎ *83–35–03–01,* FAX *83–32–86–04. 51 rooms with bath. Restaurant, bar. Restaurant reservations required. Jacket and tie. AE, DC, MC, V. $$$*

Carnot. This somewhat generic downtown hotel, with 1950s-style comforts and mostly tiny rooms, is handy to cours Léopold parking and backs up on the old town. Corner rooms are sizable, back rooms quiet. ⊞ *2 cours Léopold,* ☎ *83–36–59–58,* FAX *83–37–00–19. 33 rooms, most with bath. Breakfast room. MC, V. $*

Central. Next to the train station, the Central makes a less expensive but equally convenient alternative to the Grand Hôtel de la Reine. It is fully modernized, with double glazing to keep out the noise, and has a charming courtyard garden. There's no restaurant. ⊞ *6 rue Raymond-Poincaré, 54000,* ☎ *83–32–21–24,* FAX *83–37–84–66. 68 rooms with bath or shower. AE, MC, V. $$*

Deguise. Deep in the shuttered old town, this formerly grand mansion features a magnificent stone-floor entry and a dramatic sweeping stair that unfortunately winds up to a standard, creaky renovation job above. Breakfast on the noble main floor and an excellent location make this a good choice for bargain-hunting romantics. ⊞ *18 rue Guise,* ☎ *83–32–24–68,* FAX *83–35–75–63. 45 rooms. AE, MC, V. $*

Ottrott

DINING AND LODGING

★ **A l'Ami Fritz.** In the center of an unspoiled, half-timbered village at the foot of Mont St-Odile, this gem of a restaurant manages to gracefully combine chic, warmth, and a rustic atmosphere—and even offers the Fritz family's own *crus* from their Ottrott vineyards. The owner-chef's specialties include succulent *presskopf* (head cheese) with homemade mayonnaise; tender onion tart; breast of duck in sour apples; and seasonal game with traditional chestnut-and-red-cabbage garnish. The *cave* is deep, the counsel sound, but do drink the redolent *rouge d'Ottrott.* The weekday lunch is a great deal. Unfortunately, the all-modern hotel, a recent addition to the business, is inconveniently far (325 yards) away. Rooms are spacious, solid, and impeccable, nonetheless. ⊞ *8 rue des Châteaux, 67530,* ☎ *88–95–80–81,* FAX *88–95–84–85. 17 rooms with bath or shower. Restaurant (closed Wed.). AE, DC, MC, V. $$*

Riquewihr

DINING AND LODGING

Le Sarment d'Or. In this justifiably touristy village, among dozens of brilliantly preserved medieval buildings, this cozy little hotel stands apart for its irreproachable modern comforts tactfully dove-tailed with stone, dark timbers, and meter-thick walls. The restaurant downstairs offers firelit romance with its pastry-wrapped pâté, *presskopf*, and breast of duck in Pinot Noir. ⊞ *4 rue du Cerf, 68340,* ☎ *89–47–92–85,* FAX *89–47–99–23. 17 rooms. Restaurant. MC, V. $–$$*

Strasbourg

DINING

★ **Crocodile.** Chef Emile Jung is celebrated throughout the region for his Alsatian dishes prepared with an urbane finesse: warmed goose liver with apples and ginger; chicken breast and cock's comb in Riesling with Alsatian noodles; bitter-chocolate cherry cake with vanilla-bourbon cream. The restaurant's opulent decor makes a sophisticated backdrop for a sensual meal. ✕ *10 rue de l'Outre,* ☎ *88–32–13–02. Reserva-*

tions advised. Jacket and tie. AE, DC, MC, V. Closed Sun., Mon., second week in July–first week in Aug., and Christmas–New Year's. $$$$

Maison Kammerzell. This restaurant glories in its richly carved, wood-framed, 15th-century building—probably the most familiar house in Strasbourg, given its position on the corner of the cathedral square. The classic local menu is served on four stories: Fight your way through the tourist hordes on the terrace and ground floor to one of the atmospheric rooms above, with their gleaming wooden furniture and stained-glass windows. Foie gras and choucroute are best bets, though you may want to try the chef's pet discovery, choucroute with freshwater fish. Portions are large, but service can be slipshod. ✕ *16 pl. de la Cathédrale,* ☎ *88–32–42–14. Reservations advised. AE, DC, MC, V. $$$*

Au Gourmet Sans Chiqué. This intimate little restaurant, *sans chiqué* (unpretentious) but sophisticated, offers a procession of exquisite, if nouvelle-proportion, experiments from the soigné kitchen of chef Daniel Klein: foie gras in Szechuan pepper with caramelized choucroute, roast turbot in salsify, tenderloin of rabbit in hazelnut oil, and airy chocolate soufflé. Aim for the weekday lunch menu, and delve into the deep selection of local wines. ✕ *15 rue Ste-Barbe,* ☎ *88–32–04–07. Reservations advised. Jacket suggested. AE, DC, MC, V. Closed Sun., Mon. lunch, 1 wk in Feb. and 2 wks in Aug. $$–$$$*

★ **Au Sanglier.** Step briefly off the busy rue des Hallebardes and settle by the fireplace in this dark-timbered, lace-clothed old dining room, where you can delve into a flavorful choucroute, crisp *jambonneau* (ham shank), trout in white-wine cream sauce, or cheese-crusted onion soup. Wines are local and reasonable, and service familial. ✕ *11 rue du Sanglier,* ☎ *88–32–64–58. MC, V. $–$$*

★ **Au Tire-Bouchon.** Near the cathedral on a small backstreet, you'll find this comfortable "winstub," called "Corkscrew," offering a classic choucroute, a simple plat du jour, plus lighter options: salade de Gruyère (nutty cheese and onion bits in a rich vinaigrette), omelets, and sausages—and, of course, local wines by the carafe. ✕ *5 rue des Tailleurs-de-Pierre,* ☎ *88–32–47–86. MC, V. $*

LODGING

★ **Le Régent Contades.** This sleek, modern hotel holds forth in a revamped mansion near the old town in a residential turn-of-the-century district close to the River Ill (ask for a room with a view of St-Paul's). First-class amenities add to the appeal of the spacious rooms. There's no restaurant, but small hot meals are available through room service. 🏨 *8 av. de la Liberté, 67000,* ☎ *88–36–26–26,* FAX *88–37–13–70. 44 rooms with bath. Bar, sauna, solarium. AE, DC, MC, V. $$$*

★ **Régent Petite France.** Opposite the famous Ponts Couverts in the Petite France district stands the newest and smartest of the city's hotels. The outside of the buildings (originally an ice factory) is almost unchanged—but the inside is resolutely modern, with a spacious marble vestibule, tinkling white grand piano, and the pastel-tone Pont Tournant restaurant, where beer-based dishes are a house specialty. The best tables look out over the river, as do some of the rooms, which vary considerably in size (and price). Ask to see your room first. The only drawback here is the tortuous access; aim for Pont St-Thomas (opposite St-Thomas church) and head west on quai Finkwiller, before bearing right onto rue des Moulins. 🏨 *5 rue des Moulins, 67000,* ☎ *88–76–43–43,* FAX *88–76–43–76. 72 rooms with bath. Restaurant, piano bar. $$$$*

★ **Gutenberg.** A 200-year-old mansion is the setting of this charming hotel, just off place Gutenberg and only a few hundred yards from the cathedral. Several rooms and the reception and breakfast area have been modernized with a sleek, scrubbed decor, though enough antique oak details remain to remind you of the building's history. There's no restaurant. ⊞ *31 rue des Serruriers, 67000,* ☎ *88–32–17–15,* FAX *88–75–76–67. 50 rooms, 17 with bath, 27 with shower. MC, V. Closed first wk in Jan.* *$–$$*

Toul

DINING

Le Dauphin. The large, flower-laden dining room was once a G.I. canteen, and the setting (in an industrial section 5 kilometers, or 3 miles, from the town center) has little of the ambience of historic Toul. Yet Christophe Vohmann entices gourmets with cooking of great finesse, tapping local farm and forest sources: foie gras with artichokes, veal chop with truffled pasta. Prices à la carte run quickly out of hand. ✕ *Rte. de Villey-St-Etienne, 54200,* ☎ *83–43–13–46. Reservations advised. Jacket and tie. MC, V. Closed Sun. dinner.* *$$$*

Verdun

DINING

★ **La Tourtière.** About 23 kilometers (14 miles) northeast of Verdun in the pretty, tiny village of Senon lies an isolated culinary treasure. It offers rare authentic Lorraine cuisine, based on local products and regional traditions, prepared by a sophisticated homegrown chef, and served in an old beamed-and-firelit former monks' lodging. It's the noblest and simplest of regional fare: brilliant little wild-mushroom *tourtes,* smoked *pintadeau* (guineau fowl) in cabbage, home-preserved *confit de canard* with garlicky bean salad, rabbit stewed in musky mirabelles, and baked Brie de Meuse, from just up the road. The atmosphere is further enhanced by the beeswaxed antiques of chef Marie-Laure Becque-Moreau's brother, whose award-winning shop lies across the street, just down from the pretty Gothic-Renaissance church. Their proud matriarch, cane in hand, fusses over guests. ✕ *2 pl. Eugène-Antoine,* ☎ *29–85–98–30. Reservations advised. Jacket suggested. MC, V.* *$–$$*

DINING AND LODGING

Coq Hardi. This large, steep-roofed, half-timbered hotel, built in 1827 on the banks of the Meuse, is furnished in solid regional style. A family-style welcome pervades here and in the large, comfortable restaurant, where traditional cuisine dominates without risking stuffiness: turbot with eggplant confit, duck liver with zucchini flowers, duck in raspberry vinegar. ⊞ *8 av. de la Victoire, 55100,* ☎ *29–86–36–36,* FAX *29–86–09–21. 35 rooms, most with bath. Restaurant (closed Fri.). AE, DC, MC, V. Closed Jan.* *$$$*

Villers-le-Lac

DINING AND LODGING

France. Swiss gourmets flock across the border, just two minutes away, to savor young Hugues Droz's artichoke hearts with morels, quail pâté with beetroot, escargots in absinthe, pork jowl with fava beans and Szechuan pepper, and roast leg of pigeon with dried fruit. Hugues's family runs the hotel and will happily book you a two-hour boat trip (40 francs) along the Gorges du Doubs. Breakfasts are large, but the rooms are somewhat noisy. ⊞ *8 pl. Nationale, 25130,* ☎ *81–68–00–06,* FAX *81–68–09–22. 14 rooms with bath or shower. Restaurant (closed Sun. evening and Mon.). AE, DC, MC, V. Closed Jan.* *$$*

THE ARTS AND NIGHTLIFE

The Arts

Many regional towns and villages, especially the wine villages of Alsace, stage festivals in summer. Note the spectacular pagan-inspired burning of the three pine trees at **Thann** (late June) and the Flower Carnival at **Sélestat** (mid-August). The major regional wine fair is held at **Colmar** (first half of August); organization is chaotic. There are impressive son-et-lumière performances at the château of **Saverne.** On the **place Stanislas** in Nancy, an ambient evening of light and music takes place nightly. The Strasbourg cathedral produces an all-out son-et-lumière show every summer evening, in German and in French. A monthly handbook, *Strasbourg Actualités*, is a mine of information on local cultural events.

Concerts

The annual Festival de Musique is held in **Strasbourg** from June to early July at the modern Palais des Congrès and at the cathedral (☎ 88–32–43–10 for details or write to Société des Amis de la Musique, 24 rue de la Mésange, 67000 Strasbourg). There is a rock festival in June, organized by Strasbourg's Centre Culturel (13 pl. André-Maurois), and summer concerts at the Pavillon Joséphine in the Orangerie. For tickets to the concerts of the Orchestre Philharmonique (Palais des Congrès, ☎ 88–52–18–45), contact the box office. Tuesday evening concerts are held at **Colmar** Collegiate Church in summer. **Besançon** stages a jazz festival in June (☎ 80–83–39–09) and an international music festival in September (☎ 81–80–73–26). In Nancy, watch for concerts in the Salle Poirel (☎ 83–32–31–25), often featuring the Orchestre Symphonique & Lyrique (1 rue Ste-Catherine, ☎ 83–85–30–65).

Opera

The Opéra du Rhin (19 pl. Broglie, ☎ 88–75–48–23) in **Strasbourg** has a sizable repertoire.

Nightlife

Cabaret

In **Metz:** Le Palladium (1 en Nexirue, ☎ 87–74–80–26). In **Strasbourg:** L'Aiglon (27 rue du Vieux-Marché-Vins, ☎ 88–32–01–89).

Bars and Nightclubs

In **Nancy:** Le Blueberry (22 rue Gustave-Simon, ☎ 83–35–13–11). In **Strasbourg:** Le Bistrot (30 rue des Tonneliers, ☎ 88–23–02–71).

Jazz Clubs

The **Nancy** Jazz Festival takes place each October at the Parc de la Pepinière. In **Metz:** Caveau des Trinitaires (10 rue des Trinitaires, ☎ 87–75–04–96) peppers a little rock and folk into an 80% jazz format.

Discos

There is a good choice in **Nancy:** Métro (1 rue du Général-Hoche, ☎ 83–40–25–13); Majestique (22 rue St-Dizier, ☎ 83–32–83–42); Les Caves du Roy (9 pl. Stanislas, ☎ 83–35–24–14). Two of the best bets in **Strasbourg** are the Blue Hawaï (19 rue du Marais-Vert, ☎ 88–22–05–58) and Le Bambou (366 rte. de la Wantzeneau, ☎ 88–41–87–17). In **Besançon,** you have a choice between the young and lively Taos Club (5 Grande-Rue, ☎ 81–82–80–70) or the classier Karaoké Club (4 av. Edouard-Droz, ☎ 81–53–04–00).

Casinos

There are casinos in Besançon, Lons-le-Saunier, Salins-les-Bains, Contrexéville, Gerardmer, Plombières, and Vittel.

ALSACE AND LORRAINE ESSENTIALS

Arriving and Departing

By Plane

Most international flights to Alsace land at Mulhouse-Basel airport on the Franco-Swiss border. There are also airports at Strasbourg, Metz-Nancy, Dole, and Mirecourt (Vittel/Epinal).

By Car

The A4 toll expressway heads east from Paris to Strasbourg, via Verdun, Metz, and Saverne. It is met by A26, coming down from the English Channel, at Reims. A31 links Metz to Nancy, continuing south to Burgundy and Lyon. The quickest route from Paris to Besançon and the Jura is the A6 (to Beaune) and then the A36.

By Train

Mainline trains leave Paris (**Gare de l'Est**) every couple of hours for the four-hour, 504-kilometer (315-mile) journey to Strasbourg. Some stop at Toul and all stop at Nancy, where there are connections for Epinal, Gérardmer, and Vittel. Trains run three times daily from Paris to Verdun and more often to Metz (around 3 hours to each). Mainline trains stop at Mulhouse (four to five hours) en route to Basel. Three TGV trains leave Paris (**Gare de Lyon**) daily for Besançon (2½ to 3 hrs.).

Getting Around

By Car

N83/A35 connects Strasbourg, Colmar, and Mulhouse. The A36 expressway continues to Belfort and Besançon. The A4, linking Paris to Strasbourg, passes through Lorraine via Metz, linking Lorraine and Alsace.

By Train

Several local trains a day run between Strasbourg and Mulhouse, stopping at Sélestat and Colmar. Several continue to Belfort and Besançon. Local trains link Besançon to Lons-le-Saunier, occasionally stopping at Arbois. The Mulhouse–Strasbourg train links directly with Metz.

Guided Tours

Orientation

Strasbourg Port Authority (25 rue de la Nuée-Bleue, ☎ 88–21–74–74) organizes 75-minute boat tours along the River Ill.

Aerial

You can take a 15-minute helicopter tour of Nancy with **Tecnavia** (☎ 83–21–09–75) or a plane ride over Strasbourg and the Vosges from the Aérodrome du Polygone with **Aéroclub d'Alsace** (☎ 88–34–00–98). Balloon trips are organized by **Air Adventures** of Arc-et-Senans (☎ 81–57–45–51).

Important Addresses and Numbers

Travel Agencies

Wagons-Lits (30 pl. Kléber, Strasbourg, ☎ 88–32–16–34; 2 rue Raymond-Poincaré, Nancy, ☎ 83–35–06–97) and **Havas Voyages** (23 rue de la Haute-Montée, Strasbourg, ☎ 88–32–99–77).

Car Rental

In **Besançon:** Avis (7 pl. Flore, ☎ 81–80–91–08). In **Nancy:** Hertz (7 pl. Thiers, ☎ 83–32–13–14) and Europcar (18 rue de Serre, ☎ 83–37–57–24). In **Strasbourg:** Avis (pl. de la Gare, ☎ 88–32–30–44).

Visitor Information

The principal regional tourist offices are in **Strasbourg** (9 rue du Dôme, ☎ 88–21–01–02, and 17a pl. de la Cathédrale, ☎ 88–52–28–28), **Nancy** (14 pl. Stanislas, ☎ 83–35–22–41), and **Besançon** (9 rue de Pontarlier, ☎ 81–83–50–47). In **Strasbourg,** there is also a city tourist office (pl. de la Gare, ☎ 88–32–51–49).

Other tourist offices: **Belfort** (rue Jules-Vallès, ☎ 84–28–12–23), **Colmar** (4 rue Unterlinden, ☎ 89–20–68–92), **Guebwiller** (73 rue de la République, ☎ 89–76–10–63), **Lons-le-Saunier** (1 rue Louis-Pasteur, ☎ 84–24–65–01), **Metz** (pl. d'Armes, ☎ 87–55–53–76), **Mulhouse** (9 av. du Maréchal-Foch, ☎ 89–45–68–31), **Obernai** (59 rue du Général-Gouraud, ☎ 88–95–64–13), **Saverne** (Château des Rohan, ☎ 88–91–80–47), **Sélestat** (10 blvd. Leclerc, ☎ 88–92–02–66), **Toul** (Parvis de la Cathédrale, ☎ 83–64–11–69), and **Verdun** (pl. de la Nation, ☎ 29–86–14–18).

9 Burgundy

FOR A REGION whose powerful medieval dukes ruled over large tracts of Western Europe and whose glamorous image is closely allied to its expensive and treasured wine, Burgundy (Bourgogne in French)—just southeast of Paris—can seem a surprisingly rustic backwater. Here "life in the fast lane" refers exclusively to the Paris-bound A6 expressway. We'll travel from Sens in the north to Autun in the south, exploring central Burgundy; at the heart of this region is the dark, brooding Morvan Forest.

In the Middle Ages, Sens, Auxerre, and Troyes, in neighboring Champagne, came under the sway of the Paris-based Capetian kings, who erected mighty Gothic cathedrals in those towns. Burgundy's leading religious monument, however, is the older, Romanesque basilica at Vézelay, once one of Christianity's most important centers of pilgrimage and today a tiny village hidden in the folds of rolling, verdant hills.

Chablis is renowned for its excellent bone-dry white wine, although better values for the money can be found at St-Bris-le-Vineux and Irancy, south of Auxerre. The great wine lands of Burgundy, however, lie farther east. Dijon, the province's only city, retains something of the opulence it acquired under the rich, powerful dukes of Burgundy who ruled in the late Middle Ages but its latter-day reputation is essentially gastronomic. Burgundians like to eat well, and the number of outstanding restaurants reflects this. Game, freshwater trout, ham, goat cheese, coq au vin, and mushrooms are the bases of the region's specialties. Local industries at Dijon involve the production of mustard, cassis (blackcurrant liqueur), snails, and—of course—wine.

The famous vineyards south of Dijon—the Côte de Nuits and Côte de Beaune—are among the world's most distinguished and picturesque. Don't expect to unearth many bargains here, but a good place for sampling is the Marché aux Vins in Beaune, a charming old town clustered around the patterned-tile roofs of its medieval Hôtel-Dieu (hospital). Less expensive Burgundies can be found between Chalon and Mâcon as you head south along the Saône Valley toward the ruined Abbey of Cluny—once a religious center equal in importance to Vézelay.

EXPLORING

Orientation

Our first tour covers northern Burgundy, stretching from Sens in the north to Autun in the south and the River Loire in the west, with a rewarding detour to the interesting town of Troyes, in Champagne. Our second tour, of Burgundy's wine country, begins at Dijon before heading south to Mâcon through the Saone Valley.

Tour 1: Northern and Western Burgundy

Numbers in the margin correspond to points of interest on the Burgundy map.

★ ❶   It makes sense for **Sens** to be your first stop, since it lies just 112 kilometers (70 miles) from Paris on N6, a fast road that hugs the pretty Yonne Valley south of Fontainebleau. Sens was for centuries the ecclesiastical center of France and is still dominated by the **Cathédrale St-Etienne,** begun around 1140. You can see the cathedral's 240-foot south tower from far away; the highway forges straight past it. The pompous 19th-century buildings that line this road can give a false impression to visitors in a hurry: The streets leading off it near the cathedral (notably rue Abelard and rue Jean-Cousin) are full of half-timbered medieval houses, and within their midst sits the 13th-century church of **St-Pierre-le-Rond,** with its unusual wooden roof and 16th-century stained glass. And on Monday, the cathedral square will be crowded with stalls selling anything and everything, while the colorful covered market throbs with housewives and chefs buying meat and produce.

The cathedral's sturdy facade used to have two towers; one was destroyed in the 19th century, and the other was topped in 1532 by an elegant, though somewhat incongruous, Renaissance campanile that contains two monster bells. The gallery, with statues of former archbishops of Sens, is a 19th-century addition, but the statue of St. Stephen, between the doors of the central portal, is thought to date from the late 12th century.

The vast, harmonious interior is justly renowned for its stained-glass windows. The oldest (circa 1200) are in the north choir; those in the south transept were manufactured in 1500 at nearby Troyes and include a much-admired *Tree of Jesse.* The cathedral treasury (access near the sacristy to the south of the choir) is one of the richest in France. It contains a collection of miters, ivories, and gold plates, together with the richly woven gold-and-silver robes of the archbishops of Sens. Robes belonging to Thomas à Becket are here as well. Becket fled to Sens from England to escape the wrath of Henry II before returning to his cathedral in Canterbury where, in 1170, he was murdered. Stained-glass windows in the north of the chancel retrace his story. *Pl. de la République,* ☎ *86–64–15–27. Admission to treasury included in ticket to Palais Synodal (see below).*

The 13th-century **Palais Synodal,** alongside the cathedral, provides a first encounter with Burgundy's multicolored tiled roofs: From its courtyard, there is a fine view of the cathedral's Flamboyant Gothic south transept, constructed by master stonemason Martin Chambiges at the start of the 16th century. (Rose windows were his specialty, as you can appreciate here.) The Palais Synodal houses a museum with statues, mosaics, and tapestries, but its six grand windows and the vaulted Synodal Hall are the outstanding features. ☎ *86–64–46–27.* ☛ *18 frs adults,* ☉ *June–Sept., daily 10–noon and 2–6; Oct.–May, Wed. and weekends 10–noon and 2–6, Mon., Thurs., and Fri. 2–6.*

Numbers in the margin correspond to points of interest on the Troyes map.

★ ❷ The inhabitants of **Troyes** would be seriously insulted if you mistook them for Burgundians. This old town, 64 kilometers (40 miles) from Sens along N60, is the capital of southern Champagne; as if to prove the point, its historic town center is shaped like a champagne cork, the rounded top enclosed by a loop of the Seine. The town's phenomenal number of old buildings, magnificent churches, and fine museums will amaze visitors: Few, if any, French town centers contain so much to see and do. A wide choice of restaurants and a web of enchanting pedestrian streets with timber-framed houses add even more appeal.

The center of Troyes is divided by quai Dampierre, a broad, busy boulevard. A good place to begin exploring is **place de la Libération,** where quai Dampierre meets the rectangular artificial lake known as the Bassin de la Préfecture. Although Troyes stands on the Seine, it is the capital of the *département* named after the River Aube, adminis-
❸ tered from the elegant **Préfecture** that gazes across both the lake and place de la Libération from behind its gleaming gilt-iron railings.

Burgundy

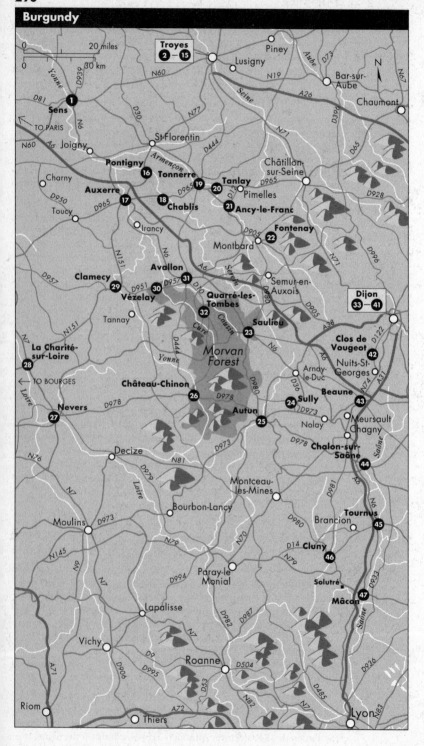

0   20 miles
0   30 km

N

Troyes 2 — 15

Piney
Lusigny
Bar-sur-Aube
Chaumont

1 Sens
TO PARIS
Joigny
Charny
St-Florentin

16 Pontigny
Tonnerre
19 **Tanlay**
20
Pimelles
Châtillon-sur-Seine

Auxerre **17**
18 **Chablis**
21 **Ancy-le-Franc**

Toucy
Irancy
Montbard
22 **Fontenay**

Clamecy
Avallon
31
Semur-en-Auxois

29 **30**
Vézelay
Quarré-les-Tombes

Tannay
32
Saulieu
23
Dijon 33 — 41

La Charité-sur-Loire
28
TO BOURGES

Morvan Forest

Clos de Vougeot **42**
Arnay-le-Duc
Nuits-St-Georges

Château-Chinon
26
Sully **24**
Beaune **43**

Nevers
27
Autun
25
Nolay
Meursault
Chagny

Decize
Chalon-sur-Saône
44

Moulins
Montceau-les-Mines
Tournus **45**
Brancion

Bourbon-Lancy

Paray-le-Monial
Cluny **46**

Lapalisse
Solutré
Mâcon **47**

Vichy
Roanne

Riom
Thiers
Lyon

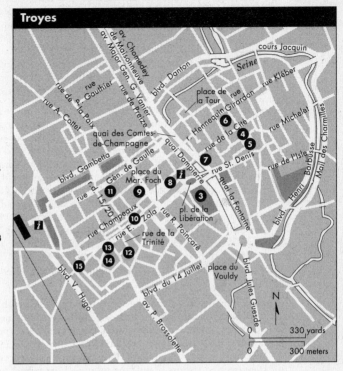

Troyes

But the most charming view from place de la Libération is undoubtedly that of the cathedral, whose 200-foot tower peeps through the trees above the statue and old lamps of the central flower garden. The **4 Cathédrale St-Pierre-St-Paul,** just a five-minute walk away, is in a tumbledown square that, like the narrow surrounding streets, has not changed for centuries.

Perhaps the first thing to strike you about the cathedral will be its resemblance to the one in Sens. You'll see this in the incomplete one-tower facade; the small Renaissance campaniles on top of the tower; and the artistry of Martin Chambiges, who worked on Troyes's facade (with its characteristic large rose window) around the same time as he did the transept of Sens. Try to see the facade at night, when its floodlit features are thrown into dramatic relief.

The cathedral's vast five-aisle interior, refreshingly light thanks to large windows and the near-whiteness of the local stone, dates mainly from the 13th century. Like Sens, it has renowned stained glass—fine examples of primitive 13th-century glass in the choir and richly colored 16th-century glass in the nave and facade rose window. The arcaded triforium above the pillars of the choir was one of the first in France to be glazed rather than filled with stone. *Pl. St-Pierre.* ☉ *Daily 10–noon and 2–6. Son-et-lumière (sound-and-light) shows are held in the cathedral at variable hours in summer months; contact the tourist office for details.* ☛ *Free.*

5 Just south of the cathedral is the **Musée d'Art Moderne** (Modern Art Museum), housed in the 16th- to 17th-century former Bishop's Palace. Its magnificent interior, with huge fireplaces, carved wood-beamed roofs, and a Renaissance staircase, plays host to the Levy Collection of modern art, featuring drawings, sculpture, and nearly 400 paintings. The assembly of Fauve works—a short-lived style that succeeded Impressionism at the start of the 20th century—is exceptional, notably the frenzied, hotly colored canvases by Maurice de Vlaminck, Georges Braque, and André Derain. *Pl. St-Pierre,* ☎ *25–80–57–30.* ☛ *15 frs adults; free Wed. Guided tours: 20 frs adults, 10 frs children 18 and under. Admission ticket is good for length of stay in town. Joint ticket covering all town museums: 20 frs.* ☉ *Wed.–Mon. 11–6.*

❻ On the other side of the cathedral square are the former abbey buildings of the **Musée St-Loup,** housing two museums. The ground-floor display is devoted to natural history, with impressive collections of birds and meteorites; the Musée des Beaux-Arts et d'Archéologie (Fine Arts and Archaeology Museum) is confusingly spread over two floors. The former abbey cellars contain local archaeological finds, especially gold-mounted 5th-century jewelry and a Gallo-Roman bronze statue of Apollo. There is also a section dedicated to medieval statuary and gargoyles. Paintings from the 15th to the 19th centuries are exhibited on the second floor and include works by Rubens, Anthony Van Dyck, Antoine Watteau, François Boucher, and Jacques-Louis David. *1 rue Chrétien-de-Troyes,* ☎ *25–42–33–33, ext. 35–92.* ☛ *15 frs adults, 5 frs children under 18. Joint ticket: 20 frs.* ☉ *Wed.–Mon. 10–noon and 2–6.*

❼ From the Musée St-Loup, the rue de la Cité, packed with restaurants, leads back to quai Dampierre, passing in front of the superb wrought-iron gates of the 18th-century **Hôtel-Dieu** (hospital), topped with the blue-and-gold fleurs-de-lis emblems of the French monarchy. Around the corner is the entrance to the **Pharmacie,** the only part of the Hôtel-Dieu open to visitors. Take time to inspect the former medical laboratory, with its quaint assortment of pewter dishes and jugs, earthenware jars, and painted wooden boxes designed to contain herbs and medicines. *Quai des Comtes-de-Champagne,* ☎ *25–42–33–33, ext. 35–92. Joint ticket: 20 frs.* ☉ *Wed.–Mon. 10–noon and 2–6.*

❽ The cathedral quarter northeast of quai Dampierre seems quiet and drowsy compared with the more upbeat, commercial southwest part of Troyes. Cross over from the Hôtel-Dieu and continue down rue Clemenceau to the **Basilique St-Urbain,** built between 1262 and 1286 by Pope Urban IV, who was born in Troyes. St-Urbain is one of the most remarkable churches in France, a perfect culmination of Gothic's quest to replace stone walls with stained glass. Huge windows, containing much of their original glass, ring the church, while the exterior bristles with the thrust-bearing flying buttresses that made this daring structure possible.

❾ Follow rue Urbain-IV down to **place du Maréchal-Foch,** the main square of central Troyes, flanked by cafés, shops, and the delightful early 17th-century facade of the **Hôtel de Ville** (Town Hall). In summer, the square throbs from morning to night as residents and tourists swarm in to drink coffee or eat crepes in the various cheap restaurants that spill into the rue Champeaux, Troyes's liveliest pedestrian street.

❿ Rue Champeaux runs parallel to **St-Jean,** a lengthy church where England's warrior king, Henry V, married Catherine of France in 1420. The church's tall 16th-century choir contrasts with the low earlier nave; the clock tower is an unmistakable landmark of downtown Troyes.

TIME OUT A good place to settle into the medieval ambience of Troyes is the friendly, unpretentious **Bouchon Champenois** (champagne cork). This restaurant serves both light lunches and generous, inexpensive evening meals in a wood-beamed dining room whose large mirrors reflect the striped timbered patterns of the cour du Mortier d'Or. *Closed Mon.*

(11) The church of **Ste-Madeleine** (rue de Général-de-Gaulle), the oldest in Troyes, is best known for its elaborate triple-arched stone rood screen separating the nave and the choir. Only six other such screens still remain in France—most were dismantled during the French Revolution—and this one was carved with panache by Jean Gailde between 1508 and 1517. The church's west tower and main door also date from the early 16th century.

Take rue des Quinze-Vingts, which runs parallel to the ruelle des Chats, as far as rue Émile-Zola. Turn right, then take the second left, onto
(12) rue de la Trinité. The private museum known as **Maison de l'Outil** stands at No. 7 in the 16th-century Hôtel de Mauroy. The upstairs holds a collection of pictures, models, and tools relevant to such traditional wood-related trades as carpentry, clog making, and barrel making. *7 rue de la Trinité,* ☎ *25–73–28–26.* ☛ *30 frs adults, 20 frs children.* ⊘ *Daily 9–noon and 2–6.*

Close to the Maison de l'Outil, via rue Bordet, is another 16th-cen-
(13) tury building: the church of **St-Pantaléon.** A number of fine stone statues, surmounted by canopies, cluster around its pillars. The tall, narrow walls are topped not by stone vaults but by a wooden roof, unusual for such a late church. Just as unexpected are the red-and-white streamers and *Solidarnosc* (Solidarity) banners sometimes found next to the altar: St-Pantaléon conducts services for the Polish community. *Rue de Turenne.* ⊘ *10–noon and 2–6 in summer months only; at other times apply to the tourist office.*

The Renaissance Hôtel de Vauluisant, opposite, houses two museums.
(14) The **Musée Historique** (History Museum) traces the development of Troyes and southern Champagne, with a section devoted to religious art. The **Musée de la Bonneterie** (Textile Museum) outlines the history and manufacturing process of the town's traditional bonnet-making industry; some of the bonnets on display are more than 200 years old. *4 rue Vauluisant,* ☎ *25–42–33–33, ext. 35–92. Joint ticket: 20 frs.* ⊘ *Wed.–Mon. 10–noon and 2–6.*

Close by, beyond place Jean-Jaurès, stands yet another church: that of
(15) **St-Nicolas.** You may not be tempted by its grimy exterior, but undaunted souls will be rewarded by the chance to scale a wide stone staircase up to an exuberantly decorated chapel and an unexpected view over the nave. Notice the funny little spiral staircase on the left of the nave that appears to vanish into mid-wall.

Numbers in the margin correspond to points of interest on the Burgundy map.

Leaving Troyes—by far the largest town on this tour—you will soon be plunged back into rural tranquillity as you drive southwest along
(16) the Auxerre-bound N77. **Pontigny,** just 21 kilometers (13 miles) short of Auxerre, can easily be mistaken for another drowsy, dusty village, but its once-proud **abbey** is as large as many cathedrals; in the 12th and 13th centuries, it sheltered three archbishops of Canterbury, including St. Thomas à Becket.

The abbey was founded in 1114, but the current church was begun in 1150. The monks belonged to the Cistercian order, which, frowning on the opulence of the rival House of Cluny, fostered buildings of intense sobriety. Small, even-spaced windows render the abbey's silhouette monotonous: The single tower, that of the facade, scrambles almost apologetically to roof level. A wooden screen divides the austere, 330-foot interior in two. The only ornament is provided by the late-17th-century wooden choir stalls, carved with garlands and angels. ☎ *86–47–54–99.* ☛ *Free.* ☉ *Daily 9–7, except during services.*

⑰ **Auxerre** is a small, peaceful town, dominated by its **Cathédrale St-Etienne,** perched on a steep hill overlooking the River Yonne. The 13th-century choir, the oldest part of the edifice, contains its original stained glass, dominated by dazzling reds and blues. Beneath the choir, the frescoed 11th-century Romanesque crypt keeps company with the Treasury, which features medieval enamels, manuscripts, and miniatures. *Pl. St-Etienne,* ☎ *86–52–31–68.* ☛ *Crypt and treasury: 5 frs each. The Passport Ticket (20 frs) gives entry to the crypt and treasury plus St-Germain (below).* ☉ *Easter–Nov., Mon.–Sat. 9–noon and 2–6, Sun. 2–6.*

Fanning out from Auxerre's main square, place des Cordeliers (just up from the cathedral), are a number of venerable streets lined with 16th-century houses. Explore these before heading north toward the town's most interesting church, the former abbey of **St-Germain,** which stands parallel to the cathedral some 300 yards away. The church's earliest section aboveground is the 11th-century Romanesque bell tower, but the extensive underground crypt dates from the 9th century and contains its original frescoes. *Pl. St-Germain,* ☎ *86–51–09–74.* ☛ *20 frs. Guided tours of the crypt, Wed.–Mon. 9–11:30 and 2–5:30.*

⑱ **Chablis,** famous for its white wine, lies just 16 kilometers (10 miles) east of Auxerre along N65 and D965. A pretty village, it nestles on the banks of the River Serein ("serene") and is protected by the massive, round, turreted towers of the Porte Noël gateway. While "Chablis" in America has become a generic name for cheap white wine, not so in France. Chablis is a fine, slightly oak-tasting wine of tremendous character, with the Premier Cru and Grand Cru wines standing head-to-head with the best French whites. Even the vin ordinaire from Chablis is eminently drinkable. Prices in the local shops tend to be inflated, and your best bet is to visit a vineyard or two and make your purchases there. You can at the same time be charmed by the surrounding vineyards' dramatic views, as their towering slopes contrast with the region's characteristic rolling hills. Remember that most vineyards are closed on Sunday.

⑲ Continue along D965 from Chablis to the village of **Tonnerre,** 16 kilometers (10 miles) away. The Armançon Valley and 16th-century houses can be surveyed from the terrace of the church of St-Pierre, rebuilt, like most of the town, after a devastating fire in 1556. Tonnerre's chief attraction, the high-roofed **Ancien Hôpital,** was built in 1293 and has survived the passing centuries—flames and all—largely intact. The main room, the Grande Salle, is 250 feet long and retains its oak ceiling; it was conceived as the hospital ward and after 1650 served as the parish church. The original hospital church leads off from the Grande Salle; in the adjoining Chapelle du Revestière a dramatic 15th-century stone group represents the *Burial of Christ. Rue du Part,* ☎ *86–54–33–00.* ☛ *22 frs.* ☉ *June–Sept., daily 10–noon and 1–6; Apr.–May and Oct., weekends 1–6.*

⑳ Ten kilometers (6 miles) east of Tonnerre lies the château of **Tanlay,** built around 1550 and betraying the classical influence of the Renaissance. The vestibule, framed by wrought-iron railings, leads to a wood-paneled salon and dining room filled with period furniture. A graceful staircase climbs to the second floor with a frescoed gallery and ornate fireplaces. A small room in the tower above was used as a secret meeting place by Huguenot Protestants during the 1562–98 Wars of Religion; its cupola boasts a fresco of scantily clad 16th-century religious personalities. ☎ 86–75–70–61. ☛ *Guided tours only, 36 frs adults, 18 frs children under 16; grounds only: 15 frs.* ☉ *Apr.–Nov. 11, Wed.–Mon. 9:30–11:30 and 2:15–5:15.*

㉑ Continue along D965 to Pimelles, then turn right onto D12. Eleven kilometers (7 miles) south is another, slightly earlier château, **Ancy-le-Franc.** The Renaissance styling here has an Italian flavor: The château was built to the designs of Sebastiano Serlio with interior decor by Primaticcio, both of whom worked at the court of French king François I (1515–47). The plain, majestic exterior contrasts with the sumptuous rooms and apartments, many—particularly the magnificent Chambre des Arts—with carved or painted walls and ceilings and their original furniture. Such grandeur won the approval of Sun King Louis XIV, no less, who once stayed in the Salon Bleu. Adjoining the château is a small Musée Automobile featuring vintage cars. *Pl. Clermont-Tonnerre,* ☎ *86–75–14–63.* ☛ *42 frs adults, 17 children 11–16.* ☉ *Late Mar.–mid-Nov.; guided tours at 10, 11, 2, 3, 4, 5, and (May–Sept.) 6.* ☛ *Musée Automobile: 20 frs, same hours.*

★ ㉒ Twenty-nine kilometers (18 miles) southeast along D905 (take D32 at Marmagne, just past Montbard) is the **Cistercian abbey** of **Fontenay,** founded by St-Bernard in 1118. The same Cistercian criteria applied to Fontenay as to Pontigny: no-frills architecture and an isolated site. By the end of the 12th century, the church and other buildings constituting the monastery were finished. The abbey's community grew to some 300 monks and prospered until the 16th century, when religious wars and administrative mayhem hastened its decline. It was dissolved during the French Revolution, and the abbey was used as a paper factory until 1906. Fortunately the historic buildings emerged unscathed and, with the help of original plans, Fontenay has since been restored.

The abbey is surrounded by extensive gardens dotted with the fountains that gave it its name. The church and cloister are the most important buildings to survive. The church's solemn interior is lit by windows in the facade and by a double row of three narrow windows, representing the Trinity, in the choir. A staircase in the south transept leads to the wood-roofed dormitory (spare a thought for the bleary-eyed monks, obliged to stagger down for services in the dead of night). The chapter house, flanked by a majestic arcade, and the scriptorium, where monks worked on their manuscripts, lead off from the adjoining cloisters. *21500 Marmagne,* ☎ *80–92–15–00.* ☛ *38 frs adults, 18 frs students.* ☉ *Daily 9–noon and 2–6; guided tours only mid-Mar.–mid-Nov.*

㉓ Head back to Montbard and take D980 south—via the picturesque old town of Semur-en-Auxois—to **Saulieu,** 48 kilometers (30 miles) away. Saulieu's reputation belies its size: It is renowned for good food (Rabelais, that roly-poly 16th-century man of letters, extolled its Gargantuan hospitality) and Christmas trees (a million are packed off from the area each year). The basilica of **St-Andoche** is almost as old as that of Vézelay, though less imposing and much restored. The adjoining **Musée François Pompon** is devoted, in part, to the work of animal-bronze sculptor Pompon (1855–1933), whose smooth, stylized creations seem contemporary but predate World War II. After renovations, the expanded museum also contains Gallo-Roman funeral stones, sacred art, and a room devoted to local gastronomic lore—historic menus and preparation techniques. *Rue Sallier,* ☎ *80–64–19–51.* ☛ *20 frs adults, 15 frs students.* ☉ *Wed.–Mon., Apr.–Sept. 10–12:30 and 2–5:30; Oct.–Mar. 10–12:30 and 2–6.*

㉔ Before going south through the brooding Morvan Forest toward Autun, detour to the Renaissance château of **Sully,** recently opened to visitors, Take N6 to Arnay-le-Duc, then D36, turning right for Sully after the village of Vellerot. The turreted château stands in a stately park and is surrounded by a moat, while a monumental staircase leads to the north front and a broad terrace. Marshal MacMahon, president of France from 1873 to 1879, was born here in 1808. ☎ 85–82–10–27. ☺ *Summer afternoons for 45-min guided tours;* ☛ *35 frs; call for precise times.* ☺ *Grounds daily 10–noon and 2–6.* ☛ *15 frs.*

㉕ D326 links Sully to D973 and, 9 kilometers (6 miles) later, **Autun**—an important town since Roman times, as you can detect from the well-preserved archways, Porte St-André and Porte d'Arroux, and the Théâtre Romain, once the largest arena in Gaul. Julius Caesar even referred to Autun as the "sister and rival of Rome itself." Another famous warrior, Napoléon, studied here in 1779 at the military academy (now the Lycée Bonaparte).

★ Autun's principal monument, however, is its **cathedral,** built from 1120 to 1146 to house the relics of St. Lazarus; the main tower, spire, and upper reaches of the chancel were added in the late 15th century. The influx of medieval pilgrims accounts for the building's size (35 yards wide and nearly 80 yards long). Lazarus's tomb was dismantled in 1766 by canons who were believers in the rationalist credo of the Enlightenment. They also did their best to transform the Romanesque-Gothic cathedral into a Classical temple at the same time, adding pilasters and classical ornament willy-nilly. Fortunately, some of the best Romanesque stonework, including the inspired nave capitals and the tympanum above the main door—a gracefully elongated *Last Judgment* sculpted by Gislebertus in the 1130s—emerged unscathed. Jean-Auguste Ingres's painting depicting the *Martyrdom of St-Symphorien* has been relegated to a dingy chapel in the north aisle of the nave. *Pl. St-Louis.*

Across from the cathedral, the **Musée Rolin** boasts several fine paintings from the Middle Ages and good examples of Burgundian sculpture, including another Gislebertus masterpiece, the *Temptation of Eve,* which originally topped one of the side doors of the cathedral. *Pl. St-Louis,* ☎ *85–52–09–76.* ☛ *14 frs.* ☺ *Nov.–Mar., Mon. and Wed.–Sat. 10–noon and 2–6, Sun. 10–noon and 2–5; Apr.–Sept., Wed.–Mon. 9:30–noon and 1:30–6; Oct., Mon. and Wed.–Sat. 10–noon and 2–5, Sun. 10–noon and 2:30–5.*

TIME OUT   The Roman amphitheater at the edge of town on the road to Chalon-sur-Saône is a historic spot for lunch. Pick up the makings in town and you can eat your picnic on the stepped seats where Gallo-Roman audiences sat two millennia ago. While you're in a classical mood, don't miss the temple to Juno. It is off in a field at the other edge of town as you leave for Château-Chinon. Keep your eyes peeled to the right for the turnoff.

㉖ Our next port of call, **Château-Chinon,** lies 37 kilometers (23 miles) west of Autun along D978. This small town has been in the news during recent years thanks to its former mayor, the past French president, François Mitterrand. One of his legacies is the brash, colorful, and controversial fountain by Niki de St-Phalle, in front of the town hall. Another is the **Musée du Septennat** (☎ 86–85–19–23), which houses an astonishing variety of gifts he received while president. The museum is at the top of the hill as you leave the town (*see* Musée du Costume, *below*).

Château-Chinon is the capital of the Morvan, and a fine view of the town and forest can be had from the Panorama du Calvaire near square d'Aligre. The dress and traditions of the Morvan are the subject of the **Musée du Costume.** *16–18 rue St-Christophe,* ☎ *86–85–18–55.* ☛ *20 frs adults, 10 frs children 6–18.* ⏲ *Nov.–May, weekends 10–6; June and Sept.–Oct., daily 10–6, July and Aug. 10–7. Combined tickets to Costume Museum and Musée du Septennat: 30 frs.*

From Château-Chinon you can either drive northwest to Clamecy or
27 continue to **Nevers,** 64 kilometers (40 miles) away—Burgundy's western outpost on the banks of the Loire. Nevers, renowned for its ceramics, has been producing earthenware since the late 16th century, promoted initially by Italian craftsmen. The French Revolution prompted a slowdown in activity, but three traditional manufacturers still remain. An extensive selection of Nevers earthenware, retracing its stylistic development, can be admired at the **Musée Municipal.** *Promenade des Remparts,* ☎ *86–68–45–62.* ☛ *10 frs adults, 5 frs children under 13.* ⏲ *Wed.–Mon., May–Sept. 10–5:15; Oct.–Apr. 10–11:45 and 2–5:15; closed Tues.*

Part of the medieval walls extend behind the museum, culminating in the intimidating gateway known as the **Porte du Croux** (built in 1393), which, thanks to its turrets and huge, sloping roof, resembles a small castle. The nearby **Cathédrale St-Cyr-Ste-Julitte,** with its 52-meter (170-foot) square tower and two apses, is another enormous building, constructed during several periods of the Middle Ages.

Beyond the cathedral stands the **Palais Ducal,** which has a sumptuous, large-windowed Renaissance facade but, unfortunately, is closed to the public. A few hundred yards north, across a park that can be entered from place Carnot, is **St-Gildard's convent,** where Saint Bernadette of Lourdes (1844–79) spent the last 13 years of her life. A small museum contains mementos and outlines her life story (she claimed to have seen the Virgin several times in 1858 and was canonized in 1933). ☎ *86–36–91–45.* ☛ *Free.* ⏲ *Daily 10–5.*

28 Unlike those of Pontigny and Fontenay, the abbey church of **La Charité-sur-Loire,** 24 kilometers (15 miles) downstream from Nevers, was dependent on Cluny; when it was consecrated by Pope Pascal II in 1107, it was the country's second-largest church after Cluny. Fire and neglect have taken their toll on the massive original edifice, and these days the church is cut in two, with the single-tower facade separated from the imposing choir and transept by the pretty place Ste-Croix (which occupies the former site of the nave). A fine view of the church's exterior can be seen from square des Bénédictins, just off Grande-Rue.

29 From La Charité, head northeast to **Clamecy,** 51 kilometers (32 miles) away. Slow-moving Clamecy is not on many tourist itineraries, but its tumbling alleyways and untouched, ancient houses epitomize *La France Profonde.* Clamecy's multishaped roofs, dominated by the majestic square tower of St-Martin's collegiate church, are best viewed from the banks of the Yonne. The river played a crucial role in Clamecy's development; trees from the nearby Morvan Forest were chopped down and floated to Paris in huge convoys. The history of this form of transport (*flottage*), which lasted until 1923, is detailed in the town museum, housed in two mansions. The **Musée d'Art et d'Histoire Romain Rolland,** is named for a native son, Nobel laureate for literature in 1915. *Av. de la République,* ☎ *86–27–17–99.* ☛ *15 frs adults.* ⏲ *Nov.–Easter, Mon. and Wed.–Sat. 10–noon and 2–6; Easter–Oct., Wed.–Mon. 10–noon and 2–6.*

In homage to the logs that used to be floated downriver from Clamecy to Paris, a log-shape, sugared-almond candy has long been chewed by Clamecycois, as the local inhabitants are called. You can find your *bûchettes* at the **Avignon** (22 rue de la Monnaie) pastry shop (which doubles as a tearoom), close to the steps leading up to the church square.

★ **30** The picturesque old town of **Vézelay** lies 24 kilometers (15 miles) east of Clamecy along D951. In the 11th and 12th centuries, its celebrated **basilica,** perched at the top of a rocky crag, was one of the focal points of Christendom. Pilgrims poured in to gasp at the relics of St. Mary Magdalene before setting off on the great medieval trek to the shrine of St. James at Santiago de Compostela in northwest Spain.

By the mid-13th century, the authenticity of St. Mary's relics was in doubt; others had been discovered in Provence. The decline continued until the French Revolution, when the basilica and adjoining monastery buildings were sold by the state. Only the basilica escaped demolition and was itself falling into ruin when ace restorer Viollet-le-Duc rode to the rescue in 1840 (he also restored the cathedrals of Laon and Amiens and Paris's Notre-Dame).

Today the basilica at Vézelay, under the patrimony of UNESCO, has recaptured its onetime glory and is considered to be France's most prestigious Romanesque showcase. Note the wonderful decoration in the nave, whose column capitals, imaginatively designed and superbly carved, represent miniature medieval men in all manner of situations— working in the fields, wielding battle swords, or undergoing the tortures of hell.

The basilica's exterior is best seen from the leafy terrace to the right of the facade. Opposite a vast, verdant panorama encompasses lush valleys and rolling hills and hedgerows. In the forefront is the Flamboyant Gothic spire of St-Père-sous-Vézelay, a tiny village a couple of miles away, which has Marc Meneau's excellent restaurant (*see* Dining and Lodging, *below*). A somewhat isolated hill town, Vézelay rarely becomes as crowded as it deserves. You can climb the cobbled streets and ramparts, admire restored private homes and eclectic (but not kitschy) shops, or relax in cloistered rose gardens with a feeling of uncluttered calm. Tourists are asked to park at the bottom of the village, but in the off-season, you can drive up to the basilica and perhaps find a spot to park in the cathedral square.

31 Another 13 kilometers (8 miles) east via D957 lies **Avallon,** spectacularly situated on a promontory jutting over the Cousin Valley. The town's old streets and ramparts are pleasant places for strolling, before or after viewing the works of medieval stone carvers whose imaginations ran riot on the portals of the venerable church of St-Lazarus.

The A6 expressway passes close to Avallon and can whisk you north to Paris or south to Dijon and the famous Burgundy vineyards that are part of our second tour. If you have time, however, we suggest that you make an excursion from Avallon to the northern part of the **Morvan Regional Park,** whose photogenic lakes, hills, and forest can be seen around every twisty corner. Take D944 out of Avallon and then ★ **32** turn left on D10 to **Quarré-les-Tombes,** so called because of the empty prehistoric stone tombs discovered locally and eerily arrayed in a ring around the church. The **Rocher de la Pérouse,** 8 kilometers (5 miles) south of Quarré-les-Tombes, is a mighty outcrop worth scrambling up for a view of the Morvan and the Cure Valley.

Tour 2: Wine Country

*Numbers in the margin correspond to points of interest on the Dijon
and Burgundy maps.*

③③ **Dijon,** linked to Paris 314 kilometers (195 miles) away by expressway
(A6/A38) and TGV train, is the age-old capital of Burgundy. Throughout the Middle Ages, Burgundy was a duchy that led a separate existence from the rest of France, culminating in the rule of the four
"Grand Dukes of the West" between 1364 and 1477. A number of monuments date from this period, including the Palais des Ducs (Ducal
Palace), now largely converted into an art museum.

Dijon's fame and fortune outlasted its dukes, and the city continued
to flourish under French rule from the 17th century on. It has remained
the major city of Burgundy—the only one, in fact, with more than
100,000 inhabitants. Its site, on the major European north–south trade
route and within striking distance of the Swiss and German borders,
has helped maintain its economic importance. It's also a cultural center—home to no fewer than 10 museums, of which a few are mentioned
below. The same can be said of its numerous gastronomic specialties:
snails, mustard, and cassis (a blackcurrant liqueur often mixed with
white wine—preferably Burgundy Aligoté—to make Kir, one of France's
most popular aperitifs).

★ ③④ The **Palais des Ducs** is Dijon's leading testimony to bygone splendor.
These days, it's home to one of France's major art museums, the **Musée
des Beaux-Arts,** where the tombs of two of the aforementioned dukes—
Philip the Bold and John the Fearless—are the center of a rich collection of medieval objects and Renaissance furniture. Among the paintings
are works by Italian Old Masters and French 19th-century artists, such
as Théodore Géricault and Gustave Courbet, and their Realist and Impressionist successors, notably Édouard Manet and Claude Monet. The
ducal kitchens (circa 1435), with their six huge fireplaces, and the 14th-
century chapter house catch the eye, as does the 15th-century **Salle des
Gardes** (Guard Room), with its richly carved and colored tombs and
late-14th-century altarpieces. The elegant, classical exterior of the former palace can best be admired from place de la Libération and cour
d'Honneur. *Pl. de la Ste-Chapelle,* ☎ *80–74–52–70.* ☛ *12 frs adults,
5 frs students; ticket valid for all town museums.* ⊙ *Wed.–Mon. 10–
6 (contemporary section closed noon–2:30).*

Further links with Dijon's medieval past are found west of the town
center, just off the avenue Albert Ier beyond the train station. Keep an
eye out for the exuberant 15th-century gateway to the Chartreuse de
Champmol—all that remains of a former charterhouse—and the adjoining **Puits de Moïse,** the so-called Well of Moses, with six large, com-
pellingly realistic medieval statues on a hexagonal base (1395–1405).

③⑤ **Notre-Dame** (rue de la Préfécture), one of the city's old churches,
stands out with its elegant towers, delicate nave stonework, 13th-cen-
③⑥ tury stained glass, and soaring chancel. The church of **St-Michel** (rue
Rameau) takes us forward 300 years with its chunky Renaissance fa-
③⑦ cade. **Cathédrale St-Bénigne** (off rue Mariotte) is comparatively austere; its chief glory is the 10th-century crypt—a forest of pillars
surmounted by a rotunda.

③⑧ The **Musée Archéologique** (Archaeological Museum), housed in the
former abbey buildings of St-Bénigne, traces the history of the region
through archaeological discoveries. *5 rue du Dr-Maret,* ☎ *80–30–*

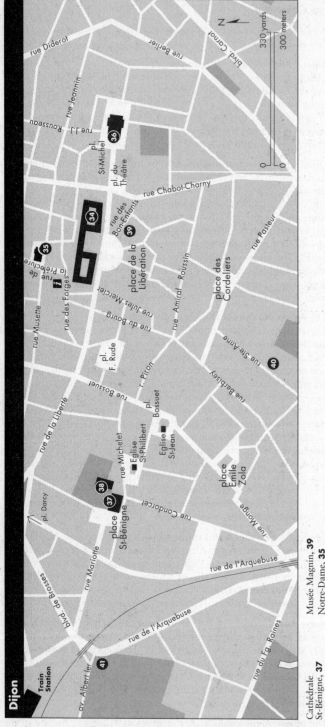

Dijon

rue Diderot

rue Berlier

blvd. Carnot

N

330 yards
300 meters

rue Jeannin

rue J.J. Rousseau

pl.
St-Michel

36

pl. du
Théâtre

rue Chabot-Charny

34

rue des
Bon-Enfants

39

rue Pasteur

35

rue de
la Préfecture

i

place de la
Libération

rue des Forges

rue Jules Mercier

rue Amiral Roussin

place des
Cordeliers

rue Musette

rue du Bourg

rue Ste-Anne

pl.
F. Rude

rue Bossuet

r. Piron

rue Berbisey

40

rue de la Liberté

rue Michelet

Eglise
St-Philibert

pl.
Bossuet

Eglise
St-Jean

place
Emile
Zola

pl. Darcy

38

37

place
St-Bénigne

rue Condorcet

rue Monge

rue Mariotte

rue de l'Arquebuse

blvd. de Brosses

rue de l'Arquebuse

rue du Fg. Raines

Train
Station

41

av. Albert ler

Cathédrale
St-Bénigne, **37**
Musée
Archéologique, **38**
Musée d'Art Sacré, **40**
Musée d'Histoire
Naturelle/Jardin
Botanique, **41**

Musée Magnin, **39**
Notre-Dame, **35**
Palais des Ducs, **34**
St-Michel, **36**

88–54. ☉ *Sept.–May, Wed.–Mon. 9–noon and 2–6; June–Aug., Wed.–Mon. 9:30–6.*

❸❾ The **Musée Magnin** is a 17th-century mansion showcasing original furnishings and a variety of paintings from the 16th to the 19th centuries. *4 rue des Bons-Enfants,* ☎ *80–67–11–10.* ☉ *June–Sept., Tues.–Sun. 10–6; Oct.–May, Tues.–Sun. 10–noon and 2–6.*

❹⓿ The **Musée d'Art Sacré,** devoted to religious art, has a collection of sculpture and altarpieces in the appropriate setting of a former church. *17 rue Ste-Anne,* ☎ *80–30–65–91.* ☉ *Wed.–Mon. 9–noon and 2–6.*

❹❶ The **Musée d'Histoire Naturelle** (☎ 80–76–82–76) and the **Jardin Botanique** (☎ 80–76–82–84), behind the train station, encompass a natural-history museum and impressive botanical gardens, with a wide variety of trees and tropical flowers. *1 av. Albert-Ier. Museum open Wed.–Mon. 9–noon and 2–6; garden open daily 7:30–6 (8 PM in summer).*

TIME OUT Place Darcy has more to recommend it than the Dijon tourist office in one corner. Gastronomically speaking, this square caters to all tastes and budgets. Choose from the bustling **Concorde** brasserie, the quiet bar of the **Hôtel de la Cloche,** the underground **Caveau de la Porte Guillaume** wine-and-snack bar, or—for those with a sweet tooth—the **Pâtisserie Darcy.**

A31 connects Dijon to Beaune, 40 kilometers (25 miles) south, but you may prefer a leisurely route through the vineyards to racing down the expressway. Chug along D122, past venerable properties with names like Gevrey-Chambertin, Chambolle-Musigny, and Morey-St-Denis, to
❹❷ **Clos de Vougeot.** The **Château du Clos de Vougeot** was constructed by Cistercian monks in the 12th century and completed during the Renaissance; it's famous as the seat of Burgundy's elite company of wine lovers, the *Confrérie des Chevaliers du Tastevin,* who gather here in November at the start of an annual three-day festival, *Les Trois Glorieuses.* You can admire the château's cellars, where ceremonies are held, and ogle the huge grape presses. ☎ *80–62–86–09.* ☛ *22 frs adults, 10 frs children 8–13.* ☉ *Apr.–Sept., weekdays and Sun. 9–7, Sat. 9–6:30; Oct.–Mar., weekdays and Sun. 9–11:30 and 2–5:30, Sat. 9–5.*

Wine has been made in nearby **Nuits-St-Georges** since Roman times; its "dry, tonic, and generous qualities" were recommended to Louis XIV for medicinal use. It is appropriate, then, that some of the region's
★ finest vineyards should be owned by the **Hospices de Beaune** (Hôtel Dieu), founded in 1443 as a hospital, which carried on its medical activities until 1971, its nurses still sporting their strange medieval uni-
❹❸ forms. A visit to the Hospices is one of the highlights of a stay in **Beaune;** it's right across from the city's tourist office. The hospital's medical history is retraced in a museum whose wide-ranging collections feature some of the weird and wonderful instruments used by doctors back in the 15th century. You can also see a collection of tapestries including Roger Van der Weyden's stirringly composed medieval Flemish masterpiece, *The Last Judgment.* A suspended magnifying glass allows you to scan the extraordinary details of the work. *Rue de l'Hôtel-Dieu,* ☎ *80–24–45–00. Museum admission: 27 frs.* ☉ *Apr.–Nov., daily 9–6:30; Dec.–Mar., daily 9–11:30 and 2–5:30.*

Another good series of tapestries, relating the life of the Virgin, can be admired in Beaune's main church, the 12th-century **Collégiale Notre-Dame,** just off avenue de la République.

Despite the hordes of tourists, Beaune remains one of the most charming and attractive French provincial towns. There are few more delightful experiences than a visit to the candle-lit cellars of the **Marché aux Vins.**
★ Here you can taste as many of the regional wines as you wish—beginning with whites and fruity Beaujolais and ending with such big reds as Gevrey-Chambertin—for the price of admission. *7 rue Nicolas Rolin,* ☎ *80–22–27–69. Admission and tasting: 40 frs.* ✆ *Feb.–mid-Dec. daily 9:30–11:30 and 2–6.*

TIME OUT A good place to find refreshment in the center of Beaune—and to drink something other than wine—is the **Bouché** tearoom opposite the old belfry. Pastries and homemade ice cream are specialties. *1 pl. Monge.*

From Beaune, another scenic route cuts through the vineyards on the way south to Chalon-sur-Saône. Take D973 from Beaune, which soon passes through Pommard, Volnay, and Meursault before continuing to Auxey-Duresses, La Rochepot and its pretty château, and Nolay. From Nolay, N6 scissors through another vineyard, Chassagne-Montrachet, on its way to Chagny. D981 runs south to Rully, past the Mercurey vineyard and the start of the Côte Chalonnaise, which links the vineyards of Burgundy and Beaujolais to Germolles and Givry, where you take D69 to Chalon.

㊹ Chalon-sur-Saône has its medieval heart near the **Eglise St-Vincent—**a former cathedral displaying a jumble of styles—close to the banks of the River Saône. This area was reconstructed to have an Old World charm, but the rest of Chalon is a modern, commercial, and cosmopolitan city, the cultural and shopping center of southern Burgundy. Chalon is the birthplace of Nicéphore Niepce (1765–1833), whose early experiments, developed further by Jacques Daguerre, qualify him as the father of photography. The **Musée Nicéphore Niepce,** occupying an 18th-century house overlooking the Saône, retraces the early history of photography and motion pictures with the help of some pioneering equipment. It also includes a selection of contemporary photographic work and a lunar camera used during the U.S. Apollo program. But the star of the museum must be the primitive camera used to take the first photographs in 1816. *20 quai des Messageries,* ☎ *85–48–41–98.* ✆ *10 frs adults, 5 frs children (free Wed.).* ✆ *Sept.–June, Wed.–Mon. 9:30–11:30 and 2:30–5:30; July–Aug., Wed.–Mon. 10–6.*

㊺ N6 continues down the Saône Valley to **Tournus** (24 kilometers, or 15 miles away), a town that retains much of the charm of the Middle Ages and the Renaissance. One of Burgundy's most spectacular and best-preserved Romanesque buildings is the **abbey of St-Philibert.** Despite its massiveness—unadorned cylindrical pillars over four feet thick support the nave—it is spacious and light. No effort was made to decorate or embellish the interior, whose sole hint of frivolity is the alternating red and white stones in the nave arches. The crypt and former abbey buildings, including the cloister and magnificent 12th-century refectory, can also be visited.

Head west from Tournus along picturesque D14 to the fortified hilltop town of Brancion, with its old castle and soaring keep. Shortly after,
㊻ turn left along D981 to **Cluny,** another 19 kilometers (12 miles) away. The **Abbey of Cluny,** founded in the 10th century, was the biggest church in Europe until the 16th century, when Michelangelo built St. Peter's in Rome. Cluny's medieval abbots were as powerful as popes. In 1098, Pope Urban II (himself a Cluniac) assured the head of his old abbey that Cluny was the "light of the world." That assertion, of dubious

religious validity, has not stood the test of time, and today Cluny stands in ruins—a reminder of the limits of human grandeur.

The ruins nonetheless suggest the size and glory of Cluny Abbey at its zenith. Only the Clocher de l'Eau-Bénite (a majestic bell tower) and the right arms of the two transepts, climbing 100 feet above-ground, remain. The 13th-century *farinier* (flour mill), with its fine chestnut roof and collection of statues, can also be seen. The gardens contain an ancient lime tree, several hundred years old, named Abélard after the controversial philosopher who sought shelter at the abbey in 1142. No one is sure the tree is quite that old, though! A small museum, with separate entry price, displays religious paintings, sculptures rescued from demolished portions of the abbey, and the remains of the *bibliothèque des moines*, or monks' library. ☎ 85–59–12–79. ✆ *29 frs adults, 15 frs senior citizens, 9 frs children 7–17. Museum only: 13 frs.* ۞ *Nov.–Mar., daily 10:30–11:30 and 2–4; Apr.–June, daily 9:30–noon and 2–6; July–Sept., daily 9–7; Oct., daily 10–noon and 2–5. Museum closed Tues.*

Head for Mâcon, a mere 25 kilometers (16 miles) southeast of Cluny via D980/N79. Stop just outside the town to admire the giant rocky outcrop of **Solutré** on your right, towering above the vineyard of Pouilly-Fuissé, renowned for its white wine. Excavations around the Rock of Solutré have revealed the presence of prehistoric man—and prehistoric horse (so many horses, in fact, that one school of thought asserts that the poor beasts were driven over the top of the cliff to crash to their death below).

47 **Mâcon** is a bustling town, best known for its wine fair in May and for its pesky stone bridge across the Saône, whose low arches are a headache for the pilots of large river barges. The two octagonal towers of the ruined cathedral of St-Vincent loom over the wide quays along the river. The Romantic poet Alphonse de Lamartine (1790–1869) was born in Mâcon.

What to See and Do with Children

Go for walks and picnics in the **Morvan Forest** (maybe along the shores of one of its small lakes) or hike up the imposing **Rock of Solutré** (Tour 2).

In Troyes (Tour 1), look for the yard-wide **ruelle des Chats** (alleyway) in the heart of town.

The beautifully restored **abbey of Fontenay** (Tour 1) shows how and where monks lived as well as worshipped.

Visit **Musée Nicéphore Niepce,** in Chalons (Tour 2), with its collection of antique camera equipment.

SHOPPING

Antiques
The auction houses at Semur-en-Auxois and Dijon are good places to prospect for antiques and works of art; the streets of Tournus are riddled with antiques shops.

Clothes
If there is an ideal place for a shopping spree, it's Troyes. Many clothing manufacturers are just outside town, so prices in stores can be 50% cheaper than elsewhere in France. Rue des Bas-Trévois, rue Bégand (leather goods also), and rue Cartalon are good places to look; the best buys on jeans can be had at the **Jeans Shop** (64 rue Émile-Zola).

Food Items

Shopping is not one of life's major activities in sleepy Burgundy, where eating and drinking are most important. Mustard, snails, and all manner of candies (including chocolate snails—*escargots de Bourgogne*) may be found without difficulty, especially in the commercial heart of Dijon, with its numerous pedestrian streets. You can get the famous Burgundy wine at a fairly good price if you buy it from an individual producer. Cassis can be bought anywhere in France for much the same price.

SPORTS AND THE OUTDOORS

Ballooning

From April to November you can float through the skies in a balloon. Most flights last an hour, but the total excursion, which includes inflation and deflation, can take three. A popular company is **Air Escargot** (71150 Remigny, ☎ 85–87–08–84, FAX 85–87–12–30), or try **Ballons de Bourgogne** (21630 Pommard, ☎ 80–24–20–32, FAX 80–24–12–87).

Bicycling

Biking through Burgundy's rolling green vineyards, hedgerowed pastures, and dense forests can be the best of all possible ways to burn off those three-hour, twice-a-day, four-course feasts. Cycle tours are organized by **La Peurtantaine** (Accueil Morvan Environment, Ecole du Bourg, 71550 Anost, ☎ 85–82–77–74). Most tourist offices will be able to give details about recommended routes and where to rent bikes (train stations are a good bet).

Horseback Riding

Burgundy's pastoral countryside is well suited to leisurely riding tours. Among the numerous establishments that provide lessons or from which you can rent horses are **Locacheval** (Martine Richard, 21540 Turcey, ☎ 80–33–21–13), **Les Grilles** (89710 St-Fargeau, ☎ 86–74–12–11), and the **Ecuries de la Sarial** (71260 La Salle, ☎ 85–37–52–44). Horses can be taken out for about 80 francs an hour.

DINING AND LODGING

Dining

The Burgundians are hearty eaters; whatever the class of restaurant, you are unlikely to go hungry. Dijon ranks with Lyon as one of the unofficial gastronomic capitals of France. Wealthy Parisian gourmets think nothing of the three-hour drive needed to sample the cuisine of Dijon's Jean-Pierre Billoux or that of Marc Meneau at Vézelay. Game, freshwater trout, garlicky *jambon persillé* (ham flavored with parsley), goat cheese, coq au vin, snails, mustard, and mushrooms number among the region's specialties. Meat is often served in rich, wine-based sauces. There is wine of all types and prices. Whites range from cheapish Aligoté to classy Chablis and legendary Meursault; and reds from light, unpretentious Mâcon to indescribable GevreyChambertin and Romanée-Conti.

CATEGORY	COST*
$$$$	over 400 frs
$$$	250–400 frs
$$	125–250 frs
$	under 125 frs

*per person for a three-course meal, including tax (18.6%) and tip, but not wine

Lodging

For all its charms, Burgundy is seldom deluged by tourists, and finding accommodations is not hard. But it is still wise to make advance reservations, especially in the wine country (from Dijon to Beaune). If you intend to visit Beaune for the Trois Glorieuses wine festival in November, make your hotel reservation several months in advance. Note that nearly all country hotels have restaurants, and you are usually expected to eat in them.

Highly recommended hotels are indicated by a star ★.

CATEGORY	COST*
$$$$	over 800 frs
$$$	550–800 frs
$$	300–550 frs
$	under 300 frs

All prices are for a standard double room for two, including tax (18.6%) and service charge.

Arnay-le-Duc

DINING AND LODGING

★ **Chez Camille.** Small, quiet, and friendly sum up this hotel on N6 between Saulieu and Beaune, though the exterior looks very ordinary and you might easily pass it by. The 16th-century house has been tastefully renovated, with period furniture and original wooden beams in many rooms. The upper floors (no elevator) are the most romantic. Room 22 (385 francs) has a wonderful beamed and gabled ceiling, and Room 23 (485 francs), the most dramatic, has a beamed ceiling that looks like spokes in a wheel. A cozy downstairs lounge leads into the light, airy, glass-roofed restaurant. Traditional Burgundian fare—duck and boar are specialties—figures high on the menu, and there is a thoughtful choice of regional wines. Monique Poinsot will greet you and guide you through the menu. You will see her husband, Armand, working with his team in the kitchen, separated from the dining room by plate glass windows. ⊞ *1 pl. Edouard-Herriot, 21230,* ☏ *80–90–01–38,* FAX *80–90–04–64. 12 rooms with bath. AE, DC, MC, V. $$*

Autun

DINING

Chalet Bleu. In the center of Autun, this restaurant serves solid traditional French cuisine. The setting, complemented by spruce white furniture, is fresh and green and resembles a converted conservatory. Foie gras and beef with shallots are trustworthy choices. ✕ *3 rue Jeannin,* ☏ *85–86–27–30. Reservations advised. AE, DC, MC, V. Closed Mon. dinner and Tues. $*

LODGING

St-Louis. This comfortable hotel dates from the 17th century; legend has it that Napoléon once slept here, and visitors can sleep here, too—it's on a quiet street away from the traffic noise. The cozily decorated guest rooms have a slightly faded charm. The hotel boasts a pleasant patio-garden and its own restaurant, La Rotonde. ⊞ *6 rue de l'Arbalète, 71400,* ☏ *85–52–21–03,* FAX *85–86–32–54. 52 rooms, some with bath. Restaurant. AE, DC, MC, V. $$*

Auxerre

DINING

★ **Jardin Gourmand.** As its name implies, this restaurant features a pretty garden where you can eat *en terrasse* during summer months; the interior, accented by light-colored oak, is equally congenial. The cuisine is innovative but simple, showcasing ingredients in their own juices—try the ravioli and foie gras or the duck with black currants. The service is discreet. ✕ *56 blvd. Vauban,* ☎ *86–51–53–52. Reservations advised. MC, V. Closed Mon. and Tues. lunch. $$*

LODGING

Le Maxime. This slightly old-fashioned, family-run hotel on the banks of the Yonne, a five-minute walk from the cathedral, the abbey, and the old town center, attracts guests who like the personal touch of René and Kelly Fortune. The guest rooms are individually decorated and refurbished with twin or double beds. Reserve a room with a river view. The bar, Le Cave de Bourgogne, with its exposed beams and copper pots, is a comfortable place to relax before trying one of the good restaurants nearby. ⊞ *2 quai de la Marine, 89000,* ☎ *86–52–14–19,* 🅵🅰🆇 *86–52–21–70. 25 rooms with bath. Bar. AE, DC, MC, V. Closed Dec. 24–Jan. 31. $$*

Normandie. The picturesque, vine-covered Normandie occupies a grand-looking building conveniently set in the center of Auxerre, a short walk from the cathedral. The guest rooms are unpretentious but of good value and spanking clean, with such pleasantries as hair dryers in the bathroom. You can relax in the charming garden, but there is no restaurant on the premises. ⊞ *41 blvd. Vauban, 89000,* ☎ *86–52–57–80,* 🅵🅰🆇 *86–51–54–33. 48 rooms with bath or shower. Bar, sauna, gym exercise room. AE, DC, MC, V. $–$$*

Avallon

DINING AND LODGING

★ **Les Capucins.** On a peaceful square 10 minutes from the center, this intimate hotel owned by M. et Mme. Aublanc offers rooms in a wide range of prices, with a few rooms at just under 300 francs. It is better known for its restaurant, however, which features four set menus dominated by regional cooking. There's a pleasing garden for breakfast and aperitifs, and small cozy rooms for a postprandial *digestif.* Dishes of especially good value are the duck, the trout in flaky pastry, and the very local *oeufs en meurette* (eggs poached in broth and red wine). The desserts are excellent. ⊞ *6 av. Paul-Doumer (also known as av. de la Gare), 89200,* ☎ *86–34–06–52,* 🅵🅰🆇 *86–34–58–47. 8 rooms, 7 with bath. AE, MC, V. Closed mid-Nov.–mid-Jan. Restaurant also closed Wed., Tues. dinner out of season. $–$$*

Moulin des Ruats. Once an old flour mill, the Moulin des Ruats became a family hotel in 1924. After several renovations it has evolved into a comfortable country inn, 4 kilometers (2 miles) southwest of Avallon. The guest rooms are decorated with a pretty country-French decor, and many have balconies that overlook the River Cousin. The new dining room has picture windows and views of the river, and the large menu is made up of traditional dishes. The 230-franc menu is the most popular, and the robust main course is a good Burgundian coq au vin. ⊞ *Vallée du Cousin, 89200,* ☎ *86–34–07–14,* 🅵🅰🆇 *86–31–65–47. 26 rooms with bath or shower. Restaurant. AE, DC, MC, V. Closed Nov.–Feb. $$*

LODGING

Château de Vault-de-Lugny. This 16th-century château (5 kilometers, or 3 miles, northeast of Avallon via D957) has its own moat and extensive grounds that include a 13th-century keep. It has been harmoniously renovated; most rooms have four-poster or canopy beds, period-style furniture, and spacious, gleaming tile bathrooms. Tranquillity is assured; meals are served to residents only. ⊞ *89200 Vault* *de Lugny,* ☎ *86–34–07–86,* FAX *86–34–16–36. 11 rooms with bath. Restaurant, tennis courts, fishing. MC, V. $$$*

Beaune

DINING

Auberge St-Vincent. Perhaps the best thing about this restaurant is its admirable setting opposite the Hospices de Beaune. Not surprisingly, it pulls in as many tourists as locals, and although the cuisine and ambience are undistinguished, the grilled lobster tails flambéed with whiskey creates a show. Service is attentive and the wine list appropriately lengthy, but order carefully, or the meal can become expensive. Good choices are the *daurade* (sea bream) in a mille-feuille shell and the roast lamb from the Pyrenees. ✗ *Pl. de la Halle,* ☎ *80–22–42–34. Reservations advised. AE, DC, MC, V. $$*

L'Ecusson. Don't be put off by its unprepossessing exterior. This is a comfortable, friendly, thick-carpeted restaurant whose four variously priced menus offer outstanding value. L'Ecusson showcases chef Jean-Pierre Senelet's sure-footed culinary mastery: duck sweetbreads with ham and spinach, rabbit terrine with tarragon, leg of duck in oxtail sauce. ✗ *Pl. Malmédy,* ☎ *80–24–03–82. Reservations advised. AE, DC, MC, V. Closed Sun. and Feb. $$*

Le Gourmandin. This is just what the center of tourist Beaune needs: a no-nonsense restaurant that serves regional fare—boeuf bourguignon, *quenelles de brochet* (a light dumpling of pike), and *tourte de canard* (duck pie), for example—at reasonable prices. Prepared under the direction of Jean Crotet (chef-owner of Hostellerie Levernois), the food is excellent. The wine list, too, has a superb selection from small vineyards at affordable prices. Decor is simple, in the style of a 1930s café, and the small dining area is on two levels. ✗ *8 pl. Carnot,* ☎ *80–24–07–88. Closed Sun. dinner and Mon. $–$$*

★ **La Grilladine.** This small restaurant deserves a recommendation on three counts. Chef Pierre Lenko's cooking, while not elaborate, produces good, hearty Burgundy dishes like boeuf bourgignon and ouefs en meurette. The prices are extremely reasonable, with three-course menus beginning at 78 francs, though for 98 francs you get a wider selection. Finally, the ambience is warm, intimate, and cheerful. Of the two rooms in the restaurant, the warmer one, on the right, has rose-pink tablecloths, exposed stone walls, and a mammoth, ancient beam supporting the ceiling. The restaurant is easy to find—it is just before the Hotel Cep as you walk left from the Hospices de Beaune. ✗ *17 rue Maufoux,* ☎ *80–22–22–36. Reservations advised. MC, V. Closed Mon. $–$$*

DINING AND LODGING

★ **Hostellerie de Levernois.** Jean Crotet won a reputation for traditional culinary finesse at a restaurant in Nuits-St-Georges. Then, in 1988, he and his wife, Christiane, opened their own marvelous hotel and restaurant in a small village 10 kilometers (6¼ miles) east of Beaune. Christiane is responsible for the decor. The main building shimmers and gleams with light from large picture windows and marble tiles, and the four traditionally furnished guest rooms upstairs have a comfortably elegant bourgeois feel. In a modern one-story building in the landscaped gardens are 12 rooms, whose contemporary interiors use lots of natural wood and warm pastel fabrics. Everything is immaculate. In the kitchen, Jean works with his son, Christophe, who, having trained under the Trois Gros brothers, is more "nouvelle" in his cooking. Their combination of talents makes one of the most exciting dining rooms in Burgundy, where meals are occasions to be savored. But they are also expensive; the menus begin at 380 francs (200 francs at lunch). ☎ *Route de Verdun-sur-le-Doubs, Levernois, 21200,* ☎ *80–24–73–58,* ꜰᴀX *80–22–78–00. 16 rooms. Restaurant (closed Tues. lunch). Closed last 2 wks of Dec. AE, DC, MC, V. $$$$*

★ **Le Cep.** Within the ramparts and a five-minute walk from the main square, Beaune's top hotel offers large, tastefully decorated rooms that are furnished with antiques and have large tiled bathrooms. (Even the standard double rooms are spacious by French standards.) The hotel is a combination of several ancient town houses—the oldest circa 1547—whose courtyards have been made into a small garden. The ground-floor rooms have exposed wood beams, and in the lounge a log fire burns during the chillier months. Choose a room facing the courtyard, such as No. 303, Romanee-Conti, and you'll have a quiet night's sleep even with the window open—rare at French hotels. All the creature comforts are offered, including CNN News, a large couch, and a table. Service is efficient if a little curt, but it's limited to basic needs and can be a little harried when tour groups check in and out. ☎ *27 rue Maufoux, 21200 Beaune,* ☎ *80–22–35–48,* ꜰᴀX *80–22–76–80. 52 rooms. Restaurant (closed Mon., and Tues. lunch). AE, DC, MC, V. $$$*

La Poste. The front rooms of this French provincial hotel look over the ramparts and the rear ones over nearby vineyards; not a bad combination! The service is briskly professional; the hotel was redecorated several years ago, so inspect the room before accepting it—some (room 205, for example) are not as good as others. The long, narrow restaurant with its gleaming silverware breathes tradition. The setting compensates somewhat for the uninventive cuisine, as does the fabulous wine list. ☎ *1 blvd. Clemenceau, 21200,* ☎ *80–22–08–11,* ꜰᴀX *80–24–19–71. 21 rooms with bath, 9 suites. Restaurant. AE, DC, MC, V. Closed winter. $$$*

Hotel Clarion. This small hotel 8 kilometers (5 miles) north of Beaune is on the slope behind the wine village of Aloxe Croton. The vines that begin at the end of the garden belong to the brother of the hotel owner, who is a marvelous source of wine gossip. The hotel has no dining room, so you are free to try the excellent nearby restaurants, but if you should want a supper tray in your room or in the garden, M. and Mme. Voarick, who speak fluent English, will happily oblige. The guest rooms are spacious for France, and their exposed-gable beams give a warm atmosphere. Beds are mostly side-by-side twins, and bedside lights on dimmer controls add to the romance. Room 44 has a private terrace and view of the garden. The least expensive rooms, on the ground floor, have French windows out to the garden. The good breakfast includes Black Forest ham (not too salty), cheese, and excellent coffee. ☎ *21420 Aloxe-Croton,* ☎ *80–26–46–70,* ꜰᴀX *80–26–47–16. 10 rooms. MC, V. $$–$$$*

Central. A well-run establishment with several enlarged and modernized rooms, the Central lives up to its name: It's just around the corner from the Hôtel-Dieu in downtown Beaune. The stone-wall restaurant is cozy—some might say cramped—and the consistently good cuisine of chef Jean Garein is popular with the local gentry. You, too, will enjoy its presentation and reliability, from the oeufs en meurette to the coq au vin *à l'Ancienne.* The service is efficient, if a little hurried. The evening meal is obligatory in July and August. ☎ *2 rue Victor-Millot, 21200,* ☎ *80–24–77–24,* ꜰᴀX *80–22–30–40. 20 rooms, most with bath. Restaurant (closed Wed., and Sun. dinner, Nov.–June). MC, V. Closed Dec.–Jan. $$*

Reality check. Call home.

—— *AT&T USADirect® and World Connect®. The fast, easy way to call most anywhere.* ——

Take out AT&T Calling Card or your local calling card.** Lift phone. Dial AT&T Access Number for country you're calling from. Connect to English-speaking operator or voice prompt. Reach the States or over 200 countries. Talk. Say goodbye. Hang up. Resume vacation.

Austria*†††.....................022-903-011	Luxembourg 0-800-0111	Turkey* 00-800-12277
Belgium* 0-800-100-10	Netherlands*...................06-022-9111	United Kingdom................0500-89-0011
Czech Republic*.............00-420-00101	Norway 800-190-11	
Denmark 8001-0010	Poland†♦'.........................0◊010-480-0111	
Finland 9800-100-10	Portugal† 05017-1-288	
France....................................19-0011	Romania*........................01-800-4288	
Germany.............................0130-0010	Russia*†(Moscow)................155-5042	
Greece*..........................00-800-1311	Slovak Rep.*...................00-420-00101	
Hungary*............00◊-800-01111	Spain●...........................900-99-00-11	
Ireland 1-800-550-000	Sweden 020-795-611	
Italy*..................................172-1011	Switzerland* 155-00-11	

AT&T
Your True Choice

**You can also call collect or use most U.S. local calling cards. Countries in bold face permit country-to-country calling in addition to calls to the U.S. World Connect® prices consist of USADirect® rates plus an additional charge based on the country you are calling. Collect calling available to the U.S. only. *Public phones require deposit of coin or phone card. †May not be available from every phone. †††Public phones require local coin payment during call. ♦Not available from public phones. ◊Await second dial tone.'Dial 010-480-0111 from major Warsaw hotels. ●Calling available to most European countries. ©1995 AT&T.

For a free wallet sized card of all AT&T Access Numbers, call: 1-800-241-5555.

All the best trips start with **Fodor's**.

EXPLORING GUIDES

At last, the color of an art book combined with the usefulness of a complete guide.

"As stylish and attractive as any guide published." —*The New York Times*

"Worth reading before, during, and after a trip." —*The Philadelphia Inquirer*

More than 30 destinations available worldwide. $19.95 each.

BERKELEY GUIDES

The budget traveler's handbook

"Berkeley's scribes put the funk back in travel."
—*Time*

"Fresh, funny, and funky as well as useful."
—*The Boston Globe*

"Well-organized, clear and very easy to read."
—*America Online*

14 destinations worldwide. Priced between $13.00 - $19.50. ($17.95 - $27.00 Canada)

AFFORDABLES

"All the maps and itinerary ideas of Fodor's established gold guides with a bonus—shortcuts to savings." —*USA Today*

"Travelers with champagne tastes and beer budgets will welcome this series from Fodor's." —*Hartfort Courant*

"It's obvious these Fodor's folk have secrets we civilians don't." —*New York Daily News*

Also available: Florida, Europe, France, London, Paris. Priced between $11.00 - $18.00 ($14.50 - $24.00 Canada)

At bookstores, or call **1-800-533-6478**

Fodor's
The name that means smart travel.™

Chablis
DINING AND LODGING

★ **Hostellerie des Clos.** The moderately priced guest rooms at this inn are quite simple and ordinary, given color by the gay floral curtains and quilts. They have twin beds or a queen-size bed and a wicker table with chairs; the TV (one English-speaking program) is hung from the ceiling above the minibar. Second-floor rooms have angled ceilings, which add a slight charm, and bathrooms are large but plain. Guests come to stay here in order to dine on Michel Vignaud's superb cuisine; though he has only one Michelin star, clearly his patrons award him two. Vignaud creates dishes whose taste does not lose its interest after the second mouthful. The sandre is served with a chicken-based sauce that stands in tasty juxtaposition to the fish. The casserole of hare is wonderfully robust. Most exciting are the *huitres d'Isgny* (small oysters) in a dill and Chablis sauce served as an appetizer. Desserts are equally splendid; perhaps try the feuille de chocolat with red fruits. ⊞ *Rue Jules-Rathier, 89800 Chablis,* ☎ *86–42–10–63,* FAX *86–42–17–11. 26 rooms with bath. Restaurant. AE, DC, MC, V. $$–$$$*

Chagny
DINING AND LODGING

Lameloise. This small hotel is on the outskirts of a small village, 14 kilometers (9 miles) south of Beaune. It may be the only Relais & Châteaux property to stock crayons for the kids. Don't be misled, though; the clientele here are well heeled and well dressed. Confident, relaxed, and consistent, chef Jacques Lameloise offers luxury without stuffiness in his stone-and-beam dining room, as well as on the garden terrace. Try scallops in black olive juice, turbot in truffle butter, or veal kidney in shallot puree, and explore the highly personal list of Burgundies. Rooms are fresh and deluxe, with token rustic touches. ⊞ *36 pl. d'Armes,* ☎ *85–87–08–85,* FAX *85–87–03–57. 8 rooms. AE, MC, V. Closed Wed. and Thurs. lunch. Hotel and restaurant closed Dec. 21–Jan. 26. $$$–$$$$*

Château de Bellecroix. The Bellecroix is just what you expect a château to be. It bristles with turrets, is draped in creepers, and is set in its own park, but you should be aware that at times the hotel can be overwhelmed by seminar groups. Some of the buildings date from 1199, and the huge dining room, with its majestic fireplace, conjures up the atmosphere of medieval feasts. Turbot with morels, beef fillet *Charolais* (a local breed in Burgundy sauce), and fruit gratins number among the latter-day specialties. Guests are expected to take at least one meal per day, besides breakfast, in the restaurant. Set menus cost 230 and 340 francs. Four of the bedrooms are round, set in the towers, and are reached by a picturesque spiral staircase. ⊞ *71150 Chagny,* ☎ *85–87–13–86,* FAX *85–91–28–62. 21 rooms with bath. Restaurant, pool. AE, DC, MC, V. Closed Wed. and Dec. 20–Jan. $$–$$$*

Chalon-sur-Saône
DINING AND LODGING

St-Georges. Close to the train station and town center, the friendly, white-walled St-Georges hotel has been tastefully modernized and has many spacious rooms. Its cozy restaurant is known locally for its efficient service and menus of outstanding value. You can't go wrong with the duck in white pepper, foie gras with truffles, or roast pigeon. ⊞ *32 av. Jean-Jaurès, 71100,* ☎ *85–48–27–05,* FAX *85–93–23–88. 48 rooms, most with bath. AE, DC, MC, V. $$*

Charny

LODGING

Château de Prunoy. Staying here is not for everyone. The building is a vast château, built by one of the finance ministers to Louis XVI. It's imposing and grand, set in parkland with avenues of trees. It has a couple of lounges, a dining room, space for seminars, and 16 mammoth guest rooms. Kept as a private house for lavish entertaining until the cost of maintaining it, albeit minimally, became overwhelming, it was transformed in the 1970s into a hotel, though "hotel" implies professional management and a degree of uniformity. That certainly is not the case here: All seems a little haphazard, but if you don't expect prompt service and have a sense of humor, you'll enjoy it. Mme. Josée Roumilhac has put together a fascinating collection, through inheritance and buying at auction; her eclectic taste runs from 17th-century museum-quality antiques to the outrageously modern. So different are the guest rooms, they defy general description, but all have an idiosyncratic flair, and comfort is not ignored. One has a pair of carved, gilded wings 7 feet tall guarding an 18th-century ivory-and-pearl-inlaid jewelry stand, and a desk with two early 19th-century Portuguese chairs. Another room is designed as a Japanese tea house, and yet another has black and cream for its color scheme. The spacious modern bathrooms vary, too: One has a clawfoot tub in the center of the room, another a marble-tile unit surrounded by mirrors. Dinner is not especially grand, rather a matter of convenience. Service is harried, and Labradors roam freely through the château. ⌂ *89120 Charny (on D950 in the direction of Prunoy),* ☎ *86–63–66–91,* ℻ *86–63–77–79. 16 rooms with bath. Restaurant, pool. AE, DC, MC, V. $$$*

Châteauneuf-en-Auxois

DINING AND LODGING

Hostellerie du Château. Lying only 10 minutes from the Paris–Dijon autoroute, the ancient village of Châteauneuf-en-Auxois is just the place for a romantic to live. It's full of old houses from the 14th century and has a village pub and store and a picturesque 12th-century feudal castle. In the shadow of the castle is the Hostellerie du Château, itself an ancient timbered building. The restaurant serves honest, classical Bourgogne fare at lunch and dinner: roasted *Epoisses* (cow's milk cheese) on a salad bed with walnuts, and noisettes of lamb with thyme makes for a delightful dinner. And coq au vin, escargots, lemon sole, and other fairly standard dishes are typical offerings. The guest rooms vary considerably from a small room with a shower (185 francs) to a much more commodious one, No. 2 for example, which has a full bath. The favored rooms have a view of the castle. ⌂ *Châteauneuf-en-Auxois, 21320 Pouilly,* 80–49–22–00, ℻ *80–49–21–27. 17 rooms with bath or shower. Restaurant (closed Tues.). Closed Nov.–mid-Mar. $–$$*

Clamecy

DINING

L'Angélus. The cuisine here is as charming as the setting—opposite the collegiate church, in a wood-beamed, listed medieval building. When young chef Thierry Lambelin escapes from the conservative eye of *patronne* Mafoy Danjean, the grande dame of Clamecy cuisine, he lets loose with such creations as perch in orange sauce and duck-and-chicken salad in raspberry vinegar. ✕ *11 pl. St-Jean,* ☎ *86–27–23–25. Reservations advised. AE, DC, MC, V. Closed Wed. evening and Thurs. $$*

DINING AND LODGING

Boule d'Or. This down-to-earth country hotel (not particularly comfortable but oh-so-cheap) boasts a delightful setting by the River

Yonne. Ask for a room facing the river for lovely views of Old Clamecy. The restaurant is housed in a former medieval chapel, which, together with absurdly cheap menus, more than compensates for the often apathetic service. ☎ *5 pl. Bethléem, 58500,* ☎ *86–27–11–55,* FAX *86–24–47–02. 12 rooms, most with bath. AE, MC, V. Closed Sun. evening, Mon. off-season. $*

Cluny

DINING AND LODGING

Bourgogne. There's no better place to get into Cluny's medieval mood than the Bourgogne. What remains of the famous abbey is just next door, and the old-fashioned hotel building, which dates from 1817, stands where other parts of the abbey used to be. There is a small garden and an atmospheric restaurant with sober pink decor and comfortable, if slightly stodgy, cuisine: foie gras, snails, and the more exotic fish with ginger. The evening meal is mandatory in July and August. ☎ *Pl. de l'Abbaye, 71250,* ☎ *85–59–00–58,* FAX *85–59–03–73. 14 rooms with bath. AE, DC, V. Closed mid-Nov.–early Mar. Restaurant also closed Tues.,Wed. lunch. $$–$$$*

Hôtel de l'Abbaye. The parents of the owner-chef, M. Lassagne, used to have a small hotel next to the abbey, but the Germans blew it up during World War II and they moved to this new location on the outskirts of the village but kept the name. It's a five-minute walk from the center. This is a modest, simple hotel. The three rooms to the right of the dining room are more recently decorated than the others and at 250 francs are an especially good value. The restaurant offers local cooking that's less elaborate than at the Bourgogne, but better (according to the chef, who did his training there). He says that his products are really fresh, and, certainly, his chicken fricassee in a white Macon sauce and his confit of rabbit are rich, hearty fare. And prices—for example, 98 francs for the three-course prix-fixe menu—are very reasonable. ☎ *Av. Charles-de-Gaulle, 71250 Cluny,* ☎ *85–59–11–14,* FAX *85–59–09–76. 16 rooms, 9 with bath. Restaurant (closed Mon., Tues. lunch, and Jan.–mid-Feb.). MC, V. Hotel closed Jan.–mid-Feb. $*

Dijon

DINING

Jean-Pierre Billoux. Chef Jean-Pierre Billoux has created a restaurant that is outstanding even in this most gastronomic of French cities. The stone-vaulted restaurant is magnificently situated in a spacious, restored town house, the Hôtel de la Cloche, complete with garden, bar, and chintz-curtained dining room. The service is refined and charming. Specialties include frogs' legs steamed and served with watercress pancakes and guinea fowl with foie gras. On pleasant days, reserve a spot in the enclosed garden. ✕ *14 pl. Darcy,* ☎ *80–30–11–00. Reservations required. Jacket and tie. AE, DC, MC, V. Closed Sun. dinner, Mon., mid-Feb., and part of Aug. $$$$*

★ **Thibert.** Like Jean-Pierre Billoux, chef Jean-Paul Thibert has no need to give his restaurant a fancy name. The severely Art Deco setting is less appealing than that of Billoux, but the cuisine is nearly as refined and imaginative. The menu changes regularly. Cabbage stuffed with snails, and prawns with peas and truffles figure among the tours de force; sorbets encased in black-and-white mixed chocolate will tempt you to indulge in dessert. Compared with Billoux, the competitive Thibert continues to represent remarkable value for the money. The Thibert is associated with, and connected by a walkway to, the Hotel Wilson (☎ 80–66–82–50, FAX 80–36–41–54), which has built 26 modern, comfortable rooms in a 17th-century posthouse. ✕ *10 pl. Wilson,*

☎ *80–67–74–64. Reservations required. Jacket and tie. AE, MC, V. Closed Sun., Mon. lunch, and early Jan. and Aug. $$–$$$*

★ **Dame Aquitaine.** A happy marriage between two of France's greatest gastronomic regions—Monique Saléra, the chef, from Aquitaine, her husband from Burgundy—has produced a wonderful blend of regional cuisines in this atmospheric medieval crypt, facing the St-Jean church. The foie gras and duck, either in confit or with cèpes, come from Saléra's native Pau; the coq au vin, boeuf bourguignon, snails, and *lapin à la moutarde* (rabbit with mustard) from her husband's region. The moderate menus—especially the *menu terroir* (of the earth, basic)—are good value. ✕ *23 pl. Boussuet,* ☎ *80–30–36–23. Reservations suggested. AE, DC, MC, V. Closed Mon. lunch, Sun. $$*

★ **Toison d'Or.** A collection of superbly restored 16th-century buildings belonging to the Burgundian Company of Winetasters forms the backdrop to this fine restaurant, which features a small wine museum in the cellar. Toison d'Or is lavishly furnished and quaint (candlelight is de rigueur in the evening), and the food is increasingly sophisticated. Try the langoustines with ginger and the nougat and honey dessert. There are also 27 moderately priced standard rooms. ✕ *18 rue Ste-Anne, 21000,* ☎ *80–30–73–52,* ℻ *80–30–95–51. Reservations accepted. Jacket required. AE, DC, MC, V. Closed Sun. eve. $$*

DINING AND LODGING

Chapeau Rouge. The thick, venerable stone walls of the Chapeau Rouge near Dijon Cathedral encase both a hotel and a newly redecorated restaurant, renowned as a haven of classic regional cuisine. Snails cooked in basil and stuffed pigeon provide the menu's robust highlights. Off the maze of corridors are the guest rooms, done with floral wallpaper and old-fashioned furniture. The bathrooms are quite large, though the toilet cabinets are cramped, and you should avoid rooms with twin beds—they are so narrow and short, six-footers must bend themselves double or fall out of bed. ▥ *5 rue Michelet, 21000,* ☎ *80–30–28–10,* ℻ *80–30–33–89. 29 rooms with bath. Restaurant, bar. AE, DC, MC, V. Reservations required for the restaurant. $$$*

Central Ibis. This central, old-established hotel, now part of a national chain, has benefited from recent modernization: Its sound-proof, air-conditioned rooms offer a degree of comfort in excess of their price. The adjoining grill room, the Central Grill Rôtisserie, presents a good alternative to the gastronomic sophistication that is difficult to avoid elsewhere in Dijon. There's carpaccio and smoked salmon in addition to heavier *abats* (organ meats). ▥ *3 pl. Grangier, 21000,* ☎ *80–30–44–00,* ℻ *80–30–77–12. 90 rooms, most with bath. AE, DC, MC, V. Restaurant closed Sun. $$*

Sens

DINING AND LODGING

Paris & Poste. The newly modernized Paris & Poste is a convenient and pleasant stopping point, should you want a city hotel on the drive down to Burgundy from Paris. The guest rooms are clean, bright, and airy, in line with the hotel's Mapotel connections. The restaurant's helpful service and sumptuous breakfasts confirm the sense of well-being created by the robust evening meal (duck, steak, and snails are high on the various set menus), served in the large, solemn restaurant. ▥ *97 rue de la République, 89100,* ☎ *86–65–17–43,* ℻ *86–64–48–45. 25 rooms with bath. Restaurant. AE, DC, MC, V. $$–$$$*

Croix Blanche. A five-minute walk from the cathedral will bring you to this calm, straightforward hotel. Its two-room restaurant (plus veranda) provides three good-value menus, headed by turbot in crayfish sauce, salmon with sorrel, and beef with Roquefort (cheese) sauce. 🏨 *9 rue Victor-Guichard, 89100,* ☎ *86–64–00–02,* 𝐅𝐀𝐗 *86–65–29–19. 25 rooms with bath or shower. Restaurant. MC, V. $*

Tournus
DINING AND LODGING
Le Rempart. An alternative to staying at the formally elegant high-priced Hotel and Restaurant Greuze, Le Rempart offers adequate rooms that are modern, functional, and kept fresh in appearance with continual refurbishing. Double glazing is effective in keeping out the traffic and train noise, but that does mean you have to rely on the air-conditioning for air circulation. At the "gastronomic" restaurant, prix-fixe dinners begin at 155 francs, and the cooking, though competently prepared by chef Daniel Rogie, doesn't live up to its reputation; you may wish to dine elsewhere. 🏨 *2 av. Gambetta, 71700 Tournus,* ☎ *85–51–10–56,* 𝐅𝐀𝐗 *85–40–77–22. 32 rooms, 6 suites. Restaurant, bar. AE, DC, MC, V. $$*

★ **Aux Terrasses.** For a most enjoyable meal that takes advantage of the region's products and seasons at reasonable prices, try Chef Pariaut's cooking. It is a light version of classic Burgundian, with such fare as coq au vin, escargots in garlic butter, and *poulet Bresse* (chicken roasted with a tasty wine sauce). Desserts are simple but good, from creamy flans to a chocolate ice with two sauces. There are two dining rooms, both comfortable and casual, and many French, German, and Dutch travelers stop here for dinner and a night's rest. The guest rooms are reasonably large, each decorated differently in muted tones, and all comfortably laid out. 🏨 *18 av. du 23-Janvier, 71700 Tournus,* ☎ *85–51–01–74,* 𝐅𝐀𝐗 *85–51–09–99. MC, V. Closed Jan. 4–Feb. 6. Restaurant also closed Sun. dinner and Mon. $$*

Le Coq d'Or. For an inexpensive meal where prix-fixe menus begin at 70 francs, this cheerful hotel restaurant is just the spot. Many of the dishes are cooked on an open-hearth grill in view of the guests, and the exposed beams, peach tablecloths, and friendly service contribute to an ambience of cozy gaiety. The traditional fare is reliable, from onion soup, grilled lamb chops, and steak to poulet Bresse and fruit tarts. The wine list offers mostly low-priced bottles from the region. And if you're looking for a place to sleep, Le Coq d'Or has bare-bones but clean rooms. The best one, with a bath and toilet en suite, is No. 8 (170 francs) at the quiet back of the building. 🏨 *1 rue Pasteur, 71700 Tournus,* ☎ *85–51–35–91. 9 rooms. Restaurant (closed Tues. Dec.–Feb.). MC, V. $*

Troyes
DINING
Valentino. Although the restaurant is housed in an old, half-timbered building on a pedestrian street next to the Hôtel de Ville, its flowery interior makes a bold effort to join the 20th century by mimicking Art Deco chic. Tables are set outside in summer. Oysters are served as a complement to the menu's fish specialties—grilled crayfish with poppy seeds and Brittany lobster in a casserole flavored with ginger, for example. There is a fine choice of wines to accompany the gastronomic menus. ✗ *11 cour de la Rencontre,* ☎ *25–73–14–14. Reservations advised. Jacket and tie. AE, DC, MC, V. Closed Sun. dinner, Mon., and mid-Aug.–early Sept. $$$*

LODGING
Relais St-Jean. This calm, stylish hotel, opened in 1990 in the heart of the old town in the pedestrian zone near the Eglise St-Jean, has good-size rooms that are fully equipped and air-conditioned, and service specializing in the personal touch. 🏨 *49 rue Paillot-de-Montabert, 10000,*

☎ *25–73–89–90,* FAX *25–73–88–60. 22 rooms with bath. Bar. AE, DC, MC, V. Closed mid-Dec.–Jan. 2. $$$*

Vézelay

DINING AND LODGING

★ **L'Espérance.** In the small neighboring village of St-Père-sous-Vézelay, this elegant spot is one of France's premier restaurants. Chef Marc Meneau may not be the most modest of men—his monogram appears everywhere—but he is renowned for the subtlety and originality of his cuisine: delicate lobster soup, sweetbreads in sorrel cream, or scallops in lemon marmalade, for example. The setting—by a stream and a large, statue-filled garden with Vézelay's hill and basilica in the background—is delightful. Be sure to distinguish between the take-out wine list and the restaurant wine list. Another restaurant, Le Pré des Marguerites, has been added near the main house, which offers much simpler, more traditional fare that's less dear (*$$$*). L'Espérance also has 40 charming rooms at varying prices in different buildings: Those in the main house are pretty but quite small; the ones in Le Pré des Marguerites are larger (1,300–2,000 francs); those in the Millhouse, priced similarly, are more rustic; and the five rooms in a small village building near the restaurant cost 400–580 francs. ⌧ *89450 Vézelay,* ☎ *86–33–39–10,* FAX *86–33–26–15. Reservations required. Jacket and tie. AE, DC, MC, V. Closed Feb. and Tues. and Wed. lunch. $$$$*

LODGING

Résidence Hôtel Le Pontot. With limited lodging in this isolated village, you would do well to book ahead, especially in this historic fortified house with 10 sumptuous little rooms and a lovely garden. ⌧ *Place Pontot,* ☎ *86–33–24–40. 10 rooms with bath. Closed Nov.–Apr. DC, MC, V. $$$*

THE ARTS AND NIGHTLIFE

The Arts

One may say that Burgundy is hotter on folklore than it is on the performing arts. Dijon stages a **Festival International de Folklore** (September), a **Bell-Ringing Festival** (mid-August), and an **International Fair of Gastronomy** (November). Beaune's famous wine festival, **Les Trois Glorieuses,** is held on the third Sunday in November, when the wine world congregates to bid at the Hospices auction.

Cultural activity is best represented by music. The ruined abbey of Cluny forms the backdrop to the **Grandes Heures de Cluny** in August (☎ 85–59–05–34 for details). Autun Cathedral provides a stunning setting for the **Musique en Morvan** festival in the second half of July, and Nevers is the base for **Musique en Nivernais** in September and October. Dijon stages **Eté Musical** in June and July. Check local tourist offices for details.

Nightlife

Nightlife to most Burgundians means staying up late to finish yet another big meal. Since the province's one and only city, Dijon, is one of the most serious eating venues on earth, it is not surprising that nightclubbers can expect a lean time. For a more sedate ambience, try **L'Iceberg** (47 rue Devosge, ☎ 80–72–41–41) or the **Bahia Brazil** piano bar (39 rue des Godrans, ☎ 80–30–90–19). **Le Messire** (3 rue Jules-Mercier, ☎ 80–30–16–40) and **L'An Fer** (8 rue Pierre-Marceau, ☎ 80–

70–03–69) cater to a slightly younger clientele. **L'Endroit** (Centre Dauphine, ☎ 80–30–60–63) is a popular new Dijon disco.

BURGUNDY ESSENTIALS

Arriving and Departing

By Plane
Dijon has Burgundy's only commercial passenger airport (☎ 80–67–67–67), which serves domestic flights between Paris and Lyon.

By Car
The A6 expressway heads southeast from Paris through Burgundy, passing Auxerre, Avallon, Beaune, and Mâcon.

By Train
The TGV has made Dijon, 290 kilometers (180 miles) away, just 1½ hours from Paris. Trains run frequently; some continue down to Lyon, though the fastest Paris–Lyon trains do not stop at Dijon or go anywhere near it. Also a cross-country service links Dijon to Reims (320 kilometers, or 200 miles) in 3½ hours. Sens is on a mainline route from Paris.

Getting Around

By Train
Train travel is unrewarding, especially since the infrequent cross-country trains chug along at the legendary speed of a Burgundian snail. You'll invariably have to change trains at La Roche-Migenne for Avallon, Auxerre, Clamecy, and Autun and at Dijon for Beaune.

By Car
Burgundy is best visited by car because its meandering country roads invite leisurely exploration. A38 provides a quick link between Dijon and A6, while A31 heads down from Dijon to Beaune (45 kilometers/27 miles).

Guided Tours

For further information on tours in Burgundy, write to the regional tourist office, **Comité Régional du Tourisme** (12 blvd. Brosses, 21000 Dijon).

Special-Interest
Gastronomic weekends, including wine tastings, are organized by **Bourgogne Tour** (11 rue de la Liberté, 21000 Dijon, ☎ 80–30–49–49). You may opt to see Burgundy from a canal barge; package tours are most often booked through a travel agent before leaving the U.S.

Aerial
In summer months, **Air Escargot** (71150 Remigny, ☎ 85–87–12–30) and the **Société Bombard** (Château de Laborde, 21200 Meursanges, ☎ 80–26–63–30) offer hot-air balloon rides over the surrounding countryside; prices begin at 1,300 francs for a leisurely flight, including champagne.

Important Addresses and Numbers

Travel Agencies
Air France (29 pl. Darcy, Dijon; ☎ 80–42–89–90) and **Wagons Lits** (8 av. du Maréchal-Foch, Dijon; ☎ 80–45–26–26).

Car Rental

Avis (5 av. Foch, Dijon; ☎ 80–43–60–76), **Hertz** (18 bis av. Foch, Dijon; ☎ 80–43–55–22), and **Europcar** (47 rue Guillaume-Tell, Dijon; ☎ 80–43–28–44).

Visitor Information

The principal regional tourist offices are found at **Dijon** (29 pl. Darcy, close to the cathedral; ☎ 80–30–35–39), **Auxerre** (1 quai de la République, ☎ 86–52–06–19), and **Mâcon** (187 rue Carnot, ☎ 85–39–71–37).

The addresses of other tourist offices in towns mentioned here are as follows: **Autun** (3 av. Charles-de-Gaulle, ☎ 85–52–20–34), **Avallon** (6 rue Bocquillot, ☎ 86–34–14–19), **Beaune** (rue de l'Hôtel-Dieu, ☎ 80–26–31–30), **Clamecy** (rue du Grand-Marché, ☎ 86–27–02–51), **Cluny** (6 rue Mercière, ☎ 85–59–05–34), **Sens** (pl. Jean-Jaurès, ☎ 86–65–19–49), **Troyes** (16 blvd. Carnot, ☎ 25–73–00–36), and **Vézelay** (rue St-Pierre, ☎ 86–33–23–69).

10 Lyon and the Alps

Beaujolais and the Rhône Valley

EVEN STATE authorities find it difficult to pin a name on this part of central-eastern France. Their solution, "Lyon-Rhône-Alpes," is hardly poetic, but at least it sums up the major features—the grand city of Lyon, the broad valley of the Rhône, and the towering Alpine mountain range on the frontier with Switzerland and Italy. Although the region is pierced by expressways and high-speed train lines, the pace of life is far from frenzied. Tiny medieval towns dot the landscape, while the only city apart from Lyon is Grenoble, in a majestic setting in the foothills of the Alps.

Lyon, often neglected, is one of the country's most appealing cities, renowned for historic buildings, quaint *traboules* (passageways), and a spectacular setting at the confluence of the Saône and Rhône rivers. Lyon has good museums, fascinating old streets, a gorgeous opera house, talented young chefs, and more good restaurants to the square mile than any European city except Paris.

Before reaching Lyon, the Saône flows between the lush hillside of the Beaujolais vineyards and the flat marshland of the Dombes. The Rhône, the great river of southern France, actually trickles to life high up in the Swiss mountains, but it's only at Lyon, where it merges with the Saône, that it truly comes into its own, plummeting due south in search of the Mediterranean. The river's progress south from Lyon is often spectacular, as steep-climbing vineyards conjure up vistas that are more readily associated with the river's Germanic cousin, the Rhine. All along the way, you'll find an abundance of small-town vintners inviting you to sample their wine, without obliging you to buy a crateful. Be warned, though: Rhône wine and the noonday sun make a heady combination.

Roman towns like Vienne and Valence reflect the Rhône's age-old importance as a trading route. To the west lies the Ardèche, a rugged, rustic area where time has stood still; away to the east, the skiing industry has hurtled once-inaccessible Alpine villages into the 20th century.

EXPLORING

Orientation

Our exploring tours use Lyon as a base and concentrate on three points of the compass: north toward Burgundy, south down the Rhône Valley, and east into the Alps.

Our first tour visits Lyon before heading north into the hilly Beaujolais vineyards, then crossing the Saône to the marshy Dombes area toward Bourg-en-Bresse. Our second tour heads south toward Vienne, Valence, and Montélimar and includes an excursion into the dramatic country of the Ardèche, to the west of the river. Last, we move east to Grenoble and the Alps, taking in Europe's highest cable car (at Chamonix), highest mountain (Mont Blanc), and highest road pass (Col de l'Iseran).

Tour 1: Lyon, Beaujolais, and La Dombes

Numbers in the margin correspond to points of interest on the Lyon and the Lyon and the Alps maps.

★ ❶ **Lyon** and Marseille both like to claim they are France's "second city." In terms of size and industrial importance, Marseille probably grabs that title. But when it comes to tourist appeal, Lyon's a clear winner. It's first of all a human-size town. You can encompass it in a glance from high on the bank of the Saône; you can walk all its pedestrian streets and see all its sights in a few days. And it would take a lifetime to discover all of its food. Diverge from our tour wherever a pedestrian street beckons or a charming corner catches your eye. La Presqu'Ile (Almost Island), lying between the rivers, and Vieux Lyon, across the Saône, are full of such seductions.

Lyon's development owes much to its position halfway between Paris and the Mediterranean and within striking distance of Switzerland, Italy, and the Alps. The city's exceptional site is physically impressive, with steep cliffs dominating the River Saône, which parallels the Rhône before the two converge south of the city center.

Because Lyon has never really had to endure hard times, a mood of untroubled content prevails. The Lyonnais bask in the knowledge that their city has been important for more than 2,000 years: The Romans made it the capital of Gaul around 43 BC. Its name derives from the Roman Lugdunum, or "Hill of the Crow."

❷ Few, if any, crows, rooks, or ravens are found these days on **place Bellecour,** where we begin our tour. This imposing tree-shaded square, midway between the Saône and the Rhône, one of the largest in France, is lent architectural distinction by the classical facades erected along its narrower sides in 1800. The large bronze statue of Louis XIV on horseback is the work of local sculptor Jean Lemot, installed in 1828.

Stop in the city's main tourist office for a city map and information leaflets. (A 30-franc day pass for admission to all municipal museums, once available here, can now be bought at the museums themselves.) Cross the square and head north along lively rue du Président-Herriot before turning left into place des Jacobins to explore along rue Mercière and the small streets off it. Take the Pont Maréchal-Juin over the Saône to the old town at the foot of Fourvière Hill, crowned by the imposing silhouette of Notre-Dame basilica.

On the right bank of the Saône lies **Vieux Lyon** (Old Lyon), an atmospheric warren of streets and alleys. Turn right after the bridge, then ❸ take the first left down a little alley to **place de la Baleine,** a small square lined with 17th-century houses.

TIME OUT At one corner of place de la Baleine is a cozy lunch spot, **Aux Trois Maries** (1 rue des Trois-Maries). The curious name comes from the carved stone niche on the wall of No. 7, holding statuettes of the Virgin Mary, Mary of Bethany, and Mary Magdalene. ☎ 78-37-67-28.

At the far end of place de la Baleine lies **rue St-Jean,** one of the many streets that weave their way around the banks of the Saône. Many of the area's elegant houses were built for the town's most illustrious denizens—bankers and silk merchants—during the French Renaissance under the 16th-century king François I. Originally, they had four stories; the upper floors were added in the last century. Look for the intricate old iron signs hanging over the shop doorways, many of which gave the streets their names.

A peculiarity of the streets of old Lyon are the *traboules,* quaint little passageways that cut under the houses from one street to another. Don't hesitate to venture in; they aren't private. There's a fine example at 24

Lyon and the Alps

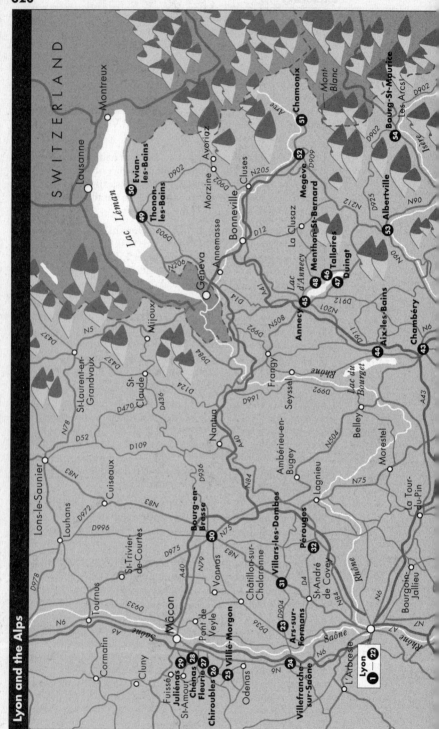

SWITZERLAND

Montreux

Lausanne

Lac Léman

Evian-les-Bains 50

Thonon-les-Bains 49

Avoriaz

Morzine

Cluses

Bonneville

Annemasse

Geneva

Mijoux

St-Laurent-en-Grandvaux

St-Claude

Nantua

Chamonix 51

Mont-Blanc

Megève 52

Menthon-St-Bernard

La Clusaz

Talloires 47
Menthon-St-Bernard 46
Duingt

Annecy 45

Lac d'Annecy

Albertville 53

Bourg-St-Maurice

Les Arcs

Albertville 54

Aix-les-Bains 44

Chambéry 43

Frangy

Seyssel

Rhône

Lac du Bourget

Belley

Lagnieu

Ambérieu-en-Bugey

Morestel

La Tour-du-Pin

Lons-le-Saunier

Louhans

Cuiseaux

St-Trivier-de-Courtes

Bourg-en-Bresse 30

Villars-les-Dombes

Pérouges 32

Châtillon-sur-Chalaronne

Villars-les-Dombes 31

Bourgoin-Jallieu

Tournus

Mâcon

Pont de Veyle

Vonnas

St-André de Covey

Ars-sur-Formans 23

Cormatin

Cluny

Fuissé
Juliénas 29
St-Amour
Chénas 28
Fleurie 27
Chiroubles 26
Villié-Morgon 25

Odenas

Villefranche-sur-Saône 24

Saône

L'Arbresle

Lyon 1 — 22

Rhône

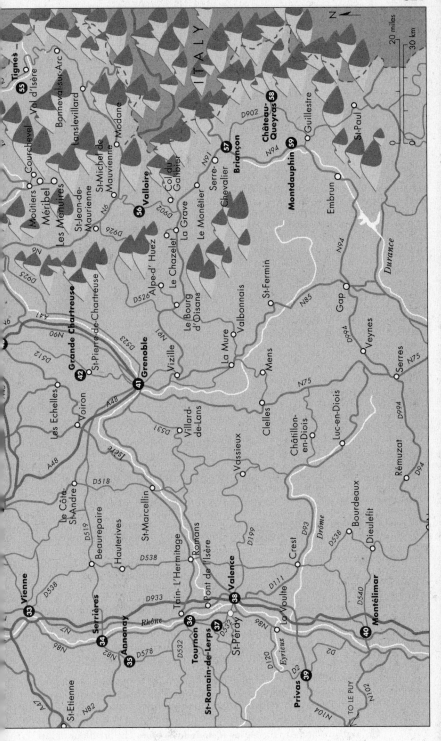

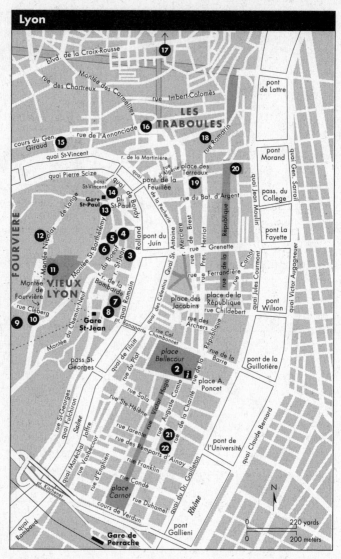

Lyon

rue St-Jean, just off place de Baleine (to the left), which leads through to 1 rue du Boeuf via an airy, restored courtyard.

Rue St-Jean was old Lyon's major thoroughfare. Stop in the elegant courtyard of No. 27 on your way north from place de la Baleine to place du Change, where money changers once operated during Lyon's medieval trade fairs. The **Loge du Change** church, on one side of the square, was built by Germain Soufflot (best known as architect of the Panthéon in Paris) in 1747.

Take rue Soufflot to one side of the church and turn left onto rue de Gadagne, where the largest Renaissance ensemble in Lyon is located: the Hôtel de Gadagne, built between the 14th and the 16th centuries and now home to the **Musée Historique de Lyon.** The first floor of this history museum contains medieval sculpture from long-gone local churches and abbeys, while other floors showcase local furniture, pottery, paintings, engravings, and antique playing cards. On the second floor is the **Musée de la Marionnette** (Puppet Museum), which traces the history of marionettes from Guignol and Madelon (Lyon's local equivalent of Punch and Judy, created by Laurent Mourguet in 1795) through contemporary hand and string puppets from across the globe. *1 pl. du Petit-Collège,* ☎ *78–42–03–61.* ☞ *20 frs.* ☉ *Wed.–Mon. 10:45–6 (until 8 Fri.).*

Continue through tiny place du Petit-Collège to rue du Boeuf.

6 One of old Lyon's finest mansions lies farther down rue du Boeuf, at No. 16: the 17th-century **Maison du Crible.** Venture into its courtyard to glimpse the original Tour Rose—an elegant, pink-washed tower—and the charming terraced garden. Close by, at the corner of place Neuve St-Jean, is one of the most famous hanging signs in old Lyon, the work of Giambologna (1529–1608), a renowned French sculptor who honed his skills in Renaissance Italy; the sign portrays the bull for which rue du Boeuf is named. Head down place Neuve and turn right onto rue St-Jean. A hundred yards farther, turn left onto rue de la Bombarde, **7** which leads to the **Jardin Archéologique** (Archaeological Gardens), with its excavated remains of the four churches that succeeded one another on the spot.

8 Alongside is one church that has withstood the onslaught of time: the **Cathédrale St-Jean,** Lyon's somewhat disappointing cathedral. You won't find any soaring roof or lofty spires here. A stumpy facade is stuck almost bashfully onto the nave, and while the interior mish-mash has its moments—the 13th-century stained-glass windows in the choir and the variety of window tracery and vaulting in the side chapels—it lacks drama and a sense of harmony. The cathedral dates from the 12th century, and the chancel is Romanesque, but construction continued over three centuries. The 14th-century astronomical clock, in the north transept, chimes a hymn to St-Jean (St. John) on the hour from noon to 3 PM as a screeching rooster and other automatons enact the Annunciation.

To the right of the cathedral facade stands the venerable 12th-century **Manécanterie** (choir school); upstairs you'll find a small treasury museum housing medieval Limoges enamels, fine ivories, and embroidered robes. *70 rue St-Jean,* ☎ *78–92–82–29.* ☞ *18 frs adults, 10 frs students and senior citizens.* ☉ *Weekdays 10–noon and 2–6:30; weekends 9–5.*

9 To continue our tour, take the *ficelle* (funicular railway) at the left of the cathedral up to the top of Fourvière Hill. At the top, head along the Montée de Fourvière to the **Théâtres Romains** (Roman ruins). There are two semicircular theaters here: the **Grand Théâtre,** the oldest Roman theater in France, built in 15 BC to seat 10,000 spectators, and the smaller **Odéon,** with its geometric-pattern tiled flooring. The best time to appreciate the theaters is September, when they are used to stage events during the Lyon International Arts Festival. *Fourvière Hill.* ☞ *Free.* ☉ *Daily 9–dusk.*

10 Since 1933, systematic excavations have unearthed many vestiges of the opulent Roman city of Lugdunum. These remains can be viewed in the **Musée de la Civilisation Gallo-Romaine** (Gallo-Roman Museum), which overlooks the theaters. The museum's semisubterranean open-plan design is an unusual showcase for the collection of statues, mosaics, vases, coins, and tombstones. One of the museum's highlights is a large bronze plaque, the **Table Claudienne,** on which is inscribed part of Emperor Claudius's speech to the Roman Senate in AD 48, conferring senatorial rights on the Roman citizens of Gaul. *17 rue Clébert,* ☏ *78–25–94–68.* ☞ *20 frs adults, 10 frs students and senior citizens.* ☉ *Wed.–Sun. 9:30–noon and 2–6.*

⑪ Head back to the spot where the ficelle dropped you off. You won't be able to miss the pompous, late-19th-century basilica of **Notre-Dame-de-Fourvière,** which has unfortunately become one of the symbols of Lyon. In terms of its mock-Byzantine architecture and hilltop site, it's a close cousin of Paris's Sacré-Coeur. Both were built for a similar reason: to underline the might of the Roman Catholic Church after the Prussian defeat of France in 1870 gave rise to the birth of the anticlerical Third Republic. The riot of interior decoration—an overkill of gilt, marble, and colorful mosaics—reveals that the Church had mind-boggling wealth to compensate for its waning political clout. *Place de Fourvière.* ☉ *Daily 8–noon and 2–6.*

One of the few places in Lyon from which you can't see the Fourvière basilica is the terrace alongside it. The plummeting panorama reveals the city laid out on either side of the Saône and Rhône rivers, with the St-Jean cathedral facade in the foreground and the huge glass towers of the reconstructed Part-Dieu business complex glistening behind. For an even more sweeping view—encompassing the surrounding hills—climb the 287 steps of the basilica's **observatory.** ☞ *6 frs.* ☉ *Easter–Oct., daily 10–noon and 2–6; Nov.–Easter, weekends 10–noon and 2–5.*

⑫ Looming beyond the basilica is a skeletal metal tower, **Tour Métallique,** built in 1893 and now used as a television transmitter. Take the stone staircase, **Montée Nicolas-de-Lange,** at the foot of the tower, which sneaks back down to old Lyon, emerging alongside the St-Paul train station ⑬ at place St-Paul. Venture briefly into rue Juiverie, to the right; the **Hôtel Paterin** at No. 4 is a splendid Renaissance mansion, and the Hôtel Bullioud (No. 8) has a courtyard with an ingenious gallery constructed in 1536 by Philibert Delorme, one of France's earliest and most accomplished exponents of Classical architecture (he worked at the châteaus of Fontainebleau and Chenonceau in the Loire Valley).

⑭ To the left of place St-Paul is the 12th-century church of **St-Paul,** whose octagonal lantern, frieze of animal heads in the chancel, and Flamboyant Gothic chapel are all worth a look. Head around the church, take the St-Vincent footbridge over the Saône, and turn left along quai St-Vin-⑮ cent. Two hundred yards along, to the right, is the **Jardin des Chartreux,** a small, leafy park. Cut through the park up to cours du Général Giraud, then turn right into place Rouville, pausing to admire the splendid view of the river and Fourvière Hill.

⑯ Rue de l'Annonciade leads from place Rouville to the **Jardin des Plantes,** 250 yards away, a haven of peace in this otherwise busy quarter. These luxurious botanical gardens contain remnants of the **Amphithéâtre des Trois Gauls,** a once-huge circular amphitheater built in AD 19. From the gardens, you'll be able to survey the hilly, surrounding **Croix Rousse** district, which once resounded to the clanking of weaving looms that churned out yards of the silk and cloth for which Lyon became famous. By the 19th century, over 30,000 *canuts* (weavers) were working in Lyon; they set up their looms on the upper floors—the brightest—of the tightly packed houses. The houses were so tightly packed, in fact, that the only way to transport the finished fabrics was through the traboules, which had the additional advantage of protecting the fabrics from bad weather.

Armed with a detailed map, you could spend hours "trabouling" your way across the Croix Rousse, still a hive of activity despite the industrialization of silk and textile production and the ensuing demise of most of the original workshops. Old-time "Jacquard" looms can still be seen in action at the **Maison des Canuts:** The weavers—many surprisingly young—are happy to show children how to operate a miniature loom. *12 rue d'Ivry,* ☎ *78–28–62–04.* ☛ *10 frs adults, 5 frs students and senior citizens.* ☉ *Weekdays 8:30–noon and 2–6:30, Sat. 9–noon and 2–6.*

For an impromptu tour of the Croix Rousse, leave the gardens and head along rue Imbert-Colomès as far as No. 20. Here, turn right through the traboule that leads to rue des Tables Claudiennes, then veer right across place Chardonnet. Take the passage Mermet alongside **St-Polycarpe** church, then turn left onto rue Leynaud. A traboule at No. 32 leads to montée St-Sébastien. Keep right, cross place Croix-Paquet, and take rue Romarin down to place des Terreaux. The north side of the sizable place des Terreaux is lined with cafés, from which you can survey on your left the facade of the **Hôtel de Ville** (Town Hall), redesigned by architects Jules Hardouin-Mansart and Robert de Cotte after a serious fire in 1674; the rest of the building dates from the early 17th century. (Groups may take a guided tour on Monday or Tuesday; ask a day ahead at the tourist office.) In the middle of the square, four majestic horses rear up from a monumental 19th-century fountain by Frédéric-Auguste Bartholdi, whose most famous creation is New York's Statue of Liberty. On the south side of the square is the elegant 17th-century front of the former Benedictine abbey, **Palais St-Pierre,** now the city's art museum.

The **Musée des Beaux-Arts** (Fine Arts Museum) showcases the country's largest collection of art after the Louvre. The cloister gardens are studded with various worthy statues, including three works by Rodin: *The Walker, The Shadow,* and *The Bronze Age.* Inside, the wide-ranging collections include enamels, Byzantine ivories, Etruscan statuettes, 4,000-year-old Cypriot ceramics, and a plethora of Egyptian archaeological finds. Amid the usual wealth of Old Master, Impressionist, and modern paintings is a unique collection of works by the tight-knit Lyon School, whose twin characteristics are exquisitely painted flowers and an overbearing religious sentimentality. Note Louis Janmot's *The Poem of the Soul,* a series of immaculately painted visions that seesaw among the heavenly, the hellish, and the downright spooky. *20 pl. des Terreaux,* ☎ *78–28–07–66.* ☛ *20 frs adults, 10 frs students.* ☉ *Wed.–Sun. 10:30–6.*

Leave the museum and walk west across place des Terreaux and through the ground floor of the Hôtel de Ville (go around if it's closed) to the **Opéra de Lyon.** This wonderful, barrel-vaulted reincarnation of a moribund building from 1831 was built in the early '90s at a cost of 478 million francs. The columned exterior and neoclassical public spaces blend beautifully with the latest in backstage high-tech magic and soaring double-glass vaulting. And above it all, looking out between heroic-size statues of the muses lined up along the parapet, sits Philippe Chavent's small restaurant, Les Muses (*see* Dining and Lodging, *below*). *Pl. de la Comédie,* ☎ *72–00–45–00 or 72–00–45–45 (seating),* FAX *72–00–45–01.*

From the opera house, head south by way of shop-lined rue de la République, which becomes rue de la Charité after place Bellecour. Some 300 yards down are two major museums. The **Musée des Arts Décoratifs** (Decorative Arts Museum) occupies an 18th-century mansion, with fine displays of silverware, furniture, objets d'art, ceramics, and tapestries.

Take time to admire the outstanding array of Italian Renaissance porcelain. *34 rue de la Charité,* ☎ *78–37–15–05.* ☛ *25 frs adults, 12 frs students (joint ticket).* ☉ *Tues.–Sun. 10–noon and 2–5:30.*

㉒ The **Musée Historique des Tissus** (Fabrics Museum) contains a stream of intricate carpets, tapestries, and silks. You'll see Oriental tapestries dating as early as the 4th century and a fabulous assembly of Turkish and Persian carpets from the 16th to the 18th century. European highlights include Italian Renaissance fabrics, Hispano-Moorish cloth from Spain, and 18th-century Lyon silks. *20 rue de la Charité,* ☎ *78–37–15–05.* ☛ *25 frs adults, 12 frs students (joint ticket).* ☉ *Tues.–Sun. 10–noon and 2–5:30.*

TIME OUT Follow rue de la Charité down to the cours de Verdun and stop in for an inexpensive lunch at **Brasserie Georges** (30 cours de Verdun); it's one of the city's largest and oldest brasseries, founded in 1836 but now housed in a palatial Art Deco building from the 1930s. Meals range from hearty veal stew or sauerkraut and sausage to more refined fare, dished up at any hour of the day or evening.

㉓ Take A6 north from Lyon to the Villefranche exit 30 kilometers (19 miles) away, then head east on D904 to nearby **Ars-sur-Formans.** This tiny village (population 719) is invaded each year by 400,000 pilgrims paying homage to the Curé d'Ars: Jean-Baptiste Vianney (1786–1859), the patron saint of parish priests. Vianney arrived in Ars in 1818, at age 32, and gradually built up a reputation as a charismatic confessor of unparalleled godliness. He was famed as a "saint" well before his death in 1859—he was canonized by the Church in 1925—and, notwithstanding the rigors of mid-19th-century transportation, the faithful poured into Ars to meet him. The village church has been enlarged to accommodate today's pilgrims and retains Vianney's confessional and embalmed body; Vianney's Saint's Day is August 4. His life is charted at the **Historial du Saint Curé-d'Ars** (opened 1994), with 17 tableaus featuring 35 waxwork figures. *Le Tonneau,* ☎ *74–00–70–22.* ☛ *28 frs adults, 12 frs children 7–17.* ☉ *Apr.–Oct., daily 10–12:30 and 1:30–7; Nov.–Mar., weekends 2–6.*

㉔ Backtrack on D904 to **Villefranche-sur-Saône.** This lively industrial town, capital of the Beaujolais wine region, is renowned for its Vin Nouveau, the youthful, fruity, red wine eagerly gulped down each year across the globe on the third Thursday of November (the date of its official "release").

Not all Beaujolais is so flippant, though. Wine classed as "Beaujolais Villages," with higher alcoholic strength, is produced from a clearly defined region northwest of Villefranche. Take D43 through part of this region to **Odenas,** and the start of a narrow strip of land, just 23 kilometers (14 miles) long, that is home to the nine deluxe Beaujolais wines, known as *crus,* that come close to rivaling the renowned wines of Burgundy, just to the north. Most villages along the Beaujolais wine road have a *cave* (communal cellar) or *co-opérative,* where you can taste and buy the local wine.

Odenas stands in the southernmost and largest vineyard of the Beaujolais crus: Brouilly, which produces soft, fruity wine that is best drunk very young. In the middle of the Brouilly vineyard is the imposing Mont Brouilly, a towering hill whose vines produce a tougher, firmer wine, classified as Côte de Brouilly. From Odenas, take D68, via St-Lager,
㉕ to **Villié-Morgon,** in the heart of the Morgon vineyard, whose robust wines age well.

TIME OUT At Monternot, a little east of Villié, is the 15th-century **Château de Corcelles,** noted for Renaissance galleries, a wrought-iron, canopied courtyard well, and medieval wood carvings in its chapel. Round off your visit with a trip to the guardroom, which has been transformed into a wine-tasting cellar, an atmospheric spot in which to sample the local wines. ☎ *74–66–72–42. Off D9 from Villié.* ☉ *Mon.–Sat. 10–noon and 2:30–6:30.*

㉖ ㉗
㉘ D68 threads its way north from Villié-Morgon through the wine villages of **Chiroubles** (rare light wines best drunk young) and **Fleurie** (noted for its elegant flowery bouquet) to **Chénas,** home of two crus: the prestigious Moulin à Vent, robust, velvety, and expensive, and Chénas, an underestimated, fruity wine that ages well.

㉙ Only two wine villages now remain. **Juliénas** is home to sturdy, deep-colored wines that can be sampled in the atmospheric cellar of the town church, decorated with Bacchanalian scenes (open Wed.–Mon., closed lunchtime). **St-Amour** produces light but firm red wine and a limited quantity of white. A more famous white wine, Pouilly-Fuissé, is produced a few miles north of St-Amour around the village of Fuissé, in the shadow of the Rock of Solutré (*see* Chapter 9, Burgundy).

㉚ From St-Amour, take N79 east to **Bourg-en-Bresse,** a cheerful town known for its production of fowl, mainly chicken. These striking-looking creatures, with plump white bodies and bright-blue feet, are a highly esteemed gastronomic luxury, and, like that of many French wines, their production is carefully regulated by the government. The town's southeast-lying district, **Brou,** is its most interesting. The church here—**Eglise de Brou,** a marvel of Flamboyant Gothic—is no longer in religious use but remains open to visitors; it was built between 1506 and 1532 by Margaret of Austria in memory of her husband Philibert le Beau, duke of Savoy, and their finely sculpted tombs are among the highlights of the richly decorated interior.

The church makes a magical setting for *son-et-lumière* (sound-and-light) performances held on Easter and Pentecost Sunday and Monday, and on Thursday, Saturday, and Sunday from early May to the end of September. The nearby **cloisters** house a museum noted for its paintings: 16th- and 17th-century Flemish and Dutch artists out in force, alongside 17th- and 18th-century French and Italian masters, 19th-century pictures from the Lyon School and by Gustave Doré, imbued with powerful melodrama, and contemporary works by local artists. *63 blvd. de Brou,* ☎ *74–45–39–00. Admission to church and museum: 32 frs.* ☉ *Apr.–Sept., daily 8:30–noon and 2–6:30; Oct.–Mar., daily 9–noon and 2–5.*

La Dombes, the area south of Bourg-en-Bresse, was once covered by an alpine glacier. The glacier gradually eroded the clay soil to create an elaborate grid of lakes and ponds that today attract both anglers (the lakes are famous for their carp) and bird-watchers. The **Parc des**
㉛ Oiseaux at **Villars-les-Dombes,** 29 kilometers (18 miles) south of Bourg-en-Bresse via N83, is one of the finest bird sanctuaries in Europe. Four hundred species of native and exotic birds live and breed here in 56 acres of lakeland. You can visit 435 open-air aviaries, housing species from waders and herons to birds of prey, and an indoor birdhouse filled with an assortment of vibrantly colored tropical birds. ☎ *74–98–05–54.* ☛ *36 frs adults, 28 frs students, 16 frs children.* ☉ *Easter–Sept., daily 8:30–7:30; Oct.–Easter, daily 8:30–dusk.*

N83 continues past the Dombes region's largest lake, the Grand Etang de Birieux, on its way to St-André de Covey, where you should turn ★ ㉜ left along D4 to **Pérouges,** 21 kilometers (13 miles) away. Pérouges is a wonderfully preserved hilltop village of medieval houses and cobbled streets, surrounded by ramparts. Hand weavers brought it prosperity, but the Industrial Revolution was their downfall; by the end of the 19th century, the population had dwindled from 1,500 to 12, and many old houses were demolished. Fortunately, local conservationists persuaded state authorities to restore and preserve the most interesting houses. Today a new influx of craftsmen (a potter, bookbinder, cabinetmaker, and weaver) has breathed life back into Pérouges.

Park your car by the main gateway, Porte d'En-Haut, alongside the 15th-century fortress-church. Rue du Prince, the town's main street, leads to the Maison des Princes de Savoie, which has a fine watchtower. Just around the corner is place de la Halle, a pretty square with great charm; in its middle is a splendid lime tree, planted in 1792. To one side of the square stands the small **town museum,** containing local historic artifacts and a reconstructed weaver's workshop. Don't miss the medieval *hortulus* garden alongside, with its array of rare medicinal plants. *Pl. de la Halle.* ☛ *15 frs.* ⊙ *Daily 10–noon and 2–6; closed Wed. and Thurs. morning Oct.–Apr.*

Pérouges is barely 200 yards across, and you should take time to explore its quaint, narrow streets. The rue des Rondes encircles the town; there are fine views over the surrounding countryside from the second gateway, the Porte d'En-Bas (on clear days, you can see the Alps).

From nearby Meximieux, N84 heads back to Lyon.

Tour 2: The Rhône Valley

㉝ Our second tour begins 27 kilometers (17 miles) south of Lyon at **Vienne;** take either N7 (more direct) or the A7 expressway, which meanders along the banks of the Rhône.

Despite being a major road and train junction, Vienne retains a lot of historic charm. It was one of the most important towns of Roman Gaul and a religious and cultural center under its count-archbishops in the Middle Ages. The tourist office stands at the river end of cours Brillier in the leafy shadow of the **Jardin Public** (Public Gardens). Begin your tour here, turning right along quai Jean-Jaurès, beside the Rhône, to the nearby church of **St-Pierre.** Note the rectangular 12th-century Romanesque bell tower with its arcaded tiers. The lower parts of the church walls date from the 6th century.

Head down the left-hand side of the church and turn left again into rue Boson, which leads to the cathedral of **St-Maurice.** Although the religious wars deprived this cathedral of many statues, much of the original decoration is intact; the arches of the portals on the 15th-century façade are carved with Old Testament scenes. The cathedral was built between the 12th and 16th centuries, with later interior additions, such as the splendid 18th-century mausoleum to the right of the altar that contains the tombs of two of Vienne's archbishops. The entrance to the vaulted passage that once led to the cloisters, but now opens onto place St-Paul, is adorned with a frieze of the zodiac.

Place St-Paul and rue Clémentine take you to place du Palais and the remains of the **Temple d'Auguste et de Livie** (Temple of Augustus and Livia), thought to date, in part, from the earliest Roman settlements in Vienne (1st century BC). The slender Corinthian columns that ring the temple were filled in with a wall during the 11th century, when the temple was used as a church; today, however, the temple has been restored to its original appearance.

Rue Brenier leads to rue Chantelouve, site of a **Roman gateway** decorated with delicate friezes (the last vestige of the city's sizable Roman baths). Continue to rue de la Charité and the **Théâtre Romain.** This was one of the largest Roman theaters in Gaul (143 yards in diameter), and it is only slightly smaller than Rome's famed Theater of Marcellus. Vienne's theater was buried under tons of rubble until 1922, but since then, the 46 rows of seating and parts of the marble flooring and frieze on the original stage have been excavated and renovated. Shows and concerts are staged here on summer evenings. *7 rue du Cirque,* ☎ *74–85–39–23.* ☛ *9 frs.* ⊙ *Apr.–mid-Oct., Wed.–Mon. 9:30–1 and 2–6; mid-Oct.–Mar., Wed.–Sat. 10–noon and 2–5, Sun. 1:30–5:30.*

Take rue de la Charité back down to rue des Orfèvres, lined with Renaissance facades, and continue on to the church of **St-André-le-Bas,** once part of a powerful abbey. Extensive restoration is in progress, but, if possible, venture inside to see the finely sculpted 12th-century capitals and the 17th-century wooden statue of St. Andrew. The adjacent cloisters are at their best during the summer music festival held here (and at the cathedral) from June to August. *Cour St-André,* ☎ *74–85–18–49.* ☛ *9 frs.* ⊙ *Apr.–mid-Oct., Wed.–Mon. 9:30–1 and 2–6; mid-Oct.–Mar., Wed.–Sat. 10–noon and 2–5; Sun. 2–6.*

Cross the nearby bridge across the Rhône to inspect the excavated Cité Gallo-Romaine, where the Romans built most of their sumptuous private villas. ☛ *Free.* ⊙ *Daily.*

㉞ Stay on this bank of the Rhône and follow N86 south 32 kilometers (20 miles) to the little town of **Serrières,** a traditional stopping point for Rhône river craft. You can see the valley boatmen's way of life from the exhibits at the **Musée des Mariniers du Rhône** (Boatmen's Museum) in the wooden-roofed Gothic chapel of St-Sornin. ☎ *75–34–01–26.* ☛ *12 frs.* ⊙ *Apr.–Oct., weekends 3–6.*

Nearly 10 kilometers (6 miles) southwest of Serrières along N82, just beyond the village of Peaugres, is the 200-acre **Safari de Peaugres.** Some 800 animals (including lions, bears, buffalo, bison, tigers, wolves, and camels) can be encountered here—from the safety of your car, with the windows firmly rolled up. Stroll along the separate pedestrian trail to admire tamer beasts, such as giraffes and ostriches, and check out the snakes, crocodiles, and lizards lounging inside their vivarium. The park also has its own bars, cafeteria, souvenir shops, and playground, making it a great place to spend an afternoon if you're traveling with children. ☎ *75–33–00–32.* ☛ *70 frs adults, 45 frs children under 12.* ⊙ *Apr.–Oct., daily 9:30–7; Nov.–Mar., daily 10–5.*

㉟ N82 shortly reaches **Annonay,** a prosperous town that grew up around the leather industry. It's best known, though, as home to the Montgolfier brothers, Joseph and Etienne, who, in 1783, invented the hot-air balloon (known in French as *une montgolfière*). The first flight took place at Annonay on June 4, 1783; it lasted half an hour, and the balloon soared to 6,500 feet. The brothers' exploit is commemorated by an obelisk on avenue Marc-Seguin, although the actual balloon launch occurred in the place des Cordeliers (close to the tourist office).

The narrow streets and passageways of central Annonay are full of character. Local history and folklore are evoked at the **Musée Vivarais César Filhol,** between the Mairie (Town Hall) and Notre-Dame church. *15*

rue Béchetoille, ☎ *75–67–67–93.* ☛ *10 frs.* ⊙ *June–Aug., Tues.–Sun.*
2–6; Sept.–May, Wed. and weekends 2–6.

36 D578/D532 head southeast to **Tournon,** 37 kilometers (23 miles) away
on the banks of the Rhône at the foot of some impressive granite hills.
Tournon's chief attraction is its hefty 15th- to 16th-century **château.**
From the château's two terraces there are sumptuous views of the old
town, river, and—towering above the village of Tain-l'Hermitage across
the Rhône—the steep-climbing vineyards that produce Hermitage
wine, one of the Rhône Valley's most refined (and costly) reds. The
château houses a museum of local history, the **Musée Rhodanien,**
which features an account of the life of Annonay-born Marc Seguin
(1786–1875), the engineer who built the first suspension bridge over
the Rhône at Tournon in 1825 (the bridge was demolished in 1965).
Pl. Auguste-Faure, ☎ *75–07–15–96.* ☛ *14 frs adults, 7 frs children.*
⊙ *June–Aug., Wed.–Mon. 10–noon and 2–6; Apr.–May and Sept.–Oct.,*
Wed.–Mon. 2–6.

If you're in the mood for an adventurous side trip, take a ride on one
of France's last steam trains—the **Chemin de Fer du Vivarais.** Trains
leave from Tournon station on a two-hour, 33-kilometer (21-mile)
trip along the narrow, rocky Doux Valley to Lamastre. ☎ *78–28–83–*
34. ☛ *Round-trip ticket: 150 frs adults, 115 frs children. Departures*
daily 10 AM June–Aug., weekends only May and Sept.

From Tournon's main square (place Jean-Jaurès), slightly inland from
the château, take the signposted **Route Panoramique** in the direction of
37 **St-Romain-de-Lerps.** There are breathtaking views at every turn along
this narrow, twisting, clambering road. At the old village of St-Romain,
you will be rewarded with an immense panorama that, in fine weather,
takes in no fewer than 13 *départements* and extends to Mont-Blanc in
the east and the whalelike bulk of arid Mont Ventoux to the south.

D287 winds its way down from St-Romain to St-Péray. Looming 650
feet above the plain is the Montagne de Crussol, a white cliff topped
38 by the 12th-century ruins of Crussol Castle. The largish town of **Va-**
lence lies just a couple of miles away along N532. Valence is capital
of the Drôme *département* and is the principal fruit-and-vegetable
market for the surrounding region. Steep-curbed alleyways—known
as *côtes*—extend from the banks of the Rhône to the heart of the old
town around the cathedral of **St-Apollinaire.** Although the cathedral
was begun in the 12th century in the Romanesque style, it's not altogether as old as it looks: Parts were rebuilt in the 17th century, and
the belfry in the 19th century. Alongside the cathedral, in the former
18th-century Bishops' Palace, is the **Musée des Beaux-Arts,** featuring
local sculpture and furniture and a collection of 96 red-chalk drawings by deft landscapist Hubert Robert (1733–1808). *Place des*
Ormeaux, ☎ *75–79–20–80.* ☛ *14 frs adults.* ⊙ *Mon.–Tues. and*
Thurs.–Fri. 2–6, Wed. and weekends 9–noon and 2–6.

Continue 16 kilometers (10 miles) south from Valence along N86 and
turn right onto D120 just before La Voulte. This attractive road follows the Eyrieux Valley as far as Les Ollières-sur-Eyrieux, where you
should turn south along D2, under the shade of horse chestnut trees,
39 toward **Privas,** capital of the spectacular Ardèche *département,* renowned
for its rocky gorges and stalagmite-bearing caves.

Privas was a Protestant stronghold during the 16th-century Wars of
Religion. In 1629, it was razed by the army of Louis XIII after a siege
lasting 16 days. The **Pont Louis XIII** over the River Ouvèze celebrates

the king's reconciliation with Privas, which rose from the dust to become a peaceful administrative town, best known for the production of that delicious French delicacy the *marron glacé* (candied chestnut).

Privas makes a good base for exploring the Ardèche, and the tourist office just off place Charles-de-Gaulle, in the center of town, will provide details of the region's beauty spots. Our tour, meanwhile, continues **40** to another town of sweet-toothed fame: **Montélimar,** the home of the *nougat,* a white or pink candy that usually contains chopped almonds and cherries.

Montélimar, 35 kilometers (22 miles) southeast of Privas (via D2) on the other side of the Rhône, is named after the 12th-century fortress of **Mont-Adhémar.** This château, enlarged in the 14th century, stands in a park surveying the town and valley. *24 rue du Château,* ☎ *75–01–07–85.* ☞ *12 frs adults, 6 frs children.* ☉ *Wed.–Mon. 9:30–11:30 and 2–5:30.*

You can buy nougat at virtually every shop in town; it makes for a mighty chew, a good idea if you want to keep the children quiet.

Tour 3: Grenoble and the Alps

Whatever the season, the Alpine mountain range is captivating. In winter, the dramatic, snow-carpeted slopes offer some of the best skiing in the world; in summer, chic spas, shimmering lakes, and breathtaking hilltop trails come into their own. The Savoie and Haute-Savoie *départements* occupy the most impressive Alpine territory, but our tour begins in the Dauphiné, with the area's only city: Grenoble.

★ **41** **Grenoble,** 104 kilometers (65 miles) southeast of Lyon via A48, is a large, cosmopolitan city whose skyscrapers and forbidding gray buildings may seem intimidating by homey French standards. Along with the city's nuclear research plant, they bear witness to Grenoble's fierce desire to move with the times. The city is also home to a large university and is the birthplace of Stendhal, one of the most famous French novelists of the 19th century.

A cable car (30 francs round-trip; operates Apr.–Oct., 9 AM–midnight, Nov.–Dec. and Feb.–Mar., 10–6) starting at quai St-Stéphane-Jay whisks you up to the hilltop and its **Fort de la Bastille,** offering splendid views of the city and the River Isère. Walk down rue Maurice-Gignoux, past gardens, cafés, and stone mansions, to the **Musée Dauphinois,** a lively regional museum in a 17th-century convent, featuring displays of local folk arts and crafts. *30 rue Maurice-Gignoux,* ☎ *76–85–19–01.* ☞ *15 frs adults, 10 frs children, free Wed.* ☉ *Wed.–Mon. 9–noon and 2–6.*

Heading left from the museum, make for the church of **St-Laurent,** which contains an atmospherically murky 6th-century crypt (one of the country's oldest Christian monuments) supported by a row of formidable marble pillars. *2 pl. St-Laurent,* ☎ *76–44–78–68.* ☞ *15 frs adults, 10 frs children.* ☉ *Wed.–Mon. 10–noon and 2–6.*

Art buffs will want to cross the river to place de Lavalette, new home to the **Musée de Peinture et de Sculpture** (Painting and Sculpture Museum), one of France's oldest museums (founded in 1796), and the first to concentrate on modern art (Picasso donated his *Femme Lisant* back in 1921). The collection now runs to 4,000 pictures and 5,500 drawings, and a new museum to house them opened in January 1994. It incorporates the medieval Tour de l'Isle, a noted Grenoble landmark, into the long and low modern section, designed to harmonize with the backcloth of the old town. The collection predating 1900 highlights the Italian Renaissance, Rubens, Flemish still lifes, Zurburan, a Canaletto view of Venice, and culminates in the Impressionists (Renoir, Monet). The 20th-century art includes works by Matisse (*Intérieur aux Aubergines* of 1911), Signac, Derain, Vlaminck, Magritte, Ernst, Miró, Dubuffet, and Hans Hoffmann. An array of modern sculpture adorns the gardens. *5 pl. de Lavalette,* ☎ *76–63–44–44.* ☛ *25 frs adults, 15 frs children and senior citizens.* ⊙ *Wed. 11–10, Thurs.–Mon. 11–7.*

TIME OUT   Head back along the river to the cable car and turn right, through the Jardin de Ville (City Gardens) to **place Grenette,** a lively, flower-strewn pedestrian mall lined with a plethora of sidewalk cafés. It makes a great place to relax and enjoy a *pastis*—an anise-flavored aperitif—while admiring the city's majestic mountain setting.

If you only have time for a brief glimpse of the Alps, take N91 from Grenoble directly to Briançon (*below*), past the spectacular mountain scenery of L'Alpe d'Huez, Les Deux Alpes and the Col du Galibier. Otherwise, follow our tour north on D512 from Grenoble through the Chartreuse mountain range. Seventeen kilometers (11 miles) from Grenoble, fork left off D512 and follow the small D57-D as far as you can (only a few miles) before leaving your car and making the 30-minute climb to the top of the 6,000-foot Charmant Som peak. Your reward: **42** a stimulating view over the **Grande Chartreuse** monastery, home of the Carthusians, 10 kilometers (6 miles) north. The monastery's 12-acre setting, enclosed by wooded heights and limestone crags, is both austere and serene.

Return to D512 and continue north, forking left 8 kilometers (5 miles) along D520-B just before **St-Pierre-de-Chartreuse:** the Grande Chartreuse is set well back to the right 2 kilometers (1 mile) along this road. The monastery, which was to spawn 24 similar charterhouses throughout Europe, was founded by St-Bruno in 1084 according to ascetic and eremetic principles. It was burned and rebuilt several times, then finally stripped of its possessions during the French Revolution, when the monks were expelled. After their return they resumed the manufacture of their sweet Chartreuse liqueur, a main source of income. Today "Green" and "Yellow" Chartreuse are marketed worldwide, though their herb-based formulas are known only to three monks. You can't visit the monastery itself, but stop in at the **Musée de La Correrie,** close by, to see exhibits on monastic life. You'll also be able to purchase some of the monks' famous distillation. ☎ *76–88–60–45.* ☛ *12 frs adults, 6 frs children.* ⊙ *Easter–Oct., daily 9:30–noon and 2–6.*

Chartreuse is now produced in nearby **Voiron,** where you can visit the cellar and distillery—and enjoy a tasting—for free. *10 blvd. Edgar-Kofler,* ☎ *76–05–81–77.* ⊙ *Daily except winter weekends, 8:30–11:30 and 2–5:30.*

Return to St-Pierre-de-Chartreuse and continue north along the windy **43** D512 and D912 roads to the elegant old town of **Chambéry,** 40 kilometers (25 miles) away. Stop for coffee on the pedestrian **place St-Léger** before walking two blocks to visit the 14th-century **Château des Ducs de Savoie.** The château's Gothic Sainte-Chapelle contains some good stained glass and houses a replica of the notorious Turin Shroud, once thought to have been the burial wrappings for the crucified Christ (but probably, according to recent scientific analysis, a medieval hoax). *Rue Basse du Château.* ☛ *20 frs. Guided tours June and Sept., daily at 10:30 and 2:30; July and Aug., daily at 10:30, 2:30, 3:30, 4:30, and 5:30; Mar.–May and Oct.–Nov., Sat. at 2:15, Sun. at 3:30.*

N201 takes you 14 kilometers (9 miles) north to the gracious spa
④ town of **Aix-les-Bains,** on the eastern shore of Lac du Bourget. Although
swimming in the lake is not advised (it's freezing cold), you can sail,
fish, play golf and tennis, or picnic on the 25 acres of parkland that
stretches along the lakefront. Visit the ruins of the original Roman baths,
underneath the present **Thermes Nationaux** (Thermal Baths), built in
1934 and renovated in 1972 (guided tours only; Apr.–Oct., Mon.–Sat.
at 3 PM; Nov.–Mar., Wed. at 3 PM). The Roman Temple of Diana
(2nd–3rd centuries AD) now houses an **archaeology museum** (entrance
via the tourist office on place Mollard).

There are half-hour boat trips from Aix-les-Bains across Lac du Bourget to the **Abbaye de Hautecombe,** where mass is celebrated with Gregorian chant. ☎ 79–54–26–12. ☞ 60 frs. *Departures from the Grand
Pont, Mar.–June and Sept.–Oct., daily at 2:30; July–Aug. at 9:30, 2,
2:30, 3, 3:30, and 4:30.*

Leaving Aix-les-Bains, follow the striking D911 some 24 kilometers
(15 miles) to La Charniaz, then turn left along D912, which snakes 24
kilometers (15 miles) farther north alongside the Montagne du Sem-
㊺ noz to **Annecy.**

Annecy stands on the shores of a crystal-clear mountain lake—the Lac
d'Annecy—and is surrounded by rugged snow-tipped peaks. The
canals, flower-covered bridges, and cobbled pedestrian streets of old
Annecy are at their liveliest on market days, Tuesday and Friday,
though the town and the tree-lined boulevard have tranquil, invigorating appeal any day of the week.

Start a meander through the old town on a small island in the River
Thiou at the 12th-century Palais de l'Isle, once home to courts of law
and a prison, now containing a small museum of local history. You may
notice that the Thiou seems to be flowing the "wrong way," i.e., out
of the lake. It does in fact drain the lake, feeding the network of Annecy's canals.

TIME OUT **Le Petit Zinc** (11 rue du Pont-Morens, near the Pont-Morens bridge, ☎
50–51–12–93), a delicious and reasonably priced bistro, is a perfect
place to stop for lunch after you've finished wandering around the old
quarter. This cozy, beamed dining room is very popular with locals, who
come for the cheese croquettes and salad, roast pork, and good carafe
wines—so come early.

There are views over the lake from the towers of the medieval **castle,** set high on a hill opposite the Palais. Put aside a morning or afternoon to make the 40-kilometer (25-mile) drive around the lake,
㊻ stopping at the picturesque village of **Talloires** and the medieval
㊼ ㊽ châteaus at **Duingt** and **Menthon-St-Bernard** (tours every afternoon
in July and Aug.; open Thurs. and weekend afternoons only in May,
June, and Sept.).

Take N201 north from Annecy and after 18 kilometers (11 miles) turn
off into D14, which follows a winding course along Mont Salève to
Annemasse 34 kilometers (21 miles) away. From Annemasse, Geneva
is just a few minutes away over the Swiss border, but we'll follow
㊾ N206/D903 northeast to **Thonon-les-Bains,** on the banks of Lake
Geneva (Lac Léman in French). Thonon and its neighboring sister-spa,
㊿ **Evian-les-Bains,** have all the trappings (restful parks and lakefront
promenades) of chic spa towns.

Many of the leading Alpine ski resorts lie south of Thonon. A river road (D902) runs 32 kilometers (20 miles) from Thonon to **Morzine,** where you can go up to **Avoriaz,** renowned for its annual Fantasy Film Festival in January, via D338 or by cable car. D902 continues south to Cluses, where the N205 heads left along the Arve Valley to the

★ ⑤ largish town of **Chamonix** (about 64 kilometers, or 40 miles, from Morzine), the oldest and biggest French winter-sports resort and site of the first Winter Olympics in 1924. The **world's highest cable car** soars 12,000 feet from Chamonix up the Aiguille du Midi, from which there are staggering views of Europe's loftiest peak, the 15,700-foot **Mont-Blanc** (open May–Sept., daily 8–4:45, Oct.–Apr., daily 8–3:45; 170 frs round-trip). Be prepared for a lengthy wait, though, to go up and come down—and take warm clothing.

⑤ N206/D909 leads back down the valley to **Megève.** This idyllic Alpine village is not only a major ski resort but also a chic winter watering hole that draws royalty, celebrities, and big wallets from all over the world. During the summer it's popular with golfers, too. From Megève, N212 runs 32 kilometers (20 miles) south through the Arly Valley to

⑤ **Albertville,** base for the 1992 Winter Olympics. Stop off at the suburb of **Conflans,** a well-preserved military town perched precariously on a rocky crag. Just south of Albertville are two other serious ski resorts, **Courchevel** and **Méribel,** where many of the 1992 Winter Olympic events were held. As a result, both towns now have some of the most up-to-date ski facilities and hotels in the French Alps.

Another spectacular road, D925 (becoming D902), heads 61 kilome-

⑤ ters (38 miles) east from Albertville to **Bourg-St-Maurice,** a cheerful base for summer vacations, with winter sports catered to at the nearby com-

⑤ plexes of **Les Arcs** and **Tignes** farther down D902. Tignes features an extensive network of chairlifts and cable cars that connect it with small resorts like La Daille, Les Boisses, and Les Brévières, and with **Val d'Isère,** a favorite among the rich and famous.

The **Route de l'Iséran** (D902) runs from Val d'Isère to Bonneval-sur-Arc, at 9,084 feet the country's highest mountain pass; it's accessible only between July and late October. Along this Iseran Way, a succession of magnificent views unfurls beneath your eyes.

At Lanslevillard, tucked in beneath its old church on a rocky outcrop, D902 broadens into N6; continue through the old frontier town of Modane (a 13-kilometer, or 9-mile, tunnel leads into Italy) as far as St-Michel de Maurienne, where the **Route du Galibier** (usually closed November–May) twists south in rugged grandeur. Follow signs for the

★ ⑤ busy ski village of **Valloire** and enjoy the spectacular views as you wind up the barren **Col du Galibier.** A short walk to the summit (follow signs), 8,900 feet up, yields a sweeping panorama of the southern Alps. Just afterward, stop to admire a monument to Henri Desgranges, founder of the Tour de France bike race, and if you're breathless, spare a thought for the hapless cyclists who pedal up here each July.

Eight kilometers (5 miles) on from the Col du Galibier, the road crosses the 6,750-foot **Col du Lautaret,** alive with wildflowers in summer (follow signs to the Jardin Alpin), before linking up with the N91 high-

★ ⑤ way bound for **Briançon.** This altitudinous town combines historic appeal with direct access to the Serre-Chevalier ski complex (take the Prorel cable car from the low town). The old town, referred to as the Ville Haute (Upper Town) or Briançon-Vauban, was remodeled by Vauban from 1692 onward. His three-tiered defensive outworks proved their worth in 1815 when, in the aftermath of Waterloo, marauding Austro-Sardinian troops were kept at bay. Enter the old town through **Porte Pignerol,** one of the four gateways. Head right along avenue Vauban to the early 18th-century **Collégiale Notre-Dame,** whose twin towers each boast a sundial, and continue down rue Carlhan to **place d'Armes,** a bustling square with two more sundials: The Briançon region is famed for its sunny microclimate (300 days of rays a year).

Place d'Armes leads to the old town's main street, **Grande Gargouille** (also called Grande Rue), with its gutter in the middle. Admire the fine doorway at No. 64, built in 1714, and the **Fontaine François I,** a fountain with whimsical spouts in the form of elephants' heads. Turn right onto rue du Pont-Asfeld, which leads past the Chapelle des Pénitents and the **Eglise des Cordeliers** (down some stone stairs), renowned for its 15th-century frescoes, to the daring **Pont d'Asfeld,** straddling the Durance River 180 feet below. Admire the view, then head left along the Chemin de Rond, beneath the citadel, to return to Porte Pignerol.

58 From Briançon take the D902 southeast to **Château-Queyras,** perched on a hilltop above the Guil Valley, where **a Fort** has stood since the 14th century. Cross the drawbridge to visit the casemates, courtyard, and 14th-century keep. ☛ *15 frs.* ⏲ *Mid-June–early Sept., Wed.–Mon. 10–7.*

Continue south on D902 along the crystal-clear Guil River, beneath pine-covered slopes and the jagged peaks of the Combe du Queyras.
59 At the market town of Guillestre, head west to **Montdauphin,** a fortified town perched on a barren promontory at 3,400 feet. Vauban chose this strategic site for a new citadel and used local pink stone to build a fortified town from scratch. He intended to attract local inhabitants, but until 1980 only soldiers lived here. Local artisans and craftsmen have since moved in. Montdauphin was not completed for nearly a century. The history of its construction is outlined in a permanent exhibit in the 18th-century **Arsenal.** Other highlights include the **Poudrière** (powder mill), with its vaulted upper chamber and larch-beam ground floor; the airy **church,** and the huge beamed roof of the **Caserne Rochambeau** (barracks). ☎ *92–45–17–80 for details of guided tours.*

What to See and Do with Children

The 300-acre **Parc de la Tête d'Or,** on the banks of the Rhône in the north of Lyon, contains a lake, botanical gardens, and a small zoo, as well as facilities for rowing, miniature golf, pony rides, and go-carting. *Take the métro from Perrache train station to Masséna.* ☛ *Free.* ⏲ *Dawn to dusk.*

Chairlift at Chamonix, Tour 3
Haut Vivarais Safari Park, Tour 2
Maison des Canuts, Lyon, Tour 1
Musée de la Marionnette, Lyon, Tour 1
Parc des Oiseaux, Villars-les-Dombes, Tour 1

Off the Beaten Track

Hauterives, 40 kilometers (25 miles) south of Vienne (D538), would be just another quaint village if it weren't for the **Palais Idéal,** one of the weirdest constructions in Western Europe. This make-believe palace, constructed entirely of stones and pebbles, was built single-handedly by a local postman, Ferdinand Cheval (1836–1924). Although Cheval was haunted by visions of faraway mosques and temples, the result is pure fantasy. It came to be Cheval's lifework: One of the many wall inscriptions reads "1879–1912: 10,000 days, 93,000 hours, 33 years of toil." ☎ 75–68–81–19. ☛ *20 frs adults, 13 frs children under 16.* ☉ *Daily 9–7 (9:30–5 in winter).*

If you're keen on modern architecture, make the trip to Eveux, just outside L'Arbresle, 16 kilometers (10 miles) northwest of Lyon, to admire the Dominican convent of **Sainte-Marie de la Tourette** (built 1957–59). This stark, blocky edifice in unadorned concrete, protruding over the hillside on slender pillars that look like stilts, bears the minimalist hallmark of Le Corbusier. A mood of meditation was his aim here; the lighting effects are subtle and intriguing. ☎ 74–01–01–03. ☛ *20 frs.* ☉ *July–Aug., daily 9–noon and 2–6; Sept.–June, weekends 2–6.*

The former mining city of **St-Etienne** (pop. 200,000), 35 miles (56 kilometers) southwest of Lyon, is better known for its soccer team than its tourist appeal, but it makes a logical stopover en route from Lyon to the Auvergne region of central France (*see* Chapter 11, The Massif Central and Auvergne). Wealthy gastronomes will head straight to Pierre Gagnaire's top-ranked restaurant (*see* Dining and Lodging, *below*), but culture vultures will stop to see the exhibits at the **Musée d'Art et d'Industrie,** ranging from paintings (Rubens, Whistler, Monet) to local industry, and swords, guns, and armor. *2 pl. Louis-Comte,* ☎ 77–33–04–85. ☛ *Free.* ☉ *Wed. 2–5, Thurs.–Mon. 10–noon and 2–5.*

From St-Etienne, head south via N88 to **Le Puy-en-Velay,** set on a high plateau broken by giant cores of sheer solidified lava called *puys.* Le Puy-en-Velay's four cores are crowned with man-made monuments: on the lowest, a statue of St. Joseph and the Infant Jesus; on the highest, the 11th-century chapel of St-Michel; on another, a huge statue of the Virgin. Most spectacular is the Romanesque cathedral, **Notre-Dame-du-Puy,** which balances at the top of the fourth narrow pinnacle, approachable only by a long flight of steps. Built of polychrome lava, the cathedral is reminiscent of an Islamic mosque; interior highlights include the statue of the Black Virgin and the Carolingian *Bible of Théodulfe.*

Some 40 kilometers (25 miles) north via N102 and D906 lies the abbey of **La Chaise-Dieu** (Chair of God), famous for its splendid red-and-black frescoes of the *Danse Macabre* (Death dancing with the nobility, bourgeoisie, and peasants). The abbey also features 16th-century Brussels and Arras tapestries and 144 carved-oak choir stalls.

SHOPPING

Clothing and Gift Ideas
Lyon makes for the region's best shopping for chic clothing; try the stores on **rue du Président Edouard-Herriot** and **rue de la République** in the center of town. Lyon has maintained its reputation as the French silks-and-textile capital, and all the big-name French and international designers have shops here; Lyonnais designer **Clémentine** (18 rue Emile-Zola) is a good bet for well-cut clothes, or, for trendy outfits for youngsters, try **Etincelle** (34 rue St-Jean) in the old town. If it's antiques you're after, wander down **rue Auguste-Comte** (from place Bellecour to Perrache); you'll find superb engravings at **Image en Cours** (26 rue du Boeuf) and authentic Lyonnais puppets on **place du Change,** both in the old town.

Food Items
Two excellent Lyon charcuteries are **Reynon** (13 rue des Archers) and **Pignol** (17 rue Émile-Zola). A wide choice can be found at **Les Halles** (102 cours Lafayette). For chocolates, try **Bernachon** (42 cours Franklin-

Roosevelt), which many people consider to be the best chocolaterie in France. **La Boîte à Dessert** (1 rue de l'Ancienne-Préfecture) is an innovative patisserie with tarts, cakes, and luscious red-peach turnovers that make a perfect snack. In the Drôme region, the town of **Montélimar** has more nougat shops than cafés; **Chabert et Guillot** (9 rue Charles-Chabert) is one of the best.

Arts and Crafts

The tiny Ardèche villages of **Thines** and **Les Vans** are popular crafts centers, with several showrooms set up by the **Compagnons de Gerboul,** an association of craftsmen. The medieval village of **Châteauneuf-de-Mazenc** (Drôme) has a particularly pretty arts-and-crafts shop with a range of handmade jewelry and trinkets. In Lyon, local textiles are offered at **La Maison des Canuts** (10–12 rue d'Ivry) and the **Boutique des Soyeux Lyonnais** (3 rue du Boeuf).

SPORTS AND THE OUTDOORS

Golf

Golf can be played in **Aix-les-Bains** (av. du Golf); **Chamonix** (rte. de Tines, Les Praz de Chamonix); **Chassieu,** north of Lyon via D29; **Evian** (Route du Golf); **Eybens,** near Grenoble; **Megève** (Mont d'Arbois); **Montélimar** (Château Le Monard, Montboucher-sur-Labron); **St-Didier de Charpey,** near Valence; **Talloires** (Echarvines) and **Villars-les-Dombes** (Le Clou).

Horseback Riding

This is a wonderful region for exploring on horseback. Try the *centres equestres* (stables) at **Aix-les-Bains** (Hippodrome Marlioz), **Chambéry** (rue Sainte-Rose), **Montélimar** (Ile Montmélian), and **Vienne** (Ecuries du Couzon, La Petite Rente).

Skiing

The ski season begins in December and lasts through April. The region's most famous ski venue is **Chamonix.** Most of the 64 slopes are for experienced skiers, but there are plenty of other things to do here: hiking, visiting the casino, or simply admiring the incredible scenery via cable cars. **Val d'Isère** ranks as one of Europe's poshest resorts, with lots of cross-country runs as well as 67 downhill slopes. Nearby **Tignes** has a range of 62 slopes for both beginners and more daring skiers. Family groups should try **Morzine,** a popular small resort whose 74 gentle slopes are geared to the inexperienced. Chic, expensive **Megève** offers a lively nightlife by way of casino, nightclubs, and restaurants; it also features a particularly impressive network of *téléfériques* (cable cars) and helicopter services. **Courchevel** is renowned for its après-ski, while across the mountain, fashionable **Méribel** boasts lots of difficult runs. **L'Alpe d'Huez** is the most extensive resort near Grenoble, while **Serre-Chevalier** is linked by cable car to Briançon.

Swimming

The Alpine lakes are pretty chilly for swimming most of the year, but can offer pleasant bathing in midsummer, with **Lac d'Annecy** and especially **Lac du Bourget** equipped with slides, diving boards, and the like. You'll also find public swimming pools in the following towns: **Aix-les-Bains** (av. Daniel-Rops), **Albertville** (av. des Chasseurs-Alpins), **Annecy** (29 rue des Marquisats), **Chambéry** (Nautiparc, rue Eugène-Ducretet), **Evian** (Centre Nautique, av. du Gal-Dupas), **Grenoble** (rue Lazare-Carnot), **Lyon** (221 rue Garibaldi), and **Valence** (av. Valensolles).

DINING AND LODGING

Dining

Lyon is a renowned capital of good cuisine. Both gourmets and gourmands will enjoy the robust local specialties, such as *saveloy* (sausage) and *quenelles* (poached fish dumplings). The choice is wide between Lyon's many topflight restaurants and the traditional, homey *bouchons* with their wooden benches, zinc counters, and paper tablecloths. Bouchons serve a wide choice of salads, pork products (try the local *rosette* sausage seasoned with garlic and pepper), and sturdy main courses like tripe, andouillette (chitterling sausage), and veal stew. If prices at the stylish Léon de Lyon are too daunting, try the Petit Léon—its bustling sister-restaurant next door. The Dombes is rich in game and fowl; chicken, cooked in any number of ways, usually with cream, is a firm favorite. Thrush, partridge, and hare feature prominently on menus as you head south along the Rhône. This part of France also offers up a splendid cheese tray, including such locally produced varieties as Saint-Marcellin, Roquefort, Beaufort, Tomme, and Cabecou, a goat cheese. The marrons glacés of Privas and the nougats of Montélimar cater to the sweet tooth. The rivers and lakes of the Alps teem with pike and trout, while the hills are a riot of wild raspberries and black currants during summer months. *Raclette* is a warming Alpine winter specialty: melted cheese served with salami, ham, and boiled potatoes. Mountain herbs form the basis of traditional drinks—try a tangy, dark Suédois or a bittersweet Suze (made from gentian), and round off your meal with a green Chartreuse.

CATEGORY	COST*
$$$$	over 400 frs
$$$	250–400 frs
$$	125–250 frs
$	under 125 frs

*per person for a three-course meal, including tax (18.6%) and tip but not wine

Lodging

The region is filled with hotels and country inns; at many, you'll be expected to take your evening meal (especially in summer), but this tends to be more a pleasure than an obligation. The Alpine region has an extensive hotel infrastructure—geared primarily to winter visitors, who are invariably expected to take *demi-pension* or *pension complète* (room with some or all meals).

CATEGORY	COST*
$$$$	over 800 frs
$$$	400–800 frs
$$	200–400 frs
$	under 200 frs

*All prices are for a standard double room for two, including tax (18.6%) and service charge.

Annecy

DINING AND LODGING

Impérial Palace. This grand hotel, in parkland just across a corner of the lake from the center of town, has been described as a "grand old white elephant sitting in stately dignity." The rooms are unusually spacious and have attractive views over the gardens or lake, although their modern blue and black decor seems out of character with the Belle Epoque exterior. Fine cuisine (good choice of fish) is served in the stylish restaurant, La Voile (jacket and tie required), and the Brasserie du Parc offers an acceptable, less costly alternative. ⬚ *32 av. Albigny, 74000,* ☎ *50–09–30–00,* ℻ *50–09–33–33. 98 rooms with bath. 2 restaurants, casino. AE, DC, MC, V. $$$$*

Bagnols

DINING AND LODGING

Château de Bagnols. This exquisite, small medieval castle began life in the 13th century and has undergone many transformations, most recently at the hands of the Amanresorts chain, which opened it in the early 1990s. No expense was spared in the decor—you may have seen pictures in *Vogue Decoration*. Period glassware, fabric, porcelain, and silver were copied to complement the antique furniture, which belongs to a private collection. The moat and the fortifications are grassy lawns nowadays, where tables are set for tea or lunch, but the walls inside are still adorned with 17th- and 18th-century mural paintings inspired by Lyon's textile industry: coats of arms, architectural trompe l'oeil, arabesques, fanciful animals, flowers, and fruit. Wine tastings are held in the beautiful stone *cuvage* (wine-pressing room). A Continental breakfast is included in the astronomical rates, each room has a safe, and you can buy the reproduced decorative items in the boutique. ⬚ *69620 Bagnols,* ☎ *74–71–40–00,* ℻ *74–71–40–49. 12 rooms and 8 suites. Restaurant, library, meeting rooms. AE, DC, MC, V. $$$$*

Bourg-en-Bresse

DINING

L'Auberge Bressane. The beauty of this restaurant's location—the terrace looks out on the elegant Brou church—makes up for the rather chilly welcome you'll receive inside. The rustic dining room is an excellent setting in which to enjoy the academic rigor of Jean-Pierre Vullin's cooking. The wine list offers more than 300 vintages. Frogs' legs and succulent Bresse chicken with morel mushroom cream sauce are house specialties. ✕ *166 blvd. de Brou,* ☎ *74–22–22–68. Reservations required. Jacket and tie. AE, DC, MC, V. Closed Mon. dinner and Tues., mid-Nov.–mid-Dec. $$$*

★ **La Petite Auberge.** This cozily informal flower-bedecked inn is set in the countryside just on the outskirts of town. Motherly Mme. Bertrand is a kindly hostess and even provides games for children on the summer terrace. Inside, you'll appreciate chef Philippe Garnier's subtle way with mullet (he grills it in saffron butter) and Bresse chicken (browned in tangy cider vinegar). ✕ *St-Just, Rte. de Ceyzeriat,* ☎ *74–22–30–04. Reservations accepted. MC, V. Closed Mon. dinner and Jan. $$–$$$*

LODGING

Terminus. The best hotel in town is a converted mansion close to the train station. The guest rooms have been renovated with considerable taste and feature traditional French decor; the best room in the house is the two-room suite. The flower garden makes a fine place to relax and sip *pastis* (an anise-flavored drink). You'll be given a hearty meal (*saveloy*—sausage—and seasonal game birds) in the unpretentious restaurant; in fine weather, you can dine outdoors on the terrace. ⬚ *19 rue Alphonse-Baudin, 01000,* ☎ *74–21–01–21,* ℻ *74–21–36–47. 50 rooms with bath or shower. Restaurant. AE, DC, MC, V. $$*

Briançon

DINING AND LODGING

★ **Vauban.** Despite its name, this is a foursquare modern building, unpretentious, comfortable, and convenient: just 300 yards from the train station and cable car in the lower town, a 10-minute walk from the historic upper town. Rooms and bathrooms are spacious, and many have balconies. The best ones are on the fourth floor, facing south. The Sémiond family provides a friendly welcome and traditional French cooking with the freshest ingredients. Try the pepper steak or trout in butter sauce. ⊞ *13 av. du Général-de-Gaulle, 05100, ☎ 92–21–12–11, ℻ 92–50–58–20. 44 rooms, 26 with bath, 12 with shower. Restaurant, bar. MC, V. Closed early Nov.–Dec. $$*

Chamonix

DINING AND LODGING

Albert I & Milan. The welcoming chalet-style Albert I & Milan is the best-value quality hotel in Chamonix. Many guest rooms were renovated in 1992; most have balconies, and all are furnished with elegant period reproductions. The dining room offers stupendous views of Mont Blanc, while Pierre Carrier's cuisine scales heights of invention and enthusiasm; try the oysters fried with asparagus. ⊞ *119 impasse du Montenvers, 74400, ☎ 50–53–05–09, ℻ 50–55–95–48. 17 rooms and 12 suites with bath. Restaurant, pool, tennis, sauna, hot tub. AE, DC, MC, V. Closed middle 2 wks of May; restaurant closed Wed. lunch. $$$*

Grenoble

DINING AND LODGING

Alpotel. This reasonably priced member of the Mercure chain is modern, functional, and air-conditioned; comfortable rather than plush; and handily situated on one of Grenoble's main boulevards within a few minutes' walk of the old town center. The bustling Magnolia restaurant has an inventive menu featuring local delicacies like crab saveloy with cress, poached salmon with pink butter, and veal with basil. ⊞ *12 blvd. du Mal-Joffre, 38000, ☎ 76–87–88–41, ℻ 76–47–58–42. 88 rooms with bath or shower. Restaurant, bar. AE, DC, MC, V. $$–$$$*

Hauterives

DINING AND LODGING

Le Relais. The local tourist wonder, the Palais Idéal, is just a stone's throw from this comfortable, rustic inn. The reasonably sized guest rooms feature an unpretentious country look, with chunky wooden desks and headboards and wicker chairs. The same warm, golden color scheme dominates the cozy restaurant, where you can enjoy such specialties as roasted partridge or delicately seasoned frogs' legs. Half-board is mandatory during summer months. ⊞ *Pl. de l'Eglise, 26390, ☎ 75–68–81–12. 13 rooms with bath. Restaurant. AE, DC, V. Closed Sun. dinner, Mon., and Jan.–Feb. $$*

Lyon

DINING

★ **Léon de Lyon.** A mix of regional ingredients (butter, cream, foie gras, olive oil) and eye-opening innovation keep this restaurant at the forefront of the city's gastronomic scene. Enlarged in 1992, it now occupies two floors in an old house full of alcoves and wood paneling (there's a room for nonsmokers). The blue-aproned waiters blend in with the old-fashioned decor, but Jean-Paul Lacombe is an innovative chef, and such dishes as fillet of veal with celery or leg of lamb with fava beans will linger in your memory. One of his latest recipes is suckling pig with foie gras and onions, served with a truffle salad with garlic/parsley vinaigrette. ✕ *1 rue Pléney,* ☎ *78–28–11–33,* 𝕱𝕬𝕏 *78–39–89–05. Reservations required. Jacket required. MC, V. Closed Sun. dinner, Mon. lunch, most of Aug., and Dec. 24–Jan. 6. $$$$*

Orsi. Pierre Orsi, a Meilleur Ouvrier de France ("Best Worker of France"), runs a truly sumptuous restaurant. It sits by a tiny tree-lined square, a pink stucco wonder with flower boxes. From its inlaid marble floors, pink silk-taffeta draperies under brocade, tubs of lilies, and posturing bronze nudes, to its mirrored cupboards with glittering glass, gilt-frame paintings, and rococo glasses, everything lends your evening a festive glow. Limp foie gras raviolis with truffles languishing in a clear, rich reduction, and mesclun with crumbled goat cheese and tiny buttered toasts are hard acts to follow, but the sliced figs (looking like sausage) with a dab of pistachio ice cream certainly holds its own. ✕ *3 pl. Kléber,* ☎ *79–89–57–68. Jacket and tie. AE, V. $$$–$$$$*

★ **Paul Bocuse.** One of the country's most celebrated gourmet temples lies 12 kilometers (7 miles) north of town in Collonges-au-Mont-d'Or. The dining room's grand decor is a fitting backdrop for the culinary expertise of larger-than-life chef Paul Bocuse. Bocuse is often away on the lecture-tour trail, but his restaurant continues to please its elegantly dressed diners, who feast on such house specialties as truffle soup and succulent sea bass. The restaurant's reputation means you'll have to reserve a table long in advance. ✕ *50 quai de la Plage, 69660 Collonges-au-Mont-d'Or,* ☎ *72–27–85–85,* 𝕱𝕬𝕏 *72–27–85–87. Reservations required. Jacket and tie. AE, DC, MC, V. $$$$*

★ **Café des Fédérations.** For the past 80 years, this sawdust-strewn café has reigned as one of the city's friendliest eating spots; expect to be treated like one of the gang. Jocular Raymond Fulchiron not only serves up such deftly prepared Lyonnaise classics as hearty *boudin blanc* (white-meat sausage), but he also comes out to chat with guests and make sure everyone feels at home. The decor is a homey mix of red-checked tablecloths, wood paneling, and old-fashioned bench seating. ✕ *8 rue du Major-Martin,* ☎ *78–28–26–00. Reservations advised. AE, DC, MC, V. Closed weekends and Aug. $$*

★ **Les Muses.** High up under the glass vault of the Opéra de Lyon is a small restaurant run by ubiquitous Philippe Chavent (when he's not tending his other irons in the fire). The restaurant's glass front looks out between the buxom statues of the muses and across the street to the splendid Hotel de Ville; but if you can drag your attention back to your plate and Chavent's classic-inspired nouvelle cuisine, you'll be hard put to choose between the salmon in butter sauce with watercress mousse and the 59-franc *plat du jour*—for example, chicken in tarragon cream with sautéed zucchini. ✕ *Opéra de Lyon,* ☎ *72–00–45–58. Reservations advised. AE, V. $$*

★ **Le Vivarais.** This simple, tidy restaurant, run by Roger Duffaud, the pupil and former colleague of superstar chef Alain Chapel, is one of the city's most outstanding gourmet good buys. Don't expect napkins folded into flower shapes here—all the excitement happens on your plate. The menu offers a perfect contemporary take on the Lyonnaise classics. Try the *lièvre royale* (hare cooked with onions, red wine, and cinnamon and then rolled and stuffed with truffles and pâté); the superb cheese tray; and the daily dessert, perhaps a pear tart. ✕ *1 pl. du Dr-Gailleton,* ☎ *78–37–85–15. Reservations advised. MC, V. Closed Sun. $$*

Chez Sylvain. The old-fashioned decor of Chez Sylvain is a delightful reminder of its days as a favorite neighborhood beanery. Little has changed since, and the huge wooden counter, turn-of-the-century wall decorations, and original spiral staircase are the ideal backdrop for this friendly bouchon's robust Lyonnaise cuisine; the tripe and andouillettes are especially good. ✕ *4 rue Tupin,* ☎ *78–42–11–98. Reservations accepted. V. Closed Sun., Mon., and Aug.* $–$$

LODGING

La Cour des Loges. A team of young Lyonnais architects and Italian interior designers worked for three years to transform four Renaissance mansions into one of the most stylish hotels in Lyon. Four stories of sand-color stone, an immense courtyard, spiral stone staircases, and exposed roof beams lend a courtly ambience; guest rooms (a bit on the small side) are furnished with the best in modern furniture design and effects. In the cellar there's an exclusive wine club, and an informal little *tapas* bar provides an array of appetizer-size snacks. ☎ *6 rue du Boeuf, 69005,* ☎ *78–42–75–75,* FAX *72–40–93–61. 63 rooms with bath. Bar, breakfast room, heated indoor pool, hot tub, sauna, health club, library, meeting room. AE, DC, MC, V.* $$$$

La Tour Rose. Philippe Chavent's silk-swathed hotel in Vieux Lyon was created from several houses around a secret courtyard overlooked by a rose-washed tower. From the court you look down into the steel- and glass-roof restaurant, built in a former chapel. Each guest room is named for one of the old silk factories and done in that house's goods—silk taffetas, plissés, and *panne de velours* (printed velvet) cover walls, windows, and beds. A discerning eye and daring taste provide surprises wherever you look. Take breakfast, for a change, around the corner at Chavent's wine bar, the Comptoir du Boeuf. ☎ *22 rue du Boeuf, 09005,* ☎ *78–37–25–90,* FAX *78–42–26–02. 12 rooms with bath. Restaurant, bar. AE, DC, V.* $$$$

Villa Florentine. High above the old town, near the Roman theater and the basilica, this pristine new hotel has been made from an old convent, with beamed and vaulted ceilings, terraces everywhere, and marvelous views over Lyon. Les Terrasses de Lyon, its restaurant, serves refined nouvelle cuisine spiced with the view. ☎ *25–27 Montée St-Barthélémy, 69005,* ☎ *72–56–56–56,* FAX *72–40–90–56. 16 rooms, 3 suites, all with bath. Restaurant, bar, breakfast room, pool, meeting rooms. AE, DC, MC, V.* $$$$

Hôtel des Artistes. An intimate little hotel on a quiet, elegant square across from the Théâtre des Célestins, this has long been a popular place for visiting artists to hang their hats; black-and-white photographs of several of them adorn the walls of the lobby. The rooms are modern and smallish but perfectly comfortable, and the friendly reception and great location make this place equally popular with those who have never picked up a paintbrush or had a go at the keyboard. ☎ *8 rue Gaspard-André, 69002,* ☎ *78–42–04–88,* FAX *78–42–93–76. 35 rooms with bath. AE, MC, V.* $$

Le Boulevardier. From the front windows you can look across the narrow street at St-Nizier church with all its Gothic glory, as if under a magnifier. You enter through a restaurant-comptoir-café hung with charcuterie that serves breakfast, meals, and snacks nonstop from 7 AM to 1 AM. Up the winding stairs are minuscule rooms, each with cable TV and telephone; downstairs is a meeting room and an after-dinner jazz club. All is clean and convenient; what more could you want? ☎ *5 rue de la Fromagerie, 69001,* ☎ *78–28–48–22,* FAX *78–27–06–09. 11 rooms with WC and basin (9 with bath or shower). Restaurant, meeting room, jazz club. MC, V.* $$

Elysée Hotel. Almost everything you'll want to see in Lyon is within a few minutes' walk of this small hotel on Presqu'Ile, just off place des Jacobins. Movies, night clubs, antiques shops, and fashion outlets are also nearby. The rooms, more functional than decorative, all have color TV, hair dryers, and phones. ☎ *92 rue Président-Edouard-*

Herriot, 69002, ☎ *78–42–03–15,* FAX *78–37–76–49. 29 single and double rooms with bath or shower. Bar, meeting room. AE, DC, MC, V. $$*

Bed et Breakfast à Lyon. This nonprofit agency can house a single or a family for one night or several. ☎ *2 Pétite rue Tramassac, 69005,* ☎ *72–41–72–00,* FAX *72–41–76–66. 120 frs–290 frs single; 170 frs–390 frs double.*

Megève

DINING AND LODGING

★ **Chalet-Hôtel du Mont d'Arbois.** This rustic-looking but luxurious mountain roost is run by Nadine de Rothschild, who also designed its quietly sophisticated interior. Overlooking Megève, the chalet offers fine views from well-appointed rooms that are furnished with antiques and beds with big down comforters. It also has the best gourmet restaurant in Megève, with delicious spit-roasted meats and fish, such as salmon steak in red-wine sauce. There's also a superb wine list that features many bottles from the Rothschilds' vineyards in Bordeaux. Special summer offers (including meals and greens fees) start at 1,540 francs per couple per weekend. ☎ *447 chem. Rocaillé, 74120,* ☎ *50–21–25–03,* FAX *50–21–24–79. 20 rooms and 1 suite, all with bath. Restaurant, pool, sauna, golf, tennis. AE, DC, MC, V. Closed Apr.–mid-June, Oct.–mid-Dec. $$$$*

Montélimar

LODGING

Les Hospitaliers. This tastefully designed modern hotel is in the center of the tiny hilltop town of Le Poët-Laval, 22 kilometers (14 miles) east of Montélimar along D540. With its stone walls and red-tile roof, the hotel blends perfectly into the medieval surroundings; there are sweeping views of the valley and mountains from the terrace. In cold weather, you can escape from the tacky '70s decor of the large guest rooms to warm yourself by the immense stone hearth in the sitting room. Local specialties are served in the airy restaurant; thrush pâté with truffles is always a good bet. ☎ *Le Vieux Village, 26160 Le Poët-Laval,* ☎ *75–46–22–32,* FAX *75–46–49–99. 20 rooms with bath. Restaurant, pool. AE, DC, MC, V. Closed mid-Nov.–Feb. $$$*

★ **Relais de l'Empéreur.** Sure enough, Napoléon spent a night here, on April 24, 1814, after his return from exile on the Mediterranean island of Elba—sufficient reason for the hotel (member of the Best Western chain) to have carved a niche in the hearts of many visitors. The grandiose Empire decor of the guest rooms does its bit as well. There's a stylish, if costly, restaurant, where the Napoleonic heart-strings are tugged to the breaking point (guinea fowl *à la Joséphine,* "imperial" thrush pâté). The bar has an exceptional choice of cocktails and the wine list is comprehensive. ☎ *1 pl. Marx-Dormoy, 26200,* ☎ *75–01–29–00,* FAX *75–01–32–21. 40 rooms, most with bath. AE, DC, MC, V. Closed mid-Nov.–Dec. 25. $$$*

Pérouges

DINING AND LODGING

★ **Ostellerie du Vieux Pérouges.** This historic Bresson inn is an extraordinary place even by French standards. Antiques are scattered throughout, and the venerable rustic tone is heightened by glossy wood floors and tables, as well as gigantic stone hearths. You'll be served your meal on chunky pewter plates, by waitresses decked out in colorful folk costume; the crayfish is particularly good. Reserve a room in the geranium-clad 15th-century manor rather than in the annex; those in the former are more spacious, with marble bathrooms and period furniture. ☎

Pl. du Tilleul, 01800 Meximieux, ☎ *74–61–00–88,* FAX *74–34–77–90. 28 rooms with bath. Restaurant (closed Thurs. lunch and Wed. Nov.–Mar.). $$$$*

Pont de l'Isère

DINING AND LODGING

Michel Chabran. This sophisticated hotel-restaurant is decidedly modern; it's on the east bank of the Rhône at Pont de l'Isère, 10 kilometers (6 miles) south of Tournon via N7. Guest rooms, lounge, and dining rooms feature slick Danish-style furniture, elaborate floral displays, and airy plate-glass windows opening onto the private garden. Chabran's cuisine is light and imaginative; try his grilled salmon in creamed butter sauce. ☎ *29 av. du 45e Parallèle, 26600 Pont de l'Isère,* ☎ *75–84–60–09,* FAX *75–84–59–65. 12 rooms with bath. Restaurant. MC, V. Closed Sun. evening and Mon. in winter. $$$*

Privas

DINING

Lous Esclos. In the countryside, just 5 kilometers (3 miles) south-east of Privas on D2, is a striking modern restaurant with more windows than walls—all looking out over the wild Ardèche landscape. Monsieur Costechareyre serves succulent French cuisine—including goose and snail *feuilleté* (in a flaky pastry)—at a price that's almost too good to be true. ✗ *Los Esclops, 07210 Alissas,* ☎ *75–65–12–73. Reservations accepted. AE, V. Closed last wk Dec.–Jan. 10. $–$$*

Serrières

DINING AND LODGING

Schaeffer. In a sophisticated setting of white wood trim and gleaming mirrors, halfway between Vienne and Tournon, chef Bernard Mathé dishes up inventive variants of traditional French dishes: smoked duck cutlet in lentil stew and lamb with eggplant in anchovy butter. Don't skimp on dessert; the choice is somewhat overwhelming, but the pistachio cake with bitter chocolate is a clear winner. There are 12 contemporary guest rooms as well. ☎ *Quai Jules Roche, 07340,* ☎ *75–34–00–07,* FAX *75–34–08–79. 12 rooms with bath. Reservations required. Jacket required. AE, DC, V. Closed Jan., restaurant closed Mon. (except July–Aug.) and Mon. dinner. $$–$$$*

St-Etienne

DINING

Pierre Gagnaire. Some would say that the main reason to come to industrial St-Etienne, southwest of Lyon, is to visit chef Pierre Gagnaire—especially since his 1992 move to a listed 1930 Art Deco mansion with fancy iron railings and large bay windows. Gagnaire spent more than $1 million doing up the interior with contemporary art, designer furniture, and colored-glass chandeliers. The stunning result (traditionalists stay clear) earned an award from the magazine *Interiors.* Beneath a shy, ponderous exterior, the fair-haired, boyish-faced Gagnaire is a born rebel. Critics have raved about his off-beat concoctions, like pigeon with crayfish flan, and lettuce stuffed with crab and small onions in a cherry and red-currant sauce. But don't be upset if these aren't on the menu; it changes whenever Gagnaire has other wacky ideas. ✗ *7 rue Richelandière,* ☎ *77–42–30–90,* FAX *77–42–30–95. Reservations essential. Jacket required. AE, DC, MC, V. Closed Sun. dinner. $$$–$$$$*

Tain-L'Hermitage

DINING

Jean-Marc Reynaud. Tain-L'Hermitage, just across the river from Tournon, is the setting for this fine restaurant, with a magnificent view over the Rhône and a comfortable, atmospheric dining room. Brilliantly prepared classic cuisine is served in the traditionally styled dining room; house specialties include poached egg with foie gras, and pigeon fillet in a black-currant sauce. ✕ *82 av. du Président-Roosevelt,* ☎ *75–08–07–96. Reservations advised. AE, DC, MC, V. Closed Sun. dinner, Mon., Jan., and 1 wk in Aug.* $$

Talloires

DINING AND LODGING

★ **Père Bise.** This deluxe auberge on the banks of Lake Annecy has a leafy veranda, marvelous views—from both the hotel rooms and the restaurant—and a classy menu. Sophie Bise, granddaughter of Père Bise, is the only three-star female chef in France, and such dishes as puff pastry with potatoes, foie gras, and truffles, and grilled lobster with a spicy tomato garnish will linger in your memory. You'll also find excellent service, a superb wine list, and a famous dessert—a *marjolaine* (a multilayer chocolate-and-nut cake). 🖫 *Rte. du Port, 74290,* ☎ *50–60–72–01,* FAX *50–60–73–05. 25 rooms and 9 suites with bath. Restaurant. AE, DC, MC, V. Closed Dec.–Mar.* $$$$

Valence

DINING AND LODGING

★ **Pic.** The Pic family are the undisputed kings among Drôme restaurateurs, with subtle and original recipes to please the most demanding gourmets; try the truffle-flavored *galettes* (pancakes) or asparagus with caviar. Comfortable, embroidered armchairs; flowering plants on all the tables; wall-to-wall carpeting; and the smiling service of Mme. Pic lend a cozy warmth to the peach-color dining room. In summer you can eat outside on the terrace. Two elegantly furnished guest rooms and two even more opulent suites are available, but you'll have to reserve well in advance. 🖫 *285 av. Victor-Hugo, 26000,* ☎ *75–44–15–32,* FAX *75–40–96–03. Reservations required. Jacket and tie. AE, DC, V. Closed Sun. dinner, Wed., and Aug.* $$$$

Vienne

DINING

Le Bec Fin. An inexpensive weekday menu makes Le Bec Fin a good lunch spot, and a serious dinner venue as well. The unpretentious eatery is just opposite the cathedral; its main dishes—steak and freshwater fish—seldom disappoint and occasionally display a deft touch (burbot cooked with saffron). The dining room has an understated elegance. ✕ *7 pl. St-Maurice,* ☎ *74–85–76–72. Reservations accepted. Jacket required. MC, V. Closed Sun. dinner and Mon.* $$

Vonnas

DINING AND LODGING

★ **Georges Blanc.** It's worth making the 19-kilometer (12-mile) trip from Bourg-en-Bresse west to Vonnas (via D936, D45, and D96), because Georges Blanc must rank as one of the world's best chefs. The simple 19th-century country inn has been embellished with flowers, rugs, grandfather clocks, and antique country furniture and makes a fine setting in which to appreciate Blanc's constantly updated menu. Try the frogs' legs any way he offers them. The wine list is extensive, the desserts are superb, and there is a separate room for nonsmokers. There are also 30 guest rooms, ranging from (relatively) simple to downright luxurious. Make your reservations well in advance. 🖫 *Place du*

Marché, 01540 Vonnas, ☎ *74–50–00–10,* FAX *74–50–08–80. 30 rooms with bath. Restaurant, pool, golf, tennis, helipad. AE, DC, MC, V. Closed Jan.–mid-Feb.; restaurant closed Wed. and Thurs. (except for dinner June–mid-Sept.).* $$$$

THE ARTS AND NIGHTLIFE

The Arts

Lyon is the region's liveliest arts center; *Lyon-Poche,* a weekly guide published on Wednesdays and sold at any newsstand, will give details of the week's cultural events. In Grenoble, pick up the monthly *Grenoble-Spectacles.*

Festivals

September in Lyon sees the internationally renowned **Biennale de la Danse** (even years). October brings the **Festival Bach** (☎ 78–72–75–31) and (odd years) the Contemporary Art Festival, **Octobre des Arts** (☎ 78–30–50–66). In September, Lyon stages a pottery fair, **Foire aux Tupiniers** (☎ 78–37–00–68), while in November and December, there's a musical **Festival du Vieux Lyon** in the old town (☎ 78–42–39–04).

Jazz fans will want to catch Grenoble's **Cinq Jours de Jazz** (Five Days of Jazz) in February or March; those with classical tastes are catered to during the **Session Internationale de Grenoble-Isère** in June and July. Vienne's cathedral and church host a **Summer Music Festival** throughout June, July, and August.

Theater

The café-theater, a Lyonnais specialty, lets you eat and drink while watching a revue: **Espace Gerson** (1 pl. Gerson, ☎ 78–27–96–99) or **Café-Théâtre de L'Accessoire** (26 rue de l'Annonciade, ☎ 78–27–84–84).

Music

Lyon's Société de Musique de Chambre performs at **Salle Molière** (18 quai Bondy, ☎ 78–28–03–11). The recently modernized **Opéra de Lyon** (1 pl. de la Comédie, ☎ 72–00–45–45) presents plays, concerts, ballets and opera in its season, October–June.

Nightlife

Lyon is your best bet for nighttime entertainment, with dozens of discos, piano bars, and nightclubs; for a full list of what's available, pick up a copy of the weekly guide *Lyon-Poche.*

Discos and Nightclubs

The low-key **Comoëdia** (30 rue Neuve) has a downstairs disco and an old-fashioned piano bar upstairs. Expect anything from the tango to rock and roll at **Palace Mobile** (2 rue René-Leynaud). Caribbean and African music are featured at **Le Club des Iles** (1 Grande Rue des Feuillants).

In Grenoble, **Le Joker** (1 Grande-Rue) is youthful and lively, while **La Soupe aux Choux** (7 rte. de Lyon) caters to jazz fans.

Bars and Pubs

Lyon's **Hot Club** (26 rue Lanterne) has been going strong for 40 years in a vaulted stone basement that features live jazz. The **Sofitel** hotel (20 quai Dr-Gailleton) has a more restrained cocktail bar catering to the city's intellectual set. For a casual game of darts and a pint of English bitter, head to the **Albion Public House** (12 rue Ste-Catherine). The **Bouchon à Vin** wine bar (64 rue Mercière) has more than 30 vintages;

for a more romantic evening, sip champagne in the intimate, wood-paneled **Métro Club** (2 rue Stella). Fifties fans should try the **Navire Night** (3 rue Terme).

LYON AND THE ALPS ESSENTIALS

Arriving and Departing

By Plane

The international airport at **Satolas,** 26 kilometers (16 miles) from Lyon, is one of France's busiest (for flight information, call 72–22–72–21).

Between the Airport and Downtown

Buses leave for the center of Lyon every 20 minutes between 5 AM and 9 PM, and for the train stations every 20 minutes between 6 AM and 11 PM; journey time is 35–45 minutes, and the fare is 37 francs adults, 18 francs children. There's also a bus from Satolas to Grenoble; journey time is just over an hour, and the fare is 100 francs.

By Train

The TGV high-speed train to Lyon leaves from Paris's Gare de Lyon station hourly and arrives in just two hours. There are also six TGVs daily between Lyon and Charles de Gaulle airport near Paris.

By Car

A6 speeds south to Lyon from Paris (463 kilometers/287 miles away), but be warned that the Tunnel de Fourvière, which cuts through Lyon, is a classic vacationers' hazard, and at peak times you may have to sit for hours.

Getting Around

By Plane

There are domestic airports at Grenoble, Valence, Annecy, Chambéry, and Aix-les-Bains.

By Train

Major rail junctions include Grenoble, Annecy, Valence, Chambéry, and Lyon. Lyon also has a good subway system that serves both the city's train stations. A single ticket costs 7.50 francs, a book of 10, 65 francs, and a day pass 20 francs.

By Car

Regional roads are fast and well maintained, though smaller mountainous routes can be difficult to navigate, and many of the higher passes are closed in winter. In Lyon, **Lyon Espace Affairés** (☎ 78–39–26–11) runs a fleet of well-kept taxi-vans.

Guided Tours

Orientation

Ask at the Tourist Office on Place Bellecour about minibus tours of the city. The **French Travel Agents' Association** offers a "Weekend Contract in Lyon," including a tour of the old city, cooking demonstrations, and hotel accommodations. The cost per person in a single room is 2,850 francs; per person in a double room, 2,500 francs. Contact **Sorotour Voyages** (18 rue de Sèze, 69006 Lyon, ☎ 78–24–01–07) for reservations.

Special-Interest

The Rhône Valley and the Alps offer a variety of special-interest tours, the most relaxing of which are by boat or barge along the region's waterways. **Navig-Inter** (13 bis quai Rambaud, 69002 Lyon, ☎ 78–42–96–81) offers daily boat trips on the Saône and Rhône, leaving from quai des Célestins. If you prefer to survey Lyon and Beaujolais from a plane, contact the **Aero-Club du Rhône et du Sud-Est** (Aeroport de Lyon-Bron, 69500 Bron, ☎ 78–26–83–97).

Walking

The **Office du Tourisme** in Lyon (pl. Bellecour, ☎ 78–42–25–75) offers guided walks of the city's sights with an English-speaking guide. **Philibert** (24 av. Barthélémy-Thimonier, B.P. 16, 69300 Caluire, ☎ 72–23–10–56, FAX 72–27–00–97) runs a cityrama coach April–October.

By Boat

Naviginter (☎ 78–42–96–81) runs year-round sightseeing (42 frs) and lunch and dinner (200 frs) cruises around La Presqu'Ile and other islands farther afield.

Important Addresses and Numbers

Travel Agencies

American Express (6 rue Childebert, 69002 Lyon, ☎ 78–37–40–69) and **Wagons-Lits** (76 rue des Alliés, 38100 Grenoble, ☎ 76–40–47–78; and 48 blvd. Vauban, 26000 Valence, ☎ 75–42–02–04).

Car Rental

Avis (1 av. du Docteur-Desfrançois, Chambéry, ☎ 79–33–58–54; and Aéroport de Lyon-Satolas, ☎ 72–22–75–25) and **Hertz** (16 rue Emile-Gueymard, Grenoble, ☎ 76–43–12–92; and 11 rue Pasteur, Valence, ☎ 75–44–39–45).

Visitor Information

Contact the **Maison du Tourisme** (14 rue de la République, B.P. 227, 38019 Grenoble cedex, ☎ 76–42–41–41) for the Isère *département* and the area around Grenoble, and the **Comité Régional du Tourisme Rhône-Alpes** (78 rte. de Paris, 69260 Charbonnières-les-Bains, ☎ 72–38–40–00) for Lyon and the Alps.

Local tourist offices in major towns covered in this chapter are **Annecy** (Clos Bonlieu, 1 rue Jean-Jaurès, ☎ 50–45–00–33) **Briançon** (1 pl. du Temple, ☎ 92–21–08–50), **Bourg-en-Bresse** (6 av. d'Alsace-Lorraine, ☎ 74–22–49–40), **Chambéry** (24 blvd. de la Colonne, ☎ 79–33–42–47), **Grenoble** (14 rue de la République, ☎ 76–42–41–41, and in the train station, ☎ 76–54–34–36), **Lyon** (pl. Bellecour, ☎ 78–42–25–75, with branches on av. Adolphe Max, near the cathedral; ☎ 78–42–25–75, and the Perrache train station), **Montélimar** (av. Rochemaure, ☎ 75–01–00–20), **Privas** (3 rue Elie-Reynier, ☎ 75–64–33–35), **Valence** (blvd. Maurice-Clerc, ☎ 75–43–04–88), and **Vienne** (cours Brillier, ☎ 74–85–12–62).

11 The Massif Central and Auvergne

The Volcanic Park, Rocamadour, and Gorges du Tarn

WINDSWEPT PLAINS, snow-capped mountains, volcanic plateaus, deep ravines, and thick forests have made the heart of the Massif Central the least discovered area of France. To outsiders the land is forbidding; for the inhabitants, it has made life hard. In the old days, it is said, people trained their dogs to lie on top of them for warmth. And dangers, real and imagined, lurked everywhere. The Evil Eye could make people sterile, take away mothers' milk, or make cows go dry. At full moon a bastard could turn into the devil's wolf. But there were also faith and hope: Amulets of toadskin or snakeskin could ward off evil; spiderwebs could stop bleeding, and chopped snails could cure corns.

Since the dawn of history the Auvergne has been a battle ground: Romans versus Arvernes (the original Celtic settlers); Gauls versus Visigoths; Charlemagne versus Saracens; Duc d'Aquitaine versus Frankish kings Pepin I and Pepin II; English Plantagenets versus French kings (the Hundred Years' War, which strewed the land with ruined fortresses); the Dukes of Bourbon versus Francis I; and Huguenots and Catholics massacring one another in the Wars of Religion. By then, it seems the Auvergnois had had enough. They kept to themselves and managed to escape most of the excesses of the Revolution. In World War II, the Nazi puppet Pétain set up a figurehead French government at Vichy, and the Massif Central was spared the bombing. Though embroiled in the tumultuous history, Auvergne has never been part of courtly France. Its heritage is its earth, its rugged geography, where life revolves around the seasons and the produce of the soil.

There are few large towns in this heartland; Clermont Ferrand (pop. 150,000) is the major metropolis. For years France's major highways bypassed the Massif Central: Roads out of Paris went southwest to Bordeaux by way of Tours and Poitiers; the route south went through Burgundy and Lyon. New highways now cut south directly into the Auvergne, linking Clermont-Ferrand to Lyon, and tourists in search of the unspoiled are discovering the region.

The best season to visit is generally the autumn. It is usually drier then, and the sun is still warm on the shimmering golden trees, on the pansies, harebells, and cranesbill. Summers can be hot, often with a cloud-covered sky. Winters are cold, and May is the prime time of the short spring, with daffodils and irises and dozens of wildflowers, from dog rose to white bladderwort and yellow crosswort.

EXPLORING

Orientation

This tour describes a backward "s," starting in Bourges before entering the Auvergne proper at Montluçon. This region is known as the Bourbonnais for the dynasty of kings that it produced, and castles, most in ruins, abound. We visit Vichy, whose thermal springs have attracted people since Roman times, then Clermont-Ferrand, home to the Michelin tire company. Southwest lie the Parc Régional des Volcans, the volcanic cones of the Monts du Dôme, and the hills of Monts du Cantal. Still farther west on the limestone plateau of Causse de Gramat we come to Rocamadour, with its miraculous medieval cathedral. We then follow the Lot Valley east and head into the rolling hills of Aveyron. This is, strictly speaking, not the Auvergne, but it shares the same feeling of untamed nature, and the grandeur at the Gorges du Tarn is challenged in its magnificence by the Corniche des Cévennes.

Numbers in the margin correspond to points of interest on the Massif Central map.

Leave Paris on the A10 autoroute, then take the A71 at Orléans to
❶ **Bourges.** If you were to drop a plumb line over France to find her center, Bourges is where the finger would point. Modern times have largely passed it by, and the result is a preserved market town with medieval streets and the 13th-century Cathédrale-St-Etienne. You'll see the towers as you approach the town, but once you've arrived, its asymmetrical facade is hidden, and it is impossible to photograph. The central portal is a masterpiece of sculpture: Cherubim, angels, saints, and prophets cluster in the archway above the tympanum, which contains an elaborate representation of the Last Judgment. The interior is unlike that of any other Gothic cathedral. The forest of tall, slender pillars rising to the vaults is remarkable enough, but the height of the side aisles flanking the nave is unique: 65 feet—high enough to allow windows to be pierced above the level of the second side aisles. The cathedral contains exquisite stained glass, some dating from its construction. *Off rue du Guichet.*

The center of Bourges, downhill from the cathedral, has been restored to its medieval state. Rue Mirabeau and rue Coursalon, pedestrian streets full of timber-frame houses, are charming places for browsing and shopping. At one end of rue Coursalon, across rue Moyenne—Bourges's busy but less distinguished main street—stands the Palais Jacques-Coeur, one of the most sumptuous Gothic dwellings in France. Notice its vaulted chapel, the wooden ceilings covered with original paintings, and the dining room with its tapestries and massive fireplace. *Rue Jacques-Coeur,* ☎ *48–24–06–87.* ☛ *26 frs adults, 17 frs senior citizens and those 18–25; 7 frs children under 18.* ☉ *Daily. Guided tours only, about 45 min, begin 15 min after the hr.*

From Bourges, you may want to meander through the countryside, admiring the rich farmland, or return to the autoroute and head south as
❷ far as **Montluçon.** The Bourbon castle here, like most others that you will see, was built during the Hundred Years' War. Unlike most, however, this fortress has been well maintained and put to good use. Down from the castle, Montluçon's old quarter of 16th- and 17th-century houses is small and cute. The **Musée du Vieux Château,** comprises a folklore exhibition and a historical account of the hurdy-gurdy, a traditional stringed instrument played in Auvergne villages. ☎ *70–05–00–06.* ☛ *15 frs.* ☉ *Tues.–Sun. 10–noon and 2:30–6.*

❸ From Montluçon take D94 to **Bourbon-l'Archambault,** passing through the delightful rural town of Cosne-d'Allier (exit 10 off A71 to D94 east). During the 17th, 18th, and 19th centuries, Bourbon-l'Archambault was a smart, well-endowed thermal spa. Talleyrand, France's powerful foreign minister, and the Marquise de Montespan, mistress of Louis XIV, took the waters here. The fleeting fancy for fashionable spas has left the town a little less noble than it once was. Hotels and restaurants now cater to middle-class pensioners, but the weathered buildings and the ruined 14th-century castle—once the quarters of the noble tourists—have an appealing faded glory. ☛ *Free.* ☉ *Mid-Apr.–mid-Oct., daily 2–6.*

Backtrack a couple of miles and pick up D1, then take D11/D75 east
❹ into **Souvigny.** In the center of this small, picturesque town is the Prieuré St-Pierre church, built in the 11th, 12th, and 15th centuries of

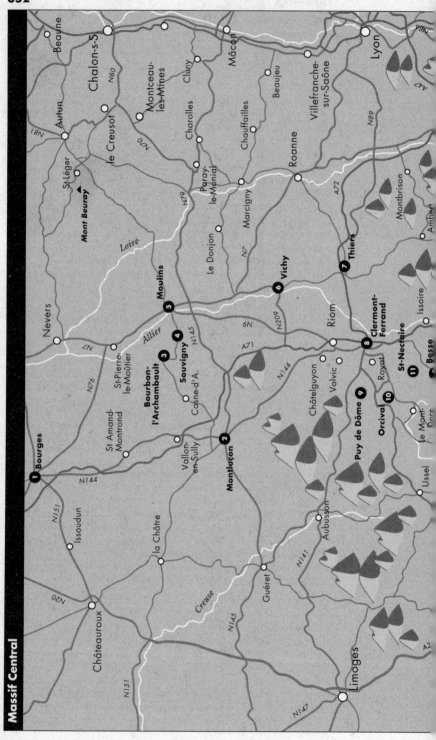

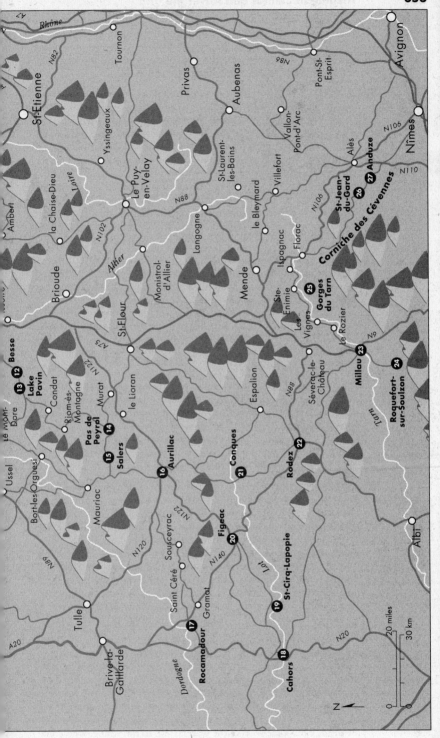

pale, golden stone. Compared to the Auvergne buildings of volcanic stone that you will see, St-Pierre is light and buoyant. But what catches you unawares is its size, for such a small village—but then, this village and its estates were the financial base of the Bourbon fortunes, solid enough to enable them to establish a royal dynasty.

5 Drive east now to **Moulins,** once the capital city for the ducs de Bourbon. It has barely grown since then. That is, of course, its charm. The center is compact and medieval, dominated by the Cathedral of Notre-Dame. The older part (1474–1507) is in the Flamboyant Gothic style, with an extremely decorative interior known for its stained-glass windows. In the 15th century such windows served as storybooks for the illiterate peasants, so, without knowing French, you can follow the story of the crusades of Louis IX much as you would read a comic book. The cathedral's other medieval treasure is the triptych of the Maître de Moulins, painted toward the end of the 15th century. Notice that the Virgin is not as richly clothed as the Duke of Bourbon and his wife, Anne of France, the couple who commissioned the painting!

Moulins also has a famous belfry, in the place de l'Hôtel. Known as the **Jacquemart,** this free-standing clock tower was built in 1232 (and rebuilt most recently in 1946 after having ignited during a fireworks display). The keepers of the hour are a uniformed grenadier and his wife; their two children manage the quarter and half hours. Next door to the tower in a 15th-century mansion is the **Musée du Folklore,** which is full of costumes, farming implements, and other reminders of Moulins past. *Pl. de l'Hôtel,* ☎ *70–44–39–03.* ✔ *10 frs.* ⊙ *Tues.–Sun. 9:30–noon and 2–5:30.*

Since most of the local wine comes from **St-Pourçain-sur-Sioule,** you may want to detour to this attractive little village on your way south to Vichy. It is one of the oldest centers of viticulture in France, with wineries that predate the Romans. Some of the wine is quite good, though it varies a great deal; it is generally not found throughout France and is often a good value for the money. Be sure to wander through the small streets along the River Sioule.

6 **Vichy** is the most elegant city in the Auvergne, although perhaps without the depth of character you'd expect of a town whose mineral waters first attracted the Romans and then, after 1,000 years, the haute society of Paris. Vichy's second coming began during the 1860s, when Napoléon III came to cure his intestinal troubles. Prior to that, when such nobles as the Marquise de Sévigné and the Duchess of Angoulême came for the waters, they stayed in local villas and were very discreet. But the arrival of Napoléon III and, later, of the railroad attracted the middle classes. In 1920, the income from Vichy's Grand Casino surpassed that of all the casinos in Europe, including Monte Carlo.

When France fell in 1940 and the country was divided, under direct and indirect German control, the Pétain government moved its quarters to Vichy, partly because the existing hotels could serve as embassies and ministries. The puppet government left a stain of infamy that, after the war, isolated the town from the new republic. Today it is making a comeback, transforming a stretch of the River Allier into a lake and promoting Vichy as a water-sports center, and building large conference facilities and new thermal baths. Vichy now appeals to the middle-aged, who come to take the waters, and to the young, who come for the water sports.

To the visitor, Vichy is attractive for its newly awakened vibrancy, its smart shops, many restaurants, and hundreds of hotels of every caliber. While there are no old, famous buildings to admire, the city has a pleasant center around the Parc des Sources; the Thermal Establishment, with its glass and mosquelike construction; and the Grand Casino, with its opera house and seasonal concerts and plays.

7 The next stop south is **Thiers,** famous for cutlery. It supplies 70% of France's cutting needs, with everything from table knives to daggers. In the old days, while the rushing waters of the Durolle turned the massive grindstones, the craftsmen would lie on their stomachs on planks over the icy water to hone their blades on the stone. In freezing weather, their dogs would lie on their masters' backs, keeping their kidneys warm. Today's factories use less exotic methods, but the tourist office still gives demonstrations of the old way.

Thiers, built on a steep hill, has a natural charm. Park your car at the top of town and be prepared for stiff walking—the attractive pedestrian streets run only up and down! Take rue Conchette, then rue Bourg to the appealing square, place du Pirou. The tourist office here has maps and information. The 15th-century Maison du Pirou, a wonderful half-timbered building, is the town's major sight. The nearby building at 11 rue de Pirou is called the House of the Seven Deadly Sins—look at the carvings on the ends of the beams and you'll see why. You should also seek out rue de la Coutellerie for its old workshops and the 15th-century **Maison des Couteliers,** which is now a small museum and workshop demonstrating five centuries of the knife-making process. *58 rue de la Coutellerie,* ☎ *73–80–58–86.* ☛ *12 frs.* ☉ *May–Oct., daily 9–noon and 2–5; Nov.–Apr., weekdays 2–6.*

8 Forty kilometers (24 miles) west of Thiers is **Clermont-Ferrand,** the only large city in the Auvergne and known to historians as the hometown of Vercingétorix, who rallied the Arvernes to defeat Julius Caesar in 52 BC. A bustling commercial center that's a hub for road, rail, and air, it is not a city that draws tourists for more than a few hours. The small old quarter is dominated by a foreboding prison (not open to the law-abiding public) and the **Cathédrale Notre-Dame-de-l'Assomption.** The construction of this monolith was the first to use the special black volcanic stone, which enabled the pillars to be thinner and the interior to soar to great heights. The 13th- and 14th-century stained-glass windows still throw marvelous patterns of illumination.

Walk east to rue Pascal, turn left and walk to rue du Port, where a right turn brings you to the Romanesque church of **Notre-Dame-du-Port,** which is entirely different in feel. Built 200 years before the cathedral of yellowish sandstone (somewhat blackened over 800 years), it has a notable raised choir with wonderful carved capitals telling old, familiar tales: the struggle of virtue and vice, the fall of Adam and Eve, the glorification of Mary. The sculptor was Robert of Clermont, and you'll see his work again at Conques (*see below*).

Clermont-Ferrand has its share of museums: the **Musée des Beaux-Arts,** housed in a former Ursuline convent, has a historical overview of painting and sculpture. Its layout is beautifully designed to lead the visitor through the progression of styles, and it has a cafeteria. *Pl. Louis-Deteix,* ☎ *73–23–08–49.* ☛ *21 frs.* ☉ *Tues.–Sun. 11–7.*

The **Musée Bargoin** is known for its Gallo-Roman wooden votive offerings. *45 rue Ballainvilliers,* ☎ *73–91–37–31.* ☛ *21 frs.* ☉ *Apr.–Oct., Wed.–Sun. 10–noon and 2–6.*

The **Musée du Ranquet** has a varied collection, from ancient musical instruments to the world's first calculating machine, invented by native son Blaise Pascal. *34 rue des Gras,* ☎ *73–37–38–63.* ☛ *12 frs.* ⊙ *Tues.–Sat. 10–noon and 2–6 (until 5 in winter) and Sun. 2–5.*

Leave Clermont-Ferrand via its western suburb, the town of **Royat,** which, in Roman times, was a popular spa. The town still hangs on to that claim, and as you drive through, you'll notice dozens of late-18th-century buildings that have been converted into hotels for guests with creaky bones. Pick up D68 out of Royat and follow the signs to

★ ❾ **Puy de Dôme,** the most revered of the volcanoes comprising the **Parc National des Volcans.** Stretching 150 kilometers (90 miles) from north to south and encompassing some 153 towns and villages, the park contains 80 or so dormant volcanoes, with all kinds of craters, dikes, domes, prismatic lava flows, caldera cones, and basaltic plateaus, all lined up to make a chain. They are extremely young, the most recent only 6,000 to 8,000 years old, which explains why their shapes are so well preserved.

Puy-de-Dôme, at 1,465 meters (4,806 feet), is the highest volcano in the Mont Dômes range. Its power and majesty gave it sacred status in the eyes of the Romans, and fittingly, they built a temple to Mercury. When the Romans left and the temple fell into disarray, looters carried off what they could. A millennium or more later (in 1872), the ruins were uncovered, and they have become a place where those with imagination see witches and devils roam. (Cynics say they would have long since been driven away by the parking lot, restaurant, and television tower.) The number of tourists, especially in July and August, is tremendous—Puy de Dôme is one of the three most visited sites in France. Give yourself the best part of the day here, and bring your walking shoes, as trails lead off from the television tower to magnificent unfolding panoramas. For those inspired by the god Mercury's wings, parasailing, hot-air ballooning, and hang-gliding give bird's-eye views. ☛ *20 frs per automobile.* ⊙ *Daily Mar. and Nov. 8–6, Apr. and Oct. 8–8, May–Sept. 7–10, weekends in Dec. 7–5:30.*

❿ When you leave the mountain, cross over N89 and take D216/D27 west to **Orcival.** The obstacle of the Mont Dôme was a major hurdle for pilgrims making the long walk to Santiago de Compostela in Spain. To house them, give them succor, and take their offerings, five major sanctuaries—St-Austremoine d'Issoire, Notre-Dame du Port, Notre-Dame d'Orcival, St-Nectaire, and St-Saturnin—were erected in the 12th century. Of these vaulted Romanesque hospices for the weary walkers, Notre-Dame d'Orcival (1146–1178) was one of the most famous. It's delightfully solid and secure. Nothing has been done to this church but a few repairs after an earthquake and some reinforcing of the spire after damage during the French Revolution. The church is original, even to the hinges on the doors. It is dark inside, but do step in; the door is always open to the pilgrim. Notice how rays of light fall upon the choir and the most unusual statue of the Virgin carrying an adult-looking child. This is a church with personality and warmth, attributes often lacking in the grander and more ornate churches of France.

From Orcival, take D27, which joins D983, for a beautiful run over the pass Col de Guery at 1,268 meters (4,160 feet). As the descent starts into Le Mont-Dore, a former Roman spa town and now a convenient but not particularly attractive summer and winter resort base, take a

⓫ left on D996 to **St-Nectaire.** Here, in the upper part of the village, stands another Romanesque hospice. You may want to stop in and give thanks after the dramatic drive over the passes. Then find a market, so you can try the local cheese. St-Nectaire produces a superb, soft, nutty-tasting cheese, named after the saint, that has been made since the 3rd century. If you are here on Monday, go to the next village, Besse-et-St-Anastiase, for the area's cheese market. Only then may you begin to understand the wheel of life in rural Auvergne!

⑫ D978 south takes you into **Besse,** an old village that's now a popular
⑬ winter-sports center and, a few miles farther, to **Lake Pavin,** one of the most beautiful, classic caldera lakes of the Auvergne. For all its perfect symmetry, it is a mysterious lake: Its name supposedly derives from the Latin *pavens,* meaning frightening. Anglers, though, don't seem to mind. They come here to fish for mammoth-size trout called *omble chevalier*—delicious in the hands of a good chef.

The route south is splendid as you take D978 over the Monts du Cantal, through Condat and Riom-les-Montagnes. It becomes even more dramatic when at Riom, instead of continuing to Mauriac, you take
⑭ D62 to climb **Pas de Peyrol,** the Auvergne's highest pass, at nearly 1,600 meters (5,249 feet). Leave your car in the parking spot here, and make
★ the 30-minute walk to the summit of **Puy Mary.** The views are tremendous: Thirteen valleys radiate from the mountain, funneling their streams to some of France's major rivers. Puy Mary's summit is surely where Satan tempted Christ, though; in fact, the mountain is named after St-Marius, who converted the locals to Christianity. Now take D680 west through the Cirque de Falgoux, another splendidly scenic route, whose twists and turns will take all the driver's attention.

★ ⑮ **Salers,** perched on a ledge above the valley of the Maronne, has become a tourist town indeed, but its medievalism is so attractive and its defensive position so secure, it cannot fail to seduce you. Isolated Salers was permitted to build ramparts against roaming brigands and, subsequently, won the right to govern itself. The compact, self-contained town prospered and has left for future generations good-looking, well-made 15th- and 16th-century houses, built in black lava stone, with turrets and gables.

The charming Grande Place, in the heart of the village, is where locals and tourists congregate, and from here narrow streets radiate to the ramparts. The town has lots of little boutiques (mostly of artisans) and small restaurants occupying the ground floor of the medieval houses. Salers is, indeed, a good choice as a base for roaming the countryside. It was once an important cattle-market town for the rough hairy-coated Salers breed, famous throughout France. On market days the population still swells, but nowadays residents are fewer than 800 and farming plays a smaller role than tourism—even though you can still be woken up on a spring or autumn night by the sound of cowbells as the herds are moved between the valleys and the mountains.

⑯ The major town of **Aurillac** is just a 30-minute drive away, at the edge of the Monts du Cantal. As the prefecture, Aurillac bustles during the day but at night becomes a sleepy country town. It is a comfortable, friendly place, but there's little to see; the old part of town is very small, with twisting narrow streets along the banks of the River Jordanne. The **Musée d'Art et d'Archéologie** exhibits finds like the remains of a Gallo-Roman temple, objects from the Middle Ages, and 17th-century religious paintings. It has also a unique collection of the plastic arts and a collection of umbrellas from the past three centuries—about half of all French umbrellas are made in Aurillac. *Centre Pierre Mendès-France, 37 rue des Carmes,* ☎ *71–45–46–10.* ☛ *12 frs.* ☉ *Apr.–Oct., Mon.–Sat. 10–noon and 2–6 (daily July and Aug.).*

Further activity will entail sitting and relaxing at a café in place du Palais-de-Justice, the main square after you call at the tourist office for information, free maps, and brochures on Cantal and the Haute-Auvergne.

From Aurillac, take N120 west as far as Laroquebrou and pick up D653 to Sousceyrac, then D673, which twists and turns attractively to St-Cléré. You are now on the Causses de Gramat, the extensive limestone plateau where stubby trees claw the white-gray earth, struggling to keep ★ ⑰ a roothold. Don't go into Gramat, but continue on D673 into **Rocamadour,** a medieval village that seems to defy the laws of gravity as it surges out of a cliff 465 meters (1,500 feet) above the Alzou River gorge.

Rocamadour got its name after the miraculous discovery in 1166 of the body of St-Amadour "quite whole" under a sanctuary. (This was a major event: Amadour had died a thousand years earlier and was allegedly none other than Zaccheus, the tax collector of Jericho, who had come to live in Gaul as a hermit after Christ persuaded him to give up his money-grubbing ways.) Amadour's body was moved into the church, displayed to pilgrims, and began to work miracles. Its fame soon spread to Portugal, Spain, and Sicily, and pilgrims flocked to the site, climbing the 216 steps up to the church on their knees. Making the climb on foot is sufficient reminder of the medieval penchant for agonizing penance, and today an elevator lifts weary souls.

In the summer the village is mobbed and cars are prohibited. Park in one of the car parks (if you're very lucky, you'll find a spot in the small lot just outside the village gates). The staircase and elevator start from place de la Carreta; those on foot can pause at a landing after the first 141 steps to admire the Fort, as the 14th-century Bishop's Palace is invitingly called. The steps and the elevator lead to tiny place St-Amadour and its seven sanctuaries: the basilica of **St-Sauveur** opposite the staircase; the **St-Amadour crypt** under the basilica; the chapel of **Notre-Dame** to the left; the chapels of **John the Baptist, St-Blaise,** and **Ste-Anne** to the right; and the Romanesque chapel of **St-Michel,** built into an overhanging cliff. St-Michel's two 12th-century frescoes—depicting the Annunciation and the Visitation—have survived in superb condition. *Centre d'Accueil Notre-Dame. English-speaking guide available. Guided tours Mon.–Sat. 9–5; tips at visitors' discretion.*

The village itself is full of beautifully restored medieval houses. One of the finest is the 15th-century **Hôtel de Ville** (Town Hall), near the Porte Salmon, which also houses the tourist office and an excellent collection of tapestries. ☞ *Free.* ⊙ *Mon.–Sat. 10–noon and 3–8.*

⑱ From Rocamadour, take D673, 19 winding kilometers (12 miles) west to Peyrac, then N20 south to **Cahors,** 41 kilometers (26 miles) farther. Once an opulent Gallo-Roman town, Cahors sits snugly within a loop of the River Lot. The town is perhaps best known for its tannic red wine—often, in fact, a deep purple—known to the Romans as black wine, which you can taste at many of the small estates nearby. The finest sight in Cahors is the Pont Valentré, a spellbinding feat of medieval engineering whose tall, elegant towers have guarded the river since 1360.

Rue du Président-Wilson cuts across town from the bridge to the old quarter of Cahors around the Cathedral of St-Etienne, easily recognized by its cupolas and fortresslike appearance. The tympanum over the north door was sculpted around 1135, with figures portraying the Ascension and the life of St-Etienne. The cloisters, to the right of the choir, contain a corner pillar embellished with a charmingly sculpted Annunciation Virgin with long, flowing hair. The cloisters connect with the courtyard of the archdeaconry, awash with Renaissance decoration and thronged with visitors looking at its temporary art exhibits.

Leave Cahors in the direction of Figeac on D653; then after 8 kilometers (5 miles) turn right on D662 and continue to follow the River Lot, until a sign for **St-Cirq-Lapopie** (pronounced "sincere") directs you over a narrow one-lane bridge. Then the climb begins to the village, 262 feet up on a rocky spur with nothing but a vertical drop below. This spot—a choice one for any baron wanting to command the valley—owes its name to young St-Cyr, who was killed with his mother in Asia Minor during the reign of Diocletian. The Lapopie part of the name was attached in the Middle Ages, when that family, the local lords, built their castle at the highest point. You can reach the castle, much of it in ruins now, by a stiff walk along the path leading from beside the town hall. The château in the village houses the tourist office. St-Cirq-Lapopie is now an artisan town with more crafts shops and studio workshops than you'll ever want to visit. But the streets are so charming—the village has not yet been renovated à la Disney—and the views so dramatic, you'll want to spend several hours here.

D662 continues to Cajarc, which will put you onto D19 for the run into **Figeac.** This charming old town, with a lively Saturday-morning market, grew up around an abbey in the 9th century, becoming, in turn, a stopping point for pilgrims slouching toward Compostela. Many houses in the old part of town, from the 13th, 14th, and 15th centuries, have been carefully restored to preserve their octagonal chimneys, rounded archways and arcades, and *soleilhos,* open attics used for drying flowers and wood. The 13th-century **Hôtel de la Monnaie,** a block from the River Célé, is a characteristic example, an elegant building probably used as a medieval money-changing office. These days it houses the tourist office and a museum displaying fragments of sculpture and religious relics found in the town. *Pl. Vival,* ☎ *65–34–06–25.* ☛ *Free.* ⊙ *July–Aug., daily 10–noon and 2:30–6:30; Sept.–June, Mon.–Sat. 3–5.*

Figeac was the birthplace of Jean-François Champollion (1790–1830), one of the men who first deciphered Egyptian hieroglyphic script. The **Musée Champollion** (leave place Vival on rue 11-Novembre, take the first left, and follow it as it bends right) contains a casting of the Rosetta stone, discovered in the Nile delta. The stone's three renderings of the same inscription—in hieroglyphic and demotic Egyptian and in ancient Greek—enabled the mysteries of the Pharaonic dialect to be penetrated for the first time. On the ground floor, a film traces Champollion's life. *5 impasse Champollion,* ☎ *65–34–66–18.* ☛ *22 frs, 14 frs children.* ⊙ *May–Sept., Tues.–Sat. 10–noon and 2:30–6:30.*

Leave Figeac on the road to Rodez and take the small D52, on your left, up the beautiful Lot Valley to D901, which goes south to **Conques.** The pretty, ocher-red houses here harmonize perfectly with the surrounding rocky gorge, but Conques is more than just a picturesque village; it holds the outstanding Romanesque church of **Ste-Foy,** one of the principal stopping points on the pilgrimage route between Le Puy and Santiago de Compostela. Begun in the early 11th century, Ste-Foy had its heyday in the 12th and 13th centuries, though the flood of pilgrims and their revenue eventually dried up. In 1561, at the onset of the Wars of Religion, it was devastated by Huguenot hordes; then it languished until the 19th century, when the writer Prosper Mérimée, a lover of historic monuments, raised the money to salvage it.

Ste-Foy clings to a hill so steep that even driving and walking—let alone building—are precarious. First note the intensely dramatic Last Judgment, carved over the main portal in the 12th century. The church's interior is high and dignified; the ambulatory was given a lot of wear by medieval pilgrims, who admired the church's most precious relic, a 10th-century wooden statue of Ste-Foy, encrusted with gold and precious stones. Latter-day visitors can see it in the treasury, off the recently restored cloister. Other gold and silver relics testify to the presence of skilled metalworkers in Conques from the 9th to the 14th century. The **Musée Docteur Joséph-Fau** (Trésor II), opposite the pilgrims' fountain near the church, houses furniture, statues, tapestries, and sculpture. ☞ *22 frs adults, 16 frs children.* ☉ *Sept.–June, Mon.–Sat. 9–noon and 2–6, Sun. 2–6; July–Aug., Mon.–Sat. 9–noon and 2–7, Sun. 2–7.*

㉒ Stay on D901 for 35 kilometers (22 miles) to **Rodez,** capital of the Aveyron, on a windswept hill between the arid Causses plateau and the verdant Ségala hills. On top of the hill towers the pink sandstone cathedral of **Notre-Dame** (13th–15th centuries). Its awesome bulk is lightened by decorative upper stories, completed in the 17th century, and by the magnificent 285-foot bell tower. The interior contains ornamental altarpieces, an elaborate 15th-century choir screen, and a 17th-century organ within an intricate wooden casing.

The renovated Cité quarter, once ruled by medieval bishops, lies behind the cathedral; attractive pedestrian zones surround place du Bourg. On tiny place de l'Olmet, just off place du Bourg, stands the 16th-century House of Armagnac, a fine Renaissance mansion with a courtyard and an ornate facade covered with medallion emblems of the counts of Rodez. The 18th-century church of **St-Amans,** at place de la Madeleine, has finely preserved Romanesque capitals and some colorful 16th-century tapestries. The extensively modernized **Musée Denys Puech,** an art gallery exhibiting works by painters and sculptors from the area, lies just east of the wide boulevard that encircles the old town. *Pl. Clemenceau,* ☎ *65–42–70–64.* ☞ *17 frs adults, 12 frs children under 18 (free Wed.).* ☉ *Mon. 2–8, Wed.–Sat. 10–noon and 3–7, Sun. 3–7.*

㉓ Leave N88 for D28, a shorter and prettier route to **Millau,** less than 60 kilometers (35 miles) away. In Roman times, Millau produced pottery, sending its vases as far afield as Scotland. Some of these artifacts, collected from the nearby archaeological site, are shown at the **Musée de Millau** along with the displays of the city's more recent glove-making industry. *Hôtel de Pégayrolles, pl. Foch,* ☎ *65–59–01–08.* ☞ *22 frs adults, 17 frs children.* ☉ *Daily Apr.–Sept., 10–noon and 2–6; Oct.–Mar., closed Sun. and holidays.*

Give yourself a little time to wander in the old quarter, especially around place du Maréchal-Foch, with its 800-year-old arcades. The later Church of Notre-Dame, built on the site of a Roman temple, is only marginally interesting. Browse through the shops around place des Mandarous and place de la Tine for leather goods. The leather trade developed as a by-product of all those sheep, exhausted from producing milk for all that Roquefort, most famous of French cheeses.

So widely sought after is this cheese that the milk from local sheep is not enough—30% of it now comes from the Pyrénées and Corsica. Foul play, you may say, but what makes Roquefort is not the milk but the place it is stored and infected with the bacteria! It becomes Roquefort and carries that name only after being stored in the seven levels of the ㉔ caves at nearby **Roquefort-sur-Soulzon.** These caves, home to the *penicillum glaucum roquefortii,* stay year-round between 7°C and 9°C, the temperature that the penicillum likes. These happy bacteria float through the air to inoculate the cheeses during their three-month stay.

Take a sweater. ☎ 65–58–59–58. ☛ *Guided tour: 15 frs adults.* ⊘ *Daily July–Aug. 9:30–6; Sept.–June 9:30–11:30 and 2–5.*

★ ㉕ Millau is a jumping-off point to a geographical splendor—the **Gorges du Tarn.** Though not as awesome as the Grand Canyon, the Gorges du Tarn has an intimate beauty and frequent dramatic sights. Fifty years ago, you could come across it only from the high plateau, seeing it as a giant crack in the earth's crust. Today a road leads you into its mouth, running along its 80 kilometers (48 miles), 600 meters (1,968 feet) below the cliff top. It's a slow run in July and August, when French families ride through bumper to bumper.

The gorge begins at **Le Rozier,** 16 kilometers (10 miles) northeast of Millau on D907. Here you take D907b, and here the Tarn, flowing out of the gorge, is joined by the Jonte, flowing out of its own gorge. Here, too, some good full-day hikes begin, to the cliffs above for marvelous views. But if you continue to Les Vignes, where the gorge opens into a little valley, you can go to the top on D995, up some arm-wrenching switchbacks to Causse de Sauveterre, and then right onto D46 to St-Georges-de-Léyéjac. Follow the sign for Point Sublime, and you'll find views that justify the name.

After Les Vignes, the gorge becomes the most dramatic, with sheer cliffs rising vertically and the rock face dappled with grays, whites, and blues. In summer, you can take a boat through this stretch. Leave your car at the disembarkation point; a bus will take you to where you board the rafts. Just before Malène, you will reach the **Cirque des Baumes,** where the cliffs form a natural amphitheater; then comes Les Détroits, the narrowest part, where the tumbling waters foam through.

After La Malène, you'll notice the medieval-looking Château de la Caze, with its imposing array of turrets, built in the 15th century. Today it is a luxury hotel (*see* Lodging, *below*). Beyond this, just before the village of St-Chély-du-Tarn, is the Cirque de Pournadoires and, diagonally opposite, a larger natural amphitheater. In summer, the gorge is floodlit nightly with a son-et-lumière show. But don't make a point of seeing it; the gorge looks far more beautiful under natural light.

The next village, **Ste-Énimie,** is the gorge's major resort, rather mired in summer by the flood of tourists and vendors. In the little church, ceramic tiles tell the charming 7th-century legend of Ste-Énimie, the beautiful sister of Dagobert, king of the Franks. When she was about to marry, she suddenly fell ill with leprosy, and her suitor no longer wanted her. Off she went in search of a cure and, on the advice of an angel, sought the fountain of Burle. She was immediately cured, but on her way home she fell sick again. Back she went to the fountain and was cured again, but each time she tried to leave, the same events occurred. Finally she understood that God wished her to stay, so she set up a convent there, devoting her life to charity until she died in AD 628. The ruins of the convent can still be seen, as can the fountain of Burle.

★ From there continue on 907b to Florac, a small market town where campers buy supplies. Pick up the road known as the **Corniche des Cévennes** for its spectacular scenery. First take D907, and then fork left on D983 to St-Laurent-de-Trèves. Now the road winds up the Col du Rey to where the Corniche rides high above the valley and, where high on this plateau, dinosaurs lived 190 million years ago. The trip is less than 50 kilometers (30 miles) but crammed with wonderful vistas until you drop down into **St-Jean-du-Gard** on the banks of the Gardon River. The small but interesting **Musée des Vallées Cévenoles,** housed in an old coaching inn, celebrates the town's silk industry and the mulberry and chestnut trees, upon which it once depended. Hard times came with imports from abroad, and today only a few bolts of Cévennes's silk make their way to the Paris couture market. ☎ *66–85–10–48.* ☛ *12 frs.* ⏲ *June–Sept., Tues.–Sat. 9–noon and 2–5. Sun. 2–5.*

27 Continue southeast to **Anduze,** once a Huguenot stronghold whose fortifications were so mighty that Louis XIII left it alone and sacked nearby Alès instead. The peace treaty stipulated that Anduze's fortifications be torn down, so only the 14th-century Tour d'Horloge remains. With its history gone, Anduze is simply the last pretty village of this tour, only 60 kilometers (36 miles) from Nîmes and the Mediterranean.

SPORTS AND THE OUTDOORS

Ballooning

From April to November you can float through the skies above the volcanoes. Most flights last a little over an hour, but the total excursion, which includes inflation and deflation, can take the better part of a morning or afternoon. Contact **Objectif** (☎ 73–35–32–01).

Bicycling

The best way to explore the real heart of the Auvergne is by following the country roads. Bicycles may be rented from railway stations and mountain bikes for the Gorges du Tarn from **William Orts** (21 blvd. de l'Ayrolle, Millau, ☎ 65–61–14–29).

Rafting

There is rafting down the Gorges de l'Allier and Gorges du Tarn from April through October. Rafts and canoes may be rented on site. For longer trips, contact **Service Loisirs** (Haute-Loire, ☎ 61–09–20–80) or **Association Le Merlet** (Route de Nîmes, St-Jean du Gard, ☎ 66–85–18–19).

DINING AND LODGING

Dining

A few Massif Central specialties are *aligot,* a puree of potatoes with Tomme de Cantal cheese, cream, garlic and butter; *cousinat,* a chestnut soup; *sanflorin,* fried pork and herbs in pastry; and *salmis de colvert Cévenole,* wild duck sautéed in red wine and onions. The region also produces Roquefort cheese; Bleu d'Auvergne, similar to Roquefort and delightfully creamy; Cantal, made from cow's milk, the best of which comes from Salers; Tomme de Cantal, from fresh, unfermented cow's milk; little-known Gaperon, made with garlic; and soft St-Nectaire, which has a delightful nutty flavor.

CATEGORY	COST*
$$$$	over 400 frs
$$$	250–400 frs
$$	125–250 frs
$	under 125 frs

**per person for a three course meal, including tax (18.6%) and tip but not wine*

Lodging

Until recently the Massif Central was off the beaten track, so the choice of accommodations is relatively small. The large towns have modest hotels whose main clientele are business travelers. The smaller tourist areas have small hotels and many bed-and-breakfast farm-houses. You'll need reservations for July and August, and you will pay premium rates. Many hotels close from November through March.

CATEGORY	COST*
$$$$	over 800 frs
$$$	550–800 frs
$$	300–550 frs
$	under 300 frs

All prices are for a standard double room for two, including tax (18.6%) and service charge.

Anduze

DINING AND LODGING

La Ranquet. A hilly, wooded setting; a swimming pool; a piano bar; and the comfortable, spacious air-conditioned rooms are just part of the reason for staying here. Annie Majourel is one of the few top-ranking female chefs in France; her menus (two moderately priced) change every two months, but you can expect such delightful meals as rillettes of rabbit, shoulder of lamb stuffed with herbs, and orange praline mousse with hot chocolate sauce. Tornac is 6 kilometers (4 miles) southwest of Anduze and is a good end or beginning for this tour. The mid-June–mid-September rate (750 frs) is rather high. ⌨ *Rte. de St-Hippolyte, 30140 Tornac,* ☎ *66–77–51–63,* ℻ *66–77–55–62. 10 rooms with bath. Restaurant, bar, pool. Closed Tues. and Wed. out of season, mid-Nov.–Dec. 25, and Feb. $$–$$$*

Aurillac

DINING

Le Bistro. For genuine local Auvergne grub come here. The decor is nonexistent (formica tables, marble-tile floors, and a long bar); the staff and clientele are young; the food is uncomplicated but good. Two fine regional specialties are *truffade* (sautéed sliced potatoes covered with melted cheese) and *choux farci* (stuffed cabbage). ✗ *23 rue Gambetta,* ☎ *71–48–01–04. No reservations. MC, V. $*

Poivre & Sel. This intimately small and friendly bistro, owned by Thierry and Cecile Perbet (Thierry in the kitchen), serves a refined version of Auvergne fare. It is a good place to try Salers beef, which rivals Charolais as the best in France, as well as other such regional dishes as *salmis de colvert Cévenole* (duck) and lightly grilled fresh trout. ✗ *4 Rte. du 14-Juillet,* ☎ *71–64–20–20. Closed Mon. MC, V. $$*

LODGING

Grand Hotel de Bordeaux. There are three advantages to this Best Western hotel: Its central location near the Palais de Justice, a private garage at its rear, and the fact that it has no restaurant. This leaves you free to try the local eateries, unless you order from the very reasonably priced room-service menu. The guest rooms are clean, functional, and adequate, even if compact. The staff is extremely helpful and very willing to inform you about the region, its foods, and the best places to explore. ⌨ *2 av. de la République, 15000,* ☎ *71–48–01–84,* ℻ *71–48–49–93. 33 rooms. bar. $$*

Bort les Orgues

LODGING

★ **Château de Bassignac.** This sturdy fortified manor from the 16th century has just four rooms, decorated with an assortment of family antiques. Bassignac is still a working farm, the running of which is left to the son. M. and Mme. Besson receive the guests and on request will prepare great farmhouse dinners, which you might eat in the kitchen with the family.

M. Besson, a painter by vocation, speaks English well. This is a place for warm Auvergne hospitality, where you sit in the evening sipping wine, chatting before a log fire, and running the risk of becoming friends with your hosts. The château is on the edge of the tiny village of Bassignac, 14½ kilometers (9 miles) southwest of Bort-les-Orgues. ⌂ *15240 Bassignac,* ☎ *71–40–82–82. 4 rooms. Table d'hôte dinner with reservations. Fishing.* ☉ *Easter–Nov., in winter by reservation. $$*

Bourges

DINING AND LODGING

Central et Angleterre. This efficient hotel in the center of town, close to the Palais Jacques Coeur, is popular with business travelers. The interior has been carefully renovated and rooms given modern conveniences, from tiled bathrooms to direct-dial telephones and minibars. The restaurant, whose menus start at 120 francs, is quite sedate, done in the style of Louis XVI. The American bar off the lobby is a comfortable place to sit before or after dinner. ⌂ *1 pl. des Quatre-Piliers, 18000 Bourges,* ☎ *48–24–68–51,* ⨳ *48–65–21–41. 31 rooms. Restaurant. AE, DC, MC, V. $$*

Cahors

DINING

Le Coq & La Pendule. This small, café-restaurant, in a pedestrian street near the cathedral, is a classic example of homey French cooking in a down-to-earth setting. Space is tight and it's all hustle-bustle, but service is friendly, portions are generous, and a five-course meal with wine and coffee won't cost much more than 70 francs. ✗ *10 rue St-James,* ☎ *65–35–28–84. No credit cards. $*

DINING AND LODGING

Château de Mercuès. The former home of the counts of Cahors, built in the 13th century, lies 6 kilometers (4 miles) west of town on the road to Villleneuve-sur-Lot. The older guest rooms display some of the baronial splendor you might expect, though the newer ones on the ground floor are simply boring modern, with paisley and pastel fabrics. The most exciting rooms are L'Evêque (bishop) and Tour (turret). The latter has a unique ceiling that slides back to expose the shaft of the turret, supported by ancient cross beams. Duck, lamb, and truffles reign in the restaurant, but the high prices lead you to expect more creativity than the kitchen produces. You should try the wine the hotel bottles under its own name, and also visit the wine cellar, which is actually under the front lawn. ⌂ *46090 Mercuès,* ☎ *65–20–00–01,* ⨳ *65–20–05–72. 25 rooms and 9 suites, all with bath. Restaurant, pool, tennis, helipad. AE, DC, MC, V. Closed Nov.–mid-Mar. $$$–$$$$*

Terminus. This small, ivy-covered hotel is deep in the heart of truffle country yet just two minutes' walk from Cahors's train station. Its restaurant, La Balandre, is the city's best. The decor is mainly Roaring '20s, and the atmosphere is comfortably traditional, emphasized by filtered light from the stained-glass windows in the lobby. Gilles Marre and his wife, Jacqueline, specialize in truffles but also serve an exceptional fresh cod *brandade* (mousse) and foie gras in flaky pastry. There is a good selection of local wines, and the service is professional yet friendly. The rooms are cozily traditional. ⌂ *5 av. Charles-de-Freycinet, 46000,* ☎ *65–35–24–50,* ⨳ *65–37–95–93. 31 rooms with bath. Restaurant: reservations advised; closed 2 wks in Feb., 1 wk in June, Sun. dinner and Mon. Jan.–Mar., and Sat. lunch July–Aug. AE, MC, V. $$*

Clermont-Ferrand

DINING

Bernard Audrieux. Chef Bernard Audrieux gained a reputation and his first Michelin star when he cooked at his Auberges des Touristes; now he has changed his location and uses his name. His dishes are deceptively simple: The salmon with a truffle sauce is visually appealing, and its juxtaposition of flavors excites your palate with every bite. Try also the *escalope de foie chaud de canard* (sliced hot duck liver) with Thai-accented herbs and the ravioli of crab and lobster with a seafood coulis. The restaurant's tasteful modern decor—cream walls, white linens, well-spaced tables—does not interfere with your concentration on the fine food. The service is similarly discreet. All this elegance contrasts with the rather dowdy suburban location 3 kilometers (2 miles) northwest of town on D641A. ✗ *Rte. de la Baroque, ☎ 73–37–00–26. Reservations advised. Closed Sat. lunch, Sun., 1 wk in Feb., first wk in May, and July 20–Aug. 20. AE, DC, MC, V. $$$*

LODGING

Hotel de Lyon. This is a very down-to-earth city hotel in the center of town. Convenience is its chief benefit, but the rooms have been recently renovated and are clean. Service is perfunctory but efficient. ☎ *16 pl. de Jaude, 63000 Clermont-Ferrand, ☎ 73–93–92–55, FAX 73–93–54–33. 32 rooms with bath. Restaurant. MC, V. $$*

Ispagnac

DINING AND LODGING

Le Vallon. In this tourist town at the edge of Gorges du Tarn, restaurants cater mostly to the summer trade. Le Vallon, though, is a local and serves the village all year. That explains why the price is so reasonable and the fare so hearty. For 85 francs you get four courses, which might include an omelet, a salad, a casserole, and cheese. For another 8 francs a half carafe of local wine will be included. In summer you can dine on the terrace, from which you look down on the valley and the village, though not the gorge. Le Vallon also has simple, clean guest rooms at reasonable prices. Choose those at the back, away from the road. ☎ *Rte. D907B, 48320 Ispagnac, ☎ 66–44–21–24. 24 rooms, most with bath. Restaurant, bar. MC, V. $*

Millau

DINING AND LODGING

Château de Creissels. In an ancient 12th-century fort 3 kilometers (2 miles) from Millau on D992, this hotel was extensively renovated and enlarged in 1990. It is now a very comfortable base for exploring the Gorges du Tarn and the Grand Causse. Guest rooms are neatly furnished in simple country style. Fifteen are in the old building; the others are modern. The charming dining room is in a vaulted cellar, full of medieval atmosphere. For relaxing, there are marvelous shaded gardens and a park. ☎ *Rte de Ste-Affrique, 12100 Millau, ☎ 65–60–31–79, FAX 65–61–24–63. 31 rooms, 26 with bath or shower. Restaurant. Closed mid-Dec.–Feb. 10. MC, V. $$*

Mont Dore

DINING

Le Boeuf dans l'Assiette. This simple restaurant, with yellow tablecloths and large plate-glass windows looking onto the center of town, does not pretend to offer more than honest fare for the skier or hiker whose appetite is ravenous. With a three-course menu, a bottle of local St-Pourçain wine, and coffee, two people can replenish their energies for less than 175 francs. Beef is the restaurant's speciality, but fish and salads are also served. ✗ *9 av. Michel-Bertrand, ☎ 73–65–01–23. MC, V. $*

Meyrueis

DINING AND LODGING

Château d'Ayres. This grand building, whose origins are from the 12th century, is surrounded by trees on 12 acres, with a small reflecting lake. The manor house of today dates from the 18th century, and, notwithstanding the fact that General de Gaulle once stayed here, the hotel is full of charm. The spacious guest rooms are furnished with antiques, and the reception rooms resemble those in a country house. Traditional family recipes are prepared by Mme. de Montjou and her son, Thibault. The cèpe quiche, the terrine of fresh duck foie gras made on the premises, and the confit of duck are fine fare after a day's exploring. ☎ *Rte. d'Ayres, 48150 Meyrueis,* ☎ *66–45–60–10,* FAX *66–45–62–26. 24 rooms and 3 suites with bath. Restaurant, pool, tennis, horseback riding. Closed mid-Nov.–late Mar. AE, DC, MC, V. $$*

Plaisance

DINING AND LODGING

★ **Les Magnolias.** This 14th-century village inn combines rustic charm with up-to-date comfort and sophisticated regional cooking from the jocular, mustached patron, Francis Roussel. Out of season he can be found lecturing Parisians on how to concoct that archetypal southwestern delicacy, foie gras. Sample his, and Roussel will be only too happy to divulge a few trade secrets. He has a flair for finding tastes that complement each other; his wonderful grilled cheese in a duck bouillon is an example, as is his *sandre* (a white fish) in a red wine sauce. Try also his cod in garlic and parsley, then walk it all off beneath the magnolias in the garden. The wine list contains excellent labels from the region, including Domaine de Labarthe, a Gailliac that can stand up to the top wines of Cahors. The ambience of Les Magnolias is wonderfully medieval, with oak beams, flagstone halls, stone staircases, and paneled walls. The comfortable guest rooms are simple and slightly eclectic—nice to come home to after exploring this beautiful part of France east of Albi. This is an exceptionally good value. ☎ *12550 Plaisance,* ☎ *65–99–77–34,* FAX *65–99–70–57. 6 rooms with bath or shower. Restaurant. AE, MC, V. Closed mid-Nov.–mid-Mar. $$*

Rocamadour

DINING AND LODGING

Le Beau Site. How often can you spend the night in a medieval village clinging to a rock face? This is the best hotel of the few in the old town (where you really want to stay), and it has ordinary but comfortable rooms, many with wonderful views, and a staff that's helpful and friendly. The antique charm of the ancient beams, exposed stone, and open hearth in the foyer ends as you climb the stairs; the bedrooms are modern and functional. (Avoid the three new rooms at the back; they have little sunlight and no view.) Staying here, with the convenience of being able to drive in and park (nonresidents can't bring in cars), and the pleasure of dinner overlooking the canyon help make Rocamadour a memorable experience. ☎ *Cité Médiévale, 46500,* ☎ *65–33–63–08,* FAX *65–33–65–23. 55 rooms with bath or shower. Restaurant. MC, V. Closed mid-Dec.–mid-Jan. $$*

Rodez

DINING AND LODGING

★ **La Diligence.** Expect to hear more about Joel Delmas, the chef and part-owner, with Jean-Claude Lausset, of this new hotel and restaurant 10 kilometers (6 miles) northwest of town. Delmas's talent and creativity have not been shaped by studying under great chefs or attending school but by the sheer joy of cooking. Of special note are the sauces that add an exciting taste to fish, where even well-known chefs often fail. Also a succulent millefeuille of lamb kidneys with a delicate, sensuous brown sauce, a suprême of volaille with a light cream dressing, and a superb banana coconut tart in an airy custard. Equally impressive are the prices: Prix-fixe lunch menus start at 89 francs and four-course dinner menus at 125 francs. La Diligence has six small guest rooms furnished in modern style, with either bath or shower—not luxurious but adequate and extremely modestly priced. ⌆ *12000 Marcillac-Vallon,* ☎ *65–72–60–20. 6 rooms with bath. Restaurant (reservations advised); closed Tues. dinner and Wed. Hotel closed Jan., first two wks of Sept. MC, V. $–$$*

St-Amand-Montrond

★ **Château de la Commanderie.** This impressive château with an ivy-clad newer house alongside was built in the 11th century, but it looks late-17th to early 18th. The interior is extremely well maintained, with new fabrics and carpets, fresh-looking bathrooms, and good-quality antiques. Rooms are large and elegantly furnished. You will meet your hosts, the Comte and Comtesse de Jouffrey-Gonsans, for an aperitif and lively conversation in the drawing room before going into the paneled dining room, hung with tapestries and portraits. The food is well-prepared family fare—often with perfectly aged Charolais beef—and the wine is always appropriate for each dish. ⌆ *Farges-Allichamps, 18200,* ☎ *48–61–04–19, ꜰᴀx 48–61–01–84. 7 rooms and 1 suite, all with bath. Reservations required for dinner. MC, V. $$$–$$$$*

Salers
DINING AND LODGING

Hostellerie de la Maronne. Six kilometers (4 miles) southwest of Salers on D35 stands this delightful, old Auvergne house converted into a hotel. The guest rooms are furnished in country style, simple and cozy. The meals pay homage to the land, with fresh summer produce, roast pigeon in wine sauce, and always the best Salers beef. If you are staying more than one day, ask for a room rate only, as there are good restaurants in the village nearby. ⌆ *St-Martin Valmeroux, 15410 Salers,* ☎ *71–69–20–33, ꜰᴀx 71–69–28–22. 24 rooms with bath. Restaurant (closed Wed. lunch). Hotel and restaurant closed mid-Nov.–late- Mar. AE, MC, V. $$–$$$*

Hotel des Remparts. This hotel, at the edge of the village on top of the ramparts, offers the best in panoramic views. The rooms are simple and functional, and those with the view command a higher price. Management likes to quote half-pension rates, but you should resist that if you are staying more than one night. ⌆ *Esplanade de Barrouze, 15410 Salers,* ☎ *71–40–70–33, ꜰᴀx 71–40–75–32. 18 rooms. Restaurant. Closed Oct. 20–Dec. 20. MC, V. $$*

Souvigny
DINING

★ **Auberge des Tilleuls.** In an old town house on a small square near the abbey, Christian Letolle and his wife, Lydia, offer an inspired cuisine and exceptionally reasonable prices. In summer, you take aperitifs on the terrace before entering the small dining room, where a pair of old oil paintings humorously depicts village scenes. A teasing sense of humor is also felt behind Christian's delightful cooking—innovative and playful. The *noix St-Jacques,* (sautéed scallops) titillate your taste buds, and the hearty beef casserole has a zesty rich sauce. Menus at lunch start at 70 francs; at dinner they begin at 118 francs. Pick a table by the window looking out on the square. ✗ *Pl. St-Eloi, 03210.* ☎ *70–43–60–70. Reservations advised. Closed Mon. MC, V. $*

Target

LODGING

Château de Boussac. Although the turrets and moat suggest its defensive past, you'll know you're in the gentrified France of today when you stay at this comfortable and fully modernized chateau. The Marquis and Marquise de Longueil entertain their guests with aperitifs before sitting down to dinner. His colonial tales of Mozambique are a bit tendentious, but she is warm and open. Lovely breakfasts are served in your room, which is furnished in heirloom antiques, with new draperies and carpets from the best Parisian stores. The property is a working Charolais cattle farm, deep in the countryside and sublimely quiet. ⊞ *Target, 03140 Chantelle,* ☎ *70–40–63–20,* FAX *70–40–60–03. 4 rooms. Table d'hôte dinner with reservations.* ☺ *Apr.–Nov. MC, V. $$$*

Vichy

DINING

L'Alambic. Jean-Jacques Barbot, chef and owner here and a bear of a man, is a master at bringing out the flavor of products from his native Auvergne. Barbot grills salmon trout from nearby streams with endives and an anise-based sauce and bakes his sandre (white fish) with a mustard coating. Be sure to try his lentil salad—the tiny *lentilles de Puy* are famous in their own right. The restaurant is tiny, intimate, and full of bonhomie created not just by the food but also by Jean-Jacques's wife, Marie-Ange. Menus, based upon what is fresh in the market that day, begin at 160 francs. ✗ *8 rue Nicolas-Larbaud,* ☎ *70–59–12–71. Closed Mon., Tues. lunch, early Mar., and early Sept. MC, V. $$*

DINING AND LODGING

Pavillon Sévigné. Named after the famous marquise, who stayed here in 1676 while visiting the thermal baths nearby (her room is still available for guests), this Relais & Châteaux property is the epitome of elegance. You do need to like Napoléon, though: His portraits are everywhere. Rooms are formal and decorated with the utmost attention to detail, to pamper the guests who have come to take the waters. The sumptuous dining room is decorated with crystal chandeliers, and the food is presented with a flourish, if not prepared with great imagination. ⊞ *50 blvd. Kennedy, 03200 Vichy,* ☎ *70–32–16–22,* FAX *70–59–97–37. 48 rooms with bath. Restaurant. AE, DC, MC, V. $$$$*

Averna Hotel. The old 18th-century structure in the center of town was completely renovated and made a modern hotel in 1991. The result is a convenient place where the price-to-value ratio is excellent. The rooms are modest but quite functional, and the bathrooms kept sparkling clean. ⊞ *12 rue Debrest, 03200 Vichy,* ☎ *70–31–31–19,* FAX *70–97–86–43. 26 rooms with bath. Closed mid-Dec.–Jan. AE, DC, MC, V. $–$$*

MASSIF CENTRAL ESSENTIALS

Arriving and Departing

By Plane

The major airport for the region, at Clermont-Ferrand (☎ 73–62–71–00), has regularly scheduled flights to Paris (Orly), Bordeaux, Dijon, Lyon, Marseille, Nantes, Nice, and Toulouse on **Air France** and **Air Inter** and direct international flights to Geneva, Milan, and London on **Air France, British Airways,** and **Swissair. TAT** (Transport Aérien Transregional) has direct flights from Paris's Orly airport to Rodez (reservations in Paris, ☎ 42–79–05–05; in Rodez, ☎ 65–42–20–30).

By Car

By the A10 autoroute from Paris to Orléans, then by the new A71, it is a fast trip into the center of France. From Paris, Bourges is 229 kilometers (137 miles) and Clermont-Ferrrand 378 kilometers (243 miles). Coming from Lyon, the A72 autoroute makes the 179-kilometer (111-mile) drive take less than 90 minutes.

By Train

The fastest way to get to the Auvergne from Paris is to take the TGV (Gare de Lyon) to Lyon and change for the regular train to Clermont-Ferrand (☎ 73–92–50–50). Regular SNCF trains go from Paris to Bourges and Clermont-Ferrand, and from Nîmes to Clermont-Ferrand.

Getting Around

By Car

There is really only one way to explore the Auvergne, and that is by car. Although national highways will get you from one place to another fairly expediently, the beauty of Auvergne will be discovered on the regional roads that twist through the mountains and along the gorges.

Important Addresses and Numbers

Travel Agencies

Centre Auvergne Tourisme (9 rue Ballainvilliers, 63000 Clermont-Ferrand, ☎ 73–90–10–20), **Voyagers Maisonneuve** (24 rue Georges-Clemenceau, 63000 Clermont-Ferrand, ☎ 73–93–16–72).

Car Rental

The main offices in the region are in Clermont-Ferrand: **Avis** (57 rue Bonnabaud, ☎ 73–93–39–90; and at the airport, ☎ 73–91–18–08); **Hertz** (71 av. de l'Union Soviétique, ☎ 73–92–36–10; and at the airport, ☎ 73–62–71–93), **Europcar** (rue Emile-Loubet and at the airport, ☎ 73–92–70–26).

Visitor Information

The main tourist office is the **Comité Regional du Tourisme** (43 av. Julien, 63011 Clermont-Ferrand, ☎ 73–93–04–03). Local offices are as follows: for **Allier** (35 rue de Bellecroix, 03402 Yzeure, ☎ 70–44–41–57; for **Aveyron** (pl. Maréchal-Foch, 12000 Rodez, ☎ 65–68–02–27); for **Cantal** (Hôtel du Départment, 15018 Aurillac, ☎ 71–46–22–00); for **Haute-Loire** (12 blvd. Phillipe-Jourde, 43005 Le Puy-en-Velay, ☎ 71–09–66–66); for **Lot** (pl. Aristide-Briand, 46000 Cahors, ☎ 65–35–09–56); for **Lozère** (14 blvd. Henri-Bourrillon, 48000 Mende, ☎ 66–65–60–00); for **Puy-de-Dome** (26 rue St-Esprit, 63000 Clermont-Ferrand, ☎ 73–42–21–21).

12 Provence

AS YOU APPROACH Provence, there is a magical moment when the north is finally left behind: Cypresses and red-tile roofs appear; you hear the screech of the cicadas and catch the scent of wild thyme and lavender. Even on the modern highway, oleanders flower on the central strip against a backdrop of harsh, brightly lit landscapes that inspired the paintings of Paul Cézanne and Vincent van Gogh.

Provence lies in the south of France, bordered by Italy to the east and the blue waters of the Mediterranean. The Romans called it Provincia—the Province—for it was the first part of Gaul they occupied. Roman remains litter the ground in well-preserved profusion. The theater and triumphal arch at Orange, the amphitheater at Nîmes, the aqueduct at Pont-du-Gard, and the mausoleum at St-Rémy-de-Provence are considered the best of their kind in existence.

Provençal life continues at an old-fashioned pace. Hot afternoons tend to mean siestas, with signs of life discernible only as the shadows under the *platanes* (plane trees) start to lengthen and lethargic locals saunter out to play *boules* (the French version of bocce) and drink long, cooling *pastis,* an anise-based aperitif.

Provence means dazzling light and rugged, rocky countryside, interspersed with vineyards, fields of lavender, and olive groves. Any Provençal market provides a glimpse of the bewildering variety of olives and herbs cultivated, and the local cuisine is pungently spiced with thyme, rosemary, basil, and garlic.

The famous mistral—a fierce, cold wind that races through the Rhône Valley—is another feature of Provence. It's claimed that the extensive network of expressways has lessened the mistral's effect, but you may have trouble believing this as the wind whistles around your ears. Thankfully, clear blue skies usually follow in its wake.

The Rhône, the great river of southern France, splits in two at Arles, 24 kilometers (15 miles) before reaching the Mediterranean: The Petit Rhône crosses the region known as the Camargue on its way to Stes-Maries-de-la-Mer, while the Grand Rhône heads off to Fos, an industrial port just along the coast from Marseille.

A number of towns have grown up along the Rhône Valley owing to its historical importance as a communications artery. The biggest is dowdy, bustling Marseille; Orange, Avignon, Tarascon, and Arles have more picturesque charm. The Camargue, on the other hand, is the realm of birds and beasts; pink flamingoes and wild horses feel more at home among its marshy wastes than people ever could.

North of Marseille lies Aix-en-Provence, whose old-time elegance reflects its former role as regional capital. We have extended Provence's traditional boundaries westward slightly into Languedoc, to include historic Nîmes and the dynamic university town of Montpellier. The Riviera, meanwhile, is part of Provence—but so full of interest that we devote an entire chapter to it.

EXPLORING

Orientation

We have divided Provence into three exploring tours, each following directly from the other. The marshy Camargue forms the heart of our first tour, which ventures briefly into the Languedoc region to visit the fine old towns of Nîmes and Montpellier before wheeling back to examine the Roman remains at Arles and St-Rémy. The second tour, which falls within the boundaries of the Vaucluse, begins at Avignon, with its papal palace, and ranges north to the Roman towns of Orange and Vaison-la-Romaine; the main natural feature is Mont Ventoux, towering above surrounding plains. The third tour begins in Aix, the historic capital of Provence, then heads south to Marseille and east along the spectacular coast to Toulon.

Tour 1: Nîmes and the Camargue

Numbers in the margin correspond to points of interest on the Provence and Nîmes maps.

★ ❶ The first tour starts with a bridge that symbolically links the 20th century to the Roman grandeur that haunts Provence: the **Pont du Gard,** midway between Avignon and Nîmes off the N86 highway (take D981 at Remoulins; if you arrive by the A9 expressway, take the Remoulins exit).

The Pont du Gard is a huge, three-tiered aqueduct, erected 2,000 years ago as part of a 30-mile canal supplying water to Roman Nîmes. It is astonishingly well preserved. Its setting, spanning a rocky gorge 150 feet above the River Gardon, is nothing less than spectacular. There is no entry fee or guide, and at certain times you can have it all to yourself: Early morning is best, when the honey-colored stone gleams in the sunlight. The best way to gauge the full majesty of the Pont du Gard is to walk right along the top.

TIME OUT In the enchanting little medieval town of Uzès, 14 kilometers (9 miles) northwest via D981, the **Alexandry** restaurant is a good choice for an inexpensive bite to eat. *6 blvd. Gambetta, ☎ 66-22-27-82.*

❷ **Nîmes** lies 20 kilometers (13 miles) southwest of the Pont du Gard (via N86) and 24 kilometers (15 miles) south of Uzès (via D979). Few towns have preserved such visible links with their Roman past: Nemausus, as the town was then known, grew to prominence during the reign of Caesar Augustus (27 BC–AD 14) and still boasts a Roman amphitheater (Arènes), temple (Maison Carrée), and watchtower (Tour Magne). Luckily, these monuments emerged relatively unscathed from the cataclysmic flash flood that devastated Nîmes in 1988, leaving thousands homeless. A 60-franc "passport" (30 frs students), available from the Tourist Office, admits you to all the town's museums and monuments and is valid three days.

★ ❸ Start out at the **Arènes,** which is more than 140 yards long and 110 yards wide, with a seating capacity of 21,000. After a checkered history—it was transformed into a fortress by the Visigoths and used for housing in medieval times—the amphitheater has been restored almost to its original look. An inflatable roof covers it in winter, when various exhibits and shows occupy the space, and bullfights and tennis tournaments are held here in summer. A smaller version of the Colosseum in Rome, this is considered the world's best-preserved Roman amphitheater. *Blvd.*

Provence

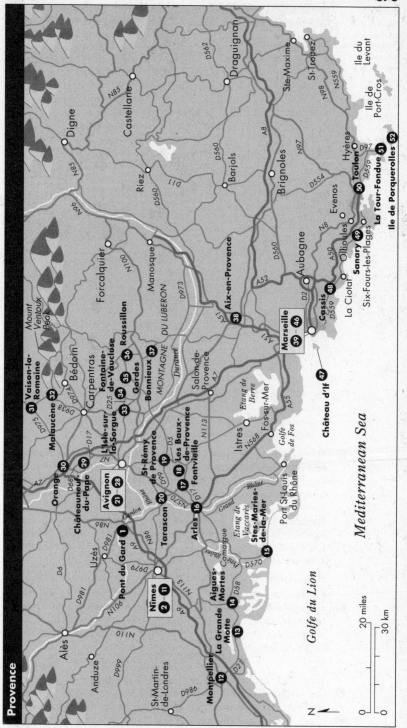

Mediterranean Sea

Golfe du Lion

Golfe de Fos

Etang de Berre

Etang de Vaccarès

MONTAGNE DU LUBERON

Mount Ventoux Peak

Île du Levant

Île de Port-Cros

Île de Porquerolles

St-Tropez
Ste-Maxime
Draguignan
Castellane
Digne
Riez
Barjols
Brignoles
Hyères
La Tour-Fondue ⑤¹
Toulon ⑤⁰
Sanary ④⁹
Ollioules
Six-Fours-les-Plages
La Ciotat
Cassis ④⁸
Aubagne
Evenos
Aix-en-Provence ㊳
Marseille ㊴ – ㊻
Château d'If ㊼
Port St-Louis du Rhône
Salon-de-Provence
Istres
Fos-sur-Mer
Forcalquier
Manosque
Roussillon ㊱
Gordes ㊲
Bonnieux ㊲
Bédoin
Fontaine-de-Vaucluse
Carpentras
L'Isle-sur-la-Sorgue ㉝
Vaison-la-Romaine ㉛
Malaucène ㉜
Orange ㉚
Châteauneuf-du-Pape ㉙
Avignon ㉑ – ㉘
St-Rémy-de-Provence ⑲
Les Baux-de-Provence ⑱
Fontvieille ⑰
Tarascon
Arles ⑯
Stes-Maries-de-la-Mer ⑮
Pont du Gard ①
Nîmes ② – ⑪
Uzès
Alès
Anduze
St-Martin-de-Londres
Montpellier ⑫
La Grande Motte ⑬
Aigues-Mortes ⑭

Camargue

Grand Rhône
Petit Rhône
Durance
Gardon

N85
N85
N85
N85
N100
N100
N100
N559
N559
N98
N97
N8
A8
A50
A52
A51
A55
A54
A9
A7
D6
D979
D981
D982
D986
D999
N110
N106
N113
N568
D570
D58
D27
D979
D281
D98N
N570
D17
N570
D99
D5
D973
D25
D942
D943
D938
D74
D17
D975
D68
N86
A7
D562
D560
D560
D560
D560
D560
D554
D559
D559
D97
D559
D2
D1

20 miles
30 km

N

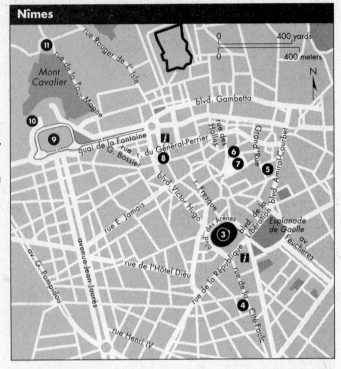

Victor-Hugo, ☎ 66–67–45–76. ☛ 22 frs adults, 16 frs students; joint ticket to Arènes and Tour Magne: 30 frs adults, 21 frs students. ☉ Mid-June–mid-Sept., daily 8–8; mid-Sept.–Oct. and Apr.–mid-June, daily 9–noon and 2–6; Nov.–Mar., daily 9–noon and 2–5.

4 Take rue de la Cité-Foulc behind the Arènes to the **Musée des Beaux-Arts** (Fine Arts Museum), where you can admire a vast Roman mosaic discovered in Nîmes during the past century; the marriage ceremony depicted in the center of the mosaic provides intriguing insights into the Roman aristocratic lifestyle. Old Masters (Nicolas Poussin, Pieter Brueghel, Peter Paul Rubens) and sculpture (Auguste Rodin and his pupil Émile Bourdelle) form the mainstay of the collection. *Rue de la Cité-Foulc, ☎ 66–67–38–21. ☛ 22 frs adults, 16 frs students. ☉ Tues.–Sat. 9:30–12:30 and 2–6, Sun. and Mon. 2–6.*

Return to the Arènes and head right, along boulevard de la Libération, which soon becomes boulevard de l'Amiral-Courbet. A hundred and **5** fifty yards down on the left is the **Musée Archéologique et d'Histoire Naturelle**, rich in local archaeological finds, mainly statues, busts, friezes, tools, glass, and pottery. It also houses an extensive collection of Greek, Roman, and medieval coins. *Blvd. de l'Amiral-Courbet, ☎ 66–67–25–57. ☛ 22 frs adults, 16 frs students. ☉ Tues.–Sun. 11–6.*

Turn north onto Grand' Rue behind the museum, then take the sec-**6** ond left up toward the **cathedral.** This uninspired 19th-century reconstruction is of less interest than either the surrounding pedestrian **7** streets or the **Musée du Vieux Nîmes** (Museum of Old Nîmes), opposite the cathedral in the 17th-century Bishop's Palace. Embroidered garments and woolen shawls fill the rooms in an exotic and vibrant display. Nîmes used to be a cloth-manufacturing center and lent its name to what has become one of the world's most popular fabrics—denim *(de Nîmes—from Nîmes). Pl. aux Herbes,* ☎ *66–36–00–64.* 🕿 *22 frs adults, 16 frs students.* ⊘ *Tues.–Sun. 11–6.*

★ **❽** Head north from the cathedral along rue des Halles, then left down rue du Général-Perrier, to reach the **Maison Carrée.** Despite its name (the "square house"), this is an oblong Roman temple, dating from the 1st century AD. Transformed down the ages into a stable, a private dwelling, a town hall, and a church, today the building is a museum that contains an imposing statue of Apollo and other antiquities. The exquisite carvings along the cornice and on the Corinthian capitals rank as some of the finest in Roman architecture. Thomas Jefferson admired the Maison Carrée's chaste lines of columns so much that he had them copied for the Virginia state capitol at Richmond. *Blvd. Victor-Hugo.* 🕿 *Free.* ⊘ *Mid-June–mid-Sept., daily 9–7; mid-Sept.–Oct. and Apr.–mid-June, daily 9–noon and 2–6; Nov.–Mar., daily 9–noon and 2–5.*

Directly opposite the Maison Carrée is the **Carrée d'Art,** a swanky, glass-fronted contemporary art museum opened in May 1993, showcasing international pictures and sculpture from 1960 onward. *Pl. de la Maison Carrée,* ☎ *66–76–35–35.* 🕿 *22 frs adults, 16 frs students.* ⊘ *Tues.–Sun. 10–6.*

❾ Rue Molière and rue Gaston-Boissier lead from the Maison Carrée to the **Jardin de la Fontaine.** This elaborate, formal garden was landscaped on the site of the Roman baths in the 18th century, when the Source de Nemausus, a once sacred spring, was channeled into pools and a canal. Close by, you'll see the shattered remnant of a Roman **❿** ruin, known as the **Temple of Diana.** At the far end of the jardin is the **⓫ Tour Magne**—a stumpy tower that was probably used as a lookout post, which, despite having lost 30 feet during the course of time, still provides fine views of Nîmes for anyone who is energetic enough to climb the 140 steps to the top. *Quai de la Fontaine,* ☎ *66–67–65–56.* 🕿 *Tour Magne: 12 frs adults, 10 frs students; joint ticket as described above at the Arènes.* ⊘ *Mid-June–mid-Sept., daily 9–7; mid-Sept.–Oct. and Apr.–mid-June, daily 9–noon and 2–6; Nov.–Mar., daily 9–noon and 2–5.*

⓬ Both N113 and the A9 expressway link Nîmes to **Montpellier,** 50 kilometers (30 miles) southwest. It's a comparatively young town, a mere 1,000 years old; no Romans settled here. Ever since medieval times, Montpellier's reputation has been linked to its university, which was founded in the 14th century. Its medical school, in particular, was so highly esteemed that François Rabelais, one of France's top 16th-century writers, left his native Loire Valley to take his doctorate here. Albanian dictator Enver Hoxha studied here in the early 1930s. Montpellier remains one of France's premier universities, and a student population of 20,000 peps things up during the school year.

The 17th-century town center has been improved by an imaginative urban planning program, and several streets and squares are banned to cars. The heart of Montpellier is place de la Comédie, a wide square now free of traffic jams, much to the benefit of the cafés and terraces laid out before the handsome 19th-century facade of the civic theater.

Boulevard Sarrail leads from the far end of the square, past the leafy Esplanade with its rows of plane trees, to the **Musée Fabre.** The museum's collection of art highlights important works by Gustave Courbet (notably *Bonjour Monsieur Courbet*) and Eugène Delacroix (*Femmes d'Alger*), as well as paintings by Frédéric Bazille (1841–70)—whose death during the Franco-Prussian War deprived Impressionism of one of its earliest exponents. Older standouts of the museum's varied collection include pictures from the English (Joshua Reynolds), Italian (Raphael), Flemish (David Teniers), and Spanish (Jusepe de Ribera) schools. *37 blvd. Sarrail,* ☎ *67–14–83–00.* ☛ *18 frs.* ☉ *Tues.–Fri. 9–5:30, weekends 9:30–5.*

Follow rue Montpelliéret, alongside the museum, into the heart of old Montpellier—a maze of crooked, bustling streets ideal for shopping and strolling. Rue Foch strikes a more disciplined note, slicing straight through to the pride of Montpellier, the **Promenade du Peyrou.** With its wrought-iron railings and majestic flights of steps, this long, broad, tree-shaded terrace has great style. An equestrian statue of Louis XIV rides triumphant, and at the far end carved friezes and columns mask a water tower. Water used to arrive along the **St-Clément aqueduct,** an imposing two-tiered structure 70 feet high and nearly 1,000 yards long. Locals still cluster beneath the aqueduct's arches to drink pastis and play boules.

Just down boulevard Henri IV from the Promenade du Peyrou is France's oldest **botanical garden,** planted by order of Henri IV in 1593. Horticulture buffs will admire the exceptional range of plants, flowers, and trees that grow here, and even nongardeners will appreciate this oasis of peace, where water lilies float among the lotus flowers. ☛ *Free.* ☉ *Gardens Mon.–Sat. 9–noon and 2–5. Greenhouses open weekdays 9–noon and 2–5, Sat. 9–noon.*

⑬ The arid, rocky Midi landscape begins to change as you head southeast from Montpellier along D21, past pools and lagoons, to **La Grande Motte,** the most lavish—and, some would say, ugliest—of a string of new resorts built along the Languedoc coast. The mosquitoes that once infested this watery area have finally been vanquished, and tourists have taken their place. La Grande Motte was only a glint in an architect's eye back in the late '60s; since then, its arresting pyramidal apartment blocks have influenced several French resorts. They host thousands of vacationers each year.

TIME OUT Thousands of tons of oysters are cultivated in the nearby Etang (lagoon) de Thau; many end up featured on the menu of the elegant **Alexandre-Amirauté.** You can eat your oysters amid impressive Louis XV surroundings while gazing out over the Mediterranean. *345 esplanade Maurice-Justin,* ☎ *67–56–63–63.*

⑭ Thirteen kilometers (8 miles) farther east is **Aigues-Mortes,** an astonishing relic of medieval town planning, created at the behest of Louis IX (Saint-Louis) in the 13th century. Medieval streets are usually crooked and higgledy-piggledy; at Aigues-Mortes, however, a grid plan was adopted, hemmed in by sturdy walls sprouting towers at regular intervals. Aigues-Mortes was originally a port, and Louis used it as a base for his Crusades to the Holy Land. The sea has long since receded, though, and Aigues-Mortes's size and importance have decreased with it.

Unlike most of the medieval buildings, the **fortifications** remain intact. Walk along the top of the city walls and admire some remarkable views across the town and salt marshes. You can also explore the powerful **Tour de Constance,** originally designed as a fortress-keep and used in the 18th century as a prison for Protestants who refused to convert to official state Catholicism. One such unfortunate, Marie Durand, languished here for 38 years. Abraham Mazel was luckier. He spent 10 months chiseling a hole in the wall, while his companions sang psalms to distract the jailers. The ruse worked: Mazel and 16 others escaped. ☎ 66–53–73–00. ☛ *27 frs adults, 18 frs students and senior citizens, 7 frs children.* ☉ *Tower and ramparts open Apr.–Oct., daily 9–7; Nov.–Mar. 9:30–noon and 2–5:30.*

Head east on D58 across the haunting, desolate **Camargue:** a marshy wilderness of endless horizons, vast pools, low flat plains, and, overhead, innumerable species of migrating birds. The Camargue is formed by the sprawling Rhône delta and extends over 300 square miles—the swollen river burst its banks in October 1993 and January 1994, flooding much of the area. Much of it is untouched by man; this is a land of black bulls and sturdy, free-roaming gray horses. There are just two towns worthy of the name: Aigues-Mortes and, 32 kilometers (20 miles) southeast via D58/D570, Saintes-Maries-de-la-Mer.

⑮ Stes-Maries-de-la-Mer is a commercialized resort, frequented mainly by British tourists in search of the Camargue's principal sandy beach. Its tiny, dark fortress-church houses caskets containing relics of the "Holy Maries" after whom the town is named. Legend has it that Mary Jacobi (the sister of the Virgin), Mary Magdalene, Mary Salome (mother of the apostles James and John), and their black servant Sarah were washed up here around AD 40 after being abandoned at sea—why, no one knows. Their adopted town rapidly became a site of pilgrimage, the most important site for Gypsies. Sarah was adopted as their patron saint, and to this day, Gypsies from all over Europe and the rest of the world stage colorful pilgrimages to Stes-Maries in late May and late October, while guitar-strumming pseudo-gypsies serenade rich-looking tourists throughout the summer.

Take D85-A north from Stes-Maries through the 30-acre **Parc Ornithologique,** itself part of the vast Réserve Nationale centered on the Etang (lagoon) de Vaccarès. The Parc Ornithologique offers a protected environment to vegetation and wildlife: Birds from northern Europe and Siberia spend the winter here, while pink flamingos flock in during the summer months. ☎ 90–97–82–62. ☛ *30 frs adults, 15 frs children under 10.* ☉ *Mar.–Oct., daily 8–dusk; Nov.–Feb., daily 9–dusk.*

⑯ Continue along D85-A until it rejoins D570, then keep north on this road for 25 kilometers (16 miles) until you reach **Arles.** The first inhabitants of Arles were probably the Greeks, who arrived from Marseille in the 6th century BC. The Romans, however, left a stronger mark, constructing the theater and amphitheater (Arènes) that remain the biggest tourist attractions. Arles used to be a thriving port before the Mediterranean receded over what is now the Camargue. It was also the site of the southernmost bridge over the Rhône, and became a commercial crossroads; merchants from as far afield as Arabia, Assyria, and Africa would linger here to do business on their way from Rome to Spain or northern Europe.

Firebrand Dutchman Vincent van Gogh produced much of his best work—and chopped off his ear—in Arles during a frenzied 15-month spell (1888–90) just before his suicide at 37. Unfortunately, the houses he lived in are no longer standing—they were destroyed during World War II—but part of one of his most famous subjects remains: the **Pont de Trinquetaille** across the Rhône. Van Gogh's rendering of the bridge, painted in 1888, was auctioned a century later for $20 million.

Local art museums, such as the **Musée Réattu,** 300 yards from the bridge along quai Marx-Dormoy, can't compete with that type of bidding—which is one reason none of Van Gogh's works are displayed there. Another is that Arles failed to appreciate him; he was jeered at and eventually packed off to the nearest lunatic asylum. To add insult to injury, Jacques Réattu, after whom the museum is named, was a local painter of dazzling mediocrity. His works fill three rooms, but of much greater interest is the collection of modern drawings and paintings by Pablo Picasso, Fernand Léger, and Maurice de Vlaminck, as well as the photography section containing images by some of the field's leading names. *Rue du Grand-Prieuré,* ☎ *90–49–37–58.* ☞ *15 frs; passport to all monuments and museums: 55 frs adults, 35 frs students.* ☉ *June–Sept., daily 9:30–7; Nov.–Mar., daily 10–12:30 and 2–5; Apr.–May and Oct., daily 9:30–12:30 and 2–6.*

The museum facade, facing the Rhône, dates from the Middle Ages and formed part of a 15th-century priory. Beside it are the ruins of

★ the **Palais Constantin** (same opening times as above), site of Provence's
★ largest Roman baths, the **Thermes de la Trouille** (entrance on rue Dominique-Maisto; admission: 12 francs adults, 7 frs students; joint ticket as above).

Most of the significant sights and museums in Arles are set well away from the Rhône. The most notable is the 26,000-capacity **Arènes,** built in the 1st century AD for circuses and gladiator combats. The amphitheater is 150 yards long and as wide as a football field, with each of its two stories composed of 60 arches; the original top tier has long since crumbled, and the three square towers were added in the Middle Ages. Climb to the upper story for some satisfying views across the town and countryside. Despite its venerable age, the amphitheater still sees a lot of action, mainly Sunday afternoon bullfights. *Rond-Point des Arènes,* ☎ *90–96–03–70.* ☞ *15 frs adults, 9 frs students; joint ticket as above.* ☉ *June–Sept., daily 8:30–7; Nov.–Mar., daily 9–noon and 2–4:30; Apr.–May and Oct., daily 9–12:30 and 2–6:30.*

Just 100 yards from the Arènes are the scanty remains of Arles's
★ **Théâtre Antique** (Roman theater); the bits of marble column scattered around the grassy enclosure hint poignantly at the theater's onetime grandeur. The capacity may have shrunk from 7,000 to a few hundred, but the orchestra pit and a few tiers of seats are still used for the city's Music and Drama festival each July. *Rue du Cloître,* ☎ *90–96–93–30 for ticket information.* ☞ *15 frs adults, 9 frs students; joint ticket as above.* ☉ *June–Sept., daily 8:30–7; Nov.–Mar., daily 9–noon and 2–4:30; Apr.–May and Oct., daily 9–12:30 and 2–6:30.*

Follow rue de la Calade to place de la République. To the left is the church of **St-Trophime,** dating mainly from the 11th and 12th centuries; subsequent additions have not spoiled its architectural harmony. Take time to admire the accomplished 12th-century sculptures flanking the main portal, featuring the *Last Judgment,* the apostles, the Nativity, and various saints. There are other well-crafted sculptures in the cloisters. *Rue de l'Hôtel-de-Ville,* ☎ *90–49–36–36.* ☞ *Cloisters: 15 frs adults, 9 frs students; joint ticket as above.* ☉ *June–Sept., daily 8:30–7; Nov.–Mar., daily 9–noon and 2–4:30; Apr.–May and Oct., daily 9–12:30 and 2–6:30.*

Opposite St-Trophime is the **Musée d'Art Païen** (Museum of Pagan Art), housed in a former church next to the 17th-century Hôtel de Ville. The "pagan art" displays encompass Roman statues, busts, mosaics, and a white marble sarcophagus. You'll also see a copy of the famous statue the *Venus of Arles;* Sun King Louis XIV waltzed off to the Louvre with the original. *Pl. de la République.* ☞ *12 frs adults, 7 frs students; joint ticket as above.* ☉ *June–Sept., daily 8:30–7; Nov.–Mar., daily 9–noon and 2–4:30; Apr.–May and Oct., 9–12:30 and 2–6:30.*

Turn left alongside the Hôtel de Ville into plan de la Cour. A hundred yards down, in a former 17th-century Jesuit chapel, is the **Musée d'Art Chrétien** (Museum of Christian Art). One of the highlights is a magnificent collection of sculpted marble sarcophagi, second only to the Vatican's, that date from the 4th century on. Downstairs, you can explore a vast Roman double gallery built in the 1st century BC as a grain store and see part of the great Roman sewer built two centuries later. *Rue Balze.* ☛ *12 frs adults, 7 frs students; joint ticket as above.* ⊗ *June–Sept., daily 8:30–7; Nov.–Mar., daily 9–noon and 2–4:30; Apr.–May and Oct., daily 9–12:30 and 2–6:30.*

The **Muséon Arlaten,** an old-fashioned folklore museum, is housed next door in a 16th-century mansion. The charming displays include costumes and headdresses, puppets, and waxworks, lovingly assembled by that great 19th-century Provençal poet Frédéric Mistral. *29 rue de la République,* ☎ *90–96–08–23.* ☛ *15 frs adults, 10 frs students; joint ticket as above.* ⊗ *June–Sept., daily 8:30–7; Nov.–Mar., Tues.–Sun. 9–noon and 2–4:30; Apr.–May and Oct., Tues.–Sun. 9–12:30 and 2–6:30.*

Head down rue du Président-Wilson opposite the museum to the **boulevard des Luces,** a broad, leafy avenue flanked by trendy shops and sidewalk cafés. Locals favor it for leisurely strolls and aperitifs.

At the east end of the boulevard is the **Jardin d'Hiver,** a public garden whose fountains figure in several of Van Gogh's paintings. Cross the gardens to rue Fassin and head left to place de la Croisière and the start of the allée des Sarcophages, which leads to the **Alyscamps,** a Provençal term meaning "mythical burial ground." This was a prestigious burial site from Roman times through the Middle Ages. A host of important finds have been excavated here, many of which are exhibited in the town's museums. Empty tombs and sarcophagi line the allée des Sarcophages, creating a powerfully gloomy atmosphere in dull weather. ☎ *90–49–36–87.* ☛ *12 frs adults, 7 frs students.* ⊗ *Daily 9–5.*

⓱ Leave Arles on Avignon-bound N570, and almost immediately turn right along D17 to the striking village of **Fontvieille,** 10 kilometers (6 miles) away and home of the **Moulin de Daudet.** Nineteenth-century author Alphonse Daudet dreamed up his short stories, *Lettres de Mon Moulin,* in this well-preserved, charmingly situated windmill just up D33 on the outskirts of the village. Inside there's a small museum devoted to Daudet, and you can walk upstairs to see the original milling system. ☎ *90–54–60–78.* ☛ *10 frs adults, 5 frs children under 12.* ⊗ *Apr.–Oct., daily 9–noon and 2–7; Nov.–Dec. and Feb.–Mar., daily 10–noon and 2–5; Jan., Sun. only, 10–noon and 2–5.*

★ ⓲ From Fontvieille, take D17 and then D78-A to **Les Baux-de-Provence,** 8 kilometers (5 miles) farther. Les Baux-de-Provence is an amazing place, perched on a mighty spur of rock high above the surrounding countryside of vines, olive trees, and quarries. The mineral bauxite was discovered here in 1821. Half of Les Baux is composed of tiny climbing streets and ancient stone houses inhabited, for the most part, by local craftsmen selling pottery, carvings, and assorted knickknacks. The other half, the Ville Morte (Dead Town), is a mass of medieval ruins, vestiges of Les Baux's glorious past, when the town boasted 6,000 inhabitants and the defensive impregnability of its rocky site far outweighed its isolation and poor access.

Cars must be left in the parking lot at the entrance to the village. Close to the 12th-century church of St-Vincent (where local shepherds continue an age-old tradition by herding their lambs to midnight mass at Christmas) is the 16th-century **Hôtel des Porcelets,** featuring some

18th-century frescoes and a small but choice collection of contemporary art. *Pl. Hervain,* ☎ *90–54–36–99.* ☛ *32 frs adults, 22 frs children under 18. (joint ticket with Musée Lapidaire and Ville Morte).* ☺ *Easter–Oct., daily 9–noon and 2–6.*

Rue Neuve leads around to the **Ville Morte.** Enter through the 14th-century Tour-de-Brau, which houses the Musée Lapidaire, displaying locally excavated sculptures and ceramics. You can wander at will amid the rocks and ruins of the Dead Town. A 13th-century castle stands at one end of the clifftop and, at the other, the Tour Paravelle and the Monument Charloun Rieu. From here, you can enjoy a magnificent view of Arles and the Camargue as far as Stes-Maries-de-la-Mer., *La Citadelle,* ☎ *90–54–37–37.* ☛ *32 frs (joint ticket with museums).* ☺ *Daily 9:15–6:15.*

Half a mile north of Les Baux, off D27, is the **Cathédrale d'Images,** where the majestic setting of the old bauxite quarries, with their towering rock faces and stone pillars, is used as a colossal screen for nature-based films (Jacques Cousteau gets frequent billing). *Rte. de Maillane,* ☎ *90–54–38–65.* ☛ *40 frs adults, 25 frs children.* ☺ *Mid-Feb.–mid-Nov., daily 10–7.*

★ ⑲ Hilly D5 heads 8 kilometers (5 miles) north from Les Baux to the small town of **St-Rémy de Provence,** founded in the 6th century BC and known as Glanum to the Romans. St-Rémy is renowned for its outstanding Roman remains: Temples, baths, forum, and houses have been excavated, while the Mausoleum and Arc Municipal (Triumphal Arch) welcome visitors as they enter the town.

The **Roman Mausoleum** was erected around AD 100 to the memory of Caius and Lucius Caesar, grandsons of the emperor Augustus; the four bas-reliefs around its base, depicting ancient battle scenes, are stunningly preserved. The Mausoleum is composed of four archways topped by a circular colonnade. The nearby **Arc Municipal** is a few decades older and has suffered heavily; the upper half has crumbled away, although you can still make out some of the stone carvings.

Excavations of **Glanum** began in 1921, and a tenth of the original Roman town has now been unearthed. The remains, spread over 300 yards along what was once the Aurelian Way between Arles and Milan, are less spectacular than the arch and mausoleum, but students of archaeology won't mind paying for the privilege of admiring what were once temples, fountains, gateways, baths, houses, and a forum. ☎ *90–92–23–79.* ☛ *32 frs adults, 10 frs children under 10.* ☺ *Apr.–Sept., daily 9–noon and 2–6; Oct.–Mar., daily 9–noon and 2–5.*

Many of the finds—statues, pottery, and jewelry—can also be examined at the town museum, **Le Musée Archéologique,** in the center of St-Rémy. *Hôtel de Sade, rue Parage,* ☎ *90–92–13–07.* ☛ *14 frs adults, 7 frs children under 10.* ☺ *June–Oct., daily 9–noon and 2–6; Apr.–May and Oct., weekends 10–noon, weekdays 3–6; closed Nov.–Mar.*

⑳ Take D99 16 kilometers (10 miles) west from St-Rémy to **Tarascon,** home of the mythical Tarasque, a monster that would emerge from the Rhône to gobble children and cattle. Luckily Saint Martha, who also washed up at Stes-Maries-de-la-Mer, allegedly tamed the beast with a sprinkle of holy water, after which the inhabitants clobbered it senseless and slashed it to pieces. This dramatic event is celebrated on the last Sunday in June with a colorful parade.

Ever since the 12th century, Tarascon has possessed a formidable **castle** to protect it from any beast or man that might be tempted to emulate the Tarasque's fiendish deeds. The castle's massive stone walls, towering 150 feet above the rocky banks of the Rhône, are among the most daunting in France, so it's not surprising that the castle was used as a prison for centuries. Since 1926, however, the chapels, vaulted royal apartments, and stone carvings of the interior have been restored to less-intimidating glory. ☎ 90–91–01–93. ☛ 26 frs adults, 18 frs senior citizens, 10 frs students. ☉ July–Aug., daily 9–7; Sept.–June, daily 9–noon and 2–6 (2–5 Oct.–Mar.).

It's just 24 kilometers (15 miles) from Tarascon to Avignon and the start of our second tour.

Tour 2: The Vaucluse

Numbers in the margin correspond to points of interest on the Provence and Avignon maps.

㉑ A warren of medieval alleys nestling behind a protective ring of stocky towers, **Avignon** is possibly best known for its Pont St-Bénezet, the Avignon bridge that many will remember singing about during their nursery-rhyme days. No one dances across the bridge these days, however; it was amputated in midstream in the 17th century, when a cataclysmic storm washed half of it away. Still, Avignon has lots to offer, starting with the Palais des Papes (Papal Palace), where seven exiled popes camped between 1309 and 1377 after fleeing from the corruption of Rome. Avignon remained papal property until 1791, and elegant mansions bear witness to the town's 18th-century prosperity.

★ **㉒** Avignon's main street, rue de la République, leads from the tourist office (41 cours Jean-Jaurès) past shops and cafés to place de l'Horloge and place du Palais, site of the colossal **Palais des Papes.** This "palace" creates a disconcertingly fortresslike impression, underlined by the austerity of its interior decor; most of the furnishings were dispersed during the French Revolution. Some imagination is required to picture it in medieval splendor, awash with color and worldly clerics enjoying what the 14th-century Italian poet Petrarch called "licentious banquets."

On close inspection, two different styles of building emerge: the severe **Palais Vieux** (Old Palace), built between 1334 and 1342 by Pope Benedict XII, a member of the Cistercian order, which frowned on frivolity, and the more decorative **Palais Nouveau** (New Palace), built in the following decade by the arty, lavish-living Pope Clement VI. The Great Court, where visitors arrive, links the two.

The main rooms of the Palais Vieux are the consistory (council hall), decorated with some excellent 14th-century frescoes by Simone Martini; the Chapelle St-Jean (original frescoes by Matteo Giovanetti); the Grand Tinel, or Salle des Festins, with a majestic vaulted roof and a series of 18th-century Gobelin tapestries; the Chapelle St-Martial (more Matteo frescoes); the Chambre du Cerf, with a richly decorated ceiling, murals featuring a stag hunt, and a delightful view of Avignon; the Chambre de Parement (papal ante-chamber); and the Chambre à Coucher (papal bedchamber).

The principal attractions of the Palais Nouveau are the Grande Audience, a magnificent two-nave hall on the ground floor, and, upstairs, the Chapelle Clémentine, where the college of cardinals gathered to elect the new pope. *Pl. du Palais-des-Papes,* ☎ 90–27–50–73. ☛ 45 frs adults, 34 frs students. Guided tours only Mar.–Oct. ☉ Apr.–Oct., daily 9–7; Nov.–Mar., daily 9–12:30 and 2–6.

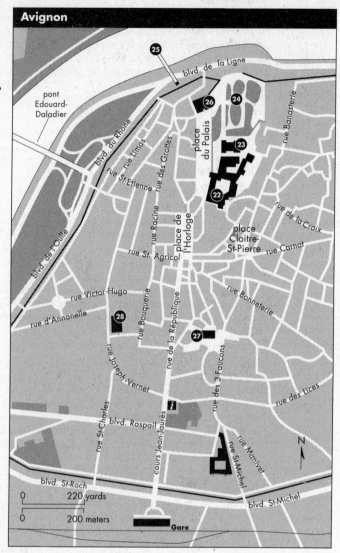

Avignon

23 The 12th-century **cathedral** nearby contains the Gothic tomb of Pope
24 John XII. Beyond is the **Rocher des Doms,** a large, attractive garden
25 offering fine views of Avignon, the Rhône, and the celebrated **Pont St-
Bénezet**—built, according to legend, by a local shepherd named Bénezet
in the 12th century. It was the first bridge to span the Rhône at Avignon and was originally 900 yards long. Though only half the bridge
remains, it's worth strolling along for the views and a visit to the tiny
Chapelle St-Nicolas that juts out over the river. ☎ 90–85–60–16. ☛
10 frs adults, 5 frs children. ☉ Apr.–Sept., daily 9–6:30; Oct.–Mar.,
Tues.–Sun. 9–1 and 2–5.

26 The medieval **Petit Palais,** situated between the bridge and the Rocher
des Doms garden, was once home to cardinals and archbishops. Nowadays it contains an outstanding collection of Old Masters, led by the
Italian schools of Venice, Siena, and Florence (note Sandro Botticelli's

Virgin and Child). 21 pl. du Palais, ☎ *90–86–44–58.* ☞ *20 frs adults, 10 frs children.* ⊘ *Wed.–Mon. 9:30–noon and 2–6.*

Double back past the Papal Palace and venture into the narrow, winding, shop-lined streets of old Avignon. Halfway down rue de la **㉗** République is the **Musée Lapidaire,** which displays a variety of archaeological finds—including the remains of Avignon's Arc de Triomphe—in a sturdy 17th-century Baroque chapel fronted by an imposing facade. *27 rue de la République,* ☎ *90–85–75–38.* ☞ *5 frs. adults.* ⊘ *Wed.–Mon. 10–noon and 2–6.*

Cross rue de la République and turn right onto rue Joseph-Vernet. A few **㉘** minutes' walk will lead you to the **Musée Calvet,** an 18th-century town house featuring an extensive collection of mainly French paintings from the 16th century on; highlights include works by Théodore Géricault, Camille Corot, Édouard Manet, Raoul Dufy, Maurice de Vlaminck, and the Italian artist Amedeo Modigliani. Greek, Roman, and Etruscan statuettes are also displayed. *65 rue Joseph-Vernet,* ☎ *90–86–33–84. At press time the museum was closed for renovation, scheduled for reopening July 1995. Probable hours: Wed.–Mon. 10–6.*

From Avignon, head north to Orange. The most picturesque route, via **㉙** N7/D17, goes by the hillside village of **Châteauneuf-du-Pape,** founded by the popes in the 14th century. The popes knew their wine: The vineyard here is still regarded as the best of the southern Rhône, even though the vines are embedded less in soil than in stones and pebbles. Several producers stage tastings in the village and sell distinctive wine bottles emblazoned with the crossed-key papal crest.

TIME OUT Inexpensive local wines, filling fare, and a cheerful welcome make **La Mule du Pape** a good choice for lunch. *2 rue de la République,* ☎ *90– 83-79-22. Closed Tues.*

㉚ **Orange,** 10 kilometers (6 miles) north of Châteauneuf via D68, is a small, pleasant town that sinks into total siesta somnolence during hot afternoons but, at other times, buzzes with visitors who are keen on admiring its Roman remains.

★ The magnificent, semicircular **Théâtre Antique,** in the center of town, is the best-preserved remains of a theater from the ancient world. It was built just before the birth of Christ, to the same dimensions as that of Arles. Orange's theater, however, has a mighty screen wall, more than 100 yards long and 120 feet high, and steeply climbing terraces carved into the hillside. Seven thousand spectators can crowd in, and regularly do, for open-air concerts and operatic performances; the acoustics are superb. This is the only Roman theater that still possesses its original Imperial statue, of Caesar Augustus, which stands in the middle of the screen. At nearly 12 feet, it's one of the tallest Roman statues in existence. *Pl. des Frères-Mounet,* ☎ *90–34–70–88.* ☞ *25 frs adults, 20 frs students and senior citizens; joint ticket with Musée Municipal.* ⊘ *Apr.–Oct., daily 9–6:30; Nov.–Mar., daily 9–noon and 1:30–5.*

The **Parc de la Colline St-Eutrope,** the banked garden behind the theater, yields a fine view of the theater and of the 6,000-foot Mont Ventoux to the east. Walk up cours Aristide-Briand, turn right at the top, then left immediately after to the venerable **Arc de Triomphe**—composed of a large central arch flanked by two smaller ones, the whole topped by a massive entablature. The 70-foot arch, the third-highest Roman arch still standing, towered over the old Via Agrippa between Arles and Lyon and was probably built around AD 25 in honor of the Gallic Wars. The carvings on the north side depict the legionnaires' battles with the Gauls and Caesar's naval showdown with the ships of Marseille. Today the arch presides over a busy traffic circle.

㉛ The D975 heads 27 kilometers (17 miles) northeast from Orange to **Vaison-la-Romaine,** which, as its name suggests, was also a Roman town. The ruins here are more extensive, though less spectacular than those at Orange; they can be explored on either side of the avenue du Général-de-Gaulle. The floors and walls of houses, villas, a basilica, and a theater have been unearthed, and the Roman street plan is partly discernible. Statues and objects are housed in a small museum near the theater. With its lush lawns and colorful flower beds, the entire site suggests a well-tended historical garden. ☎ *90–36–02–11. Admission to ruins and museum: 35 frs adults, 20 frs students, 12 frs children 12– 17. ⊗ Daily June–Sept. 10–12:30 and 2:30–5:45 (6:45 June–Aug.); in winter 10–noon and 2–4:30.*

㉜ Before leaving Vaison, pause to admire the 2,000-year-old Roman bridge over the River Ouvèze and venture briefly into the medieval town across the river. Then head 10 kilometers (6 miles) south along D938 to **Malaucène,** at the foot of **Mont Ventoux**—a huge mountain that looms incongruously above the surrounding plains. Weather conditions on this sprawling, whalelike bulk—known reverentially as "Le" Ventoux—can vary dramatically. In summer, few places in France experience such scorching heat; in winter, the Ventoux's snow-topped peak recalls the Alps. Its arid heights sometimes provide a grueling setting for the Tour de France cycling race; British bicyclist Tommy Simpson collapsed and died under the Ventoux's pitiless sun in 1967.

㉝ D974 winds its way from Malaucène up to the summit, 6,250 feet above sea level. Stay on D974 as it doubles back around the southern slopes, then from Bédoin toward Carpentras. From here, take D938 south to **L'Isle-sur-la-Sorgue,** 18 kilometers (11 miles) away, where the River Sorgue, which once turned the waterwheels of the town's silk factories, splits into a number of channels. Silkworms were cultivated locally, one reason for the profusion of mulberry trees in Provence. Some of the waterwheels are still in place, and you can admire them as you stroll along the banks of the river that encircles the town. The richly decorated 17th-century church is also of interest.

TIME OUT A good place for lunch is **Le Pescador,** an inexpensive restaurant whose shaded terrace overlooks the arms of the Sorgue. There is a wide choice and an excellent-value menu during the week. *Le Partage des Eaux,* ☎ *90–38–09–69. Closed Mon.*

㉞ Tiny D25 leads east from L'Isle-sur-la-Sorgue to **Fontaine-de-Vaucluse,** 8 kilometers (5 miles) away. The "fountain" in question is the site of the River Sorgue's emergence from underground imprisonment: Water shoots up from a cavern as the emerald-green river sprays and cascades at the foot of steep cliffs. This is the picture in springtime or after heavy rains; in the drought of summer, the scene may be less spectacular and infested with tourists.

㉟ It's just 6 kilometers (4 miles) from Fontaine-de-Vaucluse to **Gordes,** as the crow flies, but drivers have to wind their way south, east, and then north for 16 kilometers (10 miles) on D100-A, D100, D2, and D15 to skirt the impassable hillside. The golden-stone village of Gordes is perched dramatically on its own hill. At the summit sits a Renaissance **château** with a collection of mind-stretching, geometric-pattern paintings by 20th-century Hungarian-French artist Victor Vasarely. ☎

90–72–02–89. 🖝 *25 frs adults, 15 frs students 11–18.* ⊙ *Wed.–Mon. 10–noon and 2–6.*

In a wild valley some 4 kilometers (2 miles) north of Gordes (via D177) stands the beautiful 12th-century **Abbey of Sénanque.** In 1969, its Cistercian monks moved to the island of St-Honorat (*see* Chapter 13, The Riviera), off the shore of Cannes, and the admirably preserved buildings here are now a cultural center that presents concerts and exhibitions. The dormitory, refectory, church, and chapter house can be visited, along with an odd museum devoted to the Sahara's Tuareg nomads. ☎ *90–72–05–72.* 🖝 *18 frs adults, 15 frs students.* ⊙ *July–Aug., Mon.–Sat. 10–7, Sun. 2–7; Sept.–Oct. and Mar.–June, Mon.–Sat. 10–noon and 2–6, Sun. 2–6; Nov.–Feb., daily 2–6.*

Return to Gordes and strike 10 kilometers (6 miles) east along D2/D102 to another hilltop village, **Roussillon,** whose houses are built with a distinctive orange-and-pink-colored stone. This is ocher country, and local quarrying has slashed cliffs into bizarre shapes. **Bonnieux,** 11 kilometers (7 miles) south of Roussillon (D149), is equally picturesque. Climb to the terrace of the old church (not to be confused with the big 19th-century one lower down) for a sweeping view north that takes in Gordes, Roussillon, and the ruined château of Lacoste, once home to the notorious marquis de Sade.

Aix-en-Provence, starting point for our third tour, lies 48 kilometers (29 miles) southeast.

Tour 3: The Marseille Area

Numbers in the margin correspond to points of interest on the Provence and Marseille maps.

Many villages, but few towns, are as well preserved as the traditional capital of Provence: elegant **Aix-en-Provence.** The Romans were drawn here by the presence of thermal springs; the name Aix originates from *Aquae Sextiae* (the waters of Sextius) in honor of the consul who reputedly founded the town in 122 BC. Twenty years later, a vast army of Germanic barbarians invaded the region but were defeated by General Marius at a neighboring mountain, known ever since as the Montagne Sainte-Victoire. Marius remains a popular local first name to this day.

Aix-en-Provence numbers two of France's most creative geniuses among its sons: the Impressionist Paul Cézanne (1839–1906), many of whose paintings feature the nearby countryside, especially Montagne Sainte-Victoire (though Cézanne would not recognize it now, after the forest fire that ravaged its slopes in 1990), and the novelist Émile Zola (1840–1902), who, in several of his works, described Aix ("Plassans") and his boyhood friendship with Cézanne.

The celebrated **cours Mirabeau,** flanked with intertwining plane trees, is the town's nerve center, a graceful, lively avenue with the feel of a toned-down, intimate Champs-Elysées. It divides Old Aix into two, with narrow medieval streets to the north and sophisticated, haughty 18th-century mansions to the south. Begin your visit at the west end of cours Mirabeau (the tourist office is close by at 2 place du Général-de-Gaulle). Halfway down is the **Fontaine des Neuf Canons** (Fountain of the Nine Cannons), dating from 1691, and farther along is the **Fontaine d'Eau Thermale** (Thermal Water), built in 1734.

Turn left down rue Clemenceau to place St-Honoré, with another small fountain, then make a left again onto rue Espariat. The sumptuous Hôtel Boyer d'Eguilles at No. 6, erected in 1675, is worth a visit for its fine woodwork, sculpture, and murals but is best known as the **Muséum d'Histoire Naturelle.** The highlight is its rare collection of dinosaur eggs, accompanied by lifesize models of the dinosaurs that roamed locally 65 million years ago. *6 rue Espariat,* ☎ *42–26–23–67.* ☛ *15 frs adults, 9 frs students.* ☉ *Mon.–Sat. 10–noon and 2–6, Sun. 2–6.*

Continue on rue Espariat past the sculpted facade of the Hôtel d'Albertas (built in 1707) at No. 10, then turn right onto rue Aude, lined with ancient town houses. Wend your way down to the **Hôtel de Ville,** pausing to admire its 17th-century iron gates and balcony, and the 16th-century **Tour de l'Horloge** (former town belfry) alongside. Toward the far end of the street (now known as rue Gaston-de-Saporta), just past the intimate square of place des Martyrs, stands the **Cathédrale St-Sauveur.** Its mishmash of styles lacks harmony, and the interior feels gloomy and dilapidated, but there's a remarkable 15th-century triptych by Nicolas Froment, entitled *Tryptique du Buisson Ardent* (*Burning Bush*), depicting King René (duke of Anjou, count of Provence, and titular king of Sicily) and Queen Joan kneeling beside the Virgin. Ask the sacristan to spotlight it for you (he'll expect a tip) and to remove the protective shutters from the ornate 16th-century carvings on the cathedral portals. Afterward, wander into the tranquil Romanesque cloisters next door to admire the carved pillars and slender colonnades.

The adjacent Archbishop's Palace is home to the **Musée des Tapisseries** (Tapestry Museum). Its highlight is a magnificent suite of 17 tapestries made in Beauvais that date, like the palace itself, from the 17th and 18th centuries. Nine woven panels illustrate the adventures of the bumbling Don Quixote. *28 pl. des Martyrs de la Résistance,* ☎ *42–23–09–91.* ☛ *14 frs adults, 8 frs students.* ☉ *Wed.–Mon. 10–noon and 2–5:45.*

Return past the cathedral and take rue de la Roque up to the broad, leafy boulevard that encircles Old Aix. Head up avenue Pasteur, opposite, then turn right onto avenue Paul-Cézanne, which leads to the **Musée-Atelier de Paul Cézanne** (Cézanne's studio). Cézanne's pioneering work, with its interest in angular forms, paved the way for the Cubist style of the early 20th century. No major pictures are on display here, but his studio remains as he left it at the time of his death in 1906, scattered with the great man's pipe, clothing, and other personal possessions, many of which he painted in his still lifes. *9 av. Paul-Cézanne,* ☎ *42–21–06–53.* ☛ *15 frs adults, 9 frs students.* ☉ *Wed.–Mon. 10–noon and 2–5.*

TIME OUT   Good addresses for picnic provisions are the **Olivier** charcuterie (26 rue Jacques-de-Laroque near the cathedral) and the **Béchard** *traiteur* (caterer)(12 cours Mirabeau).

Make your way back to cours Mirabeau and cross into the southern half of Aix. The streets here are straight and rationally planned, flanked with symmetrical mansions imbued with classical elegance. Rue du Quatre-Septembre, three-quarters of the way down cours Mirabeau, leads to the splendid **Fontaine des Quatre Dauphins,** where sculpted dolphins play in a fountain erected in 1667. Turn left along rue Cardinale to the **Musée Granet,** named after another of Aix's artistic sons: François Granet (1775–1849), whose works are good examples of the formal, at times sentimental, style of art popular during the first half of the 19th century. Cézanne is also represented here with several oils and watercolors; there are European paintings from the 16th to the 19th century, plus archaeological finds from Egypt, Greece, and the Roman Empire. *13 rue Cardinale,* ☎ *42–38–14–70.* ☛ *18 frs adults, 10 frs students.* ☉ *Wed.–Mon. 10–noon and 2–6.*

The quickest route by car between Aix and Marseille is the toll-free A51 expressway, provided you avoid the rush hours.

㊴ **Marseille** is not crowded with tourist goodies, nor is its reputation as a big dirty city entirely unjustified, but it still has more going for it than many realize: a craggy mountain hinterland that provides a spectacular backdrop, superb coastal views of nearby islands, and the sights and smells of a Mediterranean melting pot where different peoples have mingled for centuries—ever since the Phocaean Greeks invaded in around 600 BC. The most recent immigrants come from North Africa.

This is the Mediterranean's largest port. The sizable, ugly industrial docks virtually rub shoulders with the intimate, picturesque old harbor, the **Vieux Port,** packed with fishing boats and pleasure craft: This is the heart of Marseille, with the Canebière avenue leading down to the water's edge.

Pick up your leaflets and town map at the tourist office (4 La Canebière) and peruse them on a café terrace overlooking the Vieux Port. These days, a forest of yacht and fishing-boat masts creates a scene of colorful bustle. Restaurants line the quays, and fishwives spout incomprehensible Provençal insults as they serve gleaming fresh sardines each morning. The Marseillais can be an irascible lot: Louis XIV built the Fort St-Nicolas, at the entry of the Vieux Port, with the guns facing inland to keep the citizens in order.

A short way down the right quay (as you look out to sea) is the elegant 17th-century Hôtel de Ville (Town Hall). Just behind, on rue de la Prison, is the Maison Diamantée, a 16th-century mansion with an **㊵** elaborate interior staircase. The mansion houses the **Musée du Vieux Marseille,** renovated in 1995, which displays costumes, pictures, and figurines. *2 rue de la Prison,* ☎ *91–55–10–19.* ☛ *10 frs adults, 5 frs students and senior citizens.* ☉ *Tues.–Sun. 10–5.*

㊶ Marseille's pompous, striped neo-Byzantine **cathedral** stands around the corner, its various domes looking utterly incongruous against the backdrop of industrial docks. If, however, you skirt around the colossal edifice and climb up rue du Panier behind the City Police Station, or *"archevêché"* ("archbishop's seat"), as it is irreverently known, the cathedral's Oriental silhouette, facing out over the Mediterranean, acquires fresh significance as a symbol of Marseille's role as gateway to the Levant.

The grid of narrow, tumbledown streets leading off rue du Panier is called simply *Le Panier* (The Basket). There is a claustrophobic feel here, heightened by the lines of washing strung from window to window, sometimes blotting out the sky; you can taste some of the dowdy, Naples-like essence of Marseille, and don't go wearing your best jewelry. Yet, apart from the colorful, sleazy ambience, the Panier is worth visiting for the elegantly restored 17th-century hospice now known as **㊷** the **Musée de la Vieille-Charité.** Excellent art exhibitions are held here, and the architecture—an arcaded, three-story courtyard built around a shallow-domed chapel—displays the subtlety and restraint lacking in the cathedral. *2 rue de la Charité,* ☎ *91–56–28–38.* ☛ *10 frs adults (25 frs for exhibitions).* ☉ *Tues.–Sun. 10–5.*

Now return to the Hôtel de Ville and take the barge that plows across the Vieux Port every few minutes (6 francs). Head right along the quay

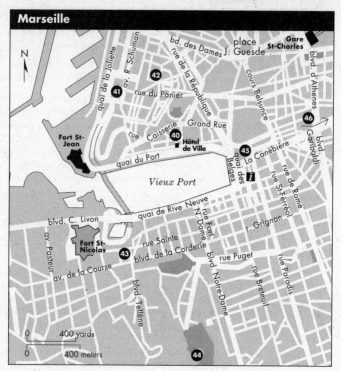

Marseille

43 toward the **Basilique St-Victor** across the water, in the shadow of the **Fort St-Nicolas** (which can't be visited). With its powerful tower and thick-set walls, the basilica resembles a fortress and boasts one of southern France's oldest doorways (circa 1140), a 13th-century nave, and a 14th-century chancel and transept. Downstairs, you'll find the murky 5th-century underground crypt, with its collection of ancient sarcophagi. *Rue Sainte.*

TIME OUT Just up the street from the basilica is the **Four des Navettes**—a bakery that has been producing slender, orange-spiced, shuttle-shape *navette* loaves for more than 200 years. Since the navettes can last for up to a year, they make good take-home presents as well as on-the-spot snacks. *136 rue Sainte,* ☎ *91–33–32–12.*

A brisk half-mile walk up boulevard Tellène, followed by a trudge up **44** a steep flight of steps, will take you to the foot of **Notre-Dame de la Garde.** This church, a flashy 19th-century cousin of the Sacré-Coeur in Paris and Fourvière in Lyon, features a similar hilltop location. The expansive view, clearest in early morning (especially if the mistral is blowing), stretches from the hinterland mountains to the sea via the Cité Radieuse, a controversial '50s housing project by Swiss-born architect Le Corbusier. The church's interior is generously endowed with bombastic murals, mosaics, and marble, while, at the top of the tower, the great gilded statue of the Virgin stands sentinel over the old port, 500 feet below. *Pl. du Colonel-Edon,* ☎ *91–13–40–80.*

Return to the Vieux Port and venture onto the legendary **La Canebière**—the "Can O' Beer" to prewar sailors—where stately mansions recall faded glory. La Canebière has been on the decline in recent years, but cafés and restaurants continue to provide an upbeat pulse. A hundred yards down on the left is the big white Palais de la Bourse (stock exchange) and, inside, the **Musée de la Marine** (Nautical Museum), with a rundown on the history of the port and an interesting display of model ships. ☎ *91–39–33–33.* ☛ *10 frs.* ☽ *Wed.–Mon. 9–noon and 2–6.*

Behind the bourse is the **Jardin des Vestiges,** a public park that holds the excavated ruins of Greek and Roman fortifications and foundations. Here you will find the little **Musée de l'Histoire de Marseille** (Town Museum), featuring exhibits related to the town's history. One of the highlights is the 60-foot Roman boat. *Centre Commercial,* ☎ *91–90–42–22.* ☛ *10 frs adults, 5 frs senior citizens and children.* ☽ *Tues.–Sat. 10–4:45.*

Continue past such busy shopping streets as rue Paradis, rue St-Ferréol, and rue de Rome, and turn right into boulevard Garibaldi to reach **cours Julien,** a traffic-free street lined with sidewalk cafés, restaurants, bookshops, and boutiques. The atmosphere is that of a scaled-down St-Germain-des-Prés wafted from Paris to the Mediterranean.

Return to La Canebière and, when you reach the undistinguished church of St-Vincent de Paul, fork left along cours Jeanne-Thierry (which becomes boulevard Longchamp) to the imposing **Palais Longchamp,** built in 1860 by Henri Espérandieu (1829–74), the same architect who built Notre-Dame de la Garde. The palais is home to the **Musée des Beaux-Arts;** its collection of paintings and sculptures includes works by 18th-century Italian artist Giovanni Battista Tiepolo, Rubens, and French caricaturist and painter Honoré Daumier. ☎ *91–62–21–17.* ☛ *10 frs adults, 5 frs students and senior citizens.* ☽ *Tues.–Sun. 10–5.*

Marseille is no seaside resort, but a scenic 5-kilometer (3-mile) coast road (corniche du Président-J.-F.-Kennedy) links the Vieux-Port to the newly created Prado beaches in the swanky parts of southern Marseille. There are breathtaking views across the sea toward the rocky Frioul Islands, which can be visited by boat.

Ninety-minute trips (40 frs) leave the Vieux-Port hourly in summer and frequently in winter to visit the **Château d'If,** a castle in which various political prisoners were held captive down the ages. Alexandre Dumas condemned his fictional hero, the count of Monte Cristo, to be shut up in a cell here, before the wily count made his celebrated escape through a hole in the wall. ☎ *91–59–02–30.* ☛ *21 frs.* ☽ *June–Sept., daily 8:30–noon and 1:30–6:30; Oct.–May, daily 8:30–noon and 1:30–4.*

Head east from Marseille along D2 to **Aubagne,** 16 kilometers (10 miles) away. The headquarters of the French Foreign Legion is on D44A (turn left off D2 just before Aubagne). The legion was created in 1831 and accepts recruits from all nations, no questions asked. The discipline and camaraderie instilled among its motley team of adventurers, criminals, and mercenaries has helped the legion forge a reputation for exceptional valor—a reputation romanticized by songs and films in which sweaty deeds of heroism are performed under the desert sun. The **Musée du Képi Blanc,** named after the *légionnaires'* distinctive white caps, does its best to polish the image by way of medals, uniforms, weapons, and photographs. *Caserne Viénot,* ☎ *42–03–03–20.* ☛ *Free.* ☽ *June–Sept., Tues.–Sun. 9–noon and 2–5; Oct.–May, Wed. and weekends, 9–noon.*

Head south from Aubagne via D559/D1 to the fishing village of **Cassis,** 11 kilometers (7 miles) away. Cafés, restaurants, and seafood shops cluster around its harbor and three beaches, at the foot of Europe's highest cliff, the 1,300-foot Cap Canaille. Boats leave the harbor from quai St-Pierre to visit the neighboring *calanques*—long creeks that weave their way between towering white-stone cliffs. The farthest of the three calanques visited by boat, **En-Vau,** is the most intimidating; you may want to walk back from here along the scenic footpath.

49 From Cassis, a daring clifftop road runs along the top of Cap Canaille to the shipbuilding base of La Ciotat, 13 kilometers (8 miles) away. Stay on D559 for another 19 kilometers (12 miles), through Bandol, to **Sanary,** whose old streets and charming seafront invite discovery. At neighboring Six-Fours-les-Plages, spin right on D616, around the Cap Sicié peninsula, in search of more fine panoramas and a colossal view across the Bay of Toulon.

50 **Toulon** is France's leading Mediterranean naval base. Leave your car in the underground parking lot at place de la Liberté, head along boulevard de Strasbourg, and turn right after the theater into rue Berthelot. This street leads into the pedestrian streets that constitute the heart of old Toulon. Shops and colorful stalls make it an attractive area by day, but avoid it at night.

TIME OUT Good-value menus and a cozy setting make **La Ferme,** situated on a small square at the harbor end of cours Lafayette, a sensible choice for lunch. *6 pl. Louis-Blanc,* ☎ *94–42–69–77. Closed Sun. and Aug.*

Avenue de la République, an ugly array of concrete apartment blocks, runs parallel to the waterfront, where yachts and pleasure boats—some available for trips to the Iles d'Hyères or around the arsenal and the bay—add bright splashes of color. At the western edge of the quay is the **Musée Naval,** with large models of old and new ships, figureheads, paintings, and other items related to Toulon's maritime history. *Pl. Monsenergue,* ☎ *94–02–02–01.* ☛ *20 frs adults, 10 frs children.* ☉ *Wed.–Mon. 9–noon and 2–5.*

Leading up from the quayside is the cours Lafayette; from Monday to Saturday it turns into a colorful street market selling glistening fish and masses of fruit.

Mighty hills surround Toulon. **Mont-Faron,** 1,600 feet, is the highest of all; its steep slopes veer up just outside the town. You can drive to the top, taking the circular route du Faron in either direction, or make the six-minute ascent by cable car from boulevard de l'Amiral Jean-Vence. ☎ *94–92–68–25. Operates daily 9:15–noon and 2:15–6; closed Mon., Sept.–May.*

51 Head east from Toulon along D559 to Hyères-Plage, then turn right along D97 to **La Tour-Fondue** at the tip of the narrow Giens peninsula. Boats leave here frequently (every half hour in July and August, every 60 or 90 minutes at other times) for the nearby island of Porquerolles. *Crossing time 20 min; round-trip fare 70 frs.*

52 **Ile de Porquerolles** is the largest of the Iles d'Hyères, an archipelago spanning some 20 miles. Although the village has several small hotels and restaurants, the main reason for coming here is simply to escape from the hustle of the modern world. Filmmakers love the island and use it as a handy base for shooting tropical or South Sea Island—type scenery. You can stroll across from the harbor to the lighthouse (*le phare*) in about 90 minutes, or head east among luxuriant flowers and thick woods. Boats for two of the other islands leave from Hyères-Plages and, farther along, from Port-de-Miramar and Le Lavandou. **Ile de Port-Cros,** a national park, has delightful, well-marked nature trails. **Ile du**

Levant is long and rocky and much less interesting; the French Navy has grabbed part of it, and much of the rest is a nudist camp.

What to See and Do with Children

The Wild West has invaded Provence at the **O.K. Corral,** a huge amusement park with roller coasters, Ferris wheels, and rootin' tootin' cowboy shows. The less than authentic flavor is more Gallic than *Gunsmoke,* but children love it nonetheless. *11 km (7 mi) west of Aubagne on N8, just beyond Cuges-les-Pins,* ☎ *42–73–80–05.* ☛ *73 frs adults, 63 frs children.* ☉ *June, daily 10:30–6:30; July–Aug., daily 10:30–7:30; Apr.–May and Sept.–Oct., Wed. and weekends 10:30–6:30.*

Just outside Stes-Maries-de-la-Mer is the **Musée de Cire** (also known as the **Musée du Boumian**), which provides an entertaining overview of local life in 18 scenes with waxwork figures. *Quartier Boumian,* ☎ *90–97–82–65.* ☛ *25 frs adults, 15 frs children.* ☉ *Apr.–Oct., daily 10–noon and 2–7; Nov.–Mar., Sun. 10–noon and 2–6.*

Wave machines, slides, water cannons, and bubble baths make up the fun at **Aquatropic** in Nîmes—an indoor swimming pool with a difference. *39 rue de la Hostellerie,* ☎ *66–38–31–00.* ☛ *30 frs.* ☉ *Weekdays 10–8, weekends 10–7.*

Boat tour of the calanques, near Cassis, Tour 3
Cathédrale d'Images, near Les Baux-de-Provence, Tour 1
Moulin de Daudet, Fontvieille, Tour 1
Muséon Arlaten, Arles, Tour 1
Parc Ornithologique, north of Stes-Maries-de-la-Mer, Tour 1 **Marseille fish market,** Tour 3 (*see also* Shopping, *below*).

Off the Beaten Track

Six-Fours-les-Plages on the dramatic Cap Sicié peninsula is a sprawling town of limited interest, but three nearby sites deserve a visit. The **Fort of Six-Fours,** at the top of a steep hill at Six-Fours itself, is a private military base that can't be visited, but the views across the Bay of Toulon are stupendous. Nearby is the former parish church of **St-Pierre,** featuring a Romanesque nave and a rich medieval altarpiece by Louis Bréa. Archaeological digs to the right of the entrance have revealed Roman walls built on the site.

Just north of Six-Fours (take D63 and turn left following signs marked *Monument Historique*) is the small stone chapel of **Notre-Dame de Pépiole,** hemmed in by pines and cypresses. It is one of the oldest Christian buildings in France, dating from the 5th century. The simple interior has survived the years in remarkably good shape, although the colorful stained glass that fills the tiny windows is modern—composed mainly of broken bottles! *Chapel open most afternoons.*

Continue 5 kilometers (3 miles) north (via D11) to Ollioules and take N8 (direction Le Beausset) through the spectacular **Gorge d'Ollioules;** the 5-kilometer (3-mile) route twists its scenic way beneath awesome chalky rock faces. Turn right along D462 to pay a visit to the village of **Evenos,** a patchwork of inhabited and ruined houses dominated by an abandoned cliff-top castle.

SHOPPING

Gift Ideas

Santons, colorful painted clay figures traditionally placed around a Christmas crib, make excellent gifts or souvenirs. There are hundreds of characters from which to choose, ranging from Mary, Joseph, and the Wise Men to fictional characters and notable personalities, both historic and contemporary. While santons can be found throughout the region (especially at Aubagne), the best place to purchase them is at **Santons Fouque** (65 cours Gambetta, Aix-en-Provence), which has 1,800 different models to offer.

Two specialties of Aix-en-Provence are deliciously fragrant soaps with natural floral scents and *calissons d'Aix,* ingeniously sculpted high-quality marzipan made of almonds and eggs. Delicately patterned beautiful Provençal print fabrics made by **Souleïado** can be bought in lengths or already fashioned into dresses, scarves, tea cozies, and other accessories. You can find the prints in Aix (8 pl. des Chapeliers), Arles (18 blvd. des Lices), Marseille (101 rue du Paradis), Montpellier (11 rue Foch), and Avignon (5 rue Joseph-Vernet),

Markets

Aix-en-Provence has several markets that are a delight to explore: the flower market on Tuesday, Thursday, and Saturday mornings at place de l'Hôtel-de-Ville; the fruit and vegetable market every morning at place Richelme; and the fruit, vegetable, and herb market on Tuesday, Thursday, and Saturday mornings at place des Prêcheurs. There is also an antiques market on Tuesday, Thursday, and Saturday mornings at place de Verdun. At **Arles,** fruit, vegetables, and household goods are sold on Wednesday and Saturday mornings in the boulevard de Lices, while **Marseille's** famous fish market is held on Monday through Saturday mornings at the Vieux Port. The flower market at **Nîmes** is open Monday mornings at boulevard Jean-Jaurès, and you can purchase fruit, herbs, honey, and truffles at **Orange** on Thursday mornings in cours Aristide-Briand. Finally, in **Toulon,** there's a celebrated fish, fruit, and household-goods market from Monday to Saturday mornings on cours Lafayette near the harbor.

SPORTS AND THE OUTDOORS

Bicycling

Bikes can be rented from train stations at Aix-en-Provence, Arles, Avignon, Marseille, Montpellier, Nîmes, and Orange; the cost is about 40 francs per day. Contact the **Comité Départemental de Cyclotourisme** (Les Passadoires, 84420 Piolenc) for a list of scenic bike paths.

Bullfighting

Provence's most popular spectator sport is bullfighting, both Spanish-style or the kinder *courses libres,* where the bulls have star billing and are often regarded as local heroes (they always live to fight another day). There are Spanish-style spectacles in the Roman arenas in **Arles** and **Nîmes.** Courses libres are also held at Nîmes and in nearly all the surrounding little villages throughout the summer.

Golf

Golf is still considered a pastime for the rich, and you will find many more golf courses on the Riviera. However, Provence has an excellent course at La Grande Motte (☎ 67–56–05–00) and another near Aix-en-Provence (**Golf International du Château de l'Arc,** Fuveau, ☎ 42–

53–28–38). Eighteen kilometers (11 miles) east of Hyéres is **Golf de Valcros** (La Londe–Les Maures, ☎ 94–66–81–02).

Hiking

This has become newly popular in France, and you'll find blazed trails (discreet paint marks on rocks) on the best routes. Contact the **Comité Départemental de la Randonnée Pédestre** (307 av. Foch, Orange, ☎ 90–51–14–86) for a detailed list of trails and outfitters.

Horseback Riding

Practically every locality in Provence has stables where horses can be rented. **Cheval Nomade** (col du Pointu, Bonnieux, ☎ 90–74–40–48) specializes in tours on horseback (*see also* Guided Tours under Essential Information, *above*). In Avignon, **Barthelasse** (Chemin du Mont Blanc, ☎ 90–85–83–48) offers lessons for children at **Le Poney Club,** a children's riding school, in addition to renting horses to more experienced equestrians. Or contact the **Association de Tourisme Equestre** (Chemin St-Julien, 30133 Les Angles, ☎ 90–25–38–91) for details.

Water Sports

You can windsurf and sail at La Grande Motte, Stes-Maries-de-la-Mer, Carry-le-Rouet and Martigues (near Marseille), Cassis, Hyères-Plage, and the island of Porquerolles, where equipment and sailboats can be rented. In Hyères, **Wanako Centre du Nautisme** (Av. du Dr-Robin, ☎ 94–57–77–20) rents sailboats starting at 300 francs for the day and Windsurfers beginning at 320 francs.

DINING AND LODGING

Dining

Provence has more than its share of France's top restaurants. Thank tourism for this: Nature didn't intend for Provence to be a gastronomic paradise. There are no deep, damp pastures for cattle and no chill rivers for salmon. In the old days, cooking was based on olive oil, fruit, and vegetables grown in valleys where summer irrigation is possible; salt cod was another staple, while the heady scent and flavor of garlic and wild herbs from stony, sunbaked hills improved the scant meat dishes. The current gastronomic scene is a far cry from this frugality: Wealthy tourists demand caviar and champagne, and Parisian chefs have created internationally renowned restaurants to satisfy them. Still, there's a lot to be said for simple Provençal food on a vine-shaded terrace. Have a *pastis,* that pale green, anise-based aperitif, accompanied by black olives, or try the *tapenade,* a delicious paste of capers, anchovies, olives, oil, and lemon juice, best smeared on chunks of garlic-rubbed bread. Follow it up with crudités (raw vegetables) served with *aïoli,* a garlicky mayonnaise, and a simple dish of grilled lamb or beef, accompanied by a bottle of chilled rosé. Locals like to end their meal with a round of goat cheese and fruit.

The Provençal image comes through in a love of color; bell peppers, eggplant, zucchini, saffron, and tomatoes crop up everywhere. Fish is very trendy these days. A trip to the fish market at Marseille will reveal the astronomical price of the fresh local catch; in the Mediterranean there are too few fish chased by too many boats. Steer clear of the multitude of cheap Marseille fish restaurants, many with brisk ladies out front who deliver throaty sales pitches; any inexpensive fish menu must use frozen imports. The Marseille specialty of bouillabaisse is a case in point: Once a fisherman's cheap stew of spanking-fresh specimens too small or bony to put on sale, it has now become a celebration dish, with such heretical additions as lobster. The high-priced versions can be delicious, but avoid the cheaper ones, undoubtedly concocted with canned, frozen, and even powdered ingredients.

CATEGORY	COST*
$$$$	over 400 frs
$$$	250–400 frs
$$	125–250 frs
$	under 125 frs

per person for a three-course meal, including tax (18.6%) and tip but not wine

Lodging

Accommodations are varied in this much-visited part of France and range from luxurious *mas* (converted farmhouses) to modest downtown hotels convenient for sightseeing. Service is often less than prompt, a casualty of the sweltering summer heat. Reservations are essential for much of the year, and many hotels are closed during winter.

CATEGORY	COST*
$$$$	over 800 frs
$$$	400–800 frs
$$	200–400 frs
$	under 200 frs

All prices are for a standard double room for two, including tax (18.6%) and service charge.

Aix-en-Provence

DINING

★ **Le Clos de la Violette.** Aix's best restaurant lies in a residential district north of the old town. You can eat under the chestnut trees or in the charming, airy pink-and-blue dining room. Chef Jean-Marc Banzo uses only fresh, local ingredients in his nouvelle and traditional recipes. Try the *saumon vapeur,* an aromatic steamed salmon, or the oyster and calamari salad. The weekday lunch menu is moderately priced and well worth the trek uptown. ✕ *10 av. de la Violette,* ☎ *42–23–30–71. Reservations advised. Jacket required. AE, MC, V. Closed Sun., Mon. lunch, early Nov., and most of Mar. $$$*

Brasserie Royale. This noisy, bustling eatery on cours Mirabeau serves up hearty Provençal dishes amid a background din of banging pots, vociferous waiters, and tumultuous cries for more wine. The best place to eat is in the glassed-in patio out front, so you can soak up the Champs-Elysées–style atmosphere of the leafy boulevard while enjoying your meal. ✕ *17 cours Mirabeau,* ☎ *42–26–01–63. Reservations advised. MC, V. $*

LODGING

★ **Mercure-Paul Cézanne.** Jean-Claude Trésy runs this stately townhouse hotel, and his taste for antiques and ornate furnishings has made it a civilized and sophisticated place. Each guest room is individually decorated with lots of marble, gilt, and period furniture. There's no restaurant. 🏨 *40 av. Victor-Hugo, 13100,* ☎ *42–26–34–73,* FAX *42–27–20–95. 56 rooms with bath. AE, DC, MC, V. $$$*

Nègre-Coste. A cours Mirabeau location makes this hotel both a convenient and an atmospheric choice; it's extremely popular, so make reservations long in advance. The elegant 18th-century town house has been completely modernized but features a luxurious Old World decor that extends to the guest rooms as well as the public areas. The views from the front rooms are worth the extra bit of noise. There's no restaurant. ⌧ *33 cours Mirabeau, 13100,* ☎ *42–27–74–22,* FAX *42–26–80–93. 37 rooms with bath. AE, DC, MC, V. \$\$–\$\$\$*

Arles

DINING

Le Vaccarès. In an upstairs restaurant overlooking place du Forum, chef Bernard Dumas serves classic Provençal dishes with a touch of invention and some particularly good seafood creations. Try his mussels dressed in herbs and garlic. The dining-room decor is as elegant as the cuisine. ✕ *11 rue Favorin,* ☎ *90–96–06–17. Reservations advised. MC, V. Closed end of Dec.–end of Jan., Sun. dinner, and Mon. \$\$*

DINING AND LODGING

Jules César. This elegant hotel was originally a Carmelite convent, and many guest rooms overlook the attractive 17th-century cloisters. The rooms are tastefully decorated with antiques, and the garden is an oasis of tranquillity. The restaurant, Lou Marquès, is the most fashionable eating place in Arles, thanks to new chef Pascal Renaud, who pleases his international clientele with both nouvelle cuisine and traditional Provençal dishes. Try his cod with lentils and fresh cream. ⌧ *Blvd. des Lices, 13200,* ☎ *90–93–43–20,* FAX *90–93–33–47. 55 rooms with bath. Restaurant, pool. AE, DC, MC, V. Closed Nov.–Dec. 23. \$\$\$*

LODGING

Arlatan. Follow the signposts from place du Forum to the picturesque street where you'll find this 15th-century house, former home of the counts of Arlatan and built on the site of a 4th-century basilica (tiled flooring dating from this period is visible below glass casing). The hotel was renovated in 1989, and antiques, pretty fabrics, and lots of tapestries and elegant furniture lend it a gracious atmosphere. There's no restaurant, but there is an attractive garden and a private bar. ⌧ *26 rue du Sauvage, 13200,* ☎ *90–93–56–66,* FAX *90–49–68–45. 51 rooms with bath. Bar. AE, DC, MC, V. \$\$\$*

Avignon

DINING

★ **Hiély-Lucullus.** According to most authorities, this establishment numbers among the top 50 restaurants in France, although André Chaussy has now taken over as chef for the legendary Pierre Hiély. The upstairs dining room has a quiet, dignified charm and is run with aplomb by Mme. Hiély. Traditional delicacies include crayfish tails in scrambled eggs hidden inside a puff-pastry case. Save room for the extensive cheese board. ✕ *5 rue de la République,* ☎ *90–86–17–07. Reservations required. AE, V. Closed most of Jan., last 2 wks in June, Mon. and Tues. lunch. \$\$\$*

DINING AND LODGING

Cloître Saint-Louis. Although close to Avignon's train station, leading monuments, and busy shopping streets, this stately hotel stands calm and serene within its sturdy 17th-century walls. The early Baroque building, fronted by pillars and ground-level arcades, was erected by the Jesuits in 1611 as a theological school and later served as a hospital. Its transformation into a hotel at the start of the decade was subtle yet stylish; much of the original open stonework has been retained, enhanced in the lobby and the vaulted dining room by modern marble flooring and contemporary furnishings. Some of the guest rooms have exposed beams, and most of those on the top floor have sloping ceilings. Snacks are served beside the small pool on the roof. There are family suites, unusual in France, for up to four people. ⌧ *20 rue du Portail-Boquier, 84000,* ☎ *90–27–55–55,* FAX *90–82–24–01. 80 rooms with bath. Restaurant, bar, pool, solarium. AE, DC, MC, V. \$\$\$*

Europe. This noble 16th-century town house became a hotel in Napoleonic times. In fact, the great man himself was one of the very first customers; since then, everyone from crowned heads of state to Robert and Elizabeth Browning has stayed here. Lovers of gracious living find it an excellent value; the spacious guest rooms, filled with period furniture, have lavishly appointed modern bathrooms. Make reservations well in advance. The restaurant, La Vieille Fontaine, serves respectable regional cuisine, and you can eat outside in the stone courtyard. Try the chicken with wild mushrooms or the duck liver. ☎ *12 pl. Crillon, 84000,* ☎ *90–82–66–92,* 𝔽𝔸𝕏 *90–85–43–66. 47 rooms with bath. Restaurant (closed Sat. lunch and Sun.). AE, DC, MC, V. $$$*

Les Frênes. The thumbnail-size town of Montfavet, 5 kilometers (3 miles) outside Avignon, is the setting for this luxurious hotel-restaurant. The country house features gardens to ramble in, splashing fountains, and individually decorated guest rooms; the styles range from subtle modern to art deco. Whatever the period of decor, each room is distinctive and equipped with every modern convenience. The excellent restaurant specializes in stylish country cuisine; the pigeon with black truffles in a puff-pastry case is always a good bet. ☎ *645 av. des Vertes-Rives, 84140 Montfavet,* ☎ *90–31–17–93,* 𝔽𝔸𝕏 *90–23–95–03. 15 rooms with bath. Pool, restaurant, sauna, golf, tennis. AE, DC, MC, V. Closed Nov.–early Mar. $$$*

Fontaine-de-Vaucluse

DINING AND LODGING

Le Parc. Handily placed in the heart of the village, with a terrace overlooking the River Sorgue, this comfortable hotel has a good choice of prix-fixe menus and specialties ranging from pasta with foie gras to salmon with mushrooms and duckling with berries. ☎ *Rue de Bourgades, 84800,* ☎ *90–20–31–57,* 𝔽𝔸𝕏 *90–20–27–03. 12 rooms with bath or shower. Restaurant. AE, DC, M, V. Closed Wed. and Jan.–mid-Feb. $$*

Gordes

DINING

Comptoir du Victuailler. You'll find only 10 tables at this tiny restaurant in the village center, which serves elegantly simple meals using only the freshest local capon, guinea fowl, asparagus, artichokes, truffles. . . . The fruit sorbets are a revelation, and there is an admirable choice of little-known Rhône wines. ✗ *Place du Château,* ☎ *90–72–01–31. Reservations required. MC, V. Closed mid-Nov.–mid-Dec., mid-Jan.–mid-Mar., Tues. dinner, and Wed. Sept.–May. $$$*

DINING AND LODGING

Domaine de l'Enclos. Small, private stone cottages make up this charming hotel just outside Gordes; they have deceptively simple exteriors, but inside you'll find them luxurious in a quaint, countrified way. The restaurant serves remarkably good nouvelle dishes; the menu varies with the seasons, but if it's offered, try the excellent aromatic duck. Both the views and the value are outstanding. ☎ *Rte. de Sénanque, 84220 Gordes,* ☎ *90–72–08–22,* 𝔽𝔸𝕏 *90–72–03–03. 14 rooms with bath. Restaurant, pool, tennis. AE, DC, MC, V. $$$*

Ile de Porquerolles

DINING AND LODGING

★ **Mas du Langoustier.** This luxurious hideout lies amid some stunningly lush terrain at the westernmost point of the island, 3 kilometers (2 miles) from the harbor. Anchor your yacht, and Mme. Richard will pick you up in a handy launch; arrive by ferry, and she'll send a car to meet you. The rooms are delightful, the views superb. Hotel guests must eat their meals here (no hardship), but the restaurant is open to nonresidents, too. Chef Michel Sarran uses a delicate nouvelle touch with his seafood dishes; try the fresh sardines in ginger or the grilled red mullet or lobster, accompanied by the rare island rosé. ⌑ *Pointe du Langoustier, 83400 Ile de Porquerolles,* ☎ *94–58–30–09,* FAX *94–58–36–02. 55 rooms with bath. Restaurant, tennis, billiards, private beach. AE, DC, MC, V. Closed Nov.–Apr. $$$*

Les Baux de Provence

DINING AND LODGING

L'Oustau de la Beaumanière. An idyllic setting under chalk-white cliffs (off D27), sumptuous guest rooms, and exquisite food make this a place of pilgrimage for lovers of the good life. The famous restaurant occupies an old Provençal farmhouse; you'll be served your meal in a cavernous room like a luxurious crypt, decked out with ornate furniture. Some say that the welcome nowadays lacks warmth and that young chef Jean-André Charial has yet to acquire the panache of his late grandfather, the legendary Raymond Thuilier. Nevertheless, you'll be splendidly housed and fed. ⌑ *Val d'Enfer, 13520,* ☎ *90–54–33–07,* FAX *90–54–40–46. 25 rooms with bath. Restaurant (reservations required, closed Wed., Thurs. lunch Sept.–June), tennis, pool, horseback riding. AE, DC, MC, V. Closed late Jan.–early Mar. $$$$*

Marseille

DINING

Chez Fonfon. The Marseillais come here for the best bouillabaisse in the world, and past diners lured by the top-quality seafood have included John Wayne and Nikita Khrushchev. "Fonfon" is the chef, sometimes known as Alphonse Mounier; he's thinking of retiring, but a successor is being trained to his rigorous standards. The restaurant is located on the corniche J.-F.-Kennedy, which twists its scenic path around the edges of the Mediterranean; the great sea views come gratis. ✕ *140 rue du Vallon des Auffes,* ☎ *91–52–14–38. Reservations advised. AE, DC, MC, V. Closed Oct., Dec. 25–Jan. 1, and weekends. $$$*

★ **Chez Madie.** Every morning Madie Minassian, the colorful *patronne,* bustles along the quayside to trade insults with the fishwives at the far end of the Vieux Port—and scour their catch for the freshest specimens. They swiftly end up in her bouillabaisse, fish soup, *favouilles* sauce (made with tiny local crabs), and other dishes you'll savor at her restaurant. ✕ *138 quai du Port,* ☎ *91–90–40–87. Reservations advised. AE, DC, MC, V. Closed Mon., Sun. dinner, and most of Aug. $$*

Dar Djerba. This is perhaps the best of the North African restaurants scattered throughout Marseille. The cozy, white-walled Dar Djerba on bustling cours Julien specializes in couscous of all kinds (with lamb, chicken, or even quail) as well as Arab coffees and pastries. The Moorish tile patterns and exotic aromas will waft you away on a Saharan breeze. ✕ *15 cours Julien,* ☎ *91–48–55–36. Reservations advised in summer. DC, MC, V. Closed Tues. and second half of Aug. $$*

DINING AND LODGING

★ **Sofitel.** Mainly because of the idyllic views across the old fort to the Vieux Port, the Sofitel possesses more appeal than most modern chain hotels. Rooms with a balcony are more expensive, but the pleasure of an outdoor breakfast in the morning sunshine—possible much of the year—is worth a splurge. The top-floor restaurant, Les Trois Forts, boasts stunning panoramic views and delicious Provençal fare; the red mullet, flavored with pepper, is superb. ⌑ *36 blvd. Charles-Livon, 13007,* ☎ *91–52–90–19,* FAX *91–31–46–52. 127 rooms and 3 suites with bath. Restaurant, pool. AE, DC, MC, V. $$$*

LODGING

★ **Pullman Beauvau.** Right on the Vieux Port, a few steps from the end of La Canebière, the Beauvau is the ideal town hotel. The 200-year-old former coaching inn was totally modernized in 1986 and its elegant facade cleaned in 1992. Its charming Old World opulence is enhanced by wood paneling, designer fabrics, fine paintings, genuine antique furniture—and exceptional service. The best rooms look out onto the Vieux Port. There's no restaurant, but you can start your day in the cozy breakfast room. ▣ *4 rue Beauvau, 13001,* ☎ *91–54–91–00 (U.S. reservations, 800/223–9868; in the U.K., 0171/621–1962),* FAX *91–54–15–76. 71 rooms with bath. Bar, breakfast room. AE, DC, MC, V. $$$*

Lutétia. There's nothing remarkable about this small hotel, but its rooms are quiet, airy, modernized, and a good value for the money, given the handy setting between La Canebière and St-Charles rail station. ▣ *38 allée Léon-Gambetta, 13001,* ☎ *91–50–81–78,* FAX *91–50–23–52. 29 rooms with bath or shower. DC, MC, V. $$*

Montpellier

DINING

★ **Le Chandelier.** The only complaints here concern the prices à la carte; the service is impeccable, the trendy pink decor is more than acceptable, and Gilbert Furlan's inventive cuisine is delicious: Try his chilled artichoke and rabbit soup or sea bass with crushed olives. Also good are the lobster in lasagna or the pigeon. There's a sound wine list, and the cinnamon-honey ice cream makes a fine end to your meal. ✕ *3 rue Albert-Leenhardt,* ☎ *67–92–61–62. Reservations advised. AE, DC, MC, V. Closed part of Feb., first 2 wks in Aug., Sun., and Mon. lunch. $$–$$$*

Petit Jardin. As the name implies, you can dine here in a charming leafy garden, within sight of the cathedral; the cheerful, flower-bedecked dining room is equally pleasant. Owner Roland Heilmann has made a rapid name for himself with such tasty regional dishes as *bourride* (garlicky fish soup made with monk- or anglerfish) and the *piperade* omelet with king-size prawns. ✕ *20 rue Jean-Jacques-Rousseau,* ☎ *67–60–78–78. Reservations advised. AE, DC, MC, V. Closed Sun. evening, Mon., and Jan.–Mar. $$*

DINING AND LODGING

Métropole. After a thorough overhaul in 1991, this venerable 19th-century hotel, halfway between the train station and city center, emerged soundproof and air-conditioned, with sumptuous 18th century–style furnishings and marble bathrooms. A courtyard garden provides a haven of calm. In La Closerie restaurant, young chef Jean-Luc Rabanel serves regional dishes like mullet with olives or lamb with thyme, accompanied by a good selection of local, fruity wines. The staff tries hard—sometimes too hard—to please, but you may find that a refreshing change. ▣ *3 rue du Clos-René, 34000,* ☎ *67–58–11–22,* FAX *67–92–13–02. 92 rooms with bath. Restaurant, bar. AE, DC, MC, V. $$$*

Nîmes

DINING

★ **Nicolas.** Locals have long known about this homey place, which is always packed; you'll hear the noise before you open the door. A friendly, frazzled staff serves up delicious bourride and other local specialties—all at unbelievably low prices. ✕ *1 rue Poise,* ☎ *66–67–50–47. Reservations advised. MC, V. Closed Mon., first 2 wks in July, and mid-Dec.–first wk in Jan. $*

DINING AND LODGING

★ **Impérator.** This little palace-hotel, just a few minutes' walk from the Jardin de la Fontaine, has been totally modernized in excellent taste. Most guest rooms retain a quaint Provençal feel, and all are cozy but spacious. The fine restaurant, L'Enclos de la Fontaine, is Nîmes's most fashionable eating place, where chef Jean-Michel Nigon provides such inventive dishes as iced, dill-perfumed *langoustine* (crayfish) soup, and calves' liver with black-currant sauce and Calvados-soaked apples. The set menus are bargains. ☎ *15 rue Gaston-Boissier, 30900, ☎ 66–21–90–30, FAX 66–67–70–25. 59 rooms with bath. Restaurant (closed Sat. lunch). AE, DC, MC, V. $$–$$$*

Lisita. There's something of a Spanish feel to this cozy hotel situated just a stone's throw from the Arènes. It's a favored haunt of Spanish matadors whenever they're in town for a bullfight. Rooms are on the small side, but some have a charming view of the plane trees that line the street, and most are tastefully decorated with regional furniture. The restaurant specializes in classic French fish and meat dishes rather than paella. ☎ *2 bis blvd. des Arènes, 30000, ☎ 66–67–66–20, FAX 66–76–22–30. 30 rooms with bath or shower. Restaurant (closed Sat. and first half of Aug.). AE, DC, MC, V. $$*

Orange

DINING

★ **Le Pigraillet.** One of Orange's best lunch spots is Le Pigraillet, on the Chemin Colline St-Eutrope at the far end of the gardens. You may want to eat in the garden, but most diners seek shelter from the mistral in the glassed-in terrace. The modern cuisine includes crab ravioli, foie gras in port, and duck breast in the muscat wine of nearby Beaumes-de-Venise. ✕ *Chemin de la Colline St-Eutrope, ☎ 90–34–44–25. Reservations advised. MC, V. Closed Jan.–Feb. and Mon. $$–$$$*

LODGING

Arène. This stylish old hotel, on a venerable, shady square lined with plane trees, prides itself on a warm welcome, attentive service, and large, air-conditioned rooms. ☎ *Pl. de Langes, 84100, ☎ 90–34–10–95, FAX 90–34–91–62. 30 rooms with bath or shower. AE, DC, MC, V. Closed Nov.–mid-Dec. $$*

St-Rémy-de-Provence

DINING AND LODGING

Vallon de Valrugues. This luxurious villa is fast making a name for itself; the arrival of chef Joël Guillet coincided with an extensive renovation. Many rooms have been enlarged and fitted with marble bathrooms. Some have a view of the rocky Alpilles hills, while others look out across olive groves. Guillet, who learned his trade at the famous Négresco in Nice, specializes in imaginative regional dishes like sea bass with calamari, pigeon roasted in lavender honey, and fricassee of scallops with cauliflower and parsley. His fruit desserts, usually made with dates, hazelnuts, pineapples, vanilla, or bananas, make a refreshing change from cream and chocolate. ☎ *Chemin Canto-Cigalo, 13210, ☎ 90–92–04–40, FAX 90–92–44–01. 34 rooms and 17 suites with bath. Restaurant, pool, sauna, hot tub. AE, MC, V. $$$–$$$$*

LODGING

Château des Alpilles. This lavishly appointed 19th-century château lords it over a fine park off D31. In its heyday, it counted statesmen and aristocrats among its guests. The crowd these days is almost as sophisticated, and the guest rooms offer the best in classic luxury. Decorators have gone wild with plush carpeting and polished wood furniture. Many rooms are equipped with kitchenettes. ☎ *Ancienne rte. du Grès,*

13210, ☎ *90–92–03–33,* FAX *90–92–45–17. 15 rooms and 4 suites with bath. AE, DC, MC, V. Pool, sauna, tennis. Closed mid-Nov.–mid-Dec. and Jan.–mid-Mar. $$$*

DINING AND LODGING

★ **Château de Roussan.** A manicured 15-acre park makes a lush setting for this 18th-century mansion, 2 kilometers (1 mile) outside town on the road to Tarascon (N99). Originally a country retreat, the château was converted into a hotel just after World War II. Today it seems so well preserved that it's almost spooky. The interior is quiet and gracious and appears virtually unaltered, save for the newly renovated bathrooms. The guest rooms are large and comfortable, and many feature pleasant parkland views. 🖪 *Rte. de Tarascon, 13210,* ☎ *90–92–11–63,* FAX *90–92–50–59. 20 rooms with bath. Restaurant, tennis. AE, MC, V. Closed mid-Nov.–Dec. 25 and Jan.–mid-Mar. $$$*

Tarascon
DINING AND LODGING

Saint-Jean. A dozen cozy, spacious, rustic rooms are hidden behind the austere facade. The wood-beam dining room serves regional dishes, including steak with shallot butter, salade niçoise, scallops, and chicken done in basil. 🖪 *24 blvd. Victor-Hugo, 13150,* ☎ *90–91–13–87,* FAX *90–91–32–42. 12 rooms with shower or bath. Restaurant (closed Fri. and Sat. lunch in winter). AE, DC, MC, V. Closed mid-Dec.–mid-Jan. $$*

Tornac
DINING AND LODGING

Le Ranquet. A hilly, wooded setting; an outdoor pool; a piano bar; and 10 stylish, spacious, air-conditioned rooms justify the 32-kilometer (20-mile) detour to Le Ranquet, northwest of Nîmes. Annie Majourel is one of France's few top-ranking female chefs; her menus (two are moderately priced) change every two months. 🖪 *Rte. de St-Hippolyte du Fort, 30140,* ☎ *66–77–51–63,* FAX *66–77–55–62. 10 rooms with bath. Restaurant, piano bar, pool. MC, V. Closed Tues. and Wed. out of season, mid-Nov.–Dec. 25, and Feb. $$–$$$*

Vaison-la-Romaine
DINING AND LODGING

Le Beffroi. This 16th-century mansion, with a nearby 17th-century annex and its own parking lot, sits on the hill in the old town. Rooms range in price from 300 to 600 francs; most are spacious and comfortable, with old furniture, and the best have an attractive view of the gardens. The restaurant offers saddle of hare, mushroom soup, and gizzard and goose-fillet salad. 🖪 *Rue de l'Evêché, 84110,* ☎ *90–36–04–71,* FAX *90–36–24–78. 20 rooms, some with bath or shower. Restaurant (closed Tues. lunch). AE, DC, MC, V. Closed Mon., mid-Nov.–Mar. $$*

LODGING

Evêché. Jean and Aude Verdier moved into this turreted, 17th-century former bishop's palace in the medieval, hilltop part of town in 1975 and spent 10 years restoring it. When they decided to rent four rooms to guests, their warm welcome and the rustic charm of the exposed beams, tile floors, and wooden bedsteads quickly earned them a loyal following from travelers who prefer architectural character to creature comfort. Breakfast is taken on a terrace overlooking the Ouvèze Valley—a good chance to try out your French, as your hosts' English is rudimentary! 🖪 *Rue de l'Evêché, 84110,* ☎ *90–36–13–46,* FAX *90–36–32–43. 2 rooms with bath, 2 rooms with shower. Reservations required. No credit cards. $$*

THE ARTS AND NIGHTLIFE

The Arts

Theater and Music

The summer music and drama festivals at Aix-en-Provence, Arles, Avignon, and Orange attract top performers. At Aix, the **International Arts and Music Festival,** with first-class opera, symphonic concerts, and chamber music, flourishes from mid-July to mid-August; its principal venue is the Théâtre de l'Archevêché in the courtyard of the Archbishop's Palace (pl. des Martyrs-de-la-Résistance). At Arles, the **International Photography Festival** takes place in July in the Théâtre Antique (rue de la Calade/rue du Cloître). Avignon's prestigious **International Music and Drama Festival,** held during the last three weeks of July, is centered on the Grand Courtyard of the Palais des Papes (pl. du Palais, ☎ 90–82–67–08). The **International Opera Festival** in Orange, during the last two weeks of July, takes place in the Théâtre Antique (pl. des Freres-Mounet).

Opera and concerts are performed throughout the year in Aix-en-Provence's 18th-century Théâtre Municipal (17 rue de l'Opéra, ☎ 42–38–44–71); Montpellier puts on concerts at the 19th-century Théâtre des Treize Vents (allée Jules-Milhau, ☎ 67–58–08–13).

Nightlife

Provence is a disappointing provincial backwater as far as razzle-dazzle nightlife goes; if you've come to the south of France hoping to paint the place red—keep heading east to the Riviera. Your best bets for clubs and discos are towns that have a major student population—such as Aix-en-Provence, Marseille, and Montpellier—or the seaside resorts of La Grande Motte and Stes-Maries-de-la-Mer. Most nightspots open and close with alarming frequency, but at press time, Marseille's major cabaret-nightclub was still going strong: **Au Son des Guitares** (18 rue Corneille). Disco lovers should try the **London Club** (73 corniche J.-F.-Kennedy). In Montpellier, we suggest **Le Rimmel** (4 bis rue de Boussairolles); in La Grande Motte, **Copacabana** (Grand Travers, allée de la Plage). Aix has a noteworthy jazz club, **Scat Club** (11 rue de la Verrerie), and Marseille has **Jazz Hot** (48 av. La Rose). Cabaret fans should try **Les Ambassadeurs** in Avignon (27 rue Bancasse). Finally, for those who thrive on roulette and blackjack, go to the **Casino** in Aix-en-Provence, open from 3 PM to 2 AM (2 bis av. Napoléon-Bonaparte).

PROVENCE ESSENTIALS

Arriving and Departing

By Plane

Marseille and Montpellier are served by frequent flights from Paris and London, and daily flights from Paris arrive at the smaller airport at Nîmes. There are direct flights from the United States to Nice, 160 kilometers (100 miles) from Aix-en-Provence.

By Car

The A6/A7 expressway (toll road) from Paris, known as the Autoroute du Soleil—the Expressway of the Sun—takes you straight to Provence, whereupon it divides at Orange.

By Train

Avignon is less than four hours from Paris's Gare de Lyon by TGV.

Getting Around

By Car
After the A7 divides at Orange, the A9 heads west to Nîmes and Montpellier (765 kilometers, or 475 miles, from Paris), extending into the Pyrénées and across the Spanish border. A7 continues southeast from Orange to Marseille on the coast (1,100 kilometers, or 680 miles, from Paris), while A8 goes to Aix-en-Provence (with a spur to Toulon) and then to the Riviera and Italy.

By Train
After the main line divides at Avignon, the westbound link heads to Nîmes, Montpellier (less than five hours from Paris by TGV), and points west. The southeast-bound link takes in Marseille (also under five hours from Paris by TGV), Toulon, and the Riviera.

By Bus
A moderately good network of bus services links places not served, or badly served, by the railway. If you plan to explore Provence by bus, Avignon is the best base. The town is well served by local buses, and excursion buses and boat trips down the Rhône start from here.

Guided Tours

The regional tourist offices' "52 Week" program pools 52 tours offered by various agencies, allowing visitors to choose from a myriad of tours throughout the year, touching on wine tasting, sailing, hang gliding, golfing, gastronomy, and cultural exploration. Contact **Loisirs-Acceuil** (Domaine de Vergon, 13370 Mallemort, ☎ 90–59–18–05) for details. In addition, local tourist offices can arrange many tours, ranging from one-hour guided walks to excursions that take a week or longer by bus, by bicycle, on horseback, or on foot.

Bus
The **Comité Départemental du Tourisme** (6 rue Jeune-Anacharsis, 13006 Marseille, ☎ 91–54–92–66) offers a five-day bus tour called "Découverte de la Provence," which includes full board in two-star hotels and entry to all places of interest. The tour starts in Marseille, continues to Cassis (from which there is a boat trip in the fjordlike waterways known as *calanques*), and includes a day in the Camargue and visits to Aix-en-Provence, Les Baux, and Arles; the cost is 2,000 francs per person. **S.A.A.F.** (110 blvd. des Dames, 13002 Marseille, ☎ 91–91–10–91) offers a "Bouillabaisse Weekend" in Marseille, taking in a trip to the harbor, the Château d'If, and Les Iles de Frioul; the cost is 2,900 francs per person. The **Arles Tourist Office** (35 pl. de la République, ☎ 90–18–41–22) employs 15 guide-lecturers to run excursions of the town and region.

Cycling
Illinois-based **Euro-Bike Tours** (Box 990, DeKalb, IL 60115, ☎ 800/321–6060) runs nine-day cycling tours of Provence in May, June, and September, to many of the towns and sights described in this chapter.

Horseback
The **Office Municipal de Tourisme** in Marseille features a six-day guided tour on horseback, during which you can stay in simple houses or tents. Beginning near Marseille in the hills of the Massif de la Sainte-Beaune, the tour continues through some wild but picturesque countryside, including Cézanne's mountain, La Sainte-Victoire; the cost, including insurance, is 2,900 francs per person. Twenty-seven kilometers (17 miles) from Aix-en-Provence off N113, lies **Sellerie Lou Mazet** (13680 Lançon-

de-Provence, ☎ 90–42–89–38), which offers horseback excursions of the Camargue that cost from 250 to 400 francs a day.

Special-Interest

S.A.A.F. offers a two-day "Wines of the Sun and Gastronomy" tour, which includes Avignon, a trip to the "Wine University" at Suze-la-Rousse, and stops at Orange and Villeneuve-les-Avignon. The price for one person is 1,400 francs, though it is lower for groups of two or more.

Important Addresses and Numbers

Travel Agencies

Wagons-Lits (2 rue Olivier, Avignon, ☎ 90–82–20–56; 225 av. du Prado, Marseille, ☎ 91–79–30–80; 3 rue des Cordeliers, Aix-en-Provence, ☎ 42–96–31–88). **Midi-Libre Voyages** (40 blvd. Victor-Hugo, Nîmes, ☎ 66–67–45–34).

Car Rental

Avis (11 cours Gambetta, Aix-en-Provence, ☎ 42–21–64–16; 267 blvd. National, Marseille, ☎ 91–50–70–11; and 92 blvd. Rabatau, Marseille, ☎ 91–80–12–00), **Europcar** (2 bis av. Victor-Hugo, Arles, ☎ 90–93–23–24; 27 av. St-Ruf, Avignon, ☎ 90–82–49–85), and **Hertz** (Parking des Gares, 18 rue Jules-Ferry, Montpellier, ☎ 67–58–65–18; 5 blvd. de Prague, Nîmes, ☎ 66–76–25–91).

Visitor Information

Provence's regional tourist offices accept written inquiries only. **Comité Régional du Tourisme du Languedoc-Roussillon** (20 rue de la République, 34000 Montpellier, ☎ 67–22–81–00) will provide information on all towns west of the River Rhône, while the remainder of towns covered in this chapter are handled by the **Comité Régional du Tourisme de Provence-Alpes-Côte d'Azur** (Immeuble C.M.C.I., 2 rue Henri-Barbusse, 13241 Marseille, ☎ 91–39–38–00) and the **Chambre Départementale de Tourisme de Vaucluse** (La Balance, Place Campana, B.P. 147, 84008 Avignon cedex, ☎ 90–86–43–42).

Local tourist offices for major towns covered in this chapter are as follows: **Aix-en-Provence** (2 pl. du Général-de-Gaulle, ☎ 42–16–11–61), **Arles** (Esplanade Charles-de-Gaulle, ☎ 90–18–41–21), **Avignon** (41 cours Jean-Jaurès, ☎ 90–82–65–11), **Marseille** (4 La Canebière, ☎ 91–13–89–00), **Montpellier** (Pl. René-Devic, ☎ 67–58–67–58), **Nîmes** (6 rue Auguste, ☎ 66–67–29–11), and **Toulon** (8 av. Colbert, ☎ 94–22–08–22).

13 The Riviera

St-Tropez to Monaco

T'S IMPORTANT to begin with a realistic sense of Riviera life so you won't spend your holiday nursing wounded expectations. The Riviera conjures up images of fabulous yachts and villas, movie stars and palaces, and budding starlets sunning themselves on ribbons of golden sand. The truth is that most beaches, at least east of Cannes, are small and pebbly. In summer, hordes of visitors are stuffed into concrete high rises or roadside campsites—on weekends it can take two hours to drive the last six miles into St-Tropez. Yes, the film stars are here—but in their private villas. When the merely wealthy come, they come off-season, in the spring and fall—the best time for you to visit, too.

That said, we can still recommend the Riviera, even in summer, as long as you're selective about the places you choose to visit. A few miles inland are fortified medieval towns perched on mountaintops, high above the sea. The light that Renoir and Matisse came to capture is as magical here as ever. Fields of roses and lavender still send their heady perfume up to these fortified towns, where craftspeople make and sell their wares, as their predecessors did in the Middle Ages. Some resorts are as exclusive as ever, and no one will argue that the chefs hereabouts have lost their touch.

It's impossible to be bored along the Riviera. You can try a different beach or restaurant every day. When you've had enough of the sun, you can visit pottery towns like Vallauris, where Picasso worked, or perfumeries at Grasse, where three-quarters of the world's essences are produced. You can drive along dizzying gorges, one almost as deep as the Grand Canyon. You can disco or gamble the night away in Monte Carlo and shop for the best Paris has to offer, right in Cannes or Nice. Only minutes from the beaches are some of the world's most famous museums of modern art, featuring the works of Fernand Léger, Henri Matisse, Pablo Picasso, Pierre-Auguste Renoir, Jean Cocteau—all the artists who were captivated by the light and color of the Côte d'Azur.

EXPLORING

Orientation

Our Riviera text covers the 75 miles between St-Tropez and the Italian border. The first tour concentrates on the Mediterranean coast from St-Tropez to Cannes and Antibes. The second begins with the inland towns of Grasse, Vence, and St-Paul-de-Vence, then rejoins the Mediterranean at Cagnes and continues to Nice and Monaco.

Tour 1. St-Tropez to Antibes

Numbers in the margin correspond to points of interest on the Riviera maps.

❶ Old money never came to **St-Tropez,** but Brigitte Bardot did. Bardot came with her director Roger Vadim in 1956 to film *And God Created Woman,* and the resort has never been the same. Actually, the village was first "discovered" by the writer Guy de Maupassant (1850–93) and again, later, by the French painter Paul Signac (1863–1935), who came in 1892 and brought his friends—Matisse, Pierre Bonnard, and others. What attracted them was the pure, radiant light and the serenity and colors of the landscape. The writer Colette moved into a villa here between the two world wars and contributed to its notoriety. When the movie people staked their claim in the 1950s, St-Tropez became St-Trop (*trop* in French means "too much").

Anything associated with the distant past almost seems absurd in St-Tropez. Still, the place has a history that predates the invention of the string bikini, and people have been finding reasons to come here for centuries. First, in AD 68 there was a Roman soldier from Pisa named Torpes who was beheaded for professing his Christian faith in the presence of the emperor Nero. The headless body was put in a boat between a dog and a cock and sent drifting out to sea. The body eventually floated ashore, perfectly preserved, still watched over by the two animals. The buried remains became a place of pilgrimage, which by the 4th century was called St-Tropez. In the late 15th century, under the Genovese, St-Tropez became a small independent republic.

Since then, people have come for the sun and the sea, and, starting in the 1950s, the celebrities. But whatever celebrities there are here stay hidden away in villas, and the people you'll see are mere mortals—lots of them. In summer, the population swells from 7,000 to 64,000 and the beaches are filled with every imaginable type of human animal, each displaying the best (or at least the most) of his or her youth, beauty, or wealth.

Off-season is the time to come, but even in summer there are reasons to stay. The soft, sandy beaches are the best on the coast. Take an early morning stroll along the harbor or down the narrow medieval streets—the rest of the town will still be sleeping off the Night Before—and you'll see just how pretty St-Tropez is, with its tiny squares and rich, pastel-colored houses bathed in light. There's a weekend's worth of trendy boutiques to explore—to be delighted or shocked by—and many cute cafés, where you can sit under colored awnings sipping wine and feel very French. Five minutes from town, you'll be in a green world of vineyards and fields, where you'll see nothing more lascivious than a butterfly fluttering around some chestnut leaves or a grapevine clinging to a farmhouse wall. Above the fertile fields are mountains crowned with medieval villages, where you can come at dusk for wild strawberry tarts and fabulous views. Perhaps it's the soft light, perhaps the rich fields and faded pastels, but nowhere else along the coast will you experience so completely the magic of the Riviera.

Two cafés on the harbor provide dress-circle seats for admiring the St-Tropez scene: **Le Gorille,** on quai Suffren, and **Sénéquier's** the café with the big terrace on quai Jean-Jaurès, beyond the tourist office. Walk along the harbor, filled with pleasure boats, and along the breakwater (the Môle), and continue to the **Musée de l'Annonciade,** a church converted into a major art museum. The collection of Impressionist paintings is filled with views of St-Tropez by Matisse, Bonnard, Paul Signac, Maurice de Vlaminck, and others. *Quai de l'Epi,* ☏ *94–97–04–01.* ☛ *25 frs adults, 13 frs children.* ☺ *June–Sept., Wed.–Mon. 10–noon and 3–7; Oct.–May, Wed.–Mon. 10–noon and 4–6.*

The tourist office is at the center of the half-moon quay surrounding the old port, at the corner of rue de la Citadelle. Less than 20 yards up the street on the left is a covered fish market—very small, but with a marvelous array of *fruits de mer* (seafood). On through the market you'll find a delightful tiny square with produce stalls and shops, which supply the myriad St-Tropez restaurants. Return to rue de la Citadelle and head inland up the hill to the **Citadel,** a 16th-century fortress with commanding views from St-Tropez across the bay to Ste-Maxime. In the keep is the **Musée de la Marine,** stocked with marine paintings and ship models. *Citadelle*, ☎ *94–97–59–43.* ☛ *25 frs.* ⊙ *Nov.–Easter, Wed.–Mon. 10–5; Easter–Oct., 10–noon and 2–4:30.*

Stroll down Montée Ringrave to **place Carnot,** site of a twice-weekly market (Saturday and Tuesday) and daily games of *boules* (like boccie). Trendy boutiques are on **rue Sibilli.**

TIME OUT Food at the **Café des Arts** may be ordinary, but the café is a popular place in which to sit and feel as if you're part of the in-crowd. *Pl. Carnot. Closed Oct.–Mar.*

Beaches close to town—**Plage des Greniers** and the **Bouillabaisse**—are great for families, but holiday people snub them, preferring a 10-kilometer (6-mile) sandy crescent at **Les Salins** and **Pampellone.** These beaches are about 3 kilometers (2 miles) from town, so it helps to have a car, motorbike, or bicycle.

❷ Visitors seem to enjoy a trip through **Port-Grimaud,** a modern architect's idea of a Provençal fishing village–cum–Venice, built out into the gulf for the yachting crowd—each house with its own mooring. Particularly appealing are the harmonious pastel colors, which have weathered nicely, and the graceful bridges over the canals.

From St-Tropez, take D93 south 11 kilometers (7 miles) to the old ❸ Provençal market town of **Ramatuelle.** The ancient houses are huddled together on the slope of a rocky spur 440 feet above the sea. The central square has a 17th-century church and a huge 300-year-old elm. Surrounding the square are narrow, twisting streets with medieval archways and vaulted passages.

❹ From Ramatuelle, follow signs to the old village of **Gassin.** The ride through vineyards and woods is lovely, and takes you over the highest point of the peninsula (1,070 feet), where you can stop and enjoy a splendid view. The perched village of Gassin, with its venerable old houses and 12th-century Romanesque church, has somehow managed to maintain its medieval appearance.

D98a runs 6 kilometers (4 miles) west from St-Tropez, joining the major coastal highway, N98, which proceeds eastward 8 kilometers (5 miles) ❺ to **Ste-Maxime**—a family resort with a fine sandy beach.

The coastline between Ste-Maxime and Cannes consists of a succession of bays and beaches. Minor resorts have sprung up wherever nature permits—curious mixtures of lush villas, campsites, and fast-food ❻ stands. **Fréjus,** 19 kilometers (12 miles) farther along N98, was founded by Julius Caesar as Forum Julii in 49 BC, and it is thought that the Roman city grew to 40,000 people—10,000 more than the population today. The Roman remains are unspectacular, if varied, and consist of part of the theater, an arena, an aqueduct, and city walls.

Fréjus Cathedral dates from the 10th century, although the richly worked choir stalls belong to the 15th century. The baptistry alongside it, square on the outside and octagonal inside, is thought to date from AD 400, making it one of France's oldest buildings. The cloisters have an unusual combination of round and pointed arches.

The rugged Massif de l'Estérel, between Fréjus and Cannes, is a hiker's joy, made up of volcanic rocks (porphyry) carved by the sea into dreamlike shapes. The harshness of the landscape is softened by patches of lavender, cane apple, and gorse. The deep gorges with sculpted, parasol pines could have inspired Tang and Sung Dynasty landscape painters. Drivers can take N7, the mountain route to the north or, as we pro-

The Riviera: St-Tropez to Cannes

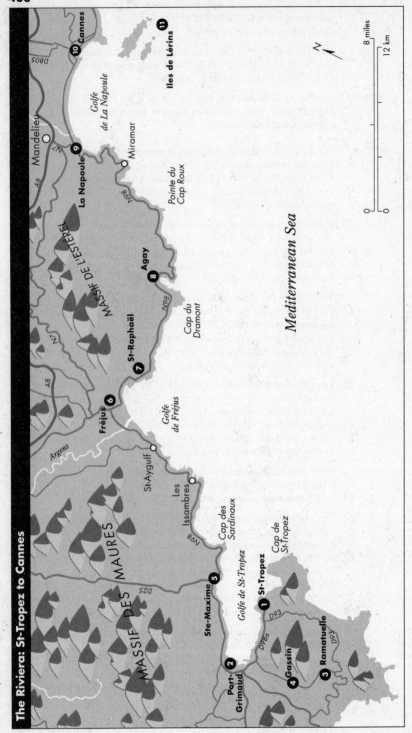

Cannes

Iles de Lérins

Golfe de La Napoule

Mandelieu

La Napoule

Miramar

MASSIF DE L'ESTÉREL

Agay

St-Raphaël

Pointe du Cap Roux

Cap du Dramont

Fréjus

Golfe de Fréjus

Argens

St-Aygulf

Les Issambres

MASSIF DES MAURES

Cap des Sardinaux

Ste-Maxime

Golfe de St-Tropez

Port-Grimaud

St-Tropez

Cap de St-Tropez

Gassin

Ramatuelle

Mediterranean Sea

N

0 — 8 miles
0 — 12 km

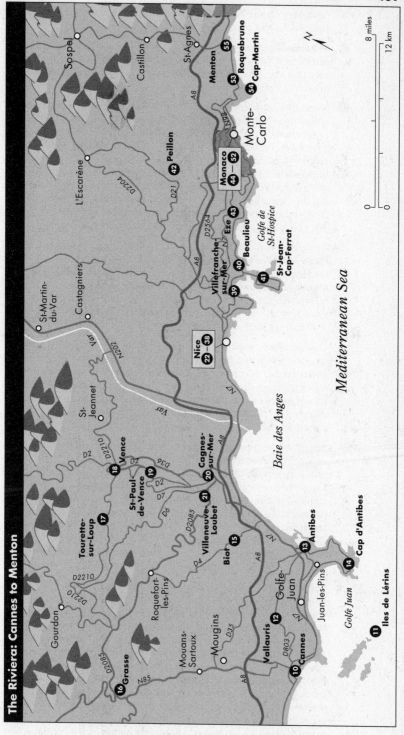

The Riviera: Cannes to Menton

Mediterranean Sea

Monte-Carlo

Roquebrune
Cap-Martin

Menton

St-Agnès

Castillon

Sospel

Peillon **42**

L'Escarène

Castagniers

St-Martin-du-Var

St-Jeannet

55

53

54

Monaco
44 — 52

Èze **43**

Beaulieu

Golfe de St-Hospice

St-Jean-Cap-Ferrat **41**

Villefranche-sur-Mer **40**

39

Nice
22 — 38

Golfe de St-Hospice

Baie des Anges

Vence **18**

St-Paul-de-Vence **19**

Tourrette-sur-Loup **17**

Cagnes-sur-Mer **20**

Villeneuve-Loubet **21**

Roquefort-les-Pins

Gourdon

Grasse **16**

Biot **15**

Antibes **13**

Cap d'Antibes **14**

Mouans-Sartoux

Mougins

Vallauris **12**

Golfe-Juan

Juan-les-Pins

Golfe Juan

Cannes **10**

Iles de Lérins **11**

N
8 miles
12 km

pose, stay on the N98 coast road past tiny rust-colored beaches and sheer rock faces plunging into the sea.

❼ **St-Raphaël,** next door to Fréjus, is another family resort with holiday camps, best known to tourists as the railway stop for St-Tropez. It was here that the Allied forces landed in their offensive against the Germans in August 1944.

❽ Some 10 kilometers (6 miles) from St-Raphaël is the resort of **Agay,** whose deep bay was once used by traders from ancient Greece. Agay has the best-protected anchorage along the coast. It was near here that writer Antoine de Saint-Exupéry (*The Little Prince*) was shot down in July 1944, having just flown over his family castle on his last mission.

❾ **La Napoule,** 24 kilometers (15 miles) from Agay, forms a unit with the older, inland village of **Mandelieu.** The village explodes with color during the Fête du Mimosa in February and boasts extensive modern sports facilities (swimming, boating, waterskiing, deep-sea diving, fishing, golf, tennis, horseback riding, and parachuting).

Art lovers will want to stop in La Napoule at the **Château de La Napoule Art Foundation** to see the eccentric work of the American sculptor Henry Clews. A cynic and reputed sadist, Clews had, as one critic remarked, a knowledge of anatomy worthy of Michelangelo and the bizarre imagination of Edgar Allen Poe. *Av. Henry-Clews,* ☎ *93–49–95–05.* ☛ *28 frs. Guided visits Mar.–Nov., Wed.–Mon. at 3, 4, and 5; Dec.–Feb., at 3 and 4.*

❿ Cosmopolitan, sophisticated, smart—these are words that describe the most lively and flourishing town on the Riviera, 6 kilometers (4 miles) farther up the coast. **Cannes** is a resort town—unlike Nice, which is a city—that exists only for the pleasure of its guests. It's a tasteful and expensive breeding ground for the upscale (and those who are already "up"), a sybaritic heaven for those who believe that life is short and sin has something to do with the absence of a tan.

Alongside the narrow beach runs a broad, elegant promenade called La Croisette, bordered by palm trees and flowers. At one end of the promenade is the modern Festival Hall, a summer casino, and an old harbor where pleasure boats are moored. At the other end is a winter casino and a modern harbor for some of the most luxurious yachts in the world. All along the promenade are cafés, boutiques, and luxury hotels like the Carlton and the Majestic. Speedboats and waterskiers glide by; little waves lick the beach, lined with prostrate bodies. Behind the promenade lies the town, filled with shops, restaurants, and hotels, and behind the town are the hills with the villas of the very rich.

★ The first thing to do is stroll along **La Croisette,** stopping at cafés and boutiques along the way. Near the eastern end, before you reach Port Canto, is the **Parc de la Roserie,** where some 14,000 roses nod their heads in the wind. Walking west takes you past the **Palais des Festivals** (Festival Hall), where the famous film festival is held each May. Just past the hall is **Place du Général-de-Gaulle,** while on your left is the **old port.** If you continue straight beyond the port on Allées de la Liberté, you'll reach a tree-shaded area, where flowers are sold in the morning, boules is played in the afternoon, and a flea market is held on Saturday. If instead of continuing straight from the square you turn inland, you'll quickly come to rue Meynadier. Turn left. This is the old main street, which has many 18th-century houses—now boutiques and specialty food shops, where you can buy exotic foods and ship them.

TIME OUT   The **Café Poet** at 7 rue Félix-Faure is the ideal spot to stop for breakfast or an ice cream alongside the bustling Allées de la Liberté.

⓫ You may want to visit the peaceful **Iles de Lérins** (Lerin Islands) to escape the crowds. The ferry leaves from Cannes harbor (near the Palais des Festivals) and takes 15 minutes and 40 francs to **Ste-Marguerite,** 30 minutes and 45 francs to **St-Honorat** (☎ 93–39–11–82 for information). Boats leave approximately every hour. A ticket to both islands costs 60 francs.

Ste-Marguerite, the larger of the two, is an island of wooded hills, with a tiny main street lined with fishermen's houses. Visitors enjoy peaceful walks through a forest of enormous eucalyptus trees and parasol pines. Paths wind through a dense undergrowth of tree heathers, rosemary, and thyme. The main attraction is the dank cell in **Fort Royal,** where the Man in the Iron Mask was imprisoned (1687–98) before going to the Bastille, where he died in 1703. The mask, which he always wore, was in fact made of velvet. Was he the illegitimate or twin brother of Louis XIV or Louis XIII's son-in-law? No one knows. The fort also contains a marine museum. ☎ 93–43–18–17. ☛ *10 frs adults; free Wed.* ☉ *Wed.–Mon., 10:30–noon and 2–4:30 (6:30 in summer). Closed Jan.*

St-Honorat is less tamed but more tranquil than its sister island. It was named for a hermit-monk who came here to escape his followers; but when the hermit founded a monastery here in AD 410, his disciples followed and the monastery became one of the most powerful in all Christendom. It's worth taking the two-hour walk around the island to the **old fortified monastery,** where noble Gothic arcades are arranged around a central courtyard. Next door to the "new" 19th-century monastery is a shop where the monks sell handicrafts, lavender scent, and a home-brewed liqueur called Lerina. *Monastère de Lérins,* ☎ 93–48–68–68. ☛ *10 frs.* ☉ *Daily 9–noon and 2–4:45. High mass at the abbey 9:45 Sun.*

⓬ From Cannes, take D803 northeast to the pottery-making center of **Vallauris,** 5 kilometers (3 miles) away. Pottery is on sale throughout the village, and several workshops can be visited. Picasso spurred a resurgence of activity when he settled here in 1947 and created some whimsically beautiful ceramics. He also decorated the tunnel-like medieval chapel of the former priory—now the **Musée National Picasso**—with a fresco entitled *War and Peace. Pl. de la Libération,* ☎ 93–64–18–05. ☛ *8 frs.* ☉ *Mid-Dec.–Oct., Wed.–Mon. 10–noon and 2–6 (until 5 in winter).*

⓭ From Vallauris, continue east to **Antibes,** founded as a Greek trading port in the 4th century BC and now a center for fishing and rose growing. Avenue de l'Amiral-Grasse runs along the seafront from the harbor to the **marketplace,** a colorful sight most mornings, and to the church of the **Immaculate Conception,** with intricately carved portals (dating from 1710) and a 1515 altarpiece by Nice artist Louis Bréa (c. 1455–1523).

★ The **Château Grimaldi,** built in the 12th century by the ruling family of Monaco and extensively rebuilt in the 16th century, is reached by nearby steps. Tear yourself away from the sun-baked terrace overlooking the sea to go inside to the Picasso Museum. There are stone Roman remains on exhibit, but the works of Picasso—who occupied the château during his most cheerful and energetic period—hold center stage; they include an array of paintings, pottery, and lithographs inspired by the sea and Greek mythology. *Pl. du Château,* ☎ 93–34–91–91.

☛ *20 frs adults, 10 frs students and senior citizens.* ☉ *Dec.–Oct., Wed.–Mon. 10–noon and 2–6 (3–7 July–Sept.).*

Continue down avenue de l'Amiral-Grasse to the St-André Bastion, constructed by the military engineer Sébastien de Vauban in the late 17th century and home to the **Musée Archéologique.** Here 4,000 years of local history are illustrated by continually expanding displays. *Bastion St-André,* ☎ *93–34–48–01.* ☛ *10 frs adults, 5 frs children and senior citizens.* ☉ *Dec.–Oct., weekdays 9–noon and 2–6.*

Antibes officially forms one town (dubbed "Juantibes") with the more recent resort of **Juan-les-Pins** to the south, where beach and nightlife attract a younger and less affluent crowd than in Cannes. In the summer, the mood is especially frenetic.

★ ⑭ The **Cap d'Antibes** peninsula is rich and residential, with beaches, views, and large villas hidden in luxurious vegetation. Barely two miles long by a mile wide, it offers a perfect day's outing. An ideal walk is along the **Sentier des Douaniers,** the customs officers' path.

From Pointe Bacon there is a striking view over the Baie des Anges (Bay of Angels) toward Nice; climb up to the nearby Plateau de la Garoupe for a sweeping view inland over the Esterel massif and the Alps. The **Sanctuaire de la Garoupe** (sailors' chapel) has a 14th-century icon, a statue of Our Lady of Safe Homecoming, and numerous frescoes and votive offerings. The lighthouse alongside, which can be visited, has a powerful beam that carries more than 40 miles out to sea. ☛ *Free.* ☉ *Nov.–Mar., daily 10:30–12:30 and 2:30–7:30; Apr.–Oct., daily 10:30–12:30 and 2–5.*

Nearby is the **Jardin Thuret,** established by botanist Gustave Thuret (1817–75) in 1856 as France's first garden for subtropical plants and trees. The garden, now run by the Ministry of Agriculture, remains a haven for rare, exotic plants. *Blvd. du Cap.* ☛ *Free.* ☉ *Weekdays 8–12:30 and 2–5:30.*

At the southwest tip of the peninsula, opposite the luxurious Grand Hôtel du Cap d'Antibes, is the **Musée Naval & Napoléonien,** a former battery, where you can spend an interesting hour scanning Napoleonic proclamations and viewing scale models of oceangoing ships. *Batterie du Grillon, av. Kennedy,* ☎ *93–61–45–32.* ☛ *15 frs adults, 7 frs children and senior citizens.* ☉ *Apr.–Sept., weekdays 10–noon and 3–7, Sat. 10–noon; Nov.–Mar., weekdays 9:30–noon and 2:15–4, Sat. 9:30–noon.*

Marineland, Europe's first aquatic zoo, is only a short distance from Antibes. Take N7 north and then head left at La Brague onto D4; Marineland is on the right. Performing dolphins leap into action every afternoon, abetted by a supporting cast of seals, penguins, and sea lions. There is also an amusement park. *309 rue Mozart,* ☎ *93–33–49–49.* ☛ *93 frs adults, 62 frs children.* ☉ *Apr.–Oct., daily 10–9; Nov.–Mar., daily 10–6; first performance at 2:30.*

⑮ Mimosa and roses for the cut-flower market are grown at the charming old village of **Biot,** 4 kilometers (2½ miles) up D4. The glassworks at the edge of the village welcomes visitors to observe its glassblowers. *Verrerie de Biot, 5 chemin des Combes,* ☎ *93–65–03–00.* ☛ *Free.* ☉ *Mon.–Sat. 9–6:30, Sun. 10:30–1 and 2:30–6:30.*

Artist Fernand Léger (1881–1955) lived in Biot, and hundreds of his paintings, ceramics, and tapestries are on display at the **Musée National Fernand Léger,** a strikingly designed museum, which opened in 1960.

Léger's stylistic evolution is traced from his early flirtation with Cubism to his ultimate preference for flat expanses of primary color and shades of gray, separated by thick black lines. The museum also houses an extensive collection of mosaics. *Chemin du Val de Pomme,* ☎ *93–65–63–61.* ☛ *32 frs adults, 15 frs students and senior citizens.* ☉ *Apr.–Oct., Wed.–Mon. 10–noon and 2–6; Nov.–Mar., Wed.–Mon. 10–noon and 2–5.*

Tour 2: Grasse to Menton

⑯   Our tour of the eastern Riviera begins a dozen miles inland at **Grasse.** If you are coming from Cannes or Antibes, stop off en route to admire the dramatic hilltop setting of **Mougins,** a quaint, fortified town just north of Cannes.

If touring a perfume factory in a tacky modern town is your idea of pleasure, by all means visit Grasse. If you had visited four centuries ago, when the town specialized in leatherwork, you would have come for gloves. In the 16th century, when scented gloves became the rage, the town began cultivating flowers and distilling essences. That was the beginning of the perfume industry. Today some three-fourths of the world's essences are made here from wild lavender, jasmine, violets, daffodils, and other sweet-smelling flowers. Five thousand producers supply some 20 factories and six cooperatives. If you've ever wondered why perfume is so expensive, consider that it takes 10,000 flowers to produce 2.2 pounds of jasmine petals and that nearly one ton of petals is needed to distill 1½ quarts of essence. Sophisticated Parisian perfumers mix Grasse essences into their own secret formulas; perfumes made and sold in Grasse are considerably less subtle. You can, of course, buy Parisian perfumes in Grasse—at Parisian prices.

Several perfume houses welcome visitors for a whiff of their products and an explanation of how the perfumes are made: Galimard (73 rte. de Cannes, ☎ 93–09–20–00); Molinard (60 blvd. Victor-Hugo, ☎ 93–36–01–62); and Fragonard (20 blvd. Fragonard, ☎ 93–36–44–65), which is conveniently central and has its own museum. ☛ *Perfume houses free.* ☉ *Daily 9–noon and 2–6.*

A new perfume museum, the **Musée International de la Parfumerie,** was opened in early 1989 and explains the history and manufacturing process of perfume. Old machinery, pots, and flasks can be admired; toiletry, cosmetics, and makeup accessories are on display; and there is a section devoted to perfume's refined marketing aids, with examples of packaging and advertising posters. *8 pl. du Cours,* ☎ *93–36–80–20.* ☛ *14 frs adults, 7 frs children and senior citizens.* ☉ *Oct.–May, daily 10–noon and 2–5; June–Sept., daily 10–7.*

The artist Jean-Honoré Fragonard (1732–1806) was born in Grasse, and many of his pictures, etchings, drawings, and sketches—plus others by his son Alexandre-Evariste and his grandson Théophile—are hung in the 17th-century **Musée Fragonard.** *23 blvd. Fragonard,* ☎ *93–36–01–61.* ☛ *10 frs adults, 5 frs children and senior citizens (joint ticket with Musée d'Art).* ☉ *Wed.–Sun. 10–noon and 2–5.*

The **Musée d'Art et d'Histoire de Provence,** 150 yards away in an 18th-century mansion, houses a collection of Provençal furniture, folk art, tools and implements, and china. *2 rue Mirabeau,* ☎ *93–36–01–61.* ☛ *10 frs adults, 5 frs children and senior citizens (joint ticket with Musée Fragonard).* ☉ *Apr.–Oct., Mon.–Sat. 10–noon and 2–6; Dec.–Mar., Mon.–Sat. 10–noon and 2–5.*

From Grasse, strike east along D2085/D2210 toward Vence, 25 kilometers (16 miles) away. About 5 kilometers (3 miles) before you reach
⑰ Vence is **Tourette-sur-Loup,** whose outer houses form a rampart on a rocky plateau, 1,300 feet above a valley full of violets. The town is much less commercialized than many others in the area; its shops are filled not with postcards and scented soaps but with the work of dedicated artisans. A rough stone path takes you on a circular route around the rim of the town, past the shops of engravers, weavers, potters, and painters. Ask any artisan for a map of the town that locates each of the shops. Also worth visiting is a single-nave 14th-century church that has a notable wooden altarpiece.

⑱ When you arrive in **Vence,** leave your car on avenue Foch and climb up to the medieval town (Vieille Ville). The Romans were the first to settle on the 1,000-foot hill; the **cathedral** (built between the 11th and 18th centuries), rising above the medieval ramparts and traffic-free streets, was erected on the site of a temple to Mars. Of special note are a mosaic by Marc Chagall of Moses in the bullrushes and the ornate 15th-century wooden choir stalls.

At the foot of the hill, on the outskirts of Vence, is the **Chapelle du Rosaire,** a small chapel decorated with beguiling simplicity and clarity by Matisse between 1947 and 1951. The walls, floor, and ceiling are gleaming white and there are small stained-glass windows in cool greens and blues. "Despite its imperfections I think it is my masterpiece . . . the result of a lifetime devoted to the search for truth," wrote Matisse, who designed and dedicated the chapel when he was in his eighties and nearly blind. *Av. Henri-Matisse,* ☎ *93–58–03–26.* ☛ *Free.* ⊙ *Tues. and Thurs. 10–11:30 and 2–5:30.*

★ ⑲ A few miles south along D2 is **St-Paul-de-Vence,** a gem of a town whose medieval atmosphere has been perfectly preserved. Not even the hordes of tourists—to which the village now caters—can destroy its ancient charm. You can walk the narrow, cobbled streets in perhaps 15 minutes, but you'll need another hour to explore the shops—mostly galleries selling second-rate landscape paintings, but also a few serious studios and gift shops offering everything from candles to dolls, dresses, and hand-dipped chocolate strawberries. Your best bet is to visit in the late afternoon, when the tour buses are gone, and enjoy a drink among the Klees and Picassos in the Colombe d'Or (*see* Dining and Lodging, *below*). Be sure to visit the remarkable 12th-century Gothic church; you'll want to light a candle to relieve its wonderful gloom. The treasury is rich in 12th–15th-century pieces, including processional crosses, reliquaries, and an enamel Virgin and Child.

★   At La Gardette, just northwest of the village, is the **Fondation Maeght** (founded in 1964 by art dealer Aimé Maeght), one of the world's most famous small museums of modern art. Monumental sculptures are scattered around its pine-tree park, and a courtyard full of Alberto Giacometti's elongated creations separates the two museum buildings. The rooms inside showcase the works of Joan Miró, Georges Braque, Wassily Kandinsky, Bonnard, Matisse, and others. Few museums blend form and content so tastefully and imaginatively. There is also a library, movie theater, and auditorium. ☎ *93–32–81–63.* ☛ *40 frs adults, 30 frs children.* ⊙ *July–Sept., daily 10–7; Oct.–June, daily 10–12:30 and 2:30–6.*

⑳ Return to D2 and continue 6 kilometers (4 miles) south to **Cagnes-sur-Mer.** An attractive **château,** once a medieval fortress, is perched high above the modern seaside resort within the walls of Haut-de-Cagnes, the old town. Much of the château's Renaissance decoration—frescoes, plasterwork, and fireplaces—remains intact, and the third floor hosts an art gallery devoted to Mediterranean artists, including Chagall and Raoul Dufy. There's an exciting panorama from the top of the tower. *Pl. Grimaldi,* ☎ *93–20–85–57.* ☛ *6 frs adults, 3 frs students.* ☉ *Easter–mid-Oct., daily 10–noon and 2:30–7; mid-Nov.–Easter, Wed.–Mon. 10–noon and 2–5.*

The painter Auguste Renoir (1841–1919) spent the last 12 years of his life at Cagnes. His home at Les Collettes has been preserved as a **Musée Renoir,** and you can see his studio, as well as some of his work. A bronze statue of Venus nestles amid the fruit trees in the colorful garden. *Av. des Collettes,* ☎ *93–20–61–07.* ☛ *22 frs adults, 11 frs children.* ☉ *June–Oct., daily 10–noon and 2–6; Nov.–May, Wed.–Mon. 10–noon and 2–5.*

㉑ A mile west of Cagnes is the tiny village of **Villeneuve-Loubet,** worth visiting for its **Fondation Escoffier:** a gourmet shrine that can be fitted in between meals because there's nothing to eat. As kitchen overlord at the London Carlton and the Paris Ritz, Auguste Escoffier (1846–1935) carved out a reputation as Europe's top chef. One of his inventions is Peach Melba. This museum, in the house where he was born, displays some elaborate *pièces montées* in sugar and marzipan and boasts a collection of 15,000 lip-smacking menus. *3 rue Escoffier,* ☎ *93–20–80–51.* ☛ *10 frs adults, 5 frs students.* ☉ *Dec.–Oct., Tues.–Sun. 2–6.*

The congested N7 from Cagnes to Nice is enough to put you off the Riviera for life. Tedious concrete constructions assault the eye; the railroad on one side and the stony shore on the other offer scant respite.
㉒ Soon, however, you'll arrive at the Queen of the Riviera—**Nice.**

Nice is less glamorous, less sophisticated, and less expensive than Cannes. It's also older—weathered-old and faded-old—like a wealthy dowager who has seen better days but still maintains a demeanor of dignity and poise. Nice is a big, sprawling city of 350,000 people—five times as many as Cannes—and has a life and vitality that survive when tourists pack their bags and go home.

Nice is worth a visit, but should you stay here? On the negative side, its beaches are cramped and pebbly. Many of its hotels are either rundown or being refurbished for the convention crowd. On the positive side, Nice is likely to have hotel space, at prices you can afford, when all other towns are full. It's also a convenient base from which to explore Monte Carlo and the medieval towns in the interior. It does have its share of first-class restaurants and boutiques, and an evening stroll through the old town or along the Promenade des Anglais is something to savor.

Numbers in the margin correspond to points of interest on the Nice map.

We suggest that you divide your visit to Nice into three minitours, with
㉓ arcaded **place Masséna,** the city's main square, as a common starting
㉔ point. First, head west through the fountains and gardens of the **Jardin Albert I** to the **Promenade des Anglais,** built, as the name indicates, by the English community in 1824. Traffic on this multilane highway can be heavy, but once you have crossed to the seafront, there are fine views, across private beaches, of the Baie des Anges.

TIME OUT   Walk west as far as the Neptune Plage (beach) and cross over to the **Hôtel Négresco.** If you can't afford to stay here, spend a few dollars on

Nice

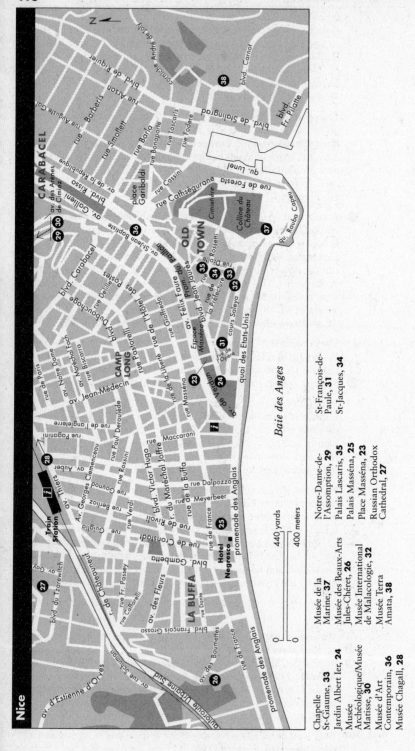

Baie des Anges

a cup of coffee and think of it as an admission charge to the palatial hotel. *37 promenade des Anglais.*

㉕ Just up rue de Rivoli from the Hôtel Négresco is the **Palais Masséna,** a museum concerned principally with the Napoleonic era and, in particular, with the life of local-born general André Masséna (1756–1817). Bonaparte rewarded the general for his heroic exploits during the Italian campaign with the sonorous sobriquet *l'Enfant chéri de la victoire* (the Cherished Child of Victory). Sections of the museum evoke the history of Nice and its carnival; there are also some fine Renaissance paintings and objects. *65 rue de France,* ☎ *93–88–11–34.* ☛ *Free. Open. Dec.–Oct., Tues.–Sun. 10–noon and 2–5 (3–6 May–Sept.).*

Head west along rue de France, then turn right up avenue des Baumettes **㉖** to the **Musée des Beaux-Arts Jules-Chéret,** Nice's fine-arts museum, built in 1878 as a palatial mansion for a Russian princess. The rich collection of paintings includes works by Auguste Renoir, Edgar Degas, Claude Monet, and Raoul Dufy; Oriental prints; sculptures by Auguste Rodin; and ceramics by Picasso. Jules Chéret (1836–1932) is best known for his Belle Epoque posters; several of his oils, pastels, and tapestries can be admired here. *33 av. des Baumettes,* ☎ *93–62–18– 12.* ☛ *Free.* ☉ *May–Sept., Tues.–Sun. 10–noon and 3–6; Oct. and Dec.–Apr., Tues.–Sun. 10–noon and 2–5.*

Nice's main shopping street, avenue Jean-Médecin, runs inland from place Masséna; all needs and most tastes are catered to in its big department stores (Nouvelles Galeries, Prisunic, and the split-level Etoile mall). Turn left at the far end into avenue Thiers, pass the train station, turn right (boulevard Gambetta) then make the first left into boule- **㉗** vard du Tzarewitch. As that name suggests, the **Russian Orthodox Cathedral**—a famously unorthodox Nice landmark, with its colorful ceramics, onion domes, and iconed interior—is waiting for you just around the corner. It was built largely with money from Czar Nicholas II (early this century, the Riviera was popular with Russian top brass, too). But within six years of its 1912 grand opening, Czar Nicholas and the "Czarevitch"—his son Alexis—were dead and the Romanov dynasty overthrown.

Return to avenue Thiers, pass the train station, turn left into avenue Malausséna, and across the railway take the first right down to the **㉘** **Musée Chagall**—built to show off the paintings of Marc Chagall (1887– 1985) in natural light. The Old Testament is the primary subject of the works, which include 17 huge canvases covering a period of 13 years, together with 195 preliminary sketches, several sculptures, and nearly 40 gouaches. In summertime, you can buy snacks and drinks in the garden. *Av. du Dr-Ménard,* ☎ *93–81–75–75.* ☛ *27 frs adults, 18 frs senior citizens.* ☉ *July–Sept., Wed.–Mon. 10–7; Oct.–July, Wed.–Mon. 10–12:30 and 2–5:30.*

Boulevard de Cimiez, just east of the museum, runs northeast to the residential quarter of Nice—the hilltop site of **Cimiez,** occupied by the Romans 2,000 years ago. The foundations of the Roman town can be seen, along with vestiges of the arena, less spectacular than those at Arles or Nîmes but still in use (notably for a summer jazz festival). Close **㉙** by is the Franciscan monastery of **Notre-Dame-de-l'Assomption,** with some outstanding late-medieval religious pictures; guided tours include the small museum and an audiovisual show on the life and work of the Franciscans. *Place du Monastère,* ☎ *93–81–00–04.* ☛ *Free.* ☉ *Mon.–Sat. 10–noon and 3–6.*

30 A 17th-century Italian villa amid the Roman remains contains two museums: the **Musée Archéologique,** with a plethora of ancient objects, and the **Musée Matisse,** with paintings and bronzes by Henri Matisse (1869–1954), illustrating the different stages of his career. The Matisse Museum reopened in 1993 after a five-year renovation program. *164 av. des Arènes-de-Cimiez,* ☎ *93–81–08–08.* ☛ *Musée Matisse 25 frs.* ⊘ *Apr.–Sept., Wed.–Mon. 11–7; Oct.–Mar., Wed.–Mon. 10–5.* ☛ *Musée Archéologique free.* ⊘ *Dec.–Oct., Tues.–Sat. 10–noon and 2–5, Sun. 2–5.*

★ The **old town** of Nice is one of the delights of the Riviera. Cars are forbidden on streets that are so narrow that their buildings crowd out the sky. The winding alleyways are lined with faded 17th- and 18th-century buildings, where families sell crafts and produce. Flowers cascade from window boxes on soft-pastel-colored walls. You wander down cobbled streets, proceeding with the logic of dreams, or sit in an outdoor café on a Venetian-looking square, basking in the purest, most transparent light.

To explore the old town, head south from place Masséna along rue de l'Opéra, and turn left into rue St-François-de-Paule, where you'll soon
31 come to the 18th-century church of **St-François-de-Paule,** renowned for its ornate Baroque interior and sculpted decoration.

TIME OUT Shop for the best crystallized fruits in Nice at **Henri Auer** (7 rue St-François-de-Paule) and have an ice cream and pastry in his cozy tearoom.

Rue St-François-de-Paule widens to become the pedestrian-only cours Saleya, which has a colorful morning market selling seafood, flowers,
32 and orange trees in tubs. Toward the far end of cours Saleya is the **Musée International de Malacologie,** with a collection of seashells from all over the world (some for sale) and a small aquarium of Mediterranean sea life. *3 cours Saleya,* ☎ *93–85–18–44.* ☛ *Free.* ⊘ *Dec.–Oct., Tues.–Sat. 10:30–1 and 2–6.*

33 Next, stroll left up rue la Poissonnerie and pop into the **Chapelle St-Giaume** to admire its gleaming Baroque interior and grand altar-pieces.
34 Continue to rue de Jésus; turn right to the church of **St-Jacques,** featuring an explosion of painted angels on the ceiling. Walk north on rue
35 Droite to the elegant **Palais Lascaris,** built in the mid-17th century and decorated with paintings and tapestries. The palace boasts a particularly grand staircase and a reconstructed 18th-century pharmacy. *15 rue Droite.* ☛ *Free.* ⊘ *Dec.–Oct., Tues.–Sun. 9:30–noon and 2–6.*

Continue up rue Droite, turn left across place St-François, then right
36 along boulevard Jean-Jaurès to reach the **Musée d'Art Contemporain.** This state-of-the-art museum (inaugurated in 1990), with four marble-fronted towers overlooking a sculpture-laden concourse, boasts an outstanding collection of French and international abstract and figurative art from the late 1950s onward: 'New Realists' like local-based Arman, Martial Raysse, and Yves Klein, American moderns like LeWitt and Stella, plus pop-art popes such as Warhol, Rauschenberg, Lichtenstein, and Wesselmann. Temporary exhibits are held on the ground floor. *Promenade des Arts,* ☎ *93–62–61–62.* ☛ *Free.* ⊘ *Wed.–Mon. 11–6 (Fri. 11–10).*

Old Nice is dominated by the **Colline du Château** (Castle Hill), a romantic cliff fortified many centuries before Christ. The ruins of a 6th-century castle can be explored and the views from the surrounding garden
37 admired. A small naval museum, the **Musée de la Marine,** is situated in the 16th-century tower known as the **Tour Bellanda,** with models,

instruments, and documents charting the history of the port of Nice. *Rue du Château,* ☎ *93–80–47–61.* ☞ *Free.* ⊙ *June–Sept., Wed.–Mon. 10–noon and 2–7; Oct.–mid-Nov. and Jan.–May, Wed.–Mon. 10–noon and 2–5.*

The elevator between Tour Bellanda and the quayside operates daily 9 until 7 in summer and 2 until 7 in winter. The back of Castle Hill overlooks the harbor, and across the water, along boulevard Carnot,
38 is the **Musée Terra Amata,** containing relics of a local settlement that was active 400,000 years ago. There are recorded commentaries in English and films explaining the life-style of prehistoric dwellers. *25 blvd. Carnot,* ☎ *93–55–59–93.* ☞ *Free.* ⊙ *Oct.–mid-Sept. Tues.–Sun. 9–noon and 2–6.*

There are three scenic roads at various heights above the coast between Nice and Monte Carlo, a distance of about 19 kilometers (12 miles). All are called "corniches"—literally, a projecting molding along the top of a building or wall. The **Basse** (lower) **Corniche** is the busiest and slowest route because it passes through all the coastal towns. The **Moyenne** (middle) **Corniche** is high enough for views and close enough for details. It passes the perched village of Eze. The **Grande** (upper) **Corniche** winds some 1,300 to 1,600 feet above the sea, offering sweeping views of the coast. The Grande Corniche follows the Via Aurelia, the great Roman military road that brought Roman legions from Italy to Gaul (France). In 1806, Napoléon rebuilt the road and sent Gallic troops into Italy. The best advice is to take the Moyenne Corniche one way and the Grande Corniche the other. The view from the upper route is best in the early morning or evening.

Numbers in the margin correspond to points of interest on the Riviera map: Cannes to Menton.

Boulevard Carnot becomes the popular, pretty Basse Corniche (N98),
39 which crawls along the coast from Nice to **Villefranche-sur-Mer,** 4 kilometers (2½ miles) east. The harbor town is a miniature version of old Marseille, with steep narrow streets—one, **rue Obscure,** an actual tunnel—winding down to the sea. The town is a stage set of brightly colored houses—orange buildings with lime-green shutters, yellow buildings with ice-blue shutters—the sort of place where *Fanny* could have been filmed. If you're staying in Nice, include Villefranche on a tour of Cap Ferrat. To see the Cocteau Chapel you'll need to arrive by 4 PM. If you skip the chapel, your best bet is to come at sundown (for dinner, perhaps) and enjoy an hour's walk around the harbor, when the sun turns the soft pastels to gold. But if you're a photographer, the sun's angle is best for pictures in the morning.

The 17th-century **St-Michel** church has a strikingly realistic Christ, carved of boxwood by an unknown convict. The chapel of St-Pierre-des-Pêcheurs, known as the **Cocteau Chapel,** is a small Romanesque chapel once used for storing fishing nets, which the French writer and painter Jean Cocteau decorated in 1957. Visitors walk through the flames of the Apocalypse (represented by staring eyes on either side of the door) and enter a room filled with frescoes of St. Peter, Gypsies, and the women of Villefranche. ☞ *15 frs.* ⊙ *May–Oct., Tues.–Sun. 9–noon and 2:30–7; Dec.–Apr., Tues.–Sun. 9:30–noon and 2:30–5.*

40 **Beaulieu** is just next door to Villefranche, a place for high society at the turn of the century. Stop and walk along the promenade, sometimes called Petite Afrique (Little Africa) because of its magnificent palm trees, to get a flavor of how things used to be.

The one thing to do in Beaulieu is visit the **Villa Kérylos.** In the early part of the century, a rich amateur archaeologist named Théodore Reinach asked an Italian architect to build an authentic Greek house for him. The villa, now open to the public, is a faithful reproduction, made from cool Carrara marble, alabaster, and rare fruitwoods. The furniture, made of wood inlaid with ivory, bronze, and leather, was copied from drawings of Greek interiors found on ancient vases and mosaics. *Rue Gustave-Eiffel,* ☎ *93–01–01–44.* ☛ *35 frs adults, 15 frs children and senior citizens.* ☉ *July–Aug., weekdays 3–7, weekends 10:30–12:30 and 3–7; Sept.–June, Tues.–Fri. 2–5:30, weekends 10:30–12:30 and 2–5:30.*

❹❶ ★ From Beaulieu, make a detour along D25 around the lush peninsula of **St-Jean-Cap-Ferrat** and visit the 17-acre gardens and richly varied art collection of the **Musée Ephrussi de Rothschild.** The museum reflects the sensibilities of its former owner, Madame Ephrussi de Rothschild, sister of Baron Edouard de Rothschild. An insatiable collector, she surrounded herself with an eclectic but tasteful collection of Impressionist paintings, Louis XIII furniture, rare Sèvres porcelain, and objets d'art from the Far East. *Villa Ile-de-France,* ☎ *93–01–33–09.* ☛ *38 frs adults, 25 frs students. Guided tours 17 frs extra.* ☉ *June–Sept., daily 10–6; Oct.–May, weekdays 2–6, weekends 10–6.*

★ **❹❷** The hill village of **Peillon** is about 20 kilometers (12 miles) inland from Nice. Take D2204, turn right on D21, and turn right again, up the mountain. Of all the perched villages along the Riviera, this fortified medieval town, on a craggy mountaintop more than 1,000 feet above the sea, is the most spectacular and the least spoiled. Unchanged since the Middle Ages, the village has only a few narrow streets and many steps and covered alleys. There's really nothing to do here but look—which is why the tour buses stay away, leaving Peillon uncommercialized for the 50 families who live there—including professionals summering away from Paris and artists who want to escape the craziness of the world below. Visit the **Chapel of the White Penitents** (key available at the Auberge); spend a half hour exploring the ancient streets, then head back down the mountain to Nice.

TIME OUT Have lunch or dinner at the charming **Auberge de la Madone** on Place Arnulf, a short walk from the chapel.

❹❸ Almost every tour from Nice to Monaco includes a visit to the medieval hill town of **Eze,** perched on a rocky spur near the Middle Corniche, some 1,300 feet above the sea. (Don't confuse Eze with the beach town of **Eze-sur-Mer,** which is down by the water.) Be warned that because of its accessibility the town is also crowded and commercial: Eze has its share of serious craftspeople, but most of its vendors make their living selling perfumed soaps and postcards to the package-tour trade.

Enter through a fortified 14th-century gate and wander down narrow, cobbled streets with vaulted passageways and stairs. The church is 18th century, but the small Chapel of the White Penitents dates from 1306 and contains a 13th-century gilded wooden Spanish Christ and some notable 16th-century paintings. Tourist and crafts shops line the streets leading to the ruins of a castle, which has a scenic belvedere. Some of the most tasteful crafts shops are in the hotel/restaurant **Chèvre d'Or.**

Near the top of the village is a garden with exotic flowers and cacti. It's worth the admission price, but if you have time for only one exotic garden, visit the one in Monte Carlo.

If you're not going to Grasse, the perfume capital of the world (*see above*), consider visiting a branch of a Grasse perfumerie, **La Parfumerie Fragonard,** in front of the public gardens.

From Eze it's just a short—albeit spectacular—drive up the coast to **④④ Monaco.** The Principality of Monaco covers just 473 acres and would fit comfortably inside New York's Central Park or a family farm in Iowa. Its 5,000 citizens would fill only a small fraction of the seats in Yankee Stadium. The country is so tiny that residents have to go to another country to play golf.

The present ruler, Rainier III, traces his ancestry to Otto Canella, who was born in 1070. The Grimaldi dynasty began with Otto's great-great-great-grandson, Francesco Grimaldi, also known as Frank the Rogue. Expelled from Genoa, Frank and his cronies disguised themselves as monks and seized the fortified medieval town known today as the Rock in 1297. Except for a short break under Napoléon, the Grimaldis have been here ever since, which makes them the oldest reigning family in Europe. On the Grimaldi coat of arms are two monks holding swords (look up and you'll see them above the main door as you enter the palace).

Back in the 1850s, a Grimaldi named Charles III made a decision that turned the Rock into a giant blue chip. Needing revenues but not wanting to impose additional taxes on his subjects, he contracted with a company to open a gambling facility. The first spin of the roulette wheel was on December 14, 1856. There was no easy way to reach Monaco then—no carriage roads or railroads—so no one came. Between March 15 and March 20, 1857, one person entered the casino—and won two francs. In 1868, however, the railroad reached Monaco, filled with wheezing Englishmen who came to escape the London fog. The effects were immediate. Profits were so great that Charles eventually abolished all direct taxes.

Almost overnight, a threadbare principality became an elegant watering hole for European society. Dukes (and their mistresses) and duchesses (and their gigolos) danced and dined their way through a world of spinning roulette wheels and bubbling champagne—preening themselves for nights at the opera, where such artists as Vaslav Nijinsky, Sarah Bernhardt, and Enrico Caruso came to perform.

Monte Carlo—the modern gambling town with elegant shops, man-made beaches, high-rise hotels, and a few Belle Epoque hotels—is actually only one of four parts of Monaco. The second is the medieval town on the Rock ("Old Monaco"), 200 feet above the sea. It's here that Prince Rainier lives.

The third area is **La Condamine,** the commercial harbor area with apartments and businesses. The fourth is **Fontvieille,** the industrial district situated on 20 acres of reclaimed land.

Numbers in the margin correspond to points of interest on the Monaco map.

Start at the Monte Carlo tourist office just north of the casino gardens (ask for the useful English booklet *Getting Around in the Principality*). ★ ④⑤ The **Casino** is a must-see, even if you don't bet a cent. You may find it fun to count the Jaguars and Rolls-Royces parked outside and breathe on the windows of shops selling Saint-Laurent dresses and fabulous jewels. Into the gold-leaf splendor of the casino, where fortunes have been won and shirts have been lost, the hopeful traipse from tour buses to tempt fate at slot machines beneath the gilt-edged rococo ceiling.

422

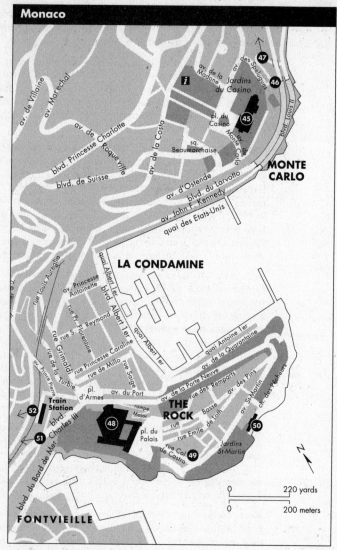

The main gambling hall, once called the European Room, has been renamed the American Room and fitted with 150 one-armed bandits from Chicago. Adjoining it is the Pink Salon, now a bar where unclad nymphs float about on the ceiling smoking cigarillos. The Salles Privées (private rooms) are for high rollers. The stakes are exalted here, so the mood is sober, and well-wishers are herded farther back from the tables.

On July 17, 1924, black came up 17 times in a row on Table 5. This was the longest run ever. A dollar left on black would have grown to $131,072. On August 7, 1913, the number 36 came up three times in a row. In those days, if a gambler went broke, the casino bought him a ticket home.

The casino opens at noon and continues until the last die is thrown. Ties and jackets are required in the back rooms, which open at 4 PM. Bring your passport (under-21s not admitted).

Place du Casino is the center of Monte Carlo, and, in the true spirit of the town, it seems that the **Opera House,** with its 18-ton gilt-bronze chandelier, is part of the casino complex. The designer, Charles Garnier, also built the Paris Opera.

46 The serious gamblers, some say, play at **Loew's Casino,** nearby. It opens weekdays at 4 PM and weekends at 1 PM. You may want to try parking here, since parking near the old casino is next to impossible in season.

From place des Moulins there is an escalator down to the Larvotto beach **47** complex, artfully created with imported sand, and the **Musée National,** housed in a Garnier villa within a rose garden. This museum has a beguiling collection of 18th- and 19th-century dolls and mechanical automatons, most in working order. *17 av. Princesse-Grace,* ☎ *93–30–91–26.* ☛ *28 frs adults, 17 frs children.* ⊘ *Daily except holidays 10–12:15 and 2:30–6:30.*

48 Prince Rainier spends much of the year in his grand Italianate **Palace** on the Rock. The changing of the guard takes place here each morning at 11:55, and the State Apartments can be visited in summer. ☎ *93–25–18–31.* ☛ *26 frs adults, 15 frs children. Joint ticket with Musée Napoléon: 40 frs adults, 20 frs children.* ⊘ *June–Oct., daily 9:30–6:30.*

One wing of the palace, open throughout the year, is taken up by a museum filled with Napoléonic souvenirs and documents related to Monaco's history. ☛ *20 frs adults, 10 frs children. Joint ticket with palace apartments as above.* ⊘ *Tues.–Sun. 9:30–6:30.*

From here, a stroll through the medieval alleyways takes you past the **49** **cathedral,** a neo-Romanesque monstrosity (1875–84), with several important paintings of the Nice school. Continue to one of Monaco's most **50** outstanding showpieces, the **Musée Océanographique**—also an important research institute headed by celebrated underwater explorer and filmmaker Jacques Cousteau (his films are shown in the museum cinema). Prince Rainier's great-grandfather Albert I (1848–1922), an accomplished marine biologist, founded the institute in 1910. It now boasts two exploration ships, laboratories, and a staff of 60 scientists. Nonscientific visitors may wish to go straight to the well-arranged and generously stocked aquarium in the basement. Other floors are devoted to Prince Albert's collection of seashells and whale skeletons and to Cousteau's diving equipment. *Av. St-Martin,* ☎ *93–15–36–00.* ☛ *60 frs adults, 30 frs children.* ⊘ *July–Aug., daily 9–8; Sept.–June; daily 9:30–7 (6 in winter).*

TIME OUT Take the museum's elevator to the roof terrace for a fine view and a restorative drink.

51 A brisk half-hour walk west from the palace takes you to the **Jardin Exotique** (Tropical Gardens), where 600 varieties of cacti and succu-**52** lents cling to a sheer rock face. The **Museum of Prehistoric Anthropology,** on the grounds, contains bones, tools, and other artifacts. Shapes of the stalactites and stalagmites in the cavernous grotto (entered from the gardens) resemble the cacti outside. *Blvd. du Jardin Exotique,* ☎ *93–15–80–06.* ☛ *39 frs adults, 26 frs senior citizens, 16 frs children.* ⊘ *Daily 9–7 (dusk in winter).*

Numbers in the margin correspond to points of interest on the Riviera map: Cannes to Menton.

Five kilometers (3 miles) northeast of Monaco is the engaging hilltop
⑤③ village of **Roquebrune,** with its Carolingian castle, its medieval houses,
⑤④ covered steps, and narrow streets. The adjacent **Cap-Martin** peninsula
is colonized by wealthy villa dwellers. Near the tip, on avenue Winston-Churchill, is the start of a coastal path—promenade Le Corbusier—that leads hardy ramblers to Monte Carlo in 1½ hours.

⑤⑤ Next door to Roquebrune is **Menton,** a comparatively quiet all-year
resort with the warmest climate on the Riviera. Lemon trees flourish
here, as do senior citizens, enticed by a long strand of beaches. Menton likes to call itself the Pearl of the Riviera—beautiful, respectable,
and not grossly expensive.

Walk eastward from the casino along promenade du Soleil to the harbor. There is a small 17th-century fort here, where writer, artist, and
filmmaker Jean Cocteau (1889–1963) once worked. The fort now houses
the **Cocteau Museum** of fantastic paintings, drawings, stage sets, and
a large mosaic. *Bastion du Port, 111 quai Napoléon-III,* ☎ *93–57–
72–30.* ☛ *Free.* ☉ *Apr.–Oct., Wed.–Sun. 10–noon and 2–6; Nov.–Mar.,
Wed.–Sun. 10–noon and 3–6.*

The quaint old town above the jetty has an Italian feel to it. Visit the
church of **St-Michel** for its ornate Baroque interior and altarpiece of
St. Michael slaying a dragon. Concerts of chamber music are held in
the square on summer nights. Higher still you come to the **Vieux
Cimetière** (old cemetery), with a magnificent view of the old town and
coast. Here lie Victorian foreigners—Russians, Germans, English—who
hoped (in vain, as the dates on the tombstones reveal) that Menton's
balmy climate would reverse the ravages of tuberculosis.

Return to the center and the pedestrian rue St-Michel. On avenue de
la République, which runs parallel, is the **Hôtel de Ville** (Town Hall).
The room in which civil marriage ceremonies are conducted has vibrant allegorical frescoes by Cocteau; a tape in English helps to in-
terpret them. *17 rue de la République.* ☛ *5 frs.* ☉ *Weekdays
8:30–12:30 and 1:30–5.*

Two other places of interest lie at opposite ends of Menton. To the west
is the **Palais Carnolès,** an 18th-century villa once used as a summer retreat by the princes of Monaco. The gardens are beautiful, and the collection of European paintings (13th- to 18th-century) is extensive. *3
av. de la Madone,* ☎ *93–35–49–71.* ☛ *Free.* ☉ *Wed.–Sun. 10–noon
and 2–6; closed holidays.*

At the other end of Menton, above the Garavan harbor, lie the **Colombières Gardens,** where follies and statues lurk among 15 acres of
hedges, yew trees, and Mediterranean flowers. *Chemin de Valleya.* ☛
20 frs. ☉ *Feb.–Sept., daily 9–noon and 3–8 (or sunset if earlier).*

The Italian frontier is just a mile away, and the first Italian town, **Ventimiglia** (Vintimille in French), lies 10 kilometers (6 miles) beyond.

What to See and Do with Children

The **Jungle des Papillons,** opposite Marineland in Antibes, hosts a fluttering "Butterfly Ballet" that must be seen to be believed. Visitors are
requested to wear colored clothing because this apparently stimulates
the butterflies into a wing-flapping frenzy. *309 av. de Mozart,* ☎ *93–
33–55–77.* ☛ *27 frs adults, 19 frs children.* ☉ *Daily 10–5.*

Automatons at the Musée Nationale, Monte-Carlo, Tour 2
Glassblowers at Biot, Tour 1

Marineland, near Antibes, Tour 1
Musée Océanographique, Monte Carlo, Tour 2

Off the Beaten Track

Consider a visit to the Italian towns of Ventimiglia and San Remo by train, bus, or car. **Ventimiglia** lies just 10 kilometers (6 miles) over the border and is best known for its colorful Friday flower market, which draws huge crowds (mostly French). If you visit on market day, take the train or bus; there will be no place to park. The elegant town of **San Remo,** just 6 kilometers (4 miles) farther down the coast, still maintains some of the glamour of its late-19th-century heyday; compare its casino with that of Monte Carlo. From October to June, you can visit Italy's most important flower market, the Mercato dei Fiori. The old town is an atmospheric warren of alleyways leading up to the piazza Castello, from which there's a splendid view.

Costumes, furniture, buildings, and even entire towns often evoke the stuff of heroes. Occasionally, so do roads—and one of the most famous roads in France is the **Route Napoléon,** taken by Napoléon Bonaparte in 1815 after his escape from imprisonment on the Mediterranean island of Elba. Napoléon landed at Golfe-Juan, near Cannes, on March 1 and forged northwest to Grasse and through dramatic, hilly countryside to Castellane, Digne, and Sisteron. In Napoléon's day, most of this "road" was little more than a winding dirt track, but now N85 allows drivers to mix history with scenery. Commemorative plaques bearing the imperial eagle stud the route, inspired by Napoléon's remark that "The eagle will fly from steeple to steeple until it reaches the towers of Notre-Dame." That prediction came true. Napoléon covered the 110 miles from the coast to Sisteron in just four days, romped north through Grenoble and Burgundy, and entered Paris in triumph on May 20.

One of the most spectacular roads in France is the **Corniche Sublime** (D71), which runs along the south side of the **Grand Canyon du Verdon** (Verdon River Gorge), France's answer to the Grand Canyon. To reach the gorge, take the Route Napoléon (N85) from Grasse; turn left after 43 kilometers (27 miles) along D21, which becomes D71 at Comps-sur-Artuby. This is not a road for anyone who is afraid of heights. The narrow lane—just wide enough for two cars to scrape by—snakes its way for 25 miles along the cliffside, 3,000 feet above the tiny River Verdon. At times the river disappears from view beneath the sheer rock face. At the far end of the gorge you'll arrive at the sparkling blue Lac de Sainte-Croix.

If you have a day or two to spare, a high-speed ferry will whisk you to Corsica: in 2½ hours to Calvi or 3½ hours to Bastia. These ferries, operated by **SNCM Ferryterranée,** depart from Nice twice a day.

SHOPPING

Clothes

Cannes is one of the Riviera's top spots for chic clothing. Some of the most exclusive shops are **Chanel** (5 La Croisette), **Alexandra** (Rond-Point Duboys-d'Angers), **Cacharel** (16 rue des Belges), **Révillon** (45 La Croisette), and **Yves St-Laurent** (44 La Croisette). For well-cut menswear, try **Cerruti** (15 rue des Serbes), **Christian Dior,** and **Francesco Smalto** (both at the Hôtel Gray Albion, 38 rue des Serbes). **Souleaido,** renowned for its clothes in printed fabrics, has shops in Nice (1 bis rue du Paradis), Cannes (17 La Croisette) and St-Tropez (Ave. du 8-mai-1945) and is recommended for helpful, courteous service. While in St-Tropez, drop in to **Cecile** (on the port) for the best in T-shirts and fun wear.

Food Items

Crystallized fruit is a Nice specialty; there's a terrific selection at **Henri Auer** (7 rue St-François-de-Paule). Locals and visitors alike buy olive oil by the gallon from tiny **Alziari,** just down the street at No. 14; the cans sport colorful, old-fashioned labels, and you can also pick up lots of Provençal herbs and spices. (From November to April you can visit Alziari's "oil mill" at 318 blvd. de la Madeleine.) For cheese, try l'**Etable** (1 rue Sade) in Antibes. **Georget** (11 rue Allard), in St-Tropez, sells delicious handmade chocolates, and **Schwartz** (75 blvd. de la République), in Cannes, is renowned for candy and macaroons. **Maison Cochet** in St-Raphaël (98 blvd. Félix-Martin) produces some of France's finest nougat.

Markets

St-Tropez's **place des Lices** has a clothing and antiques market on Tuesday and Saturday mornings. In addition to plants, Nice's famous flower market at **cours Saleya** also features mounds of fish, shellfish, and a host of other food items; on Monday, there's a flea market at the same spot. In Cannes, a market selling everything from strings of garlic to secondhand gravy boats is held Saturday on **Allées de la Liberté,** and at the **place de la Justice** on the first and third Saturday of each month, you can find an array of esoteric old books, posters, postcards, and such at the 24 stalls of the Marché du Livre Ancien et des Vieux Papiers.

SPORTS AND THE OUTDOORS

La Napoule is the best place for the sports oriented. As well as facilities for boating, golf, horseback riding, and tennis, there are eight beaches with waterskiing and jet-skiing (there's a school on the plage du Sweet) and a deep-sea diving club (Club Nautique de L'Esterel) that gives lessons to anyone over age eight. Ask for the "Star dul Siècle" brochure at tourist offices for details of canoeing, cycling, riding, climbing, rambling, hang gliding, rafting, and potholing. In **Nice,** jogging and roller blading are popular along the Promenade des Anglais, especially off-season.

Beaches

If you like your beaches sandy, stick to those between St-Tropez and Antibes; most of the others are pebbly, though Menton and Monaco have imported vast tons of sand to spread around their shores. Private beaches are everywhere. You'll have to pay to use them (between 80 and 140 francs a day), but you get value for the money—a café or restaurant, cabanas and showers, mattresses and umbrellas, and the pleasure of watching the perpetual parade of stylish swimwear and languid attitudes.

St-Tropez's best beaches are scattered along a 3-mile stretch reached by the Routes des Plages; the most fashionable are **Moorea, Tahiti Plage,** and **Club 55.** You'll see lots of topless bathers, and some beaches allow total nudity. If you're traveling with children, try the family beaches at **Ste-Maxime** and **St-Raphaël.** At **La Napoule's** eight beaches, you can indulge in almost any watersport, or just stretch out on a lounge chair. One of Cannes's most fashionable beaches, which belongs to the **Carlton Hotel** (open Mar.–Oct.), has a glassed-in terrace and heating to offset out-of-season chills. Nice's beaches extend along the Baie des Anges (the Bay of Angels); **Ruhl Plage** is one of the most popular, with a good restaurant and facilities for waterskiing, windsurfing, and children's swimming lessons. Not to be outdone, **Neptune Plage** has all that plus a sauna.

Bicycling

Bikes can be rented from train stations at **Antibes, Cannes, Juan-les-Pins,** and **Nice.** Two especially scenic trips on fairly level ground are from Nice to the area around Cap d'Antibes and around Cap Ferrat from Cannes. Bikes are ideal at St-Tropez, since the beach is a few miles from town.

Golf

There are 18-hole courses at **Cannes, La Napoule, Menton, Mougins, St-Raphaël,** and **Monte Carlo** (the last is spectacularly sited on the slopes of Mont Angel at nearby La Turbie).

Horseback Riding

Just a couple of miles inland from Mandelieu-La Napoule on N7 is the **Poney Club du Soleil** (Domaine de Barbossi); children will enjoy the small zoo, as well as the pony rides, while adults can rent horses and, if they like, take lessons.

Skiing

Nice is just 60 miles from the Alps: **Valberg** (4,600 feet), **Auron** (5,250 feet), and **Isola 2000** (6,500 feet) are the best-equipped resorts. Isola 2000 has 75 miles of *pistes* (trails) with the highest runs in the Southern Alps (8,500 feet).

Water Sports

If you want to get in some sailing, try **Sportmer** (8 pl. Blanqui) in St-Tropez, and **Yacht Club de Cannes** (Palm Beach Port) and **Camper & Nicholson's** (Port Canto) in Cannes. This is a great area for windsurfing; you can rent equipment from **Le Club Nautique La Croisette** (plage Pointe Palm-Beach, Cannes), **Centre Nautique Municipal** (9 rue Esprit-Violet, Cannes), and **Sillages** (av. Henry-Clews, Mandelieu-La Napoule).

DINING AND LODGING

Dining

Though prices often scale Parisian heights, the Riviera shares its cuisine with Provence, enjoying the same vegetable and fish dishes prepared with vivid seasonings. The most famous is bouillabaisse, a fish stew from around Marseille. Genuine bouillabaisse combines *rascasse* (scorpion fish), eel, and half a dozen other types of seafood; crab and lobster are optional. Local fish is scarce, however, so dishes like *loup flambé* (sea bass with fennel and anise liqueur), braised tuna, and even fresh sardines are priced accordingly. *Estocaficada,* a stockfish stew with garlic and olives, is a Nice specialty.

With Italy so close, it's no surprise that many menus feature such specialties as ravioli and potato gnocchi. Try vegetable *soupe au pistou,* an aromatic brew seasoned with basil, garlic, olive oil, and Parmesan cheese, or *pissaladière,* a pastry-based version of pizza, topped with tomato, olives, anchovy, and plenty of onion. Nice claims its own specialties: *pan bagna* (salad in a bun) and *poulpe à la niçoise* (octopus in a tomato sauce). Of the various vegetable dishes, the best is ratatouille, a stew of tomatoes, onions, eggplant, and zucchini.

Anise-flavored *pastis* is the Riviera's number one drink.

CATEGORY	COST*
$$$$	over 500 frs
$$$	250–500 frs
$$	150–250 frs
$	under 150 frs

per person for a three-course meal, including tax (18.6%) and tip but not wine

---

Lodging

Hotels on the Riviera can push opulence to the sublime—or the ridiculous. Pastel colors, gilt, and plush are the decorators' staples in the resort hotels catering to le beau monde. The glamour comes hand in hand with hefty price tags, however, and while inexpensive hotels do exist, they're found mainly on dull outskirts of big centers and in less fashionable "family" resorts.

CATEGORY	COST*
$$$$	over 1,000 frs
$$$	600–1,000 frs
$$	300–600 frs
$	under 300 frs

All prices are for a standard double room for two, including tax (18.6%) and service charge.

Antibes/Juan-les-Pins

DINING

★ **Bacon.** This is the Riviera's top spot for bouillabaisse or any other dish that depends on prime fish, simply and perfectly cooked. The Sordello brothers have run Bacon for more than 40 years and don't regard a fish as fresh unless it's still twitching—count on eating only the pick of the local catch. Eat outside on the airy terrace overlooking the port. ✕ *Blvd. James-Wyllie, Cap d'Antibes,* ☎ *93–61–50–02. Reservations required. Jacket required. AE, DC, MC, V. Closed Sun. dinner, Mon., and mid-Nov.–Jan. $$$*

Auberge de l'Esterel. The affable Denis Latouche runs the best moderately priced restaurant in Juan-les-Pins, lending a nouvelle twist to local dishes; try the monkfish and, for dessert, the lemon tart. The secluded garden is a romantic setting for dinner under the stars. There are 15 bedrooms (six with bath) in the small attached hotel. ✕ *21 rue des Iles, Juan-les-Pins,* ☎ *93–61–74–11. Reservations advised. MC, V. Closed mid-Nov.–mid-Dec., part of Feb., Sun. dinner, and Mon. $$–$$$*

La Bonne Auberge. Philippe Rostang took over from his father Jo in 1992, adding his own creations—lamb in thyme with kidneys, for instance—to such house specialties as lobster ravioli, salads of red mullet, and airy soufflés—though the menu changes every three months to match the season. The dining room is a flower-filled haven of exposed beams, dim lantern lighting, and rose-colored walls; huge glass windows allow diners a view of the inspired work going on in the kitchen. Rostang has introduced a *menu gastronomique* at 200 francs. ✕ *Quartier de la Brague, Antibes,* ☎ *93–33–36–65. Reservations advised. Jacket required. AE, MC, V. Closed Mon. (except for dinner mid-Apr.–Sept.), Wed. lunch (July–Aug.), and mid-Nov.–mid-Dec. $$–$$$*

DINING AND LODGING

Hôtel du Cap Eden-Roc. Crystal chandeliers, gilt mirrors, gleaming antique furniture, and lots of marble make the Cap d'Antibes a glorious testimony to the opulence of another age. Guest rooms are enormous and feature the same impressive decor as the public rooms. The glass-fronted Pavillon Eden Roc is the place for lobster thermidor, accompanied by vintage champagne. 🕾 *Blvd. Kennedy, 06600 Antibes,* 🕿 *93–61–39–01,* ꜰᴀx *93–67–76–04. 112 rooms with bath. Restaurant, pool, tennis. Closed Nov.–Easter. No credit cards. $$$$*

Juana. This luxuriously renovated '30s hotel sits opposite the casino, a couple of blocks from the beach. Towering pine trees overhang the grounds and the white marble pool. La Terrasse is one of the best restaurants on the Côte d'Azur; chef Christian Morisset wins praise for his fine seafood. Eat outside on the terrace, overlooking the palm trees in the landscaped garden. All the guest rooms are large and individually decorated. 🕾 *Av. Georges-Gallice, 06160 Juanles-Pins,* 🕿 *93–61–08–70,* ꜰᴀx *93–61–76–60. 45 rooms with bath. Restaurant, bar, pool. No credit cards. Closed late Oct.–mid-Apr. $$$$*

Djoliba. There are only 14 rooms at this converted Provençal farmhouse, all with a country-house feel. The salon features an airy bamboo-shoot motif, while the guest rooms, painted in a range of pastel shades, have antique furnishings. Choose between views of the park or the sea. The restaurant is open for dinner only. 🕾 *29 av. de Provence, 06600 Antibes,* 🕿 *93–34–02–48,* ꜰᴀx *93–34–05–81. 14 rooms with bath. Restaurant (closed Oct.–Mar.), pool. AE, DC, MC, V. Closed Jan. $$*

Manoir Castel Garoupe Axa. This old inn is known locally as Motel Axa, after owner Mme. Axa. It is not a deluxe resort by any means, but the atmosphere is friendly and the hotel is only a two-minute walk to the beach. Little English is spoken, but smiles and a minimal grasp of French are all that's needed. There is no restaurant; just breakfast is served. The rooms have a balcony with countryside views and a convenient kitchenette if you want something simpler (and less expensive) than a restaurant meal. That's a big plus in this high-priced region, where dining out every day can severely dent the budget. 🕾 *959 blvd. de la Garoupe, 06600 Cap d'Antibes,* 🕿 *93–61–36–51,* ꜰᴀx *93–67–74–88. 22 rooms with bath. Pool, tennis court. Closed Jan. MC, V. $$*

Cannes

DINING

★ **La Mère Besson.** Mix with the locals at this boisterous family eatery, which features a range of authentic Provençal fare. Go on Friday for the *aïoli,* a heaped platter of fish, seafood, and boiled vegetables in a thick garlic mayonnaise. The stuffed rabbit is equally superb. The decor borders on the frumpy, but the food is what counts here. ✕ *13 rue des Frères-Pradignac,* 🕿 *93–39–59–24. Reservations advised. AE, DC, MC, V. Closed Sun. and Mon. lunch, except July–Aug. $$–$$$*

Au Bec Fin. A devoted band of regulars will attest to the quality of this family-run restaurant near the train station. Don't look for carefully staged decor: It's the spirited local clientele and the homey food that distinguish this cheerful bistro. The fixed-price menus are a fantastic value at 90 francs—often with choucroute and fish for the main course. Try the fish cooked with fennel or the *salade niçoise.* ✕ *12 rue du 24-Août,* 🕿 *93–38–35–86. Reservations advised. AE, DC, MC, V. Closed Sat. dinner, Sun., and Dec. 25–late Jan. $*

Chez Astoux. There are hordes of restaurants along this popular people-watching street, one block from the sea on a small park dotted with flower sellers. But Chez Astou, which ranks highly for its seafood, stands out. (Indeed, it has a seafood stall next door, where locals come to buy for their own kitchens.) The ambience at Chez Astou is plain and simple, and you have the choice of sitting on the terrace (heated when necessary) or inside. The local mussels, known as *bouchots,* are strongly recommended. They're small and meaty, ideal served either marinière or à la crème. At lunch, there's a three-course menu for 98 francs—very reasonable compared to prices at the other restaurants nearby. ✗ *43 rue Felix-Faure,* ☎ *93–39–06–22. Reservations accepted. AE, DC, MC, V.* $

DINING AND LODGING

Carlton. Cannes's most elegantly old-fashioned hotel is the gleaming white Carlton, built at the turn of the century right on the seafront. The opulent public rooms feature marble floors, chandeliers, floral bouquets, and glittering mirrors. The service, though, is not what it was, and some rooms are cramped. Those in the west wing are best; they're quieter and have terrific views. There are three restaurants: La Côte serves haute cuisine in an imposingly formal atmosphere; La Belle Otéro has a terrace overlooking La Croisette; and the Grill Room is simpler but still impressive. The bar is one of *the* places for mingling with the Riviera's Beautiful People. ☎ *58 La Croisette, 06400,* ☎ *93–68–91–68,* FAX *93–38–20–90. 325 rooms with bath. 3 restaurants, bar, health club, casino, private beach. Main restaurant closed Tues., Wed., and Nov.–Dec. 25. AE, DC, MC, V.* $$$$

Gray d'Albion. This striking contemporary hotel is the last word in state-of-the-art luxury. Its white facade is austere; inside, the atmosphere is ultrasophisticated, with gray and cream walls and plenty of leather, metal, and mirrors. The guest rooms are fitted with slick, modern accessories. Comfort is the key word, making up for the lack of sea views, except for those from a few suites on the ninth floor, which look over the condominium that stands between the hotel and the seafront. There are a number of restaurants; the Royal Gray is one of Cannes's most fashionable. ☎ *38 rue des Serbes, 06400,* ☎ *92–99–79–79,* FAX *93–99–26–10. 174 rooms with bath. 3 restaurants, dance club, private beach. AE, DC, MC, V. Royal Gray closed Feb., Sun., and Mon.* $$$$

★ **Martinez.** While many of the luxury palace-hotels that cosseted kings and heads of state have receded into history, the Martinez still manages to retain that sybaritic atmosphere of indulgence, despite the fact it wasn't built until 1929–a little late for classic status. The Concorde group bought it in 1982 and revamped its Art Deco style, while a gentle renovation in 1989 redid 100 bedrooms in cool blue and salmon shades, with wooden furniture and large marble bathrooms. One of the hotel's biggest assets is the Palme d'Or restaurant, whose chef, Christian Willer, draws lavish praise for his choice line of modern cuisine. ☎ *73 La Croisette, 06400,* ☎ *92–98–73–00,* FAX *93–39–67–82. 430 rooms with bath. 3 restaurants, bar, pool, tennis, beach. Restaurants closed mid-Nov.–mid-Jan., Feb., and Mon. and Tues. lunch. Hotel closed mid-Nov.–mid-Jan. AE, DC, MC, V.* $$$$

Noga Hilton. The $150 million Noga Hilton opened in 1992, on the La Croisette site of the Palais des Festivals (original home to the famous film festival). The words *"Palais Croisette"* are unashamedly emblazoned high up the Noga's gleaming white-and-glass facade. Service and comfort are no more or less than you'd expect from the luxury Hilton chain. Chef Jean-Yves Méraud oversees four restaurants, including a Caviar House, a round-the-clock brasserie, a beach diner across the road, and the upmarket La Scala, where his penchant for Italian dishes comes to the fore. ☎ *50 La Croisette, 06400,* ☎ *92–99–70–00,* FAX *92–99–70–11. 180 rooms with bath and 45 suites, some with Jacuzzis. 4 restaurants, 3 bars, pool, private beach, health club. AE, DC, MC, V.* $$$$

LODGING

★ **Le Fouquet's.** If you're looking for a comfortable base from which to explore the beach, the shops, the bistros, and the nightclubs, this is the place, in a quiet residential area. The hotel ambience is welcoming—from the brightly lit archway, plants, and mirrors to the rooms, decorated in warm shades and decked out with lots of French flounces. All the guest rooms are large and feature covered loggias. There's no restaurant. ⊡ *2 rond-point Duboys-d'Angers, 06400,* ☎ *93–38–75–81,* FAX *92–98–03–39. 10 rooms with bath. AE, DC, MC, V. Closed Nov.–Dec. $$$*

Mondial. A three-minute walk from the beach takes you to this six-story hotel, a haven for the traveler seeking solid, unpretentious lodging in a town that tends to lean toward tinsel. Many guest rooms offer sea views and most have small terraces, though the hotel's in the heart of the commercial center, 250 yards from the train station. There's no restaurant. ⊡ *77 rue d'Antibes, 06400,* ☎ *93–68–70–00,* FAX *93–99–39–11. No credit cards. Closed Nov. $$*

Beverly. Halfway between the train station and La Croisette, this hotel, renovated in 1993, probably offers the best value in central Cannes. The quieter rooms (some with small balconies) are at the back. ⊡ *14 rue Hoche, 06400,* ☎ *93–39–10–66,* FAX *92–98–65–63. 19 rooms, 15 with shower. Closed end of Jan. AE, MC, V. $–$$*

Eze

DINING AND LODGING

★ **Château de la Chèvre d'Or.** Located in the medieval hilltop village, the Chèvre d'Or, a member of the Relais & Châteaux group, comprises a number of ancient houses whose mellow stone walls are set off by terra-cotta pots brimming with geraniums. The guest rooms, though small, are individually decorated and feature antique furnishings and attractive fabrics and wallpapers; ask for Room 9. The views of Cap Ferrat from the poolside terrace are sensational. The bar is in a medieval room with stone walls, a tall fireplace, and Louis XIII furniture. The restaurant is dignified, a far cry from some of the Riviera's flashier dining rooms. Be prepared for the prices. Luncheon menus start at 250 francs and dinner at 560. When you've swallowed that, settle in to enjoy the beautifully presented cuisine, scented, as chef Mazot likes to say, with the perfumes of Provence. ⊡ *Rue du Barri, 06360,* ☎ *93–41–12–12,* FAX *93–41–06–72. 28 rooms with bath. Restaurant, café, bar, pool. AE, DC, MC, V. Closed Dec.–Feb. $$$$*

Grasse

LODGING

Panorama. This tidy modern hotel has a pleasant, helpful staff and well-appointed, soundproof, air-conditioned rooms, where snacks can be served on request. ⊡ *2 pl. Cours, 06130,* ☎ *93–36–80–80,* FAX *93–36–92–04. 36 rooms with bath. MC, V. $$*

Menton

DINING AND LODGING

Londres. This small, central hotel, close to the beach and casino, has its own restaurant, serving solid, traditional French cuisine, and a small garden for outdoor summer dining. ⊡ *15 av. Carnot, BP 73, 06502 cedex,* ☎ *93–35–74–62,* FAX *93–41–77–78. 26 rooms with shower or bath. Restaurant (closed Wed.), bar. AE, MC, V. $$*

Monte Carlo

DINING

Port. Harbor views from the terrace and top-notch Italian food make the Port a good choice. A large, varied menu includes shrimp, lasagna, fettuccine, fish risotto, and veal with ham and cheese. ✕ *Quai Albert-Ier,* ☎ *93–50–77–21. Reservations advised. AE, DC, MC, V. Closed Mon. and Nov. $$–$$$*

★ **Polpetta.** This popular little trattoria is close enough to the Italian border to pass for the real McCoy and is excellent value for the money. If it's on the menu, go for the vegetable *soupe au pistou* and the *risotto al porcini*, a meal that will run about 130 francs per person, plus wine. ✕ *2 rue Paradis,* ☎ *93–50–67–84. Reservations required in summer. V. Closed Tues. and Sat. lunch and Feb. $–$$*

DINING AND LODGING

★ **Hôtel de Paris.** Though discreetly modernized, the Hôtel de Paris still exudes the gold-plate splendor of an era in which kings and grand dukes were regulars. Surprisingly, the rooms, all quite spacious, are done in light colors with white oak furniture—more romantic than grand. The restaurant, the Louis XV, stuns you with such royal decor that you may be distracted from the food, but make the effort to give it your attention, since Alain Ducasse is one of Europe's most celebrated chefs, with three Michelin stars. Try his ravioli de foie gras. About the other restaurants: Try Le Côte Jardin for lunch on a terrace facing the sea and Le Grill (one Michelin star), which serves Mediterrean-style cuisine on a rooftop overlooking the harbor. ▦ *Pl. du Casino, 98000,* ☎ *92–16–30–00,* ℻ *93–15–90–03. 143 rooms, 41 suites, and 19 junior suites. 4 restaurants, indoor and outdoor pool, spa. Restaurant Louis XV closed Tues., Wed. (except dinner July–Aug.), late Feb.–early Mar., and Nov.–Dec. AE, DC, MC, V. $$$$*

Loews. Big, brash, and more than a touch vulgar, Loews has a plush extravagance on a scale Donald Trump would envy. Fountains splash, contemporary rooms are decorated in ice cream shades, and celebrities mix with sheikhs in the bars, casino, and restaurants. Die-hard football fans can watch the Super Bowl by satellite; those in search of live entertainment should head for the Folie Russe, boasting lines of scantily clad showgirls and mountains of caviar. ▦ *12 av. des Spéluges, 98000,* ☎ *93–50–65–00,* ℻ *93–30–01–57. 650 rooms with bath. 3 restaurants, pool, hot tub, health club, casino. AE, DC, MC, V. $$$$*

Hermitage. For interior decor—in the public areas, at least—this Belle Epoque palace is a must-see. Even if you're not staying, come to see the glass-dome Art Nouveau vestibule at the avenue d'Ostende entrance and the white-stucco rococo corridor leading to the lavish dining room, where pink marble columns hold up a gilded, frescoed ceiling. The adjacent terrace, with a tinkling pianist in action on summer evenings, has a pleasant view over the harbor. The recently reappointed rooms are comfortable but far less stylish. ▦ *Square Beaumarchais, BP 277, 98005 cedex,* ☎ *92–16–40–00,* ℻ *93–50–47–12. 236 rooms with bath. Restaurant, bar, pool, solarium. AE, DC, MC, V. $$$$*

LODGING

Alexandra. Shades of the Belle Epoque linger in this comfortable hotel's spacious lobby and airy guest rooms. Tan and rose colors dominate the newer rooms. If you're willing to do without a private bath, this place sneaks into the $ category. The friendly proprietress, Mme. Larouquie, makes foreign visitors feel right at home. ▦ *35 blvd. Princesse-Charlotte, 98000,* ☎ *93–50–63–13,* ℻ *92–16–06–48. 55 rooms, 46 with bath. AE, DC, MC, V. $$*

Mougins
DINING AND LODGING

★ **Moulin de Mougins.** A 16th-century olive mill houses one of the country's top 20 restaurants. Chef Roger Vergé has an ever-changing repertoire and creates new dishes every season. Some of them capitalize on traditional regional cuisine; others are innovative concoctions using lobster, caviar, and other ingredients that many crave but few can afford.

The intimate beamed dining rooms, with oil paintings, plants, and porcelain tableware, are the perfect setting for world-class fare. In summer, dine outside under the awnings. There are five elegantly rustic guest rooms as well. (For a moderately priced sampling of Vergé's cuisine, try **L'Amandier,** nearby; ☎ 93–90–00–91.) ⌂ *Notre-Dame-de-Vie, 06250,* ☎ *93–75–78–24,* FAX *93–90–18–55. Reservations required. AE, DC, MC, V. Closed Feb.–Mar., Mon. and Thurs. lunch (times are variable). $$$$*

La Napoule

DINING AND LODGING

Royal Hôtel Casino. Weighing in at just over 200 rooms, this is a pocket edition of the Loews at Monte Carlo, with plenty of marble, plush, and gilt. The guest rooms have sea views and balconies and are decorated in pink and blue, with blond wooden furniture and large bathrooms. Be warned: Rooms overlooking the main road can be noisy. Diners at the restaurant can gaze out over a flood-lit swimming pool and deliberate among such textbook delicacies as caviar, lobster, and vintage champagne, but the preparation is relatively uninspiring for the prices charged—the fixed menu starts at 190 francs. ⌂ *605 av. Général-de-Gaulle, 06210,* ☎ *92–97–70–00. 211 rooms with bath. 2 restaurants, bars, pool, tennis, cabaret, casino, travel services. AE, DC, MC, V. $$$*

LODGING

Le Domaine d'Olival. There's not the slightest hint of mass production at this charming hotel, whose rooms have been individually designed by the architect-owner. It's small, so make reservations long in advance. All the guest rooms are air-conditioned and have balconies, as well as tiny kitchens. Some suites sleep six, which brings the price per couple down to $$. ⌂ *778 av. de la Mer, 06210,* ☎ *93–49–31–00,* FAX *92–97–69–28. 18 rooms with bath. AE, DC, MC, V. Closed Nov.–mid-Jan. $$$*

Nice

DINING

★ **Ane Rouge.** The Vidalots run a tight ship. Their tiny restaurant, perched right by the harbor, is always crowded and has been famous for generations as the place to go to for Nice's best fish and seafood. Best bets are the sea bass braised in champagne and the stuffed mussels. Note that you'll pay a bit extra for the Ane Rouge's reputation and for the chance to spot celebrities among your fellow guests. ✕ *7 quai des Deux-Emmanuel,* ☎ *93–89–49–63. Reservations advised. AE, DC, MC, V. Closed weekends and mid-July–Sept. $$$$*

L'Olivier. Franck Musso bakes his own bread and serves up sturdy Provençal dishes (fish soup, snail ravioli) and homemade desserts, while his brother Christian provides guests with a chirpy welcome to the small, cozy dining room lined with pictures. Locals love it, and because the restaurant seats only 20, book ahead. ✕ *2 pl. Garibaldi,* ☎ *93–26–89–09. Reservations required. AE, MC, V. Closed Sun., Mon. lunch, and most of Aug. and Dec. $$*

★ **La Mérenda.** This noisy bistro moved 200 yards across town to more spacious premises in 1992, but its down-to-earth Italo-Provençal food has remained a tremendously good value. The Giustis, who run it, have reluctantly installed a telephone but often refuse to take reservations, so go early to be sure of getting a table. House specials include pasta with *pistou* (a garlic-and-basil sauce) and succulent tripe. ✕ *5 rue Gioffredo,* ☎ *93–85–55–95. No credit cards. Closed weekends, Mon., Feb., and Aug. $$*

Le Tire Bouchon. This small restaurant in the heart of old Nice has only 10 tables, but the narrow room is made to seem wider by mirrors on the wall. Currently very popular, it serves good simple fare at very reasonable prices: Three-course menus cost 69 and 94 francs. The salade niçoise is an obvious choice; less obvious is the salad with smoked duck. Other dishes include curries, entrecôte, and grilled fish. If you cannot obtain a table here, wander up to the parallel street, rue de l'Abbaye, which is packed with mostly Italian restaurants (try the Ville de Sienna or Casa di Pompeii). ✕ *19 rue de la Préfecture,* ☎ *63–92–63–64. Reservations advised. Closed Sun. MC, V. $*

DINING AND LODGING

Elysée Palace. This glass-fronted addition to the Nice hotel scene lies close to the seafront; all guest rooms feature views of the Mediterranean. The interior is spacious and ultramodern, with plenty of marble in evidence. The large restaurant is a sound bet for nouvelle cuisine, enjoyed amid surroundings of contemporary works of art. ☎ *117 rue de France, 06000,* ☎ *93–86–06–06,* FAX *93–44–50–40. 143 rooms with bath. Restaurant, bar, pool, sauna, health club. AE, DC, MC, V. $$$$*

★ **Négresco.** Henri Négresco wanted to out-Ritz all the Ritzes when he built this place. There were eight kings at the opening ceremony in 1912, grouped on the 560,000-franc gold Aubusson carpet (the world's largest, naturally) beneath the 1-ton crystal chandelier in the great oval salon. No two rooms are the same, though each floor has its own motif based on a particular epoch from the 16th to the 20th century. The third floor, for example, has 19th-century antiques, and the second floor is decorated with opulent contemporary designs—Room 212 even has a gold-painted toilet, gold washbasins, and a gold oval bathtub. Chef Dominique le Stanc forged a name for himself in Monte Carlo and is consolidating the Chantecler restaurant's reputation as one of France's finest dining rooms. The menu translated into Japanese hints that prices are to match—550 francs for the menu gastronomique. The brasserie, decorated with charming carousel horses, serves informal, lighter, and less expensive fare. ☎ *37 promenade des Anglais, 06000,* ☎ *93–88–00–58,* FAX *93–88–35–68. 130 rooms with bath. 2 restaurants, bar, private beach. $$$$*

★ **Beau Rivage.** Occupying an imposing late-19th-century town house near the cours Saleya, the Beau Rivage is run by the same hotel group (Clef d'Or) as the Elysée Palace (*see above*). Though the rooms are decorated in a similar modern style, the overall effect is more intimate and personal here. Renowned chef Roger Vergé oversees a catering school on the premises; his nouvelle touch can be appreciated in the hotel's fine restaurant, Le Relais. ☎ *24 rue St-François-de-Paule, 06000,* ☎ *93–80–80–70,* FAX *93–80–55–77. 110 rooms with bath. Restaurant, private beach. AE, DC, MC, V. $$$–$$$$*

LODGING

Florence. This old-yet-modernized hotel, just off rue Jean-Médecin (Nice's major shopping street), is recommended for friendly service, comfort (air-conditioning) and style (marble bathrooms). ☎ *3 rue Paul-Déroulède, 06000,* ☎ *93–88–46–87,* FAX *93–88–43–65. 56 rooms with bath or shower. AE, DC, MC, V. $$*

Mirabeau. This stylishly renovated palm-tree-fronted hotel lies 200 yards from the train station on busy avenue Malausséna, a good 15-minute walk from the beach. Plants, flowers, and leather armchairs brighten up the lobby-breakfast area; the bedrooms, with floral-pattern quilts and functional modern furniture, are air-conditioned and soundproof, if scarcely large enough for a lengthy stay. ☎ *15 av. Malausséna,*

06000, ☎ 93–88–33–67, FAX 93–16–14–08. *42 rooms with shower. Bar. AE, MC, V. $$*

Little Palace. M. and Mme. Loridan run the closest thing to a country-house hotel in Nice. The old-fashioned decor, the jumble of bric-a-brac, and the heavy wooden furniture lend an Old World air; some may say it's like stepping onto a film set. ☎ *9 av. Baquis, 06000,* ☎ *93–88–70–49,* FAX *93–88–78–89. 36 rooms, 31 with bath. MC, V. Closed Nov. $*

La Mer. This small hotel is handily situated on place Masséna, close to the old town and seafront. The rooms are spartan (and carpets are sometimes frayed), but all have a minibar and represent good value. Ask for a room away from the square to be sure of a quiet night. ☎ *4 pl. Masséna, 06000,* ☎ *93–92–09–10,* FAX *93–85–00–64. 12 rooms with bath or shower. No credit cards. $*

St-Paul-de-Vence
DINING AND LODGING

★ **Colombe d'Or.** Anyone who likes the ambience of a country inn will feel right at home here. You'll pay for your room or meal with cash or credit cards; Picasso, Klee, Dufy, Utrillo—all friends of the former owner—paid with the paintings that now decorate the walls. The restaurant has a very good reputation. The Colombe d'Or is certainly on the tourist trail, but many of the tourists who stay here are rich and famous—if that's any consolation. ☎ *Pl. Général-de-Gaulle, 06570 St-Paul-de-Vence,* ☎ *93–32–80–02,* FAX *93–32–77–78. 24 rooms with bath. Restaurant, pool. AE, DC, MC, V. Closed mid-Nov.–late Dec., part of Jan. $$$*

St-Tropez
DINING

Bistrot des Lices. You'll find a mix of celebrities and locals at this popular bistro, a hot spot for interesting food, served by a staff as fashionable as the clientele. Bronzed men and glamorous women lounge in the garden or eat inside in the pastel interior. The barman is renowned for his way with a cocktail shaker, high praise in a town where cocktails are a way of life. ✕ *3 pl. des Lices,* ☎ *94–97–29–00. Reservations advised. MC, V. Closed Tues. out of season and Jan.–Mar. $$*

Le Girelier. Fish enthusiasts—especially those with a taste for garlic—will enjoy the hearty, heavily spiced dishes at this bustling restaurant, located right on the quay. The fish soup and the giant shrimp are local favorites. Of the many restaurants on the port, this is the best for seafood at reasonable prices. ✕ *Quai Jean-Jaurès,* ☎ *94–97–03–87. Reservations advised. AE, DC, MC, V. Closed mid-Jan.–early Mar. $$*

Lou Revelen. This smart restaurant has outside tables in a tiny square during the summer and an open fire in the dining room in the colder months. It serves good Provençal cooking, with menus beginning at 125 francs. Roasted shoulder of rabbit with a strong scent of thyme and a wide selection of fish, many with a robust, tomato-based sauce, are good choices. ✕ *Blvd. d'Aumale,* ☎ *94–97–41–76. Reservations advised. MC, V. $$*

DINING AND LODGING

Byblos. The Byblos resembles a Provençal village, with cottagelike suites grouped around courtyards paved with Picasso-inspired tiles and shaded by olive trees and magnolias. Inside, the atmosphere is distinctly New York Casbah, with lots of heavy damask and hammered brass, a leopard-skin bar, and Persian carpets on the dining-room ceiling. If you can't afford to stay here, at least go to use the pool (for a steep fee). The restaurant, Les Arcades, is lucky to have the talented Philippe

Audibert as chef; his grilled sardines are memorable. ☎ *Av. Paul Signac, 83990,* ☎ *94–97–00–04,* FAX *94–97–40–52. 59 rooms, 48 suites, all with bath. Restaurant, pool, exercise room, nightclub. AE, DC, MC, V. Closed mid-Oct.–Mar.* $$$$

Le Mas de Chastelas. In an old farmhouse that was once a silkworm farm, guests can enjoy a happy marriage of traditional and modern surroundings. The pink-toned facade, offset by white shutters, is half hidden behind trees and flowering shrubbery. Inside, white walls, modern furniture, and sculpture by the owner's sister combine to create a cool retreat from the blazing Mediterranean sun. The restaurant is usually filled with a congenial mélange of celebrities and well-heeled travelers, attracted by the traditional regional cuisine (asparagus with sea urchins, for example) of chef Patrick Cartier. ☎ *Quartier Bertaud, Grande Bastide, 83580 Gassin,* ☎ *94–56–09–11,* FAX *94–56–11–56. 15 rooms and 12 duplexes, all with bath. Restaurant, pool. AE, DC, MC, V. Closed Nov.–Easter.* $$$–$$$$

LODGING

★ **Ermitage.** This is the ideal town hotel, featuring an old-fashioned charm rarely found in modern-day St-Tropez. The guest rooms' white walls are offset by coordinated patterns of strong primary colors on the beds and at the windows. Rooms that look over the garden and the town with the harbor beyond are the ones to ask for—try for No. 23. There's no restaurant, but the heart of St-Tropez and its numerous eateries is only eight minutes away. A friendly bar seems always open and M. Merle ready to chat (in English) on the virtues and vices of his hometown. ☎ *Av. Paul-Signac, 83990,* ☎ *94–97–52–33,* FAX *94–97–10–43. 27 rooms with bath. AE, DC, MC, V.* $$$

Lou Cagnard. This is one of the few inexpensive hotels in St-Tropez, just two minutes' walk from place des Lices, so book well ahead. Don't expect great style or comfort, but the rooms are clean and not too cramped. ☎ *18 av. Paul-Roussel, 83990,* ☎ *94–97–04–24. 19 rooms, most with bath or shower. No credit cards. Closed Nov.–Christmas.* $

Trigance

DINING AND LODGING

Château de Trigance. Not much remains of the 9th-century original, except for the barrel vaulting in the lounge, where aperitifs are served, and in the dining room. Entertaining and hospitable M. Thomas, the current owner, has spent the last decade reconstructing the fortress to provide a unique hostelry with rooms of pleasant simplicity—very comfortable, but not fancy or elegant. The setting, on top of a bluff above a small village, gives commanding views of the surrounding hills, setting the mood for exploring the nearby Grand Canyon du Verdon and Haute Provence. The dining atmosphere is wonderful; the culinary art, average. ☎ *83840 Trigance,* ☎ *94–76–91–18,* FAX *94–85–68–99. 8 rooms and 2 suites with bath. Restaurant, helipad. Closed mid-Nov.–mid-Mar. AE, DC, MC, V.* $$–$$$

Vence

DINING AND LODGING

★ **Château St-Martin.** The secluded, elite St-Martin stands on the site of a crusader castle, surrounded by tall, shady trees and set within spacious grounds. The guest rooms are exquisitely decorated with antiques, needlepoint, and brocade; those in the tower are smaller and less expensive but show the same loving attention to detail. There's an excellent restaurant serving Provençal-inspired dishes. ☎ *Rte. de Coursegoules, 06140,* ☎ *93–58–02–02,* FAX *93–24–08–91. 25 rooms* *with bath. Restaurant, pool, tennis, helipad. AE, DC, MC, V. Closed mid-Nov.–mid.-Mar. $$$$*

La Roseraie. While there's no rose garden here, a giant magnolia spreads its venerable branches over the terrace. Chef Maurice Ganier hails from the southwest, as do the ducks that form the basis of his cooking. Polished service and sophisticated menus prove that you don't have to be rich to enjoy life in this part of France. All the rooms have a sunny southern exposure looking over the garden, and, like the entire hotel, are furnished with antiques that Maurice and his wife, Monica, have gathered over the years from auctions and fairs. The warm welcome here, plus the owners' determination to keep three-quarters of their rooms under 500 francs (including breakfasts), makes La Roseraie one of the best values in the region. ⌖ *51 av. Henri-Giraud, 06140,* ☎ *93–58–02–20,* ⓕⓐⓧ *93–58–99–31. 12 rooms with bath. Restaurant, pool. AE, MC, V. Closed Jan.; restaurant closed Tues. lunch and Wed. $$*

THE ARTS AND NIGHTLIFE

The Arts

Festivals

The Riviera's cultural calendar is splashy and star-studded, and never more so than during the region's world-famous festivals. The biggest and most celebrated is the **Cannes Film Festival** in May, rivaled by Monte Carlo's arts festival, **Printemps des Arts** (late March through late April). Antibes and Nice both host **jazz festivals** during July, drawing international performers. Menton has a **chamber music festival** in August and a **September music festival** at the Palais d'Europe.

Music and Ballet

Monte Carlo's primary venue for jazz and rock is **Le Chapiteau de Fontvieille** (☎ 93–25–18–68); the **Salle Garnier** (Casino de Monaco, ☎ 93–50–76–54) offers both classical music and ballet, as does Nice's **Acropolis** (Palais des Congrès, Esplanade John F. Kennedy, ☎ 93–92–80–00). St-Tropez's major concert hall, which doubles as a cinema, is the **Salle de la Renaissance** (pl. des Lices, ☎ 94–97–48–16). There are frequent jazz and pop concerts at Nice's **Théâtre de Verdure** (Jardin Albert Ier, ☎ 93–82–38–68), which relocates to the **Arènes de Cimiez** during summer months.

Opera

The Nice **Opéra** (4 rue St-François-de-Paul, ☎ 93–85–67–31) has a season that extends from September to June. In Monte Carlo, the **Salle Garnier** (*see above*) hosts operatic performances, most frequently during the spring arts festival.

Theater

In Nice try the **Théâtre Municipal Francis-Gag** (4 rue St-Joseph, ☎ 93–62–00–03) or the **Théâtre de Nice** (Promenade des Arts, ☎ 93–13–90–90). In Monte Carlo, the **Théâtre Princesse Grace** (12 av. d'Ostende, ☎ 93–25–32–27) stages a number of plays during the spring festival; off-season, there's usually a new show each week.

Nightlife

There's no need to go to bed before dawn in any of the Riviera's major resorts, the most fashionable of which are St-Tropez, Cannes, Juan-les-Pins, Nice, and Monte Carlo. Juan-les-Pins draws a young crowd; St-Tropez has gay appeal; and clubs in Cannes, Nice, and Monte Carlo are expensive and sophisticated. Note that to get into many of the Riviera's night spots, you'll have to dress the part—or risk being brushed aside by the burly doormen.

Discos and Nightclubs

La Siesta (rte. du Bord de Mer, Antibes) is an enormous setup, with seven dance floors, roulette, bars, and supper places—all dramatically lit by torches; it's open during the summer season only. The top spots in Cannes are **Studio-Circus** (48 blvd. de la République) and **Jimmy'z** (Palais des Festivals), which admit celebrities, stars, and starlets, but not necessarily everyone else. The cabaret shows are legendary, accompanied by lasers and deafening noise. Top-class cabaret is offered at Menton's **Club 06,** at the casino (Promenade de Soleil). In Monte Carlo, head to **Jimmy'z**; it operates from place du Casino from September to June, then moves to premises on avenue Princesse-Grace (if you can't get in, try at the neighboring, slightly younger **Parady'z**). The location may be different, but the disco remains expensive and chic, and the clientele is drawn from the elite. On the avenue des Spélugues, you'll find **The Living Room** (at No. 7) and **Tiffany's** (at No. 3); both are popular, crowded, and open year-round. **Harry's** piano bar (19 av. Charles-III) often attracts good jazz singers. **The Offshore** (29 rue Alphonse-Karr) is Nice's trendiest spot, but you'll have to dress sharp to get past the doorman. If you don't make it, try the young, lively **Bin's Discothèque** (71 blvd. Jean-Béhra). The hottest place in St-Tropez is **Les Caves du Roy** (Byblos Hotel, av. Signac); the decor is stunningly vulgar, but the *très chic* clientele don't seem to mind. It's large but always crowded, so look your best if you want to get in.

Casinos

There are casinos in **Cannes** (Carlton and Hilton hotels, Palais des Festivals, Palm Beach), **Antibes, La Napoule, Nice** (Promenade des Anglais), and **Menton** (Promenade de Soleil), but the Riviera's most famous gambling venue is at **Monte Carlo** (pl. du Casino).

RIVIERA ESSENTIALS

Arriving and Departing

By Plane

The area's only international airport is at Nice (☎ 93–21–30–12).

By Train

Mainline trains from the French capital stop at most of the major resorts; the trip to Nice takes about seven hours.

By Car

If you're traveling from Paris by car, you can avoid a lengthy drive by taking the overnight motorail (*train-auto-couchette*) service to Nice, which departs from Paris's Gare de Bercy, five minutes from the Gare de Lyon. Otherwise, leave Paris by A6 (becoming A7 after Lyon), which continues down to Avignon. Here A8 branches off east toward Italy, with convenient exit/entry points for all major towns (except St-Tropez).

Getting Around

By Train

The train is a practical and inexpensive way of getting around the Riviera and stops at dozens of stations. Note that the pretty Nice-Digne line is not run by the SNCF but by the Chemin de Fer de Provence (Gare du Sud, 33 av. Malausséna, Nice, ☎ 93–88–28–56).

By Car

If you prefer to avoid the slower, albeit spectacularly scenic, coastal roads, opt for the Italy-bound A8.

By Bus

Local buses cover a network of routes along the Riviera and stop at many out-of-the-way places that can't be reached by train. Timetables are available from tourist offices, train stations, and the local bus depots (*gares routières*).

Guided Tours

Bus

A variety of tours (most starting from the coach station, or gare routière, on Promenade du Paillon in Nice, but sometimes with pickups in Menton, Cannes, or Antibes) are organized by **Santa Azur** (11 av. Jean-Médecin, 06000 Nice, ☎ 93–85–46–81, FAX 93–87–90–08). Excursions include Cannes and Antibes (140 francs); Cannes and the Lérins Islands (165 francs); Eze and Monaco, Wednesday and Sunday from April to October (140 francs); Biot and Vallauris, Monday (110 francs); Vence and St-Paul-de-Vence, Tuesday and Thursday in July and August (175 francs); St-Tropez, Tuesday and Saturday (165 francs); the Gorges du Verdon, Sunday and Thursday from July to September (165 francs); and panoramic tours of Nice every Monday and Wednesday from May through October (95 francs). Full- or half-day minibus tours for up to eight passengers, with English-speaking driver-guides, are organized by **Joe's Sight-Seeing** (15 rue Alberti, BP 194, 06000 Nice cedex 1, ☎ 93–88–97–11, FAX 93–82–44–93), which promises a 10% discount on normal prices to Fodor's readers.

Boat

Gallus Excursions 80 (24 quai Lunel, 06000 Nice, ☎ 93–55–33–33) offers an enjoyable day-long jaunt to the Iles de Lérins; the cost is about 175 francs.

Special-Interest

Any tourist office will produce a sheaf of suggestions on gourmandizing, golfing, and walking tours, among others. **Novatour** (9 rue de Lille, 06400 Cannes, ☎ 93–69–47–47) offers tailor-made packages for its clients, though museum tours are a specialty; a three-day, two-night museum tour of Vence and Antibes, including half-board, costs about 3,000 francs.

Important Addresses and Numbers

Travel Agencies

American Express (8 rue des Belges, Cannes, ☎ 93–38–15–87; 11 promenade des Anglais, Nice, ☎ 93–16–53–53; **Wagons-Lits** (2 av. Monte-Carlo, Monaco, ☎ 93–25–01–05).

Car Rental

Avis (9 av. d'Ostende, Monaco, ☎ 93–30–17–53; and av. du 8-Mai-1945, St-Tropez, ☎ 94–97–03–10), **Europcar** (9 av. Thiers, Menton, ☎ 93–28–21–80), and **Hertz** (147 rue d'Antibes, Cannes, ☎ 93–99–04–20; and 12 av. de Suède, Nice, ☎ 93–87–11–87).

Visitor Information

The Riviera's regional tourist office is the **Comité Régional du Tourisme de Riviera—Côte d'Azur** (55 promenade des Anglais, 06000 Nice; written inquiries only). Local tourist offices in major towns covered in this chapter are as follows: **Antibes** (11 pl. Général-de-Gaulle, ☎ 93–33–

95–64), **Cannes** (Palais des Festivals, 1 La Croisette, ☎ 93–39–24–53), **Fréjus** (325 rue Jean-Jaurès, ☎ 94–17–19–19), **Juan-les-Pins** (51 blvd. Charles-Guillaumont, ☎ 93–61–04–98), **La Napoule** (272 av. Henry-Clews, ☎ 93–49–95–31), **Menton** (Palais de l'Europe, av. Boyer, ☎ 93–57–57–00), **Monte Carlo** (2a blvd. des Moulins, ☎ 92–16–61–66), **Nice** (av. Thiers, ☎ 93–87–07–07), and **St-Tropez** (quai Jean-Jaurès, ☎ 94–97–45–21).

14 Corsica

ACOMBINATION OF ANCIENT Mediterranean ports, crystalline waters, archaeological treasures, and breathtaking high mountains makes Corsica one of the most breathtakingly scenic and unspoiled regions of France. The island is roughly the shape of an inverted triangle, with the cities of Calvi and Bastia on the top corners and Bonifacio on the southern tip. The capital, Ajaccio (pronounced a-*jack*-sio), lies on the western side of the island halfway between Calvi and Bonifacio, and the lonely peninsula of Cap Corse juts north of Bastia toward France.

For thousands of years, its natural resources and strategic location, 168 kilometers (105 miles) south of the French coast and just 81 kilometers (50 miles) west of Italy, have made Corsica a prize hotly contested by many Mediterranean civilizations. You can still see vestiges of those invaders, from primitive stone statues of prehistoric warriors to exquisite Grecian urns and crumbling Roman ruins. The city-state of Genoa ruled Corsica for hundreds of years, leaving behind impressive citadels and bridges and a network of nearly 100 medieval watchtowers that still encircle the island. The Italian influence is also apparent in village architecture and in the Corsican language, a combination of Italian and Latin. Corsican is still spoken among island residents, but everyone except the oldest villagers also speaks French.

While Corsica is only 215 kilometers (133 miles) long and 81 kilometers (50 miles) wide it seems much larger—partly because rugged, mountainous terrain makes for slow traveling and partly because the landscape varies so much from region to region. Bastia and Ajaccio are big cities with urban sprawl but colorful old quarters. The area surrounding the capital is rural and hilly, while the Calvi region has sand-colored villages and cheerful crescent beaches. The eastern part of the island is a marshy plain with long sandy beaches, the southern region around Bonifacio contains austere granite hill towns, while the entire interior is a chain of dramatic mountaintops. Unlike many other Mediterranean islands, Corsica is green year-round and has plentiful supplies of fresh water; 14 rivers tumble down from the mountains through wooded valleys, full of cork-oak trees and ancient, majestic laricio pines, Europe's tallest conifer.

All of Corsica that is not wooded or cultivated is covered with a dense thicket of undergrowth called the *maquis*. The maquis is made up of a variety of sweet-smelling plants like lavender, myrtle, and heather that turn the hillsides white with tiny flowers in the spring, and gave Corsica its nickname, "the perfumed isle." It's also famous for harboring bandits and a motley assortment of other fugitives. In Corsica, you don't head for the hills, you head for the maquis.

There's always been a kind of black legend associated with the island that stems mainly from a tradition of clannishness. While Corsican clans often fought each other in endless cycles of revenge, they also took care of each other. Corsicans who emigrated always found a fellow Corsican willing to help, and this strong network of connections landed government jobs for thousands of islanders during the hard times following World War I. They still make up 15% of the French police force.

Corsica is also famous as the birthplace of Napoléon Bonaparte. Although he never returned to the island after beginning his military career, Napoléon is honored with statues in Ajaccio, where you can visit his family's home. Perhaps better suited to the individualist character of the island is Corsica's real hero, Pasquale Paoli, who framed the world's first constitution for the independent Corsican republic in 1755. Paoli's ideas greatly influenced the French Revolution as well as the founding fathers of the United States, who drew upon Corsica's constitution in writing their own version some 30 years later.

The best time to visit Corsica is the spring and the fall, when temperatures in the 60s and 70s allow for comfortable sightseeing and swimming. It's an easy side trip from the Riviera and during the off-season can be an economic alternative to the pricey Cote d'Azur. Try to avoid visiting in busy July and August, when French and Italian vacationers fill hotels and push up prices. It is also possible to see Corsica in winter, when the island will likely have the best weather in all of France, but expect to find the majority of hotels and restaurants closed. Be sure to brush up on your French before you go—outside the main hotels and restaurants it's difficult to find people who speak English.

EXPLORING

Orientation

The best way to tour the island is to drive along the coastal circuit, venturing inland to admire the remote rural regions and picturesque villages, with their fortresslike stone houses and tiny alleyways. First off, buy the yellow Michelin 1/200,000 map No. 90. Road signs are somewhat erratic, so a good map and a good navigator are essential. Despite, or possibly because of, Corsica's insular confinement, drivers circulate at consistently terrifying speeds.

Experienced Corsica hands generally agree that the northern half of the island (Haute Corse) is fresher, wilder, and more thrilling than the southern half, which is hotter, drier, and generally more barren (particularly since the forest fires of 1994). And that the least interesting part of the island is the east coast between Porto-Vecchio and Bastia.

Our tour begins in the bustling port of Bastia and moves around the island counterclockwise. You'll need a minimum of six days to complete the entire circuit: Day 1, Bastia–Calvi; Day 2, Calvi–Piana; Day 3, Piana–Ajaccio; Day 4, Ajaccio–Bonifacio; Day 5, Bonifacio–Corte; Day 6, Corte–Bastia. Be sure to allow additional days if you plan to explore the mountains, take boat rides, or spend time at the beach. Another approach is to settle in Corte, near the island's center, and sally forth each day to the different attractions around the edges. Corte is cooler than elsewhere in summer, and 90-minute train rides connect you with Bastia, Ajaccio, and Calvi.

Exploring the Island

Numbers in the margin correspond to points of interest on the Corsica and Ajaccio maps.

① We begin our tour in **Bastia,** whose name comes from *bastaglia,* or fortress. The Genoese built a prodigious one here in the 14th century as a stronghold against rebellious islanders and potential invaders from across the Tuscan Straits. Today, the city is Corsica's business center and largest town. Despite sprawling suburbs filled with supermarkets, apartment towers, and giant hardware stores, the center of Bastia retains the timeless, salty flavor of an ancient Mediterranean port.

The **Terra Vecchia** (Old Town) is small enough to be explored on foot. Start at the wide, palm-filled **place St-Nicolas** bordered on one side by

Corsica

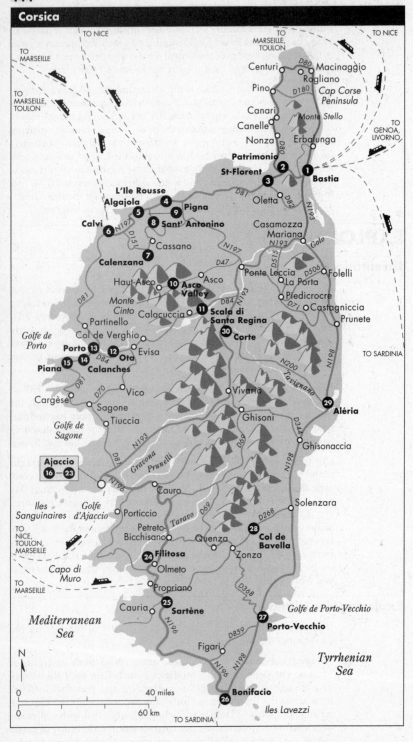

TO NICE

TO MARSEILLE, TOULON

TO NICE

TO MARSEILLE

TO MARSEILLE, TOULON

TO GENOA, LIVORNO

Centuri

Macinaggio

D80

Ragliano

Pino

D180

Cap Corse Peninsula

Canari

Monte Stello

Canelle

Nonza

D80

Erbalunga

Patrimonio

2

St-Florent

1

3

Bastia

Oletta

D81

D82

N193

L'Ile Rousse

Algajola

4

Pigna

5

9

Casamozza

Calvi

8

Sant' Antonino

Mariana

6

N197

Cassano

N193

Golo

D151

7

N197

Calenzana

D47

Ponte Leccia

D506

Folelli

Haut-Asco

10

Asco Valley

Asco

La Porta

Monte Cinto

Calacuccia

11

Scala di Santa Regina

Predicrocre

D515

D71

Castagniccia

Prunete

Partinello

D81

Col de Verghio

Evisa

30

Corte

D84

N193

Porto

13

12

Ota

TO SARDINIA

Piana

15

14

Calanches

D84

Vivario

N200

N198

Tavignano

Cargèse

D81

D70

Vico

Golfe de Porto

Sagone

Tiuccia

Ghisoni

29

Aléria

Golfe de Sagone

N193

Gravona

Prunelli

D69

D343

Ajaccio

16 — 23

D81

N196

Cauro

Ghisonaccia

N161

Iles Sanguinaires

Golfe d'Ajaccio

Porticcio

Tavaro

D59

Solenzara

TO NICE, TOULON, MARSEILLE

Petreto-Bicchisano

Quenza

D268

28

Col de Bavella

Capo di Muro

24

Filitosa

Olmeto

Zonza

TO MARSEILLE

Propriano

D368

Cauria

25

Sartène

Golfe di Porto-Vecchio

Mediterranean Sea

N196

27

Porto-Vecchio

Figari

D859

N

N196

N198

Tyrrhenian Sea

0 ___ 40 miles

0 ___ 60 km

26

Bonifacio

Iles Lavezzi

TO SARDINIA

the sea and on the other by two blocks of cafés that stretch out along boulevard Général de Gaulle. These cafés with their tables spilling into the square are the hub of Bastia's social life. A good one to try is the wood-paneled Les Palmiers.

Head south on boulevard de Gaulle, which becomes rue Napoléon, and in two blocks on the left you will see the **Church of the Conception** occupying a pebble-studded square. Step inside to admire the church's ornate 18th-century interior, although the lighting is poor and you'll need a bright day to see much. The walls are covered with a riot of wood carvings, gold, and marble, and the ceiling is painted with vibrant frescoes.

Walk around the back of the church and you will come out on the **place du Marché**—the market square where every morning except Monday black-swathed grandmothers haggle over the price of fish and fruit. Continue across the market and you'll come to a warren of tiny streets that make up the old **fishermen's quarter.** The sky disappears above the tall buildings, plaster crumbles, laundry drips from overhead, children scoot by on bikes, and sounds of family life drift out the windows into the clammy air trapped between the houses.

Continue south to the picturesque **old port,** along quai des Martyrs de la Libération, dominated by the hilltop citadel. The harbor, now lined with excellent seafood restaurants, is home to million-dollar yachts, but you can still find many bright red-and-blue fishing boats and tangles of old nets and lines. A walk around the port brings you to **Terra Nova** (New Town), a maze of not-so-new streets and houses at the base of the 15th-century fortress. Climb the stairs to the top for a sweeping view of the Italian islands of Capraia, Elba, and Montecristo. If it's a clear day you'll be able to make out the hills of Tuscany.

At the place de la Citadelle, stop in at the **Genoese Governor's Palace,** whose vaulted, colonnaded galleries now house the **Corsican Ethnographic Museum,** with collections detailing peasant life and the island's history. There are exhibits of Roman vases, opalescent glass vials, and more recent military and domestic artifacts. Be sure to look for the 18th-century rebel flag with the black head and white headband. This symbol of Corsican nationalism frequently appears nowadays throughout the island on everything from bags of cookies to political posters. Behind the ancient defense tower, a tiny stairway leads past the heroic *Casablanca,* a French submarine that refused to surrender and fought for the resistance. The swastikas on the turret are for downed Nazi aircraft. The governor's private gardens, an intimate green oasis, provide a superb view over the port to the towers of the Church of St. John the Baptist. *Pl. du Donjon,* ☎ *95–31–09–12.* 👉 *15 frs.* ☉ *Weekdays 9–noon and 2–6, weekends 10–noon and 2–5.*

Opposite the museum, a network of cobbled alleyways rambles across the citadel to the 15th-century **Cathédrale Ste-Marie** on rue Notre-Dame. Inside, classic Baroque abounds in an explosion of gilt decoration. The church's 18th-century silver statue of the Assumption is paraded at the head of a solemn religious procession through the streets of the Old Town each August 15th. Just behind the church stands the **Chapelle Sainte Croix,** with a sumptuous Baroque style that makes it look more like a theater than a church. The chapel owes its names to a blackened oak crucifix, "Christ of the Miracles," discovered by fishermen at sea in 1428 and venerated to this day by Bastia's fishing community.

With an early start from Bastia, the **Cap Corse** peninsula is an ambitious but feasible part of a day scheduled to end in Calvi, though you could easily spend a week here. The D80 coastal road runs around the Monte Stello mountains along the edge of the peninsula through pretty little towns like **Erbalunga,** whose tiny houses tumble to the water's edge, and **Macinaggio,** a fishing port. It also passes some of the most beautiful of the 90 watchtowers constructed around Corsica. The towers at Erbalunga, Agnello, and Nonza are among the best. Higher up is **Rogliano** on the road over to the 18th-century port of **Centuri,** famous for underwater scenery. You might also cross the tip of Cap Corse on D180 through the Col de Ste-Lucie past the **Tour de Sénèque,** the tower to which the luckless Seneca was exiled for having seduced the emperor Claudius's niece Julia. Along the west coast you'll hit the pretty villages of **Pino, Canari,** and **Cannelle.**

2 Near the base of the peninsula is the little town of **Patrimonio,** 18 kilometers (11 miles) from Bastia. Set among acres of vineyards that stretch into the distance, Patrimonio produces what is considered Corsica's best wine. The highly prized reds are made from unique Corsican grapes called Nielluccio. The Orenga de Gaffory label is the most famous. Stop for a tour of the family vineyard and art gallery. ☎ 95–37–11–38. ☉ *Weekdays 9–noon and 3–6.*

3 Five kilometers (3 miles) farther down D81 the postcard-perfect village of **St-Florent** nestles in the crook of the Golfe de St-Florent, between the rich Nebbio Valley and the desert of Agriates, a barren chaos of rocks sloping into the sea. St-Florent has a crumbling citadel and a popular yacht basin ringed by shops and restaurants. Before leaving, be sure to seek out one of Corsica's most interesting Romanesque churches, **Santa Maria Assunta** (open July and Aug., daily 9–noon and 3–7:30), just outside the village on rue Agostino Giustiniani. Standing in isolated splendor among the vineyards, this 12th-century limestone church is one of only two Pisan cathedrals remaining on the island. The facade and interior columns support a menagerie of sculpted human faces, snakes, snails, and mythical animals. In the apse, the gilt statue of St. Florus, a martyred Roman soldier, stands near his relics displayed in a glass case.

TIME OUT For a great seafood lunch with dreamy views of the yachts, look for a harborside table at **La Gaffe** (Le Port, ☎ 95–37–00–12; closed Mon. and Oct.–Mar.). Here you'll find bouillabaisse, grilled fish, salads, and platters of chilled oysters, lobster, or mussels.

4 Snaking west across the desert, D81 joins N197 shortly before you arrive at the resort town of **L'Ile Rousse,** 37 kilometers (22 miles) from St-Florent. The town, named for the mass of reddish rock now connected to the town by a causeway, is a favorite with French vacationers. A small two-car train runs from here along the coast to Calvi, picking up and depositing sun worshippers at beach coves not accessible by road.

5 More charming is the village of **Algajola,** 10 kilometers (6 miles) farther west on N197. This is the last and smallest of the seven citadel towns built by the Genoese on Corsica's shores. Its perfect crescent beach attracts crowds, but the tiny old town's medieval roots can still be felt.

6 Continue west along N197 through the orchards and farms of the rich Balagne region, known as the garden of Corsica, for 14 kilometers (9 miles) until you reach **Calvi,** one of Corsica's most sophisticated resort towns and the port closest to mainland France. Calvi grew rich by supplying products to Genoa. Citizens always considered themselves far superior to the rest of the Corsicans and remained loyal supporters of Genoa long after the rest of the island had declared independence. Calvi also claims to be the birthplace of Christopher Columbus, the most famous Genoese of them all. The proof is not airtight, but the crew lists from Columbus's voyages to the New World do contain the names of many Calvi residents.

Like that of Bastia, Calvi's location has made it a strategic spot for warriors and tourists alike. During the 18th century the town endured assaults from Corsican nationalists, the most prominent being the celebrated patriot Pasquale Paoli. Today's Calvi sees a summertime invasion of mainly French and Italian visitors, drawn by the resort's 6-kilometer long (4-mile-long) white sand beach flanked by graceful umbrella pines, a perfectly carved bay, and a busy marina.

The **Genoese Citadel,** perched on a rocky promontory at the tip of the bay, competes with the beach as a major attraction. The ramparts are the natural place to begin our tour of the city. As you cross the drawbridge, notice the plaque above. The inscription *Civitas Calvi semper fidelis,* "The citizens of Calvi always faithful," reflects the town's unswerving allegiance to Genoa. At the welcome center, just inside the gates, you can see a video on the city's history, and a guided tour is available in English three times a day at 10, 4:30, and 6:30 from Easter to October 1. There's also a self-guided walking tour. ☎ 95–65–36–74. *Guided tour and video show: 45 frs adults, 15 frs children 10–15.*

TIME OUT   For a pleasant salad lunch or coffee and a pastry in the heart of the old town, stop at **La Voûte** (rue St-François, ☎ 95–65–12–83) where owner-chef Pastourette cooks recipes handed down from her great-grand-mother in Provence.

From the citadel, descend to the elegant **quai Landry,** lined with attractive restaurants and cafés. Rue Clemenceau, one block behind the harbor, and boulevard Wilson are major shopping streets. As you explore, stop in at the 13th-century church of **St-Jean-Baptiste** on the place d'Armes. It contains an interesting baptismal font dating from the Renaissance. Look up to see the rows of pews screened by grillwork. The chaste young women of Calvi's upper classes would sit here to say their prayers, protected from the hot glances of any lusty peasant.

Before leaving the Calvi region make an excursion to see the rose-colored hill towns of the **Balagne.** This was the so-called land of lords and remained a feudal society right up until the French Revolution. Head back east on N197 for 5 kilometers (3 miles) and make a right turn on D151 toward Calenzana, 13 kilometers (8 miles) from Calvi.

➐ **Calenzana,** once a hideout for Corsica's notorious bandits, lies among olive groves and boasts the 11th-century **church of Ste-Restitute,** less than a mile beyond the town. The church's marble and granite altar is backed by medieval frescoes depicting the life of St. Restitute. Legend has it that the saint was martyred here in the 3rd century, and when the people of the town began building a church on another site, the stone blocks were moved here each night by two huge white bulls. Apparently, this happened several times before the townsfolk finally got the divine message and changed building sites.

The road, D151, continues to wind around hillsides dotted with picturesque villages. Most are surrounded by walls and have the same layout: a gate that opens onto a square, with a church and fountain, surrounded by streets leading out from the center like the spokes of a wheel. The short streets lined with a tumble of tall houses come to a dead end at the final house, built into the village walls. From Calenzana to **Cateri** sweeping coast and valley views spread out before you.

TIME OUT A little past the crossroads in Cateri you can find an economical lunch of tasty Corsican specialties at **Restaurant A Lataria** (☎ 95-61-71-44), a family-owned place with a flower-filled terrace.

8 After Cateri, turn onto D13 and cross the gorge to the medieval stone village of **Sant'Antonino,** believed to date from the 9th century, making it one of the oldest still-inhabited villages on the island.

9 Back on D151 continue to the unusual village of **Pigna,** dedicated to bringing back traditional Corsican music and crafts. Here you can listen to folk songs in cafés, visit workshops, and buy handmade musical instruments, as well as music boxes, pottery, paintings, baskets, ironwork, and jewelry. Don't miss the **Casa Musicale,** a music retreat house and concert hall–cum–auberge/restaurant/museum! It's full of composers and musicians who come to write and practice (*see also* Dining and Lodging, *below*).

★ 10 Another 5 kilometers (3 miles) brings you back to highway N197 near L'Ile Rousse. From here you start to move southward, first traveling east on N197, then continuing on D81 as it rounds the headlands, turns south toward Ponte Leccia and becomes N197 again. Two kilometers (1 mile) before Ponte Leccia make a right turn on D47 toward the village of Asco. The **Asco Valley** runs west to an awe-inspiring barrier of mountains crowned by Monte Cinto, rising to 2,706 meters (8,795 feet), the highest point in Corsica. The peaks shimmer with snow for part of the year and turn various colors from red-mauve to deep purple-gray, depending on the time of day. As you travel, the maquis-covered valley gives way to a sheer granite gorge hung with sweet-smelling juniper.

The Asco region is studded with beehives. Honey and cheese abound in the shops of the village, a slow 16 kilometers (10 miles) from N197. Here the granite gorge becomes a cool pine forest, perfect for picnicking and hiking. The road continues for another 12 kilometers (7 miles) past the village to end against the wall of mountains. A small ski area operates here in winter and there is a chalet for overnight stays.

★ 11 For even more dramatic scenery, get back on the main highway, N197, drive south 10 kilometers (6 miles) and just past the village of Francardo turn right on D84. This road, known as the **Scala di Santa Regina** (stairway of the holy queen), is one of the most spectacular on the island. It's also one of the wildest and most difficult to navigate. Be careful, especially in winter. The route follows the twisty path of the Golo River, which has carved its way through layers of red granite, forming dramatic gorges and waterfalls. Be prepared for herds of free-range pigs, sheep, goats, cows, or wild boar to cross the road.

12 The road passes through the forest of Valdo-Niello before climbing to the pass at **Col de Verghio,** where you once again have good views of Monte Cinto. About 11 kilometers (7 miles) past Evisa, look across the gorge to catch sight of the village of **Ota,** seemingly suspended on the mountainside. A small road on the right will take you across the gorge, where there's an ancient Genoese-built bridge at the bottom. The village is 5 kilometers (3 miles) above the flashy new resort of Porto and couldn't be more different. It's the typical safe haven sought by many Corsicans, who turned their back to life on the coast, exposed and vulnerable to invaders or pirates.

13 Descend to **Porto,** a pretty pink-granite town without much character but with a superb setting on the crystalline Gulf of Porto. There's a good place to view the gulf along the coastal highway just to the north.

★ 14 Our circuit takes us south of Porto on D81 through the **Calanches,** a jagged outcropping of red rock that ranks as one of the most extraordinary natural sites in France. There are natural arches and stelae, and rocks that seem to have faces and distorted animal shapes. Stop and follow some of the paths that wind through this strange rock garden. It's also a perfect place to watch the sunset.

⑮ Piana, 11 kilometers (7 miles) from Porto on the other side of the Calanches, offers more views of the gulf. Climb up to the old fortress at the top of Capo Rosso to admire the craggy rocks that jut out from the water and explore the crooked streets of the old town.

★ **⑯** Leaving Piana, pick up D81 and follow it along the coast past inviting beach towns and through green rural landscapes to **Ajaccio,** 72 kilometers (43 miles) away. High-rise buildings and urban sprawl announce your approach to this commercial city—Napoléon's birthplace and Corsica's modern capital.

⑰ Begin your tour at **place Maréchal-Foch,** the city's main square, planted firmly on the waterfront. Rows of stately palm trees create a tropical atmosphere and lead to a marble statue of Napoléon dressed in a **⑱** Roman toga and surrounded by four lions. Stop in at the **Hôtel de Ville** (Town Hall), whose Empire-style Grand Salon is hung with portraits of a long line of Bonapartes. You'll find a fine bust of Letizia, Napoléon's formidable mother, and a bronze death mask of the emperor himself. The frescoed ceiling portrays Napoléon's meteoric rise to fame. *Pl. Maréchal-Foch.* ☛ *5 frs.* ⊘ *Apr.–Oct., weekdays 9–noon and 2:30–5:30; Nov.–Mar., weekdays 9–noon and 2–5.*

⑲ Behind the town hall look for the **city market,** a lovely square where every morning except Monday you can ogle the enticing array of sausages, cheeses, and vegetables fresh from the city's surrounding farms. Be sure to try the unusual beignets that white-haired village women still make the traditional way, with chestnut flour and brocciu cheese.

Walk back to place Maréchal-Foch, go right up to the Napoléon statue and then left two short blocks down rue Bonaparte. Just up rue St-Charles **⑳** stands the large middle-class 18th-century **Maison Bonaparte** (Bonaparte House), where Napoléon was born on August 15, 1769. Today the building houses a museum featuring the rather spartan Louis XV and XVI interiors designed by Napoléon's mother. Glass cases display mementos, and another room contains portraits and cameos of the entire Bonaparte clan. Search out the two family trees: one spanning more than 200 years (1769–the present), the other dating from the 19th century and woven out of human hair. *Rue St-Charles.* ☛ *17 frs.* ⊘ *Mon. 2–5, Tues.–Sat. 10–noon and 2–5, Sun. 10–noon.*

Turning left outside the Maison Bonaparte down rue St-Charles, you'll come to the city's oldest houses, on the corner of rue Roi de Rome, opposite the tiny church of St. John the Baptist. These simple homes were built shortly after the town was founded in 1492. As with most buildings in Corsica, nobody has made any effort to repair the crumbling plaster. It's not a case of poverty, because the island enjoys a relatively high standard of living, nor is it squalor, since you'll notice the streets and parks are kept clean and tidy. Corsica is just now beginning to appreciate its historic buildings.

㉑ At the end of rue St-Charles stands the 16th-century baroque **cathedral** where Napoléon was baptized. The interior is covered with newly restored trompe l'oeil frescoes, and the high altar, from an old church in Lucca, Italy, was donated by Napoléon's sister Eliza after he made

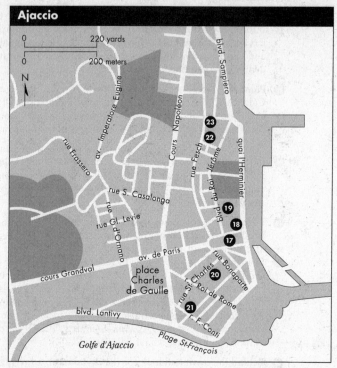

Ajaccio

her princess of Tuscany. Above the altar, look for Eugène Delacroix's famous painting *Virgin of Sacré Coeur.*

TIME OUT After visiting the old quarter, make your way down to the **plage St-François** and stop at one of the many cafés. Café Fesch is a good one, with fine views of the gulf.

22 Before leaving Ajaccio, walk back to the statue on place Maréchal-Foch and head four blocks up rue Fesch to the Renaissance-style **Chapelle Impérial,** built in 1857 by Napoléon's nephew, Napoléon III, to accommodate the tombs of the Bonaparte family. (The great man himself is buried, however, in the Hôtel des Invalides in Paris.) A Coptic crucifix taken from Egypt during the general's 1798 campaign hangs over the main altar. *50 rue Fesch.* ☛ *10 frs.* ⊙ *Tues.–Sat. 10–12:30, 3–7.*

23 Right next door is the island's finest art museum, the **Musée Fesch,** which houses what is considered the best collection of Italian masters—Botticelli, Canaletto, De Tura—outside Florence and Paris. This is just part of a collection of 30,000 paintings bought up at bargain prices following the French revolution by Napoléon's uncle, Cardinal Fesch, the archbishop of Lyon. *50 rue Fesch,* ☎ *95–21–48–17.* ☛ *25 frs.* ⊙ *Apr.–Oct., Wed.–Mon. 9:30–noon and 3–6:30 (also in July and Aug., Tues.–Sat. 9–midnight); Nov.–Mar., Wed.–Mon. 9:30–noon and 2:30–6.*

Leaving Ajaccio, N196 crosses the Prunelli River amidst quiet, pastoral scenery. The capital's beach resort, filled with good hotels, is to the right in the town of **Porticcio.** Continue southeast for 65 kilometers (39 miles) **★ 24** and turn right on D57 for the final 6 kilometers (4 miles) to **Filitosa**, site of Corsica's largest grouping of megalithic menhir statues. Bizarre, life-size stone figures of ancient warriors rise up mysteriously from the undulating terrain, many with human faces that have been eroded and flattened with time. A small museum on the site houses fascinating archaeological finds, including the menhir known as Scalsa Murta, whose delicately carved spine and rib cage make it difficult to believe the statue dates from some 3,000 years before the birth of Christ. During June, July, and August there are English-speaking guides to show you around. Be sure to buy the excellent guidebook in English (30 frs) by experts Cesari and Acquaviva. ☎ 95–74–00–91. ☛ 25 frs. ⊘ Daily 8–7.

TIME OUT There's a pleasant **museum café** at Filitosa, where you can soak up the prehistoric ambience over a light lunch or snack.

25 Following N196 about 27 kilometers (16 miles) southeast from Filitosa, you'll arrive at the hillside town of **Sartène,** often called the "most Corsican of all Corsican towns." Founded in the 16th century, Sartène has survived pirate raids and bloody feuding among the town's families. The word *vendetta* comes from here. Centuries of fighting have left the town with an almost spooky atmosphere. As you draw near, a line of fortresslike granite houses rise in surly greeting.

The most interesting part of town is **Vieux Sartène** (Old Sartène), surrounded by ancient ramparts. Start your walking tour at the place de la Libération, the main square and town meeting place. To one side of the square is the **Hôtel de Ville,** the former Genoese governor's palace, which retains a decorative coat of arms. For a taste of the Middle Ages, slip through the tunnel in the building to place du Maggiu and the old quarter of **Santa Anna,** an eerie warren of narrow, cobbled streets, lined with granite houses. Scarcely 100 yards from the Town Hall, down a steep and winding street, a 12th-century watchtower stands out in sharp contrast to the modern apartment buildings behind.

Sartène is the center for research into Corsica's prehistory, due to its proximity to a region rich in dolmens and megalithic statues just to the south. For a look at some of the island's best prehistoric relics, stop by the **Musée Départemental de la Préhistoire Corse** (Departmental Museum of Corsican Prehistory) in the town's former prison. *Rue Croce,* ☎ 95–77–01–09. ☛ 10 frs. ⊘ Apr.–Oct., Mon.–Sat. 10–noon and 2–6; Nov.–Mar., weekdays 10–noon and 2–5.

★ **26** The ancient fortress-town of **Bonifacio,** 54 kilometers (33 miles) southeast on N196, occupies a spectacular clifftop setting above a handsome fjordlike harbor carved from limestone cliffs. It is just 13 kilometers (8 miles) from Sardinia, and local speech is heavily influenced by the accent and idiom of the neighboring Italian island.

Established in the 12th century as Genoa's first Corsican stronghold against the Moors, Bonifacio remained Genoese through centuries of battles and sieges. As you wander the narrow streets of the **Haute-Ville** (Upper Village), inside the walls of the citadel, think of Homer's *Odyssey.* It was here, in the bottleneck harbor at Bonifacio, that, according to Classics scholars, Ulysses' fleet was bombarded by the vicious Laestrygonians.

From the place d'Armes at the city gate, enter the **Bastion of the Standard**; you can still see the system of weights and pulleys used to pull up the drawbridge. The chambers of the former garrison now house life-size dioramas from Bonifacio's history. ☛ 15 frs. ⊘ June 15–Sept. 15, daily 9–7.

In the center of the maze of cobbled streets that makes up the citadel you'll find the 12th-century church of **Ste-Marie-Majeure,** with buttresses attaching it to surrounding houses. Inside the church, look for the Renaissance baptismal font, carved in bas relief, and a white marble Roman sarcophagus that dates back to the 3rd century. Walk around the back to see the loggia, where town elders once held court and dispensed justice. The loggia is built above a huge cistern that contained water for use in times of siege. Also note circular silos throughout the town that were used to store food and supplies needed to sustain lengthy battles.

If the sheltered, sandy beaches surrounding Bonifacio don't hold your interest, continue northward on N198 toward **Porto-Vecchio,** 27 kilometers (16 miles) away. The walled old town features a network of medieval streets now given over to bistros, boutiques, and cafés, while the Gulf of Porto-Vecchio is lined with more beautiful beaches. Have a look at the exquisite Grand Hotel de Cala Rossa, one of Corsica's great hotels, whether you are staying or not.

Porto-Vecchio backs onto Corsica's largest cork-oak forest, l'Ospédale. An excursion across the forest on D368, climbing 49 kilometers (30 miles) to the mountain pass of Col de Bavella, is one of Corsica's not-to-be-missed itineraries.

TIME OUT   Near the top of the spectacular drive, follow signs for **La Refuge** (Cartalavonu, ☎ 95–70–00–39), 2 kilometers (1½ miles) off D368 to the left, through a lovely wood of cork oak and pine. Although you might have changed into shorts an hour earlier in Porto Vecchio, lunch by a roaring fire will be more than welcome at this little hikers' inn. The cuisine is very Corsican, inexpensive and delicious.

★ ㉘   Continue to Zonza, and turn right on D268 to reach the **Col de Bavella.** To the west, the granite peaks called the "needles of Bavella" tower overhead, higher than 2,000 meters (6,562 feet), as the narrow but mostly well-paved track winds along the Solenzara River back out to the coast. If you stop and look carefully, you will be able to see wild Corsican trout, called *macrostigma* for their unusually large black spots, dining on aquatic insects in the flat stretches of this immaculately clear stream.

㉙   Back on the coast road at Solenzara, the N198 makes fast work of the 32 kilometers (20 miles) to the ruins of the Roman city of **Aléria,** just before the village. On a pine-studded plateau you'll see the carefully restored 16th-century Fort de Matra, which houses the Jérôme-Carcopino museum of pottery and tools found on the site. Its contents—Etruscan, Greek, and Roman artifacts from as far back as 500 BC—reveal Corsica's staggeringly rich history. ☞ *10 frs.* ☉ *Apr.–Oct., daily 8–noon and 2–7; Nov.–Mar., Mon.–Sat. 8–noon and 2–5.*

㉚   From Aléria, N200 will take you to **Corte,** 48 kilometers (30 miles) northwest. Spectacularly sited among cliffs and gorges at the confluence of the Tavignano, Restonica, and Orta rivers, Corte is the spiritual heart and soul of Corsica (if there is one). It was the capital of Pasquale Paoli's government from 1755 to 1769 and where he established the Corsican University in 1765. Closed by the victorious French in 1769, the university, always a symbol of Corsican identity, was reopened in 1981 and now has more than 2,000 students. To reach the upper town, where the 15th-century château perches, looking over the rivers, walk up the cobblestone ramp from place Pasquale-Paoli to the lovely **place Gaffori.** Here there are several cafés and restaurants, and the bullet-pocked house where the Corsican hero Gian Pietro Gaffori and his wife, Faustina, held off the Genoans in 1750. Continue up, passing under a beautiful stone archway, to the Palais National (open weekdays 2–6) and the **Citadelle.** This Vauban-style fortress (1769–1778) is built

around the chateau—the "Eagle's Nest"—the original, 15th-century fortification, at the highest point of the cliff, and it also contains the **Musée
de la Corse,** on the island's history and ethnography. ☎ 95–61–00–
61. ☞ *20 frs adults, 10 frs children.* ☉ *Weekdays 9–6.*

Walk left along the Citadelle wall to the Belvedere for an unforgettable
view of the river junction and the Genoan bridge below, the tiny watchtower of the Citadelle above, and the mountains behind. Now follow
the cobblestones down, bearing right at the St-Théophile chapel through
the Quartier de Chiostra. To the left is a minuscule patio with an excellent pottery shop. Over the door to the left is a small stone carving
said to be a prehistoric goddess of fertility. Don't miss the flying stone
staircase sticking out of the opposite wall; it looks precarious, but the
treads are seated about 31 inches into the stone wall. Continue down
to the ramp back to place Pasquale-Paoli.

From Corte, the Restonica gorges are a superb drive or hike. At the
top of the drivable part, the **Bergeries Ustazzu** serves cheese and bread,
omelets and drinks. The trails up to the lakes cover some fine high country (*see* Sports and the Outdoors, *below*).

After driving the 24 kilometers (15 miles) north from Corte to Ponte
Leccia on N193, take a right turn on D71 through the **Castagniccia,**
a hilly region full of Baroque churches and named for the *chataines*
(chestnuts; in Italian, *castagna*)—a picturesque and moving piece of
Corsica, the most rural and remote part of the island. Here villagers
still wave at passing motorists and the tall houses are still roofed in
the traditional way, with beautiful blue-gray slate. There's an enchanting juxtaposition of art and architecture with unspoiled villages
and valleys where tiny roadways twist through tunnels of centuries-
old chestnut trees, and wild pigs browsing. The chestnuts are especially
picturesque when the leaves turn color in early December. Take D 405
as far as Stoppia Nova, and then D515 to **La Porta,** to see its St-Jean-
Baptiste church, a masterpiece of Corsican Baroque art. Then follow
signs for Folelli or Bastia and you will eventually find your way out
of the Castagniccia—unless you decide to spend a week.

What to See and Do with Children

Corsica's **beaches** provide the best island entertainment for children
(*see* Beaches, *below*). Or take them to the **Acqua Cyrné Gliss** water park
in Porticcio, just south of Ajaccio, which has water slides, swimming
pools, and plenty of organized aquatic games. *20166 Porticcio,* ☎ *95–
25–17–48.* ☞ *67 frs adults, 47 frs children 5–12, 30 frs children under
5.* ☉ *Mid-June–mid-Sept., daily 10:30–7, plus 2 evenings a wk (usually Tues. and Fri.).*

Off the Beaten Track

The GR 20 (Grande Randonnée 20) begins at the lighthouse off Calvi
and follows the watershed line on the crests of the mountains, northwest–southeast to Ste-Lucie de Porto Vecchio. Considered one of the
great hiking trails of Europe, comparable to those in the Tyrol, the
Dolomites or the Pyrenees, this trek requires 70 to 100 hours of walking to complete. Planned in stages from one mountain refuge to another, the well-marked GR 20 is the ultimate way to see Corsica. You
need a certain degree of fitness, equipment, and prior planning. If you
are exploring by car, short probes along the GR 20 are easily feasible.
Check with tourist offices and/or bookstores for guides.

SHOPPING

Artisans use the wood from Corsica's rich chestnut and juniper forests to craft beautifully carved letter openers, pipes, and other objects. **Pierres de Cade** in the Haute Ville of Bonifacio offers an especially good selection.

Island potters produce colorful, modern ceramics that are very popular. The **Poterie d'Olette** in Nebbio, between St-Florent and Oletta, sells a variety of handsome clay designs; and **U Tilaghju,** one of several artisan shops in Ajaccio on rue Forcioli Conti near the cathedral, has an impressive avant-garde ceramics collection. For antique ceramic reproductions try the shops near the entrance to the Roman ruins in **Aléria.**

In the Balagne region, the village of **Pigna** is good hunting grounds for local products. At the **Casa di l'Artigiani** you can buy a wide range, from local jams and honey to hand-knitted sweaters, silk scarves, knives with wood handles, and musical instruments. A branch of the same shop is in Bastia at 5 rue des Terrasses.

Small packages of herbs from the sweet-smelling maquis, chestnut cakes and cookies, local wines, or myrtle liqueur make good presents and are easy to carry home. A fun place to buy them is at the **markets** in Bastia, L'Ile Rousse, or Ajaccio.

SPORTS AND THE OUTDOORS

Beaches

The island's coastline offers astonishing variety: from the long, white stretches of sand along the eastern plain to the steep, rocky creeks of the rugged west coast; from the wild, undeveloped beaches of Cap Corse to the commercial tourist beaches near Calvi and Propriano. The most unusual and attractive beaches back onto the maquis and the forest; when the wind is offshore, the heady scent of juniper and pine is sensational. Even in July and August, when the popular beaches of seaside resorts (Calvi, L'Ile Rousse, St-Florent, Propriano, Porto-Vecchio) are swarming with tourists, you can always find privacy in one of the numerous little creeks on the west coast or north of Porto-Vecchio on the east coast.

Bicycling

Rental shops include **Corsica Loisirs** (3 Montée St-Jean, Ajaccio), **Locacycles** (40 rue César-Campinchi, Bastia), and **Avis** (Hôtel Marina Viva, Porticcio).

Hiking

In addition to the GR 20 (*see* Off the Beaten Track, *above*), hiking is a major outdoor activity all over Corsica. There is a sea-to-sea trek (*Tra mare a mare*) from Propriano to Porto Vecchio and shorter excursions that may last from an hour to a day. Watch for roadside information points with maps and suggested itineraries.

You can take a beautiful and popular day hike in an area called the **Restonica,** outside Corte. Drive up the Restonica gorge and leave your car at the end of the road. A one-hour climb will bring you to Lac de Mélo, surrounded by a circle of craggy granite peaks. Leaflets covering most walking paths are available in local tourist offices. The **Associu di Muntagnoli Corsi** (quartier Pentaniedda, 20122 Quenza, ☎ 95–78–64–05) offers two- and three-day guided hikes through the mountains and lake regions.

Horseback Riding

Corsican equestrian trails are actually former mule paths. There are numerous stables, including **Poney-Club d'Ajaccio** (Campo dell' Oro, ☎ 95–23–03–10), **Centre Equestre de Calvi** (rte. de Pietra-maggiore, ☎ 95–65–22–22), **Ferme Equestre de Baracci** (Propriano, ☎ 95–76–08–02), and **Société Hippique Urbaine de Bastia La Marana** (Bastia, ☎ 95–33–53–08 or 95–30–37–62).

Water Sports

Corsica is ideal for water sports because it offers 16 "Sub-Aqua" clubs for underwater diving, swimming, and fishing. In Ajaccio, try the **Club des Calanques** (Hôtel des Calanques, rte. des Sanguinaires, ☎ 95–21–39–65) or, in Bonifacio, the **Club Atoll** (to contact the manager, M. Ferrari, call 95–73–02–83). If you'd like to get in some sailing, contact the **Tahiti Nautic Club d'Ajaccio** (plage du Ricanto, ☎ 95–20–05–95), or, in Bastia, the **Rugby Club Bastiais** (Cala Biancah, 20290 Borgo, ☎ 95–32–73–86). Canoeing, kayaking, and rafting are popular pastimes on inland mountain rivers; for details, write the **Association Municipale de Ponte-Leccia** (20218 Ponte Leccia).

Winter Sports

Corsica's upper reaches are snowed in from December to April and sometimes earlier and later. **Asco, Col de Vergio, Ghisoni,** and **Bastelica** have lifts and Alpine skiing, while **Evisa, Soccia, Zicavo,** and **Quenza** offer cross-country tracks and equipment. Consult the Club Alpin Français in Ajaccio (☎ 95–22–73–81).

DINING AND LODGING

Dining

Although many things about Corsica may strike you as Italian, the islanders remain thoroughly French in the way they cherish their regional cooking. There are excellent restaurants, many with moderate prices. The most authentic ones are found in country inns or *auberges* nestled in the hills outside the main cities. Attractive harborside cafés offer classic French and nouvelle cuisine. Their best dishes use fresh Mediterranean seafood—lobster, oysters, mussels, and a variety of fish such as sea bream, red mullet, sole, and sardines—many of which go into a rich bouillabaisse called *aziminu*.

Corsica also offers a variety of delicious local cheeses and charcuterie. The best-known cheese is *brocciu* (pronounced *bro*-cho). Similar to ricotta, it serves as a filling in a variety of sweet and savory dishes, such as omelets with mint, cannelloni, and *fritelli* (doughnuts made with chestnut flour). Also try the mild *basteliccacis* and the *bleu de Corse*. Cold meats, including *figatelli* (pork sausages), *lonzu* (pork tenderloin), *copa* (pork shoulder), and *prisuttu* (cured ham), are all made from free-range, chestnut-fed pigs and/or wild boar and smoked with a combination of herbs from the maquis. Traditional stews of wild boar and lamb feature prominently on menus, often accompanied by slices of *pulenta* made from chestnut flour. The addition of *merle* (blackbird) is now outlawed. Fresh mountain trout is also popular in the interior. For those with a sweet tooth, *fiadoni*, a cheesecake made with brocciu, and *canistrelli* (anise cookies) make a good ending to a meal.

Corsica, with no fewer than eight AOC (*Appellations d'Origine Contrôlée*) classifications, produces many fine wines. Worth looking for are an excellent berry-flavored red wine from Ajaccio made with the local sciacarello grapes and warm full-bodied reds produced in Patrimonio. Sartène's Fiumicicoli is one of the smoothest reds, while the Domaine San Quilico from the Gaffory vineyards in Patrimonio is a top rosé. A highly prized muscatel is made on Cap Corse and local liqueurs include a curiously refreshing myrtle-flavored brandy.

CATEGORY	COST*
$$$$	over 400 frs
$$$	250–400 frs
$$	100–250 frs
$	under 100 frs

per person for a three-course meal, including tax (18.6%) and tip but not wine

Lodging

When tourism began in Corsica in the 1960s, the majority of hotels were built in a modern, boxy style. But as a second generation of hoteliers begins to take over the family businesses, more attention is being paid to decor and service. Restored country inns are emerging, and tastefully designed new hotels are being built at the rate of three or four a year. The best seaside hotels keep their prices only marginally less than the Riviera, but hotels in the interior villages remain substantially cheaper. Good prices can be found everywhere on the island during the off season; however, many hotels close from November 1st through Easter. During the peak season (July 1–Sept. 15) prices shoot up and some hotels will insist that you have breakfast and dinner.

CATEGORY	COST*
$$$$	over 750 frs
$$$	400–750 frs
$$	200–400 frs
$	under 200 frs

All prices are for a standard double room for two, including tax (18.6%) and service charge.

Ajaccio

DINING

A La Funtana. A babbling fountain greets diners at the door of this gourmet restaurant, which is named after a popular Corsican folk-song. Fresh flowers and Oriental carpets are the only touch of decoration in the simple white dining room, where the focus is clearly on food. The house specialty is homemade foie gras; other dishes worth sampling include salmon in puff pastry and iced prunes with Armagnac cream. ✕ *7 rue Notre-Dame,* ☎ *95–21–78–04. Reservations advised. AE, DC, MC, V. Closed May. $$$*

★ **Auberge de Prunelli.** This authentic Corsican inn about 11 kilometers (7 miles) south of Ajaccio has a leafy terrace overlooking the Prunelli River. There is a set five-course menu at a reasonable 155 francs, which allows you to sample the best the island has to offer—much of it produced on the owner's farm. You'll dine on brocciu omelet, trout, roast lamb, and figatelli sausage. The atmosphere is friendly and cheerful, especially in off-season, when there is often a fire blazing in the hearth. ✕ *Pisciatello,* ☎ *95–20–02–75. Reservations required. MC, V. Closed Tues. and Oct.–Nov. $$*

★ **Restaurant de France.** Locals come here, a few blocks from the touristy Old Quarter, for a tasty and inexpensive meal. The old-fashioned dining room, with starched white linens, serves up three-course menus featuring such fare as smoked salmon, steak with Roquefort sauce, and walnut torte, all for very good prices. Also available are Corsican specialties like wild boar stew and chestnut ice cream. ✕ *59 rue Fesch,* ☎ *95–21–11–00. AE, DC, MC, V.* ☉ *All year. Closed Sun. $*

DINING AND LODGING

Eden Roc. Eden Roc, built in the modern style of the '60s, overlooks the gulf and the Iles Sanguinaires from a superb location 8 kilometers (5 miles) from the center of town in Ajaccio's most exclusive suburb. Manicured gardens surround the swimming pool, a tiny beach lies across the road, and the ground floor has a health club with hot seawater whirlpool baths. Rooms are large and clean, and each comes with a terrace and sea view. The hotel's gourmet restaurant and bar attract the capital's country club set. Try the lobster ravioli or dishes with local touches like the Corsican smoked ham or fish stuffed with brocciu. ▥ *Rte. des Iles Sanguinaires, km 8, 20000,* ☎ *95–52–01–47,* FAX *95– 52–05–03. 45 rooms with bath. Restaurant, piano bar, pool, health club. AE, DC, MC, V. $$$–$$$$*

La Dolce Vita. Spread out on flower-filled terraces at the edge of the gulf of Ajaccio, La Dolce Vita has a lavish Italianate decor and a spectacular swimming pool overlooking the sea. Its restaurant ranks as one of the island's best for gourmet interpretations of traditional Corsican dishes. ▥ *Rte. des Iles Sanguinaires, km 8, 20000,* ☎ *95–52–00–93,* FAX *95–52–07–15. 32 rooms with bath. Restaurant, bar, pool. AE, DC, MC, V. Closed Nov.–Easter. $$$–$$$$*

LODGING

Stella di Mare. A low-slung, motel-style hotel, the Stella di Mare is relaxed, friendly, and unpretentious—fine for families and for those who want to spend most of their time outdoors on the white sand beach. Frequent buses will take you into the center of town about 10 minutes away. ▥ *Rte. des Iles Sanguinaires, km 7, 20000,* ☎ *95–52–01–07,* FAX *95–52–08–69. 60 rooms with bath. Restaurant, bar, pool. AE, DC, MC, V. Closed Nov.–Easter. $$*

Hotel San Carlu. This renovated building overlooking the Ajaccio citadel has wonderful views out to sea. On the edge of the old town, this is a good spot for exploring Ajaccio. The reception here is very friendly, and there is a sense of being where the action is. The rooms are clean and comfortable. ▥ *Blvd. Danielle-Casanova 8,* ☎ *95–21– 13–84,* FAX *95–21–09–99. 40 rooms with bath. AE, DC, MC, V. $$*

Algajola

DINING AND LODGING

L'Ondine. Nestled into the rocks at the edge of a sandy cove, L'Ondine is a village of single-story, beige stucco buildings pleasantly landscaped with trees and flowering shrubs. The dining room commands a million-dollar view of the beach and the 16th-century citadel town of Algajola, a low-key and friendly resort. ▥ *7 rue à Marina, 20220,* ☎ *95–60–70–02,* FAX *95–60–60–36. 55 rooms with bath. Restaurant, bar, pool. MC, V. Closed Oct. 30–Mar. 31. $$*

Bastia

DINING

★ **Lavezzi.** Diners will enjoy a view over Bastia's old port as they make their choice of a host of fish and seafood specials. The cuisine is traditional Corsican; try the mussel and oyster quiche or duck breast in honey and olives. Wall-to-wall carpeting and white, rough-cast plaster walls enhance Lavezzi's charm. ✕ *8 rue St-Jean,* ☎ *95–31–05– 73. Reservations required. AE, DC, MC, V. Closed Sun. and Feb.–Mar. $$$*

La Voûte. Kids come here for the pizza cooked in a wood-fired oven, while their parents dip into excellent fish and steaks, making La Voûte one of Bastia's most popular restaurants. Vaulted brick ceilings, exposed stone, and indirect lighting add an authentic Corsican atmosphere. The smoked salmon and rockfish soup are both superb. ✕ *6 bis rue Luce de Casabianca,* ☎ *95–32–47–11. AE, MC, V. Reservations advised. Closed Sun. lunch. $$*

LODGING

Pietracap. Perched on a hillside about five minutes north of Bastia, Pietracap is a strikingly modern hotel nestled into a fragrant garden filled with flowering shrubs and olive trees. Rooms are large with stark, white modern furnishings and balconies looking onto the garden and out to the Mediterranean. The lobby and hallways are decorated with bold canvases painted by the friendly owner's brother. ☎ *20 Rte. de San Martino, 20200 Pietranera-Bastia,* ☎ *95–31–64–63,* FAX *95–31–39–00. 42 rooms with bath. Bar, pool, bicycles. AE, DC, MC, V. Closed Dec. 15–Mar. 1. $$$*

★ **Castel Brando.** One of Bastia's most congenial hotels is about 15 minutes north of the city in a restored villa in the picturesque coastal village of Erbalunga. Owners Joëlle and Jean Paul Pieri have refurbished the 19th-century mansion with extreme good taste, using a cool buff color, dark green shutters, and terra-cotta tile. The large guest rooms are furnished with country-style antiques, dried flowers, and decorative tile in the baths, and each comes equipped with a kitchenette. The hotel's garden has a large swimming pool and a terrace where guests enjoy the breakfast included in the room rate. ☎ *B.P. 20 Erbalunga 20222,* ☎ *95–30–10–30,* FAX *95–33–98–18. 16 rooms with bath. Pool, tennis. AE, MC, V. Closed late Oct.–Apr. $$–$$$*

Posta Vecchia. An old building overlooking the port was renovated and transformed into the Posta Vecchia hotel in 1978. The unpretentious guest rooms are decorated with floral wallpaper and print bedspreads, while the wood-beam ceilings add a rustic touch. Some rooms are small; the best are in the main house, facing the port. The hotel's best feature is its location. ☎ *Quai des Martyrs, 20200,* ☎ *95–32–32–38. 49 rooms with bath. AE, DC, MC, V. $$*

Bonifacio

DINING

★ **U Ceppu.** This rustic, barn-size restaurant, about 5 kilometers (3 miles) east of Bonifacio on the road to Santa Manza beach, features grilled meats and seafood prepared in the dining room on a big open hearth. Picture windows look out on lobster pots bobbing in the bay and sprinkled on the beach. Besides local seafood, the house specialties include homemade smoked salmon, raviolis stuffed with brocciu, and wild boar stew. ✕ *L'Auberge de Santa Manza,* ☎ *95–73–02–34. Reservations advised in summer. AE, MC, V. Closed for lunch except Sun. $$*

★ **Les 4 Vents.** An informal, family-style eatery with kids and dogs running underfoot and bright flowers tumbling from a wooden balcony in the dining room, this friendly restaurant is popular with the yachting crowd. In winter, the kitchen serves up the specialties of Alsace like sauerkraut and sausages, but it concentrates on barbecued fish and meats in summer. Typical Corsican dishes change daily, but they are always cheap, delicious, and filling. ✕ *29 quai Bando di Ferro,* ☎ *95–73–07–50. Reservations advised weekends. No credit cards. Closed Tues. $–$$*

Restaurant du Pêcheur. This tiny place has only six tables, and people often line the sidewalk for a chance to dine at the most authentic seafood spot in town. True to its name, the restaurant is run by fishermen who serve the catch of the day straight from the sea. There's no written menu, but you can ask to see what's available. ✕ *14 rue Doria,* ☎ *95–73–12–56. No reservations. MC, V. Closed Nov.–Easter.* $

LODGING

Le Genovese. Built right into the ramparts of the upper town's citadel, the Genovese is a small, personal hotel with a friendly staff and lots of luxurious details. The rooms are like the inside of a jewel box with peach fabric wall coverings, and the handrails in the stairway are made from an exquisite multicolored braided rope. But the best thing about this hotel is the superb view from the upstairs rooms overlooking the fortress and the harbor. ☎ *Quartier de Citadelle, Haute Ville 20169,* ☎ *95–73–12–34,* FAX *95–73–09–03. 14 rooms with bath. Bar. AE, DC, MC, V.* $$$–$$$$

Calvi

DINING

★ **Chez Tao.** At Chez Tao, a mandatory stop on almost everyone's itinerary, you can rub elbows with French film stars and the rest of the town's glitterati. You dine in ocher-color 16th-century vaults that look out over the bay through arched picture windows. Seafood is what everyone eats here, but food and wine play second fiddle to the atmosphere, which includes Corsican folksinging and dancing until the wee hours. ✕ *Place de la Citadelle,* ☎ *95–65–00–73. Reservations advised. AE, MC, V. Closed mid-Sept.–Easter.* $$$

L'Ile de Beauté. One of Calvi's most celebrated restaurants, L'Ile de Beauté has been pulling in the crowds since 1929, but recently it changed hands and the verdict is still out. It's on the quayside, right next to the port. Metal suns adorn the walls of the dining room, while the terrace catches Calvi's festive atmosphere. The menu features a range of fish specials, including lobster fricassee; meat eaters should try the wild boar stew. ✕ *Quai Landry,* ☎ *95–65–00–46. Reservations advised. AE, DC, MC, V. Closed Wed. lunch and Oct.–Apr.* $$$

U San Carlu. Good, classic Corsican and French cooking at reasonable prices makes U San Carlu a favorite with tourists and locals alike. The restaurant, with its brick-vaulted dining room, is in a restored 16th-century building that once housed the town hospital. In summer, you can eat outdoors on a palm-shaded patio. Specialties include steak in Roquefort and prawns flamed in brandy; the warm goat cheese salad is great, and the daily menu is an excellent value. ✕ *10 place St-Charles,* ☎ *95–65–21–93. Reservations advised weekends. AE, DC, MC, V. Closed Tues. evening and Wed. in winter.* $–$$

DINING AND LODGING

La Villa. Opened in 1992 on a hill with marvelous views of the town and the citadel, this hotel has the atmosphere of a modern Italian villa. The architecture leans heavily toward arched loggias, wrought iron, and bubbling fountains, and original paintings and abstract sculpture abound. The rooms are large and floored in terra-cotta; they have walkin closets, glass and copper tables, dressing areas, and balconies. A canopied dining area overlooks the pool, surrounded by a fragrant garden of herbs and flowers. ☎ *Chemin de Notre Dame de la Serra 20260,* ☎ *95–65–10–10,* FAX *95–65–10–50. 25 rooms with bath. Restaurant, bar, pool, Turkish bath, hairdresser. AE, DC, MC, V. Closed Jan.–Mar.* $$$$

★ **Le Signoria.** This 17th-century country inn occupies a park of pine, eucalyptus, and olive trees about 5 kilometers (3 miles) outside Calvi. The manor house and annex have been fitted with homey bedrooms and large baths. The swimming pool area and patio, used for dining, offer panoramic views of the mountains and the bay. Its renowned restaurant serves a regional cuisine, creating imaginative dishes with local products fresh from the market. ☎ *Rte. de la Forêt de Bonifato 20260,* ☎ *95–65–23–73,* FAX *95–65–33–20. 10 rooms with bath. Restaurant, bar, pool, Turkish bath. AE, MC, V. Closed Nov.–Easter and for lunch, except weekends in July and Aug. $$$*

LODGING

La Balanea. This friendly place overlooking the port is filled with good cheer, good taste, and interestingly designed furniture shaped like whales and dolphins. The rooms are as impeccable as the location, across the street from Calvi's best-value restaurant, U San Carlu, and literally on top of all the movement, day and night, along the quai Landry. ☎ *Port de Plaisance, Rue Clemenceau, 20260 Calvi,* ☎ *95–65–00–45,* FAX *95–65–29–71. 38 rooms with bath. AE, DC, MC, V. $$*

Centuri

DINING AND LODGING

★ **Le Vieux Moulin.** If you're after Old World charm and an authentic Corsican flavor, Le Vieux Moulin is the place to try. The main house was built in 1870 as a private residence; the eight-room annex is more recent but no less inviting, with bougainvillea cascading from its balconies. The friendly staff will arrange boat rides and fishing trips around the coast of the wildly dramatic Cap Corse peninsula, and there's a tennis court and small golf course nearby. The restaurant specializes in seafood: Try the bouillabaisse. ☎ *Centuri Port, 20238,* ☎ *95–35–60–15,* FAX *95–35–60–24. 14 rooms with bath. Restaurant. AE, DC, MC, V. Closed Nov.–Mar. $$*

Corte

DINING AND LODGING

★ **Auberge de la Restonica–Hotel Dominique Colonna.** This fine auberge and restaurant, known for its cuisine, has created a sister ship across the parking lot. The 7 rooms in the original building, rather like a hunting lodge, are now joined by 28 modern double rooms in the functional but pleasant new hotel. The Normandy-born chef, David Verger, has a light nouvelle touch with the powerful Corsican ingredients, and owner Dominique "Dumé" Colonna, one of France's all-time-great soccer stars, is a gracious host. The Restonica torrent rushing by like a steady downpour soothes you to sleep at night. Ask for one of the more rustic rooms in the auberge. ☎ *Vallée de la Restonica, 20250,* ☎ *(auberge) 95–46–20–13; (hotel) 95–61–05–45,* FAX *95–61–03–91; (restaurant) 95–46–09–58. 35 rooms with bath. AE, DC, MC, V. $$*

L'Ile Rousse

DINING AND LODGING

A Pasturella. If you want to escape the beach crowds, try this picturesque hotel in the center of Monticello, a small village 5 kilometers (3 miles) uphill from L'Ile Rousse. The simple rooms, most of which overlook the surrounding mountains, have modern furnishings and geranium-filled window boxes. But A Pasturella is better known for its restaurant. The wood-beam dining room specializes in seafood, such as giant prawns and lotte with green peppercorns, as well as mouthwatering Corsican dishes like crepes with brocciu. A reasonably priced five-course menu makes quite a nice meal. This is one of the only hotels on the island that don't raise their rates during July and August. ☎ *20220 Monticello,* ☎ *95–60–05–65,* FAX *95–60–21–78. 14 rooms with bath. Restaurant, bar. AE, MC, V. Closed mid-Nov.–mid-Dec. $$*

Piana

DINING AND LODGING

Capo Rosso. The four-star Capo Rosso sits high in the hills overlooking the Golfe de Porto, just yards from the famous rocky outcropping. The views—whether seen from your room, the outdoor pool, or the restaurant's terrace—are stunningly dramatic. Unfortunately, the modern guest rooms are functional rather than charming. ☎ *20115 Piana,* ☎ *95–27–82–40,* FAX *95–27–80–00. 70 rooms with bath. Restaurant. AE, DC, MC, V. Closed mid-Oct.–Easter. $$–$$$*

Les Roches Rouges. On the hillside just below the Capo Rosso, this rambling old mansion caters to an essentially British clientele. Don't be misled by the crumbling facade; the current owners took over only a few years ago and are still renovating. Most guest rooms are sparse and monastic, but the irrepressible owner, Mady; the eccentric British atmosphere; and the hotel's stunning location make Les Roches Rouges a winner. The vast Imperial-style restaurant is classified as a historic monument; go for the fish soup or the grilled lobster. ☎ *Rte. de Porto, 20115 Piana,* ☎ *95–27–81–81. 20 rooms with bath. Restaurant. AE, DC, MC, V. Closed Nov.–Mar. $$*

Pigna

DINING AND LODGING

Casa Musicale. Don't miss this unique spot. It has traditional local cuisine, music of all kinds—authentic Corsican polyphonic singing more often than not—and a lovely view over the Balagne down to Calvi. The rooms are simple but elegant, with whitewashed walls and rustic furniture. ☎ *20220 Pigna,* ☎ *95–61–77–31,* FAX *95–61–77–81. 7 rooms that sleep 2, 3, or 4. MC, V. $*

Porticcio

DINING AND LODGING

★ **Le Maquis.** The evocatively named Maquis ranks as one of the island's finest *hôtels de charme*. The quaint, ivy-covered building reaches down to a private beach backed by fragrant herbs. Sea-level rooms open directly onto arch-covered patios. West-facing rooms and terraces capture the stunning sunsets over the hills beyond Ajaccio. The candlelit restaurant features hand-hewn beams and white plaster walls, decorated with an ornate gilt mirror; tile floors and wicker chairs add to the rustic elegance. The food is a blend of traditional and nouvelle: Fish tartare, scrambled eggs with truffles, *coquilles St-Jacques,* and fresh *tagliatelles* all make fine choices. ☎ *CD55, 20166 Porticcio,* ☎ *95–25–05–55,* FAX *95–25–11–70. 27 rooms with bath. Restaurant, outdoor and indoor pools, tennis, private beach, solarium. AE, DC, MC, V. $$$–$$$$*

Porto

DINING AND LODGING

Chez Felix. Perched in the hillside village of Ota, 5 kilometers (3 miles) from Porto, this homey place serves as dining room, taxi stand, and town meeting hall. The cheerful owner, Marinette Ceccaldi, cooks up heaping portions of Corsican specialties like wild boar, cannelloni stuffed with chard and brocciu, and fritters made with chestnut flour and zucchini. She also rents out rustic guest rooms, which attract a backpacking crowd and are decorated with junk-store finds and country antiques. Each has a balcony overlooking the Ota gorge. ☎ *Place de la Fontaine,* ☎ *95–26–12–92. 6 rooms that sleep 2–8 people, with kitchenette and bath. Restaurant, bar. No credit cards. $*

Porto-Vecchio

DINING AND LODGING

★ **Grand Hôtel de Cala Rossa.** This mansion-hotel is one of the island's finest, showcasing modern design at its best. Nothing jars, from the curves of the heavy white walls to the choice of contemporary paintings lining the corridors. The rooms vary greatly in price, but are all luxurious. An early morning breakfast outside under the trees, just yards from the beach, will make you forget your sightseeing plans. Corsican-style nouvelle dishes are featured in the restaurant; you can't go wrong with the roast kid or the fresh-mint omelet. ☎ *8 km (5 mi) north of town, Cala Rossa, 20137,* ☎ *95–71–61–51,* FAX *95–71–60–11. 50 rooms with bath. Restaurant, tennis. AE, DC, MC, V. Closed Nov.–Apr. $$–$$$$*

Moby Dick. The scheme here is sophisticated simplicity: white stucco walls, white marble lamps, and blue comb-painted doors. The modern hotel 8 kilometers (5 miles) south of Porto-Vecchio is virtually surrounded by water and sandy beaches, and the guest rooms offer views of the sea and mountains. The restaurant serves a good-value buffet lunch and both a "normal" and *gastronomique* (gargantuan) menu at dinner. The crayfish is delicious. ☎ *Baie de Santa Giulia, 20137 Porto-Vecchio,* ☎ *95–70–43–23,* FAX *95–70–01–54. 44 rooms with bath. Restaurant. AE, DC, MC, V. Closed Nov.–Apr. $$–$$$*

THE ARTS AND NIGHTLIFE

The Arts

Music and Festivals

Singing plays an important role in both traditional and daily island life. You'll doubtless come across impromptu café gatherings where the amateurs sing haunting polyphonies, giving impressive renderings of a traditional *paghiella* (a three-voice harmony), a *voceru* (funeral chant), or a *chjiama e rispondi* duel (in which two singers rival each other in a lyrical ping-pong match, throwing questions and answers in an attempt to outdo one another by the wit, beauty, or rhyme of their invention).

The island has two major **carnivals**—one in Bastia in April and the other in Ajaccio in May—when the towns come alive with song, costumed processions, and outdoor theater. Both towns feature similar festivities throughout the summer, reaching a climax on August 15, when Ajaccio celebrates Napoleon's birthday. Other island festivals include an **Italian Film Festival** in Bastia in February; a **Jazz Festival** in Calvi in June; a classical **International Music Meeting** in Ajaccio in July; Calvi's late-October **Festiventu,** a festival of wind-powered sports; and an **International Music Festival** in Bastia in early December, when the music varies from classical to jazz. **The Casa Musicale** in Pigna organizes **Festivoce** during the first half of July.

Nightlife

Traditional Music

For traditional Corsican singing try **Le Pavillon Bleu** (54 cours Grandval) in Ajaccio or **U-Fanale** (Le Vieux Port) in Bastia. The lively patio of the **Pub Chez Assunta** (pl. Fontaine Nueve 4) in Bastia is also filled on most summer nights with folksingers and street musicians.

Popular Music

In Ajaccio, **Le 3615** (Port de Plaisance, L'Amirauté) and **Le Brazil Cafe** (28 cours Grandval) have easy-listening piano bars. **Ricanto** (plage Ricanto) has a transvestite revue. For dancing try **Le Weekend Discothèque** (Rte. de Iles Sanguinaires) or **Le Krypton** (Porticcio). In Bastia, **L'Alba** (22 quai des Martyrs) is a piano bar for the middle-age crowd, while the younger set gathers for loud rock and roll at **Mayflower** (Port de Plaisance). In Bonifacio **Le Fa Dièse** (10 rue Portone) rages until dawn. In Calvi, the in spot to be is **Chez Tao** (pl. de la Citadelle; *see* Dining and Lodging, *above*).

CORSICA ESSENTIALS

Arriving and Departing

By Plane
Corsica has four major airports: **Ajaccio, Bastia, Calvi, and Figari. Air Inter** (☎ 45–46–90–00 Paris, 95–29–45–45 Ajaccio) offers daily service connecting Paris and Lyon with Ajaccio, Bastia, and Calvi. **Delta Airlines** connects with Air Inter for flights to Corsica May–October. In addition, **TAT** (Transport Aérian Transrégional, ☎ 42–79–05–05 Paris, 95–71–01–20 Figari) flies to Figari from Paris. **Compagnie Corse Méditérranée** (☎ 95–29–45–45 Ajaccio) connects Ajaccio and Bastia to Nice and Marseille, with several flights a day.

Between the Airports and Downtown
The airports at Ajaccio and Bastia run regular *navette* (shuttle) bus services to and from town. At Figari, a bus meets all incoming flights and will take passengers as far as Bonifacio and Porto-Vecchio for a small fee. If you arrive at Calvi, take a taxi into the town center.

By Ferry
SNCM (Société Nationale Maritime Corse-Méditérranée, ☎ 91–56–80–20 Marseille, 95–29–66–66 Ajaccio) and **CMN** (Compagnie Méridionale de Navigation, ☎ 95–21–20–34 Ajaccio) run regular car-ferries from Marseille, Nice, and Toulon to Ajaccio, Bastia, Calvi, L'Ile-Rousse, and Propriano. These spectacular and romantic crossings take from 5 to 10 hours, with sleeping cabins available. SNCM also offers package tours that include the crossing with a car, onboard cabin, and hotel accommodations in Corsica.

Getting Around

By Plane
Air Balagne (☎ 95–65–02–97), **ATM** (Air Transport Méditérranée, ☎ 95–76–04–99), and **Kyrnair** (☎ 95–20–52–29) offer inter-island flights throughout the year.

By Car
Though driving is undoubtedly the best way to explore the island's scenic stretches, note that winding, mountainous roads and uneven surfaces can actually double or triple your expected travel time.

By Train
The main line of Corsica's simple rail network runs from Ajaccio, in the west, to Corte, in the central valley, then divides at Ponte Leccia. From here, one line continues to L'Ile-Rousse and Calvi in the north and the other to Bastia in the northeast. Another daily service runs four times daily between Ajaccio and Bastia, the island's two largest cities. During the summer months, a small two-car train connects Calvi and L'Ile-Rousse, stopping at numerous beaches and resorts (for information, call 95–23–11–03 Ajaccio, 95–32–60–06 Bastia, 95–65–00–61 Calvi, or 15–46–00–87 Corte).

By Bus

The local bus network is geared to residents, who use it in the morning and evening to get to and from school and work. At least two buses a day connect all the southern towns with Ajaccio, while northern towns are connected by bus to Bastia.

Guided Tours

Orientation

Ollandini (1 rue d'Alata, Ajaccio, ☎ 95–21–10–12) is one of Corsica's largest bus-tour companies. Typical half-day bus excursions from Ajaccio visit the prehistoric site at Filitosa, taking in Porticcio and some of the scenic viewpoints in the hills around the gulf. The most attractive whole-day excursion includes a trek along the breathtaking Scala di Santa Regina, Calacuccia, the forest of Valdo-Niello, with a lunch break at the Col de Verghio.

Boat

Much of Corsica's most spectacular scenery is best viewed from the water. Boats leave Ajaccio daily (at 9 and 2), from the Bar du Golfe, below place Foch, for the three-hour trip to the Iles Sanguinaires ("Bloody Islands"—named for the red hue of the rocks in the setting sun), which lie just off the coast. Contact **Promenades en Mer** (Port de l'Amirauté 20000 Ajaccio, ☎ 95–23–23–38). From Bonifacio, you can visit the Dragon Grottoes and Venus's Bath (boats that make one-hour trips set out every 15 minutes during July and August) and the Lavezzi Islands (boats leave from outside the Hôtel La Caravelle, ☎ 95–75–05–93). Italian ferries ply between Bastia and Genoa or Livorno: **Corsica Ferries** (5 blvd. Channoine-Leschi, 20200 Bastia, ☎ 95–31–18–09) or **Corsica Maritima** (6 rue Luce-de-Casablanca, 20200 Bastia, ☎ 95–32–69–04). You can also reach Sardinia by ferry from Bastia or Bonifacio on **Navarma Lines** (4 rue Luce-de-Casablanca, 20200 Bastia, ☎ 95–31–46–29 or at the port in Bonifacio, ☎ 95–73–00–29) or **Saremar** (Gare Maritime, 20169 Bonifacio, ☎ 95–73–06–75). Whole-day tours in glass-bottom boats leave from Calvi and visit Girolata, the Scandola nature reserve, and the Golfe de Porto. Boats depart at 9 AM, mid-May through September, and return at about 4:30 (contact **Colombo Line,** Quai Landry, ☎ 95–65–32–10).

Aerial

Kyrnair (☎ 95–20–52–29) and **ATM. (Air Transport Méditérranée,** ☎ 95–76–04–99) offer sightseeing tours.

Important Addresses and Numbers

Travel Agencies

Corse Itineraries (32 cours Napoléon, Ajaccio, ☎ 95–51–01–10), **Kallistour** (6 av. Maréchal-Sebastiani, Bastia, ☎ 95–31–71–49), and **Les Beaux Voyages** (pl. de la Porteuse-d'Eau, Calvi, ☎ 95–65–11–35).

Car Rental

Hertz (Ajaccio airport, ☎ 95–22–14–84; 8 cours Grandval, Ajaccio, ☎ 95–21–70–94; Square St-Victor, Bastia, ☎ 95–31–14–24; quai du Commerce, Bonifacio, ☎ 95–73–02–47; 2 rue Maréchal Joffre, Calvi, ☎ 95–65–06–64) serves the entire island with 18 offices at all the airports, harbors, and major towns. Be sure to reserve at least two weeks in advance during July and August. **Avis Ollandini** (Ajaccio airport, ☎ 95–23–25–14) and **Europcar** (1 rue du Nouveau Port, Bastia, ☎ 95–31–59–29).

Visitor Information

The **Agence du Tourisme de la Corse** (17 Blvd. Roi-Jérome, Ajaccio, ☎ 95–21–56–56, FAX 95–51–14–40) can provide information about all areas of the island. Local tourist offices are: **Ajaccio** (Hôtel de Ville, pl. Foch, ☎ 95–21–53–39), **Bastia** (pl. St-Nicholas, ☎ 95–31–00–89), **Bonifacio** (rue des Deux Moulins, ☎ 95–73–11–88), **Calvi** (Port de Plaisance, ☎ 95–65–16–67), **Corte** (La Citadelle, ☎ 95–46–24–20), and **Sartène** (rue Borgo, ☎ 95–77–15–40).

15 Toulouse, the Midi-Pyrénées, and Roussillon

MIDI-PYRÉNÉES is France's largest region, spreading over 28,500 square miles from the Dordogne in the north to the Spanish border in the south. Mountains, plains, lakes, rivers, verdant hills, and arid limestone plateaus lend the region extreme natural variety. This is the perfect vacation spot for nature lovers and sports enthusiasts; walking, hiking, climbing, horseback riding, sailing, canoeing, skiing, windsurfing, and rafting are all possible.

The Pyrénées, Western Europe's highest mountain range after the Alps, give birth to the Garonne, the great river of Toulouse and Bordeaux. The Garonne is joined by the Aveyron and Tarn rivers, which cross the region from east to west, carving out steep gorges and wide green valleys. The Pyrenean foothills are riddled with streams, lakes, and spas established in Roman times.

The region has few large towns. Chief among them is Toulouse, an upbeat university center whose energetic nightlife smacks more of Spain (less than two hours' drive away) than of the drowsy French provinces. Toulouse, known as the Ville Rose because of its soft pink brick, is an elegant old city. The Canal du Midi, built in the 17th century, passes through Toulouse and continues east, near the medieval walls of Carcassonne, on its way from the Atlantic to the Mediterranean.

Other highlights range from the picturesque hilltop village of Cordes to the religious mecca of Lourdes (though its football-stadium-like appearance may come as a bit of a disappointment). There are two outstanding art museums: the Musée Ingres at Montauban, devoted to one of France's most accomplished pre-Impressionist painters, and the Musée Toulouse-Lautrec at Albi, with its racy testimony to the acuity of the leading observer of Belle Epoque cabaret. Albi also holds the most impressive monument in the Midi-Pyrénées: the redbrick cathedral of Ste-Cécile, with slits for windows and walls like cliffs.

The attractive Mediterranean coast between Narbonne and the Spanish border can easily be reached from Toulouse and is covered on our tour of the Roussillon region. Perpignan, its capital, has a bustling, Spanish feel: Roussillon has strong linguistic and historic ties with Catalonia, across the Pyrénées, and was ceded by Spain to France as recently as 1659. The streets of even the smallest towns are awash with the proud Catalan colors of *sang et or* (blood and gold), on buildings and on banners.

EXPLORING

Orientation

We have divided this region into four tours. The first explores Toulouse, a lively center imbued with culture and history. Tour 2 heads north and west, taking in Albi, Montauban, and verdant Gascony, known more prosaically these days as the Gers *département,* home of Armagnac brandy. The third tour plunges south to the Pyrénées, taking in snowcapped peaks, mountain passes, thermal spas, and the holy site at Lourdes. The fourth heads east to Roussillon and the Mediterranean, starting with Carcassonne and looping back toward the Pyrénées.

Tour 1: Toulouse

❶ The ebullient, pink-brick city of **Toulouse** lies just 96 kilometers (60-odd miles) from the border with Spain, and its flavor is more Spanish than French. The city's downtown sidewalks and restaurants pulse well past midnight as foreign tourists mingle with immigrant workers, college students, and technicians from the giant Airbus aviation complex headquartered outside the city. Toulouse is the most vibrant city in France's southwest. Traffic, though, is horrendous. Consider parking your car in the huge garage beneath place du Capitole; you can easily walk to the major sights. You can also use the new subway system that runs east–west; it costs 7 francs for one zone, and most of central Toulouse is within a zone.

Numbers in the margin correspond to points of interest on the Toulouse map.

Place du Capitole, a vast, open square lined with shops and cafés in the city center, is the best spot for getting your bearings. One side of
❷ the square is occupied by the 18th-century facade of the **Capitole** itself, home of the Hôtel de Ville (Town Hall) and the city's highly regarded opera company. The coats of arms of the Capitouls, the former rulers of Toulouse, can be seen on the balconies in the Capitole's courtyard, and the building's vast reception rooms are open to visitors when not in use for official functions. Halfway up the Grand Escalier (Grand Staircase) hangs a large painting of the *Jeux Floraux* (Floral Games), organized by the Compagnie du Gai-Savoir—a literary society created in 1324 to promote the local language, Langue d'Oc. The festival continues to this day: Poets give public readings here each May, the best receiving silver- and gold-plated flowers as prizes. The pompous Salle des Illustres, with its late-19th-century paintings, is used for official receptions and uppercrust wedding ceremonies. Weddings are also held in the Salle Gervaise, beneath a series of paintings inspired by the theme of Love at ages 20, 40, and 60; while the men age, the women stay young forever.

Four more giant paintings in the Salle Henri-Martin, named for the artist (1860–1943), show how important the River Garonne has always been to the region. Look out for Jean Jaurès, one of France's greatest Socialists (1859–1914), in *Les Rêveurs* (The Dreamers); he's the one who's wearing a boater and a beige-colored coat. *Pl. du Capitole,* ☎ *61–22–29–22 (ext. 3412) to check opening times.* ☞ *Free. Closed Tues. and weekends.*

Head north from place du Capitole along rue du Taur, lined with tiny
❸ shops. Half a block up, the 14th-century church of **Notre-Dame du Taur** was built on the spot where St-Saturnin (or Sernin), the martyred bishop of Toulouse, was dragged to his death in AD 257 by a rampaging bull. The church is famous for its *cloche-mur,* or wall tower; the wall looks more like an extension of the facade than a tower or steeple and has inspired many similar versions throughout the Toulouse region.

★ ❹ The basilica of **St-Sernin,** Toulouse's most famous landmark, lies at the far end of rue du Taur. The basilica once belonged to a Benedictine abbey, built in the 11th century to house pilgrims on their way to Santiago de Compostela in Spain. When illuminated at night, St-Sernin's five-tiered octagonal tower glows red against the sky, dominating the city. Not all the tiers are the same: The first three, with their rounded windows, are Romanesque; the upper two, with their pointed Gothic win-

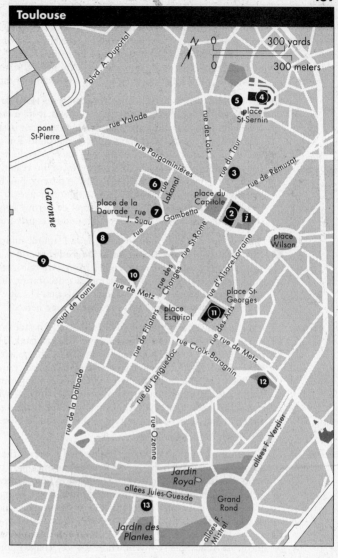

Toulouse

dows, were added around 1300. *Rue du Taur,* ☎ *61–21–70–18.* ✒
Crypt: 10 frs. ⊘ *Daily 10–11:30 and 2:30–5:30.*

❺ Opposite the basilica is the **Musée St-Raymond,** the city's archaeological museum. The ground floor has an extensive collection of imperial Roman busts, while the second floor is devoted to the applied arts, featuring ancient and medieval coins, lamps, vases, and jewelry. *Pl. St-Sernin,* ☎ *61–22–21–85.* ✒ *10 frs adults, 5 frs children.* ⊘ *Wed.–Mon. 8–noon and 2–6 (closed Sun. morning).*

❻ Retrace your steps down rue du Taur, turn right at place du Capitole and then left into rue Lakanal to arrive at the **Jacobins church,** built in the 1230s for the Dominicans; the name Jacobins was given to the Dominicans in 1217 when they set up their Paris base at the Porte St-Jacques. The church was harmoniously restored during the 1970s, its interior retaining the original orange-ocher tones. The two rows of columns running the length of the nave—to separate the monks from their congregation—is a feature of Dominican churches, though this one is special, since the column standing the farthest from the entrance is said to be the world's finest example of palm-tree vaulting. The original refectory is used for temporary art exhibitions, while the cloisters provide an atmospheric setting for the city's summer music festival.

⑦ Around the corner, on rue Gambetta, stands the **Hôtel de Bernuy,** built during the 16th century, when Toulouse was at its most prosperous. Merchant Jean de Bernuy made his fortune exporting pastel, a blue dye made from the leaves of a plant cultivated around Toulouse and Albi and used to color cloth, especially bed linen. Merchant wealth is reflected in the use of stone, a costly material in this region of brick, and by the octagonal stair tower, the highest in the city. Building such towers was a rarely bestowed privilege, and this one makes its opulent point by rising above the top floor. The Hôtel de Bernuy is now part of a school, but you may wander freely around its courtyard.

⑧ Walk down rue Jean-Suau to place de la Daurade and the 18th-century church of **Notre-Dame de la Daurade,** overlooking the River Garonne. The name Daurade comes from *doré* (gilt), referring to the golden reflection given off by the mosaics decorating the 5th-century temple to the Virgin that once stood on this site. The flowers presented to the winners of the Floral Games are blessed here.

⑨ Take time to saunter along quai de la Daurade, beside the church, and **⑩** admire the view from **Pont Neuf** across to the left bank. Then head east along rue de Metz. A hundred yards down, on the left, is the **Hôtel d'Assézat,** built in 1555 by Toulouse's top Renaissance architect, Nicolas Bachelier. The facade is particularly striking: Superimposed classical orders frame alternating arcades and rectangular windows, with ornately carved doorways lurking below. Climb to the top of the tower for splendid views over the city's rooftops. *Rue de Metz.* ☛ *Free.* ☉ *Daily 10–noon and 2–6.*

Continue along rue de Metz. The second road on the left (rue des Changes, which becomes rue St-Rome) was once part of the Roman road that sliced through Toulouse from north to south; today it's a chic pedestrian shopping area. Running parallel is the swinging rue d'Alsace-Lorraine, a center of nightlife, luxury boutiques, and department stores. On the corner of rue d'Alsace-Lorraine and rue de Metz, just **⑪** beyond busy place Esquirol, is the **Musée des Augustins,** housed in a medieval Augustinian convent whose sacristy, chapter house, and cloisters provide an attractive setting for an outstanding array of Romanesque sculpture and religious paintings by such renowned artists as Spain's Bartolomé Esteban Murillo (1618–82) and Flemish maestro Peter Paul Rubens (1577–1640). *21 rue de Metz,* ☎ *61–23–55–07.* ☛ *10 frs (free Sun.).* ☉ *Wed. 10–9, Thurs.–Mon. 10–5.*

TIME OUT Around the corner from the Musée des Augustins, on place St-Georges—a delightful little square—is the intimate **Le Père Bacchus** (20 pl. St-Georges), much frequented by locals. By night it's a popular jazz venue. This area, by the way, is popular with students. In the maze of streets, numerous inexpensive restaurants will offer a good three-course meal for around 70 francs.

From the Musée des Augustins, cross rue de Metz and head down rue des Arts, then turn left on rue Croix-Baragnin to place St-Etienne, site of both the city's oldest fountain, in marble (16th century), and of the **⑫** cathedral of **St-Etienne,** erected in stages between the 13th and 17th centuries. The nave and choir languished unfinished because of a lack of funds; they look awkward because they are not properly aligned. A fine collection of 16th- and 17th-century tapestries traces the life of St. Stephen (Etienne, in French).

The broad allée François Verdier leads to the leafy, circular Grand Rond, flanked by the **Jardin Royal** (royal gardens) and **Jardin des Plantes** (botan-
❸ ical gardens)—home of the **Muséum d'Histoire Naturelle** (Natural His-
tory Museum) and its varied collection of stuffed birds and prehistoric exhibits. *35 allée Jules-Guesde,* ☎ *61–52–00–14.* ☉ *Gardens daily dawn to dusk;* ☛ *Free.* ☉ *Museum Wed.–Mon. 10–5;* ☛ *8 frs.*

Tour 2: Albi–Montauban–Auch

*Numbers in the margin correspond to points of interest on the Midi-
Pyrénées and Roussillon map.*

Leave Toulouse by N88 and drive 53 kilometers (33 miles) northeast
❹ to **Gaillac,** an old town on the right bank of the Tarn and the center of a long-established vineyard renowned for its versatility. Dry, sweet, and lightly sparkling (*perlant*) white wine are all produced here, as are fruity reds; if you're in the mood to sample some, follow signs to a *dégustation* (tasting session). Some of the earliest winemakers, beginning in the 10th century, were Benedictine monks, whose abbey church stands alongside Pont St-Michel.

★ **❺** From Gaillac head east on N88 for **Albi.** This old town, with its narrow streets and redbrick buildings, has been tastefully preserved. Lo-
cals consider their city to be more pink than Toulouse, arguing that more of Albi's buildings are made from the rose-colored brick than their rival's. In its heyday, Albi was a major center for Cathars, members of an ascetic religious sect that rejected earthly life as evil and criticized the worldly ways of the Catholic Church. Albi's huge cathedral of **Ste-
Cécile,** with its intimidating clifflike walls, resembles a cross between a castle, a power station, and an ocean liner and was meant to sym-
bolize the Church's return to power after the crusade against the Cathars (or Albigensians) at the start of the 13th century.

The cathedral's interior is an ornate reply to the massive austerity of the ocher outer walls. Every possible surface has been painted; the lead-
ing contributors were a 16th-century team of painters from Bologna, Italy, who splattered the main vault with saints and Old Testament *venerati,* then lined the bays with religious scenes and brightly colored patterns. The most striking fresco, however, is a 15th-century depic-
tion of the Last Judgment, which extends across the west wall beneath the 18th-century organ loft. Unfortunately, its central section was de-
molished in 1693, to make the St-Clair chapel.

Between the cathedral and the Pont Vieux (Old Bridge) spanning the
★ River Tarn, is the **Palais de la Berbie.** Built in 1265 as a defensive fortress and later taken over by the bishops, it became a museum in 1905, hon-
oring Albi's most famous son: Belle Epoque painter Henri de Toulouse-
Lautrec (1864–1901).

Toulouse-Lautrec left Albi for Paris in 1882 and soon made his name with racy evocations of the bohemian glamour of the cabarets, music halls, bars, and cafés in and around Montmartre. Despite his aristocratic origins (Lautrec is a town not far from Toulouse), Henri cut a far-from-noble figure. He was less than five feet tall (due to a bone de-
ficiency that was aggravated by slipping on his bedroom floor—not by falling off a horse) and pursued a decadent life that led to an early

Midi-Pyrénées and Roussillon

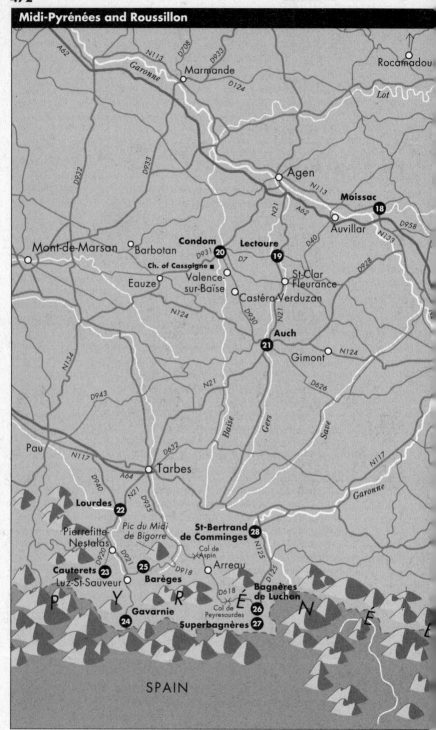

A62 · N113 · D708 · D933 · Garonne · Marmande · D124 · Lot · Rocamadou

D932 · D933 · N113 · Agen · N113 · Moissac **18** · A62 · Auvillar · D958 · D133

Mont-de-Marsan · Barbotan · **Condom 20** · **Lectoure 19** · St-Clar · D928 · D40 · D7 · Fleurance

Ch. of Cassaigne ■ · D931 · Eauze · Valence-sur-Baïse · Castéra-Verduzan · N21

N124 · **Auch 21** · Gimont · N124

N134 · D930 · Baïse · Gers · Save · D626

D943 · N21 · Pau · N117 · D632 · N117

A64 · Tarbes · Garonne

D940 · N21 · D935 · **Lourdes 22**

Pierrefitte Nestalas · *Pic du Midi de Bigorre* · **St-Bertrand de Comminges 28**

Col de l'Aspin · N125

D920 · D921 · **Cauterets 23** · **25** · D918 · Arreau

Luz-St-Sauveur · **Barèges** · D618 · **Bagnères de Luchon**

P Y R É · Col de Peyresourdes · **26** · **N É** · **E**

Gavarnie · **Superbagnères 27**

24

SPAIN

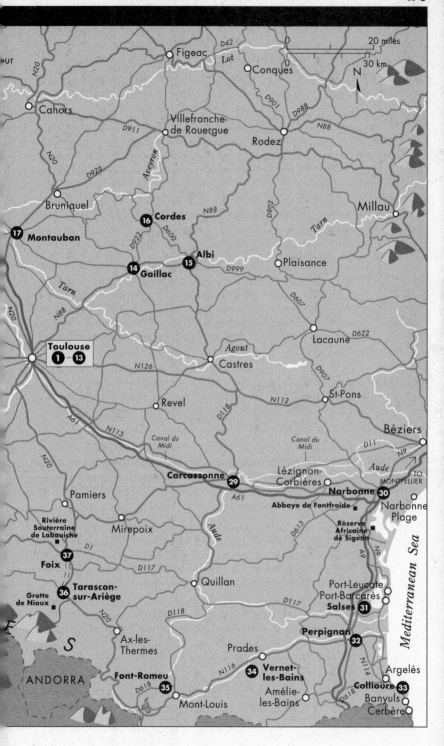

grave. The Albi exhibit is the country's largest collection of Toulouse-Lautrecs, with 600 works. These works are beautifully presented, notably in the lengthy Galérie Ambrie (holding his earliest efforts) and in the rooms leading from the Salon Rose (portraits and lithographs). *Just off pl. Ste-Cécile,* ☎ *63–54–14–09.* ☛ *22 frs adults, 12 frs children.* ☉ *Easter–Oct., daily 10–noon and 2–6; Nov.–Easter, Wed.–Mon. 10–noon and 2–5.*

Before leaving Albi, stroll around the old town to admire its pedestrian streets and elegant shops. You may also be able to visit Lautrec's birthplace, **Maison Natale de Toulouse-Lautrec** (along boulevard Sibille from the cathedral), to see more of his early works, as well as his personal possessions and memorabilia. The house is privately owned and occasionally during the summer it is opened to the public. Check with the tourist office for schedules. *14 rue Henri de Toulouse-Lautrec.*

★ ⑯ From Albi take D600 northwest to the picture-book hilltop village of **Cordes,** built in 1222 by Count Raymond VII of Toulouse. This is one of the most impressively preserved fortified medieval villages in the whole of France. When mists steal up from the Cérou Valley and enshroud the hillside, Cordes appears to hover in midair, hence its nickname, Cordes-sur-Ciel (Cordes in the Sky). It is a typical *bastide,* a fortified medieval town built to a strict grid plan. Wander around the ancient streets and admire the restored medieval houses, many of which are peopled by artisans and craftsmen; the best crafts shops are found along the main street, **Grande-Rue.** The village's venerable **covered market,** supported by 24 octagonal stone pillars, is also noteworthy, as is the nearby well, at more than 300 feet deep.

TIME OUT   Stop for a drink at one of the cafés on **Terrace de la Bride** and take in the view over the Cérou Valley. If you want something more substantial, try the delightful terrace of the **Hostellerie du Vieux Cordes** (*see* Dining and Lodging, *below*). *Pl. de la Halle.*

⑰ Leaving Cordes, continue on D600, a beautiful scenic stretch of road, and then take D115 to Bruniquel and on to **Montauban,** birthplace of the great painter Jean Auguste Dominique Ingres (1780–1867). Ingres was the last of the great French Classicists, who took their cue from Raphaël, favoring line over color and taking much of their subject matter from the antique world. Ingres's personal dislike of Eugène Delacroix (the earliest and most important French Romantic painter), his sour personality, and (for some) his arid painting style, with its worship of line and draftsmanship, led many contemporaries to ridicule his work. These days, he is undergoing a considerable revival; looking at his works, with their quasiphotographic realism, it's easy to see why.

★ The **Musée Ingres** is housed in the sturdy brick 17th-century Bishop's Palace overlooking the River Tarn. Ingres has the second floor to himself; note the contrast between his love of myth (*Ossian's Dream*) and his deadpan, uncompromising portraiture (*Madame Gonse*), underscored by a closet eroticism (silky-skinned nudes) that belies the staid reputation of academic art. Most of the paintings are from Ingres's excellent private collection, ranging from his followers (Théodore Chassériau) and precursors (Jacques-Louis David) to Old Masters. *Pl. Bourdelle,* ☎ *63–63–18–04.* ☛ *15 frs adults, 10 frs students.* ☉ *July–Aug., Mon.–Sat. 9:30–noon and 1:30–6, Sun. 1:30–6; Sept.–June, Tues.–Sat. 10–noon and 2–6.*

Explore the old streets of Montauban, especially the pedestrian zone around the restored place Nationale (home to a lively morning market).

(18) From Montauban, push on to **Moissac,** 29 kilometers (18 miles) away,
to see the wonderfully fine cloisters and one of the region's most re-
★ markable abbey churches, **St-Pierre.** Little is left of the original 7th-
century abbey, and religious wars laid waste its 11th-century replacement.
Today's abbey, dating mostly from the 15th century, narrowly escaped
demolition in this century when the Bordeaux-Sète railroad was rerouted
within feet of the cloisters, sparing the precious columns around the
arcades, carved in different shades of marble. Each of the 76 capitals
has a unique pattern of animals, geometric motifs, and religious or historical scenes. Conserved in the corner chapels of the cloisters are
local religious sculpture and photographs of similar sculpture from all
over the Quercy region. The highlight of the abbey church is the 12th-
century south portal, topped with carvings illustrating the Apocalypse. The sides and vaults of the porch are adorned with historical
scenes sculpted in intricate detail. The town museum has the regional
treasures of Auvillar and a room specializing in local costumes. *6 bis
rue de l'Abbaye,* ☎ *63–04–03–08.* ☛ *Museum and cloisters: 24 frs
joint ticket.* ☼ *Daily 9–noon and 2–5 (until 6 Apr.–June and Sept.; 7
in July and Aug.). Museum closed Mon.*

From Moissac, we now enter the rural Gers département, which occupies the heart of the former dukedom of Gascony; it's studded with
châteaus—from simple medieval fortresses to ambitious classical residences—and tiny, isolated villages. Leave Moissac on D12 toward St-
Nicholas-de-la-Grave and go to **Auvillar,** a pleasant country town, to
have a look at the restored market square and its shops. Then head
(19) south on D40 to St-Clar, where you pick up D7 for **Lectoure.** Once a
Roman city and a fortified Gallic town, it stands on a promontory above
the Gers Valley. Archaeologists have a field day combing the area for
ancient remains. Although Lectoure was ravaged in 1473, when Louis
XI attacked the fortress and established direct royal rule by killing the
last count of Armagnac, there's still plenty to see in its old arched streets:
the 13th-century **Fontaine Diane** (fountain) on rue Fontélie for starters.
Park in front of the tourist office to visit the 15th-century St-Gervais
et St-Protais cathedral and the nearby **Musée Municipal.** Installed in
the vaulted cellars of the former Episcopal Palace (now the Town
Hall), its collection contains a dramatic group of 20 pagan altars, discovered in 1640 under the choir of the cathedral. These altars feature
Latin inscriptions and heads of the sacrificed bulls (or rams). *Hôtel de
Ville,* ☎ *62–68–70–22.* ☛ *21 frs adults, 6 frs children.* ☼ *Daily 9–
noon and 2–6.*

(20) D7 heads west from Lectoure to **Condom,** a town of seven churches,
in the heart of Ténarèze, one of the three nearby regions that produce
Armagnac. Condom's location on the River Baïse made it an excellent
base for exporting the local brandy to Bordeaux or Bayonne on the
Atlantic coast. The musty **Musée de l'Armagnac,** in an 18th-century
annex of the former Bishop's Palace in the town center, details the production process from the grape harvest to the barrel. Armagnac is distilled only once (unlike cognac, which is distilled twice); you can
inspect the copper stills, or *alambics. 2 rue Jules-Ferry,* ☎ *62–28–31–
41.* ☛ *10 frs adults, 5 frs children.* ☼ *June–Sept., Tues.–Sun. 10–noon
and 2–6; Oct.–May, Tues.–Sat. 10–noon and 2–4.*

Six kilometers (4 miles) southwest of Condom (take D931/D208) is
the **château of Cassaigne,** once the country residence of the bishops
of Condom. The vineyards surrounding this 13th-century manor house
were originally cultivated for wine, with only the unconsumed leftovers
distilled to make brandy (once prescribed by local pharmacists as a dis-

infectant!). By the 17th century, the English were importing Armagnac in large quantities; ever since, brandy production has been the château's main raison d'être. Cassaigne has belonged to the same family since 1827. Today Elvire and Henri Faget organize tours of the château and visits to the 17th-century cellars, where the Armagnac is stored in oak barrels that give it an amber color. There's a small Armagnac museum, and you can taste and buy the brandy in the 16th-century vaulted kitchen. The slide show on the history of the house and the traditional methods of distillation is in English as well as French. ☎ 62–28–04–02. ☛ *Free.* ⊙ *Daily 9–noon and 2–7.*

D142 links Cassaigne to the 12th-century abbey of **Flaran,** just over 4 kilometers (2½ miles) away. In 1971, regional authorities took over the abbey, renovated it, and converted the guests' quarters into a cultural center for temporary exhibits. The abbey was built by Cistercian monks under Saint Bernard; the monks' rooms on the second floor, overlooking the cloisters, remain largely unchanged. Have a look at the impressive sacristy, with its ribbed arches resting on one central column, and at the storeroom, with its exhibit illustrating the medieval routes of pilgrims (two of which crossed the Gers) to Santiago de Compostela. *Valence-sur-Baïse,* ☎ 62–28–50–19. ☛ *18 frs adults, 9 frs children.* ⊙ *July–Aug., daily 9:30–7; Sept.–June, Wed.–Mon., 9:30–noon and 2–6.*

Return to Condom to pick up D654 into **Fleurance,** a *bastide* (fortified) town with a regimented street plan. The town's Gothic church of St-Laurent boasts three stained-glass windows by Arnaud de Moles, whose most famous windows are in Auch.

㉑ **Auch,** the capital of Gers, is best known for its Gothic cathedral and quaint alleyways, or *pousterles* (from the French for posterns—*poternes,* the gateways to the medieval fortifications). The cathedral of **Ste-Marie,** in the center of town, dates from the 15th and 16th centuries. Most of the stained-glass windows in the choir, by Arnaud de Moles, who was working here around 1513, portray biblical figures and handsome pagan sybils, or prophetesses. The oak choir stalls are especially interesting, carved with more than 1,500 figures, both biblical and mythological; they took 50 years to complete. In June, classical music concerts are held in the cathedral. *Pl. Salinis.* ☛ *6 frs.* ⊙ *Daily 8–noon and 2–6.*

Cross place Salinis to the terrace overlooking the River Gers. A monumental flight of 232 steps leads down to the riverbank, and there is a statue of D'Artagnan, the musketeer immortalized by Alexandre Dumas, halfway down. Although Dumas set the action of his historical drama *The Three Musketeers* in the 1620s, the true D'Artagnan—Charles de Batz—was born in 1620, probably at Castlemore near Lupiac, and didn't become a musketeer until 1645. Batz adopted the nobler name of D'Artagnan from his mother's family, the Montesquieus, lords of Artagnan and one of the highest-ranking families in Gascony.

On the other side of the cathedral, behind the former Archbishop's Palace (now the Préfecture), is the **Musée des Jacobins,** with a fine collection of Latin-American art and pre-Columbian pottery, gathered by 19th-century adventurer Guillaume Pujos. The museum also contains Gallo-Roman relics; look for the white-marble epitaph dedicated by a grief-stricken mistress to her dog Myia. *Rue Daumesnil,* ☎ 62–05–74–79. ☛ *10 frs adults, 5 frs children.* ⊙ *May–Oct., Tues.–Sun. 10–noon and 2–6; Nov.–Apr., Tues.–Sat. 10–noon and 2–4.*

Tour 3: The Hautes Pyrénées

Your point of entry into the Hautes-Pyrénées will probably be **Tarbes** (about 75 kilometers, or 45 miles, southwest of Auch on N21), where you should stop in the tourist office (3 cours Gambetta, ☎ 62–51–30–31) for information, brochures, and maps. The city is the commercial and administrative center of the Pyrénées region, of no particular tourist interest, but you might enjoy a stroll around the pretty Jardin Massey amid the abundance of summer flowers. Continue on N21.

②② More than 5 million pilgrims flock to **Lourdes** each year, many in quest of a miracle cure for their sickness or disability. In February 1858, Bernadette Soubirous, a 14-year-old miller's daughter, claimed the Virgin Mary had appeared to her in the **Massabielle grotto** near the Gave de Pau river. The visions were repeated. During the night, Bernadette dug at the ground in the grotto, releasing a gush of water from a spot where no spring existed. From then on, pilgrims thronged the Massabielle rock in response to the water's supposed healing powers.

Church authorities reacted skeptically. It took four years of inquiry for the miracle to be authenticated by Rome and a sanctuary erected over the grotto. In 1864, the first organized procession was held. Today there are six official annual pilgrimages, the most important on August 15. In 1958, Lourdes celebrated the centenary of the apparitions by constructing the world's largest underground church, the basilica of **St-Pie X.** The basilica looks more like a parking lot than a church, but it can accommodate 20,000 people—more than the permanent population of the entire town. Above the basilica stand the neo-Byzantine basilica of **Rosaire** (1889) and the tall, white basilica of **Supérieure** (1871). Both are open throughout the day, but their spiritual function far outweighs their aesthetic appeal.

The area surrounding the churches and grotto (situated between the basilicas and the river) is woefully lacking in beauty. Out of season, the acres of parking space beneath the basilicas echo like mournful parade grounds to the steps of solitary visitors. Shops are shuttered and restaurants are closed. In season, a milling throng jostles for postcards, tacky souvenirs, and a glimpse of the famous grotto, lurking behind a forest of votive candles struggling to remain aflicker in the breeze.

The Pavillon Notre-Dame, across from the underground basilica, houses the **Musée Bernadette,** with mementoes of her life (she died at a convent in Nevers, Burgundy, in 1879) and an illustrated history of the pilgrimages. In the basement is the **Musée d'Art Sacré du Gemmail,** *gemmail* being a modern approach to the stained-glass technique involving the assembly of broken glass, lit from behind, often by electric light. *72 rue de la Grotte,* ☎ *62–94–13–15.* ☛ *Free.* ⊙ *July–Nov., daily 9:30–11:45 and 2:30–6:15; Dec.–June, Wed.–Mon. 9:30–11:45 and 2:30–5:45.*

TIME OUT Stop in at the **Taverne de Bigorre** (21 pl. du Champ Commun); Chef Claude Moreau prepares a filling stew of cabbage and bacon and several lighter fish dishes, all worth a try.

Just across the river are the **Moulin des Boly,** where Bernadette was born on January 7, 1844 (12 rue Bernadette-Soubirous; open Easter–mid-Oct., daily 9:30–11:45 and 2:30–5:45), and, close to the parish church where she was baptized, the **Cachot,** a shabby little room where she and her family lived. *15 rue des Petits-Fossés,* ☎ *62–94–51–30.* ☛ *Free.* ⊙ *Easter–mid-Oct., daily 9:30–11:45 and 2:30–5:30; mid-Oct.–Easter, daily 2:30–5:30.*

Despite Lourdes's miraculous fame and Bernadette's compelling story, in the opinion of many, it's a tourist center to be missed. The town is lucky to have an authentic historic attraction to complement the commercialized aura of its pilgrim sites. **Lourdes Castle** stands on a hill above the town and can be reached on foot or by escalator. In the 17th and 18th centuries, the castle was used as a prison; now it contains the **Musée Pyrénéen,** one of France's best provincial museums, devoted to popular customs and arts throughout the Pyrénées region, from Bayonne to Perpignan. It's well worth the price of admission for its views and displays. *25 rue du Fort,* ☎ *62–94–02–04.* ☛ *28 frs adults, 14 frs students.* ☉ *Easter–mid-Oct., daily 9–noon and 2–7 (last admission at 6); mid-Oct.–Easter, Wed.–Mon. 9–noon and 2–7.*

㉓ Lourdes is close to several attractive Pyrenean spots. **Cauterets,** 30 kilometers (19 miles) south of Lourdes (via N21/D920), is a spa-resort set deep in the mountains, where you can sometimes ski until May. Ever since Roman times, Cauterets' thermal springs have been revered as a miracle cure for female sterility. Virile novelist Victor Hugo (1802–85) womanized here, and Lady Aurore Dudevant—better known as the writer George Sand (1804–76)—discovered her feminism. Poetic viscount François René Chateaubriand (1768–1848) stayed determinedly chaste, however, pining for his "inaccessible Occitan girl."

Continue south from Cauterets to the **Pont d'Espagne,** where steep-twisting D920 peters out. Continue on foot or by chairlift to the plateau and a view over the bright blue **Lac de Gaube,** fed by the river of the same name.

㉔ ★ Return via Cauterets to Pierrefitte-Nestalas and turn right along D921 and the Gorge de Luz to **Gavarnie,** 30 kilometers (19 miles) away at the foot of the **Cirque de Gavarnie,** one of the world's most remarkable examples of glacial erosion. When the upper snows melt, numerous streams whoosh down from the cliffs to form spectacular waterfalls; the greatest of them—the **Grande Cascade**—drops nearly 1,400 feet. The Cirque presents a daunting challenge to mountaineers; if you've forgotten your climbing boots, a horse or donkey can take you partway into the mountains from the village of Gavarnie.

㉕ Return along D921 as far as Luz-St-Sauveur and turn right along D918. The dramatic mountain scenery continues to impress. The road passes through the lively little spa town of **Barèges** and under the brow of the mighty Pic du Midi de Bigorre, towering nearly 10,000 feet above the Col du Tourmalet pass. Luz-St-Sauveur lies just 29 kilometers (18 miles) from **Arreau** as the crow flies, but 61 kilometers (38 miles) as the tortuous D918 twists. The finest views—and the sharpest curves—are found toward the Col d'Aspin pass, whose panoramic views of the Pyrénées are unequaled.

㉖ Another spectacular road, D618, covers the 32 kilometers (20 miles), via the Col de Peyresourde, from Arreau southeast to the largest and most fashionable Pyrenean spa, **Bagnères de Luchon** (better known as just plain Luchon). Thermal waters here cater to the vocal cords: Opera singers, lawyers, and politicians hoarse from electoral promises all pile in. Luchon lies at the head of a lush valley, beneath the ski re-

㉗ sort of **Superbagnères,** reached by a serpentine 19-kilometer (12-mile) road (D46); on the way up, admire the breathtaking views of the Maladeta mountain range across the border in Spain. The Romans considered Luchon to rank second as a spa only to Naples. A Roman road

㉘ led directly from Luchon to **St-Bertrand de Comminges** (then a huge town of 60,000), 32 kilometers (20 miles) north on D125/N125. This delightful village, whose inhabitants number just 500 today, is dwarfed beneath the imposing cathedral of **Ste-Marie,** largely 12th-century but extended in the 13th by Bertrand de Got (later Pope Clement V). Old houses, sloping alleyways, and crafts shops add to the charm.

Tour 4: Roussillon

★ ㉙ **Carcassonne,** 88 kilometers (55 miles) east of Toulouse along the A61 expressway, has Europe's longest **medieval town walls.** The circle of towers and battlements stands high on a hilltop above the River Aude and is said to be the setting for Charles Perrault's *Puss in Boots.* The earliest sections of wall were built by the Romans in the 1st century AD, and the Visigoths later enlarged the settlement into a true fortress during the 5th century. During the 13th century, Louis IX (Saint Louis) and his son Philip the Bold strengthened the fortifications and gave Carcassonne much of its present-day appearance. Much, but not all: In 1835, the Historic Monument Inspector (and poet) Prosper Mérimée was appalled by the dilapidated state of the walls, and by 1844 Viollet-le-Duc was at work restoring them.

Unless you are staying at a hotel in the old town, private vehicles are not permitted; park in the lot (10 frs) across the road from the drawbridge. Be aware that the train station is in the *ville basse* (lower town), and that means a cab ride or a 45-minute walk up to the old city. Plan on spending at least a couple of hours exploring the walls and peering over the battlements across sun-drenched plains toward the distant Pyrénées. The old streets inside the walls are lined with souvenir shops, crafts boutiques, and restaurants; be sure to visit the **Château Comtal,** with its drawbridge and Musée Lapidaire, home to stone sculptures found in the area. ☎ *68–25–01–66.* ✆ *26 frs adults; 17 frs students and children.* ☉ *Daily 9–noon and 2–5 (9–6 June–Sept.).*

The ville basse, built between the River Aude and the Canal du Midi, is altogether less captivating, but you may wish to visit the **Musée des Beaux-Arts,** which houses a fine collection of porcelain, 17th- and 18th-century Flemish paintings, and works by local artists—including some stirring battle scenes by Jacques Gamelin (1738–1803). *Rue Verdun,* ☎ *68–72–47–22.* ✆ *Free.* ☉ *Mon.–Sat. 10–noon and 2–5.*

㉚ Take N113 east from Carcassonne, via the wine town of Lézignan-Corbières, to bustling, industrial **Narbonne,** 55 kilometers (34 miles) away. Back in Roman times Narbonne was the second-largest town in Gaul (after Lyon) and an important port, though little remains of its Roman past. Until the sea receded during the Middle Ages, Narbonne prospered, and you will appreciate its onetime wealth when you enter the 14th-century cathedral; its vaults rise 133 feet from the floor, making it the tallest cathedral in southern France. Only Beauvais and Amiens, in Picardy, are taller, and as at Beauvais, the nave at Narbonne was never built. Richly sculpted cloisters link the cathedral to the former **Archbishop's Palace,** now home to the Museums of Archaeology, Art, and History. Note the enormous palace kitchen, with its ornate central pillar, and check out the late-13th-century keep, Donjon Gilles-Aycelin; climb the 180 steps to the top for a view of the region as well as the town. *Palais des Archevêques,* ☎ *68–90–30–30.* ✆ *25 frs (joint ticket for all town museums).* ☉ *May–Sept., daily 9–noon and 2–6; Oct.–Apr., Tues.–Sun. 10–noon and 2–5:30.*

Cross the nearby canal to visit the **Musée Lapidaire** (sculpture museum), housed in the handsome, 13th-century former church of Notre-Dame de la Mourguié. Classical busts, ancient sarcophagi, lintels, and Gallo-

Roman inscriptions await you. *Pl. Lamourguier,* ☎ *68–65–53–58. Joint admission with and same hours as Palais des Archevêques, above.*

Follow pretty D168 as it winds its way over the Montagne de la Clape to Narbonne-Plage, 15 kilometers (9 miles) away. Just up the coast at St-Pierre-sur-Mer is the curious Gouffre de l'Oeil-Doux, an inland lake fed by seawater.

Head west out of Narbonne on N113 and turn left 5 kilometers (3 miles) from the town center onto D613. Seven kilometers (4½ miles) farther, you'll see a sign for the **Abbaye de Fontfroide,** down a small road to the left. The abbey, one of the largest and best preserved in France, was founded in 1093 in this quiet, secluded spot, embellished with cypress trees, the type of setting beloved of Cistercian monks. Pope Benedict XII was abbot here from 1311 to 1317, and the finest monastic buildings—including the church, flower-bedecked cloisters, chapter house, and dormitory—date from his time. Especially noteworthy is the rose garden, with 2,000 bushes in 11 separate beds. *Abbaye de Fontfroide,* ☎ *68–45–11–08. Guided tours only:* ☛ *32 frs. adults, 20 frs children. Tours begin every 45 min in summer, every hour in winter.* ☉ *Daily 10–noon and 2–5:30; closed weekday mornings in winter.*

Return toward Narbonne, take the beltway south, and follow signs to Perpignan (N9). You can stay on this road for 30 kilometers (19 miles), passing the African Reserve at Sigean (*see* What to See and Do with Children, *below*) and the vineyards of Fitou. Then, turn left onto D627, which spins around the Etang de Leucate (becoming D83), through the ugly modern resorts of Port-Leucate and Port-Bacarès, bustling with pleasure crafts and holiday makers. Some 8 kilometers (5 miles) out of Port-Bacarès, turn right along D11 to **Salses.** Hannibal reportedly stormed through Salses with his elephants on his way to the Alps in 218 BC, but no trace of his passage remains. Instead, you'll see the colossal and well-preserved **Fort de Salses,** built by Ferdinand of Aragon in 1497. The fort—equipped for 300 horses and 1,000 soldiers—served Spain well; it fell to the French under Cardinal Richelieu in 1642, only after a three-year siege. In 1691 Sébastien de Vauban made a few improvements to make sure the Spanish would never return. Bulky round towers protected by imposing outworks ring the rectangular inner fort, with its sprawling Place d'Armes and barracks, stables, and bakery. The five-story keep, with its twisted, narrow corridors and small-scale drawbridges, was destined to keep the fort's governor safe to the last. A walk along the walls completes the visit. ☎ *68–38–60– 13.* ☛ *25 frs adults, 14 frs children.* ☉ *July–Aug., daily 9–6; Sept.–June, daily 9:30–11:30 and 2–5:30 (until 4 in winter).*

N9 continues south past Rivesaltes (home of a sweet white wine) to Roussillon's historic capital, **Perpignan,** 16 kilometers (10 miles) away. With a population of 120,000, it's the largest French town south of Toulouse. During medieval times, Perpignan was the second city of Catalonia (after Barcelona), before falling to Louis XIII's French army in 1642. Spanish influence is evident in Perpignan's leading monument, the fortified **Palais des Rois de Majorque,** begun in the 14th century by James II of Majorca. Highlights here are the majestic Cour d'Honneur, the two-tiered Flamboyant Gothic Chapel of Sainte-Croix, and the *Grande Salle* (Great Hall) with its monumental fireplaces. *Rue des Archers,* ☎ *68–34–48–29.* ☛ *10 frs.* ☉ *Daily 9–5.*

Head back across town toward the River Têt and the medieval monument **Le Castillet,** with its tall, crenellated twin towers. The Casa Pairal, a museum devoted to Catalan art and traditions, is housed here. *Pl. de Verdun,* ☎ *68–35–42–05.* ☛ *Free.* ⊙ *Wed.–Mon. 9–noon and 2–6.*

Across boulevard Wilson from Le Castillet is the **Promenade des Platanes,** a cheerful place for strolling, with its flowers, plane trees, and fountains. Perpignan may not be rich in outstanding sights, but the streets near Le Castillet and the adjacent Place de la Loge, the town's nerve center, contain interesting medieval buildings. Among them are the **Cathédrale St-Jean** (with its frilly wrought-iron campanile and dramatic medieval crucifix), the **Loge de Mer** (formerly a maritime exchange), and the **Palais de la Députation** (once home to the Spanish law courts). The **Petite Rue des Fabriques d'En Nabot,** opposite the Palais, is Perpignan's best-preserved medieval street.

Head east from Perpignan along D617, past Château-Roussillon and its ruined church, to Canet-Plage, with its casino, marina, and sandy beach. Then drive south 18 kilometers (11 miles) along D81A, past the pink flamingos in the Etang de Canet and the modern resort of St-Cyprien-Plage, to Argelès, which has France's largest campground. Here, join N114 and snake south along the clifftops to **Collioure,** with its sheltered natural harbor, originally a fishing town. Anchovies are still caught here at night using the *lamparo* technique (powerful lamps to which anchovies are irresistibly attracted). The town's setting makes it a mecca for tourists, the first of whom were painters like Henri Matisse, André Derain, Henri Martin, and Georges Braque.

The view they admired remains largely unchanged today. To the north, the rocky Ilot St-Vincent juts out into the sea, a modern lighthouse at its tip. The first building on the mainland is the 17th-century church of Notre-Dame-des-Anges—observe the exuberantly carved altarpieces—whose pink-domed bell tower doubled as the original lighthouse. Behind the church lie the tumbling streets of the old Quartier du Mouré. A slender jetty divides the Boramar beach, beneath the church, from the small landing area at the foot of the **Château Royal.** This 15th-century castle, remodeled by Vauban 200 years later, can be visited and has fine views of the bay. ☎ *68–82–06–43.* ☛ *20 frs.* ⊙ *Mar.–Oct., daily 10–noon and 2–5.*

Collioure is the prettiest village south of Perpignan, but N114 continues its windy, spectacular route south to the Spanish border, through **Port-Vendres,** once a thriving military harbor, and **Banyuls,** famous for sweet wine and as the birthplace of sculptor Aristide Maillol (1861–1944). Nearby Cap Rederis gives a panoramic view spanning the Mediterranean coastline. Tiny **Cerbère,** 10 kilometers (6 miles) from Banyuls and the last town before Spain, is etched in the heart of the many travelers who have changed trains at its "international" rail station. Few places could be less tedious when waiting for a connection, since the platform is a mere five-minute walk from the beach.

We now leave the Mediterranean and travel inland toward the Pyrénées. Return to Argelès, head west along D618 to Amélie-les-Bains, and forge north on a slow, scenic, challenging drive across the Aspres hills via St-Marsal to **Bouleternère,** stopping en route to admire the richly sculpted Romanesque priory at Serrabonne. From Bouleternère take N116 west, through ancient Marquixanes and beneath the hilltop village of Eus, to the market town of **Prades,** once home to the Spanish cellist Pablo Casals. The annual musical festival he founded in 1950 takes place at the much restored medieval Benedictine abbey of **St-Michel de Cuxa,** 3 kilometers (2 miles) south along D27. Its sturdy, crenellated, four-story bell tower is visible from afar.

34   Stay on D27 as it winds its way another 15 kilometers (9 miles) to **Vernet-les-Bains,** a long-established spa town where the English writer Rudyard Kipling came to take the waters. The hilltop village church is dwarfed by the imposing Mont Canigou behind. Leave your car in nearby Casteil, 2 kilometers (1¼ miles) farther, and complete the journey to the abbey of **St-Martin du Canigou** on foot. Brace yourself for the steep half-hour climb; the abbey is perched on a triangular promontory at an altitude of nearly 3,600 feet. Although the abbey was diligently restored by the bishop of Perpignan early this century, part of the cloisters, along with the higher (and larger) of the two churches, date from the 11th century. The capitals atop the pillars here are rustically—almost crudely—carved. The lower church, dedicated to Notre-Dame-sous-Terre, is even older. Rising above is a stocky, battlemented bell tower. ☎ 68–05–50–03. ☛ 15 frs. ☉ Daily 10–12:30 and 2:30–5.

35   Return to N116 and drive 39 kilometers (24 miles) southwest (via Mont-Louis) to **Font-Romeu,** a popular high-altitude holiday base founded in 1920 and equipped with excellent recreational facilities (ski slopes and chair lifts, an ice rink, a riding school, and a swimming pool). Visit the 17th-century Ermitage, beside a natural fountain where, legend has it, a bull once discovered a miraculous statue of the Virgin. This statue is now safely ensconced in an altarpiece inside the adjoining chapel, although it is removed for ritual bearing-aloft each September. A staircase to the right of the high altar leads to an exuberant, Spanish-style *Camaril* (carved religious scene) with musical angels in each corner. *Av. Pierre-de-Coubertin,* ☎ 68–30–00–02. ☛ *Free.*

36   An appealing drive along mountain valleys (D618, N20) leads from Font-Romeu to **Ax-les-Thermes** (a spa town) and **Tarascon-sur-Ariège,** 95 kilometers (59 miles) away, or to the new 5-kilometer (3-mile) tunnel that avoids the winding, sometimes snowbound road north to Foix. At the entrance to Tarascon, veer left along D8 to the **Grotte de Niaux,** a superb, extensive grotto containing scores of red-and-black Magdalenian rock paintings done in charcoal and iron oxide. Stylized horses, goats, deer, and bison, dating from about 20,000 BC, gallop around a naturally circular underground gallery (known as the *Salon Noir*) 1 kilometer (½ mile) inside the entrance. Now that the famous caves at Lascaux in the Dordogne can be seen only in reproduction, this is the finest assembly of prehistoric art open to the public anywhere in France. ☎ 61–05–88–37 *(call ahead for reservations and to check schedule).* ☛ *Guided tours only: 40 frs.* ☉ *Daily July–Sept. Tours every 45 min 8:30–11:30 and 1:30–5:15. Oct.–June. Tours at 11, 3, and 4:30.*

37   If you don't take the tunnel, return to Tarascon and continue 20 kilometers (12 miles) along the Ariège Valley (via N20) to **Foix,** capital of the Ariège *département.* Notice the swanky 19th-century administrative buildings to the south of avenue Fauré, the town's major thoroughfare. The narrow streets on the other side of the avenue reflect the old town's illustrious past; the Comté de Foix was a powerful medieval entity attached to France only in 1607. Its château, sitting impregnably on a promontory above the town and river, has three enormous towers (two square, one round) that reach skyward like sentinels guarding the approach to the Pyrénées, forming one of the most majestic architectural ensembles in southern France. The castle museum details regional history and archaeological finds. *Rue Mercadal,* ☎ 61–65–56–05. ☛ *20 frs adults, 10 frs children.* ☉ *Daily 10–noon and 2–5:30.*

A 5-kilometer (3-mile) drive northwest from Foix along D1 leads to the **Rivière Souterraine de Labouiche,** a mysterious underground river whose waters have tunneled a 3-mile gallery through the limestone.

The 75-minute boat trip covers a mile-long stretch, past weirdly shaped, subtly lit stalactites and stalagmites, ending with a subterranean waterfall. Dry land is 230 feet overhead. ☎ *61–65–04–11.* ☛ *38 frs.* ☯ *Daily 10–noon and 2–5 in summer (9–6 July–Aug.); Apr.–May, daily 2–5; closed Oct.–Mar.*

What to See and Do with Children

No fewer than 1,600 wild animals roam freely in the 500-acre, pond-studded **Réserve Africaine de Sigean,** 15 kilometers (9 miles) south of Narbonne. The reserve was designed by France's leading game expert, the vicomte de La Panouse, who is best known for cross-breeding lions and tigers at his country seat at Thoiry (*see* Chapter 3, Ile de France). ☎ *68–48–20–20.* ☛ *70 frs adults, 50 frs children.* ☯ *Daily 9–6:30 (until 5 in winter).*

Boat trip on the Rivière Souterraine, Labouiche, Tour 4
Grotte de Niaux, near Tarascon-sur-Ariège, Tour 4
Grande Cascade, Tour 3
Muséum d'Histoire Naturelle, Toulouse, Tour 1

SHOPPING

Gift Ideas
Don't leave the Midi-Pyrénées without buying some of the region's renowned foie gras and preserved duck (*confit de canard*). Two manufacturers in Gimont, **Aux Ducs de Gascogne** (rte. de Mauvezin) and **Comtesse de Barry** (rte. Touget) offer beautifully packaged tins that make ideal gifts. You'll also find their products in most good grocery stores and general-food shops. Excellent local ceramics can be found at the picturesque **Sant Vicens** crafts center (rue Sant Vicens, off D22 east of the town center) in Perpignan.

Spirits
Armagnac brandy is distilled throughout the Gers *département.* You'll see signs for *dégustation* (tasting) just about everywhere in the area (you can buy as well as taste), but any good wine and liquor store will have plenty in stock. For a wide selection, try **Caves de l'Hôtel de France** (rue d'Etigny) in Auch.

Stores and Boutiques
The downtown Toulouse **Centre Commercial St-Georges** (rue du Rempart St-Etienne) is a frenetic, modern shopping mall offering a vast array of clothing, jewelry, books, records—and just about anything else you could want. For upscale clothes, try the chic shops on **rue St-Rome** and **rue d'Alsace-Lorraine,** site of the department store, **Nouvelles Galeries.**

SPORTS AND THE OUTDOORS

Canoeing
Try canoe-kayaking in the rough waters of the Pyrenean torrents or the Tarn and Aveyron gorges, or make gentler progress in the peaceful Quercy rivers. The most important bases are at Millau, Rozier-Pyreleau, Najac, Penne, Midi-Pyrénées, Trébas, Burlats, Albi, St-Juéry, and Laguépie. Contact **Ligue de Canoë-Kayak** (16 rue Guillemin-Tarayre, 31000 Toulouse, ☎ 61–62–65–05).

Fishing

The rivers here teem with trout and salmon. Courses, for beginners and advanced fishermen, are run by **Loisirs Accueil** (Service Pêche, 14 rue Lazéma, 09000 Foix, ☎ 61–65–01–15).

Hiking

The Midi-Pyrénées offers more than 2,000 miles of marked paths for walkers and hikers, all designed to pass natural and historic sights. Local tourist offices have detailed maps, or, for advance information, contact **Comité de Randonnées Midi-Pyrénées** (CORAMIP, 12 rue Salammbô, 31200 Toulouse, ☎ 61–47–11–12).

Horseback Riding

There are more than 120 stables and riding centers in the region; for a full listing, get in touch with **CORAMIP** (*see* Hiking, *above*). Two that we recommend are **Poney Club** (Association Vacances, Loisirs Nature, chemin St-Jean, Colomiers, near Toulouse, ☎ 61–78–24–74) and the **Centre Equestre et Poney Club** (Degagnac, 46340 Salviac, north of Cahors via D6, ☎ 65–35–07–09).

Skiing

Skiing—both downhill and cross-country—is often more fun in the Pyrénées than in the Alps; resorts tend to be prettier and are certainly cheaper. There are 26 "stations" along the central part of the range. Contact **Comité Régional Pyrénées Est de Sports d'Hiver** (1 rue de la Charité, 31000 Toulouse, ☎ 61–62–89–25).

DINING AND LODGING

Dining

The cuisine in Toulouse and the southwest is rich and strongly seasoned, making generous use of garlic and goose fat. This is the land of foie gras, especially delicious when sautéed with grapes. The most famous regional dish is *cassoulet,* a succulent white-bean stew with *confit d'oie* (preserved goose), spicy sausage, pork, and sometimes lamb; there are a number of local versions around Toulouse and Carcassonne. Goose and duck dishes are legion: Try a *magret de canard* (a steak of duck breast). Cheaper specialties include *garbure,* mixed vegetables served as a broth or puree; *farci du lauragais,* a kind of pork pancake; and *gigot de sept heures,* a leg of lamb braised with garlic for seven hours. The local *poule au pot* of stuffed chicken poached with vegetables is memorable. Garlic and olive oil are much used along the Mediterranean, and harbor restaurants often serve lobster and *bouillinade,* a fish stew.

CATEGORY	COST*
$$$$	over 400 frs
$$$	250–400 frs
$$	125–250 frs
$	under 125 frs

*per person for a three-course meal, including tax (18.6%) and tip but not wine

Lodging

Hotels range from Mediterranean modern to Middle Ages baronial; most are small and cozy rather than luxurious. Toulouse has the usual range of big-city hotels; make reservations well ahead if you plan to visit in spring or fall. Many of the hotels have excellent restaurants.

CATEGORY	COST*
$$$$	over 800 frs
$$$	550–800 frs
$$	300–550 frs
$	under 300 frs

All prices are for a standard double room, including tax (18.6%) and service charge.

Albi

DINING

Le Jardin des Quatre Saisons. There are two reasons for this restaurant's excellent reputation: value for the money and its fish. Ask the wine waiter to help you choose a bottle from the extensive wine list to accompany one of the chef's fish dishes. House specialties include mussels baked with leeks or *suprême de sandre* (a type of perch in wine). Desserts are surprisingly light for this gastronomic region. Try for a table in the garden if the weather's fine. Service can be rather sloppy at times. ✕ *19 blvd. de Strasbourg, ☎ 63–60–77–76. Reservations advised. Jacket and tie. AE, MC, V. Closed Mon. $$*

DINING AND LODGING

La Réserve. A five-acre park surrounds this modern, hacienda-style building with arched windows and terraces extending the length of the facade. The garden stretches down to the river Tarn. This is a good retreat for those who do not want to stay in the center of Albi. All the guest rooms are spacious, but those in the main building have the most charm, with elegant reproduction furniture and lots of pretty knick-knacks. The restaurant offers tempting local specialties; the salmon with grapefruit, and foie gras lightly fried with apples is a good bet. ⌚ *Rte. de Cordes, 81000 Fonvialane (5 km, or 3 mi, outside town), ☎ 63–47–60–22. 24 rooms with bath. Restaurant, pool, tennis. Restaurant closed Nov.–Mar. AE, DC, MC, V. $$$–$$$$*

Hostellerie Saint-Antoine. Founded in 1734, this is one of the oldest hostelries in France (owned by one family for five generations), as well as the smartest hotel in the region. Though in the center of town, it is very quiet, and modern renovations (the last of which were in 1989) make it eminently comfortable. Electric Venetian blinds and terry-cloth bathrobes are just a couple of the modern conveniences, but old-fashioned luxury prevails. Room 30 has a pleasing view of the garden, and the pristine white furnishings create a spacious atmosphere. Room 15 is actually extra large, with a lounge area big enough for breakfast for four and easy chairs for relaxing. The superb restaurant offers classical cuisine with a three- or four-course menu. A good choice is the foie gras de canard or saddle of hare with a foie gras based sauce—both rich and delicious. ⌚ *17 rue St-Antoine, 81000 Albi, ☎ 63–54–04–04, FAX 63–47–10–47. 50 rooms with bath. Restaurant, parking. AE, DC, MC, V. $$–$$$*

Mercure Albi Bastides. Ask for a room with a view in this converted 18th-century mill, overlooking the River Tarn. The ones on the second and fourth floors are best; those on the third and top floors have tiny windows. Room 110, on a corner, looks one way to the 22-Août-1994 bridge and weir, and the other to the Pont Vieux and the cathedral. The rooms are functional, modern, and fairly cramped. Bathrooms are utilitarian. The hotel's restaurant is a stylish place to try Eric Sanchez's regional specialties, such as *fritons*—peanut-size chunks of duck lard in flaky pastry with capers; they're a great deal more appetizing than they sound. Dine on the terrace in summer. There is ample parking, but bear in mind that it is a stiff 10-minute walk to the old center of Albi, across the river. ⌚ *41 rue Porta, 81000, ☎ 63–47–*

66–66, FAX 63–46–18–40. *U.S. reservations,* ☎ 800–637–2873; *U.K. reservations,* ☎ 0181/741–3100. 56 *rooms with bath. Restaurant. AE, DC, MC, V.* $$

Auch

DINING AND LODGING

★ **France.** Be sure to pay a visit to this, the most celebrated restaurant in Gascony. Despite the building's sober facade, the dining room's ambience is as warm and welcoming as at any corner bistro, with a bit of extra plush thrown in for good measure. Renowned chef André Daguin creates traditional Gascon cuisine with a masterly touch; his best dishes include salad with kid's liver and cod in flaky pastry accompanied by a whipped liver sauce. Save room for dessert—chocolates in *Banyuls* (warmed wine). The limited three-course menu, Santiago Compostella, has a terrine in aspic, magret de canard (the duck dish that Daguin claims to have invented), and dessert, for 180 francs. And if you take a table at Le Bar du IXème, you can try another limited menu for 130 francs. There are 29 guest rooms as well, which André's wife, Jocelyne, has decorated with great charm and individuality, using exposed wood beams to maximum effect. Ask about two-day packages off-season. ☎ *Pl. de la Libération, 32000,* ☎ 62–61–71–71, FAX 62–61–71–81. 29 *rooms. Reservations required. Restaurant closed Jan., Sun. dinner, and Mon. AE, DC, MC, V.* $$$

Auvillar

LODGING

Château St-Roch. If you missed the château at Azay-le-Rideau, here is an opportunity to see the closest copy—and to stay in it. The neo-Renaissance château, with all the turrets and spirals that could possibly be put on one building, is an eye-stopper, especially when you see it floodlit from below. Guest rooms are huge, with coffered ceilings and (most) with French doors leading onto terraces. Room 11, a fine choice, has a canopied queen-size bed, antique mirrors galore, writing tables, and a sculptured fireplace. Small carpets cover most of the wood floors, a turret room is the closet, and the modern bathroom has a decent-size tub. Of the 55 rooms in the building, only 15 are guest rooms. The others are kept as museum pieces, on show to visitors for 25 francs. There are limitations to staying here: The barracklike bar and dining room are in a separate modern building 100 yards away. The food is only just acceptable, so consider eating elsewhere—perhaps try the Mexican food and live music at Natchez on the outskirts of Auvillar (RN 113, ☎ 63–29–02–42). On the plus side, the breakfasts brought to your room are fine, with good coffee and fresh breads. English is not spoken, though a few words of French will get you by. ☎ *82340 Le Pin (5 km east of Auvillar),* ☎ 63–95–95–22, FAX 63–94–85–54. 15 *rooms. Restaurant, bar. Closed Nov.–Mar. MC, V.* $$–$$$

Barbotan-les-Thermes

DINING AND LODGING

La Bastide Gasconne. This sumptuously decorated 18th-century manor house, converted into a fine hotel-restaurant, is located near an immense lake, close to the spa of Barbotan and 36 kilometers (21 miles) west of Condom. Monsieur Hubert cheerfully presides over the magnificent, wood-beam dining room and dishes up exceptional nouvelle cuisine; try the fresh foie gras cooked in muslin or raywing in a rich mushroom-and-parsley sauce. Cognac or Armagnac and coffee by the open hearth make a suitably grand finale. The guest rooms feature a quaint-chic touch, and there is a pool and a tennis court. ☎ *Rue des Thermes, 32150,*

☎ 62–69–52–09, FAX 62–69–51–97. *36 rooms. Reservations required. Jacket and tie. AE, DC, MC, V. Closed Nov.–Mar. $$$*

Carcassonne

DINING

Auberge du Pont-Levis. At the foot of the medieval city gateway, Porte Narbonnaise, the Pont-Levis provides a welcome shelter from the tourist crowds. Chefs Olivier and Thierry Pautard serve traditional cassoulet stews and foie gras alongside a more inventive terrine marbled with artichokes and leeks, accompanied by a truffle vinaigrette. Otherwise, try the *méli-mélo du pêcheur,* a refreshing mix of seafood. In summer, you can eat on the terrace or in the pretty garden. ✕ *Chemin des Anglais,* ☎ 68–25–55–23. *Reservations advised. Jacket required. AE, DC, MC, V. Closed Nov., Feb., Sun. dinner, and Mon. $$$*

DINING AND LODGING

★ **La Cité.** The reason for coming to Carcassonne is to see the medieval city, and staying overnight within the ancient walls lets you savor the timeless atmosphere after the visitors are gone. Of the half a dozen hotels here several are good, but without doubt the most luxurious is La Cité. Enter the ivy-covered building and you'll step into gentle civility and luxuriate in just the kind of creature comforts the Cathars would have decried. Take your afternoon tea in the library, stocked with leather-bound volumes, or in the garden, looking at the towers of the château. Change for dinner in your spacious, high-ceilinged room (No. 21, a good choice, has two queen-size beds) before taking an aperitif in the bar. Dinner is an elaborate (also read "expensive") affair. Chef Michel Del Burgo changes his menu with the seasons; you should hope that it offers the delectable slices of lobster in a butter sauce with artichokes, and the pigeon brochette with truffle sauce. On warm evenings, be sure to return to the garden to see the spotlights on the château and the lights blinking down below. Then, soak in the deep bathtub before a blissfully quiet sleep in a brass bedstead. ⊞ *Pl. de l'Église, 11000 Cité de Carcassonne,* ☎ 68–25–03–34, FAX 68–71–50–15. *23 rooms, 3 suites. Restaurant, pool. AE, DC, MC, V. $$$$*

Domaine d'Auriac. Former rugby player Bernard Rigaudis and his wife, Anne-Marie, have created a countrified atmosphere in this 19th-century manor house 4 kilometers (2½ miles) southwest of Carcassonne. Room prices vary according to the size and view; larger rooms look out over the magnificent park and vineyards. The dining room, enlarged in 1995 to accommodate 140, is festooned with copper pots and pans and offers traditional Languedoc cuisine. Feast on foie gras poached in Sauternes, anchovies with lemon in salmon carpaccio, or local game in season. This Relais & Châteaux property tends to charge even more than top dollar—a superior room runs more than 1,000 francs and a good after-dinner brandy can cost 400 francs. ⊞ *Rte. de St-Hilaire, 11330 Auriac,* ☎ 68–25–72–22, FAX 68–47–35–54. *23 rooms with bath (13 have air-conditioning). Restaurant, pool, tennis, 9-hole golf course. AE, MC, V. Closed mid-Jan.–Feb.; restaurant closed Sun. dinner and Mon. lunch. $$$$*

Hotel Montségur and **Le Languedoc.** The mother runs the hotel and the sister and brother-in-law the restaurant two blocks away. Both are in new Carcassonne, which may be more convenient than the old city if you are staying in the area for several days. The compact hotel fits into a large town house. Rooms on the first two floors feature Louis XV and Louis XVI furniture, some of it genuine, while those above are more romantic, with gilt-iron bedsteads set under the sloping oak beams. The restaurant (32 allée d'Iéna, ☎ 68–25–22–17, $$), under chef Didier

Faugeras's culinary direction, offers a light version of the region's specialties, from confit to game. The setting is quite romantic and the enthusiasm is there, but the food lacks a certain robustness and taste. 🖪 *27 allée d'Iéna, 11000,* ☎ *68–25–31–41,* 🗚 *68–47–13–22. 21 rooms with bath. Restaurant. DC, MC, V. Restaurant and hotel closed mid-Dec.–mid-Jan.; restaurant closed Sun. and Mon. Sept.–June. $$*

Castéra-Verduzan

DINING AND LODGING

Ténarèze. This hotel's restaurant, Le Florida, is fast acquiring a reputation nearly as lofty as that of André Daguin's establishment in Auch. The dining room's setting is unpretentious and completely upstaged by chef Bernard Ramounéda's creative flair. Ramounéda serves his foie gras with grapes, apples, or gooseberries and a glass of Sauternes; offers duck cooked in every possible manner; and presents a sumptuous range of desserts, including ice cream with prunes and Armagnac or peaches with spices. The hotel's inexpensive guest rooms are traditionally decorated, with heavy velvet draperies and lace trim. Castéra-Verduzan is a spa town featuring curative thermal springs, 25 kilometers (15 miles) northwest of Auch on tree-lined D930. 🖪 *32410 Castéra-Verduzan,* ☎ *62–68–10–22,* 🗚 *62–68–14–69. 24 rooms, 13 with bath. Reservations required. Jacket and tie. AE, DC, MC, V. Closed Mon., Sun. dinner, and Feb. $–$$*

Collioure

DINING AND LODGING

★ **Relais des Trois Mas.** *Patron* Jean-Pierre de Gelder provides a warm welcome for you in charming Collioure. Snuggled in the cliff that curves around the bay and looks over the harbor to the old fort, this unique hotel has charm enough to warrant staying here even if Collioure itself were not picturesque. The rooms have spectacular views, and each is named for a particular painter. A group of glazed tiles behind the whirlpool tub in each bathroom reproduces a work of that painter, and a print reproduction of another work hangs in the bedroom. Rooms are small but interestingly furnished, with antique Spanish doors for headboards. The more expensive rooms have separate sitting areas with huge armchairs; four rooms have private patios leading onto a small garden. While there is a pebble beach below the hotel, most guests linger around the small pool (hewn from rock) and, before dressing for dinner, enter the solarium to take a dip in the huge Jacuzzi. Dinner is at La Balette restaurant. Dine either on the terrace or indoors in one of the two small dining rooms, whose picture windows make the most of the harbor view. The fare, cooked by a young chef, Christian Peyre from Avignon, is varied, using local produce but with recipes from throughout France. Perhaps try the rabbit terrine and duck in a redberry sauce. 🖪 *Rte. de Port-Vendres, 66190,* ☎ *68–82–05–07,* 🗚 *68–82–38–08. 19 rooms, 4 suites, all with bath. Restaurant, pool, solarium, exercise room. Closed mid-Nov.–mid-Dec. AE, DC, MC, V. $$–$$$*

Condom

LODGING

Hotel des Trois Lys. You can recognize this hotel in the heart of Condom, by its 18th-century facade. Once a private mansion, now this small town's best traditional hotel, it reflects an age before time passed Condom by. Most of the furnishings are Empire reproductions. The high-ceiling guest rooms vary in size, the smaller ones being a little cramped. Bathrooms are modern. While there is no restaurant, a bar is open for evening aperitifs, and in summer, breakfast is served on the terrace overlooking the pool. ⚐ *38 rue Gambetta, 32100,* ☎ *62–28–33–33,* FAX *62–28–41–85. 10 rooms. Bar, pool. AE, DC, MC, V.* $$

Cordes
DINING AND LODGING

★ **Le Grand Ecuyer.** Dramatically set in one of the region's most beautiful villages, Le Grand Ecuyer is a perfectly preserved medieval mansion. The guest rooms contain period furnishings, and a few feature four-poster beds; only the bathrooms are contemporary. The best rooms, Planol, Horizon, and Ciel, have grand views of the rolling countryside. Yves Thuriès is one of the southwest's best chefs, and the dining room's elegant decor and ornate silverware provide a stylish background to his inventive recipes. Sample his salmon and sole twist in vanilla puree or the guinea fowl *suprême* in fragrant, flaky pastry. Menus begin at 180 francs and culminate in a gourmet extravaganza with seven courses at 520 francs. After dinner, take a brandy in one of the many small lounges. ⚐ *Rue Voltaire, 81170,* ☎ *63–56–01–03,* FAX *63–56–18–83. 13 rooms with bath. Restaurant. AE, DC, MC, V. Closed Nov.–Mar.; restaurant closed Mon. Sept.–June.* $$$

★ **L'Hostellerie du Vieux Cordes.** This magnificent 13th-century house, belonging to the same family as Le Grand Ecuyer, is set around a charming courtyard, shaded by a 200-year-old wisteria and dotted with tiny white tables. Inside, the 21 guest rooms are richly decorated but not nearly as opulent as the vast crimson dining rooms. Bernard Lafuente, Yves Thuriès's brother-in-law, is yet another accomplished chef, and at his restaurant, Tonin'Ty, the main products are duck and salmon prepared in a variety of ways. There are no fixed menus and each plate costs 40 francs. ⚐ *Rue St-Michel, 81170,* ☎ *63–56–00–12,* FAX *63–56–16–99. 21 rooms with bath. Reservations advised. Jacket required. AE, DC, MC, V. Closed Mon., Nov.–Easter; hotel closed in Jan.* $$

Foix
DINING AND LODGING

Lons. This former posthouse in the town center has comfortable, modernized rooms that vary in size and a reasonably priced restaurant overlooking the Ariège River. ⚐ *4 pl. Georges-Duthil, 09000,* ☎ *61–65–52–44,* FAX *61–02–68–18. 35 rooms, 24 with bath or shower. Restaurant. AE, DC, MC, V. Closed Sat. in winter and mid-Dec.–mid-Jan.* $

Font-Romeu
DINING AND LODGING

Carlit. This friendly modern resort hotel in the heart of Font-Romeu, within sight of the Pyrénées, has excellent facilities (bar, garden, solarium, pool) and is happy to arrange a ski instructor or mountain guide for you or organize a minibus excursion to nearby Spain and Andorra. It is popular with French families on vacation in the mountains, and prices are highest in the ski season and in mid-summer. The restaurant serves filling mountain fare (demi-pension is mandatory during peak periods). ⚐ *Av. du Dr-Capelle, 66120,* ☎ *68–30–80–30,* FAX *68–30–80–68. 58 rooms with bath or shower. Restaurant, bar, brasserie, pool, solarium. MC, V. Closed Nov.–mid-Dec.* $–$$

Mirepoix
DINING AND LODGING

★ **Château de Camon.** If you are within 160 kilometers (100 miles), you should make a point of staying in this medieval castle in Camon, south of delightful Mirepoix. You enter the gates, go through the heavy door, and step back into the 16th century. The flagstone floors are indented by centuries of footsteps, and your footfall echoes through time. Furnishings in most guest rooms are 18th- and 19th-century, with tapestries on the walls. The astonishing overall impression, of red velvet and tassels, seems suitable either for a Louis XVI resort or an elite bordello, depending on your perspective. "Tour One," a room furnished in a more modern style, has a four-poster bed, fabric-covered walls, Empire tables and chairs, and a gabled window looking onto far-reaching fields. Bathrooms are modern, tiled, and commodious. Aperitifs are served in the lounge, which is chock full of tapestries, antiques, and a television set that's turned on at 7 for a cartoon takeoff on French politics. At 7:30, the television goes off, wine is served, and conversation with the owner, M. Dominique du Pont, begins. His English is limited, but he will listen sympathetically to the most plebeian French. Dinner (by reservation), is served table d'hôte style in the family dining room, and as everyone becomes relaxed, guests start pouring wine for each other. Château de Camon is very much a private house, and you are the honored guest. ☎ *09500 Mirepoix,* ☎ *61–68–28–28,* 🅵🅰🆇 *61–68–81–56. 9 rooms with bath. Closed end Nov.–mid-Mar. MC, V. $$$*

Narbonne

DINING AND LODGING

Le Relais du Val d'Orbieu. Good hotels are scarce in or near Narbonne. The most commodious, though a bit overprice, is this 1982 hostelry 14 kilometers (8 miles) west of town, owned by Agnes and Jean-Pierre Gonzalvez. (He speaks fluent English and is extremely helpful.) Designed around a courtyard Mediterranean-style, most guest rooms are reached down covered arcades. The better rooms are pleasantly simple, with bare tiled floors and large French windows leading onto terraces overlooking a small garden. Bathrooms (with a separate toilet) are spacious, though the tubs are narrow. Standard rooms (100 francs less) are slightly smaller and do not have terraces or the view. The large pool is sheltered from breezes by a fence of trees. The dining room is large and without warmth or intimacy, the food is acceptable, and the wine list has very respectable local wines at reasonable prices. ☎ *D24, 11200 Ornaisons,* ☎ *68–27–10–27,* 🅵🅰🆇 *68–27–52–44. 20 rooms. Restaurant, pool, tennis. AE, DC, MC, V. $$$*

Languedoc. In this old-fashioned, turn-of-the-century hotel downtown the smallish rooms have been renovated, but they vary in style and comfort—ask to check yours out first—and you pay an extra 100 francs for a full bath. La Coupole restaurant serves inexpensive regional dishes, Sir John's Piano Bar stays open until 2 AM, and there is also a billiards-snooker parlor. The hotel is only 10 minutes' walk from the train station. ☎ *22 blvd. Gambetta, 11100,* ☎ *68–65–14–74,* 🅵🅰🆇 *68–65–81–48. 38 rooms, 34 with bath or shower, 2 suites. Restaurant (closed Sun. dinner, Mon.), piano bar. AE, DC, MC, V. $$*

Perpignan

DINING

La Serre. Such regional cuisine as artichoke in pastry with garlic, or duck with honey and grapefruit is showcased at this friendly restaurant in the old heart of town. The 90-franc menu offers good food for the price. ✕ *2 bis rue Dagobert,* ☎ *68–34–33–02. Reservations advised. AE, DC, MC, V. Closed Sat. lunch. $–$$*

DINING AND LODGING

Park. This family-run hotel, with its own garden, is without a doubt the chicest in Perpignan; although some rooms are small, most are positively luxurious, and all are soundproof and air-conditioned. Ask for one that has recently been refurbished; these have a Catalonia theme. No. 117, for example, has yellow Catalonia furniture; the bed looks startlingly new, though it's more than 100 years old. The local bourgeoisie pours into the excellent Chapon Fin restaurant to sample the subtle, understated cuisine. Chef Eric Cerf spent seven years working with Joël Robuchon in Paris before coming to Perpignan in 1993, and now he is a star in his own right. Three set menus showcase authentic Mediterranean food made with fresh produce. A second restaurant, recently added, Le Bistro du Park, is for lovers of seafood in particular. Choose from the array laid out on the ice-bar at the entrance and discuss with the maître d' how you want it prepared. Not only is the cooking excellent, but the prices are very reasonable ($$). ☎ *18 blvd. Jean-Bourrat, 66000,* ☎ *68–35–14–14,* FAX *68–35–48–18. 67 rooms with bath or shower. 2 restaurants. MC, V. Formal restaurant closed Sat. dinner, Sun., mid-Aug.–early Sept. $$–$$$*

Quillan

LODGING

Moulins du Roc. A couple of years ago Chris Colyer and his family bought an old farmhouse south of Carcassonne that still had its waterwheel for grinding wheat. From this they have created a few simple rooms and prepared a field in which to park a caravan or two. Casual meals are served, table wine flows freely, and the conversation is usually in English (most guests are Dutch). Four pack llamas will assist in portering your luggage on long hikes through this glorious countryside of hills and canyons, and overnight horseback trips can also be arranged. It's an ideal inexpensive base for exploring the area. ☎ *11500 St-Julia de Bec,* ☎ *68–20–07–15,* FAX *68–20–17–97. 4 rooms with bath (3 with kitchens). Restaurant, pool, horseback riding. MC, V. $*

Revel

LODGING

Château de Garrevaques. Halfway between Toulouse and Carcassonne and 5 kilometers (3 miles) northwest of Revel is a country house that's a charming base from which to explore the southwest. Built in 1470 and then rebuilt in the early 19th century, the château, with two roof turrets, stands on 8 acres of parkland at the edge of the tiny village of Garrevaques. It is, in fact, the home of Mme. Barande, who lives with her daughter and son-in-law, M. and Mme. Combes. Mme. Barande is a rather dominating but extremely helpful hostess, especially in planning trips. She will join you for dinner and ably encourage everyone to join in conversation. The château is full of family heirlooms and antiques; they add warmth to the ample high-ceiling bedrooms. Lunch is sometimes served around the outdoor pool, and Continental breakfast is included in the room rates. The table d'hôte dinner costs extra and is plain, dull family fare. ☎ *81700 Garrevaques,* ☎ *63–75– 04–54,* FAX *63–70–26–44. Dinner reservations required. 8 rooms and 1 suite, all with bath. Pool, tennis, billiards. English spoken.* ☾ *Mid-Apr.–Oct. (Winter on special request.) AE. $$$*

Toulouse

DINING

★ **Vanel.** French gastronomes have long rated Vanel the top restaurant in Toulouse, and one of the country's finest. Lucien Vanel has passed on his taste for innovation to the new chef, Pierre-Yves Lamaison. Roast pigeon with fried mushrooms and warm oysters with foie gras are among the house specialties. The decor was more comfortable than exciting until a recent renovation transformed its Belle Epoque fustiness into modern chic. ✕ *22 rue Maurice-Fonvieille,* ☎ *61–21–51–82. Reser-*

vations required. Jacket and tie. AE, MC, V. Closed part of Aug.,
Sun., and Mon. lunch. $$$

La Belle Epoque. Owner Pierre Roudgé's approach to cooking is novel:
Tell him what you don't like, and he'll invent your menu on the spot.
The ginger-spiced lobster in a flaky pastry is as good as it sounds, while
other dishes include cod in leek butter and a light pastry stuffed with
asparagus and foie gras. The mock Belle Epoque decor provides a suit-
ably grand stage for chef Pierre-Jean Ferrié's culinary efforts. ✕ *3 rue*
Pargaminières, ☎ *61–23–22–12. Reservations advised. AE, DC, MC,*
V. Closed Sat. and Mon. lunch, Sun., and July. $$–$$$

Chez Emile. There are two dining rooms at this restaurant overlook-
ing place St-Georges. The ground floor is modern and elegant, specializing
in light, contemporary fish dishes that change daily; if it's on the menu,
try the turbot in ginger. Upstairs is a cozy hideaway for those who ap-
preciate a more traditional taste of Toulouse: *cassoulet, magret de ca-*
nard (duck), and other filling fare. ✕ *13 pl. St-Georges,* ☎
61–21–05–56. Reservations required. AE, DC, MC, V. Closed last
wk in Aug., Sun., and Mon. $$

DINING AND LODGING

★ **Grand Hôtel de l'Opéra.** This downtown doyen is conveniently located
on Toulouse's place du Capitole. The guest rooms are comfortably plush,
with calm, soothing colors and modern conveniences; make sure you're
not given one of the smaller rooms—they are *very* small. Dominique
Toulousy and his wife, Maryse, have made the hotel's Jardins de
l'Opéra the most fashionable restaurant in town. Several intimate dining rooms and a covered terrace around a little pond make for unde-
niable, if slightly overcute, charm. The food is a successful mix of
innovation and traditional Gascon fare; try the ravioli stuffed with foie
gras and truffles or the *gambas* (jumbo shrimp) baked with artichokes
and cheese. ⊞ *1 pl. du Capitole, 31000,* ☎ *61–21–82–66,* FAX *61–*
23–41–04. 63 rooms with bath. Restaurant, café, pool, health club.
AE, DC, MC, V. Closed 2 wks in Aug. $$$

★ **Hotel Albert 1er.** The new building appears rather ordinary and the re-
ception area is just pleasant and functional, but the newly furnished
guest rooms are cheerful and as spacious as you can expect for a hotel
in the heart of Toulouse. The extremely personable owner, Mme. Hi-
laire, is on hand for a chat and to give suggestions on where to dine
and shop. Her tastes are refined, her manner professional, and her con-
versations loaded with good humor, as she runs this superb-value-for-
money hotel with panache. ⊞ *8 rue Rivals, 31000,* ☎ *61–21–17–91,*
FAX *61–21–09–64. 46 rooms, all with bath. Continental breakfast only.*
MC, V. $–$$

THE ARTS AND NIGHTLIFE

The Arts

Toulouse, the region's cultural high spot, is one of France's most arty cities.
Its classical, lyrical, and chamber music orchestras; dramatic-arts center; and ballet are all listed as national companies—no mean feat in this
arts-oriented country. So many opera singers sing here at the Théâtre du
Capitole or the Halle aux Grains that the city is known as the *capitale*
du bel canto. The performing arts season lasts from October until late
May, with occasional summer presentations. Contact **Théâtre du Capi-**
tole (pl. du Capitole, 31000 Toulouse, ☎ 61–23–21–35).

The medieval city of **Carcassonne** has a major arts festival in July, featuring dance, theater, classical music, and jazz; for details, contact the

Théâtre Municipal (B.P. 236, rue Courtejaire, 11005 Carcassonne cedex, ☎ 68–25–33–13).

Music

There are 50 music festivals a year in smaller towns throughout the region; the CRT and larger tourist offices can provide a list of dates and addresses, or contact **Délégation Musicale Régionale** (56 rue du Taur, 31000 Toulouse, ☎ 61–23–20–39).

Dance

Toulouse's **Ballet du Capitole** stages classical ballets, while the **Ballet-Théâtre Joseph Russilo** and **Compagnie Jean-Marc Matos** put on modern-dance performances. The **Centre National Chorégraphique de Toulouse** welcomes international companies each year in the St-Cyprien quarter. For a schedule of current programs, get in touch with the city tourist office (*see* Essential Information, *above*).

Theater

The main theaters in Toulouse are the **Théâtre du Capitole** (pl. du Capitole, ☎ 61–23–21–35); **Théâtre de la Digue** (3 rue de la Digue, ☎ 61–42–97–79); **Théâtre du Taur** (69 rue du Taur, ☎ 61–21–77–13); **Halle Aux Grains** (pl. Dupuy, ☎ 61–63–18–65); and **Théâtre Daniel Sorano** (35 allée Jules Guesde, ☎ 61–25–66–87).

Nightlife

Toulouse stays up late. For a complete list of clubs and discos, buy a copy of the weekly *Toulouse Pratique* at any bookshop or newsstand.

Nightclubs

L'Art Club (1 rue de l'Echarpe) is a trendy, elegant vaulted brick cellar in the Esquirol quarter; if you like a more intimate setting, try **La Cendrée** (15 rue des Tourneurs), which has lots of cozy nooks and crannies. **L'Ubu** (16 rue St-Rome) has been the city's top night spot for 20 years, where the local glitterati and concert and theater stars come to relax. **Victory Clippers Club** (Canal de Brienne, 90 allée de Barcelone) may be a bit daring for some, but liberated couples love it.

Jazz Clubs

Le Café des Allées (64 allée Charles-de-Fitte) is a regular hothouse of local musicians. **Café Le Griot** (34 rue des Blanchers) features jazz, blues, and a number of American duos and trios. **Le Père Bacchus** (20 pl. St-Georges) is the trendiest spot on the city's trendiest square.

MIDI-PYRÉNÉES ESSENTIALS

Arriving and Departing

By Plane

All international flights arrive at Toulouse's **Blagnac Airport,** a few minutes' drive from the center of town. Regular **Air France** flights link Toulouse with most European capitals, while **Air Inter** runs as many as 30 flights a day during the week between Paris and Toulouse (for reservations, call 45–39–25–25 in Paris or 61–71–11–10 in Toulouse). There are also four flights daily from Paris to Perpignan. **TAT** (Transport Aérien Transregional) offers direct flights from Paris's Orly Airport to Rodez (for reservations, call 42–79–05–05 in Paris or 65–42–20–30 in Rodez).

Between the Airport and Downtown

Buses run regularly (every half hour between 8:15 AM and 8:45 PM) from the airport to the bus station in Toulouse (fare 20 francs) and also at 9:20, 10, and 10:45 PM. From Toulouse bus station to the airport, buses leave at 5:30 AM, 6, 7, 7:30, and then every half hour until 8:30 PM.

By Train

Trains for the southwest leave from Gare d'Austerlitz in Paris. There are direct trains to Toulouse (six to seven hours), Cahors (five to six hours), Carcassonne (seven to eight hours), and Montauban (six hours). For Rodez (seven to eight hours), change in Brive, and for Auch (over eight hours), in Toulouse. Seven trains daily leave Gare de Lyon in Paris for Narbonne (six hours) and Perpignan (seven hours); a change at Montpellier is often necessary. Note that at least one TGV train per day leaves Paris for Toulouse—from Gare Montparnasse. Journey time is five hours.

By Car

The fastest route from Paris to Toulouse is via Bordeaux (on A10), then switch to A62; journey time is about nine hours. Travelers en route from Toulouse to Barcelona on N20E09 can avoid 20 minutes of the winding route between Foix and Tarascon, over the often snowbound pass, by taking the new 5 kilometer (3-mile) **Tunnel du Puymorens** (40 frs toll).

Getting Around

By Plane

From Toulouse's Blagnac Airport, you can pick up an **Air Inter** flight to Tarbes, near Lourdes (for information, call 61–71–11–10).

By Train

The French rail network in the southwest provides regular services to all towns.

By Car

The A62 expressway slices through the region on its way to the coast at Narbonne, where A9 heads south to Perpignan. At Toulouse, where A62 becomes A61, various highways fan out in all directions: N117 to Pau, N20 to Montauban and Cahors, and N88 to Albi and Rodez.

Guided Tours

Orientation

From July to September, a tour of Toulouse's monuments and historic houses leaves Monday to Saturday from the tourist office at 10 AM; the cost is 30 francs. The "Toulouse: Past and Present" bus tour, also leaving from the tourist office, departs at 3 PM and costs 40 francs. A walking tour that takes in the Jacobins church and the private mansions of the St-Rome quarter leaves from the tourist office at 3 PM; the cost is 30 francs, plus 6 francs entrance fee to the church's cloister.

Sightseeing

Day-long regional circuits run from May through September, departing from the Toulouse tourist office and costing 140 francs; stops include Rocamadour, Conques (*see* Chapter 11, The Massif Central and Auvergne), and Cordes, as well as Moissac Abbey, the Ingres museum at Montauban, and the Toulouse-Lautrec museum at Albi.

Important Addresses and Numbers

Travel Agencies

American Express (Office Catholique de Voyages, 14 chaussée du Bourg, Lourdes, ☎ 62–94–40–84), **Havas** (73 rue d'Alsace Lorraine, Toulouse, ☎ 61–23–16–35), and **Wagons-Lits** (Voyages Dépêche, 42 bis rue d'Alsace-Lorraine, Toulouse, ☎ 61–23–40–15).

Car Rental

Avis (pl. de la Gare, Lourdes, ☎ 62–34–26–76; 13 blvd. Conflent, Perpignan, ☎ 68–34–26–71; Blagnac Airport, Toulouse, ☎ 61–30–04–94), **Hertz** (pl. Lagarrasic, Auch, ☎ 62–05–26–26; 5 av. Chamier, Montauban, ☎ 63–20–29–00).

Visitor Information

The regional tourist office for the Midi-Pyrénées (written inquiries only) is the **Comité Régional du Tourisme** (CRT, 12 rue Salambo, 31200 Toulouse, ☎ 61–47–11–12) Ask for the brochure "1,001 Escapes in the Midi-Pyrénées," with descriptions of weekends and short organized package vacations. For Roussillon, contact the **Comité Départemental de Tourisme** (quai De Lattre de Tassigny, 66000 Perpignan, ☎ 68–34–29–94). Local tourist offices are as follows: **Albi** (pl. Ste-Cécile, ☎ 63–54–22–30), **Auch** (1 rue Dessoles, ☎ 62–05–22–89), **Cahors** (pl. Aristide-Briand, ☎ 65–35–09–56), **Carcassonne** (15 blvd. Camille-Pelletan, ☎ 68–25–07–04), **Lourdes** (pl. du Champ-Commun, ☎ 62–94–15–64), **Montauban** (2 rue du Collège, ☎ 63–63–60–60), **Narbonne** (pl. Roger-Salengro, ☎ 68–65–15–60), **Pau** (pl. Royale, ☎ 59–27–27–08), **Perpignan** (pl. Armand-Lanoux, ☎ 68–66–30–30), **Rodez** (pl. du Mal-Foch, ☎ 65–68–02–27), and **Toulouse** (Donjon du Capitole, pl. Charles-de-Gaulle, ☎ 61–23–32–00).

16 The Atlantic Coast

Bordeaux, Biarritz, and the Atlantic Pyrénées

IF THERE'S A FORMULA for enjoying the Atlantic coast of France and its hinterland, it should include cultural exploration, wine tasting, eating oysters, and relaxing by the sea. Swaths of sandy beaches line the coast: Well-heeled resorts, like Biarritz, are thronged with glistening bodies baking in the sun, although visitors who prefer solitude won't have any trouble discovering vast, underpopulated stretches.

For three centuries of the medieval era, this region was a battlefield in the wars between the French and the English, and the Dordogne and Périgord regions were on the front line. Castles and châteaus—some ruined, some domesticated—stud the area, with Biron, Hautefort, and Beynac among the best. Robust Romanesque architecture is more characteristic of this area than the airy Gothic style found elsewhere in France: Poitiers showcases the best examples, notably Notre-Dame-la-Grande, with its richly worked facade, but Romanesque can also be admired at nearby St-Savin abbey and at Angoulême and Périgueux. Humble village churches with distinctive, sturdy towers perch on verdant hills, and generations of painters have been inspired by La Rochelle.

It's hard not to eat well while visiting the Atlantic coast. Truffles, walnuts, plums, trout, eel, and myriad succulent species of mushrooms jostle for attention on restaurant menus. The goose market in the quaint old town of Sarlat is proof of the local addiction for foie gras. The River Dordogne is home to sturgeon, the rarest western European fish, whose caviar surpasses even foie gras as a sought-after delicacy.

The elegant 18th-century city of Bordeaux has tried to diversify its tourist appeal—its May music festival is a major crowd puller—but the city remains synonymous with the wine trade: The vineyards of Médoc, Sauternes, Graves, Entre-Deux-Mers, and St-Emilion are all within a short drive. Proud châteaus, standing resplendent among the vines, can be visited. Note that the *vendanges* (grape harvests) usually begin about mid-September in the Bordelais (though you can't visit the wineries at this time). Harvests begin two weeks later in the Cognac region to the north, famed for its brandy.

In the Gironde *département* around Bordeaux, the great Landes pine forest extends all the way from Bordeaux to Spain. Farther north lies the Marais Poitevin, an extraordinary region whose marshy network of rivers and canals is nicknamed Green Venice. And along the Spanish border rise the Atlantic Pyrénées, with their trout streams, pilgrimage churches, and high Basque villages.

EXPLORING

Orientation

We've divided the region into four tours. The first explores Poitou-Charentes, a rural area north of Bordeaux, from St-Savin to the seacoast town of La Rochelle and back inland again to Cognac country and Limoges. Our second tour explores the scenic provinces of Dordogne and Périgord. The vineyards surrounding Bordeaux form the basis of the third tour, which continues south through sand dunes and forested scenery to the coastal resort of Biarritz, and the fourth makes a loop into the Basque Pyrénées, on the Spanish border.

The Atlantic Coast

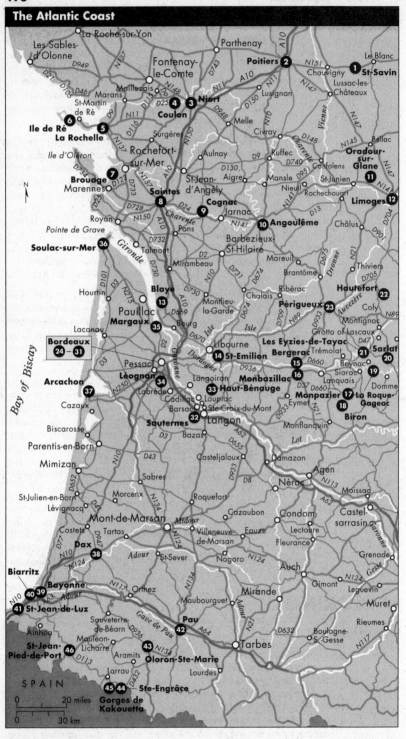

La Roche-sur-Yon

Les Sables-d'Olonne

D949

Parthenay

Poitiers ②

Le Blanc

St-Savin ①

Chauvigny

Lussac-les-Châteaux

N151

N147

Fontenay-le-Comte

D743

A10

N148

N11

Lusignan

N150

N11

Maillezais

Marans

St-Martin de Ré

Coulon

Niort ④ ③

Melle

Civray

N10

Ruffec

N147

Oradour-sur-Glane

Ile de Ré ⑥ ⑤

La Rochelle

Surgères

Aulnay

D9

Charente

D740

Confolens

N145

Bellac

St-Junien

N141

⑪

Ile d'Oléron

Rochefort-sur-Mer

St-Jean-d'Angély

D130

Aigre

Mansle

Nieuil

Rochechouart

Limoges ⑫

Brouage ⑦

Marennes

Saintes ⑧

Cognac ⑨

Jarnac

Angoulême ⑩

Châlus

N21

D704

Royan

Pons

Barbezieux-St-Hilaire

Mareuil

D675

Thiviers

D705

Pointe de Grave

Talmont

Mirambeau

D2

D731

Brantôme

Dronne

Hautefort ㉒

Soulac-sur-Mer ㊱

D730

D74

Ribérac

Périgueux ㉓

Coly

N89

Hourtin

Blaye

Montlieu-la-Garde

Chalais

Isle

Grotto of Lascaux

Montignac

D47

Pauillac

D669

Bourg

Isle

Les Eyzies-de-Tayac

Sarlat ⑳

Margaux ㉟

Libourne

St-Emilion ⑭

Bergerac

Trémolat

㉑

Lacanau

Bordeaux (24 – 31)

Pessac

Dordogne

D936

⑮

D660

Beynac

Siorac

Lanquais

⑲

Domme

Arcachon ㊲

Léognan ㉞

Labrède

Langoiran

㉝ Haut-Bénauge

Monbazillac

⑯

Monpazier ⑰ La Roque-Gageac

Cazaux

Cadillac

Laupiac

Ste-Croix-du-Mont

Eymet

Biron ⑱

Biscarosse

Sauternes

Barsac

㉜ Langon

Monflanquin

Parentis-en-Born

Bazas

Lot

Mimizan

D43

Casteljaloux

D33

Damazan

Sabres

D8

Agen

Moissac

St-Julien-en-Born

Morcenx

Roquefort

Nérac

N113

Lévignacq

Mont-de-Marsan

Midour

Gazaubon

Condom

Lectoure

Castelsarrasin

Costets

Tartas

Villeneuve-de-Marsan

Eauze

Fleurance

Garonne

Dax ㊳

Adour

St-Sever

Nogaro

N124

Auch

Grenade

Gesse

Biarritz

Bayonne ㊵ ㊴

Orthez

Maubourguet

Mirande

Gimont

N124

Leguevin

Muret

St-Jean-de-Luz ㊶

Sauveterre-de-Béarn

Gave de Pau

Pau ㊷

A64

D632

Boulogne-S.-Gesse

Rieumes

N117

Ainhoa

Mauléon-Licharre

Aramits

Oloron-Ste-Marie ㊸

Tarbes

St-Jean-Pied-de-Port ㊻

Larrau

Lourdes

SPAIN

Ste-Engrâce

㊺ ㊹ Gorges de Kakouetta

0   20 miles

0   30 km

Tour 1: Poitou-Charentes

Numbers in the margin correspond to points of interest on the Atlantic Coast map.

The region of Poitou-Charentes occupies the middle band of France's Atlantic coast. Our tour starts just about as far from the sea as regional

❶ boundaries will allow: at the tiny village of **St-Savin,** 40 kilometers (25 miles) east of Poitiers. If you are coming from Tours, it will take just over an hour on the A10.

The large **abbey of St-Savin,** which dates from the 11th century, is impressive enough from the outside. But it is the interior that beckons, partly for the sculpted ornament—monsters run riot on the column capitals—and mainly for the extensive wall paintings in restrained but skillfully contrasted hues of green and ocher. These frescoes date from the building's construction, and it's surprising that the thin film of paint has survived the centuries in such fine condition. Swaying folds of cloth and enormous hands lend life and expression to the numerous figures enacting biblical stories.

★ **❷** Leave St-Savin on N151, and head west for **Poitiers.** Thanks to its majestic hilltop setting above the River Clain and its position halfway along the Bordeaux–Paris trade route, Poitiers became an important commercial, religious, and university town in the Middle Ages. Since the 17th century nothing much has happened, but visitors will find that this is not a bad thing; stagnation equals preservation, and Poitiers' architectural heritage is correspondingly rich.

The church of **Notre-Dame-la-Grande,** in the town center, is an impressive example of the Romanesque architecture so common in western France. Its 12th-century facade is framed by rounded arches and decorated with a multitude of bas-reliefs and sculptures. The interior is dark. The painting on its walls and pillars is not original; such decoration was a frequent ploy of mid-19th-century clerics keen to brighten up their otherwise austere churches. *Rue des Cordeliers.*

Just off Grand'Rue, a few hundred yards beyond Notre-Dame-la-Grande, is the cathedral of **St-Pierre,** built during the 12th to the 14th century. The largest church in Poitiers, it has a distinctive facade featuring two asymmetrical towers, as well as the usual rose window and carved portals. The imposing interior is noted for its 13th-century stained glass, especially the Crucifixion in the chancel, and 13th-century wooden choir stalls, thought to be the oldest in France. *Pl. de la Cathédrale.*

Head down Grand'Rue, taking the second left and first right onto rue Jean-Jaurès. **Musée Ste-Croix,** a modern building, houses archaeological discoveries and European paintings from the 15th to the 19th century of good, though not outstanding, quality. *61 rue St-Simplicien,* ☎ *49–41–07–53.* ☛ *15 frs (includes the museums of Chièvre-Croix and Hypogée).* ☉ *Tues.–Sun. 10–noon and 1–5 (2–6 on weekends).*

Next to the museum is the 4th-century **Baptistère St-Jean,** the oldest Christian building in France. Its heavy stone bulk, some 12 feet beneath ground level, consists of a rectangular baptismal chamber and an eastern end added during the 6th and 7th centuries. The porch, or narthex (restored in the 10th century), is linked to the main building by three archways. Go inside to see the octagonal basin, for baptism by total immersion, and a collection of sarcophagi and sculpture. *Rue*

Jean-Jaurès. 🖝 *4 frs.* ☉ *Summer, daily 10–12:30 and 2–4:30; winter, Thurs.–Tues. 2–4:30.*

Make your way back into the town center, pausing to admire the beautifully preserved houses lining the way. Perhaps stop to pick up some nougat, for which Poitiers is famous. The best is from La Boutique du Patisserie on the north side of place M. Leclerc. Walk across the square to rue Carnot. Shortly after this street has become rue de la Tranchée, the oldest of Poitiers's churches, **St-Hilaire-le-Grand,** appears on the right. Parts of St-Hilaire date from the early 11th century, but unfortunately, the original church had to be reduced in width in the 12th century when its roof was destroyed by fire; local masons lacked the expertise to cover large expanses with the fireproof stone vaulting used in its replacement. The semicircular, mosaic-floor choir rises high above the level of the nave. Cupolas, mighty columns, frescoes, and finely carved capitals add to the church's interest. *Rue St-Hilaire.*

❸ Niort, 72 kilometers (45 miles) down A10, is a complacent, middle-class town best known as the capital of the French insurance business. The massive keep (Le Donjon), with its two square towers dominating the River Sèvre, is all that remains of the **Plantagenet castle** built at the end of the 12th century by English kings Henry II and Richard the Lionhearted. Inside there is a museum with an extensive collection of arms and local costumes. *Rue Duguesclin,* ☎ *49–28–14–28.* 🖝 *14 frs.* ☉ *Apr.–Oct., Wed.–Mon. 9–noon and 2–6; Nov.–Mar., Wed.–Mon. 9–noon and 2–5.*

Just off the nearby rue Victor-Hugo is the old town hall, a triangular building completed in 1535. It now houses the **Musée du Pilori,** with a collection of local archaeological finds and Renaissance artifacts. The highlight is an ebony chest encrusted with gold and silver. *Just off rue Victor-Hugo,* ☎ *49–28–51–73.* 🖝 *13 frs.* ☉ *Apr.–Oct., Wed.–Mon. 9–noon and 2–6; Nov.–Mar., Wed.–Mon. 9–noon and 2–5.*

Do an about-face and amble down rue St-Jean, the oldest street in Niort, to the **Musée des Beaux-Arts** (Fine Arts Museum), where tapestries, gold and enamelware, wooden statues and effigies, and 17th- to 18th-century paintings are on display. The museum is closed for renovation through 1995. *Rue St-Jean,* ☎ *49–24–97–84.*

★ **❹** West of Niort stretches the **Marais Poitevin,** an extraordinary region of canals, lush fields, and rows of hedges. **Coulon** (11 kilometers, or 7 miles west of Niort) is your best base for exploring the region; it has several hotels and restaurants, plus a lovely medieval church (whose arches are shored up with timbers) and a delightful folk museum, the **Musée Maraichi** (rue de l'Eglise, no ☎ , admission by donation). The only way to explore the marais proper is by rowboat—or, more typically, on a *pigouille* (a flat, narrow boat maneuvered with a long pole), which you can find in Coulon. They cost about 90 francs per hour per boat, maximum six persons, and the guide will fill you in on local lore as he steers sedately around the canals; be aware, though, that not all guides speak much English. To explore the region by car or bicycle, a detailed map and sense of direction are advisable (bicycles can be rented at La Ribellale, pl. de l'Eglise, Coulon, ☎ 49–35–83–42).

Willow, ash, and alder trees line the rivers and canals; artichokes, onions, melons, and garlic are grown in the fields alongside. There is little but the occasional very pretty village apart from the ruins of the once-mighty Benedictine **Abbaye de Maillezais,** 13 kilometers (8 miles) northwest of Coulon via D9. Maillezais used to be a bishop's seat and a powerful monastery. The ruins include the 14th-century cloister and refectory, the 11th-century porch, and the 15th-century transept. There is a fine view from the top of one of the towers. ☎ *51–00–70–11.* ☛ *14 frs.* ☉ *Nov.–Mar., Fri.–Wed. 9–12:30 and 2–6; Apr.–Oct., daily 9–8.*

TIME OUT   Before or after your trip on the marais, pause at the rustic café nearby, Les Mangeux de Lumas; its stone walls, wood beams, and open fireplace have great character. ☎ *49–35–93–42.*

Between Maillezais and the Atlantic coast, the Marais Mouillé (wet marsh) gradually dries up and a flat, barren, eerie landscape appears: the Marais Desséché, or dried-out marsh. From Maillezais, head south along D15, then turn right after La Ronde onto narrow D262, which hugs the straight banks of the Canal de la Branche as far as Marans, once a thriving seaport but now linked to the sea only by canal. D105 sneaks seaward from Marans. At the first major crossroad, 8 kilometers (5 miles) past Marans, turn left along D9 toward La Rochelle, 16 kilometers (10 miles) away.

★ ❺   **La Rochelle** is an appealing old town, a vibrant collection of the old and the new; its ancient streets are centered on its harbor, the remarkably picturesque Vieux Port. Standing sentinel on either side of the harbor are the fortresslike 14th-century towers known as **Tour St-Nicholas** (to the left) and **Tour de la Chaîne** (to the right). Climb to the top of Tour St-Nicholas for the view over the bay toward the Ile d'Aix. ☛ *13 frs to each tower.* ☉ *Wed.–Mon. 9:30–12:30 and 2:30–6 (5 in winter).*

Take cours des Dames, a spacious avenue lined with sturdy trees and 18th-century houses, back to the Porte de la Grosse Horloge, a massive stone gate marking the entrance to the straight, narrow, bustling streets of the old town. Head down rue du Palais and onto rue Gargoulleau. Halfway down on the left is the 18th-century Bishop's Palace, now a painting museum. Opposite is the **Musée d'Histoire Naturelle** (Museum of Natural History), housed in an elegant mansion and containing extensive collections of rocks, coral, and shellwork. Other items range from a tribal idol from Easter Island in the South Pacific to a giraffe (now stuffed) given as a gift to King Charles X (reigned 1824–30). *28 rue Albert-Ier,* ☎ *46–41–18–25.* ☛ *16 frs.* ☉ *Apr.–Oct., Tues.–Sun. 10–noon and 2–6; Nov.–Mar., Tues.–Sat. 10–noon and 2–5, Sun. 2–5.*

Farther down rue du Palais (which becomes rue Albert-Ier) is another 18th-century building containing the **Musée du Nouveau-Monde** (New World Museum). Old maps, engravings, watercolors, and even wallpaper evoke the commercial links between La Rochelle and the New World. *10 rue Fleuriau,* ☎ *46–41–46–50.* ☛ *16 frs.* ☉ *Wed.–Mon. 10:30–12:30 and 1:30–6, Sun. 3–6.*

❻   A bridge curves across from La Rochelle to a cheerful island, known as **Ile de Ré,** just 26 kilometers (16 miles) long and never more than 6 kilometers (4 miles) wide. Vineyards sweep over the eastern part of the island while oyster beds straddle the shallow waters to the west. The largest village, **St-Martin de Ré** (population 3,000), has a lively harbor and a citadel built by ace military architect Sébastien de Vauban in 1681. Many of its streets also date from the 17th century, and the villagers' low, white houses, often embellished with window boxes filled with flowers, are typical of the island as a whole.

Head down to the far end of the island to climb up the **Phare de la Baleine** (lighthouse) for sweeping views, and check out the village of **Ars,** with its black-and-white church spire and cute harbor.

TIME OUT The **Café de la Phare,** at the foot of the lighthouse, serves excellent meals and snacks in a surprising Art Deco setting full of arty '30s lamps. Try the *poutargue,* a local specialty made from smoked cod roe and served with shallots and sour cream.

La Rochelle will impress you as more than a port if you are here on a Wednesday or Saturday. Be sure to go to the market that takes place all around the covered market in the old town. A good way to get around is on a bicycle. There are several *location de vélos;* try Centre de Location Agrée (48 rue St-Jean, ☎ 46–41–84–32).

Boats leave La Rochelle harbor daily in summer for cruises to the nearby **Ile de Ré** (72 frs adults, 40 frs children, round-trip), **Ile d'Aix** and **Fort Dayard** (82 frs adults, 62 frs children, round-trip).

The wide N137 speeds down the coast from La Rochelle to Rochefort-sur-Mer, 32 kilometers (20 miles) away and home to the 400-yard-long Corderie Royale—a rope-making factory built for Louis XIV's fleet in 1666. From Rochefort head southwest along D3, via the ancient town **❼** of **Brouage,** whose 17th-century walls loom sullenly above deserted marshland. Samuel de Champlain, who founded Quebec in 1608, was born in Brouage—then a major port. You can stroll freely around the walls and gaze across the marsh toward the sea—now more than 2 miles away—and then visit the village church to learn more of Champlain's tale (Quebec flags flutter proudly in the main street). You can also muse on the fate of Louis XIV's sweetheart, Marie Mancini, who retired here in 1659 after learning that her regal suitor had wed the Infanta of Spain for reasons of state. Plan to have lunch here at an inexpensive and delightful local restaurant, the Brouage (*see* Dining, *below*).

Head toward Marennes and its mighty 280-foot spire, turning right onto D26 and crossing a modern 3-kilometer (2-mile) bridge to the **Ile d'Oléron.** Sand dunes ring the island to the north and west, while oyster beds line the eastern shores, notably along the Route des Huîtres north of the Château d'Oléron, a ruined 17th-century castle. Mainland activity is dominated by the vine; the tangy sweet aperitif known as Pineau des Charentes is produced by mixing unfermented grape juice with cognac.

Back on the mainland, take D25 across the Baie de la Seudre and its quiltlike pattern of oyster beds and continue around the coast to **Royan,** a commercialized resort town that was rebuilt—largely in concrete—after being pounded to bits by Nazi shells in 1945. The Royan skyline is dominated by the tower of the **Eglise Notre-Dame,** an enormous concrete church with a breathtaking oval interior; the huge sweep of its curved ceiling, unsupported by any pillar, is a technical tour de force.

Royan's vast seafront is packed to the gills in summer, although there are prettier beaches just north (Pontaillac and St-Palais). A car ferry (follow signs to the BAC) plows across the Gironde estuary to the Médoc peninsula several times daily from Royan Harbor (*see* Tour 3, *below*).

Head down the coast from Royan along D25 to the pleasant resort of St-Georges-de-Didonne, then continue through a landscape of pine forest and chalky grottoes (via D145) to Meschers and **Talmont,** an unspoiled village renowned for its gently proportioned 12th-century church jutting out over the waters on a rocky promontory.

TIME OUT On your way from Royan to Talmont, stop off in Meschers at **Les Grottes de Matata,** where you can sip tea or eat ice cream on a flower-be-decked terrace overlooking the estuary. ⊘ *Daily June–Sept.*

8 From Talmont head inland along D114 to **Saintes,** a city of stately seren-ity. Its **cathedral** seems to stagger beneath the weight of its stocky tower, which climbs above the red roofs of the old town. Engineering cau-tion foiled plans for the traditional pointed spire, so the tower was given a shallow dome—incongruous, perhaps, but distinctive. Angels, prophets, and saints decorate the Flamboyant Gothic main door of the cathedral, while the austere 16th-century interior is lined with circu-lar pillars of formidable circumference.

The narrow pedestrian streets clustered around the cathedral contrast with the broad boulevards that slice through the town and over the River Charente, but both are full of life and color. Just across the bridge, to the right, is the impressive Roman **Arc de Germanicus,** built in AD 19. Ahead, reached by rue de l'Arc de Triomphe, is the sturdy octag-onal tower of the **Abbaye aux Dames.** Consecrated in 1047, this abbey church is fronted by an exquisite, arcaded facade, whose portals and capitals, carved with fantastic beasts, deserve more than a quick look. Although the Romanesque choir remains largely in its original form, the rest of the interior is less harmonious, having been restored peri-odically. The abbey fell on hard times after the death of the last abbess—the 30th—in 1792. First it became a prison and then a bar-racks. It was recently converted into a cultural center for expositions. ☎ 46–97–48–48. ⊘ *June–Sept., daily 10–12:30 and 2–7; Oct.–May, Thurs. and Sat. 10–12:30 and 2–7, Mon., Tues., Fri., and Sun. 2–7.*

TIME OUT The abbey complex was reopened in 1989 after a thorough overhaul. One consequence: a brasserie opposite the abbey portals that offers state-of-the-art design and astounding lunchtime menus (60 and 100 francs). Try the broccoli flan.

Saintes owes its development to the salt marshes that first attracted the Romans to the area some 2,000 years ago. The Romans left their mark with the arch and with an impressively restored amphitheater. There are several better-preserved examples in France, but few as old. To reach the amphitheater, take the boulevard back across the river and veer left into cours Reverseaux. *Access via rue St-Eutrope.*

9 Leave Saintes going east along D24, making for the black-walled town of **Cognac,** 27 kilometers (17 miles) away. Compared with Saintes, Cognac seems dull and an unlikely hometown for one of the world's most successful drink trades. You may be disappointed initially by the town's unpretentious appearance, but, like the drink, it tends to grow on you. Cognac owed its early development to the transport of salt and wine along the River Charente. When 16th-century Dutch mer-chants discovered that the local wine was both tastier and easier to trans-port if distilled, the town became the heart of the brandy industry and remains so today.

The leading monument in Cognac is its former **castle,** now part of the premises of Otard Cognac, a leading merchant. Volatile Renaissance monarch François I was born here in 1494. The castle has changed quite a bit since then. The remaining buildings are something of a hodge-podge, though the stocky towers that survey the Charente recall the site's fortified origins. The tour of Otard Cognac combines its own pro-paganda with historical comment on the drink itself. The slick audio-visuals are tastefully done, and you will visit some interesting rooms and receive a free taste of the firm's product, which is available for sale at vastly reduced prices. ☎ *45–82–40–00.* ☛ *Free. Guided tours daily on the hour 10–noon and 2–5 (except Sun. Oct.–May).*

Most cognac houses organize visits of their premises and *chais* (warehouses). **Hennessy,** a little farther along the banks of the Charente (note the company's emblem: an ax-wielding arm carved in stone), and **Martell** both give polished guided tours, an ideal introduction to the mysteries of cognac. Martell's chais are perhaps more picturesque, but the Hennessy tour includes a cheerful jaunt across the Charente in old-fashioned boats. Wherever you decide to go, you will literally soak up the atmosphere of cognac; 3% of the precious cask-bound liquid evaporates every year! This has two consequences: Each chais smells delicious, and a small, black, funguslike mushroom, which feeds on cognac's alcoholic fumes, forms on walls throughout the town. *Hennessy, rue Richonne,* ☎ *45–82–52–22. Martell, pl. Martell,* ☎ *45–82–44–44.* ⊙ *Mid-June–mid-Sept., weekdays 9–5:30; mid-Sept.–mid-June, weekdays 8:30–11.*

Rue Saulnier, alongside the Hennessy premises, is the most atmospheric of the somber, sloping, cobbled streets that compose the core of Cognac, dominated by the tower of **St-Léger,** a church with a notably large Flamboyant Gothic rose window. Busy boulevard Denfert-Rochereau twines around the old town, passing the town hall and the neighboring **Musée du Cognac,** worth visiting mainly for its section on cognac. *48 blvd. Denfert-Rochereau,* ☎ *45–32–07–25.* ☛ *15 frs.* ⊙ *Wed.–Mon. 10–noon and 2–5:30 in summer, Wed.–Mon. 2–5:30 the rest of the year.*

Several cognac firms are found 16 kilometers (10 miles) upriver at the charming village of **Jarnac. Hine** (quai de l'Orangerie, ☎ 45–81–11–38) and **Courvoisier** (pl. du Château, ☎ 45–35–55–55) organize visits of their riverbank premises, though Hine's cozy buildings in local chalky stone have more appeal than does Courvoisier's bombastic redbrick factory by the bridge. Jarnac is also famous as the birthplace of former French president François Mitterrand.

❿ Twenty-six kilometers (16 miles) east of Jarnac along N141 is **Angoulême,** divided, like many other French towns, between an old, picturesque section perched around a hilltop cathedral and a modern, industrial part sprawling along the valley and railroad below. Don't let the outskirts deter you—the initial depression soon wears off!

Angoulême Cathedral, in place St-Pierre, bears little resemblance to the majority of its French counterparts because of the cupolas topping each of its three bays. This style was popular in the southwest, and Angoulême's cathedral was influenced by the one in Perigueux. The cathedral dates from the 12th century (the fourth construction), though it was partly destroyed by Calvinists in 1562, then restored in a heavy-handed manner in 1634 and 1866. Its main attraction is the magnificent Romanesque facade, whose layers of rounded arches boast 70 stone statues and bas-reliefs illustrating the Last Judgment. The interior is austere and massive with a few odd points of interest. Collect the free pamphlet from the tourist office, across the street, which gives a detailed description.

The cathedral dominates the *ville haute* (upper town), known as the "plateau." There are stunning views from the ramparts alongside, and a warren of quaint old streets to explore in the shadow of the Hôtel de Ville (Town Hall), with its colorful garden. The 19th-century novelist Honoré de Balzac is one of the town's adopted sons; Balzac described Angoulême in his meaty novel *Lost Illusions.*

⑪ The next stop has a quiet entirely different from that in the previous towns. The village of **Oradour-sur-Glane,** just north of N141 near Limoges, stands as a reminder of war's inhumanity. No one knows why the Germans stormed the village on the night of June 10, 1944, herded the men into a barn, the women and children into the church, and killed them. Some believe they mistook it for another town, reputed to harbor the Resistance. Nevertheless, 642 people, including 205 children, were murdered. Ten villagers survived by hiding under the corpses. A new town was established with the same name 1 kilometer (½ mile) away, leaving this village as it was on that very evening. ☛ *Donation of 30 frs.* ⊙ *Daily 9–sunset.*

⑫ The final stop is **Limoges,** 20 kilometers (12 miles) east on N141, the city famous for porcelain and the economic capital of western France. Every other shop, especially on rue Jean-Jaurès, rue du Clocher, rue du Consulat, and rue St-Michel, seems to sell porcelain. You can get a good overview of what is produced by the factories at the **Limoges-Castel Demonstration Center.** *Pavillon de la Porcelaine, 40 av. John-Kennedy, Zone Industrielle Magré,* ☏ *55–30–21–86.* ⊙ *Mid-Apr.–mid-Oct., daily 8:30–6; mid-Oct.–mid-Apr., Mon.–Sat. 8:30–6.*

To see the very best of the porcelain made over the last two centuries as well as 18th- and 19th-century ceramics from other European countries, visit the **Musée National Adrien-Dubouché.** It also has a good technical section introducing the process that gave rise to the four principal ceramic groups: terra-cotta, glazed earthenware, stoneware, and porcelain. *Pl. Winston-Churchill,* ☏ *55–77–45–58.* ☛ *17 frs.* ⊙ *Wed.–Mon. 10–noon and 1:30–5:15.*

At the **Musée Municipal de l'Evêché,** in the 18th-century Bishop's Palace, there's an even more extensive array of ceramics—from the 12th century to the 20th. The museum also has an archaeological section on Limoges Roman history. Look out, too, for the few works of Renoir. Limoges was his birthplace. *Pl. de la Cathédrale,* ☏ *55–45–61–75.* ☛ *Free.* ⊙ *Wed.–Mon. 10–11:45 and 2–6 (to 5 PM Oct.–June.)*

Just across from the museum is the **St-Etienne Cathedral,** begun in 1273, which closely resembles the cathedrals of Narbonne and Clermont-Ferrand, with their extremely high vaults—the trademark of architect Jean Deschamps.

Tour 2: Dordogne and Périgord

Numbers in the margin correspond to points of interest on the Atlantic Coast map.

The gentle hills and charming valleys, the small villages, and, of course, the replica cave paintings of Cro-Magnon people at Lascaux 2 attract the visitors to this region. Many travelers will spend a week exploring the small lanes, often picnicking for lunch and dining on foie gras and confit. Savor this region unhurriedly, rather than rushing from sight to sight.

On the first half of this tour, we follow one of the country's longest rivers, the Dordogne, as it meanders inland past Sarlat from its confluence with the River Garonne. The two rivers merge to form the

⑬ Gironde between Bourg and Blaye. The small harbor town of **Blaye** (pronounced "bly"), 48 kilometers (30 miles) north of Bordeaux, is worth a visit, chiefly for its vast riverside **citadel,** over half a mile across, erected by Sébastien de Vauban in the 1680s. From a vantage point at the top of the citadel's Tour de l'Aiguillette, the roving gaze can survey the mighty Gironde estuary and the beginnings of the Atlantic Ocean. Close by are two other towers, all that remain of the medieval Château des Rudel. Ditches and ramparts surround the citadel on the landward side. Beyond, the streets of Blaye soon give way to the Côtes de Blaye vineyard, which extends north to the limits of Cognac country.

D669 runs 14 kilometers (9 miles) along the banks of the Gironde estuary from Blaye to **Bourg,** with its once-fortified *ville haute* perched on top of a chalky cliff and linked by stone stairs to the *ville basse* (lower town), with its harbor on the River Dordogne. There is a fine wooded garden around the **Château de la Citadelle** (former summer residence of the bishops of Bordeaux) and a broad view over the Côtes de Bourg vineyard from its terrace.

Follow D670 southeast of Bourg to **Libourne,** 30 kilometers (19 miles) away and surrounded by some famous vineyards. The tiny vineyards of Fronsac and Canon-Fronsac (producing robust, spicy reds) greet you on your approach from the west.

If you are short on time, skip Blaye and Bourg and head straight to St-Emilion using Libourne's bypass. Otherwise from Libourne, take D244 east to approach the pretty town of St-Emilion across the sun-fired flatness of Pomerol, a land of tiny, twisty lanes and ubiquitous grapevines. The occasional hamlet apologetically interrupts, with scruffy gardens and scraggly dogs. All the wealth is in the earth. Locally produced Château Petrus, made exclusively from Merlot grapes, claims to be the world's most expensive red wine, while the nearby Cheval Blanc vineyard produces one of the two top-ranking St-Emilion wines.

★ ⑭ Without any warning, the flatlands break into hills to send you tumbling into **St-Emilion.** This jewel of a town has old buildings of golden stone, ruined town walls, well-kept ramparts offering charming views, and a church hewn into a cliff. Sloping vineyards invade from all sides, and lots and lots of tourists invade down the middle.

The medieval streets are filled with wine stores and crafts shops. Macaroons are a specialty. The local wines offer the twin advantages of reaching maturity earlier than other Bordeaux reds and representing better value for the money. Tours of the pretty **St-Emilion vineyard,** including wine tastings, are organized by the *Syndicat d'Initiative* (tourist office) on place des Créneaux, a bulky square with a terrace overlooking the lower part of town. A stroll along the 13th-century ramparts helps you appreciate St-Emilion's ancient, unspoiled stone-walled houses and soon takes you to the Royal Castle, or **Château du Roi,** built by occupying sovereign Henry III of England (1216–72). ☛ 26 frs. ☉ *Daily 9:30–12:30 and 2–6:30.*

Steps lead down from the ramparts to place du Marché, a wooded square where cafés remain open late into the balmy summer night. Beware of the inflated prices at the café tables, especially those managed by the Bar Le Poste ($4 for water, $6.50 for an inedible sandwich). Lining one side are the east windows of the **Eglise Monolithe,** one of France's largest underground churches, hewn out of the rock face between the 9th and 12th centuries. Visits (every 45 minutes, beginning at 10 and ending at 5) start from the tourist office (☎ 57–24–72–03) and cover the citadel, the Eglise Monolithe, the Catacombes, and the Grotte de l'Ermitage (cost: 34 frs adults, 17 frs children). You may also wish to take the tourist train for a 30-minute ride (25 frs; book through the tourist office) with informative commentary and amusing anecdotes through St-Emilion vineyards.

Just south of the town walls is **Château Ausone,** an estate that is ranked with Cheval Blanc as producing the finest wine of St-Emilion.

As you continue east along D243, you'll soon find yourself amid the vines of the Côtes de Castillon, whose wine is a cheaper and more than palatable alternative to St-Emilion. We are now at the beginning of what English speakers often refer to simply as the Dordogne, those magical words conjuring up French gastronomy and romantic castles perched above steep valleys.

⑮ D936 chugs along the north then the south bank of the river, past the old bastide town of Sainte-Foy-la-Grande, to **Bergerac.** Vines are cultivated here, too, though less expected is the presence of tobacco plantations. Learn about this local industry at the **Musée du Tabac,** a museum housed in the haughty 17th-century Maison Peyrarède near the quayside. The manufacture, uses, and history of tobacco, from its American origins to its spread worldwide, are explained with the help of maps, pictures, documents, and other exhibits, including a collection of pipes and snuff bottles. *10 rue de l'Ancien-Pont,* ☎ *53–63– 04–13.* ☛ *15 frs.* ⊙ *Tues.–Fri. 10–noon and 2–6, Sat. 10–noon and 2–5, Sun. 2:30–6:30.*

Head left from the tobacco museum, past place de la Myrpe, to the **Couvent des Récollets,** a former convent. The convent's stone-and-brick buildings range in date from the 12th to the 17th century and include galleries, a large, vaulted cellar, and a cloister, where the Maison du Vin dishes out information on—and samples of—local wines. From the first floor of the convent, treat yourself to a view of the sloping vineyards of Monbazillac across the Dordogne. *Just off pl. de la Myrpe,* ☎ *53–57–12–57.* ☛ *12 frs.* ⊙ *July–Aug., daily tours every hr 10:30– 11:30 and 1:30–5:30; mid-May–June and Sept.–mid-Oct., Tues.–Sat. at 3:30 and 4:30.*

The regional wines of Bergerac range from red and rosé to dry and sweet whites. The most famous is Monbazillac, a sweet wine made from overripe grapes that enjoyed an international reputation long before its Bordeaux rival, Sauternes. The reds of the region, however, are popular and inexpensive table wines. Guided walking tours of the old town of Bergerac lasting 90 minutes leave from the tourist office (☎ 53–57– 03–11; cost: 22 frs). You can also take an hour-long cruise on the Dordogne for 35 francs. Check the schedules with the tourist office or with the cruise company (☎ 53–24–58–06).

⑯ In fact, if you have time, take D13 south 8 kilometers (5 miles) from Bergerac to the 16th-century château of **Monbazillac.** Vines grow up to the very doors of this beautifully proportioned, gray-stone building whose squat corner towers pay tribute to the fortress tradition of the Middle Ages but whose large windows and sloping roofs reveal the domesticating influence of the Renaissance. Regional furniture and an ornate, early 17th-century bedchamber enliven the interior. A tasting is provided at the end of your tour. ☎ *53–57–06–38.* ☛ *18 frs.* ⊙ *Apr.–Oct., daily 9:30–noon and 2–6:30; Nov.–Mar., 10–noon and 2– 5 (closed Mon. Jan. 10–Mar. 30).*

From Monbazillac, head back toward Bergerac and take D37 east to the village and turreted château of **Lanquais** (15th–17th centuries), surrounded by a large garden. The interior is richly furnished throughout and features majestic Italian fireplaces on loan from the Louvre. ☎ *53– 61–24–24.* ☛ *15 frs.* ⊙ *Apr.–Oct., Fri.–Wed. 9:30–noon and 2:30–7.*

On the opposite side of the Dordogne loom the towers of Baneuil Castle. Stay on the south bank and turn right at Couze on D660, making (17) for the tiny town of **Monpazier,** 27 kilometers (17 miles) away. Monpazier is one of France's best-preserved *bastides* (fortified medieval towns with regimented street plans), built in ocher-colored stone by English king Edward I in 1284 to protect the southern flank of his French possessions. The bastide features three stone gateways (of an original six), a large central square, and the church of **St-Dominique,** housing 35 carved wooden choir stalls and a would-be relic of the True Cross. Opposite the church is the finest medieval building in Monpazier, the **Maison du Chapître** (chapter house), once used as a barn for storing grain. Its wood-beam roof is constructed of chestnut to repel web-spinning spiders.

Detour 8 kilometers (5 miles) south of Monpazier to the hilltop château (18) of **Biron**; its keep, square tower, and chapel date from the Middle Ages, while the classical buildings were completed in 1730. Highlights of a visit here include monumental staircases, the kitchen with its huge stone slabs, and the tomb of a former owner, Pons de Gontaut-Biron (who died in 1524). English Romantic poet Lord Byron (1788–1824) is claimed as a distant descendant of the Gontaut-Biron family, which lived here for 14 generations. ☎ *53–53–85–50.* ☛ *20 frs.* ☉ *Feb.–June and Sept.–Nov., Wed.–Mon. 9–11:30 and 2–6; July–Aug., daily 9–11:30 and 2–6.*

Return to Monpazier and go northeast on D53, which passes by the château of **Les Milandes,** once owned by the American-born cabaret star of Roaring Twenties Paris, Josephine Baker (open May–Oct., daily 9:30–11:30 and 2–6). D53 goes by the ruined castle of **Castlenaud** (open May–Nov., daily 10–7). From here, you cross over the Dordogne; ★ take D703 west to the 13th-century castle of **Beynac,** daringly perched atop a sheer cliff face beside an abrupt bend in the Dordogne. The restoration of this privately owned castle doesn't detract from its powerful setting. You won't quickly forget the muscular architecture and staggering views from its battlements. ☎ *53–29–50–40.* ☛ *25 frs.* ☉ *Mar.–mid-Nov., daily 10–noon and 2:30–5, 6, or 7; July and Aug., daily 10–noon and 2:30–7.*

(19) A short distance upriver, huddled beneath a towering gray cliff, is **La Roque-Gageac,** one of the prettiest and best-restored villages in the Dordogne Valley. Crafts shops line its low, narrow streets, dominated by the outlines of the 19th-century mock-medieval Château de Malartrie and the Manoir de Tarde, with its cylindrical turret. The historic clifftop village of **Domme** lies across the Dordogne from La Roque-Gageac. It is famous for its *grottes* (caves), where prehistoric bison and rhinoceros bones have been discovered. You can visit the 500-yard-long illuminated galleries, lined with stalagmites and stalactites. *Entrance on pl. de la Halle.* ☛ *25 frs.* ☉ *Apr.–Sept., daily 9:30–noon and 2–6; Mar. and Oct., daily 2–6.*

Take D46 a few miles north to another Dordogne gem, the small town ★ (20) of **Sarlat.** To do justice to its golden-stone splendor, you should wander through its medieval streets, aided by the tourist office's walking map, which briefly dates and describes virtually every building, or you may want to take the guided tour offered by the tourist office (*see Essential Information, above*). Rue de la Liberté leads to place du Payrou, occupied on one corner by the pointed-gable Renaissance house where writer-orator Etienne de la Boétie (1530–63) was born. Diagonally opposite is the entrance to **Sarlat Cathedral.** An elaborate turret-topped tower, begun in the 12th century, is the oldest part of the building and, along with the choir, all that remains of the original Romanesque church. A sloping garden behind the cathedral, the Cour de l'Evêché, affords good views of the choir and contains a strange, conical tower known as the **Lanterne des Morts** (Lantern of the Dead), which was occasionally used as a funeral chapel.

Rue d'Albusse, adjoining the garden, and rue de la Salamandre are narrow, twisty streets that head back to place de la Liberté and the 17th-century town hall. Opposite the town hall is the rickety former church of St-Marie, overlooking place des Oies and pointing the way to Sarlat's most interesting street, **rue des Consuls.** Among its medieval buildings are the Hôtel Plamon, with broad windows that resemble those of a Gothic church, and, opposite, the 15th-century Hôtel de Vassal.

TIME OUT If you feel like lunch or a snack, make your way to the **Jardin des Consuls** (4 rue des Consuls). It's part restaurant, part tearoom, serving sorbets and pancakes. The stone-walled dining room is pleasant enough, but in sunny weather, cross through it to the idyllic courtyard in back. Soups and *cassoulet* stews head the filling 100-franc menu, best accompanied by a young, *gouleyant* (fruity) Cahors.

㉑ From Sarlat, D47 twists 21 kilometers (13 miles) west to **Les Eyzies-de-Tayac,** passing the elegant **Château de Puymartin** (open July–Sept., daily 10–noon and 2–6) on the way. Many signs of prehistoric man have been discovered in the vicinity of Les Eyzies; a number of excavated caves and grottoes, some with wall paintings, are open for public viewing. Ask for details of possible visits at the **Musée Nationale de Préhistoire,** where you can also examine many artifacts. The museum's primitive sculpture, furniture, and tools are presented in an appealing setting: a restored, mainly Renaissance, château. ☎ *53–06–97–03.* ☛ *21 frs adults, 12 frs children (free Wed.).* ۞ *Apr.–Oct., Wed.–Mon. 9:30–noon and 2–6; Nov.–Mar., Wed.–Mon. 9:30–noon and 2–5.*

Take D706 up the Vézère Valley toward Montignac. Six kilometers (4 miles) away is the famous **Grotto of Lascaux,** whose hundreds of mesmerizing prehistoric wall paintings, thought to be at least 20,000 years old, were discovered by chance in 1940. Although the caves have been sealed off to prevent irreparable damage, two of the galleries and many of the paintings have been reproduced in vivid detail in the Lascaux 2 exhibition center nearby. ☎ *53–51–95–03.* ☛ *48 frs.* ۞ *Tues.–Sun. 10–noon and 2–5:30.*

㉒ Continue north via D65 and D704 until you reach the château of **Hautefort,** a vast castle surrounded by gardens, presenting a disarmingly arrogant face to the world. The castle's skyline bristles with high roofs, domes, chimneys, and cupolas. The square-lined Renaissance left wing clashes with the muscular, round towers of the right wing, as the only surviving section of the original medieval castle—the gateway and drawbridge—referees in the middle. Most of the buildings date from the 17th century, and furniture and tapestries of that period adorn the interior. ☎ *53–50–51–23.* ☛ *24 frs.* ۞ *Easter–Nov., daily 2–6; Dec.–Easter, Sun. 2–6.*

㉓ **Périgueux,** lying 40 kilometers (25 miles) west via D704/705 (which joins N21), is famous not for a château but for its weird-looking cathedral. The **Cathédrale St-Front** (finished in 1173 but comprehensively restored in the past century) might be on loan from Istanbul, given its shallow, scale-pattern domes and small, elongated, conical cupolas sprouting from the roof like baby minarets. The 200-foot Romanesque tower, one of the finest in southern France, is also topped by a conical dome. You may be struck by similarities with the Byzantine-style Sacré-Coeur in Paris; that's no coincidence—architect Paul Abadie (1812–84) worked on both sites. The interior is cool, vast, and relatively dark. *Pl. de la Clautre.*

From Périgueux, head 27 kilometers (17 miles) up D939 to the beautiful old town of **Brantôme,** with its abbey, village square, small streets, and bridges across the sparkling waters of the River Dronne.

Tour 3: Bordeaux to Biarritz

Numbers in the margin correspond to points of interest on the Atlantic Coast and Bordeaux maps.

㉔ **Bordeaux,** the capital of southwest France, is renowned worldwide for its wines. Vineyards extend on all sides: Graves and pretty Sauternes to the south; flat, dusty Médoc to the west and north; and Pomerol and St-Emilion to the east. Stylish châteaus loom above the most famous vineyards, but much of the wine-making area is unimpressive, with little sign of the extraordinary regional affluence it promotes.

Wine shippers have long based their headquarters along the banks of the Garonne. An aura of 18th-century elegance permeates the downtown area, whose fine shops and pedestrian precincts invite leisurely exploration. For the time being you may want to miss the **old dockland** to the south of the central city. The town planners promise to resurrect this area by attracting artisans and shopkeepers to the warehouse buildings connected by narrow streets, but enthusiasm for the project is still lukewarm, and nothing has happened yet. Currently, the area has a forbidding feel and, indeed, Bordeaux as a whole is a less exuberant city than most others in France, with an almost British reserve.

㉕ For a better view of the picturesque quayside, stroll across the **Pont de Pierre** bridge spanning the Garonne; built by Napoléon at the start of the 19th century, the bridge makes spectacular viewing itself, thanks to graceful curving arches.

Two blocks from the riverbank, along cours Chapeau-Rouge, is the city's
㉖ leading 18th-century monument: the **Grand Théâtre,** built between 1773 and 1780 to the plans of architect Victor Louis. Its elegant exterior is ringed by graceful Corinthian columns and pilasters. The majestic foyer, with its two-winged staircase and cupola, inspired Charles Garnier's design for the Paris Opéra. The theater-hall itself has a frescoed ceiling and a shimmering chandelier composed of 14,000 Bohemian crystals; the acoustics are said to be perfect. The theater was restored in 1991. *Pl. de la Comédie,* ☎ *57–81–90–81. Contact the Tourist Office (☎ 56–48–04–61) for guided tours.* ☛ *25 frs adults, 20 frs children.*

The allées de Tourny and cours du 30-Juillet, haughty tree-lined boulevards, reel off from the Grand Théâtre. At the start of the cours du
㉗ 30-Juillet is the **CIVB,** headquarters of the Bordeaux wine trade, where information can be had and samples tasted. The **Vinothèque,** opposite, sells Bordeaux by the bottle to suit every purse. At the far end of the cours is the **Esplanade des Quinconces,** a vast, 400-yard-long square overlooking the Garonne.

Only dedicated oenophiles should turn north from the esplanade and
㉘ head 1 kilometer (½ mile) along the quayside to the **Cité Mondiale du Vin** (entry 25 quai des Chartrons). This ambitious complex, opened in 1991, is part office block, part shopping mall, and part cultural cen-

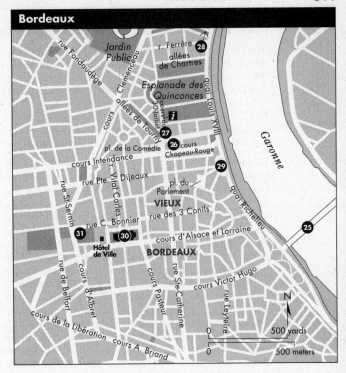

ter; a museum, bars, and exhibition hall all have a common theme: the world of wine.

29 Head back along the river, past the esplanade, as far as **place de la Bourse,** another important 18th-century landmark. A provincial reply to Paris's celebrated place Vendôme, the square (built 1730–55) features airy, large-windowed buildings designed by the country's most esteemed architect of the era, Jacques-Ange Gabriel.

TIME OUT Head two blocks down rue F-Philippart to the 18th-century **place du Parlement,** and you'll have no problem finding a promising-looking lunch spot. No fewer than six bistros and restaurants, some with outdoor tables, line the square. Among them are bustling **L'Ombrière** (No. 14); **La Ténarèze** (No. 18), providing rich dishes from Gascony; and expensive **Chez Philippe** (No. 1), one of the city's top fish restaurants. *Most restaurants closed Sun. and Mon.*

30 A maze of narrow streets wends its way from the river to the **Cathédrale St-André,** in place Pey-Berland. This hefty edifice, 135 yards long, isn't one of France's better Gothic cathedrals, and the outside has a dirty, neglected look. The interior, though, rewards your scrutiny in that the soaring 14th-century chancel makes an interesting contrast with the earlier, more severe nave. Excellent—albeit grimy—stone carvings adorn the facade (notably that of the Porte Royale, to the right) and the nearby 15th-century Pey-Berland Tower.

31 Across the tidy gardens behind the luxurious **Hôtel de Ville** (Town Hall) opposite the cathedral is the busy cours d'Albret and the **Musée des Beaux-Arts.** This fine-arts museum has a notable collection of works spanning the 15th–20th centuries, with important paintings by Paolo Veronese (*Apostle's Head*), Camille Corot (*Bath of Diana*), and Odilon

Redon (*Chariot of Apollo*) and sculptures by Auguste Rodin. *20 cours d'Albret,* ☎ *56–10–17–49.* ☛ *15 frs.* ☉ *Wed.–Mon. 10–6.*

You can find one of the region's most famous châteaus without even leaving the city. Follow N250 southwest from central Bordeaux (direction Arcachon) for a couple of miles to the district of Pessac, home to the flagship of the Graves vineyard: **Haut-Brion,** producer of the only non-Médoc wine to be ranked a *premier cru* (the most elite wine classification). The white, classical château surveys pebbly soil whose vines yield a celebrated red wine, plus tiny quantities of white. The wines produced at La Mission-Haut Brion, across the road, are almost as sought after.

Oenophiles will want to tour the vineyards all around Bordeaux, but for other travelers, it is really a very boring route. Bear in mind that though vineyards refer to themselves as châteaus, it does not mean a noble building stands on the property. Most of the better vineyards like visitors to make appointments, with the implication and expectation that a purchase will be made. Excursions to the Sauternes, Graves, and Médoc regions may be made as day trips from Bordeaux. Of all the towns and villages, Pauillac is the nicest; you may want to stroll along the riverfront and stop for refreshments at one of the restaurants. Continue from Pessac to the A630 expressway that encircles Bordeaux, then head 32 kilometers (20 miles) south via A62 as far as the **㉜** Barsac exit 13 kilometers (8 miles) north of the tiny village of **Sauternes.** Nothing here would tell you that mind-boggling wealth lurks amid the picturesque vine-laden slopes and hollows. Grubby Sauternes has a wine shop where bottles of the celebrated Château d'Yquem gather dust on rickety shelves, next to handwritten price tags demanding 1,000 francs (about $200) and more. The bottles do not seem to have been disturbed for years, which, at that price, is hardly surprising.

Making Sauternes is a tricky business. Autumn mists that steal up the valleys promote a form of rot called *pourriture noble,* which sucks moisture out of the grapes, leaving a high proportion of sugar. Not all grapes achieve the required degree of overripeness simultaneously; up to seven successive harvests are undertaken at Château d'Yquem, one mile north of Sauternes village, to assure the optimum selection. This painstaking attention to detail, added to a centuries-old reputation and soil ideally suited to making sweet white wine, enables bottles of d'Yquem to obtain prices more appropriate to liquid gold. If you do splurge on a recent vintage, you may as well lock it away; Château d'Yquem needs to wait a good 10 years before coming into its own and will reward decades of patience.

From Sauternes, take D8 to Langon, cross the Garonne, and head north up the attractive D10, sandwiched between the river and the vineyards of Sainte-Croix-du-Mont, Loupiac, and Cadillac. These picturesque villages also produce excellent sweet wines, at a fraction of the cost of prestigious Sauternes.

Meanwhile, 8 kilometers (5 miles) north of Cadillac via D11, a dif-**㉝** ferent style of wine is produced near the ruins of the Château of **Haut-Bénauge.** The vines here are too far from the Garonne to benefit from the rising early morning damp of the river valley; their grapes prove more suitable for dry white wine—excellent dry white, in fact. Officially, it's the best of the Entre-Deux-Mers region that stretches northeast toward the River Dordogne.

Cross back over the Garonne at Langoiran and head toward Bordeaux (via Labrède and Léognan) through the vineyards of the **Graves** region, so called because of its gravelly soil. The Graves encircles western Bordeaux and is the region's most historic appellation; a lightish red wine known as Clairet (origin of the word "claret," to mean red Bordeaux) was esteemed by English occupiers during the Middle Ages. White wine—both dry and sweet—is also produced, some of the best at the tiny Domaine de Chevalier in **Léognan.**

34

A630 skirts Bordeaux, with the N215 exit swiftly announcing the Wine Road, or D2, which slips off north toward **Médoc.** This is strange, dusty territory. Even the vines look dusty, and so does the ugly town of **Margaux,** the area's unofficial capital. Yet the soil hereabouts is sown with the seeds of grandeur. The small, arid communes and châteaus of Haut-Médoc feature such venerable names as Margaux, St-Julien, Pauillac, and St-Estèphe. Château Margaux, an elegant, coolly restrained classical building of 1802, and three wineries at Pauillac—Lafite-Rothschild, Latour, and Mouton-Rothschild—are recognized as producers of *premiers crus,* their wines qualifying with Graves's Haut-Brion as Bordeaux's top five reds.

35

D2 chugs through the less prestigious wine fields of northern, or Bas, Médoc, before merging with N215. **Pointe de Grave,** at the tip of the Médoc peninsula, is the site of an American memorial commemorating the landing of U.S. troops in 1917. From the surrounding sand dunes, there are views over the Gironde estuary to Royan and back across the Atlantic. A car-ferry plows across to Royan four times daily (cost: 125 frs per car, 35 frs per passenger). Another ferry, closer to Bordeaux, crosses the Gironde from Lamarque to Blaye four times a day (cost: 78 frs per car, 20 frs per passenger).

Just south of Pointe de Grave is **Soulac-sur-Mer.** The 12th-century basilica of **Notre-Dame de la Fin-des-Terres** deserves to have an outlandish history, given its name—Our Lady of the Ends of the Earth, and it does. By 1800 it had been almost completely embedded in drifting sands and was dug out and restored only 100 years ago.

36

The entire coast, which stretches down to Spain in a straight line, was once subject to drifting sands. Today the highest dunes in Europe pile up behind uninterrupted miles of sandy beach. The sands' unpredictable inland advance used to go on at the alarming rate of several yards a year. At the start of the 19th century, efforts were made to stop the sandy invasion by planting a frontline of sturdy beach grass with pine trees to the rear. The resulting forest has transformed the hinterland region. The name **Landes,** now synonymous with "enormous pine forest," originally implied a wasteland. This is precisely what the region once was: part sandy desert, part marshy wilderness, whose eccentric inhabitants sported sheepskin jackets and stomped around on stilts. Some still do, mainly for the benefit of the tourists who are attracted to the area by the healthy climate and the variety of outdoor activities—hiking, fishing, canoeing, sand-skiing, golf, tennis, surfing, sailing, bathing, and water sports of all kinds. You will find few overseas tourists here; most vacationers will be French families.

At the start of the century, the coast adopted the name Côte d'Argent, or Silver Coast, in a bid to consolidate its new image. Parallel to this silver coast, a few miles inland, is a chain of lakes connected by streams and canals. The first lake we encounter (take D101 from Soulac) is France's largest: the wild, 12-mile-long **Lac d'Hourtin-Carcans.** The small town of Hourtin, with a marina and 460-yard jetty, stands on its northern shore.

After Hourtin, D3 continues south as the Lake Road to the smaller Lac de Lacanau, which teems with pike, perch, and eel and is linked by the Canal de Lège to the Bassin d'Arcachon, a vast triangular bay named after the town on its southern flank. The bay is renowned both for its variety of migratory birds and for its excellent oysters. Many of the oyster beds cluster around the Ile aux Oiseaux, a small island in the middle of the bay.

㊲ Arcachon was "created"—at least as a resort—in the 1850s, when the new railroad connected it with Bordeaux, 64 kilometers (40 miles) away. These days, Arcachon is a lively boating center, with three jetties protruding over its sandy beaches. From boulevard de la Mer, there are good views toward Cap Ferret, across the narrow straits that mark the divide between bay and ocean.

A small lake, 13 kilometers (8 miles) south of Arcachon, the Etang de Cazaux, marks the boundary between the Gironde and Landes *départements*. Oil has been found at Parentis-en-Born, on the eastern shore of the neighboring Etang de Biscarosse. Mimizan, on the southern shore of the Etang d'Aureilhan (the next lake along), was swamped in roving sand during the 18th century; sand still surrounds its ruined Benedictine abbey. Take D652 down to St-Julien-en-Born, then D41 to the charming old village of Lévignacq, with its fortified church and low houses that are typical of the region.

D41 joins N10, which branches off toward Dax (as D947) at Castets.
㊳ Dax, known in Roman times as Aquae Tarbellicae, has been famous for 2,000 years for its thermal springs. The daughter of Caesar Augustus came here to soothe her aches and pains and was the first in a long line of seasonal guests whose numbers have swollen to 50,000 each year, making Dax the country's premier warm-water spa. Steaming water gushes out of the lion-headed Néhé fountain in the center of town.

Dax is an airy town, offering pleasant walks through its parks and gardens and along the banks of the River Adour. Eleventh-century bas-reliefs adorn the east end of the church of St-Paul-les-Dax, while the 17th-century cathedral, built in the classical style, boasts a variety of fine sculpture, some inherited from the previous Gothic building. People generally come to Dax for the waters, and unless you plan to do so, you may not want to make the stop.

㊴ Bayonne, 48 kilometers (30 miles) southwest of Dax via N124 and N10, is the gateway to Basque country, a territory stretching across the Pyrénées to Bilbao in Spain. Bayonne stands at the confluence of the Rivers Adour and Nive; the port of Bayonne extends along the valley to the sea 5 kilometers (3 miles) away. You could easily spend an enjoyable few hours here, admiring the town's 13th-century cathedral, cloisters, old houses, and 17th-century ramparts. The airy, modernized **Musée Bonnat** houses a notable collection of 19th-century paintings. *5 rue Jacques-Lafitte,* ☎ *59–59–08–52.* ☛ *15 frs.* ۞ *Wed.–Mon. 10–noon and 2:30–6:30.*

★ **㊵** The celebrated resort of **Biarritz** lies 8 kilometers (5 miles) west of Bayonne on a particularly sheltered part of the Atlantic coast. Biarritz rose to prominence in the 19th century when upstart emperor Napoléon III took to spending his holidays here on the prompting of his Spanish wife, Eugénie. You'll soon understand why: The crowded Grande Plage and neighboring Miramar Beach provide fine sand and friendly breakers amid a setting of craggy natural beauty. Biarritz would like to remain a high-brow resort, but the fashionable crowd has dispersed and many of the hotels have discounted their rooms. Once so smart and stylish, the resort struggles to keep its head above water, although there are still some smart hotels, in particular Hotel Le Palais. With a smart new casino facing the sea and a new convention center that should be completed in 1996, Biarritz may be on the road to make a comeback and challenge its rival to the south, St-Jean-de-Luz, and San Sebastian, across the border in Spain. Certainly the old down-to-earth charm of the former fishing village remains to counterbalance the resort ambience. The narrow streets around the cozy 16th-century church of St-Martin are delightful to stroll and, together with the harbor of Port des Pêcheurs, offer a tantalizing glimpse of the Biarritz of old.

★ ④ A 26-kilometer (16-mile) drive along the coast, through the pretty villages of St-Jean-de-Luz and Hendaye, leads to Irun on the Spanish border. **St-Jean-de-Luz,** in particular, deserves a visit, for its old streets, curious church, colorful harbor, and elegant beach. The tree-lined place Louis-XIV, alongside the Hôtel de Ville with its narrow courtyard and dainty statue of Louis XIV on horseback, is the quaint hub of the town. Nearby are the **Eglise St-Jean-Baptiste,** where unusual wooden galleries line the walls to create a theaterlike effect, and the **Maison de l'Infante,** where Maria Teresa of Spain stayed prior to her wedding to the Sun King. The four-square mansion contains worthy 17th-century furnishings. *Quai de l'Infante, ☎ 59–26–01–56. ☛ 25 frs. ☉ June–Sept. 10:30–noon and 3–6:30. Closed Sun.* AM.

Tour 4: The Atlantic Pyrénées

If you can arrange it, drive from Bayonne to Pau (one hour on the highway) in the late afternoon or early evening. As you go east, the views of the Pyrenean peaks to the south, illuminated by the sun sinking behind you, are unforgettable.

④ The busy and elegant town of **Pau,** 106 kilometers (63 miles) east of Bayonne, is the historic capital of Béarn, a state annexed to France in 1620. Pau rose to prominence after being "discovered" in 1815 by British officers returning from the Peninsular War in Spain, and it was soon launched as a winter resort. Fifty years later, English-speaking inhabitants made up one-third of Pau's population. They started the Pont-Long steeplechase, still one of the most challenging in Europe, in 1841; created France's first golf course here, in 1856; and introduced fox hunting to the region.

Pau's regal past is commemorated at the **château,** begun in the 14th century by Gaston Phoebus, the flamboyant count of Béarn. The building was transformed into a Renaissance palace in the 16th century by Marguerite d'Angoulême, sister of François I. Marguerite's grandson, the future King Henri IV, was born in the château in 1553. Temporary exhibits connected to Henri's life and times are staged regularly here. His cradle—a giant turtle shell—is on exhibit in his bedroom, one of the sumptuous, tapestry-lined royal apartments. Other highlights are the 16th-century kitchens and the imposing dining hall, which could seat up to 100 guests. *Rue du Château, ☎ 59–82–38–00. ☛ 26 frs (14 frs Sun.). ☉ Apr.–Oct., daily 9:30–11:30 and 2–5:45; Nov.–Mar., daily 9:30–11:30 and 2–4:30.*

On the fourth floor of the château, the **Musée Béarnais** offers an overview of the region, encompassing everything from fauna to furniture to festival costumes. There is a reconstructed Béarn house and displays of such local crafts as cheese- and béret-making. *☎ 59–27–07–36. ☛ 8 frs adults. ☉ Apr.–Oct., daily 9:30–12:30 and 2:30–6:30; Nov.–Mar., daily 9:30–12:30 and 2:30–5:30.*

43 Southwest of Pau on N-134, **Oloron–Ste-Marie** straddles the confluence of the *gave* (mountain torrent) d'Aspe and the gave d'Ossau, which join forces—much as the towns of Ste-Marie and Oloron did in 1858. Much of Oloron seems to hang over one river or the other, where trout and even the occasional Atlantic salmon are not impossible to spot when the sun illuminates the water correctly. The town, originally an Iberian and later a Roman military outpost, was made a stronghold by the viscounts of Béarn in the 11th century. The quartier Ste-Croix occupies the once fortified point between the two rivers and is the most interesting part of town. The fortresslike Église Ste-Croix, with its Moorish-influenced cupola, the two Renaissance buildings nearby, and the 14-century Grède tower are the main attractions. A walk around the Promenade Bellevue along the ramparts below the west side of the church offers a view down the Aspe Valley and into the mountains behind.

TIME OUT For a look into a real Béarn kitchen stop at **Le Corn d'Henric,** across the gave d'Ossau at 10 place de la Résistance. M. and Mme. Claverie serve excellent home-cooked *garbure,* a vegetable and duck-broth stew typical of the region, and even better *pipérade,* another hearty dish based on ham, peppers, and beans.

We now take a small circular tour through Soule, the smallest Basque province, where nearly all the inhabitants speak Euskera (Basque), a non–Indo-European language of mysterious origins, and through the rolling green hills and corn fields of the **Barétous** region, an undulating and moist transitional zone between the Basque country and Béarn.

Take D936 northwest toward Sauveterre de Béarn and after 12 kilometers (7 miles) turn left on D25. **L'Hôpital-St-Blaise,** the first village on this road, has a 12th-century church, another example of the Hispano-Moorish influence, which is rare north of the Pyrénées. Thirteen kilometers (8 miles) west you come to **Mauléon-Licharre,** the capital of Soule, on the banks of the Saison, where you should stop to see the 16th-century **Hotel de Maytie** (also known as the Château d'Andurain), the 17th-century **Hotel de Montréal,** and the remains of a 12th-century fortress. As you leave town, driving south on D918 you'll come to the rustic 11th-century Chapelle St-Jean-de-Berraute, built by the Order of Malta for pilgrims on the way to Santiago de Compostela. After just over 3 kilometers (2 miles) you'll come to **Gotein** and its characteristic *clocher-calvaire,* a three-peaked bell tower evocative of Calvary. Then you'll pass through Trois Villes, Tardets, and Lanne before your loop ends in Aramits, capital of the Barétous.

If time is short you can drive straight from Oloron-Ste-Marie to Aramits on D919 along the Vert River. This gentle valley and its meadow brook, well populated with trout, lead past the town of Féas, where you might like to do some fly-fishing.

From Aramits, take D918/D932 through Arette, which was rebuilt after a 1967 earthquake leveled most of the town, and continue south up into the Pyrénées, 22 kilometers (14 miles) through increasingly spectacular scenery to the ski station of **Arette-Pierre–St-Martin.** Just short **44** of Arette-Pierre–St-Martin, make a hairpin right turn onto D113, to **Ste-Engrâce,** a village still largely populated by Basque shepherds. There's an especially haunting **11th-century church** honoring Sancta Gracia, a young Portuguese noblewoman martyred around the year 300. Its assymetrical, slanting roof, reminiscent of the typical *maison Basque,* and its gray stone seen against the smooth green hills and fields behind seem to communicate unusual emotion. The rich ornamentation of the church interior is a surprising contrast to the stark exterior. Don't miss the stunning polychrome stone carvings on the choir capitals.

Pilgrims on the way to Santiago de Compostela flocked here to venerate the arm of the martyred saint, until Calvinists pillaging Soule in 1569 removed the cherished relic. Sancta Gracia's right-hand ring finger was then sent from Zaragoza, the scene of her martyrdom, in order to sustain the cult. Ste-Engrâce is still an important crossroads for pilgrims traveling west to Santiago and trans-Pyrenean trekkers going east across the "dragon's back." Its *gîte d'étape*, or hiker's quarters, called Elichalt, is an interesting and economical place to spend a night (in summer) with an international group of hikers, travelers, and pilgrims of one kind or another.

Just past Ste-Engrâce is the famous canyon cut through limestone cliffs by the Uhaitxa river: the **Gorges de Kakouetta.** This is one of the wonders of the Pyrénées, an all but required stop, weather permitting. At times as narrow as 12 feet across, the gorges are more than 700 feet deep. Stairways are cut into the rock, and hanging bridges cross the watercourse. A waterfall and a grotto mark the end of the climb, a two-hour walk round-trip. This hike is recommended only during low-water conditions, normally between June and October. Good hiking shoes are indispensable.

Continue for another 11 kilometers (6 miles) on D113 to the junction of the Uhaitxa and Larrau rivers, where a left turn up D26 will take you past the **Crevasses d'Holçarté.** The walk up through these gorges is another one you will be glad you took, a 90-minute round-trip highlighted by a spectacular hanging bridge 561 feet over the rocky stream bed below. **Larrau,** the next town, a cozy way station on the road over the Larrau pass into Spain, is known for its 19th-century forges.

TIME OUT Stop at **Hotel Etxemaïté** (☎ 59–28–61–45) for the excellent Basque cooking, whether you spend the night or not. If you happen through in winter there will be fires in the splendid fireplaces, (*see* Dining and Lodging, *below*).

The road down toward St-Jean-Pied-de-Port twists through mountain passes (Col de Bagargui and Col de Burdinkurutzeta) with staggeringly lovely views up into the limestone massif and the vast Iraty forest to the south, and out over the Arbailles forest and the sweeping Basque hills to the north. The Iraty forest, one of Europe's largest stands of beech, provided masts for the Spanish and French fleets up through the 18th century.

At the junction with D933, just 5 kilometers (3 miles) before St-Jean-Pied-de-Port, you come to **St-Jean-le-Vieux,** one of those villages on either side of the road out of the Haute Soule that are all worth stopping in, possibly for a lifetime. Many have perfectly acceptable, economical inns and restaurants, and nearly all have adorable farmhouses and chapels—often matching sets of sister chapels like the twin buildings in Bascassan and Alciette, a fairly common phenomenon in the Basque country.

St-Jean-Pied-de-Port, a fortified town on the river Nive, got its name from its position at the foot of the mountain pass (*port*) of Roncevaux (Roncesvalles). The pass was the setting for *La Chanson de Roland* (*The Song of Roland*), the 11th-century epic poem that's considered the real beginning of French literature. The bustling center, a major stop for pilgrims en route to Santiago de Compostela, the town, even in winter, seems like Manhattan after a tour through the Haute Soule. In summer, especially around the time of Pamplona's San Fermín blowout (the running of the bulls, July 7–14), the place is filled to the gills and is somewhere between exciting and unbearable, depending on what you're looking for.

Nevertheless, the town is charming. Walk into the old section through the Porte de France just behind and to the left of the tourist office, climb the steps on the left up to the walkway circling the ramparts, and walk around to the stone stairway down to the rue de l'Église.

TIME OUT   Chez Arbillaga (8 rue de l'Église, ☎ 59-37-06-44), a sound choice for lunch or dinner, will be to your left at the bottom of the stairs.

Rue de l'Église leads down to the magnificent doorway of the church, a characteristic Basque three-tiered structure: men below, women above, and the choir loft above that. From this church, Notre-Dame-du-Bout-du-Pont (Our Lady of the End of the Bridge), walk out on the bridge and watch the very healthy wild trout helping themselves to whatever aquatic insect is emerging at that time of day or year. The Nive is a scheduled Atlantic salmon stream. Fishing is *défendu* (forbidden) in town, and it seems that the smarter riverine subjects have gotten the word and are prospering here, protected by decree. Following the left bank upstream, you come to another wooden bridge. Cross there, noting the rounded wall of an ancient stone house on the far bank, and then walk around and back through town, crossing back to the left bank on the main road. On rue de la Citadelle, note the Arcanzola house at No. 32 (1510), the Maison des Évêques (Bishops' House) at No. 39, and the famous Prison des Évêques next door. The citadel up above, a classic Vauban fortress, is occupied by a school.

TIME OUT   At the **Relais de la Nive** (hanging over the river at the north end of the bridge in the center of town), you can admire the reflection of the Notre-Dame bridge upstream and watch the trout working in the current. It's an ideal spot for a drink or a meal, especially in summer, when the terrace is open.

Continue along the Nive northwest (D918), and after 30 kilometers (18 miles) follow signs for Itxassou and proceed past the town up to **Pas de Roland,** where legend has it that Roland, to allow Charlemagne's troops to pass, cut a breach through a boulder with his mystical sword Durandal, in the process leaving his footprint in the rock. The evidence remains, along with some charming spots along the Nive River and a cozy inn, the Hotel du Mont Roland (Rte. Laxia, Itxassou 64250, ☎ 59-29-75-23).

Backtracking, but not to the main road, take D118 near Espelette and follow signs for the classical Basque village of **Ainhoa,** officially catalogued as one of the prettiest towns in France. It is lined with one beautiful house after another: They have whitewashed walls, flowered balconies, brightly painted shutters and eaves, and carved master beams, and the town has looked this way for more than 300 years. The church at Ainhoa is another three-tiered beauty, with carved railings and woodwork.

Go back 1 kilometer (½ mile) and take the first road to the left, to **Sare,** a tiny village also listed among the most beautiful in France. Shady streets, a large *fronton* for *pala* (handball), and a lovely three-tiered church are among its chief assets, while up the Sare valley is the panoramic Col de Lizarrieta and the **Grottes de Sare** (grottoes), where you can take a guided tour (five languages) for ⅔ mile underground, guided by blue lights set in the ground and entertained by a sound-and-light show. ☎ *59–54–21–88. ☛ 30 frs. Closed Jan.–mid-Feb.*

West of Sare on D4, at the Col de St-Ignace, you can take the **Petit Train de la Rhune,** a tiny wood-paneled cogwheel train that reaches the dizzying speed of 8 kph (5 mph) while climbing up La Rhune peak. The views out over the Bay of Biscay, the Pyrénées, and the grassy hills of the Basque farmland are wonderful from here. ☛ *45 frs adults, 25 frs children. Round-trip (1 hr); Easter vacation and May–June, daily 10 and 3; July–Sept., daily every 35 min.*

Ascain, with its Roman bridge, three-tiered church, and arcaded bell tower, is the last town before following the Nivelle River down to St-Jean-de-Luz and the sea.

What to See and Do with Children

The Atlantic coast **beaches** are ideal for swimming and sunbathing (also *see* Sports and the Outdoors, *below*).

Harbor, Musée Lafaille, and **Musée du Nouveau-Monde** (New World Museum), La Rochelle, Tour 1.

Hennessy tour (including boat trip), Cognac, Tour 1.

Boat trip through the **Marais Poitevin** (*see* Guided Tours in Essential Information and Tour 1, *above*).

Futuroscope, just outside Poitiers in the suburb of Jaunay-Clan, has enjoyed tremendous success since its creation. About a million visitors a year glimpse the future from "simulated seating" (which moves, tilts, and jolts) and via interactive cinema. They also enjoy the vicarious widescreen thrills of bobsledding and a runaway train. *Futuroscope (Exit 18 off A10), 86000 Poitiers, ☎ 49–49–31–10. ☛ 125 frs adults, 90 frs children under 17. ☉ Mid-Feb.–Nov., daily 9–6 (8 PM July and Aug.).*

Sarlat Aquarium shows the fish found in the local rivers: salmon, eel, pike, perch, trout, and even sturgeon, rarely seen outside the Caspian Sea. *Rue du Commandant-Marátuel, ☎ 53–59–44–58. ☛ 32 frs adults, 20 frs children. ☉ June–mid-Sept., daily 10–7; mid-Sept.–Oct. and Apr.–May, daily 10–noon and 2–6.*

Grottes de Sare, Sare, Tour 4.

Le Petit Train de la Rhune, near Sare, Tour 4.

SHOPPING

The city of Bordeaux abounds with stylish shops in its commercial heart between the cathedral and Grand Théâtre, where you'll find numerous pleasant pedestrian streets. Serious shoppers should also keep their eyes peeled for likely-looking shops in every small town and village.

Food Items

The Périgord region owes much of its fame to such gastronomic specialties as truffles, *fruits confits* (fruit preserved in brandy), and foie gras (ask for a sealed can rather than a glass jar, and it will last for months). Similar local goods are found at **La Maison des Produits Régionaux,** in the Cestras complex on N250 outside Arcachon. For an exceptional selection of cheeses, go to **Jean d'Alos** in Bordeaux (4 rue Montesquieu). If you feel like giving yourself a present that definitely won't last, try some of "the best butter in the world"—available from the **Laiterie Co-Opérative** at Echiré, just north of Niort, a box of nougat from Poitiers, or some macaroons from St-Emilion.

Gift Ideas

Regional gifts include embroidery, wooden models, and, more exceptionally, the small green animals made from the stems of the wild angelica found around Poitiers and Niort.

Wine and Spirits

A bottle of old cognac makes a fine souvenir; try **La Cognathèque** in Cognac itself (10 pl. Jean-Monnet), though you can sometimes find the same item infinitely cheaper at a local producer. For a top-ranking Bordeaux, try the **Vinothèque** in Bordeaux (8 cours du XXX-Juillet) or the **Maison de Tourisme et du Vin** in Pauillac (north of Bordeaux), where you'll have a wide choice.

SPORTS AND THE OUTDOORS

Beaches and Water Sports

The Atlantic coast presents an outstanding stretch known as the **Côte d'Argent** (Silver Coast), but the chilly Atlantic waters do separate the men from the boys! Major resorts, offering a welter of sports facilities, are **Royan, Soulac, Carcans, Lacanau,** and **Arcachon.** The **Aquacity** complex (off N250 south of Arcachon, ☎ 56–66–39–39), with water slides, wave machine, and heated swimming pool, offers fun for the entire family (admission: 80 frs adults, 60 frs children under 12).

The lakes that dot the **Landes pine forest** some 30 kilometers (20 miles) from the coast offer various water sports (such as waterskiing and canoeing), as does the stretch of the Dordogne at **Siorac** between Bergerac and Sarlat.

Bullfighting

As you approach the Pyrénées, you step into Basque country, where bullfights are a major sporting occupation. Bullfights are held at **Dax, Mont-de-Marsan,** and **Bayonne**; if you're in the area in summer, you can't miss the colorful posters announcing them.

Golf

There are courses at **Biarritz** (☎ 59–03–71–80), **Lacanau** (☎ 56–26–35–50), **Bordeaux** (☎ 56–39–10–02), **Arcachon** (☎ 56–54–44–00), **Monestier** (near Eymet, at the Château Vigiers, ☎ 53–61–50–00), and **Cognac** (☎ 45–32–18–17). Typical greens fees are 300 francs in the summer and 200 francs during the winter.

Pelote

This Basque specialty is played in **Biarritz** on Wednesday and Saturday at 9 PM during July, August, and September, at the Parc des Sports d'Aguilera (☎ 59–23–91–09) and other locations.

DINING AND LODGING

Dining

The cuisine of this ocean-facing region centers on fish and seafood. Oysters and mussels are major industries, while carp, eel, sardines, sole, and even sturgeon form the basis of menus in fish restaurants. Béarn, around Pau, is great eating country, famous for richly marinated stews made with wood pigeon (*civet de palombes*) or wild goat (*civet d'isnard*). Heading inland into Périgord, along the Dordogne Valley, you'll find that the cooking becomes richer. Truffles and foie gras lead the way, followed by many types of game, fowl, and mushrooms. The versatile wines of Bordeaux make fine accompaniments to most regional dishes, but don't overlook their less prestigious cousins (Bergerac, Pécharmant, Fiefs Vendéens, Monbazillac, Charentes). Cognac is de rigueur to finish a meal.

CATEGORY	COST*
$$$$	over 400 frs
$$$	250–400 frs
$$	125–250 frs
$	under 125 frs

*per person for a three-course meal, including tax (18.6%) and tip but not wine

Lodging

In summer, France's western coast provides extreme contrasts of crowds and calm. Vacationers flock to La Rochelle, Royan, Arcachon, Biarritz, and the nearby islands of Ré and Oléron, and for miles around, hotels are booked solid months in advance. Farther inland the situation is easier, but note the dearth of hotel accommodations in Bordeaux. Advance booking is recommended here and in Périgord, whose few towns—Sarlat, Périgueux, and Brantôme—fill up quickly in midsummer. Many country or small-town hotels expect you to have at least one dinner there, and, in fact, if they offer a MAP plan (two meals), it will save you money if you stay several nights. Prices off-season (Oct.–May) often drop by as much as 20%.

CATEGORY	COST*
$$$$	over 800 frs
$$$	550–800 frs
$$	300–550 frs
$	under 300 frs

*All prices are for a standard double room for two, including tax (18.6%) and service charge.

Ainhoa

LODGING

Hotel Ohantzea. This classical Basque house, with a beautiful facade, was originally a 17th-century farm. The wood stairways, the original antique furniture, the many paintings by artists who traded them for lodging all make this comfortable space as much of a museum as a hotel. The garden in back is especially delicious; ask for a room with a balcony overlooking this shady retreat. 🖼 *Rue Principale (across from the church), 64250, ☎ 59–29–90–50. 9 rooms with bath. MC, V. Closed Dec. and Jan. $$*

DINING

La Tour des Valois. Of the many small restaurants in the old quarter, this one diagonally across from the market offers a good choice of food from the region. Try one of the veal dishes (*veau de Chalais*)—the one using the local mustard from Jarnac for the sauce is particularly good. Start with the locally made pâté de foie gras and finish with the *duchesses d'Angoulême*. ✕ *7 rue Massillon, ☎ 45–95–91–76. No reservations. Closed Sat. lunch and Sun. MC, V. $*

Angoulême

DINING AND LODGING

Mercure Hotel de France. Set in an old building (part 17th-century), this hotel retains a traditional atmosphere, with lots of wood and stone in evidence. It is extremely well located, on the fringe of the Ville

Haute and across from the covered market. From the garden, there are fine views of the city. The staff is professional and accustomed to English-speaking visitors. Rooms have recently been redecorated in light blues with striped curtains and bedspreads. The restaurant serves solid, unpretentious regional cuisine. ⌖ *1 pl. des Halles, 16000,* ☎ *45–95–47–95,* ℻ *45–92–02–70; in the U.K.,* ☎ *0181/741–3100; in the U.S.,* ☎ *800/637–2873. 90 rooms with bath. Restaurant, bar. AE, DC, V. Restaurant closed Christmas, New Year's, Sun. lunch; Sat. during Sept.–May.* $$

Bergerac

DINING AND LODGING

Bordeaux Hotel. Bergerac has several "three-star" hotels from which to choose. The Bordeaux, one of the better ones, has recently been refurbished with contemporary furnishings. Rooms are neat, with tiled bathrooms en suite; a good one is No. 22, which has slightly more space than the others. The restaurant is above-average—its well-prepared traditional menu of Périgord (145 francs) offers three regional courses, including confit of duck and foie gras. Though guests are not obliged to eat here, who can refuse the marinated salmon in anisette and lime or the pan-fried escalope de foie gras? The owner, M. Maury, speaks fluent English and is usually on hand for giving advice on the area. Rooms facing the garden-courtyard are preferred. ⌖ *38 pl. Gambetta, 24100,* ☎ *53–57–12–83,* ℻ *53–57–72–14. 40 rooms with bath. Restaurant, bar, pool. AE, DC, MC, V. Closed mid-Dec.–Jan.* $$

Biarritz

DINING

Les Platanes. If you recognize the style of cooking here, it's because owner-chef Arnaud Daguin is the son of André Daguin, who placed Gascony cuisine on the map with his restaurant at the Hotel de France in Auch. Arnaud, like his father, takes the country recipes and adapts them to give a lighter touch and bring out the flavors of the produce, whether it be *merlu* (hake) or lamb. Be sure to try his foie gras, which he gets from his hometown in Gers. The decor of the restaurant, in an old Basque town house, is comfortably formal. ✗ *32 av. Beau-Soleil,* ☎ *59–23–13–68. Reservations advised. Jacket and tie. Closed Mon., Tues. lunch. MC, V.* $$

Grill Eugénie. For a more substantial lunch than the pizzas, salads, or crepes you can get many other places in the old part of town, try the Grill Eugénie at the Hotel Florida. It offers three-course meals for 89 francs and four courses for 105, which can include mussels in a dill sauce, crab and avocado salad, trout in white wine, or saddle of lamb. You can sit on the glassed-in veranda and watch the action on the square. The cooking is traditional, if not inspired, and the value is good. ✗ *5 place Ste-Eugénie,* ☎ *59–24–01–76. Reservations accepted. MC, V.* $

DINING AND LODGING

★ **Palais.** This majestic redbrick hotel exudes a stylish, opulent, and aristocratic air. Empress Eugénie, wife of Nápoléon III, left her mark here a century ago. An immense driveway; lawns; and a many-mirrored, semicircular dining room overlooking the sea embody a style and luxury that stop just short of decadence. Chef Jean-Marie Gautier creates deft, innovative fare that takes full advantage of subtle herbs and textures. Informal lunch is served on the terrace facing the curved pool above the Atlantic. In all of France, the Palais has the most spacious hotel rooms. Their high ceilings, foyers for luggage, vast closets, and large bathrooms with separate toilet cabinets permit the bedrooms, already minimally furnished, to be free from clutter and seem even more grand. In 1993, a multi-million dollar refurbishing brought the comfort level back to the luxury expected in a 2,000-franc ocean-view room. ⊞ *1 av. de l'Impératrice, 64200,* ☎ *59–24–09–40. 134 rooms and 20 suites, all with bath. 3 restaurants, 2 bars, pool, sauna. AE, DC, MC, V. Annual winter closing varies. $$$$*

★ **Café de Paris.** This is the most elegant dining room in Biarritz. There is a moderately priced set menu, but most of chef Pierre Laporte's specialties, including grilled duck liver and *ris de veau* (calf's sweetbreads), can be ordered only à la carte, and you will pay handsomely for that privilege. Fish and meats are also available, served with an imaginative nouvelle touch that is now complemented by a renovated, modern decor. The reasonably priced wine list is strong on Bordeaux. Riding on the success of the restaurant are the new, luxurious and vast guest rooms, some with upper levels and all with a view of the sea. ⊞ *5 pl. Bellevue,* ☎ *59–24–19–53,* FAX *59–24–18–20. 18 rooms. Restaurant. Closed Sun. dinner, Mon. except July–Sept., and Nov.–Apr. Reservations required. Jacket and tie. AE, DC, V. $$$*

Miramar. If you can't get into the Palais or prefer less opulence, make for the modern Miramar next door. It has less atmosphere, perhaps, but the service is more informal, and you can enjoy the same sea views. The Miramar, aside from being a comfortable hotel, also has a thalassotherapy center. And in the main dining room polite regard is given to watching the waistband. The dishes, based on original recipes, are adapted to a modern, lighter diet, which indeed keeps the calorie count down, but they still have succulent taste. ⊞ *13 rue Louison-Bobet, 64200,* ☎ *59–41–30–00,* FAX *59–24–77–20. 126 rooms with bath. Restaurant, bar, pool. AE, DC, MC, V. $$$*

Windsor. Built in the 1920s, this hotel is handy for the casino and beach and boasts its own restaurant with a variety of menus that include roast lamb, turbot with grapefruit, and milk-fed baby veal. The guest rooms are modern and cozy. Those with sea views cost about twice as much (750 francs) as those facing the inner courtyard. ⊞ *19 blvd. du Général-de-Gaulle, 64200,* ☎ *59–24–08–52,* FAX *59–24–98–90. 49 rooms with bath. Restaurant. AE, MC, V. Closed mid-Nov.–mid-Mar. $$–$$$*

Bordeaux

DINING

★ **Clavel.** The recently opened sister restaurant to a center-city establishment of the same name adds a good-value gastronomic note to the undistinguished St-Jean *quartier* near the train station. It is one of the few places in town where you can sample claret by the glass, though any number of fruity young Bordeaux are available by the bottle for under 120 francs. The squeaky-clean modern-rustic decor, varied cuisine (including salmon, ravioli stuffed with lobster, duck with orange and chocolate sauces), and true bistro prices make this an excellent choice. ✕ *44 rue Charles-Domercq,* ☎ *56–92–91–52. Reservations advised. MC, V. Closed Sun., Mon. lunch, and second half of July. $$*

★ **Vieux Bordeaux.** This much-acclaimed nouvelle cuisine haunt lies on the fringe of the old town. Chef Michel Bordage concentrates on fresh produce. His menu is therefore short but of high quality, complemented by three set-price menus. His fish dishes are particularly good; try the steamed turbot. The wine is good value, the decor modern, and the ambience lively. ✕ *27 rue Buhan,* ☎ *56–52–94–36. Reservations advised. AE, MC, V. Closed Sat. lunch, Sun., Aug., and 1 wk in Feb. $$*

Ombrière. The friendly Ombrière looks out over one of the finest squares in old Bordeaux; in summer, you can eat outside. The food is pleasant in an unexciting, brasserie sort of way (steak and fries), but for central Bordeaux its set menu is fairly priced, and even a choice à la carte dinner won't seem extravagant. ✕ *14 pl. du Parlement,* ☎ *56–44–82–69. MC, V. Closed Sun., Mon., and Aug.* $

LODGING

Burdigala. Of the three luxury hotels in Bordeaux, this is the only one within walking distance of the center of town and Vieux Bordeaux. The modern (1988) exterior is extremely unappealing, but it is comfortable inside, with a small lounge area and a light, airy restaurant behind. The soundproof rooms are smart and neat, with spacious bathrooms that come with hair dryers, bathrobes, and speakers for the television. Room 416 is especially quiet and has plenty of sunlight from windows that can be safely left open at night. The deluxe rooms have marble bathrooms with whirlpool baths and separate shower stalls that have side water jets. The Jardin du Burdigala restaurant serves haute cuisine in nouvelle style. ☎ *115 rue Georges-Bonnac, 33000,* ☎ *56–90–16–16,* FAX *56–93–15–06. 76 rooms and 7 suites, all with bath. Restaurant, meeting rooms. AE, DC, MC, V.* $$$

Hôtel Sainte Catherine. This very fashionable hotel, in the heart of Vieux Bordeaux, has carved out 83 rooms from a renovated 19th-century building. Service is limited, but the reception staff is helpful and friendly. The compact rooms are neatly decorated with light floral fabrics and cane chairs, giving them a pleasant airiness. Beds are two singles placed together—better for fraternal sleeping than conjugal. Bathrooms, though immaculate, tend to be a trifle small. The dining room serves light nouvelle cuisine beautifully presented in an atmosphere made intimate by its 12th-century vaulted ceilings. Since rue Ste-Catherine is reserved for pedestrians until 8 PM, if you come by car you will need to approach the hotel along the side street, rue de Parlement. ☎ *22 rue du Ste-Catherine, 33000,* ☎ *56–81–95–12,* FAX *56–44–50–51. 83 rooms and 3 suites, all with bath. Restaurant, piano bar. AE, DC, MC, V.* $$$

Royal Médoc. This Bordeaux hotel is admirably situated near the Esplanade des Quinconces in the city center, in a building that dates from 1720. English-speaking guests form the backbone of the foreign clientele, attracted by the elegant, neoclassical architecture and cheerful, efficient service. There is no restaurant. ☎ *5 rue de Sèze, 33000,* ☎ *56–81–72–42,* FAX *56–51–74–98. 45 rooms, many with bath. AE, MC, V.* $$

Hôtel des Quatre Soeurs. This inexpensive gem, between the Grand Théâtre and the city tourist office, offers well-kept rooms of varying sizes and prices. The adjoining café, excellent for coffee and small bites, treats guests to classical music on many afternoons. The charming owner, Mme. Defalque, will help direct you to the best of Bordeaux. ☎ *6 cours du XXX-Juillet, 33000,* ☎ *56–48–16–00,* FAX *54–01–04–28. 35 rooms with bath or shower. Bar, café. MC, V.* $–$$

Brouage

DINING AND LODGING

★ **Brouage.** This cheerful, recently modernized hotel-restaurant on the main street, owned by good-humored M. Boroin, doubles as the village bar, where colorful locals put the world to rights over beer and *pastis.* You'll soon feel like one of the family—and be sure of a top-value meal featuring such regional specialties as oysters, superb mussels, and eel fricassee (with huge chunks of pâté served "while you wait"). Few places in France offer such good value, and it's worth a special detour for its wholesome freshness. Guest rooms are small, but clean with expensive contemporary fabrics, a nice change from the ubiquitous chintz. ☎ *Rue* *de Québec, 17320 Hiers-Brouage, ☎ 46–85–03–06. 8 rooms with bath or shower. Lunch reservations advised. MC, V. $*

Cognac

DINING AND LODGING

★ **Pigeons Blancs.** "White Pigeons," a converted and modernized coaching inn standing in spacious grounds, has been owned by the same family since the 17th century. The welcome is warm, and the hotel is comfortable and intimate. Each room is different; all have their charm. No. 32, a particular favorite, has a gabled ceiling supported by an ancient beam, an extremely comfortable bed, a window and a skylight, and a small bathroom en suite. Though the rooms are charming and reasonable (380 francs), the major draw is chef Jacques Tachet's cuisine, which includes milk-fed lamb with *jus d'ail doux* (sweet garlic), lightly grilled escargots with locally cured ham, chicken with *girolles* mushrooms and *pineau*. He also has a three-course menu of the day (155 francs). ⌨ *110 rue Jules-Brisson (rte de St-Jean Anjou) 16100,* ☎ *45–82–16–36,* 𝔽𝔸𝕏 *45–82–29–29. 6 rooms with bath. Restaurant (MAP offered). AE, DC, MC, V. Closed Sun. dinner and first half of Jan. $$*

Auberge. The two-story Auberge occupies an old building on a quiet street in the heart of Cognac. The emphasis is on bourgeois comfort; the restaurant, decked out in earnest Louis XVI style, sets the tone. Age has taken its toll, however, and you should inspect the room assigned to you before you register. The food has a serious ring to it: copious but unexceptional. ⌨ *13 rue Plumejeau, 16100,* ☎ *45–32–08–70. 27 rooms, 20 with bath. Restaurant. MC, V. Hotel closed Dec. 25–Jan. 1; restaurant closed Sat. $*

Hôtel d'Orleans. This 17th-century building in the center of town and not far from the train station has been turned into a most agreeable small hotel with reasonable rates (120 francs with only a toilet, 250 francs for toilet and bath). The lobby is quite splendid, with a marvelous stairway and wall mosaics. The restaurant, La Brasserie, is popular with locals as a place to hang out for a drink and listen to live music as well as to eat. ⌨ *25 rue d'Angoulême, 16100,* ☎ *45–82–01–26,* 𝔽𝔸𝕏 *45–82–20–33. 23 rooms, some with shower or bath. Restaurant. MC, V. $*

Coly

DINING AND LODGING

Manoir d'Hautegente. An old ivy-covered manor house, in Périgord Noir, 26 kilometers (16 miles) from Sarlat, is the Hamelin family's small hotel. Its pastoral setting has a lily pond, a small stream, sheep in a paddock, and a 13th-century windmill and forge. Inside, simple guest rooms have beige, patterned fabric wallpaper and colorful curtains that match the bedspreads. Impressionist prints complement the provincial antiques. On chilly days, guests gather around a roaring fire in the lounge for aperitifs. The intimate dining room offers regional fare, including homemade foie gras. The chef takes local recipes that can sometimes be heavy and greasy and gives them a balanced lightness. ⌨ *24120 Coly,* ☎ *53–51–68–03,* 𝔽𝔸𝕏 *53–50–38–52. 10 rooms with bath. Restaurant, pool. MC, V. ☉ Easter–mid-Nov. MC, V. $$*

Coulon

DINING AND LODGING

Au Marais. The old village of Coulon is a sound base for exploring the Marais Poitevin, and Au Marais is a delightful waterside inn and restaurant. The pleasant decor is simple, with contemporary photographs, pink tablecloths, and turquoise chairs; the food is light renditions of regional fare, with a set menu for 85 francs and one at 150 francs for greater variety. Try the succulent mussels, which are wonderfully sweet and are served in a light dill sauce, and then, perhaps, the veal chops in a delicate madeira sauce. Alain Merrière masterminds the kitchen, and his wife, Martine, sees to guests' needs in the dining room. Their adjacent small hotel offers plain, clean rooms at reasonable rates. ☎ *48 quai Louis-Tardy, 79510,* ☎ *49–35–90–43,* FAX *49–35–81–98. 11 rooms with bath. MC, V. Closed mid-Nov.–mid-Mar.; restaurant closed Sun. dinner and Mon. $–$$*

Domme
DINING AND LODGING
L'Esplanade. Make sure your room looks over the Dordogne, because it's the expansive view that makes this hotel special. The rooms are small but modern, and the staff English speaking. Salmon and trout top the menu, but dining à la carte can be pricey. ☎ *24250 Domme,* ☎ *53–28–31–41,* FAX *53–28–49–92. 19 rooms with bath or shower. AE, MC, V. Closed mid-Nov.–mid-Feb., Sun. dinner and Mon. out of season. $$*

Eymet
DINING AND LODGING
La Petite Auberge. Visitors to Bergerac and Monbazillac should head a few miles south to Razac d'Eymet (4 kilometers, or 2 miles, east of D933), where an English couple, Guy and Lynne Feltham, have modernized an old country house and made a small hotel full of local character. The neat and cozy rooms have all been newly painted and furnished, but for an extra 100 francs guests are frequently tempted to stay in Room 7, the spacious ground-floor suite with a fireplace in the living room. The cuisine, a light version of Périgord cooking, has been so successful that locals come to dine here for the confit de canard, the foie gras, and the walnut tart. Vegetarian dishes are offered on every menu. Altogether, La Petite Auberge is an excellent base for exploring the Périgord and Dordogne. ☎ *24500 Razac d'Eymet,* ☎ *53–24–69–27,* FAX *53–27–33–55. 9 rooms with bath and 2 service apartments. Dining room, pool. MC, V. Restaurant closed Sun. evening and Mon. $$*

Les Eyzies
DINING AND LODGING
★ **Le Centenaire.** Although its hotel is stylish, modern, comfortable and offers numerous amenities, Le Centenaire is known first and foremost as a restaurant. Roland Mazère, one of the most accomplished chefs in the whole of Périgord, adds flair and imagination to the preparation of local specialties: risotto with truffles, foie gras and scampi, and snails with ravioli and gazpacho. The dining room, with its gold-color stone and wooden beams, retains its local character, too, and commands pleasant views across the countryside. Guest rooms, especially at the lower end of the price scale, while neat and contemporary, are pretty small. ☎ *24620 Les Eyzies-de-Tayac,* ☎ *53–06–97–18,* FAX *53–06–92–41. 21 rooms with bath. Restaurant, pool, sauna, health club. Restaurant reservations advised. Jacket required. MC, V. Closed Tues. lunch and Nov.–Mar. $$$*

Féas
LODGING
In Féas, ask for directions to the Chambres d'Hôtes (bed-and-breakfast) run by Christian and Marie-France Paris, which is a bargain, especially if you're interested in fly-fishing. Christian, a registered guide,

knows every trout in the Barétous by name. ☎ *Chambre d'Hôtes Paris, Féas 64570,* ☎ *59–39–01–10. No credit cards. $*

Larrau

DINING AND LODGING

Hotel Etxemaïté. This country inn is no secret in the Basque country—it's known as one of the Haute Soule's most exquisite spots. The views over the valley and up into the Pyrenean heights are superb; ask for a room that looks southeast. The corner of the dining room seems suspended over the garden, and there are unusual ancient wood cabinets and several examples of the *susulia,* a Basque chair and table designed to allow two people to sit comfortably by the fire. You'll also find excellent Basque cooking here. ☎ *Route D26, Larrau 64560,* ☎ *59–28–61–45,* FAX *59–28–72–71. 16 rooms with bath. Closed Jan. AE, DC, MC, V. $$–$$$*

Monflanquin

DINING AND LODGING

Prince Noir. This 13th-century house in the fortified town of Monflanquin, close to the Château de Biron, offers renovated comfort and regional cuisine (foie gras and confit de canard). The second-floor restaurant has a section for nonsmokers. ☎ *Pl. des Arcades, 47150,* ☎ *53–36–50–25. 9 rooms, 1 suite. MC, V. $$*

Nieuil

DINING AND LODGING

Château de Nieuil. You approach this former hunting lodge, off N141 between Limoges and Angoulême, down an avenue of trees. Ahead you'll see the huge château, with towers on either side and steep-pitched roofs pierced by the slender chimneys that used to heat every room. A grand circular lawn flanked by two ivy-covered stone buildings sits before it, while in the back is a French garden with neat arc-shaped borders. Unfortunately, the reception area is small and lacks a comfortable lounging area. Guests rooms vary: Some have modern traditional furniture and pastel blue fabric; another might have a petit salon or a grand bathroom and garden view. Guests talk in murmurs in the formidable dining room, which has a large stone fireplace with sculpted family crests, polished paneling, and a multifaceted chandelier. It's a pleasant place to enjoy the superb lamb (a regional specialty), the fish soup, or the escalope of milk-fed veal with grapes. The wine list is also impressive, but you will need to search for an affordable bottle. ☎ *16270 Neuil,* ☎ *45–71–36–38,* FAX *45–71–46–45. 15 rooms and 3 suites, all with bath. Restaurant, pool, tennis, fishing, helipad. Closed Nov.–Mar. AE, DC, MC, V. $$$*

Oloron-Sainte-Marie

DINING

Le Biscondau. This establishment serves one of the best *garbures,* a hearty peasant vegetable soup, in Oloron. The view from the Ste-Croix district out over the river, the gave d'Ossau, is at its best from the Biscondau terrace in summer. ✕ *7 rue de la Filature, 64400,* ☎ *59–39–06–15. Closed Mon. DC, MC, V. $$*

Pau

DINING

Gousse d'Ail. Down in the Hédas district, the deep mid-city canyon in the oldest part of Pau, there is a row of restaurants and cafés from which to choose. This lovely hideaway, tucked under the stairway at the end of rue du Hédas on the left, serves traditional Béarn and international cuisine. ✕ *12 rue du Hédas,* ☎ *59–27–31–55. Reservations advised. MC, V. Closed Sun. $$–$$$*

LODGING
Hotel de Gramont. Within sight of the gardens of the castle where Henri IV was born and just above the Hédas restaurant and nightlife area, the Gramont is a convenient and comfortable base camp for exploring Pau. The hotel has no restaurant, but it does offer arrangements with nearby establishments, and it has a pleasant breakfast room. Ask for one of the *chambres mansardés* (dormered bedrooms), up under the eaves. ☎ *3 pl. de Gramont, 64000,* ☎ *59–27–84–04,* FAX *59–27–62–23. 36 rooms with bath. AE, DC, MC, V. $$*

Poitiers
DINING
Maxime. This crowd-pleaser lives up to its famous name, thanks to a wide choice of set menus, the personal recipes of chef Christian Rougier (foie gras and duck salad, for instance), and a pastel-tone decor featuring '30s-style frescoes. The reasonable prix-fixe menus have made this restaurant extremely popular with local businesspeople, so come as soon after noon as you can in order to get a table. ✕ *4 rue St-Nicolas,* ☎ *49–41–09–55. Reservations required. AE, MC, V. Closed Sat., Sun., and much of July and Aug. $$*

LODGING
Europe. An early 19th-century building in the middle of town houses this unpretentious hotel, though some rooms occupy a modern extension. Foreign visitors often stay here, attracted by the traditional decor and competitive prices. Because it is stepped back from the main street, with a forecourt, the rooms are quiet. There is also a pleasant garden in the back for a lazy tea or an evening aperitif. There is no restaurant. ☎ *39 rue Carnot, 86000,* ☎ *49–88–12–00,* FAX *49–88–97–30. 88 rooms with bath or shower. MC, V. $$*

Pons
DINING AND LODGING
★ **Moulin de Marcouze.** You, too, can feast like a brandy baron—if you take the 30-minute drive from Cognac or Saintes to the village of Mosnac (11 kilometers, or 7 miles, south of Pons). Dominique Bouchet (of Tour d'Argent in Paris) has transformed an old mill (complete with stream and waterwheel) into a sophisticated restaurant in a picturesque country setting. The style is understated: spacious layout, original paintings, and food that is innovative but not flashy (sautéed sole fillet or duck pie with truffles). At midday, local drink executives and their clients pile in for power lunches, but if you come for dinner or book one of the guestrooms, you can linger over a peaceful meal. The waiters will gladly steer you to the bargain end of the extensive wine list. ☎ *Rte de St-Georges, 17240 Mosnac,* ☎ *46–70–46–16,* FAX *46–70–48–14. 10 rooms with bath. Restaurant, pool, helipad. Jacket and tie. AE, DC, MC, V. Closed Feb. and Tues. and Wed. lunch out of season. $$–$$$*

La Rochelle
DINING
André. The salty decor is somewhat excessive—fishing nets flutter overhead and posters of ocean liners billow from the walls—but the food and service have such gusto that you'll be caught up in the mood, especially if you order the monumental seafood platter (washed down with white Charentes wine). ✕ *5 rue St-Jean,* ☎ *46–41–28–24. Reservations advised. AE, DC, MC, V. $–$$*

Maître Kanter. There are many of these restaurants throughout France, whose heritage is Alsatian and which serve choucroute and sausages—this one has an excellent shellfish bar. The location on Le Vieux Port (next door to the Hotel Mercure) and the decor of boat models and fishing nets makes chugging a plate of oysters even more pleasant. ✕ *15 Quai Valin,* ☎ *46–41–42–88.* ⊙ *Lunch and dinner. MC, V. $*

DINING AND LODGING

Hotel Mercure. There are two niceties about this member of a national hotel chain: its restaurant and its spot facing the quay of the old port. Chef Layec happily creates an innovative menu from traditional recipes, taking advantage of the abundance of fresh seafood. A good choice would be salmon and mullet tartare, lobsters with mushrooms, or tournedos of tuna with foie gras. The guest rooms, furnished with contemporary fabrics, are generally unremarkable except for those with splendid views of the old port. ☎ *23 quai Valin, 17000,* ☎ *46–41–20–68,* ℻ *46–41–81–24. 47 rooms (46 with bath), 1 suite. Restaurant. AE, DC, MC, V. $$*

★ **33 Thiers.** One would be tempted to stay here just for the welcome and charm of this inn. Actually, it's a private town house owned by the amiable Mme. Iribe, who in addition speaks fluent English, is a gourmet cook, and an enthusiast of the region. With advance notice, she will prepare a splendid dinner made from products bought at the lively market that's held twice weekly a few blocks away. You'll likely eat in the country kitchen and, if you want, pick up some cooking tips while she works. (Mme. Iribe teaches cooking classes.) She also knows the best restaurants in town for when you wish to eat out. The guest rooms are large and wonderfully furnished, expressing the owner's idiosyncrasies. The Mexican Room is gaily decorated with cheerful colors. The Blue Room is also a delight in its cool, refreshing tones. Both are at the back of the house, removed from any street noise. ☎ *33 rue Thiers, 17000,* ☎ *46–41–62–23,* ℻ *46–41–10–76. 8 rooms with bath. Dining room (by reservation). MC, V. $$*

Tour de Nesle. This 19th-century hotel is just around the corner from the quai Valin (the waterfront avenue), ideally placed for exploring the harbor and old town. While the rooms may be a bit cramped, they have recently been refurbished. Ask for a room with a view across the canal toward St-Sauveur church. There is no restaurant or lounge, but a breakfast room for petit déjeuner (Continental). ☎ *2 quai Louis-Durand, 17000,* ☎ *46–41–30–72,* ℻ *46–41–95–17. 28 rooms with shower or bath. MC, V. $$*

La Roque Gageac

DINING AND LODGING

La Plume d'Oie. In this dramatically situated village on the Dordogne is a small inn with neat bedrooms that overlook the river and the limestone cliffs. The rooms, furnished in light fabrics and wicker furniture, vary in size and are priced accordingly (275–380 francs), but all have a bath or shower, hair dryer, minibar, and telephone. La Plume d'Oie's major raison d'être, however, is the pretty beamed and stone-walled restaurant at which all hotel guests are expected to have at least one meal during their stay. Chef Marc-Pierre Walker, owner of the inn and husband of Hiddy, who will greet you on your arrival, prepares a fairly classical cuisine of the region: fillet of beef cooked in red wine and ragout of foie gras. ☎ *24250 La Roque Gageac,* ☎ *53–29–57–05,* ℻ *53–31–04–81. 4 rooms with bath or shower. Restaurant. Closed late Nov.–mid-Dec. and Feb. Restaurant closed Mon. MC, V. $–$$*

St-Emilion

DINING

Chez Germaine. Family cooking and regional dishes are featured at this central St-Emilion eatery. The stylish upstairs dining room, candlelit and adorned with flowers, is a pleasant place in which to enjoy the reasonably priced set menus. Grilled meats and fish are house specialties; for dessert, try the almond macaroons. There's also a terrace for outdoor eating. ✗ *Pl. du Clocher,* ☎ *57–24–70–88. Reservations advised. DC, V. Closed Sun., Mon., and mid-Dec.–mid-Jan. $$*

DINING AND LODGING

Grand Barrail. This turn-of-the-century estate 4 kilometers (2½ miles) northwest of the medieval town, across from the vineyards of Figeac, has been converted into a luxury hotel. All the rooms are smartly furnished with elegant modern fabrics and exposed beams, and they're unusually large for French hotels. Room 20 (in the medium price range) has our vote because of its sweeping view of the vineyards and its superb bathroom, which uses tiles, two types of wood, and mirrors as the setting for the two-person bathtub and separate glass shower stall. Another 16 rooms have been made in the former stables and are similarly furnished. The talented young chef serves traditional regional fare in the small dining room smartly done with yellow linen. St-Emilions constitute at least 60% of the very impressive carte du vin, which lists 350 wines, with only modest markups. ☎ *Rte. de Libourne, 33330,* ☎ *57–55–37–00,* ℻ *57–55–37–49. 28 rooms with bath. Restaurant, pool, wine-tasting. AE, DC, MC, V. $$$*

★ **Hostellerie de Plaisance.** Across from the tourist office in the upper part of this medieval town stands this much sought-after hotel. Its prime location affords marvelous views down on the staggered roofs of the town and the sprawling vineyards. Each of the rooms is furnished differently, but all have a warm appealing style that makes a peaceful haven in this tourist town. The one called Descault has special charm, in part because of its view of the vineyards. Dinner, in the smartly furnished dining room with upholstered chairs and a view of the town, is an occasion to match the excellence of the St-Emilion wines. If you are not staying here, make this your number one choice for a leisurely lunch. ☎ *Pl. du Clocher, 33330 St-Emilion,* ☎ *57–24–72–35,* ℻ *57–74–41–11. 12 rooms with bath. Restaurant. AE, DC, MC, V. Closed Dec., Jan. $$$*

Auberge de la Commanderie. For such a pretty town, St-Emilion is a bit short on accommodations. Luckily, this two-story, 19th-century hotel is admirable in every sense. It is close to the ramparts and has its own garden and views of the vineyards. The rooms are small but clean and individually decorated. The attractive restaurant is often frequented by nonresidents and boasts a good selection of local wines. ☎ *Rue des Cordeliers, 33300,* ☎ *57–24–70–19,* ℻ *57–74–44–53. 15 rooms, most with bath. Restaurant. MC, V. Closed late Dec.–Feb.; restaurant closed Tues. except in July and Aug. $$*

Ste-Engrâce

DINING AND LODGING

Auberge Elichalt. This cozy hikers' inn has 50 beds in varying condition, all good. There are five double rooms, 40 dormitory beds and apartments for rent, all in the shadow of the 11th-century church of Ste-Engrâce. M. and Mme. Burguburu ("town's end" in Basque) can recommend hikes into the mountains and other activities in the Haute Soule. ☎ *Ste-Engrâce 64560,* ☎ *59–28–61–63. 5 double rooms, 40 dormitory beds and apartments for rent. No credit cards. $*

St-Jean-de-Luz

DINING AND LODGING

Grand. This hotel is in the process of renovating its rooms, and when the work is completed, in late 1995, they should be very welcoming. Many of them have magnificent views of the beach and bay. Dining at its gourmet restaurant, La Coupole, is already a treat. The semicircular dining room with a panoramic view of the bay sets off the creative cuisine of Patrice Demangel, who uses the regional specialties to their best advantage: Confit of lobster, baby lamb from the Pyrénées with three sauces, and a luscious dessert of three chocolate flowers in a vanilla sauce are just part of his repertoire, which is not to be missed. ⌂ *43 blvd. Thiers, 64500,* ☎ *59–26–35–36,* Ⅲ *59–51–19–91. 43 rooms, 3 suites, all with bath. Restaurant. AE, DC, MC, V. $$–$$$*

Saintes

DINING AND LODGING

Relais du Bois. Many hotels claim that each of their guest rooms is different, though they vary only slightly, but the Relais du Bois's rooms are vastly distinct. Some are paneled, some are not; some have contemporary furnishings, some are traditional; some are miniduplexes with loft beds, some are designed with fold-down beds—one is named Count de Montecristo's Prison Cell. On the other hand, the Tower is for romantics, the Igloo is for honeymooners (perhaps), and the Chalet du Lac is for relaxed lounging. Many rooms have separate sitting areas with libraries, and some of the bathrooms have whirlpools. The hotel is unique in giving staff members input in the decorating of the rooms and the running of the hotel. The result is enthusiastic service by a staff that takes real pride in the job. The restaurant looks out over the gardens and a lake—the home of a couple of swans. The menu's specialties of the Charente region and seafood from the Atlantic become eye-catching, ambitious creations at the hands of chef Jérôme Emery. ⌂ *Rue de Royan, Cours Genet, 17100 Saintes,* ☎ *46–93–50–99,* Ⅲ *46–93–34–93. 27 rooms, 3 suites. Restaurant, bar, indoor pool, croquet, boules, tennis, meeting rooms. MC, V. $$$*

St-Jean-Pied-de-Port

DINING AND LODGING

Ramuntxo. Just inside the town walls through the Porte de France, the hotel overlooks a garden with a turretlike tower that time has transformed into an objet d'art. Ask for a room facing the garden. Ramuntxo also serves excellent Basque cuisine: Try the *ris de veau aux petits légumes* (sweetbreads with young vegetables). ⌂ *1 rue de France, 64220.* ☎ *59–37–03–91,* Ⅲ *59–37–35–17. 17 rooms with bath. Closed Nov. 20–Dec. 20. AE, DC, MC, V. $$*

Les Pyrénées. Known as the best restaurant in town, Les Pyrénées specializes in Basque cuisine with a definite nouvelle or contemporary gourmet tendency. Try the raviolis and prawns with caviar sauce or the hot wild-mushroom terrine. ⌂ *19 pl. du Général-de-Gaulle, 64220,* ☎ *59–37–01–01,* Ⅲ *59–37–19–97. 18 rooms and 2 apartments. Closed Jan. 5–25 and Nov. 20–Dec. 20. AE, DC, MC, V. $$$*

Sarlat

DINING AND LODGING

★ **Hotels St-Albert et Montaigne.** The Garrigou family has two hotels on a delightful square in the center of Sarlat. The entirely renovated Montaigne reincarnated a former manor house. Freshly decorated guest rooms have double-glazed windows to silence street noise and neatly tiled bathrooms. Room 33 with exposed beams is especially charming. The St-Albert offers another 31 rooms of varying sizes, all simply furnished with basic comforts. Bathrooms have either a shower or bath. The dining room for both hotels is in the St-Albert, where wholesome and hearty regional fare is on hand at very reasonable prices. Enjoy the three complimentary pâtés and a local aperitif as you look over the menu. The confit is very traditional and worth trying, especially when accompanied by a young Bergerac. Over dinner, discuss your next day's itinerary with M. Garrigou—Not only does he know the region well, but he is also the town's backroom politician and chairman of the rugby club. ⊞ *10 pl. Pasteur, 24200 Sarlat,* ☎ *53–31–55–55,* 𝔽𝔸𝕏 *53–59–19–99. 56 rooms, 6 suites, all with bath or shower. Restaurant (closed Sun. dinner and Mon. Nov.–mid-Apr.). AE, MC, V. $–$$*

Souillac

DINING AND LODGING

Château de la Treyne. This small château hotel outside Souillac (40 kilometers, or 25 miles, east of Sarlat) serenely guards the Dordogne River, as it has since the 14th century. Dinner is served in a delightful paneled room with old portraits on the walls and a log fire in the spring and autumn. A cozy bar for afternoon tea or mulling over an after-dinner brandy has been added. Spacious bedrooms are traditionally furnished with 19th-century paintings and country antiques. Ask for one that overlooks the river. Prices have escalated in the past year or two as Mme. Gombert-Devals, the owner, becomes less the hostess and more the hotelier, adding a professional director to her staff and joining the Relais & Châteaux chain. Nevertheless, though the Château de la Treyne has lost some of its personality and intimacy, it still has fairy-tale qualities. During high season, guests are expected to dine at the hotel. ⊞ *Lacave, 46200,* ☎ *65–32–66–66,* 𝔽𝔸𝕏 *65–37–06–57. 14 rooms with bath. Restaurant, pool, sauna, tennis. Closed mid-Nov.–Easter. MC, V. $$$–$$$$*

Tremolat

DINING AND LODGING

★ **Le Vieux Logis.** This member of the Relais & Châteaux group ranks close to the top in the contest for best hotel in the Dordogne. The rambling old stone house at the edge of the charming village has warmly decorated rooms, most of which face the well-tended garden and a rushing brook. The pool at the far end of the garden is a good place to spend a day off from touring. Guest rooms are romantic, varying in size and decor. One favorite is No. 22, on the ground floor facing the garden. The floor is polished terra-cotta tiles, the curtains are patterned with cheerful red prints, the ceiling has exposed beams, three walls are deep rose pink, and the fourth is stone. The modern brass double bed, high off the floor, has a firm, comfortable mattress and lighting is subdued. The bathroom is like a suite, with the toilet in a separate room; terry-cloth robes and a warming towel rack are nice extras. Dinner is an occasion. Start with an aperitif before the fire in a small lounge and then move to the dining room. Le Menu Vieux Logis (230 francs), the mid-priced prix-fixe dinner, comprises five courses. The hors d'oeuvres are the chef's forte—an interesting and complex pigeon terrine and the salad with veal knuckles are two delicious ways to start the dinner. Also try the duck sautéed with olives, grilled leg of lamb, or the peppered fish fillet with tomatoes and potatoes crushed with olive oil. ⊞ *24510 Tremolat,* ☎ *53–22–80–06,* 𝔽𝔸𝕏 *53–22–84–89. 19 rooms and 3 suites, all with bath. Restaurant (closed Tues. mid-Jan.–May), pool. Closed mid-Jan.–Mar. AE, DC, MC, V. $$$–$$$$*

Vieux Mareuil

DINING AND LODGING

Château de Vieux Mareuil. Off the road between Angoulême and Perigueux, just north of Brantôme, there is a well-executed modern manor built on the foundations of an ancient farmhouse. Most of the guest rooms in the attractive courtyard-style building are modern, furnished with good taste in pastels, with spacious bathrooms and small terraces. A couple of guest rooms in the old part of the building are distinctly special—the most noteworthy is named Tour 1. High ceilings and thick stone walls give it a feeling of permanence, and exposed beams and rich carpets give warmth. Dinner is well prepared, nouvelle rather than classical. A safe and delicious choice is the warm *cabecon* (local goat cheese) salad and the navarin of lamb, with a bottle of Domaine des Bertranoux 1988. There are two dining rooms, both small and intimate enough for enforced listening to other diners' conversations! The surrounding gardens and park ensure the quietness of this hotel and offer the opportunity for a wander through the woods before dinner. ☎ *Rte. d'Angoulême-Perigueux, Vieux Mareuil,* ☎ *53–60–77–15,* FAX *53–56–49–33. 14 rooms, 2 suites, all with bath. Restaurant, pool. Closed Sept.–Apr. MC, V. $$$*

THE ARTS AND NIGHTLIFE

The Arts

The major festival activities in this ocean-bordered region are inspired by the sea. "Fêtes de la Mer"—sometimes including carnival parades—are frequent, with the biggest at **La Rochelle** at Pentecost, **Royan** in late June, and **Arcachon** in mid-August. Drama and music combine to make up the **Festival International de l'Entre-Deux-Mers** (for information, call 56–71–51–35). A Bande Dessinée (comic book) festival takes place in **Angoulême** in January, and there's a Crime Film festival in **Cognac** each September. The music and arts **Festival de Pau** offers events almost every evening, nearly all of them gratis, mid-July–August 20.

Theater

The region's principal theaters—inevitably devoted to works in the French language—are at **Poitiers** (1 pl. du Maréchal-Leclerc, ☎ 49–41–28–33) and **Bordeaux** (Grand Théâtre, pl. de la Comédie, ☎ 56–90–91–60).

Concerts

Bordeaux's International Musical May is a leading event on France's cultural calendar. Smaller summer festivals are held at **Saintes** (the **Festival de la Musique Ancienne,** early July) and **Arcachon** (the **International Guitar Festival** in July). Modern music gets a week-long airing at **La Rochelle's Franco-Folies** festival in July.

Opera

There are occasional operatic performances at the **Grand Théâtre** in **Bordeaux** (*see above*).

Nightlife

Bars and Nightclubs

Try **L'Aztécal** (61 rue du Pas-St-Georges) or **Cabaret Andalucia** (7 quai Bacalan) in Bordeaux. **Le Vaudeville** (13 quai de la République) in Saintes has a homey English atmosphere and a tongue-tingling array of old whiskies. Bars, cafés, and clubs come and go in Biarritz. A comfortable hangout both day and night is the small **Le Queen's Bar** (25 pl. Clémenceau, ☎ 59–24–70–65). The young at heart gather here in the evening and the un-shy take the mike to sing to the karaoke videos.

Jazz Clubs

Les Argentiers (7 rue Teulère) is a respected and long-established Bordeaux hangout.

Rock Clubs

A late-night venue for raunchy music, complete with videos, is **Le Chat-Bleu** in Bordeaux (122 quai Bacalan).

Discos

In Bordeaux, try **Sénéchal** (57 bis quai de Paludate); in Arcachon, **Cyclone** (177 blvd. de la Plage) or **Cotton Club** (4 blvd. Mestrezat); in Niort, **Le Niagara** (469 av. de Limoges) or **Club St-Gelais** (43 rue St-Gelais); in Sarlat, **Le Bas Roc** (av. de la Dordogne); in Cognac, **New Orleans** (2 impasse du Moulin); and in Poitiers, **Black House** (195 av. du 8-mai-1945) or the split-level **La Grand' goule** (46 rue du Pigeon-Blanc).

Casinos

There are casinos in **Biarritz, Royan,** and **Arcachon** and on the island of **Oléron** (Le Château).

ATLANTIC COAST ESSENTIALS

Getting There and Getting Around

By Plane

There are frequent daily flights from Paris and weekly flights from London to Bordeaux and Biarritz and a purely domestic airport at Limoges. You can also fly daily to Pau on Air Inter (☎ 59–33–21–29).

By Car

As the capital of southwest France, Bordeaux boasts superb transport links with Paris, Spain, and even the Mediterranean (A62 expressway via Toulouse). The A10 Paris–Bordeaux expressway passes close to Poitiers, Niort (exit 23 for La Rochelle), and Saintes before continuing toward Spain as A63. The fast N137 connects La Rochelle with Saintes via Rochefort; Angoulême is linked to Bordeaux and Poitiers by the rapid N10; and D936 runs along the Dordogne Valley to Bergerac.

By Train

The new superfast TGV Atlantique service linking Paris (Gare Montparnasse) to Bordeaux—584 kilometers (365 miles) in three hours—stops at Poitiers (change for Niort, La Rochelle, and Rochefort) and Angoulême (change for Jarnac, Cognac, and Saintes). Trains run regularly from Bordeaux to Bergerac (80-minute journey), with occasional stops at St-Emilion, and, three times daily, to Sarlat (nearly three hours). The TGV covers the 800 kilometers (500 miles) from Paris to Biarritz in 4¾–5¼ hours.

Guided Tours

Bus Excursions

Horizons Européens (France Tourisme, 3 rue d'Alger, 75001 Paris, ☎ 42–60–31–25) organizes a seven-day bus tour of Dordogne and Périgord, leaving from Paris and taking in Limoges, castles, wine tastings, and grottoes; the cost is about 4,000 francs inclusive.

Boat Trips

You can tour the canal-crossed Marais Poitevin area by boat, starting at the **Abbey of Maillezais** or at Coulon, from Easter through October, for a cost of 70–90 francs per boat.

To get a feel for the historic port of **Bordeaux,** the region's largest city, take the 90-minute boat tour that leaves weekdays from the Embarcadères des Quinconces at around 3; the cost is about 50 francs.

Special-Interest

Tours of the pretty St-Emilion vineyard (including wine tastings) are organized by the **St-Emilion tourist office** (pl. du Clocher, ☎ 57–24–72–03). Tours last two hours and depart weekdays during summer months from the tourist office at 2 and 4:15; the cost is 55 francs.

Important Addresses and Numbers

Travel Agencies

American Express (14 cours de l'Intendance, Bordeaux, ☎ 56–81–70–02) and **Wagons-Lits** (43 rue Porte-Dijeaux, ☎ 56–52–92–70).

Car Rental

Avis (59 rue Peyronnet, Bordeaux, ☎ 56–92–69–38; 133 blvd. du Grand-Cerf, Poitiers, ☎ 49–58–13–00; and 166 blvd. Joffre, La Rochelle, ☎ 46–41–13–55). **Hertz** (pl. de la Gare, Bergerac, ☎ 53–57–19–27; and 107 blvd. du Grand-Cerf, Poitiers, ☎ 49–58–24–24).

Visitor Information

Suggestions about wine tours and tastings, as well as information on local and regional sights, are available at the **Bordeaux Office de Tourisme,** which also provides a round-the-clock answering service in English (12 cours du XXX-Juillet, ☎ 56–44–28–41).

The addresses of other tourist offices in towns mentioned on this tour are as follows: **Angoulême** (2 pl. St-Pierre, ☎ 45–95–16–84), **Bergerac** (97 rue Neuve d'Argenson, ☎ 53–57–03–11), **Biarritz** (1 sq. Ixelles, ☎ 59–24–20–24), **Cognac** (16 rue du XIV-Juillet, ☎ 45–82–10–71), **Niort** (rue Ernest-Pérochon, ☎ 49–24–18–79), **Pau** (pl. Royale, ☎ 59–27–27–08), **Poitiers** (15 rue Carnot, ☎ 49–41–58–22), **La Rochelle** (pl. de la Petite-Sirène, ☎ 46–41–14–68), **St-Emilion** (pl. du Clocher, ☎ 57–24–72–03), **St-Jean de Luz** (pl. Foch, ☎ 59–26–03–16), **St-Jean-Pied-de-Port** (14 pl. Charles-de-Gaulle, ☎ 59–37–03–57), **Saintes** (62 cours National, ☎ 46–74–23–82), and **Sarlat** (pl. de la Liberté, ☎ 53–59–27–67).

17 Portraits of France

FRANCE AT A GLANCE: A CHRONOLOGY

ca 3500 BC   Megalithic stone complexes erected at Carnac, Brittany

ca 1500 BC   Lascaux cave paintings executed (Dordogne, southwest France)

ca 600 BC   Greek colonists found Marseille

after 500 BC   Celts appear in France

58–51 BC   Julius Caesar conquers Gaul; writes up the war in *De Bello Gallico*

52 BC   Lutetia, later to become Paris, is built by the Gallo-Romans

46 BC   Roman amphitheater built at Arles

14 BC   The Pont du Gard, the aqueduct at Nîmes, is erected

AD 406   Invasion by the Vandals (Germanic tribes)

451   Attila invades and is defeated at Châlons

The Merovingian Dynasty

486–511   Clovis, king of the Franks (481–511), defeats the Roman governor of Gaul and founds the Merovingian Dynasty. Great monasteries, such as those at Tours, Limoges, and Chartres, become centers of culture

497   Franks converted to Christianity

567   The Frankish kingdom is divided into three parts—the eastern countries (Austrasia), later to become Belgium and Germany; the western countries (Neustria), later to become France; and Burgundy

The Carolingian Dynasty

768–778   Charlemagne (768–814) becomes king of the Franks (768); conquers northern Italy (774); and is defeated by the Moors at Roncesvalles in Spain, after which he consolidates the Pyrénées border (778)

800   The pope crowns Charlemagne Holy Roman Emperor in Rome. Charlemagne expands the kingdom of France far beyond its present borders and establishes a center for learning at his capital, Aix-la-Chapelle (Aachen, in present-day Germany)

814–987   Death of Charlemagne. The Carolingian line continues through a dozen or so monarchs, with a batch called Charles (the Bald, the Fat, the Simple) and a sprinkling of Louises. Under the Treaty of Verdun (843), the empire is divided in two—the eastern half becoming Germany, the western half France

The Capetian Dynasty

987   Hugh Capet (987–996) is elected king of France and establishes the principle of hereditary rule for his descendants. Settled conditions and the increased power of the Church see the flowering of the Romanesque style of architecture in the cathedrals of Autun and Angoulême

1066   Norman conquest of England by William the Conqueror (1028–87)

1067   Work begins on the Bayeux Tapestry, the Romanesque work of art celebrating the Norman Conquest

ca 1100	First universities in Europe include Paris. Development of European vernacular verse: *Chanson de Roland*
1140	The Gothic style of architecture first appears at St-Denis and later becomes fully developed at the cathedrals of Chartres, Reims, Amiens, and Notre-Dame in Paris
ca 1150	Struggle between the Anglo-Norman kings (Angevin Empire) and the French; when Eleanor of Aquitaine switches husbands (from Louis VII of France to Henry II of England), her extensive lands pass to English rule
1257	The Sorbonne university is founded in Paris
1270	Louis IX (1226–70), the only French king to achieve sainthood, dies in Tunis on the seventh and last Crusade
1302–07	Philippe IV (1285–1314), the Fair, calls together the first States-General, predecessor to the French Parliament. He disbands the Knights Templars to gain their wealth (1307)
1309	Pope escapes from a corrupt and disorderly Rome to Avignon in southern France, seat of the papacy for nearly 70 years

The Valois Dynasty

1337–1453	Hundred Years' War between France and England: fighting for control of those areas of France gained by the English crown following the marriage of Eleanor of Aquitaine and Henry II
1348–1350	The Black Death rages in France
1428–31	Joan of Arc (1412–31), the Maid of Orléans, sparks the revival of French fortunes in the Hundred Years' War but is captured by the English and burned at the stake at Rouen
1434	Johannes Gutenberg invents the printing press in Strasbourg, Alsace
1453	France finally defeats England, terminating the Hundred Years' War and English claims to the French throne
1475	Burgundy at the height of its power under Charles the Bold
1494	Italian wars: beginning of Franco-Habsburg struggle for hegemony in Europe
1515–47	Reign of François I, who imports Italian artists, including Leonardo da Vinci (1452–1519), and brings the Renaissance to France. The château of Fontainebleau is begun (1528)
1558	France captures Calais, England's last territory on French soil
1562–98	Wars of Religion (Catholics versus Protestants/Huguenots)

The Bourbon Dynasty

1589	The first Bourbon king, Henri IV (1589–1610), is a Protestant who converts to Catholicism and achieves peace in France. He signs the Edict of Nantes, giving limited freedom of worship to Protestants. The development of Renaissance Paris begins
ca 1610	Scientific revolution in Europe begins, marked by the discoveries of mathematician and philosopher René Descartes (1596–1650)
1643–1715	Reign of Louis XIV, the Sun King, a monarch who builds the Baroque power base of Versailles and presents Europe with a

glorious view of France. With his first minister, Colbert, Louis makes France, by force of arms, the most powerful nation-state in Europe. He persecutes the Huguenots, who emigrate in great numbers, nearly ruining the French economy

1660   Classical period of French culture: writers Molière (1622–73), Jean Racine (1639–99), Pierre Corneille (1606–84), and painter Nicolas Poussin (1594–1665)

ca 1715   Rococo art and decoration develop in Parisian boudoirs and salons, typified by the painter Antoine Watteau (1684–1721) and, later, François Boucher (1703–70) and Jean-Honoré Fragonard (1732–1806)

1700 onward   Writer and pedagogue Voltaire (1694–1778) is a central figure in the French Enlightenment, along with Jean-Jacques Rousseau (1712–78) and Denis Diderot (1713–84), who, in 1751, compiles the first modern encyclopedia. The ideals of the Enlightenment—for reason and scientific method and against social and political injustices—pave the way for the French Revolution. In the arts, painter Jacques-Louis David (1748–1825) reinforces revolutionary creeds in his neo-classical works

1756–63   The Seven Years' War results in France's losing most of her overseas possessions and England's becoming a world power

1776   The French assist in the American War of Independence. Ideals of liberty cross the Atlantic with the returning troops to reinforce new social concepts

The French Revolution

1789–1804   The Bastille is stormed on July 14, 1789. Following upon early Republican ideals comes the Terror and the administration of the Directory under Robespierre. There are widespread political executions—Louis XVI and Marie Antoinette are guillotined in 1793. Reaction sets in, and the instigators of the Terror are themselves executed (1794). Napoléon Bonaparte enters the scene as the champion of the Directory (1795–99) and is installed as First Consul during the Consulate (1799–1804)

The First Empire

1804   Napoléon crowns himself emperor of France at Notre-Dame in the presence of the pope

1805–12   Napoléon conquers most of Europe. The Napoléonic Age is marked by a neoclassical style in the arts, called Empire, as well as by the rise of Romanticism—characterized by such writers as Chateaubriand (1768–1848) and Stendhal (1783–1842), and the painters Eugène Delacroix (1798–1863) and Théodore Géricault (1791–1824)—which is to dominate the arts of the 19th century

1812–14   Winter cold and Russian determination defeat Napoléon outside Moscow. The emperor abdicates and is transported to Elba

Restoration of the Bourbons

1814–15   Louis XVIII, brother of the executed Louis XVI, regains the throne after the Congress of Vienna settles peace terms

1815 The Hundred Days: Napoléon returns from Elba and musters an army on his march to the capital, but lacks national support. He is defeated at Waterloo (June 18) and exiled to the island of St. Helena in the South Atlantic

1821 Napoléon dies in exile

1830 Bourbon king Charles X, locked into a prerevolutionary state of mind, abdicates. A brief upheaval (Three Glorious Days) brings Louis-Philippe, the Citizen King, to the throne

1840 Napoléon's remains are brought back to Paris

1846–48 Severe industrial and farming depression contributes to Louis-Philippe's abdication (1848)

Second Republic and Second Empire

1848–52 Louis-Napoléon (nephew and step-grandson of Napoléon I) is elected president of the short-lived Second Republic. He makes a successful attempt to assume supreme power and is declared emperor of France, taking the title Napoléon III

ca 1850 The ensuing period is characterized in the arts by the emergence of realist painters—Jean-François Millet (1814–75), Honoré Daumier (1808–79), Gustave Courbet (1819–77)—and late-Romantic writers—Victor Hugo (1802–85), Honoré de Balzac (1799–1850), and Charles Baudelaire (1821–87)

1863 Napoléon III inaugurates the Salon des Refusés in response to critical opinion. It includes work by Edouard Manet (1832–83), Claude Monet (1840–1926), and Paul Cézanne (1839–1906) and is commonly regarded as the birthplace of Impressionism and of modern art in general

The Third Republic

1870–71 The Franco-Prussian War sees Paris besieged, and Paris falls to the Germans. Napoléon III takes refuge in England. France loses Alsace and Lorraine to Prussia before the peace treaty is signed

1871–1914 Before World War I, France expands her industries and builds up a vast colonial empire in North Africa and Southeast Asia. Sculptor Auguste Rodin (1840–1917), musicians Maurice Ravel (1875–1937) and Claude Debussy (1862–1918), and writers such as Stéphane Mallarmé (1842–98) and Paul Verlaine (1844–96) set the stage for Modernism

1874 Emergence of the Impressionist school of painting: Claude Monet (1840–1926), Pierre Auguste Renoir (1841–1919), and Edgar Degas (1834–1917)

1889 The Eiffel Tower is built for the Paris World Exhibition. Centennial of the French Revolution

1894–1906 Franco-Russian alliance (1894). Dreyfus affair: The spy trial and its anti-Semitic backlash shock France

1904 The Entente Cordiale: England and France become firm allies

1914–18 During World War I, France fights with the Allies, opposing Germany, Austria-Hungary, and Turkey. Germany invades France; most of the big battles (Vimy Ridge, Verdun, Somme, Marne) are fought in trenches in northern France. French casualties exceed 5

million. With the Treaty of Versailles (1919), France regains Alsace and Lorraine and attempts to exact financial and economic reparations from Germany

1918–39 Between wars, Paris attracts artists and writers, including Americans—Ernest Hemingway (1899–1961) and Gertrude Stein (1874–1946). France nourishes major artistic and philosophical movements: Constructivism, Dadaism, Surrealism, and Existentialism

1939–45 At the beginning of World War II, France fights with the Allies until invaded and defeated by Germany in 1940. The French government, under Marshal Pétain (1856–1951), moves to Vichy and cooperates with the Nazis. French overseas colonies split between allegiance to the legal government of Vichy and declaration for the Free French Resistance, led (from London) by General Charles de Gaulle (1890–1970)

1944 D-Day, June 6: The Allies land on the beaches of Normandy and successfully invade France. Additional Allied forces land in Provence. Paris is liberated in August 1944, and France declares full allegiance to the Allies

1944–46 A provisional government takes power under General de Gaulle; American aid assists French recovery

The Fourth Republic

1946 France adopts a new constitution; French women gain the right to vote

1946–54 In the Indochinese War, France is unable to regain control of her colonies in Southeast Asia. The 1954 Geneva Agreement establishes two governments in Vietnam: one in the north, under the Communist leader Ho Chi Minh, and one in the south, under the emperor Bao Dai. U.S. involvement eventually leads to French withdrawal

1954–62 The Algerian Revolution achieves Algeria's independence from France. Other French African colonies gain independence

1957 The Treaty of Rome establishes the European Economic Community (now known as the European Union—EU)

The Fifth Republic

1958–68 De Gaulle is the first president under a new constitution; he resigns in 1968 after widespread disturbances begun by student riots in Paris

1976 The first supersonic transatlantic passenger service begins with the Anglo-French Concorde

1981 François Mitterrand is elected the first Socialist president of France since World War II

1988 Mitterrand is elected for a second term

1990 TGV train clocks a world record—515 kph (322 mph)—on a practice run. Channel Tunnel link-up between France and England begun

1993 After nine years of painstaking renovations by I.M. Pei, American-Chinese architect, the Richelieu Wing of the Louvre is opened to the public, doubling the museum's exhibition space.

1995 Jacques Chirac, mayor of Paris, is elected president.

THE ART OF FRENCH COOKING

By Anne Willan

Anne Willan is president and founder of the
Ecole de Cuisine La Varenne in Paris. Her food
column in the *Washington Post* is widely
syndicated and her books include *French
Regional Cooking* and *La Varenne's Cooking
Course.*

BORN BRITISH, naturalized
American, I am an unabashed
chauvinist about French food.
To wander through a French open market, the vegetables overflowing from their
crates, the fruits cascading in casual heaps
on the counter, is a sensual pleasure. To
linger outside a bakery in the early morning, watching the fresh breads and croissants being lined up in regimental rows,
must awaken the most fickle appetite. Just
to read the menu posted outside a modest café alerts the imagination to pleasures to come.

Best of all, the French are happy to share
their enthusiasm for good food with others. There are more good restaurants and
eating places in France than in any other
European country; the streets are lined
with delicatessens, butchers, cheese shops,
bakeries, and pastry shops. And I have yet
to find a Frenchman, cantankerous though
he may be, who does not warm to anyone
who shows an interest in his national passion for wines and fine cuisine.

Fine cuisine does not necessarily mean
fancy cuisine. Masters though French chefs
are of the soufflé and the butter sauce, the
salmon in aspic, and the strawberry *feuilleté,* such delicacies are reserved for celebration. Everyday fare is much more likely
to be roast chicken, steak and *frites,* omelet,
or pork chop. Bread, eaten without butter, is mandatory at main meals, while the
bottle of mineral water is almost as common as wine.

Where the French do score is in the variety and quality of their ingredients. Part
of the credit must go to climate and geography—just look at the length of the
French coastline and the part seafood
plays in the cooking of Normandy, Brit-

tany, and Provence. Count the number of
rivers with fertile valleys for cattle and
crops. Olives and fruit flourish in the
Mediterranean sun, while the region from
southwest of Paris running up north to the
Belgian border is one of the great bread-
baskets of Europe.

No one but the French identifies three
basic styles of cuisine—classical, nouvelle,
and regional—not to mention such off-
shoots as diet cooking (*cuisine minceur*)
and women's cooking (*cuisine de femme*).
No other European nation pays so much
attention to menus and recipes.

Most sophisticated are the sauces and
soufflés, the *mousselines* and *macédoines*
of classical cuisine. Starting in the 17th century, successive generations of chefs have
lovingly documented their dishes, devel-
oping an intellectual discipline from what
is an essentially practical art. As a style,
classical cuisine is now outmoded, but its
techniques form the basis of rigorous professional training in French cooking. In
some measure, all other styles of cooking
are based on its principles.

Nouvelle cuisine, for instance, is directly
descended from the classics. Launched
with great fanfare about 20 years ago, it
takes a fresh, lighter approach, with simpler sauces and a colorful, almost oriental view of presentation. First-course salads,
often with hot additions of shellfish,
chicken liver, or bacon, have become routine. For a while, cooks experimented with
such way-out combinations as vanilla with
lobster and chicken with raspberries, but
now new-style cooking has settled down,
establishing its own classics. Typical are *ma-
grets de canard* (boned duck breast) sautéed
like steak and served with a brown sauce
of wine or green peppercorns; pot-au-feu
made of fish rather than the usual beef; and
quiches made with vegetables like spinach
and zucchini.

Nouvelle cuisine has swept French restaurants, with somewhat mixed results. When
scouting out a place to dine, be wary of
such flowery adjectives as "fresh-culled"
and avoid willfully odd combinations,

such as scallops with mango and saffron. The shorter the menu, the more likely the dishes are to be fresh.

COOKS HAVE recently made a refreshing return toward the third, grass-roots style of French cooking, that of the countryside. Indeed, many cooks never left it, for classical and nouvelle cuisines are almost exclusively the concern of professionals and are dominated by men. However, regional dishes are cooked by everyone—chefs, housewives, grandma, and the café on the corner. Here women come into their own, for the best country cooking has an earthy warmth that the French prize as typical of *cuisine de femme*.

The city of Lyon exemplifies the best of regional cuisine. Restaurants are often run by women known as *mères* (mothers) and feature such local specialties as poached eggs in *meurette* (red-wine sauce), *quenelles* (fish dumplings) in crayfish sauce, sausage with pistachios, and chocolate *gâteau* (cake). The Lyonnais hotly dispute Paris's title of gastronomic capital of France, pointing to the cluster of restaurants surrounding their city that have received the prestigious Michelin stars for excellence. What is more, some of the world's finest wines are produced only 90 miles north, in Burgundy. Certainly, the Lyonnais cooking style is different from that of Paris, less refined and more robust.

Lyon may represent the best of French regional cooking, but there's plenty to look for elsewhere. Compare the sole of Normandy, cooked with mussels in cream sauce, with the sea bass of Provence, flamed with dried fennel or baked with tomatoes and thyme. Contrast the butter cakes of Brittany with the yeast breads of Alsace, the braised endive of Picardy with the gratin of cardoons (a type of artichoke) found in the south.

Authentic regional specialties are based on local products. They have a character that may depend on climate (cream cakes survive in Normandy but not in Provence) or geography (each mountain area has its own dried sausages and hams). History brought spice bread to Dijon, legacy of the days when the dukes of Burgundy controlled Flanders and the spice trade. Ethnic heritage explains ravioli around Nice on the Italian border, waffles in the north near Belgium, and dumplings close to Germany. Modern ethnic influences show up in cities, with many an Arab pastry shop started by Algerian immigrants and many a restaurant run by Vietnamese.

Fundamental to French existence is the baker, the *boulanger*. From medieval times, legislation has governed the weight and content of loaves of bread, with stringent penalties for such crimes as adulteration with sand or sawdust. Today the government pegs the price of white bread, and you'll find the famous long loaves a bargain compared with the price of brioche, croissants, or loaves of whole wheat (*pain complet*), rye (*pain de seigle*), and bran (*pain de son*). White bread can be bought as thin *flûtes* to slice for soup; as *baguettes;* or as the common, thicker loaves known simply as *pains*.

SINCE FRENCH BREAD STAYS fresh for only a few hours, it is baked in the morning for midday and baked again in the afternoon. A baker's day starts at 4 AM to give the dough time to rise. Sadly, there is a lack of recruits, so more and more French bread is being produced industrially, without the right nutty flavor and chew to the crisp crust. The clue to bread baked on the spot is the heady smell of fermenting yeast, so sniff out a neighborhood bakery before you buy.

If bread is the staff of French life, pastry is the sugar icing. The window of a city pastry shop (in the country, bakery and pastry shop are often combined) is a wonderland of éclairs and meringues, madeleines, petits fours, tartlets and puff pastry, spun sugar, and caramel. You'll find pies laden with seasonal fruit, pound cakes, nut cakes, and chocolate cakes, plus the baker's specialty, for he is certain to have one. Survey them with a sharp eye; they should be small (good ingredients are expensive) and impeccably alike in color and size (the sign of an expert craftsman). Last, the window should not be overflowing; because of the high cost, the temptation to cram the shelves with leftovers from the day before is strong.

THE *CHARCUTERIE* is almost as French an institution as the bakery. *Chair cuite* means "cooked meat," and a charcuterie is a kind of delicatessen, specializing in pâtés, terrines, ham, sausages, and all kinds of cooked and cured pork. A charcuterie also sells long-lasting salads, such as cucumber, tomato, or grated carrot vinaigrette and root celery (celeriac) *remoulade* (with mustard mayonnaise). Cooked "dishes of the day" may include coq au vin; *choucroute alsacienne* (sauerkraut with smoked pork hock); and a variety of sausages, *cassoulet* (a rich stew of goose, sausage, and beans), or stuffed cabbage. Often you'll also find such condiments as pickles, plus a modest selection of wines, cheeses, and desserts—rice pudding or baked apple, for example. Only bread is needed to complete the meal, and you're set for the world's best picnic!

French cheese deserves, and gets, close attention. Sometimes whole shops are devoted to this branch of gastronomy. Take a whiff of the pungent odor, brace yourself, and plunge into a complex display of goat, sheep, and cow's milk cheeses, of fresh and aged cheeses, low-fat and high-fat, soft, hard, and blue cheeses.

Choosing a cheese is as delicate a matter as deciding on the right wine. In a good cheese shop you will be welcome to sample any of the cut cheeses, and assistants will gladly offer advice. One cardinal rule is to look for *fromage fermier* (farmhouse cheese), a rough equivalent of château-bottled wine. If the label says *lait cru* (raw milk)—even better; only when milk is unpasteurized does the flavor of some cheeses, Camembert, for example, develop properly. Try to keep a cheese cool without refrigeration and eat it as soon as you can. Delicate soft cheeses like Brie can become overripe within a matter of hours, one reason it is rare to find a wide-ranging selection of cheeses in a restaurant.

Many other kinds of specialty stores exist, often for local products. In Dijon, for instance, you'll find shops selling mustards in ornamental pots; in Gascony (near Bordeaux), it's foie gras and canned *confit* (preserved duck or goose). The Provençal hill town of Apt goes in for preserves, and

Montélimar, close to the almond orchards of the sheltered Rhône valley, makes nougat.

The most famous concentration of food shops in the world must be clustered around the place de la Madeleine in Paris. On one corner stands Fauchon, dean of luxury food emporiums. Fauchon sells everything from wild mushrooms to handmade candies and the most exotic game pâtés, all wrapped in those gift packages at which the French excel. Just across the square stands Hédiard, specializing in spices, rare fruits, and preserves. Next door is La Maison de la Truffe and Caviar Kaspia, while for cheese, it's a step around the corner to La Ferme Saint-Hubert.

THE MADELEINE CROSSROADS may be unique, but with a bit of persistence, a more modest version can be found in most French towns in the weekly market, often held in a picturesque open hall that may be centuries old. Markets start early, typically around 8 AM, and often disband at noon. In Paris, street markets continue to thrive in almost every quarter, and although the main wholesale market of Les Halles has moved to the suburbs, the area around the rue Coquillière is still worth exploring for its maze of truffle vendors, game purveyors, and professional kitchen-equipment outlets.

A market is not just somewhere to absorb local color. You'll see what fish is available and what produce is at its best. Often you'll find little old ladies offering rabbits and herbs, honey, and spice bread baked at home. You'll come across local cheeses and, with luck, find a few specialties like the *pissaladière* onion tart of Provence or the candied chestnuts of Privas, near Lyon.

French markets are still dominated by the season—there is little or no sign of frozen produce and meats. The first baby lamb heralds Christmas, little chickens arrive around Easter, together with kid and asparagus. Autumn excitement comes with game—venison, pheasant, and wild boar. Even cheeses look and taste different according to the time of year, depending on whether the animals have been fed in or outdoors.

The French light breakfast can come as no surprise; its unbeatable wakeup combination of croissant, brioche, or crusty roll with coffee has swept much of the world. Tourists may be offered a glass of orange juice as well. Traditionally, the coffee comes as café au lait, milky and steaming in a wide two-handled bowl for dipping the bread.

IF YOU'RE AN EARLY RISER, there's a long wait until lunch, for snacks are not a French habit. The structure of a meal, its timing, and its content are taken seriously. The "grazing" phenomenon of minimeals snatched here and there throughout the day is almost unheard of, and snacks are regarded as spoiling the appetite, not to mention being nutritionally unsound.

However, at noon you'll be rewarded by what, for most Frenchmen, remains the main meal of the day. In much of the country, everything stops for two hours; children return from school, and museums and businesses lock their doors. The pattern is much the same in large provincial cities. Restaurants, bistros, and cafés are crammed with diners, most of whom eat at least two and often three or more courses.

Lunch keeps French adults going until evening, but you may want to follow the example of schoolchildren, who are allowed a treat on the way home. Often it is *pain au chocolat,* a stick of chocolate stuffed in a length of French bread or baked inside croissant dough. By 8 PM, you'll be ready for dinner and one of the greatest pleasures France has to offer.

The choice of restaurants in France is a feast in itself. At least once during your trip you may want to indulge in an outstanding occasion. But restaurants are just the beginning. You can also eat out in cafés, bistros, brasseries, fast-food outlets (they, too, have reached France), or *auberges,* which range from staid country inns to sybaritic hideaways with helicopter pads and cooking to match.

Simplest is the café (where the espresso machine is king), offering drinks and such snacks as *croque monsieur* (toasted ham and cheese sandwich), *oeuf au plat* (baked eggs), *le hot dog,* and foot-long sandwiches of French bread. Larger-city cafés serve hot meals, such dishes as onion soup and braised beef with vegetables, con-

sumed on marble-topped tables to a background of cheerful banter. Like English pubs, French cafés are a way of life, a focal point for gossip and dominoes in practically every village.

The name *bistro,* once interchangeable with café, has recently taken a fashionable turn. In cities, instead of sawdust on the floor and a zinc-topped counter, you may find that a bistro is designer-decorated, serving new-style cuisine to a trendy, chattering crowd. If you're lucky the food will be as witty and colorful as the clientele. Such spots can be great fun to visit, but watch out for the prices.

WITH FEW EXCEPTIONS, brasseries remain unchanged—great bustling places with white-aproned waiters and hearty, masculine food. Go to them for oysters on the half-shell and fine seafood, for garlic snails, *boudin* (black pudding), sauerkraut, and vast ice-cream desserts. Originally a brasserie brewed beer, and since many brewers came from Alsace on the borders of Germany, the cooking reflects their origins.

Training is an important factor in maintaining the standards of French cooking. Professional chefs begin their three-year apprenticeship at age 16, starting in baking, pastry, or cuisine and later branching out into such specialties as aspic work and sugar sculpture. To be a *chocolatier* is a career in itself. Much more than a manual trade, cooking in France aspires to being an art, and its exponents achieve celebrity status. In the 1800s, it was Carême; in the 1900s, it was Escoffier; and today, it is Paul Bocuse and his nouvelle cuisine cohorts. Each decade has its stars, their rise and fall a constant source of eager speculation in the press and at the table.

The importance placed on food in France is echoed by the number of gastronomic societies, from the *Chevaliers du Tastevin* to the *Chaîne des Rôtisseurs* and the *Confrérie des Cordons Bleus,* to mention only three. The French believe that good eating, at whatever level, is an art that merits considerable time and attention. They have done the hard work, and, as a traveler, you can reap the benefits.

AN INTRODUCTION TO FRENCH WINE

By Simon Hewitt

A wine enthusiast, Simon Hewitt has traveled extensively through France's vineyards and contributed articles to several wine trade publications. He has lived in Paris since 1984.

ALTHOUGH FRANCE marginally trails Italy as the largest wine-producing country in the world, the reputation of French wines is second to none. That's partly because of luck—the exceptional variety of France's soils and climate—and partly because of 2,000 years of know-how. Few understand better than the French which grapes produce the best wines, and where.

The credentials of individual French wines have been internationally established since at least the 18th century. Back in 1787, Thomas Jefferson went down to Bordeaux and splurged on bottles of 1784 Château Yquem and Château Margaux, for prices that were, he reported, "indeed dear." Jefferson knew his wines: In 1855, both Yquem and Margaux were officially classified among Bordeaux's top five. In 1986, Jefferson's unopened bottle of Yquem rated $56,000 at auction. The Margaux—of which Jefferson boasted "there cannot be a better bottle of Bordeaux" (in fact, it was a half-bottle)—was sold for $30,000 in 1987.

With such eminent roots, it is no surprise that the United States is the richest export market for French wines, along with Great Britain. France, like Italy, produces about 20% of the world's wine—more than double that of Spain and Russia and four times as much as the United States. Nearly a quarter of a million people in France make and sell wine, and many more produce it for their own consumption.

Bordeaux's reputation dates from the Middle Ages. From 1152 to 1453, along with much of what is now western France, Bordeaux belonged to England. The light red wine then produced was known as *clairet*, the origin of our word "claret." Champagne, on the other hand, has existed as we know it only since 1700, when—thanks to the introduction of strong bottles, cork stoppers, and the blending of wines from different vineyards—its sparkle was first captured by a blind monk, Dom Pérignon. The abbey at Hautvillers, where he lived, is a site of pilgrimage for champagne aficionados. So is the monster oak barrel languishing in the Epernay cellars of the Mercier firm: It has a mindboggling capacity of 200,000 bottles, and 24 thirsty oxen spent three weeks carting it to the Paris Exhibition in 1889.

Such publicity coups have brought champagne fame, fortune—and problems. Like cognac (a brandy produced in a strictly defined area north of Bordeaux), its name is illegally exploited worldwide by would-be imitators. Producers of the real McCoy fight such fraud in international law courts, but it is a hapless struggle. It has proved easier for French authorities to attack fraud in their own backyard. Thomas Jefferson, who cagily noted that his expensive wines were "bought on the spot and therefore genuine," would have enjoyed perusing today's legal texts. Their bureaucratic aridity may be of no succor to the thirsty tourist, but their role is essential in ensuring that the wine in your glass is precisely what the bottle says it is.

Prominently printed on any self-respecting French wine label is the term *Appellation d'Origine Contrôlée* (often abbreviated AC). Such wines have to meet stringent requirements. Yield, production methods, and geographic limits are meticulously controlled, as are the varieties of grapes that are permitted (sometimes one, sometimes several—no fewer than 13 types of grapes can be used at Châteauneuf-du-Pape), and the requisite degree of alcohol (all wines must respect a minimum, ranging from 8.5% for the sunless, sharp white Gros Plant Nantais to 13% for sweet whites like Sauternes). AC wines now account for nearly a third of production, a figure that has doubled in 20 years.

THE NEXT CATEGORY, *Vin Délim-ité de Qualité Supérieure* (VDQS), accounts for about 10% of French wines. It is a sort of second division for wines that may be promoted to the AC category if they prove their mettle and show signs of steady improvement. Then come the *Vins de Pays*, regional titles with fewer restrictions, that account for about 15% of production. The simplest classification is *Vin de Table*, a poor relation in terms of price, if not necessarily quality.

Each bottle tells a tale. Usually the fancier it is, the more it has to hide. Beware of garish labels. Also, note where the wine was bottled: If it was not bottled on the spot (*mise en bouteille à la propriété/au domaine/au château*) or at least by a local merchant (often the case with burgundies), it should be treated with suspicion.

Napoléon, incidentally, was partial to unblended burgundy and, in a fit of alcoholic lucidity, once revealed the secret of his military genius: "No wine—no soldiers!" The English took the rival view of battle before wine: General Palmer celebrated victory over Napoléon at Waterloo by galloping down to Margaux and founding Château Palmer.

The vineyards of Margaux are possibly the ugliest in France, lost amid the flat, dusty plains of Médoc. Bordeaux is better represented at historic St-Emilion, with its cascading cobbled streets, or at Sauternes, where the noble rot (a tiny mushroom that sucks water from the grapes, leaving them sweeter) steals up the riverbanks as autumn mists vanish in the sunny skies. From the chilly hills of Champagne in the north to the sun-pelted slopes of the southern Midi, vines cover France. Steep-banked terraces tower above the River Rhône. The vineyards of Alsace sway and ripple into the foothills of the Vosges. Chalky cliffs, cellars, and caves line the softly lit Loire Valley.

Names of wines can be as charming as the scenery. The Loire Valley yields Vin de Pays du Jardin de la France—Country Wine from the Garden of France. Entre-Deux-Mers quaintly translates as Between Two Seas (actually the Rivers Garonne and Dordogne). It's difficult to resist flowery Fleurie, lovable St-Amour, sober Bouzy, or—if you overindulge—an early Graves.

More than a hundred different types of grapes exist in France. Some sound delicious. Try wrapping your tongue around Mourvèdre, Bourboulenc, Gewürztraminer, or Sciacarello. Visualize a bunch of Barbarossa ("red beard"), Folle Blanche ("crazy white"), or Fer ("iron"). Some names are confusing: The Auxerrois grape is used at Cahors, not near Auxerre; the Beaunois is used near Auxerre, not near Beaune; the St-Emilion is used for making cognac, not St-Emilion; while the Melon de Bourgogne has nothing to do with melons or Burgundy (it's a white grape grown near the Atlantic coast).

AS YOU TRAVEL, LOOK AT THE VINES: Are they young and slender or old, thick, and gnarled? The older the vine, the fewer grapes and wine it yields, but the better the quality. Not that you'll come across many vines more than a hundred years old. The phylloxera bug gnawed its way through them all in the 1870s; the vineyards of France had to be replanted using bug-resistant American grafts.

You can buy local wines from a *co-opérative* (which handles wines from a number of local growers) or from an individual producer. Co-opératives account for about 45% of the total production, but rarely offer wines of top quality. If you stop at a producer's, though (as you are bidden by many an enticing sign), you can hope to find a warmer welcome and wines with more character. It is customary to buy at least three bottles, but if you don't like the wine, don't buy it.

Although the big champagne houses in Reims and Epernay organize slick, informative visits, the leading Bordeaux châteaus don't—partly because the Bordelais are notoriously reserved, mainly because they have no need to seduce passersby (bulk orders account for 99% of their sales). One shudders to think what Thomas Jefferson would have made of the gum-chewing, radio-blaring welcome at Château Lascombes, just a stone's throw from his beloved Château Margaux. You can obtain parsimonious gulps of second-string clarets at the Maison du Vin on the cours du XXX Juillet in central Bordeaux, but, unfortunately, there is nothing to match the Marché aux Vins in the Burgundian town of Beaune, where a string of fine burgundies can be sampled for a modest sum.

DIFFERENT OCCASIONS warrant different wines. If you're buying wine for a picnic, go for something simple, such as a rosé or fruity red (Beaujolais or Gamay de Touraine). Full-bodied reds from the hottest regions of France are likely to knock you out if you drink them at lunchtime. Beware of restaurant wine lists designed to beef up the price of your meal, and always go for the house wine rather than a vague description such as "Bordeaux" or "Côtes du Rhône"; if there's no year or precise origin, you can't expect quality. If wine is made locally, try it; you may not come across it elsewhere, and regional cuisine is invariably tailored to regional wines.

A wide selection of local wines can be compared at any of the special fairs that proliferate in wine regions during the summer. The year's biggest celebration, however, is the appearance of Beaujolais Nouveau on the third Thursday of November. In recent years, as cafés and restaurants from Paris to New York rush the new wine from barrel to counter amid unpalatable fuss and brouhaha, the occasion has acquired a cheap if good-natured gimmickiness that obscures the fact that Beaujolais has been drunk young in the cafés of nearby Lyon since the days of, well, Thomas Jefferson, for example. The Trois Glorieuses, three days of Burgundian jollity centering on a wine auction at the Hospices de Beaune, is also held in November. Wine villages pay tribute to their patron saint on January 22, St. Vincent's Day, and another momentous feast is held at the end of the grape harvest. The harvests, or *vendanges,* begin in September and can last into December. In Sauternes, the grapes have to rot before being picked, and at Château Yquem, up to seven successive manual harvests may be required, with each grape inspected individually and picked only after achieving the right degree of maturity (by which time it looks a foul, shriveled mess).

Other wines to look out for include two from the Jura region of eastern France. *Vin Jaune,* also made from grapes picked late, is kept in oak barrels for six years or longer while yeasts form on the surface; the result is a wine (with a unique, nutty flavor sometimes likened to sherry) that can last for more than a hundred years. The grapes that produce the strong, amber-colored *Vin de Paille* are left for two months on straw mats while the juice is drawn out and the sugar concentration intensifies.

CHAMPAGNE OFFERS tiny quantities of wine without a fizz. Still reds and whites made near Reims are known as Côteaux Champenois while, far to the south, there is even a still pink, Rosé des Riceys: rare, delicious, and expensive. Neither the truly black wine of Cahors nor the sweet white Jurançon of the Pyrénées is easy to find, unlike the sand wines (*Vins de Sable*) of Provence, which are made from vines that creep right down to the beach. There are even vines in and around Paris, at Suresnes and Montmartre, where the harvest is celebrated behind the basilica of Sacré-Coeur on the first weekend of October; unfortunately, the resultant wine is often undrinkable!

Don't be a prisoner of fashion. Marketing men have convinced the British that Muscadet is *the* dry white, while Americans jostle for Pouilly-Fumé and Sancerre—fine wines, certainly, but in overhyped demand and therefore of poor value. Try instead to ferret out unfamiliar, peasanty wines, concocted by authentic local characters. If you hunt around, you may meet someone like Marcel.

Marcel makes illegal wines out of illegal vines in a lost corner of Burgundy that is off both the beaten track and the straight and narrow. People say—maps and guidebooks, anyway—there aren't any vines in Marcel's bit of Burgundy. We ambled over the Canal du Nivernais and scrambled up a hill. The hill became a street and the street a village square. There was a large sign on the square saying "Local Wine." It was 12:15. The wine merchant was closed for lunch. Till 3. We sidled hopefully into a bar. "Local wine? Not here. Try Gaston by the church."

Gaston sold it, all right, and sloshed some into cracked glass beakers. We stared solemnly at the wine, and all the flat-hatted old men playing cards in the corner stared solemnly at us. We shared impressions. Unexpected. Perky but pale. Seemed friendly, but you never know.

Gaston leaned confidentially forward, stroked his mustache, and asked, "Want some more?" Yes. "Try that fellow there who's just gone out." Which fellow? "Marcel," said Gaston, adding helpfully, "The one in the flat hat."

Eventually—many country roads and twisty bends later—we tracked Marcel down. Who were we? We'd come about the wine. What wine? His wine. Marcel looked suspicious. His *excellent* wine. Marcel mellowed and got out the key to his cellar. We clattered down the slimy steps, tastebuds tingling. Marcel grabbed a bottle. The wine's freshness came soaring through the dinge. Its sunniness pierced the murk. Marcel tossed back a glass and belched.

We murmured a few clichés of admiration. Marcel downed another glass, receded into the darkest, dirtiest depths of his cellar and rummaged under a heap of jerricans. Out popped a bottle as black as ink. Marcel squirted some into a glass, dashed it back and said, "Let's finish the bottle!"

Drinking this thick, cloying illegality was like being half-strangled in a velvet curtain. We fought our way free and staggered to the car with a crate. Marcel turned his back on us, brandished his francs triumphantly, and watered his garden in celebration.

A SURVEY OF FRENCH ARCHITECTURE

By Simon Hewitt

As a student of art history at Oxford, Simon Hewitt wrote a thesis on French Gothic architecture.

DESPITE THE RAVAGES OF wars throughout the centuries, France is still a rich showcase of architecture, with excellent examples of nearly every historic and regional style. Ornate theaters, soaring cathedrals, imposing castles, and graceful châteaus display for us French architectural achievement through the ages.

Each region has its own characteristics. The dark red brick of the north stands in contrast to the pink brick of Toulouse, as does the white, chalky stone of the Cognac and Champagne regions when compared with the pink sandstone of the Vosges. Roofs vary as well, from the steep slopes of Alpine chalets to the flat, red-tiled expanses of the Midi and the colorful slate patterns of Burgundy.

Medieval black-and-white timber-frame houses survive in towns north of the Loire, such as Troyes, Dinan, Rennes, and the Petite France sector of Strasbourg. Castles perch grandly on cliffs throughout the southwest, while hilltop villages survey the vineyards and olive groves of Provence in the southeast. Grim gateways repel strangers in the Charente region, whereas flower-strewn balconies welcome them to Alsace. Flemish campaniles, or belltowers, and Spanish gables flourish in the north, while a heavy, German Gothic-Renaissance style makes Strasbourg resemble a western Berlin.

Although the cave paintings at Lascaux in the Dordogne and the freestanding *menhirs* of Brittany prove that Frenchmen (or their ancestors, at any rate) have created and constructed since prehistoric times, the first great builders here were the Romans. Their efforts—mostly in ruins—are found throughout France, especially in the south. The amphitheaters of Nîmes and Arles, the theater of Orange, and the Pont du Gard aqueduct in southern France are masterpieces equal to anything Italy has to offer. Towns such as Autun, Saintes, and Reims boast proud Roman arches, and even the sprawling cities of Lyon and Paris house Roman remains.

With occasional exceptions, such as the 5th-century chapel at La Pépiole, near Toulon, the next architectural style of note was the Carolingian, in the 9th and 10th centuries. Surviving examples include the Basse-Oeuvre at Beauvais and the octagonal abbey church of Ottmarsheim in Alsace.

The massive and stocky Romanesque style that succeeded Carolingian differed in various ways—with its stone (as opposed to wood) ceilings or vaults, its introduction of windows high up the walls, and its preference for stone sculpture over such superficial ornament as mosaic and painting. Many 10th- and 11th-century Romanesque buildings survive in Burgundy, Alsace, the Auvergne, and western France: The city of Poitiers is particularly rich in Romanesque architecture; notably the intricately carved west front of the church of Notre-Dame-la-Grande.

THE AIRIER GOTHIC STYLE of the great French cathedrals built between the 12th and 16th centuries represented a fundamental departure from Romanesque. The most obvious visual change was that pointed arches replaced round ones. Just as important, though, was a new vaulting structure based on intersecting ribbed vaults, which sprang across the roof from column to column. Outward thrust was borne by flying buttresses, slender arches linking the outer walls to freestanding columns, often topped by spiky pinnacles. Whereas Romanesque architecture had thick, blocky walls with little room for window space, Gothic architecture, technically more sophisticated, replaced stone with stained glass.

Most medieval churches were built in the form of a cross, with two arms, or transepts, that intersect the nave at the crossing (often topped by a tower in Romanesque churches). The nave, divided into bays (the spaces between columns) and flanked on either side by side aisles, formed the main body of the church, with the east end, known as the chancel, containing the choir and altar. Many Gothic churches also have a number of small chapels behind the high altar, forming an outline known as the *chevet*, or apse.

ROMANESQUE AND GOTHIC churches are divided into three or four distinct vertical sections, like strata. Forestlike rows of pillars, topped by carved capitals, spring from the ground either to a gallery or triforium (an arcade of small columns and arches, originally of stone, later filled with glass), then to a clerestory (row of windows) above.

The Romanesque facade was intended as an ornate screen and was sometimes fronted by a large porch (or narthex). The tympanum, a large sculpted panel above the central doorway (usually representing Christ in Judgment or Glory), was retained in the Gothic facade, which also featured huge portals, a circular rose window, a statue gallery, and lofty towers. Other towers, over the crossing or alongside the transepts, gradually lost favor: The stone bulls on top of the many-towered cathedral of Laon mourn a dying breed.

Pointed arches and ribbed vaults were first used in the Gothic style during the 1130s at Sens and at St-Denis—home of Abbot Suger, the leading political figure of his day. Within a decade, local bishops had followed Suger's lead, and huge Gothic cathedrals were under way at Noyon, Senlis, and Laon. As France expanded during the early Middle Ages from its Parisian epicenter, Gothic went with it. But the Gothic style did not displace the Romanesque overnight. Many Romanesque churches survive as crypts beneath later buildings (as at Dijon Cathedral, for example); similarly, Romanesque naves were conserved at Mont-St-Michel, Vézelay, and Le Mans despite the addition of new Gothic chancels, while at Strasbourg Cathedral, the reverse is true and a Romanesque chancel survives.

As the Gothic style evolved, less and less stone was used, and churches became delicate, almost skeletal. Paris's Sainte-Chapelle is the most famous example, though as a stained-glass showcase, its scale doesn't match that of Metz Cathedral. The circular rose window was one feature that lasted throughout the Middle Ages, evolving from 13th-century geometric splendor at St-Denis and Notre-Dame in Paris to a petal-like fluidity during the first half of the 16th century.

Height was another Gothic quest. Roofs soared higher and higher—until that at Beauvais Cathedral came crashing down in 1284. Notre-Dame of Paris is 106 feet high, but later cathedrals are even loftier: Chartres is 114 feet; Bourges, 120; Reims, 124; Amiens, 137; and Beauvais an ill-fated 153 (it was never completed, so Amiens reigns as the country's tallest).

THE CHAMBIGES family, last in a long line of great Gothic master masons and glaziers, played a major role in the development of the Flamboyant style. When the bishop of Beauvais was planning a grandiose transept for his cathedral, he sent for Martin Chambiges, tempting him away from Sens and keeping him jealously at Beauvais for 30 years. Some see in the flame-like Flamboyant style the last neurotic shrieks of Gothic decadence. But while its decorative profusion sometimes smacks of sculptural self-indulgence (St-Pierre in Caen is a good example), there are several admirable Flamboyant churches, notably St-Séverin in Paris and St-Nicolas de Port near Nancy.

In the 16th century, Gothic architecture was subject to the influx of Renaissance ideas, given official encouragement when François I (1515–47) invited the Italian painters and architects Il Rosso, Primaticcio, and Leonardo da Vinci to his court. Renaissance architecture was marked by a return to classical Roman styles, which existed side by side with Gothic throughout the 16th century; in a number of Paris churches you will see classical columns and ornaments superimposed on Gothic structures (St-Etienne-du-Mont, St-Gervais, and St-Eustache are the best examples). While Gothic was first and foremost an ecclesiastical style, many of the chief creations of Renaissance architecture had a secular setting: the châteaus of noblemen, princes, and kings. In the Loire Valley, for instance, fortified medieval castles like Chinon gradually yielded to ideals of comfort and luxury (Cheverny, for example). Along the way, Renaissance proportion and daintiness were mingled with medieval massiveness, as at the châteaus of Azay-le-Rideau and Amboise. One of the loveliest showcases of Renaissance architecture is the place des Vosges in Paris, a square whose huge, steep-sloping roofs are a recurring trait of French buildings of the 16th and 17th centuries.

TO CONTRAST THE RENAISSANCE style with the Baroque, its successor, compare the pink-brick arcades of the place des Vosges (1612) with the solemn and dignified stone of the place Vendôme, built in 1685 a couple of miles across town. A similar difference can be observed between the intimate château of Fontainebleau (mid-16th century) and the immense palace of Versailles (late 17th century).

Baroque imbued the classical style with drama and a sense of movement: Take a look at Mansart's dome surging above Paris's Hôtel des Invalides, or the powerful rhythms of Charles Perrault's Louvre facade. Yet only in northern France, under the temporary influence of Spanish occupiers, did Latin exuberance find an outlet, typified in the soaring curves and curls on the colossal belfry of St-Amand-les-Eaux near Lille. The overblown fantasies to which Baroque lent itself in Italy, Spain, southern Germany, and Austria—wild curves, broken outlines, and sculptural overkill—were held firmly in check by the French love of discipline. Whole towns survive to remind us: The rigid plan and identical houses of Richelieu, south of Chinon, are restrained and austere.

The 18th century saw several major provincial building programs in the neoclassical style—a more literal, toned-down interpretation of antique precedent. The state rooms of Strasbourg's Château des Rohan, the charming place Stanislas in Nancy, and the Grand Théâtre and place de la Bourse in Bordeaux are top exam-ples. A number of the more affluent châteaus in the Bordeaux vineyards also date from this time.

Baroque, however, continued to dominate church building until the early 19th century (witness the cathedrals of Nancy and Arras). Many clerics commissioned architects to dress up Gothic buildings in classical apparel, sticking pilasters on columns or transforming pointed arches into rounded ones. Louis XIV set the tone by remodeling the choir of Notre-Dame in Paris in 1708, but Autun Cathedral—revamped throughout—is the most extreme example of this kind of architectural rethink. Stained-glass windows were even ripped out—an act of stylistic vandalism surpassed only during the French Revolution when thousands of churches were wrecked in the name of the Age of Reason.

NAPOLÉON USHERED in the 19th century with the Arc de Triomphe, which remained unfinished for 20 years—typifying the hesitations of a century bereft of original ideas. Iron made its appearance—most obviously at the Eiffel Tower, most frequently accompanied by glass in train stations and covered markets.

The 19th century bequeathed us Paris as we know it, with Baron Haussmann carving boulevards through the city. Luckily, Haussmann's seven-story buildings have proved sufficiently large and imposing to withstand the rapacious onslaughts of modern developers, and central Paris has remained unchanged for a hundred years. But it's not surprising that the showpiece of Haussmann's Paris, the Opéra, is a pompous jumble of styles.

Things perked up in the 20th century. While such Paris landmarks as the Grand and Petit Palais and opulent town halls throughout the country were faithful to conservative taste, Emile Gallé and Hector Guimard led an artistic revolution known as Art Nouveau, with sinuous, nature-based forms. The Paris métro, ornamented by iron railings and canopies, is the most familiar example. A reaction occurred in the straighter lines of Art Deco, which first turned up at the Théâtre des Champs-Elysées in 1913. At the same time, the French developed a taste for reinforced concrete that they have never lost. Its most imaginative exponent was Swiss-born Le Corbusier, an architectural Picasso whose best work (like the chapel at Ronchamp in eastern France) obeys few established rules.

In the first half of the 20th century, much energy was spent repairing the damage of two world wars: Many towns are now lackluster copies of their former selves. Efforts were lavished on restoring cathedrals and other landmarks, a pursuit instigated a century before by Eugène Viollet-le-Duc, without whom any number of cathedrals and churches might have crumbled away.

The most visited postwar building in France is Paris's futuristic Pompidou Center. Its pipes and workings are on the outside, ensuring that the interior is uncluttered to a fault (the fault being that the exterior is going rusty).

Paris's latter-day skyscrapers have—with the exception of the Tour Montparnasse—been banished to the city outskirts, notably to La Défense. There, finished only in 1989, the giant glass and concrete arch known as La Tête Défense has cemented a vista that stretches along the avenue de la Grande Armée, past the Arc de Triomphe, down the Champs-Elysées, across the place de la Concorde, and over the Tuileries to the gleaming glass pyramid of the Louvre.

MORE PORTRAITS

THE BEST INTRODUCTION to modern France, surveying social, political, and economic developments, is John Ardagh's *France Today* (Penguin). A witty, but less complete, survey of the country and its people is Theodore Zeldin's *The French* (Pantheon); Joseph T. Carroll's *The French—How They Live and Work* (David & Charles) is in a similar vein. A newer entry on the list is Richard Bernstein's *Fragile Glory* (Knopf). An immensely popular, if slightly satiric, introduction to French country life is provided by Peter Mayle's two autobiographical books on Provence, *A Year in Provence* and *Toujours Provence* (Knopf).

Nancy Mitford's readable *The Sun King* (Crown) covers the regal grandeur of the 17th century, while Alfred Cobban's workmanlike *History of Modern France* (Pelican) describes trends and events from the death of Louis XIV up to 1962. For modern French history, particularly the Vichy Era, the best bets are Robert Paxton's *Vichy France* (Knopf) and *Vichy & the Jews* (Shocken). Herbert Lottmann has written some more journalistic accounts of the Fall of Paris in 1940 and *The Left Bank,* about French intellectuals after the war (Houghton-Mifflin).

As for books about French wine and cuisine, Patricia Wells's *The Food Lover's Guide to Paris* and *The Food Lover's Guide to France* (Workman Publishing) provide a great beginning. One wine book, Eunice Fried's *Burgundy, the Country, the Wines, the People* (Harper & Row) gives a good account of Burgundy, while Nicholas Faith's *The Winemasters*

(Hamish Hamilton) offers a full history of Bordeaux's ups and downs. Steven Spurrier's pocket-size *French Country Wines* (Putnam) is unusually thorough in its treatment of lesser-known wines, often representing good value. Alexis Lichine's *Guide to Wines and Vineyards of France* (Knopf) is still the classic wine guide.

Architecture buffs should read Henri Focillon's thoughtfully illustrated *The Art of the West* (Cornell U. Press), a scholarly study of Romanesque and Gothic architecture.

Charles Dickens, in *A Tale of Two Cities* (Bantam), George Orwell, in *Down and Out in Paris and London* (Penguin), and Ernest Hemingway, notably in *A Moveable Feast* (Scribner's), are just three authors who have written about Paris in English. The novels of Emile Zola are situated mostly in Provence or in Paris—by and large the Paris we know today, emerging from mid-19th-century reconstruction amid backstreet squalor and brash glamour, all tellingly depicted in such works as *La Curée, L'Assommoir,* and *Nana* (Penguin).

Historian and archaeologist Dorothy Carrington has written the well-documented *Granite Island: A Portrait of Corsica,* which gives a thoughtful insight into the islanders' archaic beliefs, infamous vendettas, and complicated internal politics.

Several good thrillers set in France are *Assignment in Brittany* (Fawcett), by Helen MacInnes; Pierre Salinger's *The Dossier* (Doubleday); Philip Loraine's *Death Wishes* (St. Martins); and *Most Secret* (Amereon), by Nevil Shute.

CLOTHING SIZES

Men

Suits

To change American suit sizes to French suit sizes, add 10 to the American suit size.

To change French suit sizes to American suit sizes, subtract 10 from the French suit size.

U.S.	36	38	40	42	44	46	48
French	46	48	50	52	54	56	58

Shirts

To change American collar sizes to French collar sizes, multiply the American collar size by 2 and add 8.

To change French collar sizes to American collar sizes, subtract 8 from the French collar size and divide by 2.

U.S.	14	14½	15	15½	16	16½	17	17½
French	36	37	38	39	40	41	42	43

Shoes

French shoe sizes vary in their relation to American shoe sizes.

U.S.	6½	7	8	9	10	10½	11
French	39	40	41	42	43	44	45

Women

Dresses and Coats

To change U.S. dress/coat sizes to French dress/coat sizes, add 28 to the U.S. dress/coat size.

To change French dress/coat sizes to U.S. dress/coat sizes, subtract 28 from the French dress/coat size.

U.S.	4	6	8	10	12	14	16
French	32	34	36	38	40	42	44

Blouses and Sweaters

To change U.S. blouse/sweater sizes to French blouse/sweater sizes, add 8 to the U.S. blouse/sweater size.

To change French blouse/sweater sizes to U.S. blouse/sweater sizes, subtract 8 from the French blouse/sweater size.

U.S.	30	32	34	36	38	40	42
French	38	40	42	44	46	48	50

Shoes

To change U.S. shoe sizes to French shoe sizes, add 32 to the U.S. shoe size.

To change French shoe sizes to U.S. shoe sizes, subtract 32 from the French shoe size.

U.S.	4	5	6	7	8	9	10
French	36	37	38	39	40	41	42

FRENCH VOCABULARY

One of the trickiest French sounds to pronounce is the nasal final *n* sound (whether or not the *n* is actually the last letter of the word). You should try to pronounce it as a sort of nasal grunt—as in "huh." The vowel that precedes the *n* will govern the vowel sound of the word, and in this list we precede the final *n* with an *h* to remind you to be nasal.

Another problem sound is the ubiquitous but untransliterable *eu*, as in *bleu* (blue) or *deux* (two), and the very similar sound in *je* (I), *ce* (this), and *de* (of). The closest equivalent might be the vowel sound of "stood."

Words and Phrases

English	French	Pronunciation
Basics		
Yes/no	Oui/non	wee/nohn
Please	S'il vous plaît	seel voo play
Thank you	Merci	mair-**see**
You're welcome	De rien	deh ree-**ehn**
That's all right	Il n'y a pas de quoi	eel nee ah pah de kwah
Excuse me, sorry	Pardon	pahr-**dohn**
Sorry!	Désolé(e)	day-zoh-**lay**
Good morning/ afternoon	Bonjour	bohn-**zhoor**
Good evening	Bonsoir	bohn-**swahr**
Goodbye	Au revoir	o ruh-**vwahr**
Mr. (Sir)	Monsieur	muh-**syuh**
Mrs. (Ma'am)	Madame	ma-**dam**
Miss	Mademoiselle	mad-mwa-**zel**
Pleased to meet you	Enchanté(e)	ohn-shahn-**tay**
How are you?	Comment allez-vous?	kuh-mahn-tahl-ay-**voo**
Very well, thanks	Très bien, merci	tray bee-ehn, mair-**see**
And you?	Et vous?	ay voo?
Numbers		
one	un	uhn
two	deux	deuh
three	trois	twah
four	quatre	**kaht**-ruh
five	cinq	sank
six	six	seess
seven	sept	set
eight	huit	wheat
nine	neuf	nuf

ten	dix	deess
eleven	onze	ohnz
twelve	douze	dooz
thirteen	treize	trehz
fourteen	quatorze	kah-torz
fifteen	quinze	kanz
sixteen	seize	sez
seventeen	dix-sept	deez-**set**
eighteen	dix-huit	deez-**wheat**
nineteen	dix-neuf	deez-**nuf**
twenty	vingt	vehn
twenty-one	vingt-et-un	vehnt-ay-**uhn**
thirty	trente	trahnt
forty	quarante	ka-**rahnt**
fifty	cinquante	sang-**kahnt**
sixty	soixante	swa-**sahnt**
seventy	soixante-dix	swa-sahnt-**deess**
eighty	quatre-vingts	kaht-ruh-**vehn**
ninety	quatre-vingt-dix	kaht-ruh-vehn-**deess**
one-hundred	cent	sahn
one-thousand	mille	meel

Colors

black	noir	nwahr
blue	bleu	bleuh
brown	brun/marron	bruhn/mar-**rohn**
green	vert	vair
orange	orange	o-**rahnj**
pink	rose	rose
red	rouge	rouge
violet	violette	vee-o-**let**
white	blanc	blahnk
yellow	jaune	zhone

Days of the Week

Sunday	dimanche	dee-**mahnsh**
Monday	lundi	luhn-**dee**
Tuesday	mardi	mahr-**dee**
Wednesday	mercredi	mair-kruh-**dee**
Thursday	jeudi	zhuh-**dee**
Friday	vendredi	vawn-druh-**dee**
Saturday	samedi	sahm-**dee**

Months

January	janvier	zhahn-vee-**ay**
February	février	feh-vree-**ay**
March	mars	marce
April	avril	a-**vreel**
May	mai	meh
June	juin	zhwehn
July	juillet	zhwee-**ay**
August	août	ah-**oo**
September	septembre	sep-**tahm**-bruh

October	octobre	awk-**to**-bruh
November	novembre	no-**vahm**-bruh
December	décembre	day-**sahm**-bruh

Useful Phrases

Do you speak	Parlez-vous	par-lay **voo**
English?	anglais?	ahn-**glay**
I don't speak	Je ne parle pas	zhuh nuh parl pah
French	français	frahn-**say**
I don't understand	Je ne comprends pas	zhuh nuh kohm-**prahn** pah
I understand	Je comprends	zhuh kohm-**prahn**
I don't know	Je ne sais pas	zhuh nuh say **pah**
I'm American/ British	Je suis américain/ anglais	zhuh sweez a-may-ree-**kehn**/ahn-**glay**
What's your name?	Comment vous appelez-vous?	ko-mahn voo za-pell-ay-**voo**
My name is . . .	Je m'appelle . . .	zhuh ma-**pell** . . .
What time is it?	Quelle heure est-il?	kel air eh-**teel**
How?	Comment?	ko-**mahn**
When?	Quand?	kahn
Yesterday	Hier	yair
Today	Aujourd'hui	o-zhoor-**dwee**
Tomorrow	Demain	duh-**mehn**
This morning/ afternoon	Ce matin/cet après-midi	suh ma-**tehn**/set ah-pray-mee-**dee**
Tonight	Ce soir	suh **swahr**
What?	Quoi?	kwah
What is it?	Qu'est-ce que c'est?	kess-kuh-**say**
Why?	Pourquoi?	poor-**kwa**
Who?	Qui?	kee
Where is . . .	Où est . . .	oo ay
the train station?	la gare?	la gar
the subway station?	la station de métro?	la sta-**syon** duh may-**tro**
the bus stop?	l'arrêt de bus?	la-**ray** duh **booss**
the terminal (airport)?	l'aérogare?	lay-ro-**gar**
the post office?	la poste?	la post
the bank?	la banque?	la bahnk
the . . . hotel?	l'hôtel . . .?	lo-**tel**
the store?	le magasin?	luh ma-ga-**zehn**
the cashier?	la caisse?	la **kess**
the . . . museum?	le musée . . .?	luh mew-**zay**
the hospital?	l'hôpital?	lo-pee-**tahl**
the elevator?	l'ascenseur?	la-sahn-**seuhr**
the telephone?	le téléphone?	luh tay-lay-**phone**

Where are the restrooms?	Où sont les toilettes?	oo sohn lay twah-**let**
Here/there	Ici/là	ee-**see**/la
Left/right	A gauche/à droite	a goash/a drwaht
Straight ahead	Tout droit	too drwah
Is it near/far?	C'est près/loin?	say pray/lwehn
I'd like . . .	Je voudrais . . .	zhuh voo-**dray**
a room	une chambre	ewn **shahm**-bruh
the key	la clé	la clay
a newspaper	un journal	uhn zhoor-**nahl**
a stamp	un timbre	uhn **tam**-bruh
I'd like to buy . . .	Je voudrais acheter . . .	zhuh voo-**dray** ahsh-**tay**
a cigar	un cigare	uhn see-**gar**
cigarettes	des cigarettes	day see-ga-**ret**
matches	des allumettes	days a-loo-**met**
dictionary	un dictionnaire	uhn deek-see-oh-**nare**
soap	du savon	dew sah-**vohn**
city plan	un plan de ville	uhn plahn de **veel**
road map	une carte routière	ewn cart roo-tee-**air**
magazine	une revue	ewn reh-**vu**
envelopes	des enveloppes	dayz ahn-veh-**lope**
writing paper	du papier à lettres	dew pa-pee-**ay** a **let**-ruh
airmail writing paper	du papier avion	dew pa-pee-**ay** a-vee-**ohn**
postcard	une carte postale	ewn cart pos-**tal**
How much is it?	C'est combien?	say comb-bee-**ehn**
It's expensive/cheap	C'est cher/pas cher	say share/pa share
A little/a lot	Un peu/beaucoup	uhn peuh/bo-**koo**
More/less	Plus/moins	plu/mwehn
Enough/too (much)	Assez/trop	a-say/tro
I am ill/sick	Je suis malade	zhuh swee ma-**lahd**
Call a doctor	Appelez un docteur	a-play uhn dohk-**tehr**
Help!	Au secours!	o suh-**koor**
Stop!	Arrêtez!	a-reh-**tay**
Fire!	Au feu!	o fuh
Caution!/Look out!	Attention!	a-tahn-see-**ohn**

Dining Out

A bottle of . . .	une bouteille de . . .	ewn boo-**tay** duh
A cup of . . .	une tasse de . . .	ewn tass duh
A glass of . . .	un verre de . . .	uhn vair duh
Ashtray	un cendrier	uhn sahn-dree-**ay**
Bill/check	l'addition	la-dee-see-**ohn**

Bread	du pain	dew pan
Breakfast	le petit-déjeuner	luh puh-**tee** day-zhuh-**nay**
Butter	du beurre	dew burr
Cheers!	A votre santé!	ah vo-truh sahn-**tay**
Cocktail/aperitif	un apéritif	uhn ah-pay-ree-**teef**
Dinner	le dîner	luh dee-**nay**
Dish of the day	le plat du jour	luh plah dew **zhoor**
Enjoy!	Bon appétit!	bohn a-pay-**tee**
Fixed-price menu	le menu	luh may-**new**
Fork	une fourchette	ewn four-**shet**
I am diabetic	Je suis diabétique	zhuh swee dee-ah-bay-**teek**
I am on a diet	Je suis au régime	zhuh sweez o ray-**jeem**
I am vegetarian	Je suis végétarien(ne)	zhuh swee vay-zhay-ta-ree-**en**
I cannot eat . . .	Je ne peux pas manger de . . .	zhuh nuh **puh** pah mahn-**jay** deh
I'd like to order	Je voudrais commander	zhuh voo-**dray** ko-mahn-**day**
I'm hungry/thirsty	J'ai faim/soif	zhay fahm/swahf
Is service/the tip included?	Est-ce que le service est compris?	ess kuh luh sair-**veess** ay comb-**pree**
It's good/bad	C'est bon/mauvais	say bohn/mo-**vay**
It's hot/cold	C'est chaud/froid	say sho/frwah
Knife	un couteau	uhn koo-**toe**
Lunch	le déjeuner	luh day-zhuh-**nay**
Menu	la carte	la cart
Napkin	une serviette	ewn sair-vee-**et**
Pepper	du poivre	dew **pwah**-vruh
Plate	une assiette	ewn a-see-**et**
Please give me . . .	Donnez-moi . . .	doe-nay-**mwah**
Salt	du sel	dew sell
Spoon	une cuillère	ewn kwee-**air**
Sugar	du sucre	dew **sook**-ruh
Waiter!/Waitress!	Monsieur!/Mademoiselle!	muh-**syuh**/mad-mwa-**zel**
Wine list	la carte des vins	la cart day **van**

MENU GUIDE

French	English
Garniture au choix	Choice of vegetable accompaniment
Menu à prix fixe	Set menu
Plat du jour	Dish of the day
Selon arrivage	When available
Supplément/En sus	Extra charge
Sur commande	Made to order

Breakfast

Confiture	Jam
Miel	Honey
Oeuf à la coque	Boiled egg
Oeufs au bacon	Bacon and eggs
Oeufs au jambon	Ham and eggs
Oeufs sur le plat	Fried eggs
Oeufs brouillés	Scrambled eggs
Omelette (nature)	Omelet (plain)
Petits pains	Rolls

Starters

Anchois	Anchovies
Andouille(tte)	Chitterling sausage
Assiette de charcuterie	Assorted pork products
Assiette anglaise	Assorted cold cuts
Crudités	Mixed raw vegetable salad
Escargots	Snails
Hors-d'oeuvres variés	Assorted appetizers
Jambon (de Bayonne)	Ham (Bayonne)
Jambon de Campagne	Country-style ham (air-cured or smoked)
Jambonneau	Cured pig's knuckle
Mortadelle	Bologna sausage
Oeufs à la diable	Deviled eggs
Pâté	Liver purée blended with meat
Quenelles	Light dumplings (fish, fowl, or meat)
Saucisson	Dried sausage
Terrine	Pâté sliced and served from an earthenware pot
Viande séchée	Cured dried beef

Salads

Salade d'endives	Endive salad
Salade de thon	Tuna salad
Salade mixte	Mixed salad
Salade niçoise	Riviera combination salad
Salade russe	Diced vegetable salad
Salade verte	Green salad

Soups

Bisque	Seafood stew
Bouillabaisse	Fish and seafood stew

Crême de . . .	Cream of . . .
Potage	Light soup
julienne	shredded vegetables
parmentier	potato
Pot-au-feu	Stew of meat and vegetables
Soupe	Hearty soup
du jour	of the day
à l'oignon gratinée	French onion soup
au pistou	Provençal vegetable soup
Velouté de . . .	Cream of . . .
Vichyssoise	Cold leek and potato cream soup

Fish and Seafood

Anguille	Eel
Bar	Bass
Bigorneaux	Winkles
Bourride	Fish stew from Marseilles
Brandade de morue	Creamed salt cod
Brochet	Pike
Cabillaud	Fresh cod
Calmar	Squid
Carpe	Carp
Coquille St-Jacques	Scallops in creamy sauce
Crabe	Crab
Crevettes	Shrimp
Cuisses de grenouilles	Frogs' legs
Daurade	Sea bream
Ecrevisses	Prawns
Ecrevisses	Crayfish
Eperlans	Smelt
Harengs	Herring
Homard	Lobster
Huîtres	Oysters
Langouste	Spiny lobster
Langoustines	Dublin bay prawns (scampi)
Lotte	Burbot
Lotte de mer	Angler
Loup	Catfish
Maquereau	Mackerel
Matelote	Fish stew in wine
Merlan	Whiting
Morue	Cod
Moules	Mussels
Palourdes	Clams
Perche	Perch
Poulpes	Octopus
Raie	Skate
Rascasse	Fish used in bouillabaisse
Rouget	Red mullet
Saumon	Salmon
Sole	Sole
Thon	Tuna
Truite	Trout

Meat

Agneau	Lamb
Boeuf	Beef
pavé	thick slice of boned beef
Boulettes de viande	Meatballs
Brochette	Kabob
Cassoulet toulousain	Casserole of white beans and meat
Cervelle	Brains
Chateaubriand	Double fillet steak
Chops	Côtelettes
Choucroute garnie	Sausages and cured pork served with sauerkraut
Contre-filet	Loin strip steak
Côte de boeuf	T-bone steak
Côte	Rib
Entrecôte	Rib or rib-eye steak
Epaule	Shoulder
Escalope	Cutlet
Filet	Fillet steak
Foie	Liver
Gigot	Leg
Langue	Tongue
Médaillon	Tenderloin steak
Pieds de cochon	Pig's feet
Porc	Pork
Ragoût	Stew
Ris de veau	Veal sweetbreads
Rognons	Kidneys
Saucisses	Sausages
Selle	Saddle
Steak/steack	Steak (always beef)
Tournedos	Tenderloin of T-bone steak
Veau	Veal

Methods of Preparation

A point	Medium
A l'étouffée	Stewed
Au four	Baked
Bien cuit	Well-done
Bleu	Very rare
Bouilli	Boiled
Braisé	Braised
Frit	Fried
Grillé	Grilled
Rôti	Roast
Saignant	Rare
Sauté/poêlée	Sautéed

Game and Poultry

Blanc de volaille	Chicken breast
Caille	Quail
Canard/caneton	Duck/duckling

Cerf/chevreuil	Venison (red/roe)
Coq au vin	Chicken stewed in red wine
Dinde/dindonneau	Turkey/young turkey
Faisan	Pheasant
Grive	Thrush
Lapin	Rabbit
Lièvre	Wild hare
Oie	Goose
Perdrix/perdreau	Partridge/young partridge
Pigeon/pigeonneau	Pigeon/squab
Pintade/pintadeau	Guinea fowl/young guinea fowl
Poularde	Fattened pullet
Poule au pot	Chicken stewed with vegetables
Poulet	Chicken
Poussin	Spring chicken
Sanglier/marcassin	Wild boar/young wild boar
Volaille	Fowl

Vegetables

Artichaut	Artichoke
Asperge	Asparagus
Aubergine	Eggplant
Carottes	Carrots
Champignons	Mushrooms
Chicorée	Chicory (Endive)
Chou-fleur	Cauliflower
Chou (rouge)	Cabbage (red)
Choux de Bruxelles	Brussels sprouts
Courgette	Zucchini
Cresson	Watercress
Endive	Endive
Epinard	Spinach
Fèves	Broad beans
Haricots blancs/verts	White kidney/French beans
Laitue	Lettuce
Lentilles	Lentils
Oignons	Onions
Petits pois	Peas
Poireaux	Leeks
Poivrons	Peppers
Pomme de terre	Potato
Radis	Radishes
Tomates	Tomatoes

Potatoes, Rice, and Noodles

Nouilles	Noodles
Pâtes	Pasta
Pommes (de terre)	Potatoes
allumettes	matchsticks
dauphine	mashed and deep-fried
duchesse	mashed with butter and egg yolks
en robe des champs	in their skin

frites	french fries
mousseline	mashed
nature/vapeur	boiled/steamed
Riz	Rice
pilaf	boiled in bouillon with onions

Sauces and Preparations

Béarnaise	Vinegar, egg yolks, white wine, shallots, tarragon
Béchamel	White sauce
Bordelaise	Mushrooms, red wine, shallots, beef marrow
Bourguignon	Red wine, herbs
Chasseur	Wine, mushrooms, onions, shallots
Diable	Hot pepper
Forestière	Mushrooms
Hollandaise	Egg yolks, butter, vinegar
Indienne	Curry
Madère	With Madeira wine
Marinière	White wine, mussel broth, egg yolks
Meunière	Brown butter, parsley, lemon juice
Périgueux	With goose or duck liver purée and truffles
Poivrade	Pepper sauce
Provençale	Onions, tomatoes, garlic
Tartare	Mayonnaise flavored with mustard and herbs
Vinaigrette	Vinegar dressing

Fruits and Nuts

Abricot	Apricot
Amandes	Almonds
Ananas	Pineapple
Banane	Banana
Brugnon	Nectarine
Cacahouètes	Peanuts
Cassis	Blackcurrants
Cerises	Cherries
Citron	Lemon
Citron vert	Lime
Dattes	Dates
Figues	Figs
Fraises	Strawberries
Framboises	Raspberries
Fruits secs	Dried fruit
Groseilles	Red currants
Mandarine	Tangerine
Marrons	Chestnuts
Melon	Melon
Mûres	Blackberries
Myrtilles	Blueberries
Noisettes	Hazelnuts
Noix de coco	Coconut

Noix	Walnuts
Orange	Orange
Pamplemousse	Grapefruit
Pastèque	Watermelon
Pêche	Peach
Poire	Pear
Pomme	Apple
Pruneaux	Prunes
Prunes	Plums
Raisins secs	Raisins
Raisins blancs/noirs	Grapes green/blue

Desserts

Coupe (glacée)	Sundae
Crêpe suzette	Thin pancake simmered in orange juice and flambéed with orange liqueur
Crème caramel	Caramel pudding
Crème Chantilly	Whipped cream
Flan	Custard
Gâteau au chocolat	Chocolate cake
Glace	Ice cream
Mousse au chocolat	Chocolate pudding
Sorbet	Water ice
Tarte aux pommes	Apple pie
Tourte	Layer cake
Vacherin glacé	Ice-cream cake

Alcoholic Drinks

A l'eau	With water
Avec des glaçons	On the rocks
Apéritifs	Cocktails
Kir/blanc-cassis	Chilled white wine mixed with black-currant syrup
Bière	Beer
Blonde/brune	Light/dark
Calvados	Apple brandy
Eau-de-vie	Brandy
Kirsch	Cherry brandy
Liqueur	Cordial
Poire William	Pear brandy
Porto	Port
Sec	Straight
Vin	Wine
sec	dry
brut	very dry
léger	light
doux	sweet
rouge	red
rosé	rosé
mousseux	sparkling
blanc	white

Nonalcoholic Drinks

Café	Coffee
noir	black
crème	cream
au lait	with milk
décaféiné	caffeine-free
express	espresso
Chocolat chaud	Hot chocolate
Eau minérale	Mineral water
gazeuse	carbonated
non gazeuse	still
Jus de . . .	. . . juice (see fruit)
Lait	Milk
Limonade	Lemonade
Limonade gazeuse	Ginger ale
Schweppes	Tonic water
Thé	Tea
crème/citron	with milk/lemon
glacé	iced tea
Tisane	Herb tea

INDEX

Z

Before Catching Your Flight, Catch Up With Your World.

Fueled by the global resources of CNN and available in major airports across America, CNN Airport Network provides a live source  of current domestic and international news,

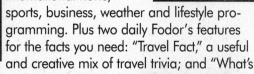

sports, business, weather and lifestyle programming. Plus two daily Fodor's features for the facts you need: "Travel Fact," a useful and creative mix of travel trivia; and "What's Happening," a comprehensive round-up of upcoming events in major cities around the world.

With CNN Airport Network, you'll never be out of the loop.

CNN Airport Network

A CNN NETWORK

HERE'S YOUR OWN PERSONAL VIEW OF THE WORLD.

Here's the easiest way to get up-to-the-minute, objective, personalized information about what's going on in the city you'll be visiting—before you leave on your trip! Unique information you could get only if you knew someone personally in each of 160 destinations around the world. Everything from special places to dine to local events only a local would know about.

It's all yours—in your Travel Update from Worldview, the leading provider of time-sensitive destination information.

Review the following order form and fill it out by indicating your destination(s)

and travel dates and by checking off up to eight interest categories. Then mail or fax your order form to us, or call your order in. (We're here to help you 24 hours a day.)

Within 48 hours of receiving your order, we'll mail your convenient, pocket-sized custom guide to you, packed with information to make your travel more fun and interesting. And if you're in a hurry, we can even fax it.

Have a great trip with your Fodor's Worldview Travel Update!

Fodor's WORLDVIEW TRAVEL UPDATE

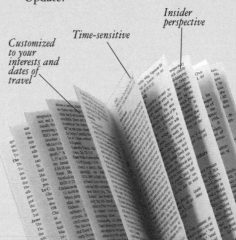

Insider perspective

Time-sensitive

Customized to your interests and dates of travel

DESTINATIONS

Worldview covers more than 160 destinations worldwide. Choose the destination(s) that match your itinerary from the list below:

Europe
Amsterdam
Athens
Barcelona
Berlin
Brussels
Budapest
Copenhagen
Dublin
Edinburgh
Florence
Frankfurt
French Riviera
Geneva
Glasgow
Lausanne
Lisbon
London
Madrid
Milan
Moscow
Munich
Oslo
Paris
Prague
Provence
Rome
Salzburg
Seville
St. Petersburg
Stockholm
Venice
Vienna
Zurich

**United States
(Mainland)**
Albuquerque
Atlanta
Atlantic City
Baltimore
Boston
Branson, MO
Charleston, SC
Chicago
Cincinnati
Cleveland
Dallas/Ft. Worth
Denver
Detroit
Houston
Indianapolis
Kansas City
Las Vegas
Los Angeles
Memphis
Miami
Milwaukee
Minneapolis/St. Paul
Nashville
New Orleans
New York City
Orlando
Palm Springs
Philadelphia
Phoenix
Pittsburgh

Portland
Reno/Lake Tahoe
St. Louis
Salt Lake City
San Antonio
San Diego
San Francisco
Santa Fe
Seattle
Tampa
Washington, DC

Alaska
Alaskan Destinations

Hawaii
Honolulu
Island of Hawaii
Kauai
Maui

Canada
Quebec City
Montreal
Ottawa
Toronto
Vancouver

Bahamas
Abaco
Eleuthera/
 Harbour Island
Exuma
Freeport
Nassau &
 Paradise Island

Bermuda
Bermuda Countryside
Hamilton

**British Leeward
Islands**
Anguilla
Antigua & Barbuda
St. Kitts & Nevis

British Virgin Islands
Tortola & Virgin
 Gorda

**British Windward
Islands**
Barbados
Dominica
Grenada
St. Lucia
St. Vincent
Trinidad & Tobago

Cayman Islands
The Caymans

Dominican Republic
Santo Domingo

Dutch Leeward Islands
Aruba
Bonaire
Curacao

**Dutch Windward
Island**
St. Maarten/St. Martin

French West Indies
Guadeloupe
Martinique
St. Barthelemy

Jamaica
Kingston
Montego Bay
Negril
Ocho Rios

Puerto Rico
Ponce
San Juan

Turks & Caicos
Grand Turk/
 Providenciales

U.S. Virgin Islands
St. Croix
St. John
St. Thomas

Mexico
Acapulco
Cancun & Isla Mujeres
Cozumel
Guadalajara
Ixtapa & Zihuatanejo
Los Cabos
Mazatlan
Mexico City
Monterrey
Oaxaca
Puerto Vallarta

South/Central America
Buenos Aires
Caracas
Rio de Janeiro
San Jose, Costa Rica
Sao Paulo

Middle East
Istanbul
Jerusalem

**Australia & New
Zealand**
Auckland
Melbourne
South Island
Sydney

China
Beijing
Guangzhou
Shanghai

Japan
Kyoto
Nagoya
Osaka
Tokyo
Yokohama

Pacific Rim/Other
Bali
Bangkok
Hong Kong & Macau
Manila
Seoul
Singapore
Taipei

INTERESTS

For your personalized Travel Update, choose the eight (8) categories you're most interested in from the following list:

1.	Business Services	Fax & Overnight Mail, Computer Rentals, Protocol, Secretarial, Messenger, Translation Services

Dining

2.	All-Day Dining	Breakfast & Brunch, Cafes & Tea Rooms, Late-Night Dining
3.	Local Cuisine	Every Price Range — from Budget Restaurants to the Special Splurge
4.	European Cuisine	Continental, French, Italian
5.	Asian Cuisine	Chinese, Far Eastern, Japanese, Other
6.	Americas Cuisine	American, Mexican & Latin
7.	Nightlife	Bars, Dance Clubs, Casinos, Comedy Clubs, Ethnic, Pubs & Beer Halls
8.	Entertainment	Theater – Comedy, Drama, Musicals, Dance, Ticket Agencies
9.	Music	Classical, Opera, Traditional & Ethnic, Jazz & Blues, Pop, Rock
10.	Children's Activites	Events, Attractions
11.	Tours	Local Tours, Day Trips, Overnight Excursions
12.	Exhibitions, Festivals & Shows	Antiques & Flower, History & Cultural, Art Exhibitions, Fairs & Craft Shows, Music & Art Festivals
13.	Shopping	Districts & Malls, Markets, Regional Specialties
14.	Fitness	Bicycling, Health Clubs, Hiking, Jogging
15.	Recreational Sports	Boating/Sailing, Fishing, Golf, Skiing, Snorkeling/Scuba, Tennis/Racket
16.	Spectator Sports	Auto Racing, Baseball, Basketball, Golf, Football, Horse Racing, Ice Hockey, Soccer
17.	Event Highlights	The best of what's happening during the dates of your trip.
18.	Sightseeing	Sights, Buildings, Monuments
19.	Museums	Art, Cultural
20.	Transportation	Taxis, Car Rentals, Airports, Public Transportation
21.	General Info	Overview, Holidays, Currency, Tourist Info

Please note that content will vary by season, destination, and length of stay.

Name

Address

City   **State**   **Country**   **ZIP**

Tel # (   )   -   **Fax #** (   )   -

Title of this Fodor's guide:

Store and location where guide was purchased:

INDICATE YOUR DESTINATIONS/DATES: You can order up to three (3) destinations from the previous page. Fill in your arrival and departure dates for each
destination. <u>**Your Travel Update itinerary (all destinations selected) cannot exceed 30 days from beginning to end.**</u>

		Month	Day	Month	Day
(Sample) **LONDON**	From:	**6** / **21**	To:	**6** / **30**
1	From:	/	To:	/	
2	From:	/	To:	/	
3	From:	/	To:	/	

CHOOSE YOUR INTERESTS: Select up to eight (8) categories from the list of
interest categories shown on the previous page and circle the numbers below:

1 2 3 4 5 6 7 8 9 10 11 12 13 14 15 16 17 18 19 20 21

CHOOSE WHEN YOU WANT YOUR TRAVEL UPDATE DELIVERED (Check one):
❑ Please send my Travel Update immediately.
❑ Please hold my order until a few weeks before my trip to include the most up-to-date
information.
Completed orders will be sent within 48 hours. Allow 7–10 days for U.S. mail delivery.

**ADD UP YOUR ORDER HERE. SPECIAL OFFER FOR FODOR'S
PURCHASERS ONLY!**

	Suggested Retail Price	Your Price	This Order
First destination ordered	$ 9.95	$ 7.95	$ 7.95
Second destination (if applicable)	$ 6.95	$ 4.95	+
Third destination (if applicable)	$ 6.95	$ 4.95	+

DELIVERY CHARGE (Check one and enter amount below)

	Within U.S. & Canada	Outside U.S. & Canada
First Class Mail	❑ $2.50	❑ $5.00
FAX	❑ $5.00	❑ $10.00
Priority Delivery	❑ $15.00	❑ $27.00

ENTER DELIVERY CHARGE FROM ABOVE: + [   ]

TOTAL: $ [   ]

METHOD OF PAYMENT IN U.S. FUNDS ONLY (Check one):
❑ AmEx ❑ MC ❑ Visa ❑ Discover ❑ Personal Check (U. S. & Canada only)
❑ Money Order/International Money Order

Make check or money order payable to: Fodor's Worldview Travel Update

Credit Card__/__/__/__/__/__/__/__/__/__/__/__/__/__/__/__/__/ **Expiration Date:**__/__

Authorized Signature

SEND THIS COMPLETED FORM WITH PAYMENT TO:
**Fodor's Worldview Travel Update, 114 Sansome Street, Suite 700,
San Francisco, CA 94104**

OR CALL OR FAX US 24-HOURS A DAY
Telephone **1-800-799-9609** • Fax **1-800-799-9619** (From within the U.S. & Canada)
(Outside the U.S. & Canada: Telephone 415-616-9988 • Fax 415-616-9989)

(Please have this guide in front of you when you call so we can verify purchase.)
Code: FTG   Offer valid until 12/31/97